Constitutional Law

Constitutional Law

Structure and Rights in Our Federal System

EIGHTH EDITION

William C. Banks
BOARD OF ADVISORS DISTINGUISHED PROFESSOR
PROFESSOR OF LAW EMERITUS
SYRACUSE UNIVERSITY COLLEGE OF LAW

Daan Braveman
PRESIDENT EMERITUS NAZARETH UNIVERSITY
FORMER DEAN SYRACUSE UNIVERSITY COLLEGE OF LAW

Rodney A. Smolla
PRESIDENT
VERMONT LAW AND GRADUATE SCHOOL

CAROLINA ACADEMIC PRESS
Durham, North Carolina

ISBN   978-1-5310-1266-3
eISBN   978-1-5310-1267-0
LCCN   2023944568

Carolina Academic Press, LLC
700 Kent Street
Durham, NC 27701
(919) 489-7486
www.cap-press.com

Printed in the United States of America

For our families

Contents

Table of Cases   xvii

Preface   xxix

Chapter 1 · The Origins: "We the People" — Where Does Power Reside
in Our Constitutional System?   3
  § 1.01 Introduction   3
  § 1.02 An Historical Prologue to the Constitution   4
    A. Pre-Colonial Constitutional Theory   4
    B. From the Colonies to the Convention   4
    C. The Constitutional Convention of 1787   6
  § 1.03 Conceptions of Sovereignty: The National Government,
    the States, and the People   8
      A Case Study of Gun Control   9
      Notes and Questions   11
  § 1.04 The Final Word? — The Judicial Review Doctrine   12
      Marbury v. Madison   13
      Notes and Questions   21
  § 1.05 Judicial Review of Executive Action   23
      United States v. Nixon   23
      Trump v. Vance   30
      Notes and Questions   33
      Problem A   36
  § 1.06 Judicial Review of State Action   37
      Martin v. Hunter's Lessee   37
      Notes and Questions   41
  § 1.07 Contemporary Sovereignty Problems   42
      Cooper v. Aaron   42
      Notes and Questions   44

Chapter 2 · Separation of Powers: Constitutional Checks and Balances   47
  § 2.01 An Historical Overview   47
    A. The English Heritage   47
    B. Bringing Separation Theory to America   49
    C. From the Convention to Current Doctrine   51

D. The Court Walks a Tightrope: Accommodating
Separation's Diverse Goals 53

§ 2.02 How Are Separation of Powers Disputes Decided? — An
Introductory Case Study 55
Youngstown Sheet & Tube Co. v. Sawyer [The Steel Seizure Case] 55
Notes and Questions 67
Problem A 69

§ 2.03 Limits on the Elected Branches: Oversight and Accountability
in the Administrative State 69
A. Introduction 69
B. Delegation of Legislative Power 70
Gundy v. United States 72
Problem B 77
Notes and Questions 78
C. Too Much Oversight: The Legislative Veto 81
Immigration and Naturalization Service v. Chadha 81
Notes and Questions 95
D. Executive Control Over the Appointment and Removal
of Officials 96
Morrison v. Olson 96
Seila Law LLC v. Consumer Financial Protection Bureau 100
Notes and Questions 103
Problem C 105
E. Line Item Veto 106
Clinton v. City of New York 106
Notes and Questions 115
F. Executive Privilege, Presidential Immunity from Lawsuit, and Con-
gress' Power of Impeachment 115
Trump v. Mazars USA, LLP 116
Notes and Questions 120
Clinton v. Jones 121
Notes and Questions 123

§ 2.04 Limits on the Elected Branches: Foreign Relations and
the War Powers 125
A. Foreign Relations Powers 125
United States v. Curtiss-Wright Export Corporation 125
Zivotofsky v. Kerry 128
Notes and Questions 136
B. War Powers 140
Prize Cases 140
Notes and Questions 142
Hamdi v. Rumsfeld 143
Problem D 159

§ 2.05 Limits on Judicial Power — The Justiciability Doctrines   159
  A. Introduction   159
   1. Legitimacy   160
   2. Efficiency   161
   3. Tyranny   162
  B. Political Questions   162
   Powell v. McCormack   164
   Nixon v. United States   166
   Notes and Questions   170
  C. Standing to Sue   170
   Notes and Questions — Citizen Plaintiffs   171
   Notes and Questions — Congressional Plaintiffs   173
   Notes and Questions — States as Plaintiffs   174
  D. Ripeness   176
   Trump v. New York   176
   Notes and Questions   181
   Problem E   181

Chapter 3 · Federalism Limits on Federal Courts   **183**
§ 3.01 Historical Overview   183
  A. The What and Why of Federalism   183
  B. The Constitutional Convention   185
   1. Federalism Concerns and the National Legislature 186
   2. Federalism Concerns and the National Judiciary   186
   3. Federalism Concerns and the National Executive   187
  C. The Ratification Debates   188
  D. Federalism From the 1780s to the Twenty-First Century   190
   1. The Pre-Civil War Period   191
   2. From the Civil War to the New Deal   192
   3. Modern Federalism   194
  E. The Role of the Tenth Amendment and "Considerations
   of Federalism" in Deciding Cases   195
§ 3.02 Introduction: Federalism and the Judiciary   196
§ 3.03 Eleventh Amendment   198
   Hans v. Louisiana   198
   Notes and Questions   200
   Ex parte Young   201
   Notes and Questions   205
   Edelman v. Jordan   205
   Notes and Questions   212
   Seminole Tribe of Florida v. Florida   216
   Notes and Questions   229
   Problem A   231

Chapter 4 · Federalism Limits on the Elected Branches and on the States   233
§ 4.01 Introduction   233
§ 4.02 Scope of Federal Power   236
    McCulloch v. Maryland   236
    Notes and Questions   243
    Problem A   244
§ 4.03 Congressional Power to Regulate Interstate Commerce   245
    A. The Emergence of Dual Sovereignty   245
    Gibbons v. Ogden   245
    Notes and Questions   248
    United States v. E.C. Knight Co.   249
    Notes and Questions   252
    Hammer v. Dagenhart   254
    Notes and Questions   258
    Problem B   259
    B. The New Deal and Beyond   259
    A.L.A. Schechter Poultry Corporation v. United States   259
    Notes and Questions   263
    United States v. Darby   266
    Katzenbach v. McClung   270
    Notes and Questions   273
    United States v. Lopez   274
    Gonzales v. Raich   284
    Notes and Questions   298
    Problem C   303
§ 4.04 Congressional Power to Enforce Civil Rights   304
    Tennessee v. Lane   309
    Notes and Questions   320
§ 4.05 Tenth Amendment Limits on Congressional Power?   320
    Garcia v. San Antonio Metropolitan Transit Authority   322
    Notes and Questions   326
    New York v. United States   326
    Notes and Questions   334
    Printz v. United States   335
    Notes and Questions   346
§ 4.06 Putting the Pieces Together: Commerce Clause, Necessary and Proper
    Clause, Spending Clause   350
    National Federation of Independent Business v. Sibelius   351
    Notes and Questions   365
    Problem D   365
§ 4.07 Constitutional Limits on State Regulation of Commerce: The Dormant
    Commerce Clause   366
    Gibbons v. Ogden   368

City of Philadelphia v. New Jersey 369
Notes and Questions 372
C & A Carbone, Ind. v. Town of Clarkstown 374
United Haulers Assn, Inc. v. Oneida-Herkimer Solid Waste Manage-
    ment Authority 376
Notes and Questions 378
Problem E 379

Chapter 5 · Public and Private Domain **381**
§ 5.01 Introduction 381
§ 5.02 Prohibiting Governmental Encroachments on Individual Rights 390
    A. The Bill of Rights 390
        Barron v. The Mayor and City Council of Baltimore 390
        Notes and Questions 392
    B. The Civil War Amendments 392
        Slaughter-House Cases 392
        Notes and Questions 404
        Problem A 407
§ 5.03 Prohibiting Encroachments on Individual Rights by Private Parties: The
State Action Doctrine 408
    The Civil Rights Cases 408
    Notes and Questions 415
    Jackson v. Metropolitan Edison Company 416
    Flagg Bros., Inc. v. Brooks 421
    Lugar v. Edmondson Oil Co. 427
    Notes and Questions 430
    Problem B 439

Chapter 6 · Exclusion and Equal Protection **441**
§ 6.01 Introduction 441
    A. "We the People" 441
        Johnson v. McIntosh 441
        Dred Scott v. Sandford 444
        Notes and Questions 448
    B. Exclusion and the Equal Protection Clause 449
§ 6.02 Social and Economic Classification: Traditional Approach 452
    Railway Express Agency v. New York 452
    Notes and Questions 453
    Massachusetts Board of Retirement v. Murgia 454
    Notes and Questions 457
    San Antonio Independent School District v. Rodriguez 459
    Notes and Questions 463
    Problem A 464

§ 6.03 Racial Classification   465
    A. Constitutional Standard   465
        Plessy v. Ferguson   465
        Korematsu v. United States   470
        Notes and Questions   477
        Brown v. Board of Education [Brown I]   479
        Notes and Questions   481
        Brown v. Board of Education [Brown II]   483
        Notes and Questions   484
        Loving v. Virginia   484
        Notes and Questions   487
    B. Discriminatory Intent or Impact?   487
        Washington v. Davis   487
        Notes and Questions   492
        Problem B   495
    C. Affirmative Action   496
        Students for Fair Admissions v. President and Fellows
          of Harvard College   498
        Notes and Questions   520
        Problem C   520
§ 6.04 Gender Classification   521
    A. Constitutional Standard   521
        Goesaert v. Cleary   521
        Notes and Questions   522
        Frontiero v. Richardson   522
        Notes and Questions   528
        United States v. Virginia   534
        Notes and Questions   543
        Romer v. Evans   546
        Notes and Questions   549
    B. Discriminatory Intent or Impact?   550
        Personnel Administrator of Massachusetts v. Feeney   550
        Notes and Questions   556
§ 6.05 Conclusion   556
        City of Cleburne v. Cleburne Living Center   557
        Notes and Questions   566
        Problem D   567

Chapter 7 · Economic and Social Rights   **569**
§ 7.01 The Rise, Fall, and Resurrection of Entrepreneurial Liberty   569
        Lochner v. New York   569
        Williamson v. Lee Optical Co.   576
        Notes and Questions   578

§ 7.02 Privacy and the Right to Be Let Alone   580
    Buck v. Bell   580
    Griswold v. Connecticut   582
    Notes and Questions   590
    Dobbs v. Jackson Women's Health Organization   597
    Notes and Questions   619
    Problem A   619
    Obergefell v. Hodges   620
    Notes and Question   635
    Problem B   635
§ 7.03 Entitlements and the Negative Constitution   636
    Dandridge v. Williams   636
    DeShaney v. Winnebago County Department of
      Social Services   642
    Notes and Questions   650
§ 7.04 Due Process in the Administrative State   651
    Goldberg v. Kelly   651
    Board of Regents v. Roth   655
    Cleveland Board of Education v. Loudermill   658
    Notes and Questions   663
    Problem C   665
§ 7.05 The Right to Bear Arms   666
    District of Columbia v. Heller   666
    Notes and Questions   680

Chapter 8 · Religion   685
§ 8.01 What Does "Religion" Mean?   685
§ 8.02 Establishment of Religion   686
    A. Rituals and Symbols in the Public Arena   686
      Town of Greece, New York v. Galloway 690
      American Legion v. American Humanist Association 702
      Notes and Questions   707
    B. Rituals and Symbols in School Settings   708
      Santa Fe Independent School District v. Doe 709
      Kennedy v. Bremerton School District 715
      Notes and Questions   721
    C. Economic Aid to Religion   725
      Everson v. Board of Education   725
      Zelman v. Simmons-Harris   730
      Notes and Questions   736
§ 8.03 Free Exercise of Religion   736
    A. Discrimination or Hostility   736
    B. Neutral Laws That Burden Religion   740

Reynolds v. United States	740
Sherbert v. Verner	742
Wisconsin v. Yoder	747
Employment Division, Department of Human Resources	
v. Smith	751
Notes and Questions	756
Problem A	762
§ 8.04 Religious Disputes in Secular Courts	762
Hosanna-Tabor Evangelical Lutheran Church & School	
v. Equal Employment Opportunity Commission	763
Notes and Questions	771
Chapter 9 · Freedom of Speech and Association	**773**
§ 9.01 Competing Conceptions of Freedom of Speech	773
A. Dueling Visions	773
B. The Order and Morality Theory	774
Chaplinsky v. New Hampshire	774
Beauharnais v. Illinois	776
C. The Marketplace Theory	782
Abrams v. United States	782
Whitney v. California	788
Notes and Questions	792
§ 9.02 Speech and Lawless Activity	797
A. Incitement	797
Brandenburg v. Ohio	797
Notes and Questions	800
Problem A	803
B. True Threats	804
Virginia v. Black	804
Notes and Questions	822
§ 9.03 Vulgar, Graphic, and Offensive Speech	824
A. Vulgarity	824
Cohen v. California	824
Federal Communications Commission v. Pacifica Foundation	829
Notes and Questions	835
B. Graphically Offensive Speech	836
Texas v. Johnson	836
United States v. Stevens	847
Notes and Questions	854
§ 9.04 Content-Based, Viewpoint-Based, and Content-Neutral Regulation	858
A. Content and Viewpoint Discrimination	858
B. Incidental Burdens on Speech and the *O'Brien* Principle	859
United States v. O'Brien	859

	C. Evidentiary Use of Speech to Prove the Elements of an Offense	864
	Wisconsin v. Mitchell	864
	Notes and Questions	869
	Problem B	870
§ 9.05	Obscene and Pornographic Speech	870
	A. Obscenity in the General Marketplace	870
	Miller v. California	870
	Paris Adult Theatre I v. Slaton	874
	Notes and Questions	877
	B. Obscenity in the Privacy of the Home	879
	Stanley v. Georgia	879
	Notes and Questions	882
	C. Pornography and the Protection of Children	882
	Ashcroft v. Free Speech Coalition	883
	Reno v. American Civil Liberties Union	889
	Notes and Questions	895
	D. Erotic Dance Clubs, Public Nudity, and the Secondary Effects Doctrine	896
§ 9.06	Free Speech and Tort Liability	898
	A. Defamation	898
	New York Times Company v. Sullivan	898
	McKee v. Cosby	908
	Notes and Questions	910
	B. False Light	913
	C. Publication of Private Facts	914
	D. Intrusion	917
	E. Appropriation and Right of Publicity	919
	F. Infliction of Emotional Distress	920
	Hustler Magazine v. Falwell	920
	Notes and Questions	929
§ 9.07	Prior Restraints	929
	New York Times Company v. United States	929
	Notes and Questions	941
	Problem C	942
§ 9.08	Commercial Speech	943
	44 Liquormart, Inc. v. Rhode Island	943
	Notes and Questions	957
§ 9.09	Campaign Finance and the Political Process	961
	Citizens United v. Federal Election Commission	961
§ 9.10	Public Forum Law	972
	Widmar v. Vincent	972
	Frisby v. Schultz	976
	Notes and Questions	983

§ 9.11 Government Speech   984
         Shurtleff v. City of Boston   985
§ 9.12 Government Funding   994
         Rust v. Sullivan   994
         Rosenberger v. Rector and Visitors of University of Virginia 1001
         Legal Services Corporation v. Valezquez   1004
§ 9.13 Government Employees   1012
         A. Discipline Against Employees   1012
         B. Political Patronage   1017
         Branti v. Finkel   1017
§ 9.14 Education   1019
         Morse v. Frederick   1019
         Notes and Questions   1030
         Problem D   1031
         Mahanoy Area School District v. B.L. by & through Levy   1031
         Notes and Questions   1041
         Problem E   1042
§ 9.15 The Legal System   1042
         A. Reporting on Judicial Proceedings   1042
         B. Controlling the Speech of Lawyers   1043
§ 9.16 Anonymous Speech   1044
§ 9.17 Forced Speech   1046
         303 Creative LLC v. Elenis   1046
         Notes and Questions   1050
§ 9.18 Freedom of Expressive Association   1052
§ 9.19 Journalism and the First Amendment   1057
         A. The Press Clause   1057
         B. Access to Institutions and Events   1060
         C. Reporters' Privilege   1061

Appendix · The Constitution of the United States of America   1063

Index   1081

Table of Cases

12 200-ft. Reels of Super 8MM. Film, United States v., 320

303 Creative LLC v. Elenis United States Supreme Court, 1046

44 Liquormart, Inc. v. Rhode Island, 943

A.L.A. Schechter Poultry Corporation v. United States, 259

Abbott Laboratories v. Gardner, 180

Ableman v. Booth, 44

Abood v. Detroit Board of Education, 1051

Abrams v. United States, 782

Adair v. United States, 579

Adarand Constructors, Inc. v. Pena, 496, 501, 507

Adkins v. Children's Hospital, 579

Allegheny, County of, v. American Civil Liberties Union Greater Pittsburgh Chapter, 689, 700

Allen v. Wright, 171, 173

Allgeyer v. Louisiana, 569

Already, LLC v. Nike, Inc., 177

Alvarez, United States v., 513, 854

American Ins. Assn. v. Garamendi, 131, 136, 137, 139

American Legion v. American Humanist Association 702

American Mfrs. Mut. Ins. Co. v. Sullivan, 437

Anderson v. Dunn, 779

Area Educ. Telcoms. Consortium v. FCC, 894

Arkansas Writers' Project, Inc. v. Ragland, 996, 1007

Arlington Heights v. Metropolitan Housing Dev. Corp., 551, 553

Arnett v. Kennedy, 659, 663

Arthrex, Inc., United States v., 104

Ashcroft v. Free Speech Coalition, 883

Associated Press v. Walker, 912

Atascadero State Hospital v. Scanlon, 213

Austin v. Michigan Chamber of Commerce, 968

Babbitt v. Farm Workers, 179

Baker v. Carr, 24, 163

Baker v. Nelson, 624

Barclay v. Florida, 866

Barnes v. Glen Theatre, Inc., 896

Barron v. The Mayor and City Council of Baltimore, 390

Barron ex rel. Tiernan v. Mayor of Baltimore, 602

Bartnicki v. Vopper, 915

Bass, United States v., 276

Bates v. State Bar of Ariz., 945

Batson v. Kentucky, 531

Baumgartner v. United States, 922

Beal v. Doe, 424

Beauharnais v. Illinois, 776

Belmont, United States v., 138

Berisha v. Lawson, 910

Bethel School Dist. No. 403 v. Fraser, 1020, 1033

Biden v. Nebraska, 79, 175

Bigelow v. Virginia, 944, 945

Bishop v. Wood, 659

Blatchford v. Native Village of Noatak, 227

Blum v. Yaretsky, 437

Board of Airport Comm'rs of Los Angeles v. Jews for Jesus, Inc., 848

Board of Directors of Rotary International v. Rotary Club of Duarte, 1053

Board of Educ. v. Earls, 1024

Board of Educ. of Okla. City Pub. Schs., Indep. Sch. Dist. No. 89 v. Dowell, 484

Board of Regents of Univ. of Wis. System v. Southworth, 710, 1006

Board of Regents v. Roth, 457, 655

Board of Trustees v. Garrett, 230, 310

Board of Trustees, State Univ. of N.Y. v. Fox, 950

Boddie v. Connecticut, 312

Boerne, City of, v. Flores, 304, 311, 316, 416, 757

Bolger v. Youngs Drug Products Corp., 894

Bolling v. Sharpe, 449, 450, 481

Bond v. Floyd, 1029

Boos v. Barry, 840

Bose Corp. v. Consumers Union of United States, Inc., 922

Bostock v. Clayton County, 549

Bowers v. DeVito, 463

Bowers v. Hardwick, 623

Bowsher v. Synar, 106, 336

Boy Scouts of America v. Dale, 1046, 1055

Bradwell v. Illinois, 407, 522

Brandenburg v. Ohio, 797, 800, 945

Branti v. Finkel, 1017

Branzburg v. Hayes, 1061

Braunfeld v. Brown, 743, 760

Bray v. Alexandria Women's Health Clinic, 601

Brentwood Academy v. Tennessee Secondary School Athletic Association, 435

Brig Aurora, The, 71

Broadrick v. Oklahoma, 888, 982

Brown v. Board of Education I, 42, 197, 460, 479, 512, 619

Brown v. Board of Education II, 194, 483, 500, 508

Brown v. EPA, 342

Brown v. North Carolina, 533

Brown, United States v., 54

Brown-Forman Distillers Corporation v. New York State Liquor Authority, 372

Buck v. Bell, 451, 580

Buckley v. Valeo, 121, 961

Bunting v. Oregon, 579

Burke, United States v., 1062

Butler, United States v., 264, 357

Byrd v. Raines, 106

C & A Carbone, Ind. v. Town of Clarkstown, 374

Caetano v. Massachusetts, 681

Cafeteria & Restaurant Workers Union v. McElroy, 652

Califano v. Webster, 536

California Federal Sav. & Loan Ass'n v. Guerra, 536

California Retail Liquor Dealers Ass'n v. Midcal Aluminum, Inc., 950

California v. Texas, 365

Calvary Chapel Dayton Valley v. Sisolak, 761

Cantrell v. Forest City Publishing Co., 914

Cantwell v. Connecticut, 407, 743, 775, 777

Capital Cities Cable, Inc. v. Crisp, 950

Capitol Square Review and Advisory Bd. v. Pinette, 807

Carey v. Brown, 976

Carey v. Population Services Int'l, 596, 894, 945, 946

Carolene Products Co., United States v., 388, 389, 451

Carroll Towing Co., United States v., 795

Carson v. Makin, 1048

Carter v. Carter Coal Co., 72, 264

Castaneda v. Partida, 492

Castle Rock, Town of, v. Gonzalez, 665

Central Hudson Gas & Elec. Corp. v. Public Serv. Comm'n of N.Y., 946, 948

Champion v. Ames (The Lottery Case), 253

Chaplinsky v. New Hampshire, 774

Chicago & Southern Air Lines, Inc. v. Waterman S.S. Corp., 137

Child Labor Tax Case (Drexel Furniture), 357

Chisholm v. Georgia, 199, 202

Christian Legal Society Chapter of the University of California, Hastings v. Martinez, 1055

Church of the Lukumi Babalu Aye, Inc. v. City of Hialeah, 718

Cincinnati v. Discovery Network, Inc., 948

Citizens United v. Federal Election Commission, 961

City of (See Name of City)

Civil Rights Cases, 307, 408, 466

Clapper v. Amnesty International USA, 171, 180

Clark v. Jeter, 533

Cleburne v. Cleburne Living Center, Inc., 312, 533, 557

Cleland's Memoirs of a Woman of Pleasure v. Attorney General of Mass., 886

Cleveland Board of Education v. Loudermill, 658

Clinton v. City of New York, 106

Clinton v. Jones, 121

Cohen v. California, 824, 831

Cohen v. Cowles Media Co., 918

Cohens v. Virginia, 22

Collins v. Yellen, 105

Committee for Public Education v. Nyquist, 973

Comstock, United States v., 350, 351

Connick v. Myers, 1012

Coombs, United States v., 292

Cooper v. Aaron, 42

Coppage v. Kansas, 579

Cornelius v. NAACP Legal Defense and Educ. Fund, 984

Counterman v. Colorado, 823

County of (See Name of County)

Cox v. Louisiana, 866

Cox Broadcasting Corp. v. Cohn, 914

Curtis Publishing Co. v. Butts, 912

Curtiss-Wright Export Corporation, United States v., 125

Cutter v. Wilkinson, 765

Dames & Moore v. Regan, 138, 158

Dandridge v. Williams, 451, 636

Darby, United States v., 191, 266, 293, 322

Dartmouth College v. Woodward, 382

Davis v. Beason, 685

Dawson v. Delaware, 866

De Jonge v. Oregon, 796

Dean Milk Co. v. Madison, 374

Debs v. United States, 793

Debs, In re, 54

Dellinger, United States v., 1029

Dellmuth v. Muth, 213

Dennis v. United States, 795, 799

Department of Commerce v. New York, 175

Department of Commerce v. United States House of Representatives, 179

DeShaney v. Winnebago County Department of Social Services, 463, 642

Dillon v. Gloss, 167

District of Columbia v. Heller, 10, 666, 684

Dobbs v. Jackson Women's Health Organization, 597, 681

Doe v. University of Michigan, 1041

Dred Scott v. Sandford, 382, 444

Drexel Furniture (Child Labor Tax Case), 357

Dun & Bradstreet, Inc. v. Greenmoss Builders, Inc., 913, 925
Duncan v. Louisiana, 623
Dunn v. Blumstein, 312

E.C. Knight Co., United States v., 249
Eastland v. United States Servicemen's Fund, 118
Edelman v. Jordan, 205
Edge Broadcasting Co., United States v., 951
Edmond v. United States, 103
Edmonson v. Leesville Concrete Company, 430, 502
Edwards v. Aguillard, 724
Eisenstadt v. Baird, 592, 596, 613
Elk v. Wilkins, 449
Elliott v. Commonwealth, 822
Elrod v. Burns, 1017
Employment Division, Department of Human Resources v. Smith, 751, 757
Engel v. Vitale, 694, 720, 722
Epperson v. Arkansas, 723
Erie, City of, v. Pap's A.M., 896
Espinoza v. Montana Department of Revenue, 740
Estate of (See Name of Deceased)
Estelle v. Gamble, 645
Eu v. San Francisco County Democratic Central Comm., 963
Evans v. Newton, 426
Everson v. Board of Education, 725
Ewing v. Mytinger & Casselberry, Inc., 660
Ex parte (See Name of Relator)

F.S. Royster Guano Co. v. Virginia, 451
Fairfax's Devisee v. Hunter's Lessee, 37
Faretta v. California, 312
FCC v. Beach Communications, Inc., 458
FCC v. Pacifica Foundation, 829, 890, 892, 924

Federal Election Comm'n v. Wisconsin Right to Life, Inc., 961
Feiner v. New York, 801, 826
FERC v. Mississippi, 278
First Nat. Bank of Boston v. Bellotti, 964, 1059
Fisher v. University of Texas at Austin (2013), 510
Fisher v. University of Texas at Austin (2016), 510, 512, 515
Fitzpatrick v. Bitzer, 219, 230, 304
Flagg Bros., Inc. v. Brooks, 421, 437
Fletcher v. Peck, 382
Florida Bar v. Went For It, Inc., 947
Florida Star v. B.J.F., 915
Food Lion v. Capital Cities/ABC, Inc., 918
Ford Motor Co. v. Department of Treasury, 207
Frazee v. Illinois Dep't of Employment Sec., 685, 759
Free Enterprise Fund v. Public Company Accounting Oversight Bd., 101
Freeman v. Pitts, 484
Friedman v. Rogers, 946
Frisby v. Schultz, 976
Frohwerk v. United States, 793
Frontiero v. Richardson, 522, 531
Frost & Frost Trucking Co. v. Railroad Comm'n of Cal., 953
Fuentes v. Shevin, 422
Fulton v. City of Philadelphia, Pennsylvania, 759

Garcetti v. Ceballos, 717, 1012
Garcia v. San Antonio Metropolitan Transit Authority, 322
Garrison v. Louisiana, 923
Gayle v. Browder, 481
Geduldig v. Aiello, 450, 601
Gentile v. State Bar of Nevada, 1043
Georgia v. McCollum, 435
Gertz v. Robert Welch, Inc., 831, 912, 922

Gibbons v. Ogden, 245, 368, 600, 667

Ginsberg v. New York (1968), 879, 890

Ginsberg v. New York (1972), 832

Gitlow v. New York, 794

Glickman v. Wileman Brothers & Elliott, Inc., 959

Goesaert v. Cleary, 521

Goldberg v. Kelly, 208, 651, 661

Goldman v. Weinberger, 761

Gonzales v. Carhart, 600

Gonzales v. O Centro Espirita Beneficente Uniao do Vegetal, 758

Gonzales v. Raich, 284

Goodridge v. Dep't of Pub. Health, 625

Graham v. Richardson, 208

Grand Jury Subpoena, Judith Miller, In re, 1062

Granholm v. Heald, 372

Gratz v. Bollinger, 500

Greece, New York, Town of, v. Galloway, 690

Green v. County School, 484

Green v. Mansour, 213

Gregory v. Ashcroft, 348

Griswold v. Connecticut, 582, 596, 613

Grutter v. Bollinger, 496, 501, 503, 505, 510, 512, 514

Guest, United States v., 416

Gundy v. United States, 72

H.P. Hood & Sons v. DuMond, 233, 234, 235

Haaland v. Brackeen, 174, 350

Hague v. CIO, 983

Haig v. Agee, 139

Hamdi v. Rumsfeld, 143

Hammer v. Dagenhart, 254

Hans v. Louisiana, 198

Harris v. McRae, 996

Haupt v. United States, 868

Hazelwood School Dist. v. Kuhlmeier, 709, 1023, 1033

Hazelwood School Dist. v. United States, 492

Healy v. James, 1002

Heart of Atlanta Motel v. United States, 270, 275, 322, 1050

Helvering v. Hallock, 220

Hernandez v. Texas, 492

Herndon v. Lowry, 796

Hess v. Indiana, 800

Hipolite Egg Co. v. United States, 255

Hirabayashi v. United States, 471

Hishon v. King & Spalding, 867

Hodel v. Virginia Surface Mining & Reclamation Assn., Inc., 275, 322, 323

Hoke v. United States, 255

Holden v. Hardy, 569

Holmes v. Atlanta, 481

Hosanna-Tabor Evangelical Lutheran Church & School v. EEOC, 763

Houchins v. KQED, Inc., 1060

Hudgens v. NLRB, 438

Humphrey's Executor v. United States, 96, 101

Hurley v. Irish-American Gay, Lesbian and Bisexual Group of Boston, Inc., 1047, 1053, 1055

Hustler Magazine v. Falwell, 920

Immigration and Naturalization Service v. Chadha, 81

In re (See Name of Party or Matter)

Iota XI Chapter of Sigma Chi Fraternity v. George Mason University, 1041

J.E.B. v. Alabama, 531, 536

J.W. Hampton, Jr. & Co. v. United States, 72

Jackson v. Indiana, 313

Jackson v. Metropolitan Edison Company, 416, 437

Jackson v. Virginia, 820

Jackson Women's Health Org. v. Currier, 600

Jacobellis v. Ohio, 879

Jacobson v. Massachusetts, 581

Jaffree v. Board of School Commissioners of Mobile County, 407

Janus v. American Federation of State, City & Municipal Employees, Council 31, 1051

Jefferson v. Hackney, 488

Jett v. Dallas Independent School Dist., 807

Johnson v. California, 501

Johnson v. McIntosh, 441

Jones v. Alfred H. Mayer Co., 416, 1050

Jones v. United States, 299

Kadrmas v. Dickinson Public Schools, 548

Kahriger, United States v., 357

Karcher v. Islamic Rep. of Iran, 159

Katzenbach v. McClung, 270, 275

Katzenbach v. Morgan, 304, 416

Kedroff v. Saint Nicholas Cathedral of Russian Orthodox Church in North America, 766

Kennedy v. Bremerton School District, 715

Keyishian v. Board of Regents, State Univ. of N.Y., 1002

Kilbourn v. Thompson, 120

Kimel v. Florida Board of Regents, 316

Kirchberg v. Feenstra, 532

Kitchen v. Herbert, 628

Klein, United States v., 54

Kois v. Wisconsin, 886

Korematsu v. United States, 470, 478

Kotch v. Board of River Pilot Commissioners, 454

Laird v. Tatum, 181

Lander v. Seaver, 1040

Landmark Communications, Inc. v. Virginia, 801

Lane Co. v. Oregon, 251

Larkin v. Grendel's Den, Inc., 707

Lassiter v. Northampton County Bd. of Elections, 305

Lawrence v. Texas, 613, 623

Lee v. Weisman, 697, 700

Legal Services Corporation v. Valezquez, 1004

Lemon v. Kurtzman, 490, 687, 973

Levy v. Louisiana, 640

Linmark Associates, Inc. v. Willingboro, 945, 946

Lochner v. New York, 564, 569, 603, 629

Locke v. Davey, 739

Logan v. Zimmerman Brush Co., 659, 660

Lopez, United States v., 274, 291, 293

Lottery Case (Champion v. Ames), 253

Louisiana v. Biden, 79

Louisiana v. United States, 539

Lovett, United States v., 54

Loving v. Virginia, 484, 605, 624

Lucia v. Securities and Exchange Commission, 104

Lugar v. Edmondson Oil Co., 427, 437

Lujan v. Defenders of Wildlife, 171, 172, 179

Lynch v. Donnelly, 688

Lyng v. Automobile Workers, 1010

M.L.B. v. S.L.J., 312

Mahanoy Area School District v. B.L. by & through Levy, 1031

Maher v. Roe, 996, 1010

Manhattan Community Access Corp. v. Halleck, 436

Marbury v. Madison, 13, 849

Marsh v. Alabama, 422, 437

Marsh v. Chambers, 336

Marshall Field & Co. v. Clark, 71, 110

Marshall v. Gordon, 26

Martin v. Hunter's Lessee, 37, 607

Martinez v. California, 645

Massachusetts Board of Retirement v. Murgia, 454

Massachusetts v. Environmental Protection Agency, 174

Masterpiece Cakeshop, Ltd. v. Colorado Civil Rights Comm'n, 737, 1048

Matal v. Tam, 987, 993

Mathews v. Eldridge, 147, 660, 664

McAuliffe v. Mayor of New Bedford, 1012

McCleskey v. Kemp, 492

McCollum v. Board of Education, 721

McConnell v. Federal Election Comm'n, 972

McCreary County Kentucky v. American Civil Liberties Union of Kentucky, 688

McCulloch v. Maryland, 26, 236, 614, 682

McDaniel v. Paty, 739

McDonald v. Chicago, 10, 602, 680, 682

McGowan v. Maryland, 707

McGrain v. Daugherty, 98, 117

McIntyre v. Ohio Elections Commission, 955, 1044

McKee v. Cosby, 908

McKesson Corp. v. Division of Alcoholic Beverages and Tobacco, 229

McLaurin v. Oklahoma State Regents, 480

Members of City Council v. Taxpayers for Vincent, 979

Metromedia, Inc. v. San Diego, 951

Meyer v. State of Nebraska, 582, 590

Miami Herald Publishing Co. v. Tornillo, 832

Milkovich v. Lorain Journal Co., 913

Miller v. California, 870, 893

Miller, United States v., 670, 672, 678, 679

Milliken v. Bradley, 539

Mills v. Commonwealth, 604

Mississippi University for Women v. Hogan, 532, 543

Missouri ex rel. Gaines v. Canada, 617

Mitchell v. Helms, 736

Mitchum v. Foster, 196

Monitor Patriot Co. v. Roy, 963

Moore v. East Cleveland, 603

Moore v. Harper, 41

Morrison v. Olson, 96, 101

Morrison, United States v., 289

Morse v. Frederick, 1019, 1033, 1037

Mt. Healthy City School District Board of Education v. Doyle, 1016

Mueller v. Allen, 732

Mugler v. Kansas, 569

Mullane v. Central Hanover Bank & Trust Co., 660

Muller v. Oregon, 579

Murphy v. National Collegiate Athletic Ass'n, 348, 350

Myers v. United States, 53, 54, 336

NAACP v. Alabama, 583

NAACP v. Button, 743

NAACP v. Claiborne Hardware Co., 866

Naim v. Naim, 485

National Collegiate Athletic Assn. v. Tarkanian, 437

National Federation of Independent Business v. Sibelius, 351

National Institute of Family & Life Advocates v. Becerra, 1050

National League of Cities v. Usery, 194, 195, 320

National Pork Producers Council v. Ross, 378

National Rifle Association v. City of Chicago, 10

Near v. Minnesota ex rel. Olson, 672, 932, 941

Nevada Department of Human Resources v. Hibbs, 230, 311

New Orleans City Park Improvement Ass'n v. Detiege, 481

New Orleans v. Dukes, 564

New State Ice Co. v. Liebmann, 10, 185, 294

New York State Rifle & Pistol Association v. Bruen, 11

New York Times Co. v. Sullivan, 898, 910

New York Times Co. v. United States, 929

New York v. Ferber, 849, 865, 886

New York v. United States, 191, 326

Nixon v. Administrator of General Services, 133

Nixon v. Condon, 437

Nixon v. Fitzgerald, 31, 120, 122

Nixon v. United States, 166

Nixon, United States v., 23

NLRB v. Jones & Laughlin Steel Corp., 265

NLRB v. Noel Canning, 133, 614

North American Cold Storage Co. v. Chicago, 660

North Georgia Finishing, Inc. v. Di-Chem, Inc., 422

Northeastern Florida Chapter, General Contractors of America v. City of Jacksonville, 170

O'Brien, United States v., 604, 837, 859, 866

O'Mara v. Commonwealth, 806

Obergefell v. Hodges, 550, 613, 620, 1049

Ohralik v. Ohio State Bar Ass'n, 946

Oklahoma v. Civil Service Comm'n, 301

Oregon v. Mitchell, 305, 416

Osborne v. Ohio, 882, 886

Our Lady of Guadalupe School v. Morrissey-Berru, 771

Palko v. Connecticut, 587

Palmer v. Thompson, 489, 495

Palmore v. Sidoti, 500

Panama Refining Co. v. Ryan, 72, 74

Papasan v. Allain, 463

Parents Involved in Community Schools v. Seattle School District No. 1, 484, 501, 507

Paris Adult Theatre I v. Slaton, 874

Pell v. Procunier, 1060

Pendergrass, State v., 1026

Pennhurst State School & Hospital v. Halderman, 216

Pennsylvania v. Union Gas Co., 219

Perez v. United States, 274

Perpich v. Department of Defense, 677, 679

Perry Educational Ass'n v. Perry Local Educators' Ass'n, 983

Perry v. Sindermann, 664, 953

Personnel Administrator of Mass. v. Feeney, 311, 532, 550

Peters, United States v., 44

Philadelphia Newspapers, Inc. v. Hepps, 913

Philadelphia, City of, v. New Jersey, 369, 376

Pickering v. Board of Ed. of Township High School Dist. 205, 717

Pierce v. Society of Sisters, 582, 590, 625, 748

Pietsch v. Bush, 172, 173

Pike v. Bruce Church, Inc., 370

Pink, United States v., 131, 138

Planned Parenthood of Southeastern Pennsylvania v. Casey, 595, 598, 599, 606, 611, 612

Planned Parenthood of the Columbia/ Wilmette, Inc. v. American Coalition of Life Activists, 823

Plaut v. Spendthrift Farm, Inc., 319

Playboy Entertainment Group, Inc., United States v., 848, 895

Pleasant Grove City v. Summum, 986, 989

Plessy v. Ferguson, 465, 617

Plyler v. Doe, 512

Poe v. Ullman, 585, 586, 615

Polk County v. Dodson, 432

Pope v. Illinois, 878

Posadas de Puerto Rico Associates v. Tourism Co. of P.R., 951

Powell v. McCormack, 52, 164

Powers v. Ohio, 435, 532

Press-Enterprise Co. v. Superior Court of Cal., County of Riverside, 312

Principality of Monaco v. Mississippi, 340

Printz v. United States, 335

Prize Cases, 140

Process Gas Consumer Group v. Consumer Energy Council, 95

Quinn v. United States, 118

R.A.V. v. City of St. Paul, 806, 858, 953

Railway Express Agency v. New York, 452

Raines v. Byrd, 106, 173, 175

Rankin v. McPherson, 1016

Red Lion Broadcasting Co. v. FCC, 832, 892

Reed v. Reed, 524, 527

Reed v. Town of Gilbert, 718, 858

Regan v. Taxation with Representation of Wash., 996

Regents of Univ. of Cal. v. Bakke, 501, 510

Rendell-Baker v. Kohn, 437

Reno v. American Civil Liberties Union, 802, 889

Reno v. Condon, 346

Renton v. Playtime Theatres, Inc., 890, 897

Reynolds v. United States United States Supreme Court 740

Rice v. Cayetano, 501, 505

Rice v. Paladin Enterprises, Inc., 802

Richmond v. J.A. Croson Co., 505

Roberts v. United States Jaycees 768, 866, 867, 1053

Roe v. Wade, 592, 598, 601, 611, 612

Roman Catholic Diocese of Brooklyn v. Cuomo, 761

Rome, City of, v. United States, 305

Romer v. Evans, 546, 623

Rosado v. Wyman, 210

Rosenberger v. Rector and Visitors of Univ. of Va., 709, 1001, 1006

Rosenbloom v. Metromedia, Inc., 912

Roth v. United States, 831, 872, 878, 879

Rubin v. Coors Brewing Co., 943

Runyon v. McCrary, 867

Rust v. Sullivan, 994

Sable Communications of Cal., Inc. v. FCC, 513

Sabri v. United States, 303

San Antonio Ind. School District v. Rodriguez, 455, 459, 511

San Francisco Arts & Athletics, Inc. v. United States Olympic Comm., 437

Santa Fe Independent School District v. Doe, 709

Saxbe v. Washington Post Co., 417 U.S. 843, 1060

Schechter Poultry Corp. v. United States, 72, 74

Schenck v. United States, 783, 792

Schlesinger v. Reservists Committee to Stop the War, 172, 173

School Dist. of Abington v. Schempp, 722

Scott v. School Board of Alachua County, 1042

Seeger, United States v., 685, 760

Seila Law LLC v. Consumer Financial Protection Bureau, 100

Seminole Tribe of Florida v. Florida, 216, 230

Serbian Eastern Orthodox Diocese for United States and Canada v. Milivo- jevich, 767

Shapiro v. Thompson, 211, 312

Shaw v. Hunt, 501, 505

Shelley v. Kraemer, 439

Sherbert v. Verner, 742

Shreveport Rate Case (W.T.R. Co. v. United States), 253, 293

Shurtleff v. City of Boston, 985

Shuttlesworth v. City of Birmingham, 941

Sipuel v. Board of Regents of Univ. of Okla., 617

Skinner v. Oklahoma ex rel. Williamson, 312, 487, 583, 590, 616

Slagle, State v., 604

Slaughter-House Cases, 392, 465

Smith v. Allwright, 437

Smith v. California, 879

Sniadach v. Family Finance Corp., 422

Snyder v. Phelps, 926

Sorrell v. IMS Health Inc., 959

South Bay United Pentecostal Church v. Newsom, 761

South Carolina v. Katzenbach, 305

South Dakota v. Dole, 300, 330

Southeastern Promotions, Ltd. v. Conrad, 892

Spence v. Washington, 866

Spokeo, Inc. v. Robins, 172

Sprague, United States v., 667

Stanley v. Georgia, 876, 879, 882

State v. (See Name of Defendant)

Sterling v. Constantin, 44

Stevens, United States v., 847

Stone v. Graham, 722

Strauder v. West Virginia, 488

Stromberg v. People of State of California, 780

Students for Fair Admissions v. President and Fellows of Harvard College, 498

Susan B. Anthony List v. Driehaus, 177, 179

Sweatt v. Painter, 479, 617

Sweezy v. New Hampshire, 1002

Swift & Co. v. United States, 280

Talley v. California, 1044

Taylor v. Louisiana, 312

Teamsters v. United States, 492

Tennessee v. Lane, 231, 309

Terminiello v. City of Chicago, 780, 865

Terry v. Adams, 437

Texas v. Johnson, 836

Texas v. United States, 365

Texas v. White, 192

Texas, United States v., 175

Thomas v. Review Bd., Ind. Empl. Sec. Div., 759

Thornhill v. State of Alabama, 780

Thornton, Estate of, v. Caldor, Inc., 760

Tilton v. Richardson, 765

Time, Inc. v. Hill, 914

Torcaso v. Watkins, 685, 694

Town of (See Name of Town)

Transportation Union v. Long Island R. Co., 323

TransUnion v. Ramirez, 172

Trinity Lutheran Church of Columbia, Inc. v. Comer, 739

Trump v. Hawaii, 478, 707

Trump v. Mazars USA, LLP, 116

Trump v. New York, 176

Trump v. Vance, 30

Tuan Anh Nguyen v. Immigration and Naturalization Service, 544

Turner Broadcasting System, Inc. v. FCC, 604, 892

Tyler Pipe Indus. v. Washington State Dep't of Revenue, 373

United Foods, Inc., United States v., 959

United Haulers Assn, Inc. v. Oneida-Herkimer Solid Waste Management Authority, 376

United Public Workers v. Mitchell, 176

United States Dept. of Agriculture v. Moreno, 464, 548

United States Forest Service v. Cowpasture River Preservation Ass'n, 299

United States Postal Service v. Council of Greenburgh Civic Associations, 984

United States v. (See Name of Defendant)

Utah v. Strieff, 514

UWM Post v. Board of Regents of the University of Wisconsin, 1041

Van Orden v. Perry, 688

Vasquez v. Hillery, 512

Virginia Bd. of Pharmacy v. Virginia Citizens Consumer Council, Inc., 944, 945, 954

Virginia v. Black, 804, 1023

Virginia v. Rives, 424

Virginia, Ex parte, 304

Virginia, United States v., 534

Vitek v. Jones, 659

W.T.R. Co. v. United States (The Shreveport Rate Case), 253, 293

Walker v. City of Birmingham, 941

Walker v. Texas Division, Sons of Confederate Veterans, Inc., 988

Wallace v. Jaffree, 407, 723

Ward v. Rock Against Racism, 983

Washington v. Davis, 487, 551

Washington v. Glucksberg, 602, 603

Watkins v. United States, 117

Watson v. Jones, 766

Wayman v. Southard, 75

Weber v. Aetna Casualty & Surety Co., 526

Welch v. Department of Highways and Public Transportation, 213

Welsh v. United States, 685

West v. Derby Unified School District No. 260, 1042

West Coast Hotel Co. v. Parrish, 579

West Virginia Board of Education v. Barnette, 959

West Virginia v. Environmental Protection Agency, 78

Whitney v. California, 788, 945

Wickard v. Filburn, 272, 273, 274, 322

Widmar v. Vincent, 972

Williamson v. Lee Optical of Okla., 454, 459, 563, 576

Williams-Yulee v. Florida Bar, 512, 513

Wisconsin v. Constantineau, 656

Wisconsin v. Mitchell, 864

Wisconsin v. Yoder, 747, 756

Witters v. Washington Dept. of Servs. for Blind, 732

Wooley v. Maynard, 959, 1050

Wyoming v. Oklahoma, 376

Yick Wo v. Hopkins, 488, 500, 645

Young v. American Mini Theatres, Inc., 831

Young, Ex parte, 197, 201, 208

Youngberg v. Romeo, 313, 646

Younger v. Harris, 41, 198

Youngstown Sheet & Tube Co. v. Sawyer, 54, 55, 129, 131, 134, 137, 138, 936

Zablocki v. Redhail, 487

Zacchini v. Scripps-Howard Broadcasting Co., 919

Zaidan v. Trump, 170

Zelman v. Simmons-Harris, 730

Zivotofsky v. Kerry, 128

Zobrest v. Catalina Foothills School Dist., 732

Zorach v. Clauson, 718, 721

Preface

More than thirty years ago we set out to create a constitutional law casebook that teaches well. We wanted to teach from a book that would engage students in learning basic constitutional law and would enable teachers to work with cases and problems relatively unencumbered by extensive secondary source materials and treatise-like notes. In preparing the eighth edition of our casebook, we have continued to develop the characteristics that distinguish our book from others. First, we continue to place heavy emphasis on the structure of government, the constitutional concepts of federalism and separation of powers. Typically, the constitutional law course has focused on three themes: judicial function, distribution of government power among the branches of the federal government and between the federal government and the states, and individual rights. The separation of powers and federalism issues, however, have been shortchanged in favor of study of the judicial function and individual rights.

Since the conception of our first edition in the early 1980's, separation of powers and federalism have retained their status as dominant themes in constitutional law as well as society generally. They continue to deserve close examination. Indeed, the renewed attention to separation of powers and federalism issues by the Supreme Court in recent years underscores the importance of structural issues in constitutional law.

Our treatment of the individual rights material also distinguishes this book from others. In prior editions, we organized the rights material around the contexts in which rights issues arise. Beginning with the third edition, we adopted a more traditional approach of presenting the individual rights materials doctrinally through separated examination of due process, equal protection, and the First Amendment. In doing so, however, we have maintained a unique focus. The chapter on equal protection, for example, begins with a consideration of the groups that were excluded from constitutional protection and then examines whether the equal protection clause has served as a vehicle of inclusion. We also omitted the electoral districting and reapportionment materials in favor of their extensive coverage in specialized texts and courses, and we relocated congressional enforcement of civil rights from what was chapter nine to the earlier chapter on congressional powers, chapter four.

Finally, we have rejected the notion that a good casebook must also be a treatise. We also have worked hard to produce a treatment of constitutional law that may reasonably be presented in a survey course. With a few exceptions, we have prepared only brief notes and comments to guide the reader through the cases and to provoke independent thought about important constitutional issues without overwhelming students with scholarly debates. In lieu of extensive excerpts from secondary sources, we rely on hypothetical problems to facilitate study of the material. In drafting problems, we have been mindful of the value of placing law students in practical situations where they may be asked to be problem solvers of concrete and realistic constitutional issues. We remain convinced that such practical problems enable students to develop a better understanding of the underlying theory and doctrine. In addition, to improve the readability of the text in this edition we have chosen not to use ellipses to indicate omitted material.

WILLIAM C. BANKS
Syracuse, New York

RODNEY A. SMOLLA
South Royalton, Vermont

DAAN BRAVEMAN
Rochester, New York
January, 2024

Constitutional Law

Chapter 1

The Origins: "We the People" — Where Does Power Reside in Our Constitutional System?

§ 1.01 Introduction

This chapter introduces what might be thought of as *the* overriding issue in U.S. constitutional law — where does ultimate sovereignty lie? In the event of a dispute involving the national government, a state, and some of the people, which legal entity holds the highest constitutional cards? Is it the national government (and if so, which of the three branches)? The state or local governments? If the people are the ultimate sovereign, which level and branch of government speaks for the people?

In the following sections, we explore these fundamental problems of sovereignty, emphasizing the role of adjudication in resolving allocation of power disputes. We begin in § 1.02 with a concise review of history bearing on the framing of the Constitution. For readers steeped in early American history, this treatment will be a cursory review. For everyone else, it is an essential primer to a study of the materials in the chapter. Section 1.03 follows with a case study of local efforts to control guns. The social and political conflicts that produced modern gun control and the opposition right to bear arms movement is presented both to illustrate how social problems may become constitutional problems, and to demonstrate, through the Supreme Court's decision striking down local gun control laws, how constitutional adjudication may resolve, at least temporarily, a fundamental question concerning sovereign power. In § 1.04 we explore the doctrine of judicial review and the Court's decision in *Marbury v. Madison*. *Marbury* raises the recurring question: Is the Supreme Court the final arbiter of the meaning of the Constitution (and thus the final say on all sovereignty questions, including those concerning the Court's own power)? In part because the *Marbury* decision concerned judicial review of an act of Congress, § 1.05 separately examines the doctrine of judicial review of executive action. Disputes from the Nixon and Trump presidencies frame some of the unique features of the sovereignty clashes that arise when executive branch action is at issue. In § 1.06 we examine Supreme Court review of the constitutionality of state laws. Finally, in § 1.07 we examine contemporary problems of sovereignty, including those concerning federal enforcement of Supreme Court decrees in the states.

§ 1.02 An Historical Prologue to the Constitution

A. Pre-Colonial Constitutional Theory

The intellectual origins of our Constitution can be traced to writers who were influenced by such classical philosophers as Plato and Aristotle. However, the classical philosophers' early writings about a constitutional political structure lay dormant until sparked by 18th century philosophical thought and the advent of the social contract theory. John Locke (1632–1704), perhaps more than any other individual, laid the intellectual foundation for the American enterprise. It was Locke's view that because people, by nature, are free, equal and independent, they can only justly be subjected to political power by their own consent. Thus, it may be advantageous for people to contract to form a social community. They must in turn, however, carry the burden of being bound by the rules of the community—the social contract.

The act of making the contractual political society into a recognizable government is central to Locke's scheme. For Locke, the essence of a constitutional system was a government where political authority consists of knowable and specifiable powers. The government would thereby have limited powers. At the same time, the basic terms of the social contract must exist prior to the operation of the government and they must establish criteria for the government's validity.

Our framers were clearly influenced by the social contract theory. In the Preamble to the Constitution, the "People of the United States" ordained and established the Constitution "in Order to form a more perfect Union." Through the Constitution they "granted" legislative powers, "vested" the President with executive powers, and "vested" the courts with judicial power. The constitutional amendments limited certain powers of the state and federal governments, and secured certain rights in the people. *See* HENRY BALDWIN, A GENERAL VIEW OF THE ORIGIN AND NATURE OF THE CONSTITUTION AND GOVERNMENT OF THE UNITED STATES (1970).

B. From the Colonies to the Convention

By the mid-eighteenth century, the American colonies had developed a character distinct from that of England. Great Britain had followed a policy of "salutary neglect" for the previous 150 years, and regulated the colonies only enough to insure steady exports of raw materials and imports of British goods. There were English governors who represented the crown but they were dependent on local assemblies for their salaries and to raise taxes. The colonies, thus, exercised a large amount of self-governance.

The colonists were bound, for the most part, by a common English heritage and a common (Calvinist) religious background. Even so, they "were reputed to be a quarrelsome, litigious, divisive lot of people." EDMUND SEARS MORGAN, THE BIRTH OF

THE REPUBLIC 4 (1977). Local governments were dominated by small groups of economic and political power-holders while the bulk of the population was comprised of small land-owners and other people who worked the soil for a living. It is not surprising that some historians have viewed the American Revolution as "more than a war between the colonies and Great Britain; it was also a struggle between those who enjoyed political privileges and those who did not." MERRILL JENSEN, THE ARTICLES OF CONFEDERATION: AN INTERPRETATION OF THE SOCIAL-CONSTITUTIONAL HISTORY OF THE AMERICAN REVOLUTION, 1774–1787, at 6–7 (1940).

England ended her long neglect of the colonies in 1764 with the Sugar Act, a duty on molasses imports, followed in March 1765, by the Stamp Act. Both were designed to alleviate England's national debt, swollen by the Seven Years War with France. The Stamp Act provided that almost anything formally written or printed would have to be on stamped paper imported from England. While the Sugar Act was tolerable because it taxed external trade, England's traditional area of regulation, the Stamp Act interfered with local, internal affairs.

The Colonists' reaction was immediate and, in some cases, violent. Mobs forced local officials to refuse to distribute the stamped paper and there was a general boycott on its use. Business went on as usual, without England's paper.

In 1765, the Stamp Act Congress met and resolved that the tax had a "manifest tendency to subvert the rights and liberties of the colonists." CARL J. FRIEDRICH, FROM THE DECLARATION OF INDEPENDENCE TO THE CONSTITUTION xviii (1954). Parliament could not accept this denial of its power and, in 1766, passed the Declaratory Act which asserted Parliament's right to make laws and statutes binding the colonists "in all cases whatsoever."

Revolution could have started with the Declaratory Act but the colonists, despite their libertarianisms, had a solid veneration for the law. "They desired liberty, which they felt was their moral due; but with equal fervor they desired to behave legally." *Id.*

Based on this dichotomy of ideas, the colonists continued to avoid revolution throughout Parliament's continuing assertions of power. The Townsend Acts, duties on various imports, were imposed in 1767. The City of Boston reacted peacefully by boycotting British goods but tempers flared in March, 1770, when five people were killed at the Boston Massacre. A period of relative peace was shattered in 1773 by the Tea Act, the Boston Tea Party, and, finally, by Britain's closing of Boston Harbor.

The first Continental Congress met in 1774 to "establish the rights and liberties of the colonies upon a just and solid foundation." ANDREW CUNNINGHAM MCLAUGHLIN, A CONSTITUTIONAL HISTORY OF THE UNITED STATES 84 (1935). After much discussion the Congress resolved that the colonists' rights were based "on the immutable law of nature, the principles of the English Constitution, and the several charters or compacts." JENSEN, *supra*, at 66. This mood of restraint did not last long. Public opinion shifted radically in January 1776, with the publication of Thomas Paine's *Common Sense*.

Paine's pamphlet was read by almost everyone in the colonies. At least 300,000 copies were sold. "It aroused public opinion, for it crystallized, in language easily understood and appreciated, the emotions and beliefs of the ordinarily inarticulate masses." JENSEN, *supra*, at 89.

Common Sense provided the impetus for the Declaration of Independence by saying that government's only justification is the freedom and security of the governed. Paine denied the supremacy of the monarchy. One small group should not be exalted above the rest; "The cause of America," Paine told them, "is in a great measure the cause of all mankind." MORGAN, *supra*, at 75.

A resolution for independence was introduced by the Virginia delegation on June 7, 1776, was adopted on July 2, and the Declaration of Independence was signed on July 4. The Continental Congress began almost immediately after declaring independence to devise a plan for joint government of the colonies. The Articles of Confederation were submitted to the states in 1777 and ratified by 1781. The government established by the Articles, however, was very similar to the informal arrangements that had developed during the Revolution. In a sense, the Articles resemble a treaty presiding over otherwise independent states.

More particularly, there was no national judiciary or independent executive branch. The powers withheld from Congress were clearly more important than those granted. It had no authority to regulate commerce or tax, while the states specifically reserved their "sovereignty, freedom, and independence." Under the Articles, each state continued to impose its own tariffs and duties. Some states with good port facilities took advantage of their less fortunate neighbors and imposed heavy fees for port usage. The need for national regulation of trade became more and more apparent. Calls for a general reform of the government began as early as 1783 and the Congress authorized the Philadelphia Convention in February, 1787.

C. The Constitutional Convention of 1787

The Convention was convened on May 26, 1787. The delegates ranged from the eighty-one-year-old "American Socrates," Benjamin Franklin, to John Dickinson, who had refused to sign the Declaration of Independence. Most of the delegates had served in Congress at some time and most were wealthy. In fact, Thomas Jefferson, who was in Paris and did not attend, called the convention "really an assembly of demi-gods." MAX FARRAND, THE FRAMING OF THE CONSTITUTION OF THE UNITED STATES 39 (1913).

Once assembled, the delegates knew that compromise was to be an important element of the convention. They formulated rules, therefore, which permitted every issue to be reopened, and which kept the proceedings secret in order to permit delegates to compromise without the fear of political repercussion. *See* 1 MERRILL JENSEN, THE DOCUMENTARY HISTORY OF THE RATIFICATION OF THE CONSTITUTION 233 (1976).

The delegates assumed from the beginning that the government would find its source of power in the people. To be sure, some of the delegates were fearful of an excess of democracy. All of the delegates' home states imposed restrictions on suffrage, usually based on property ownership. The delegates refrained from adding these restrictions to the Federal Constitution, perhaps because of their belief in the power of all the people, more likely because they feared that an attempt to prescribe a uniform standard would imperil ratification. FRIEDRICH, *supra*, at xviii–xxiv.

Although it was agreed that the power of the federal government needed strengthening in relation to the states, there was considerable discussion as to the appropriate amount of change. Some delegates advocated reducing the states to mere administrative districts of the federal government. While most delegates were not willing to go so far, they were willing to explicitly and dramatically change the nation-state relationship that had existed under the Articles. They did this by first asserting the supremacy of the national government and its laws through the Supremacy Clause in Article VI and second by arming the judiciary in Article III with the power to ensure the vitality of the national commands.

There were major disagreements, however, which needed to be resolved by compromise to save the convention and the new constitution. These disagreements primarily involved differences of opinion between the delegates of the small and large states, and between the delegates of southern and northern states.

The Virginia Plan, which included the resolution for the creation of the "supreme legislative, judiciary, and executive," provided that both houses of Congress be chosen on the basis of population. Such a scheme would have given the larger states, notably Virginia, Pennsylvania, and Massachusetts, virtual control over the new national government. The smaller states objected and countered with the New Jersey Plan, which essentially abandoned the concept of a supreme national government and called only for modification of the Articles of Confederation. In order to retain the concept of a supreme government, which many delegates thought was absolutely necessary for the survival of the new nation, compromise was needed. The resulting "Great Compromise" called for equal representation of the States in the Senate while retaining the principle of representation by population in the House.

The differences between northern and southern states primarily revolved around the slave trade and the basic differences between the agrarian economy of the South and the merchant economy of the North. Most of these differences were resolved (albeit temporarily) by compromise. For example, the northern states wanted to apportion expenses of the new government by population, including the slaves, while the southern states did not desire to include slaves in the population count. The compromise was that slaves would be counted as 3/5 persons for purposes of both taxation and representation. Art. I, Sec. 2, cl. 3.

In addition, the northern states desired to abolish the importation of slaves, while the southern states did not. A compromise was reached by which Congress could not prohibit importation until the year 1808. Art. I, Sec. 2, cl. 1. Finally, the southern states knew that expansion to the west would result in the addition of states to the union more in tune with their own agrarian interests. Therefore, they wanted the make-up of Congress to reflect that future change. The north acquiesced to the use of the decennial census to reapportion representation. Art. I, Sec. 2, cl. 3.

The delegates convened six days each week in the heat of the Philadelphia summer to compromise, where needed, and to design a new national government. The fundamental resolutions and plans were submitted by the Committee of the Whole to the Committee of Detail on July 26. The Committee of Detail produced the basic outline of the Constitution by August 6. The Committee of the Whole modified and added to this outline through September 10, when it was submitted to the Committee on Style and Arrangement. After stylistic changes, the constitution was approved by the Convention on September 17, 1787. The Constitution was then submitted to the Congress by the President of the Convention, George Washington, whose submittal letter summarized the convention's commitment to a stronger national government as well as its spirit of compromise.

The Congress sent the Constitution to the states for ratification, where the debates were far more intense than those heard in Philadelphia. Although the well-organized and politically strong Federalists succeeded in obtaining ratification in the necessary ninth state in less than a year (in 1788), popular opinion was heavily divided. In New York, where the Federalists feared defeat on ratification, Madison, Hamilton, and John Jay wrote essays in newspapers arguing the case for the Constitution. The Federalist Papers effectively marshalled support for the new charter. By 1790, all the states had ratified the Constitution. *See* GARRY WILLS, EXPLAINING AMERICA: THE FEDERALIST (1981).

§ 1.03 Conceptions of Sovereignty: The National Government, the States, and the People

Until the last decade of the twentieth century, it was thought that the fundamental questions of sovereignty in our constitutional system had been settled, first by the framers and a few early decisions of the Supreme Court, and then later by the Civil War and the post-Civil War Amendments to the Constitution. Those settled expectations will be carefully explored in this and later chapters. However, a series of developments since the 1990s has reopened an inquiry into what Justice Clarence Thomas called "first principles." We have chosen to begin our study of constitutional law with litigation over gun control precisely because the legislative measures and the Supreme Court decisions purporting to resolve the "who decides" dispute capture so well the "first principles," while they typify the way in which constitutional problems arise in our legal culture.

A Case Study of Gun Control

Ironically, the struggle over who controls the ownership and use of guns in American society began with the American Revolution, when the colonists unlawfully and violently used their weapons and seceded from the British Empire. With the Declaration of Independence as their justification, the early Americans rejected the longstanding sovereignty of the King of England over their affairs. Indeed, the early common law understanding of a right to bear arms was accompanied by the recognition that their use was subject to the control and approval of the sovereign — the King. It was the King's duty as sovereign to establish a "king's peace" that would supplant "the patchwork of local regulations" as well as "private vengeances and family feuds" that were then common. Darrell A.H. Miller, *Self-Defense, Defense of Others, and the State*, 80 Law & Contemp. Probs. 87–88 (2017).

Thus, in England, the executive decided gun rights. But the constitutional system established by the United States was decidedly different. Certain powers were through enumeration in the Constitution given to the branches of the national government, yet the sovereign states that existed before and after ratification retained the residual powers not given to the national government. When first adopted and ratified, the Constitution said next to nothing about individual rights, including a right to bear arms, at least in part because it was thought that the limited list of powers given to the national government would prevent it from being powerful enough to threaten individual rights.

A Bill of Rights soon was circulated and ratified, however, including the Second Amendment, which reads: "A well regulated Militia, being necessary to the security of a free State, the right of the people to keep and bear Arms, shall not be infringed." Until the contemporary disputes that are the subject of this case study arose, the dominant view was that the Second Amendment was designed to cement the role of state militias in society, and to ensure that local citizen soldiers could take up arms when called by the state. In contrast to the Framers' fear that a large standing army could jeopardize citizens' rights, the militias — citizen soldiers who could be called out in emergencies — did not pose the same threat. William C. Banks & Stephen Dycus, Soldiers on the Home Front: The Domestic Role of the American Military 33–36 (2016). In other words, the Second Amendment was not designed so much as a rights provision as one protecting state prerogatives over local militias.

As you will learn later in your constitutional law course, the struggle over slavery and resultant Civil War led to ratification of post-Civil War Amendments to the Constitution, the effect of which has been to selectively incorporate the protections of the original Bill of Rights to control alleged intrusions by state and local governments. For present purposes, "selectively" is the important qualifier, because until recently, it was not clear whether control over gun ownership and use was subject to state and local regulation.

Gun violence in the United States became a growing and persistent political and legal issue in recent years. In response to escalating gun-related casualties, many state and local jurisdictions enacted various forms of gun control. Then, in 2008, the Supreme Court held in *District of Columbia v. Heller*, 554 U.S. 570, that the Second Amendment protects the right to keep and bear arms for the purpose of self-defense. The Court thus struck down a District of Columbia law that banned the possession of handguns in the home. (*Heller* and the scope of the Second Amendment will be considered separately in Chapter 7.) However, *Heller* called into question only the meaning of the Second Amendment in relation to individual possession of guns in people's homes, not whether state and local control of guns was otherwise lawful. The right recognized in *Heller* was thus not absolute.

Not long after the *Heller* decision, the city of Chicago and nearby suburb Oak Park defended local ordinances banning the possession of most handguns. After local residents sued, lower federal courts upheld the local regulations. In *National Rifle Association v. City of Chicago*, 567 F. 3d 856 (2009), Seventh Circuit Judge Frank Easterbrook noted that "[o]ne function of the second amendment is to prevent the national government from interfering with state militias." Although the Constitution accomplishes this purpose by creating individual rights, "those rights may take a different shape when asserted against a state than against the national government." The court explained that "the Constitution establishes a federal republic where local differences are to be cherished as elements of liberty rather than extirpated in order to produce a single, nationally applicable rule."

The Supreme Court reversed in *McDonald v. City of Chicago*, 561 U.S. 742 (2010), and stated that "a provision of the Bill of Rights that protects a right that is fundamental from an American perspective applies equally to the Federal Government and the States." Putting aside questions about the scope of the Second Amendment, why should constitutional rights protections be the same in every state? Do states retain sovereignty to decide the scope of those rights?

Dissenting in *McDonald*, Justice Stevens maintained that "the Constitution still envisions a system of divided sovereignty, still 'establishes a federal republic where local differences are to be cherished as elements of liberty' in the vast run of cases. . . . Elementary considerations of constitutional text and structure suggest there may be legitimate reasons to hold state governments to different standards than the Federal Government in certain areas."

Justice Stevens continued: "Firearms regulation and its location is at the core of the [states'] police powers, [and] is a quintessential area in which federalism ought to be allowed to flourish without this Court's meddling. Given that relevant background conditions diverge so much across jurisdictions, the Court ought to pay particular heed to state and local legislatures' 'right to experiment.' *New State Ice* [*v. Liebmann*], 285 U.S., at 311 (Brandeis, J., dissenting)."

In the years since *Heller* and *McDonald*, it was generally understood that citizens have a constitutional right to possess a handgun in the home for self-defense, and a similar right to carry handguns publicly for the same purpose. However, states continued to require licenses to carry firearms, and in some states, including New

York, licenses were only issued when an applicant demonstrates a "proper cause" for self-defense. In *New York State Rifle & Pistol Association v. Bruen*, 142 S. Ct. 2111 (2022), the Supreme Court struck down the New York law and held that no state may require citizens to demonstrate a need for self-defense distinguishable from that of the general community in order to carry firearms outside the home. Writing for the majority, Justice Thomas noted that "we know of no other constitutional right that an individual may exercise only after demonstrating to government officers some special need. That is not how the First Amendment works when it comes to unpopular speech or the free exercise of religion. It is not how the Sixth Amendment works when it comes to a defendant's right to confront the witnesses against him. And it is not how the Second Amendment works when it comes to public carry for self-defense." Justice Thomas wrote that states remained free to ban guns in sensitive places, such as schools, government buildings, legislative assemblies, polling places and courthouses.

Dissenting, Justice Breyer, joined by Justices Sotomayor and Kagan, opined that "when courts interpret the Second Amendment, it is constitutionally proper, indeed often necessary, for them to consider the serious dangers and consequences of gun violence that lead States to regulate firearms. The question before us concerns the extent to which the Second Amendment prevents democratically elected officials from enacting laws to address the serious problem of gun violence. And yet the Court today purports to answer that question without discussing the nature or severity of that problem."

Notes and Questions

(1) The practice of incorporating the Bill of Rights guarantees against the states through the Due Process Clause of the Fourteenth Amendment will be examined separately in Chapter 5. For now, it is more important to consider whether there is something about the Second Amendment that makes it especially susceptible to local regulation of guns, or to no or only national regulation.

(2) Do you agree with Justice Stevens in *McDonald* that "elementary considerations of constitutional text and structure" justify differing state and federal standards in assessing the scope of constitutional rights? If so, what parts of the constitutional text and structure support the states or cities that wish to go their own way on gun control?

(3) In *Bruen*, might New York have had reasons unique to its population and gun violence problems to require a showing of a special need for protection before granting a gun permit? What does the *Bruen* decision teach us about where sovereignty lies in our federal system?

(4) One perspective on deciding which level of government is empowered to make gun control policy is to focus on the ultimate sovereigns in our constitutional system: "We the People." In a different setting, Justice Thurgood Marshall discussed what he regarded as the evolving meaning of "We the People" when he wrote:

For a sense of the evolving nature of the Constitution we need look no further than the first three words of the document's preamble: "We the People." When the Founding Fathers used this phrase in 1787, they did not have in mind the majority of America's citizens. "We the People" included in the words of the framers, "the whole Number of free Persons." On a matter so basic as the right to vote, for example, Negro slaves were excluded, although they were counted for representational purposes—at three-fifths each. Women did not gain the right to vote for over a hundred and thirty years.

The men who gathered in Philadelphia in 1787 could not have imagined, nor would they have accepted, that the document they were drafting would one day be construed by a Supreme Court to which had been appointed a woman and the descendant of an African slave. "We the People" no longer enslave, but the credit does not belong to the framers. It belongs to those who refused to acquiesce in outdated notions of "liberty," "justice," and "equality," and who strived to better them.[1]

What impact would Justice Marshall's interpretation of "We the People" have on how the *McDonald* or *Bruen* cases should be decided?

§ 1.04 The Final Word? — The Judicial Review Doctrine

Our constitutional structure was built in part upon the fear that accumulation of power in a single branch of government would lead to tyranny. Indeed, Madison wrote that "the accumulation of all powers, legislative, executive and judicial in the same hands, whether of one, a few, or many, and whether hereditary, self-appointed, or elective, may justly be pronounced the very definition of tyranny." The Federalist No. 47. To prevent tyranny by the national government, the Framers provided for three branches of the federal government and built into the constitutional framework a system of checks and balances. Moreover, powers not delegated to one of those branches were reserved to the states and the people.

Who should serve as the umpire, however, and determine when one of the branches exceeded the power delegated by the Constitution? Under one possible alternative, the decision of the first branch to address an issue would be conclusive on the other branches whenever that issue arose. A second alternative would allow each branch to decide constitutional issues regardless of any decision by another branch. Are either of these alternatives acceptable? *See* Learned Hand, The Bill of Rights 11–14 (1958) (rejecting both alternatives). A third option was provided by the following Supreme Court decision.

---

1. Thurgood Marshall, *Reflections on the Bicentennial of the United States Constitution*, 101 Harv. L. Rev. 1, 2, 5 (1987).

Marbury v. Madison

United States Supreme Court
5 U.S. (1 Cranch) 137, 2 L. Ed. 60 (1803)

[On March 2, 1801, one day before leaving office, President John Adams named 42 justices of the peace for the District of Columbia. These justices were confirmed by the Senate on March 3, 1801, and their commissions were signed and sealed by John Marshall, then Secretary of State. In the final moments of the Adams Administration, however, some of the commissions, including that of William Marbury, were not served.

When President Jefferson assumed office, he instructed his secretary of state, James Madison, to disregard the appointments and withhold the undelivered commissions. Invoking § 13 of the Judiciary Act of 1789, Marbury commenced a proceeding in the Supreme Court to compel Madison to deliver the commission. Section 13 provided:

> . . . the Supreme Court shall have exclusive jurisdiction of all controversies of a civil nature, where a state is a party, except between a state and its citizens; and except also between a state and citizens of other states, or aliens, in which latter case it shall have original but not exclusive jurisdiction of suits or proceedings against ambassadors, or other public ministers, or their domestics, or domestic servants, as a court of law can have or exercise consistently with the law of nations; and original, but not exclusive jurisdiction of all suits brought by ambassadors, or other public ministers, or in which a consul, or vice consul, shall be a party. And the trial of issues of fact in the Supreme Court, in all actions at law against citizens of the United States, shall be by jury. The Supreme Court shall also have appellate jurisdiction from the circuit courts and courts of the several states, in the cases herein after specially provided for; and shall have power to issue writs of prohibition to the district courts, when proceeding as courts of admiralty and maritime jurisdiction, and writs of mandamus, in cases warranted by the principles and usages of law, to any courts appointed, or persons holding office, under the authority of the United States.

Marbury began the proceeding during the Court's December Term of 1801. In February, 1803, John Marshall (at the time, Chief Justice) delivered the following opinion.

For a discussion of the historical background, see William W. Van Alstyne, *A Critical Guide to Marbury v. Madison*, 1969 DUKE L.J. 1.]

MARSHALL, C.J.

At the last term on the affidavits then read and filed with the clerk, requiring the Secretary of State to show cause why a mandamus should not issue, directing him to deliver to William Marbury his commission as a justice of the peace for the county of Washington, in the District of Columbia. . . .

The first object of inquiry is,

1st. Has the applicant a right to the commission he demands?

His right originates in an act of Congress passed in February 1801, concerning the District of Columbia.

After dividing the district into two counties, the 11th section of this law enacts, "that there shall be appointed in and for each of the said counties, such number of discreet persons to be justices of the peace as the president of the United States shall, from time to time, think expedient, to continue in office for five years."

It appears, from the affidavits, that in compliance with this law, a commission for William Marbury, as a justice of peace for the county of Washington, was signed by John Adams, then President of the United States; after which the seal of the United States was affixed to it; but the commission has never reached the person for whom it was made out.

In order to determine whether he is entitled to this commission, it becomes necessary to inquire whether he has been appointed to the office. For if he has been appointed, the law continues him in office for five years, and he is entitled to the possession of those evidences of office, which, being completed, became his property. . . .

The last act to be done by the president is the signature of the commission. He has then acted on the advice and consent of the senate to his own nomination. The time for deliberation has then passed. He has decided. His judgment, on the advice and consent of the senate concurring with his nomination, has been made, and the officer is appointed. This appointment is evidenced by an open, unequivocal act; and being the last act required from the person making it, necessarily excludes the idea of its being, so far as respects the appointment, an inchoate and incomplete transaction. . . .

It is, therefore, decidedly the opinion of the court, that when a commission has been signed by the president, the appointment is made; and that the commission is complete when the seal of the United States has been affixed to it by the secretary of state.

The discretion of the executive is to be exercised until the appointment has been made. But having once made the appointment, his power over the office is terminated in all cases, where by law the officer is not removable by him. The right to the office is *then* in the person appointed, and he has the absolute, unconditional power of accepting or rejecting it.

Mr. Marbury, then, since his commission was signed by the president, and sealed by the secretary of state, was appointed; and as the law creating the office, gave the officer a right to hold for five years, independent of the executive, the appointment was not revocable, but vested in the officer legal rights, which are protected by the laws of this country.

To withhold his commission, therefore, is an act deemed by the court not warranted by the law, but violative of a vested legal right.

This brings us to the second inquiry which is,

2dly. If he has a right, and that right has been violated, do the laws of his country afford him a remedy? The very essence of civil liberty certainly consists in the right of every individual to claim the protection of the laws, whenever he receives an injury. One of the first duties of government is to afford that protection.

The government of the United States has been emphatically termed a government of laws, and not of men. It will certainly cease to deserve this high appellation, if the laws furnish no remedy for the violation of a vested legal right.

If this obloquy is to be cast on the jurisprudence of our country, it must arise from the peculiar character of the case.

It behooves us, then, to inquire whether there be in its composition any ingredient which shall exempt it from legal investigation, or exclude the injured party from legal redress.

It follows . . . that the question, whether the legality of an act of the head of a department be examinable in a court of justice or not, must always depend on the nature of that act.

By the constitution of the United States, the president is invested with certain important political powers, in the exercise of which he is to use his own discretion, and is accountable only to his country in his political character and to his own conscience. To aid him in the performance of these duties, he is authorized to appoint certain officers, who act by his authority, and in conformity with his orders.

In such cases, their acts are his acts and whatever opinion may be entertained of the manner in which executive discretion may be used, still there exists, and can exist, no power to control that discretion. The subjects are political. They respect the nation, not individual rights, and being intrusted to the executive, the decision of the executive is conclusive. The application of this remark will be perceived by adverting to the act of congress for establishing the department of foreign affairs. This officer, as his duties were prescribed by that act, is to conform precisely to the will of the president. He is the mere organ by whom that will is communicated. The acts of such an officer, as an officer, can never be examinable by the courts.

But when the legislature proceeds to impose on that officer other duties; when he is directed preemptorily to perform certain acts; when the rights of individuals are dependent on the performance of those acts; he is so far the officer of the law; is amenable to the laws for his conduct; and cannot at his discretion sport away the vested rights of others.

The conclusion from this reasoning is, that where the heads of departments are the political or confidential agents of the executive, merely to execute the will of the president, or rather to act in cases in which the executive possesses a constitutional or legal discretion, nothing can be more perfectly clear than that their acts are only politically examinable. But where a specific duty is assigned by law, and individual rights depend upon the performance of that duty, it seems equally clear that the individual who considers himself injured, has a right to resort to the case under the consideration of the court. . . .

That, having this legal title to the office, he has a consequent right to the commission; a refusal to deliver which is a plain violation of that right, for which the laws of his country afford him a remedy.

It remains to be inquired whether,

3dly. He is entitled to the remedy for which he applies. This depends on,

1st. The nature of the writ applied for and,

2dly. The power of this court.

1st. The nature of the writ. . . .

This writ, if awarded, would be directed to an officer of government, and its mandate to him would be, to use the words of Blackstone, "to do a particular thing therein specified, which appertains to his office and duty, and which the court has previously determined, or at least supposes, to be consonant to right and justice. . . ."

These circumstances certainly concur in this case.

Still to render the mandamus a proper remedy, the officer to whom it is to be directed, must be one to whom, on legal principles, such writ may be directed; and the person applying for it must be without any other specific and legal remedy.

1st. With respect to the officer to whom it would be directed. The intimate political relation subsisting between the President of the United States and the heads of departments, necessarily renders any legal investigation of the acts of one of those high officers peculiarly irksome, as well as delicate; and excites some hesitation with respect to the propriety of entering into such investigation. Impressions are often received without much reflection or examination, and it is not wonderful that in such a case as this the assertion, by an individual, of his legal claims in a court of justice, to which claims it is the duty of that court to attend, should at first view be considered by some, as an attempt to intrude into the cabinet, and to intermeddle with the prerogatives of the executive.

It is scarcely necessary for the court to disclaim all pretensions to such jurisdiction. An extravagance, so absurd and excessive, could not have been entertained for a moment. The province of the court is, solely, to decide on the rights of individuals, not to inquire how the executive, or executive officers, perform duties in which they have a discretion. Questions in their nature political, or which are, by the constitution and laws, submitted to the executive, can never be made in this court.

But, if this be not such a question; if, so far from being an intrusion into the secrets of the cabinet, it respects a paper which, according to law, is upon record, and to a copy of which the law gives a right, on the payment of ten cents; if it be no intermeddling with a subject over which the executive can be considered as having exercised any control; what is there in exalted station of the officer, which shall bar a citizen from asserting, in a court of justice, his legal rights, or shall forbid a court to listen to the claim, or to issue a mandamus directing the performance of a duty, not depending on executive discretion, but on particular acts of congress, and the general principles of law?

If one of the heads of departments commits any illegal act, under colour of his office, by which an individual sustains an injury, it cannot be pretended that his office alone exempts him from being sued in the ordinary mode of proceeding, and being compelled to obey the judgment of the law. How, then, can his office exempt him from this particular mode of deciding on the legality of his conduct, if the case be such a case as would, were any other individual the party complained of, authorize the process?

It is not by the office of the person to whom the writ is directed, but the nature of the thing to be done, that the propriety or impropriety of issuing a mandamus is to be determined. Where the head of a department acts in a case, in which executive discretion is to be exercised; in which he is the mere organ of executive will; it is again repeated, that any application to a court to control, in any respect, his conduct would be rejected without hesitation.

But where he is directed by law to do a certain act affecting the absolute rights of individuals, in the performance of which he is not placed under the particular direction of the President, and the performance of which the President cannot lawfully forbid, and therefore is never presumed to have forbidden; as for example, to record a commission, or a patent for land, which has received all the legal solemnities; or to give a copy of such record; in such cases, it is not perceived on what ground the courts of the country are further excused from the duty of giving judgment that right be done to an injured individual, than if the same services were to be performed by a person not the head of a department. . . .

This, then, is a plain case of a mandamus, either to deliver the commission, or a copy of it from the record; and it only remains to be inquired,

Whether it can issue from this court.

. . . .

The constitution vests the whole judicial power of the United States in one supreme court, and such inferior courts as congress shall, from time to time, ordain and establish. This power is expressly extended to all cases arising under the laws of the United States; and, consequently, in some form, may be exercised over the present case; because the right claimed is given by a law of the United States.

In the distribution of this power it is declared that "the Supreme Court shall have original jurisdiction in all cases affecting ambassadors, other public ministers and consuls, and those in which a state shall be a party. In all other cases, the Supreme Court shall have appellate jurisdiction."

It has been insisted, at the bar, that as the original grant of our jurisdiction, to the supreme and inferior courts, is general, and the clause, assigning original jurisdiction to the supreme court, contains no negative or restrictive words, the power remains to the legislature, to assign original jurisdiction to that court in other cases than those specified in the article which has been recited; provided those cases belong to the judicial power of the United States.

If it had been intended to leave it in the discretion of the legislature to apportion the judicial power between the supreme and in inferior courts according to the will of that body, it would certainly have been useless to have proceeded further than to have defined the judicial power, and the tribunals in which it should be vested. The subsequent part of the section is mere surplusage, is entirely without meaning, if such is to be the construction. If congress remains at liberty to give this court appellate jurisdiction, where the constitution has declared their jurisdiction shall be original; and original jurisdiction where the constitution has declared it shall be appellate; the distribution of jurisdiction, made in the constitution, is form without substance.

To enable this court, then, to issue a mandamus, it must be shown to be an exercise of appellate jurisdiction, or to be necessary to enable them to exercise appellate jurisdiction.

It has been stated at the bar that the appellate jurisdiction may be exercised in a variety of forms, and that if it be the will of the legislature that a mandamus should be used for that purpose, that will must be obeyed. This is true, yet the jurisdiction must be appellate, not original.

It is the essential criterion of appellate jurisdiction, that it revises and corrects the proceedings in a cause already instituted, and does not create that cause. Although, therefore, a mandamus may be directed to courts, yet to issue such a writ to an officer for the delivery of that paper, is in effect the same as to sustain an original action for that paper, and, therefore, seems not to belong to appellate, but to original jurisdiction. Neither is it necessary in such a case as this, to enable the court to exercise its appellate jurisdiction.

The authority, therefore, given to the supreme court, by the act establishing the judicial courts of the United States, to issue writs of mandamus to public officers, appears not to be warranted by the constitution; and it becomes necessary to inquire whether a jurisdiction so conferred can be exercised.

The question, whether an act, repugnant to the constitution, can become law of the land, is a question deeply interesting to the United States; but, happily, not of an intricacy proportioned to its interest. It seems only necessary to recognize certain principles, supposed to have been long and well established, to decide it.

That the people have an original right to establish, for their future government, such principles as, in their opinion, shall most conduce to their own happiness is the basis on which the whole American fabric has been erected. The exercise of this original right is a very great exertion; nor can it, nor ought it, to be frequently repeated. The principles, therefore, so established, are deemed fundamental. And as the authority from which they proceed is supreme, and can seldom act, they are designed to be permanent.

This original and supreme will organizes the government, and assigns to different departments their respective powers. It may either stop here, or establish certain limits not to be transcended by those departments.

The government of the United States is of the latter description. The powers of the legislature are defined and limited; and that those limits may not be mistaken, or forgotten, the constitution is written. To what purpose are powers limited, and to what purpose is that limitation committed to writing, if these limits may, at any time, be passed by those intended to be restrained? The distinction between a government with limited and unlimited powers is abolished, if those limits do not confine the persons on whom they are imposed, and if acts prohibited and acts allowed, are of equal obligation. It is a proposition too plain to be contested, that the constitution controls any legislative act repugnant to it; or, that the legislature may alter the constitution by an ordinary act.

Between these alternatives there is no middle ground. The Constitution is either a superior paramount law, unchangeable by ordinary means, or it is on a level with ordinary legislative acts, and, like other acts, is alterable when the legislature shall please to alter it.

If the former part of the alternative be true, then a legislative act contrary to the constitution is not law; if the latter part be true, then written constitutions are absurd attempts on the part of the people, to limit a power in its own nature illimitable.

Certainly all those who have framed written constitutions contemplate them as forming the fundamental and paramount law of the nation, and, consequently, the theory of every such government must be, that an act of the legislature, repugnant to the constitution, is void.

This theory is essentially attached to a written constitution, and, is consequently, to be considered, by this court, as one of the fundamental principles of our society. It is not therefore to be lost sight of in the further consideration of this subject.

If an act of the legislature, repugnant to the constitution, is void, does it, notwithstanding its invalidity, bind the courts, and oblige them to give it effect? Or, in other words, though it be not law, does it constitute a rule as operative as it was law? . . .

It is emphatically the province and duty of the judicial department to say what the law is. Those who apply the rule to particular cases, must of necessity expound and interpret that rule. If two laws conflict with each other, the courts must decide on the operation of each.

So if a law be in opposition to the constitution, if both the law and the constitution apply to a particular case, so that the court must either decide that case conformably to the constitution, disregarding the law; the court must determine which of these conflicting rules governs the case. This is of the very essence of judicial duty.

If, then, the courts are to regard the constitution, and the constitution is superior to any ordinary act of the legislature, the constitution, and not such ordinary act, must govern the case to which they both apply.

Those, then, who controvert the principle that the constitution is to be considered, in court, as a paramount law, are reduced to the necessity of maintaining that courts must close their eyes on the constitution, and see only the law.

This doctrine would subvert the very foundation of all written constitutions. It would declare that an act which, according to the principles and theory of our government, is entirely void, is yet, in practice, completely obligatory. It would declare that if the legislature shall do what is expressly forbidden, such act, notwithstanding the express prohibition, is in reality effectual. It would be giving to the legislature a practical and real omnipotence, with the same breath which professes to restrict their powers within narrow limits. It is prescribing limits, and declaring that those limits may be passed at pleasure.

That it thus reduces to nothing what we have deemed the greatest improvement on political institutions, a written constitution, would of itself be sufficient in America, where written constitutions have been viewed with so much reverence, for rejecting the construction. But the peculiar expressions of the constitution of the United States furnish additional arguments in favour of its rejection.

The judicial power of the United States is extended to all cases arising under the constitution.

Could it be the intention of those who have this power, to say that in using it the constitution should not be looked into? That a case arising under the constitution should be decided without examining the instrument under which it arises?

This is too extravagant to be maintained.

In some cases, then, the constitution must be looked into by the judges. And if they can open it at all, what part of it are they forbidden to read or to obey? . . . [I]t is apparent, that the framers of the constitution contemplated that instrument as a rule for the government of *courts*, as well as of the legislature.

Why otherwise does it direct the judges to take an oath to support it? This oath certainly applies in an especial manner, to their conduct in their official character. How immoral to impose it on them, if they were to be used as the instruments, and the knowing instruments, for violating what they swear to support!

The oath of office, too, imposed by the legislature, is completely demonstrative of the legislative opinion on this subject. It is in these words:

> "I do solemnly swear that I will administer justice without respect to persons, and do equal right to the poor and the rich; and that I will faithfully and impartially discharge all the duties incumbent on me as _____, according to the best of my abilities and understanding, agreeably to *the constitution* and laws of the United States."

Why does a judge swear to discharge his duties agreeably to the constitution of the United States, if that constitution forms no rule for his government? If it is closed upon him, and cannot be inspected by him? . . .

It is also not entirely unworthy of observation, that in declaring what shall be the *supreme* law of the land, the *constitution* itself is first mentioned; and not the laws of the United States generally, but those only which shall be made in *pursuance* of the constitution, have that rank.

Thus, the particular phraseology of the constitution of the United States confirms and strengthens the principle, supposed to be essential to all written constitutions, that a law repugnant to the constitution is void; and that *courts*, as well as departments, are bound by that instrument.

Notes and Questions

(1) How did the Court determine that Marbury had a right to his commission? What authority supported Chief Justice Marshall's argument that Marbury had a vested right to his commission?

(2) On what basis did the Chief Justice conclude that Marbury could obtain a judicial remedy against the Secretary of State? Is it legally permissible for a federal court to order the President (through his Secretary of State) to deliver a judicial commission? Can you think of an example of a dispute involving the President and the judiciary or Congress that would not be subject to judicial review? *See* § 1.05, *infra*.

(3) Reread section 13 of the Judiciary Act of 1789. Did it authorize mandamus in the action brought by Marbury? What would have been the implications, for Marbury's claim and for the doctrine of judicial review, if the statute had been construed not to permit the lawsuit?

(4) Does the Constitution expressly confer upon the federal courts the power of "judicial review" — the authority to pass on the constitutionality of actions taken by the other branches of the federal government? If not, where did Chief Justice Marshall find the source of that power? See if you can identify and then assess each of the grounds that the Chief Justice argues in support of judicial review.

(5) Does it really make any difference whether the power of judicial review is found in the Constitution or instead is a result of important practical considerations?

(a) "[S]ince this power is not a logical deduction from the structure of the Constitution but only a practical condition upon its successful operation, it need not be exercised whenever a court sees, or thinks it sees, an invasion of the Constitution. It is always a preliminary question how importunately the occasion demands an answer. It may be better to leave the issue to be worked out without authoritative solution; or perhaps the only solution available is one that the court has no adequate means to enforce." Learned Hand, The Bill of Rights 15 (1958).

(b) "The judiciary cannot, as the legislature may, avoid a measure because it approaches the confines of the Constitution. We cannot pass it by because it is doubtful. With whatever doubts, with whatever difficulties, a case may be attended, we must decide it, if it be brought before us. We have no more right to decline the exercise of the jurisdiction which is given, than to usurp that which is not given. The one or the other would be treason to the constitution." *Cohens v. Virginia*, 19 U.S. (6 Wheat.) 264, 404, 5 L. Ed. 257, 402 (1821).

(6) Federal judges are appointed for life tenure and, thus, not directly accountable to the people. Is it undemocratic to allow them to declare invalid the acts of our elected representatives?

(a) "The root difficulty is that judicial review is a countermajoritarian force in our system. . . . [W]hen the Supreme Court declares unconstitutional a legislative act or the action of an elected executive, it thwarts the will of representatives of the actual people of the here and now; it exercises control, not in behalf of the prevailing majority, but against it." ALEXANDER M. BICKEL, THE LEAST DANGEROUS BRANCH 16–17 (1962).[2]

(b) "The attack on judicial review as undemocratic rests on the premise that the Constitution should be allowed to grow without a judicial check. The proponents of this view would have the Constitution mean what the President, the Congress, and the state legislatures say it means. In this way, they contend, the electoral process would determine the course of constitutional development, as it does in countries with plenipotentiary parliaments.

"But the Constitution of the United States does not establish a parliamentary government, and attempts to interpret American government in a parliamentary perspective break down in confusion or absurdity. . . .

"It is a grave oversimplification to contend that no society can be democratic unless its legislature has sovereign powers. . . ." Eugene Rostow, *The Democratic Character of Judicial Review*, 66 HARV. L. REV. 193, 194–196 (1952).[3]

(7) Should we fear that the politically insulated members of the federal judiciary may become too powerful?

(a) Professor Herbert Wechsler has described a number of practical avenues for limiting the federal judiciary generally and the Supreme Court specifically: (1) constitutional amendment; (2) appointment of new judges to fill vacancies; (3) increase in size of the Court; (4) congressional control over the jurisdiction of the courts; and (5) continued litigation of the issue. Herbert Wechsler, *The Courts and the Constitution*, 65 COLUM. L. REV. 1001 (1965). Are these methods effective in limiting the judiciary?

(b) Or is the judiciary's self-imposed restraint the only effective limit?

---

§ 1.05 Judicial Review of Executive Action

The relationship between the President and the Court has often been an uneasy one. On the one hand, the powers vested in the Executive by Article II are only summarily set out, leaving considerable room for growth or shrinkage of power, and ample opportunities for requests for judicial interpretations of presidential power. Thus, the task of shaping the government was largely left to the initiative of future occupants of the important constitutionally created positions. On the other hand, Article III is direct and relatively clear in its command that the federal courts decide cases and controversies arising under the Constitution. Thus, the Supreme Court's potential as the ultimate arbiter of the Constitution's meaning looms in often perilous tension with the tremendous real powers of the American presidency. Indeed, the very notion of a limited supreme power, controlled by law, the bedrock principle of American constitutionalism, is constantly threatened by a modern American presidency that is often regarded as imperial, an institution that is more a person than a branch of government, a person elected by the nation to represent the nation before the world.

United States v. Nixon

United States Supreme Court
418 U.S. 683, 94 S. Ct. 3090, 41 L. Ed. 2d 1039 (1974)

MR. CHIEF JUSTICE BURGER delivered the opinion of the Court.

[On June 17, 1972, agents of the Committee to Re-elect the President were caught as they broke into the Democratic National Headquarters at the Watergate Hotel. The agents implicated officials in President Nixon's re-election campaign, prompting the Senate and House to hold hearings on the Watergate break-in and its apparent cover-up by administration officials. After President Nixon agreed in May 1973 to name Archibald Cox as a special prosecutor to investigate any White House involvement in Watergate, former White House Counsel John Dean implicated President Nixon in the cover-up in June. By February 1974 the House Judiciary Committee had begun impeachment proceedings against the President.]

On March 1, 1974, a grand jury of the United States District Court for the District of Columbia returned an indictment charging seven named individuals [former Attorney General John Mitchell, White House advisers H.R. Haldeman and John Ehrlichman, and four others] with various offenses, including conspiracy to defraud the United States and to obstruct justice. Although he was not designated as such in the indictment, the grand jury named the President, among others, as an unindicted coconspirator. On April 18, 1974, upon motion of the Special Prosecutor, a subpoena *duces tecum* was issued pursuant to Rule 17(c) [of the Federal Rules of Criminal Procedure] to the President by the United States District Court and made returnable on May 2, 1974. This subpoena required the production, in advance of the September 9 trial date, of certain tapes, memoranda, papers, transcripts, or other writings relating to certain precisely identified meetings between the President and others. The Special Prosecutor was able to fix the time, place, and persons present at these discussions because the White House daily logs and appointment records had been delivered to him. On April 30, the President publicly released edited transcripts of 43 conversations; portions of 20 conversations subject to subpoena in the present case were included. On May 1, 1974, the President's counsel filed a "special appearance" and a motion to quash the subpoena under Rule 17(c). This motion was accompanied by a formal claim of privilege. At a subsequent hearing, further motions to expunge the grand jury's action naming the President as an unindicted coconspirator and for protective orders against the disclosure of that information were filed or raised orally by counsel for the President.

On May 20, 1974, the District Court denied the motion to quash and the motions to expunge and for protective orders. It further ordered "the President or any subordinate officer, official, or employee with custody or control of the documents or objects subpoenaed," to deliver to the District Court, on or before May 31, 1974, the originals of all subpoenaed items, as well as an index and analysis of those items, together with tape copies of those portions of the subpoenaed recordings for which transcripts had been released to the public by the President on April 30.

Justiciability

In the District Court, the President's counsel argued that the court lacked jurisdiction to issue the subpoena because the matter was an intra-branch dispute between a subordinate and superior officer of the Executive Branch and hence not subject to judicial resolution. That argument has been renewed in this Court with emphasis on the contention that the dispute does not present a "case" or "controversy" which can be adjudicated in the federal courts. The President's counsel argues that the federal courts should not intrude into areas committed to the other branches of Government. He views the present dispute as essentially a "jurisdictional" dispute within the Executive Branch which he analogizes to a dispute between two congressional committees. Since the Executive Branch has exclusive authority and absolute discretion to decide whether to prosecute a case, it is contended that a President's decision is final in determining what evidence is to be used in a given criminal case. The Special Prosecutor's demand for the items therefore presents, in the view of the President's counsel, a political question under *Baker v. Carr*, 369 U.S. 186 (1962), since it involves a "textually demonstrable" grant of power under Art. II.

The demands of and the resistance to the subpoena present an obvious controversy in the ordinary sense, but that alone is not sufficient to meet the constitutional standards. In the constitutional sense, controversy means more than disagreement and conflict; rather it means the kind of controversy courts traditionally resolve. Here at issue is the production or nonproduction of specified evidence deemed by the Special Prosecutor to be relevant and admissible in a pending criminal case. It is sought by one official of the Executive Branch within the scope of his express authority; it is resisted by the Chief Executive on the ground of his duty to preserve the confidentiality of the communications of the President. Whatever the correct answer on the merits, these issues are "of a type which are traditionally justiciable."

The independent Special Prosecutor with his asserted need for the subpoenaed material in the underlying criminal prosecution is opposed by the President with his steadfast assertion of privilege against disclosure of the material. This setting assures there is "that concrete adverseness which sharpens the presentation of issues upon which the court so largely depends for illumination of difficult constitutional questions." *Baker v. Carr.* Moreover, since the matter is one arising in the regular course of a federal criminal prosecution, it is within the traditional scope of Art. III power.

In light of the uniqueness of the setting in which the conflict arises, the fact that both parties are officers of the Executive Branch cannot be viewed as a barrier to justiciability. It would be inconsistent with the applicable law and regulation, and the unique facts of this case to conclude other than that a justiciable controversy is presented for decision.

The Claim of Privilege

A

Having determined that the requirements of Rule 17(c) were satisfied, we turn to the claim that the subpoena should be quashed because it demands "confidential conversations between a President and his close advisors that it would be inconsistent with the public interest to produce." The first contention is a broad claim that the separation of powers doctrine precludes judicial review of a President's claim of privilege.

In the performance of assigned constitutional duties each branch of the Government must initially interpret the Constitution, and the interpretation of its powers by any branch is due great respect from the others. The President's counsel, as we have noted, reads the Constitution as providing an absolute privilege of confidentiality for all Presidential communications. Many decisions of this Court, however, have unequivocally reaffirmed the holding of *Marbury v. Madison*, that "[i]t is emphatically the province and duty of the judicial department to say what the law is."

Our system of government "requires that federal courts on occasion interpret the Constitution in a manner at variance with the construction given the document by another branch." And in *Baker v. Carr*, the Court stated:

> Deciding whether a matter has in any measure been committed by the Constitution to another branch of government, or whether the action of that branch exceeds whatever authority has been committed, is itself a delicate exercise in constitutional interpretation, and is a responsibility of this Court as ultimate interpreter of the Constitution.

Notwithstanding the deference each branch must accord the others, the "judicial Power of the United States" vested in the federal courts by Art. III, Sec. 1. of the Constitution can no more be shared with the Executive Branch than the Chief Executive, for example, can share with the Judiciary the veto power, or the Congress share with the Judiciary the power to override a Presidential veto. Any other conclusion would be contrary to the basic concept of separation of powers and the checks and balances that flow from the scheme of a tripartite government. We therefore affirm that it is the province and duty of this Court "to say what the law is" with respect to the claim of privilege presented in this case. *Marbury v. Madison.*

In support of his claim of absolute privilege, the President's counsel urges two grounds, one of which is common to all governments and one of which is peculiar to our system of separation of powers. The first ground is the valid need for protection of communications between high Government officials and those who advise and assist them in the performance of their manifold duties; the importance of this confidentiality is too plain to require further discussion. Human experience teaches that those who expect public dissemination of their remarks may temper candor with a concern for appearances and for their own interest to the detriment of the decision making process. Whatever the nature of the privilege of confidentiality of Presidential communications in the exercise of Art. II powers, the privilege can be said to derive from the supremacy of each branch within its own assigned area of constitutional duties. Certain powers and privileges flow from the nature of enumerated powers;[4] the protection of the confidentiality of Presidential communications has similar constitutional underpinnings.

The second ground asserted by the President's counsel in support of the claim of absolute privilege rests on the doctrine of separation of powers. Here it is argued that the independence of the Executive Branch within its own sphere insulates a President from a judicial subpoena in an ongoing criminal prosecution, and thereby protects confidential Presidential communications.

However, neither the doctrine of separation of powers, nor the need for confidentiality of high-level communications, without more, can sustain an absolute, unqualified Presidential privilege of immunity from judicial process under all circumstances. The President's need for complete candor and objectivity from advisers calls for great deference from the courts. However, when the privilege depends solely on the broad, undifferentiated claim of public interest in the confidentiality of such conversations, a confrontation with other values arises. Absent a claim of need to protect military, diplomatic, or sensitive national security secrets, we find it difficult to accept the argument that even the very important interest in confidentiality of Presidential communications is significantly diminished by production of such material for *in camera* inspection with all the protection that a district court will be obliged to provide.

---

4. [Court's Footnote 16] The Special Prosecutor argues that there is no provision in the Constitution for a Presidential privilege as to the President's communications corresponding to the privilege of Members of Congress under the Speech or Debate Clause. But the silence of the Constitution on this score is not dispositive. "The rule of constitutional interpretation announced in *McCulloch v. Maryland*, 4 L. Ed. 579, 4 Wheat. 316, that that which was reasonably appropriate and relevant to the exercise of a granted power was to be considered as accompanying the grant, has been so universally applied that it suffices merely to state it." *Marshall v. Gordon*, 243 U.S. 521, 537 (1917).

The impediment that an absolute, unqualified privilege would place in the way of the primary constitutional duty of the Judicial Branch to do justice in criminal prosecutions would plainly conflict with the function of the courts under Art. III. In designing the structure of our Government and dividing and allocating the sovereign power among three co-equal branches, the Framers of the Constitution sought to provide a comprehensive system, but the separate powers were not intended to operate with absolute independence.

To read the Art. II powers of the President as providing an absolute privilege as against a subpoena essential to enforcement of criminal statutes on no more than a generalized claim of the public interest in confidentiality of nonmilitary and nondiplomatic discussions would upset the constitutional balance of "a workable government" and gravely impair the role of the courts under Art. III.

Since we conclude that the legitimate needs of the judicial process may outweigh Presidential privilege, it is necessary to resolve those competing interests in a manner that preserves the essential functions of each branch. The right and indeed the duty to resolve that question does not free the Judiciary from according high respect to the representations made on behalf of the President. *United States v. Burr*, 25 F. Cas. 187, 190, 191–192 (No. 14,694) (C.C. Va. 1807).

The expectation of a President to the confidentiality of his conversations and correspondence, like the claim of confidentiality of judicial deliberations, for example, has all the values to which we accord deference for the privacy of all citizens and, added to those values, is the necessity for protection of the public interest in candid, objective, and even blunt or harsh opinions in Presidential decisionmaking. A President and those who assist him must be free to explore alternatives in the process of shaping policies and making decisions and to do so in a way many would be unwilling to express except privately. These are the considerations justifying a presumptive privilege for Presidential communications. The privilege is fundamental to the operation of Government and inextricably rooted in the separation of powers under the Constitution.

But this presumptive privilege must be considered in light of our historic commitment to the rule of law. This is nowhere more profoundly manifest than in our view that "the twofold aim [of criminal justice] is that guilt shall not escape or innocence suffer." We have elected to employ an adversary system of criminal justice in which the parties contest all issues before a court of law. The need to develop all relevant facts in the adversary system is both fundamental and comprehensive. The ends of criminal justice would be defeated if judgments were to be founded on a partial or speculative presentation of the facts. The very integrity of the judicial system and public confidence in the system depend on full disclosure of all the facts, within the framework of the rules of evidence. To ensure that justice is done, it is imperative to the function of courts that compulsory process be available for the production of evidence needed either by the prosecution or by the defense.

Only recently the Court restated the ancient proposition of law, albeit in the context of a grand jury inquiry rather than a trial, "that 'the public has a right to every man's evidence,' except for those persons protected by a constitutional, common-law, or statutory privilege." The privileges referred to by the Court are designed to protect weighty and legitimate competing interests.

In this case the President challenges a subpoena served on him as a third party requiring the production of materials for use in a criminal prosecution; he does so on the claim that he has a privilege against disclosure of confidential communications. He does not place his claim of privilege on the ground they are military or diplomatic secrets. As to these areas of Art. II duties the courts have traditionally shown the utmost deference to Presidential responsibilities.

No case of the Court, however, has extended this high degree of deference to a President's generalized interest in confidentiality. Nowhere in the Constitution, as we have noted earlier, is there any explicit reference to a privilege of confidentiality, yet to the extent this interest relates to the effective discharge of a President's powers, it is constitutionally based.

The right to the production of all evidence at a criminal trial similarly has constitutional dimensions. It is the manifest duty of the courts to vindicate those guarantees, and to accomplish that it is essential that all relevant and admissible evidence be produced.

In this case we must weigh the importance of the general privilege of confidentiality of Presidential communications in performance of the President's responsibilities against the inroads of such a privilege on the fair administration of criminal justice.[5] The interest in preserving confidentiality is weighty indeed and entitled to great respect. However, we cannot conclude that advisers will be moved to temper the candor of their remarks by the infrequent occasions of disclosure because of the possibility that such conversations will be called for in the context of a criminal prosecution.

On the other hand, the allowance of the privilege to withhold evidence that is demonstrably relevant in a criminal trial would cut deeply into the guarantee of due process of law and gravely impair the basic function of the courts. A President's acknowledged need for confidentiality in the communications of his office is general in nature, whereas the constitutional need for production of relevant evidence in a criminal proceeding is specific and central to the fair adjudication of a particular criminal case in the administration of justice. Without access to specific facts

---

5. [Court's Footnote 19] We are not here concerned with the balance between the President's generalized interest in confidentiality and the need for relevant evidence in civil litigation, nor with that between the confidentiality interest and congressional demands for information, nor with the President's interest in preserving state secrets. We address only the conflict between the President's assertion of a generalized privilege of confidentiality and the constitutional need for relevant evidence in criminal trials.

a criminal prosecution may be totally frustrated. The President's broad interest in confidentiality of communications will not be vitiated by disclosure of a limited number of conversations preliminarily shown to have some bearing on the pending criminal cases.

We conclude that when the ground for asserting privilege as to subpoenaed materials sought for use in a criminal trial is based only on the generalized interest in confidentiality, it cannot prevail over the fundamental demands of due process of law in the fair administration of criminal justice. The generalized assertion of privilege must yield to the demonstrated, specific need for evidence in a pending criminal trial.

We have earlier determined that the District Court did not err in authorizing the issuance of the subpoena. If a President concludes that compliance with a subpoena would be injurious to the public interest he may properly, as was done here, invoke a claim of privilege on the return of the subpoena. Upon receiving a claim of privilege from the Chief Executive, it became the further duty of the District Court to treat the subpoenaed material as presumptively privileged and to require the Special Prosecutor to demonstrate that the Presidential material was "essential to the justice of the [pending criminal] case." *United States v. Burr*. [W]e affirm the order of the District Court that subpoenaed materials be transmitted to that court. We now turn to the important question of the District Court's responsibilities in conducting the *in camera* examination of Presidential materials or communications delivered under the compulsion of the subpoena *duces tecum*.

Enforcement of the subpoena *duces tecum* was stayed pending this Court's resolution of the issues raised by the petitions for *certiorari*. Those issues now having been disposed of, the matter of implementation will rest with the District Court. "[T]he guard, furnished to [the President] to protect him from being harassed by vexatious and unnecessary subpoenas, is to be looked for in the conduct of a [district] court after those subpoenas have issued; not in any circumstance which is to precede their being issued." *United States v. Burr*. Statements that meet the test of admissibility and relevance must be isolated; all other material must be excised. At this stage the District Court is not limited to representations of the Special Prosecutor as to the evidence sought by the subpoena; the material will be available to the District Court. It is elementary that *in camera* inspection of evidence is always a procedure calling for scrupulous protection against any release or publication of material not found by the court, at that stage, probably admissible in evidence and relevant to the issues of the trial for which it is sought. That being true of an ordinary situation, it is obvious that the District Court has a very heavy responsibility to see to it that Presidential conversations, which are either not relevant or not admissible, are accorded that high degree of respect due the President of the United States. Mr. Chief Justice Marshall, sitting as a trial judge in the *Burr* case, *supra*, was extraordinarily careful to point out that

> [i]n no case of this kind would a court be required to proceed against the President as against an ordinary individual.

Marshall's statement cannot be read to mean in any sense that a President is above the law, but relates to the singularly unique role under Art. II of a President's communications and activities, related to the performance of duties under that Article. Moreover, a President's communications and activities encompass a vastly wider range of sensitive material than would be true of any "ordinary individual." It is therefore necessary in the public interest to afford Presidential confidentiality the greatest protection consistent with the fair administration of justice. The need for confidentiality even as to idle conversations with associates in which casual reference might be made concerning political leaders within the country or foreign statesmen is too obvious to call for further treatment. We have no doubt that the District Judge will at all times accord to Presidential records that high degree of deference suggested in *United States v. Burr.*

Mr. Justice Rehnquist took no part in the consideration or decision of these cases.

In the summer of 2018, the New York County District Attorney's Office opened an investigation into what it described as "business transactions involving multiple individuals whose conduct may have violated state law." A year later, the office — acting on behalf of a grand jury — served a subpoena on the personal accounting firm of President Trump. The subpoena sought financial records relating to the President and business organizations affiliated with him, including "[t]ax returns and related schedules," from "2011 to the present."

The President, acting in his personal capacity, sued district attorney Vance and the accounting firm in Federal District Court to enjoin enforcement of the subpoena. He argued that, under Article II and the Supremacy Clause, a sitting President enjoys absolute immunity from state criminal process. He asked the court to issue a "declaratory judgment that the subpoena is invalid and unenforceable while the President is in office" and to permanently enjoin the district attorney "from taking any action to enforce the subpoena." The dispute reached the Supreme Court in 2020.

Trump v. Vance
United States Supreme Court
140 S. Ct. 2412 (2020)

Chief Justice Roberts delivered the opinion of the Court.

[This] case involves — so far as we and the parties can tell — the first state criminal subpoena directed to a President. The President contends that the subpoena is unenforceable.

[In] the summer of 1807, Aaron Burr, the former Vice President, was on trial for treason. [In] the lead-up to trial, Burr [moved] for a subpoena *duces tecum* directed at President Jefferson. The draft subpoena required the President to produce [a] letter from [Burr's accuser, General James] Wilkinson and accompanying documents. [The] prosecution opposed the request, arguing that a President could not be subjected to such a subpoena and that the letter might contain state secrets. Following four days of argument, Marshall announced his ruling to a packed chamber. The President, Marshall declared, does not "stand exempt from the general provisions of the constitution" or, in particular, the Sixth Amendment's guarantee that those accused have compulsory process for obtaining witnesses for their defense. At common law the "single reservation" to the duty to testify in response to a subpoena was "the case of the king," whose "dignity" was seen as "incompatible" with appearing "under the process of the court." But, as Marshall explained, a king is born to power and can "do no wrong." The President, by contrast, is "of the people" and subject to the law.

[In] the two centuries since the Burr trial, successive Presidents have accepted Marshall's ruling that the Chief Executive is subject to subpoena. [The] bookend to Marshall's ruling came in 1974 [in] *United States v. Nixon.* [Invoking] the common law maxim that "the public has a right to every man's evidence," the Court [concluded] that the President's "generalized assertion of privilege must yield to the demonstrated, specific need for evidence in a pending criminal trial." Two weeks later, President Nixon dutifully released the tapes.

The history surveyed above all involved federal criminal proceedings. Here we are confronted for the first time with a subpoena issued to the President by a local grand jury operating under the supervision of a state court. [We] begin with the question of absolute immunity. The President's primary contention [is] that complying with state criminal subpoenas would necessarily divert the Chief Executive from his duties. [But] *Nixon v. Fitzgerald* [457 U.S. 731 (1982) (the President is absolutely immune from defending a civil lawsuit for damages if based on his official actions)] did not hold that distraction was sufficient to confer absolute immunity. [Indeed,] we expressly rejected immunity based on distraction alone 15 years later in *Clinton v. Jones* [considered in Chapter 2].

[The] President next claims that the stigma of being subpoenaed will undermine his leadership at home and abroad. [But] even if a tarnished reputation were a cognizable impairment, there is nothing inherently stigmatizing about a President performing the citizen's normal duty of furnishing information relevant to a criminal investigation. [Finally,] the President warn[s] that subjecting Presidents to state criminal subpoenas will make them "easily identifiable targets" for harassment. But we rejected a nearly identical argument in *Clinton.*

[We] recognize [that] harassing subpoenas could, under certain circumstances, threaten the independence or effectiveness of the Executive. Even so, in *Clinton* we found that the risk of harassment was not "serious" because federal courts have the tools to deter and, where necessary, dismiss vexatious civil suits. And, while we cannot ignore the possibility that state prosecutors may have political motivations, here again the law already seeks to protect against the predicted abuse. [Grand] juries are prohibited from engaging in arbitrary fishing expeditions and initiating investigations out of malice or an intent to harass. [In] the event of such harassment, a President would be entitled to the protection of federal courts.

[And the] Supremacy Clause prohibits state judges and prosecutors from interfering with a President's official duties. [Federal] law allows a President to challenge any allegedly unconstitutional influence in a federal forum, as the President has done here. Given these safeguards and the Court's precedents, we cannot conclude that absolute immunity is necessary or appropriate under Article II or the Supremacy Clause. [On] that point the Court is unanimous.

We next consider whether a state grand jury subpoena seeking a President's private papers must satisfy a heightened need standard. [We] disagree, for three reasons. First, such a heightened standard would extend protection designed for official documents to the President's private papers. [Second,] neither the Solicitor General nor Justice Alito has established that heightened protection against state subpoenas is necessary for the Executive to fulfill his Article II functions. [Finally,] in the absence of a need to protect the Executive, the public interest in fair and effective law enforcement cuts in favor of comprehensive access to evidence. Requiring a state grand jury to meet a heightened standard of need would hobble the grand jury's ability to acquire all information that might possibly bear on its investigation.

[A] President may avail himself of the same protections available to every other citizen. These include the right to challenge the subpoena on any grounds permitted by state law, which usually include bad faith and undue burden or breadth. [A] President can raise subpoena-specific constitutional challenges, in either a state or federal forum. [In] addition, the Executive can [show] that compliance with a particular subpoena would impede his constitutional duties. [At] that point, a court should use its inherent authority to quash or modify the subpoena, if necessary to ensure that such interference with the President's duties would not occur.

JUSTICE KAVANAUGH, joined by JUSTICE GORSUCH, concurring in the judgment.

[I] would apply the longstanding *Nixon* "demonstrated, specific need" standard to this case. [In] my view, lower courts in cases of this sort involving a President will almost invariably have to begin by delving into why the State wants the information; why and how much the State needs the information, including whether the State could obtain the information elsewhere; and whether compliance with the subpoena would unduly burden or interfere with a President's official duties.

JUSTICE THOMAS, dissenting.

I agree with the majority that the President is not entitled to absolute immunity from issuance of the subpoena. But he may be entitled to relief against its enforcement. If the President can show that his duties as chief magistrate demand his whole time for national objects, he is entitled to relief from enforcement of the subpoena. [The] Burr standard places the burden on the President but also requires courts to take pains to respect the demands on the President's time. The Constitution vests the President with extensive powers and responsibilities, and courts are poorly situated to conduct a searching review of the President's assertion that he is unable to comply.

JUSTICE ALITO, dissenting.

[A] State may not block or interfere with the lawful work of the National Government. [A] sitting President may not be prosecuted by a local district attorney. [If] a sitting President were charged in New York County, would he be arrested and fingerprinted? He would presumably be required to appear for arraignment in criminal court, where the judge would set the conditions for his release. Could he be sent to Rikers Island or be required to post bail? [This] entire imagined scene is farcical. The right of all the People to a functioning government would be sacrificed.

Notes and Questions

(1) Are the results in *Nixon* and *Trump v. Vance* compelled by *Marbury*?

(a) "[A]s the Court noted, acts of Congress are declared unconstitutional notwithstanding that the power to legislate is vested exclusively in Congress. What makes the implied power of the Executive more sacrosanct than the express power of Congress? In furnishing an unequivocal answer to 'Who Decides?' the limits of the respective powers conferred by the Constitution, the Court merely affirmed a doctrine of long standing, expressed by Chief Justice Marshall in *Marbury v. Madison*: The Court is the ultimate interpreter of the Constitution; and since the Constitution sets up a Government of limited powers, it is the function of the Court to decide their parameters." Raoul Berger, *The Incarnation of Executive Privilege*, 22 UCLA L. REV. 4–5 (1974).[6]

(b) "The opinion in *United States v. Nixon* tended to merge and blur separate issues. And the linchpin in intertwining them was the excessive use of *Marbury v. Madison*. Chief Justice Burger's handling of the issue suggests that recognizing absolute executive privilege as a matter of constitutional interpretation would somehow be contrary to *Marbury v. Madison*'s view of the proper judicial role. But there is nothing in *Marbury v. Madison* that precludes a constitutional interpretation which gives final authority to another branch." Gerald Gunther, *Judicial Hegemony and Legislative Autonomy: The Nixon Case and the Impeachment Process*, 22 UCLA L. REV. 30, 34–35 (1974).[7]

(2) Should the judiciary be more reluctant to act as an umpire in disputes regarding separation of powers than in those regarding express prohibitions on Congress or the Executive? President Trump argued that Article II and the Supremacy Clause give a sitting President absolute immunity from state criminal subpoenas because compliance with those subpoenas would categorically impair a President's performance of his constitutional functions. Why did the Court reject his

---

argument? Why was President Nixon's argument that the dispute was classically political not persuasive, especially in view of the recognition by the Court in *Marbury* that some actions by the President would not be subject to judicial review? Is the more appropriate remedy for presidential misfeasance, or presidential foot-dragging, the political rather than the judicial process?

(a) "[W]hen the Court is placed in the position of umpiring between the departments of government, very special considerations attend the exercise of judicial power. The case is commonly one on which the Constitution is silent; where this is true, the Court has to work on the basis of just the sort of speculative deduction from structure and spirit. Then, too, it often appears that the matter would probably be better handled by compromise and settlement than by a clean-cut judicial declaration of right. Both these points are exhibited by the example, already mentioned, of the contest between the President and Congress on the power of the latter to subpoena Executive files. Congress has a legitimate interest, under many of its enumerated powers, in the conduct of the Executive Department. The President, on the other hand, has primary responsibility for the conduct of his own business, and is empowered to conduct it efficiently; efficiency often calls for secrecy. The Constitution gives no help at all in reconciling these contradictory considerations. For a long time now, the conflicting claims have been successfully compromised. If a case reached the Court, I should think wisdom would dictate extreme reluctance to decide, and that decision, if decision could not be avoided, should be placed on the narrowest possible grounds, so that the greatest future flexibility might be retained. This, too, can be thought of as a sort of 'judicial restraint,' but, again, it is a special sort, called into play by special considerations, and it cannot be made the basis for generalization beyond the reach of those considerations." CHARLES BLACK, JR., THE PEOPLE AND THE COURT 93–94 (1960).[8]

(b) "Question-begging aside, the Court's decision in *United States v. Nixon* is validated by all the modern justifications for judicial review.

"The possible concern, of course, is that in such a situation the judiciary may appear to be an umpire 'deciding [its] own case.' In *United States v. Nixon* itself, the Supreme Court said that the absolute privilege claimed by the President would place an impediment 'in the way of the primary constitutional duty of the Judicial Branch to do justice in criminal prosecutions,' which 'would plainly conflict with the function of the courts under Art. III.'" In the contest of powers, the judiciary ruled for the judicial power. Is judicial review less justifiable in these circumstances?

---

8. Copyright © 1960 by Charles L. Black, Jr. Reprinted by permission of Macmillan Publishing Co.

"In one perspective, judicial review seems *more* justified when the judicial branch is protecting its own function. Thus *Marbury v. Madison* has been interpreted as an example of 'defensive' judicial review, in which the Court protected the judiciary against congressional encroachment in the form of an enlargement of its original jurisdiction. Arguably judicial review is easiest to accept when the Supreme Court 'draws upon one's sympathy to maintain the Court as a co-ordinate branch of government, and not as a superior branch.' But *United States v. Nixon* goes further: it authorizes the courts not merely to refuse to take on a task unconstitutionally assigned to them, but also to command action by the President with respect to a function which the President claims to lie within his discretion. The protection-of-the-judiciary argument makes *United States v. Nixon* no stronger than the ordinary case of judicial review of the constitutionality of action by the political branches."

"Neither, however, is the case for judicial review weaker when the judiciary is one of the contending branches in a clash of claims to governmental power. In the context of *United States v. Nixon*, the chief alternative — as argued by counsel for the President — would be to allow a presidential claim of privilege to determine the issue finally. This solution obviously does not resolve the problem of the umpire 'deciding his own case': it substitutes a political umpire for a judicial one. The President would be an 'interested party' in the pejorative sense of that term." Kenneth L. Karst & Harold W. Horowitz, *Presidential Prerogative and Judicial Process*, 22 UCLA L. Rev. 47, 56–58 (1974).[9]

(3) There is no explicit grant of executive immunity in the Constitution; nor was it the subject of debate at the Convention. However, the existence of executive immunity has been asserted by Presidents since 1796, when President Washington refused a request by the House of Representatives for all correspondence relating to the Jay Treaty, although he provided it to the Senate. 5 Annals of Cong. 760 (1796). Can you see why the Jay Treaty episode may not supply good authority for a general claim of executive privilege? Former Watergate Special Prosecutor Archibald Cox reviewed 27 additional instances since the Washington administration where Presidents refused to comply with congressional requests for information. Archibald Cox, *Executive Privilege*, 122 U. Pa. L. Rev. 1383, 1395–1405 (1974). Cox concluded that "nothing appears which even approaches a solid historical practice of recognizing claims of executive privilege based upon an undifferentiated need for preserving the secrecy of internal communications within the executive branch." *Id.* at 1404. Does such historical practice help or hinder future claims by Presidents for executive privilege?

---

9. Copyright © 1974 by U.C.L.A. Law Review and Fred B. Rothman & Co. Reprinted by permission.

(4) President Nixon's first argument was that the requested privilege derived from the need for confidentiality in carrying out important Article II tasks. The Court characterized the claim as "common to all governments" derived from "the supremacy of each branch within its own assigned area of constitutional duties." Although the specific claim for privilege was denied on the facts, the Court recognized the existence of a legitimate constitutionally-based executive privilege. If not mentioned in the text, what is its source? Does the opinion imply the existence of a "necessary and proper" clause in Article II? If not, is the privilege bottomed on some extra-constitutional principle "common to all governments"? Is footnote 16 helpful in this regard?

(5) Consider this position:

> "Executive privilege" — the President's claim of constitutional authority to withhold information from Congress (or the judicial branch) — is a myth. Unlike most myths, the origins of which are lost in the mists of antiquity, "executive privilege" is a product of the nineteenth century, fashioned by a succession of presidents who created "precedents" to suit the occasion.

RAOUL BERGER, EXECUTIVE PRIVILEGE: A CONSTITUTIONAL MYTH 1 (1974). If the historical precedents are weak, as Berger suggests, did the Court persuasively pin down the constitutional legitimacy of the executive privilege? See MARK J. ROZELL, EXECUTIVE PRIVILEGE: THE DILEMMA OF SECRECY AND DEMOCRATIC ACCOUNTABILITY (1994); Symposium: United States v. Nixon, 22 UCLA L. REV. 1 (1974).

(6) The privilege recognized by the Court in Nixon is a qualified one, not the absolute privilege which the President sought. Would the judicial balancing which weighs a claim of qualified privilege be employed in a claim of privilege based on the asserted need to protect military or national security secrets? How should such a claim be decided? Why did the Trump v. Vance Court refuse to apply the "demonstrated, specific need" standard from Nixon?

(7) A qualified privilege may be appropriately conditioned. To what extent, if at all, may the Congress legislate to condition or curtail executive privilege? Recall that the Nixon Court expressly declined to address that issue in the opinion (see footnote 19).

Problem A

Assume that congressional committees investigating alleged foreign interference in the 2028 presidential election sought access to audio recordings of meetings between the President and White House staff that occurred in the first weeks of the administration, during a period when the media reported that high-level White House meetings discussed how Chinese disinformation campaigns benefited the election prospects of the incoming President. How should the Supreme Court decide the President's appeal from a lower court order that he turn the recordings over to Congress? Would your answer change if the President alleged that the materials sought by the congressional committees are part of or are intermingled with other White House conversations involving sensitive national security information?

§ 1.06 Judicial Review of State Action

Martin v. Hunter's Lessee

United States Supreme Court
14 U.S. (1 Wheat.) 304, 4 L. Ed. 97 (1816)

[*Martin v. Hunter's Lessee* arose out of a dispute regarding title to Virginia land formerly held by Lord Fairfax. Virginia claimed to have acquired the property under state law and in 1789 conveyed it to Hunter and his heirs. Hunter's lessee brought an ejectment action in state court claiming title under state law. The Fairfax heirs, including Martin, asserted their right to the property under federal treaties. The Virginia Court of Appeals decided in favor of Hunter's lessee. The Supreme Court, however, reversed, holding that a treaty of 1794 with Great Britain confirmed the title remaining in the Fairfax heirs. *Fairfax's Devisee v. Hunter's Lessee*, 3 L. Ed. 453, 7 Cranch 603 (1813). The Supreme Court remanded the case to the Virginia Court of Appeals with directions to obey the Supreme Court's mandate. The Virginia Court of Appeals, however, refused to comply, holding that § 25 of the Judiciary Act was unconstitutional to the extent it extended the appellate jurisdiction of the Supreme Court to the Virginia court. Section 25 authorized Supreme Court review of decisions by the highest state courts in three instances: (1) where the state court held invalid a federal law or treaty; (2) where the state court upheld a state law that had been challenged as contrary to the Constitution, treaties or laws of the United States; and (3) where the state court decided against a title, right, privilege, or exemption claimed under the Constitution, treaties, or federal law.]

STORY, J. delivered the opinion of the court:

This is a writ of error from the Court of Appeals of Virginia, founded upon the refusal of that court to obey the mandate of this court, requiring the judgment rendered in this very cause, at February term, 1813, to be carried into due execution. The following is the judgment of the Court of Appeals rendered on the mandate:

> The court is unanimously of opinion that the appellate power of the Supreme Court of the United States does not extend to this court, under a sound construction of the constitution of the United States; that so much of the 25th section of the act of Congress to establish the judicial courts of the United States, as extends the appellate jurisdiction of the Supreme Court to this court, is not in pursuance of the constitution of the United States; that the writ of error, in this cause, was improvidently allowed under the authority of that act; that the proceedings thereon in the Supreme Court were, *coram non judice* in relation to this court, and that obedience to its mandate be declined by the court.

Before proceeding to the principal questions, it may not be unfit to dispose of some preliminary considerations which have grown out of the arguments at the bar.

The constitution of the United States was ordained and established, not only by the states in their sovereign capacities, but emphatically, as the preamble of the constitution declares, by the people of the United States. There can be no doubt that it was competent to the people to invest the general government with all the powers which they might deem proper and necessary; to extend or restrain these powers according to their own good pleasure, and to give them a paramount and supreme authority. As little doubt can there be that the people had a right to prohibit to the states the exercise of any powers which were, in their judgment, incompatible with the objects of the general compact; to make the powers of the state governments, in given cases, subordinate to those of the nation, or to reserve to themselves those sovereign authorities which they might not choose to delegate out of existing state sovereignties, nor a surrender of powers already existing in state institutions, for the powers of the states depend upon their own constitutions; and the people of every state had the right to modify and restrain them, according to their own views of policy or principle. On the other hand, it is perfectly clear that the sovereign powers vested in the state governments, by their respective constitutions, remained unaltered and unimpaired, except so far as they were granted to the government of the United States.

These deductions do not rest upon general reasoning, plain and obvious as they seem to be. They have been positively recognized by one of the articles in amendment of the constitution, which declares that the powers not delegated to the United States by the constitution, nor prohibited by it to the states, are reserved to the states respectively, or to the people.

The government, then, of the United States, can claim no powers which are not granted to it by the constitution, and the powers actually granted, must be such as are expressly given, or given by necessary implication.

The constitution unavoidably deals in general language. It did not suit the purposes of the people, in framing this great charter of our liberties, to provide for minute specifications of its powers, or to declare the means by which those powers should be carried into execution. It was foreseen that this would be a perilous and difficult, if not an impracticable, task. The instrument was not intended to provide merely for the exigencies of a few years, but was to endure through a long lapse of ages, the events of which were locked up in the inscrutable purposes of Providence. It could not be foreseen what new changes and modifications of power might be indispensable to effectuate the general objects of the charter; and restrictions and specifications which, at the present might seem salutary, might, in the end, prove the overthrow of the system itself.

With these principles in view — principles in respect to which no difference of opinion ought to be indulged — let us now proceed to the interpretation of the constitution, so far regards the great points in controversy.

The third article of the constitution is that which must principally attract our attention.

The appellate power is not limited by the terms of the third article to any particular courts. The words are, "the judicial power (which includes appellate power) shall extend to all cases," etc., and "in all other cases before mentioned the Supreme Court shall have appellate jurisdiction." It is the case, then, and not the court, that gives the jurisdiction.

[I]t is plain that the framers of the constitution did contemplate that cases within the judicial cognizance of the United States not only might but would arise in the state courts, in the exercise of their ordinary jurisdiction. With this view the sixth article declares, that "this constitution, and the laws of the United States which shall be made in pursuance thereof, and all treaties made, or which shall be made, under the authority of the United States, shall be the supreme law of the land, and the judges in every state shall be bound thereby, anything in the constitution or laws of any state to the contrary notwithstanding." It is obvious that this obligation is imperative upon the state judges in their official, and not merely in their private, capacities. From the very nature of their judicial duties they would be called upon to pronounce the law applicable to the case in judgment. They were not to decide merely according to the laws or constitution of the state, but according to the constitution, laws and treaties of the United States — "the supreme law of the land."

It must, therefore, be conceded that the constitution not only contemplated, but meant to provide for cases within the scope of the judicial power of the United States, which might yet depend before state tribunals. It was foreseen that in the exercise of their ordinary jurisdiction, state courts would incidentally take cognizance of cases arising under the constitution, the laws and treaties of the United States. Yet to all these cases the judicial power, by the very terms of the constitution, is to extend. It cannot extend by original jurisdiction if that was already rightfully and exclusively attached in the state courts, which (as has been already shown) may occur; it must, therefore, extend by appellate jurisdiction, or not at all. It would seem to follow that the appellate power of the United States must, in such cases, extend to state tribunals; and if in such cases, there is no reason why it should not equally attach upon all others within the purview of the constitution.

It has been argued that such an appellate jurisdiction over state courts is inconsistent with the genius of our governments, and the spirit of the constitution. That the latter was never designed to act upon state sovereignties, but only upon the people, and that if the power exists, it will materially impair the sovereignty of the states, and the independence of their courts. We cannot yield to the force of this reasoning; it assumes principles which we cannot admit, and draws conclusions to which we do not yield our assent. The courts of the United States can, without question, review the proceedings of the executive and legislative authorities of the states, and if they are found to be contrary to the constitution, may declare them to be of no legal validity. Surely the exercise of the same right over judicial tribunals is not a higher or more dangerous act of sovereign power.

Nor can such a right be deemed to impair the independence of state judges. It is assuming the very ground in controversy to assert that they possess an absolute independence of the United States. In respect to the powers granted to the United States, they are not independent; they are expressly bound to obedience by the letter of the constitution; and if they should unintentionally transcend their authority, or misconstrue the constitution, there is no more reason for giving their judgments an absolute and irresistible force than for giving it to the acts of other coordinate departments of state sovereignty.

It is further argued that no great public mischief can result from a construction which shall limit the appellate power of the United States to cases in their own courts; first, because state judges are bound by an oath to support the constitution of the United States, and must be presumed to be men of learning and integrity; and secondly, because Congress must have an unquestionable right to remove all cases within the scope of the judicial power from the state courts to the courts of the United States, at any time before final judgment, though not after final judgment. As to the first reason — admitting that the judges of the state courts are, and always will be, of as much learning, integrity, and wisdom, as those of the courts of the United States (which we very cheerfully admit) — it does not aid the argument. It is manifest that the constitution has proceeded upon a theory of its own, and given or withheld powers according to the judgment of the American people, by whom it was adopted. We can only construe its powers, and cannot inquire into the policy or principles which induced the grant of them. The constitution has presumed (whether rightly or wrongly we do not inquire) that state attachments, state prejudices, state jealousies and state interests, might sometimes obstruct, or control, or be supposed to obstruct or control, the regular administration of justice. Hence, in controversies between states; between citizens of different states; between a state and its citizens, or foreigners, and between citizens and foreigners, it enables the parties, under the authority of Congress, to have the controversies heard, tried, and determined before the national tribunals. No other reason than that which has been stated can be assigned, why some, at least, of those cases would not have been left to the cognizance of the state courts. In respect to the other enumerated cases — the cases arising under the constitution, laws, and treaties of the United States, cases affecting ambassadors and other public ministers, and cases of admiralty and maritime jurisdiction — reasons of a higher and more extensive nature, touching the safety, peace, and sovereignty of the nation, might well justify a grant of exclusive jurisdiction.

This is not all. A motive of another kind, perfectly compatible with the most sincere respect for state tribunals, might induce the grant of appellate power over their decisions. That motive is the importance, and even necessity of uniformity of decisions throughout the whole United States, upon all subjects within the purview of the constitution. Judges of equal learning and integrity, in different states, might differently interpret a statute, or a treaty of the United States, or even the constitution itself. If there were no revising authority to control these jarring and discordant judgments, and harmonize them into uniformity, the laws, the treaties, and the constitution of the United States would be different in different states, and might, perhaps, never have precisely the same construction, obligation, or efficacy, in any two states. The public mischiefs that would attend such a state of things would be truly deplorable; and it cannot be believed.

On the whole, the court is of the opinion that the appellate power of the United States does extend to cases pending in the state courts; and that the 25th section of the judiciary act, which authorizes the exercise of this jurisdiction in the specified cases, by a writ of error, is supported by the letter and spirit of the constitution. We find no clause in that instrument which limits this power; and we dare not impose a limitation where the people have not been disposed to create one.

[*Reversed.*]

Notes and Questions

(1) What is the source of the Supreme Court's power to review the constitutionality of actions taken by state governments?

(2) Is the source of such power more easily found in the constitution than the power asserted in *Marbury*?

(3) Does *Martin* threaten the independence of state governments and the basic structure of "Our Federalism" which has been described as

> a system in which there is sensitivity to the legitimate interests of both State and National Governments, and in which the National Government, anxious though it may be to vindicate and to protect federal rights and federal interests, always endeavors to do so in ways that will not unduly interfere with the legitimate activities of the States?

Younger v. Harris, 401 U.S. 37 (1971).

(4) Do you agree with the following observation by Justice Holmes?

> I do not think the United States would come to an end if we lost our power to declare an Act of Congress void. I do think the Union would be imperiled if we could not make that declaration as to the laws of the several states.

OLIVER W. HOLMES, JR., COLLECTED LEGAL PAPERS 295–296 (1920).

(5) Compare the *Martin* decision with the Supreme Court's resolution of the gun control disputes in *McDonald* and *Bruen*. Were the answers to the gun control questions determined by the Court's reasoning and holding in *Martin*? Would a decision in favor of the Illinois cities or New York State have been inconsistent with *Martin*?

(6) In *Moore v. Harper*, 143 S. Ct. 2065 (2023), the Court ruled 6-3 that the North Carolina Supreme Court had authority to strike down the state legislature's gerrymandered congressional map. In doing so, the Court rejected the independent state legislature theory (ISLT), which claims that the Elections Clause in the Constitution (Art. 1, §4, cl. 1) gives state legislatures essentially complete authority over

the running of federal elections in their state and bars state courts from reviewing their districting decisions. Two state legislators argued that the ISLT barred the
North Carolina courts from hearing constitutional challenges to its congressional
maps. Citing *Marbury v. Madison*, the Court ruled that the Elections Clause "does
not insulate state legislatures from the ordinary exercise of state judicial review."
Accordingly, the North Carolina Supreme Court may continue to rule on the constitutionality of the state's congressional map, and the U.S. Supreme Court may
provide oversight to ensure that state courts do not "transgress the ordinary boundaries of judicial review." Can you see how the decision in *Moore* is a big win for the
authority of state courts, as well as a reaffirmation of the doctrine of judicial review?

§ 1.07 Contemporary Sovereignty Problems

Cooper v. Aaron

United States Supreme Court
358 U.S. 1, 78 S. Ct. 1401, 3 L. Ed. 2d 5 (1958)

Opinion of the Court by The Chief Justice [Warren], Mr. Justice Black, Mr.
Justice Frankfurter, Mr. Justice Douglas, Mr. Justice Burton, Mr. Jus-
tice Clark, Mr. Justice Harlan, Mr. Justice Brennan, and Mr. Justice
Whittaker.

As this case reaches us it raises questions of the highest importance to the maintenance of our federal system of government. It necessarily involves a claim by the
Governor and Legislature of a State that there is no duty on state officials to obey
federal court orders resting on this Court's considered interpretation of the United
States Constitution. Specifically it involves actions by the Governor and Legislature
of Arkansas upon the premise that they are not bound by our holding in *Brown v.
Board of Education*, 347 U.S. 483 [1954]. That holding was that the Fourteenth
Amendment forbids States to use their governmental powers to bar children on
racial grounds from attending schools where there is state participation through
any arrangement, management, funds or property. We are urged to uphold a suspension of the Little Rock School Board's plan to do away with segregated public
schools in Little Rock until state laws and efforts to upset and nullify our holding in
Brown v. Board of Education have been further challenged and tested in the courts.
We reject these contentions.

While the [Little Rock District] School Board was going forward with its preparation for desegregating the Little Rock school system, other state authorities, in
contrast, were actively pursuing a program designed to perpetuate in Arkansas
the system of racial segregation which this Court had held violated the Fourteenth
Amendment. First came, in November 1956, an amendment to the State Constitution flatly commanding the Arkansas General Assembly to oppose "in every Constitutional manner the un-constitutional desegregation decisions of the United
States Supreme Court," Ark.Const.Amend. 44, and, through the initiative, a pupil

assignment law. Pursuant to this state constitutional command, a law relieving school children from compulsory attendance at racially mixed schools and a law establishing a State Sovereignty Commission were enacted by the General Assembly in February 1957.

The School Board and the Superintendent of Schools nevertheless continued with preparations to carry out the first stage of the desegregation program. Nine Negro children were scheduled for admission in September 1957 to Central High School, which has more than two thousand students. Various administrative measures, designed to assure the smooth transition of this first stage of desegregation, were undertaken.

On September 2, 1957, the day before these Negro students were to enter Central High, the school authorities were met with drastic opposing action on the part of the Governor of Arkansas who dispatched units of the Arkansas National Guard to the Central High School grounds and placed the school "off limits" to colored students. As found by the District Court in subsequent proceedings, the Governor's action had not been requested by the school authorities, and was entirely unheralded.

On February 20, 1958, the School Board and the Superintendent of Schools filed a petition in the District Court seeking a postponement of their program for desegregation. Their position in essence was that because of extreme public hostility, which they stated had been engendered largely by the official attitudes and actions of the Governor and the Legislature, the maintenance of a sound educational program at Central High School, with the Negro students in attendance, would be impossible. The Board therefore proposed that the Negro students already admitted to the school be withdrawn and sent to segregated schools, and that all further steps to carry out the Board's desegregation program be postponed for a period later suggested by the Board to be two and one-half years.

The controlling legal principles are plain. [T]he constitutional rights of children not to be discriminated against in school admission on grounds of race or color declared by this Court in the *Brown* case can neither be nullified openly and directly by state legislators or state executive or judicial officers, nor nullified indirectly by them through evasive schemes for segregation whether attempted "ingeniously or ingenuously."

What has been said, in the light of the facts developed, is enough to dispose of the case. However, we should answer the premise of the actions of the Governor and Legislature that they are not bound by our holding in the *Brown* case. It is necessary only to recall some basic constitutional propositions which are settled doctrine.

Article VI of the Constitution makes the Constitution the "supreme Law of the Land." In 1803, Chief Justice Marshall, speaking for a unanimous Court, referring to the Constitution as "the fundamental and paramount law of the nation," declared in the notable case of *Marbury v. Madison*, that "It is emphatically the province and duty of the judicial department to say what the law is." This decision declared the basic principle that the federal judiciary is supreme in the exposition of the law of the Constitution, and that principle has ever since been respected by this Court and the Country as a permanent and indispensable feature of our constitutional system. It follows that the interpretation of the Fourteenth Amendment enunciated by this Court in the *Brown* case is the supreme law of the land, and Art. VI of the Constitution makes it of binding effect on the States "any Thing in the Constitution or Laws of any State to the Contrary notwithstanding." Every state legislator and executive and judicial officer is solemnly committed by oath taken pursuant to Art. VI, cl.3 "to support this Constitution." Chief Justice Taney, speaking for a unanimous Court in 1859, said that this requirement reflected the framers' "anxiety to preserve it [the Constitution] in full force, in all its powers, and to guard against resistance to or evasion of its authority, on the part of a State. . . ." *Ableman v. Booth*, 21 How. 506, 524.

No state legislator or executive or judicial officer can war against the Constitution without violating his undertaking to support it. Chief Justice Marshall spoke for a unanimous Court in saying that: "If the legislatures of the several states may, at will, annul the judgments of the courts of the United States, and destroy the rights acquired under those judgments, the constitution itself becomes a solemn mockery." *United States v. Peters*, 5 Cranch 115. A Governor who asserts a power to nullify a federal court order is similarly restrained. If he had such power, said Chief Justice Hughes, in 1932, also for a unanimous Court, "it is manifest that the fiat of a state Governor, and not the Constitution of the United States, would be the supreme law of the land; that the restrictions of the Federal Constitution upon the exercise of state power would be but impotent phrases." *Sterling v. Constantin*, 287 U.S. 378.

[The concurring opinion of Mr. Justice Frankfurter is omitted.]

Notes and Questions

(1) What precisely did the Court hold in *Cooper*? Does the holding in *Cooper* follow necessarily from *Marbury*? Former Attorney General Edwin Meese opined: "The [*Brown*] decision was binding on the parties in the case; but the implication that everyone would have to accept its judgments uncritically, that it was a decision from which there could be no appeal, was astonishing. [T]he Court seemed to reduce the Constitution to the status of ordinary constitutional law, and to equate the judge with the lawgiver. [The] logic of the dictum in *Cooper v. Aaron* was, and is, at war with the Constitution, at war with the basic principles of democratic government, and at war with the very meaning of the rule of law." Edwin Meese, *The Law of the Constitution*, 61 Tul. L. Rev. 979, 987 (1987). Did Meese correctly assess *Cooper*?

(2) The Meese challenge to the idea of the Supreme Court as the "final word" on the meaning of the Constitution spawned an outpouring by constitutional scholars and others. The reaction of Professor Laurence Tribe was typical: Meese's position "represents a grave threat to the rule of law." Stuart Taylor, Jr., *Liberties Union Denounces Meese*, N.Y. Times, Oct. 24, 1986. Journalist Anthony Lewis responded to Meese in this way: "To argue that no one owes respect to a Supreme Court decision unless he was actually a party to the case — is to invite anarchy." Anthony Lewis,

Source: Law or Power?, N.Y. Times, Oct. 27, 1986. Are these criticisms of the Meese position on the mark?

(3) Consider what does or should happen when, for example, a legislative or executive official disagrees with a Supreme Court decision declaring a federal or state statute unconstitutional. May the public official act contrary to the interpretation of the Constitution supplied by the Supreme Court so long as she is not a party to the lawsuit? What is the constitutional basis, if any, for such independence? To take an extreme example, may a federal legislator introduce a bill after *Brown* seeking to overturn its holding?

(4) History suggests that the coordinate branches and the states have often asserted the legal authority to engage in constitutional interpretation at variance with the Court. Examples include state resolutions opposing the Alien and Sedition Acts of 1798 (which criminalized criticizing the government), followed by President Jefferson's pardon of every person prosecuted under the Acts, based on his view that they were unconstitutional. Congress likewise indemnified anyone fined under the Acts, based on its view of the constitutionality of the legislation. Indeed, all public officers take the Article VI, Clause 3 oath "to support this Constitution." Louis Fisher and Neal Devins note that, "[u]nder the doctrine of 'coordinate construction,' the elected branches participate [in constitutional interpretation] before the courts decide and afterwords as well. The process is not linear, with the courts issuing the final word. The process is circular, turning back on itself again and again until society is satisfied with the outcome." Louis Fisher & Neal Devins, Political Dynamics of Constitutional Law 11 (6th ed. 2019).

Yet recent trends suggest that the Court is more often than at any other time in its history asserting its primacy. The Roberts Court has "not been favoring one branch of the government over another, or favoring states' rights over the federal government, or the rights of people over governments. Rather it is withdrawing power from all of them at once." Mark A. Lemley, *The Imperial Supreme Court*, 136 Harv. L. Rev. F. 97 (2022). If such a trend continues, what are the implications for where sovereignty resides in our constitutional system?

Chapter 2

Separation of Powers:
Constitutional Checks and Balances

§ 2.01 An Historical Overview

"The constitutional convention of 1787 is supposed to have created a government of 'separated powers.' It did nothing of the sort. Rather, it created a government of separated institutions *sharing* powers." RICHARD E. NEUSTADT, PRESIDENTIAL POWER 33 (1960).

The Constitution allocates the national government's powers into discrete Articles (I, II, III), each of which begins by "vesting" the power described in the single branch of government described there. There is, however, no explicit reference in the text to a separation of powers, no requirement that each institution do only its assigned work, no specific prohibition against sharing prerogatives and responsibilities.

Due in part to the textual ambiguity, separation of powers may today be more a political doctrine than a set of legal rules. Its conceptual content and its doctrine are hard to define with precision. Further, the intellectual history of the separation of powers doctrine complicates the picture: Separation meant different things to different theorists at different times, and it is clear that a few very divergent theories concerning separation were influential to our Framers.

Nonetheless, throughout our history separation of powers issues have found their way to the Supreme Court, resulting in decisions that have often exposed the uncertain role that separation was intended to play. Moreover, the Court has been forced to apply separation principles to a government that is vastly different in character and size from that envisioned by the Framers.

This section will first briefly trace the intellectual origins and early development of the separation idea in the United States. The evolution of separation of powers doctrine will then be reviewed briefly from the perspective of the Supreme Court's attempts to fit the doctrine's diverse meanings to the controversies it has decided.

A. The English Heritage

Separation in government was first stated by Aristotle in his *Politics* to include a tripartite government of deliberators, magistrates, and judicial functionaries; but Aristotle's division did not distinguish parts by function or institution. Nor did other ancient theorists contribute a normative theory of separated powers. In England, the origins for the separation of powers doctrine may be traced to the fifteenth century or earlier when political writers began to describe the distinction between legislative and executive functions. The sphere of government activities which we would characterize as lawmaking required that the king act only with the consent of Parliament; but there was also a sphere of government or prerogative where the king had no obligation to confer with anyone before acting. WILLIAM GWYNN, THE MEANING OF THE SEPARATION OF POWERS 28–29 (1965). The normative base for the separation of functions was, the political writers argued, that the government activity labeled as legislative was best carried out by one type of institution, while the activity labeled as executive was best performed by another.

Fortunately for the later efforts at constitution-making in America, the revolutions in seventeenth-century England created the needed furor over constitutional matters to greatly help in adapting ancient theory to modern government. In England, the problem was one of fitting the balancing of the three interests first identified by Aristotle into the two institutions of English government. (In England, the King and Parliament both had judicial functions.)

John Locke tried to achieve such a fit in his *Second Treatise* (1690). He distinguished function and institution, and divided government into three functions (legislative, executive, and judicial), assigning the functions to the two institutions of government then available. He looked to differing institutions not only to discharge different functions, but also to provide a system of mutual checks. Locke recognized that the Parliament has two branches with one function, but he sought to mesh with the three-interest government idea by arguing that the King has two functions in one branch. The King dealt with foreign nations through exercise of the federative power and he held the executive power for enforcing laws domestically. While Locke thought a balancing of powers important in government, he did not urge complete separation between the legislature and the executive. Further, Locke did not provide for an independent judiciary; he placed that function largely under the executive department.

In 1748, Montesquieu succeeded in adapting the separation idea to Locke's three functions in his *De L'Espirit des Loix (Spirit)*. He specifically called for the legislative, executive, and judicial branches, more or less in their modern form. Although his model was the British Constitution with its two institutions, Montesquieu called the King's federative power "executive" and the internal application of the laws "judicial." Montesquieu, however, chose to ignore the realities of the partisan battles of English politics in order to present a clean and uncomplicated model of separated powers. Even though Montesquieu's work succeeded in finding a way of dividing the three into the two, his system was of limited utility not only because it described an ideal government far from the English experience upon which he based his work, but also because his system had not yet been put into practice anywhere. *See* LOUIS FISHER, PRESIDENT AND CONGRESS 244–250 (1972). It was still the task for others to bring separation theory to America and to make practical the lofty goals of Montesquieu and Locke.

B. Bringing Separation Theory to America

The American constitution-makers were influenced by many sources, ranging from Gibbon's account of *The Decline and Fall of the Roman Empire*, and Adam Smith's *Wealth of Nations*, to other classical accounts of the rise and fall of governments. However, the overwhelming source of information and inspiration for the Americans was the development of the British Constitution and the relationship between the crown and parliament.

The political theory that provided an impetus for the American revolution was based on one view of the British experience offered by the Radical Whigs. The Whigs believed that a compact existed between the rulers and the people, created by the people, under which the rulers could act only so long as they did so in the interest of the nation as a whole. *See* THOMAS HOBBES, LEVIATHAN (1651). English liberty, then, took the form of the right of the collective people to check the actions of their rulers. When the crown was viewed as having breached the compact in 1688, the ensuing Revolution resulted in the House of Commons being given authority to limit the actions of both the House of Lords and the King.

By the time of the American Revolution, the colonies were again calling into question abuses of power by the English crown, and because it failed to protect the colonies, the parliament as well. To the colonists, this compact had once again been broken. But it is crucial to an understanding of the later constitution-making efforts in America to realize that the revolution was "not against the English constitution but on behalf of it." GORDON WOOD, THE CREATION OF THE AMERICAN REPUBLIC 1776–1787, at 10 (1969).

Optimism faded soon after the Revolution, as the experience of government under the Articles of Confederation and the states, dominated as they were by the legislatures, soon revealed itself as unstable and ineffective. The legislatures had been given too much power. They confiscated property, made up all sorts of paper money schemes, and changed the laws so frequently that common citizens were often heard to complain that they did not know the law. Edward Levi, *Some Aspects of Separation of Powers*, 76 COLUM. L. REV. 371, 374–375 (1976). Thus, in many senses, the constitutional convention of 1787 was again a reaction to an abuse of power, this time by the legislatures.

Again Montesquieu, Locke, and earlier theorists regained their influence. Indeed, Montesquieu's separation theory, emphasizing as it did a fairly strict separation, albeit one which ignored political realities of his time, was an important contributor to the efforts at constitution-making in several of the states after they had achieved their independence from England. Many states wrote explicit separation guarantees into their constitutions, but the concept of separation was so subject to differing interpretations that those provisions lacked any widely accepted meaning. Some states (*e.g.*, Massachusetts) had strong separation language competing with equally clear commandments in the constitution authorizing invasions of one branch's power by another branch. Other states had separation provisions in their constitutions which were ignored in practice. The New Hampshire Constitution, the last of the thirteen, may have had the most candid separation provision of the time. The departments of government were to be kept "as separate from and independent of each other, as the nature of a free government will admit, or as is consistent with that chain of connection that binds the whole fabric of the constitution in one indissoluble bond of union and amity." Fisher, *supra*, at 252–253.

It is clear that both Montesquieu and Locke heavily influenced the American version of the separation of powers. Both writers emphasized a rule of law reason for separation, where the separation of departments of government is essential for the legitimacy of the regime. One difference between Montesquieu and Locke that may be relevant to an understanding of separation of powers in America is their treatment of the doctrine of balanced government. Locke barely mentioned it. For many English constitutionalists, however, the balanced government idea was so intoxicating that they revised separation theory to have it become simply an aspect of balancing. The separation of executive and legislative functions became an arrangement to allow the two parts of the government to check one another. Montesquieu, on the other hand, relied on the balancing idea, but for him both separation and balancing were necessary for the achievement of liberty. Nor did they conflict with one another. For Montesquieu,

> [t]he legislative body being composed of two parts, the one restrains the other by the mutual power of rejection. They are both bound by the executive power, which itself is bound by the legislative. These three powers are inclined to form a state of repose or inaction. But as they are obliged to move by the necessary monument of human affairs, they are forced to move in concert.

(*Spirit*, Ch. 6.) Of course, the three powers are not the three powers familiar to later American separation. Rather he was referring to the legislative power of each chamber of the legislature and the executive power of the king, the three English institutions which, according to the Constitution, held each other in check.

Moreover, Montesquieu theorized that a separation of powers can be maintained only if there is also a system of checks and balances. He viewed the legislature as particularly dangerous since it is not limited in its powers by law. Thus, he gave the executive the power to stop a piece of legislation, while denying the legislature the power to obstruct the executive. Gwynn, *supra*, at 110–111. Indeed, this emphasis on the relationship between separation and balancing constitutes Montesquieu's real contribution to both. By emphasizing the importance of an executive check on the legislative power, Montesquieu was offering a point of view quite different from the earlier English writers.

The American constitutionalist John Adams was perhaps the best commentator on the difference between seventeenth and eighteenth century theories. Though Adams often praised the writings of the seventeenth century English republicans, he, like Montesquieu, accepted the balanced government idea which would be put into practice by a constitution. However, unlike Montesquieu, Adams included the judicial branch in the balancing. He was doubtful of its strength in relation to the legislature, but he thought the judiciary essential in preserving the governmental balance.

It was Adams' inclusion of the judicial branch in separation and balanced government that was one of probably only two uniquely American contributions to separation theory. Largely, the Americans brought the European ideas to a new land and adopted them to a country with new institutions. But the role of the courts in this mix of government is an American invention. Adams' idea was expanded by later writers who began to speak of a new role for the judiciary: reviewing the constitutionality of the actions of the other branches of government.

The second American innovation in separation theory concerned the complimentary notions that the chief executive as well as the legislature were representatives of the people and that the executive should be popularly elected. Prior to the colonial experience, separation was effected in England by parliament appointing the executive. But in the republican governments of the American states the distrust of the legislature helped to insure that the executive was popularly elected and therefore just as representative as the legislature.

C. From the Convention to Current Doctrine

. . . Madison, Wilson, and Washington had the greatest personal influences in shaping the Constitution at the Convention. Given their unanimous approval of the separation concept, it is not surprising that the principle was approved without debate. But the separation principle still had to be applied in the document. All the written plans offered at the Convention included some form of separation, usually patterned after extant state constitutional provisions. When the Committee of Detail started its work on drafting final language, an early draft included a resolution that the three departments shall be distinct, and independent of each other except in specified cases. The Committee deleted the separation language later, however, and the delegates chose to accept the implicit existence of separation of powers in the final document in favor of debating specific issues, such as the make-up of the Senate and the executive, and the subsequent Great Compromise. When the Convention's work was done Madison wrote to Jefferson that the lines separating the three branches though in general so strongly marked in themselves, consist in many instances of mere shades of differences.

Later still, in *The Federalist No. 37*, Madison wrote about the inherent difficulty of drawing the line between branches of government and the "privileges and powers of the different legislative branches. Questions daily occur in the course of practice, which prove the obscurity which reigns in these subjects, and which puzzle the greatest adepts of political science." In *No. 47* Madison sought to refute the antifederalist position that pure or complete separation was needed or wise. After recounting the incomplete separation in Britain and the American states, he said that the message of Montesquieu was nothing more than "that where the *whole* power of one department is exercised by the same hands which possess the *whole* power of another department, the fundamental principles of a free constitution are subverted."

William C. Banks, *Efficiency in Government: Separation of Powers Reconsidered*, 35 SYRACUSE L. REV. 715, 721–723 (1984)[1] (footnotes omitted).

Thus, it appears that by the late 1780s separation had lost ground as an idea to checks and balances. The text of the Constitution promotes sharing: the Senate confirms presidential appointments and ratifies treaties, the House may impeach the president, and the president may veto bills but then can be overridden. However, the two ideas are not contradictory; they are complementary. An institution cannot check unless it has some measure of independence; it cannot retain that independence without the power to check.

The sharing idea does not capture it all. There are some exclusive powers, enshrined in the text. Article I, § 6 prohibits members of Congress from holding appointive office, nor may Congress pass a bill of attainder, a judicial function. The Speech or Debate Clause was added to protect legislators from executive or judicial harassments. Congress may not reduce the compensation of the President or members of the federal judiciary; the appropriations power belongs to Congress alone; only the House may originate tax bills.

Other exclusive powers for the Congress include the House's sole power to impeach and the Senate's sole power to try; each chamber is the judge of the qualifications of its own members and each may make its own rules and expel a member. *See Powell v. McCormack*, 395 U.S. 486 (1969). The President's exclusive powers are the power to nominate, the power to negotiate with foreign countries, and the power to pardon.

But even these supposedly exclusive powers are constrained. On nominations, the Congress has a role in providing the names; it may limit the size of the list, or stipulate the qualifications of appointees. As a practical matter, for example, senators often nominate federal judges, U.S. attorneys and marshalls, while the President gives his "Advice and Consent." Also, the President can decide whom to appoint but not whether an agency or an office should exist.

---

1. Copyright © 1984 by Syracuse University Law Review. Reprinted by permission.

Even in foreign affairs, the President's primacy is conditioned by a practical sharing. For example, his power "by and with the Advice and Consent of the Senate, to make Treaties" is theoretically the President's alone until the ratification stage, but most successful treaty negotiations have included a legislative-executive partnership (*e.g.,* International Covenant on Civil and Political Rights, Exec. Rpt. 23, 102d Cong., 2d Sess. (1992), 138 Cong. Rec. S4781–4784 (daily ed. Apr. 2, 1992)).

How should separation of powers doctrine be defined, in light of its historical development in America? Separation had at least three discrete bases in its preconvention status — fear of tyranny, efficiency, and legitimacy. All were thus available to the Framers, and there is ample proof that all were thought by at least some of the delegates to be important reasons for separating powers. While the need to make an effective working government out of the shambles that then existed under the Articles of Confederation prompted Madison and others to argue for a separate legislature and executive for reasons of efficiency, the fear of concentrated power made them also stress that separation would serve the complementary end of forestalling tyranny. But we have already seen how these two seemingly harmonious versions of separation may be at odds. It may be expedient to share powers between legislature and executive, for example, but if too much power is shared, the gain in efficiency in government may be outweighed by the accumulation of power in one branch. Finally, recall that separation was sought for the purpose of insuring legitimacy, the right of the government to rule. Thus, legitimacy, efficiency, and fear of tyranny each had some influence in motivating the Framers toward separation of powers. How should we assess the relative importance of the versions of separation in deciding the contemporary meaning of the idea?

D. The Court Walks a Tightrope: Accommodating Separation's Diverse Goals

The inevitable conflicts that occur in a government of divided powers have usually been solved by compromise and accommodation, often facilitated by the exigencies of the situation. *See* Neal Devins, *Congressional-Executive Information Access Disputes: A Modest Proposal — Do Nothing,* 48 Admin. L. Rev. 109 (1996). Compromise and accommodation have been often facilitated too by the elected branches' recognition that the courts may rely on the "case or controversy" requirement of Article III to limit the occasions on which judicial review may be obtained.

In some respects, the history of separation of powers jurisprudence in America is itself full of inconsistencies. Faced with the potentially competing commands of the efficiency and checking or monitoring bases for separation, the Court has sometimes denied the existence of one theory of separation in order to stress a different version which supports the outcome in the case the Court has decided. For example, in 1926, Justice Brandeis wrote that "the doctrine of separation of powers was adopted by the Convention of 1787, not to promote efficiency, but to preclude the exercise of arbitrary power." *Myers v. United States,* 272 U.S. 52 (1926). Chief

Justice Warren repeated this view in 1965, declaring that separation was "obviously not instituted with the idea that it would promote governmental efficiency." *United States v. Brown*, 381 U.S. 437 (1965). In both cases the Court emphasized the monitoring function of the Court by downplaying the efficiency reasons for separation. On the other hand, at another time, Justice Jackson wrote "[w]hile the Constitution diffuses power the better to secure liberty, it also contemplates that practice will integrate the dispersed powers into a workable government. It enjoins upon its branches separateness but interdependence, autonomy but reciprocity." *Youngstown Sheet & Tube Co. v. Sawyer*, 343 U.S. 579, 635 (1947) (concurring).

There have been instances in our history when one branch of government has sought to encroach upon the functions of another branch. At those times, separation of powers may or may not have come to the invaded branch's rescue. *In re Debs*, 158 U.S. 564 (1895), in which the Court upheld an injunction issued by the executive without express statutory authority, may be viewed as a case in which both the Court and the executive usurped the legislative function of Congress. The *Youngstown* case (*see* § 2.02, *infra*), on the other hand, in which President Truman sought to commandeer the nation's steel mills without statutory authority, is an example of the President arrogating to himself the legislative power of the Congress. There, the Court relied on separation of powers to deny the President the authority he sought. In *United States v. Klein*, 80 U.S. (13 Wall.) 128 (1871), Congress sought to limit the effect of the President's pardon power by depriving federal courts of jurisdiction to enforce certain indemnification claims. The Court found a separation violation, holding that the statute invaded the judicial power by prescribing a rule of decision in pending cases and infringed upon the power of the President, "impairing the effect of a pardon." Similarly, in *United States v. Lovett*, 328 U.S. 303 (1946), the Court held that a statute forbidding payment of compensation to three named government employees was unconstitutional because it imposed punishment without a judicial trial and thus constituted a bill of attainder.

The Court has on occasion acted to protect the President against improper Congressional intrusion on its prerogatives. For example, in *Myers v. United States, supra*, the Court allowed the President to remove executive officers appointed with the advice and consent of the Senate. The statute which required the consent of the Senate for removal was unconstitutional because the executive power vested in Article II was held to include unlimited discretion to remove subordinates.

Thus, each branch has on occasion abused its powers by invading those entrusted to another branch. Sometimes the Court has actively performed a policing function in such cases; other times it has not; and in still other situations the Court has contributed to, or been entirely responsible for the invasion of another branch's turf. Perhaps, however, our institutions are not to be faulted for the seeming inconsistencies in their approaches to deciding where separation commands that lines be drawn or authority ceases to exist. Recall that the "doctrine" of separation of powers can probably never be stated with one voice because it was never so spoken by our Framers or by those who were influential in bringing the separation idea to this country. The reasons for separating powers in our Constitution are diverse, sometimes overlapping, often complementary, but occasionally the normally consistent notions of division of labor and separation of control are in competition and cooperation may quickly melt into conflict.

§2.02 How Are Separation of Powers Disputes Decided? — An Introductory Case Study

Youngstown Sheet & Tube Co. v. Sawyer
[The Steel Seizure Case]

United States Supreme Court
343 U.S. 579, 72 S. Ct. 863, 96 L. Ed. 1153 (1952)

MR. JUSTICE BLACK delivered the opinion of the Court.

We are asked to decide whether the President [Truman] was acting within his constitutional power when he issued an order directing the Secretary of Commerce to take possession of and operate most of the Nation's steel mills. The mill owners argue that the President's order amounts to lawmaking, a legislative function which the Constitution has expressly confided to the Congress and not to the President. The Government's position is that the order was made on findings of the President that his action was necessary to avert a national catastrophe which would inevitably result from a stoppage of steel production, and that in meeting this grave emergency the President was acting within the aggregate of his constitutional powers as the Nation's Chief Executive and the Commander-in-Chief of the Armed Forces of the United States. The issue emerges here from the following series of events:

In the latter part of 1951 [during the Korean War], a dispute arose between the steel companies and their employees over terms and conditions that should be included in new collective bargaining agreements. Long-continued conferences failed to resolve the dispute. On April 4, 1952, the Union gave notice of a nation-wide strike called to begin at 12:01 a.m. April 9. The indispensability of steel as a component of substantially all weapons and other war materials led the President to believe that the proposed work stoppage would immediately jeopardize our national defense and that governmental seizure of the steel mills was necessary in order to assure the continued availability of steel. Reciting these considerations for his action, the President, a few hours before the strike was to begin, issued Executive Order 10340, [which] directed the Secretary of Commerce [Sawyer] to take possession of most of the steel mills and keep them running. The Secretary immediately issued his own possessory orders, calling upon the presidents of the various seized companies to serve as operating managers for the United States. They were directed to carry on their activities in accordance with regulations and directions of the Secretary. The next morning the President sent a message to Congress reporting his action. Twelve days later he sent a second message. Congress has taken no action.

Obeying the Secretary's orders under protest, the companies brought proceedings against him in the District Court. Their complaints charged that the seizure was not authorized by an act of Congress or by any constitutional provisions. [T]he District Court on April 30 issued a preliminary injunction restraining the Secretary from "continuing the seizure and possession of the plants and from acting under the purported authority of Executive Order No. 10340." On the same day the Court of Appeals stayed the District Court's injunction. Deeming it best that the issues raised be promptly decided by this court, we granted certiorari on May 3 and set the cause for argument on May 12.

The President's power, if any, to issue the order must stem either from an act of Congress or from the Constitution itself. There is no statute that expressly authorizes the President to take possession of property as he did here. Nor is there any act of Congress to which our attention has been directed from which such a power can fairly be implied. Indeed, we do not understand the Government to rely on statutory authorization for this seizure. There are two statutes which do authorize the President to take both personal and real property under certain conditions. However, the Government admits that these conditions were not met and that the President's order was not rooted in either of the statutes. The Government refers to the seizure provisions of one of these statutes as "much too cumbersome, involved, and time-consuming for the crisis which was at hand."

Moreover, the use of the seizure technique to solve labor disputes in order to prevent work stoppages was not only unauthorized by any congressional enactment; prior to this controversy, Congress had refused to adopt that method of settling labor disputes. When the Taft-Hartley Act was under consideration in 1947, Congress rejected an amendment which would have authorized such government seizures in cases of emergency. Instead, the plan sought to bring about settlements by use of the customary devices of mediation, conciliation, investigation by boards of inquiry, and public reports. In some instances temporary injunctions were authorized to provide cooling-off periods. All this failing, unions were left free to strike after a secret vote by employees as to whether they wished to accept their employers' final settlement offer.

It is clear that if the President had authority to issue the order he did, it must be found in some provisions of the Constitution. And it is not claimed that express constitutional language grants this power to the President. The contention is that presidential power should be implied from the aggregate of his powers under the Constitution. Particular reliance is placed on provisions in Article II which say that "The executive Power shall be vested in a President"; that "he shall take Care that the Laws be faithfully executed"; and that he "shall be Commander-in-Chief of the Army and Navy of the United States."

The order cannot properly be sustained as an exercise of the President's military power as Commander-in-Chief of the Armed Forces. The Government attempts to do so by citing a number of cases upholding broad powers in military commanders engaged in day-to-day fighting in a theater of war. Such cases need not concern us here. Even though "theater of war" be an expanding concept, we cannot with faithfulness to our constitutional system hold that the Commander-in-Chief of the Armed Forces has the ultimate power as such to take possession of private property in order to keep labor disputes from stopping production. This is a job for the Nation's lawmakers, not for its military authorities.

Nor can the seizure order be sustained because of the several constitutional provisions that grant executive power to the President. In the framework of our Constitution, the President's power to see that the laws are faithfully executed refutes the idea that he is to be a lawmaker. The Constitution limits his functions in the lawmaking process to the recommending of laws he thinks wise and the vetoing of laws he thinks bad. And the Constitution is neither silent nor equivocal about who shall make laws which the President is to execute. The first section of the first article says that "All legislative Powers herein granted shall be vested in a Congress of the United States." After granting many powers to the Congress, Article I goes on to provide that Congress may "make all Laws which shall be necessary and proper for carrying into Execution the foregoing Powers, and all other Powers vested by this Constitution in the Government of the United States, or in any Department or Officer thereof."

The President's order does not direct that a congressional policy be executed in a manner prescribed by Congress — it directs that a presidential policy be executed in a manner prescribed by the President. The preamble of the order itself, like that of many statutes, sets out reasons why the President believes certain policies should be adopted, proclaims these policies as rules of conduct to be followed, and again, like a statute, authorizes a government official to promulgate additional rules and regulations consistent with the policy proclaimed and needed to carry that policy into execution. The power of Congress to adopt such public policies as those proclaimed by the order is beyond question. It can authorize the taking of private property for public use. It can make laws regulating the relationships between employers and employees, prescribing rules designed to settle labor disputes, and fixing wages and working conditions in certain fields of our economy. The Constitution does not subject this lawmaking power of Congress to presidential or military supervision or control.

It is said that other Presidents without congressional authority have taken possession of private business enterprises in order to settle labor disputes. But even if this be true, Congress has not thereby lost its exclusive constitutional authority to make law necessary and proper to carry out the powers vested by the Constitution "in the Government of the United States, or any Department or Officer thereof."

The Founders of this Nation entrusted the lawmaking power to the Congress alone in both good and bad times. It would do no good to recall the historical events, the fears of power and the hopes for freedom that lay behind their choice. Such a review would but confirm our holding that this seizure order cannot stand.

The judgment of the District Court is

Affirmed.

Mr. Justice Frankfurter, [concurring:]

The issue before us can be met, and therefore should be, without attempting to define the President's powers comprehensively. We must therefore put to one side consideration of what powers the President would have had if there had been no legislation whatever bearing on the authority asserted by the seizure, or if the seizure had been only for a short, explicitly temporary period, to be terminated automatically unless Congressional approval were given. These and other questions, like or unlike, are not now here.

No room for doubt remains that the proponents as well as the opponents of the bill which became the Labor Management Relations Act of 1947 clearly understood that as a result of that legislation the only recourse for preventing a shutdown in any basic industry, after failure of mediation, was Congress.

Instead of giving him even limited powers, Congress in 1947 deemed it wise to require the President, upon failure of attempts to reach a voluntary settlement, to report to Congress if he deemed the power of seizure a needed shot for his locker. The President could not ignore the specific limitations of prior seizure statutes. No more could he act in disregard of the limitation put upon seizure by the 1947 Act.

It cannot be contended that the President would have had power to issue this order had Congress explicitly negated such authority in formal legislation. Congress has expressed its will to withhold this power from the President as though it had said so in so many words. The authoritatively expressed purpose of Congress to disallow such power to the President and to require him, when in his mind the occasion arose for such a seizure, to put the matter to Congress, and ask for specific authority from it, could not be more decisive if it had been written into §§ 206–210 of the Labor Management Relations Act of 1947.

[T]he content of the three authorities of government is not to be derived from an abstract analysis. The areas are partly interacting, not wholly disjointed. The Constitution is a framework for government. Therefore the way the framework has consistently operated fairly establishes that it has operated according to its true nature. Deeply embedded traditional ways of conducting government cannot supplant the Constitution or legislation, but they give meaning to the words of a text or supply them. In short, a systematic, unbroken, executive practice, long pursued to the knowledge of the Congress and never before questioned, engaged in by Presidents who have also sworn to uphold the Constitution, making as it were such exercise of power part of the structure of our government, may be treated as a gloss on "executive Power" vested in the President by § 1 of Art. II.

[T]he record is barren of instances comparable to the one before us. Of twelve seizures by President Roosevelt prior to the enactment of the War Labor Disputes Act in June, 1943, three were sanctioned by existing law, and six others were effected after Congress, on December 8, 1941, had declared the existence of a state of war. In this case, reliance on the powers that flow from declared war has been commendably disclaimed by the Solicitor General. Thus the list of executive assertions of the power of seizure in circumstances comparable to the present reduces to three in the six-month period from June to December of 1941. We need not split hairs in comparing those actions to the one before us, though much might be said by way of differentiation. Without passing on their validity, as we are not called upon to do, it suffices to say that these three isolated instances do not add up, either in number, scope, duration or contemporaneous legal justification, to the kind of executive construction of the Constitution [required to validate his action here]. Nor do they come to us sanctioned by long-continued acquiescence of Congress giving decisive weight to a construction by the Executive of its powers.

Mr. Justice Douglas, concurring.

There can be no doubt that the emergency which caused the President to seize these steel plants was one that bore heavily on the country. But the emergency did not create power; it merely marked an occasion when power should be exercised.

The legislative nature of the action taken by the President seems to me to be clear. When the United States takes over an industrial plant to settle a labor controversy, it is condemning property. The seizure of the plant is a taking in the constitutional sense. But there is a duty to pay for all property taken by the Government. The command of the Fifth Amendment is that no "private property be taken for public use, without just compensation."

The President has no power to raise revenues. That power is in the Congress by Article I, Section 8 of the Constitution. The branch of government that has the power to pay compensation for a seizure is the only one able to authorize a seizure or make lawful one that the President has effected. Stalemates may occur when emergencies mount and the Nation suffers for lack of harmonious, reciprocal action between the White House and Capitol Hill. That is a risk inherent in our system of separation of powers. The tragedy of such stalemates might be avoided by allowing the President the use of some legislative authority. The Framers with memories of the tyrannies produced by a blending of executive and legislative power rejected that political arrangement. Some future generation may, however, deem it so urgent that the President have legislative authority that the Constitution will be amended. We could not sanction the seizures and condemnations of the steel plants in this case without reading Article II as giving the President not only the power to execute the laws but to make some.

Mr. Justice Jackson, concurring in the judgment and in the opinion of the Court.

A judge, like an executive adviser, may be surprised at the poverty of really useful and unambiguous authority applicable to concrete problems of executive power as they actually present themselves. Just what our forefathers did envision, or would have envisioned had they foreseen modern conditions, must be divined from materials almost as enigmatic as the dreams Joseph was called upon to interpret for Pharaoh. A century and a half of partisan debate and scholarly speculation yields no net result but only supplies more or less apt quotations from respected sources on each side of any question. They largely cancel each other. And court decisions are indecisive because of the judicial practice of dealing with the largest questions in the most narrow way.

The actual art of governing under our Constitution does not and cannot conform to judicial definitions of the power of any of its branches based on isolated clauses or even single Articles torn from context. While the Constitution diffuses power the better to secure liberty, it also contemplates that practice will integrate the dispersed powers into a workable government. It enjoins upon its branches separateness but interdependence, autonomy but reciprocity. Presidential powers are not fixed but fluctuate, depending upon their disjunction or conjunction with those of Congress. We may well begin by a somewhat over-simplified grouping of practical situations in which a President may doubt, or others may challenge, his powers, and by distinguishing roughly the legal consequences of this factor of relativity.

1. When the President acts pursuant to an express or implied authorization of Congress, his authority is at its maximum, for it includes all that he possesses in his own right plus all that Congress can delegate. In these circumstances, and in these only, may he be said (for what it may be worth) to personify the federal sovereignty. If his act is held unconstitutional under these circumstances, it usually means that the Federal Government as an undivided whole lacks power. A seizure executed by the President pursuant to an Act of Congress would be supported by the strongest of presumptions and the widest latitude of judicial interpretation, and the burden of persuasion would rest heavily upon any who might attack it.

2. When the President acts in absence of either a congressional grant or denial of authority, he can only rely upon his own independent powers, but there is a zone of twilight in which he and Congress may have concurrent authority, or in which its distribution is uncertain. Therefore, congressional inertia, indifference or quiescence may sometimes, at least as a practical matter, enable, if not invite, measures on independent presidential responsibility. In this area, any actual test of power is likely to depend on the imperatives of events and contemporary imponderables rather than on abstract theories of law.

3. When the President takes measures incompatible with the expressed or implied will of Congress, his power is at its lowest ebb, for then he can rely only upon his own constitutional powers minus any constitutional powers of Congress over the matter. Courts can sustain exclusive presidential control in such a case only by disabling the Congress from acting upon the subject. Presidential claim to a power at once so conclusive and preclusive must be scrutinized with caution, for what is at stake is the equilibrium established by our constitutional system.

Into which of these classifications does this executive seizure of the steel industry fit? It is eliminated from the first by admission, for it is conceded that no congressional authorization exists for this seizure. That takes away also the support of the many precedents and declarations which were made in relation, and must be confined, to this category.

Can it then be defended under flexible tests available to the second category? It seems clearly eliminated from that class because Congress has not left seizure of private property an open field but has covered it by three statutory policies inconsistent with this seizure.

This leaves the current seizure to be justified only by the severe tests under the third grouping, where it can be supported only by any remainder of executive power after subtraction of such powers as Congress may have over the subject. In short, we can sustain the President only by holding that seizure of such strike-bound industries is within his domain and beyond control by Congress.

I did not suppose, and I am not persuaded, that history leaves it open to question, at least in the courts, that the executive branch, like the Federal Government as a whole, possesses only delegated powers. The purpose of the Constitution was not only to grant power, but to keep it from getting out of hand. However, because the President does not enjoy unmentioned powers does not mean that the mentioned ones should be narrowed by a niggardly construction. Some clauses could be made almost unworkable, as well as immutable, by refusal to indulge some latitude of interpretation for changing times. I have heretofore, and do now, give to the enumerated powers the scope and elasticity afforded by what seem to be reasonable, practical implications instead of the rigidity dictated by a doctrinaire textualism.

The Solicitor General seeks the power of seizure in three clauses of the Executive Article, the first reading, "The executive Power shall be vested in a President of the United States of America."

I cannot accept the view that this clause is a grant in bulk of all conceivable executive power but regard it as an allocation to the presidential office of the generic powers thereafter stated.

The clause on which the Government next relies is that "The President shall be Commander-in-Chief of the Army and Navy of the United States." These cryptic words have given rise to some of the most persistent controversies in our constitutional history. Of course, they imply something more than an empty title. But just what authority goes with the name has plagued presidential advisors who would not waive or narrow it by nonassertion yet cannot say where it begins or ends. It undoubtedly puts the Nation's armed forces under presidential command. Hence, this loose appellation is sometimes advanced as support for any presidential action, internal or external, involving use of force, the idea being that it vests power to do anything, anywhere, that can be done with an army or navy.

That seems to be the logic of an argument tendered at our bar — that the President having, on his own responsibility, sent American troops abroad derives from that act "affirmative power" to seize the means of producing a supply of steel for them.

Nothing in our Constitution is plainer than that declaration of a war is entrusted only to Congress. Of course, a state of war may in fact exist without a formal declaration. But no doctrine that the Court could promulgate would seem to me more sinister and alarming than that a President whose conduct of foreign affairs is so largely uncontrolled, and often even is unknown, can vastly enlarge his mastery over the internal affairs of the country by his own commitment of the Nation's armed forces to some foreign venture. I do not, however, find it necessary or appropriate to consider the legal status of the Korean enterprise to discountenance argument based on it.

Assuming that we are in a war *de facto*, whether it is or is not a war *de jure*, does that empower the Commander-in-Chief to seize industries he thinks necessary to supply our army? The Constitution expressly places in Congress power "to raise and *support* Armies" and "to *provide* and *maintain* a Navy." (Emphasis supplied.) This certainly lays upon Congress primary responsibility for supplying the armed forces. Congress alone controls the raising of revenues and their appropriation and may determine in what manner and by what means they shall be spent for military and naval procurement. I suppose no one would doubt that Congress can take over war supply as a Government enterprise. On the other hand, if Congress sees fit to rely on free private enterprise collectively bargaining with free labor for support and maintenance of our armed forces, can the Executive, because of lawful disagreements incidental to the process, seize the facility for operation upon Government-imposed terms?

There are indications that the Constitution did not contemplate that the title Commander-in-Chief *of the Army and Navy* will constitute him also Commander-in-Chief of the country, its industries and its inhabitants. He has no monopoly of "war powers," whatever they are. While Congress cannot deprive the President of the command of the army and navy, only Congress can provide him an army and navy to command. It is also empowered to make rules for the "Government and Regulation of land and naval Forces," by which it may to some unknown extent impinge upon even command functions.

We should not use this occasion to circumscribe, much less to contract, the lawful role of the President as Commander-in-Chief. I should indulge the widest latitude of interpretation to sustain his exclusive function to command the instruments of national force, at least when turned against the outside world for the security of our society. But, when it is turned inward, not because of rebellion but because of a lawful economic struggle between industry and labor, it should have no such indulgence. His command power is not such an absolute as might be implied from that office in a militaristic system but is subject to limitations consistent with a constitutional Republic whose law and policy-making branch is a representative Congress.

The third clause in which the Solicitor General finds seizure powers is that "he shall take Care that the Law be faithfully executed." That authority must be matched against words of the Fifth Amendment that "No person shall be deprived of life, liberty or property, without due process of law." One gives a governmental authority that reaches so far as there is law, the other gives a private right that authority shall go no farther. These signify about all there is of the principle that ours is a government of laws, not of men, and that we submit ourselves to rulers only if under rules.

The Solicitor General lastly grounds support of the seizure upon nebulous, inherent powers never expressly granted but said to have accrued to the office from the customs and claims of preceding administrations. The plea is for a resulting power to deal with a crisis or an emergency according to the necessities of the case, the unarticulated assumption being that necessity knows no law.

Loose and irresponsible use of adjectives colors all nonlegal and much legal discussion of presidential powers. "Inherent" powers, "implied" powers, "incidental" powers, "plenary" powers, "war" powers and "emergency" powers are used, often interchangeably and without fixed or ascertainable meanings.

The vagueness and generality of the clauses that set forth presidential power afford a plausible basis for pressures within and without an administration for presidential action beyond that supported by those whose responsibility it is to defend his actions in court. The claim of inherent and unrestricted presidential powers has long been a persuasive dialectical weapon in political controversy. While it is not surprising that counsel should grasp support from such unadjudicated claims of power, a judge cannot accept self-serving press statements of the attorney for one of the interested parties as authority in answering a constitutional question, even if the advocate was himself. But prudence has counseled that actual reliance on such nebulous claims stop short of provoking a judicial test.

In view of the ease, expedition and safety with which Congress can grant and has granted large emergency powers, certainly ample to embrace this crisis, I am quite unimpressed with the argument that we should affirm possession of them without statute. Such power either has no beginning or it has no end. If it exists, it need submit to no legal restraint. I am not alarmed that it would plunge us straightway into dictatorship, but it is at least a step in that wrong direction.

As to whether there is imperative necessity for such powers, it is relevant to note the gap that exists between the President's paper powers and his real powers. The Constitution does not disclose the measure of the actual controls wielded by the modern presidential office. That instrument must be understood as an Eighteenth-Century sketch of a government hoped for, not as a blueprint of the Government that is. Vast accretions of federal power, eroded from that reserved by the States, have magnified that scope of presidential activity.

Executive power has the advantage of concentration in a single head in whose choice the whole Nation has a part, making him the focus of public hopes and expectations. In drama, magnitude and finality his decisions so far overshadow any others that almost alone he fills the public eye and ear. No other personality in public life can begin to compete with him in access to the public mind through modern methods of communications. By his prestige as head of state and his influence upon public opinion he exerts a leverage upon those who are supposed to check and balance his power which often cancels their effectiveness.

I cannot be brought to believe that this country will suffer if the Court refuses further to aggrandize the presidential office, already so potent and so relatively immune from judicial review, at the expense of Congress.

But I have no illusion that any decision by this Court can keep power in the hands of Congress if it is not wise and timely in meeting its problems. A crisis that challenges the President equally, or perhaps primarily, challenges Congress. If not good Law, there was worldly wisdom in the maxim attributed to Napoleon that "The tools belong to the man who can use them." We may say that power to legislate for emergencies belongs in the hands of Congress, but only Congress itself can prevent power from slipping through its fingers.

With all its defects, delays and inconveniences, men have discovered no technique for long preserving free government except that the Executive be under the law, and that the law be made by parliamentary deliberations.

Such institutions may be destined to pass away, but it is the duty of the Court to be last, not first, to give them up.

Mr. Justice Burton, concurring in both the opinion and judgment of the Court.

In the case before us, Congress authorized a procedure which the President declined to follow. Instead, he followed another procedure which he hoped might eliminate the need for the first. Upon its failure, he issued an executive order to seize the steel properties in the face of the reserved right of Congress to adopt or reject that course as a matter of legislative policy.

This brings us to a further crucial question. Does the President, in such a situation, have inherent constitutional power to seize private property which makes congressional action in relation thereto unnecessary? We find no such power available to him under the present circumstances. The present situation is not comparable to that of an imminent invasion or threatened attack. We do not face the issue of what might be the President's constitutional power to meet such catastrophic situations. Nor is it claimed that the current seizure is in the nature of a military command addressed by the President, as Commander-in-Chief, to a mobilized nation waging, or imminently threatened with, total war.

Mr. Justice Clark, concurring in the judgment of the Court.

The limits of presidential power are obscure. However, Article II, no less than Article I, is part of "a constitution intended to endure for ages to come, and, consequently, to be adapted to the various crises of human affairs." Some of our Presidents, such as Lincoln, "felt that measures otherwise unconstitutional might become lawful by becoming indispensable to the preservation of the Constitution through the preservation of the nation." Others, such as Theodore Roosevelt, thought the President to be capable, as a "steward" of the people, of exerting all power save that which is specifically prohibited by the Constitution or the Congress. In my view the Constitution does grant to the President extensive authority in times of grave and imperative national emergency. In fact, to my thinking, such a grant may well be necessary to the very existence of the Constitution itself. As Lincoln aptly said, "[is] it possible to lose the nation and yet preserve the Constitution?" In describing this authority I care not whether one calls it "residual," "inherent," "moral," "implied," "aggregate," "emergency," or otherwise. I am of the conviction that those who have had the gratifying experience of being the President's lawyer have used one or more of these adjectives only with the utmost of sincerity and the highest of purpose.

I conclude that where Congress has laid down specific procedures to deal with the type of crisis confronting the President, he must follow those procedures in meeting the crisis; but that in the absence of such action by Congress, the President's independent power to act depends upon the gravity of the situation confronting the nation. I cannot sustain the seizure in question because here Congress had prescribed methods to be followed by the President in meeting the emergency at hand.

Mr. Chief Justice Vinson, with whom Mr. Justice Reed and Mr. Justice Minton join, dissenting.

Those who suggest that this is a case involving extraordinary power should be mindful that these are extraordinary times. A world not yet recovered from the devastation of World War II has been forced to face the threat of another and more terrifying global conflict.

Admitting that the Government could seize the mills, plaintiffs claim that the implied power of eminent domain can be exercised only under an Act of Congress; under no circumstances, they say, can that power be exercised by the President unless he can point to an express provision in enabling legislation. This was the view adopted by the District Judge when he granted the preliminary injunction. Without an answer, without hearing evidence, he determined the issue on the basis of his "fixed conclusion that defendant's acts are illegal" because the President's only course in the face of an emergency is to present the matter to Congress and await the final passage of legislation which will enable the Government to cope with threatened disaster.

Under this view, the President is left powerless at the very moment when the need for action may be most pressing and when no one, other than he, is immediately capable of action. Under this view, he is left powerless because a power not expressly given to Congress is nevertheless found to rest exclusively with Congress.

A review of executive action demonstrates that our Presidents have on many occasions exhibited the leadership contemplated by the Framers when they made the President Commander-in-Chief, and imposed upon him the trust to "take Care that the Laws be faithfully executed." With or without explicit statutory authorization, Presidents have at such times dealt with national emergencies by acting promptly and resolutely to enforce legislative programs, at least to save those programs until Congress could act. Congress and the courts have responded to such executive initiative with consistent approval.

Beginning with the Bank Holiday Proclamation and continuing through World War II, executive leadership and initiative were characteristic of President

Franklin D. Roosevelt's administration. In 1939, upon the outbreak of war in Europe, the President proclaimed a limited national emergency for the purpose of strengthening our national defense. In May of 1941, the danger from the Axis belligerents having become clear, the President proclaimed "an unlimited national emergency" calling for mobilization of the Nation's defenses to repel aggression. The President took the initiative in strengthening our defense by acquiring rights from the British Government to establish air bases in exchange for overage destroyers.

Some six months before Pearl Harbor, a dispute at a single aviation plant at Inglewood, California, interrupted a segment of the production of military aircraft. In spite of the comparative insignificance of this work stoppage to the total defense production as contrasted with the complete paralysis now threatened by a shutdown of the entire basic steel industry, and even though our armed forces were not then engaged in combat, President Roosevelt ordered the seizure of the plant "pursuant to the powers vested in [him] by the Constitution and laws of the United States, as President of the United States of America and Commander-in-Chief of the Army and Navy of the United States." The Attorney General (Jackson) vigorously proclaimed that the President had the moral duty to keep this Nation's defense effort a "going concern."

Following the declaration of war, five additional industrial concerns were seized to avert interruption of the needed production. During the same period, the President directed seizure of the Nation's coal mines to remove an obstruction to the effective prosecution of the war.

At the time of the seizure of the coal mines, Senator Connally's bill to provide a statutory basis for seizures and for the War Labor Board was again before Congress. As stated by its sponsor, the purpose of the bill was not to augment Presidential power, but to "let the country know that the Congress is squarely behind the President."

This is but a cursory summary of executive leadership. But it amply demonstrates that Presidents have taken prompt action to enforce the laws and protect the country whether or not Congress happened to provide in advance for the particular method of execution. [T]he fact that Congress and the courts have consistently recognized and given their support to such executive action indicates that such a power of seizure has been accepted throughout our history.

History bears out the genius of the Founding Fathers, who created a Government subject to law but left no subject to inertia when vigor and initiative are required.

Much of the argument in this case has been directed at straw men. We do not now have before us the case of a President acting solely on the basis of his own notions of the public welfare. Nor is there any question of unlimited executive power in this case. The President himself closed the door to any such claim when he sent his Message to Congress stating his purpose to abide by any action of Congress, whether approving or disapproving his seizure action. Here, the President immediately made sure that Congress was fully informed of the temporary action he had taken only to preserve the legislative programs from destruction until Congress could act.

The absence of a specific statute authorizing seizure of the steel mills as a mode of executing the laws—both the military procurement program and the anti-inflation program—has not until today been thought to prevent the President from executing the laws. Unlike an administrative commission confined to the enforcement of the statute under which it was created, or the head of a department when administering a particular statute, the President is a constitutional officer charged with taking care that a "mass of legislation" be executed. Flexibility as to mode of execution to meet critical situations is a matter of practical necessity.

The diversity of views expressed in the six opinions of the majority, the lack of reference to authoritative precedent, the repeated reliance upon prior dissenting opinions, the complete disregard of the uncontroverted facts showing the gravity of the emergency and the temporary nature of the taking all serve to demonstrate how far afield one must go to affirm the order of the District Court.

The broad executive power granted by Article II to an officer on duty 365 days a year cannot, it is said, be invoked to avert disaster. Instead, the President must confine himself to sending a message to Congress recommending action. Under this messenger-boy concept of the Office, the President cannot even act to preserve legislative programs from destruction so that Congress will have something left to act upon.

Notes and Questions

(1) What is the holding of the case? Which justices agree with Justice Black that the executive has no lawmaking power unless delegated by Congress? Some justices would, in an appropriate case, have found presidential authority in the absence of prohibitory statutes. What would be the source of such a power which, although not present in the *Steel Seizure* case, may well validate a presidential action in another situation? Could the President support the exercise of lawmaking power by his obligation in Article II §3 to "take care that the laws be faithfully executed"?

(2) Does Justice Black's opinion recognize any inherent powers in the executive branch? Which justices would support a presidential power to respond to emergency situations, despite the absence of explicit statutory or constitutional authority? Many have argued that the *Steel Seizure* case effectively closed the door on the inherent powers theory, among them the Senate Foreign Relations Committee and former Supreme Court Justice Arthur Goldberg. *See* Arthur Goldberg, *The Constitutional Limitations on the President's Powers*, 22 Am. U. L. Rev. 667, 675 (1973). Others have cautioned against such a reading of the case:

> That the President does possess "residual" or "resultant" powers over and above, or in consequence of, his specifically granted powers to take temporary alleviative action in the presence of serious emergency is a proposition to which all but Justices Black and Douglas would probably have assented

in the absence of the complicating issue that was created by the president's refusal to follow the procedures laid down in the Taft-Hartley Act.

Edward S. Corwin, *The Steel Seizure Case: A Judicial Brick Without Straw*, 53 COLUM. L. REV. 53, 65 (1953).[2]

(3) What significance did Justices Frankfurter, Jackson, Burton, and Clark place on the history of congressional action or inaction concerning plant seizures? When may congressional acquiescence in executive custom empower the President? Why did the history of plant seizures described by Justice Frankfurter fail to establish an executive custom in which Congress had acquiesced?

(4) If there are some shared lawmaking powers, how should they be allocated and how should disputes about them be decided? Recall Justice Jackson's "twilight zone" analysis. Why did Justice Jackson place the steel seizure in the third category? He failed to suggest how cases falling into his third category — when the President acts contrary to statute — should be resolved. How would you resolve separation of powers disputes when presidential and congressional powers are squarely pitted against one another? Should the judiciary resolve such a dispute?

Why did President Truman's seizure not instead fall into the "twilight zone"? Which branch prevails in a "twilight zone" dispute? May presidential powers in the "twilight zone" be cut off by statutory directive from the Congress?

(5) Why did the Court reject the Commander-in-Chief Clause as authority for the seizure? Consider each opinion. Would the Commander-in-Chief Clause have legitimated the seizure if Congress had remained silent on the issue of seizure?

(6) Note the contrasting approaches to deciding the case used by Justices Black and Jackson. The two opinions offer classic examples of what may be characterized as the formal and functional approaches to separation of powers analyses. Justice Black's assertion that "the framework of the Constitution refutes the idea that [the President] is to be a lawmaker" is at once literally or formally undeniable and at the same time ignorant of the realities of modern government. Perhaps Justice Black's failure to acknowledge the legitimacy of Presidential lawmaking may be excused because the dispute came about after a congressional denial of presidential power. Justice Jackson's approach contemplates that the *Steel Seizure* holding may have less precedential value in a policy dispute with significantly different facts. Arguably, then, Justice Jackson's analysis is more consistent with the theoretical inconsistencies with which separation of powers is saddled. In a case where efficiency reasons for separating powers support an executive role in lawmaking, Jackson's analysis could support it, while Justice Black's could not. Similarly, where a tyranny or legitimacy threat emerged from an asserted executive role in lawmaking, the functional approach could deny the presidential prerogative.

---

2. Copyright © 1953 by the Directors of the Columbia Law Review Association, Inc. All rights reserved. This article originally appeared at 53 COLUM. L. REV. 53 (1953). Reprinted by permission.

Problem A

In 1986, Congress enacted the Emergency Medical Treatment and Labor Act (EMTALA) to ensure public access to emergency medical services regardless of ability to pay. The Act provides:

> If any individual comes to a hospital and the hospital determines that the individual has an emergency medical condition, the hospital must provide for such further medical examination and treatment as may be required to stabilize the medical condition. . . .

EMTALA defines "emergency medical condition" as "a medical condition manifesting itself by acute symptoms of sufficient severity (including severe pain) such that the absence of immediate medical attention could reasonably be expected to result in —

> (i) placing the health of the individual (or, with respect to a pregnant woman, the health of the woman or her unborn child) in serious jeopardy,
>
> (ii) serious impairment to bodily functions, or
>
> (iii) serious dysfunction of any bodily organ or part.

Assume that, in the wake of the 2022 Supreme Court decision in *Dobbs v. Jackson Women's Health* holding that the Constitution does not confer a right to an abortion, the President issued an Executive Order stating that

> hospitals subject to the EMTALA must provide emergency abortion services if necessary to stabilize the patient's medical condition. If a state law prohibits abortions and does not include an exception for the health or life of the pregnant person — or draws the exception more narrowly than EMTALA's emergency medical condition definition — that state law is preempted.

Does the President's Executive Order exceed his constitutional powers?

§ 2.03 Limits on the Elected Branches: Oversight and Accountability in the Administrative State

A. Introduction

As early as the first decade of the 20th century, the growing size and complexity of American society and government was forcing some, including future President Woodrow Wilson, to question the wisdom and practicality of the separation and checks and balances theory.

> The trouble with the [separation of powers] theory is that government is not a machine, but a living thing. . . . No living thing can have its organs offset

against each other as checks, and live. On the contrary, its life is dependent upon their quick cooperation, their ready response to the commands of instinct or intelligence, their amicable community of purpose. Government is not a body of blind forces; it is a body of men, with highly differentiated function, no doubt, in our modern day of specialization, but with a common task and purpose. Their cooperation is indispensable, their warfare fatal. There can be no successful government without leadership or without the intimate, almost instinctive, coordination of the organs of life and action. This is not theory but fact, and displays its force as fact, whatever theories may be thrown across its track.

WOODROW WILSON, CONSTITUTIONAL GOVERNMENT IN THE UNITED STATES 56–57 (1908).

Particularly since the New Deal era, the federal bureaucracy has grown tremendously and, with it, the share of government and governing that takes place outside the confines of our originally conceived three-branch federal government. Indeed, federal administrative agencies have become so powerful as to be commonly referred to as constituting a fourth branch of government:

> However one counts its branches, the size alone of contemporary American administrative government places strains on the eighteenth-century model. The minimalist federal government outlined in Philadelphia in 1787 envisioned a handful of cabinet departments to conduct the scanty business of government, each headed by a Secretary responsible to the President, thinly peopled with political employees. Significant regulatory responsibilities were not in view. . . . The eighteenth-century model relied heavily on the controls of politics over and among the branches of government to keep it within reach of the people, to subdue the risks of tyranny.
>
> The simple model of cabinet departments has long since been supplanted by a rich variety of governmental forms. Today, President and Congress must each deal with a continuing government whose dimensions and power were unprovided for. The civil service, largely insulated from politics, may appropriately be regarded as the fourth effective branch of government. . . .

Peter Strauss, *The Place of Agencies in Government: Separation of Powers and the Fourth Branch*, 84 COLUM. L. REV. 573, 582–583 (1984).[3]

B. Delegation of Legislative Power

Under any of the versions of separation of powers discussed in § 2.01, the Constitution assigned primary responsibility for lawmaking to the legislature, for law enforcing to the executive, and for law deciding to the courts. Indeed, under Justice

---

3. Copyright © 1984 by the Directors of the Columbia Law Review Association, Inc. All rights reserved. This article originally appeared at 84 COLUM. L. REV. 573 (1984). Reprinted by permission.

Black's view of the separation of powers in the *Steel Seizure* case, it is difficult to imagine that the President could ever be a lawmaker. The modern reality, however, is that administrative agencies, often located within one of the executive departments, frequently perform all three governmental functions.

Our immediate task is to examine the constitutional justifications for the delegation of legislative powers to the executive branch. Obviously neither the transfer of legislative power nor the existence of the agencies was contemplated by the Framers. Indeed, the Constitution's statement that "All legislative Powers herein granted shall be vested in a Congress of the United States" (Article I, §1) appears to be a textual bar to delegation, unless it may be legitimated by the power granted Congress "To make all laws which shall be necessary and proper for carrying into Execution the foregoing powers, and all other Powers vested in the Government . . . or in any Department or officer thereof" (Article I, §8).

Despite the growth in the nation and in government, during the nation's first century only two cases challenging legislative delegations reached the Supreme Court. In *The Brig Aurora*, 11 U.S. (7 Cranch) 382 (1813), the Court upheld a delegation to the President to act in the future to lift trade embargoes when the United States' neutrality in commerce was observed by England and France. The statute revived some portions of a previous trade law when triggered by the above finding by the President "which fact the President shall declare by proclamation." When President Madison issued the required proclamation, reviving the old statute, the new law was challenged on the theory that the Congress could not transfer its power to the President; because the earlier law's revival was conditional on the President's action, the proclamation had the force and effect of legislation. The Court rejected the argument summarily: "[W]e can see no sufficient reason why the legislature should not exercise its discretion either expressly or conditionally, as their judgment should direct." *Id.* at 388.

Almost eighty years later the Court relied on *The Brig Aurora* to sustain a statute which provided a retaliatory tariff schedule on imports from nations which imposed duties on American products and which the President "may deem to be reciprocally unequal and unreasonable." Although the Court in *Marshall Field & Co. v. Clark*, 143 U.S. 649 (1892), acknowledged "[t]hat Congress cannot delegate legislative power to the President," Justice Harlan's opinion found no violation of the delegation rule in the President's role under the Tariff Act of 1890:

> The act does not in any real sense invest the President with the power of legislation. Legislative power was exercised when Congress declared that the suspension should take effect upon a named contingency. What the President was required to do was simply in execution of the act of Congress. It was not the making of law. He was the mere agent of the law-making department to ascertain and declare the event upon which its expressed will was to take effect.

Id. at 692–693.

Subsequently the Supreme Court suggested that any delegation of legislative power that contains an "intelligible principle" to guide the implementing official's discretion could be sustained against a nondelegation challenge. *J.W. Hampton, Jr. & Co. v. United States*, 276 U.S. 394 (1928). During the New Deal period, the Court applied the nondelegation doctrine to strike down statutory delegations to executive officials, *Panama Refining Co. v. Ryan*, 293 U.S. 388 (1935); *Schechter Poultry Corp. v. United States*, 295 U.S. 495 (1935); *Carter v. Carter Coal Co.*, 298 U.S. 238 (1936). Since 1936, however, no federal statute has been declared unconstitutional by the Supreme Court on the basis of the nondelegation doctrine.

Despite the judicial record since 1936, there are signs that the Court has renewed interest in imposing limits on the delegation of congressional power. Consider the following case.

Gundy v. United States
United States Supreme Court
139 S. Ct. 2116 (2019)

KAGAN, J., announced the judgment of the Court and delivered an opinion, in which GINSBURG, BREYER, and SOTOMAYOR, JJ., join.

The nondelegation doctrine bars Congress from transferring its legislative power to another branch of Government. This case requires us to decide whether 34 U.S.C. § 20913(d), enacted as part of the Sex Offender Registration and Notification Act (SORNA), violates that doctrine. We hold it does not.

SORNA makes "more uniform and effective" the prior "patchwork" of sex-offender registration systems. The Act's express "purpose" is "to protect the public from sex offenders and offenders against children" by "establish[ing] a comprehensive national system for [their] registration." The basic registration scheme works as follows. A "sex offender" must register—provide his name, address, and certain other information—in every State where he resides, works, or studies. Section 20913—the disputed provision here—elaborates the "[i]nitial registration" requirements for sex offenders. Subsection (b) sets out the general rule: An offender must register "before completing a sentence of imprisonment with respect to the offense giving rise to the registration requirement" (or, if the offender is not sentenced to prison, "not later than [three] business days after being sentenced"). Two provisions down, subsection (d) addresses (in its title's words) the "[i]nitial registration of sex offenders unable to comply with subsection (b)." The provision states:

> The Attorney General shall have the authority to specify the applicability of the requirements of this subchapter to sex offenders convicted before the enactment of this chapter . . . and to prescribe rules for the registration of any such sex offenders and for other categories of sex offenders who are unable to comply with subsection (b).

Subsection (d), in other words, focuses on individuals convicted of a sex offense before SORNA's enactment—a group we will call pre-Act offenders. Many of these individuals were unregistered at the time of SORNA's enactment. Under [his] delegated authority, the Attorney General issued an interim rule in February 2007, specifying that SORNA's registration requirements apply in full to "sex offenders convicted of the offense for which registration is required prior to the enactment of that Act." That rule has remained the same to this day.

Petitioner Herman Gundy is a pre-Act offender. The year before SORNA's enactment, he pleaded guilty under Maryland law for sexually assaulting a minor. After his release from prison in 2012, Gundy came to live in New York. But he never registered there as a sex offender. A few years later, he was convicted for failing to register. He argued below (among other things) that Congress unconstitutionally delegated legislative power when it authorized the Attorney General to "specify the applicability" of SORNA's registration requirements to pre-Act offenders.

Article I of the Constitution provides that "[a]ll legislative Powers herein granted shall be vested in a Congress of the United States." But the Constitution does not "deny[] to the Congress the necessary resources of flexibility and practicality [that enable it] to perform its function[s]." Congress may "obtain the assistance of its coordinate Branches" — and in particular, may confer substantial discretion on executive agencies to implement and enforce the laws. *Mistretta v. United States*, 488 U.S. 361, 372 (1989). "[I]n our increasingly complex society, replete with ever changing and more technical problems," this Court has understood that "Congress simply cannot do its job absent an ability to delegate power under broad general directives." So we have held, time and again, that a statutory delegation is constitutional as long as Congress "lay[s] down by legislative act an intelligible principle to which the person or body authorized to [exercise the delegated authority] is directed to conform." *Id.* (quoting *J.W. Hampton, Jr., & Co. v. United States*).

Section 20913(d) does not give the Attorney General anything like the "unguided" and "unchecked" authority that Gundy says. The provision, in Gundy's view, "grants the Attorney General plenary power to determine SORNA's applicability to pre-Act offenders — to require them to register, or not, as she sees fit, and to change her policy for any reason and at any time." If that were so, we would face a nondelegation question. But it is not. The Act's legislative history [shows] that the need to register pre-Act offenders was front and center in Congress's thinking. According to the House Report, "[t]he most significant enforcement issue in the sex offender program is that over 100,000 sex offenders" are "'missing,' meaning that they have not complied with" then-current requirements. Senators struck a similar chord.

Both the title and the remaining text of section 20913(d) pinpoint one of the "practical problems" [that Congress discerned]: At the moment of SORNA's enactment, many pre-Act offenders were "unable to comply" with the Act's initial registration requirements. That was because . . . the requirements assumed that offenders would be in prison, whereas many pre-Act offenders were on the streets. In identifying that issue, § 20913(d) itself reveals the nature of the delegation to the Attorney General. It was to give him the time needed (if any) to address the various implementation issues involved in getting pre-Act offenders into the registration system. "Specify the applicability" thus does not mean "specify whether to apply SORNA" to pre-Act offenders at all, even though everything else in the Act commands their coverage. The phrase instead means "specify how to apply SORNA" to pre-Act offenders if transitional difficulties require some delay. In that way, the whole of § 20913(d) joins the rest of SORNA in giving the Attorney General only time-limited latitude to excuse pre-Act offenders from the statute's requirements. Under the law, he had to order their registration as soon as feasible.

Now that we have determined what § 20913(d) means, we can consider whether it violates the Constitution. Under this Court's long-established law, that question is easy. Its answer is no.

As noted earlier, this Court has held that a delegation is constitutional so long as Congress has set out an "intelligible principle" to guide the delegee's exercise of authority. *J.W. Hampton, Jr., & Co.* Or in a related formulation, the Court has stated that a delegation is permissible if Congress has made clear to the delegee "the general policy" he must pursue and the "boundaries of [his] authority." Those standards, the Court has made clear, are not demanding. Only twice in this country's history (and that in a single year) have we found a delegation excessive — in each case because "Congress had failed to articulate any policy or standard" to confine discretion. See *A.L.A. Schechter Poultry Corp. v. United States*, 295 U.S. 495 (1935); *Panama Refining Co. v. Ryan*, 293 U. S. 388 (1935). By contrast, we have over and over upheld even very broad delegations.

In that context, the delegation in SORNA easily passes muster . . . Indeed, if SORNA's delegation is unconstitutional, then most of Government is unconstitutional — dependent as Congress is on the need to give discretion to executive officials to implement its programs.

KAVANAUGH, J., took no part in the consideration or decision of this case.

ALITO, J., concurring in the judgment.

If a majority of this Court were willing to reconsider the approach we have taken for the past 84 years, I would support that effort. But because a majority is not willing to do that, it would be freakish to single out the provision at issue here for special treatment.

Because I cannot say that the statute lacks a discernable standard that is adequate under the approach this Court has taken for many years, I vote to affirm.

GORSUCH, J., with whom ROBERTS, C.J., and THOMAS, J., join, dissenting.

The Constitution promises that only the people's elected representatives may adopt new federal laws restricting liberty. Yet the statute before us scrambles that design. It purports to endow the nation's chief prosecutor with the power to write his own criminal code governing the lives of a half-million citizens.

At the time of SORNA's enactment, the nation's population of sex offenders exceeded 500,000, and Congress concluded that something had to be done about these "pre-Act" offenders. But it seems Congress couldn't agree what that should be. So Congress simply passed the problem to the Attorney General. The breadth of the authority Congress granted to the Attorney General in [§ 20913(d)] can only be described as vast. Congress gave the Attorney General free rein to write the rules for virtually the entire existing sex offender population in this country.

To the framers, each of the vested powers [of the three branches] had a distinct content. When it came to the legislative power, the framers understood it to mean the power to adopt generally applicable rules of conduct governing future actions by private persons — the power to "prescrib[e] the rules by which the duties and rights of every citizen are to be regulated," or the power to "prescribe general rules for the government of society." The framers understood, too, that it would frustrate "the system of government ordained by the Constitution" if Congress could merely announce vague aspirations and then assign others the responsibility of adopting legislation to realize its goals.

If Congress could pass off its legislative power to the executive branch, the vesting clauses, and indeed the entire structure of the Constitution, would "make no sense." Without the involvement of representatives from across the country or the demands of bicameralism and presentment, legislation would risk becoming nothing more than the will of the current President. And if laws could be simply declared by a single person, they would not be few in number, the product of widespread social consensus, likely to protect minority interests, or apt to provide stability and fair notice. Accountability would suffer too. Legislators might seek to take credit for addressing a pressing social problem by sending it to the executive for resolution, while at the same time blaming the executive for the problems that attend whatever measures he chooses to pursue. In turn, the executive might point to Congress as the source of the problem.

Accepting, then, that we have an obligation to decide whether Congress has unconstitutionally divested itself of its legislative responsibilities, the question follows: What's the test? The framers offered us important guiding principles. First, we know that as long as Congress makes the policy decisions when regulating private conduct, it may authorize another branch to "fill up the details." In *Wayman v. Southard*, [23 U.S. 1 (1825,] this Court upheld a statute that instructed the federal courts to borrow state-court procedural rules but allowed them to make certain "alterations and additions." Writing for the Court, Chief Justice Marshall distinguished between those "important subjects, which must be entirely regulated by the legislature itself," and "those of less interest, in which a general provision may be made, and power given to those who are to act to fill up the details." Second, once Congress prescribes the rule governing private conduct, it may make the application of that rule depend on executive fact-finding.

Third, Congress may assign the executive and judicial branches certain non-legislative responsibilities. While the Constitution vests all federal legislative power in Congress alone, Congress's legislative authority sometimes overlaps with authority the Constitution separately vests in another branch, [such as the President's

Article II power over foreign affairs or the judiciary's Article III power to regulate court practice].

Before the 1930s, federal statutes granting authority to the executive were comparatively modest and usually easily upheld. But then the federal government began to grow explosively. And with the proliferation of new executive programs came new questions about the scope of congressional delegations. Twice the Court responded by striking down statutes for violating the separation of powers [discussing *Schechter Poultry* and *Panama Refining*]. [S]ince that time the Court hasn't held another statute to violate the separation of powers in the same way. [M]aybe the most likely explanation of all lies in the story of the evolving "intelligible principle" doctrine.

This Court first used that phrase in 1928 in *J.W. Hampton, Jr., & Co. v. United States*, where it remarked that a statute "lay[ing] down by legislative act an intelligible principle to which the [executive official] is directed to conform" satisfies the separation of powers. Still, it's undeniable that the "intelligible principle" remark eventually began to take on a life of its own. This mutated version of the "intelligible principle" remark has no basis in the original meaning of the Constitution, in history, or even in the decision from which it was plucked. Judges and scholars representing a wide and diverse range of views have condemned it as resting on "misunderst[ood] historical foundations."

To determine whether a statute provides an intelligible principle, we must ask: Does the statute assign to the executive only the responsibility to make factual findings? Does it set forth the facts that the executive must consider and the criteria against which to measure them? And most importantly, did Congress, and not the Executive Branch, make the policy judgments? Only then can we fairly say that a statute contains the kind of intelligible principle the Constitution demands.

[W]hen the separation of powers is at stake, we don't just throw up our hands. In [multiple] areas, we recognize that abdication is "not part of the constitutional design." And abdication here would be no more appropriate. To leave this aspect of the constitutional structure alone undefended would serve only to accelerate the flight of power from the legislative to the executive branch, turning the latter into a vortex of authority that was constitutionally reserved for the people's representatives in order to protect their liberties.

[JUSTICE GORSUCH concluded that none of the tests just outlined could justify SORNA.]

It would be easy enough to let this case go. After all, sex offenders are one of the most disfavored groups in our society. But the rule that prevents Congress from giving the executive carte blanche to write laws for sex offenders is the same rule that protects everyone else. Nor would enforcing the Constitution's demands spell doom for what some call the "administrative state." The separation of powers does not prohibit any particular policy outcome, let alone dictate any conclusion about the proper size and scope of government. Instead, it is a procedural guarantee that requires Congress to assemble a social consensus before choosing our nation's course on policy questions like those implicated by SORNA. What is more, Congress is hardly bereft of options to accomplish all it might wish to achieve. It may always authorize executive branch officials to fill in even a large number of details, to find facts that trigger the generally applicable rule of conduct specified in a statute, or to exercise non-legislative powers. Congress can also commission agencies or other experts to study and recommend legislative language. What do the government and the plurality have to say about the constitutional concerns SORNA poses? The government invites us to reimagine SORNA as compelling the Attorney General to register pre-Act offenders "to the maximum extent feasible." And, as thus reinvented, the government insists, the statute supplies a clear statement of legislative policy, with only details for the Attorney General to clean up.

[T]he feasibility standard is a figment of the government's (very recent) imagination. The only provision addressing pre-Act offenders, § 20913(d), says nothing about feasibility. With so little in statutory text to work with, the government and the plurality [resort to] highlighting certain statements from the Act's legislative history. But "legislative history is not the law." In a future case with a full panel, I remain hopeful that the Court may yet recognize that, while Congress can enlist considerable assistance from the executive branch in filling up details and finding facts, it may never hand off to the nation's chief prosecutor the power to write his own criminal code. That "is delegation running riot."

Problem B

Congress enacted the Telecommunications Act of 1996 in part to delegate to the Federal Communications Commission (FCC) the authority to impose "surcharges" on all interstate telephone calls, which are used to provide subsidies to high-cost geographical areas, schools and libraries, certain health facilities, and low-income persons. The surcharges are paid into a Universal Service Fund by telecommunications service providers and are typically passed through by the providers and paid by consumers. The size of the surcharge has grown over two decades and now amounts to nearly 30% of the ordinary charge for each call.

The 1996 Act defines "universal service" as an "evolving level of telecommunications services that the Commission shall establish periodically, taking into account advances in telecommunications and information technologies and services." The Act requires the FCC, in directing subsidies, to consider which services are "essential to education, public health, or public safety; have, through market choices by customers been subscribed to by a substantial majority of residential customers and are consistent with the public interest."

You have been contacted by a consumer advocate group that is opposed to the surcharges program. The consumer advocate group argues that the surcharges to support the universal service subsidies violate the nondelegation doctrine because the FCC may raise and spend nearly unlimited amounts via the Universal Service Fund, at its discretion. Moreover, the surcharges are, they say, taxes because they provide benefits for the general public. As such, they should be imposed, if at all, by

Congress. They want to know if they are likely to succeed in a lawsuit claiming that the FCC exceeded its authority in creating the universal service surcharges. What arguments will you make, and what are your prospects?

Notes and Questions

(1) Is delegation of legislative authority to administrative agencies and generally to the executive branch a practical necessity, a phenomenon inherent in our modern system of government? If so, how may overly broad delegations best be controlled? Does the answer depend on which congressional power is being delegated? On the existence of a national emergency? Could Congress delegate the power to declare war? To appropriate funds?

(2) An alternative to the nondelegation doctrine for limiting the scope of delegations conferred by Congress was embraced by the Supreme Court in *West Virginia v. Environmental Protection Agency* 136 S. Ct. 1000 (2022). The Clean Air Act authorizes the Agency to prescribe standards of performance for power plants that implement "the best system of emission reduction which (taking into account the cost of achieving such reduction and any non-air quality health and environmental impact and energy requirements) the [Agency] determines has been adequately demonstrated." Over a period of years, the EPA adopted a Clean Power Plan that would have effectively required a wholesale shift in electricity production from coal to natural gas and renewables. The Supreme Court stayed implementation of the Plan in 2016, and after further litigation, in 2022, the Court ruled 6-3 that the Plan exceeded the statutory power of the EPA.

Chief Justice Roberts based the decision on what has become known as "the major questions" doctrine:

> in "extraordinary cases the history and breadth of the authority that [the agency] has asserted, and the economic and political significance" of that assertion, provide a "reason to hesitate before concluding that Congress meant to confer such authority." The agency must "point to clear congressional authorization for the authority it claims." Our decision is based on "both separation of powers principles and a practical understanding of legislative intent."

Concurring, Justice Gorsuch, joined by Justice Alito, argued that the "major questions" doctrine was meant "to ensure that the government does not inadvertently cross constitutional lines." Which constitutional lines do you suppose Justice Gorsuch has in mind?

In dissent, Justice Kagan, joined by Justices Breyer and Sotomayor, noted that "Congress has always delegated — including on important policy issues." She argued that an "anti-administrative state stance suffused the concurrence," and that the Court is textualist only when being so suits it. When that method would frustrate broader goals, special canons like the "major questions doctrine" magically appear as "get-out-of-text-free cards."

Which is more in synch with the purposes of the separation of powers — an invigorated non-delegation doctrine, or the major programs doctrine? If your answer is "none of the above," what arguments would you make to persuade the Supreme Court of the wisdom of your views?

(3) If in the future Congress delegates broad authority to an agency and tasks it with promulgating regulations in support of a "major program," how will the Court decide its constitutionality? Late in 2022, the Fifth Circuit ruled that President Biden lacked authority under the Procurement Act of 1949 to require federal contractors to mandate COVID-19 vaccines for their employees. *Louisiana v. Biden*, 55 F.4th 1017 (5th Cir. 2022). The Supreme Court denied review, 142 S. Ct. 2750 (2022). The Act authorizes the President to issue directives that provide the federal government "with an economical and efficient system" for procurement. Although the administration argued that the vaccine policy will improve economy and efficiency by reducing absenteeism and decreasing labor costs for contractors, the court applied the major programs doctrine, which it said requires Congress to speak clearly when authorizing an agency to exercise powers of "vast economic and political significance." The court saw no reason to apply the doctrine differently to agencies and a President. Do you agree?

(4) The Higher Education Relief for Students Act of 2003 (HEROES Act), enacted following the 9/11 attacks, allows the Secretary of Education to "waive or modify any statutory or regulatory provision" to protect borrowers affected by "a war or other military operation or national emergency." In 2020, President Trump declared that the COVID pandemic was a national emergency and ordered loan payments and interest charges paused. In 2022, President Biden relied on the HEROES Act and followed suit, ordering the cancellation of more than $400 billion of student debt in one of the most expensive executive actions in U.S. history. In *Biden v. Nebraska*, 143 S. Ct. 2355 (2023), the Court voted 6-3 to overturn the HEROES Act student loan forgiveness program, saying that the Biden administration was "seizing the power of the legislature" by trying to forgive loan debt for more than 40 million borrowers during the COVID pandemic. According to Chief Justice Roberts' opinion for the Court, the Secretary has authority "to make modest adjustments and additions to existing programs, not transform them." The Chief Justice quipped that the loan forgiveness program modified the federal program "only in the same sense that 'the French Revolution "modified" the status of the French nobility' — it has abolished them and supplanted them with a new regime entirely." Quoting from and relying on its 2022 decision in *West Virginia v. EPA*, the majority held that "a decision of such magnitude and consequence [as cancelling $430 billion in student loans] must rest with Congress itself, or an agency acting pursuant to a clear delegation from that representative body." Should the fact that the $430 billion debt cancellation would have been one of the most expensive executive actions in U.S. history impact its constitutionality?

But what happened to the "emergency"? The government argued that the whole point of the act "is to ensure that in the face of a national emergency that is causing financial harm to borrowers, the Secretary can do something," and that "the unprecedented nature of the Secretary's debt cancellation plan only 'reflects the pandemic's unparalleled scope.'" The majority was unmoved. "The question here is not whether something should be done; it is who has the authority to do it."

In a separate concurring opinion, Justice Barrett asserted that the major programs doctrine "should not be taken for more than it is — the familiar principle that we do not interpret a statute for all it is worth when an average person would not read it that way." Does Justice Barrett's "familiar principle" make the basis for and boundaries of the major programs doctrine more or less clear?

In her dissent, joined by Justices Sotomayor and Jackson, Justice Kagan accused the majority of applying "heightened specificity requirements, thwarting Congress's efforts to ensure adequate responses to unforeseen events. . . . [T]he Court substitutes itself for Congress and the Executive Branch in making national policy about student-loan forgiveness." Emphasizing the "capacious" power Congress delegated to the Secretary in a declared national emergency, they posed the following hypothetical:

> A terrorist organization sets off a dirty bomb in Chicago. Beyond causing deaths, the incident leads millions of residents (including many with student loans) to flee the city to escape the radiation. They must find new housing, probably new jobs. And still their student-loan bills are coming due every month. To prevent widespread loan delinquencies and defaults, the Secretary wants to discharge $10,000 for the class of affected borrowers. Is that legal? Of course it is; it is exactly what Congress provided for. The statutory preconditions are met: The President has declared a national emergency; the Secretary's proposed relief extends only to "affected individuals"; and the Secretary has deemed the action "necessary to ensure" that the attack does not place those borrowers "in a worse position" to repay their loans. And the statutory powers of waiver and modification give the Secretary the means to offer the needed assistance. He can, for purposes of this special loan forgiveness program, scratch the pre-existing conditions for discharge and specify different conditions met by the affected borrowers. That is what the congressionally delegated powers are for. If the Secretary did not use them, Congress would be appalled.

In the dissenters' view, the loan cancellation program was no different. While Congress may not have anticipated the particular emergency created by the pandemic, "Congress knew that national emergencies would continue to arise. And Congress decided that when they did, the Secretary should have the power to offer relief without waiting for another, incident-specific round of legislation. Emergencies, after all, are emergencies, where speed is of the essence."

The majority never questioned the existence of the emergency, although it did note that President Biden had declared the "epidemic" at end. Did that end the emergency for affected parties? The majority says that the issue is "who decides." But did

Congress already decide in the HEROES Act? How could it have been more specific *before* the scope of the pandemic was recognized? What does a robust major questions doctrine mean for legislative delegations of emergency powers to the executive branch, more generally?

C. Too Much Oversight: The Legislative Veto

After examining the growth of administrative government in the section on delegation, it will likely come as no surprise to learn that the Congress has sought to improve its oversight of agencies and, accordingly, to exercise greater control over agency action. The most popular and perhaps the most important of the devices relied upon by the Congress to improve oversight has been the legislative veto. The device works by attaching to the delegations to the agencies a condition that agency actions implementing the delegated powers will be effective only if not vetoed by action of one or both houses of Congress. As you read the next decision, consider the assertion from Justice White's dissenting opinion in the *Chadha* decision that the legislative veto had become so important to the Congress that without it

> Congress is faced with a Hobson's choice: either to refrain from delegating the necessary authority, leaving itself with a hopeless task of writing laws with the requisite specificity to cover endless special circumstances across the entire policy landscape, or in the alternative, to abdicate its lawmaking function to the executive branch and independent agencies.

Immigration and Naturalization Service v. Chadha

United States Supreme Court
462 U.S. 919, 103 S. Ct. 2764, 77 L. Ed. 2d 317 (1983)

CHIEF JUSTICE BURGER delivered the opinion of the Court. . . .

Chadha is an East Indian who was born in Kenya and holds a British passport. He was lawfully admitted to the United States in 1966 on a nonimmigrant student visa. His visa expired on June 30, 1972. On October 11, 1973, the District Director of the Immigration and Naturalization Service ordered Chadha to show cause why he should not be deported for having "remained in the United States for longer time than permitted." Pursuant to § 242(b) of the Immigration and Nationality Act (Act), 8 U.S.C. § 1252(b), a deportation hearing was held before an immigration judge on January 11, 1974. Chadha conceded that he was deportable for overstaying his visa and the hearing was adjourned to enable him to file an application for suspension of deportation under § 244(a)(1) of the Act. . . .

After Chadha submitted his application for suspension of deportation, the deportation hearing was resumed on February 7, 1974. On the basis of evidence adduced at the hearing, affidavits submitted with the application, and the results of a character investigation conducted by the INS, the immigration judge, on June 25, 1974, ordered that Chadha's deportation be suspended. The immigration judge found that

Chadha met the requirements of §244(a)(1): He had resided continuously in the United States for over seven years, was of good moral character, and would suffer "extreme hardship" if deported.

Pursuant to §244(c)(1) of the Act, . . . the immigration judge suspended Chadha's deportation and a report of the suspension was transmitted to Congress. Section §244(c)(1) provides:

> Upon application by any alien who is found by the Attorney General to meet the requirements of subsection (a) of this section the Attorney General may in his discretion suspend deportation of such alien. If the deportation of any alien is suspended under the provisions of this subsection, a complete and detailed statement of the facts and pertinent provisions of law in the case shall be reported to the Congress with the reasons for such suspension. Such reports shall be submitted on the first day of each calendar month in which Congress is in session.

Once the Attorney General's recommendation for suspension of Chadha's deportation was conveyed to Congress, Congress had the power under §244(c)(2) of the Act, 8 U.S.C. §1254(c)(2), to veto the Attorney General's determination that Chadha should not be deported. Section 244(c)(2) provides:

> (2) In the case of an alien specified in paragraph (1) of subsection (a) of this subsection — if during the session of the Congress at which a case is reported, or prior to the close of the session of the Congress next following the session at which a case is reported, either the Senate or the House of Representatives passes a resolution stating in substance that it does not favor the suspension of such deportation, the Attorney General shall thereupon deport such alien or authorize the alien's voluntary departure at his own expense under the order of deportation in the manner provided by law. If, within the time above specified, neither the Senate nor the House of Representatives shall pass such a resolution, the Attorney General shall cancel deportation proceedings.

The June 25, 1974 order of the immigration judge suspending Chadha's deportation remained outstanding as a valid order for a year and a half. For reasons not disclosed by the record, Congress did not exercise the veto authority reserved to it under §244(c)(2) until the first session of the 94th Congress. This was the final session in which Congress, pursuant to §244(c)(2), could act to veto the Attorney General's determination that Chadha should not be deported. The session ended on December 19, 1975. . . . Absent Congressional action, Chadha's deportation proceedings would have been cancelled after this date and his status adjusted to that of a permanent resident alien. . . .

On December 12, 1975, Representative Eilberg, Chairman of the Judiciary Subcommittee on Immigration, Citizenship, and International Law, introduced a resolution opposing "the granting of permanent residence in the United States to [six] aliens," including Chadha. . . . The resolution was referred to the House Committee on the Judiciary. On December 16, 1975, the resolution was discharged from further consideration by the House Committee on the Judiciary and submitted to the House of Representatives for a vote. The resolution had not been printed and was not made available to other Members of the House prior to or at the time it was voted on. So far as the record before us shows, the House consideration of the resolution was based on Representative Eilberg's statement from the floor that

> [i]t was the feeling of the committee, after reviewing 340 cases, that the aliens contained in the resolution [Chadha and five others] did not meet these statutory requirements, particularly as it relates to hardship; and it is the opinion of the committee that their deportation should not be suspended.

The resolution was passed without debate or recorded vote. Since the House action was pursuant to § 244(c)(2), the resolution was not treated as an Article I legislative act; it was not submitted to the Senate or presented to the President for his action.

After the House veto of the Attorney General's decision to allow Chadha to remain in the United States, the immigration judge reopened the deportation proceedings to implement the House order deporting Chadha. Chadha moved to terminate the proceedings on the ground that § 244(c)(2) is unconstitutional. The immigration judge held that he had no authority to rule on the constitutional validity of § 244(c)(2). On November 8, 1976, Chadha was ordered deported pursuant to the House action. . . .

Pursuant to § 106(a) of the Act, Chadha filed a petition for review of the deportation order in the United States Court of Appeals for the Ninth Circuit. [T]he Court of Appeals held that the House was without constitutional authority to order Chadha's deportation; accordingly it directed the Attorney General "to cease and desist from taking any steps to deport this alien based upon the resolution enacted by the House of Representatives. The essence of its holding was that § 244(c)(2) violates the constitutional doctrine of separation of powers.

We granted *certiorari* and we now affirm.

[T]he fact that a given law or procedure is efficient, convenient, and useful in facilitating functions of government, standing alone, will not save it if it is contrary to the Constitution. Convenience and efficiency are not the primary objectives — or the hallmarks — of democratic government and our inquiry is sharpened rather than blunted by the fact that Congressional veto provisions are appearing with increasing frequency in statutes which delegate authority to executive and independent agencies:

> Since 1932, when the first veto provision was enacted into law, 295 congressional veto-type procedures have been inserted in 196 different statutes as follows: from 1932 to 1939, five statutes were affected; from 1940–49, nineteen statutes; between 1950–59, thirty-four statutes; and from 1960–69, forty-nine. From the year 1970 to 1975, at least one hundred sixty-three such provisions were included in eighty-nine laws.

Abourezk, *The Congressional Veto: A Contemporary Response to Executive Encroachment on Legislative Prerogatives*, 52 Ind. L. Rev. 323, 324 (1977).

Justice White undertakes to make a case for the proposition that the one-House veto is a useful "political invention," and we need not challenge that assertion. We can even concede this utilitarian argument although the long range political wisdom of this "invention" is arguable. But policy arguments supporting even useful "political inventions" are subject to the demands of the Constitution which defines powers and, with respect to this subject, sets out just how those powers are to be exercised.

Explicit and unambiguous provisions of the Constitution prescribe and define the respective functions of the Congress and of the Executive in the legislative process. Since the precise terms of those familiar provisions are critical to the resolution of this case, we set them out verbatim. [*See* Art. I §1, Art. I, §7, cl. 2, Art. I, §7, cl. 3.]

These provisions of Art. I are integral parts of the constitutional design for the separation of powers. We have recently noted that "[t]he principle of separation of powers was not simply an abstract generalization in the minds of the Framers; it was woven into the documents that they drafted in Philadelphia in the summer of 1787." [W]e see that the purposes underlying the Presentment Clauses, Art. I, §7, cls. 2, 3, and the bicameral requirement of Art. I. §1 and §7, cl. 2, guide our resolution of the important question presented in this case. The very structure of the articles delegating and separating powers under Arts. I, II, and III exemplify the concept of separation of powers and we now turn to Art. I.

The Presentment Clause

The records of the Constitutional Convention reveal that the requirement that all legislation be presented to the President before becoming law was uniformly accepted by the Framers. Presentment to the President and the Presidential veto were considered so imperative that the draftsmen took special pains to assure that these requirements could not be circumvented. During the final debate on Art I, §7, cl. 2, James Madison expressed concern that it might easily be evaded by the simple expedient of calling a proposed law a "resolution" or "vote" rather than a "bill." 2 M. Farrand, *The Records of the Federal Convention of 1787* 301–302. As a consequence, Art. I, §7, cl. 3, was added.

The decision to provide the President with a limited and qualified power to nullify proposed legislation by veto was based on the profound conviction of the Framers that the powers conferred on Congress were the powers to be most carefully circumscribed. It is beyond doubt that lawmaking was a power to be shared by both Houses and the President. In *The Federalist No. 73* Hamilton focused on the President's role in making laws:

> If even no propensity had ever discovered itself in the legislative body to invade the rights of the Executive, the rules of just reasoning and theoretic propriety would of themselves teach us that the one ought not to be left to

the mercy of the other, but ought to possess a constitutional and effectual power of self-defense. . . .

The President's role in the lawmaking process also reflects the Framers' careful efforts to check whatever propensity a particular Congress might have to enact oppressive, improvident, or ill-considered measures. The President's veto role in the legislative process was described later during public debate on ratification:

> It establishes a salutary check upon the legislative body, calculated to guard the community against the effects of faction, precipitancy, or of any impulse unfriendly to the public good which may happen to influence a majority of that body. The primary inducement to conferring the power in question upon the Executive is to enable him to defend himself; the secondary one is to increase the chances in favor of the community against the passing of bad laws through haste, inadvertence, or design.

The Federalist No. 73 (A. Hamilton).

Bicameralism

The bicameral requirement of Art. I, §§ 1, 7 was of scarcely less concern to the Framers than was the Presidential veto and indeed the two concepts are interdependent. By providing that no law could take effect without the concurrence of the prescribed majority of the Members of both Houses, the Framers reemphasized their belief, already remarked upon in connection with the Presentment Clauses, that legislation should not be enacted unless it has been carefully and fully considered by the Nation's elected officials. In the Constitutional Convention debates on the need for a bicameral legislature, James Wilson, later to become a Justice of this Court, commented:

> Despotism comes on mankind in different shapes. Sometimes in an Executive, sometimes in a military, one. Is there danger of a Legislative despotism? Theory & practice both proclaim it. If the Legislative authority be not restrained, there can be neither liberty nor stability; and it can only be restrained by dividing it within itself, into distinct and independent branches. In a single house there is no check, but the inadequate one, of the virtue & good sense of those who compose it.

1 M. Farrand at 254.

Hamilton argued that a Congress comprised of a single House was antithetical to the very purposes of the Constitution. Were the Nation to adopt a constitution providing for only one legislative organ, he warned:

> we shall finally accumulate, in a single body, all the most important prerogatives of sovereignty, and thus entail upon our posterity one of the most execrable forms of government that human infatuation ever contrived. Thus we should create in reality that very tyranny which the adversaries of the new Constitution either are, or affect to be, solicitous to avert.

The Federalist No. 22.

These observations are consistent with what many of the Framers expressed, none more cogently than Hamilton in pointing up the need to divide and disperse power in order to protect liberty:

> In republican government, the legislative authority necessarily predominates. The remedy for this inconvenience is to divide the legislature into different branches; and to render them, by different modes of election and different principles of action, as little connected with each other as the nature of their common functions and their common dependence on the society will admit.

The Federalist No. 51. . . .

However familiar, it is useful to recall that apart from their fear that special interests could be favored at the expense of public needs, the Framers were also concerned, although not of one mind, over the apprehensions of the smaller states. Those states feared a commonality of interest among the larger states would work to their disadvantage; representatives of the larger states, on the other hand, were skeptical of a legislature that could pass laws favoring a minority of the people. It need hardly be repeated here that the Great Compromise, under which one House was viewed as representing the people and the other the states, allayed the fears of both the large and small states.

We see therefore that the Framers were acutely conscious that the bicameral requirement and the Presentment Clauses would serve essential constitutional functions. The President's participation in the legislative process was to protect the Executive Branch from Congress and to protect the whole people from improvident laws. The division of the Congress into two distinctive bodies assures that the legislative power would be exercised only after opportunity for full study and debate in separate settings. The President's unilateral veto power, in turn, was limited by the power of two-thirds of both Houses of Congress to overrule a veto thereby precluding final arbitrary action of one person. It emerges clearly that the prescription of legislative action in Art. I, §§ 1, 7 represents the Framers's decision that the legislative power of the Federal government be exercised in accord with a single finely wrought and exhaustively considered, procedure.

The Constitution sought to divide the delegated powers of the new federal government into three defined categories, legislative, executive and judicial, to assure, as nearly as possible, that each Branch of government would confine itself to its assigned responsibility. The hydraulic pressure inherent within each of the separate Branches to exceed the outer limits of its power, even to accomplish desirable objectives, must be resisted.

Although not "hermetically" sealed from one another, the powers delegated to the three Branches are functionally identifiable. When any Branch acts, it is presumptively exercising the power the Constitution has delegated to it. When the Executive acts, it presumptively acts in an executive or administrative capacity as defined in Art. II. And when, as here, one House of Congress purports to act, it is presumptively acting within its assigned sphere.

Beginning with this presumption, we must nevertheless establish that the challenged action under §244(c)(2) is of a kind to which the procedural requirements of Art. I, §7 apply. Not every action taken by either House is subject to the bicameralism and presentment requirements of Art. I. Whether actions taken by either House are, in law and fact, an exercise of legislative power depends not on their form but upon "whether they contain matter which is properly to be regarded as legislative in its character and effect.

Examination of the action taken here by one House pursuant to §244(c)(2) reveals that it was essentially legislative in purpose and effect. In purporting to exercise power defined in Art. I, §8, cl. 4 to "establish an uniform Rule of Naturalization," the House took action that had the purpose and effect of altering the legal rights, duties and relations of persons, including the Attorney General, Executive Branch officials and Chadha, all outside the legislative branch. Section 244(c)(2) purports to authorize one House of Congress to require the Attorney General to deport an individual alien whose deportation otherwise would be cancelled under §244. The one-House veto operated in this case to overrule the Attorney General and mandate Chadha's deportation; absent the House action, Chadha would remain in the United States. Congress has *acted* and its action has altered Chadha's status.

The legislative character of the one-House veto in this case is confirmed by the character of the Congressional action it supplants. Neither the House of Representatives nor the Senate contends that, absent the veto provision in §244(c)(2), either of them, or both of them acting together, could effectively require the Attorney General to deport an alien once the Attorney General, in the exercise of legislatively delegated authority had determined the alien should remain in the United States. Without the challenged provision in §244(c)(2), this could have been achieved if at all, only by legislation requiring deportation. Similarly, a veto by one House of Congress under §244(c)(2) cannot be justified as an attempt at amending the standards set out in §244(a)(1), or as a repeal of §244 as applied to Chadha. Amendment and repeal of statutes, no less than enactment, must conform with Art. I.

The nature of the decision implemented by the one-House veto in this case further manifests its legislative character. After long experience with the clumsy, time consuming private bill procedure, Congress made a deliberate choice to delegate to the Executive Branch, and specifically to the Attorney General, the authority to allow deportable aliens to remain in this country in certain specified circumstances. It is not disputed that this choice to delegate authority is precisely the kind of decision that can be implemented only in accordance with the procedures set out in Art. I. Disagreement with the Attorney General's decision on Chadha's deportation — that is, Congress' decision to deport Chadha — no less than Congress's original choice to delegate to the Attorney General the authority to make that decision, involves determinations of policy that Congress can implement in only one way; bicameral passage followed by presentment to the President. Congress must abide by its delegation of authority until that delegation is legislatively altered or revoked.

Finally, we see that when the Framers intended to authorize either House of Congress to act alone and outside of its prescribed bicameral legislative role, they narrowly and precisely defined the procedure for such action. There are but four provisions in the Constitution, explicit and unambiguous, by which one House may act alone with the unreviewable force of law, not subject to the President's veto:

> (a) The House of Representatives alone was given the power to initiate impeachments. Art. I, § 2, cl. 6;

> (b) The Senate alone was given the power to conduct trials following impeachment on charges initiated by the House and to convict following trial. Art. I, § 3, cl. 5;

> (c) The Senate alone was given final unreviewable power to approve or to disapprove presidential appointments. Art. II, § 2, cl. 2;

> (d) The Senate alone was given unreviewable power to ratify treaties negotiated by the President. Art. II, § 2, cl. 2.

Clearly, when the Draftsmen sought to confer special powers on one House, independent of the other House, or of the President, they did so in explicit, unambiguous terms. These carefully defined exceptions from presentment and bicameralism underscore the difference between the legislative functions of Congress and other unilateral but important and binding one-House acts provided for in the Constitution. These exceptions are narrow, explicit, and separately justified; none of them authorize the action challenged here. On the contrary, they provide further support for the conclusion that Congressional authority is not to be implied and of the conclusion that the veto provided for in § 244(c)(2) is not authorized by the constitutional design of the power of the Legislative Branch.

Since it is clear that the action by the House under § 244(c)(2) was not within any of the express constitutional exceptions authorizing one House to act alone, and equally clear that it was an exercise of legislative power, that action was subject to the standards prescribed in Article I. The bicameral requirement, the Presentment Clauses, the President's veto, and Congress' power to override a veto were intended to erect enduring checks on each Branch and to protect the people from the improvident exercise of power by mandating certain prescribed steps. To preserve those checks, and maintain the separation of powers, the carefully defined limits on the power of each Branch must not be eroded. To accomplish what has been attempted by one House of Congress in this case requires action in conformity with the express procedures of the Constitution's prescription for legislative action: passage by a majority of both Houses and presentment to the President.

The veto authorized by § 244(c)(2) doubtless has been in many respects a convenient shortcut; the "sharing" with the Executive by Congress of its authority over aliens in this manner is, on its face, an appealing compromise. In purely practical terms, it is obviously easier for action to be taken by one House without submission to the President; but it is crystal clear from the records of the Convention, contemporaneous writings and debates, that the Framers ranked other values higher than efficiency. The records of the Convention and debates in the States preceding ratification underscore the common desire to define and limit the exercise of the newly created federal powers affecting the states and the people. There is unmistakable expression of a determination that legislation by the national Congress be a step-by-step, deliberate and deliberative process.

The choices we discern as having been made in the Constitutional Convention impose burdens on governmental processes that often seem clumsy, inefficient, even unworkable, but those hard choices were consciously made by men who had lived under a form of government that permitted arbitrary governmental acts to go unchecked. There is no support in the Constitution or decisions of this Court for the proposition that the cumbersomeness and delays often encountered in complying with explicit Constitutional standards may be avoided, either by the Congress or by the President. See *Youngstown Sheet & Tube Co. v. Sawyer*. With all the obvious flaws of delay, untidiness, and potential for abuse, we have not yet found a better way to preserve freedom than by making the exercise of power subject to the carefully crafted restraints spelled out in the Constitution.

We hold that the Congressional veto provision in §244(c)(2) is unconstitutional. Accordingly, the judgment of the Court of Appeals is *Affirmed*.

Justice Powell, concurring in the judgment.

The Court's decision, based on the Presentment Clauses, Art. I, §7, cls. 2 and 3, apparently will invalidate every use of the legislative veto. The breadth of this holding gives one pause. Congress has included the veto in literally hundreds of statutes, dating back to the 1930s. Congress clearly views this procedure as essential to controlling the delegation of power to administrative agencies. One reasonably may disagree with Congress' assessment of the veto's utility, but the respect due its judgment as a coordinate branch of Government cautions that our holding should be no more extensive than necessary to decide this case. In my view, the case may be decided on a narrower ground. When Congress finds that a particular person does not satisfy the statutory criteria for permanent residence in this country it has assumed a judicial function in violation of the principle of separation of powers. Accordingly, I concur only in the judgment.

The Framers perceived that "[t]he accumulation of all powers legislative, executive and judiciary in the same hands, whether hereditary, self-appointed, or elective, may justly be pronounced the very definition of tyranny." *The Federalist No. 47* (James Madison). Theirs was not a baseless fear. One abuse that was prevalent during the Confederation was the exercise of judicial power by the state legislatures. The Framers were well acquainted with the danger of subjecting the determination of the rights of one person to the "tyranny of shifting majorities."

It was to prevent the recurrence of such abuses that the Framers vested the executive, legislative, and judicial powers in separate branches. Their concern that a legislature should not be able unilaterally to impose a substantial deprivation on one person was expressed not only in this general allocation of power, but also in more specific provisions, such as the Bill of Attainder Clause, Art. I, § 9, cl. 3. This Clause, and the separation of powers doctrine generally, reflect the Framers' concern that trial by a legislature lacks the safeguards necessary to prevent the abuse of power.

Functionally, the [separation of powers] doctrine may be violated in two ways. One branch may interfere impermissibly with the other's performance of its constitutionally assigned function. Alternatively, the doctrine may be violated when one branch assumes a function that more properly is entrusted to another. See *Youngstown Sheet & Tube Co. v. Sawyer.* This case presents the latter situation.

On its face, the House's action appears clearly adjudicatory. The House did not enact a general rule; rather it made its own determination that six specific persons did not comply with certain statutory criteria. It thus undertook the type of decision that traditionally has been left to other branches. Even if the House did not make a *de novo* determination, but simply reviewed the Immigration and Naturalization Service's findings, it still assumed a function ordinarily entrusted to the federal courts.

The impropriety of the Houses' assumption of this function is confirmed by the fact that its action raises the very danger the Framers sought to avoid — the exercise of unchecked power. In deciding whether Chadha deserves to be deported, Congress is not subject to any internal constraints that prevent it from arbitrarily depriving him of the right to remain in this country. Unlike the judiciary or an administrative agency, Congress is not bound by established substantive rules. Nor is it subject to the procedural safeguards, such as the right to counsel and a hearing before an impartial tribunal, that are present when a court or an agency adjudicates individual rights. The only effective constraint on Congress' power is political, but Congress is most accountable politically when it prescribes rules of general applicability. When it decides rights of specific persons, those rights are subject to "the tyranny of a shifting majority. . . ."

JUSTICE WHITE, dissenting.

Today the Court not only invalidates § 244(c)(2) of the Immigration and Naturalization Act, but also sounds the death knell for nearly 200 other statutory provisions in which Congress has reserved a "legislative veto." For this reason, the Court's decision is of surpassing importance. And it is for this reason that the Court would have been well-advised to decide the case if possible, on narrower grounds of separation of powers, leaving for full consideration the constitutionality of other congressional review statutes operating on such varied matters as war powers and agency rulemaking, some of which concern the independent regulatory agencies.

The prominence of the legislative veto mechanism in our contemporary political system and its importance to Congress can hardly be overstated. It has become a central means by which Congress secures the accountability of executive and independent agencies. Without the legislative veto, Congress is faced with a Hobson's choice: either to refrain from delegating the necessary authority leaving itself with a hopeless task of writing laws with the requisite specificity to cover endless special circumstances across the entire policy landscape, or in the alternative, to abdicate its lawmaking function to the executive branch and independent agencies. To choose the former leaves major national problems unresolved; to opt for the latter risks unaccountable policy making by those not elected to fill that role. Accordingly, over the past five decades, the legislative veto has been placed in nearly 200 statutes. The device is known in every field of governmental concern: reorganization, budgets, foreign affairs, war powers, and regulation of trade, safety, energy, the environment and the economy.

The legislative veto developed initially in response to the problems of reorganizing the sprawling government structure created in response to the Depression. The Reorganization Acts established the chief model for the legislative veto. When President Hoover requested authority to reorganize the government in 1929, he coupled his request that the "Congress be willing to delegate its authority over the problem (subject to defined principles) to the Executive" with a proposal for legislative review. He proposed that the Executive "should act upon approval of a joint committee of Congress or with the reservation of power of revision by Congress within some limited period adequate for its consideration." Congress followed President Hoover's suggestion and authorized reorganization subject to legislative review. Although the reorganization authority reenacted in 1933 did not contain a legislative veto provision, the provision returned during the Roosevelt Administration and has since been renewed numerous times. Over the years, the provision was used extensively. Presidents submitted 115 reorganization plans to Congress of which 23 were disapproved by Congress pursuant to legislative veto provisions.

During the 1970s the legislative veto was important in resolving a series of major constitutional disputes between the President and Congress over claims of the President to broad impoundment, war, and national emergency powers. [T]he legislative veto is more than "efficient, convenient, and useful." It is an important if not indispensable political invention that allows the President and Congress to resolve major constitutional and policy differences, assures the accountability of independent regulatory agencies, and preserves Congress' control over lawmaking. Perhaps there are other means of accommodation and accountability, but the increasing reliance of Congress upon the legislative veto suggests that the alternatives to which Congress must now turn are not entirely satisfactory.

The history of the legislative veto also makes clear that it has not been a sword with which Congress has struck out to aggrandize itself at the expense of the other branches — the concern of Madison and Hamilton. Rather, the veto has been a means of defense, a reservation of ultimate authority necessary if Congress is to fulfill its designated role under Article I as the nation's lawmaker. While the

President has often objected to particular legislative vetoes, generally those left in the hands of congressional committees, the Executive has more often agreed to legislative review as the price for a broad delegation of authority. To be sure, the President may have preferred unrestricted power, but that could be precisely why Congress thought it essential to retain a check on the exercise of delegated authority.

For all these reasons, the apparent sweep of the Court's decision today is regrettable. The Court's Article I analysis appears to invalidate all legislative vetoes irrespective of form or subject. Because the legislative veto is commonly found as a check upon rule-making by administrative agencies and upon broad-based policy decisions of the Executive Branch, it is particularly unfortunate that the Court reaches its decision in a case involving the exercise of a veto over deportation decisions regarding particular individuals. Courts should always be wary of striking statutes as unconstitutional; to strike an entire class of statutes based on consideration of a somewhat atypical and more-readily indictable exemplar of the class is irresponsible.

If the legislative veto were as plainly unconstitutional as the Court strives to suggest, its broad ruling today would be more comprehensible. But, the constitutionality of the legislative veto is anything but clearcut. If the veto devices so flagrantly disregarded the requirements of Article I as the Court today suggests, I find it incomprehensible that Congress, whose members are bound by oath to uphold the Constitution, would have placed these mechanisms in nearly 200 separate laws over a period of 50 years.

The reality of the situation is that the constitutional question posed today is one of immense difficulty over which the executive and legislative branches — as well as scholars and judges — have understandably disagreed. That disagreement stems from the silence of the Constitution on the precise question: The Constitution does not directly authorize or prohibit the legislative veto. Thus, our task should be to determine whether the legislative veto is consistent with the purposes of Art. I and the principles of Separation of Powers which are reflected in that Article and throughout the Constitution. We should not find the lack of a specific constitutional authorization for the legislative veto surprising, and I would not infer disapproval of the mechanism from its absence. From the summer of 1787 to the present the government of the United States has become an endeavor far beyond the contemplation of the Framers. Only within the last century has the complexity and size of the Federal Government's responsibilities grown so greatly that the Congress must rely on the legislative veto as the most effective if not the only means to insure their role as the nation's lawmakers. But the wisdom of the Framers was to anticipate that the nation would grow and new problems of governance would require different solutions. Accordingly, our Federal Government was intentionally chartered with the flexibility to respond to contemporary needs without losing sight of fundamental democratic principles. In my view, neither Article I of the

Constitution nor the doctrine of separation of powers is violated by this mechanism by which our elected representatives preserve their voice in the governance of the nation.

There is no question that a bill does not become a law until it is approved by both the House and the Senate, and presented to the President. Similarly I would not hesitate to strike an action of Congress in the form of a concurrent resolution which constituted an exercise of original lawmaking authority. I agree with the Court that the President's qualified veto power is a critical element in the distribution of powers under the Constitution, widely endorsed among the Framers, and intended to serve the President as a defense against legislative encroachment and to check the "passing of bad laws through haste, inadvertence, or design." *The Federalist No. 73* (A. Hamilton).

It does not, however, answer the constitutional question before us. The power to exercise a legislative veto is not the power to write new law without bicameral approval or presidential consideration. The veto must be authorized by statute and may only negative what an Executive department or independent agency has proposed. On its face, the legislative veto no more allows one House of Congress to make law than does the presidential veto confer such power upon the President. Accordingly, the Court properly recognizes that it "must establish that the challenged action under § 244(c)(2) is of the kind to which the procedural requirements of Art. I, § 7 apply" and admits that "not every action taken by either House is subject to the bicameralism and presentation requirements of Art. I."

The Court's holding today that all legislative-type action must be enacted through the lawmaking process ignores that legislative authority is routinely delegated to the Executive branch, to the independent regulatory agencies, and to private individuals and groups.

The wisdom and the constitutionality of these broad delegations are matters that still have not been put to rest. But for the present purposes, cases establish that by virtue of congressional delegation, legislative power can be exercised by independent agencies and Executive departments without the passage of new legislation. For some time, the sheer amount of law — the substantive rules that regulate private conduct and direct the operation of government — made by the agencies has far outnumbered the lawmaking engaged in by Congress through the traditional process. There is no question but that agency rule-making is lawmaking in any functional or realistic sense of the term. These regulations bind courts and officers of the federal government, may preempt state law and grant rights to and impose obligations on the public. In sum, they have the force of law.

If Congress may delegate lawmaking power to independent and executive agencies, it is most difficult to understand Article I as forbidding Congress from also reserving a check on legislative power for itself. Absent the veto, the agencies receiving delegations of legislative or quasi-legislative power may issue regulations having the force of law without bicameral approval and without the President's signature. It is thus not apparent why the reservation of a veto over the exercise of the legislative power must be subject to a more exacting test. In both cases, it is enough that the initial statutory authorizations comply with the Article I requirements.

The Court also takes no account of perhaps the most relevant consideration: However resolutions of disapproval under § 244(c)(2) are formally characterized, in reality, a departure from the status quo occurs only upon the concurrence of opinion among the House, Senate, and President. Reservations of legislative authority to be exercised by Congress should be upheld if the exercise of such reserved authority is consistent with the distribution of and limits upon legislative power that Article I provides.

The central concern of the presentation and bicameralism requirements of Article I is that when a departure from the legal status quo is undertaken, it is done with the approval of the President and both Houses of Congress — or, in the event of a presidential veto, a two-thirds majority in both Houses. This interest is fully satisfied by the operation of § 244(c)(2). The President's approval is found in the Attorney General's action in recommending to Congress that the deportation order for a given alien be suspended. The House and the Senate indicate their approval of the Executive's action by not passing a resolution of disapproval within the statutory period. Thus, a change in the legal status quo — the deportability of the alien — is consummated only with the approval of each of the three relevant actors. The disagreement of any one of the three maintains the alien's preexisting status: the Executive may choose not to recommend suspension; the House and Senate may each veto the recommendation. The effect on the rights and obligations of the affected individuals and upon the legislative system is precisely the same as if a private bill were introduced but failed to receive the necessary approval.

The Court of Appeals struck § 244(c)(2) as violative of the constitutional principle of separation of powers. It is true that the purpose of separating the authority of government is to prevent unnecessary and dangerous concentration of power in one branch. For that reason, the Framers saw fit to divide and balance the powers of government so that each branch would be checked by the others. Virtually every part of our constitutional system bears the mark of this judgment.

But the history of the separation of powers doctrine is also a history of accommodation and practicality. Apprehensions of an overly powerful branch have not led to undue prophylactic measures that handicap the effective working of the national government as a whole. The Constitution does not contemplate total separation of the three branches of Government.

I do not suggest that all legislative vetoes are necessarily consistent with separation of powers principles. A legislative check on an inherently executive function, for example that of initiating prosecutions, poses an entirely different question. But the legislative veto device here — and in many other settings — is far from an instance of legislative tyranny over the Executive. It is a necessary check on the unavoidably expanding power of the agencies, both executive and independent, as they engage in exercising authority delegated by Congress.

I regret that I am in disagreement with my colleagues on the fundamental questions that this case presents. But even more I regret the destructive scope of the Court's holding. Today's decision strikes down in one fell swoop provisions in more laws enacted by Congress than the Court has cumulatively invalidated in its history.

Notes and Questions

(1) The fundamental message of the *Chadha* opinion seems clear: Every "legislative" act that does not adhere to the "finely wrought and exhaustively considered procedure" of bicameral consideration and presentment to the President is unconstitutional. If there was any doubt concerning the application of the *Chadha* holding to other vetoes, it was soon dispelled by the Court's summary affirmances of decisions invalidating one- and two-house vetoes of the Federal Energy Regulatory Commission and the Federal Trade Commission. *See Process Gas Consumer Group v. Consumer Energy Council*, 463 U.S. 1216 (1983); *United States Senate v. FTC*, 463 U.S. 1216 (1983).

(2) Evaluate Chief Justice Burger's portrayal of the history and purposes of the separation of powers doctrine. Is his analysis convincing in light of the purposes of separation identified earlier in this unit? If the Burger opinion shortchanged the efficiency reasons for the separation of powers in favor of the tyranny rationale, would accounting for the efficiency reasons change the result in the *Chadha* case?

(3) How did the Court reach the conclusion that the veto in the *Chadha* case was a legislative act? If some actions of the Congress fall outside the presentment requirements of Article I, what are they?

(4) Do you agree with Justice Powell's position that the effect of the veto in the *Chadha* situation was to perform a judicial function in violation of Article III? In view of the facts surrounding the veto of the suspension decision, it may be that Chadha was simply denied the fundamental fairness of an adjudicatory proceeding before such an important decision concerning his future could be made. Why did the majority decline Justice Powell's invitation to decide the case on this narrower ground?

(5) How strong is Justice White's argument that once delegated, the power of an agency should be subject to a congressional check? In other words, if the Congress could deport Chadha by statute, why not allow the Congress to achieve the same result through their oversight of an agency?

(6) Was the Attorney General engaged in "lawmaking" here? If he was lawmaking, is there any reason to deny the Congress the right to perform an executive or, for that matter, a judicial function?

D. Executive Control Over the Appointment and Removal of Officials

Article II, § 2, cl. 2 of the Constitution provides:

[The President] shall nominate, and by and with the Advice and Consent of the Senate, shall appoint ... all other Officers of the United States, whose Appointments are not herein otherwise provided for, and which shall be established by law; but the Congress may by Law vest the Appointment of such inferior Officers, as they think proper, in the President alone, in the Courts of Law, or in the Heads of Departments.

It is thus clear that the President must appoint principal officers, with Senate advice and consent, and that Congress may choose to vest the appointment of inferior officers in the President, the courts, or agency heads. It is far from clear which officials are principal and inferior. Note as well that the Constitution says nothing about the removal of officials, once appointed. The cases below probe these issues.

Morrison v. Olson

United States Supreme Court
487 U.S. 654, 108 S. Ct. 2597, 101 L. Ed. 2d 569 (1988)

CHIEF JUSTICE REHNQUIST delivered the opinion of the Court.

[The 1978 Ethics in Government Act created a special court (the Special Division) that was authorized, in response to a request by the Attorney General, to appoint an independent counsel to investigate and prosecute possible violations of federal law by certain high ranking government officials. The Act provided that the Attorney General could remove the independent counsel, but only for "good cause." Pursuant to the procedures outlined in the Act, the Special Division appointed Alexia Morrison an independent counsel to investigate Assistant Attorney General Olson's alleged obstruction of a congressional inquiry. The Supreme Court first held that Morrison's appointment was consistent with the Appointments Clause, and then upheld the provision that protected the independent counsel from removal except for "good cause."]

[T]his case does not involve an attempt by Congress itself to gain a role in the removal of executive officials other than its established powers of impeachment and conviction. The Act instead puts the removal power squarely in the hands of the Executive Branch; an independent counsel may be removed from office, "only by the personal action of the Attorney General, and only for good cause." There is no requirement of congressional approval of the Attorney General's removal decision, though the decision is subject to judicial review. In our view, the removal provisions of the Act make this case more analogous to *Humphrey's Executor* [*v. United States*, 295 U.S. 602 (1935)].

In *Humphrey's Executor*, the issue was whether a statute restricting the President's power to remove the commissioners of the Federal Trade Commission only for "inefficiency, neglect of duty, or malfeasance in office" was consistent with the

Constitution. We stated that whether Congress can "condition the [President's power of removal] by fixing a definite term and precluding a removal except for cause, will depend upon the character of the office." The President's power to remove government officials simply was not "all-inclusive in respect of civil officers with the exception of the judiciary provided by the Constitution." At least in regard to "quasi-legislative" and "quasi-judicial" agencies such as the FTC,

> [t]he authority of Congress, in creating [such] agencies, to require them to act in discharge of their duties independently of executive control ... includes, as an appropriate incident, power to fix the period during which they shall continue in office, and to forbid their removal except for cause in the meantime.

In *Humphrey's Executor*, we found it "plain" that the Constitution did not give the President "illimitable power of removal" over the officers of independent agencies. [T]he real question is whether the removal restrictions are of such a nature that they impede the President's ability to perform his constitutional duty, and the functions of the officials in question must be analyzed in that light.

Although the counsel exercises no small amount of discretion and judgment in deciding how to carry out her duties under the Act, we simply do not see how the President's need to control the exercise of that discretion is so central to the functioning of the Executive Branch as to require as a matter of constitutional law that the counsel be terminable at will by the President.

Nor do we think that the "good cause" removal provision at issue here impermissibly burdens the President's power to control or supervise the independent counsel, as an executive official, in the execution of her duties under the Act. This is not a case in which the power to remove an executive official has been completely stripped from the President, thus providing no means for the President to ensure the "faithful execution" of the laws. Rather, because the independent counsel may be terminated for "good cause," the Executive, through the Attorney General, retains ample authority to assure that the counsel is competently performing her statutory responsibilities in a manner that comports with the provisions of the Act. Although we need not decide in this case exactly what is encompassed within the term "good cause" under the Act, the legislative history of the removal provision also makes clear that the Attorney General may remove an independent counsel for "misconduct." Here, as with the provision of the Act conferring the appointment authority of the independent counsel on the special court, the congressional determination to limit the removal power of the Attorney General was essential, in the view of Congress, to establish the necessary independence of the office. We do not think that this limitation as it presently stands sufficiently deprives the President of control over the independent counsel to interfere impermissibly with his constitutional obligation to ensure the faithful execution of the laws.

The final question to be addressed is whether the Act, taken as a whole, violates the principle of separation of powers by unduly interfering with the role of the

Executive Branch. We observe first that this case does not involve an attempt by Congress to increase its own powers at the expense of the Executive Branch. Indeed, with the exception of the power of impeachment — which applies to all officers of the United States — Congress retained for itself no powers of control or supervision over an independent counsel. The Act does empower certain members of Congress to request the Attorney General to apply for the appointment of an independent counsel, but the Attorney General has no duty to comply with the request, although he must respond within a certain time limit. Other than that, Congress' role under the Act is limited to receiving reports or other information and oversight of the independent counsel's activities, functions that we have recognized generally as being incidental to the legislative function of Congress. See *McGrain v. Daugherty*, 273 U.S. 135, 174 (1927).

Similarly, we do not think that the Act works any *judicial* usurpation of properly executive functions. As should be apparent from our discussion of the Appointments Clause above, the power to appoint inferior officers such as independent counsels is not in itself an "executive" function in the constitutional sense, at least when Congress has exercised its power to vest the appointment of an inferior office in the "courts of Law." We note nonetheless that under the Act the Special Division has no power to appoint an independent counsel *sua sponte*; it may only do so upon the specific request of the Attorney General, and the courts are specifically prevented from reviewing the Attorney General's decision not to seek appoint. In addition, once the court has appointed a counsel and defined her jurisdiction, it has no power to supervise or control the activities of the counsel. As we pointed out in our discussion of the Special Division in relation to Article III, the various powers delegated by the statute to the Division are not supervisory or administrative, nor are they functions that the Constitution requires be performed by officials within the Executive Branch. The Act does give a federal court the power to review the Attorney General's decision to remove an independent counsel, but in our view this is a function that is well within the traditional power of the judiciary.

Finally, we do not think that the Act "impermissibly undermine[s]" the powers of the Executive Branch, or "disrupts the proper balance between the coordinate branches [by] prevent[ing] the Executive Branch from accomplishing its constitutionally assigned functions." It is undeniable that the Act reduces the amount of control or supervision that the Attorney General and, through him, the President exercises over the investigation and prosecution of a certain class of alleged criminal activity. The Attorney General is not allowed to appoint the individual of his choice; he does not determine the counsel's jurisdiction; and his power to remove a counsel is limited. Nonetheless, the Act does give the Attorney General several means of supervising or controlling the prosecutorial powers that may be wielded by an independent counsel. Most importantly, the Attorney General retains the power to remove the counsel for "good cause," a power that we have already concluded provides the Executive with substantial ability to ensure that the laws are "faithfully executed" by an independent counsel. No independent counsel may be appointed without a specific request by the Attorney General, and the Attorney General's decision not to request appointment if he finds "no reasonable grounds to believe that further investigation is warranted" is committed to his unreviewable discretion. The Act thus gives the Executive a degree of control over the power to initiate an investigation by the independent counsel. In addition, the jurisdiction of the independent counsel is defined with reference to the facts submitted by the Attorney General, and once a counsel is appointed, the Act requires that the counsel abide by Justice Department policy unless it is not "possible" to do so. Notwithstanding the fact that the counsel is to some degree "independent" and free from Executive supervision to a greater extent than other federal prosecutors, in our view these features of the Act give the Executive Branch sufficient control over the independent counsel to ensure that the President is able to perform his constitutionally assigned duties.

Justice Kennedy took no part in the consideration or decision of this case.

Justice Scalia, dissenting.

The Court concedes that "[t]here is no real dispute that the functions performed by the independent counsel are 'executive'," though it qualifies that concession by adding "in the sense that they are 'law enforcement' functions that typically have been undertaken by officials within the Executive Branch." The statute before us deprives the President of exclusive control over that quintessentially executive activity: The Court does not, and could not possibly, assert that it does not. That is indeed the whole object of the statute. Instead, the Court points out that the President, through his Attorney General, has at least *some* control. That concession is alone enough to invalidate the statute, but I cannot refrain from pointing out that the Court greatly exaggerates the extent of that "some" presidential control.

It is not for us to determine, and we have never presumed to determine, how much of the purely executive powers of government must be within the full control of the President. The Constitution prescribes that they *all* are. The Court has, nonetheless, replaced the clear constitutional prescription that the executive power belongs to the President with a "balancing test." What are the standards to determine how the balance is to be struck, that is, how much removal of presidential power is too much? Once we depart from the text of the Constitution, just where short of that do we stop? The most amazing feature of the Court's opinion is that it does not even purport to give an answer. It simply *announces*, with no analysis, that the ability to control the decision whether to investigate and prosecute the President's closest advisors, and indeed the President himself, is not "so central to the functioning of the Executive Branch" as to be constitutionally required to be within the President's control. Apparently that is so because we say it is so.

Since our 1935 decision in *Humphrey's Executor*, it has been established that the line of permissible restriction upon removal of principal officers lies at the point at which the powers exercised by those officers are no longer purely executive. Thus, removal restrictions have been generally regarded as lawful for so-called "independent regulatory agencies," such as the Federal Trade Commission, which engage substantially in what has been called the "quasi-legislative activity" or rule-making, and for members of Article I courts, such as the Court of Military Appeals who engage in the "quasi-judicial" function of adjudication. It has often been observed, correctly in my view, that the line between "purely executive" functions and "quasi-legislative" or "quasi-judicial" functions is not a clear one or even a rational one. But at least it permitted the identification of certain officers, and certain agencies, whose functions were entirely within the control of the President. Congress had to be aware of that restriction in its legislation. Today, however, *Humphrey's Executor* is swept into the dustbin of repudiated constitutional principles.

The *ad hoc* approach to constitutional adjudication has real attraction, even apart from its work-saving potential. It is guaranteed to produce a result, in every case, that will make a majority of the Court happy with the law. The law is, by definition, precisely what the majority thinks, taking all things into account, it *ought* to be. I prefer to rely upon the judgment of the wise men who constructed our system, and of the people who approved it, and of two centuries of history that have shown it to be sound. Like it or not, that judgment says, quite plainly, that "[t]he executive Power shall be vested in a President of the United States."

Seila Law LLC v. Consumer Financial Protection Bureau

United States Supreme Court
140 S. Ct. 2183 (2020)

Chief Justice Roberts delivered the opinion of the Court.

[The Consumer Financial Protection Bureau (CFPB) issued a civil investigative demand to Seila Law, a California law firm that provides debt-related services to clients. The demand (essentially a subpoena) directed Seila Law to produce information and documents related to its business practices. Seila Law refused to comply, objecting on separation of powers grounds to the structure of the Bureau. The lower courts upheld the demand.]

In the wake of the 2008 financial crisis, Congress established the Consumer Financial Protection Bureau (CFPB), an independent regulatory agency tasked with ensuring that consumer debt products are safe and transparent. In organizing the CFPB, Congress deviated from the structure of nearly every other independent administrative agency in our history. Instead of placing the agency under the leadership of a board with multiple members, Congress provided that the CFPB would be led by a single Director, who serves for a longer term than the President and cannot be removed by the President except for inefficiency, neglect, or malfeasance. The CFPB Director has no boss, peers, or voters to report to. Yet the Director wields vast rulemaking, enforcement, and adjudicatory authority over a significant portion of the U.S. economy. The question before us is whether this arrangement violates the Constitution's separation of powers.

Under our Constitution, the "executive Power" — all of it — is "vested in a President," who must "take Care that the Laws be faithfully executed." Art. II,

§1, cl. 1; id., §3. Because no single person could fulfill that responsibility alone, the Framers expected that the President would rely on subordinate officers for assistance. Ten years ago, in *Free Enterprise Fund v. Public Company Accounting Oversight Bd.*, 561 U.S. 477 (2010), we reiterated that, "as a general matter," the Constitution gives the President "the authority to remove those who assist him in carrying out his duties." "Without such power, the President could not be held fully accountable for discharging his own responsibilities; the buck would stop somewhere else."

The President's power to remove—and thus supervise—those who wield executive power on his behalf follows from the text of Article II, was settled by the First Congress, and was confirmed in the landmark decision *Myers v. United States*, 272 U.S. 52 (1926). Our precedents have recognized only two exceptions to the President's unrestricted removal power. In *Humphrey's Executor v. United States*, 295 U.S. 602 (1935), we held that Congress could create expert agencies led by a group of principal officers removable by the President only for good cause. And in *Morrison v. Olson*, 487 U.S. 654 (1988), we held that Congress could provide tenure protections to certain inferior officers with narrowly defined duties. [Neither *Humphrey's Executor* nor *Morrison* resolves whether the CFPB Director's insulation from removal is constitutional.]

We are now asked to extend these precedents to a new configuration: an independent agency that wields significant executive power and is run by a single individual who cannot be removed by the President unless certain statutory criteria are met. We decline to take that step. While we need not and do not revisit our prior decisions allowing certain limitations on the President's removal power, there are compelling reasons not to extend those precedents to the novel context of an independent agency led by a single Director. Such an agency lacks a foundation in historical practice and clashes with constitutional structure by concentrating power in a unilateral actor insulated from Presidential control.

In addition to being a historical anomaly, the CFPB's single-Director configuration is incompatible with our constitutional structure. Aside from the sole exception of the Presidency, that structure scrupulously avoids concentrating power in the hands of any single individual.

To justify and check that authority—unique in our constitutional structure—the Framers made the President the most democratic and politically accountable official in Government. Only the President (along with the Vice President) is elected by the entire Nation. And the President's political accountability is enhanced by the solitary nature of the Executive Branch, which provides "a single object for the jealousy and watchfulness of the people." The resulting constitutional strategy is straightforward: divide power everywhere except for the Presidency, and render the President directly accountable to the people through regular elections. In that scheme, individual executive officials will still wield significant authority, but that authority remains subject to the ongoing supervision and control of the elected President.

The CFPB's single-Director structure contravenes this carefully calibrated system by vesting significant governmental power in the hands of a single individual accountable to no one. The Director is neither elected by the people nor meaningfully controlled (through the threat of removal) by someone who is. The Director does not even depend on Congress for annual appropriations. Yet the Director may unilaterally, without meaningful supervision, issue final regulations, oversee adjudications, set enforcement priorities, initiate prosecutions, and determine what penalties to impose on private parties. With no colleagues to persuade, and no boss or electorate looking over her shoulder, the Director may dictate and enforce policy for a vital segment of the economy affecting millions of Americans.

[S]everal other features of the CFPB combine to make the Director's removal protection even more problematic. Because the CFPB is headed by a single Director with a five-year term, some Presidents may not have any opportunity to shape its leadership and thereby influence its activities. A President elected in 2020 would likely not appoint a CFPB Director until 2023, and a President elected in 2028 may never appoint one. That means an unlucky President might get elected on a consumer-protection platform and enter office only to find herself saddled with a holdover Director from a competing political party who is dead set against that agenda.

THOMAS, J., whom GORSUCH, J., joins, concurring in part and dissenting in part.

The decision in *Humphrey's Executor* poses a direct threat to our constitutional structure and, as a result, the liberty of the American people. The Court concludes that it is not strictly necessary for us to overrule that decision. But with today's decision, the Court has repudiated almost every aspect of *Humphrey's Executor*. In a future case, I would repudiate what is left of this erroneous precedent.

KAGAN, J., with whom GINSBURG, BREYER, and SOTOMAYOR, JJ., join, dissenting in part.

Throughout the Nation's history, this Court has left most decisions about how to structure the Executive Branch to Congress and the President, acting through legislation they both agree to. In particular, the Court has commonly allowed those two branches to create zones of administrative independence by limiting the President's power to remove agency heads. The Federal Reserve Board. The Federal Trade Commission (FTC). The National Labor Relations Board. Statute after statute establishing such entities instructs the President that he may not discharge their directors except for cause—most often phrased as inefficiency, neglect of duty, or malfeasance in office. Those statutes, whose language the Court has repeatedly approved, provide the model for the removal restriction before us today. If precedent were any guide, that provision would have survived its encounter with this Court—and so would the intended independence of the Consumer Financial Protection Bureau (CFPB).

Our Constitution and history demand that result. The text of the Constitution allows these common for-cause removal limits. Nothing in it speaks of removal. And it grants Congress authority to organize all the institutions of American governance, provided only that those arrangements allow the President to perform his own constitutionally assigned duties. Still more, the Framers' choice to give the political branches wide discretion over administrative offices has played out through American history in ways that have settled the constitutional meaning.

The Court today fails to respect its proper role. It recognizes that this Court has approved limits on the President's removal power over heads of agencies much like the CFPB. Agencies possessing similar powers, agencies charged with similar missions, agencies created for similar reasons. The majority's explanation is that the heads of those agencies fall within an "exception" — one for multimember bodies and another for inferior officers — to a "general rule" of unrestricted presidential removal power. And the majority says the CFPB Director does not. That account, though, is wrong in every respect. The majority's general rule does not exist. Its exceptions, likewise, are made up for the occasion — gerrymandered so the CFPB falls outside them. And the distinction doing most of the majority's work — between multimember bodies and single directors — does not respond to the constitutional values at stake. If a removal provision violates the separation of powers, it is because the measure so deprives the President of control over an official as to impede his own constitutional functions. But with or without a for-cause removal provision, the President has at least as much control over an individual as over a commission — and possibly more.

[T]o make sense on the majority's own terms, the distinction between singular and plural agency heads must rest on a theory about why the former more easily "slip" from the President's grasp. But the majority has nothing to offer. In fact, the opposite is more likely to be true. A multimember structure reduces accountability to the President because it's harder for him to oversee, to influence — or to remove, if necessary — a group of five or more commissioners than a single director. Indeed, that is why Congress so often resorts to hydra-headed agencies. The majority says a single head is the greater threat because he may wield power "unilaterally" and "[w]ith no colleagues to persuade." [T]he majority has nothing but intuition to back up its essentially functionalist claim that the CFPB would be less capable of exercising power if it had more than one Director.

Notes and Questions

(1) Does *Morrison* represent a rejection of the formalism of *Chadha*? Can you reconcile the two decisions?

(2) On what basis could the Court approve a statute that deprives the President of control over a core executive function? What inferior officers could Congress now not authorize courts to appoint?

In *Edmond v. United States*, 520 U.S. 651 (1997), the Court upheld congressional authorization for the Secretary of Transportation to appoint civilian members of the Coast Guard Court of Criminal Appeals. The Court rejected the argument that judges of military Courts of Criminal Appeals are principal, not inferior, officers within the meaning of the Appointments Clause, which would have required that they be appointed by the President with the advice and consent of the Senate. Although the Court agreed that, in contrast to the independent counsel found to be an inferior officer in *Morrison*, the military judges are neither "limited in tenure," nor "limited in jurisdiction," and that "military appeals judges are charged with exercising significant authority on behalf of the United States," the Justices unanimously concluded that the military judges, supervised by the Judge Advocate General and the Court of Criminal Appeals for the Armed Forces, are inferior officers. Justice Scalia supplied the Court's rationale:

> Generally speaking, the term "inferior officer" connotes a relationship with some higher ranking officer or officers below the President: whether one is an "inferior officer" depends on whether he has a superior.

In *United States v. Arthrex, Inc.*, 141 S. Ct. 1970 (2021), the Court reviewed a challenge to the method of appointment to the Patent Trial and Appeal Board, an executive tribunal with the Patent and Trademark Office. The Board is composed largely of Administrative Patent Judges (APJs) appointed as inferior officers by the Secretary of Commerce. The Court applied *Edmond* and rejected the APJ appointment mechanism because the APJs have the "power to render a final decision on behalf of the United States" without review by their nominal superior or any other official in the executive branch.

(3) A different Appointments Clause issue was resolved by the Court in 2018. The Securities and Exchange Commission (SEC) has statutory authority to enforce the nation's securities laws. Often the SEC does so by instituting an administrative proceeding against an alleged wrongdoer. Usually, the SEC delegates the task of presiding over the proceeding to an administrative law judge (ALJ). SEC staff rather than the Commission itself select the ALJs. Once selected, an ALJ has authority to conduct an adversarial hearing for the accused and then render an initial decision. The SEC can review the initial decision, but if it declines review, the Commission issues an order that the initial decision becomes final.

When Raymond Lucia was charged with violating certain securities laws and an ALJ was to adjudicate the case, Lucia argued that the administrative proceeding was invalid because the ALJ had not been constitutionally appointed. Lucia argued the SEC ALJs are "Officers of the United States" and thus subject to the Appointments Clause. The SEC and Court of Appeals rejected Lucia's argument and held that SEC ALJs are not "Officers" but are instead mere employees—officials with lesser responsibilities who are not subject to the Appointments Clause. The Supreme Court reversed in *Lucia v. Securities and Exchange Commission*, 138 S. Ct. 2044 (2018). The majority reasoned that SEC ALJs hold a continuing office established by law, receive a career appointment to a position created by statute, and exercise significant discretion when carrying out important functions. In addition, because the SEC can decide against reviewing an ALJ decision, the ALJ decision may become the action of the Commission. Can you predict which agency personnel are "Officers of the

United States"? What can the SEC and similarly situated agencies do to ensure the lawfulness of ALJ appointments?

(4) Justice Scalia claimed that the Vesting Clause of Article II gives the President exclusive control over all exercises of executive power. Would any of the decisions you have read in this chapter have to be reversed if his premise was accepted? Which ones?

(5) In *Collins v. Yellen*, 141 S. Ct. 1761 (2021), the Court invalidated the structure of the Federal Housing Finance Agency (FHFA), created by Congress in 2008 as an "independent agency" tasked with regulating mortgage financing companies and, if necessary, stepping in as their conservator or receiver. Congress installed a single Director of the FHFA, whom the President could remove only "for cause." The Court was unimpressed with the efforts to distinguish the more limited authority of the FHFA Director from the CFBP in *Seila Law* — the CFPB administers 19 statutes to 1 for the FHFA, and the CFPB regulates millions of businesses and individuals while the FHFA regulates a small number of entities. The Court admonished that "the removal power helps the President maintain control over the subordinates he needs to carry out his duties," whatever the size or role of the agency. Do you think the Court would reach a different result in a challenge to removal involving a multi-member agency?

(6) The portion of the 1978 Ethics in Government Act that authorized the appointment of independent counsels expired on June 30, 1999. Paying careful attention to separation of powers concerns, see if you can outline the features of an effective and constitutional mechanism that would provide for investigating and prosecuting wrongdoing by high-ranking members of the executive branch. When the pertinent provisions of the Ethics in Government Act lapsed, Attorney General Janet Reno instructed Justice Department lawyers to draft regulations that would continue to permit the Attorney General to appoint special counsels. These internal Justice Department regulations remain in effect, 18 C.F.R. §600. In 2023, special counsel investigations were occurring simultaneously of former President Trump and President Biden, both involving alleged improper retention of classified information. Assuming the special counsels report to the Attorney General that criminal laws were likely violated by both Presidents, what guidance would you give to the Attorney General in deciding whether to indict either or both Presidents? *See* Jack Goldsmith, *Things Are Looking Pretty Weird for Merrick Garland*, N.Y. Times, Jan. 25, 2023.

Problem C

You have learned that the Appointments Clause of the Constitution is silent regarding the removal of executive appointees from office except in cases of impeachment, considered later in this Chapter. Although it has long been assumed that the President has a removal power, its scope and limits remain unclear. Is the removal power solely for the President? May Congress limit the President's removal power, and if so, to what extent? May Congress create its own mechanism for removing executive officials, separate from the impeachment procedures prescribed by Article I? *See Bowsher v. Synar*, 478 U.S. 714 (1986).

Like the CFPB in *Seila Law* and FHFA in *Collins*, the Commissioner of the Social Security Administration (SSA) is the sole head of an independent agency with for-cause removal protection by statute. A few months into his first term, President Joe Biden fired SSA Commissioner Andrew Saul, who had been appointed by President Donald Trump and who was following Trumpian policies. Commissioner Saul refused to submit his resignation as the President had requested. Would the SSA Commissioner succeed if he sued the President to get his job back?

E. Line Item Veto

Clinton v. City of New York

United States Supreme Court
524 U.S. 417, 118 S. Ct. 2091, 141 L. Ed. 2d 393 (1998)

JUSTICE STEVENS delivered the opinion of the Court.

The Line Item Veto Act (Act), 2 U.S.C. § 691 et seq., was enacted in April 1996 and became effective on January 1, 1997. The following day, six Members of Congress who had voted against the Act brought suit in the District Court for the District of Columbia challenging its constitutionality. On April 10, 1997, the District Court entered an order holding that the Act is unconstitutional. *Byrd v. Raines*, 956 F. Supp. 25. In obedience to the statutory direction to allow a direct, expedited appeal to this Court, see §§ 692(b)–(c), we promptly noted probable jurisdiction and expedited review. We determined, however, that the Members of Congress did not have standing to sue because they had not "alleged a sufficiently concrete injury to have established Article III standing," *Raines v. Byrd* [521 U.S. 811 (1997)]. [T]hus, "in . . . light of [the] overriding and time-honored concern about keeping the Judiciary's power within its proper constitutional sphere," we remanded the case to the District Court with instructions to dismiss the complaint for lack of jurisdiction.

Less than two months after our decision in that case, the President exercised his authority to cancel one provision in the Balanced Budget Act of 1997, and two provisions in the Taxpayer Relief Act of 1997, Pub. L. 105-34, 111 Stat. 788. Appellees, claiming that they had been injured by two of those cancellations, filed these cases in the District Court. That Court again held the statute invalid, and we again expedited our review. We now hold that these appellees have standing to challenge the constitutionality of the Act and, reaching the merits, we agree that the cancellation procedures set forth in the Act violate the Presentment Clause, Art. I, § 7, cl. 2, of the Constitution.

I

We begin by reviewing the canceled items that are at issue in these cases.

Section 4722(c) of the Balanced Budget Act

Title XIX of the Social Security Act, 79 Stat. 343, as amended, authorizes the Federal Government to transfer huge sums of money to the States to help finance medical care for the indigent. See 42 U.S.C. §1396d(b). In 1991, Congress directed that those federal subsidies be reduced by the amount of certain taxes levied by the States on health care providers. In 1994, the Department of Health and Human Services (HHS) notified the State of New York that 15 of its taxes were covered by the 1991 Act, and that as of June 30, 1994, the statute therefore required New York to return $955 million to the United States. The notice advised the State that it could apply for a waiver on certain statutory grounds. New York did request a waiver for those tax programs, as well as for a number of others, but HHS has not formally acted on any of those waiver requests. New York has estimated that the amount at issue for the period from October 1992 through March 1997 is as high as $2.6 billion.

Because HHS had not taken any action on the waiver requests, New York turned to Congress for relief. On August 5, 1997, Congress enacted a law that resolved the issue in New York's favor. Section 4722(c) of the Balanced Budget Act of 1997. On August 11, 1997, the President sent identical notices to the Senate and to the House of Representatives canceling "one item of new direct spending," specifying §4722(c) as that item, and stating that he had determined that "this cancellation will reduce the Federal budget deficit." He explained that §4722(c) would have permitted New York "to continue relying upon impermissible provider taxes to finance its Medicaid program" and that "[t]his preferential treatment would have increased Medicaid costs, would have treated New York differently from all other States, and would have established a costly precedent for other States to request comparable treatment."

Section 968 of the Taxpayer Relief Act

A person who realizes a profit from the sale of securities is generally subject to a capital gains tax. Under existing law, however, an ordinary business corporation can acquire a corporation, including a food processing or refining company, in a merger or stock-for-stock transaction in which no gain is recognized to the seller, see 26 U.S.C. §§354(a), 368(a); the seller's tax payment, therefore, is deferred. If, however, the purchaser is a farmers' cooperative, the parties cannot structure such a transaction because the stock of the cooperative may be held only by its members, see 26 U.S.C. §521(b)(2); thus, a seller dealing with a farmers' cooperative cannot obtain the benefits of tax deferral.

In §968 of the Taxpayer Relief Act of 1997, Congress amended §1042 of the Internal Revenue Code to permit owners of certain food refiners and processors to defer the recognition of gain if they sell their stock to eligible farmers' cooperatives. The purpose of the amendment, as repeatedly explained by its sponsors, was "to facilitate the transfer of refiners and processors to farmers' cooperatives." The amendment to §1042 was one of the 79 "limited tax benefits" authorized by the Taxpayer Relief Act of 1997 and specifically identified in Title XVII of that Act as "subject to [the] line item veto."

On the same date that he canceled the "item of new direct spending" involving New York's health care programs, the President also canceled this limited tax benefit. In his explanation of that action, the President endorsed the objective of encouraging "value-added farming through the purchase by farmers' cooperatives of refiners or processors of agricultural goods," but concluded that the provision lacked safeguards and also "failed to target its benefits to small-and-medium-size cooperatives."

II

Appellees filed two separate actions against the President and other federal officials challenging these two cancellations. The plaintiffs in the first case are the City of New York, two hospital associations, one hospital, and two unions representing health care employees. The plaintiffs in the second are a farmers' cooperative consisting of about 30 potato growers in Idaho and an individual farmer who is a member and officer of the cooperative. The District Court consolidated the two cases and determined that at least one of the plaintiffs in each had standing under Article III of the Constitution.

IV

The Line Item Veto Act gives the President the power to "cancel in whole" three types of provisions that have been signed into law: "(1) any dollar amount of discretionary budget authority; (2) any item of new direct spending; or (3) any limited tax benefit." It is undisputed that the New York case involves an "item of new direct spending" and that the Snake River case involves a "limited tax benefit" as those terms are defined in the Act. It is also undisputed that each of those provisions had been signed into law pursuant to Article I, § 7, of the Constitution before it was canceled.

The Act requires the President to adhere to precise procedures whenever he exercises his cancellation authority. In identifying items for cancellation he must consider the legislative history, the purposes, and other relevant information about the items. He must determine, with respect to each cancellation, that it will "(i) reduce the Federal budget deficit; (ii) not impair any essential Government functions; and (iii) not harm the national interest." Moreover, he must transmit a special message to Congress notifying it of each cancellation within five calendar days (excluding Sundays) after the enactment of the canceled provision. It is undisputed that the President meticulously followed these procedures in these cases.

A cancellation takes effect upon receipt by Congress of the special message from the President. If, however, a "disapproval bill" pertaining to a special message is enacted into law, the cancellations set forth in that message become "null and void." The Act sets forth a detailed expedited procedure for the consideration of a "disapproval bill," but no such bill was passed for either of the cancellations involved in these cases. A majority vote of both Houses is sufficient to enact a disapproval bill. The Act does not grant the President the authority to cancel a disapproval bill, but he does, of course, retain his constitutional authority to veto such a bill.

The effect of a cancellation is plainly stated in § 691e, which defines the principal terms used in the Act. With respect to both an item of new direct spending and a limited tax benefit, the cancellation prevents the item "from having legal force or effect." 2 U.S.C. §§ 691e(4)(B)–(C). Thus, under the plain text of the statute, the two actions of the President that are challenged in these cases prevented one section of the Balanced Budget Act of 1997 and one section of the Taxpayer Relief Act of 1997 "from having legal force or effect." The remaining provisions of those statutes, with the exception of the second canceled item in the latter, continue to have the same force and effect as they had when signed into law.

In both legal and practical effect, the President has amended two Acts of Congress by repealing a portion of each. "[R]epeal of statutes, no less than enactment, must conform with Art. I." *INS v. Chadha*. There is no provision in the Constitution that authorizes the President to enact, to amend, or to repeal statutes. Both Article I and Article II assign responsibilities to the President that directly relate to the lawmaking process, but neither addresses the issue presented by these cases. The President "shall from time to time give to the Congress Information on the State of the Union, and recommend to their Consideration such Measures as he shall judge necessary and expedient." Art. II, § 3. Thus, he may initiate and influence legislative proposals. Moreover, after a bill has passed both Houses of Congress, but "before it become[s] a Law," it must be presented to the President. If he approves it, "he shall sign it, but if not he shall return it, with his Objections to that House in which it shall have originated, who shall enter the Objections at large on their Journal, and proceed to reconsider it." Art. I, § 7, cl. 2. His "return" of a bill, which is usually described as a "veto," is subject to being overridden by a two-thirds vote in each House.

There are important differences between the President's "return" of a bill pursuant to Article I, § 7, and the exercise of the President's cancellation authority pursuant to the Line Item Veto Act. The constitutional return takes place before the bill becomes law; the statutory cancellation occurs after the bill becomes law. The constitutional return is of the entire bill; the statutory cancellation is of only a part. Although the Constitution expressly authorizes the President to play a role in the process of enacting statutes, it is silent on the subject of unilateral Presidential action that either repeals or amends parts of duly enacted statutes.

There are powerful reasons for construing constitutional silence on this profoundly important issue as equivalent to an express prohibition. The procedures governing the enactment of statutes set forth in the text of Article I were the product of the great debates and compromises that produced the Constitution itself. Familiar historical materials provide abundant support for the conclusion that the power to enact statutes may only "be exercised in accord with a single, finely wrought and exhaustively considered, procedure." *Chadha*. Our first President understood the text of the Presentment Clause as requiring that he either "approve all the parts of a Bill, or reject it in toto." What has emerged in these cases from the President's exercise of his statutory cancellation powers, however, are truncated versions of two bills that passed both Houses of Congress. They are not the product of the "finely wrought" procedure that the Framers designed.

At oral argument, the Government suggested that the cancellations at issue in these cases do not effect a "repeal" of the canceled items because under the special "lockbox" provisions of the Act, [which ensure that savings resulting from cancellation are used to reduce the deficit, rather than to offset deficit increases arising from other laws] a canceled item "retain[s] real, legal budgetary effect" insofar as it prevents Congress and the President from spending the savings that result from the cancellation. The text of the Act expressly provides, however, that a cancellation prevents a direct spending or tax benefit provision "from having legal force or effect." That a canceled item may have "real, legal budgetary effect" as a result of the lockbox procedure does not change the fact that by canceling the items at issue in these cases, the President made them entirely inoperative as to appellees.

V

The Government advances two related arguments to support its position that despite the unambiguous provisions of the Act, cancellations do not amend or repeal properly enacted statutes in violation of the Presentment Clause. First, relying primarily on *Field v. Clark*, 143 U.S. 649 (1892), the Government contends that the cancellations were merely exercises of discretionary authority granted to the President by the Balanced Budget Act and the Taxpayer Relief Act read in light of the previously enacted Line Item Veto Act. Second, the Government submits that the substance of the authority to cancel tax and spending items "is, in practical effect, no more and no less than the power to 'decline to spend' specified sums of money, or to 'decline to implement' specified tax measures." Neither argument is persuasive.

In *Field v. Clark*, the Court upheld the constitutionality of the Tariff Act of 1890. That statute contained a "free list" of almost 300 specific articles that were exempted from import duties "unless otherwise specially provided for in this act." Section 3 was a special provision that directed the President to suspend that exemption for sugar, molasses, coffee, tea, and hides "whenever, and so often" as he should be satisfied that any country producing and exporting those products imposed duties on the agricultural products of the United States that he deemed to be "reciprocally unequal and unreasonable." The section then specified the duties to be imposed on those products during any such suspension.

[There are] three critical differences between the power to suspend the exemption from import duties and the power to cancel portions of a duly enacted statute. First, the exercise of the suspension power was contingent upon a condition that did not exist when the Tariff Act was passed: the imposition of "reciprocally unequal and unreasonable" import duties by other countries. In contrast, the exercise of the cancellation power within five days after the enactment of the Balanced Budget and Tax Reform Acts necessarily was based on the same conditions that Congress evaluated when it passed those statutes. Second, under the Tariff Act, when the President determined that the contingency had arisen, he had a duty to suspend; in contrast, while it is true that the President was required by the Act to make three determinations before he canceled a provision, those determinations did not qualify his discretion to cancel or not to cancel. Finally, whenever the President suspended an exemption under the Tariff Act, he was executing the policy that Congress had embodied in the statute. In contrast, whenever the President cancels an item of new direct spending or a limited tax benefit he is rejecting the policy judgment made by Congress and relying on his own policy judgment.

Neither are we persuaded by the Government's contention that the President's authority to cancel new direct spending and tax benefit items is no greater than his traditional authority to decline to spend appropriated funds. The Government has reviewed in some detail the series of statutes in which Congress has given the Executive broad discretion over the expenditure of appropriated funds. For example, the First Congress appropriated "sum[s] not exceeding" specified amounts to be spent on various Government operations. In those statutes, as in later years, the President was given wide discretion with respect to both the amounts to be spent and how the money would be allocated among different functions. It is argued that the Line Item Veto Act merely confers comparable discretionary authority over the expenditure of appropriated funds. The critical difference between this statute and all of its predecessors, however, is that unlike any of them, this Act gives the President the unilateral power to change the text of duly enacted statutes. None of the Act's predecessors could even arguably have been construed to authorize such a change.

If there is to be a new procedure in which the President will play a different role in determining the final text of what may "become a law," such change must come not by legislation but through the amendment procedures set forth in Article V of the Constitution.

The judgment of the District Court is affirmed.

It is so ordered.

JUSTICE KENNEDY, concurring.

I write to respond to my colleague Justice Breyer, who observes that the statute does not threaten the liberties of individual citizens, a point on which I disagree. Liberty is always at stake when one or more of the branches seek to transgress the separation of powers.

In recent years, perhaps, we have come to think of liberty as defined by that word in the Fifth and Fourteenth Amendments and as illuminated by the other provisions of the Bill of Rights. The conception of liberty embraced by the Framers was not so confined. They used the principles of separation of powers and federalism to secure liberty in the fundamental political sense of the term, quite in addition to the idea of freedom from intrusive governmental acts. The idea and the promise were that when the people delegate some degree of control to a remote central authority, one branch of government ought not possess the power to shape their destiny without a sufficient check from the other two. In this vision, liberty demands limits on the ability of any one branch to influence basic political decisions.

It follows that if a citizen who is taxed has the measure of the tax or the decision to spend determined by the Executive alone, without adequate control by the citizen's Representatives in Congress, liberty is threatened.

JUSTICE SCALIA, with whom JUSTICE O'CONNOR joins, and with whom JUSTICE BREYER joins as to Part III, concurring in part and dissenting in part. . . .

III

I agree with the Court that the New York appellees have standing to challenge the President's cancellation of § 4722(c) of the Balanced Budget Act of 1997 as an "item of new direct spending." The tax liability they will incur under New York law is a concrete and particularized injury, fairly traceable to the President's action, and avoided if that action is undone. Unlike the Court, however, I do not believe that Executive cancellation of this item of direct spending violates the Presentment Clause.

There is no question that enactment of the Balanced Budget Act complied with these [Presentment Clause] requirements: the House and Senate passed the bill, and the President signed it into law. It was only after the requirements of the Presentment Clause had been satisfied that the President exercised his authority under the Line Item Veto Act to cancel the spending item. Thus, the Court's problem with the Act is not that it authorizes the President to veto parts of a bill and sign others into law, but rather that it authorizes him to "cancel" — prevent from "having legal force or effect" — certain parts of duly enacted statutes.

Article I, § 7 of the Constitution obviously prevents the President from cancelling a law that Congress has not authorized him to cancel. As much as the Court goes on about Art. I, § 7 that provision does not demand the result the Court reaches. It no more categorically prohibits the Executive reduction of congressional dispositions in the course of implementing statutes that authorize such reduction, than it categorically prohibits the Executive augmentation of congressional dispositions in the course of implementing statutes that authorize such augmentation — generally known as substantive rulemaking. There are, to be sure, limits upon the former just as there are limits upon the latter — and I am prepared to acknowledge that the limits upon the former may be much more severe. Those limits are established, however, not by some categorical prohibition of Art. I, § 7, which our cases conclusively disprove, but by what has come to be known as the doctrine of unconstitutional delegation of legislative authority: When authorized Executive reduction or augmentation is allowed to go too far, it usurps the nondelegable function of Congress and violates the separation of powers.

It is this doctrine, and not the Presentment Clause that is the issue presented by the statute before us here. Insofar as the degree of political, "law-making" power conferred upon the Executive is concerned, there is not a dime's worth of difference between Congress's authorizing the President to cancel a spending item, and Congress's authorizing money to be spent on a particular item at the President's discretion. And the latter has been done since the Founding of the Nation. From

1789–1791, the First Congress made lump-sum appropriations for the entire Government — "sum[s] not exceeding" specified amounts for broad purposes. From a very early date Congress also made permissive individual appropriations, leaving the decision whether to spend the money to the President's unfettered discretion.

Certain Presidents have claimed Executive authority to withhold appropriated funds even absent an express conferral of discretion to do so.

The short of the matter is this: Had the Line Item Veto Act authorized the President to "decline to spend" any item of spending contained in the Balanced Budget Act of 1997, there is not the slightest doubt that authorization would have been constitutional. What the Line Item Veto Act does instead — authorizing the President to "cancel" an item of spending — is technically different. But the technical difference does not relate to the technicalities of the Presentment Clause, which have been fully complied with; and the doctrine of unconstitutional delegation, which is at issue here, is preeminently not a doctrine of technicalities. The title of the Line Item Veto Act, which was perhaps designed to simplify for public comprehension, or perhaps merely to comply with the terms of a campaign pledge, has succeeded in faking out the Supreme Court. The President's action it authorizes in fact is not a line-item veto and thus does not offend Art. I, § 7; and insofar as the substance of that action is concerned, it is no different from what Congress has permitted the President to do since the formation of the Union.

Justice Breyer, with whom Justice O'Connor and Justice Scalia join as to Part III, dissenting.

III

The Court believes that the Act violates the literal text of the Constitution. A simple syllogism captures its basic reasoning:

> Major Premise: The Constitution sets forth an exclusive method for enacting, repealing, or amending laws.

> Minor Premise: The Act authorizes the President to "repea[l] or amen[d]" laws in a different way, namely by announcing a cancellation of a portion of a previously enacted law.

> Conclusion: The Act is inconsistent with the Constitution.

I find this syllogism unconvincing, however, because its Minor Premise is faulty. When the President "canceled" the two appropriation measures now before us, he did not repeal any law nor did he amend any law. He simply followed the law, leaving the statutes, as they are literally written, intact.

IV

Because I disagree with the Court's holding of literal violation, I must consider whether the Act nonetheless violates Separation of Powers principles — principles that arise out of the Constitution's vesting of the "executive Power" in "a President," U.S. Const., Art. II, § 1, and "[a]ll legislative Powers" in "a Congress," Art. I, § 1. There are three relevant Separation of Powers questions here: (1) Has Congress given the President the wrong kind of power, i.e., "non-Executive" power? (2) Has Congress given the President the power to "encroach" upon Congress' own constitutionally reserved territory? (3) Has Congress given the President too much power, violating the doctrine of "nondelegation?"

A

Viewed conceptually, the power the Act conveys is the right kind of power. It is "executive." As explained above, an exercise of that power "executes" the Act. Conceptually speaking, it closely resembles the kind of delegated authority — to spend or not to spend appropriations, to change or not to change tariff rates — that Congress has frequently granted the President, any differences being differences in degree, not kind.

B

The Act does not undermine what this Court has often described as the principal function of the Separation of Powers, which is to maintain the tripartite structure of the Federal Government — and thereby protect individual liberty — by providing a "safeguard against the encroachment or aggrandizement of one branch at the expense of the other."

[O]ne cannot say that the Act "encroaches" upon Congress' power, when Congress retained the power to insert, by simple majority, into any future appropriations bill, into any section of any such bill, or into any phrase of any section, a provision that says the Act will not apply. And it is Congress that drafts and enacts the appropriations statutes that are subject to the Act in the first place — and thereby defines the outer limits of the President's cancellation authority. Thus this Act is not the sort of delegation "without . . . sufficient check" that concerns Justice Kennedy. Indeed, the President acts only in response to, and on the terms set by, the Congress.

Nor can one say the Act's grant of power "aggrandizes" the Presidential office. The grant is limited to the context of the budget. It is limited to the power to spend, or not to spend, particular appropriated items, and the power to permit, or not to permit, specific limited exemptions from generally applicable tax law from taking effect.

C

The "nondelegation" doctrine represents an added constitutional check upon Congress' authority to delegate power to the Executive Branch. And it raises a more serious constitutional obstacle here. The Constitution permits Congress to "see[k] assistance from another branch" of Government, the "extent and character" of that assistance to be fixed "according to common sense and the inherent necessities of the governmental co-ordination." But there are limits on the way in which Congress can obtain such assistance; it "cannot delegate any part of its legislative power except under the limitation of a prescribed standard." Or, in Chief Justice Taft's more familiar words, the Constitution permits only those delegations where

Congress "shall lay down by legislative act an intelligible principle to which the person or body authorized to [act] is directed to conform."

The case before us does not involve delegation to private parties, nor does it bring all of American industry within its scope. It is limited to one area of government, the budget, and it seeks to give the President the power, in one portion of that budget, to tailor spending and special tax relief to what he concludes are the demands of fiscal responsibility.

V

In sum, I recognize that the Act before us is novel. In a sense, it skirts a constitutional edge. But that edge has to do with means, not ends. The means chosen do not amount literally to the enactment, repeal, or amendment of a law. Nor, for that matter, do they amount literally to the "line item veto" that the Act's title announces. Those means do not violate any basic Separation of Powers principle. They do not improperly shift the constitutionally foreseen balance of power from Congress to the President. Nor, since they comply with Separation of Powers principles, do they threaten the liberties of individual citizens. They represent an experiment that may, or may not, help representative government work better. The Constitution, in my view, authorizes Congress and the President to try novel methods in this way. Consequently, with respect, I dissent.

Notes and Questions

(1) The critical disagreement between the majority and dissenters concerned whether the Line Item Veto Act violates Art. I, § 7. Justice Stevens claimed that the President amended two statutes "in both legal and practical effect" when he exercised his cancellation authority. Justice Breyer opined that the President "simply followed the law, leaving the statutes . . . intact." Mindful of the approaches to separation of powers considered in this chapter, how should the Art. I, § 7 question be answered in this instance?

(2) What separation of powers problems are presented by the Line Item Veto? If the Presentment Clause concerns were not present, how should the nondelegation and other separation of powers objections to the Line Item Veto be resolved? In what respect was the authority conferred by the Line Item Veto Act different from the President's discretion to impound appropriated funds?

(3) Can you think of a way to redraft line item veto legislation that would avoid the Presentment Clause difficulties identified by the majority?

F. Executive Privilege, Presidential Immunity from Lawsuit, and Congress' Power of Impeachment

Members of Congress are "privileged from Arrest during their attendance at the Sessions of their respective Houses, and in going to and returning from the same," and "for any speech or Debate in either House, they shall not be questioned in any

Other place." Art. I, §6, cl. 1. There is no textual equivalent to the Speech or Debate Clause privilege nor any immunity for the President or members of the executive branch. Instead, the courts have recognized implied executive privileges and immunities based on the structure of the Constitution and by analogy to common law. Recall the treatment of President Richard Nixon's executive privilege claim in *United States v. Nixon* in Chapter 1.

Recall as well that President Nixon claimed that the President was not amenable to judicial process. The Court also found that the President is amenable to court orders, at least in the course of a criminal proceeding, and ruled that it was for the courts to decide the scope and content of any executive privilege. Although the Court in *Nixon* rejected the President's claim to an absolute privilege, it recognized a qualified "presumptive" privilege. You learned that such a privilege may not prevail in a contest with a state grand jury subpoena for a President's financial information in *Trump v. Vance*, Chapter 1, where the Court held that the sitting President does not enjoy absolute immunity from state criminal process. How should similar arguments for the President fare in a dispute with the House of Representatives seeking information about the finances of President Trump, his children, and affiliated businesses? Consider the following case:

Trump v. Mazars USA, LLP

United States Supreme Court
140 S. Ct. 2019 (2020)

Chief Justice Roberts delivered the opinion of the Court.

[In April 2019, three committees of the U.S. House of Representatives issued four subpoenas seeking information about the finances of President Donald Trump, his children, and affiliated businesses. The House Committee on Financial Services issued a subpoena to Deutsche Bank seeking any document related to account activity, due diligence, foreign transactions, business statements, debt schedules, statements of net worth, tax returns, and suspicious activity identified by Deutsche Bank. The Permanent Select Committee on Intelligence issued a similar subpoena to Deutsche Bank. And the House Committee on Oversight and Reform issued a subpoena to the President's personal accounting firm, Mazars, demanding information related to the President and several affiliated businesses. Although each of the committees sought overlapping sets of financial documents, each supplied different justifications for the requests, explaining that the information would help guide legislative reform in areas ranging from money laundering and terrorism to foreign involvement in U.S. elections.

President Trump contested the subpoena issued by the Oversight Committee in the District Court for the District of Columbia and the subpoenas issued by the Financial Services and Intelligence Committees in the Southern District of New York. The courts of appeals sustained the authority of the district courts to enforce the subpoenas under the regular rules for such enforcement. The Supreme Court reversed, on the ground that the courts of appeals should have applied a heightened standard, reflecting the separation of powers concerns raised by the subpoenas.]

The question presented is whether the subpoenas exceed the authority of the House under the Constitution. Historically, disputes over congressional demands for presidential documents have not ended up in court. Instead, they have been hashed out in the "hurly-burly, the give-and-take of the political process between the legislative and the executive." Hearings on S. 2170 et al. before the Subcommittee on Intergovernmental Relations of the Senate Committee on Government Operations, 94th Cong., 1st Sess., 87 (1975) (A. Scalia, Assistant Attorney General, Office of Legal Counsel).

That practice began with George Washington and the early Congress. In 1792, a House committee requested Executive Branch documents pertaining to General St. Clair's campaign against the Indians in the Northwest Territory, which had concluded in an utter rout of federal forces when they were caught by surprise near the present-day border between Ohio and Indiana. See T. Taylor, Grand Inquest: The Story of Congressional Investigations 19–23 (1955). Since this was the first such request from Congress, President Washington called a Cabinet meeting, wishing to take care that his response "be rightly conducted" because it could "become a precedent." 1 Writings of Thomas Jefferson 189 (P. Ford ed. 1892).

The meeting, attended by the likes of Alexander Hamilton, Thomas Jefferson, Edmund Randolph, and Henry Knox, ended with the Cabinet of "one mind": The House had authority to "institute inquiries" and "call for papers" but the President could "exercise a discretion" over disclosures, "communicat[ing] such papers as the public good would permit" and "refus[ing]" the rest. President Washington then dispatched Jefferson to speak to individual congressmen and "bring them by persuasion into the right channel." The discussions were apparently fruitful, as the House later narrowed its request and the documents were supplied without recourse to the courts.

[The Chief Justice provided subsequent examples where the branches had worked out demands for executive department information through a negotiated settlement. This case is the first one where the Supreme Court was called upon to resolve the legality of a congressional subpoena against the President.]

Congress has no enumerated constitutional power to conduct investigations or issue subpoenas, but we have held that each House has power "to secure needed information" in order to legislate. *McGrain v. Daugherty*, 273 U.S. 135, 161 (1927). This "power of inquiry — with process to enforce it — is an essential and appropriate auxiliary to the legislative function." Without information, Congress would be shooting in the dark, unable to legislate "wisely or effectively." The congressional power to obtain information is "broad" and "indispensable." *Watkins v. United States*, 354 U.S. 178, 187, 215 (1957). It encompasses inquiries into the administration of existing laws, studies of proposed laws, and "surveys of defects in our social, economic or political system for the purpose of enabling the Congress to remedy them." *Id.*

Because this power is "justified solely as an adjunct to the legislative process," it is subject to several limitations. *Watkins.* Most importantly, a congressional subpoena is valid only if it is "related to, and in furtherance of, a legitimate task of the Congress." The subpoena must serve a "valid legislative purpose," *Quinn v. United States,* 349 U.S. 155, 161 (1955); it must "concern[] a subject on which legislation 'could be had,'" *Eastland v. United States Servicemen's Fund,* 421 U.S. 491, 506 (1975).

Furthermore, Congress may not issue a subpoena for the purpose of "law enforcement," because "those powers are assigned under our Constitution to the Executive and the Judiciary." Thus Congress may not use subpoenas to "try" someone "before [a] committee for any crime or wrongdoing." Congress has no "'general' power to inquire into private affairs and compel disclosures," and "there is no congressional power to expose for the sake of exposure." "Investigations conducted solely for the personal aggrandizement of the investigators or to 'punish' those investigated are indefensible." Finally, recipients of legislative subpoenas retain their constitutional rights throughout the course of an investigation. And recipients have long been understood to retain common law and constitutional privileges with respect to certain materials, such as attorney-client communications and governmental communications protected by executive privilege.

[In Part II.C, the Chief Justice rejected the President's position, that the subpoena should have been governed by *Nixon's* "demonstrated, specific need" for the financial information, just as the Watergate special prosecutor was required to do in order to obtain the tapes.] Unlike the cases before us, *Nixon* involved Oval Office communications over which the President asserted executive privilege. That privilege safeguards the public interest in candid, confidential deliberations within the Executive Branch; it is "fundamental to the operation of Government." *Nixon.* As a result, information subject to executive privilege deserves "the greatest protection consistent with the fair administration of justice." We decline to transplant that protection root and branch to cases involving nonprivileged, private information, which by definition does not implicate sensitive Executive Branch deliberations. The standards proposed by the President and the Solicitor General — if applied outside the context of privileged information — would risk seriously impeding Congress in carrying out its responsibilities. The President and the Solicitor General would apply the same exacting standards to all subpoenas for the President's information, without recognizing distinctions between privileged and nonprivileged information, between official and personal information, or between various legislative objectives. Such a categorical approach would represent a significant departure from the longstanding way of doing business between the branches, giving short shrift to Congress's important interests in conducting inquiries to obtain the information it needs to legislate effectively.

[In Part II.D, the Chief Justice rejected the House's position and that of the courts of appeals, that enforcement of the subpoenas should be governed by the rules generally applicable to subpoenas. Such a rule did not take account of the sensitive separation of powers concerns presented here but not in the ordinary subpoena case.]

[In Part II.E, The Chief Justice considered the practicalities of this kind of dispute and balanced the interests of each branch to produce the following guidelines for the lower courts on remand:]

First, courts should carefully assess whether the asserted legislative purpose warrants the significant step of involving the President and his papers. "[O]ccasion[s] for constitutional confrontation between the two branches should be avoided whenever possible." *Cheney v. United States Dist. Court for D.C.*, 542 U.S. 367, 389–390 (2004) (quoting *Nixon*). Congress may not rely on the President's information if other sources could reasonably provide Congress the information it needs in light of its particular legislative objective. The President's unique constitutional position means that Congress may not look to him as a "case study" for general legislation.

Unlike in criminal proceedings, where "[t]he very integrity of the judicial system" would be undermined without "full disclosure of all the facts," *Nixon*, efforts to craft legislation involve predictive policy judgments that are "not hamper[ed] . . . in quite the same way" when every scrap of potentially relevant evidence is not available, *Cheney*. While we certainly recognize Congress's important interests in obtaining information through appropriate inquiries, those interests are not sufficiently powerful to justify access to the President's personal papers when other sources could provide Congress the information it needs.

Second, to narrow the scope of possible conflict between the branches, courts should insist on a subpoena no broader than reasonably necessary to support Congress's legislative objective. The specificity of the subpoena's request "serves as an important safeguard against unnecessary intrusion into the operation of the Office of the President."

Third, courts should be attentive to the nature of the evidence offered by Congress to establish that a subpoena advances a valid legislative purpose. The more detailed and substantial the evidence of Congress's legislative purpose, the better. That is particularly true when Congress contemplates legislation that raises sensitive constitutional issues, such as legislation concerning the Presidency. In such cases, it is "impossible" to conclude that a subpoena is designed to advance a valid legislative purpose unless Congress adequately identifies its aims and explains why the President's information will advance its consideration of the possible legislation.

Fourth, courts should be careful to assess the burdens imposed on the President by a subpoena. We have held that burdens on the President's time and attention stemming from judicial process and litigation, without more, generally do not cross constitutional lines. But burdens imposed by a congressional subpoena should be carefully scrutinized, for they stem from a rival political branch that has an ongoing relationship with the President and incentives to use subpoenas for institutional advantage.

Other considerations may be pertinent as well; one case every two centuries does not afford enough experience for an exhaustive list.

[Justice Thomas dissented, on the ground that neither chamber of Congress has subpoena power ancillary to its legislative powers under Article I. "At the time of the founding, the power to subpoena private, nonofficial documents was not included by necessary implication in any of Congress' legislative powers," a precept consistent with *Kilbourn v. Thompson*, 103 U.S. 168 (1881), which refused to enforce a subpoena against private documents. Justice Thomas would have overruled *McGrain*, which did sustain such a power, because it was inconsistent with legislative powers as understood in 1789. The House has authority under its impeachment power to issue such subpoenas, an authority not invoked for these cases.]

[Justice Alito agreed with the remand but dissented from the formulation of the standard to be applied. "Specifically, the House should provide a description of the type of legislation being considered, and while great specificity is not necessary, the description should be sufficient to permit a court to assess whether the particular records sought are of any special importance. The House should also spell out its constitutional authority to enact the type of legislation that it is contemplating, and it should justify the scope of the subpoenas in relation to the articulated legislative needs. In addition, it should explain why the subpoenaed information, as opposed to information available from other sources, is needed. Unless the House is required to make a showing along these lines, I would hold that enforcement of the subpoenas cannot be ordered."]

Notes and Questions

(1) In 1970, Department of the Air Force employee Fitzgerald provided widely publicized "whistle blower" testimony to Congress alleging abuses and cost overruns in Air Force contracts. Fitzgerald was fired, and he sought damages for violations of his First Amendment and statutory rights. President Richard Nixon was among the defendants. The Supreme Court held that "the President is absolutely immune from civil damages liability for his official acts" that lie with the "outer perimeter" of his official responsibility — at least "in the absence of explicit affirmative action by Congress." *Nixon v. Fitzgerald*, 457 U.S. 731 (1982). Writing for the Court, Justice Powell emphasized the President's "unique position in the constitutional scheme."

(2) Does the decision in *Fitzgerald* immunize a sitting President for his actions prior to assuming office? Consider the following case.

Clinton v. Jones

United States Supreme Court
520 U.S. 681, 117 S. Ct. 1636, 137 L. Ed. 2d 945 (1997)

STEVENS, J., delivered the opinion of the Court.

This case raises a constitutional and a prudential question concerning the Office of the President of the United States. Respondent, a private citizen, seeks to recover damages from the current occupant of that office based on actions allegedly taken before his term began. The President submits that in all but the most exceptional cases the Constitution requires federal courts to defer such litigation until his term ends and that, in any event, respect for the office warrants such a stay. Despite the force of the arguments supporting the President's submissions, we conclude that they must be rejected.

[The claims against President Clinton concerned alleged sexual advances and other misconduct when he was the Governor of the State of Arkansas and were brought by Paula Corbin Jones. In 1991, she lived in Arkansas, and was an employee of the Arkansas Industrial Development Commission.]

[The President's] strongest argument supporting his immunity claim is based on the text and structure of the Constitution. He does not contend that the occupant of the Office of the President is "above the law," in the sense that his conduct is entirely immune from judicial scrutiny. The President argues merely for a postponement of the judicial proceedings that will determine whether he violated any law. His argument is grounded in the character of the office that was created by Article II of the Constitution, and relies on separation of powers principles that have structured our constitutional arrangement since the founding.

As a starting premise, petitioner contends that he occupies a unique office with powers and responsibilities so vast and important that the public interest demands that he devote his undivided time and attention to his public duties. He submits that—given the nature of the office—the doctrine of separation of powers places limits on the authority of the Federal Judiciary to interfere with the Executive Branch that would be transgressed by allowing this action to proceed.

We have no dispute with the initial premise of the argument. It does not follow, however, that separation of powers principles would be violated by allowing this action to proceed. The doctrine of separation of powers is concerned with the allocation of official power among the three co-equal branches of our Government. The Framers "built into the tripartite Federal Government . . . a self-executing safeguard against the encroachment or aggrandizement of one branch at the expense of the other." *Buckley v. Valeo*, 424 U.S. at 122.

Petitioner's predictive judgment finds little support in either history or the relatively narrow compass of the issues raised in this particular case. As we have already noted, in the more than 200-year history of the Republic, only three sitting Presidents have been subjected to suits for their private actions. If the past is any indicator, it seems unlikely that a deluge of such litigation will ever engulf the Presidency. As for the case at hand, if properly managed by the District Court, it appears to us highly unlikely to occupy any substantial amount of petitioner's time.

The fact that a federal court's exercise of its traditional Article III jurisdiction may significantly burden the time and attention of the Chief Executive is not sufficient to establish a violation of the Constitution. Two long-settled propositions, first announced by Chief Justice Marshall, support that conclusion.

First, we have long held that when the President takes official action, the Court has the authority to determine whether he has acted within the law. Perhaps the most dramatic example of such a case is our holding that President Truman exceeded his constitutional authority when he issued an order directing the Secretary of Commerce to take possession of and operate most of the Nation's steel mills in order to avert a national catastrophe. *Youngstown Sheet & Tube Co. v. Sawyer*. Despite the serious impact of that decision on the ability of the Executive Branch to accomplish its assigned mission, and the substantial time that the President must necessarily have devoted to the matter as a result of judicial involvement, we exercised our Article III jurisdiction to decide whether his official conduct conformed to the law. Our holding was an application of the principle established in *Marbury v. Madison*, that "[i]t is emphatically the province and duty of the judicial department to say what the law is."

Second, it is also settled that the President is subject to judicial process in appropriate circumstances. Although Thomas Jefferson apparently thought otherwise, Chief Justice Marshall, when presiding in the treason trial of Aaron Burr, ruled that a subpoena duces tecum could be directed to the President. *United States v. Burr*, 25 F. Cas. 30 (No. 14,692d) (CC Va. 1807). We unequivocally and emphatically endorsed Marshall's position when we held that President Nixon was obligated to comply with a subpoena commanding him to produce certain tape recordings of his conversations with his aides. *United States v. Nixon*. As we explained, "neither the doctrine of separation of powers, nor the need for confidentiality of high-level communications, without more, can sustain an absolute, unqualified Presidential privilege of immunity from judicial process under all circumstances."

Sitting Presidents have responded to court orders to provide testimony and other information with sufficient frequency that such interactions between the Judicial and Executive Branches can scarcely be thought a novelty. . . .

In sum, "[i]t is settled law that the separation-of-powers doctrine does not bar every exercise of jurisdiction over the President of the United States." *Fitzgerald*, 457 U.S. at 753–754. If the Judiciary may severely burden the Executive Branch by reviewing the legality of the President's official conduct, and if it may direct appropriate process to the President himself, it must follow that the federal courts have power to determine the legality of his unofficial conduct. The burden on the President's time and energy that is a mere by-product of such review surely cannot be considered as onerous as the direct burden imposed by judicial review and the occasional invalidation of his official actions. We therefore hold that the doctrine of separation of powers does not require federal courts to stay all private actions against the President until he leaves office.

We add a final comment on two matters that are discussed at length in the briefs: the risk that our decision will generate a large volume of politically motivated harassing and frivolous litigation, and the danger that national security concerns might prevent the President from explaining a legitimate need for a continuance.

We are not persuaded that either of these risks is serious. If Congress deems it appropriate to afford the President stronger protection, it may respond with appropriate legislation.

The Federal District Court has jurisdiction to decide this case. Like every other citizen who properly invokes that jurisdiction, respondent has a right to an orderly disposition of her claims.

JUSTICE BREYER, concurring in the judgment.

I agree with the majority that the Constitution does not automatically grant the President an immunity from civil lawsuits based upon his private conduct. Nor does the "doctrine of separation of powers . . . require federal courts to stay" virtually "all private actions against the President until he leaves office." Rather, as the Court of Appeals stated, the President cannot simply rest upon the claim that a private civil lawsuit for damages will "interfere with the constitutionally assigned duties of the Executive Branch . . . without detailing any specific responsibilities or explaining how or the degree to which they are affected by the suit." To obtain a postponement the President must "bea[r] the burden of establishing its need."

In my view, however, once the President sets forth and explains a conflict between judicial proceeding and public duties, the matter changes. At that point, the Constitution permits a judge to schedule a trial in an ordinary civil damages action (where postponement normally is possible without overwhelming damage to a plaintiff) only within the constraints of a constitutional principle — a principle that forbids a federal judge in such a case to interfere with the President's discharge of his public duties. I have no doubt that the Constitution contains such a principle applicable to civil suits, based upon Article II's vesting of the entire "executive Power" in a single individual, implemented through the Constitution's structural separation of powers, and revealed both by history and case precedent. . . .

Notes and Questions

(1) Does the subsequent investigation and eventual impeachment of President Clinton change your view of the outcome in *Clinton v. Jones*? If the President could show that he was actually distracted from his duties by the lawsuit, would the Court find him immune?

(2) Is the distinction between the *Fitzgerald* grant of absolute immunity and this case persuasive? If either President deserved a break, why not give it to the sitting

President (Clinton) (who would later confront Jones under the temporary immunity grant) and not to the President (Nixon) who was out of office by the time the lawsuit against him arose?

(3) As noted above, the only immunity from judicial process enshrined in the Constitution is for Members of Congress. The immunities created for the President and other officials are thus creatures of the Court, through a sort of constitutional common law decision making. What separation of powers concerns are presented by immunities from judicial process created in such a manner?

(4) In light of the decisions in this section, do you think a sitting President may be criminally indicted? It is clear that an impeached and removed President (or other official) remains subject to criminal "Indictment, Trial, Judgment, and Punishment, according to Law." Art. I, § 3. But what about a sitting President who has not been impeached and removed? What separation of powers considerations would be important in resolving the indictment question?

(5) After the Court permitted Jones to proceed with her lawsuit, President Clinton was deposed. During the deposition, the President allegedly lied when asked whether he had "sex" with a White House intern, Monica Lewinsky, and then lied publicly after the allegation surfaced in the media. Independent Counsel Kenneth Starr then successfully broadened his original investigation of an Arkansas land deal involving the Clintons to include the newly alleged improprieties and reported his findings to Congress. After considerable debate, the House of Representatives voted articles of impeachment, relying on its authority in Article I, § 2, cl. 5.

During the House impeachment and Senate trial, one central question was whether the misconduct alleged constituted "Treason, Bribery, or other high Crimes or Misdemeanors" required for removal from office by Article II, § 4. If President Clinton's sexual improprieties did not merit removal under the constitutional standard, was the House of Representatives on firm constitutional ground in concluding that perjury during the deposition and obstruction of justice in covering up the lie were within the Article II standard? What sources should be consulted in determining the meaning of "high crimes or Misdemeanors"?

Like "all civil Officers of the United States," the President shall be "removed from Office on Impeachment for, and Conviction of, Treason, Bribery, or other high Crimes and Misdemeanors." Art. II, § 4. Only Presidents Andrew Johnson, Clinton and Trump (twice) have been impeached. The Senate failed to convict in each case. President Nixon escaped impeachment by resigning before the House voted. Most impeachments have involved federal judges.

§ 2.04 Limits on the Elected Branches: Foreign Relations and the War Powers

A. Foreign Relations Powers

United States v. Curtiss-Wright Export Corporation

United States Supreme Court
299 U.S. 304, 57 S. Ct. 216, 81 L. Ed. 255 (1936)

[In 1934 a Joint Resolution of Congress delegated broad powers to the President to prohibit arms sales to countries engaged in armed conflicts. The Court sustained President Roosevelt's embargo and the delegation in the context of upholding an indictment of Curtiss-Wright for conspiring to sell arms to Bolivia.]

Mr. Justice Sutherland delivered the opinion of the Court.

The Joint Resolution follows:

> Resolved by the Senate and House of Representatives of the United States of America in Congress assembled, That if the President finds that the prohibition of the sale of arms and munitions of war in the United States to those countries now engaged in armed conflict in the Chaco may contribute to the reestablishment of peace between those countries, and if after consultation with the governments of other American Republics and with their cooperation, as well as that of such other governments as he may deem necessary, he makes proclamation to that effect, it shall be unlawful to sell, except under such limitations and exceptions as the President prescribes, any arms or munitions of war in any place in the United States to the countries now engaged in that armed conflict, or to any person, company, or association acting in the interest of either country, until otherwise ordered by the President or by Congress.
>
> Sec. 2. Whoever sells any arms or munitions of war in violation of section 1 shall, on conviction, be punished by a fine not exceeding $10,000 or by imprisonment not exceeding two years, or both.

The President's proclamation, after reciting the terms of the Joint Resolution, declares:

> Now, therefore, I, Franklin D. Roosevelt, President of the United States of America, acting under and by virtue of the authority conferred in me by the said joint resolution of Congress, do hereby declare and proclaim that I have found that the prohibition of the sale of arms and munitions of war in the United States to those countries now engaged in armed conflict in the Chaco may contribute to the reestablishment of peace between those countries, and that I have consulted with the governments of other American Republics and have been assured of the cooperation of such governments as I have deemed necessary as contemplated by the said joint resolution;

and I do hereby admonish all citizens of the United States and every person to abstain from every violation of the provisions of the Joint Resolution above set forth, hereby made applicable to Bolivia and Paraguay, and I do hereby warn them that all violations of such provisions will be rigorously prosecuted.

And I do hereby enjoin upon all officers of the United States charged with the execution of the laws thereof, the utmost diligence in preventing violations of the said joint resolution and this my proclamation issued thereunder, and in bringing to trial and punishment any offenders against the same. And I do hereby delegate to the Secretary of State the power of prescribing exceptions and limitations to the application of the said joint resolution of May 28, 1934, as made effective by this my proclamation issued thereunder.

Whether, if the Joint Resolution had related solely to internal affairs it would be open to the challenge that it constituted an unlawful delegation of legislative power to the Executive, we find it unnecessary to determine. The whole aim of the resolution is to affect a situation entirely external to the United States, and falling within the category of foreign affairs. The determination which we are called to make, therefore, is whether the Joint Resolution, as applied to that situation, is vulnerable to attack under the rule that forbids a delegation of the law-making power. In other words, assuming (but not deciding) that the challenged delegation, if it were confined to internal affairs, would be invalid, may it nevertheless be sustained on the ground that its exclusive aim is to afford a remedy for a hurtful condition within foreign territory?

It will contribute to the elucidation of the question if we first consider the differences between the powers of the federal government in respect of foreign or external affairs and those in respect of domestic or internal affairs.

The two classes of powers are different, both in respect of their origin and their nature. The broad statement that the federal government can exercise no powers except those specifically enumerated in the Constitution, and such implied powers as are necessary and proper to carry into effect the enumerated powers, is categorically true only in respect of our internal affairs. In that field, the primary purpose of the Constitution was to carve from the general mass of legislative powers *then possessed by the states* such portions as it was thought desirable to vest in the federal government, leaving those not included in the enumeration still in the states. That this doctrine applies only to powers which the states had, is self-evident. And since the states severally never possessed international powers, such powers could not have been carved from the mass of state powers but obviously were transmitted to the United States from some other source. During the colonial period, those powers were possessed exclusively by and were entirely under the control of the Crown. By the Declaration of Independence, "the Representatives of the United States of America" declared the United [not the several] Colonies to be free and independent states, and as such have "full Power to levy War, conclude Peace, contract Alliances, establish Commerce and to do all other Acts and Things which Independent States may of right do."

As a result of the separation from Great Britain by the colonies acting as a unit, the powers of external sovereignty passed from the Crown not to the colonies severally, but to the colonies in their collective and corporate capacity as the United States of America. Even before the Declaration, the colonies were a unit in foreign affairs, acting through a common agency — namely the Continental Congress, composed of delegates from the thirteen colonies. That agency exercised the powers of war and peace, raised an army, created a navy, and finally adopted the Declaration of Independence. Rulers come and go; governments end and forms of government change; but sovereignty survives. A political society cannot endure without a supreme will somewhere. Sovereignty is never held in suspense. When, therefore, the external sovereignty of Great Britain in respect of the colonies ceased, it immediately passed to the Union. That fact was given practical application almost at once. The treaty of peace, made on September 23, 1783, was concluded between his Britanic Majesty and the "United States of America."

The Union existed before the Constitution, which was ordained and established among other things to form "a more perfect Union." Prior to that event, it is clear that the Union, declared by the Articles of Confederation to be "perpetual," was the sole possessor of external sovereignty and in the Union it remained without change save in so far as the Constitution in express terms qualified its exercise. The Framers' Convention was called and exerted its powers upon the irrefutable postulate that though the states were several their people in respect of foreign affairs were one.

It results that the investment of the federal government with the powers of external sovereignty did not depend upon the affirmative grants of the Constitution. The powers to declare and wage war, to conclude peace, to make treaties, to maintain diplomatic relations with other sovereignties, if they had never been mentioned in the Constitution, would have vested in the federal government as necessary concomitants of nationality. As a member of the family of nations, the right and power of the United States in that field are equal to the right and power of the other members of the international family. Otherwise, the United States is not completely sovereign. The power to acquire territory by discovery and occupation, the power to expel undesirable aliens, the power to make such international agreements as do not constitute treaties in the constitutional sense, none of which is expressly affirmed by the Constitution, nevertheless exist as inherently inseparable from the conception of nationality.

Not only, as we have shown, is the federal power over external affairs in origin and essential character different from that over internal affairs, but participation in the exercise of power is significantly limited. In this vast external realm, with its important, complicated, delicate and manifold problems, the President alone has the power to speak or listen as a representative of the nation. He makes treaties with the advice and consent of the Senate; but he alone negotiates. Into the field of negotiation the Senate cannot intrude; and the Congress itself is powerless to invade it.

It is important to bear in mind that we are dealing not alone with an authority vested in the President by an exertion of legislative power, but with such an authority plus the very delicate, plenary and exclusive power of the President as the sole organ of the federal government in the field of international relations — a power which does not require as a basis for its exercise an act of Congress, but which, of course, like every other governmental power, must be exercised in subordination to the applicable provisions of the Constitution. It is quite apparent that if, in the maintenance of our international relations, embarrassment — perhaps serious embarrassment — is to be avoided and success for our aims achieved, congressional legislation which is to be made effective through negotiation and inquiry within the international field must often accord to the President a degree of discretion and freedom from statutory restriction which would not be admissible were domestic affairs alone involved. Moreover, he, not Congress, has the better opportunity of knowing the conditions which prevail in foreign countries, and especially is this true in time of war. He has his confidential sources of information. He has his agents in the form of diplomatic, consular and other officials. Secrecy in respect of information gathered by them may be highly necessary, and the premature disclosure of it productive of harmful results.

This consideration, in connection with what we have already said on the subject, discloses the unwisdom of requiring Congress in this field of governmental power to lay down narrowly definite standards by which the President is to be governed.

JUSTICE MCREYNOLDS, [Dissenting, omitted].

JUSTICE STONE took no part in the consideration or decision of this case.

Zivotofsky v. Kerry

United States Supreme Court
576 U.S. 1, 135 S. Ct. 2076, 192 L. Ed. 2d 83 (2015)

Justice KENNEDY delivered the opinion of the Court. The Court addresses two questions to resolve the interbranch dispute now before it. First, it must determine whether the President has the exclusive power to grant formal recognition to a foreign sovereign. Second, if he has that power, the Court must determine whether Congress can command the President and his Secretary of State to issue a formal statement that contradicts the earlier recognition.

The President's position on Jerusalem is reflected in State Department policy regarding passports and consular reports of birth abroad. Understanding that passports will be construed as reflections of American policy, the State Department's Foreign Affairs Manual instructs its employees, in general, to record the place of birth on a passport as the "country [having] present sovereignty over the actual area of birth." Dept. of State, 7 Foreign Affairs Manual (FAM) § 1383.4 (1987). If a citizen objects to the country listed as sovereign by the State Department, he or she may list the city or town of birth rather than the country. See *id.*, § 1383.6. The FAM, however, does not allow citizens to list a sovereign that conflicts with Executive Branch policy. See generally *id.*, § 1383. Because the United States does not recognize any country as having sovereignty over Jerusalem, the FAM instructs employees to record the place of birth for citizens born there as "Jerusalem." *Id.*, § 1383.5–6.

In 2002, Congress passed the Act at issue here, the Foreign Relations Authorization Act, Fiscal Year 2003, 116 Stat. 1350. Section 214 of the Act is titled "United States Policy with Respect to Jerusalem as the Capital of Israel." The subsection that lies at the heart of this case, § 214(d), addresses passports. That subsection seeks to override the FAM by allowing citizens born in Jerusalem to list their place of birth as "Israel." Titled "Record of Place of Birth as Israel for Passport Purposes," § 214(d) states "[f]or purposes of the registration of birth, certification of nationality, or issuance of a passport of a United States citizen born in the city of Jerusalem, the Secretary shall, upon the request of the citizen or the citizen's legal guardian, record the place of birth as Israel."

When he signed the Act into law, President George W. Bush issued a statement declaring his position that § 214 would, "if construed as mandatory rather than advisory, impermissibly interfere with the President's constitutional authority to formulate the position of the United States, speak for the Nation in international affairs, and determine the terms on which recognition is given to foreign states." Statement on Signing the Foreign Relations Authorization Act, Fiscal Year 2003, *Public Papers of the Presidents*, George W. Bush, Vol. 2, Sept. 30, 2002, p. 1698 (2005). The President concluded, "U.S. policy regarding Jerusalem has not changed."

In this case the Secretary contends that § 214(d) infringes on the President's exclusive recognition power by "requiring the President to contradict his recognition position regarding Jerusalem in official communications with foreign sovereigns." In so doing the Secretary acknowledges the President's power is "at its lowest ebb." *Youngstown* [*Sheet & Tube Co. v. Sawyer*, 343 U.S. 579 (1952)], at 637. Because the President's refusal to implement § 214(d) falls into Justice Jackson's third category, his claim must be "scrutinized with caution," and he may rely solely on powers the Constitution grants to him alone. *Id.*

Recognition is a "formal acknowledgement" that a particular "entity possesses the qualifications for statehood" or "that a particular regime is the effective government of a state." *Restatement (Third) of Foreign Relations Law of the United States* § 203, Comment *a*, p. 84 (1986). It may also involve the determination of a state's territorial bounds. See 2 M. Whiteman, *Digest of International Law* § 1, p. 1 (1963) (*Whiteman*) ("[S]tates may recognize or decline to recognize territory as belonging to, or under the sovereignty of, or having been acquired or lost by, other states"). Recognition is often affected by an express "written or oral declaration." 1 J. Moore, *Digest of International Law* § 27, p. 73 (1906) (*Moore*). It may also be implied — for example, by concluding a bilateral treaty or by sending or receiving diplomatic agents.

Legal consequences follow formal recognition. Recognized sovereigns may sue in United States courts, and may benefit from sovereign immunity when they are sued. The actions of a recognized sovereign committed within its own territory also receive deference in domestic courts under the act of state doctrine. Recognition at international law, furthermore, is a precondition of regular diplomatic relations. Recognition is thus "useful, even necessary," to the existence of a state.

Despite the importance of the recognition power in foreign relations, the Constitution does not use the term "recognition," either in Article II or elsewhere. The Secretary asserts that the President exercises the recognition power based on the Reception Clause, which directs that the President "shall receive Ambassadors and other public Ministers." Art. II, § 3. As Zivotofsky notes, the Reception Clause received little attention at the Constitutional Convention.

At the time of the founding, however, prominent international scholars suggested that receiving an ambassador was tantamount to recognizing the sovereignty of the sending state. It is a logical and proper inference, then, that a Clause directing the President alone to receive ambassadors would be understood to acknowledge his power to recognize other nations. The inference that the President exercises the recognition power is further supported by his additional Article II powers. It is for the President, "by and with the Advice and Consent of the Senate," to "make Treaties, provided two thirds of the Senators present concur." Art. II, § 2, cl. 2. In addition, "he shall nominate, and by and with the Advice and Consent of the Senate, shall appoint Ambassadors" as well as "other public Ministers and Consuls." *Ibid.*

As a matter of constitutional structure, these additional powers give the President control over recognition decisions. At international law, recognition may be effected by different means, but each means is dependent upon Presidential power. In addition to receiving an ambassador, recognition may occur on "the conclusion of a bilateral treaty," or the "formal initiation of diplomatic relations," including the dispatch of an ambassador. The President has the sole power to negotiate treaties, and the Senate may not conclude a treaty without Presidential action. The President, too, nominates the Nation's ambassadors and dispatches other diplomatic agents. Congress may not send an ambassador without his involvement. Beyond that, the President himself has the power to open diplomatic channels simply by engaging in direct diplomacy with foreign heads of state and their ministers. The Constitution thus assigns the President means to effect recognition on his own initiative. Congress, by contrast, has no constitutional power that would enable it to initiate diplomatic relations with a foreign nation. Because these specific Clauses confer the recognition power on the President, the Court need not consider whether or to what extent the Vesting Clause, which provides that the "executive Power" shall be vested in the President, provides further support for the President's action here. Art. II, § 1, cl. 1.

The text and structure of the Constitution grant the President the power to recognize foreign nations and governments. The question then becomes whether that power is exclusive. The various ways in which the President may unilaterally effect recognition — and the lack of any similar power vested in Congress — suggest that it is. So, too, do functional considerations. Put simply, the Nation must have a single policy regarding which governments are legitimate in the eyes of the United States and which are not. Foreign countries need to know, before entering into diplomatic relations or commerce with the United States, whether their ambassadors will be received; whether their officials will be immune from suit in federal court; and whether they may initiate lawsuits here to vindicate their rights. These assurances cannot be equivocal.

Recognition is a topic on which the Nation must "'speak . . . with one voice.'" *American Ins. Assn. v. Garamendi,* 539 U.S. 396, 424 (2003). That voice must be the President's. Between the two political branches, only the Executive has the characteristic of unity at all times. And with unity comes the ability to exercise, to a greater degree, "[d]ecision, activity, secrecy, and dispatch." *The Federalist No. 70,* p. 424 (A. Hamilton). The President is capable, in ways Congress is not, of engaging in the delicate and often secret diplomatic contacts that may lead to a decision on recognition. See, *e.g., United States v. Pink,* 315 U.S. 203, 229 (1942). He is also better positioned to take the decisive, unequivocal action necessary to recognize other states at international law. 1 *Oppenheim's International Law* § 50, p. 169 (R. Jennings & A. Watts eds., 9th ed. 1992) (act of recognition must "leave no doubt as to the intention to grant it"). These qualities explain why the Framers listed the traditional avenues of recognition — receiving ambassadors, making treaties, and sending ambassadors — as among the President's Article II powers.

It remains true, of course, that many decisions affecting foreign relations — including decisions that may determine the course of our relations with recognized countries — require congressional action. . . .

In foreign affairs, as in the domestic realm, the Constitution "enjoins upon its branches separateness but interdependence, autonomy but reciprocity." *Youngstown,* 343 U.S., at 635 (Jackson, J., concurring). Although the President alone effects the formal act of recognition, Congress' powers, and its central role in making laws, give it substantial authority regarding many of the policy determinations that precede and follow the act of recognition itself. If Congress disagrees with the President's recognition policy, there may be consequences. Formal recognition may seem a hollow act if it is not accompanied by the dispatch of an ambassador, the easing of trade restrictions, and the conclusion of treaties. And those decisions require action by the Senate or the whole Congress.

In practice, then, the President's recognition determination is just one part of a political process that may require Congress to make laws. The President's exclusive recognition power encompasses the authority to acknowledge, in a formal sense, the legitimacy of other states and governments, including their territorial bounds. Albeit limited, the exclusive recognition power is essential to the conduct of Presidential duties. The formal act of recognition is an executive power that Congress may not qualify. If the President is to be effective in negotiations over a formal recognition determination, it must be evident to his counterparts abroad that he speaks for the Nation on that precise question.

A clear rule that the formal power to recognize a foreign government subsists in the President therefore serves a necessary purpose in diplomatic relations. All this, of course, underscores that Congress has an important role in other aspects of foreign policy, and the President may be bound by any number of laws Congress enacts. In this way ambition counters ambition, ensuring that the democratic will of the people is observed and respected in foreign affairs as in the domestic realm. *See The Federalist No. 51,* p. 322 (J. Madison).

The Secretary now urges the Court to define the executive power over foreign relations in even broader terms. He contends that under the Court's precedent the President has "exclusive authority to conduct diplomatic relations," along with "the bulk of foreign-affairs powers." In support of his submission that the President has broad, undefined powers over foreign affairs, the Secretary quotes *United States v. Curtiss-Wright Export Corp.,* which described the President as "the sole organ of the federal government in the field of international relations." This Court declines to acknowledge that unbounded power. A formulation broader than the rule that the President alone determines what nations to formally recognize as legitimate — and that he consequently controls his statements on matters of recognition — presents different issues and is unnecessary to the resolution of this case.

The *Curtiss-Wright* case does not extend so far as the Secretary suggests. [Its] description of the President's exclusive power was not necessary to the holding of *Curtiss-Wright* — which, after all, dealt with congressionally authorized action, not a unilateral Presidential determination. Indeed, *Curtiss-Wright* did not hold that the President is free from Congress' lawmaking power in the field of international relations. The President does have a unique role in communicating with foreign governments, as then-Congressman John Marshall acknowledged. *See* 10 *Annals of Cong.* 613 (1800). But whether the realm is foreign or domestic, it is still the Legislative Branch, not the Executive Branch, that makes the law.

In a world that is ever more compressed and interdependent, it is essential the congressional role in foreign affairs be understood and respected. For it is Congress that makes laws, and in countless ways its laws will and should shape the Nation's course. The Executive is not free from the ordinary controls and checks of Congress merely because foreign affairs are at issue. It is not for the President alone to determine the whole content of the Nation's foreign policy.

That said, judicial precedent and historical practice teach that it is for the President alone to make the specific decision of what foreign power he will recognize as legitimate, both for the Nation as a whole and for the purpose of making his own position clear within the context of recognition in discussions and negotiations with foreign nations. Recognition is an act with immediate and powerful significance for international relations, so the President's position must be clear. Congress cannot require him to contradict his own statement regarding a determination of formal recognition.

Having examined the Constitution's text and this Court's precedent, it is appropriate to turn to accepted understandings and practice. In separation-of-powers cases this Court has often "put significant weight upon historical practice." *NLRB v. Noel Canning,* 573 U.S. 513 (2014). This history confirms the Court's conclusion in the instant case that the power to recognize or decline to recognize a foreign state and its territorial bounds resides in the President alone.

As the power to recognize foreign states resides in the President alone, the question becomes whether § 214(d) infringes on the Executive's consistent decision to withhold recognition with respect to Jerusalem. See *Nixon v. Administrator of General Services,* 433 U.S. 425, 443 (1977) (action unlawful when it "prevents the Executive Branch from accomplishing its constitutionally assigned functions"). If the power over recognition is to mean anything, it must mean that the President not only makes the initial, formal recognition determination but also that he may maintain that determination in his and his agent's statements. This conclusion is a matter of both common sense and necessity. If Congress could command the President to state a recognition position inconsistent with his own, Congress could override the President's recognition determination.

As Justice Jackson wrote in *Youngstown,* when a Presidential power is "exclusive," it "disabl[es] the Congress from acting upon the subject." Here, the subject is quite narrow: The Executive's exclusive power extends no further than his formal recognition determination. But as to that determination, Congress may not enact a law that directly contradicts it. This is not to say Congress may not express its disagreement with the President in myriad ways. For example, it may enact an embargo, decline to confirm an ambassador, or even declare war. But none of these acts would alter the President's recognition decision.

If Congress may not pass a law, speaking in its own voice, that effects formal recognition, then it follows that it may not force the President himself to contradict his earlier statement. That congressional command would not only prevent the Nation from speaking with one voice but also prevent the Executive itself from doing so in conducting foreign relations. Although the statement required by § 214(d) would not itself constitute a formal act of recognition, it is a mandate that the Executive contradict his prior recognition determination in an official document issued by the Secretary of State. As a result, it is unconstitutional. From the face of § 214, from the legislative history, and from its reception, it is clear that Congress wanted to express its displeasure with the President's policy by, among other things, commanding the Executive to contradict his own, earlier stated position on Jerusalem. This Congress may not do.

The judgment of the Court of Appeals for the District of Columbia Circuit is *Affirmed.*

[The opinions of Justice BREYER, concurring, and Justice THOMAS, concurring in the judgment in part and dissenting in part, are omitted.]

Chief Justice ROBERTS, with whom Justice ALITO joins, dissenting. Today's decision is a first: Never before has this Court accepted a President's direct defiance of an Act of Congress in the field of foreign affairs. We have instead stressed that the President's power reaches "its lowest ebb" when he contravenes the express will of Congress, "for what is at stake is the equilibrium established by our constitutional system." *Youngstown Sheet & Tube Co. v. Sawyer,* 343 U.S. 579, 637–638 (1952) (Jackson, J., concurring).

[A]lthough the President has authority over recognition, I am not convinced that the Constitution provides the "conclusive and preclusive" power required to justify defiance of an express legislative mandate. *Youngstown,* 343 U.S., at 638 (Jackson, J., concurring). As the leading scholar on this issue has concluded, the "text, original understanding, post-ratification history, and structure of the Constitution do not support the . . . expansive claim that this executive power is plenary." Reinstein, *Is the President's Recognition Power Exclusive?* 86 Temp. L. Rev. 1, 60 (2013).

But even if the President does have exclusive recognition power, he still cannot prevail in this case, because the statute at issue *does not implicate recognition.* The relevant provision, § 214(d), simply gives an American citizen born in Jerusalem the option to designate his place of birth as Israel "[f]or purposes of" passports and other documents. Foreign Relations Authorization Act, Fiscal Year 2003, 116 Stat. 1366. The State Department itself has explained that "identification" — not recognition — "is the principal reason that U.S. passports require 'place of birth.'" Congress has not disputed the Executive's assurances that § 214(d) does not alter the longstanding United States position on Jerusalem. And the annals of diplomatic history record no examples of official recognition accomplished via optional passport designation.

I respectfully dissent.

Justice SCALIA, with whom THE CHIEF JUSTICE and Justice ALITO join, dissenting. Before this country declared independence, the law of England entrusted the King with the exclusive care of his kingdom's foreign affairs. The royal prerogative included the "sole power of sending ambassadors to foreign states, and receiving them at home," the sole authority to "make treaties, leagues, and alliances with foreign states and princes," "the sole prerogative of making war and peace," and the "sole power of raising and regulating fleets and armies." 1 W. Blackstone, *Commentaries* *253, *257, *262. The People of the United States had other ideas when they organized our Government. They considered a sound structure of balanced powers essential to the preservation of just government, and international relations formed no exception to that principle.

The Constitution contemplates that the political branches will make policy about the territorial claims of foreign nations the same way they make policy about other international matters: The President will exercise his powers on the basis of his views, Congress its powers on the basis of its views. That is just what has happened here.

Before turning to Presidential power under Article II, I think it well to establish the statute's basis in congressional power under Article I. Congress's power to "establish an uniform Rule of Naturalization," Art. I, § 8, cl. 4, enables it to grant American citizenship to someone born abroad. The naturalization power also enables Congress to furnish the people it makes citizens with papers verifying their citizenship — say a consular report of birth abroad (which certifies citizenship of an American born outside the United States) or a passport (which certifies citizenship for purposes of international travel). One would think that if Congress may grant Zivotofsky a passport and a birth report, it may also require these papers to record his birthplace as "Israel."

The Court holds that the Constitution makes the President alone responsible for recognition and that § 214(d) invades this exclusive power. I agree that the Constitution *empowers* the President to extend recognition on behalf of the United States, but I find it a much harder question whether it makes that power exclusive. The Court tells us that "the weight of historical evidence" supports exclusive executive authority over "the formal determination of recognition." But even with its attention confined to formal recognition, the Court is forced to admit that "history is not all on one side." . . . Fortunately, I have no need to confront these matters today — nor does the Court — because § 214(d) plainly does not concern recognition.

Section 214(d) does not require the Secretary to make a formal declaration about Israel's sovereignty over Jerusalem. And nobody suggests that international custom infers acceptance of sovereignty from the birthplace designation on a passport or birth report, as it does from bilateral treaties or exchanges of ambassadors. Recognition would preclude the United States (as a matter of international law) from later contesting Israeli sovereignty over Jerusalem. But making a notation in a passport or birth report does not encumber the Republic with any international obligations. It leaves the Nation free (so far as international law is concerned) to change its mind in the future. That would be true even if the statute required *all* passports to list "Israel." But in fact it requires only those passports to list "Israel" for which the citizen (or his guardian) *requests* "Israel"; all the rest, under the Secretary's policy, list "Jerusalem." It is utterly impossible for this deference to private requests to constitute an act that unequivocally manifests an intention to grant recognition.

In the end, the Court's decision does not rest on text or history or precedent. It instead comes down to "functional considerations" — principally the Court's perception that the Nation "must speak with one voice" about the status of Jerusalem. The vices of this mode of analysis go beyond mere lack of footing in the Constitution. Functionalism of the sort the Court practices today will *systematically* favor the unitary President over the plural Congress in disputes involving foreign affairs. It is possible that this approach will make for more effective foreign policy, perhaps as effective as that of a monarchy. It is certain that, in the long run, it will erode the structure of separated powers that the People established for the protection of their liberty. I dissent.

Notes and Questions

(1) The Court's decision in *Curtiss-Wright* was no doubt made easier by the absence of any legislative-executive branch conflict over the Presidential authority exercised. In fact, there was an express delegation of power to the President to prohibit the arms sales. In terms of Justice Jackson's analytic framework in the *Steel Seizure* case, the Presidential action in *Curtiss-Wright* falls within group one, backed up by all the constitutional powers of the national government. Arguably at least, *Curtiss-Wright* legitimates expansive national power to act in foreign affairs, but not necessarily expansive Presidential power to so act.

(2) Do you agree that foreign affairs decisions require broader and less precise delegations of foreign affairs authority than those concerning domestic affairs? Is it always possible to label a sphere of governmental action as "foreign" or "domestic"? Which was the *Steel Seizure* case? If you agree that the delegations may be broader, must we also recognize broader constitutional power in the President in foreign than in domestic affairs? If so, what is the source of presidential power?

(3) Justice Sutherland's view that federal power to act in foreign affairs is not dependent upon any specific enumerated power may fuel arguments that Executive power is likewise not constrained by the text of Article II. If there are inherent foreign affairs powers, by what approach should they be allocated? One possibility would be to identify "legislative" and "executive" powers and divide accordingly. But given the ambiguity of the text, how could the tasks be reliably labeled?

(4) Justice Sutherland's theory of extra-constitutional presidential power in foreign affairs has been challenged by scholars. *See, e.g.*, Charles Lofgren, *United States v. Curtiss-Wright Export Corporation: An Historical Reassessment*, 83 YALE L.J. l, 32 (1973); David M. Levitan, *The Foreign Relations Power: An Analysis of Mr. Justice Sutherland's Theory*, 55 YALE L.J. 467, 489 (1946).

(5) Does Justice Sutherland's analysis survive the *Steel Seizure* case?

(6) What provision of the Constitution vests the recognition power in the President? If the President has that power, why isn't that conclusion sufficient to decide *Zivotofsky*? If Congress shares in that power somehow, what are the practical consequences if the political branches disagree about recognizing a state?

(7) Into which of Justice Jackson's *Youngstown* categories does the *Zivotofsky* dispute fit? After the decision, is it still possible to rely on *Curtiss-Wright* to argue that the President is "the sole organ of the federal government in the field of international relations"?

(8) In *American Insurance Association v. Garamendi*, 539 U.S. 396 (2003), the Supreme Court struck down a California statute requiring insurance companies to disclose information about insurance policies that they or related companies sold to Europeans during the Holocaust era. Although there was no federal statute on point, and executive agreements between the U.S. and Germany, Austria, and France to encourage a voluntary International Commission on Holocaust Era Insurance

Claims (ICHEIC) to become the exclusive forum for such insurance claims did not expressly forbid other remedies for claimants, federal preemption was found on the basis of "interference with the foreign policy those agreements embody."

German reunification in 1990 was read by German courts as lifting previous moratoria on Holocaust claims by foreign nationals. When the victims of Nazi persecution began to file lawsuits in U.S. courts against companies doing business in Germany during the Nazi era, the Clinton Administration sought a mediated settlement mechanism as an alternative to litigation. President Clinton and German Chancellor Schroeder signed the German Foundation Agreement in July 2000. In essence, Germany agreed to fund a compensation mechanism, in return for two commitments made by President Clinton. First, when a German company was sued on a Holocaust-era claim in a court in the U.S., the U.S. would submit a statement that "it would be in the foreign policy interests of the United States for the Foundation to be the exclusive forum and remedy for the resolution of all asserted claims against German companies" arising from the Nazi activities. Second, although the U.S. could not assure Germany that U.S. foreign policy interests would "in themselves provide an independent basis for dismissal," our government promised to tell U.S. courts "that U.S. policy interests favor dismissal on any valid legal ground." *Id.*, quoting 39 INT'L LEGAL MATERIALS 1303–1304 (2000). The German Foundation agreement served as a model for similar agreements with Austria and France. *Id.*

Designed as a disclosure mechanism, the California law required "[a]ny insurer currently doing business in the state" to disclose the details of insurance policies issued "to persons in Europe, which were in effect between 1920 and 1945." Cal. Ins. Code Ann. § 13084(a). California officials issued administrative subpoenas against several companies, and demanded that the companies make the disclosures, leave the State, or lose their licenses. The insurance companies sued, challenging the constitutionality of the California statute on the basis that it "interferes with the foreign policy of the Executive Branch, as expressed principally in the executive agreements." *Id.* In the Supreme Court, Justice Souter noted for the 5-4 majority that, because of the need for uniformity, state power is preempted by national government policy in the field of foreign relations:

> Nor is there any question generally that there is executive authority to decide what that policy should be. Although the source of the President's power to act in foreign affairs does not enjoy any textual detail, the historical gloss on the "executive Power" vested in Article II of the Constitution has recognized the President's "vast share of responsibility for the conduct of our foreign relations." *Youngstown Sheet & Tube Co. v. Sawyer*, 343 U.S. 579, 610–611 (1952) (Frankfurter, J., concurring). While Congress holds express authority to regulate public and private dealings with other nations in its war and foreign commerce powers, in foreign affairs the President has a degree of independent authority to act. *See, e.g., Chicago & Southern Air Lines, Inc. v. Waterman S.S. Corp.*, 333 U.S. 103, 109 (1948) ("The President possesses in his own right certain powers conferred by the Constitution on

him as Commander-in-Chief and as the Nation's organ in foreign affairs."); *Youngstown, supra*, at 635–636, n. 2 (Jackson, J., concurring in judgment and opinion of Court) (the President can "act in external affairs without congressional authority").

At a more specific level, our cases have recognized that the President has authority to make "executive agreements" with other countries, requiring no ratification by the Senate or approval by Congress, this power having been exercised since the early years of the Republic. *See Dames & Moore v. Regan*, 453 U.S. 654, 679 (1981); *United States v. Pink*, 315 U.S. 203, 223 (1942); *United States v. Belmont*, 301 U.S. 324, 330–331 (1937); *see also* L. Henkin, Foreign Affairs and the United States Constitution 219, 496, n. 163 (2d ed. 1996) ("Presidents from Washington to Clinton have made many thousands of agreements on matters running the gamut of U.S. foreign relations."). Making executive agreements to settle claims of American nationals against foreign governments is a particularly longstanding practice, the first example being as early as 1799, when the Washington administration settled demands against the Dutch Government by American citizens who lost their cargo when Dutch privateers overtook the schooner Wilmington Packet. Given the fact that the practice goes back over 200 years to the first Presidential administration, and has received congressional acquiescence throughout its history, the conclusion "[t]hat the President's control of foreign relations includes the settlement of claims is indisputable." *Pink, supra*, at 240 (Frankfurter, J., concurring).

Generally, then, valid executive agreements are fit to preempt state law, just as treaties are, and if the agreements here had expressly preempted laws like [the California statute], the issue would be straightforward. But petitioners and the United States as amicus curiae both have to acknowledge that the agreements include no preemption clause, and so leave their claim of preemption to rest on asserted interference with the foreign policy those agreements embody.

[However,] the likelihood that state legislation will produce something more than incidental effect in conflict with express foreign policy of the National Government would require preemption of the state law. And it would be reasonable to consider the strength of the state interest, judged by standards of traditional practice, when deciding how serious a conflict must be shown before declaring the state law preempted. Judged by these standards, we think petitioners and the Government have demonstrated a sufficiently clear conflict to require finding preemption here.

[I]t is worth noting that Congress has done nothing to express disapproval of the President's policy. Legislation along the lines of [the California law] has been introduced in Congress repeatedly, but none of the bills has come close to making it into law. In sum, Congress has not acted on the matter addressed here. Given the President's independent authority "in the areas of foreign policy and national security, congressional silence is not to be equated with congressional disapproval." *Haig v. Agee*, 453 U.S. 280, 291 (1981).

American Insurance Association v. Garamendi, 539 U.S. at 414–428.

Justice Ginsburg, joined by Justices Stevens, Scalia, and Thomas dissented:

Together, *Belmont*, *Pink*, and *Dames & Moore* confirm that executive agreements directed at claims settlement may sometimes preempt state law. [A]s the Court acknowledges, no executive agreement before us expressly preempts the [the California law]. Indeed, no agreement so much as mentions the [statute's] sole concern: public disclosure. Neither would I stretch *Belmont*, *Pink*, or *Dames & Moore* to support implied preemption by executive agreement. In each of those cases, the Court gave effect to the express terms of an executive agreement. In *Dames & Moore*, for example, the Court addressed an agreement explicitly extinguishing certain suits in domestic courts. Here, however, none of the executive agreements extinguish any underlying claim for relief. The United States has agreed to file precatory statements advising courts that dismissing Holocaust-era claims accords with American foreign policy, but the German Foundation Agreement confirms that such statements have no legally binding effect. It remains uncertain, therefore, whether even litigation on Holocaust-era insurance claims must be abated in deference to the German Foundation Agreement or the parallel agreements with Austria and France.

To fill the agreements' silences, the Court points to statements by individual members of the Executive Branch. We should not do so here lest we place the considerable power of foreign affairs preemption in the hands of individual sub-Cabinet members of the Executive Branch. Executive officials of any rank may of course be expected "faithfully [to] represen[t] the President's policy," but no authoritative text accords such officials the power to invalidate state law simply by conveying the Executive's views on matters of federal policy. The displacement of state law by preemption properly requires a considerably more formal and binding federal instrument.

Sustaining the [California law] would not compromise the President's ability to speak with one voice for the Nation. To the contrary, by declining to invalidate the [statute] in this case, we would reserve foreign affairs preemption for circumstances where the President, acting under statutory or constitutional authority, has spoken clearly to the issue at hand. And judges should not be the expositors of the Nation's foreign policy, which is the role they play by acting when the President himself has not taken a clear stand. As I see it, courts step out of their proper role when they rely on no legislative or even executive text, but only on inference and implication, to preempt state laws on foreign affairs grounds.

Apply Justice Jackson's *Youngstown* framework to *Garamendi*. Into which category does this executive agreement fit? If Congress had legislated to disapprove of the executive agreement in *Garamendi*, would the statute have been constitutional?

B. War Powers

The separation of powers checking function is evident in the Constitution's allocation of powers in the military and foreign affairs sphere. Congress' Article I, §8 powers include the power "to Declare War," "To Raise and Support . . . the Army and Navy," "To make rules for the Government and Regulation of the land and naval forces," "To provide for calling forth the militia to execute the Laws of the Union, suppress Insurrections and repel Invasions," and, of course, the Necessary and Proper Clause power. The Executive's Article II powers are contained in the §2 conferral of "The President . . . [as] . . . Commander in Chief" and the §3 "take care" Clause, in addition to the general grant of executive power in §1.

However, the text of the Constitution does not enumerate specific powers adequate for the conduct of military and foreign affairs to either the President or the Congress. In light of the incompleteness of the constitutional text, how should questions regarding the allocation of the war powers between the elected branches be resolved?

Prize Cases

United States Supreme Court
67 U.S. (2 Black) 635, 17 L. Ed. 459 (1863)

Mr. Justice Grier.

[In the early days of the Civil War, during a congressional recess, President Lincoln ordered a naval blockade of Confederate ports. His proclamation provided that resisting vessels would be captured and that the captured ship and cargo could be kept by the owners of the capturing vessels. The owners of vessels that were captured as prizes sued, challenging the legality of the blockade.]

By the Constitution, Congress alone has the power to declare a national or foreign war. It cannot declare war against a State, or any number of States, by virtue of any clause in the Constitution. The Constitution confers on the President the whole Executive power. He is bound to take care that the laws be faithfully executed. He is Commander-in-Chief of the Army and Navy of the United States, and of the militia of the several States when called into the actual service of the United States. He has no power to initiate or declare a war either against a foreign nation or a domestic State. But by the Acts of Congress of February 28th, 1795, and 3d of March, 1807, he is authorized to call out the militia and use the military and naval forces of the United States in case of invasion of foreign nations, and to suppress insurrection against the government of a State or of the United States.

If a war be made by invasion of a foreign nation, the President is not only autho-rized but bound to resist force by force. He does not initiate the war, but is bound to accept the challenge without waiting for any special legislative authority. And whether the hostile party be a foreign invader, or States organized in rebellion, it is nonetheless a war, although the declaration of it be *"unilateral."*

The President was bound to meet it [the Civil War] in the shape it presented itself, without waiting for Congress to baptize it with a name; and no name given to it by him or them could change the fact.

Whether the President in fulfilling his duties, as Commander-in-Chief, in sup-pressing an insurrection, has met with such armed hostile resistance, and a civil war of such alarming proportions as will compel him to accord to them the character of belligerents, is a question to be decided *by him*, and this Court must be governed by the decisions and acts of the political department of the Government to which this power was entrusted.

If it were necessary to the technical existence of a war, that it should have a legis-lative sanction, we find it in almost every act passed at the extraordinary session of the Legislature of 1861, which was wholly employed in enacting laws to enable the Government to prosecute the war with vigor and efficiency. And finally, in 1861, we find Congress passing an act "approving, legalizing, and making valid all the acts, proclamations, and orders of the President, &c., as if they had been *issued and done under the previous express authority* and direction of the Congress of the United States."

Without admitting that such an act was necessary under the circumstances, it is plain that if the President had in any manner assumed powers which it was neces-sary should have the authority or sanction of Congress, this ratification has oper-ated to perfectly cure the defect.

[W]e are of the opinion that the President had a right, *jure belli*, to institute a blockade of ports in possession of the States in rebellion, which neutrals are bound to regard.

Mr. Justice Nelson, dissenting [in an opinion in which Chief Justice Taney and Justices Catron and Clifford concurred].

[B]efore this insurrection against the established Government can be dealt with on the footing of a civil war, within the meaning of the law of nations and the Con-stitution of the United States, and which will draw after it belligerent rights, it must be recognized or declared by the war-making power of the Government. No power short of this can change the legal status of the Government or the relations of its citizens from that of peace to a state of war, or bring into existence all those duties and obligations of neutral third parties growing out of a state of war. The war power of the Government must be exercised before this changed condition of the Govern-ment and people and of neutral third parties can be admitted. There is no difference in this respect between a civil or a public war.

The Acts of 1795 and 1807 did not, and could not under the Constitution, confer on the President the power of declaring war against a State of this Union, or of deciding that war existed, and upon that ground authorize the capture and confiscation of the property of every citizen of the State whenever it was found on the waters. The laws of war, whether the war be civil or *inter gentes* [between nations], as we have seen, convert every citizen of the hostile State into a public enemy, and treat him accordingly, whatever may have been his previous conduct. This great power over the business and property of the citizen is reserved to the legislative department by the express words of the Constitution. It cannot be delegated or surrendered to the Executive. Congress alone can determine whether war exists or should be declared; and until they have acted, no citizen of the State can be punished in his person or property, unless he has committed some offense against a law of Congress passed before the act was committed, which made it a crime, and defined the punishment. The penalty of confiscation for the acts of others with which he had no concern cannot lawfully be inflicted.

Notes and Questions

(1) Apart from any congressional authorization, where does the Court find constitutional authority for the President to use force in erecting the blockade? In some future circumstance, could a President create the conditions said to warrant a military response?

(2) How broad is the principle established by *The Prize Cases*? Under what circumstances is the President's use of military force without a declaration of war or some other form of congressional approval authorized? While the answer remains elusive, one point seems clear: In the event of an armed attack on the United States, the President has the power, indeed the obligation, to respond with all means available. But what of an attack on American persons or property abroad, or an attack on an ally or co-signatory of a defense treaty such as NATO? Assuming the existence of power somewhere in the national government to act, whose is it? Clearly a congressional declaration of war triggers broad supervisory authority in the President, but what initiative may the President take absent congressional authorization? Is such a power in the President time-limited, and if so, how is the authority limited?

(3) On what basis did the dissenters find the blockade unlawful? Did they conclude that the President's actions were prohibited by Congress? That they exceeded statutory authority? That the President lacked inherent authority to order the blockade? How would the Court in the *Steel Seizure* case have decided *The Prize Cases*?

(4) For decades, Congress acquiesced in a growing executive willingness to assume unilateral military affairs power. Then, the lingering Vietnam War and growing discontent over the executive's conduct of that war prompted the Congress to enact the War Powers Resolution (WPR) in 1973, over President Richard Nixon's veto (50 U.S.C. §§ 1541–1548). Any hope of interbranch cooperation was dashed by President Nixon's veto and by the fact that no President has conceded

the constitutionality of the WPR, nor fully complied with it. The legal and practical effects of the WPR remain unclear.

(5) Within a few days of the September 11 terrorist attacks on the World Trade Center and the Pentagon, Congress approved a joint resolution authorizing the President to

> use all necessary and appropriate force against those nations, organizations, or persons he determines planned, authorized, committed, or aided the terrorist attacks that occurred on September 11, 2001, or harbored such organizations or persons, in order to prevent any future acts of international terrorism against the United States by such nations, organizations or persons.

Joint Resolution of Congress Authorizing the Use of Force, Pub. L. No. 107-40, 115 Stat. 224 (2001) (AUMF).

President George W. Bush signed the 9/11 AUMF on September 18, 2001, and it remains on the books today. Is the AUMF the functional and legal equivalent of a declaration of war? If so, against whom is the war being waged? Does the President have constitutional authority independent of the Joint Resolution to wage war against terrorists not associated with the September 11 attacks? For how long does the authority conferred by the Joint Resolution continue?

Before attempting to answer these questions, consider the following case and the Problem that follows.

Hamdi v. Rumsfeld

United States Supreme Court
542 U.S. 507, 124 S. Ct. 2633, 159 L. Ed. 2d 578 (2004)

JUSTICE O'CONNOR announced the judgment of the Court and delivered an opinion, in which the CHIEF JUSTICE, JUSTICE KENNEDY, and JUSTICE BREYER join.

[Petitioner Yaser Hamdi was captured on the battlefield in Afghanistan during U.S. military operations following the September 11 terrorist attacks. While in military custody in Afghanistan, it was discovered that Hamdi was born in Louisiana. Once his U.S. citizenship was discovered, he was transferred to the United States as an enemy combatant and detained at a naval brig in Charleston, South Carolina. Hamdi's father filed a petition for habeas corpus on his behalf under 22 U.S.C. § 2241, alleging that his son's continuing detention violates the Fifth and Fourteenth Amendments. In the habeas proceeding, the government relied on an affidavit by Department of Defense official Michael Mobbs, who asserted the foregoing facts.]

II

The threshold question before us is whether the Executive has the authority to detain citizens who qualify as "enemy combatants." There is some debate as to the proper scope of this term, and the Government has never provided any court with the full criteria that it uses in classifying individuals as such. It has made clear, however, that, for purposes of this case, the "enemy combatant" that it is seeking to detain is an individual who, it alleges, was "'part of or supporting forces hostile to the United States or coalition partners'" in Afghanistan and who "'engaged in an armed conflict against the United States'" there. We therefore answer only the narrow question before us: whether the detention of citizens falling within that definition is authorized.

The Government maintains that no explicit congressional authorization is required, because the Executive possesses plenary authority to detain pursuant to Article II of the Constitution. We do not reach the question whether Article II provides such authority, however, because we agree with the Government's alternative position, that Congress has in fact authorized Hamdi's detention, through the AUMF.

Our analysis on that point, set forth below, substantially overlaps with our analysis of Hamdi's principal argument for the illegality of his detention. He posits that his detention is forbidden by 18 U.S.C. § 4001 (a). Section 4001(a) states that "[n]o citizen shall be imprisoned or otherwise detained by the United States except pursuant to an Act of Congress." Congress passed § 4001(a) in 1971 as part of a bill to repeal the Emergency Detention Act of 1950, which provided procedures for executive detention, during times of emergency, of individuals deemed likely to engage in espionage or sabotage. Congress was particularly concerned about the possibility that the Act could be used to reprise the Japanese internment camps of World War II. [F]or the reasons that follow, we conclude that the AUMF is explicit congressional authorization for the detention of individuals in the narrow category we describe (assuming, without deciding, that such authorization is required), and that the AUMF satisfied § 4001(a)'s requirement that a detention be "pursuant to an Act of Congress" (assuming, without deciding, that § 4001(a) applies to military detentions).

The AUMF authorizes the President to use "all necessary and appropriate force" against "nations, organizations, or persons" associated with the September 11, 2001, terrorist attacks. There can be no doubt that individuals who fought against the United States in Afghanistan as part of the Taliban, an organization known to have supported the al Qaeda terrorist network responsible for those attacks, are individuals Congress sought to target in passing the AUMF. We conclude that detention of individuals falling into the limited category we are considering, for the duration of the particular conflict in which they were captured, is so fundamental and accepted an incident to war as to be an exercise of the "necessary and appropriate force" Congress has authorized the President to use.

The capture and detention of lawful combatants and the capture, detention, and trial of unlawful combatants, by "universal agreement and practice," are "important incident[s] of war." *Ex parte Quirin*, 317 U.S. [1] [1942], at 28. The purpose of detention is to prevent captured individuals from returning to the field of battle and taking up arms once again.

There is no bar to this Nation's holding one of its own citizens as an enemy combatant. In *Quirin*, one of the detainees, Haupt, alleged that he was a naturalized

United States citizen. We held that "[c]itizens who associate themselves with the military arm of the enemy government, and with its aid, guidance and direction enter this country bent on hostile acts, are enemy belligerents within the meaning of the law of war." A citizen, no less than an alien, can be "part of or supporting forces hostile to the United States or coalition partners" and "engaged in an armed conflict against the United States"; such a citizen, if released, would pose the same threat of returning to the front during the ongoing conflict.

In light of these principles, it is of no moment that the AUMF does not use specific language of detention. Because detention to prevent a combatant's return to the battlefield is a fundamental incident of waging war, in permitting the use of "necessary and appropriate force," Congress has clearly and unmistakably authorized detention in the narrow circumstances considered here.

Hamdi contends that the AUMF does not authorize indefinite or perpetual detention. Certainly, we agree that indefinite detention for the purpose of interrogation is not authorized. Further, we understand Congress' grant of authority for the use of "necessary and appropriate force" to include the authority to detain for the duration of the relevant conflict, and our understanding is based on longstanding law-of-war principles. If the practical circumstances of a given conflict are entirely unlike those of the conflicts that informed the development of the law of war, that understanding may unravel. But that is not the situation we face as of this date. Active combat operations against Taliban fighters apparently are ongoing in Afghanistan. The United States may detain, for the duration of these hostilities, individuals legitimately determined to be Taliban combatants who "engaged in an armed conflict against the United States." If the record establishes that United States troops are still involved in active combat in Afghanistan, those detentions are part of the exercise of "necessary and appropriate force," and therefore are authorized by the AUMF.

III

Even in cases in which the detention of enemy combatants is legally authorized, there remains the question of what process is constitutionally due to a citizen who disputes his enemy-combatant status. Hamdi argues that he is owed a meaningful and timely hearing and that "extra-judicial detention [that] begins and ends with the submission of an affidavit based on third-hand hearsay" does not comport with the Fifth and Fourteenth Amendments. The Government counters that any more process than was provided below would be both unworkable and "constitutionally intolerable." Our resolution of this dispute requires a careful examination both of the writ of habeas corpus, which Hamdi now seeks to employ as a mechanism of judicial review, and of the Due Process Clause, which informs the procedural contours of that mechanism in this instance.

A

Though they reach radically different conclusions on the process that ought to attend the present proceeding, the parties begin on common ground. All agree that, absent suspension, the writ of habeas corpus remains available to every individual detained within the United States. All agree suspension of the writ has not occurred here. Thus, it is undisputed that Hamdi was properly before an Article III court to challenge his detention under 28 U.S.C. § 2241. Further, all agree that § 2241 and its companion provisions provide at least a skeletal outline of the procedures to be afforded a petitioner in federal habeas review. Most notably, § 2243 provides that "the person detained may, under oath, deny any of the facts set forth in the return or allege any other material facts," and § 2246 allows the taking of evidence in habeas proceedings by deposition, affidavit, or interrogatories.

The simple outline of § 2241 makes clear both that Congress envisioned that habeas petitioners would have some opportunity to present and rebut facts and that courts in cases like this retain some ability to vary the ways in which they do so as mandated by due process. The Government recognizes the basic procedural protections required by the habeas statute, but asks us to hold that, given both the flexibility of the habeas mechanism and the circumstances presented in this case, the presentation of the Mobbs Declaration to the habeas court completed the required factual development. It suggests two separate reasons for its position that no further process is due.

B

First, the Government urges the adoption of the Fourth Circuit's holding below-that because it is "undisputed" that Hamdi's seizure took place in a combat zone, the habeas determination can be made purely as a matter of law, with no further hearing or factfinding necessary. This argument is easily rejected. As the dissenters from the denial of rehearing en banc noted, the circumstances surrounding Hamdi's seizure cannot in any way be characterized as "undisputed," as "those circumstances are neither conceded in fact, nor susceptible to concession in law, because Hamdi has not been permitted to speak for himself or even through counsel as to those circumstances." Further, the "facts" that constitute the alleged concession are insufficient to support Hamdi's detention. Under the definition of enemy combatant that we accept today as falling within the scope of Congress' authorization, Hamdi would need to be "part of or supporting forces hostile to the United States or coalition partners" and "engaged in an armed conflict against the United States" to justify his detention in the United States for the duration of the relevant conflict. The habeas petition states only that "[w]hen seized by the United States Government, Mr. Hamdi resided in Afghanistan." An assertion that one *resided* in a country in which combat operations are taking place is not a concession that one was "*captured* in a zone of active combat operations in a foreign theater of war," and certainly is not a concession that one was "part of or supporting forces hostile to the United States or coalition partners" and "engaged in an armed conflict against the United States." Accordingly, we reject any argument that Hamdi has made concessions that eliminate any right to further process.

C

The Government's second argument requires closer consideration. This is the argument that further factual exploration is unwarranted and inappropriate in light of the extraordinary constitutional interests at stake. Under the Government's most extreme rendition of this argument, "[r]espect for separation of powers and the limited institutional capabilities of courts in matters of military decision-making in connection with an ongoing conflict" ought to eliminate entirely any individual process, restricting the courts to investigating only whether legal authorization exists for the broader detention scheme. At most, the Government argues, courts should review its determination that a citizen is an enemy combatant under a very deferential "some evidence" standard. Under this review, a court would assume the accuracy of the Government's articulated basis for Hamdi's detention, as set forth in the Mobbs Declaration, and assess only whether that articulated basis was a legitimate one. In response, Hamdi emphasizes that this Court consistently has recognized that an individual challenging his detention may not be held at the will of the Executive without recourse to some proceeding before a neutral tribunal to determine whether the Executive's asserted justifications for that detention have basis in fact and warrant in law. The ordinary mechanism that we use for balancing such serious competing interests, and for determining the procedures that are necessary to ensure that a citizen is not "deprived of life, liberty, or property, without due process of law," U.S. Const., Amdt. 5, is the test that we articulated in *Mathews v. Eldridge*, 424 U.S. 319 (1976). *Mathews* dictates that the process due in any given instance is determined by weighing "the private interest that will be affected by the official action" against the Government's asserted interest, "including the function involved" and the burdens the Government would face in providing greater process. The *Mathews* calculus then contemplates a judicious balancing of these concerns, through an analysis of "the risk of an erroneous deprivation" of the private interest if the process were reduced and the "probable value, if any, of additional or substitute safeguards." We take each of these steps in turn.

1

It is beyond question that substantial interests lie on both sides of the scale in this case. Hamdi's "private interest affected by the official action," is the most elemental of liberty interests-the interest in being free from physical detention by one's own government. "In our society liberty is the norm," and detention without trial "is the carefully limited exception." "We have always been careful not to 'minimize the importance and fundamental nature' of the individual's right to liberty," and we will not do so today.

Nor is the weight on this side of the *Mathews* scale offset by the circumstances of war or the accusation of treasonous behavior, for "[i]t is clear that commitment for *any* purpose constitutes a significant deprivation of liberty that requires due process protection." Moreover, as critical as the Government's interest may be in detaining those who actually pose an immediate threat to the national security of the United

States during ongoing international conflict, history and common sense teach us that an unchecked system of detention carries the potential to become a means for oppression and abuse of others who do not present that sort of threat. We reaffirm today the fundamental nature of a citizen's right to be free from involuntary confinement by his own government without due process of law, and we weigh the opposing governmental interests against the curtailment of liberty that such confinement entails.

2

On the other side of the scale are the weighty and sensitive governmental interests in ensuring that those who have in fact fought with the enemy during a war do not return to battle against the United States. As discussed above, the law of war and the realities of combat may render such detentions both necessary and appropriate, and our due process analysis need not blink at those realities. Without doubt, our Constitution recognizes that core strategic matters of warmaking belong in the hands of those who are best positioned and most politically accountable for making them.

The Government also argues at some length that its interests in reducing the process available to alleged enemy combatants are heightened by the practical difficulties that would accompany a system of trial-like process. In its view, military officers who are engaged in the serious work of waging battle would be unnecessarily and dangerously distracted by litigation half a world away, and discovery into military operations would both intrude on the sensitive secrets of national defense and result in a futile search for evidence buried under the rubble of war. To the extent that these burdens are triggered by heightened procedures, they are properly taken into account in our due process analysis.

3

Striking the proper constitutional balance here is of great importance to the Nation during this period of ongoing combat. But it is equally vital that our calculus not give short shrift to the values that this country holds dear or to the privilege that is American citizenship. It is during our most challenging and uncertain moments that our Nation's commitment to due process is most severely tested; and it is in those times that we must preserve our commitment at home to the principles for which we fight abroad.

We therefore hold that a citizen-detainee seeking to challenge his classification as an enemy combatant must receive notice of the factual basis for his classification, and a fair opportunity to rebut the Government's factual assertions before a neutral decisionmaker. "For more than a century the central meaning of procedural due process has been clear: 'Parties whose rights are to be affected are entitled to be heard; and in order that they may enjoy that right they must first be notified.' It is equally fundamental that the right to notice and an opportunity to be heard 'must be granted at a meaningful time and in a meaningful manner.'" These essential constitutional promises may not be eroded.

At the same time, the exigencies of the circumstances may demand that, aside from these core elements, enemy combatant proceedings may be tailored to alleviate their uncommon potential to burden the Executive at a time of ongoing military conflict. Hearsay, for example, may need to be accepted as the most reliable available evidence from the Government in such a proceeding. Likewise, the Constitution would not be offended by a presumption in favor of the Government's evidence, so long as that presumption remained a rebuttable one and fair opportunity for rebuttal were provided. Thus, once the Government puts forth credible evidence that the habeas petitioner meets the enemy-combatant criteria, the onus could shift to the petitioner to rebut that evidence with more persuasive evidence that he falls outside the criteria. A burden-shifting scheme of this sort would meet the goal of ensuring that the errant tourist, embedded journalist, or local aid worker has a chance to prove military error while giving due regard to the Executive once it has put forth meaningful support for its conclusion that the detainee is in fact an enemy combatant.

We think it unlikely that this basic process will have the dire impact on the central functions of warmaking that the Government forecasts. The parties agree that initial captures on the battlefield need not receive the process we have discussed here; that process is due only when the determination is made to *continue* to hold those who have been seized. The Government has made clear in its briefing that documentation regarding battlefield detainees already is kept in the ordinary course of military affairs. Any factfinding imposition created by requiring a knowledgeable affiant to summarize these records to an independent tribunal is a minimal one. Likewise, arguments that military officers ought not have to wage war under the threat of litigation lose much of their steam when factual disputes at enemy-combatant hearings are limited to the alleged combatant's acts. This focus meddles little, if at all, in the strategy or conduct of war, inquiring only into the appropriateness of continuing to detain an individual claimed to have taken up arms against the United States. While we accord the greatest respect and consideration to the judgments of military authorities in matters relating to the actual prosecution of a war, and recognize that the scope of that discretion necessarily is wide, it does not infringe on the core role of the military for the courts to exercise their own time-honored and constitutionally mandated roles of reviewing and resolving claims like those presented here.

In sum, while the full protections that accompany challenges to detentions in other settings may prove unworkable and inappropriate in the enemy-combatant setting, the threats to military operations posed by a basic system of independent review are not so weighty as to trump a citizen's core rights to challenge meaningfully the Government's case and to be heard by an impartial adjudicator.

D

In so holding, we necessarily reject the Government's assertion that separation of powers principles mandate a heavily circumscribed role for the courts in such circumstances. Indeed, the position that the courts must forgo any examination of the individual case and focus exclusively on the legality of the broader detention scheme cannot be mandated by any reasonable view of separation of powers, as this approach serves only to *condense* power into a single branch of government. We have long since made clear that a state of war is not a blank check for the President when it comes to the rights of the Nation's citizens. *Youngstown Sheet & Tube.* Whatever power the United States Constitution envisions for the Executive in its exchanges with other nations or with enemy organizations in times of conflict, it most assuredly envisions a role for all three branches when individual liberties are at stake. Likewise, we have made clear that, unless Congress acts to suspend it, the Great Writ of habeas corpus allows the Judicial Branch to play a necessary role in maintaining this delicate balance of governance, serving as an important judicial check on the Executive's discretion in the realm of detentions. Thus, while we do not question that our due process assessment must pay keen attention to the particular burdens faced by the Executive in the context of military action, it would turn our system of checks and balances on its head to suggest that a citizen could not make his way to court with a challenge to the factual basis for his detention by his government, simply because the Executive opposes making available such a challenge. Absent suspension of the writ by Congress, a citizen detained as an enemy combatant is entitled to this process.

Because we conclude that due process demands some system for a citizen detainee to refute his classification, the proposed "some evidence" standard is inadequate. Any process in which the Executive's factual assertions go wholly unchallenged or are simply presumed correct without any opportunity for the alleged combatant to demonstrate otherwise falls constitutionally short. This standard therefore is ill suited to the situation in which a habeas petitioner has received no prior proceedings before any tribunal and had no prior opportunity to rebut the Executive's factual assertions before a neutral decisionmaker.

Today we are faced only with such a case. Aside from unspecified "screening" processes and military interrogations in which the Government suggests Hamdi could have contested his classification, Hamdi has received no process. An interrogation by one's captor, however effective an intelligence-gathering tool, hardly constitutes a constitutionally adequate factfinding before a neutral decisionmaker. Plainly, the "process" Hamdi has received is not that to which he is entitled under the Due Process Clause.

There remains the possibility that the standards we have articulated could be met by an appropriately authorized and properly constituted military tribunal. Indeed, it is notable that military regulations already provide for such process in related instances, dictating that tribunals be made available to determine the status of enemy detainees who assert prisoner-of-war status under the Geneva Convention. In the absence of such process, however, a court that receives a petition for a writ of habeas corpus from an alleged enemy combatant must itself ensure that the minimum requirements of due process are achieved. As we have discussed, a habeas court in a case such as this may accept affidavit evidence like that contained in the Mobbs Declaration, so long as it also permits the alleged combatant to present his own factual case to rebut the Government's return. We anticipate that a District Court would proceed with the caution that we have indicated is necessary in this setting, engaging in a factfinding process that is both prudent and incremental. We have no reason to doubt that courts faced with these sensitive matters will pay proper heed both to the matters of national security that might arise in an individual case and to the constitutional limitations safeguarding essential liberties that remain vibrant even in times of security concerns.

IV

Hamdi asks us to hold that the Fourth Circuit also erred by denying him immediate access to counsel upon his detention and by disposing of the case without permitting him to meet with an attorney. Since our grant of certiorari in this case, Hamdi has been appointed counsel, with whom he has met for consultation purposes on several occasions, and with whom he is now being granted unmonitored meetings. He unquestionably has the right to access to counsel in connection with the proceedings on remand. No further consideration of this issue is necessary at this stage of the case.

The judgment of the United States Court of Appeals for the Fourth Circuit is vacated, and the case is remanded for further proceedings.

JUSTICE SOUTER, with whom JUSTICE GINSBURG joins, concurring in part, dissenting in part, and concurring in the judgment.

The plurality accept[s] the Government's position that if Hamdi's designation as an enemy combatant is correct, his detention (at least as to some period) is authorized by an Act of Congress as required by § 4001(a), that is, by the Authorization for Use of Military Force, 115 Stat. 224 (hereinafter Force Resolution). Here, I disagree and respectfully dissent. The Government has failed to demonstrate that the Force Resolution authorizes the detention complained of here even on the facts the Government claims. If the Government raises nothing further than the record now shows, the Non-Detention Act entitles Hamdi to be released.

II

The threshold issue is how broadly or narrowly to read the Non-Detention Act, the tone of which is severe: "No citizen shall be imprisoned or otherwise detained by the United States except pursuant to an Act of Congress." For a number of reasons, the prohibition within § 4001(a) has to be read broadly to accord the statute a long reach and to impose a burden of justification on the Government.

First, the circumstances in which the Act was adopted point the way to this interpretation. The provision superseded a cold-war statute, the Emergency Detention Act of 1950, which had authorized the Attorney General, in time of emergency, to detain anyone reasonably thought likely to engage in espionage or sabotage. That statute was repealed in 1971 out of fear that it could authorize a repetition of the World War II internment of citizens of Japanese ancestry.

The fact that Congress intended to guard against a repetition of the World War II internments when it repealed the 1950 statute and gave us § 4001(a) provides a powerful reason to think that § 4001(a) was meant to require clear congressional authorization before any citizen can be placed in a cell.

Second, when Congress passed § 4001(a) it was acting in light of an interpretive regime that subjected enactments limiting liberty in wartime to the requirement of a clear statement and it presumably intended § 4001(a) to be read accordingly.

Finally, even if history had spared us the cautionary example of the internments in World War II, even if there had been no principle of statutory interpretation, there would be a compelling reason to read § 4001(a) to demand manifest authority to detain before detention is authorized. The defining character of American constitutional government is its constant tension between security and liberty, serving both by partial helpings of each. In a government of separated powers, deciding finally on what is a reasonable degree of guaranteed liberty whether in peace or war (or some condition in between) is not well entrusted to the Executive Branch of Government, whose particular responsibility is to maintain security. For reasons of inescapable human nature, the branch of the Government asked to counter a serious threat is not the branch on which to rest the Nation's entire reliance in striking the balance between the will to win and the cost in liberty on the way to victory; the responsibility for security will naturally amplify the claim that security legitimately raises. A reasonable balance is more likely to be reached on the judgment of a different branch, just as Madison said in remarking that "the constant aim is to divide and arrange the several offices in such a manner as that each may be a check on the other-that the private interest of every individual may be a sentinel over the public rights." The Federalist No. 51. Hence the need for an assessment by Congress before citizens are subject to lockup, and likewise the need for a clearly expressed congressional resolution of the competing claims.

III

Under this principle of reading § 4001(a) robustly to require a clear statement of authorization to detain, none of the Government's arguments suffices to justify Hamdi's detention.

[T]here is the Government's claim, accepted by the Court, that the terms of the Force Resolution are adequate to authorize detention of an enemy combatant under the circumstances described, a claim the Government fails to support sufficiently to satisfy § 4001(a) as read to require a clear statement of authority to detain. Since the Force Resolution was adopted one week after the attacks of September 11, 2001, it naturally speaks with some generality, but its focus is clear, and that is on the use of military power. It is fairly read to authorize the use of armies and weapons, whether against other armies or individual terrorists. But it never so much as uses the word detention, and there is no reason to think Congress might have perceived any need to augment Executive power to deal with dangerous citizens within the United

States, given the well-stocked statutory arsenal of defined criminal offenses covering the gamut of actions that a citizen sympathetic to terrorists might commit.

IV

Because I find Hamdi's detention forbidden by § 4001(a) and unauthorized by the
Force Resolution, I would not reach any questions of what process he may be due
in litigating disputed issues in a proceeding under the habeas statute or prior to the
habeas enquiry itself. For me, it suffices that the Government has failed to justify
holding him in the absence of a further Act of Congress, criminal charges, a showing that the detention conforms to the laws of war, or a demonstration that § 4001(a)
is unconstitutional. I would therefore vacate the judgment of the Court of Appeals
and remand for proceedings consistent with this view.

Since this disposition does not command a majority of the Court, however, the
need to give practical effect to the conclusions of eight members of the Court rejecting the Government's position calls for me to join with the plurality in ordering
remand on terms closest to those I would impose. Although I think litigation of
Hamdi's status as an enemy combatant is unnecessary, the terms of the plurality's
remand will allow Hamdi to offer evidence that he is not an enemy combatant, and
he should at the least have the benefit of that opportunity.

It should go without saying that in joining with the plurality to produce a judgment, I do not adopt the plurality's resolution of constitutional issues that I would
not reach. It is not that I could disagree with the plurality's determinations (given
the plurality's view of the Force Resolution) that someone in Hamdi's position is
entitled at a minimum to notice of the Government's claimed factual basis for holding him, and to a fair chance to rebut it before a neutral decision maker; nor, of
course, could I disagree with the plurality's affirmation of Hamdi's right to counsel. On the other hand, I do not mean to imply agreement that the Government
could claim an evidentiary presumption casting the burden of rebuttal on Hamdi,
or that an opportunity to litigate before a military tribunal might obviate or truncate enquiry by a court on habeas.

Subject to these qualifications, I join with the plurality in a judgment of the Court
vacating the Fourth Circuit's judgment and remanding the case.

Justice Scalia, with whom Justice Stevens joins, dissenting.

Where the Government accuses a citizen of waging war against it, our constitutional tradition has been to prosecute him in federal court for treason or some other
crime. Where the exigencies of war prevent that, the Constitution's Suspension
Clause, Art. I, § 9, cl. 2, allows Congress to relax the usual protections temporarily.
Absent suspension, however, the Executive's assertion of military exigency has not
been thought sufficient to permit detention without charge. No one contends that
the congressional Authorization for Use of Military Force, on which the Government relies to justify its actions here, is an implementation of the Suspension Clause.
Accordingly, I would reverse the decision below.

I

The very core of liberty secured by our Anglo-Saxon system of separated powers has been freedom from indefinite imprisonment at the will of the Executive. Blackstone stated this principle clearly:

> "Of great importance to the public is the preservation of this personal liberty: for if once it were left in the power of any, the highest, magistrate to imprison arbitrarily whomever he or his officers thought proper there would soon be an end of all other rights and immunities. To bereave a man of life, or by violence to confiscate his estate, without accusation or trial, would be so gross and notorious an act of despotism, as must at once convey the alarm of tyranny throughout the whole kingdom. But confinement of the person, by secretly hurrying him to gaol, where his sufferings are unknown or forgotten; is a less public, a less striking, and therefore a more dangerous engine of arbitrary government.

> "To make imprisonment lawful, it must either be, by process from the courts of judicature, or by warrant from some legal officer, having authority to commit to prison; which warrant must be in writing, under the hand and seal of the magistrate, and express the causes of the commitment, in order to be examined into (if necessary) upon a *habeas corpus*. If there be no cause expressed, the gaoler is not bound to detain the prisoner. For the law judges in this respect, that it is unreasonable to send a prisoner, and not to signify withal the crimes alleged against him."

1 W. Blackstone, Commentaries on the Laws of England 132–133 (1765) [hereinafter Blackstone].

These words were well known to the Founders. Hamilton quoted from this very passage in The Federalist No. 84. The two ideas central to Blackstone's understanding-due process as the right secured, and habeas corpus as the instrument by which due process could be insisted upon by a citizen illegally imprisoned-found expression in the Constitution's Due Process and Suspension Clauses. See Amdt. 5; Art. I, § 9, cl. 2.

II

The allegations here, of course, are no ordinary accusations of criminal activity. Yaser Esam Hamdi has been imprisoned because the Government believes he participated in the waging of war against the United States. The relevant question, then, is whether there is a different, special procedure for imprisonment of a citizen accused of wrongdoing *by aiding the enemy in wartime.*

A

Justice O'Connor, writing for a plurality of this Court, asserts that captured enemy combatants (other than those suspected of war crimes) have traditionally been detained until the cessation of hostilities and then released. That is probably an accurate description of wartime practice with respect to enemy *aliens.* The tradition with respect to American citizens, however, has been quite different. Citizens aiding the enemy have been treated as traitors subject to the criminal process.

B

There are times when military exigency renders resort to the traditional criminal process impracticable. English law accommodated such exigencies by allowing legislative suspension of the writ of habeas corpus for brief periods.

Our Federal Constitution contains a provision explicitly permitting suspension, but limiting the situations in which it may be invoked: "The privilege of the Writ of Habeas Corpus shall not be suspended, unless when in Cases of Rebellion or Invasion the public Safety may require it." Art. I, § 9, cl. 2. Although this provision does not state that suspension must be effected by, or authorized by, a legislative act, it has been so understood, consistent with English practice and the Clause's placement in Article I.

III

Writings from the founding generation also suggest that, without exception, the only constitutional alternatives are to charge the crime or suspend the writ. Thus, criminal process was viewed as the primary means — and the only means absent congressional action suspending the writ — not only to punish traitors, but to incapacitate them.

The proposition that the Executive lacks indefinite wartime detention authority over citizens is consistent with the Founders' general mistrust of military power permanently at the Executive's disposal.

V

It follows from what I have said that Hamdi is entitled to a habeas decree requiring his release unless (1) criminal proceedings are promptly brought, or (2) Congress has suspended the writ of habeas corpus.

The plurality finds justification for Hamdi's imprisonment in the Authorization for Use of Military Force. This is not remotely a congressional suspension of the writ, and no one claims that it is. Contrary to the plurality's view, I do not think this statute even authorizes detention of a citizen with the clarity necessary to satisfy the interpretive canon that statutes should be construed so as to avoid grave constitutional concerns.

It should not be thought, however, that the plurality's evisceration of the Suspension Clause augments, principally, the power of Congress. As usual, the major effect of its constitutional improvisation is to increase the power of the Court. Having found a congressional authorization for detention of citizens where none clearly exists; and having discarded the categorical procedural protection of the Suspension Clause; the plurality then proceeds, under the guise of the Due Process Clause, to prescribe what procedural protections *it* thinks appropriate. It claims authority to engage in this sort of "judicious balancing" from *Mathews v. Eldridge*, a case involving *the withdrawal of disability benefits!* Whatever the merits of this technique when newly recognized property rights are at issue (and even there they are questionable), it has no place where the Constitution and the common law already supply an answer.

There is a certain harmony of approach in the plurality's making up for Congress's failure to invoke the Suspension Clause and its making up for the Executive's failure to apply what it says are needed procedures — an approach that reflects what might be called a Mr. Fix-it Mentality. The plurality seems to view it as its mission to Make Everything Come Out Right, rather than merely to decree the consequences, as far as individual rights are concerned, of the other two branches' actions and omissions. The problem with this approach is not only that it steps out of the courts' modest and limited role in a democratic society; but that by repeatedly doing what it thinks the political branches ought to do it encourages their lassitude and saps the vitality of government by the people.

VI

The Founders well understood the difficult tradeoff between safety and freedom. "Safety from external danger," Hamilton declared,

> "is the most powerful director of national conduct. Even the ardent love of liberty will, after a time, give way to its dictates. The violent destruction of life and property incident to war; the continual effort and alarm attendant on a state of continual danger, will compel nations the most attached to liberty, to resort for repose and security to institutions which have a tendency to destroy their civil and political rights. To be more safe, they, at length, become willing to run the risk of being less free."

The Federalist No. 8. The Founders warned us about the risk, and equipped us with a Constitution designed to deal with it.

Many think it not only inevitable but entirely proper that liberty give way to security in times of national crisis — that, at the extremes of military exigency, *inter arma silent leges.* Whatever the general merits of the view that war silences law or modulates its voice, that view has no place in the interpretation and application of a Constitution designed precisely to confront war and, in a manner that accords with democratic principles, to accommodate it. Because the Court has proceeded to meet the current emergency in a manner the Constitution does not envision, I respectfully dissent.

Justice Thomas, dissenting.

The Executive Branch, acting pursuant to the powers vested in the President by the Constitution and with explicit congressional approval, has determined that Yaser Hamdi is an enemy combatant and should be detained. This detention falls squarely within the Federal Government's war powers, and we lack the expertise and capacity to second-guess that decision. As such, petitioners' habeas challenge should fail, and there is no reason to remand the case. The plurality reaches a contrary conclusion by failing adequately to consider basic principles of the constitutional structure as it relates to national security and foreign affairs and by using the balancing scheme of *Mathews v. Eldridge*. I do not think that the Federal Government's war powers can be balanced away by this Court. Arguably, Congress could provide for additional procedural protections, but until it does, we have no right to insist upon them. But even if I were to agree with the general approach the plurality takes, I could not accept the particulars. The plurality utterly fails to account for the Government's compelling interests and for our own institutional inability to weigh competing concerns correctly. I respectfully dissent.

I

"It is 'obvious and unarguable' that no governmental interest is more compelling than the security of the Nation."

The Founders intended that the President have primary responsibility — along with the necessary power — to protect the national security and to conduct the Nation's foreign relations. They did so principally because the structural advantages of a unitary Executive are essential in these domains. "Energy in the executive is a leading character in the definition of good government. It is essential to the protection of the community against foreign attacks." The Federalist No. 70 (A. Hamilton). The principle "ingredien[t]" for "energy in the executive" is "unity." This is because "[d]ecision, activity, secrecy, and dispatch will generally characterise the proceedings of one man, in a much more eminent degree, than the proceedings of any greater number."

These structural advantages are most important in the national-security and foreign-affairs contexts. To this end, the Constitution vests in the President "the executive power," Art. II, §1, provides that he "shall be Commander in Chief of the" armed forces, §2, and places in him the power to recognize foreign governments, §3.

This Court has long recognized these features and has accordingly held that the President has *constitutional* authority to protect the national security and that this authority carries with it broad discretion. *Prize Cases*.

With respect to foreign affairs as well, the Court has recognized the President's independent authority and need to be free from interference. See, *e.g.*, *United States v. Curtiss-Wright Export Corp.* (explaining that the President "has his confidential sources of information. He has his agents in the form of diplomatic, consular and other officials. Secrecy in respect of information gathered by them may be highly necessary, and the premature disclosure of it productive of harmful results").

Several points are worth emphasizing. First, with respect to certain decisions relating to national security and foreign affairs, the courts simply lack the relevant information and expertise to second-guess determinations made by the President based on information properly withheld. Second, even if the courts could compel the Executive to produce the necessary information, such decisions are simply not amenable to judicial determination because "[t]hey are delicate, complex, and involve large elements of prophecy." Third, the Court has correctly recognized the primacy of the political branches in the foreign-affairs and national-security contexts.

For these institutional reasons and because "Congress cannot anticipate and legislate with regard to every possible action the President may find it necessary to take or every possible situation in which he might act," it should come as no surprise that "[s]uch failure of Congress does not, 'especially in the areas of foreign policy and national security,' imply 'congressional disapproval' of action taken by the Executive." *Dames & Moore v. Regan.* Rather, in these domains, the fact that Congress has provided the President with broad authorities does not imply-and the Judicial Branch should not infer-that Congress intended to deprive him of particular powers not specifically enumerated.

Finally, and again for the same reasons, where "the President acts pursuant to an express or implied authorization from Congress, he exercises not only his powers but also those delegated by Congress[, and i]n such a case the executive action 'would be supported by the strongest of presumptions and the widest latitude of judicial interpretation, and the burden of persuasion would rest heavily upon any who might attack it.'" *Dames & Moore, supra,* at 668 (quoting *Youngstown, supra,* at 637 (Jackson, J., concurring)). This deference extends to the President's determination of all the factual predicates necessary to conclude that a given action is appropriate.

I acknowledge that the question whether Hamdi's executive detention is lawful is a question properly resolved by the Judicial Branch, though the question comes to the Court with the strongest presumptions in favor of the Government. The plurality agrees that Hamdi's detention is lawful if he is an enemy combatant. But the question whether Hamdi is actually an enemy combatant is "of a kind for which the Judiciary has neither aptitude, facilities nor responsibility and which has long been held to belong in the domain of political power not subject to judicial intrusion or inquiry." That is, although it is appropriate for the Court to determine the judicial question whether the President has the asserted authority, we lack the information and expertise to question whether Hamdi is actually an enemy combatant, a question the resolution of which is committed to other branches.

II

Although the President very well may have inherent authority to detain those arrayed against our troops, I agree with the plurality that we need not decide that question because Congress has authorized the President to do so.

III

I agree with the plurality that the Federal Government has power to detain those that the Executive Branch determines to be enemy combatants. But I do not think that the plurality has adequately explained the breadth of the President's authority to detain enemy combatants, an authority that includes making virtually conclusive factual findings. In my view, the structural considerations discussed above, as recognized in our precedent, demonstrate that we lack the capacity and responsibility to second-guess this determination.

Problem D

In the early hours of January 3, 2020, U.S. forces launched a drone strike that killed General Qassem Soleimani, head of the Islamic Revolutionary Guard Corps-Quds Force (IRGC-QF) of Iran, as he departed the Baghdad airport. Iran has been designated by the United States as a state sponsor of terrorism, and the IRGC-QF is its expeditionary terrorist force, which has itself been designated by the United States as a Specially Designated Global Terrorist and a Foreign Terrorist Organization. The IRGC-QF "spearheaded a closely coordinated campaign to equip the [Iraqi] Shi'a militia for proxy warfare" targeting U.S. service members, among others. *Karcher v. Islamic Rep. of Iran*, 396 F. Supp. 3d 12, 22–25 (D.D.C. 2019) (describing attacks on U.S. personnel in detail). The campaign killed at least 603 U.S. soldiers and severely injured many others. *See* Kyle Rempfer, *Iran Killed More US Troops in Iraq than Previously Known, Pentagon Says*, MILITARY TIMES, Apr. 4, 2019.

Was the strike that killed General Soleimani constitutional? In addition to the President's Article II authority, consider the 2001 AUMF in addition to a 2002 AUMF, which authorized the President to use force "as he determines necessary and appropriate to defend the national security of the United States against the continuing threat posed by Iraq."

§ 2.05 Limits on Judicial Power — The Justiciability Doctrines

A. Introduction

The focus of this section is the relationship between the federal judiciary, particularly the Supreme Court, and Congress. The starting point for an examination of this relationship is *Marbury v. Madison.*

It has been suggested that there is a plausible, indeed "unanswerable," argument that judicial review "invaded 'Separation of Powers' which, as so many then believed, was the condition of all free government." LEARNED HAND, THE BILL OF RIGHTS 10–11 (1958). Judge Hand argued that the text of the Constitution did not permit even an inference that judicial review was intended by the Framers. According to Hand, only practical considerations — "to prevent the defeat of the venture at hand" — would legitimate a court decision binding upon the Congress and the president. In contrast, others have urged that a written constitution containing limited and separated powers could not survive unless some part of the government had authority to pass on the constitutionality of actions by other branches. *See* Eugene V. Rostow, *The Democratic Character of Judicial Review*, 66 HARV. L. REV. 193 (1952). Whichever position one holds, however, it is clear that judicial review was a rather remarkable innovation. Indeed, it enabled the "least dangerous branch" of the American system to emerge as the "most extraordinarily powerful court of law the world has ever known." ALEXANDER BICKEL, THE LEAST DANGEROUS BRANCH 1 (1962).

In § 2.01 we observed that separation of powers serves three goals: ensuring legitimacy, preventing tyranny and promoting efficiency. We now examine these goals in the context of the relations between the federal judiciary and the Congress.

1. Legitimacy

The power assumed by the Court in *Marbury* has serious consequences for separation of powers principles. It has the potential to both undermine and ensure the legitimacy of the national government. First, judicial review cements the legitimacy of a "government of laws" when it provides the institutional check on the government actors. On the other hand, when the Court declares a law unconstitutional it is making a determination that Congress, a popularly elected branch, has acted illegitimately. Equally important, the federal judiciary's own legitimacy is threatened when it engages in judicial review. Because the judiciary has no direct control over the "purse or the sword," its ultimate power lies in its moral force. The federal courts, including the Supreme Court, are powerful only so long as the people and the other branches of government respect their judgments. If the federal judiciary too frequently invalidates the acts of our elected representatives and renders unpopular decisions, it, and perhaps the whole government, will lose its legitimacy. Professor Bickel urged:

> The essentially important fact, so often missed, is that the Court wields a threefold power. It may strike down legislation as inconsistent with principle. It may validate, or . . . "legitimate" legislation as consistent with principle. Or it may do neither. . . . and therein lies the secret of its ability to maintain itself in the tension between principle and expediency.

> When it strikes down legislative policy, the Court must act rigorously on principle, or else it undermines the justification for its power. It must enunciate a goal, it must demonstrate that what the legislature did will not measure up, and it must proclaim its readiness to defend the goal — absolutely, if it is an absolute one. But it is not obligated to foresee all foreseeable relevant cases and to foreclose all compromise. Indeed, it cannot. It can only decide the case before it, giving reasons which rise to the dignity of principle and hence, of course, have a forward momentum and broad radiations. . . .

> Again, when the Court legitimates action, it should also act on principle. Here, the clash between judicial review and the electorally responsible institutions is less grave. Perhaps theoretically it is nonexistent. But in actual practice . . . the Court, when it legitimates a measure, does insert itself with significant consequences into the decisional process as carried on in the other institutions.

> When the Court, however, stays its hand, and makes clear that it is staying its hand and not legitimating, then the political processes are given relatively

free play. Such a decision needs relatively little justification in terms of consistency with democratic theory. It needs more to be justified as compatible with the Court's role as defender of the faith, proclaimer and protector of the goals. But in withholding constitutional judgment, the Court does not necessarily forsake an educational function, nor does it abandon principle. It seeks merely to elicit the correct answers to certain prudential questions that, in such a society as Lincoln conceived, lie in the path of ultimate issues of principle. To this end, the Court has, over the years, developed an almost inexhaustible arsenal of techniques and devices. Most of them are quite properly called techniques for eliciting answers, since so often they engage the Court in a Socratic colloquy with the other institutions of government and with society as a whole concerning the necessity for this or that measure, for this or that compromise. All the while, the issue of principle remains in abeyance and ripens. "The most important thing we do," said Brandeis, "is not doing." He had in mind all the techniques, of which he was a past master, for staying the Court's hand. They are the most important thing, because they make possible performance of the Court's grand function as proclaimer and protector of the goals. These are the techniques that allow leeway to expediency without abandoning principle. Therefore they make possible a principled government.

Alexander Bickel, The Least Dangerous Branch 69–70 (1962).[4]

The material in this section examines the Court's attempt to develop "do nothing" doctrines out of a perceived need to preserve the legitimacy of the federal judiciary. As you study the cases, consider (1) the source of the Court's power to avoid deciding the underlying dispute; (2) whether in the abstract the doctrine of judicial restraint is a useful device for limiting the business of the courts; (3) whether in the specific case the device was properly utilized; and, finally, (4) whether the federal judiciary's legitimacy is really enhanced when it avoids an issue. *See* Gerald Gunther, *The Subtle Vices of the "Passive Virtues"—A Comment on Principle and Expediency in Judicial Review*, 64 Colum. L. Rev. 1 (1964).

2. Efficiency

An examination of the relationship between the judiciary and Congress focuses as well on the second purpose of separation of powers, the desire to make the federal government more efficient. The Constitution provides that the judicial power of the United States extends only to "cases" or "controversies." U.S. Const. Art. III. One way the judiciary can avoid declaring that Congress acted illegitimately is to hold that the Court lacks power to decide the issue because there is no case or controversy. The Court may also focus on questions of efficiency when it determines the precise ingredients of a case or controversy. Underlying the cases in this section is a

---

4. Copyright © 1962 by The Bobbs-Merrill Company, Inc. Reprinted by permission.

conception of how the federal judges and the legislators best perform their respective functions.

3. Tyranny

Finally, our consideration of the relationship between the judiciary and Congress also presents a test of the proposition that separation of powers was designed to prevent tyranny by any one branch. The framers, of course, were concerned about the concentration of too much power in the legislature. They had little to fear of the courts because, as Hamilton stated in *The Federalist No. 78*, the courts must rely on the executive for the efficacy of its judgments:

> Whoever attentively considers the different departments of power must perceive, that, a government in which they are separated from each other, the judiciary, from the nature of its functions, will always be the least dangerous to the political rights of the Constitution; because it will be least in a capacity to annoy or injure them. The Executive not only dispenses the honors, but holds the sword of the community. The legislature not only commands the purse, but prescribes the rules by which the duties and rights of every citizen are to be regulated. The judiciary, on the contrary, has no influence over either the sword or the purse; no direction either of the strength or of the wealth of the society; and can take no active resolution whatever. It may truly be said to have neither FORCE nor WILL, but merely judgment; and must ultimately depend upon the aid of the executive arm even for the efficacy of its judgments.

The Federalist No. 78 (Hamilton).

The extent to which the federal courts have behaved as Hamilton predicted is widely debated. From across the political spectrum, some have charged that, far from merely exercising "the judicial Power," that the federal courts have assumed a sort of roving commission to reach out and solve social problems. As you consider the justiciability doctrines, bear in mind the ongoing argument over what constitutes the proper role for the federal courts in our constitutional system. Consider whether the judiciary has performed as Hamilton anticipated.

B. Political Questions

The courts sometimes have declined to decide a dispute after concluding that the constitutional issue is better left to the political branches for resolution. This "political question" doctrine is expressed in a holding that the dispute is not justiciable. The courts neither approve nor disapprove the action taken by the political branches.

The asserted bases for the political question doctrine are both textual and prudential. The text-based argument has been most prominently articulated by Herbert Wechsler:

[A]ll the doctrine can defensibly imply is that the courts are called upon to judge whether the constitution has committed to another agency of government the autonomous determination of the issue raised, a finding that itself requires an interpretation. . . .

. . . Difficult as it may be to make that judgment wisely, whatever factors may be rightly weighed in situations where the answer is not clear, what is involved is in itself an act of constitutional interpretation, to be made and judged by standards that should govern the interpretive process generally. That, I submit, is toto caelo different from a broad discretion to abstain or intervene.

Herbert Wechsler, *Toward Neutral Principles of Constitutional Law*, 73 Harv. L. Rev. 1, 7–9 (1959).

Alexander Bickel rejected Wechsler's argument and maintained instead that the doctrine is prudential, based on

the court's sense of lack of capacity, compounded in unequal parts of the strangeness of the issue and the suspicion that it will have to yield more often and more substantially to expediency than to principle; the sheer momentousness of it, which unbalances judgment and prevents one from subsuming the normal calculations of probabilities; the anxiety not so much that judicial judgment will be ignored, as that perhaps it should be, but won't; finally and in sum ("in a mature democracy"), the inner vulnerability of an institution which is electorally irresponsible and has no earth to draw strength from.

Alexander Bickel, *The Supreme Court, 1960 Term — Foreword: The Passive Virtues*, 75 Harv. L. Rev. 40, 75 (1961).

In *Baker v. Carr*, 369 U.S. 186 (1962), Justice Brennan summarized the formulations that the Supreme Court has utilized in deciding whether a question is nonjusticiable based on the political question doctrine:

Prominent on the surface of any case held to involve a political question is found a textual commitment of the issue to a coordinate political department; or a lack of judicially discoverable and manageable standards for resolving it; or the impossibility of deciding without an initial policy determination of a kind clearly for nonjudicial discretion; or the impossibility of a court's undertaking independent resolution without expressing lack of respect due coordinate branches of government; or an unusual need for unquestioning adherence to a political decision already made; or the potentiality of embarrassment from multifarious pronouncements by various departments on one question. 369 U.S. at 217.

The *Baker v. Carr* summary continues to frame the political question doctrine in the twenty-first century. However, nearly all of the political question outcomes have turned on application of the first two factors.

Powell v. McCormack

United States Supreme Court
393 U.S. 486 (1969)

WARREN, C.J.,

[In 1967, the House of Representatives refused to seat Rep. Adam Clayton Powell based upon a report that he had "wrongfully diverted House funds for the use of others and himself" and had made "false reports on expenditures of foreign currency to the Committee on House Administration." Powell sued, arguing that he met all the requirements for membership in the House contained in article I, section 2, clause 2 of the Constitution. The Speaker of the House answered that, based on the article I, section 5, clause 1 command that "each House shall be the Judge of the Qualifications of its own members," the question of Powell's fitness to serve was textually committed to the House. In addition, the Speaker claimed that adjudication of Powell's suit would produce a "potentially embarrassing confrontation between coordinate branches." The Supreme Court agreed to decide the controversy.]

In order to determine whether there has been a textual commitment to a coordinate department of the Government, we must interpret the Constitution. In other words, we must first determine what power the Constitution confers upon the House through Art. I, § 5, before we can determine to what extent, if any, the exercise of that power is subject to judicial review. Respondents maintain that the House has broad power under § 5, and, they argue, the House may determine which are the qualifications necessary for membership. On the other hand, petitioners allege that the Constitution provides that an elected representative may be denied his seat only if the House finds he does not meet one of the standing qualifications expressly prescribed by the Constitution.

If examination of § 5 disclosed that the Constitution gives the House judicially unreviewable power to set qualifications for membership and to judge whether prospective members meet those qualifications, further review of the House determination might well be barred by the political question doctrine. On the other hand, if the Constitution gives the House power to judge only whether elected members possess the three standing qualifications set forth in the Constitution, further consideration would be necessary to determine whether any of the other doctrines are "inextricable from the case at bar." *Baker v. Carr.*

In other words, whether there is a "textually demonstrable constitutional commitment of the issue to a coordinate political department" of government and what is the scope of such commitment are questions we must resolve for the first time in this case. In order to determine the scope of any "textual commitment" under Art. I, § 5, we necessarily must determine the meaning of the phrase to "be the Judge of the Qualifications of its own Members." Petitioners argue that the records of the debates during the Constitutional Convention; available commentary from the post-Convention, pre-ratification period; and early congressional applications of Art. I,

§ 5, support their construction of the section. Respondents insist, however, that a careful examination of the pre-Convention practices of the English Parliament and American colonial assemblies demonstrates that by 1787, a legislature's power to judge the qualifications of its members was generally understood to encompass exclusion or expulsion on the ground that an individual's character or past conduct rendered him unfit to serve. When the Constitution and the debates over its adoption are thus viewed in historical perspective, argue respondents, it becomes clear that the "qualifications" expressly set forth in the Constitution were not meant to limit the long-recognized legislative power to exclude or expel at will, but merely to establish "standing incapacities," which could be altered only by a constitutional amendment. Our examination of the relevant historical materials leads us to the conclusion that petitioners are correct and that the Constitution leaves the House without authority to *exclude* any person, duly elected by his constituents, who meets all the requirements for membership expressly prescribed in the Constitution.

Had the intent of the Framers emerged from these materials with less clarity, we would nevertheless have been compelled to resolve any ambiguity in favor of a narrow construction of the scope of Congress' power to exclude members-elect. A fundamental principle of our representative democracy is, in Hamilton's words, "that the people should choose whom they please to govern them." As Madison pointed out at the Convention, this principle is undermined as much by limiting the franchise itself. In apparent agreement with this basic philosophy, the Convention adopted his suggestion limiting the power to expel. To allow essentially that same power to be exercised under the guise of judging qualifications, would be to ignore Madison's warning, against "vesting an improper & dangerous power in the Legislature." Moreover, it would effectively nullify the Convention's decision to require a two-thirds vote for expulsion. Unquestionably, Congress has an interest in preserving its institutional integrity, but in most cases that interest can be sufficiently safeguarded by the exercise of its power to punish its members for disorderly behavior and, in extreme cases, to expel a member with the concurrence of two-thirds. In short, both the intention of the Framers, to the extent it can be determined, and an examination of the basic principles of our democratic system persuade us that the Constitution does not vest in the Congress a discretionary power to deny membership by a majority vote.

For these reasons, we have concluded that Art. I, § 5, is at most a "textually demonstrable commitment" to Congress to judge only the qualifications expressly set forth in the Constitution. Respondents' alternate contention is that the case presents a political question because judicial resolution of petitioners' claim would produce a "potentially embarrassing confrontation between coordinate branches" of the Federal Government. But, as our interpretation of Art. I, § 5, discloses, a determination of petitioner Powell's right to sit would require no more than an interpretation of the Constitution. Such a determination falls within the traditional role accorded courts to interpret the law, and does not involve a "lack of the respect due [a] coordinate [branch] of government," nor does it involve an "initial policy determination of a kind clearly for nonjudicial discretion." *Baker v. Carr.* Our system of government requires that federal courts on occasion interpret the Constitution in a manner at variance with the construction given the document by another branch. The alleged conflict that such an adjudication may cause cannot justify the courts' avoiding their constitutional responsibility.

Nor are any of the other formulations of a political question "inextricable from the case at bar." *Baker v. Carr.* Petitioners seek a determination that the House was without power to exclude Powell from the 90th Congress, which, we have seen, requires an interpretation of the Constitution — a determination for which clearly there are "judicially manageable standards." Finally, a judicial resolution of petitioners' claim will not result in "multifarious pronouncements by various departments on one question." For, as we noted in *Baker v. Carr,* it is the responsibility of this Court to act as the ultimate interpreter of the Constitution. *Marbury v. Madison.* Thus, we conclude that petitioners' claim is not barred by the political question doctrine, and, having determined generally justiciable, we hold that the case is justiciable.

Nixon v. United States

United States Supreme Court
506 U.S. 224 (1993)

[United States District Court Judge Walter L. Nixon, Jr. was convicted of perjury, based on a grand jury investigation of misconduct on his part. Nixon refused to resign his judgeship, despite his conviction and prison sentence. He was then impeached by the House and convicted by the Senate, and the Senate entered a judgment removing him from office. Nixon sued, seeking reinstatement and back pay on the ground that the Senate had not given him a trial, as required by article I, section 3, clause 6. Instead, Senate Rule XI was followed, which permits the Senate to appoint a committee to hear impeachment evidence and then act on the basis of the committee's report and any testimony the Senate may choose to hear.]

Rehnquist, C.J.,

In this case, we must examine Art. I, § 3, cl. 6, to determine the scope of authority conferred upon the Senate by the Framers regarding impeachment. It provides:

> The Senate shall have the sole Power to try all Impeachments. When sitting for that Purpose, they shall be on Oath or Affirmation. When the President of the United States is tried, the Chief Justice shall preside: And no Person shall be convicted without the Concurrence of two thirds of the Members present.

The language and structure of this Clause are revealing. The first sentence is a grant of authority to the Senate, and the word "sole" indicates that this authority is reposed in the Senate and nowhere else. The next two sentences specify requirements to which the Senate proceedings shall conform: the Senate shall be on oath or affirmation, a two-thirds vote is required to convict, and when the President is tried the Chief Justice shall preside.

Petitioner argues that the word "try" in the first sentence imposes by implication an additional requirement on the Senate in that the proceedings must be in the nature of a judicial trial. From there petitioner goes on to argue that this limitation precludes the Senate from delegating to a select committee the task of hearing the testimony of witnesses, as was done pursuant to Senate Rule XI. "'[T]ry' means more than simply 'vote on' or 'review' or 'judge.' In 1787 and today, trying a case means hearing the evidence, not scanning a cold record." Petitioner concludes from this that courts may review whether or not the Senate "tried" him before convicting him.

There are several difficulties with this position which lead us ultimately to reject it. The word "try," both in 1787 and later, has considerably broader meanings than those to which petitioner would limit it. Older dictionaries define try as "[t]o examine" or "[t]o examine as a judge." *See* 2 S. Johnson, A Dictionary of the English Language (1785). In more modern usage the term has various meanings. For example, try can mean "to examine or investigate judicially," "to conduct the trial of," or "to put to the test by experiment, investigation, or trial." Webster's Third New International Dictionary 2457 (1971). Petitioner submits that "try," as contained in T. Sheridan, Dictionary of the English Language (1796), means "to examine as a judge; to bring before a judicial tribunal." Based on the variety of definitions, however, we cannot say that the Framers used the word "try" as an implied limitation on the method by which the Senate might proceed in trying impeachments. "As a rule the Constitution speaks in general terms, leaving Congress to deal with subsidiary matters of detail as the public interests and changing conditions may require." *Dillon v. Gloss*, 256 U.S. 368, 376 (1921).

The conclusion that the use of the word "try" in the first sentence of the Impeachment Trial Clause lacks sufficient precision to afford any judicially manageable standard of review of the Senate's actions is fortified by the existence of the three very specific requirements that the Constitution does impose on the Senate when trying impeachments: the members must be under oath, a two-thirds vote is required to convict, and the Chief Justice presides when the President is tried. These limitations are quite precise, and their nature suggests that the Framers did not intend to impose additional limitations on the form of the Senate proceedings by the use of the word "try" in the first sentence.

We think that the word "sole" is of considerable significance. Indeed, the word "sole" appears only one other time in the Constitution — with respect to the House of Representatives' "*sole* Power of Impeachment." Art. I, § 2, cl. 5. The common sense meaning of the word "sole" is that the Senate alone shall have authority to determine whether an individual should be acquitted or convicted. The dictionary definition bears this out.

Petitioner argues that even if significance be attributed to the word "sole" in the first sentence of the clause, the authority granted is to the Senate, and this means that "the Senate — not the courts, not a lay jury, not a Senate Committee — shall try impeachments." It would be possible to read the first sentence of the Clause this way, but it is not a natural reading. Petitioner's interpretation would bring into judicial purview not merely the sort of claim made by petitioner, but other similar claims based on the conclusion that the word "Senate" has imposed by implication limitations on procedures which the Senate might adopt. Such limitations would be inconsistent with the construction of the Clause as a whole, which, as we have noted, sets out three express limitations in separate sentences.

The history and contemporary understanding of the impeachment provisions support our reading of the constitutional language. The parties do not offer evidence of a single word in the history of the Constitutional Convention or in contemporary commentary that even alludes to the possibility of judicial review in the context of the impeachment powers.

The Framers labored over the question of where the impeachment power should lie. Significantly, in at least two considered scenarios the power was placed with the Federal Judiciary. Indeed, Madison and the Committee of Detail proposed that the Supreme Court should have the power to determine impeachments. Despite these proposals, the Convention ultimately decided that the Senate would have "the sole Power to Try all Impeachments." Art. I, § 3, cl. 6. According to Alexander Hamilton, the Senate was the "most fit depositary of this important trust" because its members are representatives of the people. *See* The Federalist No. 65, p. 440 (J. Cooke ed., 1961). The Supreme Court was not the proper body because the Framers "doubted whether the members of that tribunal would, at all times, be endowed with so eminent a portion of fortitude as would be called for in the execution of so difficult a task" or whether the Court "would possess the degree of credit and authority" to carry out its judgment if it conflicted with the accusation brought by the Legislature — the people's representative. *See id.*, at 441. In addition, the Framers believed the Court was too small in number: "The awful discretion, which a court of impeachments must necessarily have, to doom to honor or to infamy the most confidential and the most distinguished characters of the community, forbids the commitment of the trust to a small number of persons." *Id.*, at 441–442.

There are two additional reasons why the Judiciary, and the Supreme Court in particular, were not chosen to have any role in impeachments. First, the Framers recognized that most likely there would be two sets of proceedings for individuals who commit impeachable offenses — the impeachment trial and a separate criminal trial. In fact, the Constitution explicitly provides for two separate proceedings. *See* Art. I, § 3, cl. 7. The Framers deliberately separated the two forums to avoid raising the specter of bias and to ensure independent judgments. Certainly judicial review of the Senate's "trial" would introduce the same risk of bias as would participation in the trial itself.

Second, judicial review would be inconsistent with the Framers' insistence that our system be one of checks and balances. In our constitutional system, impeachment was designed to be the only check on the Judicial Branch by the Legislature. Judicial involvement in impeachment proceedings, even if only for purposes of judicial review, is counterintuitive because it would eviscerate the "important constitutional check" placed on the Judiciary by the Framers. Nixon's argument would place final reviewing authority with respect to impeachments in the hands of the same body that the impeachment process is meant to regulate.

Nixon fears that if the Senate is given unreviewable authority to interpret the Impeachment Trial Clause, there is a grave risk that the Senate will usurp judicial power. The Framers anticipated this objection and created two constitutional safeguards to keep the Senate in check. The first safeguard is that the whole of the impeachment power is divided between the two legislative bodies, with the House given the right to accuse and the Senate given the right to judge. This split of authority "avoids the inconvenience of making the same persons both accusers and judges; and guards against the danger of persecution from the prevalence of a factious spirit in either of those branches." The second safeguard is the two-thirds supermajority vote requirement.

In addition to the textual commitment argument, we are persuaded that the lack of finality and the difficulty of fashioning relief counsel against justiciability. *See Baker v. Carr.* We agree with the Court of Appeals that opening the door of judicial review to the procedures used by the Senate in trying impeachments would "expose the political life of the country to months, or perhaps years, of chaos." This lack of finality would manifest itself most dramatically if the President were impeached. The legitimacy of any successor, and hence his effectiveness, would be impaired severely, not merely while the judicial process was running its course, but during any retrial that a differently constituted Senate might conduct if its first judgment of conviction were invalidated. Equally uncertain is the question of what relief a court may give other than simply setting aside the judgment of conviction. Could it order the reinstatement of a convicted federal judge, or order Congress to create an additional judgeship if the seat had been filled in the interim?

Petitioner finally contends that a holding of nonjusticiability cannot be reconciled with our opinion in *Powell v. McCormack.* Our conclusion in *Powell* was based on the fixed meaning of "[q]ualifications" set forth in Art. I, §2. The claim by the House that its power to "be the Judge of the Elections, Returns and Qualifications of its own Members" was a textual commitment of unreviewable authority was defeated by the existence of this separate provision specifying the only qualifications which might be imposed for House membership. The decision as to whether a member satisfied these qualifications was placed with the House, but the decision as to what these qualifications consisted of was not.

In the case before us, there is no separate provision of the Constitution which could be defeated by allowing the Senate final authority to determine the meaning of the word "try" in the Impeachment Trial Clause. We agree with Nixon that courts possess power to review either legislative or executive action that transgresses identifiable textual limits. As we have made clear, "whether the action of [either the Legislative or Executive Branch] exceeds whatever authority has been committed, is itself a delicate exercise in constitutional interpretation, and is a responsibility of this Court as ultimate interpreter of the Constitution." *Baker v. Carr; accord Powell.*

But we conclude, after exercising that delicate responsibility, that the word "try" in the Impeachment Clause does not provide an identifiable textual limit on the authority which is committed to the Senate.

Notes and Questions

(1) Do you find the Court's analysis of the Article I Qualifications Clause in *Powell v. McCormack* persuasive? Of course, the Court decided the justiciability of what congressional qualifications consisted of, not whether Powell or anyone else satisfied those qualifications. If the House voted to deny Powell his seat based on someone's false assertion that he was 23 years old, would that determination be reviewable by any court? If so, on what basis?

(2) Are you persuaded by the Court's distinction of Judge Nixon's appeal from *Powell v. McCormack*? Do you agree that the Impeachment Clause should not have been construed in this case? Can you imagine a dispute involving impeachment that would present a justiciable controversy?

(3) Most cases decided on the basis of the political question doctrine involve inter-branch disputes over the constitutional allocation of powers. Should the doctrine apply in the same way when government conduct is challenged on individual rights grounds? In *Zaidan v. Trump*, 317 F. Supp. 3d 8 (D.D.C. 2018), a citizen journalist inferred from five "near-miss" aerial attacks on him in Syria that he was wrongly included on a U.S. "kill list." He claimed that his listing violated procedures set forth in a presidential policy guidance for listing terrorist targets. The court ruled that his challenge was barred by the political question doctrine, because the guidance provided "no test or standard that must be satisfied before the government may add an individual (known or unknown) to the Kill List; it only specifies the steps and processes that the relevant defense agencies must complete." 317 F. Supp. 3d at 25. Can you think of a claim on behalf of the journalist that would not be barred by the political question doctrine?

C. Standing to Sue

In *Northeastern Florida Chapter, General Contractors of America v. City of Jacksonville*, 508 U.S. 656, 663–664 (1993), the Court declared that

> a party seeking to invoke a federal court's jurisdiction must demonstrate three things: (1) "injury in fact," by which we mean an invasion of a legally protected interest that is "(a) concrete and particularized, and (b) actual or imminent, not conjectural or hypothetical," (2) a causal relationship between the injury and the challenged conduct, by which we mean that the injury "fairly can be traced to the challenged action of the defendant," and has not resulted "from the independent action of some third party not before the court," and (3) a likelihood that the injury will be redressed by a favorable decision, by which we mean that the "prospect of obtaining relief

from the injury as a result of a favorable ruling" is not "too speculative" (internal citations omitted).

Why should the Article III "case or controversy" requirement be construed to restrict access to the federal courts on the basis of the status of the parties, as distinct from the fitness of the issues for judicial resolution?

Although the doctrinal framework for the law of citizen standing has not changed in recent years, the Supreme Court has made it increasingly clear that the doctrine of standing is "an essential and unchanging part of the case-or-controversy requirement of Article III," *Lujan v. Defenders of Wildlife*, 504 U.S. 555, 559 (1992), which defines with respect to the Judicial Branch the idea of separation of powers on which the Federal Government is founded. *Allen v. Wright*, 468 U.S. 737, 750 (1984). Should the courts be concerned about enhanced judicial power when they determine standing? Or does separation of powers counsel judicial vigilance to prevent intrusions by one elected branch into the proper domain of the other elected branch?

Alexander Hamilton suggested that the judiciary is the "least dangerous" branch because it "has no influence over either the sword or the purse." THE FEDERALIST No. 78, at 465 (Clinton Rossiter ed., 1961). Whatever the Framers intended, do you think Hamilton's statement is true today?

Notes and Questions — Citizen Plaintiffs

(1) In *Clapper v. Amnesty International USA*, 133 S. Ct. 1138 (2013), the Supreme Court held that a group of lawyers, human rights workers, labor union leaders, and journalists who regularly communicate with foreign persons outside the United States did not have standing to challenge on First and Fourth Amendment grounds provisions of the Foreign Intelligence Surveillance Act (FISA) that authorize the secret electronic interception of communications with foreign persons outside the United States, because the plaintiffs failed to persuade the Court that the harm they alleged was "certainly impending." Is that standard a fair application of the requirement that plaintiffs have an injury that is actual or threatened?

(2) The Supreme Court has emphasized that, while Congress may express its intention to allow citizens to sue to vindicate interests protected by statute, statutory grants of standing do not excuse a plaintiff from proving the constitutionally requisite injury in fact. In the *Lujan* case, noted above, the Court rejected environmental plaintiffs' claim of standing based on a statutory provision entitling "any person [to] commence a civil suit on his own behalf to enjoin any person, including the United States and any other governmental instrumentality or agency who is alleged to be in violation of any provision of this chapter." Endangered Species Act, 16 U.S.C. §1540(g)(1). Although the Court recognized that Congress in some settings may create injuries whose violation in turn creates standing, such as "where plaintiffs are seeking to enforce a procedural requirement the disregard of which could impair a separate concrete interest of theirs," the Court concluded that

> [t]o permit Congress to convert the undifferentiated public interest in exec-
> utive officers' compliance with the law into an "individual right" vindicable
> in the courts is to permit Congress to transfer from the President to the
> courts the Chief Executive's most important constitutional duty, to "take
> Care that the Laws be faithfully executed."

Lujan, 504 U.S. at 570, 573.

(3) In *Spokeo, Inc. v. Robins*, 578 U.S. 330 (2016), the Court confirmed that an injury must be both "concrete" and "particularized." These requirements are distinct: For an injury to be particularized, "it must effect the plaintiff in a personal and individual way." A "concrete injury" must "actually exist." The judgment of Congress is important on these questions, but not decisive. For example, in *TransUnion v. Ramirez*, 141 S. Ct. 2190 (2021), the Court confirmed that the "concreteness" requirement limited Congress's authority to define new injuries that lack an historical analogue. The determination of "concreteness" remains for the Court, based on Article III. *Id.*

(4) According to Justice Scalia's opinion for the Court in *Lujan*, unbridled citizen standing conferred by Congress would turn the courts into constant monitors of executive action. Judicial power would be enlarged at the expense of the Executive Branch power to "take Care that the Laws be faithfully executed." Professor Sunstein argues that the President's Take Care Clause power does not extend beyond the duties prescribed by Congress, and lawsuits to enforce compliance with those laws ensure fidelity to the legislation. Cass R. Sunstein, *What's Standing After Lujan? Of Citizen Suits, "Injuries," and Article III*, 91 Mich. L. Rev. 163, 209–215 (1992). Which view do you find more persuasive?

(5) Would a concerned citizen have standing to challenge the President's decision to commit the United States to a military conflict abroad? In *Pietsch v. Bush*, 755 F. Supp. 62 (E.D.N.Y. 1991), *aff'd without op.*, 935 F.2d 1278 (2d Cir. 1991), a citizen sought a court order preventing hostilities between the U.S. and Iraq. In concluding that Pietsch was not injured in fact, the court distinguished the interest of a concerned citizen from that of members of Congress (who "plainly have an interest in protecting their right to vote in matters entrusted to their respective chambers by the Constitution") or a member of the armed forces deployed to the potential combat area. According to the court, Pietsch's claim that he was being made "an accessory to murder against his will," a compulsion causing him emotional distress, was "too abstract" to meet Article III requirements. 755 F. Supp. at 66.

The court in *Pietsch* also rejected the argument that a citizen has standing to sue the Government to enforce obedience to the Constitution:

> [T]he Plaintiff does not have standing merely because as a citizen of the
> United States he has an "interest" in seeing the Government act constitu-
> tionally. In *Schlesinger v. Reservists Committee to Stop the War*, 418 U.S. 208
> (1974), a citizens' group challenged the membership in the National Reserve
> by United States Congressmen as violative of the Ineligibility Clause of the

Constitution (Article I, Section 6, clause 2). The plaintiffs contended that they had standing because as United States citizens they had an interest in insuring "the faithful discharge by members of Congress who are members of the Reserves of their duties as members of Congress, to which all citizens and taxpayers are entitled." (*Id.* at p. 212.) The United States Supreme Court rejected this argument, and held: "standing to sue may not be predicated upon an interest of the kind alleged here which is held in common by all members of the public, because of the necessarily abstract nature of the injury all citizens share." (*Id.* at p. 220.) The Plaintiff in this case has suffered no more cognizable injury than did the citizens in *Schlesinger*, and, therefore, does not have standing to maintain this action.

In these trying times, I understand the Plaintiff's deep concern for the loss of life in any future military action, and I appreciate the Plaintiff's altruistic purposes in bringing this lawsuit. However, this Court cannot legally alleviate these concerns. I am bound by the Constitution to solely adjudicate "cases or controversies" within the purview of our standing requirements. As the Supreme Court stated in *Schlesinger*: "Our system of government leaves many crucial decisions to the political processes. The assumption that if respondents have no standing to sue, no one would have standing, is not a reason to find standing."

Pietsch, supra, 755 F. Supp. at 67, citing *Schlesinger v. Reservists Committee to Stop the War, supra*, 418 U.S. at 227.

Is the political process the appropriate forum for redress when a citizen alleges an injury common to all citizens? Should the citizen plaintiff be satisfied that he can draft and lobby for passage of legislation to vindicate such common rights?

(6) A plaintiff who meets the Article III requirements for standing may nonetheless be unable to raise particular claims. The second prudential consideration in determining standing is "the requirement that a plaintiff's complaint fall within the zone of interests protected by the law invoked." *Allen v. Wright*, 468 U.S. 737, 751 (1984). While this concern is most prominently reflected in the requirement that taxpayer plaintiffs show a nexus between their taxpayer status and their claim, the zone of interests requirement may also bar a lawsuit when a court determines that Congress did not intend to create private rights in a statute.

Notes and Questions — Congressional Plaintiffs

(1) Should the law of legislator standing be any different from the law of citizen standing? Do legislators have a legal right to sue over deprivations of their legislative prerogatives? Clearly, legislators may sue over the loss of a personal right, such as their loss of a seat in the legislature (recall Rep. Powell). But what about when the loss is of political power?

(2) In *Raines v. Byrd*, 521 U.S. 811 (1997), the Supreme Court held that members of Congress lacked standing to challenge the constitutionality of the Line Item Veto

Act. *Raines* presented the Court with its first occasion to rule on the claim that an action causes a type of institutional injury (the diminution of legislative power) which necessarily damages all Members of Congress and both Houses of Congress equally. Although the Court recognized that the D.C. Circuit Court of Appeals has held that Members of Congress have standing to assert injury to their institutional power as legislators, the majority was unwilling to credit what it viewed as a "wholly abstract and widely dispersed" claim of injury. Thus, according to the Court, the Members of Congress lacked the necessary "personal stake" in the dispute. Chief Justice Rehnquist explained the majority's reasoning:

> The [plaintiffs] have not alleged that they voted for a specific bill, that there were sufficient votes to pass the bill, and that the bill was nonetheless deemed defeated. In the vote on the Line Item Veto Act, their votes were given full effect. They simply lost that vote. Nor can they allege that the Act will nullify their votes in the future. In the future, a majority of Senators and Congressman can pass or reject appropriations bills; the Act has no effect on this process. In addition, a majority of Senators and Congressman can vote to repeal the Act, or to exempt a given appropriations bill (or a given provision in an appropriations bill) from the Act; again, the Act has no effect on this process.

In light of the Court's opinion in *Raines*, can you think of a dispute where the Court would find legislator standing to challenge an executive branch decision?

Notes and Questions — States as Plaintiffs

(1) Under what circumstances may state governments sue the United States? In other words, when has a state government suffered an injury that satisfies the requirements of Article III? More broadly, when should the federal courts decide highly political lawsuits that typically pit the White House against state governments controlled by the other party?

(2) Lawsuits brought by states against the executive branch have proliferated in recent years. In 2007, in *Massachusetts v. Environmental Protection Agency*, 549 U.S. 497 (2007), the Court ruled 5-4 that Massachusetts had standing to challenge the EPA for failing to regulate to control climate change, noting that states are "entitled to special solicitude in our standing analysis."

However, recent decisions have applied stricter but uneven limits on standing by states, at least when challenging actions by the executive branch. In 2023, the Court ruled that Texas lacked standing to challenge provisions of the Indian Child Welfare Act that require "active efforts" by states and private parties to place Indian children requiring foster care with Indian families. Texas' argument that complying with the Act will require that it break its promise to its citizens "that it will be colorblind in child custody proceedings" is not the kind of concrete and particularized injury required by *Lujan* to satisfy the injury in fact requirement of Article III. *Haaland v. Brackeen*, 143 S. Ct. 1609 (2023).

Arising in a different context but with a similar outcome, the Court ruled in *United States v. Texas*, 143 S. Ct. 1964 (2023), that Texas and Louisiana lack standing to challenge Biden administration guidelines promulgated by the Department of Homeland Security that set priorities for which unauthorized immigrants should be detained and which to leave alone based on "national security, public safety, and border security." The plaintiff states maintained that the guidelines violate federal statutes that require, among other things, the arrest of noncitizens upon their release from prison. According to Texas and Louisiana, the effect of violating the statutes and following the guidelines was to cause the states to incur costs, which in their view conferred their standing. Relying in part on *Raines v. Byrd*, *supra*, the Court held that although monetary costs may be an injury the injury must "be legally and judicially cognizable [where] the dispute is traditionally thought to be capable of resolution through the judicial process." The states cited no precedent, history, or tradition of federal courts entertaining lawsuits similar to this one, where the states are challenging the executive's enforcement discretion. Writing for the majority, Justice Kavanaugh said that "if the court greenlighted this suit, we could anticipate complaints in future years about alleged executive branch under-enforcement of any similarly worded laws — whether they be drug laws, gun laws, obstruction of justice laws or the like. We decline to start the federal judiciary down that uncharted path." Justice Kavanaugh noted that the Court did not address the lawfulness of the guidelines, only whether Texas and Louisiana had standing to pursue their lawfulness. In his dissent, Justice Alito asked whether the 2007 *Massachusetts v. EPA* decision had "been quietly interred?"

An apparent and emphatic answer to Justice Alito was given by the Court in *Biden v. Nebraska*, 143 S. Ct. 2355 (2023), where a majority of the Court found that a Missouri student loan servicing agency had standing to challenge a nationwide cancellation of nearly $430 billion in student debt by executive order, reasoning that the Missouri agency would lose revenue as a result of the cancellations in Missouri. The Missouri agency is a student loan servicer, not a lender, and the Court did not hold that Missouri has standing as such. The agency could have sued but didn't. In her dissent Justice Kagan argued that "Missouri needs to show that the harm to [the state agency] produces harm to the State itself. Because [the agency] was set up to insulate its creator from such derivative harm, Missouri is incapable of making that showing. The separateness between [the agency] and Missouri makes the agency alone the proper party." Why do you suppose that the independent Missouri agency's costs were sufficient to confer standing while those of Texas and Louisiana, above, were not? Did the Court respect Article III limits in finding standing for the Missouri agency?

(3) In 2019, the Court ruled in *Department of Commerce v. New York*, 139 S. Ct. 2551 (2019), that states could challenge the Trump administration's decision to include a question about citizenship on census forms. However, after President Trump ordered the Secretary of Commerce to provide him two sets of census numbers for each state, one the total population as determined in the 2020 census and

the other number minus the number of "aliens who are not in a lawful immigration status," a coalition of states challenged the President's decision to exclude illegal aliens from the apportionment base for Congress. Review the Supreme Court's decision below in *Trump v New York*.

D. Ripeness

As an aspect of Article III case or controversy requirements, the ripeness doctrine maintains that "federal courts do not render advisory opinions. For adjudication of constitutional issues 'concrete legal issues, presented in actual cases, not abstractions, are requisite." *United Public Workers v. Mitchell*, 330 U.S. 75 (1947). Review the decision below.

Trump v. New York

Supreme Court of the United States
141 S. Ct. 530 (2020)

Per Curiam.

Every ten years, the Nation undertakes an "Enumeration" of its population "in such Manner" as Congress "shall by Law direct." U.S. Const., Art. I, §2, cl. 3. This census plays a critical role in apportioning Members of the House of Representatives among the States, allocating federal funds to the States, providing information for intrastate redistricting, and supplying data for numerous initiatives conducted by governmental entities, businesses, and academic researchers. Congress has given both the Secretary of Commerce and the President functions to perform in the enumeration and apportionment process. The Secretary must "take a decennial census of population in such form and content as he may determine," 13 U.S.C. §141(a), and then must report to the President "[t]he tabulation of total population by States" under the census "as required for the apportionment," §141(b). The President in turn must transmit to Congress a "statement showing the whole number of persons in each State, excluding Indians not taxed, as ascertained" under the census. 46 Stat. 26, 2 U.S.C. §2a(a). In that statement, the President must apply a mathematical formula called the "method of equal proportions" to the population counts in order to calculate the number of House seats for each State.

This past July, the President issued a memorandum to the Secretary respecting the apportionment following the 2020 census. The memorandum announced a policy of excluding "from the apportionment base aliens who are not in a lawful immigration status." To facilitate implementation "to the maximum extent feasible and consistent with the discretion delegated to the executive branch," the President ordered the Secretary, in preparing his §141(b) report, "to provide information permitting the President, to the extent practicable, to exercise the President's discretion to carry out the policy." The President directed the Secretary to include such information in addition to a tabulation of population according to the criteria promulgated by the Census Bureau for counting each State's residents.

This case arises from one of several challenges to the memorandum brought by various States, local governments, organizations, and individuals. A three-judge District Court held that the plaintiffs, appellees here, had standing to proceed in federal court because the memorandum was chilling aliens and their families from responding to the census, thereby degrading the quality of census data used to allocate federal funds and forcing some plaintiffs to divert resources to combat the chilling effect. According to the District Court, the memorandum violates § 141(b) by ordering the Secretary to produce two sets of numbers — a valid tabulation derived from the census, and an invalid tabulation excluding aliens based on administrative records outside the census. The District Court also ruled that the exclusion of aliens on the basis of legal status would contravene the requirement in § 2a(a) that the President state the "whole number of persons in each State" for purposes of apportionment. The District Court declared the memorandum unlawful and enjoined the Secretary from including the information needed to implement the memorandum in his § 141(b) report to the President. The Government appealed, and we postponed consideration of our jurisdiction.

A foundational principle of Article III is that "an actual controversy must exist not only at the time the complaint is filed, but through all stages of the litigation." *Already, LLC v. Nike, Inc.*, 568 U.S. 85, 90–91 (2013). As the plaintiffs concede, any chilling effect from the memorandum dissipated upon the conclusion of the census response period. The plaintiffs now seek to substitute an alternative theory of a "legally cognizable injury" premised on the threatened impact of an unlawful apportionment on congressional representation and federal funding. As the case comes to us, however, we conclude that it does not — at this time — present a dispute "appropriately resolved through the judicial process." *Susan B. Anthony List v. Driehaus*, 573 U.S. 149, 157 (2014).

Two related doctrines of justiciability — each originating in the case-or-controversy requirement of Article III — underlie this determination. First, a plaintiff must demonstrate standing, including "an injury that is concrete, particularized, and imminent rather than conjectural or hypothetical." Second, the case must be "ripe" — not dependent on "contingent future events that may not occur as anticipated, or indeed may not occur at all."

At present, this case is riddled with contingencies and speculation that impede judicial review. The President, to be sure, has made clear his desire to exclude aliens without lawful status from the apportionment base. But the President qualified his directive by providing that the Secretary should gather information "to the extent practicable" and that aliens should be excluded "to the extent feasible." Any prediction how the Executive Branch might eventually implement this general statement of policy is "no more than conjecture" at this time. To begin with, the policy may not prove feasible to implement in any manner whatsoever, let alone in a manner substantially likely to harm any of the plaintiffs here. Pre-apportionment litigation always "presents a moving target" because the Secretary may make (and the President may direct) changes to the census up until the President transmits his statement to the House. And as the Government recognizes, any such changes must comply with the constitutional requirement of an "actual Enumeration" of the persons in each State, as opposed to a conjectural estimate. Here the record is silent on which (and how many) aliens have administrative records that would allow the Secretary to avoid impermissible estimation, and whether the Census Bureau can even match the records in its possession to census data in a timely manner. Uncertainty likewise pervades which (and how many) aliens the President will exclude from the census if the Secretary manages to gather and match suitable administrative records. We simply do not know whether and to what extent the President might direct the Secretary to "reform the census" to implement his general policy with respect to apportionment.

While the plaintiffs agree that the dispute will take a more concrete shape once the Secretary delivers his report under § 141(b), they insist that the record already establishes a "substantial risk" of reduced representation and federal resources. That conclusion, however, involves a significant degree of guesswork. Unlike other pre-apportionment challenges, the Secretary has not altered census operations in a concrete manner that will predictably change the count. The count here is complete; the present dispute involves the apportionment process, which remains at a preliminary stage. The Government's eventual action will reflect both legal and practical constraints, making any prediction about future injury just that — a prediction.

Everyone agrees by now that the Government cannot feasibly implement the memorandum by excluding the estimated 10.5 million aliens without lawful status. Yet the only evidence speaking to the predicted change in apportionment unrealistically assumes that the President will exclude the entire undocumented population. Nothing in the record addresses the consequences of a partial implementation of the memorandum, much less supports the dissent's speculation that excluding aliens in ICE detention will impact interstate apportionment.

At the end of the day, the standing and ripeness inquiries both lead to the conclusion that judicial resolution of this dispute is premature. Consistent with our determination that standing has not been shown and that the case is not ripe, we express no view on the merits of the constitutional and related statutory claims presented. We hold only that they are not suitable for adjudication at this time.

The judgment of the District Court is vacated, and the case is remanded with instructions to dismiss for lack of jurisdiction.

It is so ordered.

JUSTICE BREYER, with whom JUSTICE SOTOMAYOR and JUSTICE KAGAN join, dissenting.

The Court argues that it is now uncertain just how fully the Secretary will implement the Presidential memorandum. In my view, that uncertainty does not warrant our waiting to decide the merits of the plaintiffs' claim. It is true that challenges to apportionment have often come *after* the President has transmitted his tabulation to the House. The Government asked us to take that approach here. But we have also reached and resolved controversies concerning the decennial census based on a substantial risk of an anticipated apportionment harm. See *Department of Commerce v. United States House of Representatives*, 525 U.S. 316, 332 (1999) (holding that it is "not necessary for this Court to wait until the census has been conducted to consider" government conduct that may affect apportionment). And that is what I believe the Court should do here. Waiting to adjudicate plaintiffs' claims until *after* the President submits his tabulation to Congress, as the Court seems to prefer, risks needless and costly delays in apportionment. Because there is a "substantial likelihood that the [plaintiffs'] requested relief . . . will redress the alleged injury," *United States House of Representatives*, 525 U.S. at 332, I would find that we can reach plaintiffs' challenge now, and affirm the lower court's holding.

The Court reasons that "standing has not been shown" because it is too soon to tell if the Government will act "in a manner substantially likely to harm any of the plaintiffs here." As I have said, I believe to the contrary. Plaintiffs have alleged a justiciable controversy, and that controversy is ripe for resolution. Begin with the threatened injury. The plaintiffs allege two forms of future injury: a loss of representation in the apportionment count and decreased federal funding tied to the census totals. For an injury to satisfy Article III, it "must be concrete and particularized and actual or imminent, not conjectural or hypothetical." *Susan B. Anthony List v. Driehaus*, 573 U.S. 149, 157 (2014) (quoting *Lujan v. Defenders of Wildlife*, 504 U.S. 555, 560 (1992). We have long said that when plaintiffs "demonstrate a realistic danger of sustaining a direct injury as a result of [a policy's] operation or enforcement," they need "'not have to await the consummation of threatened injury to obtain preventive relief. If the injury is certainly impending, that is enough.'" *Babbitt v. Farm Workers*, 442 U.S. 289, 298 (1979).

Here, inquiry into the threatened injury is unusually straightforward. The harm is clear on the face of the policy. The title of the Presidential memorandum reads: "Excluding Illegal Aliens From the Apportionment Base Following the 2020 Census." 85 Fed. Reg. 44679 (2020) (Presidential memorandum). That memorandum announces "the policy of the United States [shall be] to exclude from the apportionment base aliens who are not in a lawful immigration status . . . to the maximum extent feasible and consistent with the discretion delegated to the executive branch." Notwithstanding the "contingencies and speculation" that "riddl[e]" this case, the Government has not backed away from its stated aim to exclude aliens without lawful status from apportionment. The memorandum also announces the reason for this policy: to diminish the "political influence" and "congressional representation" of States "home to" unauthorized immigrants. 85 Fed. Reg. 44680.

Given the clarity of the Presidential memorandum, it is unsurprising the Government does not contest that plaintiffs have alleged a threatened injury. Rather, it contends that both the alleged representational and funding injuries remain "too speculative" to satisfy Article III's ripeness requirement prior to the President's actual enumeration. That is because—although the Secretary's report to the President is due in just two weeks—the Bureau's plan to implement the memorandum remains uncertain and "depends on various unknowable contingencies about the data," and until "later in December or January, the Bureau cannot predict or even estimate the results." The Government contends that given these uncertainties, "it is far from a 'virtual certainty' that any appellee will 'lose a [House] seat' when the Memorandum is implemented." It also says it is "too speculative" that plaintiffs will be disproportionately deprived of federal funding, as it is not yet certain that the tabulation the President submits to Congress for apportionment purposes will also be used as the total population for federal statutes that apportion funds on the basis of States' proportional population. At root, the Government contends that "ripeness principles support deferring judicial review of the Memorandum until it is implemented."

Whether viewed as a question of standing or ripeness, the Government's arguments are insufficient. We have said that plaintiffs need not "demonstrate that it is literally certain that the harms they identify will come about" to establish standing. *Clapper v. Amnesty Int'l USA*, 568 U.S. 398, 414, n. 5 (2013). Rather, an "allegation of future injury may suffice if the threatened injury is 'certainly impending,' or there is a '"substantial risk" that the harm will occur.'" Looking to the facts here, the memorandum presents the "substantial risk" that our precedents require.

Moreover, the statute says that "the President shall transmit to the Congress a statement showing the whole number of persons in each State . . . *as ascertained under the* . . . decennial census of the population." 2 U.S.C. §2a(a). I do not agree with the Court that the lingering uncertainty over the Government's plans renders this litigation unripe, nor that the apportionment process is at a "preliminary stage." For one thing, the Government has spent over a year collecting the administrative records that will be used to fulfill the Presidential memorandum. For another, the Government has told us in related litigation that further delays in proceeding with apportionment beyond the statutory deadline would harm "the ability to meet contingent redistricting deadlines" in the States, because "'delays would mean deadlines that are established in state constitutions or statutes will be impossible to meet.'" But even if the Secretary were to limit severely his compliance with the President's memorandum — say, by choosing to "report" only those 50,000 aliens that are estimated to be in ICE detention centers and omitting them from his census "tabulation" — that omission alone presents a "substantial risk" of affecting the census calculation for purposes of apportionment and funding. That is the very kind of injury of which plaintiffs complain. Taken together, these considerations demonstrate that now is the appropriate time to resolve this case. Cf. *Abbott Laboratories v. Gardner*, 387 U.S. 136, 149 (1967) (Harlan, J. for the Court) (explaining that the timing of judicial review turns on "the fitness of the issues for judicial decision and the hardship to the parties of withholding court consideration").

To repeat, the President's stated goal is to reduce the number of Representatives apportioned to the States that are home to a disproportionate number of aliens without lawful status. The Government has confirmed that it can identify millions of these people through administrative records. But if the Census Bureau fails to fulfill its mandate to exclude aliens without lawful status and reduce the number of Representatives to which certain States are entitled, it will be for reasons not in the record. Where, as here, the Government acknowledges it is working to achieve an allegedly illegal goal, this Court should not decline to resolve the case simply because the Government speculates that it might not fully succeed.

For these reasons, I believe that the plaintiffs have alleged a "substantial risk" that unlawfully subtracting aliens without lawful status from the tabulation of the total population that the President submits to Congress will inflict both apportionment and appropriations injuries on them. Those injuries are substantially likely to occur in the reasonably near future. This case squarely presents a concrete dispute and we should resolve it now.

Notes and Questions

(1) Do you agree that the plaintiffs in *Trump v. New York* lacked standing to sue? That their lawsuit was not ripe? Can you see how the two justiciability doctrines tend to merge in some cases? If Justice Breyer had persuaded his colleagues that the state plaintiffs had sufficient threatened injury to satisfy the standing requirements of Article III, might the dispute have been dismissed on the basis of the ripeness doctrine?

(2) The ripeness doctrine exists to prevent premature adjudication, where a dispute is speculative or insufficiently developed to justify judicial action. Intense curiosity about the legal issues does not merit a federal court deciding the merits. Most ripeness rulings are based on Article III, but sometimes courts dismiss based on equitable discretion or other prudential grounds.

(3) In *Laird v. Tatum*, 408 U.S. 1 (1972), plaintiffs sought redress against allegedly unlawful "surveillance of lawful citizen political activity" by the U.S. Army. The Court dismissed, relying on *Mitchell*, stating that the claim "rested mainly on challengers' fear of future, punitive action," and such fears did not present "threat of specific future harm."

Problem E

Assume that several recent media reports quote a reliable source inside the White House who stated that the President is very concerned about Iran's development of nuclear weapons and is considering an air strike on suspected weapons sites in Iran without first obtaining congressional authorization. In addition to believing that he has the unilateral authority to order the attack, the President is concerned that seeking congressional support would undermine the secrecy needed to ensure the operation's success. Your law firm has been approached by a group of potential plaintiffs that includes concerned citizens, members of the military who fear involvement in an unlawful conflict, and members of Congress who wish to safeguard their constitutional prerogatives to decide whether to authorize the use of military force. The group shares a belief that such an action by the President would violate the constitutional assignment to Congress of the power to declare war. What barriers, if any, would the potential plaintiffs have in bringing a federal lawsuit?

Chapter 3

Federalism Limits on Federal Courts

§ 3.01 Historical Overview

The American Constitution is much more a practical document than a theoretical statement, a point made often in the separation of powers unit. As this unit unfolds, you will see that the pragmatic problems the Framers were seeking to solve concerned the allocation of powers between the national and state governments as much as the allocations among the branches of the national government.

As a mid-point between the poles of centralization and independent colonies or states, our federalism was a political compromise which was, and still is, nothing more or less than a process for the allocation of governmental power between the national government and the states. In theory, federalism is the process of organizing separate political communities into selected arrangements for adopting joint policies and making decisions on mutual problems. In practice, not only has the American Constitution changed that basic theory by approving a federation for *all* the purposes of government, but federalism's process orientation has often been lost in our constitutional jurisprudence. Like the separation of powers "doctrine," federalism has taken on substantive doctrinal meaning in interpreting questions of constitutional power, based on limited textual authority in the Constitution.

This introductory section in the federalism unit will first examine the theoretical and historical roots of federalism prior to the American experience. Then the American federalism story will be briefly told, from the colonial period through the Articles of Confederation and the Constitutional Convention, followed by the ratification struggles. A short judicial history of the courts' treatment of federalism will follow, primarily to frame our study of how federalism considerations weigh in a judicial decision.

A. The What and Why of Federalism

There is no such thing as "pure" federalism. In fact, the varied forms which have called themselves federations or confederations throughout history range across the political spectrum. If there is any single unifying characteristic of federated political societies, it is a paradoxical one: Federalism is usually a means rather than an end.

A federal system that may have been an essential part of the deal originally made to organize a government may retard the development of a maturing nation. Once a nation survives the initial period, the national governors tend to seek to control and minimize the power of the subfederal units. *See* ARTHUR WHITTIER MACMAHON, FEDERALISM: MATURE AND EMERGENT 3–4 (1962).

Notwithstanding the diversity and ever-changing character of federal systems, they share a few common characteristics:

> *First*, the distribution of power between national and subnational governments which is the hallmark of federal arrangements cannot be changed by simple legislation. Changes may be made by constitutional amendment through a variety of means.

> *Second*, the residual powers of the subnational governments are more than menial or ministerial, whether the method of allocating them is by express delegation or residual.

> *Third*, the national government's authority reaches to control individuals directly, both to claim the legitimacy which citizen elections bring, and to insure that the national laws will be obeyed.

> *Fourth*, the subnational units have substantial discretion to establish and change their forms and procedures of government.

> *Fifth*, the subnational states are equal as legal entities, even though there will be obvious differences in size and wealth and the like.

Id. at 4–5.

Why federalism? What values does a federal system further? First, theorists have frequently argued that a federal form best insures that government will be "close to the people." By retaining significant power for the local governments, the centralization of power that could lead to tyranny may be avoided. In addition, citizens will be more likely to participate in a diffused government that is in close proximity to where they live and work. As a result, local government officials will theoretically be more in tune with the interests of local citizens and will better represent them.

Related to the idea of keeping government close to the people is the notion that federalism protects individual liberty. In America, the realities of federalism have placed this justification for the federal form in an almost constant limelight. In *theory*, federalism's division of power among national and local governments works like separating the national government into departments for the purpose of diffusing power; together, these divisions protect the individual by guarding against the concentration of power in any one level or any one branch of government.

There is, however, extensive evidence that the relationship of federalism to liberty is not all positive. The most glaring example of the federal system working to inhibit rather than protect liberty is slavery in the pre-Civil War era. Although the

Constitution itself permitted slavery, it was the local autonomy that tolerated the continuation of slavery. In contemporary times, the apparent failures of the states to guarantee civil rights for citizens has prompted extensive federal legislation and enforcement in the civil rights area, all in derogation of the theory that a large measure of local autonomy best insures individual liberty. Pay close attention to this justification for federalism as this unit unfolds.

Another justification for the federal form is governmental effectiveness. Recall that one of the three reasons for separating powers in the American Constitution was efficiency, getting the business of government done in the most effective manner. Similarly, federalism theoretically serves the end of efficiency. In contemporary America, many have argued that an overloaded federal bureaucracy is best reformed by allocating more responsibilities to state and local governments.

Still another reason for the federal form was suggested by Justice Brandeis:

> It is one of the happy incidents of the federal system that a single courageous state may, if its citizens choose, serve as a laboratory, and try novel social and economic experiments without risk to the rest of the country.

New State Ice Co. v. Liebmann, 285 U.S. 262 (1932) (dissenting). Indeed, in 19th century America, the federal system saw significant diversity in the laws, policies, and processes of the states. Harry Scheiber, *American Federalism and the Diffusion of Power: Historical and Contemporary Perspectives*, 9 U. Tol. L. Rev. 619, 636 (1978). There is evidence that local innovation continues to occur in America, in areas such as welfare reform, environmental protection, and education.

B. The Constitutional Convention

In one sense, the 1787 Convention was a continuation of the search begun in 1776 for a new form of government that would be neither wholly centralized nor fragmented. While the Articles of Confederation advanced the theory of federalism only slightly by establishing a weak national government, the ferment that existed during the 1780s helped to continue the revolutionary atmosphere that was essential to fashion the bold innovations that emerged from the Philadelphia Convention. The theoretical foundations for the new version of union had been laid by Dickinson and advanced by leaders such as Hamilton, Washington, Adams, and Madison. But there was as yet no clear picture of how to set up a government to establish and then maintain such a union. The 55 delegates who came to Philadelphia in May of 1787 faced this ominous task.

The debate at the Convention over the issues that we now regard as federalism issues was protracted, carried on by the two dominant factions, the nationalists and the federalists. In the first week of the Convention, Governor Randolph of Virginia offered a bold departure both from the Articles and from the instructions that the states had given the delegates — to revise the Articles.

1. Federalism Concerns and the National Legislature

The Virginia Plan offered a bicameral legislature that would "legislate in all cases to which the separate States are incompetent, or in which the harmony of the United States may be interrupted by the exercise of individual legislation." The Congress would also have an absolute veto over any state law which it believed to be contrary to the Constitution. State sovereignty would be a thing of the past.

The small state representatives offered the New Jersey Plan as a substitute. This Plan sought to perpetuate the states as the dominant sovereign by retaining equal state representation in the Congress. The debates over these polar positions became so emotional in June that the Convention appeared close to deadlock. But Dr. Samuel Johnson's Connecticut Compromise saved the day by providing for a lower house based on population, with that chamber to originate all appropriations bills, and an upper house with equal state representation.

The Connecticut Compromise was a watershed event in the Convention and for the future of America. Apart from expediently solving the Convention's impasse, it began the great political tradition of compromise. But the Compromise did not solve the federalism issue, the primary question of the degree of sovereignty to be exercised by the national government and state governments respectively. While the issue was temporarily hushed by the Compromise and the successful conclusion of the Convention, it soon and often reappeared until secession and the Civil War brought a painful resolution. That the resolution was only temporary will be revealed later in this chapter and throughout this unit, as the story of the unfolding struggle over sovereignty is told.

Nor did this solution to the composition of the national legislature end the Convention's concerns about federalism. One of the most important decisions made by the delegates concerned the method of describing the powers of the new national government. Recall that the Virginia Plan proposed for the Congress the vague but powerful role of legislating "in all cases in which the separate States are incompetent." Although few of the delegates expressed concern with this description of congressional authority, the Committee on Detail, which produced the draft constitution, returned the draft in a new form. This new draft replaced the general grant of legislative power with the enumerated list, which became Article I, Section 8, later approved by the delegates without debate. While the reasons for the change by the Committee on Detail are not clear, the implications have been profound for the development of American federalism. *See* Chapter 4, *infra*.

2. Federalism Concerns and the National Judiciary

Another Convention decision of major importance for federalism's future concerned the arbitrator of disputes between the national government and the states over the exercise of power. Both the Virginia and New Jersey Plans allowed for a congressional veto over state laws. But the impracticality of Congress acting affirmatively to void repugnant state laws, in addition to the arguable redundancy of having the Congress declare unconstitutional a law which the courts would not enforce, caused the delegates to abandon the proposals and substitute, from the original New Jersey Plan, essentially the existing Article VI Supremacy Clause. The Constitution and laws "made in pursuance thereof" were the "supreme law of the land" and binding on all judges. This created the possibility of a strong judicial role in developing the federalism reality. Of course, it had not yet been decided who would interpret the Constitution (recall the *Marbury* and *Martin* cases, Chapter 1, *supra*).

Even the small states supported the Supremacy Clause idea because it curbed congressional power over the states, and it was thought that the state judges would resolve most power allocation questions. But the question of how to organize the judicial system was not so easily resolved. No one objected to the creation of a Supreme Court. But the states' rights advocates wanted state courts as the uniform court of first resort, with appeals to the Supreme Court adequate in their minds to assure the uniformity needed by the new federal system. The nationalists argued for the creation of lower federal courts, both to protect against local prejudice and to diminish the number of appeals to the Supreme Court. Unable to decide, the delegates resolved to allow the Congress to establish the lower federal courts, at its discretion. Although it was not unequivocally clear at the Convention that the appeal from the state courts to the Supreme Court gave the Court a general right to review the state court's interpretation of the Constitution, the combination of the Supremacy Clause and the allowance of appeals from the state courts to the Supreme Court provided the foundation for the Supreme Court's judicial authority, which it soon asserted in *Martin v. Hunter's Lessee*.

3. Federalism Concerns and the National Executive

The delegates were overwhelmingly predisposed toward legislative power. As proponents of the separation of powers concept, however, they recognized the need for an independent executive, both to better accomplish the government's work, and to forestall any chance of tyranny or claims of the new government's illegitimacy. *See* Chapter 2, *supra*. That the delegates were hard pressed to agree on a design for the executive branch powers is evidenced by comparing the brief and relatively uncharitable grant of power in Article II with the detailed and expansive grant to the Congress in Article I.

Initially the delegates tended toward a plural executive, based on their associations of a single executive with the British monarchy. Given the weakness of the Articles of Confederation, however, and the interest in improving the effectiveness of the government, agreement on a single executive eventually was reached.

The Convention also debated whether the executive should be popularly or legislatively elected. Popular election was rejected early as impractical, given the size of the country and the capacity needed to judge the candidates. Eventually, election by the legislature was also rejected, primarily due to separation of powers concerns that the executive might join with the legislature in tyrannical acts. Faced with no ready alternative, the delegates settled on the Electoral College system in an attempt to protect against the raw democracy which they did not trust, and at the same time to give the people a voice. The electoral college concept recognized the interests of the states in matching the number of electors to the congressional delegation and by allowing their election in any way that the states preferred.

The document which the delegates approved on September 17, 1787, 109 days after they had convened, accomplished its primary mission of forming a new national government and a union between it and the states. That the nature of the union created was both unique and not fully understood by its creators is undeniable. This unprecedented federal system had each citizen become a member of two distinct political communities, those communities being assured by the Constitution that they would be distinct and possessed of separate sovereign governments.

C. The Ratification Debates

The ratification period offered still another forum for the states' rights and nationalist advocates to present their cases, either by explaining the new Constitution in a way that was most favorable to their interests, or by promoting or discouraging its ratification. During this period, the states' rights proponents, who had been the "federalists" before the Convention, became the "anti-federalists" when the nationalists were able to seize the federalist label as actually representing the system which they advocated. These anti-federalists, men such as Patrick Henry and Samuel Adams, forcefully made two telling criticisms of the new Constitution which, while not preventing ratification, provided the impetus for a Bill of Rights in one instance and sounded again the caution that the new document had really left unresolved the question of state sovereignty. On the latter, they complained that in purporting to be a compact between the people of the United States, as individuals, and not between the states as agents for the people, the Constitution would destroy state sovereignty. As to the former, if the citizens of the United States are possessed of the rights embodied in the Declaration of Independence, they should have been explicitly mentioned in the new Constitution. The rights criticism of course bore early fruit with the passage of the first eight amendments. The state sovereignty criticism, while effectively refuted for the moment by Hamilton and Madison, has always loomed large as a constitutional and political issue in America. *See* the Gun Control Case Study, *supra*, Chapter 1.

The anti-federalist arguments also stimulated preparation of *The Federalist*, a work which has generally been recognized to be among the most profound political opuses ever written. *The Federalist* was a series of 85 essays, produced rapid-fire by Hamilton, Madison, and John Jay to argue the case for ratification in New York, where approval was thought to be both essential and in doubt. Though The Federalist Papers came too late to matter much in New York (which ratified in July, 1788), the essays have become the single most important source of authority on the intended scope and operation of the new union.

The legal nature of the new union was elaborately described by Hamilton and Madison, but in somewhat different terms. Hamilton was a firm nationalist throughout. In *The Federalist No. 9*, he states, "A firm Union will be of the utmost moment to the peace and liberty of the States, as a barrier against domestic faction and insurrection." He did concede in *The Federalist No. 32* that "as the plan of the convention aims only at a partial union or consolidation, the State governments would clearly retain all the rights of sovereignty which they before had, and which were not, by that act, *exclusively* delegated to the United States." But his essays are, on the whole, strongly nationalistic: "The evils we experience do not proceed from minute or partial imperfections, but from fundamental errors in the structure of the building, which cannot be amended otherwise than by an alteration in the first principles and main pillars of the fabric." *The Federalist No. 15.*

Madison, on the other hand, spoke of the union in terms of a two-party compact:

> [T]he proposed constitution, therefore, is in strictness, neither a national nor a federal Constitution, but a composition of both. In its foundation it is federal, not national; in the sources from which ordinary powers of the government are drawn, it is partly federal and partly national; in the operation of these powers, it is national, not federal; in the extent of them, again, it is federal, not national; and finally, in the authoritative mode of introducing amendments, it is neither wholly federal nor wholly national.

The Federalist No. 39.

Also in *The Federalist No. 39*, Madison states that the federal government, while being "a people consolidated into one nation, . . . its jurisdiction extends only to certain enumerated objects only, and leaves to the several States a residuary and inviolable sovereignty over all other objects. And [t]he act, therefore, establishing the Constitution, will not be a *national*, but a *federal* act."

Later, in *The Federalist No. 45*, Madison again sounds more like a states' rights advocate:

> The powers delegated by the proposed Constitution to the federal government are few and defined. Those which are to remain in the State governments are numerous and indefinite. The former will be exercised principally on external objects, as war, peace, negotiation, and foreign commerce; with which last the power of taxation will, for the most part, be connected. The powers reserved to the several States will extend to all the objects which, on the ordinary course of affairs, concern the lives, liberties, and properties of the people; and the internal order, improvement, and prosperity of the State.
>
> The state governments may be regarded as constituent and essential parts of the federal government: whilst the latter is no wise essential to the operation or organization of the former. Without the intervention of the State Legislatures, the President of the United States cannot be elected at all.

They must in all cases have a great share in his appointment, and will, perhaps, in most cases, of themselves determine it. The Senate will be elected absolutely and exclusively by the State Legislatures.... Thus, each of the principal branches of government will owe its existence more or less to the favor of the State governments, and must consequently feel a dependence, which is much more likely to beget a disposition too obsequious than too overbearing towards them. On the other side, the component parts of the State governments will in no instances be indebted for their appointment to the direct agency of the federal government....

While it has been argued that Madison's states' rights comments are explainable primarily as sales talk to persuade his constituents in Virginia and elsewhere (GARRY WILLS, EXPLAINING AMERICA 265–270 (1981)), Madison was clearly the more moderate of the two nationalists.

In a sense, then, *The Federalist* reads with a split personality. The authors agree that a stronger national government was created, and that its purpose was to protect the individual and to check excesses of democracy in the states. For Hamilton federalism was a device to gather power in the national government, while for Madison federalism set up a balance of power. The dual persona of *The Federalist* may be a fitting legacy for the whole era of constitution building, as well as a bridge to a better understanding of the evolution of federalism in constitutional law. The disagreements between Hamilton and Madison over the meaning of the Constitution reveal the ambiguities inherent in that document. The delegates to the Philadelphia Convention were themselves neither certain nor able to speak in one voice about the exact nature of the union they were creating. Their uncertainty and lack of unanimity shows in the finished document. Looking forward from the Convention, *The Federalist* may at least have forewarned of, if not contributed to, the ongoing struggle concerning dual federalism. Because *The Federalist* was almost everywhere regarded as such an important source of the Constitution's meaning, its mixed messages may have contributed to the crisis that led to the Civil War, as well as to the courts' continuing oscillation between the various possible meanings of federalism.

D. Federalism From the 1780s to the Twenty-First Century

No sooner had the dust of the Convention settled when the first call for amendments was heard. Those who successfully argued that the Constitution was inadequate because there was no express provision for individual rights which would constrain the exercise of power by the national government, thereby achieved the first realignment of federalism by further restricting the powers of the federal government. Yet, unknowingly, the states' rights advocates such as Jefferson, who argued for a bill of rights, were effectively cementing the nationalist interpretation of the Constitution. As further expressed protections for the people, the Bill of Rights reinforced the Lockean idea that it can only be the people who are sovereign and who can form a legitimate government. Because the people of America created the compact with the new national government, and then clarified that compact with a declaration of rights, it became logically even more difficult to argue that the nature of the compact was one between the national government and the states, rather than the people.

Ironically, the inclusion of the Tenth Amendment in the Bill of Rights, at times in this century, had the same nationalizing effect. Its provision that "[t]he powers not delegated to the United States by the Constitution, nor prohibited by it to the States, are reserved to the States respectively, or to the people" was drafted in the state ratifying conventions and then forwarded to the First Congress where it was debated and formally proposed by those who were opposed to ratification. Their intent was clear: to preserve state autonomy. However, if the states had retained the autonomy to decide the extent of their own authority, no Tenth Amendment would be needed. By proposing the Amendment, the states' rights proponents unwittingly conceded the authority of the federal government to arbitrate federal-state relations. Throughout much of our history, then, the Tenth Amendment became a rule of construction, not a rule of law. Chief Justice Stone later stated that:

> the amendment states but a truism that all is retained which has not been surrendered. There is nothing in the history of its adoption to suggest that it was more than declaratory of the relationship between the national and state governments as it had been established by the Constitution before the amendment or that its purpose was other than to allay fears that the new national government might seek to exercise powers not granted, and that the states might not be able to exercise fully their reserved powers.

United States v. Darby, 312 U.S. 100, 145 (1941). On the other hand, in 1992 the Supreme Court conceded that the Tenth Amendment "is essentially a tautology [but] the Tenth Amendment confirms that the power of the Federal Government is subject to limits that may, in a given instance, reserve power to the States." *New York v. United States*, 505 U.S. 144, (1992). The meaning and significance of the Tenth Amendment remain in doubt.

1. The Pre-Civil War Period

Ratification and the addition of the Bill of Rights did not quell the debate over the meaning of federalism. While articulate nationalists such as Hamilton continued to enunciate their theories of national power, the states' rights zealots were hard at work keeping the dual sovereignty idea alive. Madison and Jefferson struck back at the nationalists promptly after the passage of the Alien and Sedition Acts arguably usurped state prerogatives. The Virginia and Kentucky Resolutions (1798–99) proclaimed that the national and state governments were each sovereign in their respective spheres:

> [T]he United States of America are not united on the principle of unlimited submission to their general government [rather it was a compact where] each state acceded as a State.

John Marshall's tenure as Chief Justice began in 1801. Although the Marshall Court is most often regarded as a nationalist Court, responsible for some of the most important decisions which affirmed the broad powers of the new government, the dual federalism theorists fared about as well during this period as the nationalists. The Supreme Court as well as the state courts recognized the dual federalism principle as a basis for deciding cases in the pre-Civil War era. The possibility that the two governments were equal when operating in their own spheres was judicially confirmed, as was the implication of dual federalism that the relationship between the federal and state governments was one of tension, not cooperation. *See* Edward Corwin, *The Passing of Dual Federalism*, 36 Va. L. Rev. 1 (1950).

During the period of Chief Justice Roger Taney's leadership (1835–63), national power was already expansively stated. The Taney Court did not cut back on the scope of federal power, but from roughly this point on, the Supreme Court began to show a greater willingness to uphold state economic regulation, perhaps due to a more general trend for the courts to defer to national and state decisions to facilitate expansion of the then fast-growing economy. The Taney Court's deference to state economic regulation was so great that it threatened to "render the supremacy clause entirely nugatory." Edward Corwin, The Commerce Power Versus States Rights 126 (1936).

Thus, the theoretical and judicial stages were set for federalism to drift either towards or away from the union contemplated by the Framers, since there was no consensus yet on the nature of that union.

2. From the Civil War to the New Deal

The Civil War provided answers to some of the questions left unanswered by the Framers. In addition to disposing of the nullification and secession issues, the War effectively put an end to the claim that the Constitution was a mere compact among sovereign states. By 1869, the Supreme Court endorsed the stronger union which the War had sought to save. In *Texas v. White*, 74 U.S. (7 Wall.) 700, 724–725 (1869), Chief Justice Chase stated:

> The Union of the States was never a purely artificial and arbitrary relation. It began among the Colonies, and grew out of common origin, mutual sympathies, kindred principles, similar interests, and geographical relations. It was confirmed and strengthened by the necessities of war, and received definite form, and character, and sanction from the Articles of Confederation. By these the Union was solemnly declared to "be perpetual." And when these Articles were found to be inadequate to the exigencies of the country, the Constitution was ordained "to form a more perfect Union." It is difficult to convey the idea of indissoluble unity more clearly than by these words. What can be indissoluble if a perpetual Union, made more perfect, is not? The Constitution, in all its provisions, looks to an indestructible Union, composed of indestructible States.

Although the Court did not deny the sovereignty of the states acting "within their own spheres," the *Texas v. White* opinion, along with the significant constitutional changes that were being engineered by the Congress, clearly directed at least the legal content of federalism toward the earlier Hamiltonian vision of national power. The ratification of the Thirteenth, Fourteenth, and Fifteenth Amendments to the Constitution, and the enactment of sweeping civil rights and jurisdiction statutes by the Congress in the years immediately after the War, promised to change dramatically the nature of the federal system. Ironically, it was the judiciary that applied the brakes to the post-War nationalism by refusing to extend most of the civil rights protections to violations by state actors. In reaffirming its supremacy by deciding allocation of governmental power questions, the Court was able to preserve its national strength as an institution while preserving the dual sovereignty idea.

From the 1890s until the crisis years surrounding the New Deal, the Court used its institutional strength to further the Congress', as well as its own, interests in nationalizing power. Particularly in the area of economic regulation, the Court worked with the Congress to greatly expand the national powers at the expense of previous strongholds of state sovereignty. *See* Chapter 4, *infra*.

In stark contrast to national legislative and judicial activity in the economic arena, the protection of civil liberties received scant attention from the federal government, even where the state governments were clearly not providing the rights guarantees. By the 1890s, the failure of the post-Civil War Amendments and related legislation in protecting civil rights was a foregone conclusion. Furthermore, between the 1890s and the 1930s conditions only worsened, as civil rights statutes were repealed, disenfranchisement in the South became widespread, and legal segregation flourished. The official federal deference to the states in the area of individual rights protection was often based on the very same "considerations of federalism" that motivated the heavy-handed nationalism in the economic regulation area.

As with the overall American experiment with constitutional government, the genesis of the New Deal was practical needs, not theoretical principle. A massive social experiment was begun soon after President Roosevelt's inauguration in 1933. The growth of national power in the Congress during this period provided the basis for the now commonly accepted assertion that a new version of federalism, "cooperative federalism," was born with the New Deal:

> In many basic respects, modern cooperative federalism was the child of the Great Depression and the New Deal. The principal dimensions of the modern system were: (a) intensive centralization of power in numerous policy areas formerly left largely or nearly exclusively to state and local government; (b) a major shift in formal constitutional doctrines; (c) the definitive and apparently permanent emergence of giantism in government, as governmental taxing, spending, and employment rose to new high levels relative to national population and income; and (d) development of new patterns in intergovernmental relations, both fiscal and administrative.

These developments occurred simultaneously with another key change in the governmental system, the expansion of Executive power in the federal government, both in the executive agencies and in the administrative-regulatory agencies.

Harry Scheiber, *American Federalism and the Diffusion of Power: Historical and Contemporary Perspectives*, 9 U. TOL. L. REV. 619, 644–45 (1978).[1]

According to the cooperative federalism which emerged, the revolution produced intergovernmental sharing of power and responsibility, not tension and heavy-handed nationalism. The provision of government services, perhaps the central component of the New Deal and cooperative federalism theory, was to be collaborative, involving all levels of government. The fact that the policies upon which the provision of services was based were made in Washington was unimportant, according to cooperative federalism theory, because the decentralized political parties and political process assures both representation and protection of state interests in the national government and its decisionmaking machinery. *See* DAVID WALKER, TOWARD A FUNCTIONING FEDERALISM 65–95 (1981).

3. Modern Federalism

The Supreme Court played an important role in shifting the content of federalism in the era that began after the failed Court-packing plan (*see* Chapter 4, *infra*). One front found the Court regularly invoking "judicial restraint" in deferring to programs of the Congress which regulated in areas that had previously been controlled by state and local governments. The other consisted of bold new activism by the Court in seeking to protect Bill of Rights freedoms against actions taken primarily by the states. At times, the Court's decisions went beyond declaring a state law unconstitutional and affirmatively ordered states to act to remedy a violation. *E.g.*, *Brown v. Board of Education* [*Brown II*], 349 U.S. 294 (1955).

Epithets for dual federalism would be premature, however. In its 1976 decision in *National League of Cities v. Usery*, 426 U.S. 833, which invalidated the Congress' attempt to extend the protections of the wage and hour laws to state employees, the Court said:

> It is one thing to recognize the authority of Congress to enact laws regulating individual businesses necessarily subject to the dual sovereignty of the government of the Nation and of the State in which they reside. It is quite another to uphold a similar exercise of congressional authority directed, not to private citizens, but to the States as States. We have repeatedly recognized that there are attributes of sovereignty attaching to every state government which may not be impaired by Congress, not because Congress may lack an affirmative grant of legislative authority to reach the matter,

---

but because the Constitution prohibits it from exercising the authority in that manner.

Id. at 845. Although the *National League* principle has since been narrowed and was finally overruled (*Garcia v. San Antonio Metropolitan Transit Authority*, 469 U.S. 528 (1985), *see* Chapter 4, *infra*), the Tenth Amendment was resurrected as a substantive bar to federal action affecting the states in *New York v. United States*, 505 U.S. 144 (1992). *See* Chapter 4, *infra*.

E. The Role of the Tenth Amendment and "Considerations of Federalism" in Deciding Cases

When studying the two chapters in this unit, pay close attention to the Court's approach to deciding the federalism issues. Also consider the relationship between the Court's approach and the result in the case. When has the Court applied "considerations of federalism" to bar an action by the Congress or to bar an assertion of jurisdiction by the lower federal courts? If dual federalism is an analytically indefensible theory, based on the text of the Constitution, why has it continued to earn respect at various times throughout our history? On the other hand, what protections exist if the political safeguards do not work?

This unit will not cover or even survey all the constitutional points of contact between the national government and the states. Nonetheless, as was the case with the separation of powers, this book maintains that structural considerations, including federalism, are increasingly important in constitutional law. As such, this unit will highlight a few federalism issues to develop your understanding of the role that federalism plays in our constitutional system.

As with the separation of powers unit, these chapters will explore the relationship between the case outcomes and the core values which federalism seeks to protect. The courts have been both contributors to, and innocent victims of, the inability to articulate federalism's constitutional content. Given the federal courts' obligation to decide cases and controversies, however, the judiciary is a principle institution responsible for supporting the core values of federalism. Thus, one important theme for the chapters that follow is the relative success or failure of the courts in supporting federalism. As you read the cases, consider what federalism values are at stake, whether they were taken into account by the legislative or executive decisionmakers, whether they were threatened by that action, and the performance of the reviewing court in protecting federalism. Also think about possible explanations for the inconsistencies in the courts' performance.

As this section has suggested, federalism's virtues are sometimes difficult to sort out in a given policy dispute. The core values may actually be in conflict, as when a more efficient allocation of power to a local government results in loss of individual liberty. In other instances, the protection of individuals may operate to concentrate national power, discourage citizen participation in local government, or stifle local experimentation. This unit considers how courts should respond to such conflicts.

Another important theme to consider in this unit is the extent to which the changes in the size and structure of our government since 1787 have affected the "considerations of federalism" that figure into case decisions. As the government has grown, particularly in this century, more of its responsibilities have been assumed by the national government. Any claim that our Framers contemplated a true system of dual federalism, as that concept was articulated in the 19th century, is hard to take seriously in current times. Recently, however, dual federalism has become a fashionable public policy. Its proponents seek more local autonomy, including a lessening of the power of federal courts to impose decisions in the individual rights area upon unwilling states. How should the Court respond to these federalism arguments?

§ 3.02 Introduction: Federalism and the Judiciary[2]

This chapter focuses on the extent to which federalism concerns limit the role of the federal judiciary in protecting constitutional rights. During our country's first century, the state courts were the principal protectors of federal constitutional rights. An exception was provided by § 25 of the Judiciary Act of 1789 which authorized Supreme Court review when a federal right was denied by a state court. *See Martin v. Hunter's Lessee* (Chapter 1).

Following the Civil War, the federal government, including the federal judiciary, was steadily transformed into the principal guarantor of federal rights. An early step in the transformation was taken in 1871 when Congress enacted the Civil Rights Act which contained the predecessor of 42 U.S.C. § 1983.[3] As the Court explained in *Mitchum v. Foster*, 407 U.S. 225, 238–239 (1972), that Act was "an important part of the basic alteration in our federal system" and was designed to open the federal courts "to private citizens offering a uniquely federal remedy against incursions under the claimed authority of state law upon rights secured by the Constitution and laws of the Nation."

---

2. Parts of the Introduction are taken from Thomas Maroney & Daan Braveman, *Averting the Flood: Henry J. Friendly, The Comity Doctrine, and the Jurisdiction of the Federal Courts — Part II*, 31 Syracuse L. Rev. 469 (1980). Copyright © 1980 by Syracuse University Law Review. Reprinted by permission.

3. In its present form, § 1983 provides:

> Every person who, under color of any statute, ordinance, regulation, custom, or usage, of any State or Territory, subjects, or causes to be subjected, any citizen of the United States or other person within the jurisdiction thereof to the deprivation of any rights, privileges, or immunities secured by the Constitution and laws, shall be liable to the party injured in an action at law, suit in equity, or other proper proceeding for redress.

The second significant development in the transformation was the passage of the Judiciary Act of March 3, 1875, which included a general grant of federal question jurisdiction. By this Act

> Congress gave the federal courts the vast range of power that had lain dormant in the Constitution since 1789. These courts ceased to be restrictive tribunals of fair dealing between citizens of different states and became the primary and powerful reliances for vindicating every right given by the Constitution, the laws and treaties of the United States.

FELIX FRANKFURTER AND JAMES LANDIS, THE BUSINESS OF THE SUPREME COURT 65 (1928).

The Civil Rights and Judiciary Acts did not produce a transformation overnight. Indeed, in the late nineteenth century the federal government, including its courts, focused its effort on protection of economic rights and maintenance of the economic status quo. This focus continued during much of the period before the New Deal. *See* John Gibbons, *Our Federalism*, 12 SUFFOLK U. L. REV. 1087 (1978). An important development in the process of transforming the federal court into the principal guarantor of constitutional rights, however, did occur during this period. In 1908, the Supreme Court rendered its decision in *Ex parte Young*, 209 U.S. 123, holding that a federal district court may enjoin a state official from enforcing a state law that is inconsistent with the federal constitution. Although today that principle may seem relatively unremarkable, in 1908 it appeared to Justice Harlan to "work a radical change in our governmental system." *Id.* at 175. Justice Harlan predicted that *Ex parte Young* "would inaugurate a new era in the American judicial system and in the relations of the national and state governments." *Id.*

The new era did not arrive until the Supreme Court's decision in the school segregation cases, *Brown v. Board of Education*, 347 U.S. 483 (1954). That landmark decision provided impetus to the federal courts as the primary guardians of federal constitutional rights and to the injunction as a remedial tool for protecting those rights. *See generally* OWEN FISS, THE CIVIL RIGHTS INJUNCTION (1978). By the late 1960s the Supreme Court had firmly established the precept that the federal courthouse doors were to be open for individuals seeking to enforce constitutional rights.

It has been argued that in recent years the Court has a different — and more limited — vision of the role of federal courts as guardians of such rights. You perhaps should withhold making any judgments on that issue until the conclusion of the course. In the meantime, and whatever your conclusions, it is clear that federalism has reemerged as a governing principle in determining the scope of the federal judiciary's power to secure constitutional liberties from infringement by the states. We say "reemerge" because to a varying extent throughout our history, federalism notions have influenced the federal judiciary's willingness to review actions taken by state officials.

Unfortunately, the Supreme Court has not carefully articulated the precise federalism concerns that are implicated when the federal court is asked to review the constitutionality of state conduct. As a general matter, Justice Black explained that the federalism concept represents

> a system in which there is sensitivity to the legitimate interests of both state and National governments and in which the National government, anxious though it may be to vindicate and to protect federal rights and federal interests, always endeavors to do so in ways that will not unduly interfere with the legitimate activities of the states.

Younger v. Harris, 401 U.S. 37, 44 (1971). A central tenet of "Our Federalism" is the notion of comity, or respect for the state governments and the ability of those governments to perform their function in separate ways. *Id.*

The material in § 3.03 examines the Eleventh Amendment which is now viewed as providing textual support for the proposition that the jurisdiction of federal courts is limited to some extent by federalism concerns. As you study this material, consider: (1) the source of the federal judiciary's authority to rely on federalism as a basis for limiting its jurisdiction or the kind of relief it will order; (2) the precise manner in which exercise of federal court jurisdiction, or the award of relief, interferes with federalism values; (3) whether the federal court is the proper institution for weighing such federalism concerns; (4) whether the federal judiciary remains as the primary guardians of constitutional rights; and (5) whether it is necessary to retain that special role for the federal courts.

§ 3.03 Eleventh Amendment

Hans v. Louisiana

United States Supreme Court
134 U.S. 1, 10 S. Ct. 504, 33 L. Ed. 842 (1890)

[Plaintiff, a citizen of Louisiana, brought suit in the federal circuit court alleging that the State failed to pay interest due on bonds and thus violated Article I, § 10 of the Constitution which bars a state from impairing the obligation of contracts.]

MR. JUSTICE BRADLEY, delivered the opinion of the court.

The question is presented, whether a State can be sued in a Circuit Court of the United States by one of its own citizens upon a suggestion that the case is one that arises under the Constitution or laws of the United States.

That a State cannot be sued by a citizen of another State, or of a foreign state, on the mere ground that the case is one arising under the Constitution or laws of the United States, is clearly established by the decisions of this court in several recent cases.

In the present case the plaintiff in error contends that he, being a citizen of Louisiana, is not embarrassed by the obstacle of the Eleventh Amendment, inasmuch as that amendment only prohibits suits against a State which are brought by the citizens of another State, or by citizens or subjects of a foreign State. It is true, the amendment does so read; and if there were no other reason or ground for abating his suit, it might be maintainable; and then we should have this anomalous result, that in cases arising under the Constitution or laws of the United States, a State may be sued in the federal courts by its own citizens, though it cannot be sued for a like cause of action by the citizens of other States, or of a foreign state; and may be thus sued in the federal courts, although not allowing itself to be sued in its own courts. If this is the necessary consequence of the language of the Constitution and the law, the result is no less startling and unexpected than was the original decision of this court, that under the language of the Constitution and the Judiciary Act of 1789, a State was liable to be sued by a citizen of another State, or of a foreign country. That decision was made in the case of *Chisholm v. Georgia*, 2 Dall. 419 (1793), and created such a shock of surprise throughout the country that, at the first meeting of Congress thereafter, the Eleventh Amendment to the Constitution was almost unanimously proposed, and was in due course adopted by the legislatures of the States. This amendment, expressing the will of the ultimate sovereignty of the whole country, superior to all legislatures and all courts, actually reversed the decision of the Supreme Court. It did not in terms prohibit suits by individuals against the States, but declared that the Constitution should not be construed to import any power to authorize the bringing of such suits. The language of the amendment is that

> the judicial power of the United States shall *not be construed to extend* to any suit in law or equity, commenced of or prosecuted against one of the United States by citizens of another State or by citizens or subjects of any foreign state.

The Supreme Court had construed the judicial power as extending to such a suit, and its decision was thus overruled.

Looking back from our present standpoint at the decision in *Chisholm v. Georgia*, we do not greatly wonder at the effect which it had upon the country. Any such power as that of authorizing the federal judiciary to entertain suits by individuals against the States, had been expressly disclaimed, and even resented, by the great defenders of the Constitution whilst it was on its trial before the American people.

The eighty-first number of *The Federalist*, written by Hamilton, has the following profound remarks:

> [It] is inherent in the nature of sovereignty not to be amenable to the suit of an individual *without its consent*. This is the general sense and the general practice of mankind; and the exemption, as one of the attributes of sovereignty, is now enjoyed by the government of every State in the Union. Unless, therefore, there is a surrender of this immunity in the plan of the convention, it will remain with the States, and the danger intimated must be merely ideal. The contracts between a nation and individuals are only binding on the conscience of the sovereign, and have no pretension to a compulsive force. They confer no right of action independent of the sovereign will.

To what purpose would it be to authorize suits against States for the debts they owe? How could recoveries be enforced? It is evident that it could not be done without waging war against the contracting State; and to ascribe to the federal courts by mere implication, and in destruction of a pre-existing right of the state government, a power which would involve such a consequence, would be altogether forced and unwarrantable.

It seems to us that these views of those great advocates and defenders of the Constitution were most sensible and just; and they apply equally to the present case as to that then under discussion. Can we suppose that, when the Eleventh Amendment was adopted, it was understood to be left open for citizens of a State to sue their own state in the federal courts, whilst the idea of suits by citizens of other states, or of foreign states, was indignantly repelled? Suppose that Congress, when proposing the Eleventh Amendment, had appended to it a provision that nothing therein contained should prevent a State from being sued by its own citizens in cases arising under the Constitution or laws of the United States; can we imagine that it would have been adopted by the states? The supposition that it would is almost an absurdity of its face.

The truth is, that the cognizance of suits and actions unknown to the law, and forbidden by the law, was not contemplated by the Constitution when establishing the judicial power of the United States.

The suability of a State without its consent was a thing unknown to the law.

But besides the presumption that no anomalous and unheard of proceedings or suits were intended to be raised up by the Constitution — anomalous and unheard of when the Constitution was adopted — an additional reason why the jurisdiction claimed for the Circuit Court does not exist, is the language of the act of Congress by which its jurisdiction is conferred. The words are these: "The circuit courts of the United States shall have original cognizance, concurrent with the courts of the several States, of all suits of a civil nature at common law or in equity arising under the Constitution or laws of the United States, or treaties," etc. — "Concurrent with the courts of the several States." Does not this qualification show that Congress, in legislating to carry the Constitution into effect, did not intend to invest its courts with any new and strange jurisdictions? The state courts have no power to entertain suits by individuals against a State without its consent. Then how does the Circuit Court, having only concurrent jurisdiction, acquire any such power?

The judgment of the Circuit Court is *Affirmed*.

Notes and Questions

(1) What are the bases for the common law doctrine that a nonconsenting sovereign is immune from a lawsuit? Does the notion that the "King can do no wrong" make any sense in a country that fought a revolutionary war against a monarchy? Are there more practical reasons for sovereign immunity?

(2) Is the result in *Hans* based on the language of Article III, the language of the Eleventh Amendment, the common law doctrine of sovereign immunity, or the language of the Judiciary Act of 1789?

(3) Does federalism lie at the heart of the decision? If so, what are the precise federalism concerns that are implicated by the exercise of federal jurisdiction in *Hans*?

(4) Was the Court concerned with not only federalism, but also the broader proposition that a nonconsenting sovereign might be forced to defend itself in any forum, state or federal?

Ex parte Young

United States Supreme Court
209 U.S. 123, 28 S. Ct. 441, 52 L. Ed. 714 (1908)

[Shareholders of the Northern Pacific Railway Company commenced an action in federal court against Edward Young, Attorney General of Minnesota, members of the Minnesota Railroad and Warehouse Commission, and other shippers of freight. The plaintiffs alleged that various legislative acts and Commission orders set maximum rates so low as to be confiscatory in violation of the Fourteenth Amendment. The complaint sought an injunction restraining enforcement of the challenged provision. The federal court entered a temporary injunction which, among other things, restrained the Attorney General from commencing a proceeding in state court to enforce the challenged laws.

Despite the injunction, the Attorney General commenced an action in state court seeking to enforce the challenged laws against the Northern Pacific Railway Company. Plaintiffs in the federal lawsuit then asked the federal court to hold the Attorney General in contempt. After a hearing the federal court concluded that the Attorney General indeed was in contempt of court, imposed a fine, and committed him to the custody of the United States Marshall until the fine was paid.

The Attorney General sought a writ of habeas corpus from the Supreme Court. He maintained that the Eleventh Amendment deprived the federal court of jurisdiction to hear the original lawsuit and that he was being held in violation of the Constitution.]

MR. JUSTICE PECKHAM delivered the opinion of the court.

We have upon this record the case of an unconstitutional act of the state legislature and an intention by the Attorney General of the State to endeavor to enforce its provision, to the injury of the company, in compelling it, at great expense, to defend legal proceedings of a complicated and unusual character, and involving questions of vast importance to all employees and officers of the company, as well as to the company itself. The question that arises is whether there is a remedy that the parties interested may resort to, by going into a Federal court of equity, in a case involving a violation of the Federal Constitution, and obtaining a judicial investigation of the problem, and pending its solution obtain freedom from suits, civil or criminal, by a temporary injunction, and if the question be finally decided favorably to the contention of the company, a permanent injunction restraining all such actions or proceedings.

This inquiry necessitates an examination of the most material and important objection made to the jurisdiction of the Circuit Court, the objection being that the suit is, in effect, one against the State of Minnesota, and that the injunction issued against the Attorney General illegally prohibits state action, either criminal or civil, to enforce obedience to the statutes of the State. The Eleventh Amendment prohibits the commencement or prosecution of any suit against one of the United States by citizens of another State or citizens or subjects of any foreign State.

It was adopted after the decision of this court in *Chisholm v. Georgia* (1793), 2 Dall. 419, where it was held that a State might be sued by a citizen of another State. Since that time there have been many cases decided in this court involving the Eleventh Amendment.

The various authorities furnish ample justification for the assertion that individuals, who, as officers of the State, are clothed with some duty in regard to the enforcement of the laws of the State, and who threaten and are about to commence proceedings, either of a civil or criminal nature, to enforce against parties affected an unconstitutional act, violating the Federal Constitution, may be enjoined by a Federal court of equity from such action.

In making an officer of the State a party defendant in a suit to enjoin the enforcement of an act alleged to be unconstitutional it is plain that such officer must have some connection with the enforcement of the act, or else it is merely making him a party as a representative of the State, and thereby attempting to make a State a party.

It is objected that as the statute does not specifically make it the duty of the Attorney General (assuming he has that general right) to enforce it, he has under such circumstances a full general discretion whether to attempt its enforcement or not, and the court cannot interfere to control him as Attorney General in the exercise of his discretion.

In our view there is no interference with his discretion under the facts herein. There is no doubt that the court cannot control the exercise of the discretion of an officer. It can only direct affirmative action where the officer having some duty to perform not involving discretion, but merely ministerial in its nature, refuses or neglects to take such action. In that case the court can direct the defendant to perform this merely ministerial duty.

The general discretion regarding the enforcement of the laws when and as he deems appropriate is not interfered with by an injunction which restrains the state officer from taking any steps towards the enforcement of an unconstitutional enactment to the injury of complainant. In such case no affirmative action of any nature is directed, and the officer is simply prohibited from doing an act which he had no legal right to do. An injunction to prevent him from doing that which he had no legal right to do is not an interference with the discretion of an officer.

It is also argued that the only proceeding which the Attorney General could take to enforce the statute, so far as his office is concerned, was one by mandamus, which would be commenced by the State in its sovereign and governmental character, and that the right to bring such action is a necessary attribute of a sovereign government. It is contended that the complainants do not complain and they care nothing about any action which Mr. Young might take or bring as an ordinary individual, but that he was complained of as an officer to whose discretion is confided the use of the name of the State of Minnesota so far as litigation is concerned, and that when or how he shall use it is a matter resting in his discretion and cannot be controlled by any court.

The answer to all this is the same as made in every case where an official claims to be acting under the authority of the State. The act to be enforced is alleged to be unconstitutional, and if it be so, the use of the name of the State to enforce an unconstitutional act to the injury of complainants is a proceeding without the authority of and one which does not affect the State in its sovereign or governmental capacity. It is simply an illegal act upon the part of a state official in attempting by the use of the name of the State to enforce a legislative enactment which is void because unconstitutional. If the act which the state Attorney General seeks to enforce be a violation of the Federal Constitution, the officer in proceeding under such enactment comes into conflict with the superior authority of that Constitution, and he is in that case stripped of his official or representative character and is subjected in his person to the consequences of his individual conduct. The State has no power to impart to him any immunity from responsibility to the supreme authority of the United States.

Mr. Justice Harlan, dissenting.

Let it be observed that the suit instituted in the Circuit Court of the United States was, as to the defendant Young, one against him *as, and only because he was*, Attorney General of Minnesota. No relief was sought against him individually but only in his capacity *as* Attorney General. And the manifest, indeed the avowed and admitted, object of seeking such relief was *to tie the hands* of the *State* so that it could not in any manner or by any mode of proceedings, *in its own courts*, test the legality of the statutes and orders in question. It would therefore seem clear that within the true meaning of the Eleventh Amendment the suit brought in the Federal court was one, in legal effect, against the State — as much so as if the State had been formally named on the record as a party — and therefore it was a suit to which, under the Amendment, so far as the State or its Attorney General was concerned, the judicial power of the United States did not and could not extend. If this proposition be sound it will follow — indeed, it is conceded that if, so far as relief is sought against the Attorney General of Minnesota, this be a suit against the State — then the order of the Federal court enjoining that officer from taking any action, suit, step or proceeding to compel the railway company to obey the Minnesota statute was beyond the jurisdiction of that court and wholly void; in which case, that officer was at liberty to proceed in the discharge of his official duties as defined by the laws of the

State, and the order adjudging him to be in contempt for bringing the mandamus proceeding in the state court was a nullity.

The fact that the Federal Circuit Court had, prior to the institution of the mandamus suit in the state court, preliminarily (but not finally) held the statutes of Minnesota and the orders of its Railroad and Warehouse Commission in question to be in violation of the Constitution of the United States, was no reason why that court should have laid violent hands upon the Attorney General of Minnesota and by its orders have deprived the State of the services of its constitutional law officer in its own courts. Yet that is what was done by the Federal Circuit Court; for, the intangible thing, called a State, however extensive its powers, can never appear or be represented or known in any court in a litigated case, except by and through its officers. When, therefore, the Federal court forbade the defendant Young, as Attorney General of Minnesota, from taking any action, suit, step or proceeding whatever looking to the enforcement of the statutes in question, it said in effect to the State of Minnesota:

> It is true that the powers not delegated to the United States by the Constitution, nor prohibited by it to the States, are reserved to the States respectively or to its people, and it is true that under the Constitution the judicial power of the United States does not extend to any suit brought against a State by a citizen of another State or by a citizen or subject of a foreign State, yet the Federal court adjudges that you, the State, although a sovereign for many important governmental purposes, shall not appear in your own courts, by your law officer, with the view of enforcing, or even for determining the validity of the state enactments which the Federal court has, upon a preliminary hearing, declared to be in violation of the Constitution of the United States.

This principle, if firmly established, would work a radical change in our governmental system. It would inaugurate a new era in the American judicial system and in the relations of the National and state governments. It would enable the subordinate Federal courts to supervise and control the official action of the States as if they were "dependencies" or provinces. It would place the States of the Union in a condition of inferiority never dreamed of when the Constitution was adopted or when the Eleventh Amendment was made a part of the Supreme Law of the Land. I cannot suppose that the great men who framed the Constitution ever thought the time would come when a subordinate Federal court, having no power to compel a State, in its corporate capacity, to appear before it as a litigant, would yet assume to deprive a State of the right to be represented in its own courts by its regular law officer. That is what the court below did, as to Minnesota, when it adjudged that the appearance of the defendant Young *in the state court*, as the Attorney General of Minnesota, representing his State as its chief law officer, was a contempt of authority of the Federal court, punishable by fine and imprisonment. Too little consequence has been attached to the fact that the courts of the States are under an obligation equally strong with that resting upon the court of the Union to respect and enforce the provisions of the Federal Constitution as the Supreme Law of the Land, and to guard rights secured or guaranteed by that instrument. We must assume — a decent respect for the States requires us to assume — that the state courts will enforce every right secured by the Constitution. If they fail to do so, the party complaining has a clear remedy for the protection of his rights; for, he can come by writ of error, in an orderly, judicial way, from the highest court of the State to this tribunal for redress in respect of every right granted or secured by that instrument and denied by the state court.

I dissent from the opinion and judgment.

Notes and Questions

(1) Did the Court reduce the Eleventh Amendment to a pleading matter: a lawsuit naming the state as a defendant is barred, but one naming a state official is not?

(2) The Court stated that Young was stripped of his official character when he performed an act in violation of the Fourteenth Amendment. If so, how did his conduct violate that amendment which limits only *state* action?

(3) Is the *Young* decision based on a legal fiction? Is it a necessary fiction to ensure that federal courts can enforce the Fourteenth Amendment?

(4) Could the Court have reached the same result in a more direct fashion? In this regard, consider the possible relationship between the Eleventh Amendment and the later ratified Fourteenth Amendment. Did the states relinquish a part of their sovereignty when they ratified a constitutional provision that states "No state shall . . ."?

(5) Did Justice Harlan exaggerate his position when he observed in dissent that the principle established in *Ex parte Young* will work a radical change in our governmental system and inaugurate a new era in the relations between the federal and state governments? Justice Harlan conceded that the state official could be sued in state court. Why did he oppose suits against state officials in federal court?

Edelman v. Jordan

United States Supreme Court
415 U.S. 651, 94 S. Ct. 1347, 39 L. Ed. 2d 662 (1974)

Mr. Justice Rehnquist delivered the opinion of the Court.

Respondent John Jordan filed a complaint in the United States District Court for the Northern District of Illinois, individually and as a representative of a class, seeking declaratory and injunctive relief against two former directors of the Illinois Department of Public Aid, the director of the Cook County Department of Public Aid, and the comptroller of Cook County. Respondent alleged that these state officials were administering the federal-state programs of Aid to the Aged, Blind, or Disabled (AABD) in a manner inconsistent with various federal regulations and with the Fourteenth Amendment of the Constitution.

AABD is one of the categorical aid programs administered by the Illinois Department of Public Aid. Under the Social Security Act, the program is funded by the State and the Federal Governments. The Department of Health, Education, and Welfare (HEW), which administers these payments for the Federal Government, issued regulations prescribing maximum permissible time standards within which States participating in the program had to process AABD applications. Those regulations, originally issued in 1968, required, at the time of the institution of this suit, that eligibility determinations must be made by the States within 30 days of receipt of applications for aid to the aged and blind, and within 45 days of receipt of applications for aid to the disabled. For those persons found eligible, the assistance check was required to be received by them within the applicable time period.

Respondent's complaint charged that the Illinois defendants were improperly authorizing grants to commence only with the month in which an application was approved and not including prior eligibility months for which an applicant was entitled to aid under federal law. The complaint also alleged that the Illinois defendants were not processing the applications within the applicable time requirements of the federal regulations. Such actions of the Illinois officials were alleged to violate federal law and deny the equal protection of the laws. Respondent's prayer requested declaratory and injunctive relief, and specifically requested a permanent injunction enjoining the defendants to award to the entire class of plaintiffs all AABD benefits wrongfully withheld.

In its judgment of March 15, 1972, the District Court declared § 4404 of the Illinois Manual to be invalid insofar as it was inconsistent with the federal regulations and granted a permanent injunction requiring compliance with the federal time limits for processing and paying AABD applicants. The District Court also ordered the state officials to

> release and remit AABD benefits wrongfully withheld to all applicants for AABD in the State of Illinois who applied between July 1, 1968 [the date of the federal regulations] and April 16, 197[1] [the date of the preliminary injunction issued by the District Court] and were determined eligible.

On appeal to the United States Court of Appeals for the Seventh Circuit, the Illinois officials contended, *inter alia*, that the Eleventh Amendment barred the award of retroactive benefits, that the judgment of inconsistency between the federal regulations and the provisions of the Illinois Categorical Assistance Manual could be given prospective effect only, and that the federal regulations in question were inconsistent with the Social Security Act itself. The Court of Appeals rejected these contentions and affirmed the judgment of the District Court. Because we believe the Court of Appeals erred in its disposition of the Eleventh Amendment claim, we reverse that portion of the Court of Appeals decision which affirmed the District Court's order that retroactive benefits be paid by the Illinois state officials.

The historical basis of the Eleventh Amendment has been oft stated, and it represents one of the more dramatic examples of this Court's effort to derive meaning from the document given to the Nation by the Framers nearly 200 years ago.

While the Amendment by its terms does not bar suits against a State by its own citizens, this Court has consistently held that an unconsenting State is immune from suits brought in federal courts by her own citizens as well as by citizens of another State. It is also well established that even though a State is not named a party to the action, the suit may nonetheless be barred by the Eleventh Amendment. In *Ford Motor Co. v. Department of Treasury*, 323 U.S. 459 (1945), the Court said:

> [W]hen the action is in essence one for the recovery of money from the state, the state is the real, substantial party in interest and is entitled to invoke its sovereign immunity from suit even though individual officials are nominal defendants.

Thus the rule has evolved that a suit by private parties seeking to impose a liability which must be paid from public funds in the state treasury is barred by the Eleventh Amendment.

The Court of Appeals in this case, while recognizing that the *Hans* line of cases permitted the State to raise the Eleventh Amendment as a defense to suit by its own citizens, nevertheless concluded that the Amendment did not bar the award of retroactive payments of the statutory benefits found to have been wrongfully withheld. The Court of Appeals held that the above-cited cases, when read in light of this Court's landmark decision in *Ex parte Young*, do not preclude the grant of such a monetary award in the nature of equitable restitution.

Petitioner concedes that *Ex parte Young* is no bar to that part of the District Court's judgment that prospectively enjoined petitioner's predecessors from failing to process applications within the time limits established by the federal regulations. Petitioner argues, however, that *Ex parte Young* does not extend so far as to permit a suit which seeks the award of an accrued monetary liability which must be met from the general revenues of a State, absent consent or waiver by the State of its Eleventh Amendment immunity, and that therefore the award of retroactive benefits by the District Court was improper.

Ex parte Young was a watershed case in which this Court held that the Eleventh Amendment did not bar an action in the federal courts seeking to enjoin the Attorney General of Minnesota from enforcing a statute claimed to violate the Fourteenth Amendment of the United States Constitution. This holding has permitted the Civil War Amendments to the Constitution to serve as a sword, rather than merely as a shield, for those whom they were designed to protect. But the relief awarded in *Ex parte Young* was prospective only; the Attorney General of Minnesota was enjoined to conform his future conduct of that office to the requirement of the Fourteenth Amendment. Such relief is analogous to that awarded by the District Court in the prospective portion of its order under review in this case.

But the retroactive portion of the District Court's order here, which requires the payment of a very substantial amount of money which that court held should have been paid, but was not, stands on quite a different footing. These funds will obviously not be paid out of the pocket of petitioner Edelman.

The funds to satisfy the award in this case must inevitably come from the general revenues of the State of Illinois, and thus the award resembles far more closely a monetary award against the State itself than it does the prospective injunctive relief awarded in *Ex parte Young*.

The Court of Appeals, in upholding the award in this case, held that it was permissible because it was in the form of "equitable restitution" instead of damages, and therefore capable of being tailored in such a way as to minimize disruptions of the state program of categorical assistance. But we must judge the award actually made in this case, and not one which might have been differently tailored in a different case, and we must judge it in the context of the important constitutional principle embodied in the Eleventh Amendment.[4]

As in most areas of the law, the difference between the type of relief barred by the Eleventh Amendment and that permitted under *Ex parte Young* will not in many instances be that between day and night. The injunction issued in *Ex parte Young* was not totally without effect on the State's revenues, since the state law which the Attorney General was enjoined from enforcing provided substantial monetary penalties against railroads which did not conform to its provisions. Later cases from this Court have authorized equitable relief which has probably had greater impact on state treasuries than did that awarded in *Ex parte Young*. In *Graham v. Richardson*, 403 U.S. 365 (1971), Arizona and Pennsylvania welfare officials were prohibited from denying welfare benefits to otherwise qualified recipients who were aliens. In *Goldberg v. Kelly*, 397 U.S. 254 (1970), New York City welfare officials were enjoined from following New York State procedures which authorized the termination of benefits paid to welfare recipients without prior hearing. But the fiscal consequences to state treasuries in these cases were the necessary result of compliance with decrees which by their terms were prospective in nature. State officials, in order to shape their official conduct to the mandate of the Court's decrees, would more likely have to spend

---

4. [Court's Footnote 11] It may be true, as stated by our Brother Douglas in dissent, that "[m]ost welfare decisions by federal courts have a financial impact on the State." But we cannot agree that such a financial impact is the same where a federal court applied *Ex parte Young* to grant prospective declaratory and injunctive relief, as opposed to an order of retroactive payments as was made in the instant case. It is not necessarily true that "[w]hether the decree is prospective only or requires payments for the weeks or months wrongfully skipped over by the state officials, the nature of the impact on the state treasury is precisely the same. . . ." This argument neglects the fact that where the State has a definable allocation to be used in the payment of public aid benefits, and pursues a certain course of action such as the processing of applications within certain time periods as did Illinois here, the subsequent ordering by a federal court of retroactive payments to correct delays in such processing will invariably mean there is less money available for payments for the continuing obligations of the public aid system.

money from the state treasury than if they had been left free to pursue their previous course of conduct. Such an ancillary effect on the state treasury is a permissible and often an inevitable consequence of the principle announced in *Ex parte Young*. But that portion of the District Court's decree which petitioner challenges on Eleventh Amendment grounds goes much further than any of the cases cited. It requires payment of state funds, not as a necessary consequence of compliance in the future with a substantive federal-question determination, but as a form of compensation to those whose applications were processed on the slower time schedule at a time when petitioner was under no court-imposed obligation to conform to a different standard. While the Court of Appeals described this retroactive award of monetary relief as a form of "equitable restitution," it is in practical effect indistinguishable in many aspects from an award of damages against the State. It will to a virtual certainty be paid from state funds, and not from the pockets of the individual state officials who were the defendants in the action. It is measured in terms of a monetary loss resulting from a part breach of a legal duty on the part of the defendant state officials.

The Court of Appeals held in the alternative that even if the Eleventh Amendment be deemed a bar to the retroactive relief awarded respondent in this case, the State of Illinois had waived its Eleventh Amendment immunity and consented to the bringing of such a suit by participating in the federal AABD program. The question of waiver or consent under the Eleventh Amendment turn[s] on whether Congress had intended to abrogate the immunity in question, and whether the State by its participation in the program authorized by Congress had in effect consented to the abrogation of that immunity.

In this case the threshold fact of congressional authorization to sue a class of defendants which literally includes States is wholly absent. The Court of Appeals held that as a matter of federal law Illinois had "constructively consented" to this suit by participating in the federal AABD program and agreeing to administer federal and state funds in compliance with federal law. Constructive consent is not a doctrine commonly associated with the surrender of constitutional rights, and we see no place for it here. In deciding where a State has waived its constitutional protection under the Eleventh Amendment, we will find waiver only where stated "by the most express language or by such overwhelming implications from the text as [will] leave no room for any other reasonable construction."

The mere fact that a State participates in a program through which the Federal Government provides assistance for the operation by the State of a system of public aid is not sufficient to establish consent on the part of the State to be sued in the federal courts. The only language in the Social Security Act which purported to provide a federal sanction against a State which did not comply with federal requirements for the distribution of federal monies was found in former 42 U.S.C. §1384 (now replaced by substantially similar provision in 42 U.S.C. §804), which provided for termination of future allocations of federal funds when a participating State failed to conform with federal law. This provision by its terms did not authorize suit against anyone, and standing alone, fell far short of a waiver by a participating State of its Eleventh Amendment immunity.

Our Brother Marshall argues in dissent, and the Court of Appeals held, that although the Social Security Act itself does not create a private cause of action, the cause of action created by 42 U.S.C. § 1983 [reprinted § 3.02, *supra*], coupled with the enactment of the AABD program, and the issuance by HEW of regulations which require the States to make corrective payments after successful "fair hearings" and provide for federal matching funds to satisfy federal court orders of retroactive payments, indicate that Congress intended a cause of action for public aid recipients such as respondent. It is, of course, true that *Rosado v. Wyman*, 397 U.S. 397 (1970), held that suits in federal court under § 1983 are proper to secure compliance with the provisions of the Social Security Act on the part of participating States. But it has not heretofore been suggested that § 1983 was intended to create a waiver of a State's Eleventh Amendment immunity merely because an action could be brought under that section against state officers, rather than against the State itself.

Respondent urges that since the various Illinois officials sued in the District Court failed to raise the Eleventh Amendment as a defense to the relief sought by respondent, petitioner is therefore barred from raising the Eleventh Amendment defense in the Court of Appeals or in this Court. The Court of Appeals apparently felt the defense was properly presented and dealt with it on the merits. We approve of this resolution, since it has been well settled that the Eleventh Amendment defense sufficiently partakes of the nature of a jurisdictional bar so that it need not be raised in the trial court.

For the foregoing reason we decide that the Court of Appeals was wrong in holding that the Eleventh Amendment did not constitute a bar to that portion of the District Court decree which ordered retroactive payment of benefits found to have been wrongfully withheld. The judgment of the Court of Appeals is therefore reversed and the cause remanded for further proceedings consistent with this opinion.

So ordered.

MR. JUSTICE DOUGLAS, dissenting.

It is said that the Eleventh Amendment is concerned, not with the immunity of States from suit, but with the jurisdiction of the federal courts to entertain the suit. The Eleventh Amendment does not speak of "jurisdiction"; it withholds the "judicial power" of federal courts "to any suit in law or equity against one of the United States." If that "judicial power," or "jurisdiction" if one prefers that concept, may not be exercised even in "any suit in equity," then *Ex parte Young* should be overruled. But there is none eager to take the step. Where a State has consented to join a federal-state cooperative project, it is realistic to conclude that the State has agreed to assume its obligations under that legislation. There is nothing in the Eleventh Amendment to suggest a difference between suits at law and suits in equity, for it treats the two without distinction. If common sense has any role to play in constitutional adjudication, once there is a waiver of immunity it must be true that it is complete so far as effective operation of the state-federal joint welfare program is concerned.

It is argued that participation in the program of federal financial assistance is not sufficient to establish consent on the part of the State to be sued in federal courts. But it is not merely participation which supports a finding of Eleventh Amendment waiver, but participation in light of the existing state of the law as exhibited in such decisions as *Shapiro v. Thompson*, 394 U.S. 618 [1969], which affirmed judgments ordering retroactive payment of benefits.

I would affirm the judgment of the Court of Appeals.

MR. JUSTICE BRENNAN, dissenting.

This suit is brought by Illinois citizens against Illinois officials. In that circumstance, Illinois may not invoke the Eleventh Amendment, since that Amendment bars only federal court suits against States by citizens of other States. Rather, the question is whether Illinois may avail itself of the nonconstitutional but ancient doctrine of sovereign immunity as a bar to respondent's claim for retroactive AABD payments. In my view Illinois may not assert sovereign immunity. The States surrendered that immunity in Hamilton's words, "in the plan of the Convention," that formed the Union, at least insofar as the States granted Congress specifically enumerated powers.

I would affirm the judgment of the Court of Appeals.

MR. JUSTICE MARSHALL, with whom MR. JUSTICE BLACKMUN joins, dissenting.

Illinois elected to participate in the AABD program and received and expended substantial federal funds in the years at issue. It thereby obligated itself to comply with federal law including the requirement of former 42 U.S.C. §1382(a)(8) that "such aid or assistance shall be furnished with reasonable promptness to all eligible individuals."

In agreeing to comply with the requirements of the Social Security Act and HEW regulations, I believe that Illinois has also agreed to subject itself to suit in the federal courts to enforce these obligations. As the Court points out the only sanction expressly provided in the Act for a participating State's failure to comply with federal requirements is the cutoff of federal funding by the Secretary of HEW.

But a cause of action is clearly provided by 42 U.S.C. §1983, which in terms authorizes suits to redress deprivations of rights secured by the "laws" of the United States.

I believe that Congress also intended the full panoply of traditional judicial remedies to be available to the federal courts in these §1983 suits.

In particular, I am firmly convinced that Congress intended the restitution of wrongfully withheld assistance payments to be a remedy available to the federal courts in these suits. Equally important, the court's power to order retroactive payments is an essential remedy to insure future state compliance with federal requirements. No other remedy can effectively deter States from the strong temptation to cut welfare budgets by circumventing the stringent requirements of federal law. The funding cutoff is a drastic sanction, one which HEW has proved unwilling or unable to employ to compel strict compliance with the Act and regulations. Moreover, the cutoff operates only prospectively; it in no way deters the States from even a flagrant violation of the Act's requirements for as long as HEW does not discover the violation and threaten to take such action.

Illinois chose to participate in the AABD program with its eyes wide open. Drawn by the lure of federal funds, it voluntarily obligated itself to comply with the Social Security Act and HEW regulations, with full knowledge that Congress had authorized assistance recipients to go into federal court to enforce these obligations and to recover benefits wrongfully denied. Any doubts on this score must surely have been removed by our decisions in *Rosado v. Wyman*, and *Shapiro v. Thompson*, where we affirmed a district court retroactive payment order. I cannot avoid the conclusion that, by virtue of its knowing and voluntary decision to nevertheless participate in the program, the State necessarily consented to subject itself to these suits. I have no quarrel with the Court's view that waiver of constitutional rights should not lightly be inferred. But I simply cannot believe that the State could have entered into this essentially contractual agreement with the Federal Government without recognizing that it was subjecting itself to the full scope of the § 1983 remedy provided by Congress to enforce the terms of the agreement.

Of course, § 1983 suits are nominally brought against state officers, rather than the State itself, and do not ordinarily raise Eleventh Amendment problems in view of this Court's decision in *Ex parte Young*. But to the extent that the relief authorized by Congress in an action under § 1983 may be open to Eleventh Amendment objections, these objections are waived when the State agrees to comply with federal requirements enforceable in such an action.

While conducting an assistance program for the needy is surely a "governmental" function, the State here has done far more than operate its own program in its sovereign capacity. It has voluntarily subordinated its sovereignty in this matter to that of the Federal Government, and agreed to comply with the conditions imposed by Congress upon the expenditure of federal funds. In entering this federal-state cooperative program, the State again "leaves the sphere that is exclusively its own," and similarly may more readily be found to have voluntarily waived its immunity.

Congress undoubtedly has the power to insist upon a waiver of sovereign immunity as a condition of its consent to such a federal-state agreement.

Notes and Questions

(1) From the state's viewpoint, is there any real difference between the prospective relief that was upheld and the retroactive relief that was barred by the Eleventh Amendment?

(2) Does the Eleventh Amendment or Article III distinguish between prospective and retroactive relief? What then was the basis for the Court's distinction? *See also Green v. Mansour*, 474 U.S. 64 (1985) (Eleventh Amendment bars declaratory judgment that past conduct by state officials violated federal law).

(3) Is *Edelman* distinguishable from *Ex parte Young*? What is left of *Ex parte Young*?

(4) The Court conceded that a state may waive its Eleventh Amendment immunity and consent to suit in federal court. Is that proposition consistent with the view that the Eleventh Amendment is a jurisdictional bar? (Consult your Civil Procedure course: Can a defendant consent to subject matter jurisdiction in the federal courts where none exists?) Did Justice Brennan offer a more defensible position when he argued that the case involves only the nonconstitutional doctrine of sovereign immunity which can be surrendered?

(5) Why did the Court hold that Illinois' participation in the federal welfare program did not constitute a waiver of the Eleventh Amendment bar?

(6) Did Justice Marshall persuasively argue that a waiver should be found because of the Social Security Act *and* 42 U.S.C. §1983? How did the majority respond to that argument?

(7) The Court has continued to rule that the Eleventh Amendment does not bar a suit if the state consents to the lawsuit in federal court, or if Congress authorizes the lawsuit pursuant to its Fourteenth Amendment enforcement power. The state's consent, or congressional authorization, however, must be unequivocal. *See, e.g., Dellmuth v. Muth*, 491 U.S. 223 (1989); *Welch v. Department of Highways and Public Transportation*, 483 U.S. 468 (1987).

The decision in *Atascadero State Hospital v. Scanlon*, 473 U.S. 234 (1985), illustrates the Court's approach. There, a closely divided Court held that the Eleventh Amendment bars a federal court lawsuit seeking damages from a state agency for violating §504 of the Rehabilitation Act of 1973, 29 U.S.C. §794. The Court rejected the argument that Congress had abrogated the state's immunity from suit in federal court. Writing for the majority, Justice Powell stated:

> Section 504 of the Rehabilitation Act provides in pertinent part:
>
> No otherwise qualified handicapped individual in the United States, as defined in section 706(7) of this title, shall, solely by reason of his handicap, be excluded from the participation in, be denied the benefits of, or be subjected to discrimination under any program or activity receiving Federal financial assistance or under any program or activity conducted by any Executive agency or by the United States Postal Service.
>
> Section 505, which was added to the Act in 1978, describes the available remedies under the Act, including the provision pertinent to this case:
>
> (a)(2) The remedies, procedures, and rights set forth in Title VI of the Civil Rights Act of 1964 [42 U.S.C. § 2000d *et seq.*] shall be available to any person

aggrieved by any act or failure to act by any recipient of Federal assistance or Federal provider of such assistance under section 794 of this title.

(b) In any action or proceeding to enforce or charge a violation of a provision of this subchapter, the court, in its discretion, may allow the prevailing party, other than the United States, a reasonable attorney's fee as part of the costs.

The statute thus provides remedies for violation of § 504 by "*any* recipient of Federal assistance." There is no claim here that the State of California is not a recipient of federal aid under the statute. But given their constitutional role, the States are not like any other class of recipients of federal aid. A general authorization for suit in federal court is not the kind of unequivocal statutory language sufficient to abrogate the Eleventh Amendment. When Congress chooses to subject the States to federal jurisdiction, it must do so specifically. Accordingly, we hold that the Rehabilitation Act does not abrogate the Eleventh Amendment bar to suits against the States.

The dissenters disagreed and urged that California, as a willing recipient of federal funds under the Rehabilitation Act, consented to suit in federal court. (*See* Blackmun, J., dissenting.) More importantly, Justice Brennan, joined by Justices Marshall, Blackmun and Stevens provided an exhaustive historical review of Eleventh Amendment jurisprudence. He observed:

If the Court's Eleventh Amendment doctrine were grounded on principles essential to the structure of our federal system or necessary to protect the cherished constitutional liberties of our people, the doctrine might be unobjectionable; the interpretation of the text of the Constitution in light of changed circumstances and unforeseen events — and with full regard for the purposes underlying the text — had always been the unique role of this Court. But the Court's Eleventh Amendment doctrine diverges from text and history virtually without regard to underlying purposes or genuinely fundamental interests. In consequence, the Court had put the federal judiciary in the unseemly position of exempting the States from compliance with laws that bind every other legal actor in our nation. Because I believe that the doctrine rests on flawed premises, misguided history, and an untenable vision of the needs of the federal system it purports to protect, I believe that the Court should take advantage of the opportunity provided by this case to re-examine the doctrine's historical and jurisprudential foundations.

Since the Court began over a decade ago aggressively to expand its doctrine of Eleventh Amendment sovereign immunity, modern scholars and legal historians have taken a critical look at the historical record that is said to support the Court's result. Recent research has discovered and collated substantial evidence that the Court's constitutional doctrine of state sovereign immunity has rested on a mistaken historical premise. The flawed underpinning is the premise that either the Constitution or the Eleventh Amendment embodied a principle of state sovereign immunity as a limit on the federal judicial power. New evidence concerning the drafting and ratification of the original Constitution indicates that the Framers never intended to constitutionalize the doctrine of state sovereign immunity. Consequently, the Eleventh Amendment could not have been, as the Court has occasionally suggested, an effort to reestablish a limitation on the federal judicial power granted in Article III. Nor, given the limited terms in which it was written, could the Amendment's narrow and technical language be understood to have instituted a sweeping new limitation on the federal judicial power whenever an individual attempts to sue a State. A close examination of the historical records reveals a rather different status for the doctrine of state sovereign immunity in federal court. There simply is no constitutional principle of state sovereign immunity, and no constitutionally mandated policy of excluding suits against States from federal court.

[The] Constitution neither abrogated nor instituted state sovereign immunity, but rather left the ancient doctrine as it found it: a state-law defense available in state-law causes of action prosecuted in federal court.

The doctrine that has thus been created is pernicious. In an era when sovereign immunity has been generally recognized by court and legislatures as an anachronistic and unnecessary remnant of a feudal legal system, the Court has aggressively expanded its scope. If this doctrine were required to enhance the liberty of our people in accordance with the Constitution's protections, I could accept it. If the doctrine were required by the structure of the federal system created by the Framers, I could accept it. Yet the current doctrine intrudes on the ideal of liberty under law by protecting the States from the consequences of their illegal conduct. And the decision obstructs the sound operation of our federal system by limiting the ability of Congress to take steps it deems necessary and proper to achieve national goals within its constitutional authority.

Justice Powell responded for the majority as follows:

We believe that our Eleventh Amendment doctrine is necessary to support the view of the federal system held by the Framers of the Constitution. The Framers believed that the States played a vital role in our system and that strong state governments were essential to serve as a "counterpoise" to the power of the federal government. *See, e.g., The Federalist No. 17*, p. 107 (J. Cooke ed., 1961); *The Federalist No. 46*, p. 316. The "new evidence," discovered by the dissent in *The Federalist* and in the records of the state ratifying conventions, has been available to historians and Justices of this Court for almost two centuries. Viewed in isolation, some of it is subject to varying interpretations. But none of the Framers questioned that the Constitution created a federal system with some authority expressly granted the federal government and the remainder retained by the several States. *See, e.g., The Federalist Nos. 39, 45.* The Constitution never would have been ratified if the States and their courts were to be stripped of their sovereign authority except as expressly provided by the Constitution itself.

The principle that the jurisdiction of the federal courts is limited by the sovereign immunity of the States "is, without question, a reflection of concern for the sovereignty of the States."

(8) As a practical matter, where should social security recipients sue if they want to recover welfare benefits that have been wrongfully denied in violation of federal law?

(9) Does the majority in *Edelman* lose sight of the fact that "Our Federalism" is a two-way street requiring states to respect the sovereignty of the federal government? What has become of the role of federal courts in protecting federal rights?

(10) In *Pennhurst State School & Hospital v. Halderman*, 465 U.S. 89 (1984), the Court further limited the *Ex parte Young* exception. The Court held that the Eleventh Amendment prevents a federal court from awarding injunctive relief against state officials on the basis of state law. The Court observed that the *Young* doctrine was necessary to ensure that federal courts are able to vindicate federal rights and promote the supremacy of federal law. That need does not exist when a plaintiff seeks relief based on a pendent state law claim.

Seminole Tribe of Florida v. Florida

United States Supreme Court
517 U.S. 44, 116 S. Ct. 1114, 134 L. Ed. 2d 252 (1996)

CHIEF JUSTICE REHNQUIST delivered the opinion of the Court.

The Indian Gaming Regulatory Act provides that an Indian tribe may conduct certain gaming activities only in conformance with a valid compact between the tribe and the State in which the gaming activities are located. 102 Stat. 2475, 25 U.S.C. § 2710(d)(1)(C). The Act, passed by Congress under the Indian Commerce Clause, U.S. Const., Art. I, § 8, cl. 3, imposes upon the States a duty to negotiate in good faith with an Indian tribe toward the formation of a compact and authorizes a tribe to bring suit in federal court against a State in order to compel performance of that duty. We hold that notwithstanding Congress' clear intent to abrogate the States' sovereign immunity, the Indian Commerce Clause does not grant Congress that power, and therefore § 2710(d)(7) cannot grant jurisdiction over a State that does not consent to be sued. We further hold that the doctrine of *Ex parte Young* may not be used to enforce § 2710(d)(3) against a state official.

I

Congress passed the Indian Gaming Regulatory Act in 1988 in order to provide a statutory basis for the operation and regulation of gaming by Indian tribes. The Act divides gaming on Indian lands into three classes — I, II, and III — and provides a different regulatory scheme for each class. Class III gaming — the type with which we are here concerned — is defined as "all forms of gaming that are not class I gaming or class II gaming," and includes such things as slot machines, casino games, banking card games, dog racing, and lotteries. It is the most heavily regulated of the three classes. The Act provides that class III gaming is lawful only where it is: (1) authorized by an ordinance or resolution that (a) is adopted by the governing body of the Indian tribe, (b) satisfies certain statutorily prescribed requirements, and (c) is approved by the National Indian Gaming Commission; (2) located in a State that permits such gaming for any purpose by any person, organization, or entity; and (3) "conducted in conformance with a Tribal-State compact entered into by the Indian tribe and the State under paragraph (3) that is in effect."

The "paragraph (3)" to which the last prerequisite of § 2710(d)(1) refers is § 2710(d)(3), which describes the permissible scope of a Tribal-State compact, and provides that the compact is effective "only when notice of approval by the Secretary [of the Interior] of such compact has been published by the Secretary in the Federal Register." More significant for our purposes, however, is that § 2710(d)(3) describes the process by which a State and an Indian tribe begin negotiations toward a Tribal-State compact: "(A) Any Indian tribe having jurisdiction over the Indian lands upon which a class III gaming activity is being conducted, or is to be conducted, shall request the State in which such lands are located to enter into negotiations for the purpose of entering into a Tribal-State compact governing the conduct of gaming activities. Upon receiving such a request, the State shall negotiate with the Indian tribe in good faith to enter into such a compact."

The State's obligation to "negotiate with the Indian tribe in good faith," is made judicially enforceable. "(A) The United States district courts shall have jurisdiction over — (i) any cause of action initiated by an Indian tribe arising from the failure of a State to enter into negotiations with the Indian tribe for the purpose of entering into a Tribal-State compact under paragraph (3) or to conduct such negotiations in good faith."

In September 1991, the Seminole Tribe of Indians, petitioner, sued the State of Florida and its Governor, Lawton Chiles. [P]etitioner alleged that respondents had "refused to enter into any negotiation for inclusion of [certain gaming activities] in a tribal-state compact," thereby violating the "requirement of good faith negotiation" contained in § 2710(d)(3). Respondents moved to dismiss the complaint, arguing that the suit violated the State's sovereign immunity from suit in federal court. The District Court denied respondents' motion, and the respondents took an interlocutory appeal of that decision.

The Court of Appeals for the Eleventh Circuit reversed the decision of the District Court, holding that the Eleventh Amendment barred petitioner's suit against respondents.

Petitioner sought our review of the Eleventh Circuit's decision, and we granted certiorari in order to consider two questions: (1) Does the Eleventh Amendment prevent Congress from authorizing suits by Indian tribes against States for prospective injunctive relief to enforce legislation enacted pursuant to the Indian Commerce Clause?; and (2) Does the doctrine of *Ex parte Young* permit suits against a State's governor for prospective injunctive relief to enforce the good faith bargaining requirement of the Act? We answer the first question in the affirmative, the second in the negative, and we therefore affirm the Eleventh Circuit's dismissal of petitioner's suit.

II

Petitioner argues that Congress through the Act abrogated the States' immunity from suit. In order to determine whether Congress has abrogated the States' sovereign immunity, we ask two questions: first, whether Congress has "unequivocally expresse[d] its intent to abrogate the immunity"; and second, whether Congress has acted "pursuant to a valid exercise of power."

A

Congress' intent to abrogate the States' immunity from suit must be obvious from "a clear legislative statement." This rule arises from a recognition of the important role played by the Eleventh Amendment and the broader principles that it reflects.

Here, we agree with the parties, with the Eleventh Circuit in the decision below, and with virtually every other court that has confronted the question that Congress has in § 2710(d)(7) provided an "unmistakably clear" statement of its intent to abrogate. § 2710(d)(7)(A)(i) vests jurisdiction in "[t]he United States district courts over any cause of action arising from the failure of a State to enter into negotiations or to conduct such negotiations in good faith."

B

Having concluded that Congress clearly intended to abrogate the States' sovereign immunity through § 2710(d)(7), we turn now to consider whether the Act was passed "pursuant to a valid exercise of power." Before we address that question here, however, we think it necessary first to define the scope of our inquiry.

Petitioner suggests that one consideration weighing in favor of finding the power to abrogate here is that the Act authorizes only prospective injunctive relief rather than retroactive monetary relief. But we have often made it clear that the relief sought by a plaintiff suing a State is irrelevant to the question whether the suit is barred by the Eleventh Amendment. We think it follows a fortiori from this proposition that the type of relief sought is irrelevant to whether Congress has power to abrogate States' immunity. The Eleventh Amendment does not exist solely in order to "preven[t] federal court judgments that must be paid out of a State's treasury"; it also serves to avoid "the indignity of subjecting a State to the coercive process of judicial tribunals at the instance of private parties."

Similarly, petitioner argues that the abrogation power is validly exercised here because the Act grants the States a power that they would not otherwise have, viz., some measure of authority over gaming on Indian lands. It is true enough that the

Act extends to the States a power withheld from them by the Constitution. Nevertheless, we do not see how that consideration is relevant to the question whether Congress may abrogate state sovereign immunity. The Eleventh Amendment immunity may not be lifted by Congress unilaterally deciding that it will be replaced by grant of some other authority.

Thus our inquiry into whether Congress has the power to abrogate unilaterally the States' immunity from suit is narrowly focused on one question: Was the Act in question passed pursuant to a constitutional provision granting Congress the power to abrogate? Previously, in conducting that inquiry, we have found authority to abrogate under only two provisions of the Constitution. In *Fitzpatrick v. Bitzer*, 427 U.S. 445 (1976), we recognized that the Fourteenth Amendment, by expanding federal power at the expense of state autonomy, had fundamentally altered the balance of state and federal power struck by the Constitution. We noted that §1 of the Fourteenth Amendment contained prohibitions expressly directed at the States and that §5 of the Amendment expressly provided that "The Congress shall have the power to enforce, by appropriate legislation, the provisions of this article." We held that through the Fourteenth Amendment, federal power extended to intrude upon the province of the Eleventh Amendment and therefore that §5 of the Fourteenth Amendment allowed Congress to abrogate the immunity from suit guaranteed by that Amendment.

In only one other case has congressional abrogation of the States' Eleventh Amendment immunity been upheld. In *Pennsylvania v. Union Gas Co.*, 491 U.S. 1 (1989), a plurality of the Court found that the Interstate Commerce Clause, Art. I, §8, cl. 3, granted Congress the power to abrogate state sovereign immunity, stating that the power to regulate interstate commerce would be "incomplete without the authority to render States liable in damages."

In arguing that Congress through the Act abrogated the States' sovereign immunity, petitioner does not challenge the Eleventh Circuit's conclusion that the Act was passed pursuant to neither the Fourteenth Amendment nor the Interstate Commerce Clause. Instead, accepting the lower court's conclusion that the Act was passed pursuant to Congress' power under the Indian Commerce Clause, petitioner now asks us to consider whether that clause grants Congress the power to abrogate the States' sovereign immunity.

Following the rationale of the *Union Gas* plurality, our inquiry is limited to determining whether the Indian Commerce Clause, like the Interstate Commerce Clause, is a grant of authority to the Federal Government at the expense of the States. The answer to that question is obvious. If anything, the Indian Commerce Clause accomplishes a greater transfer of power from the States to the Federal Government than does the Interstate Commerce Clause. This is clear enough from the fact that the States still exercise some authority over interstate trade but have been divested of virtually all authority over Indian commerce and Indian tribes. Under the rationale of *Union Gas*, if the States' partial cession of authority over a particular area includes cession of the immunity from suit, then their virtually total cession of authority over a different area must also include cession of the immunity from suit. We agree with the petitioner that the plurality opinion in *Union Gas* allows no principled distinction in favor of the States to be drawn between the Indian Commerce Clause and the Interstate Commerce Clause.

Respondents argue, however, that we need not conclude that the Indian Commerce Clause grants the power to abrogate the States' sovereign immunity. Instead, they contend that if we find the rationale of the *Union Gas* plurality to extend to the Indian Commerce Clause, then "*Union Gas* should be reconsidered and overruled." Generally, the principle of stare decisis, and the interests that it serves, viz., "the evenhanded, predictable, and consistent development of legal principles, reliance on judicial decisions, and the actual and perceived integrity of the judicial process," counsel strongly against reconsideration of our precedent. Nevertheless, we always have treated stare decisis as a "principle of policy," *Helvering v. Hallock*, 309 U.S. 106, 119 (1940), and not as an "inexorable command."

The Court in *Union Gas* reached a result without an expressed rationale agreed upon by a majority of the Court. We have already seen that Justice Brennan's opinion received the support of only three other Justices. Of the other five, Justice White, who provided the fifth vote for the result, wrote separately in order to indicate his disagreement with the majority's rationale, and four Justices joined together in a dissent that rejected the plurality's rationale. Since it was issued, *Union Gas* has created confusion among the lower courts that have sought to understand and apply the deeply fractured decision.

The plurality's rationale also deviated sharply from our established federalism jurisprudence and essentially eviscerated our decision in *Hans*. It was well established in 1989 when *Union Gas* was decided that the Eleventh Amendment stood for the constitutional principle that state sovereign immunity limited the federal courts' jurisdiction under Article III. The text of the Amendment itself is clear enough on this point: "The Judicial power of the United States shall not be construed to extend to any suit. . . ." And our decisions since *Hans* had been equally clear that the Eleventh Amendment reflects "the fundamental principle of sovereign immunity [that] limits the grant of judicial authority in Article III," *Pennhurst State School and Hospital v. Halderman*.

Never before the decision in *Union Gas* had we suggested that the bounds of Article III could be expanded by Congress operating pursuant to any constitutional provision other than the Fourteenth Amendment. Indeed, it had seemed fundamental that Congress could not expand the jurisdiction of the federal courts beyond the bounds of Article III. *Marbury v. Madison*. The plurality's citation of prior decisions for support was based upon what we believe to be a misreading of precedent.

The plurality's extended reliance upon our decision in *Fitzpatrick v. Bitzer*, that Congress could under the Fourteenth Amendment abrogate the States' sovereign immunity was also, we believe, misplaced. *Fitzpatrick* was based upon a rationale wholly inapplicable to the Interstate Commerce Clause, viz., that the Fourteenth

Amendment, adopted well after the adoption of the Eleventh Amendment and the ratification of the Constitution, operated to alter the pre-existing balance between state and federal power achieved by Article III and the Eleventh Amendment. As the dissent in *Union Gas* made clear, *Fitzpatrick* cannot be read to justify "limitation of the principle embodied in the Eleventh Amendment through appeal to antecedent provisions of the Constitution."

In the five years since it was decided, *Union Gas* has proven to be a solitary departure from established law. Reconsidering the decision in *Union Gas*, we conclude that none of the policies underlying stare decisis require our continuing adherence to its holding. The decision has, since its issuance, been of questionable precedential value, largely because a majority of the Court expressly disagreed with the rationale of the plurality. The case involved the interpretation of the Constitution and therefore may be altered only by constitutional amendment or revision by this Court. Finally, both the result in *Union Gas* and the plurality's rationale depart from our established understanding of the Eleventh Amendment and undermine the accepted function of Article III. We feel bound to conclude that *Union Gas* was wrongly decided and that it should be, and now is, overruled.

In overruling *Union Gas* today, we reconfirm that the background principle of state sovereign immunity embodied in the Eleventh Amendment is not so ephemeral as to dissipate when the subject of the suit is an area, like the regulation of Indian commerce, that is under the exclusive control of the Federal Government. Even when the Constitution vests in Congress complete law-making authority over a particular area, the Eleventh Amendment prevents congressional authorization of suits by private parties against unconsenting States. The Eleventh Amendment restricts the judicial power under Article III, and Article I cannot be used to circumvent the constitutional limitations placed upon federal jurisdiction. Petitioner's suit against the State of Florida must be dismissed for a lack of jurisdiction.

III

Petitioner argues that we may exercise jurisdiction over its suit to enforce § 2710(d)(3) against the Governor notwithstanding the jurisdictional bar of the Eleventh Amendment. Petitioner notes that since our decision in *Ex parte Young* we often have found federal jurisdiction over a suit against a state official when that suit seeks only prospective injunctive relief in order to "end a continuing violation of federal law." The situation presented here, however, is sufficiently different from that giving rise to the traditional *Ex parte Young* action so as to preclude the availability of that doctrine.

Here, the "continuing violation of federal law" alleged by petitioner is the Governor's failure to bring the State into compliance with § 2710(d)(3).

But the duty to negotiate imposed upon the State by that statutory provision does not stand alone. Rather, as we have seen, Congress passed § 2710(d)(3) in conjunction with the carefully crafted and intricate remedial scheme set forth in § 2710(d)(7).

Where Congress has created a remedial scheme for the enforcement of a particular federal right, we have, in suits against federal officers, refused to supplement that scheme with one created by the judiciary. Here, of course, the question is not whether a remedy should be created, but instead is whether the Eleventh Amendment bar should be lifted, as it was in *Ex parte Young*, in order to allow a suit against a state officer. Nevertheless, we think that the same general principle applies: therefore, where Congress has prescribed a detailed remedial scheme for the enforcement against a State of a statutorily created right, a court should hesitate before casting aside those limitations and permitting an action against a state officer based upon *Ex parte Young.*

Here, Congress intended § 2710(d)(3) to be enforced against the State in an action brought under § 2710(d)(7); the intricate procedures set forth in that provision show that Congress intended therein not only to define, but also significantly to limit, the duty imposed by § 2710(d)(3). For example, where the court finds that the State has failed to negotiate in good faith, the only remedy prescribed is an order directing the State and the Indian tribe to conclude a compact within 60 days. And if the parties disregard the court's order and fail to conclude a compact within the 60-day period, the only sanction is that each party then must submit a proposed compact to a mediator who selects the one which best embodies the terms of the Act. Finally, if the State fails to accept the compact selected by the mediator, the only sanction against it is that the mediator shall notify the Secretary of the Interior who then must prescribe regulations governing Class III gaming on the tribal lands at issue. By contrast with this quite modest set of sanctions, an action brought against a state official under *Ex parte Young* would expose that official to the full remedial powers of a federal court, including, presumably, contempt sanctions.

Here, of course, we have found that Congress does not have authority under the Constitution to make the State suable in federal court under § 2710(d)(7). Nevertheless, the fact that Congress chose to impose upon the State a liability which is significantly more limited than would be the liability imposed upon the state officer under *Ex parte Young* strongly indicates that Congress had no wish to create the latter under § 2710(d)(3). Nor are we free to rewrite the statutory scheme in order to approximate what we think Congress might have wanted had it known that § 2710(d)(7) was beyond its authority. If that effort is to be made, it should be made by Congress, and not by the federal courts. We hold that *Ex parte Young* is inapplicable to petitioner's suit against the Governor of Florida, and therefore that suit is barred by the Eleventh Amendment and must be dismissed for a lack of jurisdiction.

JUSTICE STEVENS, dissenting.

This case is about power — the power of the Congress of the United States to create a private federal cause of action against a State, or its Governor, for the violation of a federal right.

The importance of the majority's decision to overrule the Court's holding in *Pennsylvania v. Union Gas Co.* cannot be overstated. The majority's opinion does not simply preclude Congress from establishing the rather curious statutory scheme under which Indian tribes may seek the aid of a federal court to secure a State's good faith negotiations over gaming regulations. Rather, it prevents Congress from providing a federal forum for a broad range of actions against States, from those sounding in copyright and patent law, to those concerning bankruptcy, environmental law, and the regulation of our vast national economy.

In confronting the question whether a federal grant of jurisdiction is within the scope of Article III, as limited by the Eleventh Amendment, I see no reason to distinguish among statutes enacted pursuant to the power granted to Congress to regulate Commerce among the several States, and with the Indian Tribes, Art. I, § 8, cl. 3, the power to establish uniform laws on the subject of bankruptcy, Art. I, § 8, cl. 4, the power to promote the progress of science and the arts by granting exclusive rights to authors and inventors, Art. I, § 8, cl. 8, the power to enforce the provisions of the Fourteenth Amendment, § 5, or indeed any other provision of the Constitution. There is no language anywhere in the constitutional text that authorizes Congress to expand the borders of Article III jurisdiction or to limit the coverage of the Eleventh Amendment.

The Court's holdings in *Fitzpatrick v. Bitzer* and *Pennsylvania v. Union Gas Co.* do unquestionably establish, however, that Congress has the power to deny the States and their officials the right to rely on the nonconstitutional defense of sovereign immunity in an action brought by one of their own citizens. As the opinions in the latter case demonstrate, there can be legitimate disagreement about whether Congress intended a particular statute to authorize litigation against a State. Nevertheless, the Court there squarely held that the Commerce Clause was an adequate source of authority for such a private remedy.

The fundamental error that continues to lead the Court astray is its failure to acknowledge that its modern embodiment of the ancient doctrine of sovereign immunity "has absolutely nothing to do with the limit on judicial power contained in the Eleventh Amendment." It rests rather on concerns of federalism and comity that merit respect but are nevertheless, in cases such as the one before us, subordinate to the plenary power of Congress.

IV

As I noted above, for the purpose of deciding this case, it is not necessary to question the wisdom of the Court's decision in *Hans v. Louisiana*. Given the absence of precedent for the Court's dramatic application of the sovereign immunity doctrine today, it is nevertheless appropriate to identify the questionable heritage of the doctrine and to suggest that there are valid reasons for limiting, or even rejecting that doctrine altogether, rather than expanding it.

Except insofar as it has been incorporated into the text of the Eleventh Amendment, the doctrine is entirely the product of judge-made law. Three features of its English ancestry make it particularly unsuitable for incorporation into the law of this democratic Nation.

First, the assumption that it could be supported by a belief that "the King can do no wrong" has always been absurd; the bloody path trod by English monarchs both before and after they reached the throne demonstrated the fictional character of any such assumption. Even if the fiction had been acceptable in Britain, the recitation in the Declaration of Independence of the wrongs committed by George III made that proposition unacceptable on this side of the Atlantic.

Second, centuries ago the belief that the monarch served by divine right made it appropriate to assume that redress for wrongs committed by the sovereign should be the exclusive province of still higher authority. While such a justification for a rule that immunized the sovereign from suit in a secular tribunal might have been acceptable in a jurisdiction where a particular faith is endorsed by the government, it should give rise to skepticism concerning the legitimacy of comparable rules in a society where a constitutional wall separates the State from the Church.

Third, in a society where noble birth can justify preferential treatment, it might have been unseemly to allow a commoner to hale the monarch into court. Justice Wilson explained how foreign such a justification is to this Nation's principles.

In this country the sovereignty of the individual States is subordinate both to the citizenry of each State and to the supreme law of the federal sovereign. In my view, neither the majority's opinion today, nor any earlier opinion by any Member of the Court, has identified any acceptable reason for concluding that the absence of a State's consent to be sued in federal court should affect the power of Congress to authorize federal courts to remedy violations of federal law by States or their officials in actions not covered by the Eleventh Amendment's explicit text.

While I am persuaded that there is no justification for permanently enshrining the judge-made law of sovereign immunity, I recognize that federalism concerns— and even the interest in protecting the solvency of the States that was at work in *Chisholm* and *Hans*—may well justify a grant of immunity from federal litigation in certain classes of cases. Such a grant, however, should be the product of a reasoned decision by the policymaking branch of our Government. For this Court to conclude that time-worn shibboleths iterated and reiterated by judges should take precedence over the deliberations of the Congress of the United States is simply irresponsible.

For these reasons, as well as those set forth in Justice Souter's opinion, I respectfully dissent.

JUSTICE SOUTER, with whom JUSTICE GINSBURG and JUSTICE BREYER join, dissenting.

I

It is useful to separate three questions: (1) whether the States enjoyed sovereign immunity if sued in their own courts in the period prior to ratification of the National Constitution; (2) if so, whether after ratification the States were entitled to claim some such immunity when sued in a federal court exercising jurisdiction either because the suit was between a State and a non-state litigant who was not its citizen, or because the issue in the case raised a federal question; and (3) whether any state sovereign immunity recognized in federal court may be abrogated by Congress.

The answer to the first question is not clear, although some of the Framers assumed that States did enjoy immunity in their own courts. The second question was not debated at the time of ratification, except as to citizen-state diversity jurisdiction; there was no unanimity, but in due course the Court in *Chisholm* answered that a state defendant enjoyed no such immunity. As to federal question jurisdiction, state sovereign immunity seems not to have been debated prior to ratification, the silence probably showing a general understanding at the time that the States would have no immunity in such cases.

The Court's answer today to the third question is likewise at odds with the Founders' view that common law, when it was received into the new American legal systems, was always subject to legislative amendment. In ignoring the reasons for this pervasive understanding at the time of the ratification, and in holding that a nontextual common-law rule limits a clear grant of congressional power under Article I, the Court follows a course that has brought it to grief before in our history, and promises to do so again.

Whatever the scope of sovereign immunity might have been in the Colonies, however, or during the period of Confederation, the proposal to establish a National Government under the Constitution drafted in 1787 presented a prospect unknown to the common law prior to the American experience: the States would become parts of a system in which sovereignty over even domestic matters would be divided or parcelled out between the States and the Nation, the latter to be invested with its own judicial power and the right to prevail against the States whenever their respective substantive laws might be in conflict. With this prospect in mind, the 1787 Constitution might have addressed state sovereign immunity by eliminating whatever sovereign immunity the States previously had, as to any matter subject to federal law or jurisdiction; by recognizing an analogue to the old immunity in the new context of federal jurisdiction, but subject to abrogation as to any matter within that jurisdiction; or by enshrining a doctrine of inviolable state sovereign immunity in the text, thereby giving it constitutional protection in the new federal jurisdiction.

The 1787 draft in fact said nothing on the subject, and it was this very silence that occasioned some, though apparently not widespread, dispute among the Framers and others over whether ratification of the Constitution would preclude a State sued in federal court from asserting sovereign immunity as it could have done on any matter of nonfederal law litigated in its own courts. As it has come down to us, the discussion gave no attention to congressional power under the proposed Article I but focused entirely on the limits of the judicial power provided in Article III. And although the jurisdictional bases together constituting the judicial power of the national courts under section 2 of Article III included questions arising under federal law and cases between States and individuals who are not citizens, it was only upon the latter citizen-state diversity provisions that preratification questions about state immunity from suit or liability centered.

The Eleventh Amendment, of course, repudiated *Chisholm* and clearly divested federal courts of some jurisdiction as to cases against state parties. There are two plausible readings of this provision's text. Under the first, it simply repeals the Citizen-State Diversity Clauses of Article III for all cases in which the State appears as a defendant. Under the second, it strips the federal courts of jurisdiction in any case in which a state defendant is sued by a citizen not its own, even if jurisdiction might otherwise rest on the existence of a federal question in the suit. Neither reading of the Amendment, of course, furnishes authority for the Court's view in today's case, but we need to choose between the competing readings for the light that will be shed on the *Hans* doctrine and the legitimacy of inflating that doctrine to the point of constitutional immutability as the Court has chosen to do.

The history and structure of the Eleventh Amendment convincingly show that it reaches only to suits subject to federal jurisdiction exclusively under the Citizen-State Diversity Clauses. In precisely tracking the language in Article III providing for citizen-state diversity jurisdiction, the text of the Amendment does, after all, suggest to common sense that only the Diversity Clauses are being addressed. If the Framers had meant the Amendment to bar federal question suits as well, they could not only have made their intentions clearer very easily, but could simply have adopted the first post-*Chisholm* proposal, introduced in the House of Representatives by Theodore Sedgwick of Massachusetts on instructions from the Legislature of that Commonwealth. Its provisions would have had exactly that expansive effect:

> "[N]o state shall be liable to be made a party defendant, in any of the judicial courts, established, or which shall be established under the authority of the United States, at the suit of any person or persons, whether a citizen or citizens, or a foreigner or foreigners, or of any body politic or corporate, whether within or without the United States." Gazette of the United States 303 (Feb. 20, 1793).

It should accordingly come as no surprise that the weightiest commentary following the amendment's adoption described it simply as constricting the scope of the Citizen-State Diversity Clauses.

Because the plaintiffs in today's case are citizens of the State that they are suing, the Eleventh Amendment simply does not apply to them. We must therefore look elsewhere for the source of that immunity by which the Court says their suit is barred from a federal court.

II

The obvious place to look elsewhere, of course, is *Hans v. Louisiana*, and *Hans* was indeed a leap in the direction of today's holding, even though it does not take the Court all the way. The parties in *Hans* raised, and the Court in that case answered, only what I have called the second question, that is, whether the Constitution, without more, permits a State to plead sovereign immunity to bar the exercise of federal question jurisdiction. Although the Court invoked a principle of sovereign immunity to cure what it took to be the Eleventh Amendment's anomaly of barring only those state suits brought by noncitizen plaintiffs, the *Hans* Court had no occasion to consider whether Congress could abrogate that background immunity by statute.

III

Three critical errors in *Hans* weigh against constitutionalizing its holding as the majority does today. The first we have already seen: the *Hans* Court misread the Eleventh Amendment. It also misunderstood the conditions under which common-law doctrines were received or rejected at the time of the Founding, and it fundamentally mistook the very nature of sovereignty in the young Republic that was supposed to entail a State's immunity to federal question jurisdiction in a federal court. While I would not, as a matter of stare decisis, overrule *Hans* today, an understanding of its failings on these points will show how the Court today simply compounds already serious error in taking *Hans* the further step of investing its rule with constitutional inviolability against the considered judgment of Congress to abrogate it.

We said in *Blatchford v. Native Village of Noatak*, 501 U.S. 775, 779 (1991) that "the States entered the federal system with their sovereignty intact," but we surely did not mean that they entered that system with the sovereignty they would have claimed if each State had assumed independent existence in the community of nations, for even the Articles of Confederation allowed for less than that. While there is no need here to calculate exactly how close the American States came to sovereignty in the classic sense prior to ratification of the Constitution, it is clear that the act of ratification affected their sovereignty in a way different from any previous political event in America or anywhere else. For the adoption of the Constitution made them members of a novel federal system that sought to balance the States' exercise of some sovereign prerogatives delegated from their own people with the principle of a limited but centralizing federal supremacy.

[T]he ratification demonstrated that state governments were subject to a superior regime of law in a judicial system established, not by the State, but by the people through a specific delegation of their sovereign power to a National Government that was paramount within its delegated sphere. When individuals sued States to enforce federal rights, the Government that corresponded to the "sovereign" in the traditional common-law sense was not the State but the National Government, and any state immunity from the jurisdiction of the Nation's courts would have required a grant from the true sovereign, the people, in their Constitution, or from the Congress that the Constitution had empowered.

State immunity to federal question jurisdiction would, moreover, have run up against the common understanding of the practical necessity for the new federal relationship. According to Madison, the "multiplicity," "mutability," and "injustice" of then-extant state laws were prime factors requiring the formation of a new government. These concerns ultimately found concrete expression in a number of specific limitations on state power, including provisions barring the States from enacting bills of attainder or ex post facto laws, coining money or emitting bills of credit, denying the privileges and immunities of out-of-staters, or impairing the obligation of contracts. But the proposed Constitution also dealt with the old problems affirmatively by granting the powers to Congress enumerated in Article I, § 8, and by providing through the Supremacy Clause that Congress could preempt State action in areas of concurrent state and federal authority.

Given the Framers' general concern with curbing abuses by state governments, it would be amazing if the scheme of delegated powers embodied in the Constitution had left the National Government powerless to render the States judicially accountable for violations of federal rights. And of course the Framers did not understand the scheme to leave the government powerless.

IV

The Court's holding that the States' *Hans* immunity may not be abrogated by Congress leads to the final question in this case, whether federal question jurisdiction exists to order prospective relief enforcing IGRA against a state officer, respondent Chiles, who is said to be authorized to take the action required by the federal law. Just as with the issue about authority to order the State as such, this question is entirely jurisdictional, and we need not consider here whether petitioner Seminole Tribe would have a meritorious argument for relief, or how much practical relief the requested order (to bargain in good faith) would actually provide to the Tribe. Nor, of course, does the issue turn in any way on one's views about the scope of the Eleventh Amendment or *Hans* and its doctrine, for we ask whether the state officer is subject to jurisdiction only on the assumption that action directly against the State is barred. The answer to this question is an easy yes, the officer is subject to suit under the rule in *Ex parte Young*, and the case could, and should, readily be decided on this point alone.

[T]he Court suggests that it may be justified in displacing *Young* because *Young* would allow litigants to ignore the "intricate procedures" of IGRA in favor of a menu of streamlined equity rules from which any litigant could order as he saw fit. But there is no basis in law for this suggestion, and the strongest authority to reject it. *Young* did not establish a new cause of action and it does not impose any particular procedural regime in the suits it permits. It stands, instead, for a jurisdictional rule by which paramount federal law may be enforced in a federal court by substituting a nonimmune party (the state officer) for an immune one (the State itself).

Absent the application of *Ex parte Young*, I would, of course, follow *Union Gas* in recognizing congressional power under Article I to abrogate *Hans* immunity.

In being ready to hold that the relationship may still be altered, not by the Court but by Congress, I would tread the course laid out elsewhere in our cases. The Court has repeatedly stated its assumption that insofar as the relative positions of States and Nation may be affected consistently with the Tenth Amendment, they would not be modified without deliberately expressed intent. The plain statement rule, which "assures that the legislature has in fact faced, and intended to bring into issue, the critical matters involved in the judicial decision," is particularly appropriate in light of our primary reliance on "[t]he effectiveness of the federal political process in preserving the States' interests." Hence, we have required such a plain statement when Congress pre-empts the historic powers of the States, imposes a condition on the grant of federal moneys, or seeks to regulate a State's ability to determine the qualifications of its own officials.

When judging legislation passed under unmistakable Article I powers, no further restriction could be required. Nor does the Court explain why more could be demanded. In the past, we have assumed that a plain statement requirement is sufficient to protect the States from undue federal encroachments upon their traditional immunity from suit. See, e.g., *Welch v. Texas Dep't of Highways & Public Transp.*, 483 U.S. [468 (1987)], at 475; *Atascadero State Hospital v. Scanlon*, 473 U.S. [234 (1985)], at 239–240. It is hard to contend that this rule has set the bar too low, for (except in *Union Gas*) we have never found the requirement to be met outside the context of laws passed under §5 of the Fourteenth Amendment. The exception I would recognize today proves the rule, moreover, because the federal abrogation of state immunity comes as part of a regulatory scheme which is itself designed to invest the States with regulatory powers that Congress need not extend to them. This fact suggests to me that the political safeguards of federalism are working, that a plain statement rule is an adequate check on congressional overreaching, and that today's abandonment of that approach is wholly unwarranted.

Notes and Questions

(1) What is the basis for the Court's conclusion that Congress lacks power under the Commerce Clause to abrogate the state's Eleventh Amendment immunity? Why would such power exist under the Fourteenth Amendment, as suggested by the Court?

(2) What federalism values are threatened when Congress uses its Article I power to abrogate the state's immunity?

(3) Justice Stevens observed that the importance of the *Seminole* decision "cannot be overstated." Is he correct that it prevents Congress from providing a federal forum for a range of actions against the state, including those under copyright, bankruptcy, and environmental laws?

(4) Does *Seminole* prevent suits against a state in state court to enforce federal law? Would the Eleventh Amendment prevent the Supreme Court from reviewing a state court decision in a case against the state involving the interpretation of federal law? In *McKesson Corp. v. Division of Alcoholic Beverages and Tobacco*, 496 U.S. 18 (1990), the Court held that the Eleventh Amendment does not limit the appellate jurisdiction of the Supreme Court. It reasoned that a state "assents" to such appellate

review of federal issues presented in a case brought in a state court against a state. Is the notion of "assent" consistent with the Court's determination that a state's consent to suit in federal court must be clear and unequivocal?

(5) In what way does *Seminole* further limit the *Young* doctrine?

(6) It has been clear at least since *Fitzpatrick v. Bitzer*, 427 U.S. 445 (1976) (cited by the majority in *Seminole, supra*) that Section 5 of the Fourteenth Amendment altered the balance between state and federal power created by the Court's interpretation of the Eleventh Amendment. In *Kimel v. Florida Board of Regents*, 528 U.S. 62 (2000), the Court was asked to decide whether the Eleventh Amendment bars lawsuits against states for violation for the Age Discrimination in Employment Act (ADEA), 29 U.S.C. § 621, et seq. The court found that Congress relied on its Section 5 powers and unmistakably expressed its intent to abrogate the states' Eleventh Amendment immunity and to subject states to suits under the ADEA when it authorized age discrimination suits "against any employer (including a public agency)," and "public agency" was defined to include "the government of a State or political subdivision thereof." However, even though Congress unmistakably articulated its intention to abrogate state sovereign immunity in the ADEA, a majority of the Court found that Congress failed to establish a pattern of actual age discrimination constitutional violations by the states. Because the evidence that Congress did have of age discrimination by the states was anecdotal and limited to a few states, the Court viewed the remedy selected by Congress — abrogation of sovereign immunity — disproportionate to the pattern of constitutional violations and insufficient to justify use of its Section 5 authority.

In *Board of Trustees v. Garrett*, 531 U.S. 356 (2001), the Court relied on *Kimel* in holding that the Eleventh Amendment bars damage actions against the states for violating Title I of the Americans with Disabilities Act, 42 U.S.C. §§ 12111–12117. As in *Kimel*, the Court found that Congress intended to abrogate the states' immunity. It ruled, however, that Congress failed to demonstrate a widespread record of disability discrimination by state actors and thus it lacked the power under the Fourteenth Amendment to lift the immunity and subject states to lawsuits seeking damages for violations of the Act.

In contrast, the Court ruled in *Nevada Department of Human Resources v. Hibbs*, 538 U.S. 721 (2003), that the Eleventh Amendment did not bar a lawsuit for damages against the state for violating the Family and Medical Leave Act of 1993 (FMLA), 29 U.S.C. § 2612 (a)(1)(C). The FMLA allows eligible employees to take up to 12 weeks of unpaid leave to care for a spouse, child or parent. The Act authorizes a cause of action for equitable relief and monetary damages against an employer who denies rights secured by the FMLA. The statute expressly defines an employer to include the state government, a state agency, and a political subdivision. The Court found once again that Congress intended to abrogate the Eleventh Amendment immunity. Unlike in *Kimel* and *Garrett*, however, the Court also held that, based on "the States' record of unconstitutional participation in, and fostering of, gender-based discrimination in the administration of leave benefits," Congress had power under the Fourteenth Amendment to abrogate the immunity and justify enactment of prophylactic Section 5 legislation.

Problem A

Assume that the Americans with Disabilities Act (ADA) provides that "No qualified individual with a disability shall, by reason of such disability, be excluded from participation in or be denied the benefits of the services, programs, or activities of any public or private educational institution."

The Committee Reports accompanying the bill include material indicating that individuals with disabilities continue to be denied educational opportunities at the elementary, secondary, college, and university levels. Moreover, those Reports indicate that because of such exclusion individuals with disabilities are disadvantaged economically and are relegated to lesser jobs and fewer employment opportunities.

The statute includes a provision that any entity that violates the requirements of the Act may be held liable for injunctive relief, compensatory damages, punitive damages, and attorney's fees. The statute further provides that "[i]n any action in federal court against a State for a violation of the requirements of this Act, remedies are available for such violation to the same extent as such remedies are available against any public or private entity other than a State."

John Roe recently filed a lawsuit in federal court alleging that the state-operated law school violated the requirements of the Act. Specifically, he alleged that he has a handicapping condition and is required to use a wheelchair. He maintained that he was denied admission because the law school facilities are not accessible to those in wheelchairs. He named the State and the law school dean as defendants and requested (1) an injunction directing the defendants to provide an accessible facility and to admit him to the school; (2) compensatory and punitive damages; and (3) attorney's fees.

You are now employed by the State Attorney General who wants to move to dismiss the action on the ground that the court lacks power under the Eleventh Amendment to award the requested relief. He asks that you assess the likelihood of prevailing on that motion. *See Tennessee v. Lane*, 541 U.S. 509 (2004).

Chapter 4

Federalism Limits on the Elected Branches and on the States

§ 4.01 Introduction

The historical overview of federalism presented in § 3.01, *supra*, established that, while federalism may be viewed modestly as a process for the allocation of power among units of government, over time federalism in the United States has acquired considerable substantive constitutional content. Although the act of framing and ratifying the Constitution constituted a transfer of many governmental powers from the ratifying states to the new national government, those powers not granted to the national government by the Constitution were reserved to the states. During the more than two centuries experience with federalism, a few of our national crises — slavery and the Civil War, the Great Depression and New Deal, and the civil rights struggle — have developed around the central question in this unit: Where does sovereignty reside in our federal system? As revealed by our examination of the Gun Control Case Study, § 1.03, *supra*, there continues to exist among elected representatives and among the Justices of the Supreme Court fundamental disagreement concerning the nature of our federal system.

Inevitably, then, constitutional questions are presented by virtue of the federal system. One set of questions concerns the powers of the national government: What activities of government fall within the powers granted to the national government and thus enable the branches of the national government to act? We examine those questions by selecting the most prolific example of national power: the regulation of commerce. The Constitution provides that "The Congress shall have power . . . to regulate commerce with foreign Nations, and among the several States, and with the Indian Tribes." U.S. Const., Art. I, § 8. From a historical perspective those few words have immense significance. Under the Articles of Confederation, the federal government lacked power to regulate commerce, and a principal reason for calling the Constitutional Convention was to remedy that defect. *See generally* Robert L. Stern, *That Commerce Which Concerns More Than One*, 47 Harv. L. Rev. 1335 (1934). As the Court observed in *H.P. Hood & Sons v. DuMond*, 336 U.S. 525, 533–534 (1949):

> When victory relieved the Colonies from the pressure for solidarity that war had exerted, a drift toward anarchy and commercial warfare between states began. "Each state would legislate according to its estimate of its own interests, the importance of its own products, and the local advantages

or disadvantages of its position in a political or commercial view." This came "to threaten at once the peace and safety of the Union." STORY, THE CONSTITUTION §§ 259, 260. *See* FISKE, THE CRITICAL PERIOD OF AMERICAN HISTORY 144; WARREN, THE MAKING OF THE CONSTITUTION 567. The sole purpose for which Virginia initiated the movement which ultimately produced the Constitution was "to take into consideration the trade of the United States; to examine the relative situations and trade of the said states; to consider how far a uniform system in their commercial regulation may be necessary to their common interest and their permanent harmony" and for that purpose the General Assembly of Virginia in January of 1786 named commissioners and proposed their meeting with those from other states.

The desire of the Forefathers to federalize regulation of foreign and interstate commerce stands in sharp contrast to their jealous preservation of power over their internal affairs. No other federal power was so universally assumed to be necessary, no other state power was so readily relinquished. There was no desire to authorize federal interference with social conditions or legal institutions of the states. Even the Bill of Rights amendments were framed only as a limitation upon the powers of Congress. The states were quite content with their several and diverse controls over most matters but, as Madison has indicated, "want of a general power over Commerce led to an exercise of this power separately, by the States, which not only proved abortive, but engendered rival, conflicting and angry regulations.

Quite apart from its historical significance, the Commerce Clause served — and continues to serve — as "one of the most prolific sources of national powers." *H.P. Hood & Sons v. DuMond, supra,* at 534. The Framers, of course, may not have envisioned our current complex national and international economy. Indeed, when they drafted the Commerce Clause "they were thinking only in terms of the national control of trade with the European countries and the removal of barriers obstructing the physical movements of goods across state lines." Stern, *supra,* at 1344. The Framers, however, were well aware that they were writing a Constitution that must endure:

> [T]he framers of the Constitution did not use language which would restrict the federal power to regulation of the movement of physical goods, even though that was the only kind of regulation which they immediately contemplated. The history and proceedings of the Convention and of the ratifying conventions in the states indicate that the purpose of the commerce clause was to give the Federal Government as much control over commercial transactions as was and would in the future be essential to the general welfare of the union, and there is no suggestion that this power was to be limited to control over movement. The framers of the Constitution would have been exceedingly surprised if they had thought that by the language employed to accomplish that purpose — "commerce among the several states" — they had so restricted the national power as to create a union

incapable of dealing with a commercial condition even more serious than the one that had brought them together. They were acutely conscious that they were preparing an instrument for the ages, not a document adapted only for the exigencies of the time.

Id. at 1344–1345.[1]

The Commerce Clause provides an excellent vehicle for the study of federalism because, while it is a prolific source of national power, it is "an equally prolific source of conflict with legislation of the state." *H.P. Hood & Sons v. DuMond, supra.* The Clause grants the Congress power to regulate commerce among the several states but does not define "commerce" or describe what is meant by commerce "among the several States." Moreover, the Clause does not say whether or to what extent the States may regulate commerce in the absence of or overlapping with congressional legislation. Nor does the Commerce Clause, the Tenth Amendment, or any other provision in the Constitution prescribe a rule for deciding when federal regulation otherwise authorized by the Constitution may be imposed on the states. These issues must be resolved in the context of our federal system. As with other constitutional disputes, the Court often has served as the decision-maker.

We begin the study of federalism limits on the elected branches in § 4.02 by examining the Court's important decision in *McCulloch v. Maryland* where Chief Justice Marshall discussed the scope of federal power in general. We then explore in § 4.03 the Commerce Clause power, tracing the emergence of notions of dual sovereignty, and the changes in national powers and in constitutional law from the New Deal to the present. Although the Commerce Clause has been the most prolific source of congressional legislation, Congress has also relied on its power in section 5 of the Fourteenth Amendment "to enforce" by "appropriate legislation" the substantive prescriptions of the Amendment. In § 4.04 we examine the extent to which Congress may enforce the Constitution's individual rights protections through protective legislation. In § 4.05 we study the limits imposed on federal powers derived from the Tenth Amendment.

Section 4.06 provides an opportunity to review the doctrinal bases for Congress's exercises of legislative power in domestic affairs in the context of one of the most fraught and significant legal and policy disputes in modern times, leading to enactment of the Affordable Care Act. Section 4.07 briefly explores the extent to which the constitutional values underlying the Commerce Clause may stand in the way of states' economic regulation — doctrine usually referred to as the Dormant Commerce Clause.

---

§ 4.02 Scope of Federal Power

McCulloch v. Maryland

United States Supreme Court

17 U.S. (4 Wheat.) 316, 4 L. Ed. 579 (1819)

[In 1816 the Second Bank of the United States was incorporated by Congress. Two years later, Maryland enacted a law imposing a tax on banks that operated within the state but were not chartered by the State. The Bank of the United States fell within that category, but refused to pay the tax. Maryland brought a suit against McCulloch, Cashier of the Bank, for the taxes and penalties.]

MR. CHIEF JUSTICE MARSHALL delivered the opinion of the Court.

In the case now to be determined, the defendant, a sovereign State, denies the obligation of a law enacted by the legislature of the Union, and the plaintiff, on his part, contests the validity of an act which has been passed by the legislature of the State. The constitution of our country, in its most interesting and vital parts, is to be considered; the conflicting powers of the government of the Union and of its members, as marked in that constitution, are to be discussed; and an opinion given, which may essentially influence the great operations of the government. No tribunal can approach such a question without a deep sense of its importance, and of the awful responsibility involved in its decision. But it must be decided peacefully or remain a source of hostile legislation, perhaps of hostility of a still more serious nature; and if it is to be so decided, by this tribunal alone can the decision be made. On the Supreme Court of the United States has the constitution of our country devolved this important duty.

The first question made in the cause is, has Congress power to incorporate a bank?

In discussing this question, the counsel for the State of Maryland have deemed it of some importance, in the construction of the constitution, to consider that instrument not as emanating from the people, but as the act of sovereign and independent States. The powers of the general government, it has been said, are delegated by the States, who alone are truly sovereign; and must be exercised in subordination to the States, who alone possess supreme dominion.

It would be difficult to sustain this proposition. The Convention which framed the constitution was indeed elected by the State legislatures. But the instrument, when it came from their hands, was a mere proposal, without obligation, or pretensions to it. It was reported to the then existing Congress of the United States, with a request that it might "be submitted to a Convention of Delegates, chosen in each State by the people thereof, under the recommendation of its Legislature, for their assent and ratification." This mode of proceeding was adopted; and by the Convention, by Congress, and by the State Legislatures, the instrument was submitted to the people. They acted upon it in the only manner in which they can act safely, effectively, and wisely, on such a subject, by assembling in Convention. It is true, they assembled in their several States — and where else should they have assembled? No political dreamer was ever wild enough to think of breaking down the lines which separate the States, and of compounding the American people into one common mass. Of consequence, when they act, they act in their States. But the measures they adopt do not, on that account, cease to be the measures of the people themselves, or become the measures of the State governments.

From these Conventions the constitution derives its whole authority. The government proceeds directly from the people; is "ordained and established" in the name of the people; and is declared to be ordained, "in order to form a more perfect union, establish justice, ensure domestic tranquillity, and secure the blessings of liberty to themselves and to their posterity." The assent of the States, in their sovereign capacity, is implied in calling a Convention, and thus submitting that instrument to the people. But the people were at perfect liberty to accept or reject it; and their act was final. It required not the affirmance, and could not be negatived, by the State governments. The constitution, when thus adopted, was of complete obligation, and bound the State sovereignties.

It has been said, that the people had already surrendered all their powers to the State sovereignties, and had nothing more to give. But, surely, the question whether they may resume and modify the powers granted to government does not remain to be settled in this country. Much more might the legitimacy of the general government be doubted, had it been created by the States. The powers delegated to the State sovereignties were to be exercised by themselves, not by a distinct and independent sovereignty, created by themselves. To the formation of a league, such as was the confederation, the State sovereignties were certainly competent. But when, "in order to form a more perfect union," it was deemed necessary to change this alliance into an effective government, possessing great and sovereign powers, and acting directly on the people, the necessity of referring it to the people, and of deriving its powers directly from them, was felt and acknowledged by all.

The government of the Union, then, (whatever may be the influence of this fact on the case,) is emphatically, and truly, a government of the people. In form and in substance it emanates from them. Its powers are granted by them, and are to be exercised directly on them, and for their benefit.

This government is acknowledged by all to be one of enumerated powers. The principle, that it can exercise only the powers granted to it, would seem too apparent to have required to be enforced by all those arguments which its enlightened friends, while it was depending before the people, found it necessary to urge. That principle is now universally admitted. But the question respecting the extent of the powers actually granted, is perpetually arising, and will probably continue to arise, as long as our system shall exist.

In discussing these questions, the conflicting powers of the general and State governments must be brought into view, and the supremacy of their respective laws, when they are in opposition, must be settled.

If any one proposition could command the universal assent of mankind, we might expect it would be this — that the government of the Union, though limited in its powers, is supreme within its sphere of action. This would seem to result necessarily from its nature. It is the government of all; its powers are delegated by all; it represents all, and acts for all. Though any one State may be willing to control its operations, no State is willing to allow others to control them. The nation, on those subjects on which it can act, must necessarily bind its component parts. But this question is not left to mere reason: the people have, in express terms, decided it, by saying, "this constitution, and the laws of the United States, which shall be made in pursuance thereof," "shall be the supreme law of the land," and by requiring that the members of the State legislatures, and the officers of the executive and judicial departments of the States, shall take the oath of fidelity to it.

The government of the United States, then, though limited in its powers, is supreme; and its laws, when made in pursuance of the constitution, form the supreme law of the land, "any thing in the constitution or laws of any State to the contrary notwithstanding."

Among the enumerated powers, we do not find that of establishing a bank or creating a corporation. But there is no phrase in the instrument which, like the articles of confederation, excludes incidental or implied powers; and which requires that everything granted shall be expressly and minutely described. Even the 10th amendment, which was framed for the purpose of quieting the excessive jealousies which had been excited, omits the word "expressly," and declares only that the powers "not delegated to the United States, nor prohibited to the States, are reserved to the States or to the people;" thus leaving the question, whether the particular power which may become the subject of contest has been delegated to the one government, or prohibition to the other, to depend on a fair construction of the whole instrument. The men who drew and adopted this amendment had experienced the embarrassments resulting from the insertion of this word in the articles of confederation, and probably omitted it to avoid these embarrassments. A constitution, to contain an accurate detail of all the subdivisions of which its great powers will admit, and of all the means by which they may be carried into execution, would partake of the prolixity of a legal code, and could readily be embraced by the human mind. It would probably never be understood by the public. Its nature, therefore, requires, that only its great outlines should be marked, its important objects designated, and the minor ingredients which compose those objects be deduced from the nature of the objects themselves. That this idea was entertained by the framers of the American constitution, is not only to be inferred from the nature of the instrument, but from the language. Why else were some of the limitations found in the ninth section of the 1st article, introduced? It is also, in some degree, warranted by their having omitted to use any restrictive term which might prevent its receiving a fair and just interpretation. In considering this question, then, we must never forget, that it is *a constitution* we are expounding.

Although, among the enumerated powers of government, we do not find the word "bank" or "incorporation," we find the great powers to lay and collect taxes; to borrow money; to regulate commerce; to declare and conduct a war; and to raise and support armies and navies. The sword and the purse, all the external relations, and no inconsiderable portion of the industry of the nation, are entrusted to its government. It can never be pretended that these vast powers draw after them others of inferior importance, merely because they are inferior. Such an idea can never be advanced. But it may with great reason be contended, that a government, entrusted with such ample powers, on the due execution of which the happiness and prosperity of the nation so vitally depends, must also be entrusted with ample means for their execution.

But the constitution of the United States has not left the right of Congress to employ the necessary means, for the execution of the powers conferred on the government, to general reasoning. To its enumeration of powers is added that of making

> all laws which shall be necessary and proper, for carrying into execution the foregoing powers, and all other powers vested by this constitution, in the government of the United States, or in any department thereof.

The counsel for the State of Maryland have urged various arguments to prove that this clause, though in terms a grant of power, is not so in effect; but is really restrictive of the general right, which might otherwise be implied, of selecting means for executing the enumerated powers.

[T]he argument on which most reliance is placed, is drawn from the peculiar language of this clause. Congress is not empowered by it to make all laws, which may have relation to the powers conferred on the government, but such only as may be "*necessary and proper*" for carrying them into execution. The word "*necessary*" is considered as controlling the whole sentence, and as limiting the right to pass laws for the execution of the granted powers, to such as are indispensable, and without which the power would be nugatory. That it excludes the choice of means, and leaves to Congress, in each case, that only which is most direct and simple.

Is it true, that this is the sense in which the word "necessary" is always used? Does it always import an absolute physical necessity, so strong, that one thing, to which another may be termed necessary, cannot exist without that other? We think it does not. If reference be had to its use, in the common affairs of the world, or in approved authors, we find that it frequently imports no more than that one thing is convenient, or useful, or essential to another. To employ the means necessary to an end, is generally understood as employing any means calculated to produce the end, and not as being confined to those single means, without which the end would be entirely unattainable. It is, we think, impossible to compare the sentence which prohibits a State from laying "imposts, or duties on imports or exports, except what may be *absolutely* necessary for executing its inspection laws," with that which authorizes Congress "to make all laws which shall be necessary and proper for carrying into execution" the powers of the general government, without feeling a conviction that the convention understood itself to change materially the meaning of the word "necessary," by prefixing the word "absolutely." This word, then, like others, is used in various senses; and, in its construction, the subject, the context, the intention of the person using them, are all to be taken into view.

Let this be done in the case under consideration. The subject is the execution of those great powers on which the welfare of a nation essentially depends. It must have been the intention of those who gave these powers, to insure, as far as human prudence could insure, their beneficial execution. This could not be done by confiding the choice of means to such narrow limits as not to leave it in the power of Congress to adopt any which might be appropriate, and which were conducive to the end. This provision is made in a constitution intended to endure for ages to come, and, consequently, to be adapted to the various *crises* of human affairs. To have prescribed the means by which government should, in all future time, execute its powers, would have been to change, entirely, the character of the instrument, and give it the properties of a legal code. It would have been an unwise attempt to provide, by immutable rules, for exigencies which, if foreseen at all, must have been seen dimly, and which can be best provided for as they occur.

In ascertaining the sense in which the word "necessary" is used in this clause of the constitution, we may derive some aid from that with which it is associated. Congress shall have power "to make all laws which shall be necessary and *proper* to carry into execution" the powers of the government. If the word "necessary" was used in that strict and rigorous sense for which the counsel for the State of Maryland contend, it would be an extraordinary departure from the usual course of the human mind, as exhibited in composition, to add a word, the only possible effect of which is to qualify that strict and rigorous meaning; to present to the mind the idea of some choice of means of legislation not straightened and compressed within the narrow limits for which gentlemen contend.

But the argument which most conclusively demonstrates the error of the construction contended for by the counsel for the State of Maryland, is founded on the intention of the Convention, as manifested in the whole clause. This clause, as construed by the State of Maryland, would abridge, and almost annihilate this useful and necessary right of the legislature to select its means. That this could not be intended, is, we should think, had it not been already controverted, too apparent for controversy. We think so for the following reasons:

1st. The clause is placed among the powers of Congress, not among the limitations on those powers.

2nd. Its terms purport to enlarge, not to diminish the powers vested in the government. It purports to be an additional power, not a restriction on those already granted.

We admit, as all must admit, that the powers of the government are limited, and that its limits are not to be transcended. But we think the sound construction of the constitution must allow to the national legislature that discretion, with respect to the means by which the powers it confers are to be carried into execution, which will enable that body to perform the high duties assigned to it, in the manner most beneficial to the people. Let the end be legitimate, let it be within the scope of the constitution, and all means which are appropriate, which are plainly adapted to that end, which are not prohibited, but consist with the letter and spirit of the constitution, are constitutional.

If a corporation may be employed indiscriminately with other means to carry into execution the powers of the government, no particular reason can be assigned for excluding the use of a bank, if required for its fiscal operations. To use one, must be within the discretion of Congress, if it be an appropriate mode of executing the powers of government. That it is a convenient, a useful, and essential instrument in the prosecution of its fiscal operations, is not now a subject of controversy.

But, were its necessity less apparent, none can deny its being an appropriate measure; and if it is, the degree of its necessity, as has been very justly observed, is to be discussed in another place. Should Congress, in the execution of its powers, adopt measures which are prohibited by the constitution; or should Congress, under the pretext of executing its powers, pass laws for the accomplishment of objects not entrusted to the government; it would become the painful duty of this tribunal, should a case requiring such a decision come before it, to say that such an act was not the law of the land. But where the law is not prohibited, and is really calculated to effect any of the objects entrusted to the government, to undertake here to inquire into the degree of its necessity, would be to pass the line which circumscribes the judicial department, and to tread on legislative ground. This court disclaims all pretensions to such a power.

After the most deliberate consideration, it is the unanimous and decided opinion of this Court, that the act to incorporate the Bank of the United States is a law made in pursuance of the constitution, and is a part of the supreme law of the land.

It being the opinion of the Court, that the act incorporating the bank is constitutional; and that the power of establishing a branch in the State of Maryland might be properly exercised by the bank itself, we proceed to inquire —

2. Whether the State of Maryland may, without violating the constitution, tax that branch?

That the power of taxation is one of vital importance; that it is retained by the States; that it is not abridged by the grant of a similar power to the government of the Union; that it is to be concurrently exercised by the two governments: are truths which have never been denied.

The argument on the part of the State of Maryland, is, not that the States may directly resist a law of Congress, but that they may exercise their acknowledged powers upon it, and that the constitution leaves them this right in the confidence that they will not abuse it.

That the power to tax involves the power to destroy; that the power to destroy may defeat and render useless the power to create; that there is a plain repugnance, in conferring on one government a power to control the constitutional measures of another, which other, with respect to those very measures, is declared to be supreme over that which exerts the control, are propositions not be denied. But all inconsistencies are to be reconciled by the magic of the word CONFIDENCE. Taxation, it is said, does not necessarily and unavoidably destroy. To carry it to the excess of destruction would be an abuse, to presume which, would banish that confidence which is essential to all government.

But is this a case of confidence? Would the people of any one State trust those of another with a power to control the most significant operations of their State government? We know they would not. Why, then, should we suppose that the people of any one State should be willing to trust those of another with a power to control the operations of a government to which they have confided their most important and most valuable interests? In the legislature of the Union alone, are all represented. The legislature of the Union alone, therefore, can be trusted by the people with the power of controlling measures which concern all, in the confidence that it will not be abused. This, then, is not a case of confidence, and we must consider it as it really is.

If we apply the principle for which the State of Maryland contends, to the constitution generally, we shall find it capable of changing totally the character of that instrument. We shall find it capable of arresting all the measures of the government, and of prostrating it at the foot of the States. The American people have declared their constitution, and the laws made in pursuance thereof, to be supreme; but this principle would transfer the supremacy, in fact, to the States.

If the States may tax an instrument, employed by the government in the execution of its powers, they may tax any and every other instrument. They may tax the mail; they may tax the mint; they may tax patent rights; they may tax the papers of the custom-house; they may tax judicial process; they may tax all the means employed by the government, to an excess which would defeat all the ends of government. This was not intended by the American people. They did not design to make their government dependent on the States.

The Court has bestowed on this subject its most deliberate consideration. The result is a conviction that the States have no power, by taxation or otherwise, to retard, impede, burden, or in any manner control, the operations of the constitutional laws enacted by Congress to carry into execution the powers vested in the general government. This is, we think, the unavoidable consequence of that supremacy which the constitution has declared.

We are unanimously of opinion, that the law passed by the legislature of Maryland, imposing a tax on the Bank of the United States, is unconstitutional and void.

This opinion does not deprive the States of any resources which they originally possessed. It does not extend to a tax paid by the real property of the bank, in common with the other real property within the State, nor to a tax imposed on the interest which the citizens of Maryland may hold in this institution, in common with other property of the same description throughout the State. But this is a tax on the operations of the bank, and is, consequently, a tax on the operation of an instrument employed by the government of the Union to carry its powers into execution. Such a tax must be unconstitutional.

Notes and Questions

(1) On what bases did Chief Justice Marshall conclude that Congress may exercise implied, as well as expressed, powers? To what extent did he rely on constitutional text? History? Structure of government? Policy?

(2) What was Maryland's view of the "necessary and proper" clause? What meaning did the Court attach to that clause?

(3) The incorporation of a Bank was an appropriate means to accomplish which ends? Did the Court simply defer to Congress on the appropriateness of the means in accomplishing those ends? How carefully should the Court review the reasonableness of the means selected by the Congress?

(4) Are you sure you understand why Chief Justice Marshall did not rely on the General Welfare Clause, U.S. Const. Art. I, sec. 8, cl. 1?

(5) In adopting a broad view of congressional power, did the Court threaten the Constitution's distribution of power between the States and the Federal government? Is *McCulloch* consistent with the Tenth Amendment?

(6) After *McCulloch* are there any limits at all on congressional power and, if so, which institution should impose those limitations? Professor Herbert Wechsler argued that to serve the ends of federalism, the Framers gave the states a role of great importance in the composition and selection of the central government. He explained:

> The national political process in the United States — and especially the role of the states in the composition and selection of the central government — is intrinsically well adapted to retarding or restraining new intrusions by the center on the domain of the states. Far from a national authority that is expansionist by nature, the inherent tendency in our system is precisely the reverse, necessitating the widest support before intrusive measures of importance can receive significant consideration, reacting readily to opposition grounded in resistance within the states.
>
> The prime function envisaged for judicial review — in relation to federalism — was the maintenance of national supremacy against nullification or usurpation by the individual states, the national government having no part in their composition or their councils. This is not to say that the Court can decline to measure national enactments by the Constitution when it is called upon to face the question in the course of ordinary

litigation; the supremacy clause governs there as well. It is rather to say that the Court is on weakest ground when it opposes its interpretation of the Constitution to that of Congress in the interest of the states, whose representatives control the legislative process and, by hypothesis, have broadly acquiesced in sanctioning the challenged Act of Congress.

Federal intervention as against the states is thus primarily a matter for congressional determination in our system as it stands. So too, moreover, is the question whether state enactments shall be stricken down as an infringement on the national authority.

To perceive that it is Congress rather than the Court that on the whole is vested with the ultimate authority for managing our federalism is not, of course, to depreciate [sic] the role played by the Court, subordinate though it may be. It is no accident that Congress has been slow to exercise its managerial authority, remitting to the Court so much of what it could determine by a legislative rule.

Herbert Wechsler, *The Political Safeguards of Federalism: The Role of the States in the Composition and Selection of the National Government*, 54 COLUM. L. REV. 543, 544, 558–560 (1954) (footnotes omitted).[2] Are you persuaded by Professor Wechsler's position? Should the federal judiciary be especially deferent to actions taken by the elected branches of the national government, because of the role of representatives of the states in fashioning national policy?

Problem A

Assume that Committees of the United States House of Representatives and Senate are holding hearings on the problem of gun violence in the nation's schools. The Committees have found that gun violence in our nation's schools has proliferated in recent years at the same time that many state and local laws have failed to stop or even slow down an ever-expanding array of weapons available for sale to almost anyone. To remedy this problem, some representatives have introduced a bill that would raise the minimum age to 21 for all firearms purchases in the United States. The bill would also ban the sale of assault-style automatic weapons and would forbid anyone from possessing a licensed firearm within one mile of a public or private elementary or secondary school.

A member of Congress has asked you (an expert on constitutional law) whether Congress has power to enact this bill. Based on *McCulloch*, what advice would you give?

---

§ 4.03 Congressional Power to Regulate Interstate Commerce

A. The Emergence of Dual Sovereignty

Gibbons v. Ogden

United States Supreme Court
22 U.S. (9 Wheat.) 1, 6 L. Ed. 23 (1824)

[In 1803, New York granted to Fulton and Livingston the exclusive right to operate steamboats in New York waters. Subsequently, Fulton and Livingston assigned to Ogden the exclusive right to operate boats between New York and New Jersey. Notwithstanding Ogden's monopoly, Gibbons began operating steamboats between New York and Elizabethtown, New Jersey.

Ogden sued in state court to enjoin Gibbons from operating his boats. Gibbons argued that his boats were licensed under federal law and that he could operate those boats despite the monopoly granted by State laws to Ogden. The New York courts found for Ogden and enjoined Gibbons from operating his boats. The Supreme Court reversed.]

Mr. Chief Justice Marshall delivered the opinion of the Court.

The appellant [Gibbons] contends that this decree is erroneous, because the laws which purport to give the exclusive privilege it sustains, are repugnant to the constitution and laws of the United States.

They are said to be repugnant:

1st. To that clause in the constitution which authorizes Congress to regulate commerce.

As preliminary to the very able discussions of the constitution, which we have heard from the bar, and as having some influence on its construction, reference has been made to the political situation of these states, anterior to its formation. It has been said that they were sovereign, were completely independent, and were connected with each other only by a league. This is true. But when these allied sovereigns converted their league into a government, when they converted their Congress of Ambassadors, deputed to deliberate on their common concerns, and to recommend measures of general utility, into a legislature, empowered to enact laws on the most interesting subjects, the whole character in which the states appear, underwent a change, the extent of which must be determined by a fair consideration of the instrument by which that change was effected.

This instrument contains an enumeration of powers expressly granted by the people to their government. It has been said that these powers ought to be construed strictly. But why ought they to be so construed? Is there one sentence in the constitution which gives countenance to this rule? In the last of the enumerated powers, that which grants, expressly, the means of carrying all others into execution, Congress is authorized "to make all laws which shall be necessary and proper" for the purpose. But this limitation on the means which may be used, is not extended to the powers which are conferred; nor is there one sentence in the constitution which has been pointed out by the gentlemen of the bar, or which we have been able to discern, that prescribes this rule. We do not, therefore, think ourselves justified in adopting it. We know of no rule for construing the extent of such powers, other than is given by the language of the instrument which confers them, taken in connection with the purposes for which they were conferred.

The words are: "Congress shall have power to regulate commerce with foreign nations, and among the several states, and with the Indian tribes."

The subject to be regulated is commerce: and our constitution being, as was aptly said at the bar, one of enumeration, and not of definition, to ascertain the extent of the power it becomes necessary to settle the meaning of the word. The counsel for the appellee would limit it to traffic, to buying and selling, or the interchange of commodities, and do not admit that it comprehends navigation. This would restrict a general term, applicable to many objects, to one of its significations. Commerce, undoubtedly, is traffic, but it is something more; it is intercourse. It describes the commercial intercourse between nations, and parts of nations, in all its branches, and is regulated by prescribing rules for carrying on that intercourse. The mind can scarcely conceive a system for regulating commerce between nations, which shall exclude all laws concerning navigation, which shall be silent on the admission of the vessels of the one nation into the ports of the other, and be confined to prescribing rules for the conduct of individuals in the actual employment of buying and selling or of barter.

If commerce does not include navigation, the government of the Union has no direct power over the subject, and can make no law prescribing what shall constitute American vessels, or requiring that they shall be navigated by American seamen. Yet this power has been exercised from the commencement of the government, has been exercised with the consent of all, and has been understood by all to be a commercial regulation. All America understands, and has uniformly understood, the word "commerce" to comprehend navigation. It was so understood, and must have been so understood, when the constitution was framed. The power over commerce, including navigation, was one of the primary objects for which the people of America adopted their government, and must have been contemplated in forming it. The convention must have used the word in that sense: because all have understood it in that sense, and the attempt to restrict it comes too late.

If the opinion that "commerce," as the word is used in the constitution, comprehends navigation also, requires any additional confirmation, that additional confirmation is, we think, furnished by the words of the instrument itself.

The 9th section of the 1st article declares that "no preference shall be given, by any regulation of commerce or revenue, to the ports of one state over those of another." This clause cannot be understood as applicable to these laws only which are passed for the purposes of revenue, because it is expressly applied to commercial regulations; and the most obvious preference which can be given to one port over another, in regulating commerce, relates to navigation. But the subsequent part of the sentence is still more explicit. It is, "nor shall vessels bound to or from one state, be obliged to enter, clear, or pay duties, in another." These words have a direct reference to navigation.

The word used in the constitution, then, comprehends, and has been always understood to comprehend, navigation within its meaning; and a power to regulate navigation is as expressly granted as if that term had been added to the word "commerce."

The subject to which the power is applied, is to commerce "among the several states." The word "among" means intermingled with. A thing which is among others, is intermingled with them. Commerce among the states cannot stop at the external boundary line of each state, but may be introduced into the interior.

It is not intended to say that these words comprehend that commerce which is completely internal, which is carried on between man and man in a state, or between different parts of the same state, and which does not extend to or affect other states. Such a power would be inconvenient, and is certainly unnecessary.

Comprehensive as the word "among" is, it may very properly be restricted to that commerce which concerns more states than one.

The genius and character of the whole government seem to be, that its action is to be applied to all the external concerns of the nation, and to those internal concerns which affect the states generally; but not to those which are completely within a particular state, which do not affect other states, and with which it is not necessary to interfere, for the purpose of executing some of the general powers of the government. The completely internal commerce of a state, then, may be considered as reserved for the state itself.

We are now arrived at the inquiry, What is this power?

It is the power to regulate; that is, to prescribe the rule by which commerce is to be governed. This power, like all others vested in Congress, is complete in itself, may be exercised to its utmost extent, and acknowledges no limitations, other than are prescribed in the constitution. If, as has always been understood, the sovereignty of Congress, though limited to specified objects, is plenary as to those objects, the power over commerce with foreign nations, and among the several States, is vested in Congress as absolutely as it would be in a single government, having in its constitution the same restrictions on the exercise of the power as are found in the constitution of the United States. The wisdom and the discretion of Congress, their identity with the people, and the influence which their constituents possess at elections, are, in this, as in many other instances, as that, for example, of declaring war, the sole restraints on which they have relied, to secure them from its abuse. They are the restraints on which the people must often rely solely, in all representative governments.

The power of Congress, then, comprehends navigation within the limits of every state in the Union; so far as that navigation may be, in any manner, connected with "commerce with foreign nations, or among the several states, or with the Indian tribes." It may, of consequence, pass the jurisdictional line of New York, and act upon the very waters to which the prohibition now under consideration applies.

[The Court concluded that the federal statute was within Congress' commerce power. In another portion of the opinion, Chief Justice Marshall resolved the conflict between the state monopoly and the federal statute, and considered whether the state monopoly would have been constitutional if there had been no conflicting federal statute. *See* § 4.07, *infra*.]

Notes and Questions

(1) Did Ogden argue that Congress lacks power to regulate this activity? Or did he argue that while Congress has such power, it is not exclusive and the states are free to regulate commerce within their borders? Is there any textual support for the proposition that congressional power to regulate commerce is not exclusive? What did the Court hold with regard to the exclusivity of the national commerce power?

(2) Was the Court's broad interpretation of congressional power under the commerce clause compelled by *McCulloch*?

(3) What are the implications of *Gibbons* for state sovereignty? Consider Chief Justice Marshall's observation in *Gibbons* that the

> genius and character of the whole government seem to be, that its action is to be applied to all the external concerns of the nation, and to those internal concerns which affect the states generally; but not to those which are completely within a particular state, which do not affect other states, and with which it is not necessary to interfere, for the purpose of executing some of the general powers of government.

(4) Under *Gibbons*, is congressional power to regulate commerce subject to any limitations imposed by other provisions of the Constitution?

(5) Despite Marshall's view of the breadth of congressional power under the Commerce Clause, real confrontation over the exercise of such power did not occur until after enactment of the Interstate Commerce Act in 1887 and the Sherman Antitrust Act in 1890. The Sherman Antitrust Act provided that every contract, combination or conspiracy in restraint of trade among the several states is illegal and that those who monopolize trade shall be guilty of a misdemeanor. The constitutionality of that Act was considered in the following case.

United States v. E.C. Knight Co.

United States Supreme Court
156 U.S. 1, 15 S. Ct. 249, 39 L. Ed. 325 (1895)

Mr. Chief Justice Fuller delivered the opinion of the court.

By the purchase of the stock of the four Philadelphia refineries with shares of its own stock the American Sugar Refining Company acquired nearly complete control of the manufacture of refined sugar within the United States. The bill charged that the contracts under which these purchases were made constituted combinations in restraint of trade, and that in entering into them the defendants combined and conspired to restrain the trade and commerce in refined sugar among the several states and with foreign nations contrary to the [Sherman] Act of Congress of July 2, 1890.

The fundamental question is whether, conceding that the existence of a monopoly in manufacture is established by the evidence, that monopoly can be directly suppressed under the Act of Congress in the mode attempted by this bill.

It cannot be denied that the power of a state to protect the lives, health, and property of its citizens, and to preserve good order and the public morals, "the power to govern men and things within the limits of its dominion," is a power originally and always belonging to the states, not surrendered by them to the general government, nor directly restrained by the constitution of the United States, and essentially exclusive. The relief of the citizens of each state from the burden of monopoly and the evils resulting from the restraint of trade among such citizens was left with the states to deal with and this court has recognized their possession of that power even to the extent of holding that an employment or business carried on by private individuals, when it becomes a matter of such public interest and importance as to create a common charge or burden upon the citizen, — in other words, when it becomes a practical monopoly, to which the citizen is compelled to resort, and by means of which a tribute can be exacted from the community, — is subject to regulation by state legislative power. On the other hand, the power of Congress to regulate commerce among the several states is also exclusive. The constitution does not provide that interstate commerce shall be free but, by the grant of this exclusive power to regulate it, it was left free, except as Congress might impose restraints. Therefore it has been determined that the failure of Congress to exercise this exclusive power in any case is an expression of its will that the subject shall be free from restrictions or impositions upon it by the several states, and if a law passed by a state in the exercise of its acknowledged powers comes into conflict with that will, the Congress and the state cannot occupy the position of equal opposing sovereignties, because the constitution declares its supremacy, and that of the laws passed in pursuance thereof; and that which is not supreme must yield to that which is supreme. "Commerce undoubtedly is traffic," said Chief Justice Marshall, "but it is something more; it is intercourse. It describes the commercial intercourse between nations and parts of nations in all its branches, and is regulated by prescribing rules for carrying on that intercourse." That which belongs to commerce is within the jurisdiction of the United States, but that which does not belong to commerce is within the jurisdiction of the police power of the state.

The argument is that the power to control the manufacture of refined sugar is a monopoly over a necessary of life, to the enjoyment of which by a large part of the population of the United States interstate commerce is indispensable, and that, therefore, the general government, in the exercise of the power to regulate commerce, may repress such monopoly directly, and set aside the instruments which have created it. But this argument cannot be confined to necessaries of life merely, and must include all articles of general consumption. Doubtless the power to control the manufacture of a given thing involves in a certain sense, the control of its disposition, but this is a secondary, and not the primary, sense; and, although the exercise of that power may result in bringing the operation of commerce into play, it does not control it, and affects it only incidentally and indirectly. Commerce succeeds to manufacture, and is not a part of it. The power to regulate commerce is the power to prescribe the rule by which commerce shall be governed, and is a power independent of the power to suppress monopoly. But it may operate in repression of monopoly whenever that comes within the rules by which commerce is governed, or whenever the transaction is itself a monopoly of commerce.

It is vital that the independence of the commercial power and of the police power, and the delimitation between them, however sometimes perplexing, should always be recognized and observed, for, while the one furnishes the strongest bond of union, the other is essential to the preservation of the autonomy of the states as required by our dual form of government; and acknowledged evils, however grave and urgent they may appear to be, had better be borne, than the risk be run, in the effort to suppress them, of more serious consequences by resort to expedients of even doubtful constitutionality.

Contracts, combinations, or conspiracies to control domestic enterprise in manufacture, agriculture, mining, production in all its forms, or to raise or lower prices or wages, might unquestionably tend to restrain external as well as domestic trade, but the restraint would be an indirect result, however inevitable, and whatever its extent, and such result would not necessarily determine the object of the contract, combination, or conspiracy.

Again, all the authorities agree that, in order to vitiate a contract or combination, it is not essential that its result should be a complete monopoly; it is sufficient if it really tends to that end, and to deprive the public of the advantages which flow from free competition. Slight reflection will show that, if the national power extends to all contracts and combinations in manufacture, agriculture, mining, and other productive industries, whose ultimate result may affect external commerce, comparatively little of business operations and affairs would be left for state control.

It was in the light of well-settled principles that the Act of July 2, 1890, was framed. What the law struck at was combinations, contracts, and conspiracies to monopolize trade and commerce among the several states or with foreign nations;

but the contracts and acts of the defendants related exclusively to the acquisition of the Philadelphia refineries and the business of sugar refining in Pennsylvania, and bore no direct relation to commerce between the states or with foreign nations.

The circuit court declined to grant the relief prayed, and dismissed the bill.

Decree affirmed.

MR. JUSTICE HARLAN, dissenting.

The court holds it to be vital in our system of government to recognize and give effect to both the commercial power of the nation and the police powers of the states, to the end that the Union be strengthened, and the autonomy of the states preserved. In this view I entirely concur. Undoubtedly, the preservation of the just authority of the states is an object of deep concern to every lover of his country. No greater calamity could befall our free institutions than the destruction of the authority, by whatever means such a result might be accomplished. "Without the states in union," this court has said, "there could be no such political body as the United States." *Lane Co. v. Oregon*, 7 Wall. 71, 76 [1869]. But it is equally true that the preservation of the just authority of the general government is essential as well to the safety of the states as to the attainment of the important ends for which that government was ordained by the people of the United States; and the destruction of that authority would be fatal to the peace and well-being of the American people. The constitution, which enumerates the powers committed to the nation for objects of interest to the people of all the states, should not, therefore, be subjected to an interpretation so rigid, technical, and narrow that those objects cannot be accomplished.

Congress is invested with power to regulate commerce with foreign nations and among the several states. The power to regulate is the power to prescribe the rule by which the subject regulated is to be governed.

What is commerce among the states? The decisions of this court fully answer the question. "Commerce, undoubtedly, is traffic, but it is something more; it is intercourse." It does not embrace the completely interior traffic of the respective states, — that which is "carried on between man and man in a state, or between different parts of the same state, and which does not extend to or affect either states," — but it does embrace "every species of commercial intercourse" between the United States and foreign nations and among the states, and therefore it includes such traffic or trade, buying, selling, and interchange of commodities, as directly affects or necessarily involves the interests of the people of the United States. "Commerce, as the word is used in the constitution, is a unit," and "cannot stop at the external boundary line of each state, but may be introduced into the interior." "The genius and character of the whole government seem to be that its action is to be applied to all the external concerns of the nation, and to those internal concerns which affect the states generally."

In my judgment, the citizens of the several states composing the Union are entitled of right to buy goods in the state where they are manufactured, or in any other state, without being confronted by an illegal combination whose business extends throughout the whole country, which, by the law everywhere, is an enemy to the public interests, and which prevents such buying, except at prices arbitrarily fixed by it. I insist that the free course of trade among the states cannot coexist with such combinations. When I speak of trade I mean the buying and selling of articles of every kind that are recognized articles of interstate commerce. Whatever improperly obstructs the free course of interstate intercourse and trade, as involved in the buying and selling of articles to be carried from one state to another, may be reached by Congress under its authority to regulate commerce among the states. The exercise of that authority so as to make trade among the states in all recognized articles of commerce absolutely free from unreasonable or illegal restrictions imposed by combinations is justified by an express grant of power to Congress, and would rebound to the welfare of the whole country. I am unable to perceive that any such result would imperil the autonomy of the states, especially as that result cannot be attained through the action of any one state.

Undue restrictions or burdens upon the purchasing of goods in the market for sale, to be transported to other states, cannot be imposed, even by a state, without violating the freedom of commercial intercourse guaranteed by the constitution.

It may be that the means employed by Congress to suppress combinations that restrain interstate trade and commerce are not all or the best that could have been devised. But Congress, under the delegation of authority to enact laws necessary and proper to carry into effect a power granted, is not restricted to the employment of those means "without which the end would be entirely unattainable."

While the states retain, because they have never surrendered, full control of their completely internal traffic, it was not intended by the framers of the constitution that any part of interstate commerce should be excluded from the control of Congress. Each state can reach and suppress combinations so far as they unlawfully restrain its interior trade, while the national government may reach and suppress them so far as they unlawfully restrain trade among the states.

Notes and Questions

(1) The Court summarized its notion of dual sovereignty as follows:

That which belongs to commerce is within the jurisdiction of the United States, but that which does not belong to commerce is within the jurisdiction of the police power of the state.

Maintaining the independence of the commercial power and the police power, the Court observed, is essential to preservation of state autonomy. Why did the Court conclude that the power to suppress the manufacturing monopoly falls within the jurisdiction of the states, rather than Congress? Which of the federalism values were served by denying the Congress power to suppress the monopoly?

(2) The Court conceded that the monopoly "might unquestionably tend to restrain external as well as domestic trade," but concluded that such restraint would be an "indirect result" of the monopoly. Did the Court use "indirect" to mean "insubstantial" or, instead, "not proximate"?

(3) Was the Court's view of the Commerce Clause in *Knight* consistent with the approach taken in *Gibbons*?

(4) Despite the decision in *Knight*, the Court voted 5-4 to uphold the constitutionality of a federal statute that prohibited the carrying of lottery tickets across state lines, *Champion v. Ames (The Lottery Case)*, 188 U.S. 321 (1903). Speaking for the Court, Justice Harlan wrote:

> We are of opinion that lottery tickets are subjects of traffic, and therefore are subjects of commerce, and the regulation of the carriage of such tickets from state to state, at least by independent carriers, is a regulation of commerce among the several states.
>
> It is said, however, that if, in order to suppress lotteries carried on through interstate commerce, Congress may exclude lottery tickets from such commerce, that principle leads necessarily to the conclusion that Congress may arbitrarily exclude from commerce among the states any article, commodity, or thing of whatever kind or nature, or however useful or valuable, which it may choose, no matter with what motive, to declare shall not be carried from one state to another. It will be time enough to consider the constitutionality of such legislation when we must do so.

The Court also upheld the Interstate Commerce Commission's power to regulate *intrastate* railroad rates that have an effect on interstate commerce. In *Houston, E. & W.T.R. Co. v. United States (The Shreveport Rate Case)*, 234 U.S. 342, 351–353 (1914), the Court stated:

> Congress is empowered to regulate — that is, to provide the law for the government of interstate commerce; to enact "all appropriate legislation" for its "protection and advancement"; to adopt measures "to promote its growth and insure its safety"; "to foster, protect, control, and restrain." Its authority, extending to these interstate carriers as instruments of interstate commerce, necessarily embraces the right to control their operations in all matters having such a close and substantial relation to interstate traffic that the control is essential or appropriate to the security of that traffic, to the efficiency of the interstate service, and to the maintenance of conditions under which interstate commerce may be conducted upon fair terms and without molestation or hindrance. As it is competent for Congress to legislate to these ends, unquestionably it may seek their attainment by requiring that the agencies of interstate commerce shall not be used in such manner as to cripple, retard, or destroy it. The fact that carriers are instruments of intrastate commerce, as well as of interstate commerce, does not derogate from the complete and paramount authority of Congress over the latter, or preclude the Federal power from being exerted to prevent the intrastate operations of such carriers from being made a means of injury to that which has been confided to Federal care. Wherever the interstate and intrastate transactions of carriers are so related that the government of the one

involves the control of the other, it is Congress, and not the state, that is entitled to prescribe the final and dominant rule, for otherwise Congress would be denied the exercise of its constitutional authority, and the state, and not the nation, would be supreme within the national field.

Congress, in the exercise of its paramount power, may prevent the common instrumentalities of interstate and intrastate commercial intercourse from being used in their intrastate operations to the injury of interstate commerce. This is not to say that Congress possesses the authority to regulate the internal commerce of a state, as such, but that it does possess the power to foster and protect interstate commerce, and to take all measures necessary or appropriate to that end, although intrastate transactions of interstate carriers may thereby be controlled.

Are *The Lottery Case* and *Shreveport* distinguishable from *Knight*?

Hammer v. Dagenhart

United States Supreme Court
247 U.S. 251, 38 S. Ct. 529, 62 L. Ed. 1101 (1918)

MR. JUSTICE DAY delivered the opinion of the Court.

A bill was filed in the United States District Court for the Western District of North Carolina by a father in his own behalf and as next friend of his two minor sons, one under the age of fourteen years and the other between the ages of fourteen and sixteen years, employees in a cotton mill at Charlotte, North Carolina, to enjoin the enforcement of the act of Congress intended to prevent interstate commerce in the products of child labor.

The District Court held the act unconstitutional and entered a decree enjoining its enforcement. This appeal brings the case here.

The attack upon the act rests upon three propositions: First: It is not a regulation of interstate and foreign commerce; second: It contravenes the Tenth Amendment to the Constitution; third: It conflicts with the Fifth Amendment to the Constitution.

The controlling question for decision is: Is it within the authority of Congress in regulating commerce among the states to prohibit the transportation in interstate commerce of manufactured goods, the product of a factory in which, within thirty days prior to their removal therefrom, children under the age of fourteen have been employed or permitted to work, or children between the ages of fourteen and sixteen years have been employed or permitted to work more than eight hours in any day, or more than six days in any week, or after the hour of 7 o'clock p.m., or before the hour of 6 o'clock a.m.?

The power essential to the passage of this act, the government contends, is found in the commerce clause of the Constitution which authorizes Congress to regulate commerce with foreign nations and among the states.

In *Gibbons v. Ogden* Chief Justice Marshall, speaking for this court, and defining the extent and nature of the commerce power, said, "It is the power to regulate; that is, to prescribe the rule by which commerce is to be governed." In other words, the power is one to control the means by which commerce is carried on, which is directly the contrary of the assumed right to forbid commerce from moving and thus destroying it as to particular commodities. But it is insisted that adjudged cases in this court establish the doctrine that the power to regulate given to Congress incidentally includes the authority to prohibit the movement of ordinary commodities and therefore that the subject is not open for discussion. The cases demonstrate the contrary. They rest upon the character of the particular subjects dealt with and the fact that the scope of governmental authority, state or national, possessed over them is such that the authority to prohibit is as to them but the exertion of the power to regulate.

The first of these cases is *Champion v. Ames*, the so-called *Lottery Case*, in which it was held that Congress might pass a law having the effect to keep the channels of commerce free from use in the transportation of tickets used in the promotion of lottery schemes. In *Hipolite Egg Co. v. United States*, 220 U.S. 45 [1911], this court sustained the power of Congress to pass the Pure Food and Drug Act which prohibited the introduction into the states by means of interstate commerce of impure foods and drugs. In *Hoke v. United States*, 227 U.S. 308 [1913], this court sustained the constitutionality of the so-called "White Slave Traffic Act" whereby the transportation of a woman in interstate commerce for the purpose of prostitution was forbidden.

In each of these instances the use of interstate transportation was necessary to the accomplishment of harmful results. In other words, although the power over interstate transportation was to regulate, that could only be accomplished by prohibiting the use of the facilities of interstate commerce to effect the evil intended.

This element is wanting in the present case. The thing intended to be accomplished by this statute is the denial of the facilities of interstate commerce to those manufacturers in the states who employ children within the prohibited ages. The act in its effect does not regulate transportation among the states, but aims to standardize the ages at which children may be employed in mining and manufacturing within the states. The goods shipped are of themselves harmless. The act permits them to be freely shipped after thirty days from the time of their removal from the factory. When offered for shipment, and before transportation begins, the labor of their production is over, and the mere fact that they were intended for interstate commerce transportation does not make their production subject to federal control under the commerce power.

Over interstate transportation, or its incidents, the regulatory power of Congress is ample, but the production of articles, intended for interstate commerce, is a matter of local regulation. If it were otherwise, all manufacture intended for interstate shipment would be brought under federal control to the practical exclusion of the authority of the states, a result certainly not contemplated by the framers of the Constitution when they vested in Congress the authority to regulate commerce among the States.

It is further contended that the authority of Congress may be exerted to control interstate commerce in the shipment of child-made goods because of the effect of the circulation of such goods in other states where the evil of this class of labor has been recognized by local legislation, and the right to thus employ child labor has been more rigorously restrained than in the state of production. In other words, that the unfair competition, thus engendered, may be controlled by closing the channels of interstate commerce to manufacturers in those states where the local laws do not meet what Congress deems to be the more just standard of other states.

There is no power vested in Congress to require the states to exercise their police power so as to prevent possible unfair competition. Many causes may co-operate to give one state, by reason of local laws or conditions, an economic advantage over others. The commerce clause was not intended to give to Congress a general authority to equalize such conditions. In some of the states laws have been passed fixing minimum wages for women, in others the local law regulates the hours of labor of women in various employments. Business done in such states may be at an economic disadvantage when compared with states which have no such regulations; surely, this fact does not give Congress the power to deny transportation in interstate commerce to those who carry on business where the hours of labor and the rate of compensation for women have not been fixed by a standard in use in other states and approved by Congress.

The grant of power to Congress over the subject of interstate commerce was to enable it to regulate such commerce, and not to give it authority to control the states in their exercise of the police power over local trade and manufacture.

The grant of authority over a purely federal matter was not intended to destroy the local power always existing and carefully reserved to the states in the Tenth Amendment to the Constitution.

Police regulations relating to the internal trade and affairs of the states have been uniformly recognized as within such control.

That there should be limitations upon the right to employ children in mines and factories in the interest of their own and the public welfare, all will admit. That such employment is generally deemed to require regulation is shown by the fact that the brief of counsel states that every state in the Union has a law upon the subject, limiting the right to thus employ children. In North Carolina, the state wherein is located the factory in which the employment was had in the present case, no child under twelve years of age is permitted to work.

It may be desirable that such laws be uniform, but our federal government is one of enumerated powers; "this principle," declared Chief Justice Marshall in *McCulloch v. Maryland*, "is universally admitted."

The maintenance of the authority of the states over matters purely local is as essential to the preservation of our institutions as is the conservation of the supremacy of the federal power in all matters entrusted to the nation by the federal Constitution.

In interpreting the Constitution it must never be forgotten that the nation is made up of states to which are entrusted the powers of local government. And to them and to the people the powers not expressly delegated to the national government are reserved. The power of the states to regulate their purely internal affairs by such laws as seem wise to the local authority is inherent and has never been surrendered to the general government. To sustain this statute, would not be in our judgment a recognition of the lawful exertion of congressional authority over interstate commerce, but would sanction an invasion by the federal power of the control of a matter purely local in its character, and over which no authority has been delegated to Congress in conferring the power to regulate commerce among the states.

We have neither authority nor disposition to question the motives of Congress in enacting this legislation. The purposes intended must be attained consistently with constitutional limitations and not by an invasion of the powers of the states. This court has no more important function than that which devolves upon it the obligation to preserve inviolate the constitutional limitations upon the exercise of authority federal and state to the end that each may continue to discharge, harmoniously with the other, the duties entrusted to it by the Constitution.

In our view the necessary effect of this act is, by means of a prohibition against the movement in interstate commerce of ordinary commercial commodities, to regulate the hours of labor of children in factories and mines within the states, a purely state authority. Thus the act in a two-fold sense is repugnant to the Constitution. It not only transcends the authority delegated to Congress over commerce but also exerts a power as to a purely local matter to which the federal authority does not extend. The far reaching result of upholding the act cannot be more plainly indicated than by pointing out that if Congress can thus regulate matters entrusted to local authority by prohibition of the movement of commodities in interstate commerce, all freedom of commerce will be at an end, and the power of the states over local matters may be eliminated, and thus our system of government be practically destroyed.

For these reasons we hold that this law exceeds the constitutional authority of Congress. It follows that the decree of the District Court must be

Affirmed.

MR. JUSTICE HOLMES, dissenting.

The first step in my argument is to make plain what no one is likely to dispute — that the statute in question is within the power expressly given to Congress if considered only as to its immediate effects and that if invalid it is so only upon some collateral ground. The statute confines itself to prohibiting the carriage of certain goods in interstate or foreign commerce. Congress is given power to regulate such commerce in unqualified terms. It would not be argued today that the power to regulate does not include the power to prohibit. At all events it is established by the

Lottery Case and others that have followed it that a law is not beyond the regulative power of Congress merely because it prohibits certain transportation out and out.

The question then is narrowed to whether the exercise of its otherwise constitutional power by Congress can be pronounced unconstitutional because of its possible reaction upon the conduct of the State in a matter upon which I have admitted that they are free from direct control. I should have thought that that matter had been disposed of so fully as to leave no room for doubt. I should have thought that the most conspicuous decisions of this Court had made it clear that the power to regulate commerce and other constitutional powers could not be cut down or qualified by the fact that it might interfere with the carrying out of the domestic policy of any State.

The Act does not meddle with anything belonging to the States. They may regulate their internal affairs and their domestic commerce as they like. But when they seek to send their products across the State line they are no longer within their rights. If there were no Constitution and no Congress their power to cross the line would depend upon their neighbors. Under the Constitution such commerce belongs not to the States but to Congress to regulate. It may carry out its views of public policy whatever indirect effect they may have upon the activities of the States. Instead of being encountered by a prohibitive tariff at her boundaries the State encounters the public policy of the United States which it is for Congress to express. The public policy of the United States is shaped with a view to the benefit of the nation as a whole. If, as has been the case within the memory of men still living, a State should take a different view of the propriety of sustaining a lottery from that which generally prevails, I cannot believe that the fact would require a different decision from that reached in *Champion v. Ames.* Yet in that case it would be said with quite as much force as in this that Congress was attempting to intermeddle with the State's domestic affairs. The national welfare as understood by Congress may require a different attitude within its sphere from that of some self-seeking State. It seems to me entirely constitutional for Congress to enforce its understanding by all the means at its command.

MR. JUSTICE MCKENNA, MR. JUSTICE BRANDEIS, and MR. JUSTICE CLARKE concur in this opinion.

Notes and Questions

(1) How did the Court in *Hammer* attempt to distinguish *The Lottery Case, Hipolite Egg*, and *Hoke*? Are you persuaded? Are these latter cases consistent with *Knight*?

(2) Do you agree with the statement in *Hammer* (and previously in *Knight*) that the maintenance of state authority over matters purely local is essential to the preservation of our institutions? Which federalism values are served by the maintenance of such authority?

(3) Did the child labor laws regulate purely local matters? Assuming they did, could an argument be constructed on the basis of the *Shreveport Rate Case* that Congress had authority to enact such laws?

(4) Why do you suppose the Court did not rely on *Knight* to reach the result in *Hammer*? Is *Hammer* about the limitations on Congress's enumerated powers derived from the Tenth Amendment, or does it instead concern an instance where Congress exceeded its enumerated powers?

Problem B

Review Problem A, § 4.02, *supra*. A member of Congress has asked you whether Congress has power under the Commerce Clause to raise to 21 the minimum age for gun sales nationwide. Is this a "regulation" of "commerce"? Would such a law intrude on the power of states to regulate local matters and, thus, violate the Tenth Amendment?

B. The New Deal and Beyond

A.L.A. Schechter Poultry Corporation v. United States

United States Supreme Court
295 U.S. 495, 55 S. Ct. 837, 79 L. Ed. 1570 (1935)

MR. CHIEF JUSTICE HUGHES delivered the opinion of the Court.

Petitioners were convicted on eighteen counts of an indictment charging violations of what is known as the "Live Poultry Code," and on an additional count for conspiracy to commit such violations. By demurrer to the indictment and appropriate motions on the trial, the defendants contended that it [the Code] attempted to regulate intrastate transactions which lay outside the authority of Congress.

A.L.A. Schechter Poultry Corporation and Schechter Live Poultry Market are corporations conducting wholesale poultry slaughterhouse markets in Brooklyn, New York City. Defendants ordinarily purchase their live poultry from commission men at the West Washington Market in New York City or at the railroad terminals serving the city, but occasionally they purchase from commission men in Philadelphia. They buy the poultry for slaughter and resale. After the poultry is trucked to their slaughterhouse markets in Brooklyn, it is there sold, usually within twenty-four hours, to retail poultry dealers and butchers who sell directly to consumers. Defendants do not sell poultry in interstate commerce.

The "Live Poultry Code" was promulgated under section 3 of the National Industrial Recovery Act. That section authorizes the President to approve "codes of fair competition."

The "Live Poultry Code" was approved by the President on April 13, 1934.

The code fixes the number of hours for work days. It provides that no employee, with certain exceptions, shall be permitted to work in excess of forty hours in any one week, and that no employee, save as stated, "shall be paid in any pay period less than at the rate of fifty (50) cents per hour." The article containing "general labor provisions" prohibits the employment of any person under 16 years of age, and declares that employees shall have the right of "collective bargaining" and freedom of choice with respect to labor organizations, in the terms, of section 7 (a) of the act (15 USCA § 707 (a)). The minimum number of employees, who shall be employed by slaughterhouse operators, is fixed; the number being graduated according to the average volume of weekly sales.

The seventh article, containing "trade practice provisions," prohibits various practices which are said to constitute "unfair methods of competition."

The President approved the code by an executive order (No. 6675-A) in which he found that the application for his approval had been duly made in accordance with the provisions of title 1 of the National Industrial Recovery Act.

First. Two preliminary points are stressed by the government with respect to the appropriate approach to the important questions presented. We are told that the provision of the statute authorizing the adoption of codes must be viewed in the light of the grave national crisis with which Congress was confronted. Undoubtedly, the conditions to which power is addressed are always to be considered when the exercise of power is challenged. Extraordinary conditions may call for extraordinary remedies. But the argument necessarily stops short of an attempt to justify action which lies outside the sphere of constitutional authority. Extraordinary conditions do not create or enlarge constitutional power. The Constitution established a national government with powers deemed to be adequate, as they have proved to be both in war and peace, but these powers of the national government are limited by the constitutional grants. Those who act under these grants are not at liberty to transcend the imposed limits because they believe that more or different power is necessary. Such assertions of extraconstitutional authority were anticipated and precluded by the explicit terms of the Tenth Amendment — "The powers not delegated to the United States by the Constitution, nor prohibited by it to the States, are reserved to the States respectively, or to the people."

The further point is urged that the national crisis demanded a broad and intensive co-operative effort by those engaged in trade and industry, and that this necessary co-operation was sought to be fostered by permitting them to initiate the adoption of codes. But the statutory plan is not simply one for voluntary effort. It does not seek merely to endow voluntary trade or industrial associations or groups with privileges or immunities. It involves the coercive exercise of the lawmaking power. The codes of fair competition which the statute attempts to authorize are codes of laws. If valid, they place all persons within their reach under the obligation of positive law, binding equally those who assent and those who do not assent. Violations of the provisions of the codes are punishable as crimes.

The Question of the Application of the Provisions of the Live Poultry Code to Intra-state Transactions. — Although the validity of the codes rests upon the commerce clause of the Constitution, section 3(a) of the act is not in terms limited to interstate and foreign commerce. From the generality of its terms, and from the argument of the government at the bar, it would appear that section 3(a) was designed to authorize codes without the limitation. But under section 3(f) of the act penalties are confined to violations of a code provision "in any transaction in or affecting interstate or foreign commerce." This aspect of the case presents the question whether the particular provisions of the Live Poultry Code, which the defendants were convicted for violating and for having conspired to violate, were within the regulating power of congress.

These provisions relate to the hours and wages of those employed by defendants in their slaughterhouses in Brooklyn and to the sales there made to retail dealers and butchers.

(1) Were these transactions "*in*" interstate commerce? Much is made of the fact that almost all the poultry coming to New York is sent there from other states. But the code provisions, as here applied, do not concern the transportation of the poultry from other states to New York, or the transactions of the commission men or others to whom it is consigned, or the sales made by such consignees to defendants. When defendants had made their purchases, whether at the West Washington Market in New York City or at the railroad terminals serving the city, or elsewhere, the poultry was trucked to their slaughterhouses in Brooklyn for local disposition. The interstate transactions in relation to that poultry then ended. Defendants held the poultry at their slaughterhouse markets for slaughter and local sale to retail dealers and butchers who in turn sold directly to consumers. Neither the slaughtering nor the sales by defendants were transactions in interstate commerce.

(2) Did the defendants' transactions directly "*affect*" interstate commerce so as to be subject to federal regulation? The power of Congress extends, not only to the regulation of transactions which are part of interstate commerce, but to the protection of that commerce from injury. It matters not that the injury may be due to the conduct of those engaged in intrastate operations. [I]t is the "effect upon interstate commerce, not the source of the injury," which is "the criterion of congressional power."

In determining how far the federal government may go in controlling intrastate transactions upon the ground that they "affect" interstate commerce, there is a necessary and well-established distinction between direct and indirect effects. Where the effect of intrastate transactions upon interstate commerce is merely indirect, such transactions remain within the domain of state power. If the commerce clause were construed to reach all enterprises and transactions which could be said to have an indirect effect upon interstate commerce, the federal authority would embrace practically all the activities of the people, and the authority of the state over its domestic concerns would exist only by sufferance of the federal government.

The question of chief importance relates to the provisions of the code as to the hours and wages of those employed in defendants' slaughterhouse markets. It is plain that these requirements are imposed in order to govern the details of defendants' management of their local business. The persons employed in slaughtering and selling in local trade are not employed in interstate commerce. Their hours and wages have no direct relation to interstate commerce. The question of how many hours these employees should work and what they should be paid differs in no essential respect from similar questions in other local businesses which handle commodities brought into a state and there dealt in as a part of its internal commerce. This appears from an examination of the considerations urged by the government with respect to conditions in the poultry trade. Thus, the government argues that hours and wages affect prices; that slaughterhouse men sell at a small margin above operating costs; that labor represents 50 to 60 per cent of these costs; that a slaughterhouse operator paying lower wages or reducing his cost by exacting long hours of work translates his saving into lower prices; that this results in demands for a cheaper grade of goods; and that the cutting of prices brings about a demoralization of the price structure. The argument of the government proves too much. If the federal government may determine the wages and hours of employees in the internal commerce of a state, because of their relation to cost and prices and their indirect effect upon interstate commerce, it would seem that a similar control might be exerted over other elements of cost, also affecting prices, such as the number of employees, rents, advertising, methods of doing business, etc. All the processes of production and distribution that enter into cost could likewise be controlled. If the cost of doing an intrastate business is in itself the permitted object of federal control, the extent of the regulation of cost would be a question of discretion and not of power.

The government also makes the point that efforts to enact state legislation establishing high labor standards have been impeded by the belief that, unless similar action is taken generally, commerce will be diverted from the states adopting such standards, and that this fear of diversion has led to demands for federal legislation on the subject of wages and hours. The apparent implication is that the federal authority under the commerce clause should be deemed to extend to the establishment of rules to govern wages and hours in intrastate trade and industry generally throughout the country, thus overriding the authority of the states to deal with domestic problems arising from labor conditions in their internal commerce.

It is not the province of the Court to consider the economic advantages or disadvantages of such a centralized system. It is sufficient to say that the Federal Constitution does not provide for it. Our growth and development have called for wide use of the commerce power of the federal government in its control over the expanded activities of interstate commerce and in protecting that commerce from burdens, interferences, and conspiracies to restrain and monopolize it. But the authority of the federal government may not be pushed to such an extreme as to destroy the distinction, which the commerce clause itself establishes, between commerce "among the several States" and the internal concerns of a state. The same answer must be made to the contention that is based upon the serious economic situation which led to the passage of the Recovery Act—the fall in prices, the decline in wages and employment, and the curtailment of the market for commodities. Stress is laid upon the great importance of maintaining wage distributions which would provide the necessary stimulus in starting "the cumulative forces making for expanding commercial activity." Without in any way disparaging this motive, it is enough to say that the recuperative efforts of the federal government must be made in a manner consistent with the authority granted by the Constitution.

We are of the opinion that the attempt through the provisions of the code to fix the hours and wages of employees of defendants in their intrastate business was not a valid exercise of federal power.

The other violations for which defendants were convicted related to the making of local sales. Ten counts, for violation of the provision as to "straight killing," were for permitting customers to make "selections of individual chickens taken from particular coops and half coops." Whether or not this practice is good or bad for the local trade, its effect, if any, upon interstate commerce was only indirect. The same may be said of violations of the code by intrastate transactions consisting of the sale "of an unfit chicken" and of sales which were not in accord with the ordinances of the City of New York. The requirement of reports as to prices and volumes of defendants' sales was incident to the effort to control their intrastate business.

We hold the code provisions here in question to be invalid and that the judgment of conviction must be reversed.

Mr. Justice Cardozo (concurring). [Omitted.]

Notes and Questions

(1) The Court stated that the power of Congress under the Commerce Clause extends to transactions which are part of interstate commerce as well as to intrastate activities that affect interstate commerce. According to the government, how did the hours and wages of those employed in Joseph Schechter's poultry market affect interstate commerce? How did the Court respond?

(2) The decision in *Schechter* seriously threatened President Franklin D. Roosevelt's New Deal program and his Administration's attempts to fight the Great Depression. Four days after the decision was rendered, President Roosevelt summoned reporters to the White House for a news conference.

> For the next hour and a half, while reporters listened intently, Roosevelt, in an unusually somber mood, discoursed on the implications of the Court's opinion. Thumbing the copy of the *Schechter* decision as he spoke, the President argued that the Court's ruling had stripped the national government of its power to cope with critical national problems. "We are facing a very, very great national non-partisan issue," he said. "We have got to decide one way or the other whether in some way we are going to restore to the Federal Government the powers which exist in the national Governments of every other Nation in the world." Of all the words the President spoke at the extraordinary conference, newspapermen singled out one sentence which headline writers emblazoned on late afternoon newspapers: "We have been relegated to the horse-and-buggy definition of interstate commerce."

William Edward Leuchtenburg, *The Origins of Franklin D. Roosevelt's "Court-Packing" Plan*, 1966 SUP. CT. REV. 347, 357.

The Supreme Court continued to frustrate Roosevelt's efforts. On January 6, 1936, the Court rendered its decision in *United States v. Butler*, 297 U.S. 1 (1936), striking down another major New Deal program, the Agricultural Adjustment Act processing tax that was intended to establish a balance between production and consumption of agricultural commodities.

(3) In May, 1936, the Court relied on *Schechter* and invalidated New Deal legislation directed at the coal industry. In *Carter v. Carter Coal Co.*, 298 U.S. 238 (1936), the Court shattered any hope that the holding of *Schechter* might be limited to industries that were local in scope. In so doing, the Court explained that congressional power under the "affecting commerce" theory applies only to activities that have a direct impact on interstate commerce. Justice Sutherland wrote for the majority:

> Whether the effect of a given activity or condition is direct or indirect is not always easy to determine. The word "direct" implies that the activity or condition invoked or blamed shall operate proximately — not mediately, remotely, or collaterally — to produce the effect. It connotes the absence of an efficient intervening agency or condition. And the extent of the effect bears no logical relation to its character. The distinction between a direct and an indirect effect turns, not upon the magnitude of either the cause or the effect, but entirely upon the manner in which the effect has been brought about. If the production by one man of a single ton of coal intended for interstate sale and shipment, and actually so sold and shipped, affects interstate commerce indirectly, the effect does not become direct by multiplying the tonnage, or increasing the number of men employed, or adding to the expense or complexities of the business, or by all combined. It is quite true that rules of law are sometimes qualified by considerations of degree, as the government argues. But the matter of degree has no bearing upon the question here, since that question is not — What is the extent of the local activity or condition, or the extent of the effect produced upon interstate commerce? but — What is the relation between the activity or condition and the effect?

Id. at 307–308.

(4) Soon after the 1936 election, Roosevelt responded to the *Schechter* and *Carter Coal* decisions and to the constitutional vulnerability of the newly enacted National Labor Relations Act by proposing his famous "Court-packing" bill. Under this plan, when any federal judge failed to retire within six months after reaching the age of 70, the President could appoint, with the advice and consent of the Senate, an additional judge. The Supreme Court would be limited to a maximum of 15 Justices. The plan would have allowed the President to pack the Supreme Court, which in 1937 had six justices over the age of 70. Roosevelt could thus have turned the losses in *Schechter* and *Carter Coal* into victories.

Consider the legitimacy of Roosevelt's plan. Did it threaten the independence of the federal judiciary? Or, was it a legitimate (and constitutionally permissible) attempt to respond to a Court that was frustrating the will of the majority?

While opposition to Roosevelt's plan was mounting in the Congress, actions by the Supreme Court did more to thwart the plan. Although the plan was effectively defeated in Congress in June of 1937 when the Senate Judiciary Committee reported it with an unfavorable recommendation, the Court-packing plan may have had its intended effect. On April 12, 1937, the Justices who decided *Schechter* and *Carter* decided *National Labor Relations Board v. Jones & Laughlin Steel Corp.*, 301 U.S. 1 (1937), upholding the National Labor Relations Act against the Commerce Clause challenge of a large, national steel company. In an opinion by Chief Justice Hughes, the Court accepted the essence of the government's argument in favor of the constitutionality of the New Deal legislation:

> The congressional authority to protect interstate commerce from burdens and obstructions is not limited to transactions which can be deemed to be an essential part of a "flow" of interstate or foreign commerce. Although activities may be intrastate in character when separately considered, if they have such a close and substantial relation to interstate commerce that their control is essential or appropriate to protect that commerce from burdens and obstructions, Congress cannot be denied the power to exercise that control. Undoubtedly the scope of this power must be considered in the light of dual system of government and may not be extended so as to embrace effects upon interstate commerce so indirect and remote that to embrace them, in view of our complex society, would effectually obliterate the distinction between what is national and what is local and create a completely centralized government.
>
> The close and intimate effect which brings the subject within the reach of federal power may be due to activities in relation to productive industry although the industry when separately viewed is local.
>
> It is thus apparent that the fact that the employees here concerned were engaged in production is not determinative. The question remains as to the effect upon interstate commerce of the labor practice involved.
>
> Giving full weight to respondent's contention with respect to a break in the complete continuity of the "stream of commerce" by reason of respondent's manufacturing operations, the fact remains that the stoppage of those operations by industrial strife would have a most serious effect upon interstate commerce. In view of respondent's far-flung activities, it is idle to say that the effect would be indirect or remote. It is obvious that it would be immediate and might be catastrophic. We are asked to shut our eyes to the plainest facts of our national life and to deal with the question of direct and indirect effects in an intellectual vacuum. Because there may be but indirect and remote effects upon interstate commerce in connection with

a host of local enterprises throughout the country, it does not follow that other industrial activities do not have such a close and intimate relation to interstate commerce as to make the presence of industrial strife a matter of the most urgent national concern. When industries organize themselves on a national scale, making their relation to interstate commerce the dominant factor in their activities, how can it be maintained that their industrial labor relations constitute a forbidden field into which Congress may not enter when it is necessary to protect interstate commerce from the paralyzing consequences of industrial war? We have often said that interstate commerce itself is a practical conception. It is equally true that interferences with that commerce must be appraised by a judgment that does not ignore actual experience.

(5) A New Deal Court emerged after *Jones & Laughlin*. In 1937, Justice Van Devanter retired and was replaced by Justice Black. In 1938–1939, four more supporters of the New Deal were appointed to the Court: Justice Sutherland was replaced by Solicitor General Stanley Reed, Justice Cardozo by Professor Felix Frankfurter, Justice Brandeis by Securities and Exchange Commission Chair William O. Douglas, and Justice Butler by Attorney General Frank Murphy. These changes are further reflected in the next case.

United States v. Darby

United States Supreme Court
312 U.S. 100, 61 S. Ct. 451, 85 L. Ed. 609 (1941)

Mr. Justice Stone delivered the opinion of the Court.

The two principal questions raised by the record in this case are, first, whether Congress has constitutional power to prohibit the shipment in interstate commerce of lumber manufactured by employees whose wages are less than a prescribed minimum or whose weekly hours of labor at that wage are greater than a prescribed maximum, and, second, whether it has power to prohibit the employment of workmen in the production of goods "for interstate commerce" at other than prescribed wages and hours.

Appellee demurred to an indictment found in the district court for southern Georgia charging him with violation of § 15(a)(1), (2) and (3) of the Fair Labor Standards Act of 1938. The district court sustained the demurrer and quashed the indictment.

The indictment charges that appellee is engaged, in the state of Georgia, in the business of acquiring raw materials, which he manufactures into finished lumber with the intent, when manufactured, to ship it in interstate commerce to customers outside the state, and that he does in fact so ship a large part of the lumber so produced. There are numerous counts charging appellee with the shipment in interstate commerce from Georgia to points outside the State of lumber in the production of which, for interstate commerce, appellee has employed workmen at less than the prescribed minimum wage or more than the prescribed maximum hours without payment to them of any wage for overtime. Other counts charge the employment by appellee of workmen in the production of lumber for interstate commerce at wages of less than 25 cents an hour or for more than the maximum hours per week without payment to them of the prescribed overtime wage.

The prohibition of shipment of the proscribed goods in interstate commerce. Section 15(a)(1) prohibits, and the indictment charges, the shipment in interstate commerce, of goods produced for interstate commerce by employees whose wages and hours of employment do not conform to the requirements of the Act. Since this section is not violated unless the commodity shipped has been produced under labor conditions prohibited by § 6 and § 7, the only question arising under the Commerce Clause with respect to such shipments is whether Congress has the constitutional power to prohibit them.

While manufacture is not of itself interstate commerce, the shipment of manufactured goods interstate is such commerce and the prohibition of such shipment by Congress is indubitably a regulation of the commerce. The power to regulate commerce is the power "to prescribe the rule by which commerce is to be governed." *Gibbons v. Ogden.* It extends not only to those regulations which aid, foster and protect the commerce, but embraces those which prohibit it.

[I]t is said that while the prohibition is nominally a regulation of the commerce its motive or purpose is regulation of wages and hours of persons engaged in manufacture, the control of which has been reserved to the states and upon which Georgia and some of the states of destination have placed no restriction; that under the guise of a regulation of interstate commerce, it undertakes to regulate wages and hours within the state contrary to the policy of the state which has elected to leave them unregulated.

The power of Congress over interstate commerce "is complete in itself, may be exercised to its utmost extent, and acknowledges no limitations, other than as are prescribed by the constitution." *Gibbons v. Ogden.* Congress, following its own conception of public policy concerning the restrictions which may appropriately be imposed on interstate commerce, is free to exclude from the commerce articles whose use in the states for which they are destined it may conceive to be injurious to the public health, morals or welfare, even though the state has not sought to regulate their use.

Such regulation is not a forbidden invasion of state power merely because either its motive or its consequence is to restrict the use of articles of commerce within the states of destination and is not prohibited unless by other Constitutional provisions. It is no objection to the assertion of the power to regulate interstate commerce that its exercise is attended by the same incidents which attend the exercise of the police power of the states.

The motive and purpose of the present regulation is plainly to make effective the Congressional conception of public policy that interstate commerce should not be made the instrument of competition in the distribution of goods produced under substandard labor conditions, which competition is injurious to the commerce and to the states from and to which the commerce flows. The motive and purpose of a regulation of interstate commerce are matters for the legislative judgment upon the exercise of which the Constitution places no restriction and over which the courts are given no control.

In the more than a century which has elapsed since the decision of *Gibbons v. Ogden*, these principles of constitutional interpretation have been so long and repeatedly recognized by this Court as applicable to the Commerce Clause, that there would be little occasion for repeating them now were it not for the decision of this Court twenty-two years ago in *Hammer v. Dagenhart*.

Hammer v. Dagenhart has not been followed. The distinction on which the decision was rested that Congressional power to prohibit interstate commerce is limited to articles which in themselves have some harmful or deleterious property — a distinction which was novel when made and unsupported by a provision of the Constitution — has long since been abandoned. . . . The thesis of the opinion that the motive of the prohibition or its effect to control in some measure the use or production within the states of the article thus excluded from the commerce can operate to deprive the regulation of its constitutional authority has long since ceased to have force.

The conclusion is inescapable that *Hammer v. Dagenhart* was a departure from the principles which have prevailed in the interpretation of the Commerce Clause both before and since the decision and that such vitality, as a precedent, as it then had has long since been exhausted. It should be and now is overruled.

Validity of the wage and hour requirements. Section 15(a)(2) and §§ 6 and 7 require employers to conform to the wage and hour provisions with respect to all employees engaged in the production of goods for interstate commerce. As appellee's employees are not alleged to be "engaged in interstate commerce" the validity of the prohibition turns on the question whether the employment, under other than the prescribed labor standards, of employees engaged in the production of goods for interstate commerce is so related to the commerce and so affects it as to be within the reach of the power of Congress to regulate it.

There remains the question whether such restriction on the production of goods for commerce is a permissible exercise of the commerce power. The power of Congress over interstate commerce is not confined to the regulation of commerce among the states. It extends to those activities intrastate which so affect interstate commerce or the exercise of the power of Congress over it as to make regulation of them appropriate means to the attainment of a legitimate end, the exercise of the granted power of Congress to regulate interstate commerce.

Congress, having by the present Act adopted the policy of excluding from interstate commerce all goods produced for the commerce which do not conform to the specified labor standards, it may choose the means reasonably adapted to the

attainment of the permitted end, even though they involve control of intrastate activities.

We think also that §15(a)(2), now under consideration, is sustainable independently of §15(a)(1), which prohibits shipment or transportation of the proscribed goods. As we have said the evils aimed at by the Act are the spread of substandard labor conditions through the use of the facilities of interstate commerce for competition by the goods so produced with those produced under the prescribed or better labor conditions; and the consequent dislocation of the commerce itself caused by the impairment or destruction of local business by competition made effective through interstate commerce. The Act is thus directed at the suppression of a method or kind of competition in interstate commerce which it has in effect condemned as "unfair."

The means adopted by §15(a)(2) for the protection of interstate commerce by the suppression of the production of the condemned goods for interstate commerce is so related to the commerce and so affects it as to be within the reach of the commerce power. Congress, to attain its objective in the suppression of nationwide competition in interstate commerce by goods produced under substandard labor conditions, has made no distinction as to the volume or amount of shipments in the commerce or of production for commerce by any particular shipper or producer. It recognized that in present day industry, competition by a small part may affect the whole and that the total effect of the competition of many small producers may be great.

Our conclusion is unaffected by the Tenth Amendment which provides: "The powers not delegated to the United States by the Constitution, nor prohibited by it to the States, are reserved to the States respectively, or to the people." The amendment states but a truism that all is retained which has not been surrendered. There is nothing in the history of its adoption to suggest that it was more than declaratory of the relationship between the national and state governments as it had been established by the Constitution before the amendment or that its purpose was other than to allay fears that the new national government might seek to exercise powers not granted, and that the states might not be able to exercise fully their reserved powers.

From the beginning and for many years the Amendment has been construed as not depriving the national government of authority to resort to all means for the exercise of a granted power which are appropriate and plainly adapted to the permitted end.

Reversed.

Katzenbach v. McClung

United States Supreme Court
379 U.S. 294, 85 S. Ct. 377, 13 L. Ed. 2d 290 (1964)

MR. JUSTICE CLARK delivered the opinion of the Court.

This case was argued with No. 515, *Heart of Atlanta Motel v. United States*, decided this date, 379 U.S. 241, in which we upheld the constitutional validity of Title II of the Civil Rights Act of 1964 against an attack by hotels, motels, and like establishments. This complaint for injunctive relief against appellants attacks the constitutionality of the Act as applied to a restaurant. The case was heard by a three-judge United States District Court and an injunction was issued restraining appellants from enforcing the Act against the restaurant. We now reverse the judgment.

Ollie's Barbecue is a family-owned restaurant in Birmingham, Alabama, specializing in barbecued meats and homemade pies, with a seating capacity of 220 customers. It is located on a state highway 11 blocks from an interstate one and a somewhat greater distance from railroad and bus stations. The restaurant caters to a family and white-collar trade with a take-out service for Negroes. It employs 36 persons, two-thirds of whom are Negroes.

In the 12 months preceding the passage of the Act, the restaurant purchased locally approximately $150,000 worth of food, $69,683 or 46% of which was meat that it bought from a local supplier who had procured it from outside the State. The District Court expressly found that a substantial portion of the food served in the restaurant had moved in interstate commerce. The restaurant has refused to serve Negroes in its dining accommodations since its original opening in 1927, and since July 2, 1964, it has been operating in violation of the Act. The court below concluded that if it were required to serve Negroes it would lose a substantial amount of business.

Section 201(a) of Title II commands that all persons shall be entitled to the full and equal enjoyment of the goods and services of any place of public accommodation without discrimination or segregation on the ground of race, color, religion, or national origin; and 201(b) defines establishments as places of public accommodation if their operations affect commerce or segregation by them is supported by state action. Sections 201(b)(2) and (c) place any "restaurant principally engaged in selling food for consumption on the premises" under the Act "if it serves or offers to serve interstate travelers or a substantial portion of the food which it serves has moved in commerce."

Ollie's Barbecue admits that it is covered by these provisions of the Act. There is no claim that interstate travelers frequented the restaurant. The sole question, therefore, narrows down to whether Title II, as applied to a restaurant annually receiving about $70,000 worth of food which has moved in commerce, is a valid exercise of the power of Congress. The Government has contended that Congress had ample basis upon which to find that racial discrimination at restaurants which receive from out of state a substantial portion of the food served does, in fact, impose commercial burdens of national magnitude upon interstate commerce. The appellees' major argument is directed to this premise. They urge that no such basis existed. It is to that question that we now turn.

As we noted in *Heart of Atlanta Motel*, both Houses of Congress conducted prolonged hearings on the Act. And, as we said there, while no formal findings were made, which of course are not necessary, it is well that we make mention of the testimony at these hearings the better to understand the problem before Congress and determine whether the Act is a reasonable and appropriate means toward its solution. The record is replete with testimony of the burdens placed on interstate commerce by racial discrimination in restaurants. A comparison of per capita spending by Negroes in restaurants, theaters, and like establishments indicated less spending, after discounting income differences, in areas where discrimination is widely practiced. This condition, which was especially aggravated in the South, was attributed in the testimony of the Under Secretary of Commerce to racial segregation. This diminutive spending springing from a refusal to serve Negroes and their total loss as customers has, regardless of the absence of direct evidence, a close connection to interstate commerce. The fewer customers a restaurant enjoys the less food it sells and consequently the less it buys. In addition, the Attorney General testified that this type of discrimination imposed "an artificial restriction on the market" and interfered with the flow of merchandise. In addition, there were many references to discriminatory situations causing wide unrest and having a depressant effect on general business conditions in the respective communities.

Moreover there was an impressive array of testimony that discrimination in restaurants had a direct and highly restrictive effect upon interstate travel by Negroes. This resulted, it was said, because discriminatory practices prevent Negroes from buying prepared food served on the premises while on a trip, except in isolated and unkempt restaurants and under most unsatisfactory and often unpleasant conditions. This obviously discourages travel and obstructs interstate commerce for one can hardly travel without eating. Likewise, it was said, that discrimination deterred professional, as well as skilled, people from moving into areas where such practices occurred and thereby caused industry to be reluctant to establish there.

We believe that this testimony afforded ample basis for the conclusion that established restaurants in such areas sold less interstate goods because of the discrimination, that interstate travel was obstructed directly by it, that business in general suffered and that many new businesses refrained from establishing there as a result of it. Hence the District Court was in error in concluding that there was no connection between discrimination and the movement of interstate commerce. The court's conclusion that such a connection is outside "common experience" flies in the face of stubborn fact.

It goes without saying that, viewed in isolation, the volume of food purchased by Ollie's Barbecue from sources supplied from out of state was insignificant when compared with the total foodstuffs moving in commerce. But, as our late Brother Jackson said for the Court in *Wickard v. Filburn*, 317 U.S. 111 (1942):

> That appellee's own contribution to the demand for wheat may be trivial by itself is not enough to remove him from the scope of federal regulation where, as here, his contribution, taken together with that of many others similarly situated, is far from trivial.

Article I, § 8, cl. 3, confers upon Congress the power "[t]o regulate Commerce among the several States" and Clause 18 of the same Article grants it the power "[t]o make all Laws which shall be necessary and proper for carrying into Execution the foregoing Powers." This grant "extends to those activities intrastate which so affect interstate commerce, or the exertion of the power of Congress over it, as to make regulation of them appropriate means to the attainment of a legitimate end, the effective execution of the granted power to regulate interstate commerce." Much is said about a restaurant business being local but "even if appellee's activity be local and though it may not be regarded as commerce, it may still, whatever its nature, be reached by Congress if it exerts a substantial economic effect on interstate commerce." *Wickard v. Filburn*. The activities that are beyond the reach of Congress are "those which are completely within a particular State, which do not affect other States, and with which it is not necessary to interfere, for the purpose of executing some of the general powers of the government." *Gibbons v. Ogden*. This rule is as good today as it was when Chief Justice Marshall laid it down almost a century and a half ago.

Congress has determined for itself that refusals of service to Negroes have imposed burdens both upon the interstate flow of food and upon the movement of products generally. Of course, the mere fact that Congress has said when particular activity shall be deemed to affect commerce does not preclude further examination by this Court. But where we find that the legislators, in light of the facts and testimony before them, have a rational basis for finding a chosen regulatory scheme necessary to the protection of commerce, our investigation is at an end.

The power of Congress in this field is broad and sweeping; where it keeps within its sphere and violates no express constitutional limitation it has been the rule of this Court, going back almost to the founding days of the Republic, not to interfere. The Civil Rights Act of 1964, as here applied, we find to be plainly appropriate in the resolution of what the Congress found to be a national commercial problem of the first magnitude. We find it in no violation of any express limitations of the Constitution and we therefore declare it valid.

The judgment is therefore reversed.

Concurring opinions by MR. JUSTICE BLACK, MR. JUSTICE DOUGLAS and MR. JUSTICE GOLDBERG printed in No. 515, *Heart of Atlanta Motel, Inc. v. United States*, 379 U.S. 241.

[Concurring opinions by JUSTICES BLACK and GOLDBERG are omitted. JUSTICE DOUGLAS stated in his concurring opinion:]

Though I join the Court's opinions, I am somewhat reluctant to rest solely on the Commerce Clause. My reluctance is not due to any conviction that Congress lacks power to regulate commerce in the interests of human rights. It is rather my belief that the right of people to be free of state action that discriminates against them because of race "occupies a more protected position in our constitutional system than does the movement of cattle, fruit, steel and coal across state lines." The result reached by the Court is for me much more obvious as a protective measure under the Fourteenth Amendment than under the Commerce Clause. For the former deals with the constitutional status of the individuals not with the impact on commerce of local activities or vice versa.

Hence I would prefer to rest on the assertion of legislative power contained in § 5 of the Fourteenth Amendment which states: "The Congress shall have power to enforce, by appropriate legislation, the provisions of this article" — a power which the Court concedes was exercised at least in part in this Act.

A decision based on the Fourteenth Amendment would have a more settling effect, making unnecessary litigation over whether a particular restaurant or inn is within the commerce definitions of the Act or whether a particular customer is an interstate traveler. Under my construction, the Act would apply to all customers in all the enumerated places of public accommodation. And that construction would put an end to all obstructionist strategies and finally close one door on a bitter chapter in American history.

Notes and Questions

(1) In *Darby* and *McClung* did the Court return to Chief Justice Marshall's view of the Commerce Clause?

(2) Do *Darby* and *McClung* stand for the proposition that Congress has power under the Commerce Clause to regulate any activity if the cumulative effect of the activity has a substantial impact on interstate commerce? Will the Court second guess Congress on whether an activity has such an impact? To what extent did the Court rely on findings made by Congress?

(3) In *Wickard v. Filburn*, 317 U.S. 111 (1942), relied upon by Justice Clark in *McClung*, the Court upheld the Agricultural Adjustment Act quota on farm production. In the dispute before the Court, the Secretary of Agriculture limited the production of wheat, after he concluded that the supply of wheat would exceed domestic and export demand. When farmer Filburn grew modest amounts of wheat to feed the animals on his dairy farm, he was fined for violating the quota. In addition to the analysis quoted in *McClung*, the *Wickard* Court conceded that the Act forces "some farmers into the market to buy what they could provide for themselves. [However,] [i]t is of the essence of regulation that it lays a restraining hand on the self-interest of the regulated and that advantages from the regulation commonly fall to others. The conflicts of economic interest are wisely left under our system to

resolution by the Congress. Such conflicts rarely lend themselves to judicial determination." *Id.*, 317 U.S. at 155.

(4) In *Perez v. United States*, 402 U.S. 146 (1971), the Court relied on *McClung* in upholding a provision of the Consumer Credit Protection Act of 1968, which prohibits "extortionate credit transactions," or, in lay terms, loan-sharking accompanied by threats of violence. Perez was convicted under the statute, even though there was no showing that his loan-sharking affected interstate commerce. Relying in part on findings made by Congress that extortion is a national problem that, even in its intrastate applications, produced money for a national organized crime network, the Court ruled that Perez "is clearly a *member of the class* which engages in [the prohibited loan-sharking]. Where the *class of activities* is regulated and that *class* is within the reach of federal power, the courts have no power" to excuse individual members of the class. *Id.*, 402 U.S. at 154. After these decisions what Commerce Clause limits remain on congressional power?

United States v. Lopez

United States Supreme Court
514 U.S. 549, 115 S. Ct. 1624, 131 L. Ed. 2d 626 (1995)

Chief Justice Rehnquist delivered the opinion of the Court.

In the Gun-Free School Zones Act of 1990, Congress made it a federal offense "for any individual knowingly to possess a firearm at a place that the individual knows, or has reasonable cause to believe, is a school zone." 18 U.S.C. § 922(q)(1)(A). ["School zone" is defined as "in, or on the grounds of, a public, parochial or private school" or "within a distance of 1,000 feet from the grounds" of such a school.] The Act neither regulates a commercial activity nor contains a requirement that the possession be connected in any way to interstate commerce. We hold that the Act exceeds the authority of Congress "[t]o regulate Commerce among the several States." U.S. Const., Art. I, § 8, cl. 3.

On March 10, 1992, respondent, who was then a 12th-grade student, arrived at Edison High School in San Antonio, Texas, carrying a concealed .38 caliber handgun and five bullets. Acting upon an anonymous tip, school authorities confronted respondent, who admitted that he was carrying the weapon. He was arrested and charged under Texas law with firearm possession on school premises. The next day, the state charges were dismissed after federal agents charged respondent by complaint with violating the Gun-Free School Zones Act of 1990.

A federal grand jury indicted respondent on one count of knowing possession of a firearm at a school zone, in violation of § 922(q). Respondent moved to dismiss his federal indictment on the ground that § 922(q) "is unconstitutional as it is beyond the power of Congress to legislate control over our public schools." The District Court denied the motion, concluding that § 922(q) "is a constitutional exercise of Congress' well-defined power to regulate activities in and affecting commerce, and the 'business' of elementary, middle and high schools affects interstate commerce."

The District Court found him guilty of violating § 922(q), and sentenced him to six months' imprisonment and two years' supervised release.

On appeal, respondent challenged his conviction based on his claim that § 922(q) exceeded Congress' power to legislate under the Commerce Clause. The Court of Appeals for the Fifth Circuit agreed and reversed respondent's conviction. It held that, in light of what it characterized as insufficient congressional findings and legislative history, "section 922(q), in the full reach of its terms, is invalid as beyond the power of Congress under the Commerce Clause." 2 F.3d 1342(1993). Because of the importance of the issue, we granted certiorari, and we now affirm.

[W]e have identified three broad categories of activity that Congress may regulate under its commerce power. First, Congress may regulate the use of the channels of interstate commerce. See, e.g., *Darby*. Second, Congress is empowered to regulate and protect the instrumentalities of interstate commerce, or persons or things in interstate commerce, even though the threat may come only from intrastate activities. See, e.g., *Shreveport Rate Cases; Perez* ("[F]or example, the destruction of an aircraft (18 U.S.C. § 32), or thefts from interstate shipments (18 U.S.C. § 659)"). Finally, Congress' commerce authority includes the power to regulate those activities having a substantial relation to interstate commerce, *Jones & Laughlin Steel*, i.e., those activities that substantially affect interstate commerce.

Within this final category, admittedly, our case law has not been clear whether an activity must "affect" or "substantially affect" interstate commerce in order to be within Congress' power to regulate it under the Commerce Clause. We conclude, consistent with the great weight of our case law, that the proper test requires an analysis of whether the regulated activity "substantially affects" interstate commerce.

We now turn to consider the power of Congress, in the light of this framework, to enact § 922(q). The first two categories of authority may be quickly disposed of: § 922(q) is not a regulation of the use of the channels of interstate commerce, nor is it an attempt to prohibit the interstate transportation of a commodity through the channels of commerce; nor can § 922(q) be justified as a regulation by which Congress has sought to protect an instrumentality of interstate commerce or a thing in interstate commerce. Thus, if § 922(q) is to be sustained, it must be under the third category as a regulation of an activity that substantially affects interstate commerce.

First, we have upheld a wide variety of congressional Acts regulating intrastate economic activity where we have concluded that the activity substantially affected interstate commerce. Examples include the regulation of intrastate coal mining; *Hodel v. Virginia Surface Mining & Reclamation Assn., Inc.*, 452 U.S. 264 (1981); intrastate extortionate credit transactions, *Perez*, restaurants utilizing substantial interstate supplies, *Katzenbach v. McClung*, 379 U.S. 294 (1964), inns and hotels catering to interstate guests, *Heart of Atlanta Motel, Inc. v. United States*, 379 U.S. 241 (1964), and production and consumption of home-grown wheat, *Wickard v. Filburn*. These examples are by no means exhaustive, but the pattern is clear. Where economic activity substantially affects interstate commerce, legislation regulating that activity will be sustained.

Even *Wickard*, which is perhaps the most far-reaching example of Commerce Clause authority over intrastate activity, involved economic activity in a way that the possession of a gun in a school zone does not.

Section 922(q) is a criminal statute that by its terms has nothing to do with "commerce" or any sort of economic enterprise, however broadly one might define those terms. Section 922(q) is not an essential part of a larger regulation of economic activity, in which the regulatory scheme could be undercut unless the intrastate activity were regulated. It cannot, therefore, be sustained under our cases upholding regulations of activities that arise out of or are connected with a commercial transaction, which viewed in the aggregate, substantially affects interstate commerce.

Second, § 922(q) contains no jurisdictional element which would ensure, through case-by-case inquiry, that the firearm possession in question affects interstate commerce. For example, in *United States v. Bass*, 404 U.S. 336 (1971), the Court interpreted former 18 U.S.C. §1202(a), which made it a crime for a felon to "receiv[e], posses[s], or transpor[t] in commerce or affecting commerce any firearm." The Court interpreted the possession component of §1202(a) to require an additional nexus to interstate commerce both because the statute was ambiguous and because "unless Congress conveys its purpose clearly, it will not be deemed to have significantly changed the federal-state balance." The *Bass* Court set aside the conviction because although the Government had demonstrated that Bass had possessed a firearm, it had failed "to show the requisite nexus with interstate commerce." The Court thus interpreted the statute to reserve the constitutional question whether Congress could regulate, without more, the "mere possession" of firearms. Unlike the statute in *Bass*, § 922(q) has no express jurisdictional element which might limit its reach to a discrete set of firearm possessions that additionally have an explicit connection with or effect on interstate commerce.

Although as part of our independent evaluation of constitutionality under the Commerce Clause we of course consider legislative findings, and indeed even congressional committee findings, regarding effect on interstate commerce, the Government concedes that "[n]either the statute nor its legislative history contain[s] express congressional findings regarding the effects upon interstate commerce of gun possession in a school zone." We agree with the Government that Congress normally is not required to make formal findings as to the substantial burdens that an activity has on interstate commerce. See *McClung*. But to the extent that congressional findings would enable us to evaluate the legislative judgment that the activity in question substantially affected interstate commerce, even though no such substantial effect was visible to the naked eye, they are lacking here.

The Government's essential contention, in fine, is that we may determine here that § 922(q) is valid because possession of a firearm in a local school zone does indeed substantially affect interstate commerce. The Government argues that possession of a firearm in a school zone may result in violent crime and that violent crime can be expected to affect the functioning of the national economy in two ways. First, the costs of violent crime are substantial, and, through the mechanism of insurance, those costs are spread throughout the population. Second, violent crime reduces the willingness of individuals to travel to areas within the country that are perceived to be unsafe. Cf. *Heart of Atlanta Motel.* The Government also argues that the presence of guns in schools poses a substantial threat to the educational process by threatening the learning environment. A handicapped educational process, in turn, will result in a less productive citizenry. That, in turn, would have an adverse effect on the Nation's economic well-being. As a result, the Government argues that Congress could rationally have concluded that § 922(q) substantially affects interstate commerce.

We pause to consider the implications of the Government's arguments. The Government admits, under its "costs of crime" reasoning, that Congress could regulate not only all violent crime, but all activities that might lead to violent crime, regardless of how tenuously they relate to interstate commerce. Similarly, under the Government's "national productivity" reasoning, Congress could regulate any activity that it found was related to the economic productivity of individual citizens: family law (including marriage, divorce, and child custody), for example. Under the theories that the Government presents in support of § 922(q), it is difficult to perceive any limitation on federal power, even in areas such as criminal law enforcement or education where States historically have been sovereign. Thus, if we were to accept the Government's arguments, we are hard-pressed to posit any activity by an individual that Congress is without power to regulate.

The possession of a gun in a local school zone is in no sense an economic activity that might, through repetition elsewhere, substantially affect any sort of interstate commerce. Respondent was a local student at a local school; there is no indication that he had recently moved in interstate commerce, and there is no requirement that his possession of the firearm have any concrete tie to interstate commerce.

To uphold the Government's contentions here, we would have to pile inference upon inference in a manner that would bid fair to convert congressional authority under the Commerce Clause to a general police power of the sort retained by the States. Admittedly, some of our prior cases have taken long steps down that road, giving great deference to congressional action. The broad language in these opinions has suggested the possibility of additional expansion, but we decline here to proceed any further. To do so would require us to conclude that the Constitution's enumeration of powers does not presuppose something not enumerated, cf. *Gibbons v. Ogden*, and that there never will be a distinction between what is truly national and what is truly local. This we are unwilling to do.

For the foregoing reasons the judgment of the Court of Appeals is *Affirmed.*

JUSTICE KENNEDY, with whom JUSTICE O'CONNOR joins, concurring.

The history of the judicial struggle to interpret the Commerce Clause during the transition from the economic system the Founders knew to the single, national market still emergent in our own era counsels great restraint before the Court determines that the Clause is insufficient to support an exercise of the national power. That history gives me some pause about today's decision, but I join the Court's opinion with these observations on what I conceive to be its necessary though limited holding.

The history of our Commerce Clause decisions contains at least two lessons of relevance to this case. The first, as stated at the outset, is the imprecision of content-based boundaries used without more to define the limits of the Commerce Clause. The second, related to the first but of even greater consequence, is that the Court as an institution and the legal system as a whole have an immense stake in the stability of our Commerce Clause jurisprudence as it has evolved to this point. Stare decisis operates with great force in counseling us not to call in question the essential principles now in place respecting the congressional power to regulate transactions of a commercial nature. That fundamental restraint on our power forecloses us from reverting to an understanding of commerce that would serve only an 18th-century economy, dependent then upon production and trading practices that had changed but little over the preceding centuries; it also mandates against returning to the time when congressional authority to regulate undoubted commercial activities was limited by a judicial determination that those matters had an insufficient connection to an interstate system. Congress can regulate in the commercial sphere on the assumption that we have a single market and a unified purpose to build a stable national economy.

While it is doubtful that any State, or indeed any reasonable person, would argue that it is wise policy to allow students to carry guns on school premises, considerable disagreement exists about how best to accomplish that goal. In this circumstance, the theory and utility of our federalism are revealed, for the States may perform their role as laboratories for experimentation to devise various solutions where the best solution is far from clear. If a State or municipality determines that harsh criminal sanctions are necessary and wise to deter students from carrying guns on school premises, the reserved powers of the States are sufficient to enact those measures. Indeed, over 40 States already have criminal laws outlawing the possession of firearms on or near school grounds.

This is not a case where the etiquette of federalism has been violated by a formal command from the National Government directing the State to enact a certain policy, cf. *New York v. United States* [*see infra*], or to organize its governmental functions in a certain way, cf. *FERC v. Mississippi*, 456 U.S., at 781 (O' CONNOR, J., concurring in judgment in part and dissenting in part). While the intrusion on state sovereignty may not be as severe in this instance as in some of our recent Tenth Amendment cases, the intrusion is nonetheless significant. Absent a stronger connection or identification with commercial concerns that are central to the Commerce Clause, that interference contradicts the federal balance the Framers designed and that this Court is obliged to enforce.

For these reasons, I join in the opinion and judgment of the Court.

JUSTICE THOMAS, concurring.

In an appropriate case, I believe that we must further reconsider our "substantial effects" test with an eye toward constructing a standard that reflects the text and history of the Commerce Clause without totally rejecting our more recent Commerce Clause jurisprudence. At the time the original Constitution was ratified, "commerce" consisted of selling, buying, and bartering, as well as transporting for these purposes. As one would expect, the term "commerce" was used in contradistinction to productive activities such as manufacturing and agriculture.

Moreover, interjecting a modern sense of commerce into the Constitution generates significant textual and structural problems. For example, one cannot replace "commerce" with a different type of enterprise, such as manufacturing. When a manufacturer produces a car, assembly cannot take place "with a foreign nation" or "with the Indian Tribes." Parts may come from different States or other nations and hence may have been in the flow of commerce at one time, but manufacturing takes place at a discrete site. Agriculture and manufacturing involve the production of goods; commerce encompasses traffic in such articles.

The Constitution not only uses the word "commerce" in a narrower sense than our case law might suggest, it also does not support the proposition that Congress has authority over all activities that "substantially affect" interstate commerce. The Commerce Clause does not state that Congress may "regulate matters that substantially affect commerce with foreign Nations, and among the several States, and with the Indian Tribes." In contrast, the Constitution itself temporarily prohibited amendments that would "affect" Congress' lack of authority to prohibit or restrict the slave trade or to enact unproportioned direct taxation. U.S. Const., Art. V. Clearly, the Framers could have drafted a Constitution that contained a "substantially affects interstate commerce" clause had that been their objective.

The exchanges during the ratification campaign reveal the relatively limited reach of the Commerce Clause and of federal power generally. The Founding Fathers confirmed that most areas of life (even many matters that would have substantial effects on commerce) would remain outside the reach of the Federal Government. Such affairs would continue to be under the exclusive control of the States.

JUSTICE STEVENS, dissenting. [Omitted]

JUSTICE SOUTER, dissenting. [Omitted]

JUSTICE BREYER, with whom JUSTICE STEVENS, JUSTICE SOUTER, and JUSTICE GINSBURG join, dissenting.

[T]he specific question before us, as the Court recognizes, is not whether the "regulated activity sufficiently affected interstate commerce," but, rather, whether Congress could have had "a rational basis" for so concluding.

I recognize that we must judge this matter independently. And, I also recognize that Congress did not write specific "interstate commerce" findings into the law under which Lopez was convicted. Nonetheless, as I have already noted, the matter that we review independently (i.e., whether there is a "rational basis") already has considerable leeway built into it. And, the absence of findings, at most, deprives a statute of the benefit of some extra leeway. This extra deference, in principle, might change the result in a close case, though, in practice, it has not made a critical legal difference. And, it would seem particularly unfortunate to make the validity of the statute at hand turn on the presence or absence of findings. Because Congress did make findings (though not until after Lopez was prosecuted [see *infra*, Notes and Questions]), doing so would appear to elevate form over substance.

In addition there is no special need here for a clear indication of Congress' rationale. The statute does not interfere with the exercise of state or local authority. Moreover, any clear statement rule would apply only to determine Congress' intended result, not to clarify the source of its authority or measure the level of consideration that went into its decision, and here there is no doubt as to which activities Congress intended to regulate.

II

Applying these principles to the case at hand, we must ask whether Congress could have had a rational basis for finding a significant (or substantial) connection between gun-related school violence and interstate commerce. Or, to put the question in the language of the explicit finding that Congress made when it amended this law in 1994: Could Congress rationally have found that "violent crime in school zones," through its effect on the "quality of education," significantly (or substantially) affects "interstate" or "foreign commerce"? As long as one views the commerce connection, not as a "technical legal conception," but as "a practical one," *Swift & Co. v. United States*, 196 U.S. 375, 398, (1905) (Holmes, J.), the answer to this question must be yes. Numerous reports and studies—generated both inside and outside government—make clear that Congress could reasonably have found the empirical connection that its law, implicitly or explicitly, asserts.

For one thing, reports, hearings, and other readily available literature make clear that the problem of guns in and around schools is widespread and extremely serious. These materials report, for example, that four percent of American high school students (and six percent of inner-city high school students) carry a gun to school at least occasionally; that 12 percent of urban high school students have had guns fired at them; that 20 percent of those students have been threatened with guns; and that, in any 6-month period, several hundred thousand schoolchildren are victims of violent crimes in or near their schools. And, they report that this widespread violence in schools throughout the Nation significantly interferes with the quality of education in those schools. Based on reports such as these, Congress obviously could have thought that guns and learning are mutually exclusive. And, Congress could therefore have found a substantial educational problem—teachers unable to teach, students unable to learn—and concluded that guns near schools contribute substantially to the size and scope of that problem.

Having found that guns in schools significantly undermine the quality of education in our Nation's classrooms, Congress could also have found, given the effect of education upon interstate and foreign commerce, that gun-related violence in and around schools is a commercial, as well as a human, problem. Education, although far more than a matter of economics, has long been inextricably intertwined with the Nation's economy.

In recent years the link between secondary education and business has strengthened, becoming both more direct and more important. Scholars on the subject report that technological changes and innovations in management techniques have altered the nature of the workplace so that more jobs now demand greater educational skills.

The economic links I have just sketched seem fairly obvious. Why then is it not equally obvious, in light of those links, that a widespread, serious, and substantial physical threat to teaching and learning also substantially threatens the commerce to which that teaching and learning is inextricably tied? That is to say, guns in the hands of six percent of inner-city high school students and gun-related violence throughout a city's schools must threaten the trade and commerce that those schools support. The only question, then, is whether the latter threat is (to use the majority's terminology) "substantial." And, the evidence of (1) the extent of the gun-related violence problem, (2) the extent of the resulting negative effect on classroom learning, and (3) the extent of the consequent negative commercial effects, when taken together, indicate a threat to trade and commerce that is "substantial." At the very least, Congress could rationally have concluded that the links are "substantial."

Specifically, Congress could have found that gun-related violence near the classroom poses a serious economic threat (1) to consequently inadequately educated workers who must endure low paying jobs, and (2) to communities and businesses that might (in today's "information society") otherwise gain, from a well-educated work force, an important commercial advantage, of a kind that location near a railhead or harbor provided in the past. Congress might also have found these threats to be no different in kind from other threats that this Court has found within the commerce power, such as the threat that loan sharking poses to the "funds" of "numerous localities," *Perez v. United States*, and that unfair labor practices pose to instrumentalities of commerce. The violence-related facts, the educational facts, and the economic facts, taken together, make this conclusion rational. And, because under our case law, the sufficiency of the constitutionally necessary Commerce Clause link between a crime of violence and interstate commerce turns simply upon size or degree, those same facts make the statute constitutional.

To hold this statute constitutional is not to "obliterate" the "distinction of what is national and what is local," nor is it to hold that the Commerce Clause permits the Federal Government to "regulate any activity that it found was related to the economic productivity of individual citizens," to regulate "marriage, divorce, and child custody," or to regulate any and all aspects of education. For one thing, this statute is aimed at curbing a particularly acute threat to the educational process — the possession (and use) of life-threatening firearms in, or near, the classroom. The empirical evidence that I have discussed above unmistakably documents the special way in which guns and education are incompatible. For another thing, the immediacy of the connection between education and the national economic well-being is documented by scholars and accepted by society at large in a way and to a degree that may not hold true for other social institutions. It must surely be the rare case, then, that a statute strikes at conduct that (when considered in the abstract) seems so removed from commerce, but which (practically speaking) has so significant an impact upon commerce.

In sum, a holding that the particular statute before us falls within the commerce power would not expand the scope of that Clause. Rather, it simply would apply pre-existing law to changing economic circumstances.

III

The majority's holding — that § 922 falls outside the scope of the Commerce Clause — creates three serious legal problems. First, the majority's holding runs contrary to modern Supreme Court cases that have upheld congressional actions despite connections to interstate or foreign commerce that are less significant than the effect of school violence. In *Perez v. United States*, the Court held that the Commerce Clause authorized a federal statute that makes it a crime to engage in loan sharking ("[e]xtortionate credit transactions") at a local level. The Court said that Congress may judge that such transactions, "though purely intrastate affect interstate commerce." Presumably, Congress reasoned that threatening or using force, say with a gun on a street corner, to collect a debt occurs sufficiently often so that the activity (by helping organized crime) affects commerce among the States. But, why then cannot Congress also reason that the threat or use of force — the frequent consequence of possessing a gun — in or near a school occurs sufficiently often so that such activity (by inhibiting basic education) affects commerce among the States? The negative impact upon the national economy of an inability to teach basic skills seems no smaller (nor less significant) than that of organized crime.

In *Katzenbach v. McClung*, this Court upheld, as within the commerce power, a statute prohibiting racial discrimination at local restaurants, in part because that discrimination discouraged travel by African Americans and in part because that discrimination affected purchases of food and restaurant supplies from other States.

In *Wickard v. Filburn*, this Court sustained the application of the Agricultural Adjustment Act of 1938 to wheat that Filburn grew and consumed on his own local farm because, considered in its totality, (1) home-grown wheat may be "induced by rising prices" to "flow into the market and check price increases," and (2) even if it never actually enters the market, home-grown wheat nonetheless "supplies a need of the man who grew it which would otherwise be reflected by purchases in the open market" and, in that sense, "competes with wheat in commerce." To find both of these effects on commerce significant in amount, the Court had to give Congress the benefit of the doubt. Why would the Court, to find a significant (or "substantial") effect here, have to give Congress any greater leeway?

The second legal problem the Court creates comes from its apparent belief that it can reconcile its holding with earlier cases by making a critical distinction between "commercial" and noncommercial "transaction[s]." That is to say, the Court believes the Constitution would distinguish between two local activities, each of which has an identical effect upon interstate commerce, if one, but not the other, is "commercial" in nature. As a general matter, this approach fails to heed this Court's earlier warning not to turn "questions of the power of Congress" upon "formula[s]" that would give "controlling force to nomenclature such as 'production' and 'indirect' and foreclose consideration of the actual effects of the activity in question upon interstate commerce." Moreover, the majority's test is not consistent with what the Court saw as the point of the cases that the majority now characterizes. Although the majority today attempts to categorize *Perez, McClung*, and *Wickard* as involving intrastate "economic activity," the Courts that decided each of those cases did not focus upon the economic nature of the activity regulated. Rather, they focused upon whether that activity affected interstate or foreign commerce. In fact, the *Wickard* Court expressly held that Wickard's consumption of home grown wheat, "though it may not be regarded as commerce," could nevertheless be regulated — "whatever its nature" — so long as "it exerts a substantial economic effect on interstate commerce."

More importantly, if a distinction between commercial and noncommercial activities is to be made, this is not the case in which to make it. The majority clearly cannot intend such a distinction to focus narrowly on an act of gun possession standing by itself, for such a reading could not be reconciled with either the civil rights cases or *Perez* — in each of those cases the specific transaction (the race-based exclusion, the use of force) was not itself "commercial." And, if the majority instead means to distinguish generally among broad categories of activities, differentiating what is educational from what is commercial, then, as a practical matter, the line becomes almost impossible to draw. Schools that teach reading, writing, mathematics, and related basic skills serve both social and commercial purposes, and one cannot easily separate the one from the other. American industry itself has been, and is again, involved in teaching. When, and to what extent, does its involvement make education commercial? Does the number of vocational classes that train students directly for jobs make a difference? Does it matter if the school is public or private, nonprofit or profit-seeking? Does it matter if a city or State adopts a voucher plan that pays private firms to run a school? Even if one were to ignore these practical questions, why should there be a theoretical distinction between education, when it significantly benefits commerce, and environmental pollution, when it causes economic harm?

Regardless, if there is a principled distinction that could work both here and in future cases, Congress (even in the absence of vocational classes, industry involvement, and private management) could rationally conclude that schools fall on the commercial side of the line. In 1990, the year Congress enacted the statute before us, primary and secondary schools spent $230 billion — that is, nearly a quarter of a trillion dollars — which accounts for a significant portion of our $5.5 trillion Gross Domestic Product for that year.

The third legal problem created by the Court's holding is that it threatens legal uncertainty in an area of law that, until this case, seemed reasonably well settled. More importantly, in the absence of a jurisdictional element, are the courts nevertheless to take *Wickard* (and later similar cases) as inapplicable, and to judge the effect of a single noncommercial activity on interstate commerce without considering similar instances of the forbidden conduct?

Gonzales v. Raich

United States Supreme Court
545 U.S. 1, 125 S. Ct. 2195, 162 L. Ed. 2d 1 (2005)

JUSTICE STEVENS delivered the opinion of the Court.

California is one of at least nine States that authorize the use of marijuana for medicinal purposes. The question presented in this case is whether the power vested in Congress by Article I, §8, of the Constitution "[t]o make all Laws which shall be necessary and proper for carrying into Execution" its authority to "regulate Commerce with foreign Nations, and among the several States" includes the power to prohibit the local cultivation and use of marijuana in compliance with California law.

I.

California has been a pioneer in the regulation of marijuana. In 1913, California was one of the first States to prohibit the sale and possession of marijuana, and at the end of the century, California became the first State to authorize limited use of the drug for medicinal purposes. In 1996, California voters passed Proposition 215, now codified as the Compassionate Use Act of 1996. The proposition was designed to ensure that "seriously ill" residents of the State have access to marijuana for medical purposes, and to encourage Federal and State governments to take steps towards ensuring the safe and affordable distribution of the drug to patients in need. The Act creates an exemption from criminal prosecution for physician, as well as for patients and primary caregivers who possess or cultivate marijuana for medicinal purposes with the recommendation or approval of a physician.

Respondents Angel Raich and Diane Monson are California residents who suffer from a variety of serious medical conditions and have sought to avail themselves of medical marijuana pursuant to the terms of the Compassionate Use Act. They are being treated by licensed, board-certified family practitioners, who have concluded, after prescribing a host of conventional medicines to treat respondents' conditions and to alleviate their associated symptoms, that marijuana is the only drug available that provides effective treatment. Both women have been using marijuana as a medication for several years pursuant to their doctors' recommendation, and both rely heavily on cannabis to function on a daily basis. Indeed, Raich's physician believes that forgoing cannabis treatments would certainly cause Raich excruciating pain and could very well prove fatal.

Respondent Monson cultivates her own marijuana, and ingests the drug in a variety of ways including smoking and using a vaporizer. Respondent Raich, by contrast, is unable to cultivate her own, and thus relies on two caregivers, litigating as "John Does," to provide her with locally grown marijuana at no charge.

On August 15, 2002, county deputy sheriffs and agents from the federal Drug Enforcement Administration (DEA) came to Monson's home. After a thorough investigation, the county officials concluded that her use of marijuana was entirely lawful as a matter of California law. Nevertheless, after a 3-hour standoff, the federal agents seized and destroyed all six of her cannabis plants.

Respondents thereafter brought this action against the Attorney General of the United States and the head of the DEA seeking injunctive and declaratory relief prohibiting the enforcement of the federal Controlled Substances Act (CSA), 84 Stat. 1242, 21 U.S.C. § 801 *et seq.*, to the extent it prevents them from possessing, obtaining, or manufacturing cannabis for their personal medical use. In their complaint and supporting affidavits, Raich and Monson described the severity of their afflictions, their repeatedly futile attempts to obtain relief with conventional medications, and the opinions of their doctors concerning their need to use marijuana. Respondents claimed that enforcing the CSA against them would violate the Commerce Clause, the Due Process Clause of the Fifth Amendment, the Ninth and Tenth Amendments of the Constitution, and the doctrine of medical necessity.

The obvious importance of the case prompted our grant of certiorari. The case is made difficult by respondents' strong arguments that they will suffer irreparable harm because, despite a congressional finding to the contrary, marijuana does have valid therapeutic purposes. The question before us, however, is not whether it is wise to enforce the statute in these circumstances; rather, it is whether Congress' power to regulate interstate markets for medicinal substances encompasses the portions of those markets that are supplied with drugs produced and consumed locally. Well-settled law controls our answer. The CSA is a valid exercise of federal power, even as applied to the troubling facts of this case.

II.

[In 1970] Congress enacted the Comprehensive Drug Abuse Prevention and Control Act.

Title II of that Act, the CSA, repealed most of the earlier antidrug laws in favor of a comprehensive regime to combat the international and interstate traffic in illicit drugs. The main objectives of the CSA were to conquer drug abuse and to control the legitimate and illegitimate traffic in controlled substances. Congress was particularly concerned with the need to prevent the diversion of drugs from legitimate to illicit channels.

To effectuate these goals, Congress devised a closed regulatory system making it unlawful to manufacture, distribute, dispense, or possess any controlled substance except in a manner authorized by the CSA. 21 U.S.C. §§ 841(a)(1), 844(a). The CSA categorizes all controlled substances into five schedules. § 812. The drugs are grouped together based on their accepted medical uses, the potential for abuse, and their psychological and physical effects on the body. §§ 811, 812. Each schedule is associated with a distinct set of controls regarding the manufacture, distribution, and use of the substances listed therein. §§ 821–830. The CSA and its implementing regulations set forth strict requirements regarding registration, labeling and packaging, production quotas, drug security, and recordkeeping. *Ibid.* 21 CFR § 1301 *et seq.* (2004).

In enacting the CSA, Congress classified marijuana as a Schedule I drug. 21 U.S.C. § 812(c). This preliminary classification was based, in part, on the recommendation of the Assistant Secretary of HEW "that marijuana be retained within schedule I at least until the completion of certain studies now underway." Schedule I drugs are categorized as such because of their high potential for abuse, lack of any accepted medical use, and absence of any accepted safety for use in medically supervised treatment. § 812(b)(1). By classifying marijuana as a Schedule I drug, as opposed to listing it on a lesser schedule, the manufacture, distribution, or possession of marijuana became a criminal offense, with the sole exception being use of the drug as part of a Food and Drug Administration pre-approved research study. §§ 823(f), 841(a)(1), 844(a).

The CSA provides for the periodic updating of schedules and delegates authority to the Attorney General, after consultation with the Secretary of Health and Human Services, to add, remove, or transfer substances to, from, or between schedules. § 811. Despite considerable efforts to reschedule marijuana, it remains a Schedule I drug.

III.

Respondents in this case do not dispute that passage of the CSA, as part of the Comprehensive Drug Abuse Prevention and Control Act, was well within Congress' commerce power. Nor do they contend that any provision or section of the CSA amounts to an unconstitutional exercise of congressional authority. Rather, respondents' challenge is actually quite limited; they argue that the CSA's categorical prohibition of the manufacture and possession of marijuana as applied to the intrastate manufacture and possession of marijuana for medical purposes pursuant to California law exceeds Congress' authority under the Commerce Clause.

In assessing the validity of congressional regulation, none of our Commerce Clause cases can be viewed in isolation. Our decision in *Wickard*, is of particular relevance. In *Wickard*, we upheld the application of regulations promulgated under the Agricultural Adjustment Act of 1938, 52 Stat. 31, which were designed to control the volume of wheat moving in interstate and foreign commerce in order to avoid surpluses and consequent abnormally low prices. The regulations established an allotment of 11.1 acres for Filburn's 1941 wheat crop, but he sowed 23 acres, intending to use the excess by consuming it on his own farm. Filburn argued that even though we had sustained Congress' power to regulate the production of goods for commerce, that power did not authorize "federal regulation [of] production not intended in any part for commerce but wholly for consumption on the farm." Justice Jackson's opinion for a unanimous Court rejected this submission. He wrote:

> The effect of the statute before us is to restrict the amount which may be produced for market and the extent as well to which one may forestall resort to the market by producing to meet his own needs. That appellee's own contribution to the demand for wheat may be trivial by itself is not enough to remove him from the scope of federal regulation where, as here, his contribution, taken together with that of many others similarly situated, is far from trivial. *Id.* at 127–128.

Wickard thus establishes that Congress can regulate purely intrastate activity that is not itself "commercial," in that it is not produced for sale, if it concludes that failure to regulate that class of activity would undercut the regulation of the interstate market in that commodity.

The similarities between this case and *Wickard* are striking. Like the farmer in *Wickard*, respondents are cultivating, for home consumption, a fungible commodity for which there is an established, albeit illegal, interstate market. Just as the Agricultural Adjustment Act was designed "to control the volume [of wheat] moving in interstate and foreign commerce in order to avoid surpluses" and consequently control the market price, a primary purpose of the CSA is to control the supply and demand of controlled substances in both lawful and unlawful drug markets. In *Wickard*, we had no difficulty concluding that Congress had a rational basis for believing that, when viewed in the aggregate, leaving home-consumed wheat outside the regulatory scheme would have a substantial influence on price and market conditions. Here too, Congress had a rational basis for concluding that leaving home-consumed marijuana outside federal control would similarly affect price and market conditions.

More concretely, one concern prompting inclusion of wheat grown for home consumption in the 1938 Act was that rising market prices could draw such wheat into the interstate market, resulting in lower market prices. The parallel concern making it appropriate to include marijuana grown for home consumption in the CSA is the likelihood that the high demand in the interstate market will draw such marijuana into that market. While the diversion of homegrown wheat tended to frustrate the federal interest in stabilizing prices by regulating the volume of commercial transactions in the interstate market, the diversion of homegrown marijuana tends to frustrate the federal interest in eliminating commercial transactions in the interstate market in their entirety. In both cases, the regulation is squarely within Congress' commerce power because production of the commodity meant for home consumption, be it wheat or marijuana, has a substantial effect on supply and demand in the national market for that commodity.

Nonetheless, respondents suggest that *Wickard* differs from this case in three respects: (1) the Agricultural Adjustment Act, unlike the CSA, exempted small farming operations; (2) *Wickard* involved a "quintessential economic activity" — a commercial farm — whereas respondents do not sell marijuana; and (3) the *Wickard* record made it clear that the aggregate production of wheat for use on farms had a significant impact on market prices. Those differences, though factually accurate, do not diminish the precedential force of this Court's reasoning.

The fact that Wickard's own impact on the market was "trivial by itself" was not a sufficient reason for removing him from the scope of federal regulation. That the Secretary of Agriculture elected to exempt even smaller farms from regulation does not speak to his power to regulate all those whose aggregated production was significant, nor did that fact play any role in the Court's analysis. Moreover, even though Wickard was indeed a commercial farmer, the activity he was engaged in — the cultivation of wheat for home consumption — was not treated by the Court as part of his commercial farming operation. And while it is true that the record in the *Wickard* case itself established the causal connection between the production for local use and the national market, we have before us findings by Congress to the same effect.

Findings in the introductory sections of the CSA explain why Congress deemed it appropriate to encompass local activities within the scope of the CSA. The submissions of the parties and the numerous amici all seem to agree that the national, and international, market for marijuana has dimensions that are fully comparable to those defining the class of activities regulated by the Secretary pursuant to the 1938 statute. Respondents nonetheless insist that the CSA cannot be constitutionally applied to their activities because Congress did not make a specific finding that the intrastate cultivation and possession of marijuana for medical purposes based on the recommendation of a physician would substantially affect the larger interstate marijuana market. Be that as it may, we have never required Congress to make particularized findings in order to legislate, see *Lopez.*

In assessing the scope of Congress' authority under the Commerce Clause, we stress that the task before us is a modest one. We need not determine whether respondents' activities, taken in the aggregate, substantially affect interstate commerce in fact, but only whether a "rational basis" exists for so concluding. Given the enforcement difficulties that attend distinguishing between marijuana cultivated locally and marijuana grown elsewhere, 21 U.S.C. § 801(5), and concerns about diversion into illicit channels, we have no difficulty concluding that Congress had a rational basis for believing that failure to regulate the intrastate manufacture and possession of marijuana would leave a gaping hole in the CSA. Thus, as in *Wickard,* when it enacted comprehensive legislation to regulate the interstate market in a fungible commodity, Congress was acting well within its authority to "make all Laws which shall be necessary and proper" to "regulate Commerce among the several States." U.S. Const., Art. I, § 8. That the regulation ensnares some purely intrastate activity is of no moment. As we have done many times before, we refuse to excise individual components of that larger scheme.

IV.

To support their contrary submission, respondents rely heavily on two of our more recent Commerce Clause cases. In their myopic focus, they overlook the larger context of modern-era Commerce Clause jurisprudence preserved by those cases. Moreover, even in the narrow prism of respondents' creation, they read those cases far too broadly. Those two cases, of course, are *Lopez* and *United States v. Morrison*, 529 U.S. 598 (2000). [In *Morrison*, the Court held that Congress lacked authority under the Commerce Clause to enact the civil remedy in the Violence Against Women Act because the regulated activity—criminal justice—is not economic in nature.] As an initial matter, the statutory challenges at issue in those cases were markedly different from the challenge respondents pursue in the case at hand. Here, respondents ask us to excise individual applications of a concededly valid statutory scheme. In contrast, in both *Lopez* and *Morrison*, the parties asserted that a particular statute or provision fell outside Congress' commerce power in its entirety. This distinction is pivotal for we have often reiterated that "[w]here the class of activities is regulated and that class is within the reach of federal power, the courts have no power 'to excise, as trivial, individual instances' of the class." *Perez.*

The statutory scheme that the Government is defending in this litigation is at the opposite end of the regulatory spectrum [from the legislation at issue in *Lopez*]. As explained above, the CSA was a lengthy and detailed statute creating a comprehensive framework for regulating the production, distribution, and possession of five classes of "controlled substances." Most of those substances—those listed in Schedules II through V—"have a useful and legitimate medical purpose and are necessary to maintain the health and general welfare of the American people." 21 U.S.C. § 801(1). The regulatory scheme is designed to foster the beneficial use of those medications, to prevent their misuse, and to prohibit entirely the possession or use of substances listed in Schedule I, except as a part of a strictly controlled research project.

While the statute provided for the periodic updating of the five schedules, Congress itself made the initial classifications. It identified 42 opiates, 22 opium derivatives, and 17 hallucinogenic substances as Schedule I drugs. 84 Stat. 1248. Marijuana was listed as the 10th item in the third subcategory. That classification, unlike the discrete prohibition established by the Gun-Free School Zones Act of 1990, was merely one of many "essential part[s] of a larger regulation of economic activity, in which the regulatory scheme could be undercut unless the intrastate activity were regulated." *Lopez.* Our opinion in *Lopez* casts no doubt on the validity of such a program.

Unlike those at issue in *Lopez* and *Morrison*, the activities regulated by the CSA are quintessentially economic. "Economics" refers to "the production, distribution, and consumption of commodities." Webster's Third New International Dictionary 720 (1966). The CSA is a statute that regulates the production, distribution, and consumption of commodities for which there is an established, and lucrative, interstate market. Prohibiting the intrastate possession or manufacture of an article of commerce is a rational (and commonly utilized) means of regulating commerce in that product. Such prohibitions include specific decisions requiring that a drug be withdrawn from the market as a result of the failure to comply with regulatory requirements as well as decisions excluding Schedule I drugs entirely from the market. Because the CSA is a statute that directly regulates economic, commercial activity, our opinion in *Morrison* casts no doubt on its constitutionality.

The Court of Appeals was able to conclude otherwise only by isolating a "separate and distinct" class of activities that it held to be beyond the reach of federal power, defined as "the intrastate, noncommercial cultivation, possession and use of marijuana for personal medical purposes on the advice of a physician and in accordance with state law." 352 F.3d at 1229. The court characterized this class as "different in kind from drug trafficking." The differences between the members of a class so defined and the principal traffickers in Schedule I substances might be sufficient to justify a policy decision exempting the narrower class from the coverage of the CSA. The question, however, is whether Congress' contrary policy judgment, i.e., its decision to include this narrower "class of activities" within the larger regulatory scheme, was constitutionally deficient. We have no difficulty concluding that Congress acted rationally in determining that none of the characteristics making up the purported class, whether viewed individually or in the aggregate, compelled an exemption from the CSA; rather, the subdivided class of activities defined by the Court of Appeals was an essential part of the larger regulatory scheme.

First, the fact that marijuana is used "for personal medical purposes on the advice of a physician" cannot itself serve as a distinguishing factor. The CSA designates marijuana as contraband for *any* purpose; in fact, by characterizing marijuana as a Schedule I drug, Congress expressly found that the drug has no acceptable medical uses. Moreover, the CSA is a comprehensive regulatory regime specifically designed to regulate which controlled substances can be utilized for medicinal purposes, and in what manner. Indeed, most of the substances classified in the CSA "have a useful and legitimate medical purpose." 21 U.S.C. § 801(1). Thus, even if respondents are correct that marijuana does have accepted medical uses and thus should be redesignated as a lesser schedule drug, the CSA would still impose controls beyond what is required by California law. The CSA requires manufacturers, physicians, pharmacies, and other handlers of controlled substances to comply with statutory and regulatory provisions mandating registration with the DEA, compliance with specific production quotas, security controls to guard against diversion, recordkeeping and reporting obligations, and prescription requirements. See 21 U.S.C. §§ 821–830; 21 CFR § 1301 *et seq.* (2004). Furthermore, the dispensing of new drugs, even when doctors approve their use, must await federal approval. Accordingly, the mere fact that marijuana — like virtually every other controlled substance regulated by the CSA — is used for medicinal purposes cannot possibly serve to distinguish it from the core activities regulated by the CSA.

Nor can it serve as an "objective marke[r]" or "objective facto[r]" to arbitrarily narrow the relevant class as the dissenters suggest. More fundamentally, if, as the principal dissent contends, the personal cultivation, possession, and use of marijuana for medicinal purposes is beyond the "'outer limits' of Congress' Commerce Clause authority," it must also be true that such personal use of marijuana (or any other homegrown drug) for recreational purposes is also beyond those "'outer limits,'" whether or not a State elects to authorize or even regulate such use. That is, the dissenters' rationale logically extends to place *any* federal regulation (including quality, prescription, or quantity controls) of *any* locally cultivated and possessed controlled substance for *any* purpose beyond the "'outer limits'" of Congress' Commerce Clause authority. One need not have a degree in economics to understand why a nationwide exemption for the vast quantity of marijuana (or other drugs) locally cultivated for personal use (which presumably would include use by friends, neighbors, and family members) may have a substantial impact on the interstate market for this extraordinarily popular substance. The congressional judgment that an exemption for such a significant segment of the total market would undermine the orderly enforcement of the entire regulatory scheme is entitled to a strong presumption of validity. Indeed, that judgment is not only rational, but "visible to the naked eye," *Lopez*, 514 U.S. at 563 under any commonsense appraisal of the probable consequences of such an open-ended exemption.

Second, limiting the activity to marijuana possession and cultivation "in accordance with state law" cannot serve to place respondents' activities beyond congressional reach. The Supremacy Clause unambiguously provides that if there is any conflict between federal and state law, federal law shall prevail.

So, from the "separate and distinct" class of activities identified by the Court of Appeals (and adopted by the dissenters), we are left with "the intrastate, non-commercial cultivation, possession and use of marijuana." Thus the case for the exemption comes down to the claim that a locally cultivated product that is used domestically rather than sold on the open market is not subject to federal regulation. Given the findings in the CSA and the undisputed magnitude of the commercial market for marijuana, our decisions in *Wickard v. Filburn* and the later cases endorsing its reasoning foreclose that claim.

V.

Respondents also raise a substantive due process claim and seek to avail themselves of the medical necessity defense. These theories of relief were set forth in their complaint but were not reached by the Court of Appeals. We therefore do not address the question whether judicial relief is available to respondents on these alternative bases. We do note, however, the presence of another avenue of relief. As the Solicitor General confirmed during oral argument, the statute authorizes procedures for the reclassification of Schedule I drugs. But perhaps even more important than these legal avenues is the democratic process, in which the voices of voters allied with these respondents may one day be heard in the halls of Congress.

Under the present state of the law, however, the judgment of the Court of Appeals must be vacated. The case is remanded for further proceedings consistent with this opinion.

It is so ordered.

Justice SCALIA, concurring in the judgment.

I agree with the Court's holding that the Controlled Substances Act (CSA) may validly be applied to respondents' cultivation, distribution, and possession of marijuana for personal, medicinal use. I write separately because my understanding of the doctrinal foundation on which that holding rests is, if not inconsistent with that of the Court, at least more nuanced.

[U]nlike the channels, instrumentalities, and agents of interstate commerce, activities that substantially affect interstate commerce are not themselves part of interstate commerce, and thus the power to regulate them cannot come from the Commerce Clause alone. Rather, as this Court has acknowledged since at least *United States v. Coombs*, 9 L. Ed. 1004, 12 Pet. 72 (1838), Congress's regulatory authority over intrastate activities that are not themselves part of interstate commerce (including activities that have a substantial effect on interstate commerce) derives from the Necessary and Proper Clause. And the category of "activities that substantially affect interstate commerce," *Lopez, supra*, at 559, is *incomplete* because the authority to enact laws necessary and proper for the regulation of interstate commerce is not limited to laws governing intrastate activities that substantially affect interstate commerce. Where necessary to make a regulation of interstate commerce effective, Congress may regulate even those intrastate activities that do not themselves substantially affect interstate commerce.

I.

As we implicitly acknowledged in *Lopez* Congress's authority to enact laws necessary and proper for the regulation of interstate commerce is not limited to laws directed against economic activities that have a substantial effect on interstate commerce. Though the conduct in Lopez was not economic, the Court nevertheless recognized that it could be regulated as "an essential part of a larger regulation of economic activity, in which the regulatory scheme could be undercut unless the intrastate activity were regulated." This statement referred to those cases permitting the regulation of intrastate activities "which in a substantial way interfere with or obstruct the exercise of the granted power."

Although this power "to make regulation effective" commonly overlaps with the authority to regulate economic activities that substantially affect interstate commerce, and may in some cases have been confused with that authority, the two are distinct. The regulation of an intrastate activity may be essential to a comprehensive regulation of interstate commerce even though the intrastate activity does not itself "substantially affect" interstate commerce. Moreover, as the passage from *Lopez* quoted above suggests, Congress may regulate even noneconomic local activity if that regulation is a necessary part of a more general regulation of interstate commerce. The relevant question is simply whether the means chosen are "reasonably adapted" to the attainment of a legitimate end under the commerce power.

In *Darby*, for instance, the Court explained that "Congress, having adopted the policy of excluding from interstate commerce all goods produced for the commerce which do not conform to the specified labor standards," 312 U.S. at 121, could not only require employers engaged in the production of goods for interstate commerce to conform to wage and hour standards, but could also require those employers to keep employment records in order to demonstrate compliance with the regulatory scheme, *id.* at 125. While the Court sustained the former regulation on the alternative ground that the activity it regulated could have a "great effect" on interstate commerce, *id.* at 122–123 it affirmed the latter on the sole ground that "[t]he requirement for records even of the intrastate transaction is an appropriate means to a legitimate end," *id.* at 125.

As the Court said in the *Shreveport R. Co.*, the Necessary and Proper Clause does not give "Congress the authority to regulate the internal commerce of a State, as such," but it does allow Congress "to take all measures necessary or appropriate to" the effective regulation of the interstate market, "although intrastate transactions may thereby be controlled." 234 U.S. at 353; see also *Jones & Laughlin Steel Corp.*, 301 U.S. at 38 (the logic of the *Shreveport Rate Cases* is not limited to instrumentalities of commerce).

II.

Today's principal dissent objects that, by permitting Congress to regulate activities necessary to effective interstate regulation, the Court reduces *Lopez* and *Morrison* to "little more than a drafting guide." I think that criticism unjustified. Unlike the power to regulate activities that have a substantial effect on interstate commerce, the power to enact laws enabling effective regulation of interstate commerce can only be exercised in conjunction with congressional regulation of an interstate market, and it extends only to those measures necessary to make the interstate regulation effective.

Lopez and *Morrison* affirm that Congress may not regulate certain "purely local" activity within the States based solely on the attenuated effect that such activity may have in the interstate market. But those decisions do not declare noneconomic intrastate activities to be categorically beyond the reach of the Federal Government. Neither case involved the power of Congress to exert control over intrastate activities in connection with a more comprehensive scheme of regulation; *Lopez* expressly disclaimed that it was such a case, 514 U.S. at 561 and *Morrison* did not even discuss the possibility that it was.

And there are other restraints upon the Necessary and Proper Clause authority. As Chief Justice Marshall wrote in *McCulloch v. Maryland*, even when the end is constitutional and legitimate, the means must be "appropriate" and "plainly adapted" to that end. Moreover, they may not be otherwise "prohibited" and must be "consistent with the letter and spirit of the constitution." *Ibid.*

JUSTICE O'CONNOR, with whom THE CHIEF JUSTICE and JUSTICE THOMAS join as to all but Part III, dissenting.

One of federalism's chief virtues is that it promotes innovation by allowing for the possibility that "a single courageous State may, if its citizens choose, serve as a laboratory; and try novel social and economic experiments without risk to the rest of the country." *New State Ice Co. v. Liebmann*, 285 U.S. 262, 311, (1932) (Brandeis, J., dissenting).

This case exemplifies the role of States as laboratories. The States' core police powers have always included authority to define criminal law and to protect the health, safety, and welfare of their citizens. Exercising those powers, California (by ballot initiative and then by legislative codification) has come to its own conclusion about the difficult and sensitive question of whether marijuana should be available to relieve severe pain and suffering. Today the Court sanctions an application of the federal Controlled Substances Act that extinguishes that experiment, without any proof that the personal cultivation, possession, and use of marijuana for medicinal purposes, if economic activity in the first place, has a substantial effect on inter-state commerce and is therefore an appropriate subject of federal regulation. In so doing, the Court announces a rule that gives Congress a perverse incentive to legis-late broadly pursuant to the Commerce Clause — nestling questionable assertions of its authority into comprehensive regulatory schemes — rather than with precision. That rule and the result it produces in this case are irreconcilable with our decisions in *Lopez* and *Morrison*. Accordingly I dissent.

The Court's principal means of distinguishing *Lopez* from this case is to observe that the Gun-Free School Zones Act of 1990 was a "brief, single-subject statute," whereas the CSA is "a lengthy and detailed statute creating a comprehensive frame-work for regulating the production, distribution, and possession of five classes of 'controlled substances,'" *ibid.* Thus, according to the Court, it was possible in *Lopez* to evaluate in isolation the constitutionality of criminalizing local activity (there gun possession in school zones), whereas the local activity that the CSA targets (in this case cultivation and possession of marijuana for personal medicinal use) can-not be separated from the general drug control scheme of which it is a part.

Today's decision allows Congress to regulate intrastate activity without check, so long as there is some implication by legislative design that regulating intrastate activity is essential (and the Court appears to equate "essential" with "necessary") to the interstate regulatory scheme. Seizing upon our language in *Lopez* that the stat-ute prohibiting gun possession in school zones was "not an essential part of a larger regulation of economic activity, in which the regulatory scheme could be undercut unless the intrastate activity were regulated," the Court appears to reason that the placement of local activity in a comprehensive scheme confirms that it is essential to that scheme. If the Court is right, then *Lopez* stands for nothing more than a drafting guide: Congress should have described the relevant crime as "transfer or possession of a firearm anywhere in the nation" — thus including commercial and noncom-mercial activity, and clearly encompassing some activity with assuredly substantial effect on interstate commerce. Had it done so, the majority hints, we would have sustained its authority to regulate possession of firearms in school zones. Furthermore, today's decision suggests we would readily sustain a congressional decision to attach the regulation of intrastate activity to a pre-existing comprehensive (or even not-so-comprehensive) scheme. If so, the Court invites increased federal regulation of local activity even if, as it suggests, Congress would not enact a new interstate scheme exclusively for the sake of reaching intrastate activity.

Lopez and *Morrison* did not indicate that the constitutionality of federal regulation depends on superficial and formalistic distinctions. Likewise I did not understand our discussion of the role of courts in enforcing outer limits of the Commerce Clause for the sake of maintaining the federalist balance our Constitution requires, see *Lopez*, as a signal to Congress to enact legislation that is more extensive and more intrusive into the domain of state power. If the Court always defers to Congress as it does today, little may be left to the notion of enumerated powers.

The hard work for courts, then, is to identify objective markers for confining the analysis in Commerce Clause cases. Here, respondents challenge the constitutionality of the CSA as applied to them and those similarly situated. I agree with the Court that we must look beyond respondents' own activities. Otherwise, individual litigants could always exempt themselves from Commerce Clause regulation merely by pointing to the obvious — that their personal activities do not have a substantial effect on interstate commerce. The task is to identify a mode of analysis that allows Congress to regulate more than nothing (by declining to reduce each case to its litigants) and less than everything (by declining to let Congress set the terms of analysis). The analysis may not be the same in every case, for it depends on the regulatory scheme at issue and the federalism concerns implicated.

A number of objective markers are available to confine the scope of constitutional review here. Both federal and state legislation — including the CSA itself, the California Compassionate Use Act, and other state medical marijuana legislation — recognize that medical and nonmedical (*i.e.*, recreational) uses of drugs are realistically distinct and can be segregated, and regulate them differently. Moreover, because fundamental structural concerns about dual sovereignty animate our Commerce Clause cases, it is relevant that this case involves the interplay of federal and state regulation in areas of criminal law and social policy, where "States lay claim by right of history and expertise." *Lopez*.

B.

Having thus defined the relevant conduct, we must determine whether, under our precedents, the conduct is economic and, in the aggregate, substantially affects interstate commerce. Even if intrastate cultivation and possession of marijuana for one's own medicinal use can properly be characterized as economic, and I question whether it can, it has not been shown that such activity substantially affects interstate commerce. Similarly, it is neither self-evident nor demonstrated that regulating such activity is necessary to the interstate drug control scheme.

The Court's definition of economic activity is breathtaking. It defines as economic any activity involving the production, distribution, and consumption of commodities. And it appears to reason that when an interstate market for a commodity exists, regulating the intrastate manufacture or possession of that commodity is constitutional either because that intrastate activity is itself economic, or because regulating it is a rational part of regulating its market. Putting to one side the problem endemic to the Court's opinion — the shift in focus from the activity at issue in this case to the entirety of what the CSA regulates, see *Lopez*, ("depending on the level of generality, any activity can be looked upon as commercial") — the Court's definition of economic activity for purposes of Commerce Clause jurisprudence threatens to sweep all of productive human activity into federal regulatory reach.

The Court uses a dictionary definition of economics to skirt the real problem of drawing a meaningful line between "what is national and what is local," *Jones & Laughlin Steel*. It will not do to say that Congress may regulate noncommercial activity simply because it may have an effect on the demand for commercial goods, or because the noncommercial endeavor can, in some sense, substitute for commercial activity. Most commercial goods or services have some sort of privately producible analogue. Home care substitutes for daycare. Charades games substitute for movie tickets. Backyard or windowsill gardening substitutes for going to the supermarket. To draw the line wherever private activity affects the demand for market goods is to draw no line at all, and to declare everything economic. We have already rejected the result that would follow — a federal police power. *Lopez*.

In *Lopez* and *Morrison*, we suggested that economic activity usually relates directly to commercial activity. See *Morrison* (intrastate activities that have been within Congress' power to regulate have been "of an apparent commercial character"); *Lopez* (distinguishing the Gun-Free School Zones Act of 1990 from "activities that arise out of or are connected with a commercial transaction"). The homegrown cultivation and personal possession and use of marijuana for medicinal purposes has no apparent commercial character. Everyone agrees that the marijuana at issue in this case was never in the stream of commerce, and neither were the supplies for growing it. (Marijuana is highly unusual among the substances subject to the CSA in that it can be cultivated without any materials that have traveled in interstate commerce.) *Lopez* makes clear that possession is not itself commercial activity. And respondents have not come into possession by means of any commercial transaction; they have simply grown, in their own homes, marijuana for their own use, without acquiring, buying, selling, or bartering a thing of value.

The Court suggests that *Wickard*, which we have identified as "perhaps the most far reaching example of Commerce Clause authority over intrastate activity," *Lopez*, established federal regulatory power over any home consumption of a commodity for which a national market exists. I disagree. In contrast to the CSA's limitless assertion of power, Congress provided an exemption within the AAA for small producers. When Filburn planted the wheat at issue in *Wickard*, the statute exempted plantings less than 200 bushels (about six tons), and when he harvested his wheat it exempted plantings less than six acres. *Wickard*, then, did not extend Commerce Clause authority to something as modest as the home cook's herb garden. This is not to say that Congress may never regulate small quantities of commodities possessed or produced for personal use, or to deny that it sometimes needs to enact a zero tolerance regime for such commodities. It is merely to say that *Wickard* did not hold or imply that small-scale production of commodities is always economic, and automatically within Congress' reach.

Even assuming that economic activity is at issue in this case, the Government has made no showing in fact that the possession and use of homegrown marijuana for medical purposes, in California or elsewhere, has a substantial effect on interstate commerce. Similarly, the Government has not shown that regulating such activity is necessary to an interstate regulatory scheme. Whatever the specific theory of "substantial effects" at issue (*i.e.*, whether the activity substantially affects interstate commerce, whether its regulation is necessary to an interstate regulatory scheme, or both), a concern for dual sovereignty requires that Congress' excursion into the traditional domain of States be justified.

That is why characterizing this as a case about the Necessary and Proper Clause does not change the analysis significantly. Congress must exercise its authority under the Necessary and Proper Clause in a manner consistent with basic constitutional principles. As Justice Scalia recognizes, Congress cannot use its authority under the Clause to contravene the principle of state sovereignty embodied in the Tenth Amendment. Likewise, that authority must be used in a manner consistent with the notion of enumerated powers — a structural principle that is as much part of the Constitution as the Tenth Amendment's explicit textual command. Accordingly, something more than mere assertion is required when Congress purports to have power over local activity whose connection to an intrastate market is not self-evident. Otherwise, the Necessary and Proper Clause will always be a back door for unconstitutional federal regulation.

III.

We would do well to recall how James Madison, the father of the Constitution, described our system of joint sovereignty to the people of New York: "The powers delegated by the proposed constitution to the federal government are few and defined. Those which are to remain in the State governments are numerous and indefinite. The powers reserved to the several States will extend to all the objects which, in the ordinary course of affairs, concern the lives, liberties, and properties of the people, and the internal order, improvement, and prosperity of the State." The Federalist No. 45, pp. 292–293 (C. Rossiter ed. 1961).

Relying on Congress' abstract assertions, the Court has endorsed making it a federal crime to grow small amounts of marijuana in one's own home for one's own medicinal use. This overreaching stifles an express choice by some States, concerned for the lives and liberties of their people, to regulate medical marijuana differently. If I were a California citizen, I would not have voted for the medical marijuana ballot initiative; if I were a California legislator I would not have supported the Compassionate Use Act. But whatever the wisdom of California's experiment with medical marijuana, the federalism principles that have driven our Commerce Clause cases require that room for experiment be protected in this case. For these reasons I dissent.

JUSTICE THOMAS, dissenting.

Respondents Diane Monson and Angel Raich use marijuana that has never been bought or sold, that has never crossed state lines, and that has had no demonstrable effect on the national market for marijuana. If Congress can regulate this under the Commerce Clause, then it can regulate virtually anything — and the Federal Government is no longer one of limited and enumerated powers.

Notes and Questions

(1) The Gun-Free School Zones Act regulated private activity. The decision in *Lopez* is thus striking in that it represents the first occasion since 1936 where the Court has found that Congress lacks the Commerce Clause authority to regulate private conduct.

(2) On what basis did the Chief Justice conclude that the Gun-Free School Zones Act is unconstitutional? Did the majority utilize a new rule or standard for measuring compliance with the Commerce Clause? If so, what is the new rule? If not, why did the statute fail to survive the usual inquiry, asking merely whether Congress had a "rational basis" for concluding that gun possession near schools has "a significant effect on interstate commerce"? In a similar vein, how do you explain the pro-government outcome in *Gonzales*?

(3) Chief Justice Rehnquist maintained that the Gun-Free School Zones Act "has nothing to do with 'commerce'." In *Morrison* he asserted that violent gender-motivated crimes "are not, in any sense of the phrase, economic activity." What evidence led the majority to such conclusions? Consider the possible commercial effects of gun possession in the schools assessed in Justice Breyer's dissent in *Lopez*. Consider also Justice Thomas's assertion in *Gonzales* that the medical marijuana at issue had nothing to do with commerce. Which side has the better of the argument on the question of the existence of an economic dimension to the regulation in the three cases?

Consider the earlier decisions in *Wickard* and *Perez*. Were the statutes upheld in those cases directed at activities having a more significant effect on interstate commerce? Did the Court apply the same standard to these two Acts as the earlier Courts applied to the wheat farming and loan-sharking activities?

(4) An alternative interpretation of the *Lopez* and *Morrison* opinions is that the majority returned to the approaches of *Knight* and *Hammer* and the formal categorization and labelling of activities as "commercial" or not, and as logically "directly" or "indirectly" related to interstate commerce. Is this a fair assessment of the majority opinions? If it is, is the return to such an approach consistent with federalism values?

(5) According to the majority, did the two federal statutes fail because there was an insufficient demonstration in the statute or its legislative history of the connections between gun possession in the schools and gender-motivated violence and interstate commerce? Are such "findings" required of Congress when it exercises its constitutional powers? Would the presence of findings have made a difference in the outcome of *Lopez*? A veritable mountain of findings was made in support of the VWA. Why didn't they suffice? Which institution is better equipped to determine the effects of an activity on interstate commerce, Congress or the judiciary?

On September 13, 1994, President Clinton signed the Violent Crime Control and Law Enforcement Act of 1994, Pub. L. No. 103-322, 108 Stat. 1796. Section 320904 of the Act amends § 922 to include congressional findings regarding the effects of firearm possession in and around schools upon interstate commerce.

(6) May *Lopez* be viewed as a "clear statement" case, where the position of the Court is not necessarily that the Congress lacks the constitutional power to act in this sphere, but that if it wishes to act, it must make its constitutional case clearly and explicitly? In 1996, legislation was enacted that makes it unlawful for anyone to possess or discharge a firearm in a school zone "that has moved in or that otherwise affects interstate or foreign commerce." 18 U.S.C. § 922(q)(2)(A). Is this rewrite of the Gun-Free School Zones Act constitutional after *Lopez*?

(7) The Court has also stated that Congress must use "exceedingly clear language if it wishes to significantly alter the balance between federal and state power." *United States Forest Service v. Cowpasture River Preservation Ass'n*, 140 S. Ct. 1837 (2020). Perhaps *Lopez* and *Morrison* were decided against Congress simply because it regulated in areas traditionally reserved for local control — education and criminal justice. Is the subject matter of regulation a constitutionally adequate or important basis for deciding the scope of congressional Commerce Clause power? Does this perspective explain the outcome in *Gonzales*?

(8) Consider the outcomes of *Lopez* in light of the values of federalism. Perhaps the 1990 Gun-Free School Zones Act was simply unnecessary, considering the more than 40 state laws in force regulating the same or similar conduct. Is federalism served best by having federal judges overturn congressional efforts like these, or by leaving it to the political processes to determine whether there should be federal regulation? Do you agree with Justice Breyer that the inherent subjectivity of a judicial inquiry into whether an activity has a "substantial effect on interstate commerce" should cause the reviewing courts to err on the side of deference to Congress?

(9) In light of *Lopez* and *Gonzales*, can you identify what otherwise local, intrastate activity has a sufficient "effect" on interstate commerce to permit congressional regulation? Are other federal criminal laws now vulnerable to constitutional challenge on the theory that they target intrastate activities? What about federal environmental regulation, for example, that controls development of wetlands areas?

In *Jones v. United States*, 529 U.S. 848 (2000), the Court unanimously ruled that the federal arson law "does not reach an owner-occupied residence that is not used for any commercial purpose." Construing the statute's text, the Court found that the private residence was not "used in" commerce or commerce-affecting activity. The Court thus avoided what it considered a "constitutionally doubtful construction" of the arson law.

The United States defended the law's broad application on the ground that private homes were connected to interstate commerce through their receipt of natural gas through interstate lines as well as through interstate mortgage and insurance markets. Writing for the Court, Justice Ginsburg said that the Government's claim defied the "common perception" of what it means to "use" something in interstate commerce. In this instance, she said, the owner "used the property as his home, the center of his family life."

In addition, Justice Ginsburg referred to *Lopez* and its concern with federal imposition in an area like arson, "a paradigmatic common-law state crime." If the Government's interpretation of the arson law were adopted, "hardly a building in the land would fall outside the federal statute's domain."

(10) To what extent may Congress achieve its policy objectives through financial inducements, particularly in areas where more coercive regulation may be found to exceed Commerce Clause powers or threaten federalism interests? In *South Dakota v. Dole*, 483 U.S. 203 (1987), the state challenged a federal law, 23 U.S.C. §158, which directs the Secretary of Transportation to withhold a percentage of federal highway funds from those states that permit the purchase and possession of alcoholic beverages by persons under 21. South Dakota argued that section 158 violates constitutional limitations on congressional exercise of the spending power and violates the Twenty-first Amendment. Chief Justice Rehnquist, writing for the Court, rejected these arguments and upheld the law:

> The Constitution empowers Congress to "lay and collect Taxes, Duties, Imposts, and Excises, to pay the Debts and provide for the common Defense and general Welfare of the United States." Art. I, §8, cl. 1. Incident to this power, Congress may attach conditions on the receipt of federal funds, and has repeatedly employed the power "to further broad policy objectives by conditioning receipt of federal moneys upon compliance by the recipient with federal statutory and administrative directives." Thus, objectives not thought to be within Article I's "enumerated legislative fields," may nevertheless be attained through the use of the spending power and the conditional grant of federal funds.
>
> The spending power is of course not unlimited but is instead subject to several general restrictions articulated in our cases. The first of these limitations is derived from the language of the Constitution itself: the exercise of the spending power must be in pursuit of "the general welfare." In considering whether a particular expenditure is intended to serve general public purposes, courts should defer substantially to the judgment of Congress. Second, we have required that if Congress desires to condition the States'

receipt of federal funds, it "must do so unambiguously, enabl[ing] the States to exercise their choice knowingly, cognizant of the consequences of their participation." Third, our cases have suggested (without significant elaboration) that conditions on federal grants might be illegitimate if they are unrelated "to the federal interest in particular national projects or programs." Finally, we have noted that other constitutional provisions may provide an independent bar to the conditional grant of federal funds.

South Dakota does not seriously claim that § 158 is inconsistent with any of the first three restrictions mentioned above. We can readily conclude that the provision is designed to serve the general welfare, especially in light of the fact that "the concept of welfare or the opposite is shaped by Congress." Congress found that the differing drinking ages in the States created particular incentives for young persons to combine their desire to drink with their ability to drive, and that this interstate problem required a national solution. The means it chose to address this dangerous situation were reasonably calculated to advance the general welfare. The conditions upon which States receive the funds, moreover, could not be more clearly stated by Congress. And the condition imposed by Congress is directly related to one of the main purposes for which highway funds are expended — safe interstate travel. This goal of the interstate highway system had been frustrated by varying drinking ages among the States. A presidential commission appointed to study alcohol-related accidents and fatalities on the Nation's highways concluded that the lack of uniformity in the States' drinking ages created "an incentive to drink and drive" because "young persons commut[e] to border States where the drinking age is lower." By enacting § 158, Congress conditioned the receipt of federal funds in a way reasonably calculated to address this particular impediment to a purpose for which the funds are expended.

The remaining question about the validity of § 158 — and the basic point of disagreement between the parties — is whether the Twenty-first Amendment constitutes an "independent constitutional bar" to the conditional grant of federal funds. Petitioner, relying on its view that the Twenty-first Amendment prohibits *direct* regulation of drinking ages by Congress, asserts that "Congress may not use the spending power to regulate that which it is prohibited from regulating directly under the Twenty-first Amendment." But our cases show that this "independent constitutional bar" limitation on the spending power is not of the kind petitioner suggests. [T]he constitutional limitations on Congress when exercising its spending power are less exacting than those on its authority to regulate directly.

We have also held that a perceived Tenth Amendment limitation on congressional regulation of state affairs did not concomitantly limit the range of conditions legitimately placed on federal grants. In *Oklahoma v. Civil Service Comm'n*, 330 U.S. 127 (1947), the Court considered the validity of the Hatch Act insofar as it was applied to political activities of state officials whose employment was financed in whole or in part with federal funds. The State contended that an order under this provision to withhold certain federal funds unless a state official was removed invaded its sovereignty in violation of the Tenth Amendment. Though finding that "the United States is not concerned with, and has no power to regulate, local political activities as such of state officials," the Court nevertheless held that the Federal Government "does have power to fix the terms upon which its money allotments to states shall be disbursed." The Court found no violation of the State's sovereignty because the State could, and did, adopt "the 'simple expedient' of not yielding to what she urges is federal coercion. The offer of benefits to a state by the United States dependent upon cooperation by the state with federal plans, assumedly for the general welfare, is not unusual."

These cases establish that the "independent constitutional bar" limitation on the spending power is not, as petitioner suggests, a prohibition on the indirect achievement of objectives which Congress is not empowered to achieve directly. Instead, we think that the language in our earlier opinions stands for the unexceptionable proposition that the power may not be used to induce the States to engage in activities that would themselves be unconstitutional. Thus, for example, a grant of federal funds conditioned on invidiously discriminatory state action or the infliction of cruel and unusual punishment would be an illegitimate exercise of the Congress' broad spending power. But no such claim can be or is made here. Were South Dakota to succumb to the blandishments offered by Congress and raise its drinking age to 21, the State's action in so doing would not violate the constitutional rights of anyone.

Our decisions have recognized that in some circumstances the financial inducement offered by Congress might be so coercive as to pass the point at which "pressure turns into compulsion." Here, however, Congress has directed only that a State desiring to establish a minimum drinking age lower than 21 lose a relatively small percentage of certain federal highway funds. Petitioner contends that the coercive nature of this program is evident from the degree of success it has achieved. We cannot conclude, however, that a conditional grant of federal money of this sort is unconstitutional simply by reason of its success in achieving the congressional objective.

Here Congress has offered relatively mild encouragement to the States to enact higher minimum drinking ages than they would otherwise choose. But the enactment of such laws remains the prerogative of the States not merely in theory but in fact. Even if Congress might lack the power to impose a national minimum drinking age directly, we conclude that encouragement to state action found in § 158 is a valid use of the spending power.

In *Sabri v. United States*, 541 U.S. 600 (2004), the Court upheld a federal statute that proscribes bribery of state, local, and tribal officials of entities that receive at least $10,000 in federal funds. Sabri argued that the statute is unconstitutional for failure to require proof of a connection between the federal funds and the alleged bribe. The Supreme Court determined that the Spending Clause and the Necessary and Proper Clause provide authority for Congress to "see to it that taxpayer dollars appropriated are in fact spent for the general welfare, and not frittered away in graft or on projects undermined when funds are siphoned off or corrupt public officers are derelict about demanding value for dollars." Why would the Court not insist on a jurisdictional hook between the federal money and the crime? Is *Sabri* consistent with *Dole*?

Based on *Dole* and *Sabri*, can you outline the elements of a federal program based on spending inducements that would exceed Congress's constitutional power?

Problem C

The Freedom of Access to Clinic Entrances Act (FACE), 18 U.S.C. § 248, imposes criminal penalties for those who "by force or threat of force or by physical obstruction, intentionally interfere with any person because that person is" entering or leaving a family planning clinic. The stated purpose of the FACE Act is to "protect and promote the public safety and health and activities affecting interstate commerce" by establishing remedies for conduct that interferes with persons seeking to obtain or provide reproductive health services. In support of FACE and as part of the statute's preamble, Congress found that family planning clinics operate within the stream of interstate commerce because they purchase supplies, employ staff, own and lease office space, and generate income. Congress also found that some individuals travel across state lines in order to obtain family planning clinic services, that obstructing access to clinics decreases the number of abortions performed and thus has a negative effect on interstate commerce, and that the problems addressed by FACE are nationwide in scope and are beyond the ability of the states to control.

Members of Operation Rescue, a pro-life, anti-abortion group, emboldened by the Supreme Court's 2022 decision in *Dobbs v. Jackson Women's Health Organization* holding that there is no constitutional right to an abortion, seek your advice concerning the likelihood of success of a constitutional challenge to FACE. They point out that the criminal prohibition in FACE amounts to nothing more than regulation of non-violent trespass. How would you advise Operation Rescue? Does FACE exceed Congress's Commerce Clause powers? Is the FACE Act more likely to survive constitutional scrutiny if it contains an express jurisdictional element that limits the regulation to conduct affecting interstate commerce, and if there are express congressional findings regarding the effects of the regulated activity on interstate commerce? Would you answer differently if FACE was based on the spending power rather than the Commerce Clause, and the access protections outlined above were prescribed in any state that agreed to be a recipient of federal family planning block grants?

§ 4.04 Congressional Power to Enforce Civil Rights

After *Lopez*, most observers agreed that the Commerce Clause was no longer the source of limitless power for Congress to exercise an effective national police power. The provisions of the Civil Rights Act of 1964 upheld in *McClung* and *Heart of Atlanta* were anchored in the Commerce Clause to enable Congress to reach pervasive discrimination in the private sector. In those cases, the commercial transactions at issue provided a clear link to the national economy. In many instances, however, Congress has relied on its authority "to enforce" by "appropriate legislation" the post-Civil War amendments to regulate the non-economic rights of persons, and to create causes of action against state and private misconduct.

A wide range of civil rights legislation has been enacted pursuant to the post-Civil War amendment authorities, from the immediate aftermath of the Civil War to the present. We examine the scope of congressional authority to enforce civil rights in selected and controversial areas. Note that one important limit on congressional authority to enforce civil rights — the Eleventh Amendment — has been considered in Chapter 3. The Eleventh Amendment principles, along with separation of powers considerations of which branch should decide the civil rights questions presented here, should be recalled while studying the materials that follow.

In *City of Boerne v. Flores*, 521 U.S. 507 (1997), the Court reviewed the historical development of the doctrine interpreting the scope of congressional authority in § 5 of the Fourteenth Amendment "to enforce" by "appropriate legislation" the amendment's substantive provisions:

> All must acknowledge that § 5 is "a positive grant of legislative power" to Congress, *Katzenbach v. Morgan*, 384 U.S. 641, 651 (1966). In *Ex parte Virginia*, 100 U.S. 339, 345–346 (1879), we explained the scope of Congress' § 5 power in the following broad terms:

> "Whatever legislation is appropriate, that is, adapted to carry out the objects the amendments have in view, whatever tends to enforce submission to the prohibitions they contain, and to secure to all persons the enjoyment of perfect equality of civil rights and the equal protection of the laws against State denial or invasion, if not prohibited, is brought within the domain of congressional power."

> Legislation which deters or remedies constitutional violations can fall within the sweep of Congress' enforcement power even if in the process it prohibits conduct which is not itself unconstitutional and intrudes into "legislative spheres of autonomy previously reserved to the States." *Fitzpatrick v. Bitzer*, 427 U.S. 445, 455 (1976). For example, the Court upheld a suspension of literacy tests and similar voting requirements under Congress' parallel power to enforce the provisions of the Fifteenth Amendment, see U.S. Const., Amdt. 15, § 2, as a measure to combat racial discrimination in

voting, *South Carolina v. Katzenbach*, 383 U.S. 301, 308 (1966), despite the facial constitutionality of the tests under *Lassiter v. Northampton County Bd. of Elections*, 360 U.S. 45 (1959). We have also concluded that other measures protecting voting rights are within Congress' power to enforce the Fourteenth and Fifteenth Amendments, despite the burdens those measures placed on the States. *South Carolina v. Katzenbach* (upholding several provisions of the Voting Rights Act of 1965); *Katzenbach v. Morgan* (upholding ban on literacy tests that prohibited certain people schooled in Puerto Rico from voting); *Oregon v. Mitchell*, 400 U.S. 112 (1970) (upholding 5-year nationwide ban on literacy tests and similar voting requirements for registering to vote); *City of Rome v. United States*, 446 U.S. 156, 161 (1980) (upholding 7-year extension of the Voting Rights Act's requirement that certain jurisdictions preclear any change to a "'standard, practice, or procedure with respect to voting'").

It is also true, however, that "[a]s broad as the congressional enforcement power is, it is not unlimited." *Oregon v. Mitchell* (opinion of Black, J.). In assessing the breadth of § 5's enforcement power, we begin with its text. Congress has been given the power "to enforce" the "provisions of this article." Congress' power under § 5, however, extends only to "enforcing" the provisions of the Fourteenth Amendment. The Court has described this power as "remedial," *South Carolina v. Katzenbach*. The design of the Amendment and the text of § 5 are inconsistent with the suggestion that Congress has the power to decree the substance of the Fourteenth Amendment's restrictions on the States. Congress does not enforce a constitutional right by changing what the right is. It has been given the power "to enforce," not the power to determine what constitutes a constitutional violation. Were it not so, what Congress would be enforcing would no longer be, in any meaningful sense, the "provisions of [the Fourteenth Amendment]."

While the line between measures that remedy or prevent unconstitutional actions and measures that make a substantive change in the governing law is not easy to discern, and Congress must have wide latitude in determining where it lies, the distinction exists and must be observed. There must be a congruence and proportionality between the injury to be prevented or remedied and the means adopted to that end. Lacking such a connection, legislation may become substantive in operation and effect. History and our case law support drawing the distinction, one apparent from the text of the Amendment.

1

The Fourteenth Amendment's history confirms the remedial, rather than substantive, nature of the Enforcement Clause. The Joint Committee on Reconstruction of the 39th Congress began drafting what would become the Fourteenth Amendment in January 1866. The objections to the Committee's first draft of the Amendment, and the rejection of the draft, have a direct bearing on the central issue of defining Congress' enforcement power. In February, Republican Representative John Bingham of Ohio reported the following draft amendment to the House of Representatives on behalf of the Joint Committee:

"The Congress shall have power to make all laws which shall be necessary and proper to secure to the citizens of each State all privileges and immunities of citizens in the several States, and to all persons in the several States equal protection in the rights of life, liberty, and property." Cong. Globe, 39th Cong., 1st Sess., 1034 (1866).

The proposal encountered immediate opposition, which continued through three days of debate. Members of Congress from across the political spectrum criticized the Amendment, and the criticisms had a common theme: The proposed Amendment gave Congress too much legislative power at the expense of the existing constitutional structure. As a result of these objections having been expressed from so many different quarters, the House voted to table the proposal. The Amendment in its early form was not again considered. Instead, the Joint Committee began drafting a new article of Amendment, which it reported to Congress on April 30, 1866.

Section 1 of the new draft Amendment imposed self-executing limits on the States. Section 5 prescribed that "[t]he Congress shall have power to enforce, by appropriate legislation, the provisions of this article." See Cong. Globe, 39th Cong., 1st Sess., at 2286. Under the revised Amendment, Congress' power was no longer plenary but remedial. [T]he new measure passed both Houses and was ratified in July 1868 as the Fourteenth Amendment.

The significance of the defeat of the Bingham proposal was apparent even then. During the debates over the Ku Klux Klan Act only a few years after the Amendment's ratification, Representative James Garfield argued there were limits on Congress' enforcement power, saying "unless we ignore both the history and the language of these clauses we cannot, by any reasonable interpretation, give to [§ 5] the force and effect of the rejected [Bingham] clause." Cong. Globe, 42d Cong., 1st Sess., at App. 151; see also id., at App. 115–116 (statement of Rep. Farnsworth). Scholars of successive generations have agreed with this assessment. See H. Flack, The Adoption of the Fourteenth Amendment 64 (1908); Bickel, The Voting Rights Cases, 1966 Sup. Ct. Rev. 79, 97.

The design of the Fourteenth Amendment has proved significant also in maintaining the traditional separation of powers between Congress and the Judiciary. The first eight Amendments to the Constitution set forth self-executing prohibitions on governmental action, and this Court has had primary authority to interpret those prohibitions. The Bingham draft, some thought, departed from that tradition by vesting in Congress primary power to interpret and elaborate on the meaning of the new Amendment through legislation. Under it, "Congress, and not the courts, was to judge whether or not any of the privileges or immunities were not secured to citizens in the several States." While this separation of powers aspect did not occasion the widespread resistance which was caused by the proposal's threat to the federal balance, it nonetheless attracted the attention of various Members. See Cong. Globe, 39th Cong., 1st Sess., at 1064 (statement of Rep. Hale) (noting that Bill of Rights, unlike the Bingham proposal, "provide safeguards to be enforced by the courts, and not to be exercised by the Legislature"); *id.*, at App. 133 (statement of Rep. Rogers) (prior to Bingham proposal it "was left entirely for the courts to enforce the privileges and immunities of the citizens"). As enacted, the Fourteenth Amendment confers substantive rights against the States which, like the provisions of the Bill of Rights, are self-executing.

2

The remedial and preventive nature of Congress' enforcement power, and the limitation inherent in the power, were confirmed in our earliest cases on the Fourteenth Amendment. In the *Civil Rights Cases*, 109 U.S. 3 (1883), the Court invalidated sections of the Civil Rights Act of 1875 which prescribed criminal penalties for denying to any person "the full enjoyment of" public accommodations and conveyances, on the grounds that it exceeded Congress' power by seeking to regulate private conduct. The Enforcement Clause, the Court said, did not authorize Congress to pass "general legislation upon the rights of the citizen, but corrective legislation; that is, such as may be necessary and proper for counteracting such laws as the States may adopt or enforce, and which, by the amendment, they are prohibited from making or enforcing."

Recent cases have continued to revolve around the question of whether § 5 legislation can be considered remedial. In *South Carolina v. Katzenbach*, we emphasized that "[t]he constitutional propriety of [legislation adopted under the Enforcement Clause] must be judged with reference to the historical experience it reflects." There we upheld various provisions of the Voting Rights Act of 1965, finding them to be "remedies aimed at areas where voting discrimination has been most flagrant," and necessary to "banish the blight of racial discrimination in voting, which has infected the electoral process in parts of our country for nearly a century." We noted evidence in the record reflecting the subsisting and pervasive discriminatory — and therefore unconstitutional — use of literacy tests. The Act's new remedies, which used the administrative resources of the Federal Government, included the suspension of both literacy tests and, pending federal review, all new voting regulations in covered jurisdictions, as well as the assignment of federal examiners to list qualified applicants enabling those listed to vote. The new, unprecedented remedies were deemed necessary given the ineffectiveness of the existing voting rights laws, and the slow costly character of case-by-case litigation.

After *South Carolina v. Katzenbach*, the Court continued to acknowledge the necessity of using strong remedial and preventive measures to respond to the widespread and persisting deprivation of constitutional rights resulting from this country's history of racial discrimination. *See Oregon v. Mitchell; City of Rome.*

3

Any suggestion that Congress has a substantive, non-remedial power under the Fourteenth Amendment is not supported by our case law. In *Oregon v. Mitchell*, a majority of the Court concluded Congress had exceeded its enforcement powers by enacting legislation lowering the minimum age of voters from 21 to 18 in state and local elections. The five Members of the Court who reached this conclusion explained that the legislation intruded into an area reserved by the Constitution to the States. Four of these five were explicit in rejecting the position that § 5 endowed Congress with the power to establish the meaning of constitutional provisions.

There is language in our opinion in *Katzenbach v. Morgan* which could be interpreted as acknowledging a power in Congress to enact legislation that expands the rights contained in § 1 of the Fourteenth Amendment. This is not a necessary interpretation, however, or even the best one. In *Morgan*, the Court considered the constitutionality of § 4(e) of the Voting Rights Act of 1965, which provided that no person who had successfully completed the sixth primary grade in a public school in, or a private school accredited by, the Commonwealth of Puerto Rico in which the language of instruction was other than English could be denied the right to vote because of an inability to read or write English. New York's Constitution, on the other hand, required voters to be able to read and write English. The Court provided two related rationales for its conclusion that § 4(e) could "be viewed as a measure to secure for the Puerto Rican community residing in New York nondiscriminatory treatment by government." Under the first rationale, Congress could prohibit New York from denying the right to vote to large segments of its Puerto Rican community, in order to give Puerto Ricans "enhanced political power" that would be "helpful in gaining nondiscriminatory treatment in public services for the entire Puerto Rican community." Section 4(e) thus could be justified as a remedial measure to deal with "discrimination in governmental services." The second rationale, an alternative holding, did not address discrimination in the provision of public services but "discrimination in establishing voter qualifications." The Court perceived a factual basis on which Congress could have concluded that New York's literacy requirement "constituted an invidious discrimination in violation of the Equal Protection Clause." Both rationales for upholding § 4(e) rested on unconstitutional discrimination by New York and Congress' reasonable attempt to combat it. As Justice Stewart explained in *Oregon v. Mitchell*, interpreting *Morgan* to give Congress the power to interpret the Constitution "would require an enormous extension of that decision's rationale."

If Congress could define its own powers by altering the Fourteenth Amendment's meaning, no longer would the Constitution be "superior paramount law, unchangeable by ordinary means." It would be "on a level with ordinary legislative acts, and, like other acts, alterable when the legislature shall please to alter it." *Marbury v. Madison*. Under this approach, it is difficult to conceive of a principle that would limit congressional power. Shifting legislative majorities could change the Constitution and effectively circumvent the difficult and detailed amendment process contained in Article V.

Tennessee v. Lane

United States Supreme Court
541 U.S. 509, 124 S. Ct. 1978, 158 L. Ed. 2d 820 (2004)

Mr. Justice Stevens delivered the opinion of the Court.

Title II of the Americans with Disabilities Act of 1990 (ADA or Act), 104 Stat. 337, 42 U.S.C. §§ 12131–12165, provides that "no qualified individual with a disability shall, by reason of such disability, be excluded from participation in or be denied the benefits of the services, programs or activities of a public entity, or be subjected to discrimination by any such entity." § 12132. The question presented in this case is whether Title II exceeds Congress' power under § 5 of the Fourteenth Amendment.

I

In August 1998, respondents George Lane and Beverly Jones filed this action against the State of Tennessee and a number of Tennessee counties, alleging past and ongoing violations of Title II. Respondents, both of whom are paraplegics who use wheelchairs for mobility, claimed that they were denied access to, and the services of, the state court system by reason of their disabilities. Lane alleged that he was compelled to appear to answer a set of criminal charges on the second floor of a county courthouse that had no elevator. At his first appearance, Lane crawled up two flights of stairs to get to the courtroom. When Lane returned to the courthouse for a hearing, he refused to crawl again or to be carried by officers to the courtroom; he consequently was arrested and jailed for failure to appear. Jones, a certified court reporter, alleged that she has not been able to gain access to a number of county courthouses, and, as a result, has lost both work and an opportunity to participate in the judicial process. Respondents sought damages and equitable relief.

The State moved to dismiss the suit on the ground that it was barred by the Eleventh Amendment. The District Court denied the motion without opinion, and the State appealed. The United States intervened to defend Title II's abrogation of the States' Eleventh Amendment immunity. On April 28, 2000, after the appeal had been briefed and argued, the Court of Appeals for the Sixth Circuit entered an order holding the case in abeyance pending our decision in *Board of Trustees of Univ. of Ala. v. Garrett*, 531 U.S. 356 (2001).

In *Garrett*, we concluded that the Eleventh Amendment bars private suits seeking money damages for state violations of Title I of the ADA. We left open, however, the question whether the Eleventh Amendment permits suits for money damages under Title II.

II

The ADA was passed by large majorities in both Houses of Congress after decades of deliberation and investigation into the need for comprehensive legislation to address discrimination against persons with disabilities. In the years immediately preceding the ADA's enactment, Congress held 13 hearings and created a special task force that gathered evidence from every State in the Union. The conclusions Congress drew from this evidence are set forth in the task force and Committee Reports, described in lengthy legislative hearings, and summarized in the preamble to the statute. Central among these conclusions was Congress' finding that:

> individuals with disabilities are a discrete and insular minority who have been faced with restrictions and limitations, subjected to a history of purposeful unequal treatment, and relegated to a position of political powerlessness in our society, based on characteristics that are beyond the control of such individuals and resulting from stereotypic assumptions not truly indicative of the individual ability of such individuals to participate in, and contribute to, society.42 U.S.C. § 12101(a)(7).

Invoking "the sweep of congressional authority, including the power to enforce the fourteenth amendment and to regulate commerce," the ADA is designed "to provide a clear and comprehensive national mandate for the elimination of discrimination against individuals with disabilities." §§ 12101(b)(1), (b)(4). It forbids discrimination against persons with disabilities in three major areas of public life: employment, which is covered by Title I of the statute; public services, programs, and activities, which are the subject of Title II; and public accommodations, which are covered by Title III.

Title II, §§ 12131–12134, prohibits any public entity from discriminating against "qualified" persons with disabilities in the provision or operation of public services, programs, or activities. The Act defines the term "public entity" to include state and local governments, as well as their agencies and instrumentalities. § 12131(1). Persons with disabilities are "qualified" if they, "with or without reasonable modifications to rules, policies, or practices, the removal of architectural, communication, or transportation barriers, or the provision of auxiliary aids and services, mee[t] the essential eligibility requirements for the receipt of services or the participation in programs or activities provided by a public entity." § 12131(2). Title II's enforcement provision incorporates by reference § 505 of the Rehabilitation Act of 1973, 92 Stat.

2982, as added, 29 U.S.C. §794a, which authorizes private citizens to bring suits for money damages. 42 U.S.C. §12133.

III

[The Court first found that Congress unequivocally expressed its intent to abrogate the States' Eleventh Amendment immunity.] We have repeatedly affirmed that "Congress may enact so-called prophylactic legislation that proscribes facially constitutional conduct, in order to prevent and deter unconstitutional conduct." *Nevada Dep't of Human Res. v. Hibbs*, 538 U.S. 721, 727–728 (2003). The most recent affirmation of the breadth of Congress' §5 power came in *Hibbs*, in which we considered whether a male state employee could recover money damages against the State for its failure to comply with the family-care leave provision of the Family and Medical Leave Act of 1993 (FMLA), 107 Stat. 6, 29 U.S.C. §2601 *et seq*. We upheld the FMLA as a valid exercise of Congress' §5 power to combat unconstitutional sex discrimination, even though there was no suggestion that the State's leave policy was adopted or applied with a discriminatory purpose that would render it unconstitutional under the rule of *Personnel Administrator of Mass. v. Feeney*, 442 U.S. 256 (1979). When Congress seeks to remedy or prevent unconstitutional discrimination, §5 authorizes it to enact prophylactic legislation proscribing practices that are discriminatory in effect, if not in intent, to carry out the basic objectives of the Equal Protection Clause.

Congress' §5 power is not, however, unlimited. While Congress must have a wide berth in devising appropriate remedial and preventative measures for unconstitutional actions, those measures may not work a "substantive change in the governing law." *Boerne*, 521 U.S., at 519. In *Boerne*, we recognized that the line between remedial legislation and substantive redefinition is "not easy to discern," and that "Congress must have wide latitude in determining where it lies." *Id.*, at 519–520. But we also confirmed that "the distinction exists and must be observed," and set forth a test for so observing it: Section 5 legislation is valid if it exhibits "a congruence and proportionality between the injury to be prevented or remedied and the means adopted to that end." *Id.*, at 520.

Applying the *Boerne* test in *Garrett*, we concluded that Title I of the ADA was not a valid exercise of Congress' §5 power to enforce the Fourteenth Amendment's prohibition on unconstitutional disability discrimination in public employment. [W]e concluded Congress' exercise of its prophylactic §5 power was unsupported by a relevant history and pattern of constitutional violations. Although the dissent pointed out that Congress had before it a great deal of evidence of discrimination by the States against persons with disabilities, the Court's opinion noted that the "overwhelming majority" of that evidence related to "the provision of public services and public accommodations, which areas are addressed in Titles II and III," rather than Title I. We also noted that neither the ADA's legislative findings nor its legislative history reflected a concern that the States had been engaging in a pattern of unconstitutional employment discrimination. We emphasized that the House and Senate Committee Reports on the ADA focused on "'discrimination [in] *employment in the private sector,*'" and made no mention of discrimination in public employment. Finally, we concluded that Title I's broad remedial scheme was insufficiently targeted to remedy or prevent unconstitutional discrimination in public employment. Taken together, the historical record and the broad sweep of the statute suggested that Title I's true aim was not so much to enforce the Fourteenth Amendment's prohibitions against disability discrimination in public employment as it was to "rewrite" this Court's Fourteenth Amendment jurisprudence.

In view of the significant differences between Titles I and II, however, *Garrett* left open the question whether Title II is a valid exercise of Congress' §5 enforcement power. It is to that question that we now turn.

IV

The first step of the *Boerne* inquiry requires us to identify the constitutional right or rights that Congress sought to enforce when it enacted Title II. In *Garrett* we identified Title I's purpose as enforcement of the Fourteenth Amendment's command that "all persons similarly situated should be treated alike." *Cleburne v. Cleburne Living Center, Inc.*, 473 U.S. 432, 439 (1985). As we observed, classifications based on disability violate that constitutional command if they lack a rational relationship to a legitimate governmental purpose.

Title II, like Title I, seeks to enforce this prohibition on irrational disability discrimination. But it also seeks to enforce a variety of other basic constitutional guarantees, infringements of which are subject to more searching judicial review. See, *e.g., Dunn v. Blumstein*, 405 U.S. 330, 336 (1972); *Shapiro v. Thompson*, 394 U.S. 618, 634 (1969); *Skinner v. Oklahoma ex rel. Williamson*, 316 U.S. 535, 541 (1942). These rights include some, like the right of access to the courts at issue in this case, that are protected by the Due Process Clause of the Fourteenth Amendment. The Due Process Clause and the Confrontation Clause of the Sixth Amendment, as applied to the States via the Fourteenth Amendment, both guarantee to a criminal defendant such as respondent Lane the "right to be present at all stages of the trial where his absence might frustrate the fairness of the proceedings." *Faretta v. California*, 422 U.S. 806, 819, n. 15 (1975). The Due Process Clause also requires the States to afford certain civil litigants a "meaningful opportunity to be heard" by removing obstacles to their full participation in judicial proceedings. *Boddie v. Connecticut*, 401 U.S. 371, 379 (1971); *M.L.B. v. S.L.J.*, 519 U.S. 102 (1996). We have held that the Sixth Amendment guarantees to criminal defendants the right to trial by a jury composed of a fair cross section of the community, noting that the exclusion of "identifiable segments playing major roles in the community cannot be squared with the constitutional concept of jury trial." *Taylor v. Louisiana*, 419 U.S. 522, 530 (1975). And, finally, we have recognized that members of the public have a right of access to criminal proceedings secured by the First Amendment. *Press-Enterprise Co. v. Superior Court of Cal., County of Riverside*, 478 U.S. 1, 8–15 (1986).

Whether Title II validly enforces these constitutional rights is a question that "must be judged with reference to the historical experience which it reflects." While

§ 5 authorizes Congress to enact reasonably prophylactic remedial legislation, the appropriateness of the remedy depends on the gravity of the harm it seeks to prevent. "Difficult and intractable problems often require powerful remedies," but it is also true that "[s]trong measures appropriate to address one harm may be an unwarranted response to another, lesser one."

It is not difficult to perceive the harm that Title II is designed to address. Congress enacted Title II against a backdrop of pervasive unequal treatment in the administration of state services and programs, including systematic deprivations of fundamental rights. For example, "[a]s of 1979, most States categorically disqualified 'idiots' from voting, without regard to individual capacity." The majority of these laws remain on the books, and have been the subject of legal challenge as recently as 2001. Similarly, a number of States have prohibited and continue to prohibit persons with disabilities from engaging in activities such as marrying and serving as jurors. The historical experience that Title II reflects is also documented in this Court's cases, which have identified unconstitutional treatment of disabled persons by state agencies in a variety of settings, including unjustified commitment, *e.g., Jackson v. Indiana*, 406 U.S. 715 (1972); the abuse and neglect of persons committed to state mental health hospitals, *Youngberg v. Romeo*, 457 U.S. 307 (1982); and irrational discrimination in zoning decisions, *Cleburne v. Cleburne Living Center, Inc.*, 473 U.S. 432 (1985). The decisions of other courts, too, document a pattern of unequal treatment in the administration of a wide range of public services, programs, and activities, including the penal system, public education, and voting. Notably, these decisions also demonstrate a pattern of unconstitutional treatment in the administration of justice.

This pattern of disability discrimination persisted despite several federal and state legislative efforts to address it. In the deliberations that led up to the enactment of the ADA, Congress identified important shortcomings in existing laws that rendered them "inadequate to address the pervasive problems of discrimination that people with disabilities are facing." S. Rep. No. 101-116, at 18. See also H.R. Rep. No. 101-485, pt. 2, at 47, U.S. Code Cong. & Admin. News 1990, pp. 303, 329. It also uncovered further evidence of those shortcomings, in the form of hundreds of examples of unequal treatment of persons with disabilities by States and their political subdivisions. As the Court's opinion in *Garrett* observed, the "overwhelming majority" of these examples concerned discrimination in the administration of public programs and services.

With respect to the particular services at issue in this case, Congress learned that many individuals, in many States across the country, were being excluded from courthouses and court proceedings by reason of their disabilities. A report before Congress showed that some 76% of public services and programs housed in state-owned buildings were inaccessible to and unusable by persons with disabilities, even taking into account the possibility that the services and programs might be restructured or relocated to other parts of the buildings. U.S. Civil Rights Commission, Accommodating the Spectrum of Individual Abilities 39 (1983). Congress itself heard testimony from persons with disabilities who described the physical inaccessibility of local courthouses. Oversight Hearing on H.R. 4468 before the House Subcommittee on Select Education of the Committee on Education and Labor, 100th Cong., 2d Sess., 40–41, 48 (1988). And its appointed task force heard numerous examples of the exclusion of persons with disabilities from state judicial services and programs, including exclusion of persons with visual impairments and hearing impairments from jury service, failure of state and local governments to provide interpretive services for the hearing impaired, failure to permit the testimony of adults with developmental disabilities in abuse cases, and failure to make courtrooms accessible to witnesses with physical disabilities.

Given the sheer volume of evidence demonstrating the nature and extent of unconstitutional discrimination against persons with disabilities in the provision of public services, the dissent's contention that the record is insufficient to justify Congress' exercise of its prophylactic power is puzzling, to say the least. Just last Term in *Hibbs*, we approved the family-care leave provision of the FMLA as valid §5 legislation based primarily on evidence of disparate provision of parenting leave, little of which concerned unconstitutional state conduct. We explained that because the FMLA was targeted at sex-based classifications, which are subject to a heightened standard of judicial scrutiny, "it was easier for Congress to show a pattern of state constitutional violations" than in *Garrett* or *Kimel* [*v. Florida Board of Regents*, 528 U.S. 62 (2000)], both of which concerned legislation that targeted classifications subject to rational-basis review. Title II is aimed at the enforcement of a variety of basic rights, including the right of access to the courts at issue in this case, that call for a standard of judicial review at least as searching, and in some cases more searching, than the standard that applies to sex-based classifications. And in any event, the record of constitutional violations in this case—including judicial findings of unconstitutional state action, and statistical, legislative, and anecdotal evidence of the widespread exclusion of persons with disabilities from the enjoyment of public services—far exceeds the record in *Hibbs*.

The conclusion that Congress drew from this body of evidence is set forth in the text of the ADA itself: "[D]iscrimination against individuals with disabilities persists in such critical areas as education, transportation, communication, recreation, institutionalization, health services, voting, and *access to public services*." 42 U.S.C. §12101(a)(3). This finding, together with the extensive record of disability discrimination that underlies it, makes clear beyond peradventure that inadequate provision of public services and access to public facilities was an appropriate subject for prophylactic legislation.

V

The only question that remains is whether Title II is an appropriate response to this history and pattern of unequal treatment. At the outset, we must determine the scope of that inquiry. Title II reaches a wide array of official conduct in an effort to enforce an equally wide array of constitutional guarantees. Petitioner urges us both to examine the broad range of Title II's applications all at once, and to treat that breadth as a mark of the law's invalidity. According to petitioner, the fact that Title II applies not only to public education and voting-booth access but also to seating at state-owned hockey rinks indicates that Title II is not appropriately tailored to serve its objectives. But nothing in our case law requires us to consider Title II, with its wide variety of applications, as an undifferentiated whole. Whatever might be said about Title II's other applications, the question presented in this case is not whether Congress can validly subject the States to private suits for money damages for failing to provide reasonable access to hockey rinks, or even to voting booths, but whether Congress had the power under § 5 to enforce the constitutional right of access to the courts. Because we find that Title II unquestionably is valid § 5 legislation as it applies to the class of cases implicating the accessibility of judicial services, we need go no further.

Congress' chosen remedy for the pattern of exclusion and discrimination described above, Title II's requirement of program accessibility, is congruent and proportional to its object of enforcing the right of access to the courts. The unequal treatment of disabled persons in the administration of judicial services has a long history, and has persisted despite several legislative efforts to remedy the problem of disability discrimination. Faced with considerable evidence of the shortcomings of previous legislative responses, Congress was justified in concluding that this "difficult and intractable proble[m]" warranted "added prophylactic measures in response." *Hibbs.*

The remedy Congress chose is nevertheless a limited one. Recognizing that failure to accommodate persons with disabilities will often have the same practical effect as outright exclusion, Congress required the States to take reasonable measures to remove architectural and other barriers to accessibility. 42 U.S.C. § 12131(2). But Title II does not require States to employ any and all means to make judicial services accessible to persons with disabilities, and it does not require States to compromise their essential eligibility criteria for public programs. It requires only "reasonable modifications" that would not fundamentally alter the nature of the service provided, and only when the individual seeking modification is otherwise eligible for the service. As Title II's implementing regulations make clear, the reasonable modification requirement can be satisfied in a number of ways. In the case of facilities built or altered after 1992, the regulations require compliance with specific architectural accessibility standards. 28 CFR § 35.151 (2003). But in the case of older facilities, for which structural change is likely to be more difficult, a public entity may comply with Title II by adopting a variety of less costly measures, including relocating services to alternative, accessible sites and assigning aides to assist persons with disabilities in accessing services. § 35.150(b)(1). Only if these measures are ineffective in achieving accessibility is the public entity required to make reasonable structural changes. *Ibid.* And in no event is the entity required to undertake measures that would impose an undue financial or administrative burden, threaten historic preservation interests, or effect a fundamental alteration in the nature of the service. §§ 35.150(a)(2), (a)(3).

This duty to accommodate is perfectly consistent with the well-established due process principle that, "within the limits of practicability, a State must afford to all individuals a meaningful opportunity to be heard" in its courts. *Boddie.* Our cases have recognized a number of affirmative obligations that flow from this principle: the duty to waive filing fees in certain family-law and criminal cases, the duty to provide transcripts to criminal defendants seeking review of their convictions, and the duty to provide counsel to certain criminal defendants. Each of these cases makes clear that ordinary considerations of cost and convenience alone cannot justify a State's failure to provide individuals with a meaningful right of access to the courts. Judged against this backdrop, Title II's affirmative obligation to accommodate persons with disabilities in the administration of justice cannot be said to be "so out of proportion to a supposed remedial or preventive object that it cannot be understood as responsive to, or designed to prevent, unconstitutional behavior." *Boerne,* 521 U.S., at 532; *Kimel,* 528 U.S., at 86. It is, rather, a reasonable prophylactic measure, reasonably targeted to a legitimate end.

For these reasons, we conclude that Title II, as it applies to the class of cases implicating the fundamental right of access to the courts, constitutes a valid exercise of Congress' §5 authority to enforce the guarantees of the Fourteenth Amendment. The judgment of the Court of Appeals is therefore affirmed.

It is so ordered.

JUSTICE SOUTER, with whom JUSTICE GINSBURG joins, concurring [Omitted].

JUSTICE GINSBURG, with whom JUSTICE SOUTER and JUSTICE BREYER join, concurring [Omitted].

CHIEF JUSTICE REHNQUIST, with whom JUSTICE KENNEDY and JUSTICE THOMAS join, dissenting.

Rather than limiting its discussion of constitutional violations to the due process rights on which it ultimately relies, the majority sets out on a wide-ranging account of societal discrimination against the disabled. This digression recounts historical discrimination against the disabled through institutionalization laws, restrictions on marriage, voting, and public education, conditions in mental hospitals, and various other forms of unequal treatment in the administration of public programs and services. Some of this evidence would be relevant if the Court were considering the constitutionality of the statute as a whole; but the Court rejects that approach in favor of a narrower "as-applied" inquiry. We discounted much the same type of outdated, generalized evidence in *Garrett* as unsupportive of Title I's ban on employment discrimination. The evidence here is likewise irrelevant to Title II's purported enforcement of Due Process access-to-the-courts rights.

Even if it were proper to consider this broader category of evidence, much of it does not concern *unconstitutional* action by the *States.* The bulk of the Court's evidence concerns discrimination by nonstate governments, rather than the States themselves. We have repeatedly held that such evidence is irrelevant to the inquiry whether Congress has validly abrogated Eleventh Amendment immunity, a privilege enjoyed only by the sovereign States.

With respect to the due process "access to the courts" rights on which the Court ultimately relies, Congress' failure to identify a pattern of actual constitutional violations by the States is even more striking. Indeed, there is *nothing* in the legislative record or statutory findings to indicate that disabled persons were systematically denied the right to be present at criminal trials, denied the meaningful opportunity to be heard in civil cases, unconstitutionally excluded from jury service, or denied the right to attend criminal trials.

The Court's attempt to disguise the lack of congressional documentation with a few citations to judicial decisions cannot retroactively provide support for Title II, and in any event, fails on its own terms. Indeed, because this type of constitutional violation occurs in connection with litigation, it is particularly telling that the majority is able to identify only *two* reported cases finding that a disabled person's federal constitutional rights were violated.

Lacking any real evidence that Congress was responding to actual due process violations, the majority relies primarily on three items to justify its decision: (1) a 1983 U.S. Civil Rights Commission Report showing that 76% of "public services and programs housed in state-owned buildings were inaccessible" to persons with disabilities; (2) testimony before a House subcommittee regarding the "physical inaccessibility" of local courthouses; and (3) evidence submitted to Congress' designated ADA task force that purportedly contains "numerous examples of the exclusion of persons with disabilities from state judicial services and programs."

On closer examination, however, the Civil Rights Commission's finding consists of a single conclusory sentence in its report, and it is far from clear that its finding even includes courthouses. The House subcommittee report, for its part, contains the testimony of two witnesses, neither of whom reported being denied the right to be present at constitutionally protected court proceedings. Indeed, the witnesses' testimony, like the U.S. Civil Rights Commission Report, concerns only physical barriers to access, and does not address whether States either provided means to overcome those barriers or alternative locations for proceedings involving disabled persons.

Based on the majority's description, the report of the ADA Task Force on the Rights and Empowerment of Americans with Disabilities sounds promising. But the report itself says nothing about any disabled person being denied access to court. The Court thus apparently relies solely on a general citation to the Government's Lodging in *Garrett*, which, amidst thousands of pages, contains only a few anecdotal handwritten reports of physically inaccessible courthouses, again with no mention of whether States provided alternate means of access.

Even if the anecdotal evidence and conclusory statements relied on by the majority could be properly considered, the mere existence of an architecturally "inaccessible" courthouse — i.e., one a disabled person cannot utilize without assistance — does not state a constitutional violation. A violation of due process occurs only when a person is actually denied the constitutional right to access a given judicial proceeding. We have never held that a person has a *constitutional* right to make his way into a courtroom without any external assistance. Indeed, the fact that the State may need to assist an individual to attend a hearing has no bearing on whether the individual successfully exercises his due process right to be present at the proceeding. Nor does an "inaccessible" courthouse violate the Equal Protection Clause, unless it is irrational for the State not to alter the courthouse to make it "accessible." But financial considerations almost always furnish a rational basis for a State to decline to make those alterations.

The third step of our congruence-and-proportionality inquiry removes any doubt as to whether Title II is valid § 5 legislation. By requiring special accommodation and the elimination of programs that have a disparate impact on the disabled, Title II prohibits far more state conduct than does the equal protection ban on irrational discrimination. We invalidated Title I's similar requirements in *Garrett*, observing that "[i]f special accommodations for the disabled are to be required, they have to come from positive law and not through the Equal Protection Clause." Title II fails for the same reason. Like Title I, Title II may be laudable public policy, but it cannot be seriously disputed that it is also an attempt to legislatively "redefine the States' legal obligations" under the Fourteenth Amendment.

The majority, however, claims that Title II also vindicates fundamental rights protected by the Due Process Clause—in addition to access to the courts—that are subject to heightened Fourteenth Amendment scrutiny. But Title II is not tailored to provide prophylactic protection of these rights; instead, it applies to any service, program, or activity provided by any entity. Its provisions affect transportation, health, education, and recreation programs, among many others, all of which are accorded only rational-basis scrutiny under the Equal Protection Clause. A requirement of accommodation for the disabled at a state-owned amusement park or sports stadium, for example, bears no permissible prophylactic relationship to enabling disabled persons to exercise their fundamental constitutional rights.

The majority concludes that Title II's massive overbreadth can be cured by considering the statute only "as it applies to the class of cases implicating the accessibility of judicial services." Our § 5 precedents do not support this as-applied approach. In each case, we measured the full breadth of the statute or relevant provision that Congress enacted against the scope of the constitutional right it purported to enforce. If we had arbitrarily constricted the scope of the statutes to match the scope of a core constitutional right, those cases might have come out differently. In *Garrett*, for example, Title I might have been upheld "as applied" to irrational employment discrimination.

I fear that the Court's adoption of an as-applied approach eliminates any incentive for Congress to craft § 5 legislation for the purpose of remedying or deterring actual constitutional violations. Congress can now simply rely on the courts to sort out which hypothetical applications of an undifferentiated statute, such as Title II, may be enforced against the States. All the while, States will be subjected to substantial litigation in a piecemeal attempt to vindicate their Eleventh Amendment rights. The majority's as-applied approach simply cannot be squared with either our recent precedent or the proper role of the Judiciary.

For the foregoing reasons, I respectfully dissent.

JUSTICE SCALIA, dissenting.

The "congruence and proportionality" standard, like all such flabby tests, is a standing invitation to judicial arbitrariness and policy-driven decisionmaking. Worse still, it casts this Court in the role of Congress's taskmaster. Under it, the courts (and ultimately this Court) must regularly check Congress's homework to make sure that it has identified sufficient constitutional violations to make its remedy congruent and proportional. As a general matter, we are ill advised to adopt or adhere to constitutional rules that bring us into constant conflict with a coequal branch of Government. And when conflict is unavoidable, we should not come to do battle with the United States Congress armed only with a test ("congruence and proportionality") that has no demonstrable basis in the text of the Constitution and cannot objectively be shown to have been met or failed. As I wrote for the Court in an earlier case, "low walls and vague distinctions will not be judicially defensible in the heat of interbranch conflict." *Plaut v. Spendthrift Farm, Inc.*, 514 U.S. 211, 239 (1995).

I would replace "congruence and proportionality" with another test — one that provides a clear, enforceable limitation supported by the text of § 5. Section 5 grants Congress the power "to *enforce*, by appropriate legislation," the other provisions of the Fourteenth Amendment. U.S. Const., Amdt. 14 (emphasis added). *Morgan* notwithstanding, one does not, within any normal meaning of the term, "enforce" a prohibition by issuing a still broader prohibition directed to the same end. One does not, for example, "enforce" a 55-mile-per-hour speed limit by imposing a 45-mile-per-hour speed limit — even though that is indeed directed to the same end of automotive safety and will undoubtedly result in many fewer violations of the 55-mile-per-hour limit. And one does not "enforce" the right of access to the courts at issue in this case, by requiring that disabled persons be provided access to *all* of the "services, programs, or activities" furnished or conducted by the State, 42 U.S.C. § 12132. That is simply not what the power to enforce means — or ever meant. The 1860 edition of Noah Webster's American Dictionary of the English Language, current when the Fourteenth Amendment was adopted, defined "enforce" as: "To put in execution; to cause to take effect; as, to *enforce* the laws." *Id.*, at 396. See also J. Worcester, Dictionary of the English Language 484 (1860) ("To put in force; to cause to be applied or executed; as, 'To *enforce* a law'"). Nothing in § 5 allows Congress to go *beyond* the provisions of the Fourteenth Amendment to proscribe, prevent, or "remedy" conduct that does not *itself* violate any provision of the Fourteenth Amendment. So-called "prophylactic legislation" is reinforcement rather than enforcement.

Requiring access for disabled persons to all public buildings cannot remotely be considered a means of "enforcing" the Fourteenth Amendment. The considerations of long accepted practice and of policy that sanctioned such distortion of language where state racial discrimination is at issue do not apply in this field of social policy far removed from the principal object of the Civil War Amendments. "The seductive plausibility of single steps in a chain of evolutionary development of a legal rule is often not perceived until a third, fourth, or fifth 'logical' extension occurs. Each step, when taken, appeared a reasonable step in relation to that which preceded it, although the aggregate or end result is one that would never have been seriously considered in the first instance. This kind of gestative propensity calls for the 'line drawing' familiar in the judicial, as in the legislative process: 'thus far but not beyond.'" *United States v. 12 200-ft. Reels of Super 8MM. Film*, 413 U.S. 123, 127 (1973) (Burger, C.J., for the Court) (footnote omitted). It is past time to draw a line limiting the uncontrolled spread of a well-intentioned textual distortion. For these reasons, I respectfully dissent from the judgment of the Court.

Justice Thomas, dissenting [omitted].

Notes and Questions

(1) What is the justification for allowing Congress to sometimes enact remedial legislation that prohibits conduct which is not itself unconstitutional?

(2) Why can Congress not provide a remedy against private actors if state remedial systems are inadequate?

(3) What is the scope of the holding in *Lane*? Are states vulnerable to suit for discriminating on the basis of disability in access to their "services, programs or activities" other than access to courts?

(4) Did the Court in *Lane* adequately distinguish the result in *Garrett*, the earlier Americans With Disabilities Act case? What factors best explain the outcomes in *Garrett*, *Hibbs*, and *Lane*?

§ 4.05 Tenth Amendment Limits on Congressional Power?

In the 40 years following the Supreme Court's conversion in support of the New Deal programs, the Court relied on the proposition that the Tenth Amendment is a "truism" and does not operate as a federalism limitation on congressional power. In 1976, however, the Court, in the words of the dissenters, repudiated principles "settled since the time of Chief Justice John Marshall." In *National League of Cities v. Usery*, 426 U.S. 833 (1976), the Court struck down the 1974 Amendments to the Fair Labor Standards Act (FLSA) which imposed minimum wage and maximum hour provisions on state and local governments. The application of the FLSA to private employers had been upheld in *Darby*. The majority in *National League* conceded that the amendments were within the scope of the Congress' commerce powers. It held, however, that congressional power was limited by the Tenth Amendment:

> Appellants in no way challenge these decisions establishing the breadth of authority granted Congress under the commerce power. Their contention, on the contrary, is that when Congress seeks to regulate directly the activities of States as public employers, it transgresses an affirmative limitation on the exercise of its power akin to other commerce power affirmative limitations contained in the Constitution. Congressional enactments which may be fully within the grant of legislative authority contained in the Commerce Clause may nonetheless be invalid because found to offend against the right to trial by jury contained in the Sixth Amendment. Appellants' essential contention is that the 1974 amendments to the Act, while undoubtedly within the scope of the Commerce Clause, encounter a similar constitutional barrier because they are to be applied directly to the States and subdivision of States as employers.

> This court has never doubted that there are limits upon the power of Congress to override state sovereignty, even when exercising its otherwise plenary powers to tax or to regulate commerce which are conferred by Art. I of the Constitution. [T]he Court recognized that an express declaration of this limitation is found in the Tenth Amendment.

> It is one thing to recognize the authority of Congress to enact laws regulating individual businesses necessarily subject to the dual sovereignty of the government of the Nation and of the State in which they reside. It is quite another to uphold a similar exercise of congressional authority directed, not to private citizens, but to the States as States. We have repeatedly recognized that there are attributes of sovereignty attaching to every state government which may not be impaired by Congress, not because Congress may lack an affirmative grant of legislative authority to reach the matter, but because the Constitution prohibits it from exercising the authority in that manner.

> One undoubted attribute of state sovereignty is the States' power to determine the wages which shall be paid to those whom they employ in order to carry out their governmental functions, what hours those persons will work, and what compensation will be provided whether these employees may be called upon to work overtime. The question we must resolve here then, is whether these determinations are "functions essential to separate and independent existence," so that Congress may not abrogate the States' otherwise plenary authority to make them.

The Court then concluded that the challenged Amendments to the FLSA do indeed displace functions that are essential to the separate and independent existence of the states.

As the following decision reveals, the doctrine announced in *National League of Cities* survived for only nine years.

Garcia v. San Antonio Metropolitan Transit Authority

United States Supreme Court
469 U.S. 528, 105 S. Ct. 1005, 83 L. Ed. 2d 1016 (1985)

JUSTICE BLACKMUN delivered the opinion of the Court.

We revisit in these cases an issue raised in *National League of Cities v. Usery*. In that litigation, this Court, by a sharply divided vote, ruled that the Commerce Clause does not empower Congress to enforce the minimum-wage and overtime provisions of the Fair Labor Standards Act (FLSA) against the States "in areas of traditional governmental functions." Although *National League of Cities* supplied some examples of "traditional governmental functions," it did not offer a general explanation of how a "traditional" function is to be distinguished from a "nontraditional" one. Since then, federal and state courts have struggled with the task, thus imposed, of identifying a traditional function for purposes of state immunity under the Commerce Clause.

In the present case, a Federal District Court concluded that municipal ownership and operation of a mass-transit system is a traditional governmental function and thus, under *National League of Cities*, is exempt from the obligations imposed by the FLSA.

Our examination of this "function" standard applied in these and other cases over the last eight years now persuades us that the attempt to draw the boundaries of state regulatory immunity in terms of "traditional governmental function" is not only unworkable but is inconsistent with established principles of federalism and, indeed, with those very federalism principles on which *National League of Cities* purported to rest. The case, accordingly, is overruled.

The present controversy concerns the extent to which SAMTA [San Antonio Metropolitan Transit Authority] may be subjected to the minimum-wage and overtime requirements of the FLSA.

Appellees have not argued that SAMTA is immune from regulation under the FLSA on the ground that it is a local transit system engaged in intrastate commercial activity. In a practical sense, SAMTA's operations might well be characterized as "local." Nonetheless, it long has been settled that Congress' authority under the Commerce Clause extends to intrastate economic activities that affect interstate commerce. See, *e.g.*, *Hodel v. Virginia Surface Mining & Recl. Assn.*, 452 U.S. 264, 276–277 (1981); *Heart of Atlanta Motel, Inc. v. United States*, 379 U.S. 241, 258 (1964); *Wickard v. Filburn*, 317 U.S. 111, 125 (1942); *United States v. Darby*, 312 U.S. 100 (1941). Were SAMTA a privately owned and operated enterprise, it could not credibly argue that Congress exceeded the bounds of its Commerce Clause powers in prescribing minimum wages and overtime rates for SAMTA's employees. Any constitutional exemption from the requirements of the FLSA therefore must rest on SAMTA's status as a governmental entity rather than on the "local" nature of its operations.

The prerequisites for governmental immunity under *National League of Cities* were summarized by this Court in *Hodel, supra*. Under that summary, four conditions must be satisfied before a state activity may be deemed immune from a particular federal regulation under the Commerce Clause. First, it is said that the federal statute at issue must regulate "the 'States as States.'" Second, the statute must "address matters that are indisputably 'attribute[s] of state sovereignty.'" Third, state compliance with the federal obligation must "directly impair [the States'] ability 'to structure integral operations in areas of traditional governmental functions.'" Finally, the relation of state and federal interests must not be such that "the nature of the federal interest justifies state submission."

The controversy in the present cases has focused on the third *Hodel* requirement — that the challenged federal statute trench on "traditional governmental functions." The District Court voiced a common concern: "Despite the abundance of adjectives, identifying which particular state functions are immune remains difficult."

Thus far, this Court itself has made little headway in defining the scope of the governmental functions deemed protected under *National League of Cities*. In that case the Court set forth examples of protected and unprotected functions, but provided no explanation of how those examples were identified. The only other case in which the Court has had occasion to address the problem is [*Transportation Union v.*] *Long Island* [*R. Co.*, 455 U.S. 678 (1982) (commuter service provided by state owned Long Island Railroad is not a traditional governmental function)]. We there observed: "The determination of whether a federal law impairs a state's authority with respect to 'areas of traditional [state] functions' may at times be a difficult one."

The accuracy of that statement is demonstrated by this Court's own difficulties in *Long Island* in developing a workable standard for "traditional government functions." We relied in large part there on "the *historical reality* that the operation of railroads is not among the functions *traditionally* performed by state and local governments," but we simultaneously disavowed "a static historical view of state functions generally immune from federal regulation."

We believe that there is a more fundamental problem at work here, a problem that explains why the Court was never able to provide a basis for the governmental/proprietary distinction and why an attempt to draw similar distinctions with respect to federal regulatory authority under *National League of Cities* is unlikely to succeed regardless of how the distinctions are phrased. The problem is that neither the government/proprietary distinction nor any other that purports to separate out important governmental functions can be faithful to the role of federalism in a democratic society. The essence of our federal system is that within the realm of authority left open to them under the Constitution, the States must be equally free to engage in any activity that their citizens choose for the common weal, no matter how unorthodox or unnecessary anyone else — including the judiciary — deems state involvement to be. Any rule of state immunity that looks to the "traditional," "integral," or "necessary" nature of governmental functions inevitably invites an unelected federal judiciary to make decisions about which state policies it favors and which ones it dislikes. "The science of government is the science of experiment," and the States cannot serve as laboratories for social and economic experiment, if they must pay an added price when they meet the changing needs of their citizenry by taking up functions that an earlier day and a different society left in private hands.

We therefore now reject, as unsound in principle and unworkable in practice, a rule of state immunity from federal regulation that turns on a judicial appraisal of whether a particular governmental function is "integral" or "traditional." Any such rule leads to inconsistent results at the same time that it disserves principles of democratic self-governance, and it breeds inconsistency precisely because it is divorced from those principles. If there are to be limits on the Federal Government's power to interfere with state functions — as undoubtedly there are — we must look elsewhere to find them. We accordingly return to the underlying issue that confronted this Court in *National League of Cities* — the manner in which the Constitution insulates States from the reach of Congress' power under the Commerce Clause.

The States unquestionably do "retai[n] a significant measure of sovereign authority. They do so, however, only to the extent that the Constitution has not divested them of their original powers and transferred those powers to the Federal Government.

As a result, to say that the Constitution assumes the continued role of the States is to say little about the nature of that role. With rare exceptions, like the guarantee, in Article IV, § 3, of state territorial integrity, the Constitution does not carve out express elements of state sovereignty that Congress may not employ its delegated powers to displace.

Apart from the limitation on federal authority inherent in the delegated nature of Congress' Article I powers, the principal means chosen by the Framers to ensure the role of the States in the federal system lies in the structure of the Federal Government itself. It is no novelty to observe that the composition of the Federal Government was designed in large part to protect the States from overreaching by Congress. The Framers thus gave the States a role in the selection both of the Executive and the Legislative Branches of the Federal Government. The States were vested with indirect influence over the House of Representatives and the Presidency by their control of electoral qualifications and their role in presidential elections. U.S. Const., Art. I, § 2, and Art. II, § 1. They were given more direct influence in the Senate, where each State received equal representation and each Senator was to be selected by the legislature of his State. Art. I, § 3. The significance attached to the States' equal representation in the Senate is underscored by the prohibition of any constitutional amendment divesting a State of equal representation without the State's consent. Art. V.

The effectiveness of the federal political process in preserving the States' interests is apparent even today in the course of federal legislation. [T]he States have been able to direct a substantial proportion of federal revenues into their own treasuries in the form of general and program-specific grants in aid.

We realize that changes in the structure of the Federal Government have taken place since 1789, not the least of which has been the substitution of popular election of Senators by the adoption of the Seventeenth Amendment in 1913, and that these changes may work to alter the influence of the States in the federal political process. Nonetheless, against this background, we are convinced that the fundamental limitation that the constitutional scheme imposes on the Commerce Clause to protect the "States as States" is one of process rather than one of result.

Insofar as the present cases are concerned, then, we need go no further than to state that we perceive nothing in the overtime and minimum-wage requirements of the FLSA, as applied to SAMTA, that is destructive of state sovereignty or violative of any constitutional provision. SAMTA faces nothing more than the same minimum-wage and overtime obligations that hundreds of thousands of other employers, public as well as private, have to meet.

Of course, we continue to recognize that the States occupy a special and specific position in our constitutional system and that the scope of Congress' authority under the Commerce Clause must reflect that position. But the principal and basic limit on the federal commerce power is that inherent in all congressional action — the built-in restraints that our system provides through state participation in federal governmental action. The political process ensures that laws that unduly burden the States will not be promulgated. In the factual setting of these cases the internal safeguards of the political process have performed as intended.

JUSTICE POWELL, with whom THE CHIEF JUSTICE [BURGER], JUSTICE REHNQUIST, and JUSTICE O'CONNOR join, dissenting.

More troubling than the logical infirmities in the Court's reasoning is the result of its holding, *i.e.*, that federal political officials, invoking the Commerce Clause, are the sole judges of the limits of their own power. This result is inconsistent with the fundamental principles of our constitutional system. At least since *Marbury v. Madison* it has been the settled province of the federal judiciary "to say what the law is" with respect to the constitutionality of acts of Congress. In rejecting the role of the judiciary in protecting the States from federal overreaching, the Court's opinion offers no explanation for ignoring the teaching of the most famous case in our history.

In our federal system, the States have a major role that cannot be preempted by the national government. As contemporaneous writings and the debates at the ratifying conventions make clear, the States' ratification of the Constitution was predicated on this understanding of federalism. Indeed, the Tenth Amendment was adopted specifically to ensure that the important role promised the States by the proponents of the Constitution was realized.

Much of the initial opposition to the Constitution was rooted in the fear that the national government would be too powerful and eventually would eliminate the

States as viable political entities. This concern was voiced repeatedly until proponents of the Constitution made assurances that a bill of rights, including a provision explicitly reserving powers in the States, would be among the first business of the new Congress.

Notes and Questions

(1) Does the majority's view of federalism impede the ability of local governments to provide essential governmental services, as charged by the dissent?

(2) Indeed, are any federalism values threatened by the majority's view?

(3) Is the Court or the Congress better equipped to protect federalism values? Why? *See* Herbert Wechsler, *The Political Safeguards of Federalism — The Role of the States in the Composition and Selection of the National Government*, 54 COLUM. L. REV. 543, 544, 558–560 (1954) (quoted § 4.02, *supra*). Did the *Garcia* majority duck its duty under *Marbury v. Madison* to say what the law is?

(4) If *Garcia* is constitutionally unacceptable to you, can you envision an alternative model for judicial review that does not present the difficulties of *National League of Cities*? Consider the next case.

New York v. United States

United States Supreme Court
505 U.S. 144, 112 S. Ct. 2408, 120 L. Ed. 2d 120 (1992)

JUSTICE O'CONNOR delivered the opinion of the Court.

This case implicates one of our Nation's newest problems of public policy and perhaps our oldest question of constitutional law. The public policy issue involves the disposal of radioactive waste: In this case, we address the constitutionality of three provisions of the Low-Level Radioactive Waste Policy Amendments Act of 1985, Pub. L. 99-240, 99 Stat. 1842, 42 U.S.C. § 2021b *et seq.* The constitutional question is as old as the Constitution: It consists of discerning the proper division of authority between the Federal Government and the States. We conclude that while Congress has substantial power under the Constitution to encourage the States to provide for the disposal of the radioactive waste generated within their borders, the Constitution does not confer upon Congress the ability simply to compel the States to do so. We therefore find that only two of the Act's three provisions at issue are consistent with the Constitution's allocation of power to the Federal Government.

I

We live in a world full of low level radioactive waste. Radioactive material is present in luminous watch dials, smoke alarms, measurement devices, medical fluids, research materials, and the protective gear and construction materials used by workers at nuclear power plants. Low level radioactive waste is generated by the Government, by hospitals, by research institutions, and by various industries. The waste must be isolated from humans for long periods of time, often for hundreds of years. Millions of cubic feet of low level radioactive waste must be disposed of each year.

The 1985 Act was based largely on a proposal submitted by the National Governors' Association. In broad outline, the Act embodies a compromise among the sited [those with sites for disposal of nuclear waste] and unsited States. The sited States agreed to extend for seven years the period in which they would accept low level radioactive waste from other States. In exchange, the unsited States agreed to end their reliance on the sited States by 1992.

The Act provides three types of incentives to encourage the States to comply with their statutory obligation to provide for the disposal of waste generated within their borders.

1. Monetary incentives. One quarter of the surcharges collected by the sited States must be transferred to an escrow account held by the Secretary of Energy. The Secretary then makes payments from this account to each State that has complied with a series of deadlines. By July 1, 1986, each State was to have ratified legislation either joining a regional compact or indicating an intent to develop a disposal facility within the State. By January 1, 1988, each unsited compact was to have identified the State in which its facility would be located, and each compact or stand-alone State was to have developed a siting plan and taken other identified steps. By January 1, 1990, each State or compact was to have filed a complete application for a license to operate a disposal facility, or the Governor of any State that had not filed an application was to have certified that the State would be capable of disposing of all waste generated in the State after 1992. The rest of the account is to be paid out to those States or compacts able to dispose of all low level radioactive waste generated within their borders by January 1, 1993. Each State that has not met the 1993 deadline must either take title to the waste generated within its borders or forfeit to the waste generators the incentive payments it has received.

2. Access incentives. The second type of incentive involves the denial of access to disposal sites. States that fail to meet the July 1986 deadline may be charged twice the ordinary surcharge for the remainder of 1986 and may be denied access to disposal facilities thereafter. States that fail to meet the 1988 deadline may be charged double surcharges for the first half of 1988 and quadruple surcharges for the second half of 1988, and may be denied access thereafter. States that fail to meet the 1990 deadline may be denied access. Finally, States that have not filed complete applications by January 1, 1992, for a license to operate a disposal facility, or States belonging to compacts that have not filed such applications, may be charged triple surcharges.

3. The take title provision. The third type of incentive is the most severe. The Act provides: "If a State (or, where applicable, a compact region) in which low-level radioactive waste is generated is unable to provide for the disposal of all such waste generated within such State or compact region by January 1, 1996, each State in which such waste is generated, upon the request of the generator or owner of the waste, shall take title to the waste, be obligated to take possession of the waste, and

shall be liable for all damages directly or indirectly incurred by such generator or owner as a consequence of the failure of the State to take possession of the waste as soon after January 1, 1996, as the generator or owner notifies the State that the waste is available for shipment." These three incentives are the focus of petitioners' constitutional challenge.

Petitioners — the State of New York and the two counties — filed this suit against the United States in 1990. They sought a declaratory judgment that the Act is inconsistent with the Tenth and Eleventh Amendments to the Constitution, with the Due Process Clause of the Fifth Amendment, and with the Guarantee Clause of Article IV of the Constitution. The States of Washington, Nevada, and South Carolina intervened as defendants. The District Court dismissed the complaint. The Court of Appeals affirmed. Petitioners have abandoned their Due Process and Eleventh Amendment claims on their way up the appellate ladder; as the case stands before us, petitioners claim only that the Act is inconsistent with the Tenth Amendment and the Guarantee Clause.

II

A

[Federalism] questions can be viewed in either of two ways. In some cases the Court has inquired whether an Act of Congress is authorized by one of the powers delegated to Congress in Article I of the Constitution. In other cases the Court has sought to determine whether an Act of Congress invades the province of state sovereignty reserved by the Tenth Amendment. *See, e.g., Garcia v. San Antonio Metropolitan Transit Authority.* In a case like this one, involving the division of authority between federal and state governments, the two inquiries are mirror images of each other. If a power is delegated to Congress in the Constitution, the Tenth Amendment expressly disclaims any reservation of that power to the States; if a power is an attribute of state sovereignty reserved by the Tenth Amendment, it is necessarily a power the Constitution has not conferred on Congress.

It is in this sense that the Tenth Amendment "states but a truism that all is retained which has not been surrendered." *United States v. Darby.* Congress exercises its conferred powers subject to the limitations contained in the Constitution. Thus, for example, under the Commerce Clause Congress may regulate publishers engaged in interstate commerce, but Congress is constrained in the exercise of that power by the First Amendment. The Tenth Amendment likewise restrains the power of Congress, but this limit is not derived from the text of the Tenth Amendment itself, which, as we have discussed, is essentially a tautology. Instead, the Tenth Amendment confirms that the power of the Federal Government is subject to limits that may, in a given instance, reserve power to the States. The Tenth Amendment thus directs us to determine, as in this case, whether an incident of state sovereignty is protected by a limitation on an Article I power.

The actual scope of the Federal Government's authority with respect to the States has changed over the years, therefore, but the constitutional structure underlying and limiting that authority has not. In the end, just as a cup may be half empty or half full, it makes no difference whether one views the question at issue in this case as one of ascertaining the limits of the power delegated to the Federal Government under the affirmative provisions of the Constitution or one of discerning the core of sovereignty retained by the States under the Tenth Amendment. Either way, we must determine whether any of the three challenged provisions of the Low-Level Radioactive Waste Policy Amendments Act of 1985 oversteps the boundary between federal and state authority.

B

Petitioners do not contend that Congress lacks the power to regulate the disposal of low level radioactive waste. Space in radioactive waste disposal sites is frequently sold by residents of one State to residents of another. Regulation of the resulting interstate market in waste disposal is therefore well within Congress' authority under the Commerce Clause. Petitioners likewise do not dispute that under the Supremacy Clause Congress could, if it wished, pre-empt state radioactive waste regulation. Petitioners contend only that the Tenth Amendment limits the power of Congress to regulate in the way it has chosen. Rather than addressing the problem of waste disposal by directly regulating the generators and disposers of waste, petitioners argue, Congress has impermissibly directed the States to regulate in this field.

Most of our recent cases interpreting the Tenth Amendment have concerned the authority of Congress to subject state governments to generally applicable laws. The Court's jurisprudence in this area has traveled an unsteady path. This case presents no occasion to apply or revisit the holdings of any of these cases, as this is not a case in which Congress has subjected a State to the same legislation applicable to private parties.

This case instead concerns the circumstances under which Congress may use the States as implements of regulation; that is, whether Congress may direct or otherwise motivate the States to regulate in a particular field or a particular way.

While Congress has substantial powers to govern the Nation directly, including in areas of intimate concern to the States, the Constitution has never been understood to confer upon Congress the ability to require the States to govern according to Congress' instructions.

Indeed, the question whether the Constitution should permit Congress to employ state governments as regulatory agencies was a topic of lively debate among the Framers. In providing for a stronger central government, therefore, the Framers explicitly chose a Constitution that confers upon Congress the power to regulate individuals, not States. As we have seen, the Court has consistently respected this choice. We have always understood that even where Congress has the authority under the Constitution to pass laws requiring or prohibiting certain acts, it lacks the power directly to compel the States to require or prohibit those acts. The allocation of power contained in the Commerce Clause, for example, authorizes Congress to regulate interstate commerce directly; it does not authorize Congress to regulate state governments' regulation of interstate commerce.

This is not to say that Congress lacks the ability to encourage a State to regulate in a particular way, or that Congress may not hold out incentives to the States as a method of influencing a State's policy choices. Our cases have identified a variety of methods, short of outright coercion, by which Congress may urge a State to adopt a legislative program consistent with federal interests. Two of these methods are of particular relevance here.

First, under Congress' spending power, "Congress may attach conditions on the receipt of federal funds." *South Dakota v. Dole*, 483 U.S. at 206. Such conditions must (among other requirements) bear some relationship to the purpose of the federal spending, *id.*, otherwise, of course, the spending power could render academic the Constitution's other grants and limits of federal authority. Where the recipient of federal funds is a State, as is not unusual today, the conditions attached to the funds by Congress may influence a State's legislative choices.

Second, where Congress has the authority to regulate private activity under the Commerce Clause, we have recognized Congress' power to offer States the choice of regulating that activity according to federal standards or having state law preempted by federal regulation. This arrangement, which has been termed "a program of cooperative federalism," is replicated in numerous federal statutory schemes.

By either of these two methods, as by any other permissible method of encouraging a State to conform to federal policy choices, the residents of the State retain the ultimate decision as to whether or not the State will comply. If a State's citizens view federal policy as sufficiently contrary to local interests, they may elect to decline a federal grant. If state residents would prefer their government to devote its attention and resources to problems other than those deemed important by Congress, they may choose to have the Federal Government rather than the State bear the expense of a federally mandated regulatory program, and they may continue to supplement that program to the extent state law is not preempted. Where Congress encourages state regulation rather than compelling it, state governments remain responsive to the local electorate's preferences; state officials remain accountable to the people.

By contrast, where the Federal Government compels States to regulate, the accountability of both state and federal officials is diminished. If the citizens of New York, for example, do not consider that making provision for the disposal of radioactive waste is in their best interest, they may elect state officials who share their view. That view can always be preempted under the Supremacy Clause if is contrary to the national view, but in such a case it is the Federal Government that makes the decision in full view of the public, and it will be federal officials that suffer the consequences if the decision turns out to be detrimental or unpopular. But where the Federal Government directs the States to regulate, it may be state officials who will bear the brunt of public disapproval, while the federal officials who devised the regulatory program may remain insulated from the electoral ramifications of their decision. Accountability is thus diminished when, due to federal coercion, elected state officials cannot regulate in accordance with the views of the local electorate in matters not pre-empted by federal regulation.

III

[The Court first held that the monetary and access incentives did not violate the Tenth Amendment. It then considered the take title provision.]

The take title provision is of a different character. This third so-called "incentive" offers States, as an alternative to regulating pursuant to Congress' direction, the option of taking title to and possession of the low level radioactive waste generated within their borders and becoming liable for all damages waste generators suffer as a result of the States' failure to do so promptly. In this provision, Congress has crossed the line distinguishing encouragement from coercion.

The take title provision offers state governments a "choice" of either accepting ownership of waste or regulating according to the instructions of Congress. Respondents do not claim that the Constitution would authorize Congress to impose either option as a freestanding requirement. On one hand, the Constitution would not permit Congress simply to transfer radioactive waste from generators to state governments. Such a forced transfer, standing alone, would in principle be no different than a congressionally compelled subsidy from state governments to radioactive waste producers. The same is true of the provision requiring the States to become liable for the generators' damages. Standing alone, this provision would be indistinguishable from an Act of Congress directing the States to assume the liabilities of certain state residents. Either type of federal action would "commandeer" state governments into the service of federal regulatory purposes, and would for this reason be inconsistent with the Constitution's division of authority between federal and state governments. On the other hand, the second alternative held out to state governments — regulating pursuant to Congress' direction — would, standing alone, present a simple command to state governments to implement legislation enacted by Congress. As we have seen, the Constitution does not empower Congress to subject state governments to this type of instruction.

Because an instruction to state governments to take title to waste, standing alone, would be beyond the authority of Congress, and because a direct order to regulate, standing alone, would also be beyond the authority of Congress, it follows that Congress lacks the power to offer the States a choice between the two. Unlike the first two sets of incentives, the take title incentive does not represent the conditional exercise of any congressional power enumerated in the Constitution. In this provision, Congress has not held out the threat of exercising its spending power or its commerce power; it has instead held out the threat, should the States not regulate according to one federal instruction, of simply forcing the States to submit to another federal instruction. A choice between two unconstitutionally coercive regulatory techniques is no choice at all.

The take title provision appears to be unique. No other federal statute has been cited which offers a state government no option other than that of implementing legislation enacted by Congress. Whether one views the take title provision as lying outside Congress' enumerated powers, or as infringing upon the core of state sovereignty reserved by the Tenth Amendment, the provision is inconsistent with the federal structure of our Government established by the Constitution.

IV

Respondents raise a number of objections to this understanding of the limits of Congress' power.

A

First, the United States argues that the Constitution's prohibition of congressional directives to state governments can be overcome where the federal interest is sufficiently important to justify state submission. This argument contains a kernel of truth: In determining whether the Tenth Amendment limits the ability of Congress to subject state governments to generally applicable laws, the Court has in some cases stated that it will evaluate the strength of federal interests in light of the degree to which such laws would prevent the State from functioning as a sovereign; that is, the extent to which such generally applicable laws would impede a state government's responsibility to represent and be accountable to the citizens of the State. But whether or not a particularly strong federal interest enables Congress to bring state governments within the orbit of generally applicable federal regulation, no Member of the Court has ever suggested that such a federal interest would enable Congress to command a state government to enact state regulation. No matter how powerful the federal interest involved, the Constitution simply does not give Congress the authority to require the States to regulate. The Constitution instead gives Congress the authority to regulate matters directly and to pre-empt contrary state regulation. Where a federal interest is sufficiently strong to cause Congress to legislate, it must do so directly; it may not conscript state governments as its agents.

Second, the United States argues that the Constitution does, in some circumstances, permit federal directives to state governments. Various cases are cited for this proposition, but none support it. In sum, the cases relied upon by the United States hold only that federal law is enforceable in state courts and that federal courts may in proper circumstances order state officials to comply with federal law, propositions that by no means imply any authority on the part of Congress to mandate state regulation.

Third, the United States argues that the Constitution envisions a role for Congress as an arbiter of interstate disputes. The United States observes that federal courts, and this Court in particular, have frequently resolved conflicts among States. Many of these disputes have involved the allocation of shared resources among the States, a category perhaps broad enough to encompass the allocation of scarce disposal space for radioactive waste. The United States suggests that if the Court may resolve such interstate disputes, Congress can surely do the same under the Commerce Clause.

While the Framers no doubt endowed Congress with the power to regulate interstate commerce in order to avoid further instances of the interstate trade disputes that were common under the Articles of Confederation, the Framers did not intend that Congress should exercise that power through the mechanism of mandating state regulation. The Constitution established Congress as "a superintending authority over the reciprocal trade" among the States, The Federalist No. 42, by empowering Congress to regulate that trade directly, not by authorizing Congress to issue trade-related orders to state governments.

B

The sited State respondents focus their attention on the process by which the Act was formulated. They correctly observe that public officials representing the State of New York lent their support to the Act's enactment. Respondents note that the Act embodies a bargain among the sited and unsited States, a compromise to which New York was a willing participant and from which New York has reaped much benefit. Respondents then pose what appears at first to be a troubling question: How can a federal statute be found an unconstitutional infringement of State sovereignty when state officials consented to the statute's enactment?

The answer follows from an understanding of the fundamental purpose served by our Government's federal structure. The Constitution does not protect the sovereignty of States for the benefit of the States or state governments as abstract political entities, or even for the benefit of the public officials governing the States. To the contrary, the Constitution divides authority between federal and state governments for the protection of individuals. State sovereignty is not just an end in itself: "Rather, federalism secures to citizens the liberties that derive from the diffusion of sovereign power." State officials thus cannot consent to the enlargement of the powers of Congress beyond those enumerated in the Constitution.

JUSTICE WHITE, with whom JUSTICE BLACKMUN and JUSTICE STEVENS join, concurring in part and dissenting in part.

The Court's distinction between a federal statute's regulation of States and private parties for general purposes, as opposed to a regulation solely on the activities of States, is unsupported by our recent Tenth Amendment cases. In no case has the Court rested its holding on such a distinction. Moreover, the Court makes no effort to explain why this purported distinction should affect the analysis of Congress' power under general principles of federalism and the Tenth Amendment. The distinction, facilely thrown out, is not based on any defensible theory. Certainly one would be hard-pressed to read the spirited exchanges between the Court and dissenting Justices in *National League of Cities*, and in *Garcia v. San Antonio Metropolitan Transit Authority*, as having been based on the distinction now drawn by the Court. An incursion on state sovereignty hardly seems more constitutionally acceptable if the federal statute that "commands" specific action also applies to private parties. The alleged diminution in state authority over its own affairs is not any less because the federal mandate restricts the activities of private parties.

It is clear, therefore, that even under the precedents selectively chosen by the Court, its analysis of the take title provision's constitutionality in this case falls far short of being persuasive. I would also submit, in this connection, that the Court's attempt to carve out a doctrinal distinction for statutes that purport solely to regulate State activities is especially unpersuasive after *Garcia*. It is true that in that case we considered whether a federal statute of general applicability—the Fair Labor Standards Act—applied to state transportation entities but our most recent statements have explained the appropriate analysis in a more general manner. Just last Term, for instance, Justice O'Connor wrote that "this Court in *Garcia* has left primarily to the political process the protection of the States against intrusive exercises of Congress' Commerce Clause powers."

[T]he more appropriate analysis should flow from *Garcia*, even if this case does not involve a congressional law generally applicable to both States and private parties. In *Garcia*, we stated the proper inquiry: "[W]e are convinced that the fundamental limitation that the constitutional scheme imposes on the Commerce Clause to protect the 'States as States' is one of process rather than one of result. Any substantive restraint on the exercise of Commerce Clause powers must find its justification in the procedural nature of this basic limitation, and it must be tailored to compensate for possible failings in the national political process rather than to dictate a 'sacred province of state autonomy.'" Where it addresses this aspect of respondents' argument, the Court tacitly concedes that a failing of the political process cannot be shown in this case because it refuses to rebut the unassailable arguments that the States were well able to look after themselves in the legislative process that culminated in the 1985 Act's passage. Indeed, New York acknowledges that its "congressional delegation participated in the drafting and enactment of both the 1980 and the 1985 Acts." The Court rejects this process-based argument by resorting to generalities and platitudes about the purpose of federalism being to protect individual rights.

Ultimately, I suppose, the entire structure of our federal constitutional government can be traced to an interest in establishing checks and balances to prevent the exercise of tyranny against individuals. But these fears seem extremely far distant to me in a situation such as this. We face a crisis of national proportions in the disposal of low-level radioactive waste, and Congress has acceded to the wishes of the States by permitting local decisionmaking rather than imposing a solution from Washington. New York itself participated and supported passage of this legislation at both the gubernatorial and federal representative levels, and then enacted state laws specifically to comply with the deadlines and timetables agreed upon by the States in the 1985 Act. For me, the Court's civics lecture has a decidedly hollow ring at a time when action, rather than rhetoric, is needed to solve a national problem.

JUSTICE STEVENS, concurring in part and dissenting in part. [Omitted]

Notes and Questions

(1) Compare the approaches for the protection of federalism interests in *National League of Cities, Garcia*, and *New York*. How do the approaches differ

from each other? Which is easiest to apply? Which is most protective of the values of federalism?

(2) Reconsider the potential for congressional spending initiatives and the result in *South Dakota v. Dole*. Could Congress provide financial inducements to provide states a "choice" of taking title to waste or losing federal funds? If so, of what utility is the rule announced in *New York*?

(3) Is the likely effect of the decision in *New York* that every state will produce waste and no state will develop disposal sites or methods? Taking federalism values into account, at which level(s) of government should the waste disposal problem be solved?

Printz v. United States

United States Supreme Court
521 U.S. 898, 117 S. Ct. 2365, 138 L. Ed. 2d 914 (1997)

JUSTICE SCALIA delivered the opinion of the Court.

The question presented in these cases is whether certain interim provisions of the Brady Handgun Violence Prevention Act, Pub. L. 103-159, 107 Stat. 1536, commanding state and local law enforcement officers to conduct background checks on prospective handgun purchasers and to perform certain related tasks, violate the Constitution.

I

The Gun Control Act of 1968 (GCA), 18 U.S.C. § 921 *et seq.* prohibits firearms dealers from transferring handguns to any person under 21, not resident in the dealer's State, or prohibited by state or local law from purchasing or possessing firearms. It also forbids possession of a firearm by, and transfer of a firearm to, convicted felons, fugitives from justice, unlawful users of controlled substances, persons adjudicated as mentally defective or committed to mental institutions, aliens unlawfully present in the United States, persons dishonorably discharged from the Armed Forces, persons who have renounced their citizenship, and persons who have been subjected to certain restraining orders or been convicted of a misdemeanor offense involving domestic violence.

In 1993, Congress amended the GCA by enacting the Brady Act. The Act requires the Attorney General to establish a national instant background check system by November 30, 1998, and immediately puts in place certain interim provisions until that system becomes operative. Under the interim provisions, a firearms dealer who proposes to transfer a handgun must first: (1) receive from the transferee a statement (the Brady Form), containing the name, address and date of birth of the proposed transferee along with a sworn statement that the transferee is not among any of the classes of prohibited purchasers; (2) verify the identity of the transferee by examining an identification document; and (3) provide the "chief law enforcement officer" (CLEO) of the transferee's residence with notice of the contents (and a copy) of the

Brady Form. With some exceptions, the dealer must then wait five business days before consummating the sale, unless the CLEO earlier notifies the dealer that he has no reason to believe the transfer would be illegal.

The Brady Act creates two significant alternatives to the foregoing scheme. A dealer may sell a handgun immediately if the purchaser possesses a state handgun permit issued after a background check, or if state law provides for an instant background check. In States that have not rendered one of these alternatives applicable to all gun purchasers, CLEOs must "make a reasonable effort to ascertain within 5 business days whether receipt or possession would be in violation of the law. The Act does not require the CLEO to take any particular action if he determines that a pending transaction would be unlawful; he may notify the firearms dealer to that effect, but is not required to do so. If, however, the CLEO notifies a gun dealer that a prospective purchaser is ineligible to receive a handgun, he must, upon request, provide the would-be purchaser with a written statement of the reasons for that determination.

Petitioners Jay Printz and Richard Mack, the CLEOs for Ravalli County, Montana, and Graham County, Arizona, respectively, filed separate actions challenging the constitutionality of the Brady Act's interim provisions. We granted certiorari.

II

Because there is no constitutional text speaking to this precise question, the answer to the CLEOs' challenge must be sought in historical understanding and practice, in the structure of the Constitution, and in the jurisprudence of this Court. We treat those three sources, in that order, in this and the next two sections of this opinion.

Petitioners contend that compelled enlistment of state executive officers for the administration of federal programs is, until very recent years at least, unprecedented. The Government contends, to the contrary, that "the earliest Congresses enacted statutes that required the participation of state officials in the implementation of federal laws." The Government's contention demands our careful consideration, since early congressional enactments "provid[e] 'contemporaneous and weighty evidence' of the Constitution's meaning," *Bowsher v. Synar*, 478 U.S. 714, 723–724 (1986) (quoting *Marsh v. Chambers*, 463 U.S. 783, 790 (1983)). Indeed, such "contemporaneous legislative exposition of the Constitution, acquiesced in for a long term of years, fixes the construction to be given its provisions." *Myers v. United States*, 272 U.S. 52, 175 (1926). Conversely if, as petitioners contend, earlier Congresses avoided use of this highly attractive power, we would have reason to believe that the power was thought not to exist.

The Government observes that statutes enacted by the first Congresses required state courts to record applications for citizenship, Act of Mar. 26, 1790, ch. 3, §1, 1 Stat. 103, to transmit abstracts of citizenship applications and other naturalization records to the Secretary of State, Act of June 18, 1798, ch. 54, §2, 1 Stat. 567, and to register aliens seeking naturalization and issue certificates of registry, Act of Apr. 14,

1802, ch. 28, § 2, 2 Stat. 154–155. It may well be, however, that these requirements applied only in States that authorized their courts to conduct naturalization proceedings. Other statutes of that era apparently or at least arguably required state courts to perform functions unrelated to naturalization, such as resolving controversies between a captain and the crew of his ship concerning the seaworthiness of the vessel, Act of July 20, 1790, ch. 29, § 3, 1 Stat. 132, hearing the claims of slave owners who had apprehended fugitive slaves and issuing certificates authorizing the slave's forced removal to the State from which he had fled, Act of Feb. 12, 1793, ch. 7, § 3, 1 Stat. 302–305, taking proof of the claims of Canadian refugees who had assisted the United States during the Revolutionary War, Act of Apr. 7, 1798, ch. 26, § 3, 1 Stat. 548, and ordering the deportation of alien enemies in times of war, Act of July 6, 1798, ch. 66, § 2, 1 Stat. 577–578.

These early laws establish, at most, that the Constitution was originally understood to permit imposition of an obligation on state judges to enforce federal prescriptions, insofar as those prescriptions related to matters appropriate for the judicial power. That assumption was perhaps implicit in one of the provisions of the Constitution, and was explicit in another. In accord with the so-called Madisonian Compromise, Article III, § 1, established only a Supreme Court, and made the creation of lower federal courts optional with the Congress — even though it was obvious that the Supreme Court alone could not hear all federal cases throughout the United States. See C. Warren, The Making of the Constitution 325–327 (1928). And the Supremacy Clause, Art. VI, cl. 2, announced that "the Laws of the United States — shall be the supreme Law of the Land; and the Judges in every State shall be bound thereby." It is understandable why courts should have been viewed distinctively in this regard; unlike legislatures and executives, they applied the law of other sovereigns all the time. The principle underlying so-called "transitory" causes of action was that laws which operated elsewhere created obligations in justice that courts of the forum state would enforce. The Constitution itself, in the Full Faith and Credit Clause, Art. IV, § 1, generally required such enforcement with respect to obligations arising in other States.

For these reasons, we do not think the early statutes imposing obligations on state courts imply a power of Congress to impress the state executive into its service.

In addition to early legislation, the Government also appeals to other sources we have usually regarded as indicative of the original understanding of the Constitution. It points to portions of The Federalist which reply to criticisms that Congress's power to tax will produce two sets of revenue officers — for example, "Brutus's" assertion in his letter to the New York Journal of December 13, 1787, that the Constitution "opens a door to the appointment of a swarm of revenue and excise officers to prey upon the honest and industrious part of the community, eat up their substance, and riot on the spoils of the country," reprinted in 1 Debate on the Constitution 502 (B. Bailyn ed. 1993). "Publius" responded that Congress will probably "make use of the State officers and State regulations, for collecting" federal taxes, The Federalist No. 36, p. 221 (C. Rossiter ed. 1961) (A. Hamilton) (hereinafter The Federalist), and predicted that "the eventual collection [of internal revenue] under the immediate authority of the Union, will generally be made by the officers, and according to the rules, appointed by the several States," *id.*, No. 45, at 292 (J. Madison). The Government also invokes the Federalist's more general observations that the Constitution would "enable the [national] government to employ the ordinary magistracy of each [State] in the execution of its laws," *id.*, No. 27, at 176 (A. Hamilton), and that it was "extremely probable that in other instances, particularly in the organization of the judicial power, the officers of the States will be clothed in the correspondent authority of the Union," id., No. 45, at 292 (J. Madison). But none of these statements necessarily implies — what is the critical point here — that Congress could impose these responsibilities without the consent of the States. They appear to rest on the natural assumption that the States would consent to allowing their officials to assist the Federal Government, an assumption proved correct by the extensive mutual assistance the States and Federal Government voluntarily provided one another in the early days of the Republic, including voluntary federal implementation of state law.

Another passage of The Federalist reads as follows: "It merits particular attention, that the laws of the Confederacy as to the enumerated and legitimate objects of its jurisdiction will become the SUPREME LAW of the land; to the observance of which all officers, legislative, executive, and judicial in each State will be bound by the sanctity of an oath. Thus, the legislatures, courts, and magistrates, of the respective members will be incorporated into the operations of the national government as far as its just and constitutional authority extends; and will be rendered auxiliary to the enforcement of its laws." The Federalist No. 27, at 177 (A. Hamilton). The Government does not rely upon this passage, but Justice Souter (with whose conclusions on this point the dissent is in agreement) makes it the very foundation of his position; so we pause to examine it in some detail. Justice Souter finds "[t]he natural reading" of the phrases "will be incorporated into the operations of the national government" and "will be rendered auxiliary to the enforcement of its laws" to be that the National Government will have "authority, when exercising an otherwise legitimate power (the commerce power, say), to require state 'auxiliaries' to take appropriate action." There are several obstacles to such an interpretation. First, the consequences in question ("incorporated into the operations of the national government" and "rendered auxiliary to the enforcement of its laws") are said in the quoted passage to flow automatically from the officers' oath to observe the "laws of the Confederacy as to the enumerated and legitimate objects of its jurisdiction." Thus, if the passage means that state officers must take an active role in the implementation of federal law, it means that they must do so without the necessity for a congressional directive that they implement it. But no one has ever thought, and no one asserts in the present litigation, that that is the law. The second problem with Justice Souter's reading is that it makes state legislatures subject to federal direction. We have held, however, that state legislatures are not subject to federal direction. *New York v. United States.*

These problems are avoided, of course, if the calculatedly vague consequences the passage recites — "incorporated into the operations of the national government" and "rendered auxiliary to the enforcement of its laws" — are taken to refer to nothing more (or less) than the duty owed to the National Government, on the part of all state officials, to enact, enforce, and interpret state law in such fashion as not to obstruct the operation of federal law, and the attendant reality that all state actions constituting such obstruction, even legislative acts, are ipso facto invalid.

Justice Souter contends that his interpretation of Federalist No. 27 is "supported by No. 44," written by Madison, wherefore he claims that "Madison and Hamilton" together stand opposed to our view. In fact, Federalist No. 44 quite clearly contradicts Justice Souter's reading. In that Number, Madison justifies the requirement that state officials take an oath to support the Federal Constitution on the ground that they "will have an essential agency in giving effect to the federal Constitution." If the dissent's reading of Federalist No. 27 were correct (and if Madison agreed with it), one would surely have expected that "essential agency" of state executive officers (if described further) to be described as their responsibility to execute the laws enacted under the Constitution. Instead, however, Federalist No. 44 continues with the following description: "The election of the President and Senate will depend, in all cases, on the legislatures of the several States. And the election of the House of Representatives will equally depend on the same authority in the first instance; and will, probably, forever be conducted by the officers and according to the laws of the States." *Id.*, at 287. It is most implausible that the person who labored for that example of state executive officers' assisting the Federal Government believed, but neglected to mention, that they had a responsibility to execute federal laws. If it was indeed Hamilton's view that the Federal Government could direct the officers of the States, that view has no clear support in Madison's writings, or as far as we are aware, in text, history, or early commentary elsewhere.[3]

III

The constitutional practice we have examined above tends to negate the existence of the congressional power asserted here, but is not conclusive. We turn next

---

3. [Court's Footnote 9] Even if we agreed with Justice Souter's reading of the Federalist No. 27, it would still seem to us most peculiar to give the view expressed in that one piece, not clearly confirmed by any other writer, the determinative weight he does. That would be crediting the most expansive view of federal authority ever expressed, and from the pen of the most expansive expositor of federal power. Hamilton was "from first to last the most nationalistic of all nationalists in his interpretation of the clauses of our federal Constitution." C. Rossiter, Alexander Hamilton and the Constitution 199 (1964). More specifically, it is widely recognized that "The Federalist reads with a split personality" on matters of federalism. See D. Braveman, W. Banks, & R. Smolla, Constitutional Law: Structure and Rights in Our Federal System 198–199 (3d ed. 1996). While overall The Federalist reflects a "large area of agreement between Hamilton and Madison," Rossiter, *supra*, at 58, that is not the case with respect to the subject at hand, see Braveman, *supra*, at 198–199. To choose Hamilton's view, as Justice Souter would, is to turn a blind eye to the fact that it was Madison's — not Hamilton's — that prevailed, not only at the Constitutional Convention and in popular sentiment, see Rossiter, *supra*, at 44–47, 194, 196; 1 Records of the Federal Convention (M. Farrand ed. 1911) 366, but in the subsequent struggle to fix the meaning of the Constitution by early congressional practice.

to consideration of the structure of the Constitution, to see if we can discern among its "essential postulate[s]," *Principality of Monaco v. Mississippi*, 292 U.S. 313, 322 (1934), a principle that controls the present cases.

It is incontestible that the Constitution established a system of "dual sovereignty." This separation of the two spheres is one of the Constitution's structural protections of liberty. "Just as the separation and independence of the coordinate branches of the Federal Government serve to prevent the accumulation of excessive power in any one branch, a healthy balance of power between the States and the Federal Government will reduce the risk of tyranny and abuse from either front." To quote Madison once again: "In the compound republic of America, the power surrendered by the people is first divided between two distinct governments, and then the portion allotted to each subdivided among distinct and separate departments. Hence a double security arises to the rights of the people. The different governments will control each other, at the same time that each will be controlled by itself." The Federalist No. 51, at 323. See also The Federalist No. 28, at 180–181 (A. Hamilton). The power of the Federal Government would be augmented immeasurably if it were able to impress into its service — and at no cost to itself — the police officers of the 50 States.

[F]ederal control of state officers would also have an effect upon separation and equilibration of powers between the three branches of the Federal Government itself. The Constitution does not leave to speculation who is to administer the laws enacted by Congress; the President, it says, "shall take Care that the Laws be faithfully executed," Art. II, § 3, personally and through officers whom he appoints (save for such inferior officers as Congress may authorize to be appointed by the "Courts of Law" or by "the Heads of Departments" who are themselves presidential appointees), Art. II, § 2. The Brady Act effectively transfers this responsibility to thousands of CLEOs in the 50 States, who are left to implement the program without meaningful Presidential control (if indeed meaningful Presidential control is possible without the power to appoint and remove). The insistence of the Framers upon unity in the Federal Executive — to insure both vigor and accountability — is well known. See The Federalist No. 70 (A. Hamilton); 2 Documentary History of the Ratification of the Constitution 495 (M. Jensen ed. 1976) (statement of James Wilson). That unity would be shattered, and the power of the President would be subject to reduction, if Congress could act as effectively without the President as with him, by simply requiring state officers to execute its laws.

The dissent of course resorts to the last, best hope of those who defend *ultra vires* congressional action, the Necessary and Proper Clause. It reasons that the power to regulate the sale of handguns under the Commerce Clause, coupled with the power to "make all Laws which shall be necessary and proper for carrying into Execution the foregoing Powers," Art. I, § 8, conclusively establishes the Brady Act's constitutional validity, because the Tenth Amendment imposes no limitations on the exercise of delegated powers but merely prohibits the exercise of powers "not delegated to the United States." What destroys the dissent's Necessary and Proper Clause argument, however, is not the Tenth Amendment but the Necessary and Proper Clause itself. When a "La[w] for carrying into Execution" the Commerce Clause violates the principle of state sovereignty reflected in the various constitutional provisions we mentioned earlier, it is not a "La[w] proper for carrying into Execution the Commerce Clause," and is thus, in the words of The Federalist, "merely [an] ac[t] of usurpation" which "deserve[s] to be treated as such." The Federalist No. 33, at 204 (A. Hamilton). We in fact answered the dissent's Necessary and Proper Clause argument in *New York*: "[E]ven where Congress has the authority under the Constitution to pass laws requiring or prohibiting certain acts, it lacks the power directly to compel the States to require or prohibit those acts. [T]he Commerce Clause, for example, authorizes Congress to regulate interstate commerce directly; it does not authorize Congress to regulate state governments' regulation of interstate commerce."

The Government contends that *New York* is distinguishable on the following ground: unlike the "take title" provisions invalidated there, the background-check provision of the Brady Act does not require state legislative or executive officials to make policy, but instead issues a final directive to state CLEOs. It is permissible, the Government asserts, for Congress to command state or local officials to assist in the implementation of federal law so long as "Congress itself devises a clear legislative solution that regulates private conduct" and requires state or local officers to provide only "limited, non-policymaking help in enforcing that law." "[T]he constitutional line is crossed only when Congress compels the States to make law in their sovereign capacities."

The Government's distinction between "making" law and merely "enforcing" it, between "policymaking" and mere "implementation," is an interesting one. It is perhaps not meant to be the same as, but it is surely reminiscent of, the line that separates proper congressional conferral of Executive power from unconstitutional delegation of legislative authority for federal separation-of-powers purposes. This Court has not been notably successful in describing the latter line; indeed, some think we have abandoned the effort to do so. We are doubtful that the new line the Government proposes would be any more distinct. Executive action that has utterly no policymaking component is rare, particularly at an executive level as high as a jurisdiction's chief law-enforcement officer. Is it really true that there is no policymaking involved in deciding, for example, what "reasonable efforts" shall be expended to conduct a background check? It may well satisfy the Act for a CLEO to direct that (a) no background checks will be conducted that divert personnel time from pending felony investigations, and (b) no background check will be permitted to consume more than one-half hour of an officer's time. But nothing in the Act requires a CLEO to be so parsimonious; diverting at least some felony-investigation time, and permitting at least some background checks beyond one-half hour would certainly not be unreasonable. Is this decision whether to devote maximum "reasonable efforts" or minimum "reasonable efforts" not preeminently a matter of policy? It is quite impossible, in short, to draw the Government's proposed line at "no policymaking," and we would have to fall back upon a line of "not too much policymaking." How much is too much is not likely to be answered precisely; and an imprecise barrier against federal intrusion upon state authority is not likely to be an effective one.

Even assuming, moreover, that the Brady Act leaves no "policymaking" discretion with the States, we fail to see how that improves rather than worsens the intrusion upon state sovereignty. Preservation of the States as independent and autonomous political entities is arguably less undermined by requiring them to make policy in certain fields than (as Judge Sneed aptly described it over two decades ago) by "reduc[ing] [them] to puppets of a ventriloquist Congress," *Brown v. EPA*, 521 F. 2d, at 839. It is an essential attribute of the States' retained sovereignty that they remain independent and autonomous within their proper sphere of authority. It is no more compatible with this independence and autonomy that their officers be "dragooned" (as Judge Fernandez put it in his dissent below, 66 F. 3d, at 1035) into administering federal law, than it would be compatible with the independence and autonomy of the United States that its officers be impressed into service for the execution of state laws.

The Government also maintains that requiring state officers to perform discrete, ministerial tasks specified by Congress does not violate the principle of *New York* because it does not diminish the accountability of state or federal officials. This argument fails even on its own terms. By forcing state governments to absorb the financial burden of implementing a federal regulatory program, Members of Congress can take credit for "solving" problems without having to ask their constituents to pay for the solutions with higher federal taxes. And even when the States are not forced to absorb the costs of implementing a federal program, they are still put in the position of taking the blame for its burdensomeness and for its defects. Under the present law, for example, it will be the CLEO and not some federal official who stands between the gun purchaser and immediate possession of his gun. And it will likely be the CLEO, not some federal official, who will be blamed for any error (even one in the designated federal database) that causes a purchaser to be mistakenly rejected.

Finally, the Government puts forward a cluster of arguments that can be grouped under the heading: "The Brady Act serves very important purposes, is most efficiently administered by CLEOs during the interim period, and places a minimal and only temporary burden upon state officers." There is considerable disagreement over the extent of the burden, but we need not pause over that detail. Assuming all the mentioned factors were true, they might be relevant if we were evaluating whether the incidental application to the States of a federal law of general applicability excessively interfered with the functioning of state governments. See, e.g., *National League of Cities v. Usery*. But where, as here, it is the whole object of the law to direct the functioning of the state executive, and hence to compromise the structural framework of dual sovereignty, such a "balancing" analysis is inappropriate. It is the very principle of separate state sovereignty that such a law offends, and no comparative assessment of the various interests can overcome that fundamental defect.

We conclude categorically, as we concluded categorically in *New York*: "The Federal Government may not compel the States to enact or administer a federal regulatory program." The mandatory obligation imposed on CLEOs to perform background checks on prospective handgun purchasers plainly runs afoul of that rule.

What we have said makes it clear enough that the central obligation imposed upon CLEOs by the interim provisions of the Brady Act is unconstitutional. Extinguished with it, of course, is the duty implicit in the background-check requirement that the CLEO accept notice of the contents of, and a copy of, the completed Brady Form, which the firearms dealer is required to provide to him.

It is so ordered.

Justice O'Connor, concurring. [Omitted]

Justice Thomas, concurring. [Omitted]

Justice Stevens, with whom Justice Souter, Justice Ginsburg, and Justice Breyer join, dissenting.

There is not a clause, sentence, or paragraph in the entire text of the Constitution of the United States that supports the proposition that a local police officer can ignore a command contained in a statute enacted by Congress pursuant to an express delegation of power enumerated in Article I.

Under the Articles of Confederation the National Government had the power to issue commands to the several sovereign states, but it had no authority to govern individuals directly. Thus, it raised an army and financed its operations by issuing requisitions to the constituent members of the Confederacy, rather than by creating federal agencies to draft soldiers or to impose taxes.

That method of governing proved to be unacceptable, not because it demeaned the sovereign character of the several States, but rather because it was cumbersome and inefficient. Indeed, a confederation that allows each of its members to determine the ways and means of complying with an overriding requisition is obviously more deferential to state sovereignty concerns than a national government that uses its own agents to impose its will directly on the citizenry. The basic change in the character of the government that the Framers conceived was designed to enhance the power of the national government, not to provide some new, unmentioned immunity for state officers. Because indirect control over individual citizens ("the only proper objects of government") was ineffective under the Articles of Confederation, Alexander Hamilton explained that "we must extend the authority of the Union to the persons of the citizens." The Federalist No. 15, at 101.

Indeed, the historical materials strongly suggest that the Founders intended to enhance the capacity of the federal government by empowering it — as a part of the new authority to make demands directly on individual citizens — to act through local officials. Hamilton made clear that the new Constitution, "by extending the authority of the federal head to the individual citizens of the several States, will enable the government to employ the ordinary magistracy of each, in the execution of its laws." The Federalist No. 27, at 180.

More specifically, during the debates concerning the ratification of the Constitution, it was assumed that state agents would act as tax collectors for the federal government. Opponents of the Constitution had repeatedly expressed fears that the new federal government's ability to impose taxes directly on the citizenry would result in an overbearing presence of federal tax collectors in the States. Federalists rejoined that this problem would not arise because, as Hamilton explained, "the United States will make use of the State officers and State regulations for collecting" certain taxes. Id., No. 36, at 235. Similarly, Madison made clear that the new central government's power to raise taxes directly from the citizenry would "not be resorted to, except for supplemental purposes of revenue and that the eventual collection, under the immediate authority of the Union, will generally be made by the officers appointed by the several States." Id., No. 45, at 318.

Bereft of support in the history of the founding, the Court rests its conclusion on the claim that there is little evidence the National Government actually exercised such a power in the early years of the Republic. This reasoning is misguided in principle and in fact. [W]e have never suggested that the failure of the early Congresses to address the scope of federal power in a particular area or to exercise a particular authority was an argument against its existence. That position, if correct, would undermine most of our post-New Deal Commerce Clause jurisprudence.

Recent developments demonstrate that the political safeguards protecting Our Federalism are effective. The majority expresses special concern that were its rule not adopted the Federal Government would be able to avail itself of the services of state government officials "at no cost to itself." But this specific problem of federal actions that have the effect of imposing so-called "unfunded mandates" on the States has been identified and meaningfully addressed by Congress in recent legislation.

Perversely, the majority's rule seems more likely to damage than to preserve the safeguards against tyranny provided by the existence of vital state governments. By limiting the ability of the Federal Government to enlist state officials in the implementation of its programs, the Court creates incentives for the National Government to aggrandize itself. In the name of State's rights, the majority would have the Federal Government create vast national bureaucracies to implement its policies. This is exactly the sort of thing that the early Federalists promised would not occur, in part as a result of the National Government's ability to rely on the magistracy of the states. See, e.g., The Federalist No. 36, at 234–235 (Hamilton); id., No. 45, at 318 (Madison).

With colorful hyperbole, the Court suggests that the unity in the Executive Branch of the Federal Government "would be shattered, and the power of the President would be subject to reduction, if Congress could require state officers to execute its laws." Putting to one side the obvious tension between the majority's claim that impressing state police officers will unduly tip the balance of power in favor of the federal sovereign and this suggestion that it will emasculate the Presidency, the Court's reasoning contradicts *New York v. United States*.

That decision squarely approved of cooperative federalism programs, designed at the national level but implemented principally by state governments. *New York* disapproved of a particular method of putting such programs into place, not the existence of federal programs implemented locally. Indeed, nothing in the majority's holding calls into question the three mechanisms for constructing such programs that *New York* expressly approved. Congress may require the States to implement its programs as a condition of federal spending, in order to avoid the threat of unilateral federal action in the area, or as a part of a program that affects States and private parties alike. The majority's suggestion in response to this dissent that Congress' ability to create such programs is limited, is belied by the importance and sweep of the federal statutes that meet this description, some of which we described in *New York*.

Nor is there force to the assumption undergirding the Court's entire opinion that if this trivial burden on state sovereignty is permissible, the entire structure of federalism will soon collapse. These cases do not involve any mandate to state legislatures to enact new rules. When legislative action, or even administrative rule-making, is at issue, it may be appropriate for Congress either to pre-empt the State's lawmaking power and fashion the federal rule itself, or to respect the State's power to fashion its own rules. But this case, unlike any precedent in which the Court has held that Congress exceeded its powers, merely involves the imposition of modest duties on individual officers. The Court seems to accept the fact that Congress could require private persons, such as hospital executives or school administrators, to provide arms merchants with relevant information about a prospective purchaser's fitness to own a weapon; indeed, the Court does not disturb the conclusion that flows directly from our prior holdings that the burden on police officers would be permissible if a similar burden were also imposed on private parties with access to relevant data. A structural problem that vanishes when the statute affects private individuals as well as public officials is not much of a structural problem.

Our statements [in *New York*], taken in context, clearly did not decide the question presented here, whether state executive officials — as opposed to state legislators — may in appropriate circumstances be enlisted to implement federal policy. The "take title" provision at issue in New York was beyond Congress' authority to enact because it was "in principle no different than a congressionally compelled subsidy from state governments to radioactive waste producers," almost certainly a legislative act.

The majority relies upon dictum in *New York* to the effect that "[t]he Federal Government may not compel the States to enact or administer a federal regulatory program." But that language was wholly unnecessary to the decision of the case. It is, of course, beyond dispute that we are not bound by the dicta of our prior opinions. To the extent that it has any substance at all, *New York*'s administration language may have referred to the possibility that the State might have been able to take title to and devise an elaborate scheme for the management of the radioactive waste through purely executive policymaking. But despite the majority's effort to suggest that similar activities are required by the Brady Act, it is hard to characterize the minimal requirement that CLEOs perform background checks as one involving the exercise of substantial policymaking discretion on that essentially legislative scale.

In response to this dissent, the majority asserts that the difference between a federal command addressed to individuals and one addressed to the State itself "cannot be a constitutionally significant one." But there is abundant authority in our Eleventh Amendment jurisprudence recognizing a constitutional distinction between local government officials, such as the CLEO's who brought this action, and State entities that are entitled to sovereign immunity. To my knowledge, no one has previously thought that the distinction "disembowels," the Eleventh Amendment.

JUSTICE SOUTER, dissenting. [Omitted]

JUSTICE BREYER, with whom JUSTICE STEVENS joins, dissenting. [Omitted]

Notes and Questions

(1) Did the interim provisions of the Brady Act threaten the values of federalism? If so, which ones?

(2) See if you can piece together from Justice Scalia's opinion the textual and other bases for the principle protecting the integrity of state governments. How do you react to this original-intent method of constitutional interpretation?

(3) What has happened to *Garcia*? Why should the Court actively police state sovereignty when the states are formally represented in the national government? Do the decisions in *New York* and *Printz* suggest that *Garcia* should be overruled? Do these decisions call into question the continuing vitality of any other precedents you have read in this unit?

(4) In *Reno v. Condon*, 528 U.S. 141 (2000), the Court unanimously upheld the Drivers Privacy Protection Act, which bars states from selling their databases of personal information on licensed drivers and automobile owners. States had been earning millions of dollars each year by selling drivers' personal information to a variety of direct marketers, charities, and political campaigns. Sometimes, however, the information was obtained by stalkers or those interested in tracking down the identity of doctors or patients at abortion clinics. The 1994 DPPA requires that drivers consent to disclosure of personal information, although there are exceptions for law enforcement, safety, and a few other purposes.

After concluding that the information was "an article of commerce" and thus "its sale or release into the interstate stream of business is sufficient to support Congressional regulation," Chief Justice Rehnquist responded to South Carolina's argument that the DPPA violates the Tenth Amendment because it "thrusts upon the States all of the day-to-day responsibility for administering its complex provisions" and thereby makes "state officials unwilling implementors of federal policy." According to South Carolina, the DPPA requires State workers to learn and apply the Act's substantive restrictions, which will consume workers' time and cost the State money. According to the Chief Justice, the DPPA does not suffer the fatal flaws of the laws invalidated in *New York* and *Printz*: "[T]he DPPA does not require the States in their sovereign capacity to regulate their own citizens." Instead the States are regulated "as owners of databases." The States are not required "to enact any laws or regulations, [or] to assist in the enforcement of federal statutes regulating private individuals."

Finally, the Court avoided answering South Carolina's argument that the States may be subject to federal regulation only pursuant to "generally applicable" laws, or laws that apply to individuals as well as States. Because the DPPA also regulates "private resellers or redisclosers," it is a generally applicable law.

(5) In 2018, the Court revisited its anticommandeering doctrine from *New York* and *Printz*. As lotteries and various forms of casino gambling were authorized in many states in the last decades of the 20th century, the National Collegiate Athletic Association (NCAA) and professional sports leagues spearheaded opposition to legalized sports gambling. Arguing that it is particularly addictive and especially attractive to young people with a strong interest in sports, and leads to corruption and reputational damage of professional and amateur sports, the groups successfully persuaded Congress to enact the Professional and Amateur Sports Protection Act (PASPA) in 1991. 28 U.S.C. § 3701 *et. seq.* A key provision of PASPA makes it "unlawful" for a state or any of its subdivisions "to sponsor, operate, advertise, promote, license, or authorize a lottery, sweepstakes, or other betting, gambling, or wagering scheme based on" competitive sporting events. Instead of making sports gambling a federal crime, PASPA allows the Justice Department as well as professional and amateur sports organizations to bring civil actions to enjoin violations.

In 2011, with Atlantic City facing stiff competition from newly opened casinos in the region, New Jersey voters approved an amendment to the State Constitution making it lawful for the legislature to authorize sports gambling, and in 2012 the legislature enacted such a law. Unsurprisingly, the NCAA and major professional sports leagues sued New Jersey in federal court and sought to enjoin the new state law on the ground that it violated PASPA. Does PASPA unconstitutionally infringe New Jersey's sovereignty to end its sports gambling ban?

Does PASPA commandeer the state by regulating its exercise of lawmaking power? Do *New York* and *Printz* require overturning PASPA? Or is PASPA different from the commandeering cases because it does not command the states to take *any* affirmative act? Is PASPA nonetheless coercive? After one round of litigation in the lower courts found no commandeering, in 2014, the New Jersey legislature enacted a law repealing the provisions of state law prohibiting sports gambling at a horseracing track or a casino or gambling house in Atlantic City, effective only as to wagers on sporting events not involving a New Jersey college team or collegiate event taking place in New Jersey. The same parties sued again.

In *Murphy v. National Collegiate Athletic Ass'n*, 138 S. Ct. 1461 (2018), the Supreme Court came down firmly in New Jersey's favor. Justice Alito wrote for the majority:

> The anticommandeering doctrine may sound arcane, but it is simply the expression of a fundamental structural decision incorporated into the Constitution, *i.e.,* the decision to withhold from Congress the power to issue orders directly to the States. When the original States declared their independence, they claimed the powers inherent in sovereignty — in the words of the Declaration of Independence, the authority "to do all Acts and Things which Independent States may of right do." ¶ 32. The Constitution limited but did not abolish the sovereign powers of the States, which retained "a residuary and inviolable sovereignty." The Federalist No. 39, p. 245 (C. Rossiter ed. 1961). Thus, both the Federal Government and the States wield sovereign powers, and that is why our system of government is said to be one of "dual sovereignty." *Gregory v. Ashcroft,* 501 U.S. 452, 457 (1991).
>
> Our opinions in *New York* and *Printz* explained why adherence to the anticommandeering principle is important. Without attempting a complete survey, we mention several reasons that are significant here.
>
> First, the rule serves as "one of the Constitution's structural protections of liberty." *Printz.* "The Constitution does not protect the sovereignty of States for the benefit of the States or state governments as abstract political entities." *New York.* "To the contrary, the Constitution divides authority between federal and state governments for the protection of individuals." *Ibid.* "'[A] healthy balance of power between the States and the Federal Government [reduces] the risk of tyranny and abuse from either front.'" *Id.*
>
> Second, the anticommandeering rule promotes political accountability. When Congress itself regulates, the responsibility for the benefits and burdens of the regulation is apparent. Voters who like or dislike the effects of the regulation know who to credit or blame. By contrast, if a State imposes regulations only because it has been commanded to do so by Congress, responsibility is blurred.
>
> Third, the anticommandeering principle prevents Congress from shifting the costs of regulation to the States. If Congress enacts a law and requires enforcement by the Executive Branch, it must appropriate the funds needed to administer the program. It is pressured to weigh the expected benefits of the program against its costs. But if Congress can compel the States to enact and enforce its program, Congress need not engage in any such analysis.
>
> The PASPA provision at issue here — prohibiting state authorization of sports gambling — violates the anticommandeering rule. That provision unequivocally dictates what a state legislature may and may not do. And this is true under either our interpretation or that advocated by respondents and the United States. In either event, state legislatures are put under the direct control of Congress. It is as if federal officers were installed in state

legislative chambers and were armed with the authority to stop legislators from voting on any offending proposals. A more direct affront to state sovereignty is not easy to imagine.

Neither respondents nor the United States contends that Congress can compel a State to enact legislation, but they say that prohibiting a State from enacting new laws is another matter. Noting that the laws challenged in *New York* and *Printz* "told states what they must do instead of what they must not do," respondents contend that commandeering occurs "only when Congress goes beyond precluding state action and affirmatively commands it."

This distinction is empty. It was a matter of happenstance that the laws challenged in *New York* and *Printz* commanded "affirmative" action as opposed to imposing a prohibition. The basic principle — that Congress cannot issue direct orders to state legislatures — applies in either event.

Here is an illustration. PASPA includes an exemption for States that permitted sports betting at the time of enactment, but suppose Congress did not adopt such an exemption. Suppose Congress ordered States with legalized sports betting to take the affirmative step of criminalizing that activity and ordered the remaining States to retain their laws prohibiting sports betting. There is no good reason why the former would intrude more deeply on state sovereignty than the latter.

Respondents and the United States claim that prior decisions of this Court show that PASPA's anti-authorization provision is constitutional, but they misread those cases. In none of them did we uphold the constitutionality of a federal statute that commanded state legislatures to enact or refrain from enacting state law.

In *South Carolina v. Baker,* 485 U.S. 505 (1988), the federal law simply altered the federal tax treatment of private investments. Specifically, it removed the federal tax exemption for interest earned on state and local bonds unless they were issued in registered rather than bearer form. This law did not order the States to enact or maintain any existing laws. Rather, it simply had the indirect effect of pressuring States to increase the rate paid on their bearer bonds in order to make them competitive with other bonds paying taxable interest.

In any event, even if we assume that removal of the tax exemption was tantamount to an outright prohibition of the issuance of bearer bonds, the law would simply treat state bonds the same as private bonds. The anticommandeering doctrine does not apply when Congress evenhandedly regulates an activity in which both States and private actors engage.

That principle formed the basis for the Court's decision in *Reno v. Condon,* which concerned a federal law restricting the disclosure and dissemination of personal information provided in applications for driver's licenses.

The law applied equally to state and private actors. It did not regulate the States' sovereign authority to "regulate their own citizens."

In sum, none of the prior decisions on which respondents and the United States rely involved federal laws that commandeered the state legislative process. None concerned laws that directed the States either to enact or to refrain from enacting a regulation of the conduct of activities occurring within their borders. Therefore, none of these precedents supports the constitutionality of the PASPA provision at issue here.

138 S. Ct. 1478-80. Justice Alito concluded by stating that "Congress can regulate sports gambling directly, but if it elects not to do so, each State is free to act on its own." 138 S. Ct. 1484-85. Are you persuaded by Justice Alito's application of the commandeering cases to PASPA? Is there any doubt that Congress could regulate gambling on a nationwide basis? What case law supports such congressional power?

(6) In 2023, with Justices Alito and Thomas in dissent, the Court distinguished *Printz* and *Murphy* and rejected commandeering challenges to requirements of the Indian Child Welfare Act (ICWA) that apply in child custody proceedings. Writing for the Court in *Haaland v. Brackeen*, 142 S. Ct. 1205 (2023), Justice Barrett found that requirements of the ICWA for "active efforts" to keep an Indian family together by "any party" in an involuntary proceeding to place a child in foster care or terminate parental rights, including private individuals and organizations as well as state agencies, does not "require the use of sovereign power" in ways that were fatal in *Printz* and *Murphy*. As with other requirements of the ICWA that apply to state and private parties, the petitioners "failed to show that the 'active efforts' requirement commands the States to deploy their executive or legislative power to implement federal Indian policy." Similarly, that the ICWA requires state courts to apply placement preferences and comply with recordkeeping requirements established by the Act in making custody determinations is not forbidden commandeering because "Congress can require state courts, unlike state executives and legislatures, to enforce federal law." Citing *Printz* and *New York v. U.S.*, Justice Barrett characterized this aspect of the ICWA as simple federal preemption, authorized by the Supremacy Clause. Would you say that the commandeering doctrine is less or more clear after *Brackeen*?

§ 4.06 Putting the Pieces Together:
Commerce Clause, Necessary and
Proper Clause, Spending Clause

In *United States v. Comstock*, 560 U.S. 126 (2010), the Supreme Court held that the federal government has authority under the Necessary and Proper Clause to impose civil commitment for mental health reasons on incarcerated individuals whose criminal punishment is nearing its end. Relying heavily on the broad dicta in

McCullough v. Maryland that recognizes congressional power to enact laws that are "convenient" or "useful" or "conducive" to the exercise of an enumerated power, the Court in *Comstock* found that it is up to Congress to choose how to further its long-standing interest in mental health and its custodial interest in protecting members of society from violent acts by mentally ill persons:

> Neither Congress' power to criminalize conduct, nor its power to imprison individuals who engage in that conduct, nor its power to enact laws governing prisons and prisoners, is explicitly mentioned in the Constitution. But Congress nonetheless possesses broad authority to do each of those things in the course of "carrying into Execution" the enumerated powers "vested by" the "Constitution in the Government of the United States," Art. I, § 8, cl. 18 — authority granted by the Necessary and Proper Clause. 560 U.S. at 137.

The seven Justices in the majority rejected the contention that its opinion had endorsed a general police power in the Congress and instead insisted that its holding was limited to the unique circumstances of mental health civil commitment.

After *Comstock,* is it fair to characterize the Necessary and Proper Clause as an independent source of congressional power under the Constitution? How direct must the connections be between an enumerated power and the challenged legislation? Consider the next case.

National Federation of Independent Business v. Sibelius

United States Supreme Court
567 U.S. 519, 132 S. Ct. 2566, 183 L. Ed. 2d 450 (2012)

[In 2010, Congress enacted the Patient Protection and Affordable Care Act (ACA). The objective of the ACA was to increase the number of Americans covered by health insurance and decrease the overall cost of health care. An individual mandate required most Americans to maintain "minimum essential" health insurance coverage, either through their employers, or from Medicaid or Medicare. For individuals who were not exempt and did not maintain health insurance in one of the above ways, individuals could satisfy the requirement by purchasing private insurance. Individuals who did not comply with the mandate had to make a "shared responsibility payment" to the Federal Government. The ACA described the payment as a "penalty," paid to the Internal Revenue Service (IRS) with an individual's taxes, and "shall be assessed and collected in the same manner" as tax penalties.]

CHIEF JUSTICE ROBERTS announced the judgment of the Court.

On the day the President signed the Act into law, Florida and 12 other States filed a complaint in the Federal District Court for the Northern District of Florida. Those plaintiffs — who are both respondents and petitioners here, depending on the issue — were subsequently joined by 13 more States, several individuals, and the National Federation of Independent Business. The plaintiffs alleged, among other things, that the individual mandate provisions of the Act exceeded Congress's powers under Article I of the Constitution.

The second provision of the Affordable Care Act directly challenged here is the Medicaid expansion. Enacted in 1965, Medicaid offers federal funding to States to assist pregnant women, children, needy families, the blind, the elderly, and the disabled in obtaining medical care. See 42 U.S.C. §1396a(a)(10). In order to receive that funding, States must comply with federal criteria governing matters such as who receives care and what services are provided at what cost. By 1982 every State had chosen to participate in Medicaid. Federal funds received through the Medicaid program have become a substantial part of state budgets, now constituting over 10 percent of most States' total revenue.

The Affordable Care Act expands the scope of the Medicaid program and increases the number of individuals the States must cover. For example, the Act requires state programs to provide Medicaid coverage to adults with incomes up to 133 percent of the federal poverty level, whereas many States now cover adults with children only if their income is considerably lower, and do not cover childless adults at all. See §1396a(a)(10)(A)(i)(VIII). The Act increases federal funding to cover the States' costs in expanding Medicaid coverage, although States will bear a portion of the costs on their own. §1396d(y)(1). If a State does not comply with the Act's new coverage requirements, it may lose not only the federal funding for those requirements, but all of its federal Medicaid funds. See §1396c.

Along with their challenge to the individual mandate, the state plaintiffs in the Eleventh Circuit argued that the Medicaid expansion exceeds Congress's constitutional powers. The Court of Appeals unanimously held that the Medicaid expansion is a valid exercise of Congress's power under the Spending Clause. U.S. Const., Art. I, §8, cl. 1. And the court rejected the States' claim that the threatened loss of all federal Medicaid funding violates the Tenth Amendment by coercing them into complying with the Medicaid expansion. 648 F.3d, at 1264, 1268.

We granted certiorari.

III

A

The Government's first argument is that the individual mandate is a valid exercise of Congress's power under the Commerce Clause and the Necessary and Proper Clause. According to the Government, the health care market is characterized by a significant cost-shifting problem. Everyone will eventually need health care at a time and to an extent they cannot predict, but if they do not have insurance, they often will not be able to pay for it. Because state and federal laws nonetheless require hospitals to provide a certain degree of care to individuals without regard to their ability to pay, hospitals end up receiving compensation for only a portion of the services they provide. To recoup the losses, hospitals pass on the cost to insurers through higher rates, and insurers, in turn, pass on the cost to policy holders in the form of higher premiums. Congress estimated that the cost of uncompensated care raises family health insurance premiums, on average, by over $1,000 per year.

In the Affordable Care Act, Congress addressed the problem of those who cannot obtain insurance coverage because of preexisting conditions or other health issues. It did so through the Act's "guaranteed-issue" and "community-rating" provisions. The guaranteed-issue and community-rating reforms do not, however, address the issue of healthy individuals who choose not to purchase insurance to cover potential health care needs. In fact, the reforms sharply exacerbate that problem, by providing an incentive for individuals to delay purchasing health insurance until they become sick, relying on the promise of guaranteed and affordable coverage. The reforms also threaten to impose massive new costs on insurers, who are required to accept unhealthy individuals but prohibited from charging them rates necessary to pay for their coverage. This will lead insurers to significantly increase premiums on everyone.

The individual mandate was Congress's solution to these problems. By requiring that individuals purchase health insurance, the mandate prevents cost shifting by those who would otherwise go without it. In addition, the mandate forces into the insurance risk pool more healthy individuals, whose premiums on average will be higher than their health care expenses. This allows insurers to subsidize the costs of covering the unhealthy individuals the reforms require them to accept.

The Government contends that the individual mandate is within Congress's power because the failure to purchase insurance "has a substantial and deleterious effect on interstate commerce" by creating the cost-shifting problem. Given its expansive scope, it is no surprise that Congress has employed the commerce power in a wide variety of ways to address the pressing needs of the time. But Congress has never attempted to rely on that power to compel individuals not engaged in commerce to purchase an unwanted product. Legislative novelty is not necessarily fatal; there is a first time for everything. But sometimes "the most telling indication of [a] severe constitutional problem is the lack of historical precedent" for Congress's action. At the very least, we should "pause to consider the implications of the Government's arguments" when confronted with such new conceptions of federal power. *Lopez.*

... The power to *regulate* commerce presupposes the existence of commercial activity to be regulated. If the power to "regulate" something included the power to create it, many of the provisions in the Constitution would be superfluous. For example, the Constitution gives Congress the power to "coin Money," in addition to the power to "regulate the Value thereof." *Id.,* cl. 5. And it gives Congress the power to "raise and support Armies" and to "provide and maintain a Navy," in addition to the power to "make Rules for the Government and Regulation of the land and naval Forces." *Id.,* cls. 12–14. If the power to regulate the Armed Forces or the value of money included the power to bring the subject of the regulation into existence, the specific grant of such powers would have been unnecessary. The language of the Constitution reflects the natural understanding that the power to regulate assumes there is already something to be regulated.

Our precedent also reflects this understanding. As expansive as our cases construing the scope of the commerce power have been, they all have one thing in common: They uniformly describe the power as reaching "activity." Applying the Government's logic to the familiar case of *Wickard v. Filburn* shows how far that logic would carry us from the notion of a government of limited powers. Under *Wickard* it is within Congress's power to regulate the market for wheat by supporting its price. But price can be supported by increasing demand as well as by decreasing supply. The aggregated decisions of some consumers not to purchase wheat have a substantial effect on the price of wheat, just as decisions not to purchase health insurance have on the price of insurance. Congress can therefore command that those not buying wheat do so, just as it argues here that it may command that those not buying health insurance do so. The farmer in *Wickard* was at least actively engaged in the production of wheat, and the Government could regulate that activity because of its effect on commerce. The Government's theory here would effectively override that limitation, by establishing that individuals may be regulated under the Commerce Clause whenever enough of them are not doing something the Government would have them do.

Indeed, the Government's logic would justify a mandatory purchase to solve almost any problem. To consider a different example in the health care market, many Americans do not eat a balanced diet. That group makes up a larger percentage of the total population than those without health insurance. The failure of that group to have a healthy diet increases health care costs, to a greater extent than the failure of the uninsured to purchase insurance. Those increased costs are borne in part by other Americans who must pay more, just as the uninsured shift costs to the insured. Congress addressed the insurance problem by ordering everyone to buy insurance. Under the Government's theory, Congress could address the diet problem by ordering everyone to buy vegetables.

To an economist, perhaps, there is no difference between activity and inactivity; both have measurable economic effects on commerce. But the distinction between doing something and doing nothing would not have been lost on the Framers, who were "practical statesmen," not metaphysical philosophers. The Framers gave Congress the power to *regulate* commerce, not to *compel* it, and for over 200 years both our decisions and Congress's actions have reflected this understanding. There is no reason to depart from that understanding now.

The Government next contends that Congress has the power under the Necessary and Proper Clause to enact the individual mandate because the mandate is an "integral part of a comprehensive scheme of economic regulation"—the guaranteed-issue and community-rating insurance reforms. Under this argument, it is not necessary to consider the effect that an individual's inactivity may have on interstate commerce; it is enough that Congress regulate commercial activity in a way that requires regulation of inactivity to be effective. Although the Clause gives Congress authority to "legislate on that vast mass of incidental powers which must be involved in the constitution," it does not license the exercise of any "great substantive and independent power[s]" beyond those specifically enumerated.

The Government relies primarily on our decision in *Gonzales v. Raich*. In *Raich,* we considered "comprehensive legislation to regulate the interstate market" in marijuana. Certain individuals sought an exemption from that regulation on the ground that they engaged in only intrastate possession and consumption. We denied any exemption, on the ground that marijuana is a fungible commodity, so that any marijuana could be readily diverted into the interstate market. Congress's attempt to regulate the interstate market for marijuana would therefore have been substantially undercut if it could not also regulate intrastate possession and consumption. Accordingly, we recognized that "Congress was acting well within its authority" under the Necessary and Proper Clause even though its "regulation ensnare[d] some purely intrastate activity." *Raich* thus did not involve the exercise of any "great substantive and independent power," *McCulloch,* of the sort at issue here. Instead, it concerned only the constitutionality of "individual *applications* of a concededly valid statutory scheme."

That is not the end of the matter. Because the Commerce Clause does not support the individual mandate, it is necessary to turn to the Government's second argument: that the mandate may be upheld as within Congress's enumerated power to "lay and collect Taxes." Art. I, § 8, cl. 1.

The Government's tax power argument asks us to view the statute differently than we did in considering its commerce power theory. In making its Commerce Clause argument, the Government defended the mandate as a regulation requiring individuals to purchase health insurance. The Government does not claim that the taxing power allows Congress to issue such a command. Instead, the Government asks us to read the mandate not as ordering individuals to buy insurance, but rather as imposing a tax on those who do not buy that product.

Under the mandate, if an individual does not maintain health insurance, the only consequence is that he must make an additional payment to the IRS when he pays his taxes. That, according to the Government, means the mandate can be regarded as establishing a condition — not owning health insurance — that triggers a tax — the required payment to the IRS. Under that theory, the mandate is not a legal command to buy insurance. Rather, it makes going without insurance just another thing the Government taxes, like buying gasoline or earning income. And if the mandate is in effect just a tax hike on certain taxpayers who do not have health insurance, it may be within Congress's constitutional power to tax.

The exaction the Affordable Care Act imposes on those without health insurance looks like a tax in many respects. The "[s]hared responsibility payment," as the statute entitles it, is paid into the Treasury by "taxpayer[s]" when they file their tax returns. It does not apply to individuals who do not pay federal income taxes because their household income is less than the filing threshold in the Internal Revenue Code. For taxpayers who do owe the payment, its amount is determined by such familiar factors as taxable income, number of dependents, and joint filing status. The requirement to pay is found in the Internal Revenue Code and enforced by the IRS, which — as we previously explained — must assess and collect it "in the same manner as taxes." This process yields the essential feature of any tax: It produces at least some revenue for the Government.

The same analysis here suggests that the shared responsibility payment may for constitutional purposes be considered a tax, not a penalty: First, for most Americans the amount due will be far less than the price of insurance, and, by statute, it can never be more. It may often be a reasonable financial decision to make the payment rather than purchase insurance. Second, the individual mandate contains no scienter requirement. Third, the payment is collected solely by the IRS through the normal means of taxation — except that the Service is *not* allowed to use those means most suggestive of a punitive sanction, such as criminal prosecution.

The joint dissenters argue that we cannot uphold § 5000A as a tax because Congress did not "frame" it as such. In effect, they contend that even if the Constitution permits Congress to do exactly what we interpret this statute to do, the law must be struck down because Congress used the wrong labels. An example may help illustrate why labels should not control here. Suppose Congress enacted a statute providing that every taxpayer who owns a house without energy efficient windows must pay $50 to the IRS. The amount due is adjusted based on factors such as taxable income and joint filing status, and is paid along with the taxpayer's income tax return. Those whose income is below the filing threshold need not pay. The required payment is not called a "tax," a "penalty," or anything else. No one would doubt that this law imposed a tax, and was within Congress's power to tax. That conclusion should not change simply because Congress used the word "penalty" to describe the payment. Interpreting such a law to be a tax would hardly "[i]mpos[e] a tax through judicial legislation." Rather, it would give practical effect to the Legislature's enactment.

There may, however, be a more fundamental objection to a tax on those who lack health insurance. Even if only a tax, the payment under § 5000A(b) remains a burden that the Federal Government imposes for an omission, not an act. If it is troubling to interpret the Commerce Clause as authorizing Congress to regulate those who abstain from commerce, perhaps it should be similarly troubling to permit Congress to impose a tax for not doing something.

Three considerations allay this concern. First, and most importantly, it is abundantly clear the Constitution does not guarantee that individuals may avoid taxation through inactivity. A capitation, after all, is a tax that everyone must pay simply for existing, and capitations are expressly contemplated by the Constitution. The Court today holds that our Constitution protects us from federal regulation under the Commerce Clause so long as we abstain from the regulated activity. But from its creation, the Constitution has made no such promise with respect to taxes.

Whether the mandate can be upheld under the Commerce Clause is a question about the scope of federal authority. Its answer depends on whether Congress can exercise what all acknowledge to be the novel course of directing individuals to purchase insurance. Congress's use of the Taxing Clause to encourage buying something is, by contrast, not new. Tax incentives already promote, for example, purchasing homes and professional educations. Sustaining the mandate as a tax depends only on whether Congress *has* properly exercised its taxing power to encourage purchasing health insurance, not whether it *can*. Upholding the individual mandate under the Taxing Clause thus does not recognize any new federal power. It determines that Congress has used an existing one.

Second, Congress's ability to use its taxing power to influence conduct is not without limits. A few of our cases policed these limits aggressively, invalidating punitive exactions obviously designed to regulate behavior otherwise regarded at the time as beyond federal authority. See, *e.g., United States v. Butler,* 297 U.S. 1 (1936); *Drexel Furniture* [*Child Labor Tax Case*], 259 U.S. 20 [(1922)]. More often and more recently we have declined to closely examine the regulatory motive or effect of revenue-raising measures. See [*United States v.*] *Kahriger,* 345 U.S., at 27–31 [(1953)]. We have nonetheless maintained that "'there comes a time in the extension of the penalizing features of the so-called tax when it loses its character as such and becomes a mere penalty with the characteristics of regulation and punishment.'"

Third, although the breadth of Congress's power to tax is greater than its power to regulate commerce, the taxing power does not give Congress the same degree of control over individual behavior. Once we recognize that Congress may regulate a particular decision under the Commerce Clause, the Federal Government can bring its full weight to bear. Congress may simply command individuals to do as it directs. An individual who disobeys may be subjected to criminal sanctions. Those sanctions can include not only fines and imprisonment, but all the attendant consequences of being branded a criminal: deprivation of otherwise protected civil rights, such as the right to bear arms or vote in elections; loss of employment opportunities; social stigma; and severe disabilities in other controversies, such as custody or immigration disputes.

By contrast, Congress's authority under the taxing power is limited to requiring an individual to pay money into the Federal Treasury, no more. If a tax is properly paid, the Government has no power to compel or punish individuals subject to it. We do not make light of the severe burden that taxation — especially taxation motivated by a regulatory purpose — can impose. But imposition of a tax nonetheless leaves an individual with a lawful choice to do or not do a certain act, so long as he is willing to pay a tax levied on that choice.

The Affordable Care Act's requirement that certain individuals pay a financial penalty for not obtaining health insurance may reasonably be characterized as a tax. Because the Constitution permits such a tax, it is not our role to forbid it, or to pass upon its wisdom or fairness.

Justice Ginsburg questions the necessity of rejecting the Government's commerce power argument, given that § 5000A can be upheld under the taxing power. But the statute reads more naturally as a command to buy insurance than as a tax, and I would uphold it as a command if the Constitution allowed it. It is only because the Commerce Clause does not authorize such a command that it is necessary to reach the taxing power question. And it is only because we have a duty to construe a statute to save it, if fairly possible, that § 5000A can be interpreted as a tax. Without deciding the Commerce Clause question, I would find no basis to adopt such a saving construction.

The Federal Government does not have the power to order people to buy health insurance. Section 5000A would therefore be unconstitutional if read as a command. The Federal Government does have the power to impose a tax on those without health insurance. Section 5000A is therefore constitutional, because it can reasonably be read as a tax.

IV

A

The States also contend that the Medicaid expansion exceeds Congress's authority under the Spending Clause. They claim that Congress is coercing the States to adopt the changes it wants by threatening to withhold all of a State's Medicaid grants, unless the State accepts the new expanded funding and complies with the conditions that come with it. This, they argue, violates the basic principle that the "Federal Government may not compel the States to enact or administer a federal regulatory program." *New York*.

There is no doubt that the Act dramatically increases state obligations under Medicaid. The current Medicaid program requires States to cover only certain discrete categories of needy individuals — pregnant women, children, needy families, the blind, the elderly, and the disabled. There is no mandatory coverage for most childless adults, and the States typically do not offer any such coverage. The States also enjoy considerable flexibility with respect to the coverage levels for parents of needy families. On average States cover only those unemployed parents who make less than 37 percent of the federal poverty level, and only those employed parents who make less than 63 percent of the poverty line.

The Medicaid provisions of the Affordable Care Act, in contrast, require States to expand their Medicaid programs by 2014 to cover *all* individuals under the age of 65 with incomes below 133 percent of the federal poverty line. The Act also establishes a new "[e]ssential health benefits" package, which States must provide to all new Medicaid recipients — a level sufficient to satisfy a recipient's obligations under the individual mandate. The Affordable Care Act provides that the Federal Government will pay 100 percent of the costs of covering these newly eligible individuals through 2016. In the following years, the federal payment level gradually decreases, to a minimum of 90 percent. In light of the expansion in coverage mandated by the Act, the Federal Government estimates that its Medicaid spending will increase by approximately $100 billion per year, nearly 40 percent above current levels.

The Spending Clause grants Congress the power "to pay the Debts and provide for the . . . general Welfare of the United States." U.S. Const., Art. I, § 8, cl. 1. We have long recognized that Congress may use this power to grant federal funds to the States, and may condition such a grant upon the States' "taking certain actions that Congress could not require them to take." At the same time, our cases have recognized limits on Congress's power under the Spending Clause to secure state compliance with federal objectives. . . . The legitimacy of Congress's exercise of the spending power "thus rests on whether the State voluntarily and knowingly accepts the terms of the 'contract.'" Respecting this limitation is critical to ensuring that Spending Clause legislation does not undermine the status of the States as independent sovereigns in our federal system. . . . For this reason, "the Constitution has never been understood to confer upon Congress the ability to require the States to govern according to Congress' instructions." *New York.* Otherwise the two-government system established by the Framers would give way to a system that vests power in one central government, and individual liberty would suffer.

In South Dakota v. Dole, we considered a challenge to a federal law that threatened to withhold five percent of a State's federal highway funds if the State did not raise its drinking age to 21. The Court found that the condition was "directly related to one of the main purposes for which highway funds are expended — safe interstate travel." At the same time, the condition was not a restriction on how the highway funds — set aside for specific highway improvement and maintenance efforts — were to be used.

We found that the inducement was not impermissibly coercive, because Congress was offering only "relatively mild encouragement to the States." In this case, the financial "inducement" Congress has chosen is much more than "relatively mild encouragement" — it is a gun to the head. Section 1396c of the Medicaid Act provides that if a State's Medicaid plan does not comply with the Act's requirements, the Secretary of Health and Human Services may declare that "further payments will not be made to the State." A State that opts out of the Affordable Care Act's expansion in health care coverage thus stands to lose not merely "a relatively small percentage" of its existing Medicaid funding, but *all* of it.

Here, the Government claims that the Medicaid expansion is properly viewed merely as a modification of the existing program because the States agreed that Congress could change the terms of Medicaid when they signed on in the first place. The Government observes that the Social Security Act, which includes the original Medicaid provisions, contains a clause expressly reserving "[t]he right to alter, amend, or repeal any provision" of that statute. So it does. A State confronted with statutory language reserving the right to "alter" or "amend" the pertinent provisions of the Social Security Act might reasonably assume that Congress was entitled to make adjustments to the Medicaid program as it developed. Congress has in fact done so, sometimes conditioning only the new funding, other times both old and new.

The Medicaid expansion, however, accomplishes a shift in kind, not merely degree. Indeed, the manner in which the expansion is structured indicates that while Congress may have styled the expansion a mere alteration of existing Medicaid, it recognized it was enlisting the States in a new health care program.

The Court in *Steward Machine* did not attempt to "fix the outermost line" where persuasion gives way to coercion. The Court found it "[e]nough for present purposes that wherever the line may be, this statute is within it." We have no need to fix a line either. It is enough for today that wherever that line may be, this statute is surely beyond it.

B

Nothing in our opinion precludes Congress from offering funds under the Affordable Care Act to expand the availability of health care, and requiring that States accepting such funds comply with the conditions on their use. What Congress is not free to do is to penalize States that choose not to participate in that new program by taking away their existing Medicaid funding. In light of the Court's holding, the Secretary cannot apply § 1396c to withdraw existing Medicaid funds for failure to comply with the requirements set out in the expansion.

That fully remedies the constitutional violation we have identified. The chapter of the United States Code that contains § 1396c includes a severability clause confirming that we need go no further.

The judgment of the Court of Appeals for the Eleventh Circuit is affirmed in part and reversed in part.

It is so ordered.

Justice GINSBURG, with whom Justice SOTOMAYOR joins, and with whom Justice BREYER and Justice KAGAN join, concurring in part, concurring in the judgment in part, and dissenting in part.

[E]ven assuming, for the moment, that Congress lacks authority under the Commerce Clause to "compel individuals not engaged in commerce to purchase an unwanted product," such a limitation would be inapplicable here. Everyone will, at some point, consume health-care products and services. Thus, if The Chief Justice is correct that an insurance-purchase requirement can be applied only to those who "actively" consume health care, the minimum coverage provision fits the bill.

[C]ontrary to The Chief Justice's contention, our precedent does indeed support "[t]he proposition that Congress may dictate the conduct of an individual today because of prophesied future activity." In *Wickard,* the Court upheld a penalty the Federal Government imposed on a farmer who grew more wheat than he was permitted to grow under the Agricultural Adjustment Act of 1938 (AAA). He could not be penalized, the farmer argued, as he was growing the wheat for home consumption, not for sale on the open market. The Court rejected this argument. Wheat intended for home consumption, the Court noted, "overhangs the market and, if induced by rising prices, tends to flow into the market and check price increases [intended by the AAA]."

The Chief Justice could certainly uphold the individual mandate without giving Congress *carte blanche* to enact any and all purchase mandates. As several times noted, the unique attributes of the health-care market render everyone active in that market and give rise to a significant free-riding problem that does not occur in other markets.

Nor would the commerce power be unbridled, absent The Chief Justice's "activity" limitation. Congress would remain unable to regulate noneconomic conduct that has only an attenuated effect on interstate commerce and is traditionally left to state law. *In Lopez,* for example, the Court held that the Federal Government lacked power, under the Commerce Clause, to criminalize the possession of a gun in a local school zone. Possessing a gun near a school, the Court reasoned, "is in no sense an economic activity that might, through repetition elsewhere, substantially affect any sort of interstate commerce." Relying on similar logic, the Court concluded in *Morrison* that Congress could not regulate gender-motivated violence, which the Court deemed to have too "attenuated [an] effect upon interstate commerce."

An individual's decision to self-insure, I have explained, is an economic act with the requisite connection to interstate commerce. Asserting that the Necessary and Proper Clause does not authorize the minimum coverage provision, The Chief Justice focuses on the word "proper." A mandate to purchase health insurance is not "proper" legislation, The Chief Justice urges, because the command "undermine[s] the structure of government established by the Constitution." If long on rhetoric, The Chief Justice's argument is short on substance.

The Chief Justice cites only two cases in which this Court concluded that a federal statute impermissibly transgressed the Constitution's boundary between state and federal authority: *Printz* and *New York*. The statutes at issue in both cases, however, compelled *state officials* to act on the Federal Government's behalf. The minimum coverage provision, in contrast, acts "directly upon individuals, without employing the States as intermediaries."

Ultimately, the Court upholds the individual mandate as a proper exercise of Congress' power to tax and spend "for the . . . general Welfare of the United States." I concur in that determination, which makes The Chief Justice's Commerce Clause essay all the more puzzling. Why should The Chief Justice strive so mightily to hem in Congress' capacity to meet the new problems arising constantly in our ever-developing modern economy? I find no satisfying response to that question in his opinion.

A majority of the Court buys the argument that prospective withholding of funds formerly available exceeds Congress' spending power. Given that holding, I entirely agree with The Chief Justice as to the appropriate remedy. It is to bar the withholding found impermissible — not, as the joint dissenters would have it, to scrap the expansion altogether. Because The Chief Justice finds the withholding — not the granting — of federal funds incompatible with the Spending Clause, Congress' extension of Medicaid remains available to any State that affirms its willingness to participate.

This litigation does not present the concerns that led the Court in *Dole* even to consider the prospect of coercion. In *Dole,* the condition — set 21 as the minimum drinking age — did not tell the States how to use funds Congress provided for highway construction. Further, in view of the Twenty-First Amendment, it was an open question whether Congress could directly impose a national minimum drinking age.

The ACA, in contrast, relates solely to the federally funded Medicaid program; if States choose not to comply, Congress has not threatened to withhold funds earmarked for any other program. Nor does the ACA use Medicaid funding to induce States to take action Congress itself could not undertake. The Federal Government undoubtedly could operate its own health-care program for poor persons, just as it operates Medicare for seniors' health care.

For the reasons stated, I agree with The Chief Justice that, as to the validity of the minimum coverage provision, the judgment of the Court of Appeals for the Eleventh Circuit should be reversed. In my view, the provision encounters no constitutional obstruction. Further, I would uphold the Eleventh Circuit's decision that the Medicaid expansion is within Congress' spending power.

Justice SCALIA, Justice KENNEDY, Justice THOMAS, and Justice ALITO, dissenting.

The Act before us here exceeds federal power both in mandating the purchase of health insurance and in denying nonconsenting States all Medicaid funding. These parts of the Act are central to its design and operation, and all the Act's other provisions would not have been enacted without them. In our view it must follow that the entire statute is inoperative.

The case upon which the Government principally relies to sustain the Individual Mandate under the Necessary and Proper Clause is *Gonzales v. Raich*. That case's prohibition of growing, and of possession (cf. innumerable federal statutes) did not represent the expansion of the federal power to direct into a broad new field. The mandating of economic activity does, and since it is a field so limitless that it converts the Commerce Clause into a general authority to direct the economy, that mandating is not "consist[ent] with the letter and spirit of the constitution." *McCulloch.*

Moreover, Raich is far different from the Individual Mandate in another respect. The Court's opinion in *Raich* pointed out that the growing and possession prohibitions were the only practicable way of enabling the prohibition of interstate traffic in marijuana to be effectively enforced. Intrastate marijuana could no more be distinguished from interstate marijuana than, for example, endangered-species trophies obtained before the species was federally protected can be distinguished from trophies obtained afterwards — which made it necessary and proper to prohibit the sale of all such trophies.

With the present statute, by contrast, there are many ways other than this unprecedented Individual Mandate by which the regulatory scheme's goals of reducing insurance premiums and ensuring the profitability of insurers could be achieved. For instance, those who did not purchase insurance could be subjected to a surcharge when they do enter the health insurance system. Or they could be denied a full income tax credit given to those who do purchase the insurance.

[Justice GINSBURG's] dissent dismisses the conclusion that the power to compel entry into the health-insurance market would include the power to compel entry into the new-car or broccoli markets. The latter purchasers, it says, "will be obliged to pay at the counter before receiving the vehicle or nourishment," whereas those refusing to purchase health-insurance will ultimately get treated anyway, at others' expense. "[T]he unique attributes of the health-care market give rise to a significant free-riding problem that does not occur in other markets." And "a vegetable-purchase mandate" (or a car-purchase mandate) is not "likely to have a substantial effect on the health-care costs" borne by other Americans. Those differences make a very good argument by the dissent's own lights, since they show that the failure to purchase health insurance, unlike the failure to purchase cars or broccoli, creates a national, social-welfare problem that is (in the dissent's view) included among the unenumerated "problems" that the Constitution authorizes the Federal Government to solve. But those differences do not show that the failure to enter the health-insurance market, unlike the failure to buy cars and broccoli, is an *activity* that Congress can "regulate." (Of course one day the failure of some of the public to purchase American cars may endanger the existence of domestic automobile manufacturers; or the failure of some to eat broccoli may be found to deprive them of a newly discovered cancer-fighting chemical which only that food contains, producing health-care costs that are a burden on the rest of us — in which case, under the theory of Justice Ginsburg's dissent, moving against those inactivities will also come within the Federal Government's unenumerated problem-solving powers.)

[T]he legitimacy of attaching conditions to federal grants to the States depends on the voluntariness of the States' choice to accept or decline the offered package. Therefore, if States really have no choice other than to accept the package, the offer is coercive, and the conditions cannot be sustained under the spending power. And as our decision in *South Dakota v. Dole* makes clear, theoretical voluntariness is not enough.

When a heavy federal tax is levied to support a federal program that offers large grants to the States, States may, as a practical matter, be unable to refuse to participate in the federal program and to substitute a state alternative. Even if a State believes that the federal program is ineffective and inefficient, withdrawal would likely force the State to impose a huge tax increase on its residents, and this new state tax would come on top of the federal taxes already paid by residents to support subsidies to participating States.

Acceptance of the Federal Government's interpretation of the anticoercion rule would permit Congress to dictate policy in areas traditionally governed primarily at the state or local level. We should not accept the Government's invitation to attempt to solve a constitutional problem by rewriting the Medicaid Expansion so as to allow States that reject it to retain their pre-existing Medicaid funds. Worse, the Government's remedy, now adopted by the Court, takes the ACA and this Nation in a new direction and charts a course for federalism that the Court, not the Congress, has chosen; but under the Constitution, that power and authority do not rest with this Court.

The Court today decides to save a statute Congress did not write. It rules that what the statute declares to be a requirement with a penalty is instead an option subject to a tax. And it changes the intentionally coercive sanction of a total cut-off of Medicaid funds to a supposedly noncoercive cut-off of only the incremental funds that the Act makes available.

The Court regards its strained statutory interpretation as judicial modesty. It is not. It amounts instead to a vast judicial overreaching. It creates a debilitated, inoperable version of health-care regulation that Congress did not enact and the public does not expect. It makes enactment of sensible health-care regulation more difficult, since Congress cannot start afresh but must take as its point of departure a jumble of now senseless provisions, provisions that certain interests favored under the Court's new design will struggle to retain. And it leaves the public and the States to expend vast sums of money on requirements that may or may not survive the necessary congressional revision.

The Court's disposition, invented and atextual as it is, does not even have the merit of avoiding constitutional difficulties. It creates them. The holding that the Individual Mandate is a tax raises a difficult constitutional question (what is a direct tax?) that the Court resolves with inadequate deliberation. And the judgment on the Medicaid Expansion issue ushers in new federalism concerns and places an unaccustomed strain upon the Union. Those States that decline the Medicaid Expansion must subsidize, by the federal tax dollars taken from their citizens, vast grants to the States that accept the Medicaid Expansion. If that destabilizing political dynamic, so antagonistic to a harmonious Union, is to be introduced at all, it should be by Congress, not by the Judiciary.

The values that should have determined our course today are caution, minimalism, and the understanding that the Federal Government is one of limited powers. But the Court's ruling undermines those values at every turn. In the name of restraint, it overreaches. In the name of constitutional avoidance, it creates new constitutional questions. In the name of cooperative federalism, it undermines state sovereignty.

The Constitution, though it dates from the founding of the Republic, has powerful meaning and vital relevance to our own times. The constitutional protections that this case involves are protections of structure. Structural protections — notably, the restraints imposed by federalism and separation of powers — are less romantic and have less obvious a connection to personal freedom than the provisions of the Bill of Rights or the Civil War Amendments. Hence they tend to be undervalued or even forgotten by our citizens. It should be the responsibility of the Court to teach otherwise, to remind our people that the Framers considered structural protections of freedom the most important ones, for which reason they alone were embodied in the original Constitution and not left to later amendment. The fragmentation of power produced by the structure of our Government is central to liberty, and when we destroy it, we place liberty at peril. Today's decision should have vindicated, should have taught, this truth; instead, our judgment today has disregarded it.

For the reasons here stated, we would find the Act invalid in its entirety. We respectfully dissent.

Justice Thomas, dissenting. [omitted]

Notes and Questions

(1) Chief Justice Roberts' opinion in *NFIB* asserts that the Commerce Clause enables Congress to regulate only pre-existing economic activity. How persuasive is the distinction between economic activity and inactivity? How much is such a distinction likely to matter in the future? As Justice Ginsburg noted in her dissent, Congress could have simply created a health insurance plan akin to Social Security, pursuant to its taxing and spending powers.

(2) Does the Court's rejection of Commerce Clause authority for the Affordable Care Act matter in light of the decision to uphold the individual mandate as a matter within Congress's Taxing and Spending Clause power? Are you persuaded by the majority's argument that the mandate constitutes a tax? In some ways, the Roberts and Scalia opinions rely on formalist distinctions, such as activity/inactivity, rather than the practical considerations emphasized by the dissenters. It is not a stretch to analogize to the early different approaches of the Court in *Gibbons*, on the one hand, and *Knight* and *Hammer* on the other.

(3) Why wasn't the ACA simply a permissible exercise of the commerce power under precedents such as *Wickard* and *Gonzales v. Raich*?

(4) Does it matter whether Congress labels a provision a tax or penalty? Does reliance on the taxing power in *NFIB* suggest that federal regulation may expand through the taxing power even as it constricts under the Commerce Clause? If there are limits on the taxing power, what are they? Will they be judicially enforced?

(5) In 2017, Congress lowered the tax on those without insurance to $0, effectively eliminating the individual mandate in the ACA. Twenty states sued, claiming that the mandate was no longer supportable under the taxing power because there was no tax. A federal district court then ruled that, absent the unconstitutional mandate, the entire ACA was unconstitutional. *Texas v. United States*, 340 F. Supp. 3d 579 (2018). After further appeals, however, in 2021, the Supreme Court voted 7-2 to uphold the amended ACA without reaching the merits in *California v. Texas*, 141 S. Ct. 2104 (2021). The Court ruled that the state and individual plaintiffs were not injured by the repeal of the mandate and thus did not meet the requirements of Article III standing.

Problem D

Assume that Congress has been holding hearings on gun violence in our nation's schools. Among other things, the hearings have revealed wide disparity among the states in the regulation of firearms. In Massachusetts, for example, which has some of the nation's most restrictive gun laws, three people per 100,000 are killed annually by guns, while in Louisiana, a state with weak firearms regulation, the death rate from gun violence is six times higher. Hearings testimony also confirmed that, compared to twenty-two other developed nations, Americans are ten times more likely to be killed by guns.

A recent spate of mass killings in our schools has prompted Congress to take action, relying in part on the hearings and social science data they compiled. Despite intense lobbying and threats of political reprisals by the National Rifle Association, the House has passed and the Senate is considering the Safe Schools Act. The Act recites findings about the rise in gun violence in the schools, the disparity among the states in protecting students against gun violence, and the impact of gun violence on public health and the national economy. The Act would withhold federal education subsidies to any state that fails to enact a law banning gun sales to anyone under 21, and it would forbid the presence of firearms by anyone other than a licensed law enforcement officer within 5,000 feet of a school.

Assume that you are counsel to your home state senator. She wants to know whether the Safe Schools Act would be constitutional if enacted. Does Congress have authority under the Commerce Clause, Necessary and Proper Clause, and/or the Spending Clause to enact the Safe Schools Act?

§ 4.07 Constitutional Limits on State Regulation of Commerce: The Dormant Commerce Clause

In the cases in this section, the Congress has not legislated concerning the disputed subject matter. Must the states nonetheless temper their regulatory actions out of respect for national interests, because of federalism? To the extent limits exist, they are imposed by the unexercised, or "dormant" Commerce Clause, in particular by the free trade values which the Clause embodies. Thus, the dormant Commerce Clause doctrine has evolved not from the exercise of the Commerce Clause by the Congress, but from its negative implications.

The national government under the Articles of Confederation was ineffective, in part because neither the power to tax nor the power to regulate trade was given to the Congress. The trade and currency disputes which then weakened the nation were a major impetus for calling the Constitutional Convention. While the scope of the Article I commerce power was not clearly fixed by the Framers, the delegates were united in their decision to confer the national power to regulate trade. The goal, however, was to put an end to the interstate trade wars, not to encourage regulation by the Congress. To be sure, the Framers believed that if the states were prohibited from enacting protectionist measures, free trade would return. Thus, there would be no need for national regulation. This history was captured by

Justice Jackson in his opinion for the Court in *H.P. Hood & Sons v. DuMond*, 336 U.S. 525 (1949):

> When victory relieved the Colonies from the pressure for solidarity that war had exerted, a drift toward anarchy and commercial warfare between states began. "[E]ach state would legislate according to its estimate of its own interests, the importance of its own products, and the local advantages or disadvantages of its position in a political or commercial view." This came "to threaten at once the peace and safety of the Union." The sole purpose for which Virginia initiated the movement which ultimately produced the Constitution was "to take into consideration the trade of the United States; to examine the relative situations and trade of the said states; to consider how far a uniform system in their commercial regulation may be necessary to their common interest and their permanent harmony," and for that purpose the General Assembly of Virginia in January of 1786 named commissioners and proposed their meeting with those from other states.
>
> The desire of the Forefathers to federalize regulation of foreign and interstate commerce stands in sharp contrast to their jealous preservation of power over their internal affairs. No other federal power was so universally assumed to be necessary, no other state power was so readily relinquished. There was no desire to authorize federal interference with social conditions or legal institutions of the states. Even the Bill of Rights amendments were framed only as a limitation upon the powers of Congress. The states were quite content with their several and diverse controls over most matters but, as Madison has indicated, "want of a general power over Commerce led to an exercise of this power separately, by the States, which not only proved abortive, but engendered rival, conflicting and angry regulations." The necessity of centralized regulation of commerce among the states was so obvious and so fully recognized that the few words of the Commerce Clause were little illuminated by debate.

We begin by returning to a portion of Chief Justice Marshall's opinion for the Court in *Gibbons v. Ogden*, § 4.03[A], *supra*. Recall that the Court held that the Commerce Clause permitted Congress to adopt the federal statute which licensed Gibbons' boats. In the following portion of Marshall's opinion, he resolved the conflict between the federal licensing statute and the state monopoly.

Gibbons v. Ogden

United States Supreme Court

22 U.S. (9 Wheat.) 1, 6 L. Ed. 23 (1824)

[I]t has been urged with great earnestness, that although the power of Congress to regulate commerce with foreign nations, and among the several states, be co-extensive with the subject itself, and have no other limits than are prescribed in the constitution, yet the states may severally exercise the same power within their respective jurisdictions. In support of this argument, it is said that they possessed it as an inseparable attribute of sovereignty, before the formation of the constitution, and still retain it, except so far as they have surrendered it by that instrument; that this principle results from the nature of the government, and is secured by the tenth amendment; that an affirmative grant of power is not exclusive, unless in its own nature it be such that the continued exercise of it by the former possessor is inconsistent with the grant, and that this is not of that description.

In discussing the question, whether this power is still in the states, in the case under consideration, we may dismiss from it the inquiry, whether it is surrendered by the mere grant to Congress, or is retained until Congress shall exercise the power. We may dismiss that inquiry, because it has been exercised, and the regulations which Congress deemed it proper to make, are now in full operation. The sole question is, can a state regulate commerce with foreign nations and among the states, while Congress is regulating it?

The counsel for the respondent answer this question in the affirmative, and rely very much on the restrictions in the tenth section, as supporting their opinion. They say, very truly, that limitations of a power furnish a strong argument in favor of the existence of that power, and that the section which prohibits the states from laying duties on imports or exports, proves that this power might have been exercised, had it not been expressly forbidden; and, consequently, that any other commercial regulation, not expressly forbidden, to which the original power of the state was competent, may still be made.

In our complex system, presenting the rare and difficult scheme of one general government, whose action extends over the whole, but which possesses only certain enumerated powers, and of numerous state governments, which retain and exercise all powers not delegated to the Union, contests respecting power must arise. Were it even otherwise, the measures taken by the respective governments to execute their acknowledged powers, would often be of the same description, and might, sometimes interfere. This, however, does not prove that the one is exercising, or has a right to exercise, the powers of the other.

It has been contended by the counsel for the appellant, that, as the word "to regulate" implies in its nature, full power over the thing to be regulated, it excludes, necessarily, the action of all others that would perform the same operation of the same thing. That regulation is designed for the entire result, applying to those parts which remain as they were, as well as to those which are altered. It produces a uniform whole, which is as much disturbed and deranged by changing what the regulating power designs to leave untouched, as that on which it has operated.

There is a great force in this argument, and the court is not satisfied that it has been refuted.

Since, however, in exercising the power of regulating their own purely internal affairs, whether of trading or police, the states may sometimes enact laws, the validity of which depends on their interfering with, and being contrary to, an act of Congress passed in pursuance of the constitution, the court will enter upon the inquiry, whether the laws of New York, as expounded by the highest tribunal of that state, have, in their application to this case, come into collision with an act of Congress, and deprived a citizen of a right to which that act entitles him. Should this collision exist, it will be immaterial whether those laws were passed in virtue of a concurrent power "to regulate commerce with foreign nations and among the several states," or in virtue of a power to regulate their domestic trade and police. In one case and the other, the acts of New York must yield to the law of Congress; and the decision sustaining the privilege they confer, against a right given by a law of the Union, must be erroneous.

The framers of our constitution foresaw this state of things, and provided for it, by declaring the supremacy not only of itself, but of the laws made in pursuance of it. The nullity of any act, inconsistent with the constitution, is produced by the declaration that the constitution is the supreme law. The appropriate application of that part of the clause which confers the same supremacy on laws and treaties, is to such acts of the state legislatures as do not transcend their powers, but, though enacted in the execution of acknowledged state powers, interfere with, or are contrary to the laws of Congress, made in pursuance of the constitution, or some treaty made under the authority of the United States. In every such case, the act of Congress, or the treaty, is supreme; and the law of the state though enacted in the exercise of powers not controverted, must yield to it.

City of Philadelphia v. New Jersey

United States Supreme Court

437 U.S. 617, 98 S. Ct. 2531, 57 L. Ed. 2d 475 (1978)

Mr. Justice Stewart delivered the opinion of the Court.

New Jersey law prohibits the importation of most "solid or liquid waste which originated or was collected outside the territorial limits of the State." In this case we are required to decide whether this statutory prohibition violates the Commerce Clause.

Immediately affected were the operators of private landfills in New Jersey, and several cities in other States that had agreements with these operators for waste disposal. They brought suit against New Jersey and its Department of Environmental Protection in state court, attacking the statute and regulations on a number of state and federal grounds. In an oral opinion granting the plaintiffs' motion for summary judgment, the trial court declared the law unconstitutional because it discriminated against interstate commerce. The New Jersey Supreme Court reversed. It found that ch. 363 advanced vital health and environmental objectives with no economic discrimination against, and with little burden upon, interstate commerce, and that the law was therefore permissible under the Commerce Clause.

The opinions of the Court through the years have reflected an alertness to the evils of "economic isolation" and protectionism, while at the same time recognizing that incidental burdens on interstate commerce may be unavoidable when a State legislates to safeguard the health and safety of its people. Thus, where simple economic protectionism is effected by state legislation, a virtually *per se* rule of invalidity has been erected. The clearest example of such legislation is a law that overtly blocks the flow of interstate commerce at a State's borders. But where other legislative objectives are credibly advanced and there is no patent discrimination against interstate trade, the Court has adopted a much more flexible approach, the general contours of which were outlined in *Pike v. Bruce Church, Inc.*397 U.S. 137 (1970), [when a balancing formula was framed:

> Where the statute regulates even-handedly to effectuate a legitimate local public interest, and its effects on interstate commerce are only incidental, it will be upheld unless the burden imposed on such commerce is clearly excessive in relation to the putative local benefits. If a legitimate local purpose is found, then the question becomes one of degree. And the extent of the burden that will be tolerated will of course depend on the nature of the local interest involved, and on whether it could be promoted as well with a lesser impact on interstate activities. Occasionally the Court has candidly undertaken a balancing approach in resolving these issues, but more frequently it has spoken in terms of "direct" and "indirect" effects and burdens.]

The crucial inquiry, therefore, must be directed to determining whether ch. 363 is basically a protectionist measure, or whether it can fairly be viewed as a law directed to legitimate local concerns, with effects upon interstate commerce that are only incidental.

Th[e] dispute about ultimate legislative purpose need not be resolved, because its resolution would not be relevant to the constitutional issue to be decided in this case. Contrary to the evident assumption of the state court and the parties, the evil of protectionism can reside in legislative means as well as legislative ends. Thus, it does not matter whether the ultimate aim of ch. 363 is to reduce the waste disposal costs of New Jersey residents or to save remaining open lands from pollution, for we assume New Jersey has every right to protect its residents' pocketbooks as well as their environment. And it may be assumed as well that New Jersey may pursue those ends by slowing the flow of *all* waste into the State's remaining landfills, even though interstate commerce may incidentally be affected. But whatever New Jersey's ultimate purpose, it may not be accomplished by discriminating against articles of commerce coming from outside the State unless there is some reason, apart from their origin, to treat them differently. Both on its face and in its plain effect, ch. 363 violates this principle of nondiscrimination.

The New Jersey law at issue in this case falls squarely within the area that the Commerce Clause puts off limits to state regulation. On its face, it imposes on out-of-state commercial interests the full burden of conserving the States' remaining landfill space. It is true that in our previous cases the scarce natural resource was in itself the article of commerce, whereas here the scarce resource and the article of commerce are distinct. But that difference is without consequence. In both instances, the State has overtly moved to slow or freeze the flow of commerce for protectionist reasons. It does not matter that the State has shut the article of Commerce inside the State in one case and outside the State in the other. What is crucial is the attempt by one State to isolate itself from a problem common to many by erecting a barrier against the movement of interstate trade.

The appellees argue that not all laws which facially discriminate against out-of-state commerce are forbidden protectionist regulations. In particular, they point to quarantine laws, which this Court has repeatedly upheld even though they appear to single out interstate commerce for special treatment. It is true that certain quarantine laws have not been considered forbidden protection-ist measures, even though they were directed against out-of-state commerce. But those quarantine laws banned the importation of articles such as diseased livestock that required destruction as soon as possible because their very movement risked contagion and other evils. Those laws thus did not discriminate against interstate commerce as such, but simply prevented traffic in noxious articles, whatever their origin.

The New Jersey statute is not such a quarantine law. There has been no claim here that the very movement of waste into or through New Jersey endangers health, or that waste must be disposed of as soon and as close to its point of generation as possible. The harms caused by waste are said to arise after its disposal in landfill sites, and at that point, as New Jersey concedes, there is no basis to distinguish out-of-state waste from domestic waste. If one is inherently harmful, so is the other. Yet New Jersey has banned the former while leaving its landfill sites open to the latter. The New Jersey law blocks the importation of waste in an obvious effort to saddle those outside the State with the entire burden of slowing the flow of refuse into New Jersey's remaining landfill sites. That legislative effort is clearly impermissible.

Today, cities in Pennsylvania and New York find it expedient or necessary to send their waste into New Jersey for disposal, and New Jersey claims the right to close its borders to such traffic. Tomorrow cities in New Jersey may find it expedient or necessary to send their waste into Pennsylvania or New York for disposal, and those States might then claim the right to close their borders. The Commerce Clause will protect New Jersey in the future, just as it protects her neighbors now, from efforts by one State to isolate itself in the stream of interstate commerce from a problem shared by all. The judgment is Reversed.

MR. JUSTICE REHNQUIST, with whom THE CHIEF JUSTICE [BURGER] joins, dissenting.

In my opinion, the [quarantine] cases are dispositive of the present one. Under them, New Jersey may require germ-infected rags or diseased meat to be disposed of as best as possible within the State, but at the same time prohibit the *importation* of such items for disposal at the facilities that are set up within New Jersey for disposal of such material generated *within* the State. The physical fact of life that New Jersey must somehow dispose of its own noxious items does not mean that it must serve as a depository for those of every other State. Similarly, New Jersey should be free under our past precedents to prohibit the importation of solid waste because of the health and safety problems that such waste poses to its citizens. The fact that New Jersey continues to, and indeed must continue to, dispose of its own solid waste does not mean that New Jersey may not prohibit the importation of even more solid waste into the State. I simply see no way to distinguish solid waste, on the record of this case, from germ-infected rags, diseased meat, and other noxious items.

Notes and Questions

(1) In *City of Philadelphia*, the Court concluded that state legislation which discriminates against interstate commerce is virtually *per se* invalid. Why should the Court avoid the *Pike* balancing approach in such circumstances? Consider whether the state's political process would protect those who most feel the burden of such discriminatory legislation. Should the Court play an active role in reviewing state legislation that discriminates against interstate commerce?

(2) In *Brown-Forman Distillers Corporation v. New York State Liquor Authority*, 476 U.S. 573 (1986), the Court observed that "there is no clear line separating the category of state regulation that is virtually *per se* invalid under the Commerce Clause, and the category subject to the *Pike v. Bruce Church* balancing approach." Plaintiff in *Brown-Forman* challenged New York's requirement that liquor distillers and producers that sell to wholesalers within the state must sell at a price no higher than the lowest priced distiller charges anywhere else in the United States. Twenty other states had similar laws. The Court concluded that this law is the sort of economic protectionism that is *per se* invalid under the Commerce Clause. In so doing the Court stated:

> While New York may regulate the sale of liquor within its borders, and may seek low prices for its residents, it may not "project its legislation into (other States) by regulating the price to be paid" for liquor in those States.

> That the [New York] Law is addressed only to sales of liquor in New York is irrelevant if the "practical effect" of the law is to control liquor prices in other states.

In *Granholm v. Heald*, 544 U.S. 460 (2005), the Court ruled that states must permit in-state and out-of-state wineries to be subject to the same legal rules when it comes to shipping their products directly to consumers. By 5-4 margins, the Court overturned state laws in Michigan and New York that gave preferential treatment to in-state wineries, allowing them to bypass wholesalers and retailers. The majority concluded that these state laws and others like them that discriminate against interstate commerce fall under the "per se rule of invalidity" announced in *Philadelphia v. New Jersey*. The four dissenters maintained that the admitted discrimination was saved by § 2 of the Twenty-First Amendment, which provides: "The transportation or importation into any State, Territory, or possession of the United States for delivery or use therein of intoxicating liquors, in violation of the laws thereof, is hereby prohibited." According to the majority, precedents such as *Brown-Forman* underscore that the state regulation of alcohol is limited by the nondiscrimination principle of the Commerce Clause.

(3) Should the Court abandon the notion that the dormant Commerce Clause operates as a limit on state power? Consider Justice Scalia's observations in *Tyler Pipe Indus. v. Washington State Dep't of Revenue*, 483 U.S. 232 (1987) (concurring in part and dissenting in part), where the Court held that Washington's manufacturing tax, which exempted certain local manufacturers, violated the Commerce Clause:

> The fact is that in the 114 years since the doctrine of the negative Commerce Clause was formally adopted as holding of this Court and in the 50 years prior to that in which it was alluded to in various dicta of the Court, see *Gibbons v. Ogden*, our applications of the doctrine have, not to put too fine a point on the matter, made no sense.

> That uncertainty in application has been attributable in no small part to the lack of any clear theoretical underpinning for judicial "enforcement" of the Commerce Clause. The text of the Clause states that "Congress shall have Power To regulate Commerce with foreign Nations, and among the several States, and with the Indian Tribes." On its face, this is a charter for Congress, not the courts, to ensure "an area of trade free from interference by the States." The pre-emption of state legislation would automatically follow, of course, if the grant of power to Congress to regulate interstate commerce were exclusive, as Charles Pinckney's draft constitution would have provided, and as John Marshall at one point seemed to believe it was. *See Gibbons v. Ogden*. However, unlike the District Clause, which empowers Congress "To exercise exclusive Legislation," Art. I § 8, cl. 17, the language of the Commerce Clause gives no indication of exclusivity. Nor can one assume generally that Congress' Article I powers are exclusive; many of them plainly coexist with concurrent authority in the States. Furthermore, there is no correlative denial of power over commerce to the States in Art. I, § 10, as there is, for example, with the power to coin money or make treaties. And both the States and Congress assumed from the date of ratification that at least some state laws regulating commerce were valid. The exclusivity rationale is infinitely less attractive today than it was in 1847.

> The least plausible theoretical justification of all is the idea that in enforcing the negative Commerce Clause the Court is not applying a constitutional command at all, but is merely interpreting the will of Congress,

whose silence in certain fields of interstate commerce (but not in others) is to be taken as a prohibition of regulation. There is no conceivable reason why congressional inaction under the Commerce Clause should be deemed to have the same pre-emptive effect elsewhere accorded only to congressional action. There, as elsewhere, "Congress' silence is just that—silence."

C & A Carbone, Ind. v. Town of Clarkstown

United States Supreme Court

511 U.S. 383, 114 S. Ct. 1677, 128 L. Ed. 2d 399 (1994)

JUSTICE KENNEDY delivered the opinion of the Court.

The town of Clarkstown, New York, agreed to close its landfill and build a new solid waste transfer station on the same site. The cost of building the transfer station was estimated at $1.4 million. A local private contractor agreed to construct the facility and operate it for five years, after which the town would buy it for one dollar. During those five years, the town guaranteed a minimum waste flow of 120,000 tons per year, for which the contractor could charge the hauler a so-called tipping fee of $81 per ton. The object of this arrangement was to amortize the cost of the transfer station: The town would finance its new facility with the income generated by the tipping fees. The problem, of course, was how to meet the yearly guarantee. The solution the town adopted was the flow control ordinance here in question. The ordinance requires all nonhazardous solid waste within the town to be deposited at the transfer station.

The petitioners in this case are C & A Carbone, Inc., a company engaged in the processing of solid waste, and various related companies or persons, all of whom we designate Carbone. Carbone operates a recycling center in Clarkstown, where it receives bulk solid waste, sorts and bales it, and then ships it to other processing facilities—much as occurs at the town's new transfer station. While the flow control ordinance permits recyclers like Carbone to continue receiving solid waste, it requires them to bring the nonrecyclable residue from that waste to the Route 303 station. It thus forbids Carbone to ship the nonrecyclable waste itself, and it requires Carbone to pay a tipping fee on trash that Carbone has already sorted.

While the immediate effect of the ordinance is to direct local transport of solid waste to a designated site within the local jurisdiction, its economic effects are interstate in reach. By prevent[ing] everyone except the favored local operator from performing the initial processing step, the ordinance deprives out-of-state businesses of access to a local market.

The ordinance is no less discriminatory because in-state or in-town processors are also covered by the prohibition. In *Dean Milk Co. v. Madison*, 340 U.S. 349 (1951), we struck down a city ordinance that required all milk sold in the city to be pasteurized within five miles of the city lines. We found it "immaterial that Wisconsin milk from outside the Madison area is subjected to the same proscription as that moving in interstate commerce."

In this light, the flow control ordinance is just one more instance of local processing requirements that we long have held invalid. The essential vice in laws of this sort is that they bar the import of the processing service. Out-of-state meat inspectors, or shrimp hullers, or milk pasteurizers, are deprived of access to local demand for their services. Put another way, the offending local laws hoard a local resource — be it meat, shrimp, or milk — for the benefit of local businesses that treat it.

The flow control ordinance has the same design and effect. It hoards solid waste, and the demand to get rid of it, for the benefit of the preferred processing facility. The only conceivable distinction from the cases cited above is that the flow control ordinance favors a single local proprietor. But this difference just makes the protectionist effect of the ordinance more acute.

Here Clarkstown has any number of nondiscriminatory alternatives for addressing the health and environmental problems alleged to justify the ordinance in question. The most obvious would be uniform safety regulations enacted without the object to discriminate. The regulations would ensure that competitors like Carbone do not underprice the market by cutting corners on environmental safety.

Clarkstown maintains that special financing is necessary to ensure the long-term survival of the designated facility. If so, the town may subsidize the facility through general taxes or municipal bonds. But having elected to use the open market to earn revenues for its project, the town may not employ discriminatory regulation to give that project an advantage over rival businesses from out of State.

Though the Clarkstown ordinance may not in explicit terms seek to regulate interstate commerce, it does so nonetheless by its practical effect and design.

Justice O'Connor, concurring in the judgment. [omitted]

Justice Souter, with whom The Chief Justice and Justice Blackmun join, dissenting.

The law does not differentiate between all local and all out-of-town providers of a service, but instead between the one entity responsible for ensuring that the job gets done and all other enterprises, regardless of their location. The ordinance thus falls outside that class of tariff or protectionist measures that the Commerce Clause has traditionally been thought to bar States from enacting against each other, and when the majority subsumes the ordinance within the class of laws this Court has struck down as facially discriminatory (and so avails itself of our "virtually per se rule" against such statutes, the majority is in fact greatly extending the Clause's dormant reach).

The justification for subjecting the local processing laws and the broader class of clearly discriminatory commercial regulation to near-fatal scrutiny is the virtual certainty that such laws, at least in their discriminatory aspect, serve no legitimate, nonprotectionist purpose. *See Philadelphia v. New Jersey.* In the clear import of specific statutory provisions or in the legislature's ultimate purpose, the discriminatory scheme is almost always designed either to favor local industry, as such, or to achieve some other goal while exporting a disproportionate share of the burden of attaining it, which is merely a subtler form of local favoritism.

On the other hand, in a market served by a municipal facility, a law that favors that single facility over all others is a law that favors the public sector over all private-sector processors, whether local or out of State. Because the favor does not go to local private competitors of out-of-state firms, out-of-state governments will at the least lack a motive to favor their own firms in order to equalize the positions of private competitors. While a preference in favor of the government may incidentally function as local favoritism as well, a more particularized inquiry is necessary before a court can say whether such a law does in fact smack too strongly of economic protectionism.

United Haulers Assn, Inc. v. Oneida-Herkimer Solid Waste Management Authority

United States Supreme Court

550 U.S. 330, 127 S. Ct. 1786, 167 L. Ed. 2d 655 (2007)

ROBERTS, C.J., delivered the opinion of the Court.

The flow control ordinances in this case benefit a clearly public facility, while treating all private companies exactly the same. Because the question is now squarely presented on the facts of the case before us, we decide that such flow control ordinances do not discriminate against interstate commerce for purposes of the dormant Commerce Clause.

Compelling reasons justify treating these laws differently from laws favoring particular private businesses over their competitors. But States and municipalities are not private businesses-far from it. Unlike private enterprise, government is vested with the responsibility of protecting the health, safety, and welfare of its citizens.

Given these differences, it does not make sense to regard laws favoring local government and laws favoring private industry with equal skepticism. As our local processing cases demonstrate, when a law favors in-state business over out-of-state competition, rigorous scrutiny is appropriate because the law is often the product of "simple economic protectionism." *Wyoming v. Oklahoma*, 502 U.S. 437, 454 (1992); *Philadelphia v. New Jersey*, 437 U.S., at 626–627. Laws favoring local government, by contrast, may be directed toward any number of legitimate goals unrelated to protectionism. Here the flow control ordinances enable the Counties to pursue particular policies with respect to the handling and treatment of waste generated in the Counties, while allocating the costs of those policies on citizens and businesses according to the volume of waste they generate.

The contrary approach of treating public and private entities the same under the dormant Commerce Clause would lead to unprecedented and unbounded interference by the courts with state and local government. The dormant Commerce Clause is not a roving license for federal courts to decide what activities are appropriate for state and local government to undertake, and what activities must be the province of private market competition. In this case, the citizens of Oneida and Herkimer Counties have chosen the government to provide waste management services, with a limited role for the private sector in arranging for transport of waste from the curb to the public facilities. The citizens could have left the entire matter for the private sector, in which case any regulation they undertook could not discriminate against interstate commerce. But it was also open to them to vest responsibility for the matter with their government, and to adopt flow control ordinances to support the government effort. It is not the office of the Commerce Clause to control the decision of the voters on whether government or the private sector should provide waste management services.

Finally, it bears mentioning that the most palpable harm imposed by the ordinances — more expensive trash removal — is likely to fall upon the very people who voted for the laws. Our dormant Commerce Clause cases often find discrimination when a State shifts the costs of regulation to other States, because when "the burden of state regulation falls on interests outside the state, it is unlikely to be alleviated by the operation of those political restraints normally exerted when interests within the state are affected." *Southern Pacific Co. v. Arizona ex rel. Sullivan*, 325 U.S. 761, 767–768, n. 2 (1945). Here, the citizens and businesses of the Counties bear the costs of the ordinances. There is no reason to step in and hand local businesses a victory they could not obtain through the political process.

JUSTICE ALITO, with whom JUSTICE STEVENS and JUSTICE KENNEDY join, dissenting.

The fact that the flow control laws at issue discriminate in favor of a government-owned enterprise does not meaningfully distinguish this case from *Carbone*. The preferred facility in *Carbone* was, to be sure, nominally owned by a private contractor who had built the facility on the town's behalf, but it would be misleading to describe the facility as private. In exchange for the contractor's promise to build the facility for the town free of charge and then to sell it to the town five years later for $1, the town guaranteed that, during the first five years of the facility's existence, the contractor would receive "a minimum waste flow of 120,000 tons per year" and that the contractor could charge an above-market tipping fee. If the facility "received less than 120,000 tons in a year, the town [would] make up the tipping fee deficit." To prevent residents, businesses, and trash haulers from taking their waste elsewhere in pursuit of lower tipping fees (leaving the town responsible for covering any shortfall in the contractor's guaranteed revenue stream), the town enacted an ordinance "requir[ing] all nonhazardous solid waste within the town to be deposited at" the preferred facility.

The only real difference between the facility at issue in *Carbone* and its counterpart in this case is that title to the former had not yet formally passed to the municipality. The Court exalts form over substance in adopting a test that turns on this technical distinction, particularly since, barring any obstacle presented by state law, the transaction in *Carbone* could have been restructured to provide for the passage of title at the beginning, rather than the end, of the 5-year period.

For this very reason, it is not surprising that in *Carbone* the Court did not dispute the dissent's observation that the preferred facility was for all practical purposes owned by the municipality. To the contrary, the Court repeatedly referred to the transfer station in terms suggesting that the transfer station did in fact belong to the town.

I see no basis for the Court's assumption that discrimination in favor of an in-state facility owned by the government is likely to serve "legitimate goals unrelated to protectionism." Discrimination in favor of an in-state government facility serves "local economic interests," inuring to the benefit of local residents who are employed at the facility, local businesses that supply the facility with goods and services, and local workers employed by such businesses. It is therefore surprising to read in the opinion of the Court that state discrimination in favor of a state-owned business is not likely to be motivated by economic protectionism.

Equally unpersuasive is the Court's suggestion that the flow-control laws do not discriminate against interstate commerce because they "treat in-state private business interests exactly the same as out-of-state ones." Again, the critical issue is whether the challenged legislation discriminates against interstate commerce. If it does, then regardless of whether those harmed by it reside entirely outside the State in question, the law is subject to strict scrutiny.

Notes and Questions

(1) The *Carbone* Court found it unimportant that a town rather than the state had passed the flow control ordinance. Did *United Haulers* reject *Carbone* in emphasizing that the county flow-control law applied alike to in-state and out-of-state competitors? Is the more apt distinction between public and private actors rather than local and state laws?

(2) In *United Haulers*, the Chief Justice emphasized that waste hauling is a traditional function of local governments. Should the existence of such a tradition have any impact on the constitutionality of an ordinance under the dormant Commerce Clause?

(3) California Proposition 12 forbids the in-state sale of pork that comes from the offspring of sows that are "confined in a cruel manner" (in a space of less than 24 square feet). Because California imports almost all the pork it consumes, the compliance costs of Proposition 12 will be disproportionately borne by out-of-state firms. In 2023, a majority of the Court agreed with the lower courts that the Pork Producers Council failed to state a claim when it did not allege the law *purposefully* discriminates against out-of-state economic interests. *National Pork Producers Council v. Ross*, 142 S. Ct. 1413 (2023). The majority reiterated the longstanding principle that laws which have the practical effect of controlling commerce outside the state do not violate the Constitution unless the state law purposefully discriminates against the out-of-state interests.

Problem E

Assume your state legislature enacted a law requiring that all private and public employers of 100 or more workers within the state provide health insurance for employees without charge to the employees.

You are now employed as a lawyer by a large law firm that represents Widgets, Inc., a corporation employing people throughout the United States, including over 5,000 employees in your state. The company is subject to a union contract stating that "all Widgets employees shall be granted the same benefits nationwide." Thus, if employees in your state must be granted health insurance benefits, employees in all other states must also be given free insurance.

The President of Widgets is concerned because the annual cost of health insurance will be five million dollars above the Company's current operating expenses.

He has asked you whether the company is likely to succeed in a lawsuit challenging the constitutionality of the law. What advice would you give him?

Chapter 5

Public and Private Domain

§ 5.01 Introduction

In Chapter 1, we observed that the protection of individual rights is one of the essential characteristics of a constitutional form of government. It has been stated that "[e]very system of constitutional government worthy of the name embodies . . . a 'system of ordered liberty,' in which the people are guaranteed certain fundamental rights and immunities against the exercise of arbitrary power by the state." Alfred Kelly, *Where Constitutional Liberty Came From, in* FOUNDATIONS OF FREEDOM 23 (Alfred Kelly, ed., 1958). Our constitutional system is no exception.

The idea that the American constitutional system should protect individual freedoms was firmly established by 1787. It thus may come as a surprise that the Constitution, as originally ratified, had no bill of rights. The document, of course, was not devoid of any protections for individual rights. It guaranteed the right of a representative government (Art. I § 2; Art. II § 1) and prohibited certain abuses by the federal government. The privilege of the writ of habeas corpus could not be suspended and Congress could not enact ex post facto laws or bills of attainder. (Art. I § 9.) Moreover, Article III guaranteed the right of jury trials for federal crimes. Similarly, the Constitution restricted the states from passing bills of attainder, ex post facto laws or laws impairing the obligation of contracts. (Art. I § 10.) Article IV provided that the citizens of each state shall be entitled to all the privileges and immunities of citizens in the several states.

A number of explanations have been offered for the absence of a more detailed declaration of individual freedoms in the Constitution. First, after the Revolution, the Founders focused most immediately on establishing a structure of government. It was believed that the structure itself would protect against the invasion of individual rights. Second, the structure that was adopted contemplated a central government of limited, enumerated powers. As Madison argued, because the powers of Congress were limited to those enumerated it was unnecessary to include a bill of rights that set forth in further detail what Congress could not do. Third, state constitutions already contained protections for civil liberties and those protections were not controversial. Finally, some suggested that incorporation of a bill of rights would be dangerous because, as James Wilson urged, it might be assumed improperly that rights not expressly mentioned were purposely omitted.

Notwithstanding the arguments of Hamilton, Wilson, Madison and others, it soon became clear that a bill of rights was necessary, at the very least for political reasons. To ensure ratification of the Constitution, the Federalists had won over some of the Anti-Federalists by promising constitutional amendments that included a bill of rights. Moreover, opponents of the constitution had indicated that they would seek a second constitutional convention for the stated purpose of adopting a bill of rights but for the real purpose of destroying the plan of the first convention. Accordingly, even the supporters of the Constitution saw the need for a bill of rights and, thus, President Washington in his inaugural address asked that Congress consider suggestions for amendments. Madison, a member of the House of Representatives, introduced proposed amendments and, after extended debate, the House and Senate produced twelve amendments that were ratified by Congress in September, 1789. These amendments were submitted to the states, and ten of them were added to the Constitution in 1791. One of the amendments that was not ratified provided that there should not be less than one representative for every 50,000 people; the other provided that any change in salaries of Senators and representatives would not take effect until an election had intervened.

The Bill of Rights caused no immediate alteration of federal power but rather formally recognized rights that would have been assumed to exist even without the amendments. In the period prior to the Civil War, there were relatively few occasions when the bill of rights was relied on as protection for individual freedom. This was due in part to the decision in *Barron v. Mayor and City Council of Baltimore* (§ 5.02), where the Supreme Court held that the bill of rights operated as a limitation on the federal government only and not the state governments.

A second reason for the relatively infrequent reliance on the bill of rights during the first half of the nineteenth century is derived from the laissez faire political, social and economic philosophies that gained popularity during this period. The prevailing view was that government should play a minor role in managing the affairs of the people. The emphasis was on the individual and private enterprise.

It is not surprising then that the individual freedom issues during the first half of the nineteenth century focused on the preservation of vested property rights. Even the slavery issue was framed in terms of such rights. *See Dred Scott v. Sandford*, 60 U.S. (19 How.) 393 (1856). One of the important vehicles for protection of property rights was the Contract Clause, and on various occasions in this period the Court was asked to declare that a state had impaired the obligation of contracts in violation of Article I § 10. *See, e.g., Dartmouth College v. Woodward*, 17 U.S. (4 Wheat.) 518 (1819); *Fletcher v. Peck*, 10 U.S. (6 Cranch) 87 (1810).

The slavery crisis and the Civil War profoundly altered the development and character of our nation. As one commentator has observed,

> the Civil War was a kind of telophase. A new world had been created. There were fundamentally new assumptions. Legal rights and remedies were redefined. The character of the nation, the role of federal power and . . . the appropriate role of Congress underwent significant alterations.

Aviam Soifer, *Protecting Civil Rights: A Critique of Raoul Berger's History*, 54 N.Y.U. L. Rev. 651, 686 (1979).[1] The constitutional structure for protecting individual rights was very much a part of this new world.

We do not intend to review the vast literature on the slavery crisis, the Civil War, or the resulting reconstruction efforts. It is sufficient to note that a concept of national citizenship emerged after the War.

> Before the Civil War, American citizenship was an ill-defined and largely insignificant concept. For most purposes, state citizenship was far more significant. The Civil War changed all that by establishing that a citizen's primary allegiance was to the federal government. Thus, the concept of national citizenship became triumphant. But it was not enough simply to proclaim the existence of citizenship, it was also necessary to give content to that citizenship.

Daniel Farber & John Muench, *The Ideological Origins of the Fourteenth Amendment*, 1 Const. Comment. 235, 276–277 (1984).[2]

The Amendments adopted in the wake of the Civil War gave content to the idea of national citizenship. The Thirteenth Amendment, ratified in December, 1865, fundamentally restructured the federal system and for the first time provided for federal authority in the area of personal liberty, an area previously within the exclusive power of the states. The Thirteenth Amendment was designed to achieve a "revolution in federalism." Jacobus Ten Broek, Equal Under Law 158 (1951).

By its terms, the Amendment declares that neither slavery nor involuntary servitude shall exist and that Congress shall have power to enforce that prohibition. The immense significance of the language has been ignored. Professor Jacobus Ten Broek wrote in his account of the Civil War Amendments that the few words of the Thirteenth Amendment embody basic concepts of liberty and equality. Underlying these words are the theories of Locke, the Declaration of Independence, the state constitutions and the principles of common law. *Id.* at 197.

Despite the Thirteenth Amendment, the Southern states began to enact black codes that discriminated on the basis of race. These codes controlled the movement of blacks through a system of passes, prohibited the congregation of groups of blacks, prohibited blacks from residing in certain areas, forbade blacks from pursuing certain jobs and prohibited racial intermarriage. Moreover, the codes made certain conduct criminal only if done by blacks. For example, they prohibited blacks from directing insulting language at whites and provided for the death penalty when a black raped a white woman but not when a white raped a black woman. In addition, some codes prohibited blacks from voting, sitting on juries, and holding public office. *See* Harold Hyman & William Wiecek, Equal Justice Under Law 319 (1982).

---

1. Copyright © 1979 by New York University Law Review. Reprinted with permission.
2. Copyright © 1984 by University of Minnesota Law School. Reprinted by permission.

The black codes and the actions of southern state officials persuaded the Republicans that legislation was necessary. A broad interpretation of the Thirteenth Amendment provided a convenient source of congressional power. In February, 1866, Congress passed a Freedmen's Bureau bill which gave the military authority to protect the civil rights of the blacks in the southern states. Opponents of the bill argued that Congress lacked power to protect civil rights; proponents relied on §2 of the Thirteenth Amendment. The bill passed, but President Johnson vetoed it and the veto was sustained.

The Republicans also proposed a Civil Rights Act which not only prohibited discrimination against blacks but also guaranteed them certain rights — the right to make and enforce contracts, the right to inherit, buy, and sell real and personal property, the right to sue, be parties and give evidence, and the right to the full and equal benefit of all laws for the security of person and property, as is enjoyed by whites. The bill also gave federal courts jurisdiction to hear cases involving rights that could not be enforced in state courts. The non-discrimination provision was removed from the final version and the bill as amended was enacted over President Johnson's veto.

Although the sponsors insisted that the Thirteenth Amendment gave Congress power to enact the far-reaching Civil Rights Act, considerable doubt remained about the sufficiency of that basis. To remove any doubt about the power to enact such civil rights legislation and in order to ensure that the statutory rights would be beyond the control of later congressional majorities, members of the 39th Congress proposed the Fourteenth Amendment. On June 13, 1866, both houses passed the amendment, and two years later, in July 1868, the amendment became part of the Constitution after being ratified by the states.

Since the 1950s, the Fourteenth Amendment has emerged as the primary constitutional vehicle for protection of individual rights from intrusion by the states, and much of the remainder of the book will focus on the Amendment, particularly §1 which provides:

> All persons born or naturalized in the United States and subject to the jurisdiction thereof, are citizens of the United States and of the State wherein they reside. No State shall make or enforce any law which shall abridge the privileges or immunities of citizens of the United States; nor shall any State deprive any person of life, liberty, or property, without due process of law; nor deny to any person within its jurisdiction the equal protection of the laws.

In 1866 there was relatively little debate over the language of that section. One point, however, is clear — the Fourteenth Amendment was intended to place the constitutionality of the civil rights bills beyond doubt. *See* JACOBUS TEN BROEK, *supra* at 201.

Modern day constitutional scholars have devoted considerable effort to ascertaining whether the framers of the Fourteenth Amendment intended to accomplish more than that limited purpose. Did the 39th Congress intend that the Amendment might prohibit a state from maintaining segregated schools? Did the framers intend to use the Amendment as a vehicle for incorporating all the provisions of the Bill of Rights as limits on the states? Did they contemplate that the Amendment might be used to require states to allow women the right to choose an abortion? Was the Amendment intended to prohibit public schools from beginning the day with a prayer? Was it intended to limit a state's ability to reapportion its own legislature?

The debate over the intentions of the 39th Congress has much more than historical significance. Indeed, it raises two fundamental issues that we have already touched on regarding constitutional interpretation. First, to what extent should the Constitution's modern day meaning depend on the original intentions of the framers? Second, if the text and history do not provide answers to specific constitutional questions, how do we resolve contemporary constitutional issues? We will return to these questions throughout the remainder of the book, but it is worthwhile at this point to make a few introductory observations.

Reliance on the framers' intentions, while certainly relevant to constitutional interpretation, may not provide answers to contemporary constitutional questions. It may be difficult to ascertain the intentions of the drafters of the language and even more difficult to determine the reasons that state legislators voted to ratify the amendment.

> ... [T]*he most important datum bearing on what was intended is the constitutional language itself.* This is especially true where—as is emphatically the case respecting the fourteenth amendment (understandably, given the cataclysm of the times)—the legislative history is in usual disarray, but the validity of the point extends beyond. In the first place, and this is also true of statutes and for the matter of other sorts of group products, not everyone will feel called upon to place in the "legislative history" her precise understanding, assuming she has one, of the meaning of the provision for which she is voting or to rise to correct every interpretation that does not agree with hers. One of the reasons the debate culminates in a vote on an authoritative text is precisely to generate a record of just what there was sufficient agreement on to gain majority consent. Beyond that, however the constitutional situation is special in a way that makes going over the statements of members of Congress in an effort to pin down their intention doubly ill-advised. For Congress' role in the process of constitutional amendment is solely, to use the Constitution's word, one of "proposing" provisions to the states: to become law such a provision must be ratified by three quarters of the state legislatures. Now obviously there is no principled basis on which the intent of those voting to ratify can be counted less crucial in determining the "true meaning" of a constitutional provision than the intent of those in Congress who proposed it. That, however, gets to be so many different people in so many different circumstances that one cannot hope to gather a reliable picture of their intention from any perusal of the legislative history. (To complicate matters further, state ratification debates,

assuming there are debates, often are not even recorded.) Thus the only reliable evidence of what "the ratifiers" thought they were ratifying is obviously the language of the provision they approved. . . .

John Hart Ely, *Constitutional Interpretivism: Its Allure and Impossibility*, 53 IND. L.J. 339, 418–419 (1978) (footnotes omitted).[3]

There remains a more fundamental objection to the notion that one can turn to the framers of the Fourteenth Amendment for answers to specific questions of constitutional interpretation. The members of the 39th Congress were well aware that they were proposing not a statute but rather a *constitutional* provision that would endure and govern future generations. The drafters, thus, used language that was open-ended and capable of growth. Alexander Bickel, *The Original Understanding and the Segregation Decision*, 69 HARV. L. REV. 1, 63 (1955). We may focus on the wrong issue if we direct our inquiry at the framers' understanding of the immediate effects of the amendment.

> It is thus quite apparent that to seek in historical materials relevant to the framing of the Constitution, or in the language of the Constitution itself, specific answers to specific present problems is to ask the wrong questions. With adequate scholarship, the answer that must emerge in the vast majority of cases is no answer. . . . It is not true that the Framers intended the Fourteenth Amendment to outlaw segregation or to make applicable to the states all restrictions on government that may be evolved under the Bill of Rights; but they did not foreclose such policies and may indeed have invited them. It is not true that the Framers intended to forbid the issuance of money as legal tender; but they did not foreclose such a policy and may indeed have invited it and hoped rather strongly that it would prove feasible. And it is not true that the Framers intended that trials by court martial be conducted in most respects as if they were civilian trials, although, again, they far from foreclosed such a policy and quite possibly invited it.
>
> No answer is what the wrong question begets, for the excellent reason that the Constitution was not framed to be a catalogue of answers to such questions. And, indeed, how could it have been, consistently with the intention to write a charter for the governance of generations to come — for a period, it was hoped, stretching far into the future?

ALEXANDER BICKEL, THE LEAST DANGEROUS BRANCH 102–103 (1962).[4]

Ronald Dworkin has urged that constitutional interpretation of open-ended phrases like those in the Fourteenth Amendment should focus not on the framers'

---

3. Copyright © 1978 by John Hart Ely and the Indiana Law Journal, Indiana University. Reprinted by permission.

4. Copyright © 1962 by The Bobbs-Merrill Company, Inc. Reprinted by permission.

specific "conceptions" but rather on the "concepts" embodied by the language. He described the critical distinction between "concepts" and "conceptions" as follows:

> Suppose I tell my children simply that I expect them not to treat others unfairly. I no doubt have in mind examples of the conduct I mean to discourage, but I would not accept that my "meaning" was limited to these examples, for two reasons. First I would expect my children to apply my instructions to situations I had not and could not have thought about. Second, I stand ready to admit that some particular act I had thought was fair when I spoke was in fact unfair, or vice versa, if one of my children is able to convince me of that later; in that case I should want to say that my instructions covered the case he cited, not that I had changed my instructions. I might say that I meant the family to be guided by the *concept* of fairness, not by any specific *conception* of fairness I might have had in mind.

RONALD DWORKIN, TAKING RIGHTS SERIOUSLY 134 (1977).[5]

If we must look beyond the text and history in order to give meaning to open-ended constitutional phrases, to what sources should we turn? It is too often overlooked that this question must be confronted not only by judges but also by lawyers who frame arguments and by elected officials who take an oath to uphold the Constitution. *See generally* Paul Brest, *The Conscientious Legislator's Guide to Constitutional Interpretation*, 27 STAN. L. REV. 585 (1975). Judges, of course, must confront the question of constitutional interpretation when presented with a specific case. *See Marbury v. Madison* (§ 1.04, *supra*). Although we will focus on the approach used by legislators and lawyers, our principal concern will be with the methodology used by courts, particularly the Supreme Court, in attaching meaning to open-textured constitutional provisions.

Absent specific "answers" in the text or from history, the judge might decide cases by imposing his or her own personal views on the language. A federal judge who is personally opposed to abortions, for example, might hold that a state ban on abortion is not prohibited by the Fourteenth Amendment. As we study the cases on individual rights, we should consider whether this is the approach used by the Court and whether such an approach is consistent with the proper role of the appointed federal judiciary in our system of government. Recall that under *Marbury*, the judiciary has the power to declare that our political representatives have violated the Constitution and to strike down their actions. If judges exercise that power by relying on their personal views, do they run the risk of losing whatever force they have?

Another theory of constitutional interpretation provides that because of the antimajoritarian nature of judicial review, the judiciary should uphold the constitutionality of official conduct unless the conduct intrudes on fundamental values. Content is given to the open-ended phrases by reference to these values. *See* Thomas

---

5. Copyright © 1977 by Harvard University Press. Reprinted by permission.

Grey, *Do We Have an Unwritten Constitution?*, 27 STAN. L. REV. 703 (1975). A judge, whatever his personal views, might hold that anti-abortion legislation denies a woman her liberty without due process because the right to choose an abortion is a fundamental right that cannot be limited even by popular will. The difficulty under this methodology lies in determining the sources of such fundamental values. Can the source be found in natural law principles? Tradition? Reason? Consensus of the people? *Compare* JOHN HART ELY, DEMOCRACY AND DISTRUST 43–72 (1980).

A separate theory of constitutional interpretation has been constructed on the basis of the famous footnote 4 in *United States v. Carolene Products Co.*, 304 U.S. 144, 152–153 n.4 (1938). There, Justice Stone wrote:

> There may be narrower scope for operation of the presumption of constitutionality when legislation appears on its face to be within a specific prohibition of the Constitution, such as those of the first ten amendments, which are deemed equally specific when held to be embraced within the Fourteenth. . . .

> It is unnecessary to consider now whether legislation which restricts those political processes which can ordinarily be expected to bring about repeal of undesirable legislation, is to be subjected to more exacting judicial scrutiny under the general prohibitions of the Fourteenth Amendment than are most other types of legislation. . . .

> Nor need we enquire whether similar considerations enter into the review of statutes directed at particular religious, . . . or racial minorities[;] whether prejudice against discrete and insular minorities may be a special condition, which tends seriously to curtail the operation of those political processes ordinarily to be relied upon to protect minorities and which may call for a correspondingly more searching judicial inquiry. . . .

Relying on this footnote, John Hart Ely has argued that the accommodation of substantive values is the task for the political process. Preserving fundamental values, he urged, is not an appropriate constitutional task for the judiciary. Instead, the court's role is to ensure that the *process* which selected and accommodated certain values was a fair one. The themes of *Carolene Products*

> are concerned with participation: they ask us to focus not on whether this or that substantive value is unusually important or fundamental, but rather on whether the opportunity to participate either in the political processes by which values are appropriately identified and accommodated, or in the accommodation those processes have readied, has been unduly constricted.

John Hart Ely, *Toward a Representation-Reinforcing Mode of Judicial Review*, 37 MD. L. REV. 457, 456 (1978).[6] Ely explained further:

---

6. Copyright © 1978 by Maryland Law Review, Inc. Reprinted by permission.

In a representative democracy, value determinations are to be made by our elected representatives, and if in fact most of us disapprove we can kick them out of office. Malfunction occurs whenever the *process* cannot be trusted, whenever: (1) the in's are choking off the channels of political change to ensure they will stay in and the out's will stay out, or (2) though no one is actually denied a voice or a vote, an effective majority, with the necessary and understandable cooperation of its representatives, is systematically advantaging itself at the expense of one or more minorities whose reciprocal support it does not need and thereby effectively denying them the protection afforded other groups by a representative system.

Id. at 486–487.[7] Under Ely's approach the judiciary should declare a statute in violation of the Fourteenth Amendment when the law was a product of a malfunctioning political process. *See generally* JOHN HART ELY, DEMOCRACY AND DISTRUST (1980). (For criticism of Ely's approach, see Laurence Tribe, *The Puzzling Persistence of Process-Based Constitutional Theories*, 89 YALE L.J. 1063 (1980); Mark Tushnet, *Darkness on the Edge of Town: The Contributions of John Hart Ely to Constitutional Theory*, 89 YALE L.J. 1037 (1980)).

The debate over the proper methodology for giving content to the open-ended phrases like those in the Fourteenth Amendment has produced a vast body of scholarly literature. An important aspect of the study of constitutionally protected individual liberties concerns this methodological issue.

Consideration of the method of constitutional interpretation, however, should not obscure another important aspect of our study: Which substantive individual liberties are protected from governmental intrusion? Subsequent Chapters will examine the content and scope of our constitutionally protected freedoms.

We begin by examining a basic proposition that is central to the study of the individual rights. As a general matter, the Constitution protects individual freedoms only from intrusion by the government. "The Constitution structures the National Government, confines its actions, and in regard to certain individual liberties and other specified matters, confines the actions of the States. With a few exceptions, . . . constitutional guarantees of individual liberty and equal protection do not apply to the actions of private entities." *Edmonson v. Leesville Concrete Company, Inc.*, 500 U.S. 614, 619 (1991). In this regard, the Constitution creates a distinction between the public and private domains. As we will see, it is sometimes difficult to draw the precise line between private behavior that is not subject to constitutional limits and governmental conduct that is restrained by the Constitution.

---

7. Copyright © 1978 by Maryland Law Review, Inc. Reprinted by permission.

§ 5.02 Prohibiting Governmental Encroachments on Individual Rights

A. The Bill of Rights

Barron v. The Mayor and City Council of Baltimore

United States Supreme Court

32 U.S. (7 Pet.) 243 (1833)

[Barron was the owner of a wharf in Baltimore. In the process of constructing streets, the City diverted the flow of certain streams, causing large masses of sand and earth to be deposited in front of Barron's wharf. As a result, the water became so shallow that it ceased to be useful for most vessels.

Barron sued the City claiming that it violated the Fifth Amendment by taking his property without just compensation. The trial court awarded Barron $4,500. The state appellate court reversed and review was sought in the Supreme Court. The first issue was whether the Court had jurisdiction to review the state court judgment. Resolution of that issue turned on whether a federal right was involved. The Court, therefore, had to decide whether the Fifth Amendment protects an individual from the state.]

Mr. Chief Justice Marshall delivered the opinion of the court.

... The plaintiff in error contends that it comes within the clause in the fifth amendment to the constitution, which inhibits the taking of private property for public use, without just compensation. He insists that this amendment, being in favour of the liberty of the citizen, ought to be so construed as to restrain the legislative power of a state, as well as that of the United States. If this proposition be untrue, the court can take no jurisdiction of the cause.

The question thus presented is, we think, of great importance, but not of much difficulty.

The constitution was ordained and established by the people of the United States for themselves, for their own government, and not for the government of the individual states. Each state established a constitution for itself, and, in the constitution, provided such limitations and restrictions on the powers of its particular government as its judgment dictated. The people of the United States framed such a government for the United States as they supposed best adapted to their situation and best calculated to promote their interests. The powers they conferred on this government were to be exercised by itself; and the limitations on power, if expressed in general terms, are naturally, and, we think, necessarily applicable to the government created by the instrument. They are limitations of power granted in the instrument itself; not of distinct governments, framed by different persons and for different purposes.

If these propositions be correct, the fifth amendment must be understood as restraining the power of the general government, not as applicable to the states. In their several constitutions they have imposed such restrictions on their respective governments as their own wisdom suggested; such as they deemed most proper for themselves. It is a subject on which they judge exclusively, and with which others interfere no farther than they are supposed to have common interest.

The counsel for the plaintiff in error insists that the constitution was intended to secure the people of the several states against the undue exercise of power by their respective state governments; as well as against that which might be attempted by their general government. In support of this argument he relies on the inhibitions contained in the tenth section of the first article.

We think that section affords a strong if not conclusive argument in support of the opinion already indicated by the court. . . .

The ninth section having enumerated, in the nature of a bill of rights, the limitations intended to be imposed on the powers of the general government, the tenth proceeds to enumerate those which were to operate on the state legislatures. These restrictions are brought together in the same section, and are by express words applied to the states. "No state shall enter into any treaty," &c. Perceiving that in a constitution framed by the people of the United States for the government of all, no limitation of the action of government on the people would apply to the state government, unless expressed in terms; the restrictions contained in the tenth section are in direct words so applied to the states.

It is worthy of remark, too, that these inhibitions generally restrain state legislation on subjects entrusted to the general government, or in which the people of all the states feel an interest.

A state is forbidden to enter into any treaty, alliance or confederation. If these compacts are with foreign nations, they interfere with the treaty making power which is conferred entirely on the general government; if with each other, for political purposes, they can scarcely fail to interfere with the general purpose and intent of the constitution. To grant letters of marque and reprisal, would lead directly to war; the power of declaring which is expressly given to congress. To coin money is also the exercise of power conferred on congress. It would be tedious to recapitulate the several limitations on the powers of the states which are contained in this section. They will be found, generally, to restrain state legislation on subjects entrusted to the government of the union, in which the citizens of all the states are interested. In these alone were the whole people concerned. The question of their application to states is not left to construction. It is averred in positive words. . . .

[I]t is a part of the history of the day, that the great revolution which established the constitution of the United States, was not effected without immense opposition. Serious fears were extensively entertained that those powers which the patriot statesmen, who then watched over the interest of our country, deemed essential to union, and to the attainment of those invaluable objects for which union was sought, might be exercised in a manner dangerous to liberty. In almost every convention, by which the constitution was adopted, amendments demanded security against the apprehended encroachments of the general government—not against those of the local governments.

In compliance with a sentiment thus generally expressed, to quiet fears thus extensively entertained, amendments were proposed by the required majority in congress, and adopted by the states. These amendments contain no expression indicating an intention to apply them to the state governments. This court cannot so apply them.

We are of opinion that the provision in the fifth amendment to the constitution, declaring that private property shall not be taken for public use without just compensation, is intended solely as a limitation on the exercise of power by the government of the United States, and is not applicable to the legislation of the states. We are therefore of opinion that there is no repugnancy between the several acts of the general assembly of Maryland, given in evidence by the defendants at the trial of this cause, in the court of that state, and the constitution of the United States. This court, therefore, has no jurisdiction of the cause; and it is dismissed. . . .

Notes and Questions

(1) Was the Court's conclusion based on the text of the Fifth Amendment? Could one argue that the language of the Fifth Amendment limits the exercise of power by the state, as well as the federal, governments?

(2) To what extent did the Court rely on the structure of the Constitution?

(3) The Court stated that its holding is supported by the "history of the day." Should historical evidence be given controlling, or at least significant, weight in construing a constitution designed to endure for centuries?

B. The Civil War Amendments

Slaughter-House Cases
United States Supreme Court
83 U.S. (16 Wall.) 36, 21 L. Ed. 394 (1873)

Mr. Justice Miller delivered the opinion of the court.

These cases are brought here by writs of error to the Supreme Court of the State of Louisiana. They arise out of the efforts of the butchers of New Orleans to resist the Crescent City Live-Stock Landing and Slaughter-House Company in the exercise of certain powers conferred by the charter which created it, and which was granted by the legislature of the State.

The records show that the plaintiffs in error relied upon, and asserted throughout the entire course of the litigation in the State courts, that the grant of privileges in the charter of defendant, which they were contesting, was a violation of the most important provisions of the thirteenth and fourteenth articles of amendment of the Constitution of the United States.

The statute thus assailed as unconstitutional was passed March 8th, 1869, and is entitled "An act to protect the health of the city of New Orleans, to locate the stock-landings and slaughter-houses, and to incorporate the Crescent City Live-Stock Landing and Slaughter-House Company."

The first section forbids the landing or slaughtering of animals whose flesh is intended for food, within the city of New Orleans and other parishes and boundaries named and defined, or the keeping or establishing any slaughter-houses or within those limits except by the corporation thereby created, which is also limited to certain places afterwards mentioned. Suitable penalties are enacted for violations of this prohibition.

The second section designates the corporators, gives the name to the corporation, and confers on it the usual corporate powers.

The third and fourth sections authorize the company to establish and erect within certain territorial limits, therein defined, one or more stock-yards, stock-landings, and slaughter-houses, and imposes upon it the duty of erecting, on or before the first day of June, 1869, one grand slaughter-house of sufficient capacity for slaughtering five hundred animals per day.

It declares that the company, after it shall have prepared all the necessary buildings, yards, and other conveniences for that purpose, shall have the sole and exclusive privilege of conducting and carrying on the live-stock landing and slaughter-house business within the limits and privilege granted by the act, and that all such animals shall be landed at the stock-landings and slaughtered at the slaughter-houses of the company, and nowhere else. Penalties are enacted for infractions of this provision, and prices fixed for the maximum charges of the company for each steamboat and for each animal landed.

Section five orders the closing up of all other stock-landings and slaughter-houses after the first day of June, in the parishes of Orleans, Jefferson, and St. Bernard, and makes it the duty of the company to permit any person to slaughter animals in their slaughter-houses under a heavy penalty for each refusal. Another section fixes a limit to the charges to be made by the company for each animal so slaughtered in their building, and another provides for an inspection of all animals intended to be so slaughtered, by an officer appointed by the governor of the State for that purpose.

The power here exercised by the legislature of Louisiana is, in its essential nature, one which has been, up to the present period in the constitutional history of this country, always conceded to belong to the States.

This [police] power is, and must be from its very nature, incapable of any very exact definition or limitation. Upon it depends the security of social order, the life and health of the citizen, the comfort of an existence in a thickly populated community, the enjoyment of private and social life, and the beneficial use of property. "It extends," says another eminent judge, — "to the protection of the lives, limbs, health, comfort, and quiet of all persons, and the protection of all property within the State; and persons and property are subjected to all kinds of restraints and burdens in order to secure the general comfort, health, and prosperity of the State. Of the perfect right of the legislature to do this no question ever was, or, upon acknowledged general principles, ever can be made, so far as natural persons are concerned."

The regulation of the place and manner of conducting the slaughtering of animals, and the business of butchering within a city, and the inspection of the animals to be killed for meat, and of the meat afterwards, are among the most necessary and frequent exercises of this power.

It may, therefore, be considered as established, that the authority of the legislature of Louisiana to pass the present statute is ample, unless some restraint in the exercise of that power be found in the constitution of that State or in the amendments to the Constitution of the United States.

The plaintiffs in error accepting this issue, allege that the statute is a violation of the Constitution of the United States in these several particulars:

That it creates an involuntary servitude forbidden by the thirteenth article of amendment;

That it abridges the privileges and immunities of citizens of the United States;

That it denies to the plaintiffs the equal protection of the laws; and,

That it deprives them of their property without due process of law; contrary to the provisions of the first section of the fourteenth article of amendment.

Twelve articles of amendment were added to the Federal Constitution soon after the original organization of the government under it in 1789. Of these, all but the last were adopted so soon afterwards as to justify the statement that they were practically contemporaneous with the adoption of the original; and the twelfth, adopted in eighteen hundred and three, was so nearly so as to have become, like all the others, historical and of another age. But within the last eight years three other articles of amendment of vast importance have been added by the voice of the people to that now venerable instrument.

The most cursory glance at these articles discloses a unity of purpose, when taken in connection with the history of the times, which cannot fail to have an important bearing on any question of doubt concerning their true meaning. Nor can such doubts, when any reasonably exist, be safely and rationally solved without a reference to that history; for in it is found the occasion and the necessity for recurring again to the great source of power in this country, the people of the States, for additional guarantees of human rights; additional powers to the Federal government; additional restraints upon those of the States. Fortunately that history is fresh within the memory of us all, and its leading features, as they bear upon the matter before us, free from doubt.

The institution of African slavery, as it existed in about half the States of the Union, and the contests pervading the public mind for many years, between those who desired its curtailment and ultimate extinction and those who desired additional safeguards for its security and perpetuation, culminated in the effort, on the part of most of the States in which slavery existed, to separate from the Federal government, and to resist its authority. This constituted the war of the rebellion, and whatever auxiliary causes may have contributed to bring about this war, undoubtedly the overshadowing and efficient cause was African slavery.

In that struggle slavery, as a legalized social relation, perished. The proclamation of President Lincoln expressed an accomplished fact as to a large portion of the insurrectionary districts, when he declared slavery abolished in them all. But the war being over, those who had succeeded in re-establishing the authority of the Federal government were not content to permit this great act of emancipation to rest on the actual results of the contest or the proclamation of the Executive, both of which might have been questioned in after times, and they determined to place this main and most valuable result in the Constitution of the restored Union as one of its fundamental articles. Hence the thirteenth article of amendment of that instrument. Its two short sections seem hardly to admit of construction, so vigorous is their expression and so appropriate to the purpose we have indicated.

To withdraw the mind from the contemplation of this grand yet simple declaration of the personal freedom of all the human race within the jurisdiction of this government — a declaration designed to establish the freedom of four million slaves — and with a microscopic search endeavor to find in it a reference to servitudes, which may have been attached to property in certain localities, requires an effort, to say the least of it.

That a personal servitude was meant is proved by the use of the word "involuntary," which can only apply to human beings. The exception of servitude as a punishment for crime gives an idea of the class of servitude that is meant. The word servitude is of larger meaning than slavery, as the latter is popularly understood in this country, and the obvious purpose was to forbid all shades and conditions of African slavery. It was very well understood that in the form of apprenticeship for long terms, as it had been practiced in the West India Islands, on the abolition of slavery by the English government, or by reducing the slaves to the condition of serfs attached to the plantation, the purpose of the article might have been evaded, if only the word slavery had been used. And it is all that we deem necessary to say on the application of that article to the statute of Louisiana, now under consideration.

The process of restoring to their proper relations with the Federal government and with the other States those which had sided with the rebellion, undertaken under the proclamation of President Johnson in 1865, and before the assembling of Congress, developed the fact that, notwithstanding the formal recognition by those States of the abolition of slavery, the condition of the slave race would, without further protection of the Federal government, be almost as bad as it was before. Among the first acts of legislation adopted by several of the States in the legislative bodies which claimed to be in their normal relations with the Federal government, were laws which imposed upon the colored race onerous disabilities and burdens, and curtailed their rights in the pursuit of life, liberty, and property to such an extent that their freedom was of little value, while they had lost the protection which they had received from their former owners from motives both of interest and humanity.

They were in some States forbidden to appear in the towns in any other character than menial servants. They were required to reside on and cultivate the soil without the right to purchase or own it. They were excluded from many occupations of gain, and were not permitted to give testimony in the courts in any case where a white man was a party. It was said that their lives were at the mercy of bad men, either because the laws for their protection were insufficient or were not enforced.

These circumstances, whatever of falsehood or misconception may have been mingled with their presentation, forced upon the statesmen who had conducted the Federal government in safety through the crisis of the rebellion, and who supposed that by the thirteenth article of amendment they had secured the result of their labors, the conviction that something more was necessary in the way of constitutional protection to the unfortunate race who had suffered so much. They accordingly passed through Congress the proposition for the fourteenth amendment, and they declined to treat as restored to their full participation in the government of the Union the States which had been in insurrection, until they ratified that article by a formal vote of their legislative bodies.

Before we proceed to examine more critically the provisions of this amendment, on which the plaintiffs in error rely, let us complete and dismiss the history of the recent amendments, as that history relates to the general purpose which pervades them all. A few years' experience satisfied the thoughtful men who had been the authors of the other two amendments that, notwithstanding the restraints of those articles on the States, and the laws passed under the additional powers granted to Congress, these were inadequate for the protection of life, liberty, and property, without which freedom to the slave was no boon. They were in all those States denied the right of suffrage. The laws were administered by the white man alone. It was urged that a race of men distinctively marked as was the negro, living in the midst of another and dominant race, could never be fully secured in their person and their property without the right of suffrage.

Hence the fifteenth amendment, which declares that "the right of a citizen of the United States to vote shall not be denied or abridged by any State on account of race, color, or previous condition of servitude." The negro having, by the fourteenth amendment, been declared to be a citizen of the United States, is thus made a voter in every State of the Union.

We repeat, then, in the light of this recapitulation of events, almost too recent to be called history, but which are familiar to us all; and on the most casual examination of the language of these amendments, no one can fail to be impressed with the one pervading purpose found in them all, lying at the foundation of each, and without which none of them would have been even suggested; we mean the freedom of the slave race, the security and firm establishment of that freedom, and the protection of the newly-made freeman and citizen from the oppressions of those who had formerly exercised unlimited dominion over him. It is true that only the fifteenth amendment, in terms, mentions the negro by speaking of his color and his slavery. But it is just as true that each of the other articles was addressed to the grievances of that race, and designed to remedy them as the fifteenth.

We do not say that no one else but the negro can share in this protection. Both the language and spirit of these articles are to have their fair and just weight in any question of construction. Undoubtedly while negro slavery alone was in the mind of the Congress which proposed the thirteenth article, it forbids any other kind of slavery, now or hereafter. If Mexican peonage or the Chinese coolie labor system shall develop slavery of the Mexican or Chinese race within our territory, this amendment may safely be trusted to make it void. And so if other rights are assailed by the States which properly and necessarily fall within the protection of these articles, that protection will apply, though the party interested may not be of African descent. But what we do say, and what we wish to be understood is, that in any fair and just construction of any section or phrase of these amendments, it is necessary to look to the purpose which we have said was the pervading spirit of them all, the evil which they were designed to remedy, and the process of continued addition to the Constitution, until that purpose was supposed to be accomplished, as far as constitutional law can accomplish it.

The first section of the fourteenth article, to which our attention is more specially invited, opens with a definition of citizenship — not only citizenship of the United States, but citizenship of the States. No such definition was previously found in the Constitution, nor had any attempt been made to define it by act of Congress. It had been the occasion of much discussion in the courts, by the executive departments, and in the public journals. It had been said by eminent judges that no man was a citizen of the United States, except as he was a citizen of one of the States composing the Union. Those, therefore, who had been born and resided always in the District of Columbia or in the Territories, though within the United States, were not citizens. Whether this proposition was sound or not had never been judicially decided. But it had been held by this court, in the celebrated [*Dred Scott*] case, only a few years before the outbreak of the civil war, that a man of African descent, whether a slave or not, was not and could not be a citizen of a State or of the United States. This decision, while it met the condemnation of some of the ablest statesmen and constitutional lawyers of the country, had never been overruled; and if it was to be accepted as a constitutional limitation of the right of citizenship, then all the negro race who had recently been made freemen, were still, not only not citizens, but were incapable of becoming so by anything short of an amendment in the Constitution.

To remove this difficulty primarily, and to establish a clear and comprehensive definition of citizenship which should declare what should constitute citizenship of the United States, and also citizenship of a State, the first clause of the first section was framed.

All persons born or naturalized in the United States, and subject to the jurisdiction thereof, are citizens of the United States and of the State wherein they reside.

The first observation we have to make on this clause is, that it puts at rest both the questions which we stated to have been the subject of differences of opinion. It declares that persons may be citizens of the United States without regard to their citizenship of a particular State, and it overturns the *Dred Scott* decision by making *all persons* born within the United States and subject to its jurisdiction citizens of the United States. That its main purpose was to establish the citizenship of the negro can admit of no doubt. The phrase, "subject to its jurisdiction" was intended to exclude from its operation children of ministers, consuls, and citizens or subjects of foreign States born within the United States

The next observation is more important in view of the arguments of counsel in the present case. It is, that the distinction between citizenship of the United States and citizenship of a State is clearly recognized and established. Not only may a man be a citizen of the United States without being a citizen of a State, but an important element is necessary to convert the former into the latter. He must reside within the State to make him a citizen of it, but it is only necessary that he should be born or naturalized in the United States to be a citizen of the Union.

It is quite clear, then, that there is a citizenship of the United States, and a citizenship of a State, which are distinct from each other, and which depend upon different characteristics or circumstances in the individual.

We think this distinction and its explicit recognition in this amendment of great weight in this argument, because the next paragraph of this same section, which is the one mainly relied on by the plaintiffs in error, speaks only of privileges and immunities of citizens of the United States, and does not speak of those of citizens of the several States. The argument, however, in favor of the plaintiffs rests wholly on the assumption that the citizenship is the same, and the privileges and immunities guaranteed by the clause are the same.

The language is, "No State shall make or enforce any law which shall abridge the privileges or immunities of citizens of *the United States*." It is a little remarkable, if this clause was intended as a protection to the citizen of a State against the legislative power of his own State, that the word citizens of the State should be left out when it is so carefully used, and used in contradistinction to citizens of the United States, in the very sentence which precedes it. It is too clear for argument that the change in phraseology was adopted understandingly and with a purpose.

Of the privileges and immunities of the citizen of the United States, and of the privileges and immunities of the citizen of the State, and what they respectively are, we will presently consider; but we wish to state here that it is only the former which are placed by this clause under the protection of the Federal Constitution, and that the latter, whatever they may be, are not intended to have any additional protection by this paragraph of the amendment.

In the Constitution of the United States [t]he provision is found in section two of the fourth article, "The citizens of each State shall be entitled to all the privileges and immunities of citizens of the several States."

The constitutional provision [Article IV] did not create those rights, which it called privileges and immunities of citizens of the States.

Its sole purpose was to declare to the several States, that whatever those rights, as you grant or establish them to your own citizens, or as you limit or qualify, or impose restrictions on their exercise, the same, neither more or less, shall be the measure of the rights of citizens of other States within your jurisdiction.

Was it the purpose of the fourteenth amendment, by the simple declaration that no State should make or enforce any law which shall abridge the privileges and immunities of *citizens of the United States*, to transfer the security and protection of all the civil rights which we have mentioned, from the States to the Federal government? And where it is declared that Congress shall have the power to enforce that article, was it intended to bring within the power of Congress the entire domain of civil rights heretofore belonging exclusively to the States?

All this and more must follow, if the proposition of the plaintiffs in error be sound. [S]uch a construction followed by the reversal of the judgments of the Supreme Court of Louisiana in these cases, would constitute this court a perpetual censor upon all legislation of the States, on the civil rights of their own citizens, with authority to nullify such as it did not approve as consistent with those rights, as they existed at the time of the adoption of this amendment. The argument we admit is not always the most conclusive which is drawn from the consequences urged against the adoption of a particular construction of an instrument. But when, as in the case before us, these consequences are so serious, so far-reaching and pervading, so great a departure from the structure and spirit of our institutions; when the effect is to fetter and degrade the State governments by subjecting them to the control of Congress, in the exercise of powers heretofore universally conceded to them of the most ordinary and fundamental character; when in fact it radically changes the whole theory of the relations of the State and Federal governments to each other and of both these governments to the people; the argument has a force that is irresistible, in the absence of language which expresses such a purpose too clearly to admit of doubt.

We are convinced that no such results were intended by the Congress which proposed these amendments, nor by the legislatures of the States which ratified them.

Having shown that the privileges and immunities relied on in the argument are those which belong to citizens of the States as such, and that they are left to the State governments for security and protection, and not by this article placed under the special care of the Federal government, we may hold ourselves excused from defining the privileges and immunities of citizens of the United States which no State can abridge, until some case involving those privileges may make it necessary to do so.

But lest it should be said that no such privileges and immunities are to be found if those we have been considering are excluded, we venture to suggest some which owe their existence to the Federal government, its National character, its Constitution, or its laws.

It is said to be the right of the citizen of this great country, protected by implied guarantees of its Constitution, "to come to the seat of government to assert any claim he may have upon that government, to transact any business he may have with it, to seek its protection, to share its offices, to engage in administering its functions. He has the right of free access to its seaports, through which all operation of foreign commerce are conducted, to the sub-treasuries, land offices, and courts of justice in the several States."

Another privilege of a citizen of the United States is to demand the care and protection of the Federal government over his life, liberty, and property when on the high seas or within the jurisdiction of a foreign government. The right to peaceably assemble and petition for redress of grievances, the privilege of the writ of *habeas corpus*, are rights of the citizen guaranteed by the Federal Constitution. The right to use the navigable waters of the United States, however they may penetrate the territory of the several States, all rights secured to our citizens by treaties with foreign nations, are dependent upon citizenship of the United States, and not citizenship of a State. One of these privileges is conferred by the very article under consideration. It is that a citizen of the United States can, of his own volition, become a citizen of any State of the Union by a *bona fide* residence therein, with the same rights as other citizens of that State. To these may be added the rights secured by the thirteenth and fifteenth articles of amendment, and by the other clause of the fourteenth, next to be considered.

But it is useless to pursue this branch of the inquiry, since we are of opinion that the rights claimed by these plaintiffs in error, if they have any existence, are not privileges and immunities of citizens of the United States within the meaning of the clause of the fourteenth amendment under consideration.

The argument has not been much pressed in these cases that the defendant's charter deprives the plaintiffs of their property without due process of law, or that it denies to them the equal protection of the law. The first of these paragraphs has been in the Constitution since the adoption of the fifth amendment, as a restraint upon the Federal power. It is also to be found in some form of expression in the constitutions of nearly all the States, as a restraint upon the power of the States. This law, then, has practically been the same as it now is during the existence of the government, except so far as the present amendment may place the restraining power over the States in this matter in the hands of the Federal government.

We are not without judicial interpretation, therefore, both State and National, of the meaning of this clause. And it is sufficient to say that under no construction of that provision that we have ever seen, or any that we deem admissible, can the restraint imposed by the State of Louisiana upon the exercise of their trade by the butchers of New Orleans be held to be a deprivation of property within the meaning of that provision.

"Nor shall any State deny to any person within its jurisdiction the equal protection of the laws."

In the light of the history of these amendments, and the pervading purpose of them, which we have already discussed, it is not difficult to give a meaning to this clause. The existence of laws in the States where the newly emancipated negroes resided, which discriminated with gross injustice and hardship against them as a class, was the evil to be remedied by this clause, and by it such laws are forbidden.

The adoption of the first eleven amendments to the Constitution so soon after the original instrument was accepted, shows a prevailing sense of danger at that time from the Federal power. And it cannot be denied that such a jealousy continued to exist with many patriotic men until the breaking out of the late civil war. It was then discovered that the true danger to the perpetuity of the Union was in the capacity of the State organizations to combine and concentrate all the powers of the State and of contiguous States, for a determined resistance to the General Government.

Unquestionably this has given great force to the argument, and added largely to the number of those who believe in the necessity of a strong National government.

But, however pervading this sentiment, and however it may have contributed to the adoption of the amendments we have been considering, we do not see in those amendments any purpose to destroy the main features of the general system. Under the pressure of all the excited feeling growing out of the war, our statesmen have still believed that the existence of the States with powers for domestic and local government, including the regulation of civil rights—the rights of person and of property—was essential to the perfect working of our complex form of government, though they have thought proper to impose additional limitations on the States, and to confer additional power on that of the Nation.

But whatever fluctuations may be seen in the history of public opinion on this subject during the period of our national existence, we think it will be found that this court, so far as its functions required, has always held with a steady and an even hand the balance between State and Federal power, and we trust that such may continue to be the history of its relation to that subject so long as it shall have duties to perform which demand of it a construction of the Constitution, or of any of its parts.

The judgments of the Supreme Court of Louisiana in these cases are *Affirmed*.

Mr. Justice Field, dissenting:

The question presented is one of the gravest importance, not merely to the parties here, but to the whole country. It is nothing less than the question whether the recent amendments to the Federal Constitution protect the citizens of the United States against the deprivation of their common rights by State legislation. In my judgment the fourteenth amendment does afford such protection, and was so intended by the Congress which framed and the States which adopted it.

The first clause of the fourteenth amendment recognizes in express terms, if it does not create, citizens of the United States, and it makes their citizenship dependent upon the place of their birth, or the fact of their adoption, and not upon the constitution or laws of any State or the condition of their ancestry. A citizen of a State is now only a citizen of the United States residing in that State. The fundamental rights, privileges, and immunities which belong to him as a free man and a free citizen, now belong to him as a citizen of the United States, and are not dependent upon his citizenship of any State.

The amendment does not attempt to confer any new privileges or immunities upon citizens, or to enumerate or define those already existing. It assumes that there are such privileges and immunities which belong of right to citizens as such, and ordains that they shall not be abridged by State legislation. If this inhibition has no reference to privileges and immunities of this character, but only refers, as held by the majority of the court in their opinion, to such privileges and immunities as were before its adoption specially designated in the Constitution or necessarily implied as belonging to citizens of the United States, it was a vain and idle enactment, which accomplished nothing, and most unnecessarily excited Congress and the people on its passage. With privileges and immunities thus designated or implied no State could ever have interfered by its laws, and no new constitutional provision was required to inhibit such interference. The supremacy of the Constitution and the laws of the United States always controlled any State legislation of that character. But if the amendment refers to the natural and inalienable rights which belong to all citizens, the inhibition has a profound significance and consequence.

What, then, are the privileges and immunities which are secured against abridgment by State legislation?

In the first section of the Civil Rights Act Congress has given its interpretation to these terms, or at least has stated some of the rights which, in its judgment, these terms include; it has there declared that they include the right "to make and enforce contracts, to sue, be parties and give evidence, to inherit, purchase, lease, sell, hold, and convey real and personal property, and to full and equal benefit of all laws and proceedings for the security of person and property." That act, it is true, was passed before the fourteenth amendment, but the amendment was adopted to obviate objections to the act, or speaking more accurately, I should say, to obviate objections to legislation of a similar character, extending the protection of the National government over the common rights of all citizens of the United States. Accordingly, after its ratification, Congress re-enacted the act under the belief that whatever doubts may have previously existed of its validity, they were removed by the amendment.

The terms, privileges and immunities, are not new in the amendment; they were in the Constitution before the amendment was adopted. They are found in the second section of the fourth article, which declares that "the citizens of each State shall be entitled to all privileges and immunities of citizens in the several States."

The privileges and immunities designated in the second section of the fourth article of the Constitution are those which of right belong to the citizens of all free governments, and they can be enjoyed under that clause by the citizens of each State in the several States upon the same terms and conditions as they are enjoyed by the citizens of the latter States. No discrimination can be made by one State against the citizens of other States in their enjoyment, nor can any greater imposition be levied than such as is laid upon its own citizens. It is a clause which insures equality in the enjoyment of those rights between citizens of the several States whilst in the same State.

What the clause in question did for the protection of the citizens of one State against hostile and discriminating legislation of other States, the fourteenth amendment does for the protection of every citizen of the United States against hostile and discriminating legislation against him in favor of others, whether they reside in the same or in different States. If under the fourth article of the Constitution equality of privileges and immunities is secured between citizens of different States, under the fourteenth amendment the same equality is secured between citizens of the United States.

It will not be pretended that under the fourth article of the Constitution any State could create a monopoly in any known trade or manufacture in favor of her own citizens, or any portion of them, which would exclude an equal participation in the trade or manufacture monopolized by citizens of other States. She could not confer, for example, upon any of her citizens the sole right to manufacture shoes, or boots, or silk, or the sole right to sell those articles in the State so as to exclude non-resident citizens from engaging in a similar manufacture or sale. The non-resident citizens could claim equality of privilege under the provisions of the fourth article with the citizens of the State exercising the monopoly as well as with others, and thus, as respects them, the monopoly would cease. If this were not so it would be in the power of the State to exclude at any time the citizens of other States from participation in particular branches of commerce or trade, and extend the exclusion from time to time so as effectually to prevent any traffic with them.

Now, what the clause in question does for the protection of citizens of one State against the creation of monopolies in favor of citizens of other States, the fourteenth amendment does for the protection of every citizen of the United States against the creation of any monopoly whatever. The privileges and immunities of citizens of the United States, of every one of them, is secured against abridgment in any form by any State. The fourteenth amendment places them under the guardianship of the National authority. All monopolies in any known trade or manufacture are an invasion of these privileges, for they encroach upon the liberty of citizens to acquire property and pursue happiness.

[The] equality of right in the lawful pursuits of life, throughout the whole country, is the distinguishing privilege of citizens of the United States. The State may prescribe such regulations for every pursuit and calling of life as will promote the public health, secure the good order and advance the general prosperity of society, but when once prescribed, the pursuit or calling must be free to be followed by every citizen who is within the conditions designated, and will conform to the regulations. This is the fundamental idea upon which our institutions rest, and unless adhered to in the legislation of the country our government will be a republic only in name. The fourteenth amendment, in my judgment, makes it essential to the validity of the legislation of every State that this equality of right should be respected.

I am authorized by the CHIEF JUSTICE, MR. JUSTICE SWAYNE, and MR. JUSTICE BRADLEY, to state that they concur with me in this dissenting opinion.

MR. JUSTICE BRADLEY, also dissenting:

Admitting that formerly the States were not prohibited from infringing any of the fundamental privileges and immunities of citizens of the United States, except in a few specified cases, that cannot be said now, since the adoption of the fourteenth amendment. In my judgment, it was the intention of the people of this country in adopting that amendment to provide National security against violation by the States of the fundamental rights of the citizen.

The amendment prohibits any State from depriving any person (citizen or otherwise) of life, liberty, or property, without due process of law.

In my view, a law which prohibits a large class of citizens from adopting a lawful employment, or from following a lawful employment previously adopted, does deprive them of liberty as well as property, without due process of law. Their right of choice is a portion of their liberty; their occupation is their property. Such a law also deprives those citizens of the equal protection of the laws, contrary to the last clause of the section.

It is futile to argue that none but persons of the African race are intended to be benefited by this amendment. They may have been the primary cause of the amendment, but its language is general, embracing all citizens, and I think it was purposely so expressed.

The mischief to be remedied was not merely slavery and its incidents and consequences; but that spirit of insubordination and disloyalty to the National government which had troubled the country for so many years in some of the States, and that intolerance of free speech and free discussion which often rendered life and property insecure, and led to much unequal legislation. The amendment was an attempt to give voice to the strong National yearning for that time and that condition of things, in which American citizenship should be a sure guaranty of safety, and in which every citizen of the United States might stand erect on every portion of its soil, in the full enjoyment of every right and privilege belonging to a freeman, without fear of violence or molestation.

MR. JUSTICE SWAYNE, dissenting. [Omitted.]

Notes and Questions

(1) What rights are guaranteed by the Privileges and Immunities Clause of the Fourteenth Amendment? By Article IV? How did Justice Field's view of these clauses differ from that of the majority?

(2) What was the plaintiffs' due process argument? Were plaintiffs complaining about the absence of procedures or about the substance of the law? How did the Court dispose of the claim?

(3) The language of the Equal Protection Clause and the Thirteenth Amendment is not limited to racial discrimination. Why then did the Court hold that the Louisiana statute violated neither of these provisions?

(4) It has been argued that the majority's interpretation of the Amendments, particularly the Privileges and Immunities Clause, is not supported by the historical evidence. *See, e.g.*, RAOUL BERGER, GOVERNMENT BY JUDICIARY 46 (1977) ("The notion that by conferring dual citizenship the framers were separating said rights of a citizen of the United States from those of a State citizen not only is without historical warrant but actually does violence to their intentions."); HAROLD HYMAN & WILLIAM WIECEK, EQUAL JUSTICE UNDER LAW 437–438 (1982) (A review of the appropriate historical evidence "may justify doubts about the accuracy of Justice Miller's *Slaughterhouse* comment that in 1872–73 the history of the Thirteenth and Fourteenth Amendments was 'fresh within the memory of us all.' Instead it appears that Miller's memory and those of the majority of the robed brethren were dimming when the Supreme Court considered *Slaughterhouse*.").

Professors Hyman and Wiecek described the significant judicial setback for blacks:

> *Slaughterhouse* has become the major source of definitions for both the Thirteenth and the Fourteenth Amendments. The men seeking federal protection in *Slaughterhouse* were not beleaguered freedmen or Unionists, but rather white butchers being victimized by what they alleged was monopolistic legislation greased through the Louisiana legislature by bribery. The 5-4 decision in *Slaughterhouse* gave a permanently narrow reading to the new privileges and immunities clause; it began blighting the constitutional hopes of the freedmen, leading to the nadir of legally enforced segregation and discrimination. Its dissenters, Field and Bradley, disclosed embryonic doctrines — liberty of contract and substantive due process — that were, after Chase's death, to dominate American jurisprudence for two generations.
>
> Turning to the Fourteenth Amendment, Miller analyzed its section 1 clause by clause. He declared that there were two sorts of privileges and immunities, federal and state, and that "the latter must rest for their security and protection where they had heretofore rested [that is, in the states, not the federal government]; for they are not embraced by this paragraph of the amendment." The privileges and immunities of state citizenship included the most significant substantive rights of citizens, black and white, in the day-to-day conduct of their lives.
>
> Herein lay a terrible irony for blacks. After having construed the "pervading purpose" of the Civil War amendments to be the freedom of black

people, Miller relegated freedmen, for the effective protection of their new freedom, to precisely those governments — the southern states — least likely to respect either their rights or their freedom should the Republican regimes fall from power. The federal government could protect only the privileges and immunities of federal citizenship. As enumerated by Miller, these included the right of access to Washington, D.C., and the coastal seaports; the right to protection on the high seas and abroad; the right to use navigable waters of the United States; the right of assembly and petition; the privilege of habeas corpus. Of these, only the last two would be significant for most blacks.

Miller's orthodoxy made it impossible for him to imagine that the postwar Amendments made any significant change in the federal system. Miller could not share the vision of the framers of the Thirteenth and Fourteenth Amendments — a vision of federal privileges and immunities defined not by the nation but by the states, and so involving no centralization or loss of state initiatives. He concluded: "we do not see in those amendments any purpose to destroy the main features of the general system."

Miller then summarily dispensed with the arguments of due process and equal protection. Pointing out that the due process clause had existed in the Fifth Amendment since 1791, he argued that more than two generations' experience with it furnished "no construction of that provision that we have ever seen, or any that we deem admissible," that would support the position of the butchers. To make such a statement, Miller had to shut his eyes to Taney's dictum in *Dred Scott*, and to the entire rich history of the due process or law-of-the-land clauses in the state Constitutions before the war.

Miller shrugged off the equal-protection argument as abruptly: "we doubt very much whether any action of a State not directed by way of discrimination against the negroes as a class, or on account of their race, will ever be held to come within the purview of this provision." Thus, though seeming to protect blacks, Miller consigned them to the ingenuities, subterfuges, and legal chicane of white Democrats already returning to power in the South. The process of "Redemption" had begun, and it would be consolidated within a decade. *Slaughterhouse* was the first great judicial setback suffered by blacks in their quest for effective constitutional protection of their liberties.

HYMAN & WIECEK, *supra* at 475, 477–478.[8]

---

8. Copyright © 1982 by Harper & Row Publisher, Inc. Reprinted by permission.

Problem A

Assume that state law prohibits women from practicing law. You have been contacted by a group of women who want to challenge the constitutionality of the statute.

Based on the *Slaughter-House Cases*, what is the likelihood they will prevail? Does the state law abridge their privileges and immunities within the meaning of the Fourteenth Amendment? Does it deprive them of life, liberty or property without due process? Does it deny them equal protection of the laws? (In *Bradwell v. Illinois*, 83 U.S. (16 Wall.) 130 (1873), the Court upheld such a law. For the Court's modern approach, see § 6.04[B], *infra*.)

––––––––––

Recall that in *Barron v. Mayor and City Council of Baltimore*, the Court concluded that the first eight amendments operate as limits on the exercise of federal, not state, power. The Fourteenth Amendment was adopted twenty-five years after *Barron* and, of course, applies directly to the states. In the *Slaughter-House Cases*, however, the Court applied a narrow construction of the amendment, relying heavily on the drafters' original intention to address problems of racial discrimination.

We will find in subsequent chapters that the Fourteenth Amendment has been extended well beyond racial matters. Moreover, to some extent, the Court has avoided *Barron* by reading the Fourteenth Amendment to "incorporate" those rights enumerated in the first eight amendments as restrictions on the exercise of state power. In 1940, for example, the Court held that the liberty embodied in the Fourteenth Amendment embraces the liberties protected by the First Amendment. *Cantwell v. Connecticut*, 310 U.S. 296, 323 (1940). In 1983, a district court relied on what it perceived to be newly discovered evidence in concluding that the Fourteenth Amendment does not prohibit a state from establishing a religion, *Jaffree v. Board of School Commissioners of Mobile County*, 554 F. Supp. 1104 (S.D. Ala. 1983). The court held, therefore, that an Alabama law authorizing a period of silence for meditation or prayer is constitutional. The Supreme Court emphatically rejected the lower court's conclusion. In *Wallace v. Jaffree*, 472 U.S. 38 (1985), the Court stated:

> [W]hen the Constitution was amended to prohibit any State from depriving any person of liberty without due process of laws, that Amendment imposed the same limitations on the State's power to legislate that the First Amendment had always imposed on the Congress' power. This Court has confirmed and endorsed this elementary proposition of law time and time again.

§ 5.03 Prohibiting Encroachments on Individual Rights by Private Parties: The State Action Doctrine

The Civil Rights Cases

Supreme Court of the United States
109 U.S. 3, 3 S. Ct. 18, 27 L. Ed. 835 (1883)

BRADLEY, J.

These cases are all founded on the first and second sections of the act of congress known as the "Civil Rights Act," passed March 1, 1875, entitled "An act to protect all citizens in their civil and legal rights." 18 Stat. 335. Two of the cases, those against Stanley and Nichols, are indictments for denying to persons of color the accommodations and privileges of an inn or hotel; two of them, those against Ryan and Singleton, are for denying to individuals the privileges and accommodations of a theater, the information against Ryan being for refusing a colored person a seat in the dress circle of Maguire's theater in San Francisco; and the indictment against Singleton being for denying to another person, whose color is not stated, the full enjoyment of the accommodations of the theater known as the Grand Opera House in New York, "said denial not being made for any reasons by law applicable to citizens of every race and color, and regardless of any previous condition of servitude." The case of Robinson and wife against the Memphis Charleston Railroad Company was an action brought in the circuit court of the United States for the western district of Tennessee, to recover the penalty of $500 given by the second section of the act; and the *gravamen* was the refusal by the conductor of the railroad company to allow the wife to ride in the ladies' car, for the reason, as stated in one of the counts, that she was a person of African descent.

It is obvious that the primary and important question in all the cases is the constitutionality of the law; for if the law is unconstitutional none of the prosecutions can stand.

[I]t is the purpose of the law to declare that, in the enjoyment of the accommodations and privileges of inns, public conveyances, theaters, and other places of public amusement, no distinction shall be made between citizens of different race or color, or between those who have, and those who have not, been slaves. Its effect is to declare that in all inns, public conveyances, and places of amusement, colored citizens, whether formerly slaves or not, and citizens of other races, shall have the same accommodations and privileges in all inns, public conveyances, and places of amusement, as are enjoyed by white citizens; and *vice versa*. The second section makes it a penal offense in any person to deny to any citizen of any race or color, regardless of previous servitude, any of the accommodations or privileges mentioned in the first section.

Has congress constitutional power to make such a law? Of course, no one will contend that the power to pass it was contained in the constitution before the adoption of the last three amendments. The power is sought, first, in the fourteenth amendment.

The first section of the fourteenth amendment, — which is the one relied on, — after declaring who shall be citizens of the United States, and of the several states, is prohibitory in its character, and prohibitory upon the states. . . . It is state action of a particular character that is prohibited. Individual invasion of individual rights is not the subject-matter of the amendment. It has a deeper and broader scope. It nullifies and makes void all state legislation, and state action of every kind, which impairs the privileges and immunities of citizens of the United States, or which injures them in life, liberty, or property without due process of law, or which denies to any of them the equal protection of the laws. It not only does this, but the last section of the amendment invests congress with power to enforce it by appropriate legislation. To adopt appropriate legislation for correcting the effects of such prohibited state law and state acts, and thus to render them effectually null, void, and innocuous. This is the legislative power conferred upon congress, and this is the whole of it.

And so in the present case, until some state law has been passed, or some state action through its officers or agents has been taken, adverse to the rights of citizens sought to be protected by the fourteenth amendment, no legislation of the United States under said amendment, nor any proceeding under such legislation, can be called into activity, for the prohibitions of the amendment are against state laws and acts done under state authority. Of course, legislation may and should be provided in advance to meet the exigency when it arises, but it should be adapted to the mischief and wrong which the amendment was intended to provide against; and that is, state laws or state action of some kind adverse to the rights of the citizen secured by the amendment. Such legislation cannot properly cover the whole domain of rights appertaining to life, liberty, and property, defining them and providing for their vindication. That would be to establish a code of municipal law regulative of all private rights between man and man in society. It would be to make congress take the place of the state legislatures and to supersede them.

An inspection of the law shows that it makes no reference whatever to any supposed or apprehended violation of the fourteenth amendment on the part of the states. It is not predicated on any such view. It proceeds *ex directo* to declare that certain acts committed by individuals shall be deemed offenses, and shall be prosecuted and punished by proceedings in the courts of the United States. It does not profess to be corrective of any constitutional wrong committed by the states; it does not make its operation to depend upon any such wrong committed. It applies equally to cases arising in states which have the justest laws respecting the personal rights of citizens, and whose authorities are ever ready to enforce such laws as to those which arise in states that may have violated the prohibition of the amendment. In other words, it steps into the domain of local jurisprudence, and lays down rules for the conduct of individuals in society towards each other, and imposes sanctions for the enforcement of those rules, without referring in any manner to any supposed action of the state or its authorities.

The wrongful act of an individual, unsupported by state authority, is simply a private wrong, or a crime of that individual. An individual cannot deprive a man of his right to vote, to hold property, to buy and to sell, to sue in the courts, or to be a witness or a juror; he may, by force or fraud, interfere with the enjoyment of the right in a particular case; he may commit an assault against the person, or commit murder, or use ruffian violence at the polls, or slander the good name of a fellow-citizen; but unless protected in these wrongful acts by some shield of state law or state authority, he cannot destroy or injure the right; he will only render himself amenable to satisfaction or punishment; and amenable therefor to the laws of the state where the wrongful acts are committed. Hence, in all those cases where the constitution seeks to protect the rights of the citizen against discriminative and unjust laws of the state by prohibiting such laws, it is not individual offenses, but abrogation and denial of rights, which it denounces, and for which it clothes the congress with power to provide a remedy. This abrogation and denial of rights, for which the states alone were or could be responsible, was the great seminal and fundamental wrong which was intended to be remedied. And the remedy to be provided must necessarily be predicated upon that wrong. It must assume that in the cases provided for, the evil or wrong actually committed rests upon some state law or state authority for its excuse and perpetration.

[I]t is clear that the law in question cannot be sustained by any grant of legislative power made to congress by the fourteenth amendment. [It] is not corrective legislation; it is primary and direct; it takes immediate and absolute possession of the subject of the right of admission to inns, public conveyances, and places of amusement. It supersedes and displaces state legislation on the same subject, or only allows it permissive force. It ignores such legislation, and assumes that the matter is one that belongs to the domain of national regulation. Whether it would not have been a more effective protection of the rights of citizens to have clothed congress with plenary power over the whole subject, is not now the question. What we have to decide is, whether such plenary power has been conferred upon congress by the fourteenth amendment, and, in our judgment, it has not.

But the power of congress to adopt direct and primary, as distinguished from corrective, legislation on the subject in hand, is sought, in the second place, from the thirteenth amendment, which abolishes slavery. This amendment, as well as the fourteenth, is undoubtedly self-executing without any ancillary legislation, so far as its terms are applicable to any existing state of circumstances. By its own unaided force and effect it abolished slavery, and established universal freedom. Still, legislation may be necessary and proper to meet all the various cases and circumstances to be affected by it, and to prescribe proper modes of redress for its violation in letter or spirit. And such legislation may be primary and direct in its character; for the amendment is not a mere prohibition of state laws establishing or upholding slavery, but an absolute declaration that slavery or involuntary servitude shall not exist in any part of the United States.

[I]t is assumed that the power vested in congress to enforce the article by appropriate legislation, clothes congress with power to pass all laws necessary and proper for abolishing all badges and incidents of slavery in the United States; and upon this assumption it is claimed that this is sufficient authority for declaring by law that all persons shall have equal accommodations and privileges in all inns, public conveyances, and places of public amusement; the argument being that the denial of such equal accommodations and privileges is in itself a subjection to a species of servitude within the meaning of the amendment. Conceding the major proposition to be true, that congress has a right to enact all necessary and proper laws for the obliteration and prevention of slavery, with all its badges and incidents, is the minor proposition also true, that the denial to any person of admission to the accommodations and privileges of an inn, a public conveyance, or a theater, does subject that person to any form of servitude, or tend to fasten upon him any badge of slavery? If it does not, then power to pass the law is not found in the thirteenth amendment.

The long existence of African slavery in this country gave us very distinct notions of what it was, and what were its necessary incidents. Compulsory service of the slave for the benefit of the master, restraint of his movements except by the master's will, disability to hold property, to make contracts, to have standing in court, to be a witness against a white person, and such like burdens and incapacities were the inseparable incidents of the institution. Severer punishments for crimes were imposed on the slave than on free persons guilty of the same offenses. [C]ongress did not assume, under the authority given by the thirteenth amendment, to adjust what may be called the social rights of men and races in the community; but only to declare and vindicate those fundamental rights which appertain to the essence of citizenship, and the enjoyment or deprivation of which constitutes the essential distinction between freedom and slavery.

The only question under the present head, therefore, is, whether the refusal to any persons of the accommodations of an inn, or a public conveyance, or a place of public amusement, by an individual, and without any sanction or support from any state law or regulations, does inflict upon such persons any manner of servitude, or form of slavery, as those terms are understood in this country?

[W]e are forced to the conclusion that such an act of refusal has nothing to do with slavery or involuntary servitude, and that if it is violative of any right of the party, his redress is to be sought under the laws of the state; or, if those laws are adverse to his rights and do not protect him, his remedy will be found in the corrective legislation which congress has adopted, or may adopt, for counteracting the effect of state laws, or state action, prohibited by the fourteenth amendment. It would be running the slavery argument into the ground to make it apply to every act of discrimination which a person may see fit to make as to the guests he will entertain, or as to the people he will take into his coach or cab or car, or admit to his concert or theater, or deal with in other matters of intercourse or business.

Mere discriminations on account of race or color were not regarded as badges of slavery.

On the whole, we are of the opinion that no countenance of authority for the passage of the law in question can be found in either the thirteenth or fourteenth amendment of the constitution; and no other ground of authority for its passage being suggested, it must necessarily be declared void, at least so far as its operation in the several states is concerned.

HARLAN, J., dissenting.

That there are burdens and disabilities which constitute badges of slavery and servitude, and that the express power delegated to congress to enforce, by appropriate legislation, the thirteenth amendment, may be exerted by legislation of a direct and primary character, for the eradication, not simply of the institution, but of its badges and incidents, are propositions which ought to be deemed indisputable. They lie at the very foundation of the civil rights act of 1866. I do not contend that the thirteenth amendment invests congress with authority, by legislation, to regulate the entire body of the civil rights which citizens enjoy, or may enjoy, in the several states. But I do hold that since slavery, as the court has repeatedly declared, was the moving or principal cause of the adoption of that amendment, and since that institution rested wholly upon the inferiority, as a race, of those held in bondage, their freedom necessarily involved immunity from, and protection against, all discrimination against them, because of their race, in respect of such civil rights as belong to freemen of other races. Congress, therefore, under its express power to enforce that amendment, by appropriate legislation, may enact laws to protect that people against the deprivation, *on account of their race*, of any civil rights enjoyed by other freemen in the same state; and such legislation may be of a direct and primary character, operating upon states, their officers and agents, and also upon, at least, such individuals and corporations as exercise public functions and wield power and authority under the state.

It remains now to consider these cases with reference to the power congress has possessed since the adoption of the fourteenth amendment. [T]his court, in the *Slaughter-House Cases*, declared that the one pervading purpose found in all the recent amendments, lying at the foundation of each, and without which none of them would have been suggested, was "the freedom of the slave race, the security and firm establishment of that freedom, and the protection of the newly-made freeman and citizen from the oppression of those who had formerly exercised unlimited dominion over him"; that each amendment was addressed primarily to the grievances of that race.

The assumption that the amendment consists wholly of prohibitions upon state laws and state proceedings in hostility to its provisions, is unauthorized by its language. The first clause of the first section — "all persons born or naturalized in the United States, and subject to the jurisdiction thereof, are citizens of the United States, and of the state wherein they reside" — is of a distinctly affirmative character. In its application to the colored race, previously liberated, it created and granted, as well citizenship of the United States, as citizenship of the state in which they respectively resided. It introduced all of that race, whose ancestors had been imported and sold as slaves, at once, into the political community known as the "People of the United States." They became, instantly, citizens of the United States, and of their respective states. Further, they were brought, by this supreme act of the nation, within the direct operation of the provision of the constitution which declares that "the citizens of each state shall be entitled to all privileges and immunities of citizens in the several states." Article 4, § 2.

It is, therefore, an essential inquiry what, if any, right, privilege, or immunity was given by the nation to colored persons when they were made citizens of the state in which they reside? That they became entitled, upon the adoption of the fourteenth amendment, "to all privileges and immunities of citizens in the several states," within the meaning of section 2 of article 4 of the constitution, no one, I suppose, will for a moment question. What are the privileges and immunities to which, by that clause of the Constitution, they became entitled? To this it may be answered, generally, upon the authority of the adjudged cases, that they are those which are fundamental in citizenship in a free government, "common to the citizens in the latter states under their constitutions and laws by virtue of their being citizens."

Although this court has wisely forborne any attempt, by a comprehensive definition, to indicate all the privileges and immunities to which the citizens of each state are entitled of right to enjoy in the several states, I hazard nothing, in view of former adjudications, in saying that no state can sustain her denial to colored citizens of other states, while within her limits, of privileges or immunities, fundamental in republican citizenship, upon the ground that she accords such privileges and immunities only to her white citizens and withholds them from her colored citizens. The colored citizens of other states, within the jurisdiction of that state, could claim, under the constitution, every privilege and immunity which that state secures to her white citizens.

But what was secured to colored citizens of the United States — as between them and their respective states — by the grant to them of state citizenship? With what rights, privileges, or immunities did this grant from the nation invest them? There is one, if there be no others — exemption from race discrimination in respect of any civil right belonging to citizens of the white race in the same state. That, surely, is their constitutional privilege when within the jurisdiction of other states. And such must be their constitutional right, in their own state, unless the recent amendments be "splendid baubles," thrown out to delude those who deserved fair and generous treatment at the hands of the nation. Citizenship in this country necessarily imports equality of civil rights among citizens of every race in the same state. It is fundamental in American citizenship that, in respect of such rights, there shall be no discrimination by the state, or its officers, or by individuals, or corporations exercising public functions or authority, against any citizen because of his race or previous condition of servitude.

If, then, exemption from discrimination in respect of civil rights is a new constitutional right, secured by the grant of state citizenship to colored citizens of the

United States, why may not the nation, by means of its own legislation of a primary direct character, guard, protect, and enforce that right?

This court has always given a broad and liberal construction to the constitution, so as to enable congress, by legislation, to enforce rights secured by that instrument. The legislation congress may enact, in execution of its power to enforce the provisions of this amendment, is that which is appropriate to protect the right granted. [I]t is for congress, not the judiciary, to say which is best adapted to the end to be attained *McCulloch v. Maryland*.

It was said of *Dred Scott v. Sandford* that this court in that case overruled the action of two generations, virtually inserted a new clause in the constitution, changed its character, and made a new departure in the workings of the federal government. I may be permitted to say that if the recent amendments are so construed that congress may not, in its own discretion, and independently of the action or non-action of the states, provide, by legislation of a primary and direct character, for the security of rights created by the national constitution; if it be adjudged that the obligation to protect the fundamental privileges and immunities granted by the Fourteenth Amendment to citizens residing in the several states, rests, primarily, not on the nation, but on the states; if it be further adjudged that individuals and corporations exercising public functions may, without liability to direct primary legislation on the part of congress, make the race of citizens the ground for denying them that equality of civil rights which the Constitution ordains as a principle of republican citizenship; then, not only the foundations upon which the national supremacy has always securely rested will be materially disturbed, but we shall enter upon an era of constitutional law when the rights of freedom and American citizenship cannot receive from the nation that efficient protection which heretofore was accorded to slavery and the rights of the master.

But if it were conceded that the power of congress could not be brought into activity until the rights specified in the act of 1875 had been abridged or denied by some state law or state action, I maintain that the decision of the court is erroneous. There has been adverse state action within the Fourteenth Amendment.

In every material sense applicable to the practical enforcement of the fourteenth amendment, railroad corporations, keepers of inns, and managers of places of public amusement are agents of the state, because amenable, in respect of their public duties and functions, to public regulation. It seems to me that a denial by these instrumentalities of the state to the citizen, because of his race, of that equality of civil rights secured to him by law, is a denial by the state within the meaning of the fourteenth amendment. If it be not, then that race is left, in respect of the civil rights under discussion, practically at the mercy of corporations and individuals wielding power under public authority.

I agree that government has nothing to do with social, as distinguished from technically legal, rights of individuals. No government ever has brought, or ever can bring, its people into social intercourse against their wishes. Whether one person

will permit or maintain social relations with another is a matter with which government has no concern. I agree that if one citizen chooses not to hold social intercourse
with another, he is not and cannot be made amenable to the law for his conduct in
that regard; for no legal right of a citizen is violated by the refusal of others to maintain merely social relations with him, even upon grounds of race. What I affirm is
that no state, nor the officers of any state, nor any corporation or individual wielding power under state authority for the public benefit or the public convenience, can,
consistently either with the freedom established by the fundamental law, or with
that equality of civil rights which now belongs to every citizen, discriminate against
freemen or citizens, in their civil rights, because of their race, or because they once
labored under disabilities imposed upon them as a race. The rights which congress,
by the act of 1875, endeavored to secure and protect are legal, not social, rights.

For the reasons stated I feel constrained to withhold my assent to the opinion of
the court.

Notes and Questions

(1) Does the language of the Fourteenth Amendment support the Court's conclusion that only "state action" is prohibited by §1? Consider the following:

> [T]he Equal Protection Clause says that no state shall "deny" to any person
> the equal protection of the laws. Emphasis on the word "deny" is impor-
> tant. The problem is often stated in terms of "state action," that is, has the
> state acted in such a way as to offend the Equal Protection Clause? While
> the term "state action" is useful as a convenient expression for designating
> the basic problem, it is important to observe that the Constitution does not
> use the word "action," a word which is really misleading because it suggests
> that a violation of the Equal Protection Clause can arise only when the state
> acts in some affirmative way. It is well to emphasize the use of the word
> "deny," since denial of equal rights may occur either by positive action or by
> failure of the state to act in an appropriate way in a given situation.

Paul Kauper, Civil Liberties and the Constitution 128–130 (1962).

(2) Under the majority's view, state action would be present if a state legislature
enacted a law requiring racial discrimination by inns and other places of public
accommodation. Would the majority agree that state action is also present when
the state tolerates the discrimination by failing to enact legislation prohibiting the
conduct? Should the Fourteenth Amendment extend to a state's tolerance of a discriminatory practice?

> It should be clear that a state may be connected to the asserted depriva-
> tion by its tolerance of the challenged practice as well as by its positive acts.
> To illustrate, assuming that a right to do something is protected by "due
> process," how may a state "deprive any person" of that right? Obviously
> it could do so in three formally different but substantively similar ways.
> First, it could act to end the right by simply outlawing activities involving

exercises of that right. Second, it could create or explicitly approve activities by some nongovernmental entities which would limit or eliminate the right. Third, observing that absent laws to the contrary, a practice of some nongovernmental persons will exist in a form which limits or eliminates the right, the state could do nothing. Despite traditional theory it seems hard to contend that the state has done less "depriving" of the right in the third alternative. The state has acted to set a priority between the two conflicting private rights if the challenged practice is lawful within the state.

Robert Glennon, Jr. & John Nowak, *A Functional Analysis of the Fourteenth Amendment "State Action" Requirement*, 1976 SUP. CT. REV. 221, 229–230.[9]

(3) The majority's narrow interpretation of the Thirteenth Amendment was rejected in *Jones v. Alfred Mayer Co.*, 392 U.S. 409 (1968). Similarly the precise scope of congressional power under §5 of the Fourteenth Amendment has been the subject of much debate. *See, e.g., City of Boerne v. Flores*, 521 U.S. 507 (1997); *Oregon v. Mitchell*, 400 U.S. 112 (1970); *Katzenbach v. Morgan*, 384 U.S. 641 (1966); *United States v. Guest*, 383 U.S. 745 (1966); *Symposium: Reflections on City of Boerne v. Flores*, 39 WM. & MARY L. REV. 597 (1998); Robert Burt, *Miranda and Title II: A Morgantic Marriage*, 1969 SUP. CT. REV. 81; William Cohen, *Congressional Power to Interpret Due Process and Equal Protection*, 27 STAN. L. REV. 603 (1975).

(4) Does the decision in the *Civil Rights Cases* suggest that Congress wisely based the 1964 Civil Rights Act on the Commerce Clause and not on the Fourteenth Amendment? *See* Ch. 4, *supra*.

(5) The basic proposition of the *Civil Rights Cases* — that the Fourteenth Amendment reaches only "state action" — has not been abandoned during the past century. Indeed, the state action requirement remains very much a part of Fourteenth Amendment jurisprudence.

Jackson v. Metropolitan Edison Company

United States Supreme Court
419 U.S. 345, 95 S. Ct. 449, 42 L. Ed. 2d 477 (1974)

MR. JUSTICE REHNQUIST delivered the opinion of the Court.

Respondent Metropolitan Edison Co. is a privately owned and operated Pennsylvania corporation which holds a certificate of public convenience issued by the Pennsylvania Public Utility Commission empowering it to deliver electricity to a service area which includes the city of York, Pa. As a condition of holding its certificate, it is subject to extensive regulation by the Commission. Under a provision of its general tariff filed with the Commission, it has the right to discontinue service to any customer on reasonable notice of nonpayment of bills.

---

9. Copyright © 1976 by The University of Chicago Press. Reprinted by permission.

Petitioner Catherine Jackson is a resident of York, who has received electricity in the past from respondent. Until September 1970, petitioner received electric service to her home in York under an account with respondent in her own name. When her account was terminated because of asserted delinquency in payments due for service, a new account with respondent was opened in the name of one James Dodson, another occupant of the residence, and service to the residence was resumed. There is a dispute as to whether payments due under the Dodson account for services provided during this period were ever made. In August 1971, Dodson left the residence. Service continued thereafter but concededly no payments were made. Petitioner states that no bills were received during this period.

On October 6, 1971, employees of Metropolitan came to the residence and inquired as to Dodson's present address. Petitioner stated that it was unknown to her. On the following day, another employee visited the residence and informed petitioner that the meter had been tampered with so as not to register amounts used. She disclaimed knowledge of this and requested that the service account for her home be shifted from Dodson's name to that of one Robert Jackson, later identified as her 12-year-old son. Four days later on October 11, 1971, without further notice to petitioner, Metropolitan employees disconnected her service.

Petitioner then filed suit against Metropolitan in the United States District Court under the Civil Rights Act of 1871, 42 U.S.C. § 1983, seeking damages for the termination and an injunction requiring Metropolitan to continue providing power to her residence until she had been afforded notice, a hearing, and an opportunity to pay any amounts found due. She urged that under state law she had an entitlement to reasonably continuous electrical service to her home and that Metropolitan's termination of her service for alleged nonpayment, action allowed by a provision of its general tariff filed with the Commission, constituted "state action" depriving her of property in violation of the Fourteenth Amendment's guarantee of due process of law.

The District Court granted Metropolitan's motion to dismiss petitioner's complaint on the ground that the termination did not constitute state action and hence was not subject to judicial scrutiny under the Fourteenth Amendment. On appeal, the United States Court of Appeals for the Third Circuit affirmed, also finding an absence of state action. We granted certiorari to review this judgment.

The Due Process Clause of the Fourteenth Amendment provides: "[N]or shall any State deprive any person of life, liberty, or property, without due process of law." In 1883, this Court in the *Civil Rights Cases* affirmed the essential dichotomy set forth in that Amendment between deprivation by the State, subject to scrutiny under its provisions, and private conduct, "however discriminatory or wrongful," against which the Fourteenth Amendment offers no shield.

While the principle that private action is immune from the restrictions of the Fourteenth Amendment is well established and easily stated, the question whether particular conduct is "private," on the one hand, or "state action," on the other, frequently admits of no easy answer.

Here the action complained of was taken by a utility company which is privately owned and operated, but which in many particulars of its business is subject to extensive state regulation. The mere fact that a business is subject to state regulation does not by itself convert its action into that of the State for purposes of the Fourteenth Amendment. Nor does the fact that the regulation is extensive and detailed, as in the case of most public utilities, do so. It may well be that acts of a heavily regulated utility with at least something of a governmentally protected monopoly will more readily be found to be "state" acts than will the acts of an entity lacking these characteristics. But the inquiry must be whether there is a sufficiently close nexus between the State and the challenged action of the regulated entity so that the action of the latter may be fairly treated as that of the State itself.

Petitioner first argues that "state action" is present because of the monopoly status allegedly conferred upon Metropolitan by the State of Pennsylvania. As a factual matter, it may well be doubted that the State ever granted or guaranteed Metropolitan a monopoly. But assuming that it had, this fact is not determinative in considering whether Metropolitan's termination of service to petitioner was "state action" for purposes of the Fourteenth Amendment.

Petitioner next urges that state action is present because respondent provides an essential public service required to be supplied on a reasonably continuous basis by Pa. Stat. Ann., Tit. 66, § 1171 (1959), and hence performs a "public function." We have, of course, found state action present in the exercise by a private entity of powers traditionally exclusively reserved to the State. If we were dealing with the exercise by Metropolitan of some power delegated to it by the State which is traditionally associated with sovereignty, such as eminent domain, our case would be quite a different one. But while the Pennsylvania statute imposes an obligation to furnish service on regulated utilities, it imposes no such obligation on the State.

Perhaps in recognition of the fact that the supplying of utility service is not traditionally the exclusive prerogative of the State, petitioner invites the expansion of the doctrine of this limited line of cases into a broad principle that all businesses "affected with the public interest" are state actors in all their actions.

Doctors, optometrists, lawyers, Metropolitan, and [an] upstate New York grocery selling a quart of milk are all in regulated businesses, providing arguably essential goods and services, "affected with a public interest." We do not believe that such a status converts their every action, absent more, into that of the State.

We also reject the notion that Metropolitan's termination is state action because the State "has specifically authorized and approved" the termination practice. In the instant case, Metropolitan filed with the Public Utility Commission a general tariff — a provision of which states Metropolitan's right to terminate service for nonpayment. This provision has appeared in Metropolitan's previously filed tariffs for many years and has never been the subject of a hearing or other scrutiny by the Commission. Although the Commission did hold hearings on portions of Metropolitan's general tariff relating to a general rate increase, it never even considered the reinsertion of this provision in the newly filed general tariff. The provision became effective 60 days after filing when not disapproved by the Commission.

The nature of governmental regulation of private utilities is such that a utility may frequently be required by the state regulatory scheme to obtain approval for practices a business regulated in less detail would be free to institute without any approval from a regulatory body. Approval by a state utility commission of such a request from a regulated utility, where the commission has not put its own weight on the side of the proposed practice by ordering it, does not transmute a practice initiated by the utility and approved by the commission into "state action." At most, the Commission's failure to overturn this practice amounted to no more than a determination that a Pennsylvania utility was authorized to employ such a practice if it so desired. Respondent's exercise of the choice allowed by state law where the initiative comes from it and not from the State, does not make its action in doing so "state action" for purposes of the Fourteenth Amendment.

All of petitioner's arguments taken together show no more than that Metropolitan was a heavily regulated, privately owned utility, enjoying at least a partial monopoly in the providing of electrical service within its territory, and that it elected to terminate service to petitioner in a manner which the Pennsylvania Public Utility Commission found permissible under state law. Under our decision this is not sufficient to connect the State of Pennsylvania with respondent's action so as to make the latter's conduct attributable to the State for purposes of the Fourteenth Amendment.

The judgment of the Court of Appeals for the Third Circuit is therefore Affirmed.

Mr. Justice Douglas, dissenting.

A particularized inquiry into the circumstances of each case is necessary in order to determine whether a given factual situation falls within "the variety of individual-state relationships which the [Fourteenth] Amendment was designed to embrace." [T]he dispositive question in any state-action case is not whether any single fact or relationship presents a sufficient degree of state involvement, but rather whether the aggregate of all relevant factors compels a finding of state responsibility.

In the aggregate, these factors depict a monopolist providing essential public services as a licensee of the State and within a framework of extensive state supervision and control. The particular regulations at issue, promulgated by the monopolist, were authorized by state law and were made enforceable by the weight and authority of the State. Moreover, the State retains the power of oversight to review and amend the regulations if the public interest so requires. Respondent's actions are sufficiently intertwined with those of the State, and its termination-of-service provisions are sufficiently buttressed by state law to warrant a holding that respondent's actions in terminating this householder's service were "state action."

Mr. Justice Marshall, dissenting.

The pattern of cooperation between Metropolitan Edison and the State has led to significant state involvement in virtually every phase of the company's business. The majority, however, accepts the relevance of the State's regulatory scheme only to the extent that it demonstrates state support for the challenged termination procedure. Moreover, after concluding that the State in this case had not approved the company's termination procedures, the majority suggests that even state authorization and approval would not be sufficient: the State would apparently have to *order* the termination practice in question to satisfy the majority's state-action test.

I question the wisdom of giving such short shrift to the extensive interaction between the company and the State, and focusing solely on the extent of state support for the particular activity under challenge. In cases where the State's only significant involvement is through financial support or limited regulation of the private entity, it may be well to inquire whether the State's involvement suggests state approval of the objectionable conduct. But where the State has so thoroughly insinuated itself into the operations of the enterprise, it should not be fatal if the State has not affirmatively sanctioned the particular practice in question.

[I]n any event that the State *has* given its approval to Metropolitan Edison's termination procedures. The State Utility Commission approved a tariff provision under which the company reserved the right to discontinue its service on reasonable notice for nonpayment of bills.

The fact that the Metropolitan Edison Co. supplies an essential public service that is in many communities supplied by the government weighs more heavily for me than for the majority. The Court concedes that state action might be present if the activity in question were "traditionally associated with sovereignty," but it then undercuts that point by suggesting that a particular service is not a public function if the State in question has not required that it be governmentally operated. This reads the "public function" argument too narrowly. The whole point of the "public function" cases is to look behind the State's decision to provide public services through private parties. In my view, utility service is traditionally identified with the State through universal public regulation or ownership to a degree sufficient to render it a "public function."

What is perhaps most troubling about the Court's opinion is that it would appear to apply to a broad range of claimed constitutional violations by the company. The Court has not adopted the notion, accepted elsewhere, that different standards should apply to state action analysis when different constitutional claims are presented. . . . Thus, the majority's analysis would seemingly apply as well to a company that refused to extend service to Negroes, welfare recipients, or any other group that the company preferred, for its own reasons, not to serve. I cannot believe that the State's involvement with the utility company was not sufficient to impose upon the company an obligation to meet the constitutional mandate of nondiscrimination. Yet nothing in the analysis of the majority opinion suggests otherwise.

I dissent.

Flagg Bros., Inc. v. Brooks

United States Supreme Court
436 U.S. 149, 98 S. Ct. 1729, 56 L. Ed. 2d 185 (1978)

Mr. Justice Rehnquist delivered the opinion of the Court.

The question presented by this litigation is whether a warehouseman's proposed sale of goods entrusted to him for storage, as permitted by New York Uniform Commercial Code §7-210 (McKinney 1964), is an action properly attributable to the State of New York. The District Court found that the warehouseman's conduct was not that of the State, and dismissed this suit for want of jurisdiction under 28 U.S.C. §1343(3). The Court of Appeals for the Second Circuit, in reversing the judgment of the District Court, found sufficient state involvement with the proposed sale to invoke the provisions of the Due Process Clause of the Fourteenth Amendment. We agree with the District Court, and we therefore reverse.

I

According to her complaint, the allegations of which we must accept as true, respondent Shirley Brooks and her family were evicted from their apartment in Mount Vernon, N.Y., on June 13, 1973. The city marshal arranged for Brooks' possessions to be stored by petitioner Flagg Brothers, Inc., in its warehouse. Brooks was informed of the cost of moving and storage, and she instructed the workmen to proceed, although she found the price too high. On August 25, 1973, after a series of disputes over the validity of the charges being claimed by petitioner Flagg Brothers, Brooks received a letter demanding that her account be brought up to date within 10 days "or your furniture will be sold." A series of subsequent letters from respondent and her attorneys produced no satisfaction.

Brooks thereupon initiated this class action in the District Court under 42 U.S.C. §1983, seeking damages, an injunction against the threatened sale of her belongings, and the declaration that such a sale pursuant to §7-210 would violate the Due Process and Equal Protection Clauses of the Fourteenth Amendment. She was later joined in her action by Gloria Jones, another resident of Mount Vernon whose goods had been stored by Flagg Brothers following her eviction. The American Warehousemen's Association and the International Association of Refrigerated Warehouses, Inc., moved to intervene as defendants, as did the Attorney General of New York, and others seeking to defend the constitutionality of the challenged statute. On July 7, 1975, the District Court, relying primarily on our decision in *Jackson v. Metropolitan Edison Co.* dismissed the complaint for failure to state a claim for relief under §1983.

A divided panel of the Court of Appeals reversed. The court concluded that this delegation of power [traditionally exercised by a sheriff] constituted sufficient state action to support federal jurisdiction under 28 U.S.C. § 1343(3).

We granted certiorari to resolve the conflict over this provision of the Uniform Commercial Code, in effect in 49 States and the District of Columbia, and to address the important question it presents concerning the meaning of "state action" as that term is associated with the Fourteenth Amendment.

It must be noted that respondents have named no public officials as defendants in this action. The City Marshal, who supervised their evictions, was dismissed from the case by the consent of all the parties. This total absence of overt official involvement plainly distinguishes this case from earlier decisions imposing procedural restrictions on creditors' remedies such as *North Georgia Finishing, Inc. v. Di-Chem, Inc.*, 419 U.S. 601 (1975); *Fuentes v. Shevin*, 407 U.S. 67 (1972); *Sniadach v. Family Finance Corp.*, 395 U.S. 337 (1969). In those cases, the Court was careful to point out that the dictates of the Due Process Clause "attac[h] only to the deprivation of an interest encompassed within the Fourteenth Amendment's protection." While as a factual matter any person with sufficient physical power may deprive a person of his property, only a State or a private person whose action "may be fairly treated as that of the State itself," may deprive him of "an interest encompassed within the Fourteenth Amendment's protection." Thus, the only issue presented by this case is whether Flagg Brothers' action may fairly be attributed to the State of New York. We conclude that it may not.

III

Respondents' primary contention is that New York has delegated to Flagg Brothers a power "traditionally exclusively reserved to the State." *Jackson.* They argue that the resolution of private disputes is a traditional function of civil government, and that the State in § 7-210 has delegated this function to Flagg Brothers. Respondents, however, have read too much into the language of our previous cases. While many functions have been traditionally performed by governments, very few have been "exclusively reserved to the State."

One such area has been elections. While the Constitution protects private rights of association and advocacy with regard to the election of public officials, our cases make it clear that the conduct of the elections themselves is an exclusively public function. The doctrine does not reach to all forms of private political activity, but encompasses only state-regulated elections or elections conducted by organizations which in practice produce "the uncontested choice of public officials."

A second line of cases under the public-function doctrine originated with *Marsh v. Alabama*, 326 U.S. 501 (1946). [T]he Gulf Shipbuilding Corp. performed all the necessary municipal functions in the town of Chickasaw, Ala., which it owned. Under those circumstances, the Court concluded it was bound to recognize the right of a group of Jehovah's Witnesses to distribute religious literature on its streets.

These two branches of the public-function doctrine have in common the feature of exclusivity. [T]he proposed sale by Flagg Brothers under § 7-210 is not the only means of resolving this purely private dispute. Respondent Brooks has never alleged that state law barred her from seeking a waiver of Flagg Brothers' right to sell her goods at the time she authorized their storage. Presumably, respondent Jones, who alleges that she never authorized the storage of her goods, could have sought to replevy her goods at any time under state law. The challenged statute itself provides a damages remedy against the warehouseman for violations of its provisions. This system of rights and remedies, recognizing the traditional place of private arrangements in ordering relationships in the commercial world, can hardly be said to have delegated to Flagg Brothers an exclusive prerogative of the sovereign.

Whatever the particular remedies available under New York law, we do not consider a more detailed description of them necessary to our conclusion that the settlement of disputes between debtors and creditors is not traditionally an exclusive public function. Creditors and debtors have had available to them historically a far wider number of choices than has one who would be an elected public official, or a member of Jehovah's Witnesses who wished to distribute literature in Chickasaw, Ala., at the time *Marsh* was decided.

Thus, even, if we were inclined to extend the sovereign-function doctrine outside of its present carefully confined bounds, the field of private commercial transactions would be a particularly inappropriate area into which to expand it. We conclude that our sovereign-function cases do not support a finding of state action here.

[W]e would be remiss if we did not note that there are a number of state and municipal functions not covered by our election cases or governed by the reasoning of *Marsh* which have been administered with a greater degree of exclusivity by States and municipalities than has the function of so-called "dispute resolution." Among these are such functions as education, fire and police protection, and tax collection. We express no view as to the extent, if any, to which a city or State might be free to delegate to private parties the performance of such functions and thereby avoid the strictures of the Fourteenth Amendment. The mere recitation of these possible permutations and combinations of factual situations suffices to caution us that their resolution should abide the necessity of deciding them.

IV

Respondents further urge that Flagg Brothers' proposed action is properly attributable to the State because the State has authorized and encouraged it in enacting § 7-210. Our cases state "that a State is responsible for the act of a private party when the State, by its law, has compelled the act." This Court, however, has never held that a State's mere acquiescence in a private action converts that action into that of the State. [See] *Jackson.*

It is quite immaterial that the State has embodied its decision not to act in statutory form. If New York had no commercial statutes at all, its courts would still be faced with the decision whether to prohibit or to permit the sort of sale threatened here the first time an aggrieved bailor came before them for relief. A judicial decision to deny relief would be no less an "authorization" or "encouragement" of that sale than the legislature's decision embodied in this statute. It was recognized in the earliest interpretations of the Fourteenth Amendment "that a State may act through different agencies, — either by its legislative, its executive, or its judicial authorities; and the prohibitions of the amendment extend to all action of the State" infringing rights protected thereby. *Virginia v. Rives*, 100 U.S. 313, 318 (1880). If the mere denial of judicial relief is considered sufficient encouragement to make the State responsible for those private acts, all private deprivations of property would be converted into public acts whenever the State, for whatever reason, denies relief sought by the putative property owner.

Here, the State of New York has not compelled the sale of a bailor's goods, but has merely announced the circumstances under which its courts will not interfere with a private sale. Indeed, the crux of respondents' complaint is not that the State has acted, but that it has refused to act. This statutory refusal to act is no different in principle from an ordinary statute of limitations whereby the State declines to provide a remedy for private deprivations of property after the passage of a given period of time.

We conclude that the allegations of these complaints do not establish a violation of these respondents' Fourteenth Amendment rights by either petitioner Flagg Brothers or the State of New York.

Reversed.

MR. JUSTICE MARSHALL, dissenting.

Although I join my Brother Stevens' dissenting opinion, I write separately to emphasize certain aspects of the majority opinion that I find particularly disturbing.

I cannot remain silent as the Court demonstrates, not for the first time, an attitude of callous indifference to the realities of life for the poor. See, e.g., *Beal v. Doe*, 432 U.S. 438, 455–457 (1977) (Marshall, J., dissenting); *United States v. Kras*, 409 U.S. 434, 458–460 (1973) (Marshall, J., dissenting). It blandly asserts that "respondent Jones could have sought to replevy her goods at any time under state law." In order to obtain replevin in New York, however, respondent Jones would first have had to present to a sheriff an "undertaking" from a surety by which the latter would be bound to pay "not less than twice the value" of the goods involved and perhaps substantially more, depending in part on the size of the potential judgment against the debtor. Sureties do not provide such bonds without receiving both a substantial payment in advance and some assurance of the debtor's ability to pay any judgment awarded.

Respondent Jones, according to her complaint, took home $87 per week from her job, had been evicted from her apartment, and faced a potential liability to the warehouseman of at least $335, an amount she could not afford. The Court's assumption that respondent would have been able to obtain a bond, and thus secure return of her household goods, must under the circumstances be regarded as highly questionable. While the Court is technically correct that respondent "could have sought" replevin, it is also true that, given adequate funds, respondent could have paid her rent and remained in her apartment, thereby avoiding eviction and the seizure of her household goods by the warehouseman. But we cannot close our eyes to the realities that led to this litigation. Just as respondent lacked the funds to prevent eviction, it seems clear that, once her goods were seized, she had no practical choice but to leave them with the warehouseman, where they were subject to forced sale for nonpayment of storage charges.

I am also troubled by the Court's cavalier treatment of the place of historical factors in the "state action" inquiry. While we are, of course, not bound by what occurred centuries ago in England, the test adopted by the Court itself requires us to decide what functions have been "*traditionally* exclusively reserved to the State," *Jackson*. Such an issue plainly cannot be resolved in a historical vacuum. New York's highest court has stated that "[i]n [New York] the execution of a lien traditionally has been the function of the Sheriff."

By ignoring this history, the Court approaches the question before us as if it can be decided without reference to the role that the State has always played in lien execution by forced sale. The state-action doctrine, as developed in our past cases, requires that we come down to earth and decide the issue here with careful attention to the State's traditional role.

I dissent.

MR. JUSTICE STEVENS, with whom MR. JUSTICE WHITE and MR. JUSTICE MARSHALL join, dissenting.

There is no question in this case but that respondents have a property interest in the possessions that the warehouseman proposes to sell. It is also clear that, whatever power of sale the warehouseman has, it does not derive from the consent of the respondents. The claimed power derives solely from the State, and specifically from § 7-210 of the New York Uniform Commercial Code. The question is whether a state statute which authorizes a private party to deprive a person of his property without his consent must meet the requirements of the Due Process Clause of the Fourteenth Amendment. This question must be answered in the affirmative unless the State has virtually unlimited power to transfer interests in private property without any procedural protections.

In determining that New York's statute cannot be scrutinized under the Due Process Clause, the Court reasons that the warehouseman's proposed sale is solely private action because the state statute "*permits* but does not compel" the sale, and because the warehouseman has not been delegated a power "*exclusively* reserved to the State". Under this approach a State could enact laws authorizing private citizens to use self-help in countless situations without any possibility of federal challenge. A state statute could authorize the warehouseman to retain all proceeds of the lien sale, even if they far exceeded the amount of the alleged debt; it could authorize finance companies to enter private homes to repossess merchandise; or indeed, it could authorize "any person with sufficient physical power," to acquire and sell the property of his weaker neighbor. An attempt to challenge the validity of any such outrageous statute would be defeated by the reasoning the Court uses today: The Court's rationale would characterize action pursuant to such a statute as purely private action, which the State permits but does not compel, in an area not exclusively reserved to the State.

As these examples suggest, the distinctions between "permission" and "compulsion" on the one hand, and "exclusive" and "nonexclusive," on the other, cannot be determinative factors in state-action analysis. [T]here are many intervening levels of state involvement in private conduct that may support a finding of state action. In this case, the State of New York, by enacting § 7-210 of the Uniform Commercial Code, has acted in the most effective and unambiguous way a State can act. This section specifically authorizes petitioner Flagg Brothers to sell respondents' possessions; it details the procedures that petitioner must follow; and it grants petitioner the power to convey good title to goods that are now owned by respondents to a third party.

New York has authorized the warehouseman to perform what is clearly a state function. The test of what is a state function for purposes of the Due Process Clause has been variously phrased. Most frequently the issue is presented in terms of whether the State has delegated a function traditionally and historically associated with sovereignty. See, e.g., *Jackson v. Metropolitan Edison Co.*; *Evans v. Newton*, 382 U.S. 296, 299 [1965]. In this Court, petitioners have attempted to argue that the nonconsensual transfer of property rights is not a traditional function of the sovereign. The overwhelming historical evidence is to the contrary, however, and the Court wisely does not adopt this position. Instead, the Court reasons that state action cannot be found because the State has not delegated to the warehouseman an *exclusive* sovereign function. This distinction, however, is not consistent with our prior decisions on state action; is not even adhered to by the Court in this case; and, most importantly, is inconsistent with the line of cases beginning with *Sniadach v. Family Finance Corp.*

Whether termed "traditional," "exclusive," or "significant," the state power to order binding, nonconsensual resolution of a conflict between debtor and creditor is exactly the sort of power with which the Due Process Clause is concerned. And the State's delegation of that power to a private party is, accordingly, subject to due process scrutiny.

It is important to emphasize that, contrary to the Court's apparent fears, this conclusion does not even remotely suggest that "all private deprivations of property [will] be converted into public acts whenever the State, for whatever reason, denies relief sought by the putative property owner." The focus is not on the private deprivation but on the state authorization. The State's conduct in this case takes the concrete form of a statutory enactment, and it is that statute that may be challenged.

[I]t is obviously true that the overwhelming majority of disputes in our society are resolved in the private sphere. But it is no longer possible, if it ever was, to believe that a sharp line can be drawn between private and public actions. The Court today holds that our examination of state delegations of power should be limited to those rare instances where the State has ceded one of its "exclusive" powers. As indicated, I believe that this limitation is neither logical nor practical. More troubling, this description of what is state action does not even attempt to reflect the concerns of the Due Process Clause, for the state-action doctrine is, after all, merely one aspect of this broad constitutional protection.

In the broadest sense, we expect government "to provide a reasonable and fair framework of rules which facilitate commercial transactions." This "framework of rules" is premised on the assumption that the State will control nonconsensual deprivations of property and that the State's control will, in turn, be subject to the restrictions of the Due Process Clause. The power to order legally binding surrenders of property and the constitutional restrictions on that power are necessary correlatives in our system. In effect, today's decision allows the State to divorce these two elements by the simple expedient of transferring the implementation of its policy to private parties. Because the Fourteenth Amendment does not countenance such a division of power and responsibility, I respectfully dissent.

Lugar v. Edmondson Oil Co.

United States Supreme Court
457 U.S. 922, 102 S. Ct. 2744, 73 L. Ed. 2d 482 (1982)

JUSTICE WHITE delivered the opinion of the Court.

In 1977, petitioner, a lessee-operator of a truckstop in Virginia, was indebted to his supplier, Edmondson Oil Co., Inc. Edmondson sued on the debt in Virginia state court. Ancillary to that action and pursuant to state law, Edmondson sought prejudgment attachment of certain of petitioner's property. The prejudgment attachment procedure required only that Edmondson allege, in an *ex parte* petition, a belief that petitioner was disposing of or might dispose of his property in order to defeat his creditors. Acting upon that petition, a Clerk of the state court issued a writ of attachment, which was then executed by the County Sheriff. This effectively sequestered petitioner's property, although it was left in his possession. Pursuant to the statute, a hearing on the propriety of the attachment and levy was later conducted. Thirty-four days after the levy, a state trial judge ordered the attachment dismissed because Edmondson had failed to establish the statutory grounds for attachment alleged in the petition.

Petitioner subsequently brought this action under 42 U.S.C. §1983 against Edmondson and its president. His complaint alleged that in attaching his property respondents had acted jointly with the State to deprive him of his property without due process of law. The lower courts construed the complaint as alleging a due process violation both from a misuse of the Virginia procedure and from the statutory procedure itself. He sought compensatory and punitive damages for specified financial loss allegedly caused by the improvident attachment.

[T]he District Court held that the alleged actions of the respondents did not constitute state action as required by the Fourteenth Amendment and that the complaint therefore did not state a claim upon which relief could be granted under §1983. Petitioner appealed; the Court of Appeals for the Fourth Circuit, sitting en banc, affirmed, with three dissenters.

As a matter of substantive constitutional law the state-action requirement reflects judicial recognition of the fact that "most rights secured by the Constitution are protected only against infringement by governments." Careful adherence to the "state action" requirement reserves an area of individual freedom by limiting the reach of federal law and federal judicial power. It also avoids imposing on the State, its agencies or officials, responsibility for conduct for which they cannot fairly be blamed. A major consequence is to require the courts to respect the limits of their own power as directed against state governments and private interests. Whether this is good or bad policy, it is a fundamental fact of our political order.

Our cases have accordingly insisted that the conduct allegedly causing the deprivation of a federal right be fairly attributable to the State. These cases reflect a two-part approach to this question of "fair attribution." First, the deprivation must be caused by the exercise of some right or privilege created by the State or by a rule of conduct imposed by the state or by a person for whom the State is responsible. Second, the party charged with the deprivation must be a person who may fairly be said to be a state actor. This may be because he is a state official, because he has acted together with or has obtained significant aid from state officials, or because his conduct is otherwise chargeable to the State. Without a limit such as this, private parties could face constitutional litigation whenever they seek to rely on some state rule governing their interactions with the community surrounding them.

Although related, these two principles are not the same. They collapse into each other when the claim of a constitutional deprivation is directed against a party whose official character is such as to lend the weight of the State to his decisions. The two principles diverge when the constitutional claim is directed against a party without such apparent authority, i.e., against a private party.

Turning to this case, the first question is whether the claimed deprivation has resulted from the exercise of a right or privilege having its source in state authority. The second question is whether, under the facts of this case, respondents, who are private parties, may be appropriately characterized as "state actors."

Count one [in the complaint] describes the procedures followed by respondents in obtaining the prejudgment attachment as well as the fact that the state court subsequently ordered the attachment dismissed because respondents had not met their burden under state law. Petitioner then summarily states that this sequence of events deprived him of his property without due process. Although it is not clear whether petitioner is referring to the state-created procedure or the misuse of that procedure by respondents, we agree with the lower courts that the better reading of the complaint is that petitioner challenges the state statute as procedurally defective under the Fourteenth Amendment.

While private misuse of a state statute does not describe conduct that can be attributed to the State, the procedural scheme created by the statute obviously is the product of state action. This is subject to constitutional restraints and properly may be addressed in a § 1983 action, if the second element of the state-action requirement is met as well.

[W]e have consistently held that a private party's joint participation with state officials in the seizure of disputed property is sufficient to characterize that party as a "state actor" for purposes of the Fourteenth Amendment. The Court of Appeals erred in holding that in this context "joint participation" required something more than invoking the aid of state officials to take advantage of state-created attachment procedures. That holding is contrary to the conclusions we have reached as to the applicability of due process standards to such procedures. Whatever may be true in other contexts, this is sufficient when the State has created a system whereby state officials will attach property on the *ex parte* application of one party to a private dispute.

Chief Justice Burger, dissenting. [Omitted.]

Justice Powell, with whom Justice Rehnquist and Justice O'Connor join, dissenting.

Today's decision is a disquieting example of how expansive judicial decisionmaking can ensnare a person who had every reason to believe he was acting in strict accordance with law. The case began nearly five years ago as the outgrowth of a simple suit on a debt in a Virginia state court. Respondent — a small wholesale oil dealer in Southside, Va. — brought suit against petitioner Lugar, a truckstop owner who had failed to pay a debt. The suit was to collect this indebtedness. Fearful that petitioner might dissipate his assets before the debt was collected, respondent also filed a petition in state court seeking sequestration of certain of Lugar's assets. He did so under a Virginia statute, traceable at least to 1819, that permits creditors to seek prejudgment attachment of property in the possession of debtors. No court had questioned the validity of the statute, and it remains presumptively valid. The Clerk of the state court duly issued a writ of attachment, and the County Sheriff then executed it. There is no allegation that respondent conspired with the state officials to deny petitioner the fair protection of state or federal law.

This Court holds that respondent, a private citizen who did no more than commence a legal action of a kind traditionally initiated by private parties, thereby engaged in "state action." This decision is as unprecedented as it is implausible. It is plainly unjust to the respondent, and the Court makes no argument to the contrary. Respondent, who was represented by counsel, could have had no notion that his filing of a petition in state court, in the effort to secure payment of a private debt, made him a "state actor" liable in damages for allegedly unconstitutional action by the Commonwealth of Virginia.

Notes and Questions

(1) Professor Tribe has written that the state action requirement is generally thought to serve two primary purposes:

> First, by exempting private action from the reach of the Constitution's prohibitions, it stops the Constitution short of preempting individual liberty — of denying to individuals the freedom to make certain choices, such as choices of the persons with whom they will associate. Such freedom is basic under any conception of liberty, but it would be lost if individuals had to conform their conduct to the Constitution's demands. Second, the state action requirement reinforces the two chief principles of division which organize the governmental structure that the Constitution creates: federalism and the separation of powers. By limiting the scope of the rights which the Constitution guarantees, the state action requirement limits the range of wrongs which the federal judiciary may right in the absence of congressional action, and thus creates a zone of action which, in the absence of valid congressional legislation, is reserved to the states unencumbered by the constraints of federal supremacy.

LAURENCE TRIBE, AMERICAN CONSTITUTIONAL LAW § 18-2 (2d ed. 1988).

(2) Does the present Court agree that those are the purposes of the state action requirement? Were those purposes served by the results in *Jackson, Flagg Brothers,* and *Lugar?*

(3) In *Edmonson v. Leesville Concrete Company*, 500 U.S. 614 (1991), the Court held that a private litigant's use of peremptory challenges to exclude jurors based on race violates the equal protection component of the Fifth Amendment Due Process Clause. The Court first considered whether a private party's exercise of peremptory challenges constitutes state action. The Court found the requisite state action and, in so doing, said:

> The Constitution structures the National Government, confines its actions, and, in regard to certain individual liberties and other specified matters, confines the actions of the States. With a few exceptions, such as the provisions of the Thirteenth Amendment, constitutional guarantees of individual liberty and equal protection do not apply to the actions of private entities. This fundamental limitation on the scope of constitutional guarantees "preserves an area of individual freedom by limiting the reach of federal law" and "avoids imposing on the State, its agencies or officials, responsibility for conduct for which they cannot fairly be blamed." One great object of the Constitution is to permit citizens to structure their private relations as they choose subject only to the constraints of statutory or decisional law.
>
> To implement these principles, courts must consider from time to time where the governmental sphere ends and the private sphere begins. Although the conduct of private parties lies beyond the Constitution's scope in most instances, governmental authority may dominate an activity to such an

extent that its participants must be deemed to act with the authority of the government and, as a result, be subject to constitutional constraints. This is the jurisprudence of state action, which explores the "essential dichotomy" between the private sphere and the public sphere, with all its attendant constitutional obligations.

We begin our discussion within the framework for state action analysis set forth in *Lugar*. . . . We asked first whether the claimed constitutional deprivation resulted from the exercise of a right or privilege having its source in state authority, and second, whether the private party charged with the deprivation could be described in all fairness as a state actor.

There can be no question that the first part of the *Lugar* inquiry is satisfied here. By their very nature, peremptory challenges have no significance outside a court of law. Their sole purpose is to permit litigants to assist the government in the selection of an impartial trier of fact. Peremptory challenges are permitted only when the government, by statute or decisional law, deems it appropriate to allow parties to exclude a given number of persons who otherwise would satisfy the requirements for service on the petit jury.

Given that the statutory authorization for the challenges exercised in this case is clear, the remainder of our state action analysis centers around the second part of the *Lugar* test, whether a private litigant in all fairness must be deemed a government actor in the use of peremptory challenges. Although we have recognized that this aspect of the analysis is often a fact-bound inquiry, our cases disclose certain principles of general application. Our precedents establish that, in determining whether a particular action or course of conduct is governmental in character, it is relevant to examine the following: the extent to which the actor relies on governmental assistance and benefits; whether the actor is performing a traditional governmental function; and whether the injury caused is aggravated in a unique way by the incidents of governmental authority. Based on our application of these three principles to the circumstances here, we hold that the exercise of peremptory challenges by the defendant in the District Court was pursuant to a course of state action.

Although private use of state-sanctioned private remedies or procedures does not rise, by itself, to the level of state action, our cases have found state action when private parties make extensive use of state procedures with "the overt, significant assistance of state officials." It cannot be disputed that, without the overt, significant participation of the government, the peremptory challenge system, as well as the jury trial system of which it is a part, simply could not exist.

[A] private party could not exercise its peremptory challenges absent the overt, significant assistance of the court. The government summons jurors, constrains their freedom of movement, and subjects them to public scrutiny and examination. The party who exercises a challenge invokes the formal authority of the court, which must discharge the prospective juror, thus effecting the "final and practical denial" of the excluded individual's opportunity to serve on the petit jury. Without the direct and indispensable participation of the judge, who beyond all question is a state actor, the peremptory challenge system would serve no purpose. By enforcing a discriminatory peremptory challenge, the court "has not only made itself a party to the [biased act], but has elected to place its power, property and prestige behind the [alleged] discrimination." In so doing, the government has "create[d] the legal framework governing the [challenged] conduct," and in a significant way has involved itself with invidious discrimination.

In determining Leesville's state-actor status, we next consider whether the action in question involves the performance of a traditional function of the government. A traditional function of government is evident here. The peremptory challenge is used in selecting an entity that is a quintessential governmental body, having no attributes of a private actor. The jury exercises the power of the court and of the government that confers the court's jurisdiction.

If a government confers on a private body the power to choose the government's employees or officials, the private body will be bound by the constitutional mandate of race-neutrality.

We find respondent's reliance on *Polk County v. Dodson*, 454 U.S. 312 (1981), unavailing. In that case, we held that a public defender is not a state actor in his general representation of a criminal defendant, even though he may be in his performance of other official duties. While recognizing the employment relation between the public defender and the government, we noted that the relation is otherwise adversarial in nature.

In the ordinary context of civil litigation in which the government is not a party, an adversarial relation does not exist between the government and a private litigant. In the jury-selection process, the government and private litigants work for the same end. Just as a government employee was deemed a private actor because of his purpose and functions in *Dodson*, so here a private entity becomes a government actor for the limited purpose of using peremptories during jury selection. The selection of jurors represents a unique governmental function delegated to private litigants by the government and attributable to the government for purposes of invoking constitutional protections against discrimination by reason of race.

Finally, we note that the injury caused by the discrimination is made more severe because the government permits it to occur within the courthouse itself. Few places are a more real expression of the constitutional authority of the government than a courtroom, where the law itself unfolds.

Within the courtroom, the government invokes its laws to determine the rights of those who stand before it. In full view of the public, litigants press their cases, witnesses give testimony, juries render verdicts, and judges act with the utmost care to ensure that justice is done.

Race discrimination within the courtroom raises serious questions as to the fairness of the proceedings conducted there. Racial bias mars the integrity of the judicial system and prevents the idea of democratic government from becoming a reality. In the many times we have addressed the problem of racial bias in our system of justice, we have not 'questioned the premise that racial discrimination in the qualification or selection of jurors offends the dignity of persons and the integrity of the courts." To permit racial exclusion in this official forum compounds the racial insult inherent in judging a citizen by the color of his or her skin.

Justice O'Connor, joined by Chief Justice Rehnquist and Justice Scalia, dissented:

Not everything that happens in a courtroom is state action. A trial, particularly a civil trial, is by design largely a stage on which private parties may act; it is a forum through which they can resolve their disputes in a peaceful and ordered manner. The government erects the platform; it does not thereby become responsible for all that occurs upon it. As much as we would like to eliminate completely from the courtroom the specter of racial discrimination, the Constitution does not sweep that broadly. Because I believe that a peremptory strike by a private litigant is fundamentally a matter of private choice and not state action, I dissent.

The entirety of the Government's actual participation in the peremptory process boils down to a single fact: "When a lawyer exercises a peremptory challenge, the judge advises the juror he or she has been excused." This is not significant participation. The judge's action in "advising" a juror that he or she has been excused is state action to be sure. It is, however, if not *de minimis*, far from what our cases have required in order to hold the government "responsible" for private action or to find that private actors "represent" the government. The government "normally can be held responsible for a private decision only when it has exercised coercive power or has provided such significant encouragement, either overt or covert, that the choice must in law be deemed to be that of the State."

As an initial matter, the judge does not "encourage" the use of a peremptory challenge at all. The decision to strike a juror is entirely up to the litigant, and the reasons for doing so are of no consequence to the judge. It is the attorney who strikes. The judge does little more than acquiesce in this decision by excusing the juror. In point of fact, the government has virtually no role in the use of peremptory challenges. Indeed, there are jurisdictions in which, with the consent of the parties, *voir dire* and jury selection may take place in the absence of any court personnel.

Jackson is a more appropriate analogy to this case. The termination was not state action because the State had done nothing to encourage the particular termination practices. The similarity to this case is obvious. The Court's "overt, significant" government participation amounts to the fact that the government provides the mechanism whereby a litigant can choose to exercise a peremptory challenge. That the government allows this choice and that the judge approves it, does not turn this private decision into state action.

To the same effect is *Flagg Bros., Inc. v. Brooks*. We held that "the State of New York is in no way responsible for Flagg Brothers' decision, a decision which the State in § 7-210 permits but does not compel, to threaten to sell these respondents' belongings." Similarly, in the absence of compulsion, or at least encouragement, from the government in the use of peremptory challenges, the government is not responsible.

The Court errs also when it concludes that the exercise of a peremptory challenge is a traditional government function. Whatever reason a private litigant may have for using a peremptory challenge, it is not the government's reason. The government otherwise establishes its requirements for jury service, leaving to the private litigant the unfettered discretion to use the strike for any reason. This is not part of the government's function in establishing the requirements for jury service. The peremptory challenge forms no part of the government's responsibility in selecting a jury.

A peremptory challenge by a private litigant does not meet the Court's standard; it is not a traditional government function. Beyond this, the Court has misstated the law. In order to constitute state action under this doctrine, private conduct must not only comprise something that the government traditionally does, but something that only the government traditionally does. Even if one could fairly characterize the use of a peremptory strike as the performance of the traditional government function of jury selection, it has never been exclusively the function of the government to select juries; peremptory strikes are older than the Republic.

Beyond "significant participation" and "traditional function," the Court's final argument is that the exercise of a peremptory challenge by a private litigant is state action because it takes place in a courtroom. In the end, this is all the Court is left with. The Court is also wrong in its ultimate claim. If *Dodson* stands for anything, it is that the actions of a lawyer in a courtroom do not become those of the government by virtue of their location. This is true even if those actions are based on race.

Racism is a terrible thing. It is irrational, destructive, and mean. Arbitrary discrimination based on race is particularly abhorrent when manifest in a courtroom, a forum established by the government for the resolution of disputes through "quiet rationality." But not every opprobrious and inequitable act is a constitutional violation. The Fifth Amendment's Due Process Clause prohibits only actions for which the Government can be held responsible. The Government is not responsible for everything that occurs in a courtroom. The Government is not responsible for a peremptory challenge by a private litigant. I respectfully dissent.

In a separate dissenting opinion, JUSTICE SCALIA observed:

> The concrete costs of today's decision are not at all doubtful; and they are enormous. We have now added to the duties of already-submerged state and federal trial courts the obligation to assure that race is not included among the other factors (sex, age, religion, political views, economic status) used by private parties in exercising their peremptory challenges. That responsibility would be burden enough if it were not to be discharged through the adversary process; but of course it is. When combined with our decision this Term in *Powers v. Ohio*, 499 U.S. 400 (1991), which held that the party objecting to an allegedly race-based peremptory challenge need not be of the same race as the challenged juror, today's decision means that both sides, in all civil jury cases, no matter what their race (and indeed, even if they are artificial entities such as corporations), may lodge racial-challenged objections and, after those objections have been considered and denied, appeal the denials — with the consequence, if they are successful, of having the judgments against them overturned. Thus, yet another complexity is added to an increasingly Byzantine system of justice that devotes more and more of its energy to sideshows and less and less to the merits of the case. That time will be diverted from other matters, and the overall system of justice will certainly suffer. Alternatively, of course, the States and Congress may simply abolish peremptory challenges, which would cause justice to suffer in a different fashion.

(4) In *Georgia v. McCollum*, 505 U.S. 42 (1992), the Court extended *Edmonson* and held that the Constitution prohibits a criminal defendant from engaging in purposeful discrimination on the ground of race in the exercise of peremptory challenges. Although *McCollum* was decided 7-2, Chief Justice Rehnquist and Justice Thomas suggested that, but for the precedent of *Edmonson*, they would have found no state action in *McCollum*, and Justices O'Connor and Scalia dissented, finding no state action.

(5) Can you distinguish *Edmonson* from *Jackson*? *Flagg Brothers*? *Lugar*?

(6) The issue in *Brentwood Academy v. Tennessee Secondary School Athletic Association*, 531 U.S. 288 (2001), was whether the Association is engaged in state action when it enforces a rule against a member school. The Court described the Association as

> a not-for-profit membership corporation organized to regulate interscholastic sport among the public and private high schools in Tennessee that

belong to it. No school is forced to join, but without any other authority actually regulating interscholastic athletics, it enjoys the memberships of almost all the State's public high schools (some 290 of them or 84% of the Association's voting membership), far outnumbering the 55 private schools that belong. A member school's team may play or scrimmage only against the team of another member, absent a dispensation.

The Court held that the "association's regulatory activity may and should be regarded as state action owing to the pervasive entwinement of state officials in the structure of the association, there being no offsetting reason to see the association's acts in any other way."

This prompted Justice Thomas to respond on behalf of the four dissenting Justices:

> We have never found state action based upon mere "entwinement." Until today, we have found a private organization's acts to constitute state action only when the organization performed a public function; was created, coerced, or encouraged by the government; or acted in a symbiotic relationship with the government. The majority's holding — that the Tennessee Secondary School Athletic Association's (TSSAA) enforcement of its recruiting rule is state action — not only extends state-action doctrine beyond its permissible limits but also encroaches upon the realm of individual freedom that the doctrine was meant to protect.

(7) In *Manhattan Community Access Corp. v. Halleck*, 139 S. Ct. 1921 (2019), the Court held by 5-4 that private operators of public access cable channels are not state actors subject to the First Amendment. Justice Kavanaugh wrote for the majority:

> The New York State Public Service Commission regulates cable franchising in New York State and requires cable operators in the State to set aside channels on their cable systems for public access. 16 N.Y. Codes, Rules & Regs. §§ 895.1(f), 895.4(b) (2018). State law requires that use of the public access channels be free of charge and first-come, first-served. Under state law, the cable operator operates the public access channels unless the local government in the area chooses to itself operate the channels or designates a private entity to operate the channels.
>
> Time Warner (now known as Charter) operates a cable system in Manhattan. Under state law, Time Warner must set aside some channels on its cable system for public access. New York City (the City) has designated a private nonprofit corporation named Manhattan Neighborhood Network, commonly referred to as MNN, to operate Time Warner's public access channels in Manhattan. This case involves a complaint against MNN regarding its management of the public access channels.
>
> Under this Court's cases, a private entity can qualify as a state actor in a few limited circumstances — including, for example, (i) when the private entity performs a traditional, exclusive public function, see, e.g., *Jackson*; (ii) when the government compels the private entity to take a particular

action, see, e.g., *Blum v. Yaretsky*, 457 U.S. 991 (1982); or (iii) when the government acts jointly with the private entity, see, e.g., *Lugar v. Edmondson Oil Co.*, 457 U.S. 922 (1982). The producers' primary argument here falls into the first category: The producers contend that MNN exercises a traditional, exclusive public function when it operates the public access channels on Time Warner's cable system in Manhattan. We disagree.

To qualify as a traditional, exclusive public function within the meaning of our state-action precedents, the government must have traditionally *and* exclusively performed the function. The Court has stressed that "very few" functions fall into that category. *Flagg Bros.* Under the Court's cases, those functions include, for example, running elections and operating a company town. See *Terry v. Adams*, 345 U.S. 461 (1953) (elections); *Marsh v. Alabama*, 326 U.S. 501 (1946) (company town); *Smith v. Allwright*, 321 U.S. 649 (1944) (elections); *Nixon v. Condon*, 286 U.S. 73 (1932) (elections). The Court has ruled that a variety of functions do not fall into that category, including, for example: running sports associations and leagues, administering insurance payments, operating nursing homes, providing special education, representing indigent criminal defendants, resolving private disputes, and supplying electricity. See *American Mfrs. Mut. Ins. Co. v. Sullivan*, 526 U.S. 40 (1999) (insurance payments); *National Collegiate Athletic Assn. v. Tarkanian*, 488 U.S. 179 (1988) (college sports); *San Francisco Arts & Athletics, Inc. v. United States Olympic Comm.*, 483 U.S. 522 (1987) (amateur sports); *Blum*, 457 U.S., at 1011–1012 (nursing home); *Rendell-Baker* [*v. Kohn*], 457 U.S., at 842 (special education); *Polk County v. Dodson*, 454 U.S. 312 (1981) (public defender); *Flagg Bros.*, 436 U.S., at 157–163 (private dispute resolution); *Jackson*, 419 U.S., at 352–354 (electric service).

The relevant function in this case is operation of public access channels on a cable system. That function has not traditionally and exclusively been performed by government. To avoid that conclusion, the producers widen the lens and contend that the relevant function here is not simply the operation of public access channels on a cable system, but rather is more generally the operation of a public forum for speech. And according to the producers, operation of a public forum for speech is a traditional, exclusive public function.

That analysis mistakenly ignores the threshold state-action question. When the government provides a forum for speech (known as a public forum), the government may be constrained by the First Amendment, meaning that the government ordinarily may not exclude speech or speakers from the forum on the basis of viewpoint, or sometimes even on the basis of content.

By contrast, when a private entity provides a forum for speech, the private entity is not ordinarily constrained by the First Amendment because the private entity is not a state actor. The private entity may thus exercise editorial discretion over the speech and speakers in the forum. This Court so ruled in its 1976 decision in *Hudgens v. NLRB*. [424 U.S. 507 (1976)] There, the Court held that a shopping center owner is not a state actor subject to First Amendment requirements such as the public forum doctrine.

The *Hudgens* decision reflects a commonsense principle: Providing some kind of forum for speech is not an activity that only governmental entities have traditionally performed. Therefore, a private entity who provides a forum for speech is not transformed by that fact alone into a state actor. The producers retort that this case differs from *Hudgens* because New York City has designated MNN to operate the public access channels on Time Warner's cable system, and because New York State heavily regulates MNN with respect to the public access channels. Under this Court's cases, however, those facts do not establish that MNN is a state actor.

New York City's designation of MNN to operate the public access channels is analogous to a government license, a government contract, or a government-granted monopoly. But as the Court has long held, the fact that the government licenses, contracts with, or grants a monopoly to a private entity does not convert the private entity into a state actor — unless the private entity is performing a traditional, exclusive public function.

It is sometimes said that the bigger the government, the smaller the individual. Consistent with the text of the Constitution, the state-action doctrine enforces a critical boundary between the government and the individual, and thereby protects a robust sphere of individual liberty. Expanding the state-action doctrine beyond its traditional boundaries would expand governmental control while restricting individual liberty and private enterprise. We decline to do so in this case.

Justice Sotomayor wrote for the dissenters:

This is a case about an organization appointed by the government to administer a constitutional public forum. (It is not, as the Court suggests, about a private property owner that simply opened up its property to others.) New York City (the City) secured a property interest in public-access television channels when it granted a cable franchise to a cable company. State regulations require those public-access channels to be made open to the public on terms that render them a public forum. The City contracted out the administration of that forum to a private organization, petitioner Manhattan Community Access Corporation (MNN). By accepting that agency relationship, MNN stepped into the City's shoes and thus qualifies as a state actor, subject to the First Amendment like any other.

The *Jackson* line of cases is inapposite here. MNN is not a private entity that simply ventured into the marketplace. It occupies its role because it was asked to do so by the City, which secured the public-access channels in exchange for giving up public rights of way, opened those channels up (as required by the State) as a public forum, and then deputized MNN to administer them. That distinguishes MNN from a private entity that simply sets up shop against a regulatory backdrop.

She concluded:

> This is not a case about bigger governments and smaller individuals; it is a case about principals and agents. New York City opened up a public forum on public access channels in which it has a property interest. It asked MNN to run that public forum, and MNN accepted the job. That makes MNN subject to the First Amendment, just as if the City had decided to run the public forum itself. While the majority emphasizes that its decision is narrow and fact bound, that does not make it any less misguided. It is crucial that the Court does not continue to ignore the reality, fully recognized by our precedents, that private actors who have been delegated constitutional responsibilities like this one should be accountable to the Constitution's demands.

(8) Assume that a state hired a private company to operate its prisons. This company employs the guards and other personnel who run the institutions, which is populated by prisoners sentenced by the state courts. Would (should) the courts regard the company's activities in operating the prisons as state action and, thus, subject to the Fourteenth Amendment?

Problem B

Assume that a New York State law provides that "any citizen may bring a civil action against an individual who is carrying a firearm in a public place without a state license to carry a concealed weapon and recover $25,000 in damages as well as the cost of attorney's fees." Relying on this statute, Jane Smith filed a lawsuit against Ron Doe, alleging that he carried a gun in a local shopping mall and did not have a state license to carry the weapon.

Doe has moved to dismiss the lawsuit arguing that it violates his rights under the Second and Fourteenth Amendments. You are clerking for a judge who asks whether he should grant the motion to dismiss. Your research reveals that the Supreme Court recently reviewed a challenge to a New York criminal statute that makes it a crime to possess a firearm without a license, whether inside or outside the home. The Court held that New York's license requirement violated the right to bear arms as protected by the Second and Fourteenth Amendments. The judge tells you that he would be compelled by the recent Supreme Court case to dismiss this lawsuit if it had been brought by the state. Here, however, it is brought by a private citizen and the judge is concerned whether there is the requisite state action to trigger application of the Fourteenth Amendment. What advice would you give him? Compare *Shelley v. Kraemer*, 334 U.S. 1 (1948).

Chapter 6

Exclusion and Equal Protection

§ 6.01 Introduction

A. "We the People"

The Constitution states in the Preamble: "We the People of the United States, in Order to form a more perfect Union, establish Justice, insure domestic Tranquility, provide for the common defense, promote the general Welfare, and secure the Blessings of Liberty to ourselves and our Posterity, do ordain and establish this Constitution for the United States of America." As the following two cases reveal, however, the framers did not intend to include certain groups of peoples within "We the People."

Johnson v. McIntosh

United States Supreme Court
21 U.S. (8 Wheat.) 543, 5 L. Ed. 681 (1823)

MARSHALL, CH. J., delivered the opinion of the court.

The plaintiffs in this cause claim the land in their declaration mentioned, under two grants, purporting to be made, the first in 1773, and the last in 1775, by the chiefs of certain Indian tribes, constituting the Illinois and the Piankeshaw nations; and the question is, whether this title can be recognised in the courts of the United States? The facts, as stated in the case agreed, show the authority of the chiefs who executed this conveyance, so far as it could be given by their own people; and likewise show, that the particular tribes for whom these chiefs acted were in rightful possession of the land they sold. The inquiry, therefore, is, in a great measure, confined to the power of Indians to give, and of private individuals to receive, a title, which can be sustained in the courts of this country.

As the right of society to prescribe those rules by which property may be acquired and preserved is not, and cannot, be drawn into question; as the title to lands, especially, is, and must be, admitted, to depend entirely on the law of the nation in which they lie; it will be necessary, in pursuing this inquiry, to examine, not simply those principles of abstract justice, which the Creator of all things has impressed on the mind of his creature man, and which are admitted to regulate, in a great degree, the rights of civilized nations, whose perfect independence is acknowledged; but those principles also which our own government has adopted in the particular case, and given us as the rule for our decision.

On the discovery of this immense continent, the great nations of Europe were eager to appropriate to themselves so much of it as they could respectively acquire. Its vast extent offered an ample field to the ambition and enterprise of all; and the character and religion of its inhabitants afforded an apology for considering them as a people over whom the superior genius of Europe might claim an ascendancy. The potentates of the old world found no difficulty in convincing themselves, that they made ample compensation to the inhabitants of the new, by bestowing on them civilization and Christianity, in exchange for unlimited independence. But as they were all in pursuit of nearly the same object, it was necessary, in order to avoid conflicting settlements, and consequent war with each other, to establish a principle, which all should acknowledge as the law by which the right of acquisition, which they all asserted, should be regulated, as between themselves. This principle was, that discovery gave title to the government by whose subjects, or by whose authority, it was made, against all other European governments, which title might be consummated by possession. The exclusion of all other Europeans, necessarily gave to the nation making the discovery the sole right of acquiring the soil from the natives, and establishing settlements upon it. It was a right with which no Europeans could interfere. It was a right which all asserted for themselves, and to the assertion of which, by others, all assented. Those relations which were to exist between the discoverer and the natives, were to be regulated by themselves. The rights thus acquired being exclusive, no other power could interpose between them.

In the establishment of these relations, the rights of the original inhabitants were, in no instance, entirely disregarded; but were, necessarily, to a considerable extent, impaired. They were admitted to be the rightful occupants of the soil, with a legal as well as just claim to retain possession of it, and to use it according to their own discretion; but their rights to complete sovereignty, as independent nations, were necessarily diminished, and their power to dispose of the soil, at their own will, to whomsoever they pleased, was denied by the original fundamental principle, that discovery gave exclusive title to those who made it. . . .

By the treaty which concluded the war of our revolution, Great Britain relinquished all claim, not only to the government, but to the "propriety and territorial rights of the United States," whose boundaries were fixed in the second article. By this treaty, the powers of government, and the right to soil, which had previously been in Great Britain, passed definitively to these states. We had before taken possession of them, by declaring independence; but neither the declaration of independence, nor the treaty confirming it, could give us more than that which we before possessed, or to which Great Britain was before entitled. It has never been doubted, that either the United States, or the several states, had a clear title to all the lands within the boundary lines described in the treaty, subject only to the Indian right of occupancy, and that the exclusive power to extinguish that right, was vested in that government which might constitutionally exercise it. . . .

Although we do not mean to engage in the defence of those principles which Europeans have applied to Indian title, they may, we think, find some excuse, if not justification, in the character and habits of the people whose rights have been wrested from them. The title by conquest is acquired and maintained by force. The conqueror prescribes its limits. Humanity, however, acting on public opinion, has established, as a general rule, that the conquered shall not be wantonly oppressed, and that their condition shall remain as eligible as is compatible with the objects of the conquest. Most usually, they are incorporated with the victorious nation, and become subjects or citizens of the government with which they are connected. The new and old members of the society mingle with each other; the distinction between them is gradually lost, and they make one people. Where this incorporation is practicable, humanity demands, and a wise policy requires, that the rights of the conquered to property should remain unimpaired; that the new subjects should be governed as equitably as the old, and that confidence in their security should gradually banish the painful sense of being separated from their ancient connections, and united by force to strangers. When the conquest is complete, and the conquered inhabitants can be blended with the conquerors, or safely governed as a distinct people, public opinion, which not even the conqueror can disregard, imposes these restraints upon him; and he cannot neglect them, without injury to his fame, and hazard to his power.

But the tribes of Indians inhabiting this country were fierce savages, whose occupation was war, and whose subsistence was drawn chiefly from the forest. To leave them in possession of their country, was to leave the country a wilderness; to govern them as a distinct people, was impossible, because they were as brave and as high-spirited as they were fierce, and were ready to repel by arms every attempt on their independence. . . .

That law which regulates, and ought to regulate in general, the relations between the conqueror and conquered, was incapable of application to a people under such circumstances. The resort to some new and different rule, better adapted to the actual state of things, was unavoidable. Every rule which can be suggested will be found to be attended with great difficulty. However extravagant the pretension of converting the discovery of an inhabited country into conquest may appear; if the principle has been asserted in the first instance, and afterwards sustained; if a country has been acquired and held under it; if the property of the great mass of the community originates in it, it becomes the law of the land, and cannot be questioned. So too, with respect to the concomitant principle, that the Indian inhabitants are to be considered merely as occupants, to be protected, indeed, while in peace, in the possession of their lands, but to be deemed incapable of transferring the absolute title to others. However this restriction may be opposed to natural right, and to the usages of civilized nations, yet, if it be indispensable to that system under which the country has been settled, and be adapted to the actual condition of the two people, it may, perhaps, be supported by reason, and certainly cannot be rejected by courts of justice. . . .

After bestowing on this subject a degree of attention which was more required by the magnitude of the interest in litigation, and the able and elaborate arguments of the bar, than by its intrinsic difficulty, the court is decidedly of opinion, that the plaintiffs do not exhibit a title which can be sustained in the courts of the United States; and that there is no error in the judgment which was rendered against them in the district court of Illinois.

Dred Scott v. Sandford

United States Supreme Court
60 U.S. (19 How.) 393, 15 L. Ed. 691 (1857)

MR. CHIEF JUSTICE TANEY delivered the opinion of the court. . . .

The plaintiff in error, who was also the plaintiff in the court below, was, with his wife and children, held as slaves by the defendant, in the State of Missouri; and he brought this action in the Circuit Court of the United States for that district, to assert the title of himself and his family to freedom.

The declaration . . . contains the averment necessary to give the court jurisdiction; that he and the defendant are citizens of different States; that is, that he is a citizen of Missouri, and the defendant a citizen of New York. . . .

The question is simply this: Can a negro, whose ancestors were imported into this country, and sold as slaves, become a member of the political community formed and brought into existence by the Constitution of the United States, and as such become entitled to all the rights, and privileges, and immunities, guarantied by that instrument to the citizen? One of which rights is the privilege of suing in a court of the United States in the cases specified in the Constitution.

It will be observed, that the plea applies to that class of persons only whose ancestors were negroes of the African race, and imported into this country, and sold and held as slaves. The only matter in issue before the court, therefore, is, whether the descendants of such slaves, when they shall be emancipated, or who are born of parents who had become free before their birth, are citizens of a State, in the sense in which the word citizen is used in the Constitution of the United States. And this being the only matter in dispute on the pleadings, the court must be understood as speaking in this opinion of that class only, that is, of those persons who are the descendants of Africans who were imported into this country, and sold as slaves. . . .

The words "people of the United States" and "citizens" are synonymous terms, and mean the same thing. They both describe the political body who, according to our republican institutions, form the sovereignty, and who hold the power and conduct the Government through their representatives. They are what we familiarly call the "sovereign people," and every citizen is one of this people, and a constituent member of this sovereignty. The question before us is, whether the class of persons described in the plea in abatement compose a portion of this people, and are constituent members of this sovereignty? We think they are not, and that they are not included, and were not intended to be included, under the word "citizens" in the Constitution, and can therefore claim none of the rights and privileges which that instrument provides for and secures to citizens of the United States. On the contrary, they were at that time considered as a subordinate and inferior class of beings, who had been subjugated by the dominant race, and, whether emancipated or not, yet remained subject to their authority, and had no rights or privileges but such as those who held the power and the Government might choose to grant them.

It is not the province of the court to decide upon the justice or injustice, the policy or impolicy, of these laws. The decision of that question belonged to the political or law-making power; to those who formed the sovereignty and framed the Constitution. The duty of the court is, to interpret the instrument they have framed, with the best lights we can obtain on the subject, and to administer it as we find it, according to its true intent and meaning when it was adopted.

In discussing this question, we must not confound the rights of citizenship which a State may confer within its own limits, and the rights of citizenship as a member of the Union. . . .

It is very clear . . . that no State can, by any act or law of its own, passed since the adoption of the Constitution, introduce a new member into the political community created by the Constitution of the United States. It cannot make him a member of this community by making him a member of its own. And for the same reason it cannot introduce any person, or description of persons, who were not intended to be embraced in this new political family, which the Constitution brought into existence, but were intended to be excluded from it.

The question then arises, whether the provisions of the Constitution, in relation to the personal rights and privileges to which the citizen of a State should be entitled, embraced the negro African race, at that time in this country, or who might afterwards be imported, who had then or should afterwards be made free in any State; and to put it in the power of a single State to make him a citizen of the United States, and endue him with the full rights of citizenship in every other State without their consent? Does the Constitution of the United States act upon him whenever he shall be made free under the laws of a State, and raised there to the rank of a citizen, and immediately clothe him with all the privileges of a citizen in every other State, and in its own courts?

The court thinks the affirmative of these propositions cannot be maintained. And if it cannot, the plaintiff in error could not be a citizen of the State of Missouri, within the meaning of the Constitution of the United States, and, consequently, was not entitled to sue in its courts.

It is true, every person, and every class and description of persons, who were at the time of the adoption of the Constitution recognised as citizens in the several States, became also citizens of this new political body; but none other; it was formed by them, and for them and their posterity, but for no one else. And the personal rights and privileges guaranteed to citizens of this new sovereignty were intended to embrace those only who were then members of the several State communities, or who should afterwards by birthright or otherwise become members, according to the provisions of the Constitution and the principles on which it was founded. It was the union of those who were at that time members of distinct and separate political communities into one political family, whose power, for certain specified purposes, was to extend over the whole territory of the United States. And it gave to each citizen rights and privileges outside of his State which he did not before possess, and placed him in every other State upon a perfect equality with its own citizens as to rights of person and rights of property; it made him a citizen of the United States.

It becomes necessary, therefore, to determine who were citizens of the several States when the Constitution was adopted. And in order to do this, we must recur to the Governments and institutions of the thirteen colonies, when they separated from Great Britain and formed new sovereignties, and took their places in the family of independent nations. We must inquire who, at that time, were recognised as the people or citizens of a State, whose rights and liberties had been outraged by the English Government; and who declared their independence, and assumed the powers of Government to defend their rights by force of arms.

In the opinion of the court, the legislation and histories of the times, and the language used in the Declaration of Independence, show, that neither the class of persons who had been imported as slaves, nor their descendants, whether they had become free or not, were then acknowledged as a part of the people, nor intended to be included in the general words used in that memorable instrument.

It is difficult at this day to realize the state of public opinion in relation to that unfortunate race, which prevailed in the civilized and enlightened portions of the world at the time of the Declaration of Independence, and when the Constitution of the United States was framed and adopted. But the public history of every European nation displays it in a manner too plain to be mistaken.

They had for more than a century before been regarded as beings of an inferior order, and altogether unfit to associate with the white race, either in social or political relations; and so far inferior, that they had no rights which the white man was bound to respect; and that the negro might justly and lawfully be reduced to slavery for his benefit. He was bought and sold, and treated as an ordinary article of merchandise and traffic, whenever a profit could be made by it. This opinion was at that time fixed and universal in the civilized portion of the white race. It was regarded as an axiom in morals as well as in politics, which no one thought of disputing, or supposed to be open to dispute; and men in every grade and position in society daily and habitually acted upon it in their private pursuits, as well as in matters of public concern, without doubting for a moment the correctness of this opinion.

And in no nation was this opinion more firmly fixed or more uniformly acted upon than by the English Government and English people. They not only seized them on the coast of Africa, and sold them or held them in slavery for their own use; but they took them as ordinary articles of merchandise to every country where they could make a profit on them, and were far more extensively engaged in this commerce than any other nation in the world.

Mr. Justice McLean dissenting.

. . . Being born under our Constitution and laws, no naturalization is required, as one of foreign birth, to make him a citizen. The most general and appropriate definition of the term citizen is "a freeman." Being a freeman, and having his domicil in a State different from that of the defendant, he is a citizen within the act of Congress, and the courts of the Union are open to him. . . .

In the argument, it was said that a colored citizen would not be an agreeable member of society. This is more a matter of taste than of law. Several of the States have admitted persons of color to the right of suffrage, and in this view have recognised them as citizens; and this has been done in the slave as well as the free States. . . . Our independence was a great epoch in the history of freedom; and while I admit the Government was not made especially for the colored race, yet many of them were citizens of the New England States, and exercised, the rights of suffrage when the Constitution was adopted, and it was not doubted by any intelligent person that its tendencies would greatly ameliorate their condition.

Many of the States, on the adoption of the Constitution, or shortly afterward, took measures to abolish slavery within their respective jurisdictions; and it is a well-known fact that a belief was cherished by the leading men, South as well as North, that the institution of slavery would gradually decline, until it would become extinct. The increased value of slave labor, in the culture of cotton and sugar, prevented the realization of this expectation. Like all other communities and States, the South were influenced by what they considered to be their own interests.

But if we are to turn our attention to the dark ages of the world, why confine our view to colored slavery? On the same principles, white men were made slaves. All slavery has its origin in power, and is against right. . . .

Mr. Justice Curtis dissenting.

It has been often asserted that the Constitution was made exclusively by and for the white race. It has already been shown that in five of the thirteen original States, colored persons then possessed the elective franchise, and were among those by whom the Constitution was ordained and established. If so, it is not true, in point of fact, that the Constitution was made exclusively by the white race. And that it was made exclusively for the white race is, in my opinion, not only an assumption not warranted by anything in the Constitution, but contradicted by its opening declaration, that it was ordained and established by the people of the United States, for themselves and their posterity. And as free colored persons were then citizens of at least five States, and so in every sense part of the people of the United States, they were among those for whom and whose posterity the Constitution was ordained and established. . . .

It has been further objected, that if free colored persons, born within a particular State, and made citizens of that State by its Constitution and laws, are thereby made citizens of the United States, then, under the second section of the fourth article of the Constitution, such persons would be entitled to all the privileges and immunities of citizens in the several States; and if so, then colored persons could vote, and be eligible to not only Federal offices, but offices even in those States whose Constitution and laws disqualify colored persons from voting or being elected to office.

But this position rests upon an assumption which I deem untenable. Its basis is, that no one can be deemed a citizen of the United States who is not entitled to enjoy all the privileges and franchises which are conferred on any citizen. That this is not true, under the Constitution of the United States, seems to me clear.

A naturalized citizen cannot be President of the United States, nor a Senator till after the lapse of nine years, nor a Representative till after the lapse of seven years, from his naturalization. Yet, as soon as naturalized, he is certainly a citizen of the United States. Nor is any inhabitant of the District of Columbia, or of either of the Territories, eligible to the office of Senator or Representative in Congress, though they may be citizens of the United States. So, in all the States, numerous persons, though citizens, cannot vote, or cannot hold office, either on account of their age, or sex, or the want of the necessary legal qualifications. The truth is, that citizenship, under the Constitution of the United States, is not dependent on the possession of any particular political or even of all civil rights; and any attempt so to define it must lead to error. To what citizens the elective franchise shall be confided, is a question to be determined by each State, in accordance with its own views of the necessities or expediencies of its condition. What civil rights shall be enjoyed by its citizens, and whether all shall enjoy the same, or how they may be gained or lost, are to be determined in the same way. . . .

The conclusions at which I have arrived . . . are:

First. That the free native-born citizens of each State are citizens of the United States.

Second. That as free colored persons born within some of the States are citizens of those States, such persons are also citizens of the United States.

Third. That every such citizen, residing in any State, has the right to sue and is liable to be sued in the Federal courts, as a citizen of that State in which he resides.

Fourth. That as the plea to the jurisdiction in this case shows no facts, except that the plaintiff was of African descent, and his ancestors were sold as slaves, and as these facts are not inconsistent with his citizenship of the United States, and his residence in the State of Missouri. . . .

I dissent, therefore, from that part of the opinion of the majority of the court, in which it is held that a person of African descent cannot be a citizen of the United States. . . .

Notes and Questions

(1) On what basis did the Court conclude that Indians did not have power to convey title to their own land? "We the People" was certainly meant to exclude the

Native Americans. Article I provides that in apportioning representatives, "Indians, not taxed" would be excluded from the count. U.S. Const. art. I, §2. In *Elk v. Wilkins*, 112 U.S. 94 (1884), the Court held that an Indian, who had been born in the United States and had severed ties with his tribe, was not a citizen within the meaning of the Fourteenth Amendment. Congress enacted a general grant of citizenship for Indians in 1924. 8 U.S.C. §1401(a)(2).

(2) To what extent did the Court in *Dred Scott* rely on assumptions and techniques of exclusion similar to those used in *Johnson*?

(3) Professors Hyman and Wiecek described the important historical significance of *Dred Scott*:

> *Dred Scott* was a major historical event in its own right, and as such a shoal in the river of history around which events swirled for a time. The decision did not seriously diminish the prestige or power of the United States Supreme Court as an institution. On the contrary the Court continued to play a vital role as a coordinate branch of government throughout the war and Reconstruction. But the Court's majority did politicize itself. . . .

HAROLD HYMAN & WILLIAM WIECEK, EQUAL JUSTICE UNDER LAW 190–192, 201–202 (1982).[1]

B. Exclusion and the Equal Protection Clause

This Chapter examines the concept of equality and the extent to which the Constitution guarantees equal protection of the laws, thereby expanding the scope of "We the People." As ratified, the Constitution did not include an Equal Protection Clause. Even the Bill of Rights did not include a guarantee of equality, although the Fifth Amendment Due Process Clause has been interpreted to encompass principles of equality. *See Bolling v. Sharpe*, 347 U.S. 497 (1954).

The Fourteenth Amendment specifically provides that no state shall "deny any person within its jurisdiction the equal protection of the laws." There are important threshold problems with the Equal Protection Clause. By their nature, nearly all laws classify, imposing obligations or conferring benefits on some but not others. Even a traffic ordinance that requires vehicles to stop at a red light includes exceptions for emergency vehicles. Thus, discrimination is an integral component of legislation. What discrimination is the Equal Protection Clause intended to forbid?

Second, what is meant by "equal protection?" It could mean "equal treatment, which is the right to an equal distribution of some opportunity or resource or burden." RONALD DWORKIN, TAKING RIGHTS SERIOUSLY 227 (1977). Or, it might refer to "treatment as an equal, which is the right, not to receive the same distribution of some burden or benefit, but to be treated with the same respect and concern as

---

1. Copyright © 1982 by Harper & Row Publishers, Inc.

anyone else." *Id.* To appreciate this distinction, consider whether the state violates equal protection when it opens public buildings to all but does not provide ramps for those who use wheelchairs.

Another problem in equal protection cases is to determine precisely the nature of the classification, those who are benefited and those who are not. How do we define the categories of those being excluded? Consider, for example, the "Sesame Street" problem. (We are indebted to Professor Martha Minow for reminding us of the value of that show. *See* Martha Minow, Making All the Difference: Inclusion, Exclusion, and American Law 1 (1990)). Which of the following items is not like the others: a chair, a table, a lamp, and a cow? The answer depends on how the items are categorized. If, for example, the category is inanimate objects, then the cow is different. If the category is four-legged objects, the lamp is different. Finally, if the category consists of words ending in a consonant, the table is out of place. The categorization problem frequently appears in equal protection cases. *See, e.g., Geduldig v. Aiello*, 417 U.S. 484 (1974) (Is discrimination against pregnant women gender-based discrimination?).

A related threshold issue concerns the norm against which we measure equality. Something is "unequal" only in relationship to something else. What is the standard? Consider the following:

> "Difference" is only meaningful as a comparison. I am no more different from you than you are from me. A short person is different only in relation to a tall one. Legal treatment of difference tends to take for granted an assumed point of comparison: women are compared to the unstated norm of men, "minority" races to whites, handicapped persons to the able-bodied, and "minority" religions to "majorities." Such assumptions work in part through the very structure of our language, which embeds the unstated points of comparison inside categories that bury their perspective and wrongly imply a natural fit with the world. The term "working mother," modifies the general category "mother," revealing that the general term carries some unstated common meanings (that is, a woman who cares for her children full-time without pay), which, even if unintended, must expressly be modified. Legal treatment of difference thus tends to treat as unproblematic the point of view from which difference is seen, assigned, or ignored, rather than acknowledging that the problem of difference can be described and understood from multiple points of view.

Martha Minow, *Supreme Court — Forward: Justice Engendered*, 101 Harv. L. Rev. 10, 13–14 (1987).

The early view of the Equal Protection Clause was that it extended only to race discrimination. In the *Slaughter-House Cases*, the Court said: "We doubt very much whether any action of a State not directed by way of discrimination against the negroes as a class, or on account of their race, will ever be held to come within the purview" of equal protection. As the materials in this section suggest, there is continuing debate about the meaning of equal protection even in the area of race discrimination. Beyond race, the clause was little-invoked by the Court before the 1950's. Due process was the Court's primary doctrinal device for protecting individual rights, and, according to Justice Holmes, equal protection was "the usual last resort of constitutional arguments." *Buck v. Bell*, 274 U.S. 200, 208 (1927). Not surprisingly, the Court's stated standard for equal protection was quite similar to the prevailing due process standard: "[T]he classification must be reasonable, not arbitrary, and must rest upon some ground of difference having a fair and substantial relation to the object of the legislation, so that persons similarly circumstanced shall be treated alike." *F.S. Royster Guano Co. v. Virginia*, 253 U.S. 412 (1920). Accordingly, as the due process standard of judicial review of social and economic legislation has become ever more lax since 1937, so has the classic equal protection standard. By 1970, the Court rejected an equal protection challenge with these words: "A statutory discrimination will not be set aside if any state of facts reasonably may be conceived to justify it." *Dandridge v. Williams*, 397 U.S. 471 (1970).

Thus, traditional equal protection review provided almost certain victory for the government. If there was any rational connection between the classification imbedded in the law and any permissible governmental objective, equal protection commands had been satisfied. As with due process challenges, the burden was on the challengers to show a lack of rationality.

Beginning with race discrimination cases in the 1950's, a double standard emerged. While continuing to defer to social and economic legislation, the Court applied "strict scrutiny" and carefully examined legislation when the government had created a "suspect classification," such as race, or had burdened the exercise of a "fundamental right." *See United States v. Carolene Products*, 304 U.S. 144, 152–153 n.4 (1938). Under strict scrutiny, the government was an almost certain loser.

In the 1970s and 1980s, the equal protection picture was less clear. Strict scrutiny was still applied to suspect classifications and fundamental rights. Generally, however, the Court has rebelled against the claimed rigidity of the prior two-tiered review and in some instances has used an intermediate review. Because these various standards of review are not self-defining, there are significant doctrinal problems in ascertaining the purpose of a law, in seeking to measure its reasonableness, and in defining the classifications that are "suspect" and the rights that are "fundamental."

§ 6.02 Social and Economic Classification: Traditional Approach

Railway Express Agency v. New York

United States Supreme Court
336 U.S. 106, 69 S. Ct. 463, 93 L. Ed. 533 (1949)

Mr. Justice Douglas delivered the opinion of the Court.

Section 124 of the Traffic Regulations of the City of New York promulgated by the Police Commissioner provides:

> No person shall operate, or cause to be operated, in or upon any street an advertising vehicle; provided that nothing herein contained shall prevent the putting of business notices upon business delivery vehicles, so long as such vehicles are engaged in the usual business or regular work of the owner and not used merely or mainly for advertising.

Appellant is engaged in a nation-wide express business. It operates about 1,900 trucks in New York City and sells the space on the exterior sides of these trucks for advertising. That advertising is for the most part unconnected with its own business. It was convicted [and] fined.

The question of equal protection of the laws is pressed . . . on us. It is pointed out that the regulation draws the line between advertisements of products sold by the owner of the truck and general advertisements. It is argued that unequal treatment on the basis of such a distinction is not justified by the aim and purpose of the regulation. It is said, for example, that one of appellant's trucks carrying the advertisement of a commercial house would not cause any greater distraction of pedestrians and vehicle drivers than if the commercial house carried the same advertisement on its own truck. Yet the regulation allows the latter to do what the former is forbidden from doing. It is therefore contended that the classification which the regulation makes has no relation to the traffic problem since a violation turns not on what kind of advertisements are carried on trucks but on whose trucks they are carried.

That, however, is a superficial way of analyzing the problem, even if we assume that it is premised on the correct construction of the regulation. The local authorities may well have concluded that those who advertised their own wares on their trucks do not present the same traffic problem in view of the nature or extent of the advertising which they use. It would take a degree of omniscience which we lack to say that such is not the case. If that judgment is correct, the advertising displays that are exempt have less incidence on traffic than those of appellants.

We cannot say that that judgment is not an allowable one. Yet if it is, the classification has relation to the purpose for which it is made and does not contain the kind of discrimination against which the Equal Protection Clause affords protection. It is by such practical considerations based on experience rather than by theoretical inconsistencies that the question of equal protection is to be answered. And the fact that New York City sees fit to eliminate from traffic this kind of distraction but does not touch what may be even greater ones in a different category, such as the vivid displays on Times Square, is immaterial. It is no requirement of equal protection that all evils of the same genus be eradicated or none at all. . . .

Affirmed.

MR. JUSTICE JACKSON, concurring.

My philosophy as to the relative readiness with which we should resort to [the due process and equal protection] clauses is almost diametrically opposed to the philosophy which prevails on this Court. While claims of denial of equal protection are frequently asserted, they are rarely sustained. But the Court frequently uses the due process clause to strike down measures taken by municipalities to deal with activities in their streets and public places which the local authorities consider to create hazards, annoyances or discomforts to their inhabitants.

[The] burden should rest heavily upon one who would persuade us to use the due process clause to strike down a substantive law or ordinance. Even its provident use against municipal regulations frequently disables all government — state, municipal and federal — from dealing with the conduct in question because the requirement of due process is also applicable to State and Federal Governments. Invalidation of a statute or an ordinance on due process grounds leaves ungoverned and ungovernable conduct which many people find objectionable.

Invocation of the equal protection clause, on the other hand, does not disable any governmental body from dealing with the subject at hand. It merely means that the prohibition or regulation must have a broader impact. I regard it as a salutary doctrine that cities, states and the Federal Government must exercise their powers so as not to discriminate between their inhabitants except upon some reasonable differentiation fairly related to the object of regulation. This equality is not merely abstract justice. The framers of the Constitution knew, and we should not forget today, that there is no more effective practical guaranty against arbitrary and unreasonable government than to require that the principles of law which officials would impose upon a minority must be imposed generally. Conversely, nothing opens the door to arbitrary action so effectively as to allow those officials to pick and choose only a few to whom they will apply legislation and thus to escape the political retribution that might be visited upon them if larger numbers were affected. Courts can take no better measure to assure that laws will be just than to require that laws be equal in operation.

Notes and Questions

(1) What was the classification in *REA*? To what extent were like persons treated alike? Was the law over- or under-inclusive?

(2) Recall that equal protection review, like due process review, examines the rationality of the relationship of the means or classification to some permissible purpose or end. What was the purpose of the law according to the majority? How

did Justice Jackson redefine it? How was the purpose of the law determined by the Court? Did the Court look to the legislative purpose at the time the law was enacted or when the law was challenged or when the case was argued? Did the Court look to legislative history? Identifying legislative purpose is one of the most difficult and most sensitive of judicial inquiries. If purpose is not plainly stated in the legislation, how may an appellate court divine purpose? On the other hand, if the purpose inquiry is not taken seriously, the rationality test loses its meaning if the government may defend its actions by arguing any purpose which will most likely support the classification. We will return to this dilemma again.

(3) The *REA* decision is a typical resolution of equal protection challenges to economic regulation. *See, e.g., Kotch v. Board of River Pilot Commissioners*, 330 U.S. 552 (1947); *Williamson v. Lee Optical of Okla.*, 348 U.S. 483 (1955). The failed equal protection argument in *Lee Optical* challenged Oklahoma's list of specific exemptions from a general ban on the advertising of eyeware. The Court found that the law was "rational," and, in so doing, observed: "[T]he reform may take one step at a time, addressing itself to the phase of the problem which seems most acute to the legislative mind." This "one step at a time" justification is potentially quite broad. Would it justify a law which benefited whites only, on the theory that the benefit is important, and since whites are a majority in society, providing them with the benefit is a legitimate first step?

Massachusetts Board of Retirement v. Murgia

United States Supreme Court
427 U.S. 307, 96 S. Ct. 2562, 49 L. Ed. 2d 520 (1976)

PER CURIAM.

This case presents the question whether the provision of Mass. Gen. Laws Ann. c. 32 § 26(3)(a) (1969), that a uniformed state police officer "shall be retired . . . upon his attaining age fifty," denies appellee police officer equal protection of the laws in violation of the Fourteenth Amendment.

Appellee Robert Murgia was an officer in the Uniformed Branch of the Massachusetts State Police. The Massachusetts Board of Retirement retired him upon his 50th birthday. . . .

The primary function of the Uniformed Branch of the Massachusetts State Police is to protect persons and property and maintain law and order. Specifically, uniformed officers participate in controlling prison and civil disorders, respond to emergencies and natural disasters, patrol highways in marked cruisers, investigate crime, apprehend criminal suspects, and provide backup support for local law enforcement personnel. As the District Court observed, "service in this branch is, or can be, arduous." "[H]igh versatility is required, with few, if any, backwaters available for the partially superannuated." Thus, "even [appellee's] experts concede that there is a general relationship between advancing age and decreasing physical ability to respond to the demands of the job."

These considerations prompt the requirement that uniformed state officers pass a comprehensive physical examination biennially until age 40. After that, until mandatory retirement at age 50, uniformed officers must pass annually a more rigorous examination, including an electrocardiogram and tests for gastro-intestinal bleeding. Appellee Murgia had passed such an examination four months before he was retired, and there is no dispute that, when he retired, his excellent physical and mental health still rendered him capable of performing the duties of a uniformed officer.

The record includes the testimony of three physicians: that of the State Police Surgeon, who testified to the physiological and psychological demands involved in the performance of uniformed police functions; that of an associate professor of medicine, who testified generally to the relationship between aging and the ability to perform under stress; and that of a surgeon, who also testified to aging and the ability safely to perform police functions. The testimony clearly established that the risk of physical failure, particularly in the cardiovascular system, increases with age, and that the number of individuals in a given age group incapable of performing stress functions increases with the age of the group. The testimony also recognized that particular individuals over 50 could be capable of safely performing the functions of uniformed officers. The associate professor of medicine, who was a witness for the appellee, further testified that evaluating the risk of cardiovascular failure in a given individual would require a number of detailed studies. . . .

We need state only briefly our reasons for agreeing that strict scrutiny is not the proper test for determining whether the mandatory retirement provision denies appellee equal protection. *San Antonio Ind. School District v. Rodriguez*, 411 U.S. 1 (1973), reaffirmed that equal protection analysis requires strict scrutiny of a legislative classification only when the classification impermissibly interferes with the exercise of a fundamental right or operates to the peculiar disadvantage of a suspect class. Mandatory retirement at age 50 under the Massachusetts statute involves neither situation.

This Court's decisions give no support to the proposition that a right of governmental employment per se is fundamental. Accordingly, we have expressly stated that a standard less than strict scrutiny "has consistently been applied to state legislation restricting the availability of employment opportunities."

Nor does the class of uniformed state police officers over 50 constitute a suspect class for purposes of equal protection analysis. [While] the treatment of the aged in this Nation has not been wholly free of discrimination, such persons, unlike, say, those who have been discriminated against on the basis of race or national origin, have not experienced a "history of purposeful unequal treatment" or been subjected to unique disabilities on the basis of stereotyped characteristics not truly indicative of their abilities. The class subject to the compulsory retirement feature of the Massachusetts statute consists of uniformed state police officers over the age of 50. It cannot be said to discriminate only against the elderly. Rather, it draws the line at a certain age in middle life. But even old age does not define a "discrete and insular" group, *Carolene Products*, in need of "extraordinary protection from the majoritarian political process." Instead, it marks a stage that each of us will reach if we live out our normal span. Even if the statute could be said to impose a penalty upon a class defined as the aged, it would not impose a distinction sufficiently akin to those classifications that we have found suspect to call for strict judicial scrutiny.

Under the circumstances, it is unnecessary to subject the State's resolution of competing interests in this case to the degree of critical examination that our cases under the Equal Protection Clause recently have characterized as "strict judicial scrutiny."

In this case, the Massachusetts statute clearly meets the requirements of the Equal Protection Clause, for the State's classification rationally furthers the purpose identified by the State. Through mandatory retirement at age 50, the legislature seeks to protect the public by assuring physical preparedness of its uniformed police. Since physical ability generally declines with age, mandatory retirement at 50 serves to remove from police service those whose fitness for uniformed work presumptively has diminished with age. This clearly is rationally related to the State's objective. There is no indication that § 26(3)(a) has the effect of excluding from service so few officers who are in fact unqualified as to render age 50 a criterion wholly unrelated to the objective of the statute.

That the State chooses not to determine fitness more precisely through individualized testing after age 50 is not to say that the objective of assuring physical fitness is not rationally furthered by a maximum-age limitation. It is only to say that with regard to the interest of all concerned, the State perhaps has not chosen the best means to accomplish this purpose. . . .

We do not make light of the substantial economic and psychological effects premature and compulsory retirement can have on an individual; nor do we denigrate the ability of elderly citizens to continue to contribute to society. The problems of retirement have been well documented and are beyond serious dispute. But "[w]e do not decide today that the [Massachusetts statute] is wise, that it best fulfills the relevant social and economic objectives that [Massachusetts] might ideally espouse, or that a more just and humane system could not be devised." We decide only that the system enacted by the Massachusetts Legislature does not deny appellee equal protection of the laws.

The judgment is reversed.

MR. JUSTICE MARSHALL, dissenting. . . .

Although there are signs that its grasp on the law is weakening, the rigid two-tier model still holds sway as the Court's articulated description of the equal protection test. Again, I must object to its perpetuation. The model's two fixed modes of analysis, strict scrutiny and mere rationality, simply do not describe the inquiry the Court has undertaken — or should undertake — in equal protection cases. Rather, the inquiry has been much more sophisticated and the Court should admit as much. It has focused upon the character of the classification in question, the relative importance to individuals in the class discriminated against of the governmental benefits that they do not receive, and the state interests asserted in support of the classification. . . .

The danger of the Court's verbal adherence to the rigid two-tier test, despite its effective repudiation of that test in the cases, is demonstrated by its efforts here. There is simply no reason why a statute that tells able-bodied police officers, ready and willing to work, that they no longer have the right to earn a living in their chosen profession merely because they are 50 years old should be judged by the same minimal standards of rationality that we use to test economic legislation that discriminates against business interests. Yet, the Court today not only invokes the minimal level of scrutiny, it wrongly adheres to it. Analysis of the three factors I have identified above — the importance of the governmental benefits denied, the character of the class, and the asserted state interests — demonstrates the Court's error.

Whether "fundamental" or not, "the right of the individual . . . to engage in any of the common occupations of life" has been repeatedly recognized by this Court as falling within the concept of liberty guaranteed by the Fourteenth Amendment. . . . *Board of Regents v. Roth*, 408 U.S. 564 (1972).

[I] agree that the purpose of the mandatory retirement law is legitimate, and indeed compelling. The Commonwealth has every reason to assure that its state police officers are of sufficient physical strength and health to perform their jobs. In my view, however, the means chosen, the forced retirement of officers at age 50, is so over-inclusive that it must fall.

[The] only members of the state police still on the force at age 50 are those who have been determined — repeatedly — by the Commonwealth to be physically fit for the job. Yet, all of these physically fit officers are automatically terminated at age 50. Appellants do not seriously assert that their testing is no longer effective at age 50, nor do they claim that continued testing would serve no purpose because officers over 50 are no longer physically able to perform their jobs. Thus the Commonwealth is in the position of already individually testing its police officers for physical fitness, conceding that such testing is adequate to determine the physical ability of an officer to continue on the job, and conceding that that ability may continue after age 50. In these circumstances, I see no reason at all for automatically terminating those officers who reach the age of 50; indeed, that action seems the height of irrationality. . . .

Notes and Questions

(1) Why was "strict scrutiny" not the proper standard of review in *Murgia?* Consider the *Carolene Products* footnote (*supra*, at § 5.01). Was the group burdened in *Murgia* "discrete and insular," in need of "extraordinary protection from the majoritarian political process"? *See generally* John Hart Ely, Democracy and Distrust (1980). Is it surprising that the troopers were found not to have a "fundamental right" to governmental employment? Does the idea of equal respect for the

individual support their claim? *See generally* Kenneth Karst, *Why Equality Matters*, 17 GA. L. REV. 245 (1983).

(2) Did the Court examine the Massachusetts law more carefully than it examined the New York City ordinance in *REA*?

(3) The rigidity of the two-tiered approach to equal protection was attacked in Justice Marshall's dissent. What was the "danger" in that approach, according to Marshall? What standard would he apply?

(4) In *FCC v. Beach Communications, Inc.*, 508 U.S. 307 (1993), the Court described the traditional rational basis review used in assessing whether laws violate the equal protection clause:

> Whether embodied in the Fourteenth Amendment or inferred from the Fifth, equal protection is not a license for courts to judge the wisdom, fairness or logic of legislative choices. In areas of social and economic policy, a statutory classification that neither proceeds along suspect lines nor infringes fundamental constitutional rights must be upheld against equal protection challenge if there is any reasonably conceivable state of facts that could provide a rational basis for the classification. Where there are "plausible reasons" for Congress' action, "our inquiry is at an end." This standard of review is a paradigm of judicial restraint. "The Constitution presumes that, absent some reason to infer antipathy, even improvident decisions will eventually be rectified by the democratic process and that judicial intervention is generally unwarranted no matter how unwisely we may think a political branch has acted."

> On rational-basis review a classification in a statute . . . comes to us bearing a strong presumption of validity and those attacking the rationality of the legislative classification have the burden "to negative every conceivable basis which might support it." Moreover, because we never require a legislature to articulate its reasons for enacting a statute, it is entirely irrelevant for constitutional purposes whether the conceived reason for the challenged distinction actually motivated the legislature. Thus, the absence of "legislative facts" explaining the distinction "[on] the record," has no significance in rational-basis analysis. In other words, a legislative choice is not subject to courtroom fact-finding and may be based on rational speculation unsupported by evidence or empirical data. "Only by faithful adherence to this guiding principle of judicial review of legislation is it possible to preserve to the legislative branch its rightful independence and its ability to function."

> These restraints on judicial review have added force "where the legislature must necessarily engage in a process of line-drawing." Defining the class of persons subject to a regulatory requirement — much like classifying governmental beneficiaries — "inevitably requires that some persons who have an almost equally strong claim to favored treatment be placed on different sides of the line, and the fact [that] the line might have been drawn

differently at some points is a matter for legislative, rather than judicial, consideration." This necessity renders the precise coordinates of the resulting legislative judgment virtually unreviewable, since the legislature must be allowed leeway to approach a perceived problem incrementally. *See, e.g., Williamson v. Lee Optical of Okla., Inc.* [348 U.S. 483 (1955)].

San Antonio Independent School District v. Rodriguez

United States Supreme Court
411 U.S. 1, 93 S. Ct. 1278, 36 L. Ed. 2d 16 (1973)

Mr. Justice Powell delivered the opinion of the Court.

[This class action was brought by Mexican-American parents of children attending schools in the Edgewood School District in San Antonio, suing on behalf of children of poor families living in districts having a low property tax base. The suit attacked the Texas scheme for financing public education, which relied heavily on district property taxes and thus resulted in large differences in per-pupil expenditures due to differences in taxable property values among school districts. Like most states, Texas supplements local spending with state aid and thus reduces local disparities. Nonetheless, substantial spending differences existed in Texas. Plaintiffs' Edgewood District raised $26 per pupil by taxing its property at the highest rate in the metropolitan area, while Alamo Heights, an affluent district, raised $333 per pupil by taxing at a lower rate.]

I

... The District Court held that the Texas system discriminates on the basis of wealth in the manner in which education is provided for its people. Finding that wealth is a "suspect" classification and that education is a "fundamental" interest, the District Court held that the Texas system could be sustained only if the State could show that it was premised upon some compelling state interest. On this issue the court concluded that "[n]ot only are defendants unable to demonstrate compelling state interests ... they fail even to establish a reasonable basis for these classifications. . . ."

II

A

Only appellees' first possible basis for describing the class disadvantaged by the Texas school-financing system — discrimination against a class of definably "poor" persons — might arguably meet the criteria established in ... prior cases. Even a cursory examination, however, demonstrates that neither of the two distinguishing characteristics of wealth classifications can be found here. First, in support of their charge that the system discriminates against the "poor," appellees have made no effort to demonstrate that it operates to the peculiar disadvantage of any class fairly definable as indigent, or as composed of persons whose incomes are beneath any designated poverty level. Indeed, there is reason to believe that the poorest families are not necessarily clustered in the poorest property districts. A recent and exhaustive study of school districts in Connecticut concluded . . . that the poor were clustered around commercial and industrial areas—those same areas that provide the most attractive sources of property tax income for school districts. Whether a similar pattern would be discovered in Texas is not known, but there is no basis on the record in this case for assuming that the poorest people—defined by reference to any level of absolute impecunity—are concentrated in the poorest districts.

Second, neither appellees nor the District Court addressed the fact . . . that lack of personal resources has not occasioned an absolute deprivation of the desired benefit. The argument here is not that the children in districts having relatively low assessable property values are receiving no public education; rather, it is that they are receiving a poorer quality education than that available to children in districts having more assessable wealth. Apart from the unsettled and disputed question whether the quality of education may be determined by the amount of money expended for it, a sufficient answer to appellees' argument is that, at least where wealth is involved, the Equal Protection Clause does not require absolute equality or precisely equal advantages. . . .

For these two reasons—the absence of any evidence that the financing system discriminates against any definable category of "poor" people or that it results in the absolute deprivation of education—the disadvantaged class is not susceptible of identification in traditional terms. . . .

We thus conclude that the Texas system does not operate to the peculiar disadvantage of any suspect class. But in recognition of the fact that this Court has never heretofore held that wealth discrimination alone provides an adequate basis for invoking strict scrutiny, appellees have not relied solely on this contention. They also assert that the State's system impermissibly interferes with the exercise of a "fundamental" right and that accordingly the prior decisions of this Court require the application of the strict standard of judicial review. . . .

B

In *Brown v. Board of Education*, 347 U.S. 483 (1954), a unanimous Court recognized that "education is perhaps the most important function of state and local governments. . . ."

Nothing this Court holds today in any way detracts from our historic dedication to public education. We are in complete agreement with the conclusion of the three-judge panel below that "the grave significance of education both to the individual and to our society" cannot be doubted. But the importance of a service performed by the State does not determine whether it must be regarded as fundamental for purposes of examination under the Equal Protection Clause. . . .

Education, of course, is not among the rights afforded explicit protection under our Federal Constitution. Nor do we find any basis for saying it is implicitly so protected. . . . Furthermore, the logical limitations on appellees' nexus theory are difficult to perceive. How, for instance, is education to be distinguished from the significant personal interests in the basics of decent food and shelter? Empirical examination might well buttress an assumption that the ill-fed, ill-clothed, and ill-housed are among the most ineffective participants in the political process, and that they derive the least enjoyment from the benefits of the First Amendment. . . .

We have carefully considered each of the arguments supportive of the District Court's finding that education is a fundamental right or liberty and have found those arguments unpersuasive. . . .

C

. . . We need not rest our decision, however, solely on the inappropriateness of the strict-scrutiny test. A century of Supreme Court adjudication under the Equal Protection Clause affirmatively supports the application of the traditional standard of review, which requires only that the State's system be shown to bear some rational relationship to legitimate state purposes. . . .

It must be remembered . . . that every claim arising under the Equal Protection Clause has implications for the relationship between national and state power under our federal system. Questions of federalism are always inherent in the process of determining whether a State's laws are to be accorded the traditional presumption of constitutionality, or are to be subjected instead to rigorous judicial scrutiny. While "[t]he maintenance of the principles of federalism is a foremost consideration in interpreting any of the pertinent constitutional provisions under which this Court examines state action," it would be difficult to imagine a case having a greater potential impact on our federal system than the one now before us, in which we are urged to abrogate systems of financing public education presently in existence in virtually every State.

The foregoing considerations buttress our conclusion that Texas' system of public school finance is an inappropriate candidate for strict judicial scrutiny. These same considerations are relevant to the determination whether that system, with its conceded imperfections, nevertheless bears some rational relationship to a legitimate state purpose. It is to this question that we next turn our attention.

III

. . . While assuring a basic education for every child in the State, . . . [the Texas public school finance system] permits and encourages a large measure of participation in and control of each district's schools at the local level. In an era that has witnessed a consistent trend toward centralization of the functions of government, local sharing of responsibility for public education has survived. . . .

In part, local control means . . . the freedom to devote more money to the education of one's children. Equally important, however, is the opportunity it offers for participation in the decisionmaking process that determines how those local tax dollars will be spent. Each locality is free to tailor local programs to local needs. Pluralism also affords some opportunity for experimentation, innovation, and a healthy competition for educational excellence. . . .

In sum, to the extent that the Texas system of school financing results in unequal expenditures between children who happen to reside in different districts, we cannot say that such disparities are the product of a system that is so irrational as to be invidiously discriminatory. . . .

[Opinions of JUSTICE STEWART, concurring, and BRENNAN, dissenting, are omitted.]

MR. JUSTICE WHITE, with whom MR. JUSTICE DOUGLAS and MR. JUSTICE BRENNAN join, dissenting. . . .

I cannot disagree with the proposition that local control and local decisionmaking play an important part in our democratic system of government. Much may be left to local option, and this case would be quite different if it were true that the Texas system, while insuring minimum educational expenditures in every district through state funding, extended a meaningful option to all local districts to increase their per-pupil expenditures and so to improve their children's education to the extent that increased funding would achieve that goal. The system would then arguably provide a rational and sensible method of achieving the stated aim of preserving an area for local initiative and decision.

The difficulty with the Texas system, however, is that it provides a meaningful option to Alamo Heights and like school districts but almost none to Edgewood and those other districts with a low per-pupil real estate tax base. In these latter districts, no matter how desirous parents are of supporting their schools with greater revenues, it is impossible to do so through the use of the real estate property tax. In these districts, the Texas system utterly fails to extend a realistic choice to parents because the property tax, which is the only revenue-raising mechanism extended to school districts, is practically and legally unavailable. . . .

The Equal Protection Clause permits discriminations between classes but requires that the classification bear some rational relationship to a permissible object sought to be attained by the statute. It is not enough that the Texas system before us seeks to achieve the valid, rational purpose of maximizing local initiative; the means chosen by the State must also be rationally related to the end sought to be achieved. . . .

Neither Texas nor the majority heeds this rule. If the State aims at maximizing local initiative and local choice, by permitting school districts to resort to the real property tax if they choose to do so, it utterly fails in achieving its purpose in districts with property tax bases so low that there is little if any opportunity for interested parents, rich or poor, to augment school district revenues. Requiring the State to establish only that unequal treatment is in furtherance of a permissible goal, without also requiring the State to show that the means chosen to effectuate that goal are rationally related to its achievement, makes equal protection analysis no more than an empty gesture. In my view, the parents and children in Edgewood, and in like districts, suffer from an invidious discrimination violative of the Equal Protection Clause.

This does not, of course, mean that local control may not be a legitimate goal of a school-financing system. Nor does it mean that the State must guarantee each district an equal per-pupil revenue from the state school-financing system. . . . On the contrary, it would merely mean that the State must fashion a financing scheme which provides a rational basis for the maximization of local control. . . .

MR. JUSTICE MARSHALL, with whom MR. JUSTICE DOUGLAS concurs, dissenting. . . .

I

The Court acknowledges that "substantial interdistrict disparities in school expenditures" exist in Texas, and that these disparities are "largely attributable to differences in the amounts of money collected through local property taxation." But instead of closely examining the seriousness of these disparities and the invidiousness of the Texas financing scheme, the Court undertakes an elaborate exploration of the efforts Texas has purportedly made to close the gaps between its districts in terms of levels of district wealth and resulting educational funding. Yet, however praiseworthy Texas' equalizing efforts, the issue in this case is not whether Texas is doing its best to ameliorate the worst features of a discriminatory scheme but, rather, whether the scheme itself is in fact unconstitutionally discriminatory in the face of the Fourteenth Amendment's guarantee of equal protection of the laws. . . .

Notes and Questions

(1) Should the classification in *Rodriguez* be treated the same as the one in *Railway Express*? On what basis could you argue that the Court should review the law in *Rodriguez* more carefully?

(2) Is the Fourteenth Amendment designed to protect against wealth discrimination? Consider the *Carolene Products* criteria. Are the poor a "discrete and insular" minority? Is poverty, like race, an unalterable trait? Are the poor able to protect themselves in the political process?

(3) Should there be a constitutional right to a "minimum level" of basic needs like food and education? *See Papasan v. Allain*, 478 U.S. 265, 285 (1986) ("This Court has not yet definitively settled the questions whether a minimally adequate education is a fundamental right and whether a statute alleged to discriminatorily infringe that right should be accorded heightened equal protection review").

It has been said that the Constitution is a "charter of negative liberties; it tells the state to let people alone; it does not require the federal government or the state to provide services." *Bowers v. DeVito*, 686 F.2d 616, 618 (7th Cir. 1982). *See also DeShaney v. Winnebago County Department of Social Services*, 489 U.S. 189 (1989). Is this a helpful distinction? In *Rodriguez*, were plaintiffs arguing that the state had an affirmative obligation to provide an adequate education? Or were they arguing that the state could not provide education in a way that discriminates?

(4) Did the "Sesame Street" problem appear in *Rodriguez*? How did the Court describe the category of people who were the victims of discrimination? How else might you define the category?

(5) Consider the question of remedy. Given the limited remedial powers of the courts, how could the Court have enforced a decree in *Rodriguez*? Are issues raised concerning separation of powers between the judicial and legislative branches?

(6) To what extent did federalism influence the *Rodriguez* outcome? What federalism values are served by the Texas school financing scheme? For an account of the history of the San Antonio school litigation, see Jonathan Kozol, Savage Inequalities 213–229 (1991).

(7) In *United States Dept. of Agriculture v. Moreno*, 413 U.S. 528 (1973), the Court considered the constitutionality of § 3(e) of the Food Stamp Act of 1964, 7 U.S.C. § 2012(e), which excluded from participation in the food stamp program any household containing an individual who is unrelated to any other member of the household. As the Court stated, "in practical effect, § 3(e) creates two classes of persons for food stamp purposes: one class is composed of those individuals who live in households all of whose members are related to one another, and the other class consists of those individuals who live in households containing one or more members who are unrelated to the rest."

The Court applied the deferential rational basis test but held that the law was an unconstitutional denial of equal protection. The government argued that "Congress might rationally have thought (1) that households with one or more unrelated members are more likely than 'fully related' households to contain individuals who abuse the program by fraudulently failing to report sources of income or by voluntarily remaining poor; and (2) that such households are 'relatively unstable,' thereby increasing the difficulty of detecting such abuses."

In rejecting that argument, the Court stated: "Even if we were to accept as rational the Government's wholly unsubstantiated assumptions concerning the differences between 'related' and 'unrelated' households, we still could not agree with the Government's conclusion that the denial of essential federal food assistance to all otherwise eligible households containing unrelated members constitutes a rational effort to deal with these concerns."

The Court referenced legislative history, which indicated that that § 3(e) was intended to prevent so-called "hippies" and "hippie communes" from participating in the food stamp program. It concluded that "the challenged classification clearly cannot be sustained by reference to this congressional purpose. For if the constitutional conception of 'equal protection of the laws' means anything, it must, at the very least, mean that a bare congressional desire to harm a politically unpopular group cannot constitute a *legitimate* governmental interest."

Problem A

A pending bill before the state legislature provides that public assistance to a family will be terminated if the mother gives birth to a child while the family is receiving public assistance benefits. You have been asked to testify at a legislative committee hearing on whether the bill violates the Equal Protection Clause. What would you say?

§ 6.03 Racial Classification

A. Constitutional Standard

Plessy v. Ferguson
United States Supreme Court
163 U.S. 537, 16 S. Ct. 1138, 41 L. Ed. 256 (1896)

MR. JUSTICE BROWN delivered the opinion of the court.

This case turns upon the constitutionality of an act of the general assembly of the state of Louisiana, passed in 1890, providing for separate railway carriages for the white and colored races. . . .

The petition for the writ of prohibition averred that petitioner was seven-eighths Caucasian and one-eighth African blood; that the mixture of colored blood was not discernible in him; and that he was entitled to every right, privilege, and immunity secured to citizens of the United States of the white race; and that, upon such theory, he took possession of a vacant seat in a coach where passengers of the white race were accommodated, and was ordered by the conductor to vacate said coach, and take a seat in another, assigned to persons of the colored race, and, having refused to comply with such demand, he was forcibly ejected, with the aid of a police officer, and imprisoned in the parish jail to answer a charge of having violated the above act.

The constitutionality of this act is attacked upon the ground that it conflicts both with the Thirteenth Amendment of the constitution, abolishing slavery, and the Fourteenth Amendment, which prohibits certain restrictive legislation on the part of the states.

1. That it does not conflict with the Thirteenth Amendment, which abolished slavery and involuntary servitude, except as a punishment for crime, is too clear for argument. Slavery implies involuntary servitude, a state of bondage; the ownership of mankind as a chattel, or, at least, the control of the labor and services of one man for the benefit of another, and the absence of a legal right to the disposal of his own person, property, and services. This Amendment was said in the *Slaughter House Cases*, 16 Wall. 36, to have been intended primarily to abolish slavery, as it had been previously known in this country, and that it equally forbade Mexican peonage or the Chinese coolie trade, when they amounted to slavery or involuntary servitude, and that the use of the word "servitude" was intended to prohibit the use of all forms of involuntary slavery, of whatever class or name. It was intimated, however, in that case, that this Amendment was regarded by the statesmen of that day as insufficient

to protect the colored race from certain laws which had been enacted in the Southern states, imposing upon the colored race onerous disabilities and burdens, and curtailing their rights in the pursuit of life, liberty, and property to such an extent that their freedom was of little value; and that the Fourteenth Amendment was devised to meet this exigency.

So, too, in the *Civil Rights Cases*, 109 U.S. 3, it was said that the act of a mere individual, the owner of an inn, a public conveyance or place of amusement, refusing accommodations to colored people, cannot be justly regarded as imposing any badge of slavery or servitude upon the applicant, but only as involving an ordinary civil injury, properly cognizable by the laws of the state, and presumably subject to redress by those laws until the contrary appears. "It would be running the slavery question into the ground," said Mr. Justice Bradley, "to make it apply to every act of discrimination which a person may see fit to make as to the guests he will entertain, or as to the people he will take into his coach or cab or car, or admit to his concert or theater, or deal with in other matters of intercourse or business."

A statute which implies merely a legal distinction between the white and colored races a distinction which is founded in the color of the two races, and which must always exist so long as white men are distinguished from the other race by color has no tendency to destroy the legal equality of the two races, or re-establish a state of involuntary servitude. . . .

2. By the Fourteenth Amendment, all persons born or naturalized in the United States, and subject to the jurisdiction thereof, are made citizens of the United States and of the state wherein they reside; and the states are forbidden from making or enforcing any law which shall abridge the privileges or immunities of citizens of the United States, or shall deprive any person of life, liberty, or property without due process of law, or deny to any person within their jurisdiction the equal protection of the laws. . . .

The object of the Amendment was undoubtedly to enforce the absolute equality of the two races before the law, but, in the nature of things, it could not have been intended to abolish distinctions based upon color, or to enforce social, as distinguished from political, equality, or a commingling of the two races upon terms unsatisfactory to either. Laws permitting, and even requiring, their separation, in places where they are liable to be brought into contact, do not necessarily imply the inferiority of either race to the other, and have been generally, if not universally, recognized as within the competency of the state legislatures in the exercise of their police power. The most common instance of this is connected with the establishment of separate schools for white and colored children, which have been held to be a valid exercise of the legislative power even by courts of states where the political rights of the colored race have been longest and most earnestly enforced. . . .

Laws forbidding the intermarriage of the two races may be said in a technical sense to interfere with the freedom of contract, and yet have been universally recognized as within the police power of the state.

The distinction between laws interfering with the political equality of the negro and those requiring the separation of the two races in schools, theaters, and railway carriages has been frequently drawn by this court. . . .

It is claimed by the plaintiff in error that, in any mixed community, the reputation of belonging to the dominant race, in this instance the white race, is "property," in the same sense that a right of action or of inheritance is property. Conceding this to be so, for the purposes of this case, we are unable to see how this statute deprives him of, or in any way affects his right to, such property. If he be a white man, and assigned to a colored coach, he may have his action for damages against the company for being deprived of his so-called "property." Upon the other hand, if he be a colored man, and be so assigned, he has been deprived of no property, since he is not lawfully entitled to the reputation of being a white man.

In this connection, it is also suggested by the learned counsel for the plaintiff in error that the same argument that will justify the state legislature in requiring railways to provide separate accommodations for the two races will also authorize them to require separate cars to be provided for people whose hair is of a certain color, or who are aliens, or who belong to certain nationalities, or to enact laws requiring colored people to walk upon one side of the street, and white people upon the other, or requiring white men's houses to be painted white, and colored men's black, or their vehicles or business signs to be of different colors, upon the theory that one side of the street is as good as the other, or that a house or vehicle of one color is as good as one of another color. The reply to all this is that every exercise of the police power must be reasonable, and extend only to such laws as are enacted in good faith for the promotion of the public good, and not for the annoyance or oppression of a particular class. . . .

So far, then, as a conflict with the Fourteenth Amendment is concerned, the case reduces itself to the question whether the statute of Louisiana is a reasonable regulation, and with respect to this there must necessarily be a large discretion on the part of the legislature. In determining the question of reasonableness, it is at liberty to act with reference to the established usages, customs, and traditions of the people, and with a view to the promotion of their comfort, and the preservation of the public peace and good order. Gauged by this standard, we cannot say that a law which authorizes or even requires the separation of the two races in public conveyances is unreasonable, or more obnoxious to the Fourteenth Amendment than the acts of congress requiring separate schools for colored children in the District of Columbia, the constitutionality of which does not seem to have been questioned, or the corresponding acts of state legislatures.

We consider the underlying fallacy of the plaintiff's argument to consist in the assumption that the enforced separation of the two races stamps the colored race with a badge of inferiority. If this be so, it is not by reason of anything found in the act, but solely because the colored race chooses to put that construction upon it. The argument necessarily assumes that if, as has been more than once the case, and is not unlikely to be so again, the colored race should become the dominant power in the state legislature, and should enact a law in precisely similar terms, it would thereby relegate the white race to an inferior position. We imagine that the white race, at least, would not acquiesce in this assumption. The argument also assumes that social prejudices may be overcome by legislation, and that equal rights cannot be secured to the negro except by an enforced commingling of the two races. We cannot accept this proposition. If the two races are to meet upon terms of social equality, it must be the result of natural affinities, a mutual appreciation of each other's merits, and a voluntary consent of individuals. . . . Legislation is powerless to eradicate racial instincts, or to abolish distinctions based upon physical differences, and the attempt to do so can only result in accentuating the difficulties of the present situation. If the civil and political rights of both races be equal, one cannot be inferior to the other civilly or politically. If one race be inferior to the other socially, the constitution of the United States cannot put them upon the same plane.

It is true that the question of the proportion of colored blood necessary to constitute a colored person, as distinguished from a white person, is one upon which there is a difference of opinion in the different states; some holding that any visible admixture of black blood stamps the person as belonging to the colored race; others, that it depends upon the preponderance of blood, and still others, that the predominance of white blood must only be in the proportion of three-fourths. But these are questions to be determined under the laws of each state, and are not properly put in issue in this case. Under the allegations of his petition, it may undoubtedly become a question of importance whether, under the laws of Louisiana, the petitioner belongs to the white or colored race. . . .

Mr. Justice Harlan dissenting.

. . . In respect of civil rights, common to all citizens, the constitution of the United States does not, I think, permit any public authority to know the race of those entitled to be protected in the enjoyment of such rights. Every true man has pride of race, and under appropriate circumstances, when the rights of others, his equals before the law, are not to be affected, it is his privilege to express such pride and to take such action based upon it as to him seems proper. But I deny that any legislative body or judicial tribunal may have regard to the race of citizens when the civil rights of those citizens are involved. Indeed, such legislation as that here in question is inconsistent not only with that equality of rights which pertains to citizenship, national and state, but with the personal liberty enjoyed by every one within the United States. . . .

These notable additions [Civil War Amendments] to the fundamental law were welcomed by the friends of liberty throughout the world. They removed the race line from our governmental systems. They had, as this court has said, a common purpose, namely, to secure "to a race recently emancipated, a race that through many generations have been held in slavery, all the civil rights that the superior race enjoy." They declared, in legal effect, this court has further said, "that the law in the states shall be the same for the black as for the white; that all persons, whether colored or white, shall stand equal before the laws of the states; and in regard to the colored race, for whose protection the Amendment was primarily designed, that no discrimination shall be made against them by law because of their color." . . .

It was said in argument that the statute of Louisiana does not discriminate against either race, but prescribes a rule applicable alike to white and colored citizens. But this argument does not meet the difficulty. Every one knows that the statute in question had its origin in the purpose, not so much to exclude white persons from railroad cars occupied by blacks, as to exclude colored people from coaches occupied by or assigned to white persons. . . .

The white race deems itself to be the dominant race in this country. And so it is, in prestige, in achievements, in education, in wealth, and in power. So, I doubt not, it will continue to be for all time, if it remains true to its great heritage, and holds fast to the principles of constitutional liberty. But in view of the constitution, in the eye of the law, there is in this country no superior, dominant, ruling class of citizens. There is no caste here. Our constitution is color-blind, and neither knows nor tolerates classes among citizens. In respect of civil rights, all citizens are equal before the law. The humblest is the peer of the most powerful. The law regards man as man, and takes no account of his surroundings or of his color when his civil rights as guarantied by the supreme law of the land are involved. It is therefore to be regretted that this high tribunal, the final expositor of the fundamental law of the land, has reached the conclusion that it is competent for a state to regulate the enjoyment by citizens of their civil rights solely upon the basis of race.

In my opinion, the judgment this day rendered will, in time, prove to be quite as pernicious as the decision made by this tribunal in the *Dred Scott Case*. . . .

The present decision, it may well be apprehended, will not only stimulate aggressions, more or less brutal and irritating, upon the admitted rights of colored citizens, but will encourage the belief that it is possible, by means of state enactments, to defeat the beneficent purposes which the people of the United States had in view when they adopted the recent amendments of the constitution, by one of which the blacks of this country were made citizens of the United States and of the states in which they respectively reside, and whose privileges and immunities, as citizens, the states are forbidden to abridge. Sixty millions of whites are in no danger from the presence here of eight millions of blacks. The destinies of the two races, in this country, are indissolubly linked together, and the interests of both require that the common government of all shall not permit the seeds of race hate to be planted under the sanction of law. What can more certainly arouse race hate, what more certainly create and perpetuate a feeling of distrust between these races, than state enactments which, in fact, proceed on the ground that colored citizens are so inferior and degraded that they cannot be allowed to sit in public coaches occupied by white citizens? That, as all will admit, is the real meaning of such legislation as was enacted in Louisiana. . . .

The arbitrary separation of citizens, on the basis of race, while they are on a public highway, is a badge of servitude wholly inconsistent with the civil freedom and the equality before the law established by the constitution. It cannot be justified upon any legal grounds.

If evils will result from the commingling of the two races upon public highways established for the benefit of all, they will be infinitely less than those that will surely come from state legislation regulating the enjoyment of civil rights upon the basis of race. We boast of the freedom enjoyed by our people above all other peoples. But it is difficult to reconcile that boast with a state of the law which, practically, puts the brand of servitude and degradation upon a large class of our fellow citizens, our equals before the law. The thin disguise of "equal" accommodations for passengers in railroad coaches will not mislead any one, nor atone for the wrong this day done. . . .

If laws of like character should be enacted in the several states of the Union, the effect would be in the highest degree mischievous. Slavery, as an institution tolerated by law, would, it is true, have disappeared from our country; but there would remain a power in the states, by sinister legislation, to interfere with the full enjoyment of the blessings of freedom, to regulate civil rights, common to all citizens, upon the basis of race, and to place in a condition of legal inferiority a large body of American citizens, now constituting a part of the political community, called the "People of the United States," for whom, and by whom through representatives, our government is administered. Such a system is inconsistent with the guaranty given by the constitution to each state of a republican form of government, and may be stricken down by congressional action, or by the courts in the discharge of their solemn duty to maintain the supreme law of the land, anything in the constitution or laws of any state to the contrary notwithstanding. . . .

Korematsu v. United States

United States Supreme Court
323 U.S. 214, 65 S. Ct. 193, 89 L. Ed. 194 (1944)

MR. JUSTICE BLACK delivered the opinion of the Court.

The petitioner, an American citizen of Japanese descent, was convicted in a federal district court for remaining in San Leandro, California, a "Military Area", contrary to Civilian Exclusion Order No. 34 of the Commanding General of the Western Command, U.S. Army, which directed that after May 9, 1942, all persons of Japanese ancestry should be excluded from that area. No question was raised as to petitioner's loyalty to the United States. . . .

It should be noted, to begin with, that all legal restrictions which curtail the civil rights of a single racial group are immediately suspect. That is not to say that all such restrictions are unconstitutional. It is to say that courts must subject them to the most rigid scrutiny. Pressing public necessity may sometimes justify the existence of such restrictions; racial antagonism never can. . . .

Exclusion Order No. 34, which the petitioner knowingly and admittedly violated was one of a number of military orders and proclamations, all of which were substantially based upon Executive Order No. 9066, 7 Fed. Reg. 1407. That order, issued after we were at war with Japan, declared that "the successful prosecution of the war requires every possible protection against espionage and against sabotage to national-defense material, national-defense premises, and national-defense utilities."

One of the series of orders and proclamations, a curfew order, which like the exclusion order here was promulgated pursuant to Executive Order 9066, subjected all persons of Japanese ancestry in prescribed West Coast military areas to remain in their residences from 8 p.m. to 6 a.m. As is the case with the exclusion order here, that prior curfew order was designed as a "protection against espionage and against sabotage." In *Hirabayashi v. United States*, 320 U.S. 81 [(1943)], we sustained a conviction obtained for violation of the curfew order. The *Hirabayashi* conviction and this one thus rest on the same 1942 Congressional Act and the same basic executive and military orders, all of which orders were aimed at the twin dangers of espionage and sabotage.

The 1942 Act was attacked in the *Hirabayashi* case as an unconstitutional delegation of power; it was contended that the curfew order and other orders on which it rested were beyond the war powers of the Congress, the military authorities and of the President, as Commander in Chief of the Army; and finally that to apply the curfew order against none but citizens of Japanese ancestry amounted to a constitutionally prohibited discrimination solely on account of race. To these questions, we gave the serious consideration which their importance justified. We upheld the curfew order as an exercise of the power of the government to take steps necessary to prevent espionage and sabotage in an area threatened by Japanese attack.

In the light of the principles we announced in the *Hirabayashi* case, we are unable to conclude that it was beyond the war power of Congress and the Executive to exclude those of Japanese ancestry from the West Coast war area at the time they did. True, exclusion from the area in which one's home is located is a far greater deprivation than constant confinement to the home from 8 p.m. to 6 a.m. Nothing short of apprehension by the proper military authorities of the gravest imminent danger to the public safety can constitutionally justify either. But exclusion from a threatened area, no less than curfew, has a definite and close relationship to the prevention of espionage and sabotage. The military authorities, charged with the primary responsibility of defending our shores, concluded that curfew provided inadequate protection and ordered exclusion. They did so, as pointed out in our *Hirabayashi* opinion, in accordance with Congressional authority to the military to say who should, and who should not, remain in the threatened areas.

In this case the petitioner challenges the assumptions upon which we rested our conclusions in the *Hirabayashi* case. He also urges that by May 1942, when Order No. 34 was promulgated, all danger of Japanese invasion of the West Coast had disappeared. After careful consideration of these contentions we are compelled to reject them.

Here, as in the *Hirabayashi* case, "we cannot reject as unfounded the judgment of the military authorities and of Congress that there were disloyal members of that population, whose number and strength could not be precisely and quickly ascertained. We cannot say that the war-making branches of the Government did not have ground for believing that in a critical hour such persons could not readily be isolated and separately dealt with, and constituted a menace to the national defense and safety, which demanded that prompt and adequate measures be taken to guard against it."

Like curfew, exclusion of those of Japanese origin was deemed necessary because of the presence of an unascertained number of disloyal members of the group, most of whom we have no doubt were loyal to this country. It was because we could not reject the finding of the military authorities that it was impossible to bring about an immediate segregation of the disloyal from the loyal that we sustained the validity of the curfew order as applying to the whole group. In the instant case, temporary exclusion of the entire group was rested by the military on the same ground. The judgment that exclusion of the whole group was for the same reason a military imperative answers the contention that the exclusion was in the nature of group punishment based on antagonism to those of Japanese origin. That there were members of the group who retained loyalties to Japan has been confirmed by investigations made subsequent to the exclusion. Approximately five thousand American citizens of Japanese ancestry refused to swear unqualified allegiance to the United States and to renounce allegiance to the Japanese Emperor, and several thousand evacuees requested repatriation to Japan.

We uphold the exclusion order as of the time it was made and when the petitioner violated it. In doing so, we are not unmindful of the hardships imposed by it upon a large group of American citizens. But hardships are part of war, and war is an aggregation of hardships. All citizens alike, both in and out of uniform, feel the impact of war in greater or lesser measure. Citizenship has its responsibilities as well as its privileges, and in time of war the burden is always heavier. Compulsory exclusion of large groups of citizens from their homes, except under circumstances of direst emergency and peril, is inconsistent with our basic governmental institutions. But when under conditions of modern warfare our shores are threatened by hostile forces, the power to protect must be commensurate with the threatened danger. . . .

It is said that we are dealing here with the case of imprisonment of a citizen in a concentration camp solely because of his ancestry, without evidence or inquiry concerning his loyalty and good disposition towards the United States. Our task would be simple, our duty clear, were this a case involving the imprisonment of a loyal citizen in a concentration camp because of racial prejudice. Regardless of the true nature of the assembly and relocation centers — and we deem it unjustifiable to call them concentration camps with all the ugly connotations that term implies — we are dealing specifically with nothing but an exclusion order. To cast this case into outlines of racial prejudice, without reference to the real military dangers which were presented, merely confuses the issue. Korematsu was not excluded from the Military Area because of hostility to him or his race. He was excluded because we are at war with the Japanese Empire, because the properly constituted military authorities feared an invasion of our West Coast and felt constrained to take proper security measures, because they decided that the military urgency of the situation demanded that all citizens of Japanese ancestry be segregated from the West Coast temporarily, and finally, because Congress, reposing its confidence in this time of war in our military leaders as inevitably it must determined that they should have the power to do just this. There was evidence of disloyalty on the part of some, the military authorities considered that the need for action was great, and time was short. We cannot by availing ourselves of the calm perspective of hindsight now say that at that time these actions were unjustified.

Affirmed.

Mr. Justice Frankfurter, concurring. [Omitted]

Mr. Justice Roberts, dissenting.

I dissent, because I think the indisputable facts exhibit a clear violation of Constitutional rights.

This is not a case of keeping people off the streets at night as was *Hirabayashi v. United States*, nor a case of temporary exclusion of a citizen from an area for his own safety or that of the community, nor a case of offering him an opportunity to go temporarily out of an area where his presence might cause danger to himself or to his fellows. On the contrary, it is the case of convicting a citizen as a punishment for not submitting to imprisonment in a concentration camp, based on his ancestry, and solely because of his ancestry, without evidence or inquiry concerning his loyalty and good disposition towards the United States. If this be a correct statement of the facts disclosed by this record, and facts of which we take judicial notice, I need hardly labor the conclusion that Constitutional rights have been violated. . . .

Mr. Justice Murphy, dissenting.

This exclusion of "all persons of Japanese ancestry, both alien and non-alien," from the Pacific Coast area on a plea of military necessity in the absence of martial law ought not to be approved. Such exclusion goes over "the very brink of constitutional power" and falls into the ugly abyss of racism.

In dealing with matters relating to the prosecution and progress of a war, we must accord great respect and consideration to the judgments of the military authorities who are on the scene and who have full knowledge of the military facts. The scope of their discretion must, as a matter of necessity and common sense, be wide. And their judgments ought not to be overruled lightly by those whose training and duties ill-equip them to deal intelligently with matters so vital to the physical security of the nation.

At the same time, however, it is essential that there be definite limits to military discretion, especially where martial law has not been declared. Individuals must not be left impoverished of their constitutional rights on a plea of military necessity that has neither substance nor support. Thus, like other claims conflicting with the asserted constitutional rights of the individual, the military claim must subject itself to the judicial process of having its reasonableness determined and its conflicts with other interests reconciled. "What are the allowable limits of military discretion, and whether or not they have been overstepped in a particular case, are judicial questions."

The judicial test of whether the Government, on a plea of military necessity, can validly deprive an individual of any of his constitutional rights is whether the deprivation is reasonably related to a public danger that is so "immediate, imminent, and impending" as not to admit of delay and not to permit the intervention of ordinary constitutional processes to alleviate the danger. Civilian Exclusion Order No. 34, banishing from a prescribed area of the Pacific Coast "all persons of Japanese ancestry, both alien and non-alien," clearly does not meet that test. Being an obvious racial discrimination, the order deprives all those within its scope of the equal protection of the laws as guaranteed by the Fifth Amendment. It further deprives these individuals of their constitutional rights to live and work where they will, to establish a home where they choose and to move about freely. In excommunicating them without benefit of hearings, this order also deprives them of all their constitutional rights to procedural due process. Yet no reasonable relation to an "immediate, imminent, and impending" public danger is evident to support this racial restriction which is one of the most sweeping and complete deprivations of constitutional rights in the history of this nation in the absence of martial law.

It must be conceded that the military and naval situation in the spring of 1942 was such as to generate a very real fear of invasion of the Pacific Coast, accompanied by fears of sabotage and espionage in that area. The military command was therefore justified in adopting all reasonable means necessary to combat these dangers. In adjudging the military action taken in light of the then apparent dangers, we must not erect too high or too meticulous standards; it is necessary only that the action have some reasonable relation to the removal of the dangers of invasion, sabotage and espionage. But the exclusion, either temporarily or permanently, of all persons with Japanese blood in their veins has no such reasonable relation. And that relation is lacking because the exclusion order necessarily must rely for its reasonableness upon the assumption that all persons of Japanese ancestry may have a dangerous tendency to commit sabotage and espionage and to aid our Japanese enemy in other ways. It is difficult to believe that reason, logic or experience could be marshalled in support of such an assumption.

That this forced exclusion was the result in good measure of this erroneous assumption of racial guilt rather than bona fide military necessity is evidenced by the Commanding General's Final Report on the evacuation from the Pacific Coast area. In it he refers to all individuals of Japanese descent as "subversive," as belonging to "an enemy race" whose "racial strains are undiluted," and as constituting "over 112,000 potential enemies * * * at large today" along the Pacific Coast. In support of this blanket condemnation of all persons of Japanese descent, however, no reliable evidence is cited to show that such individuals were generally disloyal or had generally so conducted themselves in this area as to constitute a special menace to defense installations or war industries, or had otherwise by their behavior furnished reasonable ground for their exclusion as a group. . . .

Justification for the exclusion is sought, instead, mainly upon questionable racial and sociological grounds not ordinarily within the realm of expert military judgment, supplemented by certain semi-military conclusions drawn from an unwarranted use of circumstantial evidence. Individuals of Japanese ancestry are condemned because they are said to be "a large, unassimilated, tightly knit racial group, bound to an enemy nation by strong ties of race, culture, custom and religion." They are claimed to be given to "emperor worshipping ceremonies" and to "dual citizenship." Japanese language schools and allegedly pro-Japanese organizations are cited as evidence of possible group disloyalty, together with facts as to certain persons being educated and residing at length in Japan. It is intimated that many of these individuals deliberately resided "adjacent to strategic points," thus enabling them "to carry into execution a tremendous program of sabotage on a mass scale should any considerable number of them have been inclined to do so." The need for protective custody is also asserted. The report refers without identity to "numerous incidents of violence" as well as to other admittedly unverified or cumulative incidents. From this, plus certain other events not shown to have been connected with the Japanese Americans, it is concluded that the "situation was fraught with danger to the Japanese population itself" and that the general public "was ready to take matters into its own hands." Finally, it is intimated, though not directly charged or proved, that persons of Japanese ancestry were responsible for three minor isolated shellings and bombings of the Pacific Coast area, as well as for unidentified radio transmissions and night signalling.

The main reasons relied upon by those responsible for the forced evacuation, therefore, do not prove a reasonable relation between the group characteristics of Japanese Americans and the dangers of invasion, sabotage and espionage. The reasons appear, instead, to be largely an accumulation of much of the misinformation, half-truths and insinuations that for years have been directed against Japanese Americans by people with racial and economic prejudices the same people who have been among the foremost advocates of the evacuation. A military judgment based upon such racial and sociological considerations is not entitled to the great weight ordinarily given the judgments based upon strictly military considerations. Especially is this so when every charge relative to race, religion, culture, geographical location, and legal and economic status has been substantially discredited by independent studies made by experts in these matters.

The military necessity which is essential to the validity of the evacuation order thus resolves itself into a few intimations that certain individuals actively aided the enemy, from which it is inferred that the entire group of Japanese Americans could not be trusted to be or remain loyal to the United States. No one denies, of course, that there were some disloyal persons of Japanese descent on the Pacific Coast who did all in their power to aid their ancestral land. Similar disloyal activities have been engaged in by many persons of German, Italian and even more pioneer stock in our country. But to infer that examples of individual disloyalty prove group disloyalty and justify discriminatory action against the entire group is to deny that under our system of law individual guilt is the sole basis for deprivation of rights. Moreover, this inference, which is at the very heart of the evacuation orders, has been used in support of the abhorrent and despicable treatment of minority groups by the dictatorial tyrannies which this nation is now pledged to destroy. To give constitutional sanction to that inference in this case, however well-intentioned may have been the military command on the Pacific Coast, is to adopt one of the cruelest of the rationales used by our enemies to destroy the dignity of the individual and to encourage and open the door to discriminatory actions against other minority groups in the passions of tomorrow.

No adequate reason is given for the failure to treat these Japanese Americans on an individual basis by holding investigations and hearings to separate the loyal from the disloyal, as was done in the case of persons of German and Italian ancestry. . . .

I dissent, therefore, from this legalization of racism. Racial discrimination in any form and in any degree has no justifiable part whatever in our democratic way of life. It is unattractive in any setting but it is utterly revolting among a free people who have embraced the principles set forth in the Constitution of the United States. All residents of this nation are kin in some way by blood or culture to a foreign land. Yet they are primarily and necessarily a part of the new and distinct civilization of the United States. They must accordingly be treated at all times as the heirs of the American experiment and as entitled to all the rights and freedoms guaranteed by the Constitution.

MR. JUSTICE JACKSON, dissenting.

Korematsu was born on our soil, of parents born in Japan. The Constitution makes him a citizen of the United States by nativity and a citizen of California by residence. No claim is made that he is not loyal to this country. There is no suggestion that apart from the matter involved here he is not law-abiding and well disposed. Korematsu, however, has been convicted of an act not commonly a crime. It consists merely of being present in the state whereof he is a citizen, near the place where he was born, and where all his life he has lived. . . .

A citizen's presence in the locality, however, was made a crime only if his parents were of Japanese birth. Had Korematsu been one of four the others being, say, a German alien enemy, an Italian alien enemy, and a citizen of American-born ancestors, convicted of treason but out on parole only Korematsu's presence would have violated the order. The difference between their innocence and his crime would result, not from anything he did, said, or thought, different than they, but only in that he was born of different racial stock.

Now, if any fundamental assumption underlies our system, it is that guilt is personal and not inheritable. Even if all of one's antecedents had been convicted of treason, the Constitution forbids its penalties to be visited upon him. . . . But here is an attempt to make an otherwise innocent act a crime merely because this prisoner is the son of parents as to whom he had no choice, and belongs to a race from which there is no way to resign. . . .

Much is said of the danger to liberty from the Army program for deporting and detaining these citizens of Japanese extraction. But a judicial construction of the due process clause that will sustain this order is a far more subtle blow to liberty than the promulgation of the order itself. A military order, however unconstitutional, is not apt to last longer than the military emergency. Even during that period a succeeding commander may revoke it all. But once a judicial opinion rationalizes such an order to show that it conforms to the Constitution, or rather rationalizes the Constitution to show that the Constitution sanctions such an order, the Court for all time has validated the principle of racial discrimination in criminal procedure and of transplanting American citizens. The principle then lies about like a loaded weapon ready for the hand of any authority that can bring forward a plausible claim of an urgent need. Every repetition imbeds that principle more deeply in our law and thinking and expands it to new purposes. . . .

Notes and Questions

(1) After the *Dred Scott* decision and the Civil War, the Constitution was amended to include the Thirteenth Amendment, which abolished slavery, and the Fourteenth Amendment, which provided that all persons born or naturalized in the United States are citizens of the U.S. and the state where they reside. Yet, despite the Amendments, the Court upheld the "separate, but equal" law challenged in *Plessy*. Is *Plessy* similar to *Scott*?

(2) Does the Court in *Plessy* view the core equality principle as "equal treatment" or "equal respect and concern?"

(3) It is interesting to note that Plessy argued that he was not "colored," but rather was really "white" and, thus, had a property right to the privileges flowing to members of that group. Why do you think he adopted this strategy, rather than one that conceded membership in the targeted group? For an analysis of the property concept of whiteness, see Cheryl Harris, *Whiteness as Property*, 106 HARV. L. REV. 1709 (1993).

Plessy was seven-eighths Caucasian, and you may be wondering how the Railroad officials knew he was "colored." For a fascinating account of the design of the case as a test case, see CHARLES LOFGREN, THE PLESSY CASE (1987).

(4) How does the majority in *Korematsu* define the excluded category of people? Can you define it differently? What was the basis for the military order if it was not race?

(5) What did Justice Jackson mean when he wrote that a judicial construction of the Constitution that sustains the military order is a "far more subtle blow to liberty than the promulgation of the order itself"?

(6) Do you see any similarities between *Plessy* and *Korematsu*?

(7) Ironically, the principle that racial classifications are "suspect" and subject to close judicial scrutiny originated in *Korematsu*. Recall that Justice Black stated that "all legal restrictions which curtail the civil rights of a single racial group are immediately suspect. . . . [C]ourts must subject them to the most rigid scrutiny. . . ." Why should racial classifications be treated as suspect and subject to the most rigid judicial scrutiny?

(8) For subsequent history of *Korematsu*, see *Korematsu v. United States*, 584 F. Supp. 1406 (N.D. Calif. 1984) (vacating conviction). *See also* Peter Irons, Justice at War (1983).

(9) While the decision in *Korematsu* came to be broadly repudiated in American politics, law, and culture, the Supreme Court of the United States did not formally declare *Korematsu* overruled until 2018. In *Trump v. Hawaii*, 138 S. Ct. 2392, 2423 (2018), the Supreme Court upheld an immigration ban imposed by President Donald Trump through an Executive Order. Those who challenged the ban characterized it as an "anti-Muslim" ban, and the dissenters in the Supreme Court likened President Trump's actions to *Korematsu*. The opinion of the Court, written by Chief Justice Roberts, rejected the analogy to *Korematsu*. The Chief Justice also took advantage of the invocation of *Korematsu* to declare the case repdudiated:

> Finally, the dissent invokes *Korematsu v. United States*. Whatever rhetorical advantage the dissent may see in doing so, *Korematsu* has nothing to do with this case. The forcible relocation of U.S. citizens to concentration camps, solely and explicitly on the basis of race, is objectively unlawful and outside the scope of Presidential authority. But it is wholly inapt to liken that morally repugnant order to a facially neutral policy denying certain foreign nationals the privilege of admission. The entry suspension is an act that is well within executive authority and could have been taken by any other President — the only question is evaluating the actions of this particular President in promulgating an otherwise valid Proclamation.

> The dissent's reference to *Korematsu*, however, affords this Court the opportunity to make express what is already obvious: *Korematsu* was gravely wrong the day it was decided, has been overruled in the court of history, and — to be clear — "has no place in law under the Constitution." 323 U.S., at 248, 65 S.Ct. 193 (Jackson, J., dissenting).

Brown v. Board of Education [Brown I]

United States Supreme Court
347 U.S. 483, 74 S. Ct. 686, 98 L. Ed. 873 (1954)

MR. CHIEF JUSTICE WARREN delivered the opinion of the Court.

These cases come to us from the States of Kansas, South Carolina, Virginia, and Delaware. . . .

In each of the cases, minors of the Negro race, through their legal representatives, seek the aid of the courts in obtaining admission to the public schools of their community on a nonsegregated basis. In each instance, they have been denied admission to schools attended by white children under laws requiring or permitting segregation according to race. . . .

The plaintiffs contend that segregated public schools are not "equal" and cannot be made "equal," and that hence they are deprived of the equal protection of the laws. Because of the obvious importance of the question presented, the Court took jurisdiction. Argument was heard in the 1952 Term, and reargument was heard this Term on certain questions propounded by the Court.

Reargument was largely devoted to the circumstances surrounding the adoption of the Fourteenth Amendment in 1868. It covered exhaustively consideration of the Amendment in Congress, ratification by the states, then existing practices in racial segregation, and the views of proponents and opponents of the Amendment. This discussion and our own investigation convince us that, although these sources cast some light, it is not enough to resolve the problem with which we are faced. At best, they are inconclusive. The most avid proponents of the post-War Amendments undoubtedly intended them to remove all legal distinctions among "all persons born or naturalized in the United States." Their opponents, just as certainly, were antagonistic to both the letter and the spirit of the Amendments and wished them to have the most limited effect. What others in Congress and the state legislatures had in mind cannot be determined with any degree of certainty. . . .

In the first cases in this Court construing the Fourteenth Amendment, decided shortly after its adoption, the Court interpreted it as proscribing all state-imposed discriminations against the Negro race. The doctrine of "separate but equal" did not make its appearance in this Court until 1896 in the case of *Plessy v. Ferguson*, involving not education but transportation. American courts have since labored with the doctrine for over half a century. . . .

Here, unlike *Sweatt v. Painter* [339 U.S. 629 (1950)], there are findings below that the Negro and white schools involved have been equalized, or are being equalized, with respect to buildings, curricula, qualifications and salaries of teachers, and other "tangible" factors. Our decision, therefore, cannot turn on merely a comparison of these tangible factors in the Negro and white schools involved in each of the cases. We must look instead to the effect of segregation itself on public education.

In approaching this problem, we cannot turn the clock back to 1868 when the Amendment was adopted, or even to 1896 when *Plessy v. Ferguson* was written. We must consider public education in the light of its full development and its present place in American life throughout the Nation. Only in this way can it be determined if segregation in public schools deprives these plaintiffs of the equal protection of the laws.

Today, education is perhaps the most important function of state and local governments. Compulsory school attendance laws and the great expenditures for education both demonstrate our recognition of the importance of education to our democratic society. It is required in the performance of our most basic public responsibilities, even service in the armed forces. It is the very foundation of good citizenship. Today it is a principal instrument in awakening the child to cultural values, in preparing him for later professional training, and in helping him to adjust normally to this environment. In these days, it is doubtful that any child may reasonably be expected to succeed in life if he is denied the opportunity of an education. Such an opportunity, where the state has undertaken to provide it, is a right which must be made available to all on equal terms.

We come then to the question presented: Does segregation of children in public schools solely on the basis of race, even though the physical facilities and other "tangible" factors may be equal, deprive the children of the minority group of equal educational opportunities? We believe that it does.

In *Sweatt v. Painter*, in finding that a segregated law school for Negroes could not provide them equal educational opportunities, this Court relied in large part on "those qualities which are incapable of objective measurement but which make for greatness in a law school." In *McLaurin v. Oklahoma State Regents* [339 U.S. 637 (1950)], the Court, in requiring that a Negro admitted to a white graduate school be treated like all other students, again resorted to intangible considerations: ". . . his ability to study, to engage in discussions and exchange views with other students, and, in general, to learn his profession." Such considerations apply with added force to children in grade and high schools. To separate them from others of similar age and qualifications solely because of their race generates a feeling of inferiority as to their status in the community that may affect their hearts and minds in a way unlikely ever to be undone. The effect of this separation on their educational opportunities was well stated by a finding in the Kansas case by a court which nevertheless felt compelled to rule against the Negro plaintiffs:

> Segregation of white and colored children in public schools has a detrimental effect upon the colored children. The impact is greater when it has the sanction of the law; for the policy of separating the races is usually interpreted as denoting the inferiority of the negro group. A sense of inferiority affects the motivation of a child to learn. Segregation with the sanction of law, therefore, has a tendency to [retard] the educational and mental development of Negro children and to deprive them of some of the benefits they would receive in a racial[ly] integrated school system.

Whatever may have been the extent of psychological knowledge at the time of *Plessy v. Ferguson*, this finding is amply supported by modern authority.[2] Any language in *Plessy v. Ferguson* contrary to this finding is rejected.

We conclude that in the field of public education the doctrine of "separate but equal" has no place. Separate educational facilities are inherently unequal. Therefore, we hold that the plaintiffs and others similarly situated for whom the actions have been brought are, by reason of the segregation complained of, deprived of the equal protection of the laws guaranteed by the Fourteenth Amendment. This disposition makes unnecessary any discussion whether such segregation also violates the Due Process Clause of the Fourteenth Amendment.

Because these are class actions, because of the wide applicability of this decision, and because of the great variety of local conditions, the formulation of decrees in these cases presents problems of considerable complexity. On reargument, the consideration of appropriate relief was necessarily subordinate to the primary question — the constitutionality of segregation in public education. We have now announced that such segregation is a denial of the equal protection of the laws. In order that we may have the full assistance of the parties in formulating decrees, the cases will be restored to the docket, and the parties are requested to present further argument. . . .

Notes and Questions

(1) What did the Court hold in *Brown I*? Was the holding limited to state imposed racial segregation in education? Another possibility is that the holding was broader, invalidating racial segregation in every context. Indeed, after *Brown I*, the Court struck down racial segregation in, e.g., beaches (*Mayor of Baltimore v. Dawson*, 350 U.S. 877 (1955)); golf courses (*Holmes v. Atlanta*, 350 U.S. 879 (1955)); buses (*Gayle v. Browder*, 352 U.S. 903 (1956)); and parks (*New Orleans City Park Improvement Ass'n v. Detiege*, 358 U.S. 54 (1958)). Did *Brown I* thus stand for the proposition that all racial classifications are unconstitutional?

(2) In a companion case to *Brown I*, *Bolling v. Sharpe*, 347 U.S. 497 (1954), the Court invalidated the segregated school system in the District of Columbia on the basis of the Due Process Clause of the Fifth Amendment:

> The Fifth Amendment [does] not contain an equal protection clause. [But] the concepts of equal protection and due process, both stemming from our American ideal of fairness, are not mutually exclusive. The "equal

---

2. [Court's Footnote 11] K. B. Clark, *Effect of Prejudice and Discrimination on Personality Development* (Midcentury White House Conference on Children and Youth, 1950); Witmer and Kotinsky, *Personality in the Making* (1952), c. VI; Deutscher and Chein, *The Psychological Effects of Enforced Segregation: A Survey of Social Science Opinion*, 26 J. Psychol. 259 (1948); Chein, *What are the Psychological Effects of Segregation Under Conditions of Equal Facilities?*, 3 Int. J. Opinion and Attitude Res. 229 (1949); Brameld, Educational Costs, in Discrimination and National Welfare (MacIver, ed., 1949), 44–48; Frazier, The Negro in the United States (1949), 674–681. And see generally Myrdal, An American Dilemma (1944).

protection of the laws" is a more explicit safeguard of prohibited unfairness than "due process of law," and, therefore, we do not imply that the two are always interchangeable phrases. But, as this Court has recognized, discrimination may be so unjustifiable as to be violative of due process. Classifications based solely upon race must be scrutinized with particular care, since they are contrary to our traditions and hence constitutionally suspect.

(3) Recall the materials on the history of the Fourteenth Amendment and the "original understanding" from Chapter 5. Is the *Brown I* holding consistent with the history? If not, what weight should the "original understanding" be given in 1954? *See* Alexander Bickel, *The Original Understanding and the Segregation Decision*, 69 Harv. L. Rev. 1 (1955).

(4) Note the references to social science authorities in the Court's footnote 11 in *Brown I.* How important was the social science evidence to the holding? Would the result have changed without the empirical proof?

(5) Given the social and political environment of the early 1950s and the special constraints facing the Supreme Court as it pondered a decision in *Brown*, the tremendous impact that the *Brown* decision has had is all the more remarkable:

> Every colored American knew that *Brown* did not mean he would be invited to lunch with the Rotary the following week. It meant something more basic and more important. It meant that black rights had suddenly been redefined; black bodies had suddenly been reborn under a new law. Blacks' value as human beings had been changed overnight by the declaration of the nation's highest court. At a stroke, the Justices had severed the remaining cords of *de facto* slavery. The Negro could no longer be fastened with the status of official pariah. No longer could the white man look right through him as if he were, in the title words of Ralph Ellison's stunning 1952 novel, *Invisible Man.* No more would he be a grinning supplicant for the benefactions and discards of the master class; no more would he be a party to his own degradation. He was both thrilled that the signal for the demise of his caste status had come from on high and angry that it had taken so long and first exacted so steep a price in suffering.

Richard Kluger, Simple Justice 749 (1976).[3]

(6) It has been argued that the *Brown* Court's willingness to abandon its tolerance of segregation "cannot be understood without some consideration of the decision's value to whites," those in power who would see the "political advances at home and abroad that would follow abandonment of segregation." Derrick Bell, *Brown v. Board of Education and the Interest-Convergence Dilemma*, 93 Harv. L. Rev. 518 (1980). As Professor Bell noted, *Brown* provided credibility to our attempts to win support of third world countries. It also offered reassurance to black war veterans

---

3. Copyright © 1976 by Random House, Inc., Alfred A. Knopf, Inc. Reprinted by permission.

"that the precepts of equality and freedom so heralded during World War II might yet be given meaning at home." *Id.* at 524. Finally, it helped pave the way for the industrialization of the South.

Brown v. Board of Education [Brown II]

United States Supreme Court
349 U.S. 294, 75 S. Ct. 753, 99 L. Ed. 1083 (1955)

Mr. Chief Justice Warren delivered the opinion of the Court.

These cases were decided on May 17, 1954. The opinions of that date, declaring the fundamental principle that racial discrimination in public education is unconstitutional, are incorporated herein by reference. All provisions of federal, state, or local law requiring or permitting such discrimination must yield to this principle. There remains for consideration the manner in which relief is to be accorded. . . .

Full implementation of these constitutional principles may require solution of varied local school problems. School authorities have the primary responsibility for elucidating, assessing, and solving these problems; courts will have to consider whether the action of school authorities constitutes good faith implementation of the governing constitutional principles. Because of their proximity to local conditions and the possible need for further hearings, the courts which originally heard these cases can best perform this judicial appraisal. Accordingly, we believe it appropriate to remand the cases to those courts.

In fashioning and effectuating the decrees, the courts will be guided by equitable principles. Traditionally, equity has been characterized by a practical flexibility in shaping its remedies and by a facility for adjusting and reconciling public and private needs. These cases call for the exercise of these traditional attributes of equity power. At stake is the personal interest of the plaintiffs in admission to public schools as soon as practicable on a nondiscriminatory basis. To effectuate this interest may call for elimination of a variety of obstacles in making the transition to school systems operated in accordance with the constitutional principles set forth in our May 17, 1954, decision. Courts of equity may properly take into account the public interest in the elimination of such obstacles in a systematic and effective manner. But it should go without saying that the vitality of these constitutional principles cannot be allowed to yield simply because of disagreement with them. While giving weight to these public and private considerations, the courts will require that the defendants make a prompt and reasonable start toward full compliance with our May 17, 1954, ruling. Once such a start has been made, the courts may find that additional time is necessary to carry out the ruling in an effective manner. The burden rests upon the defendants to establish that such time is necessary in the public interest and is consistent with good faith compliance at the earliest practicable date. To that end, the courts may consider problems related to administration, arising from the physical condition of the school plant, the school transportation system, personnel, revision of school districts and attendance areas into compact units to achieve a system of determining admission to the public schools on a nonracial basis, and revision of local laws and regulations which may be necessary in solving the foregoing problems. They will also consider the adequacy of any plans the defendants may propose to meet these problems and to effectuate a transition to a racially nondiscriminatory school system. During this period of transition, the courts will retain jurisdiction of these cases.

The judgments below . . . are accordingly reversed and the cases are remanded to the District Courts to take such proceedings and enter such orders and decrees consistent with this opinion as are necessary and proper to admit to public schools on a racially nondiscriminatory basis with all deliberate speed the parties to these cases.

Notes and Questions

(1) What was the meaning of "with all deliberate speed"? Why did the Court fashion a remedy which presumed delay? Did this approach invite federal courts to take over the schools from local school boards?

(2) Invited or not, the lower federal courts did soon assume a supervisory role over local school districts. The *Brown* decisions did not end Northern neighborhood schools or dual systems in the South. Thus, eventually the Court was called upon to clarify the extent of lower court authority to carry out the remedial aspects of the *Brown* mandate. *See, e.g., Swann v. Charlotte-Mecklenburg Board of Education*, 402 U.S. 1 (1971); *Green v. County School*, 391 U.S. 430 (1968).

(3) Decades after *Brown*, the Court continues in its attempts to define the limits of judicial authority to remedy school segregation. *See, e.g., Parents Involved in Community Schools v. Seattle School District No. 1*, 551 U.S. 701 (2007); *Freeman v. Pitts*, 503 U.S. 467 (1992); *Board of Education of Oklahoma City Public Schools, Independent School District No. 89 v. Dowell*, 498 U.S. 237 (1991).

Loving v. Virginia

United States Supreme Court
388 U.S. 1, 87 S. Ct. 1817, 18 L. Ed. 2d 1010 (1967)

Mr. Chief Justice Warren delivered the opinion of the Court.

This case presents a constitutional question never addressed by this Court: whether a statutory scheme adopted by the State of Virginia to prevent marriages between persons solely on the basis of racial classifications violates the Equal Protection and Due Process Clauses of the Fourteenth Amendment. For reasons which seem to us to reflect the central meaning of those constitutional commands, we conclude that these statutes cannot stand consistently with the Fourteenth Amendment.

In June 1958, two residents of Virginia, Mildred Jeter, a Negro woman, and Richard Loving, a white man, were married in the District of Columbia pursuant to its laws. Shortly after their marriage, the Lovings returned to Virginia and established their marital abode in Caroline County. At the October Term, 1958, of the Circuit

Court of Caroline County, a grand jury issued an indictment charging the Lovings with violating Virginia's ban on interracial marriages. On January 6, 1959, the Lovings pleaded guilty to the charge and were sentenced to one year in jail; however, the trial judge suspended the sentence for a period of 25 years on the condition that the Lovings leave the State and not return to Virginia together for 25 years. He stated in an opinion that:

> Almighty God created the races white, black, yellow, malay and red, and he placed them on separate continents. And but for the interference with his arrangement there would be no cause for such marriages. The fact that he separated the races shows that he did not intend for the races to mix.

After their convictions, the Lovings took up residence in the District of Columbia. On November 6, 1963, they filed a motion in the state trial court to vacate the judgment and set aside the sentence on the ground that the statutes which they had violated were repugnant to the Fourteenth Amendment. . . .

I

In upholding the constitutionality of these provisions in the decision below, the Supreme Court of Appeals of Virginia referred to its 1955 decision in *Naim v. Naim*, 197 Va. 80, 87 S.E.2d 749, as stating the reasons supporting the validity of these laws. In *Naim* the state court concluded that the State's legitimate purposes were "to preserve the racial integrity of its citizens," and to prevent "the corruption of blood," "a mongrel breed of citizens," and "the obliteration of racial pride," obviously an endorsement of the doctrine of White Supremacy. The court also reasoned that marriage has traditionally been subject to state regulation without federal intervention, and, consequently, the regulation of marriage should be left to exclusive state control by the Tenth Amendment. While the state court is no doubt correct in asserting that marriage is a social relation subject to the State's police power, the State does not contend in its argument before this Court that its powers to regulate marriage are unlimited notwithstanding the commands of the Fourteenth Amendment. . . .

Because we reject the notion that the mere "equal application" of a statute containing racial classifications is enough to remove the classifications from the Fourteenth Amendment's proscription of all invidious racial discriminations, we do not accept the State's contention that these statutes should be upheld if there is any possible basis for concluding that they serve a rational purpose. The mere fact of equal application does not mean that our analysis of these statutes should follow the approach we have taken in cases involving no racial discrimination. . . .

In . . . cases involving distinctions not drawn according to race, the Court has merely asked whether there is any rational foundation for the discriminations, and has deferred to the wisdom of the state legislatures. In the case at bar, however, we deal with statutes containing racial classifications, and the fact of equal application does not immunize the statute from the very heavy burden of justification which the Fourteenth Amendment has traditionally required of state statutes drawn according to race.

The State argues that statements in the Thirty-ninth Congress about the time of the passage of the Fourteenth Amendment indicate that the Framers did not intend the Amendment to make unconstitutional state miscegenation laws. Many of the statements alluded to by the State concern the debates over the Freedmen's Bureau Bill, which President Johnson vetoed, and the Civil Rights Act of 1866, enacted over his veto. While these statements have some relevance to the intention of Congress in submitting the Fourteenth Amendment, it must be understood that they pertained to the passage of specific statutes and not to the broader, organic purpose of a constitutional amendment. As for the various statements directly concerning the Fourteenth Amendment, we have said in connection with a related problem, that although these historical sources "cast some light" they are not sufficient to resolve the problem; "[a]t best, they are inconclusive. The most avid proponents of the post-War Amendments undoubtedly intended them to remove all legal distinctions among 'all persons born or naturalized in the United States.' Their opponents, just as certainly, were antagonistic to both the letter and the spirit of the Amendments and wished them to have the most limited effect." We have rejected the proposition that the debates in the Thirty-ninth Congress or in the state legislatures which ratified the Fourteenth Amendment supported the theory advanced by the State, that the requirement of equal protection of the laws is satisfied by penal laws defining offenses based on racial classifications so long as white and Negro participants in the offense were similarly punished. . . .

There can be no question but that Virginia's miscegenation statutes rest solely upon distinctions drawn according to race. The statutes proscribe generally accepted conduct if engaged in by members of different races. Over the years, this Court has consistently repudiated "[d]istinctions between citizens solely because of their ancestry" as being "odious to a free people whose institutions are founded upon the doctrine of equality." At the very least, the Equal Protection Clause demands that racial classifications, especially suspect in criminal statutes, be subjected to the "most rigid scrutiny," *Korematsu v. United States*, and, if they are ever to be upheld, they must be shown to be necessary to the accomplishment of some permissible state objective, independent of the racial discrimination which it was the object of the Fourteenth Amendment to eliminate. . . .

There is patently no legitimate overriding purpose independent of invidious racial discrimination which justifies this classification. The fact that Virginia prohibits only interracial marriages involving white persons demonstrates that the racial classifications must stand on their own justification, as measures designed to maintain White Supremacy. We have consistently denied the constitutionality of measures which restrict the rights of citizens on account of race. There can be no doubt that restricting the freedom to marry solely because of racial classifications violates the central meaning of the Equal Protection Clause.

II

These statutes also deprive the Lovings of liberty without due process of law in violation of the Due Process Clause of the Fourteenth Amendment. The freedom to marry has long been recognized as one of the vital personal rights essential to the orderly pursuit of happiness by free men.

Marriage is one of the "basic civil rights of man," fundamental to our very existence and survival. *Skinner v. Oklahoma*, 316 U.S. 535, 541 (1942). To deny this fundamental freedom on so unsupportable a basis as the racial classifications embodied in these statutes, classifications so directly subversive of the principle of equality at the heart of the Fourteenth Amendment, is surely to deprive all the State's citizens of liberty without due process of law. The Fourteenth Amendment requires that the freedom of choice to marry not be restricted by invidious racial discriminations. Under our Constitution, the freedom to marry, or not marry, a person of another race resides with the individual and cannot be infringed by the State.

Reversed.

Mr. Justice Stewart, concurring [Omitted].

Notes and Questions

(1) Did the Court apply strict scrutiny in *Loving* because the law discriminated based on race, or because it interfered with a fundamental right? Was there a "fundamental right" to marriage recognized in *Loving*? In *Zablocki v. Redhail*, 434 U.S. 374 (1978), the Court invalidated a Wisconsin law prohibiting marriage by a state resident who was obligated to support a minor not in his custody, unless he demonstrated that the support had been paid and that the supported children are not, and are not likely to become, public charges. Justice Marshall's opinion for the Court made reference to *Loving* and other opinions of the Court which recognized marriage as a fundamental right in support of his conclusion that equal protection requires "critical examination" of a classification interfering with marriage rights.

(2) If the miscegenation laws apply to all individuals, why does the Court find that they discriminate based on race?

B. Discriminatory Intent or Impact?

Washington v. Davis

United States Supreme Court
426 U.S. 229, 96 S. Ct. 2040, 48 L. Ed. 2d 597 (1976)

Mr. Justice White delivered the opinion of the Court.

This case involves the validity of a qualifying test administered to applicants for positions as police officers in the District of Columbia Metropolitan Police Department. The test was sustained by the District Court but invalidated by the Court of Appeals. We are in agreement with the District Court and hence reverse the judgment of the Court of Appeals. . . .

["Test 21" was developed by the Civil Service Commission to test "verbal ability, vocabulary, reading, and comprehension." The Court of Appeals declared that lack of discriminatory intent in designing and administering Test 21 was irrelevant; the critical fact was rather that a far greater proportion of blacks—four times as many—failed the test than did whites. This disproportionate impact, standing alone and without regard to whether it indicated a discriminatory purpose, was held sufficient to establish a constitutional violation, absent proof by petitioners that the test was an adequate measure of job performance in addition to being an indicator of probable success in the training program, a burden which the court ruled petitioners had failed to discharge. That the Department had made substantial efforts to recruit blacks was held beside the point and the fact that the racial distribution of recent hirings and of the Department itself might be roughly equivalent to the racial makeup of the surrounding community, broadly conceived, was put aside as a "comparison [not] material to this appeal."]

The central purpose of the Equal Protection Clause of the Fourteenth Amendment is the prevention of official conduct discriminating on the basis of race. It is also true that the Due Process Clause of the Fifth Amendment contains an equal protection component prohibiting the United States from invidiously discriminating between individuals or groups. But our cases have not embraced the proposition that a law or other official act, without regard to whether it reflects a racially discriminatory purpose, is unconstitutional *solely* because it has a racially disproportionate impact.

Almost 100 years ago, *Strauder* [*v. West Virginia*, 100 U.S. 303 (1880)] established that the exclusion of Negroes from grand and petit juries in criminal proceedings violated the Equal Protection Clause, but the fact that a particular jury or a series of juries does not statistically reflect the racial composition of the community does not in itself make out an invidious discrimination forbidden by the Clause. . . .

The essential element of *de jure* segregation is "a current condition of segregation resulting from intentional state action." The differentiating factor between *de jure* segregation and so-called *de facto* segregation . . . "is *purpose* or *intent* to segregate." The Court has also recently rejected allegations of racial discrimination based solely on the statistically disproportionate racial impact of various provisions of the Social Security Act because "[t]he acceptance of appellants' constitutional theory would render suspect each difference in treatment among the grant classes, however lacking in racial motivation and however otherwise rational the treatment might be." *Jefferson v. Hackney*, 406 U.S. 535 (1972).

This is not to say that the necessary discriminatory racial purpose must be express or appear on the face of the statute, or that a law's disproportionate impact is irrelevant in cases involving Constitution-based claims of racial discrimination. A statute, otherwise neutral on its face, must not be applied so as invidiously to discriminate on the basis of race. *Yick Wo v. Hopkins*, 118 U. S. 356 (1886). It is also clear from the cases dealing with racial discrimination in the selection of juries that the systematic exclusion of Negroes is itself such an "unequal application of the law . . . as to show intentional discrimination." A prima facie case of discriminatory purpose may be proved as well by the absence of Negroes on a particular jury combined with the failure of the jury commissioners to be informed of eligible Negro jurors in a community, or with racially non-neutral selection procedures. With a prima facie case made out, "the burden of proof shifts to the State to rebut the presumption of unconstitutional action by showing that permissible racially neutral selection criteria and procedures have produced the monochromatic result."

Necessarily, an invidious discriminatory purpose may often be inferred from the totality of the relevant facts, including the fact, if it is true, that the law bears more heavily on one race than another. It is also not infrequently true that the discriminatory impact — in the jury cases for example, the total or seriously disproportionate exclusion of Negroes from jury venues — may for all practical purposes demonstrate unconstitutionality because in various circumstances the discrimination is very difficult to explain on nonracial grounds. Nevertheless, we have not held that a law, neutral on its face and serving ends otherwise within the power of government to pursue, is invalid under the Equal Protection Clause simply because it may affect a greater proportion of one race than of another. Disproportionate impact is not irrelevant, but it is not the sole touchstone of an invidious racial discrimination forbidden by the Constitution. Standing alone, it does not trigger the rule that racial classifications are to be subjected to the strictest scrutiny and are justifiable only by the weightiest of considerations.

There are some indications to the contrary in our cases. In *Palmer v. Thompson*, 403 U.S. 217 (1971), the city of Jackson, Miss., following a court decree to this effect, desegregated all of its public facilities save five swimming pools which had been operated by the city and which, following the decree, were closed by ordinance pursuant to a determination by the city council that closure was necessary to preserve peace and order and that integrated pools could not be economically operated. Accepting the finding that the pools were closed to avoid violence and economic loss, this Court rejected the argument that the abandonment of this service was inconsistent with the outstanding desegregation decree and that the otherwise seemingly permissible ends served by the ordinance could be impeached by demonstrating that racially invidious motivations had prompted the city council's action. The holding was that the city was not overtly or covertly operating segregated pools and was extending identical treatment to both whites and Negroes. The opinion warned against grounding decision on legislative purpose or motivation, thereby lending support for the proposition that the operative effect of the law rather than its purpose is the paramount factor. But the holding of the case was that the legitimate purposes of the ordinance — to preserve peace and avoid deficits — were not open to impeachment by evidence that the councilmen were actually motivated by racial considerations. Whatever dicta the opinion may contain, the decision did not involve, much less invalidate, a statute or ordinance having neutral purposes but disproportionate racial consequences.[4] . . .

_____

4. [Court's Footnote 11] To the extent that *Palmer* suggests a generally applicable proposition that legislative purpose is irrelevant in constitutional adjudication, our prior cases — as indicated

Both before and after *Palmer v. Thompson*, however, various Courts of Appeals have held in several contexts, including public employment, that the substantially disproportionate racial impact of a statute or official practice standing alone and without regard to discriminatory purpose, suffices to prove racial discrimination violating the Equal Protection Clause absent some justification going substantially beyond what would be necessary to validate most other legislative classifications. The cases impressively demonstrate that there is another side to the issue; but, with all due respect, to the extent that those cases rested on or expressed the view that proof of discriminatory racial purpose is unnecessary in making out an equal protection violation, we are in disagreement. . . .

Test 21 . . . seeks to ascertain whether those who take it have acquired a particular level of verbal skill; and it is untenable that the Constitution prevents the Government from seeking modestly to upgrade the communicative abilities of its employees rather than to be satisfied with some lower level of competence, particularly where the job requires special ability to communicate orally and in writing. Respondents, as Negroes, could no more successfully claim that the test denied them equal protection than could white applicants who also failed. The conclusion would not be different in the face of proof that more Negroes than whites had been disqualified by Test 21. That other Negroes also failed to score well would, alone, not demonstrate that respondents individually were being denied equal protection of the laws by the application of an otherwise valid qualifying test being administered to prospective police recruits.

Nor on the facts of the case before us would the disproportionate impact of Test 21 warrant the conclusion that it is a purposeful device to discriminate against Negroes and hence an infringement of the constitutional rights of respondents as well as other black applicants. As we have said, the test is neutral on its face and rationally may be said to serve a purpose the Government is constitutionally empowered to pursue. Even agreeing with the District Court that the differential racial effect of Test 21 called for further inquiry, we think the District Court correctly held that the affirmative efforts of the Metropolitan Police Department to recruit black officers, the changing racial composition of the recruit classes and of the force in general, and the relationship of the test to the training program negated any inference that the Department discriminated on the basis of race or that "a police officer qualifies on the color of his skin rather than ability. . . ."

A rule that a statute designed to serve neutral ends is nevertheless invalid, absent compelling justification, if in practice it benefits or burdens one race more than

---

in the text—are to the contrary; and very shortly after *Palmer* all Members of the Court majority in that case joined the Court's opinion in *Lemon v. Kurtzman*, 403 U.S. 602 (1971), which dealt with the issue of public financing for private schools and which announced, as the Court had several times before, that the validity of public aid to church-related schools includes close inquiry into the purpose of the challenged statute.

another would be far-reaching and would raise serious questions about, and perhaps invalidate, a whole range of tax, welfare, public service, regulatory, and licensing statutes that may be more burdensome to the poor and to the average black than to the more affluent white.[5]

Given that rule, such consequences would perhaps be likely to follow. However, in our view, extension of the rule beyond those areas where it is already applicable by reason of statute, such as in the field of public employment, should await legislative prescription. . . .

Mr. Justice Stevens, concurring.

[The] requirement of purposeful discrimination is a common thread running through the cases summarized . . . These cases include criminal convictions which were set aside because blacks were excluded from the grand jury, a reapportionment case in which political boundaries were obviously influenced to some extent by racial considerations, a school desegregation case, and a case involving the unequal administration of an ordinance purporting to prohibit the operation of laundries in frame buildings. Although it may be proper to use the same language to describe the constitutional claim in each of these contexts, the burden of proving a prima facie case may well involve differing evidentiary considerations. The extent of deference that one pays to the trial court's determination of the factual issue, and indeed, the extent to which one characterizes the intent issue as a question of fact or a question of law, will vary in different contexts.

Frequently the most probative evidence of intent will be objective evidence of what actually happened rather than evidence describing the subjective state of mind of the actor. For normally the actor is presumed to have intended the natural consequences of his deeds. This is particularly true in the case of governmental action which is frequently the product of compromise, of collective decisionmaking, and of mixed motivation. It is unrealistic, on the one hand, to require the victim of alleged discrimination to uncover the actual subjective intent of the decisionmaker or, conversely, to invalidate otherwise legitimate action simply because an improper motive affected the deliberation of a participant in the decisional process. A law conscripting clerics should not be invalidated because an atheist voted for it.

---

5. [Court's Footnote 14] Goodman, *De Facto School Segregation: A Constitutional and Empirical Analysis*, 60 Calif. L. Rev. 275, 300 (1972), suggests that disproportionate-impact analysis might invalidate "tests and qualifications for voting, draft deferment, public employment, jury service, and other government-conferred benefits and opportunities . . . ; [s]ales taxes, bail schedules, utility rates, bridge tolls, license fees, and other state-imposed charges." It has also been argued that minimum wage and usury laws as well as professional licensing requirements would require major modifications in light of the unequal-impact rule. Silverman, *Equal Protection, Economic Legislation, and Racial Discrimination*, 25 Vand. L. Rev. 1183 (1972). See also Demsetz, *Minorities in the Market Place*, 43 N.C. L. Rev. 271 (1965).

My point in making this observation is to suggest that the line between discriminatory purpose and discriminatory impact is not nearly as bright, and perhaps not quite as critical, as the reader of the Court's opinion might assume. I agree, of course, that a constitutional issue does not arise every time some disproportionate impact is shown. On the other hand, when the disproportion is as dramatic as in *Yick Wo v. Hopkins*, it really does not matter whether the standard is phrased in terms of purpose or effect. Therefore, although I accept the statement of the general rule in the Court's opinion, I am not yet prepared to indicate how that standard should be applied in the many cases which have formulated the governing standard in different language.

My agreement with the conclusion reached [rests] on a ground narrower than the Court describes. I do not rely at all on the evidence of good-faith efforts to recruit black police officers. In my judgment, neither those efforts nor the subjective good faith of the District administration, would save Test 21 if it were otherwise invalid.

There are two reasons why I am convinced that the challenge to Test 21 is insufficient. First, the test serves the neutral and legitimate purpose of requiring all applicants to meet a uniform minimum standard of literacy. Reading ability is manifestly relevant to the police function, there is no evidence that the required passing grade was set at an arbitrarily high level, and there is sufficient disparity among high schools and high school graduates to justify the use of a separate uniform test. Second, the same test is used throughout the federal service. The applicants for employment in the District of Columbia Police Department represent such a small fraction of the total number of persons who have taken the test that their experience is of minimal probative value in assessing the neutrality of the test itself. That evidence, without more, is not sufficient to overcome the presumption that a test which is this widely used by the Federal Government is in fact neutral in its effect as well as its "purpose" as that term is used in constitutional adjudication.

[STEWART, J. joined the opinion of the Court on the constitutional issue. BRENNAN, J. and MARSHALL, J. dissented on a statutory issue.]

Notes and Questions

(1) The technique of inferring purposeful discrimination from data regarding an apparently neutral law's administration started with jury selection cases (e.g., *Hernandez v. Texas*, 347 U.S. 475 (1954), *Castaneda v. Partida*, 430 U.S. 482 (1977)), and spread to electoral and employment discrimination (e.g., *Hazelwood School Dist. v. United States*, 433 U.S. 299 (1977); *Teamsters v. United States*, 431 U.S. 324 (1977)). *But see McCleskey v. Kemp*, 481 U.S. 279 (1987). *See generally* DAVID BARNES, STATISTICS AS PROOF: FUNDAMENTALS OF QUANTITATIVE EVIDENCE (1983); DAVID BARNES & JOHN M. CONLEY, STATISTICAL EVIDENCE IN LITIGATION: METHODOLOGIES, PROCEDURE, AND PRACTICE (1986).

(2) The Court in *Davis* made it clear that purposeful discrimination must be proved to establish an equal protection violation. What proof will satisfy the plaintiff's burden?

(3) Should a law's disproportionate impact on racial minorities, standing alone, cause courts to invoke more than the traditional rationality review in equal protection cases? Why did the Court reject such an approach? Consider these views:

Americans share a common historical and cultural heritage in which racism has played and still plays a dominant role. Because of this shared experience, we also inevitably share many ideas, attitudes, and beliefs that attach significance to an individual's race and induce negative feelings and opinions about nonwhites. To the extent that this cultural belief system has influenced all of us, we are all racist. At the same time, most of us are unaware of our racism. We do not recognize the ways in which our cultural experience has influenced our beliefs about race or the occasions on which those beliefs affect our actions. In other words, a large part of the behavior that produces racial discrimination is influenced by unconscious racial motivation.

There are two explanations for the unconscious nature of our racially discriminatory beliefs and ideas. First, Freudian theory states that the human mind defends itself against the discomfort of guilt by denying or refusing to recognize those ideas, wishes, and beliefs that conflict with what the individual has learned is good or right. While our historical experience has made racism an integral part of our culture, our society has more recently embraced an ideal that rejects racism as immoral. When an individual experiences conflict between racist ideas and the societal ethic that condemns those ideas, the mind excludes his racism from consciousness.

Second, the theory of cognitive psychology states that the culture — including, for example, the media and an individual's parents, peers, and authority figures — transmits certain beliefs and preferences. Because these beliefs are so much a part of the culture, they are not experienced as explicit lessons. Instated, they seem part of the individual's rational ordering of her perceptions of the world. The individual is unaware, for example, that the ubiquitous presence of a cultural stereotype has influenced her perception that blacks are lazy or unintelligent. Because racism is so deeply ingrained in our culture, it is likely to be transmitted by tacit understandings: Even if a child is not told that blacks are inferior, he learns that lesson by observing the behavior of others. These tacit understandings, because they have never been articulated, are less likely to be experienced at a conscious level.

In short, requiring proof of conscious or intentional motivation as a prerequisite to constitutional recognition that a decision is race-dependent ignores much of what we understand about how the human mind works. It also disregards both the irrationality of racism and the profound effect that the history of American race relations has had on the individual and collective unconscious.

Charles Lawrence, *The Id, the Ego, and Equal Protection: Reckoning with Unconscious Racism*, 39 STAN. L. REV. 317, 322–323 (1987).[6]

> Laws employing a racial criterion of selection are inherently more dangerous than laws involving no racial criterion. The former, unlike the latter, directly encourage racialism. Moreover, laws employing a racial criterion are usually difficult if not impossible to justify on legitimate grounds. By contrast, laws having a disproportionate racial impact are quite easy to explain on legitimate grounds because such laws serve a legitimate function in addition to the function of racial selection. Accordingly, the standard of review [should be] more rigorous than that required by the rational relationship test but less rigorous than that required by the strict scrutiny test. [In] determining whether a disproportionate disadvantage is justified, a court would weigh several factors: (1) the degree of disproportion in the impact; (2) the private interest disadvantaged; (3) the efficiency of the challenged law in achieving its objective and the availability of alternative means having a less disproportionate impact; and (4) the government objective sought to be advanced.

Michael Perry, *The Disproportionate Impact Theory of Racial Discrimination*, 125 U. PA. L. REV. 540, 559–560 (1977).[7]

> One relatively simple explanation for the stability of the requirement of discriminatory purpose is its intuitive appeal, or more precisely the appeal of the principles it embodies. Colorblindness is extremely attractive to white liberals, and process theory's promise to regulate only the inputs to legislative decisionmaking, but not the substance of the resulting decisions, is extremely attractive to jurists confronting the countermajoritarian difficulty. But there is, I think, another explanation: the *Davis* rule reflects a distinctively white way of thinking about race. . . .

> There is a profound cognitive dimension to the material and social privilege that attaches to whiteness in this society, in that the white person has an everyday option not to think of herself in racial terms at all. In fact, whites appear to pursue that option so habitually that it may be a defining characteristic of whiteness: to be white is not to think about it. I label the tendency for whiteness to vanish from whites' self-perception the transparency phenomenon. . . .

> At a minimum, transparency counsels that we not accept seemingly neutral criteria of decision at face value. Most whites live and work in settings that are wholly or predominantly white. Thus whites rely on primarily white referents in formulating the norms and expectations that become criteria of decision for white decisionmakers. Given whites' tendency not to be

---

aware of whiteness, it's unlikely that white decisionmakers do not similarly misidentify as race-neutral personal characteristics, traits, and behaviors that are in fact closely associated with whiteness. . . .

Barbara Flagg, *"Was Blind, But Now I See": White Race Consciousness and the Requirement of Discriminatory Intent*, 91 Mich. L. Rev. 953, 968–969, 973 (1993).[8]

(4) In the purpose inquiry, is it proper to probe the minds of the legislators to search for motive when a law is otherwise facially neutral in its application to the races? In *Palmer v. Thompson*, discussed in *Davis*, Justice Black stated:

> It is difficult or impossible for any court to determine the "sole" or "dominant" motivation behind the choices of a group of legislators. Furthermore, there is an element of futility in a judicial attempt to invalidate a law because of the bad motives of its supporters. If the law is struck down for this reason, rather than because of its facial content or effect, it would presumably be valid as soon as the legislature or relevant governing body repassed it for different reasons.

403 U.S. 217, 225 (1971). Did the *Davis* Court agree with Justice Black? What is wrong with a court looking behind a facially neutral law? Can the equality principle be protected without examining motive? *See generally* Paul Brest, *Palmer v. Thompson: An Approach to the Problem of Unconstitutional Legislative Motive*, 1971 Sup. Ct. Rev. 95; Theodore Eisenberg, *Disproportionate Impact and Illicit Motive: Theories of Constitutional Adjudication*, 52 N.Y.U. L. Rev. 36 (1977); Symposium, *Legislative Motivation*, 15 San Diego L. Rev. 925 (1978).

(5) Because of the racial and economic structure of society, many seemingly neutral laws disproportionately impact racial minorities. What are the problems associated with close judicial scrutiny of such laws?

Problem B

Assume that a state law school provides $10,000 in annual scholarships to children of the school's alumni. You have been contacted by a group of black law students who believe this policy is racially discriminatory and benefits white students. They point out that until 1954, state law prohibited blacks from attending the school. After the *Brown* decision, the state desegregated the law school and eliminated any discriminatory admission practices. Nevertheless, relatively few black students have enrolled in the past seven decades since *Brown*. Does the school's policy violate equal protection?

---

8. Copyright © 1993 by Michigan Law Review. Reprinted by permission.

C. Affirmative Action

Over recent decades, the Court has considered on several occasions how to apply equal protection doctrine to affirmative action programs that use racial classifications to benefit members of minority groups. In *Adarand Constructors, Inc. v. Pena*, 515 U.S. 200 (1995), the Petitioner "claimed that the Federal Government's practice of giving general contractors on Government projects a financial incentive to hire subcontractors controlled by 'socially and economically disadvantaged individuals,' and in particular, the Government's use of race-based presumptions in identifying such individuals, violates the equal protection component of the Fifth Amendment's Due Process Clause." The Court held that "all racial classifications, imposed by whatever federal, state, or local governmental actor must be analyzed by a reviewing court under strict scrutiny. In other words, such classifications are constitutional only if they are narrowly tailored measures that further compelling interests."

Several cases involved affirmative action programs in higher education. In 2003, for example, the Supreme Court decided *Grutter v. Bollinger*, 539 U.S. 306 (2003), which considered the constitutionality of the affirmative action admissions policy used by the University of Michigan Law School. That policy gave weight to an applicant's contribution to diversity. The Court noted:

> The policy does not restrict the types of diversity contributions eligible for "substantial weight" in the admissions process, but instead recognizes "many possible bases for diversity admissions." The policy does, however, reaffirm the Law School's longstanding commitment to "one particular type of diversity," that is, "racial and ethnic diversity with special reference to the inclusion of students from groups which have been historically discriminated against, like African-Americans, Hispanics and Native Americans, who without this commitment might not be represented in our student body in meaningful numbers." The policy does not define diversity "solely in terms of racial and ethnic status." Nor is the policy "insensitive to the competition among all students for admission to the [L]aw [S]chool." Rather, the policy seeks to guide admissions officers in "producing classes both diverse and academically outstanding, classes made up of students who promise to continue the tradition of outstanding contribution by Michigan Graduates to the legal profession."

Grutter, a white applicant who was denied admission, claimed that the Law School violated equal protection by relying on race in the admissions process. Initially, the Court stated that all governmental uses of race are subject to strict scrutiny. It then concluded that the policy was constitutional under that standard. The Court held that the Law School's interest in attaining a diverse student body satisfies the compelling interest requirement. Moreover, it stressed that the "Law School's judgment that such diversity is essential to its mission is one to which we defer." It described the value of diversity in higher education as follows:

As part of its goal of "assembling a class that is both exceptionally academically qualified and broadly diverse," the Law School seeks to "enroll a 'critical mass' of minority students." The Law School's interest is not simply "to assure within its student body some specified percentage of a particular group merely because of its race or ethnic origin." That would amount to outright racial balancing, which is patently unconstitutional. Rather, the Law School's concept of critical mass is defined by reference to the educational benefits that diversity is designed to produce.

These benefits are substantial. As the District Court emphasized, the Law School's admissions policy promotes "cross-racial understanding," helps to break down racial stereotypes, and "enables [students] to better understand persons of different races." These benefits are "important and laudable," because "classroom discussion is livelier, more spirited, and simply more enlightening and interesting" when the students have "the greatest possible variety of backgrounds."

The Law School's claim of a compelling interest is further bolstered by its *amici*, who point to the educational benefits that flow from student body diversity. In addition to the expert studies and reports entered into evidence at trial, numerous studies show that student body diversity promotes learning outcomes, and "better prepares students for an increasingly diverse workforce and society, and better prepares them as professionals."

These benefits are not theoretical but real, as major American businesses have made clear that the skills needed in today's increasingly global marketplace can only be developed through exposure to widely diverse people, cultures, ideas, and viewpoints. What is more, high-ranking retired officers and civilian leaders of the United States military assert that, "[b]ased on [their] decades of experience," a "highly qualified, racially diverse officer corps . . . is essential to the military's ability to fulfill its principle mission to provide national security."

The Court also held that the policy is narrowly tailored to meet the diversity goals.

Here, the Law School engages in a highly individualized, holistic review of each applicant's file, giving serious consideration to all the ways an applicant might contribute to a diverse educational environment. The Law School affords this individualized consideration to applicants of all races. There is no policy, either *de jure* or *de facto*, of automatic acceptance or rejection based on any single "soft" variable. [T]he Law School's admissions policy "is flexible enough to consider all pertinent elements of diversity in light of the particular qualifications of each applicant, and to place them on the same footing for consideration, although not necessarily according them the same weight."

We also find that the Law School's race-conscious admissions program adequately ensures that all factors that may contribute to student body diversity are meaningfully considered alongside race in admissions decisions.

Students for Fair Admissions v. President and Fellows of Harvard College

United States Supreme Court
600 U.S. ___, 143 S. Ct. 2141, 216 L. Ed. 2d 857 (2023)

CHIEF JUSTICE ROBERTS delivered the opinion of the Court.

In these cases we consider whether the admissions systems used by Harvard College and the University of North Carolina, two of the oldest institutions of higher learning in the United States, are lawful under the Equal Protection Clause of the Fourteenth Amendment.

The admissions process at Harvard works as follows. Every application is initially screened by a "first reader," who assigns scores in six categories: academic, extracurricular, athletic, school support, personal, and overall. A rating of "1" is the best; a rating of "6" the worst. In the academic category, for example, a "1" signifies "near perfect standardized test scores and grades"; in the extracurricular category, it indicates "truly unusual achievement"; and in the personal category, it denotes "outstanding" attributes like maturity, integrity, leadership, kindness, and courage. A score of "1" on the overall rating—a composite of the five other ratings—"signifies an exceptional candidate with >90% chance of admission." In assigning the overall rating, the first readers "can and do take an applicant's race into account."

Once the first read process is complete, Harvard convenes admissions subcommittees. Each subcommittee meets for three to five days and evaluates all applicants from a particular geographic area. The subcommittees are responsible for making recommendations to the full admissions committee. The subcommittees can and do take an applicant's race into account when making their recommendations.

The next step of the Harvard process is the full committee meeting. The committee has 40 members, and its discussion centers around the applicants who have been recommended by the regional subcommittees. At the beginning of the meeting, the committee discusses the relative breakdown of applicants by race. The "goal," according to Harvard's director of admissions, "is to make sure that [Harvard does] not hav[e] a dramatic drop-off" in minority admissions from the prior class. Each applicant considered by the full committee is discussed one by one, and every member of the committee must vote on admission. Only when an applicant secures a majority of the full committee's votes is he or she tentatively accepted for admission. At the end of the full committee meeting, the racial composition of the pool of tentatively admitted students is disclosed to the committee.

The final stage of Harvard's process is called the "lop," during which the list of tentatively admitted students is winnowed further to arrive at the final class. Any applicants that Harvard considers cutting at this stage are placed on a "lop list," which contains only four pieces of information: legacy status, recruited athlete status, financial aid eligibility, and race. The full committee decides as a group which students to lop. In doing so, the committee can and does take race into account. Once the lop process is complete, Harvard's admitted class is set. In the Harvard admissions process, "race is a determinative tip for" a significant percentage "of all admitted African American and Hispanic applicants."

Like Harvard, UNC's "admissions process is highly selective": In a typical year, the school "receives approximately 43,500 applications for its freshman class of 4,200." Every application the University receives is initially reviewed by one of approximately 40 admissions office readers, each of whom reviews roughly five applications per hour. Readers are required to consider "[r]ace and ethnicity . . . as one factor" in their review. Other factors include academic performance and rigor, standardized testing results, extracurricular involvement, essay quality, personal factors, and student background. Readers are responsible for providing numerical ratings for the academic, extracurricular, personal, and essay categories. During the years at issue in this litigation, underrepresented minority students were "more likely to score [highly] on their personal ratings than their white and Asian American peers," but were more likely to be "rated lower by UNC readers on their academic program, academic performance, . . . extracurricular activities," and essays.

After assessing an applicant's materials along these lines, the reader "formulates an opinion about whether the student should be offered admission" and then "writes a comment defending his or her recommended decision." In making that decision, readers may offer students a "plus" based on their race, which "may be significant in an individual case." The admissions decisions made by the first readers are, in most cases, "provisionally final."

Following the first read process, "applications then go to a process called 'school group review' where a committee composed of experienced staff members reviews every [initial] decision." The review committee receives a report on each student which contains, among other things, their "class rank, GPA, and test scores; the ratings assigned to them by their initial readers; and their status as residents, legacies, or special recruits." The review committee either approves or rejects each admission recommendation made by the first reader, after which the admissions decisions are finalized. In making those decisions, the review committee may also consider the applicant's race.

Petitioner, Students for Fair Admissions (SFFA), is a nonprofit organization founded in 2014 whose purpose is "to defend human and civil rights secured by law, including the right of individuals to equal protection under the law." In November 2014, SFFA filed separate lawsuits against Harvard College and the University of North Carolina, arguing that their race-based admissions programs violated, respectively, Title VI of the Civil Rights Act of 1964, 78 Stat. 252, 42 U.S.C. § 2000d *et seq.*, and the Equal Protection Clause of the Fourteenth Amendment.[9] The District Courts in both cases held [that the admissions programs were permissible under the Equal Protection Clause. In the Harvard case, the First Circuit affirmed].

We granted certiorari in the Harvard case and certiorari before judgment in the UNC case.

In the wake of the Civil War, Congress proposed and the States ratified the Fourteenth Amendment, providing that no State shall "deny to any person . . . the equal protection of the laws." Amdt. 14, §1. To its proponents, the Equal Protection Clause represented a "foundation[al] principle" — "the absolute equality of all citizens of the United States politically and civilly before their own laws." Cong. Globe, 39th Cong., 1st Sess., 431 (1866) (statement of Rep. Bingham) (Cong. Globe). The Constitution, they were determined, "should not permit any distinctions of law based on race or color," Supp. Brief for United States on Reargument in *Brown v. Board of Education*, O.T. 1953, No. 1 etc., p. 41 (detailing the history of the adoption of the Equal Protection Clause), because any "law which operates upon one man [should] operate *equally* upon all," Cong. Globe 2459 (statement of Rep. Stevens).

The conclusion reached by the *Brown [v. Board of* Education] Court was thus unmistakably clear: the right to a public education "must be made available to all on equal terms." As the plaintiffs had argued, "no State has any authority under the equal-protection clause of the Fourteenth Amendment to use race as a factor in affording educational opportunities among its citizens." The Court reiterated that rule just one year later, holding that "full compliance" with *Brown* required schools to admit students "on a racially nondiscriminatory basis." *Brown v. Board of Education*, 349 U.S. 294, 300–301 (1955). The time for making distinctions based on race had passed. *Brown*, the Court observed, "declar[ed] the fundamental principle that racial discrimination in public education is unconstitutional."

In the decades that followed, this Court continued to vindicate the Constitution's pledge of racial equality. These decisions reflect the "core purpose" of the Equal Protection Clause: "do[ing] away with all governmentally imposed discrimination based on race." *Palmore v. Sidoti*, 466 U.S. 429, 432 (1984) (footnote omitted).

Eliminating racial discrimination means eliminating all of it. And the Equal Protection Clause, we have accordingly held, applies "without regard to any differences of race, of color, or of nationality" — it is "universal in [its] application." *Yick Wo*, 118 U.S., at 369. For "[t]he guarantee of equal protection cannot mean one thing when applied to one individual and something else when applied to a person of another

---

9. [Court's Footnote 2] Title VI provides that "[n]o person in the United States shall, on the ground of race, color, or national origin, be excluded from participation in, be denied the benefits of, or be subjected to discrimination under any program or activity receiving Federal financial assistance." 42 U.S.C. §2000d. "We have explained that discrimination that violates the Equal Protection Clause of the Fourteenth Amendment committed by an institution that accepts federal funds also constitutes a violation of Title VI." *Gratz v. Bollinger*, 539 U.S. 244, 276, n. 23 (2003). Although

color." *Regents of Univ. of Cal. v. Bakke*, 438 U.S. 265, 289–290 (1978) (opinion of Powell, J.). "If both are not accorded the same protection, then it is not equal."

Any exception to the Constitution's demand for equal protection must survive a daunting two-step examination known in our cases as "strict scrutiny." *Adarand Constructors, Inc. v. Peña*, 515 U.S. 200, 227 (1995). Under that standard we ask, first, whether the racial classification is used to "further compelling governmental interests." *Grutter v. Bollinger*, 539 U.S. 306, 326 (2003). Second, if so, we ask whether the government's use of race is "narrowly tailored"—meaning "necessary"—to achieve that interest.

Outside the circumstances of these cases, our precedents have identified only two compelling interests that permit resort to race-based government action. One is remediating specific, identified instances of past discrimination that violated the Constitution or a statute. See, *e.g.*, *Parents Involved in Community Schools v. Seattle School Dist. No. 1*, 551 U.S. 701, 720 (2007); *Shaw v. Hunt*, 517 U.S. 899, 909–910 (1996); *post*, at 19–20, 30–31 (opinion of THOMAS, J.). The second is avoiding imminent and serious risks to human safety in prisons, such as a race riot. See *Johnson v. California*, 543 U.S. 499, 512–513 (2005).

Our acceptance of race-based state action has been rare for a reason. "Distinctions between citizens solely because of their ancestry are by their very nature odious to a free people whose institutions are founded upon the doctrine of equality." *Rice v. Cayetano*, 528 U.S. 495, 517 (2000) (quoting *Hirabayashi v. United States*, 320 U.S. 81, 100 (1943)). That principle cannot be overridden except in the most extraordinary case.

These cases involve whether a university may make admissions decisions that turn on an applicant's race. Our Court first considered that issue in *Regents of University of California v. Bakke*, which involved a set-aside admissions program used by the University of California, Davis, medical school. In a deeply splintered decision that produced six different opinions—none of which commanded a majority of the Court—we ultimately ruled in part in favor of the school and in part in favor of Bakke.

In the years that followed our "fractured decision in *Bakke*," lower courts "struggled to discern whether Justice Powell's" opinion [in *Bakke*] constituted "binding precedent." We accordingly took up the matter again in 2003, in the case *Grutter v. Bollinger*, which concerned the admissions system used by the University of Michigan law school. There, in another sharply divided decision, the Court for the first time "endorse[d] Justice Powell's view that student body diversity is a compelling state interest that can justify the use of race in university admissions."

The Court's analysis tracked Justice Powell's in many respects. As for compelling interest, the Court held that "[t]he Law School's educational judgment that such diversity is essential to its educational mission is one to which we defer." In achieving that goal, however, the Court made clear—just as Justice Powell had—that the law school was limited in the means that it could pursue. The school could not "establish quotas for members of certain racial groups or put members of those groups on separate admissions tracks." Neither could it "insulate applicants who belong to certain racial or ethnic groups from the competition for admission." Nor still could it desire "some specified percentage of a particular group merely because of its race or ethnic origin."

These limits, *Grutter* explained, were intended to guard against two dangers that all race-based government action portends. The first is the risk that the use of race will devolve into "illegitimate . . . stereotyp[ing]." *Richmond v. J.A. Croson Co.*, 488 U.S. 469, 493 (1989) (plurality opinion). Universities were thus not permitted to operate their admissions programs on the "belief that minority students always (or even consistently) express some characteristic minority viewpoint on any issue." The second risk is that race would be used not as a plus, but as a negative — to discriminate *against* those racial groups that were not the beneficiaries of the race-based preference. A university's use of race, accordingly, could not occur in a manner that "unduly harm[ed] nonminority applicants." But even with these constraints in place, *Grutter* expressed marked discomfort with the use of race in college admissions. The Court stressed the fundamental principle that "there are serious problems of justice connected with the idea of [racial] preference itself." It observed that all "racial classifications, however compelling their goals," were "dangerous." And it cautioned that all "race-based governmental action" should "remai[n] subject to continuing oversight to assure that it will work the least harm possible to other innocent persons competing for the benefit."

To manage these concerns, *Grutter* imposed one final limit on race-based admissions programs. At some point, the Court held, they must end. *Grutter* thus concluded with the following caution: "It has been 25 years since Justice Powell first approved the use of race to further an interest in student body diversity in the context of public higher education. . . . We expect that 25 years from now, the use of racial preferences will no longer be necessary to further the interest approved today."

Twenty years later, no end is in sight. "Harvard's view about when [race-based admissions will end] doesn't have a date on it." Neither does UNC's. Yet both insist that the use of race in their admissions programs must continue.

But we have permitted race-based admissions only within the confines of narrow restrictions. University programs must comply with strict scrutiny, they may never use race as a stereotype or negative, and — at some point — they must end. Respondents' admissions systems — however well intentioned and implemented in good faith — fail each of these criteria. They must therefore be invalidated under the Equal Protection Clause of the Fourteenth Amendment.

Because "[r]acial discrimination [is] invidious in all contexts," *Edmonson v. Leesville Concrete Co.*, 500 U.S. 614, 619 (1991), we have required that universities operate their race-based admissions programs in a manner that is "sufficiently measurable to permit judicial [review]" under the rubric of strict scrutiny, Respondents have fallen short of satisfying that burden.

First, the interests they view as compelling cannot be subjected to meaningful judicial review. Harvard identifies the following educational benefits that it is pursuing: (1) "training future leaders in the public and private sectors"; (2) preparing graduates to "adapt to an increasingly pluralistic society"; (3) "better educating its students through diversity"; and (4) "producing new knowledge stemming from diverse outlooks." UNC points to similar benefits, namely, "(1) promoting the robust exchange of ideas; (2) broadening and refining understanding; (3) fostering innovation and problem-solving; (4) preparing engaged and productive citizens and leaders; [and] (5) enhancing appreciation, respect, and empathy, cross-racial understanding, and breaking down stereotypes."

Second, respondents' admissions programs fail to articulate a meaningful connection between the means they employ and the goals they pursue. To achieve the educational benefits of diversity, UNC works to avoid the underrepresentation of minority groups, while Harvard likewise "guard[s] against inadvertent drop-offs in representation" of certain minority groups from year to year, To accomplish both of those goals, in turn, the universities measure the racial composition of their classes using the following categories: (1) Asian; (2) Native Hawaiian or Pacific Islander; (3) Hispanic; (4) White; (5) African-American; and (6) Native American. It is far from evident, though, how assigning students to these racial categories and making admissions decisions based on them furthers the educational benefits that the universities claim to pursue.

For starters, the categories are themselves imprecise in many ways. Some of them are plainly overbroad: by grouping together all Asian students, for instance, respondents are apparently uninterested in whether *South* Asian or *East* Asian students are adequately represented, so long as there is enough of one to compensate for a lack of the other. Meanwhile other racial categories, such as "Hispanic," are arbitrary or undefined. And still other categories are underinclusive. When asked at oral argument "how are applicants from Middle Eastern countries classified, [such as] Jordan, Iraq, Iran, [and] Egypt," UNC's counsel responded, "[I] do not know the answer to that question."

The universities' main response to these criticisms is, essentially, "trust us." None of the questions recited above need answering, they say, because universities are "owed deference" when using race to benefit some applicants but not others. It is true that our cases have recognized a "tradition of giving a degree of deference to a university's academic decisions." *Grutter*, 539 U.S., at 328. But we have been unmistakably clear that any deference must exist "within constitutionally prescribed limits," *ibid.*, and that "deference does not imply abandonment or abdication of judicial review."

The race-based admissions systems that respondents employ also fail to comply with the twin commands of the Equal Protection Clause that race may never be used as a "negative" and that it may not operate as a stereotype. First, our cases have stressed that an individual's race may never be used against him in the admissions process. Here, however, the First Circuit found that Harvard's consideration of race has led to an 11.1% decrease in the number of Asian-Americans admitted to Harvard. And the District Court observed that Harvard's "policy of considering applicants' race . . . overall results in fewer Asian American and white students being admitted."

Respondents nonetheless contend that an individual's race is never a negative factor in their admissions programs, but that assertion cannot withstand scrutiny. Harvard, for example, draws an analogy between race and other factors it considers in admission. "[W]hile admissions officers may give a preference to applicants likely to excel in the Harvard-Radcliffe Orchestra," Harvard explains, "that does not mean it is a 'negative' not to excel at a musical instrument." But on Harvard's logic, while it gives preferences to applicants with high grades and test scores, "that does not mean it is a 'negative'" to be a student with lower grades and lower test scores. This understanding of the admissions process is hard to take seriously. College admissions are zero-sum. A benefit provided to some applicants but not to others necessarily advantages the former group at the expense of the latter.

Respondents also suggest that race is not a negative factor because it does not impact many admissions decisions. Yet, at the same time, respondents also maintain that the demographics of their admitted classes would meaningfully change if race-based admissions were abandoned. And they acknowledge that race is determinative for at least some — if not many — of the students they admit. How else but "negative" can race be described if, in its absence, members of some racial groups would be admitted in greater numbers than they otherwise would have been? The "[e]qual protection of the laws is not achieved through indiscriminate imposition of inequalities."

Respondents' admissions programs are infirm for a second reason as well. We have long held that universities may not operate their admissions programs on the "belief that minority students always (or even consistently) express some characteristic minority viewpoint on any issue." Yet by accepting race-based admissions programs in which some students may obtain preferences on the basis of race alone, respondents' programs tolerate the very thing that *Grutter* foreswore: stereotyping. The point of respondents' admissions programs is that there is an inherent benefit in race *qua* race — in race for race's sake. Respondents admit as much. Harvard's admissions process rests on the pernicious stereotype that "a black student can usually bring something that a white person cannot offer."

We have time and again forcefully rejected the notion that government actors may intentionally allocate preference to those "who may have little in common with one another but the color of their skin." The entire point of the Equal Protection Clause is that treating someone differently because of their skin color is *not* like treating them differently because they are from a city or from a suburb, or because they play the violin poorly or well.

"One of the principal reasons race is treated as a forbidden classification is that it demeans the dignity and worth of a person to be judged by ancestry instead of by his or her own merit and essential qualities." *Rice*, 528 U.S., at 517. But when a university admits students "on the basis of race, it engages in the offensive and demeaning assumption that [students] of a particular race, because of their race, think alike," at the very least alike in the sense of being different from nonminority students. In doing so, the university furthers "stereotypes that treat individuals as the product of their race, evaluating their thoughts and efforts — their very worth as citizens — according to a criterion barred to the Government by history and the Constitution."

If all this were not enough, respondents' admissions programs also lack a "logical end point." *Grutter*, 539 U.S., at 342. By promising to terminate their use of race only when some rough percentage of various racial groups is admitted, respondents turn that principle on its head. Their admissions programs "effectively assure[] that race will always be relevant . . . and that the ultimate goal of eliminating" race as a criterion "will never be achieved." *Croson*, 488 U.S., at 495.

The dissenting opinions resist these conclusions. They would instead uphold respondents' admissions programs based on their view that the Fourteenth Amendment permits state actors to remedy the effects of societal discrimination through explicitly race-based measures. Although both opinions are thorough and thoughtful in many respects, this Court has long rejected their core thesis.

In the years after *Bakke*, the Court repeatedly held that ameliorating societal discrimination does not constitute a compelling interest that justifies race-based state action. "[A]n effort to alleviate the effects of societal discrimination is not a compelling interest," we said plainly in *Hunt*, a 1996 case about the Voting Rights Act. 517 U.S., at 909–910.

For the reasons provided above, the Harvard and UNC admissions programs cannot be reconciled with the guarantees of the Equal Protection Clause. Both programs lack sufficiently focused and measurable objectives warranting the use of race, unavoidably employ race in a negative manner, involve racial stereotyping, and lack meaningful end points. We have never permitted admissions programs to work in that way, and we will not do so today.

At the same time, as all parties agree, nothing in this opinion should be construed as prohibiting universities from considering an applicant's discussion of how race affected his or her life, be it through discrimination, inspiration, or otherwise. But, despite the dissent's assertion to the contrary, universities may not simply establish through application essays or other means the regime we hold unlawful today. A benefit to a student who overcame racial discrimination, for example, must be tied to *that student's* courage and determination. Or a benefit to a student whose heritage or culture motivated him or her to assume a leadership role or attain a particular goal must be tied to *that student's* unique ability to contribute to the university. In other words, the student must be treated based on his or her experiences as an individual — not on the basis of race. Many universities have for too long done just the opposite. And in doing so, they have concluded, wrongly, that the touchstone of an individual's identity is not challenges bested, skills built, or lessons learned but the color of their skin. Our constitutional history does not tolerate that choice.

The judgments of the Court of Appeals for the First Circuit and of the District Court for the Middle District of North Carolina are reversed.

JUSTICE THOMAS, concurring

[Justice Thomas began with a lengthy historical analysis, which he offered as an "originalist defense of the colorblind Constitution." He stated:]

Despite the extensive evidence favoring the colorblind view, it appears increasingly in vogue to embrace an "antisubordination" view of the Fourteenth Amendment: that the Amendment forbids only laws that hurt, but not help, blacks. Such a theory lacks any basis in the original meaning of the Fourteenth Amendment. Respondents cite a smattering of federal and state statutes passed during the years surrounding the ratification of the Fourteenth Amendment. And, JUSTICE SOTO-MAYOR's dissent argues that several of these statutes evidence the ratifiers' understanding that the Equal Protection Clause "permits consideration of race to achieve its goal." Upon examination, however, it is clear that these statutes are fully consistent with the colorblind view.

[The following are excerpts from the remainder of his opinion.]

The Constitution's colorblind rule reflects one of the core principles upon which our Nation was founded: that "all men are created equal." [T]he Fourteenth Amendment reflected that vision, affirming that equality and racial discrimination cannot coexist. Under that Amendment, the color of a person's skin is irrelevant to that individual's equal status as a citizen of this Nation. To treat him differently on the basis of such a legally irrelevant trait is therefore a deviation from the equality principle and a constitutional injury.

Respondents and the dissents argue that the universities' race-conscious admissions programs ought to be permitted because they accomplish positive social goals. I would have thought that history had by now taught a "greater humility" when attempting to "distinguish good from harmful uses of racial criteria." From the Black Codes, to discriminatory and destructive social welfare programs, to discrimination by individual government actors, bigotry has reared its ugly head time and again. Anyone who today thinks that some form of racial discrimination will prove "helpful" should thus tread cautiously, lest racial discriminators succeed (as they once did) in using such language to disguise more invidious motives.

Even taking the desire to help on its face, what initially seems like aid may in reality be a burden, including for the very people it seeks to assist. Take, for example, the college admissions policies here. "Affirmative action" policies do nothing to increase the overall number of blacks and Hispanics able to access a college education. Rather, those racial policies simply redistribute individuals among institutions of higher learning, placing some into more competitive institutions than they otherwise would have attended.

These policies may harm even those who succeed academically. I have long believed that large racial preferences in college admissions "stamp [blacks and Hispanics] with a badge of inferiority." They thus "tain[t] the accomplishments of all those who are admitted as a result of racial discrimination" as well as "all those who are the same race as those admitted as a result of racial discrimination" because "no one can distinguish those students from the ones whose race played a role in their admission." Consequently, "[w]hen blacks" and, now, Hispanics "take positions in the highest places of government, industry, or academia, it is an open question . . . whether their skin color played a part in their advancement." "The question itself is the stigma—because either racial discrimination did play a role, in which case the person may be deemed 'otherwise unqualified,' or it did not, in which case asking the question itself unfairly marks those . . . who would succeed without discrimination."

Finally, it is not even theoretically possible to "help" a certain racial group without causing harm to members of other racial groups. "It should be obvious that every racial classification helps, in a narrow sense, some races and hurts others." *Adarand*, 515 U.S., at 241, n. * (opinion of Thomas, J.). And, even purportedly benign race-based discrimination has secondary effects on members of other races. The anti-subordination view thus has never guided the Court's analysis because "whether a law relying upon racial taxonomy is 'benign' or 'malign' either turns on 'whose ox is gored' or on distinctions found only in the eye of the beholder." Courts are not suited to the impossible task of determining which racially discriminatory programs are helping which members of which races—and whether those benefits outweigh the burdens thrust onto other racial groups.

Justice Jackson has a different view. Rather than focusing on individuals as individuals, her dissent focuses on the historical subjugation of black Americans, invoking statistical racial gaps to argue in favor of defining and categorizing individuals by their race. As she sees things, we are all inexorably trapped in a fundamentally racist society, with the original sin of slavery and the historical subjugation of black Americans still determining our lives today. The panacea, she counsels, is to unquestioningly accede to the view of elite experts and reallocate society's riches by racial means as necessary to "level the playing field," all as judged by racial metrics.

I, of course, agree that our society is not, and has never been, colorblind. People discriminate against one another for a whole host of reasons. But, under the Fourteenth Amendment, the law must disregard all racial distinctions.

Though Justice Jackson seems to think that her race based theory can somehow benefit everyone, it is an immutable fact that "every time the government uses racial criteria to 'bring the races together,' someone gets excluded, and the person excluded suffers an injury solely because of his or her race." *Parents Involved*, 551 U.S., at 759 (Thomas, J., concurring) (citation omitted). Indeed, Justice Jackson seems to have no response—no explanation at all—for the people who will shoulder that burden. How, for example, would Justice Jackson explain the need for race-based preferences to the Chinese student who has worked hard his whole life, only to be denied college admission in part because of his skin color? If such a burden would seem difficult to impose on a bright-eyed young person, that's because it should be. History has taught us to abhor theories that call for elites to pick racial winners and losers in the name of sociological experimentation. Nor is it clear what another few generations of race-conscious college admissions may be expected to accomplish. Even today, affirmative action programs that offer an admissions boost to black and Hispanic students discriminate against those who identify themselves as members of other races that do not receive such preferential treatment. Must others in the future make sacrifices to relevel the playing field for this new phase of racial subordination? And then, out of whose lives should the debt owed to those further victims be repaid? This vision of meeting social racism with government-imposed racism is thus self-defeating, resulting in a never-ending cycle of victimization. There is no reason to continue down that path. In the wake of the Civil War, the Framers of the Fourteenth Amendment charted a way out: a colorblind Constitution that requires the government to, at long last, put aside its citizens' skin color and focus on their individual achievements.

The great failure of this country was slavery and its progeny. And, the tragic failure of this Court was its misinterpretation of the Reconstruction Amendments, as Justice Harlan predicted in *Plessy*. We should not repeat this mistake merely because we think, as our predecessors thought, that the present arrangements are superior to the Constitution.

The Court's opinion rightly makes clear that *Grutter* is, for all intents and purposes, overruled. And, it sees the universities' admissions policies for what they are: rudderless, race-based preferences designed to ensure a particular racial mix in their entering classes. Those policies fly in the face of our colorblind Constitution and our Nation's equality ideal. In short, they are plainly — and boldly — unconstitutional. See *Brown II*, 349 U.S., at 298 (noting that the *Brown* case one year earlier had "declare[d] the fundamental principle that racial discrimination in public education is unconstitutional").

While I am painfully aware of the social and economic ravages which have befallen my race and all who suffer discrimination, I hold out enduring hope that this country will live up to its principles so clearly enunciated in the Declaration of Independence and the Constitution of the United States: that all men are created equal, are equal citizens, and must be treated equally before the law.

JUSTICE GORSUCH, with whom JUSTICE THOMAS joins, concurring. [omitted] [This concurring opinion focuses on Title VI of the Civil Rights Act and argues that it "bears independent force beyond the Equal Protection Clause. Nothing in it endorses racial discrimination to any degree or for any purpose."]

JUSTICE KAVANAUGH, concurring.

I join the Court's opinion in full. I add this concurring opinion to further explain why the Court's decision today is consistent with and follows from the Court's equal protection precedents, including the Court's precedents on race-based affirmative action in higher education.

In allowing race-based affirmative action in higher education for another generation — and only for another generation — the Court in *Grutter* took into account competing considerations. The Court recognized the barriers that some minority applicants to universities still faced as of 2003, notwithstanding the progress made since *Bakke*. The Court stressed, however, that "there are serious problems of justice connected with the idea of preference itself." And the Court added that a "core purpose of the Fourteenth Amendment was to do away with all governmentally imposed discrimination based on race."

The *Grutter* Court also emphasized the equal protection principle that racial classifications, even when otherwise permissible, must be a "'temporary matter,'" and "must be limited in time." The requirement of a time limit "reflects that racial classifications, however compelling their goals, are potentially so dangerous that they may be employed no more broadly than the interest demands. Enshrining a permanent justification for racial preferences would offend this fundamental equal protection principle."

Harvard and North Carolina would prefer that the Court now ignore or discard *Grutter*'s 25-year limit on race-based affirmative action in higher education, or treat it as a mere aspiration. But the 25-year limit constituted an important part of Justice O'Connor's nuanced opinion for the Court in *Grutter*. Indeed, four of the separate opinions in *Grutter* discussed the majority opinion's 25-year limit, which belies any suggestion that the Court's reference to it was insignificant or not carefully considered.

In short, the Court in *Grutter* expressly recognized the serious issues raised by racial classifications — particularly permanent or long-term racial classifications. And the Court "assure[d] all citizens" throughout America that "the deviation from the norm of equal treatment" in higher education could continue for another generation, and only for another generation.

JUSTICE SOTOMAYOR, with whom JUSTICE KAGAN and JUSTICE JACKSON join [Justice Jackson did not participate in the decision in the Harvard case] dissenting.

Today, this Court stands in the way and rolls back decades of precedent and momentous progress. It holds that race can no longer be used in a limited way in college admissions to achieve such critical benefits. In so holding, the Court cements a superficial rule of colorblindness as a constitutional principle in an endemically segregated society where race has always mattered and continues to matter. The Court subverts the constitutional guarantee of equal protection by further entrenching racial inequality in education, the very foundation of our democratic government and pluralistic society. Because the Court's opinion is not grounded in law or fact and contravenes the vision of equality embodied in the Fourteenth Amendment, I dissent.

[Justice Sotomayor offers her historical analysis, which (contrary to Justice Thomas') concludes that "the Fourteenth Amendment does not impose a blanket ban on race-conscious policies. Simultaneously with the passage of the Fourteenth Amendment, Congress enacted a number of race-conscious laws to fulfill the Amendment's promise of equality, leaving no doubt that the Equal Protection Clause permits consideration of race to achieve its goal."]

Two decades after *Brown*, in *Bakke*, a plurality of the Court held that "the attainment of a diverse student body" is a "compelling" and "constitutionally permissible goal for an institution of higher education." Race could be considered in the college admissions process in pursuit of this goal, the plurality explained, if it is one factor of many in an applicant's file, and each applicant receives individualized review as part of a holistic admissions process.

Since *Bakke*, the Court has reaffirmed numerous times the constitutionality of limited race-conscious college admissions. First, in *Grutter v. Bollinger*, 539 U.S. 306 (2003), a majority of the Court endorsed the *Bakke* plurality's "view that student body diversity is a compelling state interest that can justify the use of race in university admissions," and held that race may be used in a narrowly tailored manner to achieve this interest. Later, in the *Fisher* litigation, the Court twice reaffirmed that a limited use of race in college admissions is constitutionally permissible if it satisfies strict scrutiny. In *Fisher v. University of Texas at Austin*, 570 U.S. 297 (2013) (*Fisher I*), seven Members of the Court concluded that the use of race in college admissions comports with the Fourteenth Amendment if it "is narrowly tailored to obtain the educational benefits of diversity." Several years later, in *Fisher v. University of Texas at Austin*, 579 U.S. 365, 376 (2016) (*Fisher II*), the Court upheld the admissions program at the University of Texas under this framework.

Bakke, *Grutter*, and *Fisher* are an extension of *Brown*'s legacy. Those decisions recognize that "'experience lend[s] support to the view that the contribution of diversity is substantial.'" *Grutter*, 539 U.S., at 324 (quoting *Bakke*, 438 U.S., at 313). Racially integrated schools improve cross-racial understanding, "break down racial stereotypes," and ensure that students obtain "the skills needed in today's increasingly global marketplace . . . through exposure to widely diverse people, cultures, ideas, and viewpoints." 539 U.S., at 330. More broadly, inclusive institutions that are "visibly open to talented and qualified individuals of every race and ethnicity" instill public confidence in the "legitimacy" and "integrity" of those institutions and the diverse set of graduates that they cultivate. *Id.*, at 332. That is particularly true in the context of higher education, where colleges and universities play a critical role in "maintaining the fabric of society" and serve as "the training ground for a large number of our Nation's leaders." *Id.*, at 331–332. It is thus an objective of the highest order, a "compelling interest" indeed, that universities pursue the benefits of racial diversity and ensure that "the diffusion of knowledge and opportunity" is available to students of all races. *Id.*, at 328–333.

In short, for more than four decades, it has been this Court's settled law that the Equal Protection Clause of the Fourteenth Amendment authorizes a limited use of race in college admissions in service of the educational benefits that flow from a diverse student body. From *Brown* to *Fisher*, this Court's cases have sought to equalize educational opportunity in a society structured by racial segregation and to advance the Fourteenth Amendment's vision of an America where racially integrated schools guarantee students of all races the equal protection of the laws.

Today, the Court concludes that indifference to race is the only constitutionally permissible means to achieve racial equality in college admissions. That interpretation of the Fourteenth Amendment is not only contrary to precedent and the entire teachings of our history. But is also grounded in the illusion that racial inequality was a problem of a different generation. Entrenched racial inequality remains a reality today. That is true for society writ large and, more specifically, for Harvard and the University of North Carolina (UNC), two institutions with a long history of racial exclusion. Ignoring race will not equalize a society that is racially unequal. What was true in the 1860s, and again in 1954, is true today: Equality requires acknowledgment of inequality.

After more than a century of government policies enforcing racial segregation by law, society remains highly segregated. About half of all Latino and Black students attend a racially homogeneous school with at least 75% minority student enrollment. The share of intensely segregated minority schools (i.e., schools that enroll 90% to 100% racial minorities) has sharply increased. To this day, the U.S. Department of Justice continues to enter into desegregation decrees with schools that have failed to "eliminat[e] the vestiges of *de jure* segregation."

Moreover, underrepresented minority students are more likely to live in poverty and attend schools with a high concentration of poverty. When combined with residential segregation and school funding systems that rely heavily on local property taxes, this leads to racial minority students attending schools with fewer resources. See *San Antonio Independent School Dist. v. Rodriguez*, 411 U.S. 1, 72–86 (1973) (Marshall, J., dissenting) (noting school funding disparities that result from local property taxation). In turn, underrepresented minorities are more likely to attend schools with less qualified teachers, less challenging curricula, lower standardized test scores, and fewer extracurricular activities and advanced placement courses. It is thus unsurprising that there are achievement gaps along racial lines, even after controlling for income differences.

Systemic inequities disadvantaging underrepresented racial minorities exist beyond school resources. Students of color, particularly Black students, are disproportionately disciplined or suspended, interrupting their academic progress and increasing their risk of involvement with the criminal justice system. Underrepresented minorities are less likely to have parents with a postsecondary education who may be familiar with the college application process. Further, low-income children of color are less likely to attend preschool and other early childhood education programs that increase educational attainment. All of these interlocked factors place underrepresented minorities multiple steps behind the starting line in the race for college admissions.

Put simply, society remains "inherently unequal." *Brown*, 347 U.S., at 495. Racial inequality runs deep to this very day. That is particularly true in education, the "'most vital civic institution for the preservation of a democratic system of government.'" *Plyler v. Doe*, 457 U.S. 202, 221, 223 (1982). As I have explained before, only with eyes open to this reality can the Court "carry out the guarantee of equal protection."

The Court concludes that Harvard's and UNC's policies are unconstitutional because they serve objectives that are insufficiently measurable, employ racial categories that are imprecise and overbroad, rely on racial stereotypes and disadvantage nonminority groups, and do not have an end point. In reaching this conclusion, the Court claims those supposed issues with respondents' programs render the programs insufficiently "narrow" under the strict scrutiny framework that the Court's precedents command. In reality, however, "the Court today cuts through the kudzu" and overrules its "higher education precedents" following *Bakke*.

There is no better evidence that the Court is overruling the Court's precedents than those precedents themselves. "Every one of the arguments made by the majority can be found in the dissenting opinions filed in [the] cases" the majority now overrules. see, *e.g.*, *Grutter*, 539 U.S., at 354 (THOMAS, J., concurring in part and dissenting in part) ("Unlike the majority, I seek to define with precision the interest being asserted"); *Fisher II*, 579 U.S., at 389 (THOMAS, J., dissenting) (race-conscious admissions programs "res[t] on pernicious assumptions about race"); *id.*, at 403 (ALITO, J., joined by ROBERTS, C.J., and THOMAS, J., dissenting) (diversity interests "are laudable goals, but they are not concrete or precise"); *id.*, at 413 (race-conscious college admissions plan "discriminates against Asian-American students"); *id.*, at 414 (race-conscious admissions plan is unconstitutional because it "does not specify what it means to be 'African-American,' 'Hispanic,' 'Asian American,' 'Native American,' or 'White'"); *id.*, at 419 (race-conscious college admissions policies rest on "pernicious stereotype[s]").

Lost arguments are not grounds to overrule a case. When proponents of those arguments, greater now in number on the Court, return to fight old battles anew, it betrays an unrestrained disregard for precedent. It fosters the People's suspicions that "bedrock principles are founded . . . in the proclivities of individuals" on this Court, not in the law, and it degrades "the integrity of our constitutional system of government." *Vasquez v. Hillery*, 474 U.S. 254, 265 (1986). Nowhere is the damage greater than in cases like these that touch upon matters of representation and institutional legitimacy.

To avoid public accountability for its choice, the Court seeks cover behind a unique measurability requirement of its own creation. None of this Court's precedents, however, requires that a compelling interest meet some threshold level of precision to be deemed sufficiently compelling. In fact, this Court has recognized as compelling plenty of interests that are equally or more amorphous, including the "intangible" interest in preserving "public confidence in judicial integrity," an interest that "does not easily reduce to precise definition." *Williams-Yulee v.*

Florida Bar, 575 U.S. 433, 447, 454 (2015) (Roberts, C.J., for the Court); see also, *e.g.*, *Ramirez v. Collier*, 595 U.S. ___, ___ (2022) (Roberts, C.J., for the Court) (slip op., at 18) ("[M]aintaining solemnity and decorum in the execution chamber" is a "compelling" interest); *United States v. Alvarez*, 567 U.S. 709, 725 (2012) (plurality opinion) ("[P]rotecting the integrity of the Medal of Honor" is a "compelling interes[t]"); *Sable Communications of Cal., Inc. v. FCC*, 492 U.S. 115, 126 (1989) ("[P]rotecting the physical and psychological wellbeing of minors" is a "compelling interest"). Thus, although the Members of this majority pay lip service to respondents' "commendable" and "worthy" racial diversity goals, they make a clear value judgment today: Racial integration in higher education is not sufficiently important to them. "Today, the proclivities of individuals rule." The majority offers no response to any of this. Instead, it attacks a straw man, arguing that the Court's cases recognize that remedying the effects of "societal discrimination" does not constitute a compelling interest. Yet as the majority acknowledges, while *Bakke* rejected that interest as insufficiently compelling, it upheld a limited use of race in college admissions to promote the educational benefits that flow from diversity. It is that narrower interest, which the Court has reaffirmed numerous times since *Bakke* and as recently as 2016 in *Fisher II*, see *supra*, at 14–15, that the Court overrules today.

The Court argues that Harvard's and UNC's programs must end because they unfairly disadvantage some racial groups. According to the Court, college admissions are a "zero-sum" game and respondents' use of race unfairly "advantages" underrepresented minority students "at the expense of" other students. That is not the role race plays in holistic admissions. Consistent with the Court's precedents, respondents' holistic review policies consider race in a very limited way. Race is only one factor out of many. That type of system allows Harvard and UNC to assemble a diverse class on a multitude of dimensions. Respondents' policies allow them to select students with various unique attributes, including talented athletes, artists, scientists, and musicians. They also allow respondents to assemble a class with diverse viewpoints, including students who have different political ideologies and academic interests, who have struggled with different types of disabilities, who are from various socioeconomic backgrounds, who understand different ways of life in various parts of the country, and — yes — students who self-identify with various racial backgrounds and who can offer different perspectives because of that identity. That type of multidimensional system benefits all students. In fact, racial groups that are not underrepresented tend to benefit disproportionately from such a system.

In the end, the Court merely imposes its preferred college application format on the Nation, not acting as a court of law applying precedent but taking on the role of college administrators to decide what is better for society. The Court's course reflects its inability to recognize that racial identity informs some students' viewpoints and experiences in unique ways. The Court goes as far as to claim that *Bakke*'s recognition that Black Americans can offer different perspectives than white people amounts to a "stereotype."

It is not a stereotype to acknowledge the basic truth that young people's experiences are shaded by a societal structure where race matters. Acknowledging that there is something special about a student of color who graduates valedictorian from a predominantly white school is not a stereotype. Nor is it a stereotype to acknowledge that race imposes certain burdens on students of color that it does not impose on white students. "For generations, black and brown parents have given their children 'the talk'—instructing them never to run down the street; always keep your hands where they can be seen; do not even think of talking back to a stranger—all out of fear of how an officer with a gun will react to them." *Utah* v. *Strieff*, 579 U. S. 232, 254 (2016) (SOTOMAYOR, J., dissenting). Those conversations occur regardless of socioeconomic background or any other aspect of a student's self-identification. They occur because of race. As Andrew Brennen, a UNC alumnus, testified, "running down the neighborhood . . . people don't see [him] as someone that is relatively affluent; they see [him] as a black man." The absence of racial diversity, by contrast, actually contributes to stereotyping. "[D]iminishing the force of such stereotypes is both a crucial part of [respondents'] mission, and one that [they] cannot accomplish with only token numbers of minority students." *Grutter*, 539 U.S., at 333. When there is an increase in underrepresented minority students on campus, "racial stereotypes lose their force" because diversity allows students to "learn there is no 'minority viewpoint' but rather a variety of viewpoints among minority students." *Id.*, at 319–320. By preventing respondents from achieving their diversity objectives, it is the Court's opinion that facilitates stereotyping on American college campuses.

The Court also holds that Harvard's and UNC's race conscious programs are unconstitutional because they rely on racial categories that are "imprecise," "opaque," and "arbitrary." To start, the racial categories that the Court finds troubling resemble those used across the Federal Government for data collection, compliance reporting, and program administration purposes, including, for example, by the U.S. Census Bureau. See, *e.g.*, 62 Fed. Reg. 58786–58790 (1997). Surely, not all "'federal grant-in-aid benefits, drafting of legislation, urban and regional planning, business planning, and academic and social studies'" that flow from census data collection.

Cherry-picking language from *Grutter*, the Court also holds that Harvard's and UNC's race-conscious programs are unconstitutional because they do not have a specific expiration date. This new durational requirement is also not grounded in law, facts, or common sense. *Grutter* simply announced a general "expect[ation]" that "the use of racial preferences [would] no longer be necessary" in the future.

True, *Grutter* referred to "25 years," but that arbitrary number simply reflected the time that had elapsed since the Court "first approved the use of race" in college admissions in *Bakke*. *Grutter*, 539 U.S., at 343. It is also true that *Grutter* remarked that "race-conscious admissions policies must be limited in time," but it did not do so in a vaccum, as the Court suggests. Rather than impose a fixed expiration date, the Court tasked universities with the responsibility of periodically assessing whether their race-conscious programs "are still necessary." *Grutter* offered as examples sunset provisions, periodic reviews, and experimenting with "race-neutral alternatives as they develop." That is precisely how this Court has previously interpreted *Grutter*'s command. See *Fisher II*, 579 U.S., at 388 ("It is the University's ongoing obligation to engage in constant deliberation and continued reflection regarding its admissions policies").

Justice Thomas, for his part, offers a multitude of arguments for why race-conscious college admissions policies supposedly "burden" racial minorities. None of them has any merit. He first renews his argument that the use of race in holistic admissions leads to the "inevitable" "underperformance" by Black and Latino students at elite universities "because they are less academically prepared than the white and Asian students with whom they must compete." Justice Thomas speaks only for himself. The Court previously declined to adopt this so-called "mismatch" hypothesis for good reason: It was debunked long ago. The decades-old "studies" advanced by the handful of authors upon whom Justice Thomas relies, have "major methodological flaws," are based on unreliable data, and do not "meet the basic tenets of rigorous social science research." Brief for Empirical Scholars as *Amici Curiae* 3, 9–25. By contrast, "[m]any social scientists have studied the impact of elite educational institutions on student outcomes, and have found, among other things, that attending a more selective school is associated with higher graduation rates and higher earnings for [underrepresented minority] students — conclusions directly contrary to mismatch." This extensive body of research is supported by the most obvious data point available to this institution today: The three Justices of color on this Court graduated from elite universities and law schools with race conscious admissions programs, and achieved successful legal careers, despite having different educational backgrounds than their peers. A discredited hypothesis that the Court previously rejected is no reason to overrule precedent.

Citing no evidence, Justice Thomas also suggests that race-conscious admissions programs discriminate against Asian American students. It is true that SFFA "allege[d]" that Harvard discriminates against Asian American students. Specifically, SFFA argued that Harvard discriminates against Asian American applicants vis-à-vis white applicants through the use of the personal rating, an allegedly "highly subjective" component of the admissions process that is "susceptible to stereotyping and bias." It is also true, however, that there was a lengthy trial to test those allegations, which SFFA lost. Justice Thomas points to no legal or factual error below, precisely because there is none.

The costly result of today's decision harms not just respondents and students but also our institutions and democratic society more broadly. Dozens of *amici* from nearly every sector of society agree that the absence of race-conscious college admissions will decrease the pipeline of racially diverse college graduates to crucial professions. Those *amici* include the United States, which emphasizes the need for diversity in the Nation's military, and in the federal workforce more generally, including the Federal Bureau of Investigation and the Office of the Director of National Intelligence. The United States explains that "the Nation's military strength and readiness depend on a pipeline of officers who are both highly qualified and racially diverse—and who have been educated in diverse environments that prepare them to lead increasingly diverse forces."

Amici also tell the Court that race-conscious college admissions are critical for providing equitable and effective public services. State and local governments require public servants educated in diverse environments who can "identify, understand, and respond to perspectives" in "our increasingly diverse communities." Brief for Southern Governors as *Amici Curiae* 5–8 (Southern Governors Brief). Likewise, increasing the number of students from underrepresented backgrounds who join "the ranks of medical professionals" improves "healthcare access and health outcomes in medically underserved communities." Brief for Massachusetts et al. as *Amici Curiae* 10; see Brief for Association of American Medical Colleges et al. as *Amici Curiae* 5 (noting also that *all* physicians become better practitioners when they learn in a racially diverse environment). So too, greater diversity within the teacher workforce improves student academic achievement in primary public schools. Brief for Massachusetts et al. as *Amici Curiae* 15–17; see Brief for American Federation of Teachers as *Amicus Curiae* 8 ("[T]here are few professions with broader social impact than teaching"). A diverse pipeline of college graduates also ensures a diverse legal profession, which demonstrates that "the justice system serves the public in a fair and inclusive manner." Brief for American Bar Association as *Amicus Curiae* 18; see also Brief for Law Firm Antiracism Alliance as *Amicus Curiae* 1, 6 (more than 300 law firms in all 50 States supporting race-conscious college admissions in light of the "influence and power" that lawyers wield "in the American system of government"). Examples of other industries and professions that benefit from race-conscious college admissions abound.

True equality of educational opportunity in racially diverse schools is an essential component of the fabric of our democratic society. It is an interest of the highest order and a foundational requirement for the promotion of equal protection under the law. *Brown* recognized that passive race neutrality was inadequate to achieve the constitutional guarantee of racial equality in a Nation where the effects of segregation persist. In a society where race continues to matter, there is no constitutional requirement that institutions attempting to remedy their legacies of racial exclusion must operate with a blindfold.

Today, this Court overrules decades of precedent and imposes a superficial rule of race blindness on the Nation. The devastating impact of this decision cannot be overstated. The majority's vision of race neutrality will entrench racial segregation in higher education because racial inequality will persist so long as it is ignored.

Notwithstanding this Court's actions, however, society's progress toward equality cannot be permanently halted. Diversity is now a fundamental American value, housed in our varied and multicultural American community that only continues to grow. The pursuit of racial diversity will go on. Although the Court has stripped out almost all uses of race in college admissions, universities can and should continue to use all available tools to meet society's needs for diversity in education. Despite the Court's unjustified exercise of power, the opinion today will serve only to highlight the Court's own impotence in the face of an America whose cries for equality resound. As has been the case before in the history of American democracy, "the arc of the moral universe" will bend toward racial justice despite the Court's efforts today to impede its progress. Martin Luther King "Our God is Marching On!" Speech (Mar. 25, 1965).

Justice Jackson, with whom Justice Sotomayor and Justice Kagan join, dissenting.

I write separately to expound upon the universal benefits of considering race in this context, in response to a suggestion that has permeated this legal action from the start. Students for Fair Admissions (SFFA) has maintained, both subtly and overtly, that it is *unfair* for a college's admissions process to consider race as one factor in a holistic review of its applicants. This contention blinks both history and reality in ways too numerous to count. But the response is simple: Our country has never been colorblind. Given the lengthy history of state-sponsored race-based preferences in America, to say that anyone is now victimized if a college considers whether that legacy of discrimination has unequally advantaged its applicants fails to acknowledge the well documented "intergenerational transmission of inequality" that still plagues our citizenry. It is *that* inequality that admissions programs such as UNC's help to address, to the benefit of us all. Because the majority's judgment stunts that progress without any basis in law, history, logic, or justice, I dissent.

History speaks. In some form, it can be heard forever. The race-based gaps that first developed centuries ago are echoes from the past that still exist today. By all accounts, they are still stark.

Start with wealth and income. Just four years ago, in 2019, Black families' median wealth was approximately $24,000. For White families, that number was approximately eight times as much (about $188,000). These wealth disparities "exis[t] at every income and education level," so, "[o]n average, white families with college degrees have over $300,000 more wealth than black families with college degrees." This disparity has also accelerated over time — from a roughly $40,000 gap between White and Black household median net worth in 1993 to a roughly $135,000 gap in 2019. Median income numbers from 2019 tell the same story: $76,057 for White households, $98,174 for Asian households, $56,113 for Latino households, and $45,438 for Black households.

These financial gaps are unsurprising in light of the link between home ownership and wealth. Today, as was true 50 years ago, Black home ownership trails White home ownership by approximately 25 percentage points. Moreover, Black Americans' homes (relative to White Americans') constitute a greater percentage of household wealth, yet tend to be worth less, are subject to higher effective property taxes, and generally lost more value in the Great Recession.

From those markers of social and financial unwellness flow others. In most state flagship higher educational institutions, the percentage of Black undergraduates is lower than the percentage of Black high school graduates in that State. Black Americans in their late twenties are about half as likely as their White counterparts to have college degrees. And because lower family income and wealth force students to borrow more, those Black students who do graduate college find themselves four years out with about $50,000 in student debt — nearly twice as much as their White compatriots.

As for postsecondary professional arenas, despite being about 13% of the population, Black people make up only about 5% of lawyers. Such disparity also appears in the business realm: Of the roughly 1,800 chief executive officers to have appeared on the well-known Fortune 500 list, fewer than 25 have been Black (as of 2022, only six are Black). Furthermore, as the COVID–19 pandemic raged, Blackowned small businesses failed at dramatically higher rates than White-owned small businesses, partly due to the disproportionate denial of the forgivable loans needed to survive the economic downturn.

Health gaps track financial ones. When tested, Black children have blood lead levels that are twice the rate of White children — "irreversible" contamination working irremediable harm on developing brains. Black (and Latino) children with heart conditions are more likely to die than their White counterparts. Race-linked mortality-rate disparity has also persisted, and is highest among infants. So, too, for adults: Black men are twice as likely to die from prostate cancer as White men and have lower 5-year cancer survival rates. Uterine cancer has spiked in recent years among all women — but has spiked highest for Black women, who die of uterine cancer at nearly twice the rate of "any other racial or ethnic group." Black mothers are up to four times more likely than White mothers to die as a result of childbirth. And COVID killed Black Americans at higher rates than White Americans.

"Across the board, Black Americans experience the highest rates of obesity, hypertension, maternal mortality, infant mortality, stroke, and asthma." These and other disparities — the predictable result of opportunity disparities lead to at least 50,000 excess deaths a year for Black Americans vis-à-vis White Americans. That is 80 million excess years of life lost from just 1999 through 2020.

Amici tell us that "race-linked health inequities pervad[e] nearly every index of human health" resulting "in an overall reduced life expectancy for racial and ethnic minorities that cannot be explained by genetics." Meanwhile — tying health and wealth together — while she lays dying, the typical Black American "pay[s] more for medical care and incur[s] more medical debt."

The majority seems to think that race blindness solves the problem of race-based disadvantage. But the irony is that requiring colleges to ignore the initial race-linked opportunity gap between applicants will inevitably widen that gap, not narrow it. It will delay the day that every American has an equal opportunity to thrive, regardless of race.

Universal benefits ensue from holistic admissions programs that allow consideration of *all* factors material to merit (including race), and that thereby facilitate diverse student populations. Once trained, those UNC students who have thrived in the university's diverse learning environment are well equipped to make lasting contributions in a variety of realms and with a variety of colleagues, which, in turn, will steadily decrease the salience of race for future generations. Fortunately, UNC and other institutions of higher learning are already on this beneficial path. In fact, all that they have needed to continue moving this country forward (toward full achievement of our Nation's founding promises) is for this Court to get out of the way and let them do their jobs. To our great detriment, the majority cannot bring itself to do so.

With let-them-eat-cake obliviousness, today, the majority pulls the ripcord and announces "colorblindness for all" by legal fiat. But deeming race irrelevant in law does not make it so in life. And having so detached itself from this country's actual past and present experiences, the Court has now been lured into interfering with the crucial work that UNC and other institutions of higher learning are doing to solve America's real-world problems. No one benefits from ignorance. Although formal race linked legal barriers are gone, race still matters to the lived experiences of all Americans in innumerable ways, and today's ruling makes things worse, not better. The best that can be said of the majority's perspective is that it proceeds (ostrich-like) from the hope that preventing consideration of race will end racism. But if that is its motivation, the majority proceeds in vain. If the colleges of this country are required to ignore a thing that matters, it will not just go away. It will take *longer* for racism to leave us. And, ultimately, ignoring race just makes it matter more.[10]

The only way out of this morass — for all of us — is to stare at racial disparity unblinkingly, and then do what evidence and experts tell us is required to level the playing field and march forward together, collectively striving to achieve true equality for all Americans. It is no small irony that the judgment the majority

---

10. [Court's Footnote 103] JUSTICE THOMAS's prolonged attack, responds to a dissent I did not write in order to assail an admissions program that is not the one UNC has crafted. He does not dispute any historical or present fact about the origins and continued existence of race-based disparity (nor could he), yet is somehow persuaded that these realities have no bearing on a fair assessment of "individual achievement." JUSTICE THOMAS's opinion also demonstrates an obsession with race consciousness that far outstrips my or UNC's holistic understanding that race can be a factor that affects applicants' unique life experiences. How else can one explain his detection of "an organizing principle based on race," a claim that our society is "fundamentally racist," and a desire for Black "victimhood" or racial "silo[s]," in this dissent's approval of an admissions program that advances all Americans' shared pursuit of true equality by treating race "on par with" other aspects of identity? JUSTICE THOMAS ignites too many more straw men to list, or fully extinguish, here. The takeaway is that those who demand that no one think about race (a classic pink-elephant paradox) refuse to see, much less solve for, the elephant in the room — the race-linked disparities that continue to impede achievement of our great Nation's full potential. Worse still, by insisting that obvious truths be ignored, they prevent our problem-solving institutions from directly addressing the real import and impact of "social racism" and "government-imposed racism," thereby deterring our collective progression toward becoming a society where race no longer matters.

hands down today will forestall the end of race-based disparities in this country, making the colorblind world the majority wistfully touts much more difficult to accomplish.

Notes and Questions

(1) The majority and dissent differ fundamentally over the issue of whether the Constitution is "colorblind." Both rely on *Brown v. Board of Education* to support their arguments about colorblindness. Who has the more convincing position? Should the continuing effects of racism in our society (as described by the dissenting opinions) be relevant to the debate over whether the Constitution is colorblind?

(2) Why does the majority conclude that the colleges' diversity goals do not satisfy the "compelling interest" required under strict scrutiny? Is the Court's application of strict scrutiny consistent with *Grutter*?

(3) The majority relies heavily on the statement in *Grutter* that the need for affirmative action may no longer exist in 25 years. Why is that time relevant to the constitutionality of the Harvard and UNC policies?

(4) In a footnote, the majority states: "The United States as *amicus curiae* contends that race-based admissions programs further compelling interests at our Nation's military academies. No military academy is a party to these cases, however, and none of the courts below addressed the propriety of race-based admissions systems in that context. This opinion also does not address the issue, in light of the potentially distinct interests that military academies may present." On what basis might the Court hold that race based affirmative action policies are constitutional at military academies but not at other institutions of higher education?

(5) What has changed in the 20 years since *Grutter* to justify the different result?

(6) How should a school redesign its admissions policies to comply with the decision and continue to further its diversity goals?

(7) Affirmative action programs also are used in other contexts, such as employment and governmental contracts. Will they survive future constitutional challenges?

Problem C

Assume that the Dean of a state law school has consulted you for advice about the design of the school's financial aid policy. The Dean tells you that the school has no history of intentional discrimination against people of color. Nevertheless, the school enrolls relatively small numbers of such applicants. The Dean believes quite strongly that a diversified student body is necessary for the school, as well as the profession. The Dean wants to develop a financial aid policy that includes scholarships to enhance diversity. Could the school designate certain scholarships for people of color? If not, how might the school design a policy to reach its goal?

§ 6.04 Gender Classification

A. Constitutional Standard

Goesaert v. Cleary

United States Supreme Court
335 U.S. 464, 69 S. Ct. 198, 93 L. Ed. 163 (1948)

MR. JUSTICE FRANKFURTER delivered the opinion of the Court.

As part of the Michigan system for controlling the sale of liquor, bartenders are required to be licensed in all cities having a population of 50,000, or more, but no female may be so licensed unless she be "the wife or daughter of the male owner" of a licensed liquor establishment. [The] claim [is] that Michigan cannot forbid females generally from being barmaids and at the same time make an exception in favor of the wives and daughters of the owners of liquor establishments. Beguiling as the subject is, it need not detain us long. To ask whether or not the Equal Protection of the Laws Clause of the Fourteenth Amendment barred Michigan from making the classification the State has made between wives and daughters of owners of liquor places and wives and daughters of non-owners, is one of those rare instances where to state the question is in effect to answer it.

We are, to be sure, dealing with a historic calling. We meet the alewife, sprightly and ribald, in Shakespeare, but centuries before him she played a role in the social life of England. The Fourteenth Amendment did not tear history up by the roots, and the regulation of the liquor traffic is one of the oldest and most untrammeled of legislative powers. Michigan could, beyond question, forbid all women from working behind a bar. This is so despite the vast changes in the social and legal position of women. The fact that women may now have achieved the virtues that men have long claimed as their prerogatives and now indulge in vices that men have long practiced, does not preclude the States from drawing a sharp line between the sexes. . . .

While Michigan may deny to all women opportunities for bartending, Michigan cannot play favorites among women without rhyme or reasons. . . . Since bartending by women may, in the allowable legislative judgment, give rise to moral and social problems against which it may devise preventive measures, the legislature need not go to the full length of prohibition if it believes that as to a defined group of females other factors are operating which either eliminate or reduce the moral and social problems otherwise calling for prohibition. Michigan evidently believes that the oversight assured through ownership of a bar by a barmaid's husband or father minimizes hazards that may confront a barmaid without such protecting oversight. This Court is certainly not in a position to gainsay such belief by the Michigan legislature. . . .

Judgment affirmed.

MR. JUSTICE RUTLEDGE, with whom MR. JUSTICE DOUGLAS and MR. JUSTICE MURPHY join, dissenting. . . .

The statute arbitrarily discriminates between male and female owners of liquor establishments. A male owner, although he himself is always absent from his bar, may employ his wife and daughter as barmaids. A female owner may neither work as a barmaid herself nor employ her daughter in that position, even if a man is always present in the establishment to keep order. This inevitable result of the classification belies the assumption that the statute was motivated by a legislative solicitude for the moral and physical well-being of women who, but for the law, would be employed as barmaids. Since there could be no other conceivable justification for such discrimination against women owners of liquor establishments, the statute should be held invalid as a denial of equal protection.

Notes and Questions

(1) Initially, the Court found little protection for women in the ratified Fourteenth Amendment. In *Bradwell v. Illinois*, 83 U.S. (16 Wall.) 130 (1873), the Court upheld an Illinois law that prohibited women from practicing law. A majority of the Court held that the state law did not deprive women of the privileges and immunities of United State citizenship. Justice Bradley, joined by Justices Swayne and Feld, observed in a concurring opinion: "The natural and proper timidity and delicacy which belongs to the female sex evidently unfits it for many of the occupations of civil life."

(2) Should the Court use a rationality standard in assessing the constitutionality of laws that discriminate against women? Or, should the Court closely scrutinize such laws like it does in race discrimination cases?

(3) The rationality standard was typically relied upon to sustain so-called protective laws which in fact operated to seriously restrict women's occupational opportunities. Further, when wage and hour laws were enacted for women only, they were sustained only because of the sexist approach evident in *Bradwell* and *Goesaert. See generally* Mary Jo Frug, *Securing Job Equality for Women: Labor Market Hostility to Working Mothers*, 59 B.U. L. Rev. 55 (1979). By the early 1970s, the Court's approach to gender discrimination equal protection challenges was changing.

Frontiero v. Richardson

United States Supreme Court
411 U.S. 677, 93 S. Ct. 1764, 36 L. Ed. 2d 583 (1973)

Mr. Justice Brennan announced the judgment of the Court in an opinion in which Mr. Justice Douglas, Mr. Justice White, and Mr. Justice Marshall join.

The question before us concerns the right of a female member of the uniformed services to claim her spouse as a "dependent" for the purposes of obtaining increased quarters allowances and medical and dental benefits under 37 U.S.C. §§ 401, 403, and 10 U.S.C. §§ 1072, 1076, on an equal footing with male members. Under these statutes, a serviceman may claim his wife as a "dependent" without regard to whether she is in fact dependent upon him for any part of her support.

A servicewoman, on the other hand, may not claim her husband as a "dependent" under these programs unless he is in fact dependent upon her for over one-half of his support. Thus, the question for decision is whether this difference in treatment constitutes an unconstitutional discrimination against servicewomen in violation of the Due Process Clause of the Fifth Amendment. . . .

In an effort to attract career personnel through reenlistment, Congress established a scheme for the provision of fringe benefits to members of the uniformed services on a competitive basis with business and industry. Thus a member of the uniformed services with dependents is entitled to an increased "basic allowance for quarters" and a member's dependents are provided comprehensive medical and dental care.

Appellant Sharron Frontiero, a lieutenant in the United States Air Force, sought increased quarters allowances, and housing and medical benefits for her husband, appellant Joseph Frontiero, on the ground that he was her "dependent." Although such benefits would automatically have been granted with respect to the wife of a male member of the uniformed services, appellant's application was denied because she failed to demonstrate that her husband was dependent on her for more than one-half of his support. Appellants then commenced this suit, contending that, by making this distinction, the statutes unreasonably discriminate on the basis of sex in violation of the Due Process clause of the Fifth Amendment. In essence, appellants asserted that the discriminatory impact of the statutes is twofold: first, as a procedural matter a female member is required to demonstrate her spouse's dependency, while no such burden is imposed upon male members; and, second, as a substantive matter, a male member who does not provide more than one-half of his wife's support receives benefits, while a similarly situated female member is denied such benefits. Appellants therefore sought a permanent injunction against the continued enforcement of these statutes and an order directing the appellees to provide Lieutenant Frontiero with the same housing and medical benefits that a similarly situated male member would receive.

Although the legislative history of these statutes sheds virtually no light on the purposes underlying the differential treatment accorded male and female members, a majority of the three-judge District Court surmised that Congress might reasonably have concluded that, since the husband in our society is generally the "breadwinner" in the family — and the wife typically the "dependent" partner — "it would be more economical to require married female members claiming husbands to prove actual dependency than to extend the presumption of dependency to such members." . . . Indeed, given the fact that approximately 99% of all members of the uniformed services are male, the District Court speculated that such differential treatment might conceivably lead to a "considerable saving of administrative expense and manpower."

At the outset, appellants contend that classifications based upon sex, like classifications based upon race, alienage, and national origin, are inherently suspect and must therefore be subjected to close judicial scrutiny. We agree and, indeed, find at least implicit support for such an approach in our unanimous decision only last Term in *Reed v. Reed*, 404 U.S. 71 (1971).

In *Reed*, the Court considered the constitutionality of an Idaho statute providing that, when two individuals are otherwise equally entitled to appointment as administrator of an estate, the male applicant must be preferred to the female. Appellant, the mother of the deceased, and appellee, the father, filed competing petitions for appointment as administrator of their son's estate. Since the parties, as parents of the deceased, were members of the same entitlement class the statutory preference was invoked and the father's petition was therefore granted. Appellant claimed that this statute, by giving a mandatory preference to males over females without regard to their individual qualifications, violated the Equal Protection Clause of the Fourteenth Amendment.

The Court noted that the Idaho statute "provides that different treatment be accorded to the applicants on the basis of their sex; it thus establishes a classification subject to scrutiny under the Equal Protection Clause." Under "traditional" equal protection analysis, a legislative classification must be sustained unless it is "patently arbitrary" and bears no rational relationship to a legitimate governmental interest.

In an effort to meet this standard, appellee contended that the statutory scheme was a reasonable measure designed to reduce the workload on probate courts by eliminating one class of contests. Moreover, appellee argued that the mandatory preference for male applicants was in itself reasonable since "men [are] as a rule more conversant with business affairs than . . . women." Indeed, appellee maintained that "it is a matter of common knowledge, that women still are not engaged in politics, the professions, business or industry to the extent that men are." And the Idaho Supreme Court, in upholding the constitutionality of this statute, suggested that the Idaho Legislature might reasonably have "concluded that in general men are better qualified to act as an administrator than are women."

Despite these contentions, however, the Court held the statutory preference for male applicants unconstitutional. In reaching this result, the Court implicitly rejected appellee's apparently rational explanation of the statutory scheme, and concluded that, by ignoring the individual qualifications of particular applicants, the challenged statute provides "dissimilar treatment for men and women who are . . . similarly situated." The Court therefore held that, even though the State's interest in achieving administrative efficiency "is not without some legitimacy," "[t]o give a mandatory preference to members of either sex over members of the other, merely to accomplish the elimination of hearings on the merits, is to make the very kind of arbitrary legislative choice forbidden by the [Constitution]. . . ." This departure from "traditional" rational-basis analysis with respect to sex-based classifications is clearly justified.

There can be no doubt that our Nation has had a long and unfortunate history of sex discrimination. Traditionally, such discrimination was rationalized by an attitude of "romantic paternalism" which, in practical effect, put women, not on a pedestal, but in a cage. Indeed, this paternalistic attitude became so firmly rooted in our national consciousness that, 100 years ago, a distinguished Member of this Court was able to proclaim:

> Man is, or should be, woman's protector and defender. The natural and proper timidity and delicacy which belongs to the female sex evidently unfits it for many of the occupations of civil life. The constitution of the family organization, which is founded in the divine ordinance, as well as in the nature of things, indicates the domestic sphere as that which properly belongs to the domain and functions of womanhood. The harmony, not to say identity, of interests and views which belong, or should belong, to the family institution is repugnant to the idea of a woman adopting a distinct and independent career from that of her husband. . . .
>
> The paramount destiny and mission of woman are to fulfill the noble and benign offices of wife and mother. This is the law of the Creator.

Bradwell v. State of Illinois.

As a result of notions such as these, our statute books gradually became laden with gross, stereotyped distinctions between the sexes and, indeed, throughout much of the 19th century the position of women in our society was, in many respects, comparable to that of blacks under the pre-Civil War slave codes. Neither slaves nor women could hold office, serve on juries, or bring suit in their own names, and married women traditionally were denied the legal capacity to hold or convey property or to serve as legal guardians of their own children. And although blacks were guaranteed the right to vote in 1870, women were denied even that right — which is itself "preservative of other basic civil and political rights" — until adoption of the Nineteenth Amendment half a century later.

It is true, of course, that the position of women in America has improved markedly in recent decades. Nevertheless, it can hardly be doubted that, in part because of the high visibility of the sex characteristic, women still face pervasive, although at times more subtle, discrimination in our educational institutions, in the job market and, perhaps most conspicuously, in the political arena.[11]

Moreover, since sex, like race and national origin, is an immutable characteristic determined solely by the accident of birth, the imposition of special disabilities upon the members of a particular sex because of their sex would seem to violate "the basic concept of our system that legal burdens should bear some relationship

---

11. [Court's Footnote 17] It is true, of course, that when viewed in the abstract, women do not constitute a small and powerless minority. Nevertheless, in part because of past discrimination, women are vastly underrepresented in this Nation's decision making councils. There has never been a female President, nor a female member of this Court. Not a single woman presently sits in the United States Senate, and only 14 women hold seats in the House of Representatives. And, as appellants point out, this underrepresentation is present throughout all levels of our State and Federal Government.

to individual responsibility. . . ." *Weber v. Aetna Casualty & Surety Co.,* 406 U.S. 164 (1972). And what differentiates sex from such non-suspect statuses as intelligence or physical disability, and aligns it with the recognized suspect criteria, is that the sex characteristic frequently bears no relation to ability to perform or contribute to society. As a result, statutory distinctions between the sexes often have the effect of invidiously relegating the entire class of females to inferior legal status without regard to the actual capabilities of its individual members. . . .

With these considerations in mind, we can only conclude that classifications based upon sex, like classifications based upon race, alienage, or national origin, are inherently suspect, and must therefore be subjected to strict judicial scrutiny. Applying the analysis mandated by that stricter standard of review, it is clear that the statutory scheme now before us is constitutionally invalid.

The sole basis of the classification established in the challenged statutes is the sex of the individuals involved. . . . [T]he statutes operate so as to deny benefits to a female member, such as appellant Sharron Frontiero, who provides less than one-half of her spouse's support, while at the same time granting such benefits to a male member who likewise provides less than one-half of his spouse's support. Thus, to this extent at least, it may fairly be said that these statutes command "dissimilar treatment for men and women who are . . . similarly situated." *Reed v. Reed.*

Moreover, the Government concedes that the differential treatment accorded men and women under these statutes serves no purpose other than mere "administrative convenience." In essence, the Government maintains that, as an empirical matter, wives in our society frequently are dependent upon their husbands, while husbands rarely are dependent upon their wives. Thus, the Government argues that Congress might reasonably have concluded that it would be both cheaper and easier simply conclusively to presume that wives of male members are financially dependent upon their husbands, while burdening female members with the task of establishing dependency in fact.[12]

The Government offers no concrete evidence, however, tending to support its view that such differential treatment in fact saves the Government any money. In order to satisfy the demands of strict judicial scrutiny, the Government must demonstrate, for example, that it is actually cheaper to grant increased benefits with respect to *all* male members, than it is to determine which male members are in fact entitled to such benefits and to grant increased benefits only to those members whose wives actually meet the dependency requirement. Here, however, there is substantial evidence that, if put to the test, many of the wives of male members would fail to qualify for benefits. And in light of the fact that the dependency determination with

---

12. [Court's Footnote 22] It should be noted that these statutes are not in any sense designed to rectify the effects of past discrimination against women. On the contrary, these statutes seize upon a group — women — who have historically suffered discrimination in employment, and rely on the effects of this past discrimination as a justification for heaping on additional economic disadvantages.

respect to the husbands of female members is presently made solely on the basis of affidavits rather than through the more costly hearing process, the Government's explanation of the statutory scheme is, to say the least, questionable.

In any case, our prior decisions make clear that, although efficacious administration of governmental programs is not without some importance, "the Constitution recognizes higher values than speed and efficiency." And when we enter the realm of "strict judicial scrutiny," there can be no doubt that "administrative convenience" is not a shibboleth, the mere recitation of which dictates constitutionality. On the contrary, any statutory scheme which draws a sharp line between the sexes, *solely* for the purpose of achieving administrative convenience, necessarily commands "dissimilar treatment for men and women who are . . . similarly situated," and therefore involves the "very kind of arbitrary legislative choice forbidden by the [Constitution]. . . ." *Reed v. Reed*. We therefore conclude that, by according differential treatment to male and female members of the uniformed services for the sole purpose of achieving administrative convenience, the challenged statutes violate the Due Process Clause of the Fifth Amendment insofar as they require a female member to prove the dependency of her husband.

Reversed.

Mr. Justice Stewart concurs in the judgment, agreeing that the statutes before us work an invidious discrimination in violation of the Constitution.

Mr. Justice Powell, with whom The Chief Justice [Burger] and Mr. Justice Blackmun join, concurring in the judgment.

I agree that the challenged statutes constitute an unconstitutional discrimination against servicewomen in violation of the Due Process Clause of the Fifth Amendment but I cannot join the opinion of Mr. Justice Brennan, which would hold that all classifications based upon sex, "like classifications based upon race, alienage, and national origin," are "inherently suspect and must therefore be subjected to close judicial scrutiny." It is unnecessary for the Court in this case to characterize sex as a suspect classification, with all of the far-reaching implications of such a holding. *Reed v. Reed*, 404 U.S. 71 (1971), which abundantly supports our decision today, did not add sex to the narrowly limited group of classifications which are inherently suspect. In my view, we can and should decide this case on the authority of *Reed* and reserve for the future any expansion of its rationale.

There is another, and I find compelling, reason for deferring a general categorizing of sex classifications as invoking the strictest test of judicial scrutiny. The Equal Rights Amendment, which if adopted will resolve the substance of this precise question, has been approved by the Congress and submitted for ratification by the States. If this Amendment is duly adopted, it will represent the will of the people accomplished in the manner prescribed by the Constitution. By acting prematurely and unnecessarily, as I view it, the Court has assumed a decisional responsibility at the very time when state legislatures, functioning within the traditional democratic process, are debating the proposed Amendment. It seems to me that this reaching out to pre-empt by judicial action a major political decision which is currently in process of resolution does not reflect appropriate respect for duly prescribed legislative processes.

There are times when this Court, under our system, cannot avoid a constitutional decision on issues which normally should be resolved by the elected representatives of the people. But democratic institutions are weakened, and confidence in the restraint of the Court is impaired, when we appear unnecessarily to decide sensitive issues of broad social and political importance at the very time they are under consideration within the prescribed constitutional processes.

MR. JUSTICE REHNQUIST dissents. . . . [Omitted.]

Notes and Questions

(1) Why should sex-based classifications invoke any special scrutiny by the courts that is more probing than traditional rationality review? Does the *Carolene Products* footnote (*see* § 5.01) and the "discrete and insular minorities" theory apply? Consider these views:

> It is even clearer in the case of sex than in the case of race that one's sexual identity is a centrally important, crucially relevant category within our culture. I think, in fact, that it is more important and more fundamental than one's race. It is evident that there are substantially different role expectations and role assignments to persons in accordance with their sexual physiology, and that the positions of the two sexes in the culture are distinct. We do have a patriarchal society in which it matters enormously whether one is a male or a female. By almost all important measures it is more advantageous to be a male rather than a female. . . .
>
> As is true for race, it is also a significant social fact that to be a female is to be an entity or creature viewed as different from the standard, fully developed person who is male as well as white. But to be female, as opposed to being black, is not to be conceived of as simply a creature of less worth. That is one important thing that differentiates sexism from racism: The ideology of sex, as opposed to the ideology of race, is a good deal more complex and confusing. Women are both put on a pedestal and deemed not fully developed persons. They are idealized; their approval and admiration is sought; and they are at the same time regarded as less competent than men and less able to live fully developed, fully human lives — for that is what men do. At best, they are viewed and treated as having properties and attributes that are valuable and admirable for humans of this type. For example, they may be viewed as especially empathetic, intuitive, loving, and nurturing. At best, these qualities are viewed as good properties for women to have, and, provided they are properly muted, are sometimes valued within the more well-rounded male. Because the sexual ideology is complex, confusing, and variable, it does not unambiguously proclaim the lesser value attached to

being female rather than being male, nor does it unambiguously correspond to the existing social realities. For these, among other reasons, sexism could plausibly be regarded as a deeper phenomenon than racism. It is more deeply embedded in the culture, and thus less visible. Being harder to detect, it is harder to eradicate. Moreover, it is less unequivocally regarded as unjust and unjustifiable. . . .

Richard Wasserstrom, *Racism, Sexism, and Preferential Treatment*, 24 UCLA L. Rev. 581, 587–590 (1977).[13]

The degree of contact between men and women could hardly be greater, and neither, of course, are women "in the closet" as homosexuals historically have been. Finally, lest you think I missed it, women have about half the votes, apparently more. As if it weren't enough that they're not discrete and insular, they're not even a minority! . . .

The very stereotypes that gave rise to laws "protecting" women by barring them from various activities are under daily and publicized attack, and are the subject of equally spirited defense. (That the common stereotypes are so openly described and debated, as they are not in the case of racial minorities, is itself some evidence of the comparatively free and nonthreatening nature of the interchange.) Given such open discussion of the traditional stereotypes, the claim that the numerical majority is being "dominated," that women are in effect "slaves" who have no realistic choice but to assimilate the stereotypes, is one it has become impossible to maintain except at the most inflated rhetorical level. . . .

In fact I may be wrong in supposing that because women now are in a position to protect themselves they will, that we are thus unlikely to see in the future the sort of official gender discrimination that has marked our past. But if women don't protect themselves from sex discrimination in the future, it won't be because they can't. It will rather be because for one reason or another — substantive disagreement or most likely the assignment of a low priority to the issue — they don't choose to. Many of us may condemn such a choice as benighted on the merits, but that is not a constitutional argument.

John Hart Ely, Democracy and Distrust 164–170 (1980).[14]

Imagine, if you will, explaining to a woman who is excluded from a "man's job" for which she is qualified, "Well you had a choice to vote down this legislation but you didn't choose to." Who didn't choose to? Suppose that *she* did what she could to vote it down, but other women embrace the stereotype it embodies. There is an uncomfortable similarity between lumping all women, or any class of people, together in this way and praising someone as "a credit to his race."

Laws of this sort, which treat people based on certain stereotypes, inflict a *dignitary* harm, an insult, a stigma. And this injury to the individual is not mitigated by the observation that most other women, or blacks, or whoever, accept the stereotype. If anything, this exacerbates the harm by making the victim feel even more powerless and frustrated.

Paul Brest, *The Substance of Process*, 42 Ohio St. L. J. 131 (1981).[15]

The legal mandate of equal treatment — which is both a systemic norm and a specific legal doctrine — becomes a matter of treating likes alike and unlikes unlike; and the sexes are defined as such by their mutual unlikeness. Put another way, gender is socially constructed as difference epistemologically; sex discrimination law bounds gender equality by difference doctrinally. A built-in tension exists between this concept of equality, which presupposes sameness, and this concept of sex, which presupposes difference. Sex equality thus becomes a contradiction in terms, something of an oxymoron, which may suggest why we are having such a difficult time getting it. . . .

There is an alternative approach, one that threads its way through existing law and expresses, I think, the reason equality law exists in the first place. It provides a second answer, a dissident answer in law and philosophy, to both the equality question and the gender question. In this approach, an equality question is a question of the distribution of power. Gender is also a question of power, specifically of male supremacy and female subordination. The question of equality, from the standpoint of what it is going to take to get it, is at root a question of hierarchy, which — as power succeeds in constructing social perception and social reality — derivatively becomes a categorical distinction, a difference. . . .

I call this the dominance approach. . . . To summarize the argument: seeing sex equality questions as matters of reasonable or unreasonable classification is part of the way male dominance is expressed in law. If you follow my shift in perspective from gender as difference to gender as dominance, gender changes from a distinction that is presumptively valid to a detriment that is presumptively suspect. The difference approach tries to map reality; the dominance approach tries to challenge and change it. In the dominance approach, sex discrimination stops being a question of morality and starts being a question of politics.

Catherine MacKinnon, Feminism Unmodified 40, 44 (1987).[16]

---

(2) In *J.E.B. v. Alabama*, 511 U.S. 127 (1994), the Court extended its 1986 decision in *Batson v. Kentucky*, 476 U.S. 79, which held that the Equal Protection Clause
governs the exercise of peremptory challenges by a prosecutor in a criminal trial. In
a paternity and child support trial, the state used nine of its ten peremptory challenges to remove male jurors. An all-female jury found petitioner to be the father of
the child in question and ordered him to pay child support. In reversing the Alabama court, the Supreme Court refused to limit the *Batson* rule to race and commented on the similarities between race and sex discrimination:

> Despite the heightened scrutiny afforded distinctions based on gender,
> respondent argues that gender discrimination in the selection of the petit
> jury should be permitted, though discrimination on the basis of race is not.
> Respondent suggests that "gender discrimination in this country . . . has
> never reached the level of discrimination" against African-Americans, and
> therefore gender discrimination, unlike racial discrimination, is tolerable
> in the courtroom.

> While the prejudicial attitudes toward women in this country have
> not been identical to those held toward racial minorities, the similarities
> between the experiences of racial minorities and women, in some contexts,
> "overpower those differences." Note, *Beyond Batson: Eliminating Gender-
> Based Peremptory Challenges*, 105 Harv. L. Rev. 1920, 1921 (1992). As a plu-
> rality of this Court observed in *Frontiero v. Richardson*, 411 U.S. 677, 685
> (1973):

>> "[T]hroughout much of the 19th century the position of women in our
>> society was, in many respects, comparable to that of blacks under the
>> pre-Civil War slave codes. Neither slaves nor women could hold office,
>> serve on juries, or bring suit in their own names, and married women
>> traditionally were denied the legal capacity to hold or convey property
>> or to serve as legal guardians of their own children. . . . And although
>> blacks were guaranteed the right to vote in 1870, women were denied
>> even that right — until adoption of the Nineteenth Amendment half a
>> century later." (Footnotes omitted.)

> Certainly, with respect to jury service, African-Americans and women
> share a history of total exclusion, a history which came to an end for women
> many years after the embarrassing chapter in our history came to an end
> for African-Americans.

> We need not determine, however, whether women or racial minorities
> have suffered more at the hands of discriminatory state actors during the
> decades of our Nation's history. It is necessary only to acknowledge that
> "our Nation has had a long and unfortunate history of sex discrimination,"
> a history which warrants the heightened scrutiny we afford all gender-based
> classifications today. Under our equal protection jurisprudence, gender-
> based classifications require "an exceedingly persuasive justification" in

order to survive constitutional scrutiny. *See Personnel Administrator of Mass. v. Feeney*, 442 U.S. 256, 273 (1979). *See also Mississippi University for Women v. Hogan*, 458 U.S. 718, 724 (1982); *Kirchberg v. Feenstra*, 450 U.S. 455, 461 (1981). Thus, the only question is whether discrimination on the basis of gender in jury selection substantially furthers the State's legitimate interest in achieving a fair and impartial trial. In making this assessment, we do not weigh the value of peremptory challenges as an institution against our asserted commitment to eradicate invidious discrimination from the courtroom. Instead, we consider whether peremptory challenges based on gender stereotypes provide substantial aid to a litigant's effort to secure a fair and impartial jury.

Far from proffering an exceptionally persuasive justification for its gender-based peremptory challenges, respondent maintains that its decision to strike virtually all the males from the jury in this case "may reasonably have been based upon the perception, supported by history, that men otherwise totally qualified to serve upon a jury might be more sympathetic and receptive to the arguments of a man alleged in a paternity action to be the father of an out-of-wedlock child, while women equally qualified to serve upon a jury might be more sympathetic and receptive to the arguments of the complaining witness who bore the child."

We shall not accept as a defense to gender-based peremptory challenges "the very stereotype the law condemns." *Powers v. Ohio*, 499 U.S. 400, 410 (1991)....

Discrimination in jury selection, whether based on race or on gender, causes harm to the litigants, the community, and the individual jurors who are wrongfully excluded from participation in the judicial process. The litigants are harmed by the risk that the prejudice which motivated the discriminatory selection of the jury will infect the entire proceedings. The community is harmed by the State's participation in the perpetuation of invidious group stereotypes and the inevitable loss of confidence in our judicial system that state-sanctioned discrimination in the courtroom engenders.

When state actors exercise peremptory challenges in reliance on gender stereotypes, they ratify and reinforce prejudicial views of the relative abilities of men and women. Because these stereotypes have wreaked injustice in so many other spheres of our country's public life, active discrimination by litigants on the basis of gender during jury selection "invites cynicism respecting the jury's neutrality and its obligation to adhere to the law." *Powers v. Ohio*, 499 U.S., at 412. The potential for cynicism is particularly acute in cases where gender-related issues are prominent, such as cases involving rape, sexual harassment, or paternity. Discriminatory use of peremptory challenges may create the impression that the judicial system has acquiesced in suppressing full participation by one gender or that the "deck has been stacked" in favor of one side....

IV

Our conclusion that litigants may not strike potential jurors solely on the basis of gender does not imply the elimination of all peremptory challenges. Neither does it conflict with a State's legitimate interest in using such challenges in its effort to secure a fair and impartial jury. Parties still may remove jurors whom they feel might be less acceptable than others on the panel; gender simply may not serve as a proxy for bias. Parties may also exercise their peremptory challenges to remove from the venire any group or class of individuals normally subject to "rational basis" review. *See Cleburne v. Cleburne Living Center, Inc.*, 473 U.S. 432, 439–442 (1985); *Clark v. Jeter*, 486 U.S. 456, 461 (1988). Even strikes based on characteristics that are disproportionately associated with one gender could be appropriate, absent a showing of pretext. . . . When an explanation is required, it need not rise to the level of a "for cause" challenge; rather, it merely must be based on a juror characteristic other than gender, and the proffered explanation may not be pretextual. . . .

CHIEF JUSTICE REHNQUIST, dissenting:

Batson is best understood as a recognition that race lies at the core of the commands of the Fourteenth Amendment. Not surprisingly, all of our post-*Batson* cases have dealt with the use of peremptory strikes to remove black or racially identified venirepersons, and all have described *Batson* as fashioning a rule aimed at preventing purposeful discrimination against a cognizable racial group. As Justice O'Connor once recognized, *Batson* does not apply "[o]utside the uniquely sensitive area of race." *Brown v. North Carolina*, 479 U.S. 940, 942 (1986) (opinion concurring in denial of certiorari).

Under the Equal Protection Clause, . . . the balance should tilt in favor of peremptory challenges when sex, not race, is the issue. Unlike the Court, I think the State has shown that jury strikes on the basis of gender "substantially further" the State's legitimate interest in achieving a fair and impartial trial through the venerable practice of peremptory challenges. The two sexes differ, both biologically and, to a diminishing extent, in experience. It is not merely "stereotyping" to say that these differences may produce a difference in outlook which is brought to the jury room. Accordingly, use of peremptory challenges on the basis of sex is generally not the sort of derogatory and invidious act which peremptory challenges directed at black jurors may be. . . .

The core of the Court's reasoning is that peremptory challenges on the basis of any group characteristic subject to heightened scrutiny are inconsistent with the guarantee of the Equal Protection Clause. That conclusion can be reached only be focusing unrealistically upon individual exercises of the peremptory challenge, and ignoring the totality of the practice. Since all groups are subject to the peremptory challenge (and will be made the object of it, depending upon the nature of the particular case) it is hard to see how any group is denied equal protection.

(3) How should the Court treat laws that discriminate against black women? Should they be viewed as gender based classifications, or racial classifications? Consider the following:

> Black women also have a strong argument that they are a "discrete and insular" minority, that they are the object of historical prejudice and stereotypes, and that this prejudice and insularity affect their ability to use the political processes to protect their interests. From the colonial period to the present, various state and private actors have singled them out for treatment different than that meted out to white women or black men. This has resulted in the creation of a group which is overrepresented among those living in poverty, and underrepresented among those who influence the political process. It is a group which carries the degraded statuses of both blacks and women, and finds its life chances thereby doubly limited. Any state action which burdens this group should be subject to at least strict scrutiny under the Equal Protection Clause.

Judith Scales-Trent, *Black Women and the Constitution: Finding Our Place, Asserting Our Rights*, 24 HARV. C.R.-C.L. L. REV. 9, 39 (1989).[17]

United States v. Virginia

United States Supreme Court
518 U.S. 515, 116 S. Ct. 2264, 135 L. Ed. 2d 735 (1996)

JUSTICE GINSBURG delivered the opinion of the Court.

Virginia's public institutions of higher learning include an incomparable military college, Virginia Military Institute (VMI). The United States maintains that the Constitution's equal protection guarantee precludes Virginia from reserving exclusively to men the unique educational opportunities VMI affords. We agree.

I

Founded in 1839, VMI is today the sole single-sex school among Virginia's 15 public institutions of higher learning. VMI's distinctive mission is to produce "citizen-soldiers," men prepared for leadership in civilian life and in military service. VMI pursues this mission through pervasive training of a kind not available anywhere else in Virginia. Assigning prime place to character development, VMI uses an "adversative method" modeled on English public schools and once characteristic of military instruction. VMI constantly endeavors to instill physical and mental discipline in its cadets and impart to them a strong moral code. The school's graduates

---

17. Copyright © 1989 by Harvard Civil Rights Civil Liberties Law Review. Reprinted by permission.

leave VMI with heightened comprehension of their capacity to deal with duress and stress, and a large sense of accomplishment for completing the hazardous course.

VMI has notably succeeded in its mission to produce leaders; among its alumni are military generals, Members of Congress, and business executives. The school's alumni overwhelmingly perceive that their VMI training helped them to realize their personal goals. VMI's endowment reflects the loyalty of its graduates; VMI has the largest per-student endowment of all undergraduate institutions in the Nation.

Neither the goal of producing citizen-soldiers nor VMI's implementing methodology is inherently unsuitable to women. And the school's impressive record in producing leaders has made admission desirable to some women. Nevertheless, Virginia has elected to preserve exclusively for men the advantages and opportunities a VMI education affords.

II

A

. . . VMI today enrolls about 1,300 men as cadets. Its academic offerings in the liberal arts, sciences, and engineering are also available at other public colleges and universities in Virginia. But VMI's mission is special. It is the mission of the school "'to produce educated and honorable men, prepared for the varied work of civil life, imbued with love of learning, confident in the functions and attitudes of leadership, possessing a high sense of public service, advocates of the American democracy and free enterprise system, and ready as citizen-soldiers to defend their country in time of national peril.'" In contrast to the federal service academies, institutions maintained "to prepare cadets for career service in the armed forces," VMI's program "is directed at preparation for both military and civilian life"; "[o]nly about 15% of VMI cadets enter career military service."

VMI produces its "citizen-soldiers" through "an adversative, or doubting, model of education" which features "[p]hysical rigor, mental stress, absolute equality of treatment, absence of privacy, minute regulation of behavior, and indoctrination in desirable values." As one Commandant of Cadets described it, the adversative method "dissects the young student," and makes him aware of his "limits and capabilities," so that he knows "how far he can go with his anger . . . how much he can take under stress . . . exactly what he can do when he is physically exhausted."

VMI cadets live in spartan barracks where surveillance is constant and privacy nonexistent; they wear uniforms, eat together in the mess hall, and regularly participate in drills. Entering students are incessantly exposed to the rat line, "an extreme form of the adversative model," comparable in intensity to Marine Corps boot camp. Tormenting and punishing, the rat line bonds new cadets to their fellow sufferers and, when they have completed the 7-month experience, to their former tormentors.

VMI's "adversative model" is further characterized by a hierarchical "class system" of privileges and responsibilities, a "dyke system" for assigning a senior class mentor to each entering class "rat," and a stringently enforced "honor code," which prescribes that a cadet "'does not lie, cheat, steal nor tolerate those who do.'"

VMI attracts some applicants because of its reputation as an extraordinarily challenging military school, and "because its alumni are exceptionally close to the school." "[W]omen have no opportunity anywhere to gain the benefits of [the system of education at VMI]."

B

In 1990, prompted by a complaint filed with the Attorney General by a female high-school student seeking admission to VMI, the United States sued the Commonwealth of Virginia and VMI, alleging that VMI's exclusively male admission policy violated the Equal Protection Clause of the Fourteenth Amendment. . . .

III

The cross-petitions in this case present two ultimate issues. First, does Virginia's exclusion of women from the educational opportunities provided by VMI—extraordinary opportunities for military training and civilian leadership development—deny to women "capable of all of the individual activities required of VMI cadets," the equal protection of the laws guaranteed by the Fourteenth Amendment? Second, if VMI's "unique" situation—as Virginia's sole single-sex public institution of higher education—offends the Constitution's equal protection principle, what is the remedial requirement?

IV

We note, once again, the core instruction of this Court's pathmarking decisions in *J.E.B. v. Alabama* [511 U.S. 127 (1994)], and *Mississippi Univ. for Women* [458 U.S. 718 (1982)]: Parties who seek to defend gender-based government action must demonstrate an "exceedingly persuasive justification" for that action. . . . The burden of justification is demanding and it rests entirely on the State. See *Mississippi Univ. for Women*. The State must show "at least that the [challenged] classification serves 'important governmental objectives and that the discriminatory means employed' are 'substantially related to the achievement of those objectives.'"

The heightened review standard our precedent establishes does not make sex a proscribed classification. Supposed "inherent differences" are no longer accepted as a ground for race or national origin classifications. See *Loving v. Virginia* [*supra*, at § 6.03]. Physical differences between men and women, however, are enduring: "[T]he two sexes are not fungible; a community made up exclusively of one [sex] is different from a community composed of both."

"Inherent differences" between men and women, we have come to appreciate, remain cause for celebration, but not for denigration of the members of either sex or for artificial constraints on an individual's opportunity. Sex classifications may be used to compensate women "for particular economic disabilities [they have] suffered," *Califano v. Webster* [430 U.S. 313 (1977)], to "promot[e] equal employment opportunity," see *California Federal Sav. & Loan Ass'n v. Guerra*, 479 U.S. 272, 289 (1987), to advance full development of the talent and capacities of our Nation's people. But such classifications may not be used, as they once were, see *Goesaert*, to create or perpetuate the legal, social, and economic inferiority of women.

Measuring the record in this case against the review standard just described, we conclude that Virginia has shown no "exceedingly persuasive justification" for excluding all women from the citizen-soldier training afforded by VMI. We therefore affirm the Fourth Circuit's initial judgment, which held that Virginia had violated the Fourteenth Amendment's Equal Protection Clause. Because the remedy proffered by Virginia — the Mary Baldwin VWIL program [Virginia Women's Institute for Leadership, a four-year, state-sponsored undergraduate program, located at the private Mary Baldwin College] does not cure the constitutional violation, *i.e.*, it does not provide equal opportunity, we reverse the Fourth Circuit's final judgment in this case.

V

The Fourth Circuit initially held that Virginia had advanced no state policy by which it could justify, under equal protection principles, its determination "to afford VMI's unique type of program to men and not to women." Virginia challenges that "liability" ruling and asserts two justifications in defense of VMI's exclusion of women. First, the Commonwealth contends, "single-sex education provides important educational benefits," and the option of single-sex education contributes to "diversity in educational approaches." Second, the Commonwealth argues, "the unique VMI method of character development and leadership training," the school's adversative approach, would have to be modified were VMI to admit women. We consider these two justifications in turn.

A

Single-sex education affords pedagogical benefits to at least some students, Virginia emphasizes, and that reality is uncontested in this litigation. Similarly, it is not disputed that diversity among public educational institutions can serve the public good. But Virginia has not shown that VMI was established, or has been maintained, with a view to diversifying, by its categorical exclusion of women, educational opportunities within the State. In cases of this genre, our precedent instructs that "benign" justifications proffered in defense of categorical exclusions will not be accepted automatically; a tenable justification must describe actual state purposes, not rationalizations for actions in fact differently grounded. . . .

Neither recent nor distant history bears out Virginia's alleged pursuit of diversity through single-sex educational options. In 1839, when the State established VMI, a range of educational opportunities for men and women was scarcely contemplated. Higher education at the time was considered dangerous for women; reflecting widely held views about women's proper place, the Nation's first universities and colleges — for example, Harvard in Massachusetts, William and Mary in Virginia — admitted only men. See E. Farello, A History of the Education of Women in the United States 163 (1970). VMI was not at all novel in this respect: In admitting no women, VMI followed the lead of the State's flagship school, the University of Virginia, founded in 1819. . . .

Virginia describes the current absence of public single-sex higher education for women as "an historical anomaly." But the historical record indicates action more deliberate than anomalous: First, protection of women against higher education; next, schools for women far from equal in resources and stature to schools for men; finally, conversion of the separate schools to coeducation. . . . A purpose genuinely to advance an array of educational options . . . is not served by VMI's historic and constant plan—a plan to "affor[d] a unique educational benefit only to males." However "liberally" this plan serves the State's sons, it makes no provision whatever for her daughters. That is not equal protection.

B

Virginia next argues that VMI's adversative method of training provides educational benefits that cannot be made available, unmodified, to women. Alterations to accommodate women would necessarily be "radical," so "drastic," Virginia asserts, as to transform, indeed "destroy," VMI's program. Neither sex would be favored by the transformation, Virginia maintains: Men would be deprived of the unique opportunity currently available to them; women would not gain that opportunity because their participation would "eliminat[e] the very aspects of [the] program that distinguish [VMI] from—other institutions of higher education in Virginia." . . .

The United States does not challenge any expert witness estimation on average capacities or preferences of men and women. Instead, the United States emphasizes that time and again since this Court's turning point decision in *Reed v. Reed*, [404 U.S. 71 (1971)], we have cautioned reviewing courts to take a "hard look" at generalizations or "tendencies" of the kind pressed by Virginia. . . . State actors controlling gates to opportunity, we have instructed, may not exclude qualified individuals based on "fixed notions concerning the roles and abilities of males and females." *Mississippi Univ. for Women; see J.E.B.*.

It may be assumed, for purposes of this decision, that most women would not choose VMI's adversative method. As Fourth Circuit Judge Motz observed, however, in her dissent from the Court of Appeals' denial of rehearing en banc, it is also probable that "many men would not want to be educated in such an environment." (On that point, even our dissenting colleague might agree.) Education, to be sure, is not a "one size fits all" business. The issue, however, is not whether "women—or men—should be forced to attend VMI"; rather, the question is whether the State can constitutionally deny to women who have the will and capacity, the training and attendant opportunities that VMI uniquely affords.

The notion that admission of women would downgrade VMI's stature, destroy the adversative system and, with it, even the school, is a judgment hardly proved, a prediction hardly different from other "self-fulfilling prophec[ies]," see *Mississippi Univ. for Women*, once routinely used to deny rights or opportunities. When women first sought admission to the bar and access to legal education, concerns of the same order were expressed. . . .

Women's successful entry into the federal military academies, and their participation in the Nation's military forces, indicate that Virginia's fears for the future of VMI may not be solidly grounded. The State's justification for excluding all women from "citizen-soldier" training for which some are qualified, in any event, cannot rank as "exceedingly persuasive," as we have explained and applied that standard. . . .

Virginia and VMI trained their argument on "means" rather than "end," and thus misperceived our precedent. Single-sex education at VMI serves an "important governmental objective," they maintained, and exclusion of women is not only "substantially related," it is essential to that objective. By this notably circular argument, the "straightforward" test *Mississippi Univ. for Women* described, was bent and bowed. . . .

VI

In the second phase of the litigation, Virginia presented its remedial plan—maintain VMI as a male-only college and create VWIL as a separate program for women. The plan met District Court approval. The Fourth Circuit, in turn, deferentially reviewed the State's proposal and decided that the two single-sex programs directly served Virginia's reasserted purposes: single-gender education, and "achieving the results of an adversative method in a military environment." Inspecting the VMI and VWIL educational programs to determine whether they "afford[ed] to both genders benefits comparable in substance, [if] not in form and detail," the Court of Appeals concluded that Virginia had arranged for men and women opportunities "sufficiently comparable" to survive equal protection evaluation. The United States challenges this "remedial" ruling as pervasively misguided.

A

A remedial decree, this Court has said, must closely fit the constitutional violation; it must be shaped to place persons unconstitutionally denied an opportunity or advantage in "the position they would have occupied in the absence of [discrimination]." See *Milliken v. Bradley*, 433 U.S. 267, 280 (1977). The constitutional violation in this case is the categorical exclusion of women from an extraordinary educational opportunity afforded men. A proper remedy for an unconstitutional exclusion, we have explained, aims to "eliminate [so far as possible] the discriminatory effects of the past" and to "bar like discrimination in the future." *Louisiana v. United States*, 380 U.S. 145, 154 (1965).

Virginia chose not to eliminate, but to leave untouched, VMI's exclusionary policy. For women only, however, Virginia proposed a separate program, different in kind from VMI and unequal in tangible and intangible facilities. . . .

VWIL affords women no opportunity to experience the rigorous military training for which VMI is famed. Instead, the VWIL program "deemphasize[s]" military education, and uses a "cooperative method" of education "which reinforces self-esteem."

VWIL students participate in ROTC and a "largely ceremonial" Virginia Corps of Cadets, but Virginia deliberately did not make VWIL a military institute. The

VWIL House is not a military-style residence and VWIL students need not live together throughout the 4-year program, eat meals together, or wear uniforms during the school day. VWIL students thus do not experience the "barracks" life "crucial to the VMI experience," the spartan living arrangements designed to foster an "egalitarian ethic." "[T]he most important aspects of the VMI educational experience occur in the barracks," . . . yet Virginia deemed that core experience nonessential, indeed inappropriate, for training its female citizen-soldiers.

VWIL students receive their "leadership training" in seminars, externships, and speaker series, episodes and encounters lacking the "[p]hysical rigor, mental stress, . . . minute regulation of behavior, and indoctrination in desirable values" made hallmarks of VMI's citizen-soldier training. Kept away from the pressures, hazards, and psychological bonding characteristic of VMI's adversative training, VWIL students will not know the "feeling of tremendous accomplishment" commonly experienced by VMI's successful cadets. . . .

As earlier stated . . . generalizations about "the way women are," estimates of what is appropriate for most women, no longer justify denying opportunity to women whose talent and capacity place them outside the average description. Notably, Virginia never asserted that VMI's method of education suits most men. It is also revealing that Virginia accounted for its failure to make the VWIL experience "the entirely militaristic experience of VMI" on the ground that VWIL "is planned for women who do not necessarily expect to pursue military careers." By that reasoning, VMI's "entirely militaristic" program would be inappropriate for men in general or as a group, for "[o]nly about 15% of VMI cadets enter career military service." . . .

B

. . . Virginia, in sum, while maintaining VMI for men only, has failed to provide any "comparable single-gender women's institution." Instead, the Commonwealth has created a VWIL program fairly appraised as a "pale shadow" of VMI in terms of the range of curricular choices and faculty stature, funding, prestige, alumni support and influence. . . .

C

. . . The Fourth Circuit plainly erred in exposing Virginia's VWIL plan to a deferential analysis, for "all gender-based classifications today" warrant "heightened scrutiny." See *J.E.B.* Valuable as VWIL may prove for students who seek the program offered, Virginia's remedy affords no cure at all for the opportunities and advantages withheld from women who want a VMI education and can make the grade. In sum, Virginia's remedy does not match the constitutional violation; the State has shown no "exceedingly persuasive justification" for withholding from women qualified for the experience premier training of the kind VMI affords. . . .

Justice Thomas took no part in the consideration or decision of this case.

Chief Justice Rehnquist, concurring in judgment. . . .

Two decades ago in *Craig v. Boren*, we announced that "[t]o withstand constitutional challenge . . . classifications by gender must serve important governmental objectives and must be substantially related to achievement of those objectives." . . . While the majority adheres to this test today, it also says that the State must demonstrate an "exceedingly persuasive justification" to support a gender-based classification. It is unfortunate that the Court thereby introduces an element of uncertainty respecting the appropriate test.

While terms like "important governmental objective" and "substantially related" are hardly models of precision, they have more content and specificity than does the phrase "exceedingly persuasive justification." That phrase is best confined, as it was first used, as an observation on the difficulty of meeting the applicable test, not as a formulation of the test itself. . . .

Our cases dealing with gender discrimination also require that the proffered purpose for the challenged law be the actual purpose. It is on this ground that the Court rejects the first of two justifications Virginia offers for VMI's single-sex admissions policy, namely, the goal of diversity among its public educational institutions. While I ultimately agree that the State has not carried the day with this justification, I disagree with the Court's method of analyzing the issue. . . .

Before this Court, Virginia has sought to justify VMI's single-sex admissions policy primarily on the basis that diversity in education is desirable, and that while most of the public institutions of higher learning in the State are coeducational, there should also be room for single-sex institutions. I agree with the Court that there is scant evidence in the record that this was the real reason that Virginia decided to maintain VMI as men only. But, unlike the majority, I would consider only evidence that postdates our decision in *Hogan*, and would draw no negative inferences from the State's actions before that time. I think that after *Hogan*, the State was entitled to reconsider its policy with respect to VMI, and to not have earlier justifications, or lack thereof, held against it. . . .

Even if diversity in educational opportunity were the State's actual objective, the State's position would still be problematic. The difficulty with its position is that the diversity benefitted only one sex; there was single-sex public education available for men at VMI, but no corresponding single-sex public education available for women. When *Hogan* placed Virginia on notice that VMI's admissions policy possibly was unconstitutional, VMI could have dealt with the problem by admitting women; but its governing body felt strongly that the admission of women would have seriously harmed the institution's educational approach. Was there something else the State could have done to avoid an equal protection violation? Since the State did nothing, we do not have to definitively answer that question.

I do not think, however, that the State's options were as limited as the majority may imply. The Court cites, without expressly approving it, a statement from the opinion of the dissenting judge in the Court of Appeals, to the effect that the State could have "simultaneously opened single-gender undergraduate institutions having substantially comparable curricular and extra-curricular programs, funding, physical plant, administration and support services, and faculty and library resources." If this statement is thought to exclude other possibilities, it is too stringent a requirement. . . . Had Virginia made a genuine effort to devote comparable public resources to a facility for women, and followed through on such a plan, it might well have avoided an equal protection violation. I do not believe the State was faced with the stark choice of either admitting women to VMI, on the one hand, or abandoning VMI and starting from scratch for both men and women, on the other. . . .

JUSTICE SCALIA, dissenting.

Today the Court shuts down an institution that has served the people of the Commonwealth of Virginia with pride and distinction for over a century and a half. To achieve that desired result, it rejects (contrary to our established practice) the factual findings of two courts below, sweeps aside the precedents of this Court, and ignores the history of our people. As to facts: it explicitly rejects the finding that there exist "gender-based developmental differences" supporting Virginia's restriction of the "adversative" method to only a men's institution, and the finding that the all-male composition of the Virginia Military Institute (VMI) is essential to that institution's character. As to precedent: it drastically revises our established standards for reviewing sex-based classifications. And as to history: it counts for nothing the long tradition, enduring down to the present, of men's military colleges supported by both States and the Federal Government.

Much of the Court's opinion is devoted to deprecating the closed-mindedness of our forebears with regard to women's education, and even with regard to the treatment of women in areas that have nothing to do with education. Closed-minded they were — as every age is, including our own, with regard to matters it cannot guess, because it simply does not consider them debatable. The virtue of a democratic system with a First Amendment is that it readily enables the people, over time, to be persuaded that what they took for granted is not so, and to change their laws accordingly. That system is destroyed if the smug assurances of each age are removed from the democratic process and written into the Constitution. So to counterbalance the Court's criticism of our ancestors, let me say a word in their praise: they left us free to change. The same cannot be said of this most illiberal Court, which has embarked on a course of inscribing one after another of the current preferences of the society (and in some cases only the counter-majoritarian preferences of the society's law-trained elite) into our Basic Law. Today it enshrines the notion that no substantial educational value is to be served by an all-men's military academy — so that the decision by the people of Virginia to maintain such an institution denies equal protection to women who cannot attend that institution but can attend others. Since it is entirely clear that the Constitution of the United States — the old one — takes no sides in this educational debate, I dissent. . . .

I have no problem with a system of abstract tests such as rational-basis, intermediate, and strict scrutiny (though I think we can do better than applying strict scrutiny and intermediate scrutiny whenever we feel like it). Such formulas are essential to evaluating whether the new restrictions that a changing society constantly imposes upon private conduct comport with that "equal protection" our society has always accorded in the past. But in my view the function of this Court is to preserve our society's values regarding (among other things) equal protection, not to revise them; to prevent backsliding from the degree of restriction the Constitution imposed upon democratic government, not to prescribe, on our own authority, progressively higher degrees. For that reason it is my view that, whatever abstract tests we may choose to devise, they cannot supersede — and indeed ought to be crafted so as to reflect — those constant and unbroken national traditions that embody the people's understanding of ambiguous constitutional texts. More specifically, it is my view that "when a practice not expressly prohibited by the text of the Bill of Rights bears the endorsement of a long tradition of open, widespread, and unchallenged use that dates back to the beginning of the Republic, we have no proper basis for striking it down." . . .

[T]he rationale of today's decision is sweeping: for sex-based classifications, a redefinition of intermediate scrutiny that makes it indistinguishable from strict scrutiny. Indeed, the Court indicates that if any program restricted to one sex is "uniqu[e]," it must be opened to members of the opposite sex "who have the will and capacity" to participate in it. I suggest that the single-sex program that will not be capable of being characterized as "unique" is not only unique but nonexistent.

In any event, regardless of whether the Court's rationale leaves some small amount of room for lawyers to argue, it ensures that single-sex public education is functionally dead. The costs of litigating the constitutionality of a single-sex education program, and the risks of ultimately losing that litigation, are simply too high to be embraced by public officials. . . . Should the courts happen to interpret that vacuous phrase as establishing a standard that is not utterly impossible of achievement, there is considerable risk that whether the standard has been met will not be determined on the basis of the record evidence — indeed, that will necessarily be the approach of any court that seeks to walk the path the Court has trod today. No state official in his right mind will buy such a high-cost, high-risk lawsuit by commencing a single-sex program. The enemies of single-sex education have won; by persuading only seven Justices (five would have been enough) that their view of the world is enshrined in the Constitution, they have effectively imposed that view on all 50 States. . . .

Notes and Questions

(1) What standard of review does the Court use? Did the Court refine the *Craig* standard?

(2) What justifications did the state offer for the men only policy at VMI? Why did these justifications fail to meet the constitutional standard?

(3) In *Mississippi University for Women v. Hogan*, 458 U.S. 718 (1982), the Court confronted the question of whether a state law that excludes men from a state-supported

nursing school violates the Equal Protection Clause. The state attempted to justify the law as compensation for past discrimination against women. The Court held, however, that the law was unconstitutional, finding that the state made no showing that women lacked opportunities to obtain training in the nursing field when the MUW opened its doors. The Court observed, "Rather than compensate for discriminatory barriers faced by women, MUW's policy of excluding males from admission to the School of Nursing tends to perpetuate the stereotyped view of nursing as an exclusively women's job."

(4) Do the *VMI* and *MUW* cases preclude a state from establishing a single-sex high school for girls?

(5) In *Tuan Anh Nguyen v. Immigration and Naturalization Service*, 533 U.S. 53 (2001), the Court considered the constitutionality of a federal statute, 8 U.S.C. § 1409, which governs the acquisition of U.S. citizenship by persons born to one U.S. citizen parent and one noncitizen parent when the child is born outside of the United States and the parents are unmarried. The statute imposes different obligations depending on whether the citizen parent is the mother or father. If the citizen parent is the father, the child must establish one of the following: (1) that the child was legitimated; (2) that the father acknowledged paternity in writing under oath; or (3) that paternity was established by court order. If the citizen parent is the mother, however, none of these affirmative steps are required. 8 U.S.C. § 1409 (a).

The closely divided Court found that the gender-based classification is constitutional because it serves two important governmental objectives and the discriminatory means are substantially related to the objectives. The Court stated:

> The first governmental interest to be served is the importance of assuring that a biological parent-child relationship exists. In the case of the mother, the relation is verifiable from the birth itself. The mother's status is documented in most instances by the birth certificate or hospital records and the witnesses who attest to her having given birth. In the case of the father, the uncontestable fact is that he need not be present at birth. If he is present, furthermore, that circumstance is not incontrovertible proof of fatherhood. Fathers and mothers are not similarly situated with regard to the proof of biological parenthood. The imposition of a different set of rules for making that legal determination with respect to fathers and mothers is neither surprising nor troublesome from a constitutional perspective. . . .
>
> The second important governmental interest furthered in a substantial manner by 8 U.S.C. § 1409 (a) (4) is the determination to ensure that the child and the citizen parent have some demonstrated opportunity or potential to develop not just a relationship that is recognized, as a formal matter, by the law, but one that consists of the real, everyday ties that provide a connection between child and citizen parent and, in turn, the United States. In the case of a citizen mother and a child born overseas, the opportunity or a meaningful relationship between citizen parent and child inheres in

the very event of birth, an event so often critical to our constitutional and statutory understandings of citizenship. The mother knows that the child is in being and is hers and has an initial point of contact with him. There is at least an opportunity for mother and child to develop a real, meaningful relationship.

The same opportunity does not result from the event of birth, as a matter of biological inevitability, in the case of the unwed father. Given the 9-month interval between conception and birth, it is not always certain that a father will know that a child was conceived, nor is it always clear that even the mother will be sure of the father's identity. . . .

Having concluded that facilitation of a relationship between parent and child is an important governmental interest, the question remains whether the means Congress chose to further its objective — the imposition of certain additional requirements upon an unwed father — substantially to that end. Under this test, the means Congress adopted must be sustained.

First, it should be unsurprising that Congress decided to require that an opportunity for a parent-child relationship occur during the formative years of the child's minority. . . .

Second, petitioners argue that § 1409(a)(4) is not effective. In particular, petitioners assert that, although a mother will know of her child's birth, "knowledge that one is a parent, no matter how it is acquired, does not guarantee a relationship with one's child." They thus maintain that the imposition of the additional requirements of § 1409(a)(4) only on the children of citizen fathers must reflect a stereotype that women are more likely than men to actually establish a relationship with their children.

This line of argument misconceives the nature of both the governmental interest at issue and the manner in which we examine statutes alleged to violate equal protection. As to the former, Congress would of course be entitled to advance the interest of ensuring an actual, meaningful relationship in every case before citizenship is conferred. Or Congress could excuse compliance with the formal requirements when an actual father-child relationship is proved. It did neither here, perhaps because of the subjectivity, intrusiveness, and difficulties of proof that might attend an inquiry into any particular bond or tie. Instead, Congress enacted an easily administered scheme to promote the different but still substantial interest of ensuring at least an opportunity for a parent-child relationship to develop. . . .

Justice O'Connor's dissenting opinion, joined by Justices Souter, Ginsburg, and Breyer, argued that the majority only paid lip-service to the heightened scrutiny standard and applied a far less rigorous evaluation to the statute:

The Court recites the governing substantive standard for heightened scrutiny of sex-based classifications, but departs from the guidance of our precedents concerning such classifications in several ways. In the first sentence of its equal protection analysis, the majority glosses over the crucial matter of the burden of justification. . . .

For example, the majority hypothesizes about the interests served by the statute and fails adequately to inquire into the actual purposes of § 1409(a)(4). The Court also does not always explain adequately the importance of the interests that it claims to be served by the provision. The majority also fails carefully to consider whether the sex-based classification is being used impermissibly "as a 'proxy for other, more germane basis of classification,'" and instead casually dismisses the relevance of available sex-neutral alternatives. And, contrary to the majority's conclusion, the fit between the means and ends of § 1409(a)(4) is far too attenuated for the provision to survive heightened scrutiny. In all, the majority opinion represents far less than the rigorous application of heightened scrutiny that our precedents require.

Romer v. Evans

United States Supreme Court
517 U.S. 620, 116 S. Ct. 1620, 134 L. Ed. 2d 855 (1996)

KENNEDY, J., delivered the opinion of the Court.

The enactment challenged in this case is an amendment to the Constitution of the State of Colorado, adopted in a 1992 statewide referendum. Amendment 2 prohibits all legislative, executive or judicial action at any level of state or local government designed to protect the named class, a class we shall refer to as homosexual persons or gays and lesbians. The amendment reads:

> "No Protected Status Based on Homosexual, Lesbian or Bisexual Orientation. Neither the State of Colorado, through any of its branches or departments, nor any of its agencies, political subdivisions, municipalities or school districts, shall enact, adopt or enforce any statute, regulation, ordinance or policy whereby homosexual, lesbian or bisexual orientation, conduct, practices or relationships shall constitute or otherwise be the basis of or entitle any person or class of persons to have or claim any minority status, quota preferences, protected status or claim of discrimination. This Section of the Constitution shall be in all respects self-executing."

Soon after Amendment 2 was adopted, this litigation to declare its invalidity and enjoin its enforcement was commenced. The State Supreme Court held that Amendment 2 was subject to strict scrutiny under the Fourteenth Amendment because it infringed the fundamental right of gays and lesbians to participate in the political process. We granted certiorari and now affirm the judgment.

The State's principal argument in defense of Amendment 2 is that it puts gays and lesbians in the same position as all other persons. So, the State says, the measure does no more than deny homosexuals special rights. This reading of the amendment's language is implausible. We rely not upon our own interpretation of the amendment but upon the authoritative construction of Colorado's Supreme Court. The state court, deeming it unnecessary to determine the full extent of the amendment's reach, found it invalid even on a modest reading of its implications. The critical discussion of the amendment is as follows: "The immediate objective of Amendment 2 is, at a minimum, to repeal existing statutes, regulations, ordinances, and policies of state and local entities that barred discrimination based on sexual orientation. The 'ultimate effect' of Amendment 2 is to prohibit any governmental entity from adopting similar, or more protective statutes, regulations, ordinances, or policies in the future unless the state constitution is first amended to permit such measures."

The Fourteenth Amendment's promise that no person shall be denied the equal protection of the laws must coexist with the practical necessity that most legislation classifies for one purpose or another, with resulting disadvantage to various groups or persons. We have attempted to reconcile the principle with the reality by stating that, if a law neither burdens a fundamental right nor targets a suspect class, we will uphold the legislative classification so long as it bears a rational relation to some legitimate end. Amendment 2 fails, indeed defies, even this conventional inquiry. First, the amendment has the peculiar property of imposing a broad and undifferentiated disability on a single named group, an exceptional and, as we shall explain, invalid form of legislation. Second, its sheer breadth is so discontinuous with the reasons offered for it that the amendment seems inexplicable by anything but animus toward the class it affects; it lacks a rational relationship to legitimate state interests.

Taking the first point, even in the ordinary equal protection case calling for the most deferential of standards, we insist on knowing the relation between the classification adopted and the object to be attained. The search for the link between classification and objective gives substance to the Equal Protection Clause; it provides guidance and discipline for the legislature, which is entitled to know what sorts of laws it can pass; and it marks the limits of our own authority. In the ordinary case, a law will be sustained if it can be said to advance a legitimate government interest, even if the law seems unwise or works to the disadvantage of a particular group, or if the rationale for it seems tenuous.

Amendment 2 confounds this normal process of judicial review. It is at once too narrow and too broad. It identifies persons by a single trait and then denies them protection across the board. The resulting disqualification of a class of persons from the right to seek specific protection from the law is unprecedented in our jurisprudence. It is not within our constitutional tradition to enact laws of this sort. Central both to the idea of the rule of law and to our own Constitution's guarantee of equal protection is the principle that government and each of its parts remain open on impartial terms to all who seek its assistance. Respect for this principle explains why laws singling out a certain class of citizens for disfavored legal status or general hardships are rare. A law declaring that in general it shall be more difficult for one group of citizens than for all others to seek aid from the government is itself a denial of equal protection of the laws in the most literal sense.

A second and related point is that laws of the kind now before us raise the inevitable inference that the disadvantage imposed is born of animosity toward the class of persons affected. "[I]f the constitutional conception of 'equal protection of the laws' means anything, it must at the very least mean that a bare . . . desire to harm a politically unpopular group cannot constitute a *legitimate* governmental interest." *Department of Agriculture v. Moreno,* 413 U.S. 528, 534 (1973). Even laws enacted for broad and ambitious purposes often can be explained by reference to legitimate public policies which justify the incidental disadvantages they impose on certain persons. Amendment 2, however, in making a general announcement that gays and lesbians shall not have any particular protections from the law, inflicts on them immediate, continuing, and real injuries that outrun and belie any legitimate justifications that may be claimed for it. We conclude that, in addition to the far-reaching deficiencies of Amendment 2 that we have noted, the principles it offends, in another sense, are conventional and venerable; a law must bear a rational relationship to a legitimate governmental purpose, *Kadrmas v. Dickinson Public Schools,* 487 U.S. 450, 462 (1988), and Amendment 2 does not.

The primary rationale the State offers for Amendment 2 is respect for other citizens' freedom of association, and in particular the liberties of landlords or employers who have personal or religious objections to homosexuality. Colorado also cites its interest in conserving resources to fight discrimination against other groups. The breadth of the amendment is so far removed from these particular justifications that we find it impossible to credit them. We cannot say that Amendment 2 is directed to any identifiable legitimate purpose or discrete objective. It is a status-based enactment divorced from any factual context from which we could discern a relationship to legitimate state interests; it is a classification of persons undertaken for its own sake, something the Equal Protection Clause does not permit. We must conclude that Amendment 2 classifies homosexuals not to further a proper legislative end but to make them unequal to everyone else. This Colorado cannot do. A State cannot so deem a class of persons a stranger to its laws. Amendment 2 violates the Equal Protection Clause, and the judgment of the Supreme Court of Colorado is affirmed.

JUSTICE SCALIA, with whom THE CHIEF JUSTICE and JUSTICE THOMAS join, dissenting.

The constitutional amendment before us here is not the manifestation of a "'bare . . . desire to harm'" homosexuals, but is rather a modest attempt by seemingly tolerant Coloradans to preserve traditional sexual mores against the efforts of a politically powerful minority to revise those mores through use of the laws. That objective, and the means chosen to achieve it, are not only unimpeachable under any constitutional doctrine hitherto pronounced (hence the opinion's heavy reliance upon principles of righteousness rather than judicial holdings); they have been specifically approved by the Congress of the United States and by this Court.

The central thesis of the Court's reasoning is that any group is denied equal protection when, to obtain advantage (or, presumably, to avoid disadvantage), it must have recourse to a more general and hence more difficult level of political decision-making than others. The world has never heard of such a principle, which is why the Court's opinion is so long on emotive utterance and so short on relevant legal citation. And it seems to me most unlikely that any multilevel democracy can function under such a principle. For *whenever* a disadvantage is imposed, or conferral of a benefit is prohibited, at one of the higher levels of democratic decisionmaking (*i.e.,* by the state legislature rather than local government, or by the people at large in the state constitution rather than the legislature), the affected group has (under this theory) been denied equal protection.

No principle set forth in the Constitution, nor even any imagined by this Court in the past 200 years, prohibits what Colorado has done here. But the case for Colorado is much stronger than that. What it has done is not only unprohibited, but eminently reasonable, with close, congressionally approved precedent in earlier constitutional practice.

First, as to its eminent reasonableness. The Court's opinion contains grim, disapproving hints that Coloradans have been guilty of "animus" or "animosity" toward homosexuality, as though that has been established as un-American. Of course it is our moral heritage that one should not hate any human being or class of human beings. But I had thought that one could consider certain conduct reprehensible-murder, for example, or polygamy, or cruelty to animals-and could exhibit even "animus" toward such conduct. Surely that is the only sort of "animus" at issue here: moral disapproval of homosexual conduct. . . .

Today's opinion has no foundation in American constitutional law, and barely pretends to. The people of Colorado have adopted an entirely reasonable provision which does not even disfavor homosexuals in any substantive sense, but merely denies them preferential treatment. Amendment 2 is designed to prevent piecemeal deterioration of the sexual morality favored by a majority of Coloradans, and is not only an appropriate means to that legitimate end, but a means that Americans have employed before. Striking it down is an act, not of judicial judgment, but of political will. I dissent.

Notes and Questions

(1) What standard of review did the Court use in *Romer*?

(2) What standard of review should the Court apply in considering the constitutionality of laws that discriminate against individuals for being homosexual or transgender? Do such laws create a suspect or quasi-suspect classification?

(3) In *Bostock v. Clayton County*, 140 S. Ct. 1731 (2020), the Court held that discrimination against an individual for being homosexual or transgender is sex based under Title VII of the Civil Rights Act of 1964, which prohibits discrimination in employment based on sex. Should the same conclusion apply to equal protection claims?

(4) For further discussion, see *Obergefell v. Hodges*, 576 U.S. 644 (2015) (Chapter 7.03, *infra*), relying on the Due Process Clause to strike down a law prohibiting same sex marriages).

B. Discriminatory Intent or Impact?

Personnel Administrator of Massachusetts v. Feeney

United States Supreme Court
442 U.S. 256, 99 S. Ct. 2282, 60 L. Ed. 2d 870 (1979)

Mr. Justice Stewart delivered the opinion of the Court.

This case presents a challenge to the constitutionality of the Massachusetts veterans' preference statute, Mass. Gen. Laws Ann., ch. 31, § 23, on the ground that it discriminates against women in violation of the Equal Protection Clause of the Fourteenth Amendment. Under ch. 31, § 23, all veterans who qualify for state civil service positions must be considered for appointment ahead of any qualifying nonveterans. The preference operates overwhelmingly to the advantage of males. . . .

The Federal Government and virtually all of the States grant some sort of hiring preference to veterans. The Massachusetts preference, which is loosely termed an "absolute lifetime" preference, is among the most generous. It applies to all positions in the State's classified civil service, which constitute approximately 60% of the public jobs in the State. . . .

The veterans' hiring preference in Massachusetts, as in other jurisdictions, has traditionally been justified as a measure designed to reward veterans for the sacrifice of military service, to ease the transition from military to civilian life, to encourage patriotic service, and to attract loyal and well-disciplined people to civil service occupations. . . .

[T]he statute today benefits an overwhelmingly male class. This is attributable in some measure to the variety of federal statutes, regulations, and policies that have restricted the number of women who could enlist in the United States Armed Forces, and largely to the simple fact that women have never been subjected to a military draft. When this litigation was commenced, then, over 98% of the veterans in Massachusetts were male; only 1.8% were female. And over one-quarter of the Massachusetts population were veterans. . . .

Classifications based upon gender, not unlike those based upon race, have traditionally been the touchstone for pervasive and often subtle discrimination. This Court's recent cases teach that such classifications must bear a close and substantial relationship to important governmental objectives, *Craig v. Boren*, and are in many settings unconstitutional. Although public employment is not a constitutional right, *Massachusetts Bd. of Retirement v. Murgia*, and the States have wide discretion in framing employee qualifications, these precedents dictate that any state law overtly or covertly designed to prefer males over females in public employment would require an exceedingly persuasive justification to withstand a constitutional challenge under the Equal Protection Clause of the Fourteenth Amendment.

The cases of *Washington v. Davis*, and *Arlington Heights v. Metropolitan Housing Dev. Corp.*, 429 U.S. 252 (1977), recognize that when a neutral law has a disparate impact upon a group that has historically been the victim of discrimination, an unconstitutional purpose may still be at work. But those cases signaled no departure from the settled rule that the Fourteenth Amendment guarantees equal laws, not equal results. *Davis* upheld a job-related employment test that white people passed in proportionately greater numbers than Negroes, for there had been no showing that racial discrimination entered into the establishment or formulation of the test. *Arlington Heights* upheld a zoning board decision that tended to perpetuate racially segregated housing patterns, since, apart from its effect, the board's decision was shown to be nothing more than an application of a constitutionally neutral zoning policy. Those principles apply with equal force to a case involving alleged gender discrimination.

When a statute gender-neutral on its face is challenged on the ground that its effects upon women are disproportionably adverse, a twofold inquiry is thus appropriate. The first question is whether the statutory classification is indeed neutral in the sense that it is not gender-based. If the classification itself, covert or overt, is not based upon gender, the second question is whether the adverse effect reflects invidious gender-based discrimination. In this second inquiry, impact provides an "important starting point," but purposeful discrimination is "the condition that offends the Constitution." *Arlington Heights*.

It is against this background of precedent that we consider the merits of the case before us. The question whether ch. 31, §23, establishes a classification that is overtly or covertly based upon gender must first be considered. The appellee has conceded that ch. 31, §23, is neutral on its face. She has also acknowledged that state hiring preferences for veterans are not *per se* invalid, for she has limited her challenge to the absolute lifetime preference that Massachusetts provides to veterans. The District Court made two central findings that are relevant here: first, that ch. 31, §23, serves legitimate and worthy purposes; second, that the absolute preference was not established for the purpose of discriminating against women. The appellee has thus acknowledged and the District Court has thus found that the distinction between veterans and nonveterans drawn by ch. 31, §23, is not a pretext for gender discrimination. The appellee's concession and the District Court's finding are clearly correct.

If the impact of this statute could not be plausibly explained on a neutral ground, impact itself would signal that the real classification made by the law was in fact not neutral. See *Washington v. Davis*; *Arlington Heights*. But there can be but one answer to the question whether this veteran preference excludes significant numbers of women from preferred state jobs because they are women or because they are nonveterans. Apart from the facts that the definition of "veterans" in the statute has always been neutral as to gender and that Massachusetts has consistently defined veteran status in a way that has been inclusive of women who have served in the military, this is not a law that can plausibly be explained only as a gender-based classification. Indeed, it is not a law that can rationally be explained on that ground. . . . Too many men are affected by ch. 31, § 23, to permit the inference that the statute is but a pretext for preferring men over women. . . .

The dispositive question, then, is whether the appellee has shown that a gender-based discriminatory purpose has, at least in some measure, shaped the Massachusetts veterans' preference legislation. As did the District Court, she points to two basic factors which in her view distinguish ch. 31, § 23, from the neutral rules at issue in the *Washington v. Davis* and *Arlington Heights* cases. The first is the nature of the preference, which is said to be demonstrably gender-biased in the sense that it favors a status reserved under federal military policy primarily to men. The second concerns the impact of the absolute lifetime preference upon the employment opportunities of women, an impact claimed to be too inevitable to have been unintended. The appellee contends that these factors, coupled with the fact that the preference itself has little if any relevance to actual job performance, more than suffice to prove the discriminatory intent required to establish a constitutional violation.

The contention that this veterans' preference is "inherently nonneutral" or "gender-biased" presumes that the State, by favoring veterans, intentionally incorporated into its public employment policies the panoply of sex-based and assertedly discriminatory federal laws that have prevented all but a handful of women from becoming veterans. There are two serious difficulties with this argument. First, it is wholly at odds with the District Court's central finding that Massachusetts has not offered a preference to veterans for the purpose of discriminating against women. Second, it cannot be reconciled with the assumption made by both the appellee and the District Court that a more limiting hiring preference for veterans could be sustained. Taken together, these difficulties are fatal.

To the extent that the status of veteran is one that few women have been enabled to achieve, every hiring preference for veterans, however, modest or extreme, is inherently gender-biased. If Massachusetts by offering such a preference can be said intentionally to have incorporated into its state employment policies the historical gender-based federal military personnel practices, the degree of the preference would or should make no constitutional difference. Invidious discrimination does not become less so because the discrimination accomplished is of a lesser magnitude. Discriminatory intent is simply not amenable to calibration. It either is a factor that has influenced the legislative choice or it is not. The District Court's conclusion that the absolute veterans' preference was not originally enacted or subsequently reaffirmed for the purpose of giving an advantage to males as such necessarily compels the conclusion that the State intended nothing more than to prefer "veterans." Given this finding, simple logic suggests that an intent to exclude women from significant public jobs was not at work in this law. To reason that it was, by describing the reference as "inherently nonneutral" or "gender-biased," is merely to restate the fact of impact, not to answer the question of intent.

To be sure, this case is unusual in that it involves a law that by design is not neutral. The law overtly prefers veterans as such. As opposed to the written test at issue in *Davis*, it does not purport to define a job-related characteristic. To the contrary, it confers upon a specifically described group — perceived to be particularly deserving — a competitive headstart. But the District Court found, and the appellee has not disputed, that this legislative choice was legitimate. The basic distinction between veterans and nonveterans, having been found not gender-based, and the goals of the preference having been found worthy, ch. 31 must be analyzed as is any other neutral law that casts a greater burden upon women as a group than upon men as a group. The enlistment policies of the Armed Services may well have discrimination on the basis of sex. See *Frontiero v. Richardson*. But the history of discrimination against women in the military is not on trial in this case.

The appellee's ultimate argument rests upon the presumption, common to the criminal and civil law, that a person intends the natural and foreseeable consequences of his voluntary actions. . . . The decision to grant a preference to veterans was of course "intentional." So, necessarily, did an adverse impact upon nonveterans follow from that decision. And it cannot seriously be argued that the Legislature of Massachusetts could have been unaware that most veterans are men. It would thus be disingenuous to say that the adverse consequences of this legislation for women were unintended, in the sense that they were not volitional or in the sense that they were not foreseeable.

"Discriminatory purpose," however, implies more than intent as volition or intent as awareness of consequences.[18] It implies that the decision maker, in this case a state legislature, selected or reaffirmed a particular course of action at least in part "because of," not merely "in spite of," its adverse effects upon an identifiable group.[19] Yet, nothing in the record demonstrates that this preference for veterans was originally devised or subsequently re-enacted because it would accomplish the collateral goal of keeping women in a stereotypic and predefined place in the Massachusetts Civil Service.

---

18. [Court's Footnote 24] Proof of discriminatory intent must necessarily usually rely on objective factors, several of which were outlined in *Arlington Heights*, 429 U.S. 252, 266. The inquiry is practical. What a legislature or any official entity is "up to" may be plain from the results its actions achieve, or the results they avoid. Often it is made clear from what has been called, in a different context, "the give and take of the situation."

19. [Court's Footnote 25] This is not to say that the inevitability or foreseeability of consequences of a neutral rule has no bearing upon the existence of discriminatory intent. Certainly, when the adverse consequences of a law upon an identifiable group are as inevitable as the gender-based consequences of ch. 31, § 23, a strong inference that the adverse effects were desired can reasonably be drawn. But in this inquiry — made as it is under the Constitution — an inference is a working tool, not a synonym for proof. When, as here, the impact is essentially an unavoidable consequence of a legislative policy that has in itself always been deemed to be legitimate, and when, as here, the statutory history and all of the available evidence affirmatively demonstrate the opposite, the inference simply fails to ripen into proof.

To the contrary, the statutory history shows that the benefit of the preference was consistently offered to "any person" who was a veteran. That benefit has been extended to women under a very broad statutory definition of the term veteran. When the totality of legislative actions establishing and extending the Massachusetts veterans' preference are considered, the law remains what it purports to be: a preference for veterans of either sex over nonveterans of either sex, not for men over women. . . .

MR. JUSTICE STEVENS, with whom MR. JUSTICE WHITE joins, concurring.

While I concur in the Court's opinion, I confess that I am not at all sure that there is any difference between the two questions posed. If a classification is not overtly based on gender, I am inclined to believe the question whether it is covertly gender based is the same as the question whether its adverse effects reflect invidious gender-based discrimination. However the question is phrased, for me the answer is largely provided by the fact that the number of males disadvantaged by Massachusetts' veterans' preference (1,867,000) is sufficiently large — and sufficiently close to the number of disadvantaged females (2,954,000) — to refute the claim that the rule was intended to benefit males as a class over females as a class.

MR. JUSTICE MARSHALL, with whom MR. JUSTICE BRENNAN joins, dissenting.

Although acknowledging that in some circumstances, discriminatory intent may be inferred from the inevitable or foreseeable impact of a statute, the Court concludes that no such intent has been established here. I cannot agree. In my judgment, Massachusetts' choice of an absolute veterans' preference system evinces purposeful gender-based discrimination. And because the statutory scheme bears no substantial relationship to a legitimate governmental objective, it cannot withstand scrutiny under the Equal Protection Clause.

The District Court found that the "prime objective" of the Massachusetts veterans' preference statute was to benefit individuals with prior military service. . . . That a legislature seeks to advantage one group does not, as a matter of logic or of common sense, exclude the possibility that it also intends to disadvantage another. Individuals in general and lawmakers in particular frequently act for a variety of reasons. . . . The critical constitutional inquiry is not whether an illicit consideration was the primary or but-for cause of a decision, but rather whether it had an appreciable role in shaping a given legislative enactment. Where there is "proof that a discriminatory purpose has been a motivating factor in the decision, . . . judicial deference is no longer justified." *Arlington Heights.*

Moreover, since reliable evidence of subjective intentions is seldom obtainable, resort to inference based on objective factors is generally unavoidable. To discern the purposes underlying facially neutral policies, this Court has therefore considered the degree, inevitability, and foreseeability of any disproportionate impact as well as the alternatives reasonably available.

In the instant case, the impact of the Massachusetts statute on women is undisputed. . . . Because less than 2% of the women in Massachusetts are veterans, the absolute-preference formula has rendered desirable state civil service employment an almost exclusively male prerogative. As the District Court recognized, this consequence follows foreseeably, indeed inexorably, from the long history of policies severely limiting women's participation in the military. Although neutral in form, the statute is anything but neutral in application. . . . Where the foreseeable impact of a facially neutral policy is so disproportionate, the burden should rest on the State to establish that sex-based considerations played no part in the choice of the particular legislative scheme.

Clearly, that burden was not sustained here. The legislative history of the statute reflects the Commonwealth's patent appreciation of the impact the preference system would have on women, and an equally evident desire to mitigate that impact only with respect to certain traditionally female occupations. Until 1971, the statute and implementing civil service regulations exempted from operation of the preference any job requisitions "especially calling for women." In practice, this exemption, coupled with the absolute preference for veterans, has created a gender-based civil service hierarchy, with women occupying low-grade clerical and secretarial jobs and men holding more responsible and remunerative positions.

Thus, for over 70 years, the Commonwealth has maintained, as an integral part of its veterans' preference system, an exemption relegating female civil service applicants to occupations traditionally filled by women. Such a statutory scheme both reflects and perpetuates precisely the kind of archaic assumptions about women's roles which we have previously held invalid. Particularly when viewed against the range of less discriminatory alternatives available to assist veterans, Massachusetts' choice of a formula that so severely restricts public employment opportunities for women cannot reasonably be thought gender-neutral. . . .

To survive challenge under the Equal Protection Clause, statutes reflecting gender-based discrimination must be substantially related to the achievement of important governmental objectives. Appellants here advance three interests in support of the absolute-preference system: (1) assisting veterans in their readjustment to civilian life; (2) encouraging military enlistment; and (3) rewarding those who have served their country. . . .

With respect to the first interest, facilitating veterans' transition to civilian status, the statute is plainly overinclusive. By conferring a permanent preference, the legislation allows veterans to invoke their advantage repeatedly, without regard to their date of discharge. . . .

Nor is the Commonwealth's second asserted interest, encouraging military service, a plausible justification for this legislative scheme. In its original and subsequent re-enactments, the statute extended benefits retroactively to veterans who had served during a prior specified period. . . . Moreover, even if such influence could be presumed, the statute is still grossly overinclusive in that it bestows benefits on men drafted as well as those who volunteered.

Finally, the Commonwealth's third interest, rewarding veterans, does not "adequately justify the salient features" of this preference system. Where a particular statutory scheme visits substantial hardship on a class long subject to discrimination, the legislation cannot be sustained unless "carefully tuned to alternative considerations." Here, there are a wide variety of less discriminatory means by which Massachusetts could effect its compensatory purposes. For example, a point preference system, such as that maintained by many States and the Federal Government, or an absolute preference for a limited duration, would reward veterans without excluding all qualified women from upper level civil service positions. Apart from public employment, the Commonwealth, can, and does, afford assistance to veterans in various ways, including tax abatements, educational subsidies, and special programs for needy veterans. Unlike these and similar benefits, the costs of which are distributed across the taxpaying public generally, the Massachusetts statute exacts a substantial price from a discrete group of individuals who have long been subject to employment discrimination, and who, "because of circumstances totally beyond their control, have [had] little if any chance of becoming members of the preferred class."

Notes and Questions

(1) According to the *Feeney* majority, foreseeability of adverse gender effects may provide "a working tool, [but it is] not a synonym for proof." Why not allow purpose to be inferred from knowledge of the consequences?

(2) Does the fact that a law was enacted "in spite of" its adverse effects on women provide evidence that it was based in part on impermissible considerations?

(3) What problems, if any, would result from closer judicial scrutiny of laws that have an adverse impact on women?

§ 6.05 Conclusion

In this Chapter we have examined equal protection challenges to laws that exclude on the basis of social and economic considerations, race, and gender. Can you identify the criteria that the Court will use to determine whether it will closely scrutinize some laws or instead defer to the legislative judgment? Are there sound explanations for deference in some instances and not in others? What are the core values protected by the Equal Protection Clause? How far have we come in defining "We the People?" By way of conclusion, consider the following case and the subsequent Problem, which deal with two other forms of exclusion.

City of Cleburne v. Cleburne Living Center

United States Supreme Court
473 U.S. 432, 105 S. Ct. 3249, 87 L. Ed. 2d 313 (1985)

Justice White delivered the opinion of the Court. . . .

In July, 1980, respondent Jan Hannah purchased a building at 201 Featherston Street in the city of Cleburne, Texas, with the intention of leasing it to Cleburne Living Centers, Inc. (CLC), for the operation of a group home for the mentally retarded. It was anticipated that the home would house 13 retarded men and women, who would be under the constant supervision of CLC staff members. . . .

The city informed CLC that a special use permit would be required for the operation of a group home at the site, and CLC accordingly submitted a permit application. In response to a subsequent inquiry from CLC, the city explained that under the zoning regulations applicable to the site, a special use permit, renewable annually, was required for the construction of "[h]ospitals for the insane or feeble-minded, or alcoholic [sic] or drug addicts, or penal or correctional institutions." The city had determined that the proposed group home should be classified as a "hospital for the feeble-minded." After holding a public hearing on CLC's application, the city council voted three to one to deny a special use permit.

CLC then filed suit in Federal District Court against the city and a number of its officials, alleging that the zoning ordinance was invalid on its face and as applied because it discriminated against the mentally retarded in violation of the equal protection rights of CLC and its potential residents. . . . [T]he District Court held the ordinance and its application constitutional. Concluding that no fundamental right was implicated and that mental retardation was neither a suspect nor a quasi-suspect classification, the court employed the minimum level of judicial scrutiny applicable to equal protection claims. The court deemed the ordinance, as written and applied, to be rationally related to the City's legitimate interests in "the legal responsibility of CLC and its residents, . . . the safety and fears of residents in the adjoining neighborhood," and the number of people to be housed in the home.

The Court of Appeals for the Fifth Circuit reversed, determining that mental retardation was a quasi-suspect classification and that it should assess the validity of the ordinance under intermediate-level scrutiny. Because mental retardation was in fact relevant to many legislative actions, strict scrutiny was not appropriate. But in light of the history of "unfair and often grotesque mistreatment" of the retarded, discrimination against them was "likely to reflect deep-seated prejudice." In addition, the mentally retarded lacked political power, and their condition was immutable. The court considered heightened scrutiny to be particularly appropriate in this case, because the City's ordinance withheld a benefit which, although not fundamental, was very important to the mentally retarded. Without group homes, the court stated, the retarded could never hope to integrate themselves into the community. Applying the test that it considered appropriate, the court held that the ordinance was invalid on its face because it did not substantially further any important governmental interests.

III

... [W]e conclude for several reasons that the Court of Appeals erred in holding mental retardation a quasi-suspect classification calling for a more exacting standard of judicial review than is normally accorded economic and social legislation. First, it is undeniable, and it is not argued otherwise here, that those who are mentally retarded have a reduced ability to cope with and function in the everyday world. Nor are they all cut from the same pattern: as the testimony in this record indicates, they range from those whose disability is not immediately evident to those who must be constantly cared for. They are thus different, immutably so, in relevant respects, and the states' interest in dealing with and providing for them is plainly a legitimate one.[20] How this large and diversified group is to be treated under the law is a difficult and often a technical matter, very much a task for legislators guided by qualified professionals and not by the perhaps ill-informed opinions of the judiciary. Heightened scrutiny inevitably involves substantive judgments about legislative decisions, and we doubt that the predicate for such judicial oversight is present where the classification deals with mental retardation.

Second, the distinctive legislative response, both national and state, to the plight of those who are mentally retarded demonstrates not only that they have unique problems, but also that the lawmakers have been addressing their difficulties in a manner that belies a continuing antipathy or prejudice and a corresponding need for more intrusive oversight by the judiciary. Thus, the federal government has not only outlawed discrimination against the mentally retarded in federally funded programs, see § 504 of the Rehabilitation Act of 1972, 29 U.S.C. § 794, but it has also provided the retarded with the right to receive "appropriate treatment, services, and habilitation" in a setting that is "least restrictive of [their] personal liberty." Developmental Disabilities Assistance and Bill of Rights Act, 42 U.S.C. §§ 6010(1), (2). In addition, the government has conditioned federal education funds on a State's assurance that retarded children will enjoy an education that, "to the maximum extent appropriate," is integrated with that of non-mentally retarded children. Education of the Handicapped Act, 20 U.S.C. § 1412(5)(B). The government has also facilitated the hiring of the mentally retarded into the federal civil service by exempting them from the requirement of competitive examination. See 5 CFR § 213.3102(5) (1984).

---

20. [Court's Footnote 10] As Dean Ely has observed:

"Surely one has to feel sorry for a person disabled by something he or she can't do anything about, but I'm not aware of any reason to suppose that elected officials are unusually unlikely to share that feeling. Moreover, classifications based on physical disability and intelligence are typically accepted as legitimate, even by judges and commentators who assert that *those* characteristics (unlike the one the commentator is trying to render suspect) are often relevant to legitimate purposes. At that point there's not much left on the immutability theory, is there?"

J. ELY, DEMOCRACY AND DISTRUST 150 (1980) (footnote omitted). See also *id.*, at 154–155.

The State of Texas has similarly enacted legislation that acknowledges the special status of the mentally retarded by conferring certain rights upon them, such as "the right to live in the least restrictive setting appropriate to [their] individual needs and abilities," including "the right to live . . . in a group home." Mentally Retarded Persons Act of 1977, Tex. Rev. Civ. Stat. Ann., Art. 5547-300, § 7.

Such legislation thus singling out the retarded for special treatment reflects the real and undeniable differences between the retarded and others. That a civilized and decent society expects and approves such legislation indicates that governmental consideration of those differences in the vast majority of situations is not only legitimate but desirable. It may be, as CLC contends, that legislation designed to benefit, rather than disadvantage, the retarded would generally withstand examination under a test of heightened scrutiny. The relevant inquiry, however, is whether heightened scrutiny is constitutionally mandated in the first instance. Even assuming that many of these laws could be shown to be substantially related to an important governmental purpose, merely requiring the legislature to justify its efforts in these terms may lead it to refrain from acting at all. Much recent legislation intended to benefit the retarded also assumes the need for measures that might be perceived to disadvantage them. The Education of the Handicapped Act, for example, requires an "appropriate" education, not one that is equal in all respects to the education of non-retarded children; clearly, admission to a class that exceeded the abilities of a retarded child would not be appropriate. Similarly, the Developmental Disabilities Assistance Act and the Texas act give the retarded the right to live only in the "least restrictive setting" appropriate to their abilities, implicitly assuming the need for at least some restrictions that would not be imposed on others. Especially given the wide variation in the abilities and needs of the retarded themselves, governmental bodies must have a certain amount of flexibility and freedom from judicial oversight in shaping and limiting their remedial efforts.

Third, the legislative response, which could hardly have occurred and survived without public support, negates any claim that the mentally retarded are politically powerless in the sense that they have no ability to attract the attention of the lawmakers. Any minority can be said to be powerless to assert direct control over the legislature, but if that were a criterion for higher level scrutiny by the courts, much economic and social legislation would now be suspect.

Fourth, if the large and amorphous class of the mentally retarded were deemed quasi-suspect for the reasons given by the Court of Appeals, it would be difficult to find a principled way to distinguish a variety of other groups who have perhaps immutable disabilities setting them off from others, who cannot themselves mandate the desired legislative responses, and who can claim some degree of prejudice from at least part of the public at large. One need mention in this respect only the aging, the disabled, the mentally ill, and the infirm. We are reluctant to set out on that course, and we decline to do so. Doubtless, there have been and there will continue to be instances of discrimination against the retarded that are in fact invidious, and that are properly subject to judicial correction under constitutional norms.

But the appropriate method of reaching such instances is not to create a new quasi-suspect classification and subject all governmental action based on that classification to more searching evaluation. Rather, we should look to the likelihood that governmental action premised on a particular classification is valid as a general matter, not merely to the specifics of the case before us. Because mental retardation is a characteristic that the government may legitimately take into account in a wide range of decisions, and because both state and federal governments have recently committed themselves to assisting the retarded, we will not presume that any given legislative action, even one that disadvantages retarded individuals, is rooted in considerations that the Constitution will not tolerate.

Our refusal to recognize the retarded as a quasi-suspect class does not leave them entirely unprotected from invidious discrimination. To withstand equal protection review, legislation that distinguishes between the mentally retarded and others must be rationally related to a legitimate governmental purpose. This standard, we believe, affords government the latitude necessary both to pursue policies designed to assist the retarded in realizing their full potential, and to freely and efficiently engage in activities that burden the retarded in what is essentially an incidental manner. The State may not rely on a classification whose relationship to an asserted goal is so attenuated as to render the distinction arbitrary or irrational. Furthermore, some objectives — such as "a bare . . . desire to harm a politically unpopular group," are not legitimate state interests. Beyond that, the mentally retarded, like others, have and retain their substantive constitutional rights in addition to the right to be treated equally by the law.

IV

We turn to the issue of the validity of the zoning ordinance insofar as it requires a special use permit for homes for the mentally retarded. . . .

The constitutional issue is clearly posed. The City does not require a special use permit in an R-3 zone for apartment houses, multiple dwellings, boarding and lodging houses, fraternity or sorority houses, dormitories, apartment hotels, hospitals, sanitariums, nursing homes for convalescents or the aged (other than for the insane or feeble-minded or alcoholics or drug addicts), private clubs or fraternal orders, and other specified uses. It does, however, insist on a special permit for the Featherston home, and it does so, as the District Court found, because it would be a facility for the mentally retarded. May the city require the permit for this facility when other care and multiple dwelling facilities are freely permitted?

It is true, as already pointed out, that the mentally retarded as a group are indeed different from others not sharing their misfortune, and in this respect they may be different from those who would occupy other facilities that would be permitted in an R-3 zone without a special permit. But this difference is largely irrelevant unless the Featherston home and those who would occupy it would threaten legitimate interests of the city in a way that other permitted uses such as boarding houses and hospitals would not. Because in our view the record does not reveal any rational basis for believing that the Featherston home would pose any special threat to the city's legitimate interests, we affirm the judgment below insofar as it holds the ordinance invalid as applied in this case.

The District Court found that the City Council's insistence on the permit rested on several factors. First, the Council was concerned with the negative attitude of the majority of property owners located within 200 feet of the Featherston facility, as well as with the fears of elderly residents of the neighborhood. But mere negative attitudes, or fear, unsubstantiated by factors which are properly cognizable in a coding proceeding, are not permissible bases for treating a home for the mentally retarded differently from apartment houses, multiple dwellings, and the like. It is plain that the electorate as a whole, whether by referendum or otherwise, could not order city action violative of the Equal Protection Clause, and the City may not avoid the strictures of that Clause by deferring to the wishes or objections of some fraction of the body politic. "Private biases may be outside the reach of the law, but the law cannot, directly or indirectly, give them effect."

Second, the Council had two objections to the location of the facility. It was concerned that the facility was across the street from a junior high school, and it feared that the students might harass the occupants of the Featherston home. But the school itself is attended by about 30 mentally retarded students, and denying a permit based on such vague, undifferentiated fears is again permitting some portion of the community to validate what would otherwise be an equal protection violation. The other objection to the home's location was that it was located on "a five hundred year flood plain." This concern with the possibility of a flood, however, can hardly be based on a distinction between the Featherston home and, for example, nursing homes, homes for convalescents or the aged, or sanitariums or hospitals, any of which could be located on the Featherston site without obtaining a special use permit. The same may be said of another concern of the Council — doubts about the legal responsibility for actions which the mentally retarded might take. If there is no concern about legal responsibility with respect to other uses that would be permitted in the area, such as boarding and fraternity houses, it is difficult to believe that the groups of mildly or moderately mentally retarded individuals who would live at 201 Featherston would present any different or special hazard.

Fourth, the Council was concerned with the size of the home and the number of people that would occupy it. The District Court found, and the Court of Appeals repeated, that "[i]f the potential residents of the Featherston Street home were not mentally retarded, but the home was the same in all other respects, its use would be permitted under the city's zoning ordinance." Given this finding, there would be no restrictions on the number of people who could occupy this home as a boarding house, nursing home, family dwelling, fraternity house, or dormitory. The question is whether it is rational to treat the mentally retarded differently. It is true that they suffer disability not shared by others; but why this difference warrants a density regulation that others need not observe is not at all apparent. At least this record does not clarify how, in this connection, the characteristics of the intended occupants of the Featherston home rationally justify denying to those occupants what would be permitted to groups occupying the same site for different purposes. Those who would live in the Featherston home are the type of individuals who, with supporting staff, satisfy federal and state standards for group housing in the community; and there is no dispute that the home would meet the federal square-footage-per-resident requirement for facilities of this type. . . .

The short of it is that requiring the permit in this case appears to us to rest on an irrational prejudice against the mentally retarded, including those who would occupy the Featherston facility and who would live under the closely supervised and highly regulated conditions expressly provided for by state and federal law. . . .

JUSTICE STEVENS, with whom THE CHIEF JUSTICE [BURGER] joins, concurring. . . .

I have never been persuaded that these so called [judicial review] "standards" adequately explain the decisional process. Cases involving classifications based on alienage, illegal residency, illegitimacy, gender, age, or — as in this case — mental retardation, do not fit well into sharply defined classifications.

"I am inclined to believe that what has become known as the [tiered] analysis of equal protection claims does not describe a completely logical method of deciding cases, but rather is a method the Court has employed to explain decisions that actually apply a single standard in a reasonably consistent fashion." *Craig v. Boren*, 429 U.S. 190, 212 (1976) (Stevens, J., concurring). In my own approach to these cases, I have always asked myself whether I could find a "rational basis" for the classification at issue. The term "rational," of course, includes a requirement that an impartial lawmaker could logically believe that the classification would serve a legitimate public purpose that transcends the harm to the members of the disadvantaged class. Thus, the word "rational" — for me at least — includes elements of legitimacy and neutrality that must always characterize the performance of the sovereign's duty to govern impartially.

The rational basis test, properly understood, adequately explains why a law that deprives a person of the right to vote because his skin has a different pigmentation than that of other voters violates the Equal Protection Clause. It would be utterly irrational to limit the franchise on the basis of height or weight; it is equally invalid to limit it on the basis of skin color. None of these attributes has any bearing at all on the citizen's willingness or ability to exercise that civil right. We do not need to apply a special standard, or to apply "strict scrutiny," or even "heightened scrutiny," to decide such cases.

In every equal protection case, we have to ask certain basic questions. What class is harmed by the legislation, and has it been subjected to a "tradition of disfavor" by our laws? What is the public purpose that is being served by the law? What is the characteristic of the disadvantaged class that justifies the disparate treatment? In most cases the answer to these questions will tell us whether the statute has a "rational basis." The answers will result in the virtually automatic invalidation of racial classifications and in the validation of most economic classifications, but they will provide differing results in cases involving classifications based on alienage, gender, or illegitimacy. But that is not because we apply an "intermediate standard of review" in these cases; rather it is because the characteristics of these groups are sometimes relevant and sometimes irrelevant to a valid public purpose, or, more specifically, to the purpose that the challenged laws purportedly intended to serve.

Every law that places the mentally retarded in a special class is not presumptively irrational. The differences between mentally retarded persons and those with greater mental capacity are obviously relevant to certain legislative decisions. An impartial lawmaker — indeed, even a member of a class of persons defined as mentally retarded — could rationally vote in favor of a law providing funds for special education and special treatment for the mentally retarded. A mentally retarded person could also recognize that he is a member of a class that might need special supervision in some situations, both to protect himself and to protect others. Restrictions on his right to drive cars or to operate hazardous equipment might well seem rational even though they deprived him of employment opportunities and the kind of freedom of travel enjoyed by other citizens. "That a civilized and decent society expects and approves such legislation indicates that governmental consideration of those differences in the vast majority of situations is not only legitimate but desirable." . . .

JUSTICE MARSHALL, with whom JUSTICE BRENNAN and JUSTICE BLACKMUN join, concurring in the judgment in part and dissenting in part. . . .

The Court holds the ordinance invalid on rational basis grounds and disclaims that anything special, in the form of heightened scrutiny, is taking place. Yet Cleburne's ordinance surely would be valid under the traditional rational basis test applicable to economic and commercial regulation. In my view, it is important to articulate, as the Court does not, the facts and principles that justify subjecting this zoning ordinance to the searching review — the heightened scrutiny — that actually leads to its invalidation. . . .

I

. . . [T]he Court's heightened scrutiny discussion is . . . puzzling given that Cleburne's ordinance is invalidated only after being subjected to precisely the sort of probing inquiry associated with heightened scrutiny. To be sure, the Court does not label its handiwork heightened scrutiny, and perhaps the method employed must hereafter be called "second order" rational basis review rather than "heightened scrutiny." But however labeled, the rational basis test invoked today is most assuredly not the rational basis test of *Williamson v. Lee Optical* [348 U.S. 483 (1955)].

The Court, for example, concludes the legitimate concerns for fire hazards or the serenity of the neighborhood do not justify singling out respondents to bear the burdens of these concerns, for analogous permitted uses appear to pose similar threats. Yet under the traditional and most minimal version of the rational basis test, "reform may take one step at a time, addressing itself to the phase of the problem which seems most acute to the legislative mind." *Williamson v. Lee Optical Co.*

The "record" is said not to support the ordinance's classifications, but under the traditional standard we do not sift through the record to determine whether policy decisions are squarely supported by a firm factual foundation. Finally, the Court further finds it "difficult to believe" that the retarded present different or special hazards than other groups. In normal circumstances, the burden is not on the legislature to convince the Court that the lines it has drawn are sensible; legislation is presumptively constitutional, and a State "is not required to resort to close distinctions or to maintain a precise, scientific uniformity with reference" to its goals.

I share the Court's criticisms of the overly broad lines that Cleburne's zoning ordinance has drawn. But if the ordinance is to be invalidated for its imprecise classifications, it must be pursuant to more powerful scrutiny than the minimal rational-basis test used to review classifications affecting only economic and commercial matters. The same imprecision in a similar ordinance that required opticians but not optometrists to be licensed to practice, see *Williamson v. Lee Optical Co.*, or that excluded new but not old businesses from parts of a community, see *New Orleans v. Dukes* [427 U.S. 297 (1976)], would hardly be fatal to the statutory scheme.

The refusal to acknowledge that something more than minimum rationality review is at work here is, in my view, unfortunate in at least two respects. The suggestion that the traditional rational basis test allows this sort of searching inquiry creates precedent for this Court and lower courts to subject economic and commercial classifications to similar and searching "ordinary" rational basis review—a small and regrettable step back toward the days of *Lochner v. New York* [198 U.S. 45 (1905)]. Moreover, by failing to articulate the factors that justify today's "second order" rational basis review, the Court provides no principled foundation for determining when more searching inquiry is to be invoked. Lower courts are thus left in the dark on this important question, and this Court remains unaccountable for its decisions employing, or refusing to employ, particularly searching scrutiny. . . .

II

I have long believed the level of scrutiny employed in an equal protection case should vary with "the constitutional and societal importance of the interest adversely affected and the recognized invidiousness of the basis upon which the particular classification is drawn." When a zoning ordinance works to exclude the retarded from all residential districts in a community, these two considerations require that the ordinance be convincingly justified as substantially furthering legitimate and important purposes.

First, the interest of the retarded in establishing group homes is substantial. The right to "establish a home" has long been cherished as one of the fundamental liberties embraced by the Due Process Clause. See *Meyer v. Nebraska.* For retarded adults, this right means living together in group homes, for as deinstitutionalization has progressed, group homes have become the primary means by which retarded adults can enter life in the community. . . .

Second, the mentally retarded have been subject to a "lengthy and tragic history," of segregation and discrimination that can only be called grotesque. . . .

In light of the importance of the interest at stake and the history of discrimination the retarded have suffered, the Equal Protection Clause requires us to do more than review the distinctions drawn by Cleburne's zoning ordinance as if they appeared in a taxing statute or in economic or commercial legislation. The searching scrutiny I would give to restrictions on the ability of the retarded to establish community group homes leads me to conclude that Cleburne's vague generalizations for classifying the "feeble minded" with drug addicts, alcoholics, and the insane, and excluding them where the elderly, the ill, the boarder, and the transient are allowed, are not substantial or important enough to overcome the suspicion that the ordinance rests on impermissible assumptions or outmoded and perhaps invidious stereotypes.

III

In its effort to show that Cleburne's ordinance can be struck down under no "more exacting standard . . . than is normally accorded economic and social legislation," the Court offers several justifications as to why the retarded do not warrant heightened judicial solicitude. These justifications, however, find no support in our heightened scrutiny precedents and cannot withstand logical analysis.

The Court downplays the lengthy "history of purposeful unequal treatment" of the retarded, by pointing to recent legislative action that is said to "beli[e] a continuing antipathy or prejudice." Building on this point, the Court similarly concludes that the retarded are not "politically powerless" and deserve no greater judicial protection than "any minority" that wins some political battles and loses others. The import of these conclusions, it seems, is that the only discrimination courts may remedy is the discrimination they alone are perspicacious enough to see. Once society begins to recognize certain practices as discriminatory, in part because previously stigmatized groups have mobilized politically to lift this stigma, the Court would refrain from approaching such practices with the added skepticism of heightened scrutiny.

Courts, however, do not sit or act in a social vacuum. Moral philosophers may debate whether certain inequalities are absolute wrongs, but history makes clear that constitutional principles of equality, like constitutional principles of liberty, property, and due process, evolve over time; what once was a "natural" and "self-evident" ordering later comes to be seen as an artificial and invidious constraint on human potential and freedom. Shifting cultural, political, and social patterns at times come to make past practices appear inconsistent with fundamental principles upon which American society rests, an inconsistency legally cognizable under the Equal Protection Clause. It is natural that evolving standards of equality come to be embodied in legislation. When that occurs, courts should look to the fact of such change as a source of guidance on evolving principles of equality. . . .

Moreover, even when judicial action *has* catalyzed legislative change, that change certainly does not eviscerate the underlying constitutional principle. The Court, for example, has never suggested that race-based classifications became any less suspect once extensive legislation had been enacted on the subject. . . .

The fact that retardation may be deemed a constitutional irrelevancy in *some* circumstances is enough, given the history of discrimination the retarded have suffered, to require careful judicial review of classifications singling out the retarded for special burdens. Although the Court acknowledges that many instances of invidious discrimination against the retarded still exist, the Court boldly asserts that "in the vast majority of situations" special treatment of the retarded is "not only legitimate but desirable." That assertion suggests the Court would somehow have us calculate the percentage of "situations" in which a characteristic is validly and invalidly invoked before determining whether heightened scrutiny is appropriate. But heightened scrutiny has not been "triggered" in our past cases only after some undefined numerical threshold of invalid "situations" has been crossed. An inquiry into constitutional principle, not mathematics, determines whether heightened scrutiny is appropriate. Whenever evolving principles of equality, rooted in the Equal Protection Clause, require that certain classifications be viewed as *potentially* discriminatory, and when history reveals systemic unequal treatment, more searching, judicial inquiry than minimum rationality becomes relevant. . . .

By invoking heightened scrutiny, the Court recognizes, and compels lower courts to recognize, that a group may well be the target of the sort of prejudiced, thoughtless, or stereotyped action that offends principles of equality found in the Fourteenth Amendment. Where classifications based on a particular characteristic have done so in the past, and the threat that they may do so remains, heightened scrutiny is appropriate.

As the history of discrimination against the retarded and its continuing legacy amply attest, the mentally retarded have been, and in some areas may still be, the targets of action the Equal Protection Clause condemns. With respect to a liberty so valued as the right to establish a home in the community, and so likely to be denied on the basis of irrational fears and outright hostility, heightened scrutiny is surely appropriate. . . .

Notes and Questions

(1) Did the Court adequately justify its refusal to confer "suspect" or "quasi-suspect" status on classifications involving mental retardation? Is retardation an immutable characteristic, like race? Would the *Carolene Products* footnote and Justice Stone's regard for "discrete and insular" minorities have changed the Court's analysis? (*See* § 5.01, *supra*.)

(2) Did the standard of review matter in light of the Court's decision to strike down the local ordinance? If not, why were there the separate concurring opinions? Did the Court really apply the rationality test of *Lee Optical*?

(3) How do you respond to the Court's argument that it should not extend quasi-suspect status to the mentally retarded because doing so would require it to provide

similar treatment to many other groups? For an analysis of discrimination against groups, such as the mentally retarded, that urges sustaining discriminatory legislation only if it does "not express or confirm the distribution of power in ways that harm the less powerful and benefit the more powerful," see Martha Minow, *When Difference Has Its Home: Group Homes for the Mentally Retarded, Equal Protection, and Legal Treatment of Difference*, 22 HARV. C.R.-C.L. L. REV. 111, 128 (1987).

Problem D

Roberta Jones applied for a position as a state trooper, and scored very well on the written and physical tests. Following the exams, the state police department conducted a routine background check. The investigation revealed very favorable information about Jones' abilities and character. It also disclosed that Jones is transgender. Roberta was born a biological male. She now presents as a female. At an interview, Jones confirmed that she is a transgender person. Shortly after the interview, the department notified Jones that it has a policy of not employing transgender persons and that she would not be offered a position.

Jones has consulted you (an expert on the Equal Protection Clause) for advice on whether she is likely to prevail on a challenge to the department's policy. What advice would you give?

Chapter 7

Economic and Social Rights

§ 7.01 The Rise, Fall, and Resurrection of Entrepreneurial Liberty

Lochner v. New York

United States Supreme Court

198 U.S. 45, 25 S. Ct. 539, 49 L. Ed. 937 (1905)

Mr. Justice Peckham delivered the opinion of the court:

The indictment, it will be seen, charges that the plaintiff in error [Lochner, the baker] violated . . . the labor law of the state of New York, in that he wrongfully and unlawfully required and permitted an employee working for him to work more than sixty hours in one week. . . .

The statute necessarily interferes with the right of contract between the employer and employees, concerning the number of hours in which the latter may labor in the bakery of the employer. The general right to make a contract in relation to his business is part of the liberty of the individual protected by the 14th Amendment of the Federal Constitution. *Allgeyer v. Louisiana*, 165 U.S. 578 (1897). Under that provision no state can deprive any person of life, liberty, or property without due process of law. The right to purchase or to sell labor is part of the liberty protected by this amendment, unless there are circumstances which exclude the right. There are, however, certain powers, existing in the sovereignty of each state in the Union, somewhat vaguely termed police powers, the exact description and limitation of which have not been attempted by the courts. Those powers, broadly stated, and without, at present, any attempt at a more specific limitation, relate to the safety, health, morals, and general welfare of the public. Both property and liberty are held on such reasonable conditions as may be imposed by the governing power of the state in the exercise of those powers, and with such conditions the 14th Amendment was not designed to interfere. *Mugler v. Kansas*, 123 U.S. 623 (1887). . . .

This court has recognized the existence and upheld the exercise of the police powers of the states in many cases which might fairly be considered as border ones, and it [has] been guided by rules of a very liberal nature, the application of which has resulted, in numerous instances, in upholding the validity of state statutes thus assailed. Among the later cases where the state law has been upheld by this court is that of *Holden v. Hardy*, 169 U.S. 366 (1898). . . . A provision in the act of the legislature of Utah was there under consideration, the act limiting the employment of

569

workmen in all underground mines or workings, to eight hours per day, "except in cases of emergency, where life or property is in imminent danger." It also limited the hours of labor in smelting and other institutions for the reduction or refining of ores or metals to eight hours per day, except in like cases of emergency. . . . It was held that the kind of employment, mining, smelting, etc., and the character of the employees in such kinds of labor, were such as to make it reasonable and proper for the state to interfere to prevent the employees from being constrained by the rules laid down by the proprietors in regard to labor. . . . There is nothing in *Holden v. Hardy* which covers the case now before us. . . .

It must, of course, be conceded that there is a limit to the valid exercise of the police power by the state. There is no dispute concerning this general proposition. Otherwise the 14th Amendment would have no efficacy and the legislatures of the states would have unbounded power, and it would be enough to say that any piece of legislation was enacted to conserve the morals, the health, or the safety of the people; such legislation would be valid, no matter how absolutely without foundation the claim might be. The claim of the police power would be a mere [pretext]. In every case that comes before this court, therefore, where legislation of this character is concerned, and where the protection of the Federal Constitution is sought, the question necessarily arises: Is this a fair, reasonable, and appropriate exercise of the police power of the state, or is it an unreasonable, unnecessary, and arbitrary interference with the right of the individual to his personal liberty, or to enter into those contracts in relation to labor which may seem to him appropriate or necessary for the support of himself and his family? Of course the liberty of contract relating to labor includes both parties to it. The one has as much right to purchase as the other to sell labor.

This is not a question of substituting the judgment of the court for that of the legislature. If the act be within the power of the state it is valid, although the judgment of the court might be totally opposed to the enactment of such a law. But the question would still remain: Is it within the police power of the state? and that question must be answered by the court.

The question whether this act is valid as a labor law, pure and simple, may be dismissed in a few words. There is no reasonable ground for interfering with the liberty of person or the right of free contract, by determining the hours of labor, in the occupation of a baker. There is no contention that bakers as a class are not equal in intelligence and capacity to men in other trades or manual occupations, or that they are not able to assert their rights and care for themselves without the protecting arm of the state, interfering with their independence of judgment and of action. They are in no sense wards of the state. Viewed in the light of a purely labor law, with no reference whatever to the question of health, we think that a law like the one before us involves neither the safety, the morals, nor the welfare, of the public, and that the interest of the public is not in the slightest degree affected by such an act. The law must be upheld, if at all, as a law pertaining to the health of the individual engaged in the occupation of a baker. It does not affect any other portion of the public other than those who are engaged in that occupation. Clean and wholesome bread does not depend upon whether the baker works but ten hours per day or only sixty hours a week. The limitation of the hours of labor does not come within the police power on that ground.

[The] mere assertion that the subject relates, though but in a remote degree, to the public health, does not necessarily render the enactment valid. The act must have a more direct relation, as a means to an end, and the end itself must be appropriate and legitimate, before an act can be held to be valid which interferes with the general right of an individual to be free in his person and in his power to contract in relation to his own labor. . . .

We think the limit of the police power has been reached and passed in this case. There is, in our judgment, no reasonable foundation for holding this to be necessary or appropriate as a health law to safeguard the public health, or the health of the individuals who are following the trade of a baker. If this statute be valid, [there] would seem to be no length to which legislation of this nature might not go. . . .

We think that there can be no fair doubt that the trade of a baker, in and of itself, is not an unhealthy one to that degree which would authorize the legislature to interfere with the right to labor, and with the right of free contract on the part of the individual, either as employer or employee. In looking through statistics regarding all trades and occupations, it may be true that the trade of a baker does not appear to be as healthy as some other trades, and is also vastly more healthy than still others. To the common understanding the trade of baker has never been regarded as an unhealthy one. Very likely physicians would not recommend the exercise of that or of any other trade as a remedy for ill health. Some occupations are more healthy than others, but we think there are none which might not come under the power of the legislature to supervise and control the hours of working therein, if the mere fact that the occupation is not absolutely and perfectly healthy is to confer that right upon the legislative department of the government. It might be safely affirmed that almost all occupations more or less affect the health. There must be more than the mere fact of the possible existence of some small amount of unhealthiness to warrant legislative interference with liberty. It is unfortunately true that labor, even in any department, may possibly carry with it the seeds of unhealthiness. But are we all, on that account, at the mercy of legislative majorities? . . .

It is also urged, pursuing the same line of argument, that it is to the interest of the state that its population should be strong and robust, and therefore any legislation which may be said to tend to make people healthy must be valid as health laws, enacted under the police power. If this be a valid argument and a justification for this kind of legislation, it follows that the protection of the Federal Constitution from undue interference with liberty of person and freedom of contract is visionary, wherever the law is sought to be justified as a valid exercise of the police power. Scarcely any law but might find shelter under such assumptions, and conduct, properly so called, as well as contract, would come under the restrictive sway of the legislature. Not only the hours of employees, but the hours of employers, could be regulated, and doctors, lawyers, scientists, all professional men, as well as athletes and artisans, could be forbidden to fatigue their brains and bodies by prolonged hours of exercise, lest the fighting strength of the state be impaired. We mention these extreme cases because the contention is extreme. We do not believe in the soundness of the views which uphold this law. On the contrary, we think that such a law as this, although passed in the assumed exercise of the police power, and as relating to the public health, or the health of the employees named, is not within that power, and is invalid. The act is not, within any fair meaning of the term, a health law, but is an illegal interference with the rights of individuals, both employers and employees, to make contracts regarding labor upon such terms as they may think best, or which they may agree upon with the other parties to such contracts. Statutes of the nature of that under review, limiting the hours in which grown and intelligent men may labor to earn their living, are mere meddlesome interferences with the rights of the individual, and they are not saved from condemnation by the claim that they are passed in the exercise of the police power and upon the subject of the health of the individual whose rights are interfered with, unless there be some fair ground, reasonable in and of itself, to say that there is material danger to the public health, or to the health of the employees, if the hours of labor are not curtailed. If this be not clearly the case, the individuals whose rights are thus made the subject of legislative interference are under the protection of the Federal Constitution regarding their liberty of contract as well as of person; and the legislature of the state has no power to limit their right as proposed in this statute. All that it could properly do has been done by it with regard to the conduct of bakeries, as provided for in the other section of the act, above set forth. These several sections provide for the inspection of the premises where the bakery is carried on, with regard to furnishing proper wash rooms and waterclosets, apart from the bake room, also with regard to providing proper drainage, plumbing, and painting; the sections, in addition, provide for the height of the ceiling, the cementing or tiling of floors, where necessary in the opinion of the factory inspector, and for other things of that nature. . . .

It was further urged on the argument that restricting the hours of labor in the case of bakers was valid because it tended to cleanliness on the part of the workers, as a man was more apt to be cleanly when not overworked, and if cleanly then his "output" was also more likely to be so. . . . In our judgment it is not possible in fact to discover the connection between the number of hours a baker may work in the bakery and the healthful quality of the bread made by the workman. The connection, if any exist, is too shadowy and thin to build any argument for the interference of the legislature. If the man works ten hours a day it is all right, but if ten and a half or eleven his health is in danger and his bread may be unhealthy, and, therefore, he shall not be permitted to do it. This, we think, is unreasonable and entirely arbitrary. When assertions such as we have adverted to become necessary in order to give, if possible, a plausible foundation for the contention that the law is a "health law," it gives rise to at least a suspicion that there was some other motive dominating the legislature than the purpose to subserve the public health or welfare.

This interference on the part of the legislatures of the several states with the ordinary trades and occupations of the people seems to be on the increase. . . . [It] is impossible for us to shut our eyes to the fact that many of the laws of this character, while passed under what is claimed to be the police power for the purpose of protecting the public health or welfare, are, in reality, passed from other motives. We are justified in saying so when, from the character of the law and the subject upon which it legislates, it is apparent that the public health or welfare bears but the most remote relation to the law. The purpose of a statute must be determined from the natural and legal effect of the language employed; and whether it is or is not repugnant to the Constitution of the United States must be determined from the natural effect of such statutes when put into operation, and not from their proclaimed purpose.

[It] is manifest to us that the limitation of the hours of labor as provided for in this section of the statute under which the indictment was found, and the plaintiff in error convicted, has no such direct relation to, and no such substantial effect upon, the health of the employee, as to justify us in regarding the section as really a health law. It seems to us that the real object and purpose were simply to regulate the hours of labor between the master and his employees (all being men, *sui juris*), in a private business, not dangerous in any degree to morals, or in any real and substantial degree to the health of the employees. Under such circumstances the freedom of master and employee to contract with each other in relation to their employment, and in defining the same, cannot be prohibited or interfered with, without violating the Federal Constitution.

[*Reversed.*]

Mr. Justice Holmes dissenting. . . .

This case is decided upon an economic theory which a large part of the country does not entertain. If it were a question whether I agreed with that theory, I should desire to study it further and long before making up my mind. But I do not conceive that to be my duty, because I strongly believe that my agreement or disagreement has nothing to do with the right of a majority to embody their opinions in law. It is settled by various decisions of this court that state constitutions and state laws may regulate life in many ways which we as legislators might think as injudicious, or if you like as tyrannical, as this, and which equally with this, interfere with the liberty to contract. Sunday laws and usury laws are ancient examples. A more modern one is the prohibition of lotteries. The liberty of the citizen to do as he likes so long as he does not interfere with the liberty of others to do the same, which has been a shibboleth for some well-known writers, is interfered with by school laws, by the post office, by every state or municipal institution which takes his money for purposes thought desirable, whether he likes it or not. The 14th Amendment does not enact Mr. Herbert Spencer's *Social Statics*. . . . United States and state statutes and decisions cutting down the liberty to contract by way of combination are familiar to this court. . . . Some of these laws embody convictions or prejudices which judges are likely to share. Some may not. But a Constitution is not intended to embody a particular economic theory, whether of paternalism and the organic relation of the citizen to the state or of *laissez faire*. It is made for people of fundamentally differing views, and the accident of our finding certain opinions natural and familiar, or novel, and even shocking, ought not to conclude our judgment upon the question whether statutes embodying them conflict with the Constitution of the United States.

General propositions do not decide concrete cases. The decision will depend on a judgment or intuition more subtle than any articulate major premise. But I think that the proposition just stated, if it is accepted, will carry us far toward the end. Every opinion tends to become a law. I think that the word "liberty," in the 14th Amendment, is perverted when it is held to prevent the natural outcome of a dominant opinion, unless it can be said that a rational and fair man necessarily would admit that the statute proposed would infringe fundamental principles as they have been understood by the traditions of our people and our law. It does not need research to show that no such sweeping condemnation can be passed upon the statute before us. A reasonable man might think it a proper measure on the score of health. Men whom I certainly could not pronounce unreasonable would uphold it as a first installment of a general regulation of the hours of work. Whether in the latter aspect it would be open to the charge of inequality I think it unnecessary to discuss.

Mr. Justice Harlan (with whom Mr. Justice White and Mr. Justice Day concurred) dissenting:

[There] is a liberty of contract which cannot be violated even under the sanction of direct legislative enactment, but assuming, as according to settled law we may assume, that such liberty of contract is subject to such regulations as the state may reasonably prescribe for the common good and the well-being of society, what are the conditions under which the judiciary may declare such regulations to be in excess of legislative authority and void? . . .

It is plain that this statute was enacted in order to protect the physical well-being of those who work in bakery and confectionery establishments. It may be that the statute had its origin, in part, in the belief that employers and employees in such establishments were not upon an equal footing, and that the necessities of the latter often compelled them to submit to such exactions as unduly taxed their strength. Be this as it may, the statute must be taken as expressing the belief of the people of New York that, as a general rule, and in the case of the average man, labor in excess of sixty hours during a week in such establishments may endanger the health of those who thus labor. Whether or not this be wise legislation it is not the province of the court to inquire. Under our systems of government the courts are not concerned with the wisdom or policy of legislation. So that, in determining the question of power to interfere with liberty of contract, the court may inquire whether the means devised by the state are germane to an end which may be lawfully accomplished and have a real or substantial relation to the protection of health, as involved in the daily work of the persons, male and female, engaged in bakery and confectionery establishments. But when this inquiry is entered upon I find it impossible, in view of common experience, to say that there is here no real or substantial relation between the means employed by the state and the end sought to be accomplished by its legislation. . . . Still less can I say that the statute is, beyond question, a plain, palpable invasion of rights secured by the fundamental law. . . .

Professor Hirt in his treatise on the *Diseases of the Workers* has said: "The labor of the bakers is among the hardest and most laborious imaginable, because it has to be performed under conditions injurious to the health of those engaged in it. It is hard, very hard, work, not only because it requires a great deal of physical exertion in an overheated workshop and during unreasonably long hours, but more so because of the erratic demands of the public, compelling the baker to perform the greater part of his work at night, thus depriving him of an opportunity to enjoy the necessary rest and sleep, — a fact which is highly injurious to his health." Another writer says:

> The constant inhaling of flour dust causes inflammation of the lungs and of the bronchial tubes. The eyes also suffer through this dust, which is responsible for the many cases of running eyes among the bakers. The long hours of toil to which all bakers are subjected produce rheumatism, cramps and swollen legs. The intense heat in the workshops induces the workers to resort to cooling drinks, which, together with their habit of exposing the greater part of their bodies to the change in the atmosphere, is another source of a number of diseases of various organs. Nearly all bakers are palefaced and of more delicate health than the workers of other crafts, which is chiefly due to their hard work and their irregular and unnatural mode of living, whereby the power of resistance against disease is greatly diminished. The average age of a baker is below that of other workmen; they seldom live over their fiftieth year. . . .

We judicially know that the question of the number of hours during which a workman should continuously labor has been, for a long period, and is yet, a subject of serious consideration among civilized peoples, and by those having special knowledge of the laws of health. . . .

We also judicially know that the number of hours that should constitute a day's labor in particular occupations involving the physical strength and safety of workmen has been the subject of enactments by Congress and by nearly all of the states. Many, if not most, of those enactments fix eight hours as the proper basis of a day's labor.

I do not stop to consider whether any particular view of this economic question presents the sounder theory. What the precise facts are it may be difficult to say. It is enough for the determination of this case, and it is enough for this court to know, that the question is one about which there is room for debate and for an honest difference of opinion. There are many reasons of a weighty, substantial character, based upon the experience of mankind, in support of the theory that, all things considered, more than ten hours' steady work each day, from week to week, in a bakery or confectionery establishment, may endanger the health and shorten the lives of the workmen, thereby diminishing their physical and mental capacity to serve the state and to provide for those dependent upon them.

If such reasons exist that ought to be the end of this case, for the state is not amenable to the judiciary, in respect of its legislative enactments, unless such enactments are plainly, palpably, beyond all question, inconsistent with the Constitution of the United States. . . .

A decision that the New York statute is void under the 14th Amendment will, in my opinion, involve consequences of a far-reaching and mischievous character; for such a decision would seriously cripple the inherent power of the states to care for the lives, health, and well-being of their citizens. Those are matters which can be best controlled by the states. . . .

Williamson v. Lee Optical Co.

United States Supreme Court
348 U.S. 483, 75 S. Ct. 461, 99 L. Ed. 563 (1955)

Mr. Justice Douglas delivered the opinion of the Court.

[The] District Court held unconstitutional portions of three sections of [an Oklahoma law]. First, it held invalid under the Due Process Clause of the Fourteenth Amendment the portions of § 2 which make it unlawful for any person not a licensed optometrist or ophthalmologist to fit lenses to a face or to duplicate or replace into frames lenses or other optical appliances, except upon written prescriptive authority of an Oklahoma licensed ophthalmologist or optometrist.

An ophthalmologist is a duly licensed physician who specializes in the care of the eyes. An optometrist examines eyes for refractive error, recognizes (but does not treat) diseases of the eye, and fills prescriptions for eyeglasses. The optician is an artisan qualified to grind lenses, fill prescriptions, and fit frames.

The effect of § 2 is to forbid the optician from fitting or duplicating lenses without a prescription from an ophthalmologist or optometrist. In practical effect, it means that no optician can fit old glasses into new frames or supply a lens, whether it be a new lens or one to duplicate a lost or broken lens, without a prescription. The District Court conceded that it was within the competence of the police power of a State to regulate the examination of the eyes. But it rebelled at the notion that a State could require a prescription from an optometrist or ophthalmologist "to take old lenses and place them in new frames and then fit the completed spectacles to the *face* of the eyeglass wearer." [The] court found that through mechanical devices and ordinary skills the optician could take a broken lens or a fragment thereof, measure its power, and reduce it to prescriptive terms. The court held that "although on this precise issue of duplication, the legislature in the instant regulation was dealing with a matter of public interest, the particular means chosen are neither reasonably necessary nor reasonably related to the end sought to be achieved. . . ."

The Oklahoma law may exact a needless, wasteful requirement in many cases. But it is for the legislature, not the courts, to balance the advantages and disadvantages of the new requirement. It appears that in many cases the optician can easily supply the new frames or new lenses without reference to the old written prescription. It also appears that many written prescriptions contain no directive data in regard to fitting spectacles to the face. But in some cases the directions contained in the prescription are essential, if the glasses are to be fitted so as to correct the particular defects of vision or alleviate the eye condition. The legislature might have concluded that the frequency of occasions when a prescription is necessary was sufficient to justify this regulation of the fitting of eyeglasses. Likewise, when it is necessary to duplicate a lens, a written prescription may or may not be necessary. But the legislature might have concluded that one was needed often enough to require one in every case. Or the legislature may have concluded that eye examinations were so critical, not only for correction of vision but also for detection of latent ailments or diseases, that every change in frames and every duplication of a lens should be accompanied by a prescription from a medical expert. To be sure, the present law does not require a new examination of the eyes every time the frames are changed or the lenses duplicated. For if the old prescription is on file with the optician, he can go ahead and make the new fitting or duplicate the lenses. But the law need not be in every respect logically consistent with its aims to be constitutional. It is enough that there is an evil at hand for correction, and that it might be thought that the particular legislative measure was a rational way to correct it. . . .

The District Court [also] held unconstitutional, as violative of the Due Process Clause of the Fourteenth Amendment, that portion of §3 which makes it unlawful "to solicit the sale of . . . frames, mountings . . . or any other optical appliances." [R]egulation of the advertising of eyeglass frames was said to intrude "into a mercantile field only casually related to the visual care of the public" and restrict "an activity which in no way can detrimentally affect the people."

[An] eyeglass frame, considered in isolation, is only a piece of merchandise. But an eyeglass frame is not used in isolation, [it] is used with lenses; and lenses, pertaining as they do to the human eye, enter the field of health. Therefore, the legislature might conclude that to regulate one effectively it would have to regulate the other. Or it might conclude that both the sellers of frames and the sellers of lenses were in a business where advertising should be limited or even abolished in the public interest. [The] advertiser of frames may be using his ads to bring in customers who will buy lenses. If the advertisement of lenses is to be abolished or controlled, the advertising of frames must come under the same restraints; or so the legislature might think. We see no constitutional reason why a State may not treat all who deal with the human eye as members of a profession who should use no merchandising methods for obtaining customers.

[T]he District Court [also] held unconstitutional, as violative of the Due Process Clause of the Fourteenth Amendment, the provision of §4 of the Oklahoma Act which reads as follows:

No person, firm, or corporation engaged in the business of retailing merchandise to the general public shall rent space, sublease departments, or otherwise permit any person purporting to do eye examination or visual care to occupy space in such retail store. . . .

[This regulation] is an attempt to free the profession, to as great an extent as possible, from all taints of commercialism. It certainly might be easy for an optometrist with space in a retail store to be merely a front for the retail establishment. In any case, the opportunity for that nexus may be too great for safety, if the eye doctor is allowed inside the retail store. Moreover, it may be deemed important to effective regulation that the eye doctor be restricted to geographical locations that reduce the temptations of commercialism. Geographical location may be an important consideration in a legislative program which aims to raise the treatment of the human eye to a strictly professional level. We cannot say that the regulation has no rational relation to that objective and therefore is beyond constitutional bounds. . . .

[*Reversed.*]

Notes and Questions

(1) How did Justice Peckham arrive at his conclusion in *Lochner* that the right to buy and sell labor is protected as part of Fourteenth Amendment "liberty" and "property"? At English common law, "liberty" meant freedom from physical restraint, and "property" was limited to real and personal property. Why should their constitutional meaning be different? *See* Charles Warren, *The "New Liberty" Under the Fourteenth Amendment*, 39 HARV. L. REV. 431 (1926). Is Justice Peckham's interpretation of the Constitution consistent with the *Slaughter-House Cases* (§ 5.02, *supra*)?

(2) According to Justice Peckham, what were the permissible objectives for exercise of the state's police power? What is wrong with "a labor law, pure and simple"? Did the state's bargaining inequality rationale fail because it is not one of the permissible exercises of the police power, or because the wage and hour law is not likely to further that end? Recall from cases such as *McCulloch v. Maryland* (§ 4.02, *supra*) that legislation is constitutional if it employs a "rational" means to further a "legitimate" end. Is the means-ends analysis applied in *Lochner*?

(3) Why did the health objective fail to persuade the Court? Consider Justice Harlan's dissent. What exactly was his disagreement with the majority regarding the law as a health measure? Was it over the role of judicial review? Which opinion favors the more active judicial review? Does federalism explain their differences?

(4) Did Justice Peckham simply substitute his judgment for that of the legislature? In that regard, recall that legislators take an oath to uphold the Constitution. Is a court better equipped than a legislature to determine the constitutionality of laws? Bear this question in mind throughout the individual rights chapters.

(5) Did the Court in *Lochner* review the motives of the legislature? How is legislative motive discoverable? Should courts consider legislative motive?

(6) Three years after *Lochner*, the Court unanimously upheld a state law limiting a woman's workday in laundries and factories to ten hours. *Muller v. Oregon*, 208 U.S. 412 (1908). The Court reasoned that a "woman's physical structure and the performance of maternal function place her at a disadvantage in the struggle for subsistence," and that "because healthy mothers are essential to vigorous offspring, the physical well-being of woman becomes an object of public interest." Thus "she is properly placed in a class by herself." Then, in 1917, the Court upheld a law setting a ten-hour day for male workers, *Bunting v. Oregon*, 243 U.S. 426 (1917). *Lochner* was not mentioned; the state law was characterized by the Court as a real health measure.

Perhaps the outcomes in *Muller* and *Bunting* were influenced by the pathbreaking lawyering in the cases: Louis Brandeis submitted a massive brief in *Muller* relating socio-economic data on the harm to women from long work hours. Felix Frankfurter submitted a two-volume "Brandeis Brief" in *Bunting*. For an assessment of the contribution of the "Brandeis Brief," see David Bryden, *Brandeis's Facts*, 1 Const. Comment. 281 (1984).

(7) In other cases, however, the "Lochnerizing" continued. In *Adair v. United States*, 208 U.S. 161 (1908), the Court found a "liberty of contract" in Fifth Amendment due process in striking down a federal law which made it criminal for an interstate carrier to discharge an employee because of his union membership. Then, in *Coppage v. Kansas*, 236 U.S. 1 (1915), the Court struck down a similar state law. Finally, in 1923, the Court held unconstitutional the District of Columbia minimum wage law for women based on the *Lochner* "freedom of contract." *Adkins v. Children's Hospital*, 261 U.S. 525 (1923). Justice Holmes dissented in each instance, in terms like these from *Adkins*: "Contract is not . . . mentioned [in the Constitution]. . . . It is merely an example of doing what you want to do . . . but pretty much all law consists in forbidding men to do some things that they want to do. . . ."

(8) In *West Coast Hotel Co. v. Parrish*, 300 U.S. 379 (1937), the Court upheld a state law that mandated minimum wages for women and overruled *Adkins*. The Court stated: "The Constitution does not speak of freedom of contract. It speaks of liberty and prohibits the deprivation of liberty without due process of law. Liberty under the Constitution is thus necessarily subject to the restraints of due process, and regulation which is reasonable in relation to its subject and is adopted in the interests of the community is due process."

(9) How should we account for the extraordinary leap from *Lochner* to *Lee Optical*? Notice that the standard for the state law has evolved to one of "minimum rationality." Is there any protection for private economic interests remaining in the Due Process Clause after *Lee Optical*? Why did the Court withdraw to such an apparent extreme?

§ 7.02 Privacy and the Right to Be Let Alone

Buck v. Bell

United States Supreme Court
274 U.S. 200, 47 S. Ct. 584, 71 L. Ed. 1000 (1927)

MR. JUSTICE HOLMES delivered the opinion of the Court.

This is a writ of error to review a judgment of the Supreme Court of Appeals of the State of Virginia, affirming a judgment of the Circuit Court of Amherst County, by which the defendant in error, the superintendent of the State Colony for Epileptics and Feeble Minded, was ordered to perform the operation of salpingectomy upon Carrie Buck, the plaintiff in error, for the purpose of making her sterile. The case comes here upon the contention that the statute authorizing the judgment is void under the Fourteenth Amendment as denying to the plaintiff in error due process of law and the equal protection of the laws.

Carrie Buck is a feeble minded white woman who was committed to the State Colony above mentioned in due form. She is the daughter of a feeble minded mother in the same institution, and the mother of an illegitimate feeble minded child. She was eighteen years old at the time of the trial of her case in the Circuit Court, in the latter part of 1924. An Act of Virginia, approved March 20, 1924, recites that the health of the patient and the welfare of society may be promoted in certain cases by the sterilization of mental defectives, under careful safeguard, etc.; that the sterilization may be effected in males by vasectomy and in females by salpingectomy, without serious pain or substantial danger to life; that the Commonwealth is supporting in various institutions many defective persons who if now discharged would become a menace but if incapable of procreating might be discharged with safety and become self-supporting with benefit to themselves and to society; and that experience has shown that heredity plays an important part in the transmission of insanity, imbecility, etc. The statute then enacts that whenever the superintendent of certain institutions including the above named State Colony shall be of opinion that it is for the best interests of the patients and of society that an inmate under his care should be sexually sterilized, he may have the operation performed upon any patient afflicted with hereditary forms of insanity, imbecility, etc., on complying with the very careful provisions by which the act protects the patients from possible abuse.

The superintendent first presents a petition to the special board of directors of his hospital or colony, stating the facts and the grounds for his opinion, verified by affidavit. Notice of the petition and of the time and place of the hearing in the institution is to be served upon the inmate, and also upon his guardian, and if there is no guardian the superintendent is to apply to the Circuit Court of the County to appoint one. If the inmate is a minor notice also is to be given to his parents if any with a copy of the petition. The board is to see to it that the inmate may attend the hearings if desired by him or his guardian. The evidence is all to be reduced to writing, and after the board has made its order for or against the operation, the superintendent, or the inmate, or his guardian, may appeal to the Circuit Court of the County. The Circuit Court may consider the record of the board and the evidence before it and such other admissible evidence as may be offered, and may affirm, revise, or reverse the order of the board and enter such order as it deems just. Finally any party may apply to the Supreme Court of Appeals, which, if it grants the appeal, is to hear the case upon the record of the trial in the Circuit Court and may enter such order as it thinks the Circuit Court should have entered. There can be no doubt that so far as procedure is concerned the rights of the patient are most carefully considered, and as every step in this case was taken in scrupulous compliance with the statute and after months of observation, there is no doubt that in that respect the plaintiff in error has had due process of law.

The attack is not upon the procedure but upon the substantive law. It seems to be contended that in no circumstances could such an order be justified. It certainly is contended that the order cannot be justified upon the existing grounds. The judgment finds the facts that have been recited and that Carrie Buck "is the probable potential parent of socially inadequate offspring, likewise afflicted, that she may be sexually sterilized without detriment to her general health and that her welfare and that of society will be promoted by her sterilization," and thereupon makes the order. In view of the general declarations of the legislature and the specific findings of the Court, obviously we cannot say as matter of law that the grounds do not exist, and if they exist they justify the result. We have seen more than once that the public welfare may call upon the best citizens for their lives. It would be strange if it could not call upon those who already sap the strength of the State for these lesser sacrifices, often not felt to be such by those concerned, in order to prevent our being swamped with incompetence. It is better for all the world, if instead of waiting to execute degenerate offspring for crime, or to let them starve for their imbecility, society can prevent those who are manifestly unfit from continuing their kind. The principle that sustains compulsory vaccination is broad enough to cover cutting the Fallopian tubes. *Jacobson v. Massachusetts*, 197 U.S. 11 (1905). Three generations of imbeciles are enough.

But, it is said, however it might be if this reasoning were applied generally, it fails when it is confined to the small number who are in the institutions named and is not applied to the multitudes outside. It is the usual last resort of constitutional arguments to point out shortcomings of this sort. But the answer is that the law does all that is needed when it does all that it can, indicates a policy, applies it to all within the lines, and seeks to bring within the lines all similarly situated so far and so fast as its means allow. Of course so far as the operations enable those who otherwise must be kept confined to be returned to the world, and thus open the asylum to others, the equality aimed at will be more nearly reached.

Judgment affirmed.

MR. JUSTICE BUTLER dissents.

Griswold v. Connecticut

United States Supreme Court
381 U.S. 479, 85 S. Ct. 1678, 14 L. Ed. 2d 510 (1965)

MR. JUSTICE DOUGLAS delivered the opinion of the Court.

Appellant Griswold is Executive Director of the Planned Parenthood League of Connecticut. Appellant Buxton is a licensed physician and a professor at the Yale Medical School who served as Medical Director for the League at its Center in New Haven — a center open and operating from November 1 to November 10, 1961, when appellants were arrested. They gave information, instruction, and medical advice to *married persons* as to the means of preventing conception. They examined the wife and prescribed the best contraceptive device or material for her use. Fees were usually charged, although some couples were serviced free.

The statutes whose constitutionality is involved . . . provid[e]:

> Any person who uses any drug, medicinal article or instrument for the purpose of preventing conception shall be fined not less than fifty dollars or imprisoned not less than sixty days nor more than one year or be both fined and imprisoned. . . .

> Any person who assists, abets, counsels, causes, hires or commands another to commit any offense may be prosecuted and punished as if he were the principal offender.

The appellants were found guilty as accessories and fined $100 each. . . .

[W]e are met with a wide range of questions that implicate the Due Process Clause of the Fourteenth Amendment. Overtones of some arguments suggest that *Lochner* should be our guide. But we decline that invitation. . . . We do not sit as a super-legislature to determine the wisdom, need, and propriety of laws that touch economic problems, business affairs, or social conditions. This law, however, operates directly on an intimate relation of husband and wife and their physician's role in one aspect of that relation.

The association of people is not mentioned in the Constitution nor in the Bill of Rights. The right to educate a child in a school of the parents' choice — whether public or private or parochial — is also not mentioned. Nor is the right to study any particular subject or any foreign language. Yet the First Amendment has been construed to include certain of those rights.

By *Pierce v. Society of Sisters*, 268 U.S. 510 (1925), the right to educate one's children as one chooses is made applicable to the States by the force of the First and Fourteenth Amendments. By *Meyer v. State of Nebraska*, 262 U.S. 390 (1923), the same dignity is given the right to study the German language in a private school. In other words, the State may not, consistently with the spirit of the First Amendment, contract the spectrum of available knowledge. . . . Without those peripheral rights the specific rights would be less secure. And so we reaffirm the principle of the *Pierce* and the *Meyer* cases.

In *NAACP v. Alabama*, 357 U.S. 449, 462 (1958), we protected the "freedom to associate and privacy in one's associations," noting that freedom of association was a peripheral First Amendment right. Disclosure of membership lists of a constitutionally valid association, we held, was invalid "as entailing the likelihood of a substantial restraint upon the exercise by petitioner's members of their right to freedom of association." In other words, the First Amendment has a penumbra where privacy is protected from government intrusion. . . .

The foregoing cases suggest that specific guarantees in the Bill of Rights have penumbras, formed by emanations from those guarantees that help give them life and substance. Various guarantees create zones of privacy. The right of association contained in the penumbra of the First Amendment is one, as we have seen. The Third Amendment in its prohibition against the quartering of soldiers "in any house" in time of peace without the consent of the owner is another facet of that privacy. The Fourth Amendment explicitly affirms the "right of the people to be secure in their persons, houses, papers, and effects against unreasonable searches and seizures." The Fifth Amendment in its Self-Incrimination Clause enables the citizen to create a zone of privacy which government may not force him to surrender to his detriment. The Ninth Amendment provides: "The enumeration in the Constitution, of certain rights, shall not be construed to deny or disparage others retained by the people. . . ." We have had many controversies over these penumbral rights of "privacy and repose." *Skinner v. Oklahoma*, 316 U.S. 535, 541 (1942). These cases bear witness that the right of privacy which presses for recognition here is a legitimate one.

The present case, then, concerns a relationship lying within the zone of privacy created by several fundamental constitutional guarantees. And it concerns a law which, in forbidding the *use* of contraceptives rather than regulating their manufacture or sale, seeks to achieve its goals by means having a maximum destructive impact upon that relationship. Such a law cannot stand in light of the familiar principle, so often applied by this Court, that a "governmental purpose to control or prevent activities constitutionally subject to state regulation may not be achieved by means which sweep unnecessarily broadly and thereby invade the area of protected freedoms." *NAACP v. Alabama*. Would we allow the police to search the sacred precincts of marital bedrooms for telltale signs of the use of contraceptives? The very idea is repulsive to the notions of privacy surrounding the marriage relationship.

We deal with a right of privacy older than the Bill of Rights — older than our political parties, older than our school system. Marriage is a coming together for better or for worse, hopefully enduring, and intimate to the degree of being sacred. It is an association that promotes a way of life, not causes; a harmony in living, not political faiths; a bilateral loyalty, not commercial or social projects. Yet it is an association for as noble a purpose as any involved in our prior decisions.

Reversed.

Mr. Justice Goldberg, whom The Chief Justice [Warren] and Mr. Justice Brennan join, concurring. . . .

In reaching the conclusion that the right of marital privacy is protected, as being within the protected penumbra of specific guarantees of the Bill of Rights, the Court refers to the Ninth Amendment. I add these words to emphasize the relevance of that Amendment to the Court's holding. . . .

This Court, in a series of decisions, has held that the Fourteenth Amendment absorbs and applies to the States those specifics of the first eight amendments which express fundamental personal rights. The language and history of the Ninth Amendment reveal that the Framers of the Constitution believed that there are additional fundamental rights, protected from governmental infringement, which exist alongside those fundamental rights specifically mentioned in the first eight constitutional amendments. . . .

The Amendment is almost entirely the work of James Madison. It was introduced in Congress by him and passed the House and Senate with little or no debate and virtually no change in language. It was proffered to quiet expressed fears that a bill of specifically enumerated rights could not be sufficiently broad to cover all essential rights and that the specific mention of certain rights would be interpreted as a denial that others were protected. . . .

While this Court has had little occasion to interpret the Ninth Amendment, "[i]t cannot be presumed that any clause in the constitution is intended to be without effect." *Marbury v. Madison.* In interpreting the Constitution, "real effect should be given to all the words it uses." The Ninth Amendment to the Constitution may be regarded by some as a recent discovery and may be forgotten by others, but since 1791 it had been a basic part of the Constitution which we are sworn to uphold. To hold that a right so basic and fundamental and so deep-rooted in our society as the right of privacy in marriage may be infringed because that right is not guaranteed in so many words by the first eight amendments to the Constitution is to ignore the Ninth Amendment and to give it no effect whatsoever. Moreover, a judicial construction that this fundamental right is not protected by the Constitution because it is not mentioned in explicit terms by one of the first eight amendments or elsewhere in the Constitution would violate the Ninth Amendment, which specifically states that "[t]he enumeration in the Constitution, of certain rights shall not be *construed* to deny or disparage others retained by the people." (Emphasis added.)

A dissenting opinion suggests that my interpretation of the Ninth Amendment somehow "broaden[s] the powers of this Court. . . ." [I] do not mean to imply that the Ninth Amendment is applied against the States by the Fourteenth. Nor do I mean to state that the Ninth Amendment constitutes an independent source of rights protected from infringement by either the States or the Federal Government. Rather, the Ninth Amendment shows a belief of the Constitution's authors that fundamental rights exist that are not expressly enumerated in the first eight amendments and an intent that the list of rights included there not be deemed exhaustive. . . . I do not see how this broadens the authority of the Court; rather it serves to support what this Court has been doing in protecting fundamental rights.

Nor am I turning somersaults with history in arguing that the Ninth Amendment is relevant in a case dealing with a *State's* infringement of a fundamental right. While the Ninth Amendment — and indeed the entire Bill of Rights — originally concerned restrictions upon *federal* power, the subsequently enacted Fourteenth Amendment prohibits the States as well from abridging fundamental personal liberties. And, the Ninth Amendment, in indicating that not all such liberties are specifically mentioned in the first eight amendments, is surely relevant in showing the existence of other fundamental personal rights, now protected from state, as well as federal, infringement. In sum, the Ninth Amendment simply lends strong support to the view that the "liberty" protected by the Fifth and Fourteenth Amendments from infringement by the Federal Government or the States is not restricted to rights specifically mentioned in the first eight amendments.

In determining which rights are fundamental, judges are not left at large to decide cases in light of their personal and private notions. Rather, they must look to the "traditions and [collective] conscience of our people" to determine whether a principle is "so rooted [there] . . . as to be ranked as fundamental." The inquiry is whether a right involved "is of such a character that it cannot be denied without violating those 'fundamental principles of liberty and justice which lie at the base of all our civil and political institutions. . . .'" "Liberty" also "gains content from the emanations of . . . specific [constitutional] guarantees" and "from experience with the requirements of a free society." *Poe v. Ullman*, 367 U.S. 497, 517 [1961] (dissenting opinion of Mr. Justice Douglas).

I agree fully with the Court that, applying these tests, the right of privacy is a fundamental personal right, emanating "from the totality of the constitutional scheme under which we live. . . ."

The Connecticut statutes here involved deal with a particularly important and sensitive area of privacy — that of the marital relation and the marital home. This Court recognized in *Meyer v. Nebraska* that the right "to marry, establish a home and bring up children" was an essential part of the liberty guaranteed by the Fourteenth Amendment. . . .

I agree with Mr. Justice Harlan's statement in his dissenting opinion in *Poe v. Ullman*:

> Certainly the safeguarding of the home does not follow merely from the sanctity of property rights. The home derives its pre-eminence as the seat of family life. And the integrity of that life is something so fundamental that it has been found to draw to its protection the principles of more than one explicitly granted Constitutional right. . . . Of this whole "private realm of family life" it is difficult to imagine what is more private or more intimate than a husband and wife's marital relations. . . .

The logic of the dissents would sanction federal or state legislation that seems to me even more plainly unconstitutional than the statute before us. Surely the Government, absent a showing of a compelling subordinating state interest, could not decree that all husbands and wives must be sterilized after two children have been born to them. Yet by their reasoning such an invasion of marital privacy would not be subject to constitutional challenge because, while it might be "silly," no provision of the Constitution specifically prevents the Government from curtailing the marital right to bear children and raise a family. While it may shock some of my Brethren that the Court today holds that the Constitution protects the right of marital privacy, in my view it is far more shocking to believe that the personal liberty guaranteed by the Constitution does not include protection against such totalitarian limitation of family size, which is at complete variance with our constitutional concepts. Yet, if upon a showing of a slender basis of rationality, a law outlawing voluntary birth control by married persons is valid, then, by the same reasoning, a law requiring compulsory birth control also would seem to be valid. In my view, however, both types of law would unjustifiably intrude upon rights of marital privacy which are constitutionally protected. . . .

Although the Connecticut birth-control law obviously encroaches upon a fundamental personal liberty, the State does not show that the law serves any "subordinating [state] interest which is compelling" or that it is "necessary . . . to the accomplishment of a permissible state policy." The State, at most, argues that there is some rational relation between this statute and what is admittedly a legitimate subject of state concern — the discouraging of extra-marital relations. It says that preventing the use of birth-control devices by married persons helps prevent the indulgence by some in such extra-marital relations. The rationality of this justification is dubious, particularly in light of the admitted widespread availability to all persons in the State of Connecticut, unmarried as well as married, of birth-control devices for the prevention of disease, as distinguished from the prevention of conception. But, in any event, it is clear that the state interest in safeguarding marital fidelity can be served by a more discriminately tailored statute, which does not, like the present one, sweep unnecessarily broadly, reaching far beyond the evil sought to be dealt with and intruding upon the privacy of all married couples. . . . "[P]recision of regulation must be the touchstone in an area so closely touching our most precious freedoms." The State of Connecticut does have statutes, the constitutionality of which is beyond doubt, which prohibit adultery and fornication. These statutes demonstrate that means for achieving the same basic purpose of protecting marital fidelity are available to Connecticut without the need to "invade the area of protected freedoms."

Finally, it should be said of the Court's holding today that it in no way interferes with a State's proper regulation of sexual promiscuity or misconduct. As my Brother Harlan so well stated in his dissenting opinion in *Poe v. Ullman*, *supra*:

> Adultery, homosexuality and the like are sexual intimacies which the State
> forbids . . . but the intimacy of husband and wife is necessarily an essential

and accepted feature of the institution of marriage, an institution which the State not only must allow, but which always and in every age it has fostered and protected. It is one thing when the State exerts its power either to forbid extra-marital sexuality . . . or to say who may marry, but it is quite another when, having acknowledged a marriage and the intimacies inherent in it, it undertakes to regulate by means of the criminal law the details of the intimacy. . . .

Mr. Justice Harlan, concurring in the judgment. . . .

In my view, the proper constitutional inquiry in this case is whether this Connecticut statute infringes the Due Process Clause of the Fourteenth Amendment because the enactment violates basic values "implicit in the concept of ordered liberty," *Palko v. Connecticut*, 302 U.S. 319, 325 (1937). For reasons stated at length in my dissenting opinion in *Poe v. Ullman*, I believe that it does. While the relevant inquiry may be aided by resort to one or more of the provisions of the Bill of Rights, it is not dependent on them or any of their radiations. The Due Process Clause of the Fourteenth Amendment stands, in my opinion, on its own bottom.

A further observation seems in order respecting the justification of my Brothers Black and Stewart for their "incorporation" approach to this case. Their approach does not rest on historical reasons, which are of course wholly lacking, but on the thesis that by limiting the content of the Due Process Clause of the Fourteenth Amendment to the protection of rights which can be found elsewhere in the Constitution, in this instance in the Bill of Rights, judges will thus be confined to "interpretation" of specific constitutional provisions, and will thereby be restrained from introducing their own notions of constitutional right and wrong into the "vague contours of the Due Process Clause."

While I could not more heartily agree that judicial "self restraint" is an indispensable ingredient of sound constitutional adjudication, I do submit that the formula suggested for achieving it is more hollow than real. "Specific" provisions of the Constitution, no less than "due process," lend themselves as readily to "personal" interpretations by judges whose constitutional outlook is simply to keep the Constitution in supposed "tune with the times. . . ."

Judicial self-restraint will not, I suggest, be brought about in the "due process" area by the historically unfounded incorporation formula long advanced by my Brother Black, and now in part espoused by my Brother Stewart. It will be achieved in this area, as in other constitutional areas, only by continual insistence upon respect for the teachings of history, solid recognition of the basic values that underlie our society, and wise appreciation of the great roles that the doctrines of federalism and separation of powers have played in establishing and preserving American freedoms. . . .

Mr. Justice White, concurring in the judgment. . . .

An examination of the justification offered . . . cannot be avoided by saying that the Connecticut anti-use statute invades a protected area of privacy and association or that it demands the marriage relationship. The nature of the right invaded is pertinent, to be sure, for statutes regulating sensitive areas of liberty do, under the cases of this Court, require "strict scrutiny," *Skinner v. State of Oklahoma*, and "must be viewed in the light of less drastic means for achieving the same basic purpose. . . ."

I find nothing in this record justifying the sweeping scope of this statute, with its telling effect on the freedoms of married persons, and therefore conclude that it deprives such persons of liberty without due process of law.

MR. JUSTICE BLACK, with whom MR. JUSTICE STEWART joins, dissenting. . . .

The Court talks about a constitutional "right of privacy" as though there is some constitutional provision or provisions forbidding any law ever to be passed which might abridge the "privacy" of individuals. But there is not. There are, of course, guarantees in certain specific constitutional provisions which are designed in part to protect privacy at certain times and places with respect to certain activities. Such, for example, is the Fourth Amendment's guarantee against "unreasonable searches and seizures." But I think it belittles that Amendment to talk about it as though it protects nothing but "privacy." To treat it that way is to give it a niggardly interpretation, not the kind of liberal reading I think any Bill of Rights provision should be given. The average man would very likely not have his feelings soothed any more by having his property seized openly than by having it seized privately and by stealth. He simply wants his property left alone. And a person can be just as much, if not more, irritated, annoyed and injured by an unceremonious public arrest by a policeman as he is by a seizure in the privacy of his office or home.

One of the most effective ways of diluting or expanding a constitutionally guaranteed right is to substitute for the crucial word or words of a constitutional guarantee another word or words, more or less flexible and more or less restricted in meaning. This fact is well illustrated by the use of the term "right of privacy" as a comprehensive substitute for the Fourth Amendment's guarantee against "unreasonable searches and seizures. . . ." I like my privacy as well as the next one, but I am nevertheless compelled to admit that government has a right to invade it unless prohibited by some specific constitutional provision. For these reasons I cannot agree with the Court's judgment and the reasons it gives for holding this Connecticut law unconstitutional. . . .

The due process argument which my Brothers Harlan and White adopt here is based, as their opinions indicate, on the premise that this Court is vested with power to invalidate all state laws that it considers to be arbitrary, capricious, unreasonable, or oppressive, or this Court's belief that a particular state law under scrutiny has no "rational or justifying" purpose, or is offensive to a "sense of fairness and justice." If these formulas based on "natural justice," or others which mean the same thing, are to prevail, they require judges to determine what is or is not constitutional on the basis of their own appraisal of what laws are unwise or unnecessary. The power to make such decisions is of course that of a legislative body. . . .

Of the cases on which my Brothers White and Goldberg rely so heavily, undoubt-edly the reasoning of two of them supports their result here — as would that of a number of others which they do not bother to name, e.g., *Lochner*. . . . The two they do cite and quote from, *Meyer* and *Pierce*, were both decided in opinions by Mr. Jus-tice McReynolds which elaborated the same natural law due process philosophy found in *Lochner*, one of the cases on which he relied in *Meyer*. . . .

My Brother Goldberg has adopted the recent discovery that the Ninth Amend-ment as well as the Due Process Clause can be used by this Court as authority to strike down all state legislation which this Court thinks violates "fundamental principles of liberty and justice," or is contrary to the "traditions and [collective] conscience of our people." He also states, without proof satisfactory to me, that in making decisions on this basis judges will not consider "their personal and private notions." One may ask how they can avoid considering them. Our Court certainly has no machinery with which to take a Gallup Poll. And the scientific miracles of this age have not yet produced a gadget which the Court can use to determine what traditions are rooted in the "[collective] conscience of our people." Moreover, one would certainly have to look far beyond the language of the Ninth Amendment to find that the Framers vested in this Court any such awesome veto powers over law-making, either by the States or by the Congress. Nor does anything in the history of the Amendment offer any support for such a shocking doctrine. The whole history of the adoption of the Constitution and Bill of Rights points the other way, and the very material quoted by my Brother Goldberg shows that the Ninth Amendment was intended to protect against the idea that "by enumerating particular exceptions to the grant of power" to the Federal Government, "those rights which were not singled out, were intended to be assigned into the hands of the General Government [the United States], and were consequently insecure." That Amendment was passed, not to broaden the powers of this Court or any other department of "the General Government," but, as every student of history knows, to assure the people that the Constitution in all its provisions was intended to limit the Federal Government to the powers granted expressly or by necessary implication. If any broad, unlimited power to hold laws unconstitutional because they offend what this Court conceives to be the "[collective] conscience of our people" is vested in this Court by the Ninth Amendment, the Fourteenth Amendment, or any other provision of the Constitu-tion, it was not given by the Framers, but rather has been bestowed on the Court by the Court. This fact is perhaps responsible for the peculiar phenomenon that for a period of a century and a half no serious suggestion was ever made that the Ninth Amendment, enacted to protect state powers against federal invasion, could be used as a weapon of federal power to prevent state legislatures from passing laws they consider appropriate to govern local affairs. . . .

I cannot rely on the Due Process Clause or the Ninth Amendment or any mys-terious and uncertain natural law concept as a reason for striking down this state law. The Due Process Clause with an "arbitrary and capricious" or "shocking to the conscience" formula was liberally used by this Court to strike down economic legislation in the early decades of this century, threatening, many people thought, the tranquility and stability of the Nation. See, e.g., *Lochner*. That formula, based on subjective considerations of "natural justice," is no less dangerous when used to enforce this Court's views about personal rights than those about economic rights. . . .

Mr. Justice Stewart, whom Mr. Justice Black joins, dissenting.

Since 1879 Connecticut has had on its books a law which forbids the use of contraceptives by anyone. I think this is an uncommonly silly law. . . . But we are not asked in this case to say whether we think this law is unwise, or even asinine. We are asked to hold that it violates the United States Constitution. And that I cannot do. . . . It is the essence of judicial duty to subordinate our own personal views, our own ideas of what legislation is wise and what is not. If, as I should surely hope, the law before us does not reflect the standards of the people of Connecticut, the people of Connecticut can freely exercise their true Ninth and Tenth Amendment rights to persuade their elected representatives to repeal it. That is the constitutional way to take this law off the books.

Notes and Questions

(1) Would *Buck v. Bell* be decided the same way today? Do you agree with Justice Holmes that "[t]he principle that sustains compulsory vaccination is broad enough to cover cutting the Fallopian tubes"? In *Skinner v. Oklahoma*, 316 U.S. 535 (1942), the Supreme Court struck down, as a violation of the Equal Protection Clause, Oklahoma's Habitual Criminal Sterilization Act, which authorized the sterilization of persons previously convicted and imprisoned two or more times of felonies "involving moral turpitude." The law exempted from its coverage embezzlement, political offenses, and revenue act violations. Thus a three-time chicken thief could be sterilized but a three time embezzler could not. The Court observed: "We are dealing here with legislation which involves one of the basic civil rights of man. Marriage and procreation are fundamental to the very existence and survival of the race." The Court applied "strict scrutiny," stating that when the law "lays an unequal hand on those who have committed intrinsically the same quality of offense and sterilizes one and not the other, it has made as invidious a discrimination, as if it had selected a particular race or nationality for oppressive treatment." The Court in *Skinner* distinguished *Buck v. Bell*, but did not purport to overrule it.

(2) In two early cases, *Meyer v. Nebraska*, 262 U.S. 390 (1923), and *Pierce v. Society of Sisters*, 268 U.S. 510 (1925), the Supreme Court, without explicitly talking about a "right of privacy," struck down statutes that limited rights of personal autonomy with regard to important individual life choices. In *Pierce*, the Court struck down a law that required students to attend public rather than private schools. In *Meyer* the Court invalidated a statute forbidding all grade schools, public or private, from teaching subjects in any language other than English. In a celebrated passage, the Court through Justice McReynolds spoke expansively in *Meyer* of the "liberty" protected by the Due Process Clause:

While this court has not attempted to define with exactness the liberty thus guaranteed, the term has received much consideration and some of the included things have been definitely stated. Without doubt, it denotes not merely freedom from bodily restraint but also the right of the individual to contract, to engage in any of the common occupations of life, to acquire useful knowledge, to marry, establish a home and bring up children, to worship God according to the dictates of his own conscience, and generally to enjoy those privileges long recognized at common law as essential to the orderly pursuit of happiness by free men.

The Court held that this liberty "may not be interfered with, under the guise of protecting the public interest, by legislative action which is arbitrary or without reasonable relation to some purpose within the competency of the state to effect." The Court rejected Nebraska's argument that the law was justified by the state's interest in promoting civic development "by inhibiting training and education of the immature in foreign tongues and ideals . . ." After discussing Plato and the history of Sparta, the Court stated that "[a]lthough such measures have been deliberately approved by men of great genius their ideas touching the relation between the individual and state were wholly different from those upon which our institutions rest . . ." Nebraska could not, the Court held, forbid instruction in foreign languages "to foster a homogeneous people with American ideals . . ."

(3) Search the various opinions in *Griswold* for the sources of the liberty interest recognized by the Court. What were they and how were they found, that is, by what method was meaning given to the Due Process Clause? Which approach is best?

(4) Why is "privacy" protected by the Constitution? What is the function that privacy serves in society? Consider this view:

> Privacy . . . has two general aspects. First, it provides the individual with the opportunities he needs for sharing confidences and intimacies with those he trusts — spouse, "the family," personal friends, and close associates at work. The individual discloses because he knows that his confidences will be held, and because he knows that breach of confidence violates social norms in a civilized society. . . . In addition, the individual often wants to secure counsel from persons with whom he does not have to live daily after disclosing his confidences. He seeks professionally objective advice from persons whose status in society promises that they will not later use his distress to take advantage of him. To protect freedom of limited communication, such relationships — with doctors, lawyers, ministers, psychiatrists, psychologists, and others — are given varying but important degrees of legal privilege against forced disclosure. . . .

ALAN WESTIN, PRIVACY AND FREEDOM, 33–38 (1967).[1]

---

1. Alan F. Westin, excerpted from *Privacy and Freedom*. Copyright © 1967 The Association of the Bar of the City of New York.

(5) What was the scope and nature of the protected "privacy" interest in *Griswold*? Which of Professor Westin's privacy functions are served by the right recognized in *Griswold*? Consider also the locational interest (the home) and the interest in the marriage relationship. Did the *Griswold* opinions recognize a privacy right in the home?

(6) Was *Griswold* a "natural law" decision? Consider this position:

> The intellectual framework against which these [privacy] rights have developed is different from the natural-rights tradition of the founding fathers — its rhetorical reference points are the Anglo-American tradition and basic American ideals, rather than human nature, the social contract, or the rights of man. But it is the modern offspring, in a direct and traceable line of legitimate descent, of the natural-rights tradition that is so deeply embedded in our constitutional origins.

Thomas Grey, *Do We Have An Unwritten Constitution?*, 27 STAN. L. REV. 703, 706 (1975).[2]

(7) Did *Meyer* and *Pierce* provide adequate support for finding the marital privacy right in *Griswold*?

(8) Consider the standard of review in *Griswold*. What was it? Why was it less deferential than the review of economic due process claims?

(9) For a sampling of views on the Ninth Amendment, see *Symposium on Interpreting the Ninth Amendment*, 64 CHI.-KENT L. REV. 37 (1988).

(10) In *Eisenstadt v. Baird*, 405 U.S. 438 (1972), the Court extended *Griswold*, invalidating a state law which prohibited the distribution of contraceptives to unmarried persons. The Court's opinion made it clear that the privacy right was not limited to the marriage relationship: "[T]he marital couple is not an independent entity with a mind and heart of its own, but an association of two individuals. . . . If the right of privacy means anything, it is the right of the individual, married or single, to be free from unwarranted governmental intrusion into matters so fundamentally affecting a person as the decision whether to bear or beget a child."

(11) In *Roe v. Wade*, 410 U.S. 113 (1973), the Court held that the Texas abortion statute, which prohibited obtaining or attempting an abortion except for the purpose of saving the mother's life, violated Due Process. Justice Blackmun, writing for the Court, stated:

> We forthwith acknowledge our awareness of the sensitive and emotional nature of the abortion controversy, of the vigorous opposing views, even among physicians, and of the deep and seemingly absolute convictions that the subject inspires. One's philosophy, one's experiences, one's exposure to the raw edges of human existence, one's religious training, one's attitudes

---

2. Copyright © 1975 by Stanford University School of Law. Reprinted by permission.

toward life and seeks to observe, are all likely to influence and to color one's thinking and conclusions about abortion. In addition, population growth, pollution, poverty, and racial overtones tend to complicate and not to simplify the problem.

Our task, of course, is to resolve the issue by constitutional measurement, free of emotion and of predilection. We seek earnestly to do this, and, because we do, we have inquired into, and in this opinion place some emphasis upon, medical and medical-legal history and what that history reveals about man's attitudes toward the abortion procedure over the centuries. We bear in mind, too, Mr. Justice Holmes' admonition in his now-vindicated dissent in *Lochner*:

> [The Constitution] is made for people of fundamentally differing views, and the accident of our finding certain opinions natural and familiar, or novel, and even shocking, ought not to conclude our judgment upon the question whether statutes embodying them conflict with the Constitution of the United States.

The principal thrust of appellant's attack on the Texas statutes is that they improperly invade a right, said to be possessed by the pregnant woman, to choose to terminate her pregnancy. Appellant would discover this right in the concept of personal "liberty" embodied in the Fourteenth Amendment's Due Process Clause; or in personal, marital, familial, and sexual privacy said to be protected by the Bill of Rights or its penumbras, see Griswold, or among those rights reserved to the people by the Ninth Amendment.

After reviewing the history of abortion, the Court stated:

> It is thus apparent that at common law, at the time of the adoption of our Constitution, and throughout the major portion of the 19th century, abortion was viewed with less disfavor than under most American statutes currently in effect. Phrasing it another way, a woman enjoyed a substantially broader right to terminate a pregnancy than she does in most States today. At least with respect to the early stage of pregnancy, and very possibly without such a limitation, the opportunity to make this choice was present in this country well into the 19th century. Even later, the law continued for some time to treat less punitively an abortion procured in early pregnancy.

The Court held that the right of personal privacy includes the abortion decision:

> The Constitution does not explicitly mention any right of privacy. In a line of decisions, however, . . . the Court has recognized that a right of personal privacy, or a guarantee of certain areas or zones of privacy, does exist under the Constitution. In varying contexts, the Court or individual Justices have, indeed, found at least the roots of that right in the First Amendment, in the Fourth and Fifth Amendments, . . . in the penumbras of the Bill of Rights, or in the concept of liberty guaranteed by the first section of the Fourteenth Amendment. These decisions make it clear that only

personal rights that can be deemed "fundamental" or "implicit in the concept of ordered liberty," are included in this guarantee of personal privacy. They also make it clear that the right has some extension to activities relating to marriage, procreation, contraception, family relationships, and child rearing and education.

This right of privacy, whether it be founded in the Fourteenth Amendment's concept of personal liberty and restrictions upon state action, as we feel it is, or, as the District Court determined, in the Ninth Amendment's reservation of rights to the people, is broad enough to encompass a woman's decision whether or not to terminate her pregnancy. The detriment that the State would impose upon the pregnant woman by denying this choice altogether is apparent. Specific and direct harm medically diagnosable even in early pregnancy may be involved. Maternity or additional offspring, may force upon the woman a distressful life and future. Psychological harm may be imminent. Mental and physical health may be taxed by child care. There is also the distress, for all concerned, associated with the unwanted child, and there is the problem of bringing a child into a family already unable, psychologically and otherwise, to care for it. In other cases, as in this one, the additional difficulties and continuing stigma of unwed motherhood may be involved. All these are factors the woman and her responsible physician necessarily will consider in consultation.

On the basis of elements such as these, appellant and some amici argue that the woman's right is absolute and that she is entitled to terminate her pregnancy at whatever time, in whatever way, and for whatever reason she alone chooses. With this we do not agree. Appellant's arguments that Texas either has no valid interest at all in regulating the abortion decision, or no interest strong enough to support any limitation upon the woman's sole determination, are unpersuasive. The Court's decisions recognizing a right of privacy also acknowledge that some state regulation in areas protected by that right is appropriate. As noted above, a State may properly assert important interests in safeguarding health, in maintaining medical standards, and in protecting potential life. At some point in pregnancy, these respective interests become sufficiently compelling to sustain regulation of the factors that govern the abortion decision. The privacy right involved, therefore, cannot be said to be absolute. . . .

We . . . conclude that the right of personal privacy includes the abortion decision, but that this right is not unqualified and must be considered against important state interests in regulation. . . .

Where certain "fundamental rights" are involved, the Court has held that regulation limiting these rights may be justified only by a "compelling state interest," and that legislative enactments must be narrowly drawn to express only the legitimate state interests at stake. *Griswold v. Connecticut.*

The Court summarized its decision as follows:

> A state criminal abortion statute of the current Texas type, that excepts from criminality only a *life-saving* procedure on behalf of the mother, without regard to pregnancy stage and without recognition of the other interests involved, is violative of the Due Process Clause of the Fourteenth Amendment.
>
> > (a) For the stage prior to approximately the end of the first trimester, the abortion decision and its effectuation must be left to the medical judgment of the pregnant woman's attending physician.
> >
> > (b) For the stage subsequent to approximately the end of the first trimester, the State, in promoting its interest in the health of the mother, may, if it chooses, regulate the abortion procedure in ways that are reasonably related to maternal health.
> >
> > (c) For the stage subsequent to viability, the State in promoting its interest in the potentiality of human life may, if it chooses, regulate, and even proscribe, abortion except where it is necessary, in appropriate medical judgment, for the preservation of the life or health of the mother.

(12) Despite *Roe,* the public debate about abortions intensified and many states continued to find ways to limit access to the procedure. Nineteen years after *Roe,* the Court refused to overrule the decision. The Court was divided, but Justice O'Connor wrote for the Court in *Planned Parenthood of Southeastern Pennsylvania v. Casey,* 505 U.S. 833 (1992):

> After considering the fundamental constitutional questions resolved by *Roe*, principles of institutional integrity, and the rule of stare decisis, we are led to conclude this: the essential holding of *Roe v. Wade* should be retained and once again reaffirmed.
>
> Men and women of good conscience can disagree, and we suppose always shall disagree, about the profound moral and spiritual implications of terminating a pregnancy, even in its earliest stage. Some of us as individuals find abortion offensive to our most basic principles of morality, but that cannot control our decision. Our obligation is to define the liberty of all, not to mandate our own moral code. The underlying constitutional issue is whether the State can resolve these philosophic questions in such a definitive way that a woman lacks all choice in the matter, except perhaps in those rare circumstances in which the pregnancy is itself a danger to her own life or health, or is the result of rape or incest. . . .
>
> Our cases recognize "the right of the individual, married or single, to be free from unwarranted governmental intrusion into matters so fundamentally affecting a person as the decision whether to bear or beget a child." *Eisenstadt v. Baird.* Our precedents "have respected the private realm of family life which the state cannot enter." *Prince v. Massachusetts*, 321 U.S.

158, 166 (1944). These matters, involving the most intimate and personal choices a person may make in a lifetime, choices central to personal dignity and autonomy, are central to the liberty protected by the Fourteenth Amendment. At the heart of liberty is the right to define one's own concept of existence, of meaning, of the universe, and of the mystery of human life. Beliefs about these matters could not define the attributes of personhood were they formed under compulsion of the State.

These considerations begin our analysis of the woman's interest in terminating her pregnancy but cannot end it, for this reason: though the abortion decision may originate within the zone of conscience and belief, it is more than a philosophic exercise. Abortion is a unique act. It is an act fraught with consequences for others: for the woman who must live with the implications of her decision; for the persons who perform and assist in the procedure; for the spouse, family, and society which must confront the knowledge that these procedures exist, procedures some deem nothing short of an act of violence against innocent human life; and, depending on one's beliefs, for the life or potential life that is aborted. Though abortion is conduct, it does not follow that the State is entitled to proscribe it in all instances. That is because the liberty of the woman is at stake in a sense unique to the human condition and so unique to the law. The mother who carries a child to full term is subject to anxieties, to physical constraints, to pain that only she must bear. That these sacrifices have from the beginning of the human race been endured by woman with a pride that ennobles her in the eyes of others and gives to the infant a bond of love cannot alone be grounds for the State to insist she make the sacrifice. Her suffering is too intimate and personal for the State to insist, without more, upon its own vision of the woman's role, however dominant that vision has been in the course of our history and our culture. The destiny of the woman must be shaped to a large extent on her own conception of her spiritual imperatives and her place in society.

It should be recognized, moreover, that in some critical respects the abortion decision is of the same character as the decision to use contraception, to which *Griswold v. Connecticut, Eisenstadt v. Baird*, and *Carey v. Population Services International*, 431 U.S. 678 (1977), afford constitutional protection. We have no doubt as to the correctness of those decisions.

Justice O' Connor's opinion, however, rejected *Roe*'s trimester approach in favor of an "undue burden" test:

[W]e reject the trimester framework, which we do not consider to be part of the essential holding of *Roe*. Measures aimed at ensuring that a woman's choice contemplates the consequences for the fetus do not necessarily interfere with the right recognized in *Roe*, although those measures have been found to be inconsistent with the rigid trimester framework announced in that case. A logical reading of the central holding in *Roe* itself, and a necessary reconciliation of the liberty of the woman and the interest of the State in promoting prenatal life, require, in our view, that we abandon the trimester framework as a rigid prohibition on all previability regulation aimed at the protection of fetal life. The trimester framework suffers from these basic flaws: in its formulation it misconceives the nature of the pregnant woman's interest; and in practice it undervalues the State's interest in potential life, as recognized in *Roe*. . . .

The very notion that the State has a substantial interest in potential life leads to the conclusion that not all regulations must be deemed unwarranted. Not all burdens on the right to decide whether to terminate a pregnancy will be undue. In our view, the undue burden standard is the appropriate means of reconciling the State's interest with the woman's constitutionally protected liberty.

Dobbs v. Jackson Women's Health Organization

United States Supreme Court
597 U.S.___, 142 S. Ct. 2228 (2022)

Justice Alito delivered the opinion of the Court.

Abortion presents a profound moral issue on which Americans hold sharply conflicting views. Some believe fervently that a human person comes into being at conception and that abortion ends an innocent life. Others feel just as strongly that any regulation of abortion invades a woman's right to control her own body and prevents women from achieving full equality. Still others in a third group think that abortion should be allowed under some but not all circumstances, and those within this group hold a variety of views about the particular restrictions that should be imposed.

For the first 185 years after the adoption of the Constitution, each State was permitted to address this issue in accordance with the views of its citizens. Then, in 1973, this Court decided *Roe v. Wade*, 410 U.S. 113. Even though the Constitution makes no mention of abortion, the Court held that it confers a broad right to obtain one. It did not claim that American law or the common law had ever recognized such a right, and its survey of history ranged from the constitutionally irrelevant (*e.g.*, its discussion of abortion in antiquity) to the plainly incorrect (*e.g.*, its assertion that abortion was probably never a crime under the common law). After cataloging a wealth of other information having no bearing on the meaning of the Constitution, the opinion concluded with a numbered set of rules much like those that might be found in a statute enacted by a legislature.

Under this scheme, each trimester of pregnancy was regulated differently, but the most critical line was drawn at roughly the end of the second trimester, which, at the time, corresponded to the point at which a fetus was thought to achieve "viability," *i.e.*, the ability to survive outside the womb. Although the Court acknowledged that States had a legitimate interest in protecting "potential life," it found that this interest could not justify any restriction on pre-viability abortions. The Court did not explain the basis for this line, and even abortion supporters have found it hard to defend *Roe*'s reasoning. One prominent constitutional scholar wrote that he "would vote for a statute very much like the one the Court end[ed] up drafting" if he were "a legislator," but his assessment of *Roe* was memorable and brutal: *Roe* was "not constitutional law" at all and gave "almost no sense of an obligation to try to be."

At the time of *Roe*, 30 States still prohibited abortion at all stages. In the years prior to that decision, about a third of the States had liberalized their laws, but *Roe* abruptly ended that political process. It imposed the same highly restrictive regime on the entire Nation, and it effectively struck down the abortion laws of every single State. As Justice Byron White aptly put it in his dissent, the decision represented the "exercise of raw judicial power," 410 U. S., at 222, and it sparked a national controversy that has embittered our political culture for a half century.

Eventually, in *Planned Parenthood of Southeastern Pa. v. Casey*, 505 U.S. 833 (1992), the Court revisited *Roe*, but the Members of the Court split three ways. Two Justices expressed no desire to change *Roe* in any way. Four others wanted to overrule the decision in its entirety. And the three remaining Justices, who jointly signed the controlling opinion, took a third position. Their opinion did not endorse *Roe*'s reasoning, and it even hinted that one or more of its authors might have "reservations" about whether the Constitution protects a right to abortion. But the opinion concluded that *stare decisis*, which calls for prior decisions to be followed in most instances, required adherence to what it called *Roe*'s "central holding" — that a State may not constitutionally protect fetal life before "viability" — even if that holding was wrong. Anything less, the opinion claimed, would undermine respect for this Court and the rule of law.

Paradoxically, the judgment in *Casey* did a fair amount of overruling. Several important abortion decisions were overruled *in toto*, and *Roe* itself was overruled in part. *Casey* threw out *Roe*'s trimester scheme and substituted a new rule of uncertain origin under which States were forbidden to adopt any regulation that imposed an "undue burden" on a woman's right to have an abortion. The decision provided no clear guidance about the difference between a "due" and an "undue" burden. But the three Justices who authored the controlling opinion "call[ed] the contending sides of a national controversy to end their national division" by treating the Court's decision as the final settlement of the question of the constitutional right to abortion.

As has become increasingly apparent in the intervening years, *Casey* did not achieve that goal. Americans continue to hold passionate and widely divergent views on abortion, and state legislatures have acted accordingly. Some have recently enacted laws allowing abortion, with few restrictions, at all stages of pregnancy. Others have tightly restricted abortion beginning well before viability. And in this case, 26 States have expressly asked this Court to overrule *Roe* and *Casey* and allow the States to regulate or prohibit pre-viability abortions.

Before us now is one such state law. The State of Mississippi asks us to uphold the constitutionality of a law that generally prohibits an abortion after the 15th week of pregnancy — several weeks before the point at which a fetus is now regarded as "viable" outside the womb. In defending this law, the State's primary argument is that we should reconsider and overrule *Roe* and *Casey* and once again allow each State to regulate abortion as its citizens wish. On the other side, respondents and the Solicitor General ask us to reaffirm *Roe* and *Casey*, and they contend that the Mississippi law cannot stand if we do so. Allowing Mississippi to prohibit abortions after 15 weeks of pregnancy, they argue, "would be no different than overruling *Casey* and *Roe* entirely." They contend that "no half-measures" are available and that we must either reaffirm or overrule *Roe* and *Casey*.

We hold that *Roe* and *Casey* must be overruled. The Constitution makes no reference to abortion, and no such right is implicitly protected by any constitutional provision, including the one on which the defenders of *Roe* and *Casey* now chiefly rely — the Due Process Clause of the Fourteenth Amendment. That provision has been held to guarantee some rights that are not mentioned in the Constitution, but any such right must be "deeply rooted in this Nation's history and tradition" and "implicit in the concept of ordered liberty." *Washington v. Glucksberg,* 521 U.S. 702, 721 (1997).

The right to abortion does not fall within this category. Until the latter part of the 20th century, such a right was entirely unknown in American law. Indeed, when the Fourteenth Amendment was adopted, three quarters of the States made abortion a crime at all stages of pregnancy. The abortion right is also critically different from any other right that this Court has held to fall within the Fourteenth Amendment's protection of "liberty." *Roe*'s defenders characterize the abortion right as similar to the rights recognized in past decisions involving matters such as intimate sexual relations, contraception, and marriage, but abortion is fundamentally different, as both *Roe* and *Casey* acknowledged, because it destroys what those decisions called "fetal life" and what the law now before us describes as an "unborn human being."

Stare decisis, the doctrine on which *Casey*'s controlling opinion was based, does not compel unending adherence to *Roe*'s abuse of judicial authority. *Roe* was egregiously wrong from the start. Its reasoning was exceptionally weak, and the decision has had damaging consequences. And far from bringing about a national settlement of the abortion issue, *Roe* and *Casey* have enflamed debate and deepened division.

It is time to heed the Constitution and return the issue of abortion to the people's elected representatives. "The permissibility of abortion, and the limitations, upon it, are to be resolved like most important questions in our democracy: by citizens trying to persuade one another and then voting." *Casey*, 505 U.S., at 979 (Scalia, J., concurring in judgment in part and dissenting in part). That is what the Constitution and the rule of law demand.

The law at issue in this case, Mississippi's Gestational Age Act, see Miss. Code Ann. § 41-41-191 (2018), contains this central provision: "Except in a medical emergency or in the case of a severe fetal abnormality, a person shall not intentionally or knowingly perform . . . or induce an abortion of an unborn human being if the probable gestational age of the unborn human being has been determined to be greater than fifteen (15) weeks." § 4(b).

To support this Act, the legislature made a series of factual findings. It began by noting that, at the time of enactment, only six countries besides the United States "permit[ted] nontherapeutic or elective abortion-on-demand after the twentieth week of gestation." § 2(a). The legislature then found that at 5 or 6 weeks' gestational age an "unborn human being's heart begins beating"; at 8 weeks the "unborn human being begins to move about in the womb"; at 9 weeks "all basic physiological functions are present"; at 10 weeks "vital organs begin to function," and "[h]air, fingernails, and toenails . . . begin to form"; at 11 weeks "an unborn human being's diaphragm is developing," and he or she may "move about freely in the womb"; and at 12 weeks the "unborn human being" has "taken on 'the human form' in all relevant respects." § 2(b)(i) (quoting *Gonzales v. Carhart*, 550 U.S. 124, 160 (2007)). It found that most abortions after 15 weeks employ "dilation and evacuation procedures which involve the use of surgical instruments to crush and tear the unborn child," and it concluded that the "intentional commitment of such acts for nontherapeutic or elective reasons is a barbaric practice, dangerous for the maternal patient, and demeaning to the medical profession." § 2(b)(i)(8).

Respondents are an abortion clinic, Jackson Women's Health Organization, and one of its doctors. On the day the Gestational Age Act was enacted, respondents filed suit in Federal District Court against various Mississippi officials, alleging that the Act violated this Court's precedents establishing a constitutional right to abortion. The District Court granted summary judgment in favor of respondents and permanently enjoined enforcement of the Act, reasoning that "viability marks the earliest point at which the State's interest in fetal life is constitutionally adequate to justify a legislative ban on nontherapeutic abortions" and that 15 weeks' gestational age is "prior to viability." *Jackson Women's Health Org. v. Currier*, 349 F. Supp. 3d 536, 539–540 (SD Miss. 2019) (internal quotation marks omitted). The Fifth Circuit affirmed. 945 F.3d 265 (2019).

We granted certiorari to resolve the question whether "all pre-viability prohibitions on elective abortions are unconstitutional."

We begin by considering the critical question whether the Constitution, properly understood, confers a right to obtain an abortion.

Constitutional analysis must begin with "the language of the instrument," *Gibbons v. Ogden*, 9 Wheat. 1, 186–189 (1824), which offers a "fixed standard" for ascertaining what our founding document means, 1 J. Story, Commentaries on the Constitution of the United States § 399, p. 383 (1833). The Constitution makes no express reference to a right to obtain an abortion, and therefore those who claim that it protects such a right must show that the right is somehow implicit in the constitutional text.

Roe, however, was remarkably loose in its treatment of the constitutional text. It held that the abortion right, which is not mentioned in the Constitution, is part of a right to privacy, which is also not mentioned. See 410 U.S., at 152–153. And that privacy right, *Roe* observed, had been found to spring from no fewer than five different constitutional provisions — the First, Fourth, Fifth, Ninth, and Fourteenth Amendments.

The Court's discussion left open at least three ways in which some combination of these provisions could protect the abortion right. One possibility was that the right was "founded . . . in the Ninth Amendment's reservation of rights to the people." *Id.,* at 153. Another was that the right was rooted in the First, Fourth, or Fifth Amendment, or in some combination of those provisions, and that this right had been "incorporated" into the Due Process Clause of the Fourteenth Amendment just as many other Bill of Rights provisions had by then been incorporated. *Ibid*; see also *McDonald v. Chicago*, 561 U.S. 742, 763–766 (2010) (majority opinion) (discussing incorporation). And a third path was that the First, Fourth, and Fifth Amendments played no role and that the right was simply a component of the "liberty" protected by the Fourteenth Amendment's Due Process Clause. *Roe*, 410 U.S., at 153. *Roe* expressed the "feel[ing]" that the Fourteenth Amendment was the provision that did the work, but its message seemed to be that the abortion right could be found *somewhere* in the Constitution and that specifying its exact location was not of paramount importance. The *Casey* Court did not defend this unfocused analysis and instead grounded its decision solely on the theory that the right to obtain an abortion is part of the "liberty" protected by the Fourteenth Amendment's Due Process Clause.

We discuss this theory in depth below, but before doing so, we briefly address one additional constitutional provision that some of respondents' *amici* have now offered as yet another potential home for the abortion right: the Fourteenth Amendment's Equal Protection Clause. See Brief for United States as *Amicus Curiae* 24 (Brief for United States); see also Brief for Equal Protection Constitutional Law Scholars as *Amici Curiae*. Neither *Roe* nor *Casey* saw fit to invoke this theory, and it is squarely foreclosed by our precedents, which establish that a State's regulation of abortion is not a sex-based classification and is thus not subject to the "heightened scrutiny" that applies to such classifications. The regulation of a medical procedure that only one sex can undergo does not trigger heightened constitutional scrutiny unless the regulation is a "mere pretex[t] designed to effect an invidious discrimination against members of one sex or the other." *Geduldig v. Aiello*, 417 U.S. 484, 496, n. 20 (1974). And as the Court has stated, the "goal of preventing abortion" does not constitute "invidiously discriminatory animus" against women. *Bray v. Alexandria Women's Health Clinic*, 506 U.S. 263, 273–274 (1993) (internal quotation marks omitted). Accordingly, laws regulating or prohibiting abortion are not subject to heightened scrutiny. Rather, they are governed by the same standard of review as other health and safety measures.

With this new theory addressed, we turn to *Casey*'s bold assertion that the abortion right is an aspect of the "liberty" protected by the Due Process Clause of the Fourteenth Amendment.

The underlying theory on which this argument rests — that the Fourteenth Amendment's Due Process Clause provides substantive, as well as procedural, protection for "liberty" — has long been controversial. But our decisions have held that the Due Process Clause protects two categories of substantive rights.

The first consists of rights guaranteed by the first eight Amendments. Those Amendments originally applied only to the Federal Government, *Barron ex rel. Tiernan v. Mayor of Baltimore*, 7 Pet. 243, 247–251 (1833) (opinion for the Court by Marshall, C.J.), but this Court has held that the Due Process Clause of the Fourteenth Amendment "incorporates" the great majority of those rights and thus makes them equally applicable to the States. See *McDonald*, 561 U.S., at 763–767, and nn. 12–13. The second category — which is the one in question here — comprises a select list of fundamental rights that are not mentioned anywhere in the Constitution.

In deciding whether a right falls into either of these categories, the Court has long asked whether the right is "deeply rooted in [our] history and tradition" and whether it is essential to our Nation's "scheme of ordered liberty." *Timbs v. Indiana*, 586 U.S. ___, ___ (2019) (slip op., at 3) (internal quotation marks omitted); *McDonald*, 561 U.S., at 764, 767 (internal quotation marks omitted); *Glucksberg*, 521 U.S., at 721 (internal quotation marks omitted). And in conducting this inquiry, we have engaged in a careful analysis of the history of the right at issue.

Historical inquiries of this nature are essential whenever we are asked to recognize a new component of the "liberty" protected by the Due Process Clause because the term "liberty" alone provides little guidance. "Liberty" is a capacious term. As Lincoln once said: "We all declare for Liberty; but in using the same word we do not all mean the same thing." In a well-known essay, Isaiah Berlin reported that "[h]istorians of ideas" had cataloged more than 200 different senses in which the term had been used.

In interpreting what is meant by the Fourteenth Amendment's reference to "liberty," we must guard against the natural human tendency to confuse what that Amendment protects with our own ardent views about the liberty that Americans should enjoy. That is why the Court has long been "reluctant" to recognize rights that are not mentioned in the Constitution. *Collins v. Harker Heights*, 503 U.S. 115, 125 (1992). "Substantive due process has at times been a treacherous field for this Court," *Moore v. East Cleveland*, 431 U.S. 494, 503 (1977) (plurality opinion), and it has sometimes led the Court to usurp authority that the Constitution entrusts to the people's elected representatives. See *Regents of Univ. of Mich. v. Ewing*, 474 U.S. 214, 225–226 (1985). As the Court cautioned in *Glucksberg*, "[w]e must . . . exercise the utmost care whenever we are asked to break new ground in this field, lest the liberty protected by the Due Process Clause be subtly transformed into the policy preferences of the Members of this Court." 521 U.S., at 720 (internal quotation marks and citation omitted).

On occasion, when the Court has ignored the "[a]ppropriate limits" imposed by "'respect for the teachings of history,'" *Moore,* 431 U.S., at 503 (plurality opinion), it has fallen into the freewheeling judicial policymaking that characterized discredited decisions such as *Lochner v. New York*, 198 U.S. 45 (1905). The Court must not fall prey to such an unprincipled approach. Instead, guided by the history and tradition that map the essential components of our Nation's concept of ordered liberty, we must ask what the *Fourteenth Amendment* means by the term "liberty." When we engage in that inquiry in the present case, the clear answer is that the Fourteenth Amendment does not protect the right to an abortion.

Until the latter part of the 20th century, there was no support in American law for a constitutional right to obtain an abortion. No state constitutional provision had recognized such a right. Until a few years before *Roe* was handed down, no federal or state court had recognized such a right. Nor had any scholarly treatise of which we are aware. And although law review articles are not reticent about advocating new rights, the earliest article proposing a constitutional right to abortion that has come to our attention was published only a few years before *Roe*.

Not only was there no support for such a constitutional right until shortly before *Roe*, but abortion had long been a *crime* in every single State. At common law, abortion was criminal in at least some stages of pregnancy and was regarded as unlawful and could have very serious consequences at all stages. American law followed the common law until a wave of statutory restrictions in the 1800s expanded criminal liability for abortions. By the time of the adoption of the Fourteenth Amendment, three-quarters of the States had made abortion a crime at any stage of pregnancy, and the remaining States would soon follow.

Roe either ignored or misstated this history, and *Casey* declined to reconsider *Roe's* faulty historical analysis. It is therefore important to set the record straight.

We begin with the common law, under which abortion was a crime at least after "quickening" — *i.e.*, the first felt movement of the fetus in the womb, which usually occurs between the 16th and 18th week of pregnancy.

The "eminent common-law authorities (Blackstone, Coke, Hale, and the like)," *Kahler v. Kansas*, 589 U.S. ___, ___ (2020) (slip op., at 7), *all* describe abortion after quickening as criminal.

In this country during the 19th century, the vast majority of the States enacted statutes criminalizing abortion at all stages of pregnancy. By 1868, the year when the Fourteenth Amendment was ratified, three-quarters of the States, 28 out of 37, had enacted statutes making abortion a crime even if it was performed before quickening. Of the nine States that had not yet criminalized abortion at all stages, all but one did so by 1910.

The inescapable conclusion is that a right to abortion is not deeply rooted in the Nation's history and traditions. On the contrary, an unbroken tradition of prohibiting abortion on pain of criminal punishment persisted from the earliest days of the common law until 1973.

Neither respondents nor the Solicitor General disputes the fact that by 1868 the vast majority of States criminalized abortion at all stages of pregnancy. Instead, respondents are forced to argue that it "does [not] matter that some States prohibited abortion at the time *Roe* was decided or when the Fourteenth Amendment was adopted." Brief for Respondents 21. But that argument flies in the face of the standard we have applied in determining whether an asserted right that is nowhere mentioned in the Constitution is nevertheless protected by the Fourteenth Amendment.

The Solicitor General next suggests that history supports an abortion right because the common law's failure to criminalize abortion before quickening means that "at the Founding and for decades thereafter, women generally could terminate a pregnancy, at least in its early stages." But the insistence on quickening was not universal, see *Mills* [*v. Commonwealth*, 13 Pa. 631 (1850),] at 633; *State v. Slagle*, 83 N.C. 630, 632 (1880), and regardless, the fact that many States in the late 18th and early 19th century did not criminalize pre-quickening abortions does not mean that anyone thought the States lacked the authority to do so. When legislatures began to exercise that authority as the century wore on, no one, as far as we are aware, argued that the laws they enacted violated a fundamental right. That is not surprising since common-law authorities had repeatedly condemned abortion and described it as an "unlawful" act without regard to whether it occurred before or after quickening.

Another *amicus* brief relied upon by respondents (see Brief for Respondents 21) tries to dismiss the significance of the state criminal statutes that were in effect when the Fourteenth Amendment was adopted by suggesting that they were enacted for illegitimate reasons. According to this account, which is based almost entirely on statements made by one prominent proponent of the statutes, important motives for the laws were the fear that Catholic immigrants were having more babies than Protestants and that the availability of abortion was leading White Protestant women to "shir[k their] maternal duties." Brief for American Historical Association et al. as *Amici Curiae* 20.

Resort to this argument is a testament to the lack of any real historical support for the right that *Roe* and *Casey* recognized. This Court has long disfavored arguments based on alleged legislative motives. See, *e.g., Erie v. Pap's A.M.*, 529 U.S. 277, 292 (2000) (plurality opinion); *Turner Broadcasting System, Inc. v. FCC*, 512 U.S. 622, 652 (1994); *United States v. O'Brien*, 391 U.S. 367, 383 (1968); *Arizona v. California*, 283 U.S. 423, 455 (1931) (collecting cases). The Court has recognized that inquiries into legislative motives "are a hazardous matter." *O'Brien*, 391 U.S., at 383. Even when an argument about legislative motive is backed by statements made by legislators who voted for a law, we have been reluctant to attribute those motives to the legislative body as a whole. "What motivates one legislator to make a speech about a statute is not necessarily what motivates scores of others to enact it." *Id.,* at 384.

Instead of seriously pressing the argument that the abortion right itself has deep roots, supporters of *Roe* and *Casey* contend that the abortion right is an integral part of a broader entrenched right. *Roe* termed this a right to privacy, and *Casey* described it as the freedom to make "intimate and personal choices" that are "central to personal dignity and autonomy." *Casey* elaborated: "At the heart of liberty is the right to define one's own concept of existence, of meaning, of the universe, and of the mystery of human life."

The Court did not claim that this broadly framed right is absolute, and no such claim would be plausible. While individuals are certainly free *to think* and *to say* what they wish about "existence," "meaning," the "universe," and "the mystery of human life," they are not always free *to act* in accordance with those thoughts. License to act on the basis of such beliefs may correspond to one of the many under standings of "liberty," but it is certainly not "ordered liberty."

Ordered liberty sets limits and defines the boundary between competing interests. *Roe* and *Casey* each struck a particular balance between the interests of a woman who wants an abortion and the interests of what they termed "potential life." But the people of the various States may evaluate those interests differently. In some States, voters may believe that the abortion right should be even more extensive than the right that *Roe* and *Casey* recognized. Voters in other States may wish to impose tight restrictions based on their belief that abortion destroys an "unborn human being." Miss. Code Ann. § 41-41-191(4)(b). Our Nation's historical understanding of ordered liberty does not prevent the people's elected representatives from deciding how abortion should be regulated.

Nor does the right to obtain an abortion have a sound basis in precedent. *Casey* relied on cases involving the right to marry a person of a different race, *Loving v. Virginia*, 388 U.S. 1 (1967); the right to marry while in prison, *Turner v. Safley*, 482 U.S. 78 (1987); the right to obtain contraceptives, *Griswold v. Connecticut*, 381 U.S. 479 (1965), *Eisenstadt v. Baird*, 405 U.S. 438 (1972), *Carey v. Population Services Int'l*, 431 U.S. 678 (1977); the right to reside with relatives, *Moore v. East Cleveland*, 431 U.S. 494 (1977); the right to make decisions about the education of one's children, *Pierce v. Society of Sisters*, 268 U.S. 510 (1925), *Meyer v. Nebraska*, 262 U.S. 390 (1923); the right not to be sterilized without consent, *Skinner v. Oklahoma ex rel. Williamson*, 316 U.S. 535 (1942); and the right in certain circumstances not to undergo involuntary surgery, forced administration of drugs, or other substantially similar procedures, *Winston v. Lee*, 470 U.S. 753 (1985), *Washington v. Harper*, 494 U.S. 210 (1990), *Rochin v. California*, 342 U.S. 165 (1952). Respondents and the Solicitor General also rely on post-*Casey* decisions like *Lawrence v. Texas*, 539 U.S. 558 (2003) (right to engage in private, consensual sexual acts), and *Obergefell v. Hodges*, 576 U.S. 644 (2015) (right to marry a person of the same sex).

What sharply distinguishes the abortion right from the rights recognized in the cases on which *Roe* and *Casey* rely is something that both those decisions acknowledged: Abortion destroys what those decisions call "potential life" and what the law at issue in this case regards as the life of an "unborn human being." See *Roe*, 410

U.S., at 159 (abortion is "inherently different"); *Casey*, 505 U.S., at 852 (abortion is "a unique act"). None of the other decisions cited by *Roe* and *Casey* involved the critical moral question posed by abortion. They are therefore inapposite. They do not support the right to obtain an abortion, and by the same token, our conclusion that the Constitution does not confer such a right does not undermine them in any way.

In drawing this critical distinction between the abortion right and other rights, it is not necessary to dispute *Casey*'s claim (which we accept for the sake of argument) that "the specific practices of States at the time of the adoption of the Fourteenth Amendment" do not "mar[k] the outer limits of the substantive sphere of liberty which the Fourteenth Amendment protects." 505 U.S., at 848. Abortion is nothing new. It has been addressed by lawmakers for centuries, and the fundamental moral question that it poses is ageless.

Defenders of *Roe* and *Casey* do not claim that any new scientific learning calls for a different answer to the underlying moral question, but they do contend that changes in society require the recognition of a constitutional right to obtain an abortion. Without the availability of abortion, they maintain, people will be inhibited from exercising their freedom to choose the types of relationships they desire, and women will be unable to compete with men in the workplace and in other endeavors.

Americans who believe that abortion should be restricted press countervailing arguments about modern developments. They note that attitudes about the pregnancy of unmarried women have changed drastically; that federal and state laws ban discrimination on the basis of pregnancy; that leave for pregnancy and childbirth are now guaranteed by law in many cases; that the costs of medical care associated with pregnancy are covered by insurance or government assistance; that States have increasingly adopted "safe haven" laws, which generally allow women to drop off babies anonymously; and that a woman who puts her newborn up for adoption today has little reason to fear that the baby will not find a suitable home. They also claim that many people now have a new appreciation of fetal life and that when prospective parents who want to have a child view a sonogram, they typically have no doubt that what they see is their daughter or son.

Both sides make important policy arguments, but supporters of *Roe* and *Casey* must show that this Court has the authority to weigh those arguments and decide how abortion may be regulated in the States. They have failed to make that showing, and we thus return the power to weigh those arguments to the people and their elected representatives.

[T]he dissent is forced to rely solely on the fact that a constitutional right to abortion was recognized in *Roe* and later decisions that accepted *Roe*'s interpretation. Under the doctrine of *stare decisis*, those precedents are entitled to careful and respectful consideration, and we engage in that analysis below. But as the Court has reiterated time and time again, adherence to precedent is not "'an inexorable command.'" There are occasions when past decisions should be overruled, and as we will explain, this is one of them.

Stare decisis plays an important role in our case law, and we have explained that it serves many valuable ends. It protects the interests of those who have taken action in reliance on a past decision. It "reduces incentives for challenging settled precedents, saving parties and courts the expense of endless relitigation." It fosters "evenhanded" decisionmaking by requiring that like cases be decided in a like manner. It "contributes to the actual and perceived integrity of the judicial process." And it restrains judicial hubris and reminds us to respect the judgment of those who have grappled with important questions in the past. "Precedent is a way of accumulating and passing down the learning of past generations, a font of established wisdom richer than what can be found in any single judge or panel of judges."

We have long recognized, however, that *stare decisis* is "not an inexorable command," and it "is at its weakest when we interpret the Constitution." [W]hen it comes to the interpretation of the Constitution — the "great charter of our liberties," which was meant "to endure through a long lapse of ages," *Martin v. Hunter's Lessee,* 1 Wheat. 304, 326 (1816) (opinion for the Court by Story, J.) — we place a high value on having the matter "settled right." In addition, when one of our constitutional decisions goes astray, the country is usually stuck with the bad decision unless we correct our own mistake. An erroneous constitutional decision can be fixed by amending the Constitution, but our Constitution is notoriously hard to amend. Therefore, in appropriate circumstances we must be willing to reconsider and, if necessary, overrule constitutional decisions.

Some of our most important constitutional decisions have overruled prior precedents.

In this case, five factors weigh strongly in favor of overruling *Roe* and *Casey*: the nature of their error, the quality of their reasoning, the "workability" of the rules they imposed on the country, their disruptive effect on other areas of the law, and the absence of concrete reliance.

The nature of the Court's error. An erroneous interpretation of the Constitution is always important, but some are more damaging than others.

The infamous decision in *Plessy v. Ferguson,* was one such decision. It betrayed our commitment to "equality before the law."

Roe was also egregiously wrong and deeply damaging. For reasons already explained, *Roe*'s constitutional analysis was far outside the bounds of any reasonable interpretation of the various constitutional provisions to which it vaguely pointed.

Roe was on a collision course with the Constitution from the day it was decided, *Casey* perpetuated its errors, and those errors do not concern some arcane corner of the law of little importance to the American people.

The quality of the reasoning. Under our precedents, the quality of the reasoning in a prior case has an important bearing on whether it should be reconsidered. [W]e explained why *Roe* was incorrectly decided, but that decision was more than just wrong. It stood on exceptionally weak grounds.

Roe found that the Constitution implicitly conferred a right to obtain an abortion, but it failed to ground its decision in text, history, or precedent. It relied on an erroneous historical narrative; it devoted great attention to and presumably relied on matters that have no bearing on the meaning of the Constitution; it disregarded the fundamental difference between the precedents on which it relied and the question before the Court; it concocted an elaborate set of rules, with different restrictions for each trimester of pregnancy, but it did not explain how this veritable code could be teased out of anything in the Constitution, the history of abortion laws, prior precedent, or any other cited source; and its most important rule (that States cannot protect fetal life prior to "viability") was never raised by any party and has never been plausibly explained. *Roe*'s reasoning quickly drew scathing scholarly criticism, even from supporters of broad access to abortion.

Workability. Our precedents counsel that another important consideration in deciding whether a precedent should be overruled is whether the rule it imposes is workable — that is, whether it can be understood and applied in a consistent and predictable manner. *Casey*'s "undue burden" test has scored poorly on the workability scale.

Effect on other areas of law. Roe and *Casey* have led to the distortion of many important but unrelated legal doctrines, and that effect provides further support for overruling those decisions.

The Court's abortion cases have diluted the strict standard for facial constitutional challenges. They have ignored the Court's third-party standing doctrine. They have disregarded standard *res judicata* principles. They have flouted the ordinary rules on the severability of unconstitutional provisions, as well as the rule that statutes should be read where possible to avoid unconstitutionality. And they have distorted First Amendment doctrines.

Reliance interests. We last consider whether overruling *Roe* and *Casey* will upend substantial reliance interests.

[T]he controlling opinion in *Casey* perceived a more intangible form of reliance. It wrote that "people [had] organized intimate relationships and made choices that define their views of themselves and their places in society . . . in reliance on the availability of abortion in the event that contraception should fail" and that "[t]he ability of women to participate equally in the economic and social life of the Nation has been facilitated by their ability to control their reproductive lives." But this Court is ill-equipped to assess "generalized assertions about the national psyche."

When a concrete reliance interest is asserted, courts are equipped to evaluate the claim, but assessing the novel and intangible form of reliance endorsed by the *Casey* plurality is another matter. That form of reliance depends on an empirical question that is hard for anyone — and in particular, for a court — to assess, namely, the effect of the abortion right on society and in particular on the lives of women.

Our decision returns the issue of abortion to those legislative bodies, and it allows women on both sides of the abortion issue to seek to affect the legislative process by influencing public opinion, lobbying legislators, voting, and running for office. Women are not without electoral or political power.

Having shown that traditional *stare decisis* factors do not weigh in favor of retaining *Roe* or *Casey*, we must address one final argument that featured prominently in the *Casey* plurality opinion.

The argument was cast in different terms, but stated simply, it was essentially as follows. The American people's belief in the rule of law would be shaken if they lost respect for this Court as an institution that decides important cases based on principle, not "social and political pressures." There is a special danger that the public will perceive a decision as having been made for unprincipled reasons when the Court overrules a controversial "watershed" decision, such as *Roe*. A decision overruling *Roe* would be perceived as having been made "under fire" and as a "surrender to political pressure," and therefore the preservation of public approval of the Court weighs heavily in favor of retaining *Roe*.

[W]e cannot allow our decisions to be affected by any extraneous influences such as concern about the public's reaction to our work.

We do not pretend to know how our political system or society will respond to today's decision overruling *Roe* and *Casey*. And even if we could foresee what will happen, we would have no authority to let that knowledge influence our decision. We can only do our job, which is to interpret the law, apply longstanding principles of *stare decisis*, and decide this case accordingly.

We therefore hold that the Constitution does not confer a right to abortion. *Roe* and *Casey* must be overruled, and the authority to regulate abortion must be returned to the people and their elected representatives.

We must now decide what standard will govern if state abortion regulations undergo constitutional challenge and whether the law before us satisfies the appropriate standard.

Under our precedents, rational-basis review is the appropriate standard for such challenges. As we have explained, procuring an abortion is not a fundamental constitutional right because such a right has no basis in the Constitution's text or in our Nation's history.

It follows that the States may regulate abortion for legitimate reasons, and when such regulations are challenged under the Constitution, courts cannot "substitute their social and economic beliefs for the judgment of legislative bodies."

A law regulating abortion, like other health and welfare laws, is entitled to a "strong presumption of validity." It must be sustained if there is a rational basis on which the legislature could have thought that it would serve legitimate state interests. These legitimate interests include respect for and preservation of prenatal life at all stages of development; the protection of maternal health and safety; the elimination of particularly gruesome or barbaric medical procedures; the preservation of the integrity of the medical profession; the mitigation of fetal pain; and the prevention of discrimination on the basis of race, sex, or disability.

We end this opinion where we began. Abortion presents a profound moral question. The Constitution does not prohibit the citizens of each State from regulating or prohibiting abortion. *Roe* and *Casey* arrogated that authority. We now overrule those decisions and return that authority to the people and their elected representatives.

The judgment of the Fifth Circuit is reversed, and the case is remanded for further proceedings consistent with this opinion.

It is so ordered.

JUSTICE THOMAS, concurring.

I write separately to emphasize a second, more fundamental reason why there is no abortion guarantee lurking in the Due Process Clause. [T]he Due Process Clause at most guarantees *process*. It does not, as the Court's substantive due process cases suppose, "forbi[d] the government to infringe certain 'fundamental' liberty interests *at all*, no matter what process is provided."

For that reason, in future cases, we should reconsider all of this Court's substantive due process precedents, including *Griswold*, *Lawrence*, and *Obergefell*.

Because the Court properly applies our substantive due process precedents to reject the fabrication of a constitutional right to abortion, and because this case does not present the opportunity to reject substantive due process entirely, I join the Court's opinion. But, in future cases, we should "follow the text of the Constitution, which sets forth certain substantive rights that cannot be taken away, and adds, beyond that, a right to due process when life, liberty, or property is to be taken away." Substantive due process conflicts with that textual command and has harmed our country in many ways. Accordingly, we should eliminate it from our jurisprudence at the earliest opportunity.

JUSTICE KAVANAUGH, concurring.

Some *amicus* briefs argue that the Court today should not only overrule *Roe* and return to a position of judicial neutrality on abortion but should go further and hold that the Constitution *outlaws* abortion throughout the United States. No Justice of this Court has ever advanced that position. I respect those who advocate for that position, just as I respect those who argue that this Court should hold that the Constitution legalizes pre-viability abortion throughout the United States. But both positions are wrong as a constitutional matter, in my view. The Constitution neither outlaws abortion nor legalizes abortion.

To be clear, then, the Court's decision today *does not outlaw* abortion throughout the United States. On the contrary, the Court's decision properly leaves the question of abortion for the people and their elected representatives in the democratic process.

The Constitution does not grant the nine unelected Members of this Court the unilateral authority to rewrite the Constitution to create new rights and liberties based on our own moral or policy views. This Court therefore does not possess the authority either to declare a constitutional right to abortion *or* to declare a constitutional prohibition of abortion. See *Casey*, 505 U.S., at 953 (Rehnquist, C.J., concurring in judgment in part and dissenting in part); *id.*, at 980 (opinion of Scalia, J.); *Roe v. Wade*, 410 U.S. 113, 177 (1973) (Rehnquist, J., dissenting); *Doe v. Bolton*, 410 U.S. 179, 222 (1973) (White, J., dissenting).

In sum, the Constitution is neutral on the issue of abortion and allows the people and their elected representatives to address the issue through the democratic process. In my respectful view, the Court in *Roe* therefore erred by taking sides on the issue of abortion.

After today's decision, the nine Members of this Court will no longer decide the basic legality of pre-viability abortion for all 330 million Americans. That issue will be resolved by the people and their representatives in the democratic process in the States or Congress. But the parties' arguments have raised other related questions, and I address some of them here.

First is the question of how this decision will affect other precedents involving issues such as contraception and marriage — in particular, the decisions in *Griswold v. Connecticut*, 381 U.S. 479 (1965); *Eisenstadt v. Baird*, 405 U.S. 438 (1972); *Loving v. Virginia*, 388 U.S. 1 (1967); and *Obergefell v. Hodges*, 576 U.S. 644 (2015). I emphasize what the Court today states: Overruling *Roe* does *not* mean the overruling of those precedents, and does *not* threaten or cast doubt on those precedents.

Second, as I see it, some of the other abortion-related legal questions raised by today's decision are not especially difficult as a constitutional matter. For example, may a State bar a resident of that State from traveling to another State to obtain an abortion? In my view, the answer is no based on the constitutional right to interstate travel. May a State retroactively impose liability or punishment for an abortion that occurred before today's decision takes effect? In my view, the answer is no based on the Due Process Clause or the *Ex Post Facto* Clause.

CHIEF JUSTICE ROBERTS, concurring in the judgment.

I would take a more measured course. I agree with the Court that the viability line established by *Roe* and *Casey* should be discarded under a straightforward *stare decisis* analysis. That line never made any sense. Our abortion precedents describe the right at issue as a woman's right to choose to terminate her pregnancy. That right should therefore extend far enough to ensure a reasonable opportunity to choose, but need not extend any further — certainly not all the way to viability. Mississippi's law allows a woman three months to obtain an abortion, well beyond the point at which it is considered "late" to discover a pregnancy.

But that is all I would say, out of adherence to a simple yet fundamental principle of judicial restraint: If it is not necessary to decide more to dispose of a case, then it is necessary *not* to decide more. Perhaps we are not always perfect in following that command, and certainly there are cases that warrant an exception. But this is not one of them. Surely we should adhere closely to principles of judicial restraint here, where the broader path the Court chooses entails repudiating a constitutional right we have not only previously recognized, but also expressly reaffirmed applying the doctrine of *stare decisis*. The Court's opinion is thoughtful and thorough, but those virtues cannot compensate for the fact that its dramatic and consequential ruling is unnecessary to decide the case before us.

JUSTICE BREYER, JUSTICE SOTOMAYOR, and JUSTICE KAGAN, dissenting.

For half a century, *Roe v. Wade*, 410 U.S. 113 (1973), and *Planned Parenthood of Southeastern Pa. v. Casey*, 505 U.S. 833 (1992), have protected the liberty and equality of women. *Roe* held, and *Casey* reaffirmed, that the Constitution safeguards a woman's right to decide for herself whether to bear a child. *Roe* held, and *Casey* reaffirmed, that in the first stages of pregnancy, the government could not make that choice for women. The government could not control a woman's body or the course of a woman's life: It could not determine what the woman's future would be. See *Casey*, 505 U.S., at 853; *Gonzales v. Carhart*, 550 U.S. 124, 171–172 (2007) (Ginsburg, J., dissenting). Respecting a woman as an autonomous being, and granting her full equality, meant giving her substantial choice over this most personal and most consequential of all life decisions.

Roe and *Casey* well understood the difficulty and divisiveness of the abortion issue. The Court knew that Americans hold profoundly different views about the "moral[ity]" of "terminating a pregnancy, even in its earliest stage." *Casey*, 505 U.S., at 850. And the Court recognized that "the State has legitimate interests from the outset of the pregnancy in protecting" the "life of the fetus that may become a child." *Id.*, at 846. So the Court struck a balance, as it often does when values and goals compete. It held that the State could prohibit abortions after fetal viability, so long as the ban contained exceptions to safeguard a woman's life or health. It held that even before viability, the State could regulate the abortion procedure in multiple and meaningful ways. But until the viability line was crossed, the Court held, a State could not impose a "substantial obstacle" on a woman's "right to elect the procedure" as she (not the government) thought proper, in light of all the circumstances and complexities of her own life. *Ibid.*

Today, the Court discards that balance. It says that from the very moment of fertilization, a woman has no rights to speak of. A State can force her to bring a pregnancy to term, even at the steepest personal and familial costs. An abortion restriction, the majority holds, is permissible whenever rational, the lowest level of scrutiny known to the law. And because, as the Court has often stated, protecting fetal life is rational, States will feel free to enact all manner of restrictions. The Mississippi law at issue here bars abortions after the 15th week of pregnancy. Under the majority's ruling, though, another State's law could do so after ten weeks, or five or three or one—or, again, from the moment of fertilization. States have already passed such laws, in anticipation of today's ruling. More will follow. Some States have enacted laws extending to all forms of abortion procedure, including taking medication in one's own home. They have passed laws without any exceptions for when the woman is the victim of rape or incest. Under those laws, a woman will have to bear her rapist's child or a young girl her father's—no matter if doing so will destroy her life. So too, after today's ruling, some States may compel women to carry to term a fetus with severe physical anomalies—for example, one afflicted with Tay-Sachs disease, sure to die within a few years of birth. States may even argue that a prohibition on abortion need make no provision for protecting a woman from risk of death or physical harm. Across a vast array of circumstances, a State will be able to impose its moral choice on a woman and coerce her to give birth to a child.

Whatever the exact scope of the coming laws, one result of today's decision is certain: the curtailment of women's rights, and of their status as free and equal citizens.

And no one should be confident that this majority is done with its work. The right *Roe* and *Casey* recognized does not stand alone. To the contrary, the Court has linked it for decades to other settled freedoms involving bodily integrity, familial relationships, and procreation. Most obviously, the right to terminate a pregnancy arose straight out of the right to purchase and use contraception. See *Griswold v. Connecticut*, 381 U.S. 479 (1965); *Eisenstadt v. Baird*, 405 U.S. 438 (1972). In turn, those rights led, more recently, to rights of same-sex intimacy and marriage. See *Lawrence v. Texas*, 539 U.S. 558 (2003); *Obergefell v. Hodges*, 576 U.S. 644 (2015). They are all part of the same constitutional fabric, protecting autonomous decisionmaking over the most personal of life decisions. The majority (or to be more accurate, most of it) is eager to tell us today that nothing it does "cast[s] doubt on precedents that do not concern abortion (Thomas, J., concurring) (advocating the overruling of *Griswold*, *Lawrence*, and *Obergefell*). But how could that be? The lone rationale for what the majority does today is that the right to elect an abortion is not "deeply rooted in history": Not until *Roe*, the majority argues, did people think abortion fell within the Constitution's guarantee of liberty. The same could be said, though, of most of the rights the majority claims it is not tampering with.

Stare decisis is the Latin phrase for a foundation stone of the rule of law: that things decided should stay decided unless there is a very good reason for change. It is a doctrine of judicial modesty and humility. Those qualities are not evident in today's opinion. The majority has no good reason for the upheaval in law and society it sets off. *Roe* and *Casey* have been the law of the land for decades, shaping women's expectations of their choices when an unplanned pregnancy occurs. Women have relied on the availability of abortion both in structuring their relationships and in planning their lives. The legal framework *Roe* and *Casey* developed to balance the competing interests in this sphere has proved workable in courts across the country.

No recent developments, in either law or fact, have eroded or cast doubt on those precedents. Nothing, in short, has changed. Indeed, the Court in *Casey* already found all of that to be true. *Casey* is a precedent about precedent. It reviewed the same arguments made here in support of overruling *Roe*, and it found that doing so was not warranted. The Court reverses course today for one reason and one reason only: because the composition of this Court has changed. *Stare decisis*, this Court has often said, "contributes to the actual and perceived integrity of the judicial process" by ensuring that decisions are "founded in the law rather than in the proclivities of individuals." Today, the proclivities of individuals rule. The Court departs from its obligation to faithfully and impartially apply the law. We dissent.

The majority makes this change based on a single question: Did the reproductive right recognized in *Roe* and *Casey* exist in "1868, the year when the Fourteenth Amendment was ratified"? The majority says (and with this much we agree) that the answer to this question is no: In 1868, there was no nationwide right to end a pregnancy, and no thought that the Fourteenth Amendment provided one.

The majority's core legal postulate, then, is that we in the 21st century must read the Fourteenth Amendment just as its ratifiers did. And that is indeed what the majority emphasizes over and over again. See *ante*, at 47 ("[T]he most important historical fact [is] how the States regulated abortion when the Fourteenth Amendment was adopted"); see also *ante*, at 5, 16, and n. 24, 23, 25, 28. If the ratifiers did not understand something as central to freedom, then neither can we. Or said more particularly: If those people did not understand reproductive rights as part of the guarantee of liberty conferred in the Fourteenth Amendment, then those rights do not exist.

As an initial matter, note a mistake in the just preceding sentence. We referred there to the "people" who ratified the Fourteenth Amendment: What rights did those "people" have in their heads at the time? But, of course, "people" did not ratify the Fourteenth Amendment. Men did. So it is perhaps not so surprising that the ratifiers were not perfectly attuned to the importance of reproductive rights for women's liberty, or for their capacity to participate as equal members of our Nation. Those responsible for the original Constitution, including the Fourteenth Amendment, did not perceive women as equals, and did not recognize women's rights. When the majority says that we must read our foundational charter as viewed at the time of ratification (except that we may also check it against the Dark Ages), it consigns women to second-class citizenship.

[T]his Court has rejected the majority's pinched view of how to read our Constitution. "The Founders," we recently wrote, "knew they were writing a document designed to apply to ever-changing circumstances over centuries." *NLRB v. Noel Canning*, 573 U.S. 513, 533–534 (2014). Or in the words of the great Chief Justice John Marshall, our Constitution is "intended to endure for ages to come," and must adapt itself to a future "seen dimly," if at all. *McCulloch v. Maryland*, 4 Wheat. 316, 415 (1819). That is indeed why our Constitution is written as it is. The Framers (both in

1788 and 1868) understood that the world changes. So they did not define rights by reference to the specific practices existing at the time. Instead, the Framers defined rights in general terms, to permit future evolution in their scope and meaning. And over the course of our history, this Court has taken up the Framers' invitation. It has kept true to the Framers' principles by applying them in new ways, responsive to new societal understandings and conditions.

That does not mean anything goes. The majority wishes people to think there are but two alternatives: (1) accept the original applications of the Fourteenth Amendment and no others, or (2) surrender to judges' "own ardent views," ungrounded in law, about the "liberty that Americans should enjoy." [A]pplications of liberty and equality can evolve while remaining grounded in constitutional principles, constitutional history, and constitutional precedents. The second Justice Harlan discussed how to strike the right balance when he explained why he would have invalidated a State's ban on contraceptive use. Judges, he said, are not "free to roam where unguided speculation might take them." *Poe v. Ullman*, 367 U.S. 497, 542 (1961) (dissenting opinion). Yet they also must recognize that the constitutional "tradition" of this country is not captured whole at a single moment. *Ibid.* Rather, its meaning gains content from the long sweep of our history and from successive judicial precedents — each looking to the last and each seeking to apply the Constitution's most fundamental commitments to new conditions. That is why Americans, to go back to *Obergefell*'s example, have a right to marry across racial lines. And it is why, to go back to Justice Harlan's case, Americans have a right to use contraceptives so they can choose for themselves whether to have children.

[T]he Court has "vindicated [the] principle" over and over that (no matter the sentiment in 1868) "there is a realm of personal liberty which the government may not enter" — especially relating to "bodily integrity" and "family life." In reviewing decades and decades of constitutional law, *Casey* could draw but one conclusion: Whatever was true in 1868, "[i]t is settled now, as it was when the Court heard arguments in *Roe v. Wade*, that the Constitution places limits on a State's right to interfere with a person's most basic decisions about family and parenthood."

The Court's precedents about bodily autonomy, sexual and familial relations, and procreation are all interwoven — all part of the fabric of our constitutional law, and because that is so, of our lives. Especially women's lives, where they safeguard a right to self-determination.

Roe and *Casey* fit neatly into a long line of decisions protecting from government intrusion a wealth of private choices about family matters, child rearing, intimate relationships, and procreation. Those cases safeguard particular choices about whom to marry; whom to have sex with; what family members to live with; how to raise children — and crucially, whether and when to have children. In varied cases, the Court explained that those choices — "the most intimate and personal" a person can make — reflect fundamental aspects of personal identity; they define the very "attributes of personhood." And they inevitably shape the nature and future course of a person's life (and often the lives of those closest to her). So, the Court held, those choices belong to the individual, and not the government. That is the essence of what liberty requires.

And liberty may require it, this Court has repeatedly said, even when those living in 1868 would not have recognized the claim — because they would not have seen the person making it as a full-fledged member of the community. Throughout our history, the sphere of protected liberty has expanded, bringing in individuals formerly excluded. In that way, the constitutional values of liberty and equality go hand in hand; they do not inhabit the hermetically sealed containers the majority portrays.

Faced with all these connections between *Roe/Casey* and judicial decisions recognizing other constitutional rights, the majority tells everyone not to worry. It can (so it says) neatly extract the right to choose from the constitutional edifice without affecting any associated rights.

[T]he assurance in today's opinion does not work. Or at least that is so if the majority is serious about its sole reason for overturning *Roe* and *Casey*: the legal status of abortion in the 19th century. According to the majority, no liberty interest is present — because (and only because) the law offered no protection to the woman's choice in the 19th century. But here is the rub. The law also did not then (and would not for ages) protect a wealth of other things. It did not protect the rights recognized in *Lawrence* and *Obergefell* to same-sex intimacy and marriage. It did not protect the right recognized in *Loving* to marry across racial lines. It did not protect the right recognized in *Griswold* to contraceptive use. For that matter, it did not protect the right recognized in *Skinner v. Oklahoma ex rel. Williamson*, 316 U.S. 535 (1942), not to be sterilized without consent. So if the majority is right in its legal analysis, all those decisions were wrong, and all those matters properly belong to the States too — whatever the particular state interests involved. And if that is true, it is impossible to understand (as a matter of logic and principle) how the majority can say that its opinion today does not threaten — does not even "undermine" — any number of other constitutional rights.

Anyway, today's decision, taken on its own, is catastrophic enough. As a matter of constitutional method, the majority's commitment to replicate in 2022 every view about the meaning of liberty held in 1868 has precious little to recommend it. Our law in this constitutional sphere, as in most, has for decades upon decades proceeded differently. It has considered fundamental constitutional principles, the whole course of the Nation's history and traditions, and the step-by-step evolution of the Court's precedents. It is disciplined but not static. It relies on accumulated judgments, not just the sentiments of one long-ago generation of men (who themselves believed, and drafted the Constitution to reflect, that the world progresses). And by doing so, it includes those excluded from that olden conversation, rather than perpetuating its bounds.

By overruling *Roe*, *Casey*, and more than 20 cases reaffirming or applying the constitutional right to abortion, the majority abandons *stare decisis*, a principle central to the rule of law. The majority today lists some 30 of our cases as overruling precedent, and argues that they support overruling *Roe* and *Casey*. But none does. In some, the Court only partially modified or clarified a precedent. And in the rest, the Court relied on one or more of the traditional *stare decisis* factors in reaching its conclusion. The Court found, for example, (1) a change in legal doctrine that undermined or made obsolete the earlier decision; (2) a factual change that had the same effect; or (3) an absence of reliance because the earlier decision was less than a decade old. None of those factors apply here: Nothing — and in particular, no significant legal or factual change — supports overturning a half-century of settled law giving women control over their reproductive lives.

Contrary to the majority's view, there is nothing unworkable about *Casey*'s "undue burden" standard. Its primary focus on whether a State has placed a "substantial obstacle" on a woman seeking an abortion is "the sort of inquiry familiar to judges across a variety of contexts." And it has given rise to no more conflict in application than many standards this Court and others unhesitatingly apply every day.

In support of its holding, the majority invokes two watershed cases overruling prior constitutional precedents: *West Coast Hotel Co. v. Parrish* and *Brown v. Board of Education*. But those decisions, unlike today's, responded to changed law and to changed facts and attitudes that had taken hold throughout society.

Brown v. Board of Education overruled *Plessy v. Ferguson*, 163 U.S. 537 (1896), along with its doctrine of "separate but equal." By 1954, decades of Jim Crow had made clear what *Plessy*'s turn of phrase actually meant: "inherent[] [in]equal[ity]." Segregation was not, and could not ever be, consistent with the Reconstruction Amendments, ratified to give the former slaves full citizenship. Whatever might have been thought in *Plessy*'s time, the *Brown* Court explained, both experience and "modern authority" showed the "detrimental effect[s]" of state-sanctioned segregation: It "affect[ed] [children's] hearts and minds in a way unlikely ever to be undone." By that point, too, the law had begun to reflect that understanding. In a series of decisions, the Court had held unconstitutional public graduate schools' exclusion of black students. See, *e.g.*, *Sweatt v. Painter*, 339 U.S. 629 (1950); *Sipuel v. Board of Regents of Univ. of Okla.*, 332 U.S. 631 (1948) (*per curiam*); *Missouri ex rel. Gaines v. Canada*, 305 U.S. 337 (1938). The logic of those cases, *Brown* held, "appl[ied]" with added force to children in grade and high schools." Changed facts and changed law required *Plessy*'s end.

The reasons for retaining *Roe* and *Casey* gain further strength from the overwhelming reliance interests those decisions have created. Today the majority refuses to face the facts. "The most striking feature of the [majority] is the absence of any serious discussion" of how its ruling will affect women. By characterizing *Casey*'s reliance arguments as "generalized assertions about the national psyche," it reveals how little it knows or cares about women's lives or about the suffering its decision will cause.

The disruption of overturning *Roe* and *Casey* will be profound. Abortion is a common medical procedure and a familiar experience in women's lives. About 18 percent of pregnancies in this country end in abortion, and about one quarter of American women will have an abortion before the age of 45. Those numbers reflect the predictable and life-changing effects of carrying a pregnancy, giving birth, and becoming a parent. As *Casey* understood, people today rely on their ability to control and time pregnancies when making countless life decisions: where to live, whether and how to invest in education or careers, how to allocate financial resources, and how to approach intimate and family relationships. Women may count on abortion access for when contraception fails. They may count on abortion access for when contraception cannot be used, for example, if they were raped. They may count on abortion for when something changes in the midst of a pregnancy, whether it involves family or financial circumstances, unanticipated medical complications, or heartbreaking fetal diagnoses. Taking away the right to abortion, as the majority does today, destroys all those individual plans and expectations. In so doing, it diminishes women's opportunities to participate fully and equally in the Nation's political, social, and economic life.

That is especially so for women without money In States that bar abortion, women of means will still be able to travel to obtain the services they need.

"Power, not reason, is the new currency of this Court's decisionmaking." *Roe* has stood for fifty years. *Casey*, a precedent about precedent specifically confirming *Roe*, has stood for thirty. And the doctrine of *stare decisis* — a critical element of the rule of law — stands foursquare behind their continued existence. The right those decisions established and preserved is embedded in our constitutional law, both originating in and leading to other rights protecting bodily integrity, personal autonomy, and family relationships. The abortion right is also embedded in the lives of women — shaping their expectations, influencing their choices about relationships and work, supporting (as all reproductive rights do) their social and economic equality. Since the right's recognition (and affirmation), nothing has changed to support what the majority does today. Neither law nor facts nor attitudes have provided any new reasons to reach a different result than *Roe* and *Casey* did. All that has changed is this Court.

Now a new and bare majority of this Court — acting at practically the first moment possible — overrules *Roe* and *Casey*. It converts a series of dissenting opinions expressing antipathy toward *Roe* and *Casey* into a decision greenlighting even total abortion bans. It eliminates a 50-year-old constitutional right that safeguards women's freedom and equal station. It breaches a core rule-of-law principle, designed to promote constancy in the law. In doing all of that, it places in jeopardy other rights, from contraception to same-sex intimacy and marriage. And finally, it undermines the Court's legitimacy.

With sorrow — for this Court, but more, for the many millions of American women who have today lost a fundamental constitutional protection — we dissent.

Notes and Questions

(1) What, if anything changed in the 50 years since *Roe* to justify the Court's determination to overrule that decision?

(2) The *Dobbs'* majority relied heavily on the history of abortions, stating: "The inescapable conclusion is that a right to abortion is not deeply rooted in the Nation's history and traditions. On the contrary, an unbroken tradition of prohibiting abortion on pain of criminal punishment persisted from the earliest days of the common law until 1973." In contrast, the majority in *Roe* reviewed the history and found: "It is thus apparent that at common law, at the time of the adoption of our Constitution, and throughout the major portion of the 19th century, abortion was viewed with less disfavor than under most American statutes currently in effect. Phrasing it another way, a woman enjoyed a substantially broader right to terminate a pregnancy than she does in most States today."

How easy is it to discern the relevant history? How can you explain the different understandings of the relevant history?

(3) Even assuming that the historical evidence is clear, should it control the resolution of contemporary constitutional issues? Consider the fact that at the time of the ratification of the Fourteenth Amendment, many states mandated racially segregated schools and some did not allow blacks to attend any school. School segregation persisted in some states well into the 20th century. Does this history mean that the Court wrongly decided in *Brown v. Board of Education*, 347 U.S. 483 (1954), that a state violates the Fourteenth Amendment by mandating racially segregated schools?

(4) The majority opinion as well as Justice Kavanaugh's concurring opinion observe that the *Dobbs* decision does not cast doubt on such previous decisions such as *Griswold* and *Eisenstadt*. What is the basis for concluding that those decisions survive after *Dobbs*?

Problem A

Assume that following *Dobbs*, a Texas State legislator introduced a bill that would prevent sale or use of Plan B, an emergency contraceptive also known as the "morning-after pill," which is designed to prevent ovulation. The Food and Drug Administration says that the morning-after pill also could keep a fertilized zygote from implanting in the uterine lining, although the American College of Obstetricians and Gynecologists says this is unlikely. In promoting the bill, the legislator points to historical support for a ban on contraceptives. Indeed, he notes that the federal Comstock Act of 1873 prohibited the interstate transfer of contraceptive medicine, and many states adopted similar measures prohibiting the sale of contraceptives. He believes that based on *Dobbs* and the historical evidence, there is a strong argument that such a bill is constitutional and that the Court would overrule *Griswold*. Is he correct?

Obergefell v. Hodges
United States Supreme Court
135 S. Ct. 2584, 192 L. Ed. 2d 609 (2015)

JUSTICE KENNEDY delivered the opinion of the Court.

The Constitution promises liberty to all within its reach, a liberty that includes certain specific rights that allow persons, within a lawful realm, to define and express their identity. The petitioners in these cases seek to find that liberty by marrying someone of the same sex and having their marriages deemed lawful on the same terms and conditions as marriages between persons of the opposite sex. . . .

II

Before addressing the principles and precedents that govern these cases, it is appropriate to note the history of the subject now before the Court.

A

From their beginning to their most recent page, the annals of human history reveal the transcendent importance of marriage. The lifelong union of a man and a woman always has promised nobility and dignity to all persons, without regard to their station in life. Marriage is sacred to those who live by their religions and offers unique fulfillment to those who find meaning in the secular realm. Its dynamic allows two people to find a life that could not be found alone, for a marriage becomes greater than just the two persons. Rising from the most basic human needs, marriage is essential to our most profound hopes and aspirations.

The centrality of marriage to the human condition makes it unsurprising that the institution has existed for millennia and across civilizations. Since the dawn of history, marriage has transformed strangers into relatives, binding families and societies together. Confucius taught that marriage lies at the foundation of government. 2 Li Chi: Book of Rites 266 (C. Chai & W. Chai eds., J. Legge transl. 1967). This wisdom was echoed centuries later and half a world away by Cicero, who wrote, "The first bond of society is marriage; next, children; and then the family." See De Officiis 57 (W. Miller transl. 1913). There are untold references to the beauty of marriage in religious and philosophical texts spanning time, cultures, and faiths, as well as in art and literature in all their forms. It is fair and necessary to say these references were based on the understanding that marriage is a union between two persons of the opposite sex.

That history is the beginning of these cases. The respondents say it should be the end as well. To them, it would demean a timeless institution if the concept and lawful status of marriage were extended to two persons of the same sex. Marriage, in their view, is by its nature a gender-differentiated union of man and woman. This view long has been held — and continues to be held — in good faith by reasonable and sincere people here and throughout the world. The petitioners acknowledge this history but contend that these cases cannot end there. Were their intent to demean the revered idea and reality of marriage, the petitioners' claims would be of a different order. But that is neither their purpose nor their submission. To the contrary, it is the enduring importance of marriage that underlies the petitioners' contentions. This, they say, is their whole point. Far from seeking to devalue marriage, the petitioners seek it for themselves because of their respect — and need — for its privileges and responsibilities. And their immutable nature dictates that same-sex marriage is their only real path to this profound commitment.

Recounting the circumstances of three of these cases illustrates the urgency of the petitioners' cause from their perspective. Petitioner James Obergefell, a plaintiff in the Ohio case, met John Arthur over two decades ago. They fell in love and started a life together, establishing a lasting, committed relation. In 2011, however, Arthur was diagnosed with amyotrophic lateral sclerosis, or ALS. This debilitating disease is progressive, with no known cure. Two years ago, Obergefell and Arthur decided to commit to one another, resolving to marry before Arthur died. To fulfill their mutual promise, they traveled from Ohio to Maryland, where same-sex marriage was legal. It was difficult for Arthur to move, and so the couple were wed inside a medical transport plane as it remained on the tarmac in Baltimore. Three months later, Arthur died. Ohio law does not permit Obergefell to be listed as the surviving spouse on Arthur's death certificate. By statute, they must remain strangers even in death, a state-imposed separation Obergefell deems "hurtful for the rest of time." App. in No. 14–556 etc., p. 38. He brought suit to be shown as the surviving spouse on Arthur's death certificate.

April DeBoer and Jayne Rowse are co-plaintiffs in the case from Michigan. They celebrated a commitment ceremony to honor their permanent relation in 2007. They both work as nurses, DeBoer in a neonatal unit and Rowse in an emergency unit. In 2009, DeBoer and Rowse fostered and then adopted a baby boy. Later that same year, they welcomed another son into their family. The new baby, born prematurely and abandoned by his biological mother, required around-the-clock care. The next year, a baby girl with special needs joined their family. Michigan, however, permits only opposite-sex married couples or single individuals to adopt, so each child can have only one woman as his or her legal parent. If an emergency were to arise, schools and hospitals may treat the three children as if they had only one parent. And, were tragedy to befall either DeBoer or Rowse, the other would have no legal rights over the children she had not been permitted to adopt. This couple seeks relief from the continuing uncertainty their unmarried status creates in their lives.

Army Reserve Sergeant First Class Ijpe DeKoe and his partner Thomas Kostura, co-plaintiffs in the Tennessee case, fell in love. In 2011, DeKoe received orders to deploy to Afghanistan. Before leaving, he and Kostura married in New York. A week later, DeKoe began his deployment, which lasted for almost a year. When he returned, the two settled in Tennessee, where DeKoe works full-time for the Army Reserve. Their lawful marriage is stripped from them whenever they reside in Tennessee, returning and disappearing as they travel across state lines. DeKoe, who served this Nation to preserve the freedom the Constitution protects, must endure a substantial burden.

The cases now before the Court involve other petitioners as well, each with their own experiences. Their stories reveal that they seek not to denigrate marriage but rather to live their lives, or honor their spouses' memory, joined by its bond.

B

The ancient origins of marriage confirm its centrality, but it has not stood in isolation from developments in law and society. The history of marriage is one of both continuity and change. That institution — even as confined to opposite-sex relations — has evolved over time.

For example, marriage was once viewed as an arrangement by the couple's parents based on political, religious, and financial concerns; but by the time of the Nation's founding it was understood to be a voluntary contract between a man and a woman. See N. Cott, Public Vows: A History of Marriage and the Nation 9–17 (2000); S. Coontz, Marriage, A History 15–16 (2005). As the role and status of women changed, the institution further evolved. Under the centuries-old doctrine of coverture, a married man and woman were treated by the State as a single, male-dominated legal entity. See 1 W. Blackstone, Commentaries on the Laws of England 430 (1765). As women gained legal, political, and property rights, and as society began to understand that women have their own equal dignity, the law of coverture was abandoned. See Brief for Historians of Marriage et al. as Amici Curiae 16–19. These and other developments in the institution of marriage over the past centuries were not mere superficial changes. Rather, they worked deep transformations in its structure, affecting aspects of marriage long viewed by many as essential. See generally N. Cott, Public Vows; S. Coontz, Marriage; H. Hartog, Man & Wife in America: A History (2000).

These new insights have strengthened, not weakened, the institution of marriage. Indeed, changed understandings of marriage are characteristic of a Nation where new dimensions of freedom become apparent to new generations, often through perspectives that begin in pleas or protests and then are considered in the political sphere and the judicial process.

This dynamic can be seen in the Nation's experiences with the rights of gays and lesbians. Until the mid–20th century, same-sex intimacy long had been condemned as immoral by the state itself in most Western nations, a belief often embodied in the criminal law. For this reason, among others, many persons did not deem homosexuals to have dignity in their own distinct identity. A truthful declaration by same-sex couples of what was in their hearts had to remain unspoken. Even when a greater awareness of the humanity and integrity of homosexual persons came in the period after World War II, the argument that gays and lesbians had a just claim to dignity was in conflict with both law and widespread social conventions. Same-sex intimacy remained a crime in many States. Gays and lesbians were prohibited from most government employment, barred from military service, excluded under immigration laws, targeted by police, and burdened in their rights to associate. See Brief for Organization of American Historians as Amicus Curiae 5–28.

For much of the 20th century, moreover, homosexuality was treated as an illness. When the American Psychiatric Association published the first Diagnostic and Statistical Manual of Mental Disorders in 1952, homosexuality was classified as a mental disorder, a position adhered to until 1973. See *Position Statement on Homosexuality and Civil Rights, 1973*, in 131 Am. J. Psychiatry 497 (1974). Only in more recent years have psychiatrists and others recognized that sexual orientation is both a normal expression of human sexuality and immutable. See Brief for American Psychological Association et al. as Amici Curiae 7–17.

In the late 20th century, following substantial cultural and political developments, same-sex couples began to lead more open and public lives and to establish families. This development was followed by a quite extensive discussion of the issue in both governmental and private sectors and by a shift in public attitudes toward greater tolerance. As a result, questions about the rights of gays and lesbians soon reached the courts, where the issue could be discussed in the formal discourse of the law.

This Court first gave detailed consideration to the legal status of homosexuals in *Bowers v. Hardwick*, 478 U.S. 186 (1986). There it upheld the constitutionality of a Georgia law deemed to criminalize certain homosexual acts. Ten years later, in *Romer v. Evans*, 517 U.S. 620 (1996), the Court invalidated an amendment to Colorado's Constitution that sought to foreclose any branch or political subdivision of the State from protecting persons against discrimination based on sexual orientation. Then, in 2003, the Court overruled Bowers, holding that laws making same-sex intimacy a crime "demea[n] the lives of homosexual persons." *Lawrence v. Texas*, 539 U.S. 558 (2003).

Against this background, the legal question of same-sex marriage arose. . . .

After years of litigation, legislation, referenda, and the discussions that attended these public acts, the States are now divided on the issue of same-sex marriage. . . .

III

Under the Due Process Clause of the Fourteenth Amendment, no State shall "deprive any person of life, liberty, or property, without due process of law." The fundamental liberties protected by this Clause include most of the rights enumerated in the Bill of Rights. See *Duncan v. Louisiana*, 391 U.S. 145, 147–149 (1968). In addition these liberties extend to certain personal choices central to individual dignity and autonomy, including intimate choices that define personal identity and beliefs. . . .

The identification and protection of fundamental rights is an enduring part of the judicial duty to interpret the Constitution. . . . That process is guided by many of the same considerations relevant to analysis of other constitutional provisions that set forth broad principles rather than specific requirements. History and tradition guide and discipline this inquiry but do not set its outer boundaries. That method respects our history and learns from it without allowing the past alone to rule the present.

The nature of injustice is that we may not always see it in our own times. The generations that wrote and ratified the Bill of Rights and the Fourteenth Amendment did not presume to know the extent of freedom in all of its dimensions, and so they entrusted to future generations a charter protecting the right of all persons to enjoy liberty as we learn its meaning. When new insight reveals discord between the Constitution's central protections and a received legal stricture, a claim to liberty must be addressed.

Applying these established tenets, the Court has long held the right to marry is protected by the Constitution. In *Loving v. Virginia*, 388 U.S. 1, 12 (1967), which invalidated bans on interracial unions, a unanimous Court held marriage is "one of the vital personal rights essential to the orderly pursuit of happiness by free men." . . .

It cannot be denied that this Court's cases describing the right to marry presumed a relationship involving opposite-sex partners. The Court, like many institutions, has made assumptions defined by the world and time of which it is a part. This was evident in *Baker v. Nelson*, 409 U.S. 810 (1972), a one-line summary decision issued in 1972, holding the exclusion of same-sex couples from marriage did not present a substantial federal question.

Still, there are other, more instructive precedents. This Court's cases have expressed constitutional principles of broader reach. In defining the right to marry these cases have identified essential attributes of that right based in history, tradition, and other constitutional liberties inherent in this intimate bond. . . .

This analysis compels the conclusion that same-sex couples may exercise the right to marry. The four principles and traditions to be discussed demonstrate that the reasons marriage is fundamental under the Constitution apply with equal force to same-sex couples.

A first premise of the Court's relevant precedents is that the right to personal choice regarding marriage is inherent in the concept of individual autonomy. This abiding connection between marriage and liberty is why *Loving* invalidated interracial marriage bans under the Due Process Clause. . . .

Choices about marriage shape an individual's destiny. As the Supreme Judicial Court of Massachusetts has explained, because "it fulfils yearnings for security, safe haven, and connection that express our common humanity, civil marriage is an esteemed institution, and the decision whether and whom to marry is among life's momentous acts of self-definition." *Goodridge* [*v. Dep't of Pub. Health*], 440 Mass., at 322, 798 N.E.2d, at 955 [(Mass. 2003)].

The nature of marriage is that, through its enduring bond, two persons together can find other freedoms, such as expression, intimacy, and spirituality. This is true for all persons, whatever their sexual orientation. . . . There is dignity in the bond between two men or two women who seek to marry and in their autonomy to make such profound choices. . . .

A second principle in this Court's jurisprudence is that the right to marry is fundamental because it supports a two-person union unlike any other in its importance to the committed individuals. . . .

As this Court held in *Lawrence*, same-sex couples have the same right as opposite-sex couples to enjoy intimate association. Lawrence invalidated laws that made same-sex intimacy a criminal act. . . .

A third basis for protecting the right to marry is that it safeguards children and families and thus draws meaning from related rights of childrearing, procreation, and education. See *Pierce v. Society of Sisters*, 268 U.S. 510 (1925); *Meyer*, 262 U.S., at 399. . . .

As all parties agree, many same-sex couples provide loving and nurturing homes to their children, whether biological or adopted. And hundreds of thousands of children are presently being raised by such couples. See Brief for Gary J. Gates as Amicus Curiae 4. Most States have allowed gays and lesbians to adopt, either as individuals or as couples, and many adopted and foster children have same-sex parents, see *id.*, at 5. This provides powerful confirmation from the law itself that gays and lesbians can create loving, supportive families.

Excluding same-sex couples from marriage thus conflicts with a central premise of the right to marry. Without the recognition, stability, and predictability marriage offers, their children suffer the stigma of knowing their families are somehow lesser. They also suffer the significant material costs of being raised by unmarried parents, relegated through no fault of their own to a more difficult and uncertain family life. The marriage laws at issue here thus harm and humiliate the children of same-sex couples.

That is not to say the right to marry is less meaningful for those who do not or cannot have children. An ability, desire, or promise to procreate is not and has not been a prerequisite for a valid marriage in any State. In light of precedent protecting the right of a married couple not to procreate, it cannot be said the Court or the States have conditioned the right to marry on the capacity or commitment to procreate. The constitutional marriage right has many aspects, of which childbearing is only one.

Fourth and finally, this Court's cases and the Nation's traditions make clear that marriage is a keystone of our social order. Alexis de Tocqueville recognized this truth on his travels through the United States almost two centuries ago:

> "There is certainly no country in the world where the tie of marriage is so much respected as in America. . . . [W]hen the American retires from the turmoil of public life to the bosom of his family, he finds in it the image of order and of peace. . . . [H]e afterwards carries [that image] with him into public affairs." 1 Democracy in America 309 (H. Reeve transl., rev. ed. 1990).

. . . For that reason, just as a couple vows to support each other, so does society pledge to support the couple, offering symbolic recognition and material benefits to protect and nourish the union. Indeed, while the States are in general free to vary the benefits they confer on all married couples, they have throughout our history made marriage the basis for an expanding list of governmental rights, benefits, and responsibilities. These aspects of marital status include: taxation; inheritance and property rights; rules of intestate succession; spousal privilege in the law of evidence; hospital access; medical decisionmaking authority; adoption rights; the rights and benefits of survivors; birth and death certificates; professional ethics rules; campaign finance restrictions; workers' compensation benefits; health insurance; and child custody, support, and visitation rules. . . . The States have contributed to the fundamental character of the marriage right by placing that institution at the center of so many facets of the legal and social order.

There is no difference between same- and opposite-sex couples with respect to this principle. Yet by virtue of their exclusion from that institution, same-sex couples are denied the constellation of benefits that the States have linked to marriage. This harm results in more than just material burdens. Same-sex couples are consigned to an instability many opposite-sex couples would deem intolerable in their own lives. As the State itself makes marriage all the more precious by the significance it attaches to it, exclusion from that status has the effect of teaching that gays and lesbians are unequal in important respects. It demeans gays and lesbians for the State to lock them out of a central institution of the Nation's society. Same-sex couples, too, may aspire to the transcendent purposes of marriage and seek fulfillment in its highest meaning.

The limitation of marriage to opposite-sex couples may long have seemed natural and just, but its inconsistency with the central meaning of the fundamental right to marry is now manifest. With that knowledge must come the recognition that laws excluding same-sex couples from the marriage right impose stigma and injury of the kind prohibited by our basic charter. . . .

The right to marry is fundamental as a matter of history and tradition, but rights come not from ancient sources alone. They rise, too, from a better informed understanding of how constitutional imperatives define a liberty that remains urgent in our own era. Many who deem same-sex marriage to be wrong reach that conclusion based on decent and honorable religious or philosophical premises, and neither they nor their beliefs are disparaged here. But when that sincere, personal opposition becomes enacted law and public policy, the necessary consequence is to put the imprimatur of the State itself on an exclusion that soon demeans or stigmatizes those whose own liberty is then denied. Under the Constitution, same-sex couples seek in marriage the same legal treatment as opposite-sex couples, and it would disparage their choices and diminish their personhood to deny them this right.

The right of same-sex couples to marry that is part of the liberty promised by the Fourteenth Amendment is derived, too, from that Amendment's guarantee of the equal protection of the laws. The Due Process Clause and the Equal Protection Clause are connected in a profound way, though they set forth independent principles. Rights implicit in liberty and rights secured by equal protection may rest on different precepts and are not always co-extensive, yet in some instances each may be instructive as to the meaning and reach of the other. In any particular case one Clause may be thought to capture the essence of the right in a more accurate and comprehensive way, even as the two Clauses may converge in the identification and definition of the right. . . .

This dynamic also applies to same-sex marriage. It is now clear that the challenged laws burden the liberty of same-sex couples, and it must be further acknowledged that they abridge central precepts of equality. Here the marriage laws enforced by the respondents are in essence unequal: same-sex couples are denied all the benefits afforded to opposite-sex couples and are barred from exercising a fundamental right. Especially against a long history of disapproval of their relationships, this denial to same-sex couples of the right to marry works a grave and continuing harm. The imposition of this disability on gays and lesbians serves to disrespect and subordinate them. And the Equal Protection Clause, like the Due Process Clause, prohibits this unjustified infringement of the fundamental right to marry.

These considerations lead to the conclusion that the right to marry is a fundamental right inherent in the liberty of the person, and under the Due Process and Equal Protection Clauses of the Fourteenth Amendment couples of the same-sex may not be deprived of that right and that liberty. The Court now holds that same-sex couples may exercise the fundamental right to marry. No longer may this liberty be denied to them. *Baker v. Nelson* must be and now is overruled, and the State laws challenged by Petitioners in these cases are now held invalid to the extent they exclude same-sex couples from civil marriage on the same terms and conditions as opposite-sex couples.

IV

. . . The respondents also argue allowing same-sex couples to wed will harm marriage as an institution by leading to fewer opposite-sex marriages. This may occur, the respondents contend, because licensing same-sex marriage severs the connection between natural procreation and marriage. That argument, however, rests on a counterintuitive view of opposite-sex couple's decisionmaking processes regarding marriage and parenthood. Decisions about whether to marry and raise children are based on many personal, romantic, and practical considerations; and it is unrealistic to conclude that an opposite-sex couple would choose not to marry simply because same-sex couples may do so. See *Kitchen v. Herbert*, 755 F.3d 1193, 1223 (C.A.10 2014) ("[I]t is wholly illogical to believe that state recognition of the love and commitment between same-sex couples will alter the most intimate and personal decisions of opposite-sex couples"). The respondents have not shown a foundation for the conclusion that allowing same-sex marriage will cause the harmful outcomes they describe. Indeed, with respect to this asserted basis for excluding same-sex couples from the right to marry, it is appropriate to observe these cases involve only the rights of two consenting adults whose marriages would pose no risk of harm to themselves or third parties.

Finally, it must be emphasized that religions, and those who adhere to religious doctrines, may continue to advocate with utmost, sincere conviction that, by divine precepts, same-sex marriage should not be condoned. The First Amendment ensures that religious organizations and persons are given proper protection as they seek to teach the principles that are so fulfilling and so central to their lives and faiths, and to their own deep aspirations to continue the family structure they have long revered. The same is true of those who oppose same-sex marriage for other reasons. In turn, those who believe allowing same-sex marriage is proper or indeed essential, whether as a matter of religious conviction or secular belief, may engage those who disagree with their view in an open and searching debate. The Constitution, however, does not permit the State to bar same-sex couples from marriage on the same terms as accorded to couples of the opposite sex.

V

. . . No union is more profound than marriage, for it embodies the highest ideals of love, fidelity, devotion, sacrifice, and family. In forming a marital union, two people become something greater than once they were. As some of the petitioners in these cases demonstrate, marriage embodies a love that may endure even past death. It would misunderstand these men and women to say they disrespect the idea of marriage. Their plea is that they do respect it, respect it so deeply that they seek to find its fulfillment for themselves. Their hope is not to be condemned to live in loneliness, excluded from one of civilization's oldest institutions. They ask for equal dignity in the eyes of the law. The Constitution grants them that right.

The judgment of the Court of Appeals for the Sixth Circuit is reversed.

It is so ordered.

CHIEF JUSTICE ROBERTS, with whom JUSTICE SCALIA and JUSTICE THOMAS join, dissenting.

Petitioners make strong arguments rooted in social policy and considerations of fairness. They contend that same-sex couples should be allowed to affirm their love and commitment through marriage, just like opposite-sex couples. That position has undeniable appeal; over the past six years, voters and legislators in eleven States and the District of Columbia have revised their laws to allow marriage between two people of the same sex.

But this Court is not a legislature. Whether same-sex marriage is a good idea should be of no concern to us. Under the Constitution, judges have power to say what the law is, not what it should be. The people who ratified the Constitution authorized courts to exercise "neither force nor will but merely judgment." The Federalist No. 78, p. 465 (C. Rossiter ed. 1961) (A. Hamilton) (capitalization altered).

Although the policy arguments for extending marriage to same-sex couples may be compelling, the legal arguments for requiring such an extension are not. The fundamental right to marry does not include a right to make a State change its definition of marriage. And a State's decision to maintain the meaning of marriage that has persisted in every culture throughout human history can hardly be called irrational. In short, our Constitution does not enact any one theory of marriage. The people of a State are free to expand marriage to include same-sex couples, or to retain the historic definition.

Today, however, the Court takes the extraordinary step of ordering every State to license and recognize same-sex marriage. Many people will rejoice at this decision, and I begrudge none their celebration. But for those who believe in a government of laws, not of men, the majority's approach is deeply disheartening. Supporters of same-sex marriage have achieved considerable success persuading their fellow citizens — through the democratic process — to adopt their view. That ends today. Five lawyers have closed the debate and enacted their own vision of marriage as a matter of constitutional law. Stealing this issue from the people will for many cast a cloud over same-sex marriage, making a dramatic social change that much more difficult to accept.

The majority's decision is an act of will, not legal judgment. The right it announces has no basis in the Constitution or this Court's precedent. The majority expressly disclaims judicial "caution" and omits even a pretense of humility, openly relying on its desire to remake society according to its own "new insight" into the "nature of injustice." As a result, the Court invalidates the marriage laws of more than half the States and orders the transformation of a social institution that has formed the basis of human society for millennia, for the Kalahari Bushmen and the Han Chinese, the Carthaginians and the Aztecs. Just who do we think we are?

It can be tempting for judges to confuse our own preferences with the requirements of the law. But as this Court has been reminded throughout our history, the Constitution "is made for people of fundamentally differing views." *Lochner v. New York*, 198 U.S. 45 (1905) (Holmes, J., dissenting). Accordingly, "courts are not concerned with the wisdom or policy of legislation." *Id.*, at 69 (Harlan, J., dissenting). The majority today neglects that restrained conception of the judicial role. It seizes for itself a question the Constitution leaves to the people, at a time when the people are engaged in a vibrant debate on that question. And it answers that question based not on neutral principles of constitutional law, but on its own "understanding of what freedom is and must become." I have no choice but to dissent.

Understand well what this dissent is about: It is not about whether, in my judgment, the institution of marriage should be changed to include same-sex couples. It is instead about whether, in our democratic republic, that decision should rest with the people acting through their elected representatives, or with five lawyers who happen to hold commissions authorizing them to resolve legal disputes according to law. The Constitution leaves no doubt about the answer. . . .

Federal courts are blunt instruments when it comes to creating rights. They have constitutional power only to resolve concrete cases or controversies; they do not have the flexibility of legislatures to address concerns of parties not before the court or to anticipate problems that may arise from the exercise of a new right. Today's decision, for example, creates serious questions about religious liberty. Many good and decent people oppose same-sex marriage as a tenet of faith, and their freedom to exercise religion is — unlike the right imagined by the majority — actually spelled out in the Constitution. Amdt. 1.

Respect for sincere religious conviction has led voters and legislators in every State that has adopted same-sex marriage democratically to include accommodations for religious practice. The majority's decision imposing same-sex marriage cannot, of course, create any such accommodations. The majority graciously suggests that religious believers may continue to "advocate" and "teach" their views of marriage. The First Amendment guarantees, however, the freedom to "exercise" religion. Ominously, that is not a word the majority uses.

Hard questions arise when people of faith exercise religion in ways that may be seen to conflict with the new right to same-sex marriage — when, for example, a religious college provides married student housing only to opposite-sex married couples, or a religious adoption agency declines to place children with same-sex married couples. Indeed, the Solicitor General candidly acknowledged that the tax exemptions of some religious institutions would be in question if they opposed same-sex marriage. There is little doubt that these and similar questions will soon be before this Court. Unfortunately, people of faith can take no comfort in the treatment they receive from the majority today.

Perhaps the most discouraging aspect of today's decision is the extent to which the majority feels compelled to sully those on the other side of the debate. The majority offers a cursory assurance that it does not intend to disparage people who, as a matter of conscience, cannot accept same-sex marriage. That disclaimer is hard to square with the very next sentence, in which the majority explains that "the necessary consequence" of laws codifying the traditional definition of marriage is to "demea[n] or stigmatiz[e]" same-sex couples. The majority reiterates such characterizations over and over. By the majority's account, Americans who did nothing more than follow the understanding of marriage that has existed for our entire history — in particular, the tens of millions of people who voted to reaffirm their States' enduring definition of marriage—have acted to "lock . . . out," "disparage," "disrespect and subordinate," and inflict "[d]ignitary wounds" upon their gay and lesbian neighbors. . . . Moreover, they are entirely gratuitous. It is one thing for the majority to conclude that the Constitution protects a right to same-sex marriage; it is something else to portray everyone who does not share the majority's "better informed understanding" as bigoted.

In the face of all this, a much different view of the Court's role is possible. That view is more modest and restrained. It is more skeptical that the legal abilities of judges also reflect insight into moral and philosophical issues. It is more sensitive to the fact that judges are unelected and unaccountable, and that the legitimacy of their power depends on confining it to the exercise of legal judgment. It is more attuned to the lessons of history, and what it has meant for the country and Court when Justices have exceeded their proper bounds. And it is less pretentious than to suppose that while people around the world have viewed an institution in a particular way for thousands of years, the present generation and the present Court are the ones chosen to burst the bonds of that history and tradition.

. . . If you are among the many Americans—of whatever sexual orientation— who favor expanding same-sex marriage, by all means celebrate today's decision. Celebrate the achievement of a desired goal. Celebrate the opportunity for a new expression of commitment to a partner. Celebrate the availability of new benefits. But do not celebrate the Constitution. It had nothing to do with it.

I respectfully dissent.

JUSTICE SCALIA, with whom JUSTICE THOMAS joins, dissenting.

. . . I write separately to call attention to this Court's threat to American democracy.

The substance of today's decree is not of immense personal importance to me. The law can recognize as marriage whatever sexual attachments and living arrangements it wishes, and can accord them favorable civil consequences, from tax treatment to rights of inheritance. Those civil consequences—and the public approval that conferring the name of marriage evidences—can perhaps have adverse social effects, but no more adverse than the effects of many other controversial laws. So it is not of special importance to me what the law says about marriage. It is of overwhelming importance, however, who it is that rules me. Today's decree says that my Ruler, and the Ruler of 320 million Americans coast-to-coast, is a majority of the nine lawyers on the Supreme Court. The opinion in these cases is the furthest extension in fact—and the furthest extension one can even imagine—of the Court's claimed power to create "liberties" that the Constitution and its Amendments neglect to mention. This practice of constitutional revision by an unelected committee of nine, always accompanied (as it is today) by extravagant praise of liberty, robs the People of the most important liberty they asserted in the Declaration of Independence and won in the Revolution of 1776: the freedom to govern themselves.

I

Until the courts put a stop to it, public debate over same-sex marriage displayed American democracy at its best. Individuals on both sides of the issue passionately, but respectfully, attempted to persuade their fellow citizens to accept their views. Americans considered the arguments and put the question to a vote. The electorates of 11 States, either directly or through their representatives, chose to expand the traditional definition of marriage. Many more decided not to. Win or lose, advocates for both sides continued pressing their cases, secure in the knowledge that an electoral loss can be negated by a later electoral win. That is exactly how our system of government is supposed to work. . . .

JUSTICE THOMAS, with whom JUSTICE SCALIA joins, dissenting.

The Court's decision today is at odds not only with the Constitution, but with the principles upon which our Nation was built. Since well before 1787, liberty has been understood as freedom from government action, not entitlement to government benefits. The Framers created our Constitution to preserve that understanding of liberty. Yet the majority invokes our Constitution in the name of a "liberty" that the Framers would not have recognized, to the detriment of the liberty they sought to protect. Along the way, it rejects the idea — captured in our Declaration of Independence — that human dignity is innate and suggests instead that it comes from the Government. This distortion of our Constitution not only ignores the text, it inverts the relationship between the individual and the state in our Republic. I cannot agree with it. . . .

JUSTICE ALITO, with whom JUSTICE SCALIA and JUSTICE THOMAS joins, dissenting.

Until the federal courts intervened, the American people were engaged in a debate about whether their States should recognize same-sex marriage. The question in these cases, however, is not what States should do about same-sex marriage but whether the Constitution answers that question for them. It does not. The Constitution leaves that question to be decided by the people of each State.

I

The Constitution says nothing about a right to same-sex marriage, but the Court holds that the term "liberty" in the Due Process Clause of the Fourteenth Amendment encompasses this right. Our Nation was founded upon the principle that every person has the unalienable right to liberty, but liberty is a term of many meanings. For classical liberals, it may include economic rights now limited by government regulation. For social democrats, it may include the right to a variety of government benefits. For today's majority, it has a distinctively postmodern meaning. . . .

II

Attempting to circumvent the problem presented by the newness of the right found in these cases, the majority claims that the issue is the right to equal treatment. Noting that marriage is a fundamental right, the majority argues that a State has no valid reason for denying that right to same-sex couples. This reasoning is dependent upon a particular understanding of the purpose of civil marriage. Although the Court expresses the point in loftier terms, its argument is that the fundamental purpose of marriage is to promote the well-being of those who choose to marry. Marriage provides emotional fulfillment and the promise of support in times of need. And by benefiting persons who choose to wed, marriage indirectly benefits society because persons who live in stable, fulfilling, and supportive relationships make better citizens. It is for these reasons, the argument goes, that States encourage and formalize marriage, confer special benefits on married persons, and also impose some special obligations. This understanding of the States' reasons for recognizing marriage enables the majority to argue that same-sex marriage serves the States' objectives in the same way as opposite-sex marriage.

This understanding of marriage, which focuses almost entirely on the happiness of persons who choose to marry, is shared by many people today, but it is not the traditional one. For millennia, marriage was inextricably linked to the one thing that only an opposite-sex couple can do: procreate.

Adherents to different schools of philosophy use different terms to explain why society should formalize marriage and attach special benefits and obligations to persons who marry. Here, the States defending their adherence to the traditional understanding of marriage have explained their position using the pragmatic vocabulary that characterizes most American political discourse. Their basic argument is that States formalize and promote marriage, unlike other fulfilling human relationships, in order to encourage potentially procreative conduct to take place within a lasting unit that has long been thought to provide the best atmosphere for raising children. They thus argue that there are reasonable secular grounds for restricting marriage to opposite-sex couples.

If this traditional understanding of the purpose of marriage does not ring true to all ears today, that is probably because the tie between marriage and procreation has frayed. Today, for instance, more than 40% of all children in this country are born to unmarried women. This development undoubtedly is both a cause and a result of changes in our society's understanding of marriage.

While, for many, the attributes of marriage in 21st-century America have changed, those States that do not want to recognize same-sex marriage have not yet given up on the traditional understanding. They worry that by officially abandoning the older understanding, they may contribute to marriage's further decay. It is far beyond the outer reaches of this Court's authority to say that a State may not adhere to the understanding of marriage that has long prevailed, not just in this country and others with similar cultural roots, but also in a great variety of countries and cultures all around the globe.

III

Today's decision usurps the constitutional right of the people to decide whether to keep or alter the traditional understanding of marriage. The decision will also have other important consequences.

It will be used to vilify Americans who are unwilling to assent to the new orthodoxy. In the course of its opinion, the majority compares traditional marriage laws to laws that denied equal treatment for African-Americans and women. E.g., *ante*, at 2598–2599. The implications of this analogy will be exploited by those who are determined to stamp out every vestige of dissent.

Perhaps recognizing how its reasoning may be used, the majority attempts, toward the end of its opinion, to reassure those who oppose same-sex marriage that their rights of conscience will be protected. We will soon see whether this proves to be true. I assume that those who cling to old beliefs will be able to whisper their thoughts in the recesses of their homes, but if they repeat those views in public, they will risk being labeled as bigots and treated as such by governments, employers, and schools.

The system of federalism established by our Constitution provides a way for people with different beliefs to live together in a single nation. If the issue of same-sex marriage had been left to the people of the States, it is likely that some States would recognize same-sex marriage and others would not. It is also possible that some States would tie recognition to protection for conscience rights. The majority today makes that impossible. By imposing its own views on the entire country, the majority facilitates the marginalization of the many Americans who have traditional ideas. Recalling the harsh treatment of gays and lesbians in the past, some may think that turnabout is fair play. But if that sentiment prevails, the Nation will experience bitter and lasting wounds.

Today's decision will also have a fundamental effect on this Court and its ability to uphold the rule of law. If a bare majority of Justices can invent a new right and impose that right on the rest of the country, the only real limit on what future majorities will be able to do is their own sense of what those with political power and cultural influence are willing to tolerate. Even enthusiastic supporters of same-sex marriage should worry about the scope of the power that today's majority claims.

Today's decision shows that decades of attempts to restrain this Court's abuse of its authority have failed. A lesson that some will take from today's decision is that preaching about the proper method of interpreting the Constitution or the virtues of judicial self-restraint and humility cannot compete with the temptation to achieve what is viewed as a noble end by any practicable means. I do not doubt that my colleagues in the majority sincerely see in the Constitution a vision of liberty that happens to coincide with their own. But this sincerity is cause for concern, not comfort. What it evidences is the deep and perhaps irremediable corruption of our legal culture's conception of constitutional interpretation.

Most Americans—understandably—will cheer or lament today's decision because of their views on the issue of same-sex marriage. But all Americans, whatever their thinking on that issue, should worry about what the majority's claim of power portends.

Notes and Question

(1) The principal quarrel between the majority and the dissents in *Obergefell* was over the role of the Supreme Court in our constitutional system. The majority emphasized evolving conceptions of liberty and equality. The dissents emphasized the importance of reserving fundamental questions of public policy on issues as divisive as same-sex marriage to the democratic process. Which of the two positions has the better argument?

(2) In *Dobbs*, Justice Kavanaugh underscored the majority's statement that over-ruling *Roe* does not threaten or cast doubt on such precedents as *Obergefell*. What is the basis for that conclusion?

Problem B

Joe Dean was a seventh grade Social Studies teacher in the public schools in a rural school district in upstate New York. He was a very popular teacher and always received excellent evaluations from his colleagues and administrators. Two months ago, the marriage column in the local newspaper had a story about Joe's marriage to Dave, his longtime partner. Several parents saw the article and were very upset. These vocal individuals came to a School Board meeting and demanded that the Board fire Joe. They reluctantly conceded that a recent Supreme Court decision held that states cannot deny marriage licenses to gay couples. They argued, however, that while Dean may have a right to marry whomever he wants, he has no right to teach at their schools. His marriage, they urged, was inconsistent with the community values that the School District should be instilling in its students. The School Board eventually agreed and terminated Joe's employment.

Joe has contacted your law firm to represent him. A senior partner asks whether Joe is likely to prevail on a claim that the School District has denied him rights under the Fourteenth Amendment.

§ 7.03 Entitlements and the Negative Constitution

Dandridge v. Williams

United States Supreme Court

397 U.S. 471, 90 S. Ct. 1153, 25 L. Ed. 2d 491 (1970)

MR. JUSTICE STEWART delivered the opinion of the Court.

This case involves the validity of a method used by Maryland, in the administration of an aspect of its public welfare program, to reconcile the demands of its needy citizens with the finite resources available to meet those demands. Like every other State in the Union, Maryland participates in the Federal Aid to Families With Dependent Children which originated with the Social Security Act of 1935. Under this jointly financed program, a State computes the so-called "standard of need" of each eligible family unit within its borders. Some States provide that every family shall receive grants sufficient to meet fully the determined standard of need. Other States provide that each family unit shall receive a percentage of the determined need. Still others provide grants to most families in full accord with the ascertained standard of need, but impose an upper limit on the total amount of money any one family unit may receive. Maryland, through administrative adoption of a "maximum grant regulation," has followed this last course. This suit was brought by several AFDC recipients to enjoin the application of the Maryland maximum grant regulation on the ground that it is in conflict with the Social Security Act of 1935 and with the Equal Protection Clause of the Fourteenth Amendment. . . .

The operation of the Maryland welfare system is not complex. By statute the State participates in the AFDC program. It computes the standard of need for each eligible family based on the number of children in the family and the circumstances under which the family lives. In general, the standard of need increases with each additional person in the household, but the increments become proportionately smaller. The regulation here in issue imposes upon the grant that any single family may receive an upper limit of $250 per month in certain counties and Baltimore City, and of $240 per month elsewhere in the State. The appellees all have large families, so that their standards of need as computed by the State substantially exceed the maximum grants that they actually receive under the regulation. . . .

Although a State may adopt a maximum grant system in allocating its funds available for AFDC payments without violating the Act, it may not, of course, impose a regime of invidious discrimination in violation of the Equal Protection Clause of the Fourteenth Amendment. Maryland says that its maximum grant regulation is wholly free of any invidiously discriminatory purpose or effect, and that the regulation is rationally supportable on at least four entirely valid grounds. The regulation can be clearly justified, Maryland argues, in terms of legitimate state interests in encouraging gainful employment, in maintaining an equitable balance in economic status as between welfare families and those supported by a wage-earner, in providing incentives for family planning, and in allocating available public funds in such a way as fully to meet the needs of the largest possible number of families. The District Court, while apparently recognizing the validity of at least some of these state concerns, nonetheless held that the regulation "is invalid on its face for over-reaching, — that it violates the Equal Protection Clause" (b)ecause it cuts too broad a swath on an indiscriminate basis as applied to the entire group of AFDC eligibles to which it purports to apply.

If this were a case involving government action claimed to violate the First Amendment guarantee of free speech, a finding of "overreaching" would be significant and might be crucial. For when otherwise valid governmental regulation sweeps so broadly as to impinge upon activity protected by the First Amendment, its very overbreadth may make it unconstitutional. But the concept of "overreaching" has no place in this case. For here we deal with state regulation in the social and economic field, not affecting freedoms guaranteed by the Bill of Rights, and claimed to violate the Fourteenth Amendment only because the regulation results in some disparity in grants of welfare payments to the largest AFDC families. For this Court to approve the invalidation of state economic or social regulation as "overreaching" would be far too reminiscent of an era when the Court thought the Fourteenth Amendment gave it power to strike down state laws "because they may be unwise, improvident, or out of harmony with a particular school of thought." That era long ago passed into history.

In the area of economics and social welfare, a State does not violate the Equal Protection Clause merely because the classifications made by its laws are imperfect. If the classification has some "reasonable basis," it does not offend the Constitution simply because the classification "is not made with mathematical nicety or because in practice it results in some inequality." "The problems of government are practical ones and may justify, if they do not require, rough accommodations — illogical, it may be, and unscientific." "A statutory discrimination will not be set aside if any state of facts reasonably may be conceived to justify it."

To be sure, the cases cited, and many others enunciating this fundamental standard under the Equal Protection Clause, have in the main involved state regulation of business or industry. The administration of public welfare assistance, by contrast, involves the most basic economic needs of impoverished human beings. We recognize the dramatically real factual difference between the cited cases and this one, but we can find no basis for applying a different constitutional standard. It is a standard that has consistently been applied to state legislation restricting the availability of employment opportunities. And it is a standard that is true to the principle that the Fourteenth Amendment gives the federal courts no power to impose upon the States their views of what constitutes wise economic or social policy.

Under this long-established meaning of the Equal Protection Clause, it is clear that the Maryland maximum grant regulation is constitutionally valid. We need not explore all the reasons that the State advances in justification of the regulation. It is enough that a solid foundation for the regulation can be found in the State's legitimate interest in encouraging employment and in avoiding discrimination between welfare families and the families of the working poor. By combining a limit on the recipient's grant with permission to retain money earned, without reduction in the amount of the grant, Maryland provides an incentive to seek gainful employment. And by keying the maximum family AFDC grants to the minimum wage a steadily employed head of a household receives, the State maintains some semblance of an equitable balance between families on welfare and those supported by an employed breadwinner.

It is true that in some AFDC families there may be no person who is employable. It is also true that with respect to AFDC families whose determined standard of need is below the regulatory maximum, and who therefore receive grants equal to the determined standard, the employment incentive is absent. But the Equal Protection Clause does not require that a State must choose between attacking every aspect of a problem or not attacking the problem at all. It is enough that the State's action be rationally based and free from invidious discrimination. The regulation before us meets that test.

We do not decide today that the Maryland regulation is wise, that it best fulfills the relevant social and economic objectives that Maryland might ideally espouse, or that a more just and humane system could not be devised. Conflicting claims of morality and intelligence are raised by opponents and proponents of almost every measure, certainly including the one before us. But the intractable economic, social, and even philosophical problems presented by public welfare assistance programs are not the business of this Court. The Constitution may impose certain procedural safeguards upon systems of welfare administration. But the Constitution does not empower this Court to second-guess state officials charged with the difficult responsibility of allocating limited public welfare funds among the myriad of potential recipients. *The judgment is reversed.*

[Concurring opinions omitted.]

[Dissenting opinion of JUSTICE DOUGLAS omitted.]

MR. JUSTICE MARSHALL, whom MR. JUSTICE BRENNAN joins, dissenting.

For the reasons stated by Mr. Justice Douglas, to which I add some comments of my own, I believe that the Court has erroneously concluded that Maryland's maximum grant regulation is consistent with the federal statute. In my view, that regulation is fundamentally in conflict with the basic structure and purposes of the Social Security Act.

More important in the long run than this misreading of a federal statute, however, is the Court's emasculation of the Equal Protection Clause as a constitutional principle applicable to the area of social welfare administration. The Court holds today that regardless of the arbitrariness of a classification it must be sustained if any state goal can be imagined that is arguably furthered by its effects. This is so even though the classification's underinclusiveness or overinclusiveness clearly demonstrates that its actual basis is something other than that asserted by the State, and even though the relationship between the classification and the state interests which it purports to serve is so tenuous that it could not seriously be maintained that the classification tends to accomplish the ascribed goals.

The Court recognizes, as it must, that this case involves "the most basic economic needs of impoverished human beings," and that there is therefore a "dramatically real factual difference" between the instant case and those decisions upon which the Court relies. The acknowledgment that these dramatic differences exist is a candid recognition that the Court's decision today is wholly without precedent. I cannot subscribe to the Court's sweeping refusal to accord the Equal Protection Clause any role in this entire area of the law, and I therefore dissent from both parts of the Court's decision.

This classification process effected by the maximum grant regulation produces a basic denial of equal treatment. Persons who are concededly similarly situated (dependent children and their families), are not afforded equal, or even approximately equal, treatment under the maximum grant regulation. Subsistence benefits are paid with respect to some needy dependent children; nothing is paid with respect to others. Some needy families receive full subsistence assistance as calculated by the State; the assistance paid to other families is grossly below their similarly calculated needs.

Yet, as a general principle, individuals should not be afforded different treatment by the State unless there is a relevant distinction between them and "a statutory discrimination must be based on differences that are reasonably related to the purposes of the Act in which it is found." Consequently, the State may not, in the provision of important services or the distribution of governmental payments, supply benefits to some individuals while denying them to others who are similarly situated.

In the instant case, the only distinction between those children with respect to whom assistance is granted and those children who are denied such assistance is the size of the family into which the child permits himself to be born. The class of individuals with respect to whom payments are actually made (the first four or five eligible dependent children in a family), is grossly underinclusive in terms of the class that the AFDC program was designed to assist, namely, all needy dependent children. Such underinclusiveness manifests "a prima facie violation of the equal protection requirement of reasonable classification," compelling the State to come forward with a persuasive justification for the classification.

The Court never undertakes to inquire for such a justification; rather it avoids the task by focusing upon the abstract dichotomy between two different approaches to equal protection problems that have been utilized by this Court.

Under the so-called "traditional test," a classification is said to be permissible under the Equal Protection Clause unless it is "without any reasonable basis." On the other hand, if the classification affects a "fundamental right," then the state interest in perpetuating the classification must be "compelling" in order to be sustained.

This case simply defies easy characterization in terms of one or the other of these "tests." The cases relied on by the Court, in which a "mere rationality" test was actually used, are most accurately described as involving the application of equal protection reasoning to the regulation of business interests. The extremes to which the Court has gone in dreaming up rational bases for state regulation in that area may in many instances be ascribed to a healthy revulsion from the Court's earlier excesses in using the Constitution to protect interests that have more than enough power to protect themselves in the legislative halls. This case, involving the literally vital interests of a powerless minority — poor families without breadwinners — is far removed from the area of business regulation, as the Court concedes. Why then is the standard used in those cases imposed here? We are told no more than that this case falls in "the area of economics and social welfare," with the implication that from there the answer is obvious.

In my view, equal protection analysis of this case is not appreciably advanced by the a priori definition of a "right," fundamental or otherwise. Rather, concentration must be placed upon the character of the classification in question, the relative importance to individuals in the class discriminated against of the governmental benefits that they do not receive, and the asserted state interests in support of the classification. As we said only recently, "In determining whether or not a state law violates the Equal Protection Clause, we must consider the facts and circumstances behind the law, the interests which the State claims to be protecting, and the interests of those who are disadvantaged by the classification."

It is the individual interests here at stake that, as the Court concedes, most clearly distinguish this case from the "business regulation" equal protection cases. AFDC support to needy dependent children provides the stuff that sustains those children's lives: food, clothing, shelter. And this Court has already recognized several times that when a benefit, even a "gratuitous" benefit, is necessary to sustain life, stricter constitutional standards, both procedural and substantive, are applied to the deprivation of that benefit.

Nor is the distinction upon which the deprivation is here based — the distinction between large and small families — one that readily commends itself as a basis for determining which children are to have support approximating subsistence and which are not. Indeed, governmental discrimination between children on the basis of a factor over which they have no control — the number of their brothers and sisters — bears some resemblance to the classification between legitimate and illegitimate children which we condemned as a violation of the Equal Protection Clause in *Levy v. Louisiana*, 391 U.S. 68 (1968). . . .

. . . Maryland has urged that the maximum grant regulation serves to maintain a rough equality between wage earning families and AFDC families, thereby increasing the political support for — or perhaps reducing the opposition to — the AFDC program. It is questionable whether the Court really relies on this ground, especially when in many States the prescribed family maximum bears no such relation to the minimum wage. But the Court does not indicate that a different result might obtain in other cases. Indeed, whether elimination of the maximum would produce welfare incomes out of line with other incomes in Maryland is itself open to question on this record. It is true that government in the United States, unlike certain other countries, has not chosen to make public aid available to assist families generally in raising their children. Rather, in this case Maryland, with the encouragement and assistance of the Federal Government, has elected to provide assistance at a subsistence level for those in particular need — the aged, the blind, the infirm, and the unemployed and unemployable, and their children. The only question presented here is whether, having once undertaken such a program, the State may arbitrarily select from among the concededly eligible those to whom it will provide benefits. And it is too late to argue that political expediency will sustain discrimination not otherwise supportable.

Vital to the employment-incentive basis found by the Court to sustain the regulation is, of course, the supposition that an appreciable number of AFDC recipients are in fact employable. For it is perfectly obvious that limitations upon assistance cannot reasonably operate as a work incentive with regard to those who cannot work or who cannot be expected to work. In this connection, Maryland candidly notes that "only a very small percentage of the total universe of welfare recipients are employable." The State, however, urges us to ignore the "total universe" and to concentrate attention instead upon the heads of AFDC families. Yet the very purpose of the AFDC program since its inception has been to provide assistance for dependent children. The State's position is thus that the State may deprive certain needy children of assistance to which they would otherwise be entitled in order to provide an arguable work incentive for their parents. But the State may not wield its economic whip in this fashion when the effect is to cause a deprivation to needy dependent children in order to correct an arguable fault of their parents. . . .

Finally, it should be noted that, to the extent there is a legitimate state interest in encouraging heads of AFDC households to find employment, application of the maximum grant regulation is also grossly underinclusive because it singles out and affects only large families. No reason is suggested why this particular group should be carved out for the purpose of having unusually harsh "work incentives" imposed upon them. Not only has the State selected for special treatment a small group from among similarly situated families, but it has done so on a basis — family size — that bears no relation to the evil that the State claims the regulation was designed to correct. There is simply no indication whatever that heads of large families, as opposed to heads of small families, are particularly prone to refuse to seek or to maintain employment. . . .

In the final analysis, Maryland has set up an AFDC program structured to calculate and pay the minimum standard of need to dependent children. Having set up that program, however, the State denies some of those needy children the minimum subsistence standard of living, and it does so on the wholly arbitrary basis that they happen to be members of large families. One need not speculate too far on the actual reason for the regulation, for in the early stages of this litigation the State virtually conceded that it set out to limit the total cost of the program along the path of least resistance. Now, however, we are told that other rationales can be manufactured to support the regulation and to sustain it against a fundamental constitutional challenge.

However, these asserted state interests, which are not insignificant in themselves, are advanced either not at all or by complete accident by the maximum grant regulation. Clearly they could be served by measures far less destructive of the individual interests at stake. Moreover, the device assertedly chosen to further them is at one and the same time both grossly underinclusive — because it does not apply at all to a much larger class in an equal position — and grossly overinclusive — because it applies so strongly against a substantial class as to which it can rationally serve no end. Were this a case of pure business regulation, these defects would place it beyond what has heretofore seemed a borderline case, and I do not believe that the regulation can be sustained even under the Court's "reasonableness" test.

In any event, it cannot suffice merely to invoke the spectre of the past and to recite from *Lindsley v. Natural Carbonic Gas Co.* and *Williamson v. Lee Optical of Oklahoma, Inc.* to decide the case. Appellees are not a gas company or an optical dispenser; they are needy dependent children and families who are discriminated against by the State. The basis of that discrimination — the classification of individuals into large and small families — is too arbitrary and too unconnected to the asserted rationale, the impact on those discriminated against — the denial of even a subsistence existence — too great, and the supposed interests served too contrived and attenuated to meet the requirements of the Constitution. In my view Maryland's maximum grant regulation is invalid under the Equal Protection Clause of the Fourteenth Amendment.

I would affirm the judgment of the District Court.

DeShaney v. Winnebago County Department of Social Services

United States Supreme Court
489 U.S. 189, 109 S. Ct. 998, 103 L. Ed. 2d 249 (1989)

Chief Justice Rehnquist delivered the opinion of the Court.

Petitioner is a boy who was beaten and permanently injured by his father, with whom he lived. Respondents are social workers and other local officials who received complaints that petitioner was being abused by his father and had reason to believe that this was the case, but nonetheless did not act to remove petitioner from his father's custody. Petitioner sued respondents claiming that their failure to act deprived him of his liberty in violation of the Due Process Clause of the Fourteenth Amendment to the United States Constitution. We hold that it did not.

I

The facts of this case are undeniably tragic. Petitioner Joshua DeShaney was born in 1979. In 1980, a Wyoming court granted his parents a divorce and awarded custody of Joshua to his father, Randy DeShaney. The father shortly thereafter moved to Neenah, a city located in Winnebago County, Wisconsin, taking the infant Joshua with him. There he entered into a second marriage, which also ended in divorce.

The Winnebago County authorities first learned that Joshua DeShaney might be a victim of child abuse in January 1982, when his father's second wife complained to the police, at the time of their divorce, that he had previously "hit the boy causing marks and [was] a prime case for child abuse." The Winnebago County Department of Social Services (DSS) interviewed the father, but he denied the accusations, and DSS did not pursue them further. In January 1983, Joshua was admitted to a local hospital with multiple bruises and abrasions. The examining physician suspected child abuse and notified DSS, which immediately obtained an order from a Wisconsin juvenile court placing Joshua in the temporary custody of the hospital. Three days later, the county convened an ad hoc "Child Protection Team" — consisting of a pediatrician, a psychologist, a police detective, the county's lawyer, several DSS caseworkers, and various hospital personnel — to consider Joshua's situation. At this meeting, the Team decided that there was insufficient evidence of child abuse to retain Joshua in the custody of the court. The Team did, however, decide to recommend several measures to protect Joshua, including enrolling him in a preschool program, providing his father with certain counselling services, and encouraging his father's girlfriend to move out of the home. Randy DeShaney entered into a voluntary agreement with DSS in which he promised to cooperate with them in accomplishing these goals.

Based on the recommendation of the Child Protection Team, the juvenile court dismissed the child protection case and returned Joshua to the custody of his father. A month later, emergency room personnel called the DSS caseworker handling Joshua's case to report that he had once again been treated for suspicious injuries. The caseworker concluded that there was no basis for action. For the next six months, the caseworker made monthly visits to the DeShaney home, during which she observed a number of suspicious injuries on Joshua's head; she also noticed that he had not been enrolled in school, and that the girlfriend had not moved out. The caseworker dutifully recorded these incidents in her files, along with her continuing suspicions that someone in the DeShaney household was physically abusing Joshua, but she did nothing more. In November 1983, the emergency room notified DSS that Joshua had been treated once again for injuries that they believed to be caused by child abuse. On the caseworker's next two visits to the DeShaney home, she was told that Joshua was too ill to see her. Still DSS took no action.

In March 1984, Randy DeShaney beat 4-year-old Joshua so severely that he fell into a life-threatening coma. Emergency brain surgery revealed a series of hemorrhages caused by traumatic injuries to the head inflicted over a long period of time. Joshua did not die, but he suffered brain damage so severe that he is expected to spend the rest of his life confined to an institution for the profoundly retarded. Randy DeShaney was subsequently tried and convicted of child abuse. . . .

Because of the inconsistent approaches taken by the lower courts in determining when, if ever, the failure of a state or local governmental entity or its agents to provide an individual with adequate protective services constitutes a violation of the individual's due process rights and the importance of the issue to the administration of state and local governments, we granted certiorari. We now affirm.

II

The Due Process Clause of the Fourteenth Amendment provides that "[n]o State shall . . . deprive any person of life, liberty, or property, without due process of law." Petitioners contend that the State deprived Joshua of his liberty interest in "free[dom] from . . . unjustified intrusions on personal security," by failing to provide him with adequate protection against his father's violence. The claim is one invoking the substantive rather than the procedural component of the Due Process Clause; petitioners do not claim that the State denied Joshua protection without according him appropriate procedural safeguards, but that it was categorically obligated to protect him in these circumstances.

But nothing in the language of the Due Process Clause itself requires the State to protect the life, liberty, and property of its citizens against invasion by private actors. The Clause is phrased as a limitation on the State's power to act, not as a guarantee of certain minimal levels of safety and security. It forbids the State itself to deprive individuals of life, liberty, or property without "due process of law," but its language cannot fairly be extended to impose an affirmative obligation on the State to ensure that those interests do not come to harm through other means. Nor does history support such an expansive reading of the constitutional text. Like its counterpart in the Fifth Amendment, the Due Process Clause of the Fourteenth Amendment was intended to prevent government "from abusing [its] power, or employing it as an instrument of oppression." . . . Its purpose was to protect the people from the State, not to ensure that the State protected them from each other. The Framers were content to leave the extent of governmental obligation in the latter area to the democratic political processes.

Consistent with these principles, our cases have recognized that the Due Process Clauses generally confer no affirmative right to governmental aid, even where such aid may be necessary to secure life, liberty, or property interests of which the government itself may not deprive the individual. . . . As we said in *Harris v. McRae*: "Although the liberty protected by the Due Process Clause affords protection against unwarranted government interference . . . , it does not confer an entitlement to such [governmental aid] as may be necessary to realize all the advantages of that freedom." If the Due Process Clause does not require the State to provide its citizens with particular protective services, it follows that the State cannot be held liable under the Clause for injuries that could have been averted had it chosen to provide them.[3] As a general matter, then, we conclude that a State's failure to protect an individual against private violence simply does not constitute a violation of the Due Process Clause.

Petitioners contend, however, that even if the Due Process Clause imposes no affirmative obligation on the State to provide the general public with adequate protective services, such a duty may arise out of certain "special relationships" created or assumed by the State with respect to particular individuals. Petitioners argue that such a "special relationship" existed here because the State knew that Joshua faced a special danger of abuse at his father's hands, and specifically proclaimed, by word and by deed, its intention to protect him against that danger. Having actually undertaken to protect Joshua from this danger — which petitioners concede the State played no part in creating — the State acquired an affirmative "duty," enforceable through the Due Process Clause, to do so in a reasonably competent fashion. Its failure to discharge that duty, so the argument goes, was an abuse of governmental power that so "shocks the conscience," as to constitute a substantive due process violation.[4]

We reject this argument. It is true that in certain limited circumstances the Constitution imposes upon the State affirmative duties of care and protection with respect to particular individuals. In *Estelle v. Gamble*, 429 U.S. 97 (1976), we recognized that the Eighth Amendment's prohibition against cruel and unusual punishment, made applicable to the States through the Fourteenth Amendment's Due Process Clause, requires the State to provide adequate medical care to incarcerated prisoners. We reasoned that because the prisoner is unable "by reason of the

---

3. [Court's Footnote 3] The State may not, of course, selectively deny its protective services to certain disfavored minorities without violating the Equal Protection Clause. See *Yick Wo v. Hopkins*, 118 U.S. 356 (1886). But no such argument has been made here.

4. [Court's Footnote 4] The genesis of this notion appears to lie in a statement in our opinion in *Martinez v. California*, 444 U.S. 277 (1980). In that case, we were asked to decide, inter alia, whether state officials could be held liable under the Due Process Clause of the Fourteenth Amendment for the death of a private citizen at the hands of a parolee. Rather than squarely confronting the question presented here — whether the Due Process Clause imposed upon the State an affirmative duty to protect — we affirmed the dismissal of the claim on the narrower ground that the causal connection between the state officials' decision to release the parolee from prison and the murder was too attenuated to establish a "deprivation" of constitutional rights within the meaning of 1983. But we went on to say: "[T]he parole board was not aware that appellants' decedent, as distinguished from the public at large, faced any special danger. We need not and do not decide that a parole officer could never be deemed to 'deprive' someone of life by action taken in connection with the release of a prisoner on parole. But we do hold that at least under the particular circumstances of this parole decision, appellants' decedent's death is too remote a consequence of the parole officers' action to hold them responsible under the federal civil rights law." Several of the Courts of Appeals have read this language as implying that once the State learns that a third party poses a special danger to an identified victim, and indicates its willingness to protect the victim against that danger, a "special relationship" arises between State and victim, giving rise to an affirmative duty, enforceable through the Due Process Clause, to render adequate protection.

deprivation of his liberty [to] care for himself," it is only "just" that the State be required to care for him.

In *Youngberg v. Romeo*, 457 U.S. 307 (1982), we extended this analysis beyond the Eighth Amendment setting, holding that the substantive component of the Fourteenth Amendment's Due Process Clause requires the State to provide involuntarily committed mental patients with such services as are necessary to ensure their "reasonable safety" from themselves and others. (dicta indicating that the State is also obligated to provide such individuals with "adequate food, shelter, clothing, and medical care"). As we explained: "If it is cruel and unusual punishment to hold convicted criminals in unsafe conditions, it must be unconstitutional [under the Due Process Clause] to confine the involuntarily committed — who may not be punished at all — in unsafe conditions." (holding that the Due Process Clause requires the responsible government or governmental agency to provide medical care to suspects in police custody who have been injured while being apprehended by the police).

But these cases afford petitioners no help. Taken together, they stand only for the proposition that when the State takes a person into its custody and holds him there against his will, the Constitution imposes upon it a corresponding duty to assume some responsibility for his safety and general well-being. See *Youngberg v. Romeo* ("When a person is institutionalized — and wholly dependent on the State[,] ... a duty to provide certain services and care does exist"). The rationale for this principle is simple enough: when the State by the affirmative exercise of its power so restrains an individual's liberty that it renders him unable to care for himself, and at the same time fails to provide for his basic human needs — e.g., food, clothing, shelter, medical care, and reasonable safety — it transgresses the substantive limits on state action set by the Eighth Amendment and the Due Process Clause. The affirmative duty to protect arises not from the State's knowledge of the individual's predicament or from its expressions of intent to help him, but from the limitation which it has imposed on his freedom to act on his own behalf. ...

The *Estelle-Youngberg* analysis simply has no applicability in the present case. Petitioners concede that the harms Joshua suffered occurred not while he was in the State's custody, but while he was in the custody of his natural father, who was in no sense a state actor. While the State may have been aware of the dangers that Joshua faced in the free world, it played no part in their creation, nor did it do anything to render him any more vulnerable to them. That the State once took temporary custody of Joshua does not alter the analysis, for when it returned him to his father's custody, it placed him in no worse position than that in which he would have been had it not acted at all; the State does not become the permanent guarantor of an individual's safety by having once offered him shelter. Under these circumstances, the State had no constitutional duty to protect Joshua.

It may well be that, by voluntarily undertaking to protect Joshua against a danger it concededly played no part in creating, the State acquired a duty under state tort law to provide him with adequate protection against that danger. *See Restatement*

(Second) of Torts § 323 (1965) (one who undertakes to render services to another may in some circumstances be held liable for doing so in a negligent fashion); see generally W. Keeton, D. Dobbs, R. Keeton, & D. Owen, Prosser and Keeton on *The Law of Torts* § 56 (5th ed. 1984) (discussing "special relationships" which may give rise to affirmative duties to act under the common law of tort). But the claim here is based on the Due Process Clause of the Fourteenth Amendment, which, as we have said many times, does not transform every tort committed by a state actor into a constitutional violation. A State may, through its courts and legislatures, impose such affirmative duties of care and protection upon its agents as it wishes. But not "all common-law duties owed by government actors were . . . constitutionalized by the Fourteenth Amendment." Because, as explained above, the State had no constitutional duty to protect Joshua against his father's violence, its failure to do so — though calamitous in hindsight — simply does not constitute a violation of the Due Process Clause.

Judges and lawyers, like other humans, are moved by natural sympathy in a case like this to find a way for Joshua and his mother to receive adequate compensation for the grievous harm inflicted upon them. But before yielding to that impulse, it is well to remember once again that the harm was inflicted not by the State of Wisconsin, but by Joshua's father. The most that can be said of the state functionaries in this case is that they stood by and did nothing when suspicious circumstances dictated a more active role for them. In defense of them it must also be said that had they moved too soon to take custody of the son away from the father, they would likely have been met with charges of improperly intruding into the parent-child relationship, charges based on the same Due Process Clause that forms the basis for the present charge of failure to provide adequate protection.

The people of Wisconsin may well prefer a system of liability which would place upon the State and its officials the responsibility for failure to act in situations such as the present one. They may create such a system, if they do not have it already, by changing the tort law of the State in accordance with the regular lawmaking process. But they should not have it thrust upon them by this Court's expansion of the Due Process Clause of the Fourteenth Amendment.

Affirmed.

JUSTICE BRENNAN, with whom JUSTICE MARSHALL and JUSTICE BLACKMUN join, dissenting.

"The most that can be said of the state functionaries in this case," the Court today concludes, "is that they stood by and did nothing when suspicious circumstances dictated a more active role for them." Because I believe that this description of respondents' conduct tells only part of the story and that, accordingly, the Constitution itself "dictated a more active role" for respondents in the circumstances presented here, I cannot agree that respondents had no constitutional duty to help Joshua DeShaney. . . .

Wisconsin has established a child-welfare system specifically designed to help children like Joshua. Wisconsin law places upon the local departments of social services such as respondent (DSS or Department) a duty to investigate reported instances of child abuse. While other governmental bodies and private persons are largely responsible for the reporting of possible cases of child abuse, Wisconsin law channels all such reports to the local departments of social services for evaluation and, if necessary, further action. Even when it is the sheriff's office or police department that receives a report of suspected child abuse, that report is referred to local social services departments for action, the only exception to this occurs when the reporter fears for the child's immediate safety. In this way, Wisconsin law invites — indeed, directs — citizens and other governmental entities to depend on local departments of social services such as respondent to protect children from abuse.

The specific facts before us bear out this view of Wisconsin's system of protecting children. Each time someone voiced a suspicion that Joshua was being abused, that information was relayed to the Department for investigation and possible action. When Randy DeShaney's second wife told the police that he had "hit the boy causing marks and [was] a prime case for child abuse," the police referred her complaint to DSS. When, on three separate occasions, emergency room personnel noticed suspicious injuries on Joshua's body, they went to DSS with this information. When neighbors informed the police that they had seen or heard Joshua's father or his father's lover beating or otherwise abusing Joshua, the police brought these reports to the attention of DSS. And when respondent Kemmeter, through these reports and through her own observations in the course of nearly 20 visits to the DeShaney home, compiled growing evidence that Joshua was being abused, that information stayed within the Department — chronicled by the social worker in detail that seems almost eerie in light of her failure to act upon it. (As to the extent of the social worker's involvement in, and knowledge of, Joshua's predicament, her reaction to the news of Joshua's last and most devastating injuries is illuminating: "I just knew the phone would ring some day and Joshua would be dead.")

Even more telling than these examples is the Department's control over the decision whether to take steps to protect a particular child from suspected abuse. While many different people contributed information and advice to this decision, it was up to the people at DSS to make the ultimate decision (subject to the approval of the local government's Corporation Counsel) whether to disturb the family's current arrangements. When Joshua first appeared at a local hospital with injuries signaling physical abuse, for example, it was DSS that made the decision to take him into temporary custody for the purpose of studying his situation — and it was DSS, acting in conjunction with the corporation counsel, that returned him to his father. Unfortunately for Joshua DeShaney, the buck effectively stopped with the Department.

In these circumstances, a private citizen, or even a person working in a government agency other than DSS, would doubtless feel that her job was done as soon as she had reported her suspicions of child abuse to DSS. Through its child-welfare program, in other words, the State of Wisconsin has relieved ordinary citizens and governmental bodies other than the Department of any sense of obligation to do anything more than report their suspicions of child abuse to DSS. If DSS ignores or dismisses these suspicions, no one will step in to fill the gap. Wisconsin's child-protection program thus effectively confined Joshua DeShaney within the walls of Randy DeShaney's violent home until such time as DSS took action to remove him. Conceivably, then, children like Joshua are made worse off by the existence of this program when the persons and entities charged with carrying it out fail to do their jobs.

It simply belies reality, therefore, to contend that the State "stood by and did nothing" with respect to Joshua. Through its child-protection program, the State actively intervened in Joshua's life and, by virtue of this intervention, acquired ever more certain knowledge that Joshua was in grave danger. These circumstances, in my view, plant this case solidly within the tradition of cases like *Youngberg* and *Estelle*. . . .

JUSTICE BLACKMUN, dissenting.

Today, the Court purports to be the dispassionate oracle of the law, unmoved by "natural sympathy." But, in this pretense, the Court itself retreats into a sterile formalism which prevents it from recognizing either the facts of the case before it or the legal norms that should apply to those facts. As Justice Brennan demonstrates, the facts here involve not mere passivity, but active state intervention in the life of Joshua DeShaney — intervention that triggered a fundamental duty to aid the boy once the State learned of the severe danger to which he was exposed.

The Court fails to recognize this duty because it attempts to draw a sharp and rigid line between action and inaction. But such formalistic reasoning has no place in the interpretation of the broad and stirring Clauses of the Fourteenth Amendment. Indeed, I submit that these Clauses were designed, at least in part, to undo the formalistic legal reasoning that infected antebellum jurisprudence, which the late Professor Robert Cover analyzed so effectively in his significant work entitled *Justice Accused* (1975).

Like the antebellum judges who denied relief to fugitive slaves, the Court today claims that its decision, however harsh, is compelled by existing legal doctrine. On the contrary, the question presented by this case is an open one, and our Fourteenth Amendment precedents may be read more broadly or narrowly depending upon how one chooses to read them. Faced with the choice, I would adopt a "sympathetic" reading, one which comports with dictates of fundamental justice and recognizes that compassion need not be exiled from the province of judging. Cf. A. Stone, *Law,*

Psychiatry, and Morality 262 (1984) ("We will make mistakes if we go forward, but doing nothing can be the worst mistake. What is required of us is moral ambition. Until our composite sketch becomes a true portrait of humanity we must live with our uncertainty; we will grope, we will struggle, and our compassion may be our only guide and comfort").

Poor Joshua! Victim of repeated attacks by an irresponsible, bullying, cowardly, and intemperate father, and abandoned by respondents who placed him in a dangerous predicament and who knew or learned what was going on, and yet did essentially nothing except, as the Court revealingly observes, "dutifully recorded these incidents in [their] files." It is a sad commentary upon American life, and constitutional principles — so full of late of patriotic fervor and proud proclamations about "liberty and justice for all" — that this child, Joshua DeShaney, now is assigned to live out the remainder of his life profoundly retarded. Joshua and his mother, as petitioners here, deserve — but now are denied by this Court — the opportunity to have the facts of their case considered in the light of the constitutional protection that 42 U.S.C. § 1983 is meant to provide.

Notes and Questions

(1) Should the equal protection standard used in cases involving the regulation of business (*see* 7.01, *supra*) be used to resolve cases involving the "most basic economic needs of impoverished human beings"?

(2) Should the poor be treated as a suspect class? *See* Bertral Ross & Su Li, *Measuring Political Power: Suspect Class Determination and the Poor,* 104 CALIF. L. REV. 341 (2016).

(3) How does the holding in *DeShaney* compare with the traditional common-law tort doctrines regarding the situations in which the law imposes a "duty to rescue?" If the Department of Social Services had been a privately run and privately financed for-profit agency, would Joshua DeShaney have had a plausible cause of action in tort against the agency? *DeShaney* is a graphic example of the principle that our Constitution is primarily a repository of "negative" rather than "positive" rights. It imposes negative restraints on governmental power, but it does not impose affirmative obligations on government. Is this a sound interpretation of our Constitution? Would society be better off with the recognition that certain affirmative obligations are part of our constitutional system? What would have been the consequences of a ruling in *DeShaney* in favor of "poor Joshua?" *See* Susan Bandes, *The Negative Constitution: A Critique,* 88 MICH. L. REV. 2271 (1990).

§ 7.04 Due Process in the Administrative State

Goldberg v. Kelly

United States Supreme Court
397 U.S. 254, 90 S. Ct. 1011, 25 L. Ed. 2d 287 (1970)

Mr. Justice Brennan delivered the opinion of the Court.

The question for decision is whether a State that terminates public assistance payments to a particular recipient without affording him the opportunity for an evidentiary hearing prior to termination denies the recipient procedural due process in violation of the Due Process Clause of the Fourteenth Amendment.

This action was brought in the District Court for the Southern District of New York by residents of New York City receiving financial aid under the federally assisted program of Aid to Families with Dependent Children (AFDC) or under New York State's general Home Relief program. Their complaint alleged that the New York State and New York City officials administering these programs terminated, or were about to terminate, such aid without prior notice and hearing, thereby denying them due process of law. At the time the suits were filed there was no requirement of prior notice or hearing of any kind before termination of financial aid. . . .

The constitutional issue to be decided, therefore, is the narrow one, whether the Due Process Clause requires that the recipient be afforded an evidentiary hearing *before* the termination of benefits. . . .

Appellant does not contend that procedural due process is not applicable to the termination of welfare benefits. Such benefits are a matter of statutory entitlement for persons qualified to receive them.[5]

Their termination involves state action that adjudicates important rights. The constitutional challenge cannot be answered by an argument that public assistance benefits are "a 'privilege' and not a 'right.'" Relevant constitutional restraints apply

---

5. [Court's Footnote 8] It may be realistic today to regard welfare entitlements as more like "property" than a "gratuity." Much of the existing wealth in this country takes the form of rights that do not fall within traditional common-law concepts of property. It has been aptly noted that:

> "[s]ociety today is built around entitlement. The automobile dealer has his franchise, the doctor and lawyer their professional licenses, the worker his union membership, contract, and pension rights, the executive his contract and stock options; all are devices to aid security and independence. Many of the most important of these entitlements now flow from government: subsidies to farmers and businessmen, routes for airlines and channels for television stations; long term contracts for defense, space, and education; social security pensions for individuals. Such sources of security, whether private or public, are no longer regarded as luxuries or gratuities; to the recipients they are essentials, fully deserved, and in no sense a form of charity. It is only the poor whose entitlements, although recognized by public policy, have not been effectively enforced."

Reich, Individual Rights and Social Welfare: The Emerging Legal Issues, 74 Yale L.J. 1245, 1255 (1965).

as much to the withdrawal of public assistance benefits as to disqualification for unemployment compensation, or to denial of a tax exemption, or to discharge from public employment. The extent to which procedural due process must be afforded the recipient is influenced by the extent to which he may be "condemned to suffer grievous loss," and depends upon whether the recipient's interest in avoiding that loss outweighs the governmental interest in summary adjudication. Accordingly, as we said in *Cafeteria & Restaurant Workers Union, etc. v. McElroy*, 367 U.S. 886, 895 (1961), "consideration of what procedures due process may require under any given set of circumstances must begin with a determination of the precise nature of the government function involved as well as of the private interest that has been affected by governmental action."

It is true, of course, that some governmental benefits may be administratively terminated without affording the recipient a pre-termination evidentiary hearing. But we agree with the District Court that when welfare is discontinued, only a pre-termination evidentiary hearing provides the recipient with procedural due process. Thus the crucial factor in this context — a factor not present in the case of the black-listed government contractor, the discharged government employee, the taxpayer denied a tax exemption, or virtually anyone else whose governmental entitlements are ended — is that termination of aid pending resolution of a controversy over eligibility may deprive an *eligible* recipient of the very means by which to live while he waits. Since he lacks independent resources, his situation becomes immediately desperate. His need to concentrate upon finding the means for daily subsistence, in turn, adversely affects his ability to seek redress from the welfare bureaucracy. . . . The same governmental interests that counsel the provision of welfare, counsel as well its uninterrupted provision to those eligible to receive it; pre-termination evidentiary hearings are indispensable to that end.

Appellant does not challenge the force of these considerations but argues that they are outweighed by countervailing governmental interests in conserving fiscal and administrative resources. These interests, the argument goes, justify the delay of any evidentiary hearing until after discontinuance of the grants. Summary adjudication protects the public fisc by stopping payments promptly upon discovery of reason to believe that a recipient is no longer eligible. Since most terminations are accepted without challenge, summary adjudication also conserves both the fisc and administrative time and energy by reducing the number of evidentiary hearings actually held.

We agree with the District Court, however, that these governmental interests are not overriding in the welfare context. The requirement of a prior hearing doubtless involves some greater expense, and the benefits paid to ineligible recipients pending decision at the hearing probably cannot be recouped, since these recipients are likely to be judgment-proof. But the State is not without weapons to minimize these increased costs. Much of the drain on fiscal and administrative resources can be reduced by developing procedures for prompt pre-termination hearings and by skillful use of personnel and facilities. . . .

[The Court then held that the "pre-termination hearing need not take the form of a judicial or quasi-judicial trial." The Court required that "a recipient have timely and adequate notice detailing the reasons for a proposed termination, and an effective opportunity to defend by bringing counsel to confront any adverse witnesses, and by presenting his own arguments and evidence orally."]

MR. JUSTICE BLACK, dissenting. . . .

The more than a million names on the relief rolls in New York and the more than nine million names on the rolls of all the 50 States were not put there at random. The names are there because state welfare officials believed that those people were eligible for assistance. Probably in the officials' haste to make out the lists many names were put there erroneously in order to alleviate immediate suffering, and undoubtedly some people are drawing relief who are not entitled under the law to do so. Doubtless some draw relief checks from time to time who know they are not eligible, either because they are not actually in need or for some other reason. Many of those who thus draw undeserved gratuities are without sufficient property to enable the government to collect back from them any money they wrongfully receive. But the Court today holds that it would violate the Due Process Clause of the Fourteenth Amendment to stop paying those people weekly or monthly allowances unless the government first affords them a full "evidentiary hearing" even though welfare officials are persuaded that the recipients are not rightfully entitled to receive a penny under the law. In other words, although some recipients might be on the lists for payment wholly because of deliberate fraud on their part, the Court holds that the government is helpless and must continue, until after an evidentiary hearing, to pay money that it does not owe, never has owed, and never could owe. I do not believe there is any provision in our Constitution that should thus paralyze the government's efforts to protect itself against making payments to people who are not entitled to them. . . .

The Court, however, relies upon the Fourteenth Amendment and in effect says that failure of the government to pay a promised charitable installment to an individual deprives that individual of *his own property*, in violation of the Due Process Clause of the Fourteenth Amendment. It somewhat strains credulity to say that the government's promise of charity to an individual is property belonging to that individual when the government denies that the individual is honestly entitled to receive such a payment.

I would have little, if any, objection to the majority's decision in this case if it were written as the report of the House Committee on Education and Labor, but as an opinion ostensibly resting on the language of the Constitution I find it woefully deficient. Once the verbiage is pared away it is obvious that this Court today adopts the views of the District Court "that to cut off a welfare recipient in the face of . . .

'brutal need' without a prior hearing of some sort is unconscionable," and therefore, says the Court, unconstitutional. The majority reaches this result by a process of weighing "the recipient's interest in avoiding" the termination of welfare benefits against "the governmental interest in summary adjudication." Today's balancing act requires a "pre-termination evidentiary hearing," yet there is nothing that indicates what tomorrow's balance will be. Although the majority attempts to bolster its decision with limited quotations from prior cases, it is obvious that today's result doesn't depend on the language of the Constitution itself or the principles of other decisions, but solely on the collective judgment of the majority as to what would be a fair and humane procedure in this case. This decision is thus only another variant of the view often expressed by some members of this Court that the Due Process Clause forbids any conduct that a majority of the Court believes "unfair," "indecent," or "shocking to their consciences." Neither these words nor any like them appear anywhere in the Due Process Clause. If they did, they would leave the majority of Justices free to hold any conduct unconstitutional that they should conclude on their own to be unfair or shocking to them. Had the drafters of the Due Process Clause meant to leave judges such ambulatory power to declare laws unconstitutional, the chief value of a written constitution, as the Founders saw it, would have been lost. In fact, if that view of due process is correct, the Due Process Clause could easily swallow up all other parts of the Constitution. And truly the Constitution would always be "what the judges say it is" at a given moment, not what the Founders wrote into the document. A written constitution, designed to guarantee protection against governmental abuses, including those of judges, must have written standards that mean something definite and have an explicit content. I regret very much to be compelled to say that the Court today makes a drastic and dangerous departure from a Constitution written to control and limit the government and the judges and moves toward a constitution designed to be no more and no less than what the judges of a particular social and economic philosophy declare on the one hand to be fair or on the other hand to be shocking and unconscionable. . . .

[The dissenting opinions of CHIEF JUSTICE BURGER and JUSTICE STEWART are omitted.]

Board of Regents v. Roth

United States Supreme Court
408 U.S. 564, 92 S. Ct. 2701, 33 L. Ed. 2d 548 (1972)

Mr. Justice Stewart delivered the opinion of the Court.

In 1968 [David] Roth, was hired for his first teaching job as assistant professor of political science at Wisconsin State University-Oshkosh. He was hired for a fixed term of one academic year. . . . Respondent [Roth] completed that term. . . .

[The] President of [the] University informed the respondent before February 1, 1969, that he would not be rehired for the 1969–1970 academic year. He gave the respondent no reason for the decision and no opportunity to challenge it at any sort of hearing.

The respondent then brought this action in Federal District Court alleging that the decision not to rehire him for the next year infringed his Fourteenth Amendment rights. . . .

The District Court decided that procedural due process guarantees apply in this case by assessing and balancing the weights of the particular interests involved. It concluded that the respondent's interest in re-employment at Wisconsin State University-Oshkosh outweighed the University's interest in denying him re-employment summarily. Undeniably, the respondent's re-employment prospects were of major concern to him — concern that we surely cannot say was insignificant. And a weighing process has long been a part of any determination of the *form* of hearing required in particular situations by procedural due process. But, to determine whether due process requirements apply in the first place, we must look not to the "weight" but to the *nature* of the interest at stake. We must look to see if the interest is within the Fourteenth Amendment's protection of liberty and property. . . .

[T]he Court has fully and finally rejected the wooden distinction between "rights" and "privileges" that once seemed to govern the applicability of procedural due process rights. The Court has also made clear that the property interests protected by procedural due process extend well beyond actual ownership of real estate, chattels, or money. By the same token, the Court has required due process protection for deprivations of liberty beyond the sort of formal constraints imposed by the criminal process.

Yet, while the Court has eschewed rigid or formalistic limitations on the protection of procedural due process, it has at the same time observed certain boundaries. For the words "liberty" and "property" in the Due Process Clause of the Fourteenth Amendment must be given some meaning.

II

While this court has not attempted to define with exactness the liberty . . . guaranteed [by the Fourteenth Amendment], the term has received much consideration and some of the included things have been definitely stated. Without doubt, it denotes not merely freedom from bodily restraint but also the right of the individual to contract, to engage in any of the common occupations of life, to acquire useful knowledge, to marry, establish a home and bring up children, to worship God according to the dictates of his own conscience, and generally to enjoy those privileges long recognized . . . as essential to the orderly pursuit of happiness by free men. In a Constitution for a free people, there can be no doubt that the meaning of "liberty" must be broad indeed.

There might be cases in which a State refused to re-employ a person under such circumstances that interests in liberty would be implicated. But this is not such a case.

The State, in declining to rehire the respondent, did not make any charge against him that might seriously damage his standing and associations in his community. It did not base the nonrenewal of his contract on a charge, for example, that he had been guilty of dishonesty, or immorality. Had it done so, this would be a different case. For "[w]here a person's good name, reputation, honor, or integrity is at stake because of what the government is doing to him, notice and an opportunity to be heard are essential." *Wisconsin v. Constantineau*, 400 U.S. 433, 437 [1971]. In such a case, due process would accord an opportunity to refute the charge before University officials. In the present case, however, there is no suggestion whatever that the respondent's "good name, reputation, honor, or integrity" is at stake.

Similarly, there is no suggestion that the State, in declining to re-employ the respondent, imposed on him a stigma or other disability that foreclosed his freedom to take advantage of other employment opportunities. The State, for example, did not invoke any regulations to bar the respondent from all other public employment in state universities. Had it done so, this, again, would be a different case. . . .

Hence, on the record before us, all that clearly appears is that the respondent was not rehired for one year at one university. It stretches the concept too far to suggest that a person is deprived of "liberty" when he simply is not rehired in one job but remains as free as before to seek another. . . .

Certain attributes of "property" interests protected by procedural due process emerge from [our] decisions. To have a property interest in a benefit, a person clearly must have more than an abstract need or desire for it. He must have more than a unilateral expectation of it. He must, instead, have a legitimate claim of entitlement to it. It is a purpose of the ancient institution of property to protect those claims upon which people rely in their daily lives, reliance that must not be arbitrarily undermined. It is a purpose of the constitutional right to a hearing to provide an opportunity for a person to vindicate those claims.

Property interests, of course, are not created by the Constitution. Rather they are created and their dimensions are defined by existing rules or understandings that stem from an independent source such as state law — rules or understandings that secure certain benefits and that support claims of entitlement to those benefits. Thus, the welfare recipients in *Goldberg v. Kelly* had a claim of entitlement to welfare payments that was grounded in the statute defining eligibility for them. The recipients had not yet shown that they were, in fact, within the statutory terms of eligibility. But we held that they had a right to a hearing at which they might attempt to do so.

Just as the welfare recipients' "property" interest in welfare payments was created and defined by statutory terms, so the respondent's "property" interest in employment at Wisconsin State University-Oshkosh was created and defined by the terms of his appointment. Those terms secured his interest in employment up to June 30, 1969. But the important fact in this case is that they specifically provided that the respondent's employment was to terminate on June 30. They did not provide for contract renewal absent "sufficient cause." Indeed, they made no provision for renewal whatsoever.

Thus, the terms of the respondent's appointment secured absolutely no interest in re-employment for the next year. They supported absolutely no possible claim of entitlement to re-employment. Nor, significantly, was there any state statute or University rule or policy that secured his interest in re-employment or that created any legitimate claim to it. In these circumstances, the respondent surely had an abstract concern in being rehired, but he did not have a *property* interest sufficient to require the University authorities to give him a hearing when they declined to renew his contract of employment.

MR. JUSTICE MARSHALL, dissenting. . . .

. . . In my view, every citizen who applies for a government job is entitled to it unless the government can establish some reason for denying the employment. This is the "property" right that I believe is protected by the Fourteenth Amendment and that cannot be denied "without due process of law." And it is also liberty — liberty to work — which is the "very essence of the personal freedom and opportunity" secured by the Fourteenth Amendment.

This Court has often had occasion to note that the denial of public employment is a serious blow to any citizen. Thus, when an application for public employment is denied or the contract of a government employee is not renewed, the government must say why for it is only when the reasons underlying government action are known that citizens feel secure and protected against arbitrary government action.

Employment is one of the greatest, if not the greatest, benefits that governments offer in modern-day life. When something as valuable as the opportunity to work is at stake, the government may not reward some citizens and not others without demonstrating that its actions are fair and equitable. And it is procedural due process that is our fundamental guarantee of fairness, our protection against arbitrary, capricious, and unreasonable government action. . . .

[JUSTICES DOUGLAS and BRENNAN also wrote dissenting opinions.]

Cleveland Board of Education v. Loudermill

United States Supreme Court
470 U.S. 532, 105 S. Ct. 1487, 84 L. Ed. 2d 494 (1985)

JUSTICE WHITE delivered the opinion of the Court.

In these cases we consider what pretermination process must be accorded a public employee who can be discharged only for cause.

I

In 1979 the Cleveland Board of Education [hired] respondent James Loudermill as a security guard. On his job application, Loudermill stated that he had never been convicted of a felony. Eleven months later, as part of a routine examination of his employment records, the Board discovered that in fact Loudermill had been convicted of grand larceny in 1968. By letter dated November 3, 1980, the Board's Business Manager informed Loudermill that he had been dismissed because of his dishonesty in filling out the employment application. Loudermill was not afforded an opportunity to respond to the charge of dishonesty or to challenge his dismissal. On November 13, the Board adopted a resolution officially approving the discharge.

Under Ohio law, Loudermill was a "classified civil servant." Such employees can be terminated only for cause, and may obtain administrative review if discharged. Pursuant to this provision, Loudermill filed an appeal with the Cleveland Civil Service Commission on November 12. The Commission appointed a referee, who held a hearing on January 29, 1981. Loudermill argued that he had thought that his 1968 larceny conviction was for a misdemeanor rather than a felony. The referee recommended reinstatement. On July 20, 1981, the full Commission heard argument and orally announced that it would uphold the dismissal. Proposed findings of fact and conclusions of law followed on August 10, and Loudermill's attorneys were advised of the result by mail on August 21.

Although the Commission's decision was subject to judicial review in the state courts, Loudermill instead brought the present suit in the Federal District Court for the Northern District of Ohio. The complaint alleged that [the statute] was unconstitutional on its face because it did not provide the employee an opportunity to respond to the charges against him prior to removal. As a result, discharged employees were deprived of liberty and property without due process. The complaint also alleged that the provision was unconstitutional as applied because discharged employees were not given sufficiently prompt post-removal hearings.

Before a responsive pleading was filed, the District Court dismissed for failure to state a claim on which relief could be granted. It held that because the very statute that created the property right in continued employment also specified the procedures for discharge, and because those procedures were followed, Loudermill was, by definition, afforded all the process due. The post-termination hearing also adequately protected Loudermill's liberty interests. Finally, the District Court concluded that, in light of the Commission's crowded docket, the delay in processing Loudermill's administrative appeal was constitutionally acceptable. . . .

[The] Court of Appeals found that [Loudermill] had been deprived of due process. . . .

Respondents' federal constitutional claim depends on their having had a property right in continued employment. *Roth*. If they did, the State could not deprive them of this property without due process.

Property interests are not created by the Constitution, "they are created and their dimensions are defined by existing rules or understandings that stem from an independent source such as state law. . . ." *Roth*. The Ohio statute plainly creates such an interest. Respondents were "classified civil service employees," entitled to retain their positions "during good behavior and efficient service," who could not be dismissed "except . . . for . . . misfeasance, malfeasance, or nonfeasance in office." The statute plainly supports the conclusion, reached by both lower courts, that respondents possessed property rights in continued employment. Indeed, this question does not seem to have been disputed below. . . .

[The argument], accepted by the District Court, has its genesis in the plurality opinion in *Arnett v. Kennedy* 416 U.S. 134 (1974). The plurality reasoned that where the legislation conferring the substantive right also sets out the procedural mechanism for enforcing that right, the two cannot be separated:

> The employee's statutorily defined right is not a guarantee against removal without cause in the abstract, but such a guarantee as enforced by the procedures which Congress has designated for the determination of cause.
>
> . . . [W]here the grant of a substantive right is inextricably intertwined with the limitations on the procedures which are to be employed in determining that right, a litigant in the position of appellee must take the bitter with the sweet.

This view garnered three votes in *Arnett*, but was specifically rejected by the other six Justices. Since then, this theory has at times seemed to gather some additional support. See *Bishop v. Wood*, 426 U.S. 341 (1976). More recently, however, the Court has clearly rejected it. In *Vitek v. Jones*, 445 U.S. 480, 491 (1980), we pointed out that "minimum [procedural] requirements [are] a matter of federal law, they are not diminished by the fact that the State may have specified its own procedures that it may deem adequate for determining the preconditions to adverse official action." This conclusion was reiterated in *Logan v. Zimmerman Brush Co.*, 455 U.S. 422, 432 (1982), where we reversed the lower court's holding that because the entitlement arose from a state statute, the legislature had the prerogative to define the procedures to be followed to protect that entitlement.

In light of these holdings, it is settled that the "bitter with the sweet" approach misconceives the constitutional guarantee. If a clearer holding is needed, we provide it today. The point is straightforward: the Due Process Clause provides that certain substantive rights — life, liberty, and property — cannot be deprived except pursuant to constitutionally adequate procedures. The categories of substance and procedure are distinct. Were the rule otherwise, the Clause would be reduced to a mere tautology. "Property" cannot be defined by the procedures provided for its deprivation any more than can life or liberty. The right to due process "is conferred, not by legislative grace, but by constitutional guarantee. While the legislature may elect not to confer a property interest in [public] employment, it may not constitutionally authorize the deprivation of such an interest, once conferred, without appropriate procedural safeguards." *Arnett v. Kennedy* (Powell, J. concurring in part and concurring in result in part); *see id.*, (White, J., concurring in part and dissenting in part).

In short, once it is determined that the Due Process Clause applies, "the question remains what process is due." The answer to that question is not to be found in the Ohio statute.

An essential principle of due process is that a deprivation of life, liberty, or property "be preceded by notice and opportunity for hearing appropriate to the nature of the case." *Mullane v. Central Hanover Bank & Trust Co.*, 339 U.S. 306, 313 (1950). We have described "the root requirement" of the Due Process Clause as being "that an individual be given an opportunity for a hearing *before* he is deprived of any significant property interest."[6] This principle requires "some kind of a hearing" prior to the discharge of an employee who has a constitutionally protected property interest in his employment. . . . Even decisions finding no constitutional violation in termination procedures have relied on the existence of some pretermination opportunity to respond. . . .

The need for some form of pretermination hearing, recognized in these cases, is evident from a balancing of the competing interests at stake. These are the private interest in retaining employment, the governmental interest in the expeditious removal of unsatisfactory employees and the avoidance of administrative burdens, and the risk of an erroneous termination. See *Mathews v. Eldridge*, 424 U.S. 319, 335 (1976).

First, the significance of the private interest in retaining employment cannot be gainsaid. We have frequently recognized the severity of depriving a person of the means of livelihood. . . .

Second, some opportunity for the employee to present his side of the case is recurringly of obvious value in reaching an accurate decision. Dismissals for cause will often involve factual disputes. Even where the facts are clear, the appropriateness or necessity of the discharge may not be; in such cases, the only meaningful

---

6. [Court's Footnote 7] There are, of course, some situations in which a post-deprivation hearing will satisfy due process requirements. See *Ewing v. Mytinger & Casselberry, Inc.*, 339 U.S. 594 (1950); *North American Cold Storage Co. v. Chicago*, 211 U.S. 306 (1908).

opportunity to invoke the discretion of the decisionmaker is likely to be before the termination takes effect.

The case before us illustrates these considerations. [The] respondent had [a] plausible argument to make that might have prevented [his] discharge. [In evaluating the claim made by] Loudermill, given the Commission's ruling we cannot say that the discharge was mistaken. Nonetheless, in light of the referee's recommendation, neither can we say that a fully informed decisionmaker might not have exercised its discretion and decided not to dismiss him, notwithstanding its authority to do so. In any event, the termination involved arguable issues and the right to a hearing does not depend on a demonstration of certain success.

The governmental interest in immediate termination does not outweigh these interests. As we shall explain, affording the employee an opportunity to respond prior to termination would impose neither a significant administrative burden nor intolerable delays. Furthermore, the employer shares the employee's interest in avoiding disruption and erroneous decisions; and until the matter is settled, the employer would continue to receive the benefit of the employee's labors. It is preferable to keep a qualified employee on than to train a new one. A governmental employer also has an interest in keeping citizens usefully employed rather than taking the possibly erroneous and counter-productive step of forcing its employees onto the welfare rolls. Finally, in those situations where the employer perceives a significant hazard in keeping the employee on the job, it can avoid the problem by suspending with pay.

The foregoing considerations indicate that the pretermination "hearing," though necessary, need not be elaborate. We have pointed out that "[t]he formality and procedural requisites for the hearing can vary, depending upon the importance of the interests involved and the nature of the subsequent proceedings." In general, "something less" than a full evidentiary hearing is sufficient prior to adverse administrative action. Under state law, respondents were later entitled to a full administrative hearing and judicial review. The only question is what steps were required before the termination took effect.

In only one case, *Goldberg v. Kelly*, 397 U.S. 254 (1970), has the Court required a full adversarial evidentiary hearing prior to adverse governmental action. However, as the *Goldberg* Court itself pointed out, that case presented significantly different considerations than are present in the context of public employment. Here, the pretermination hearing need not definitively resolve the propriety of the discharge. It should be an initial check against mistaken decisions — essentially, a determination of whether there are reasonable grounds to believe that the charges against the employee are true and support the proposed action.

The essential requirements of due process, and all that respondents seek or the Court of Appeals required, are notice and an opportunity to respond. The opportunity to present reasons, either in person or in writing, why proposed action should not be taken is a fundamental due process requirement. The tenured public employee is entitled to oral or written notice of the charges against him, an explanation of the employer's evidence, and an opportunity to present his side of the story. To require more than this prior to termination would intrude to an unwarranted extent on the government's interest in quickly removing an unsatisfactory employee. . . .

The judgment of the Court of Appeals is affirmed. . . .

JUSTICE MARSHALL, concurring in part and concurring in the judgment. . . .

I write separately . . . to reaffirm my belief that public employees who may be discharged only for cause are entitled, under the Due Process Clause of the Fourteenth Amendment, to more than respondents sought in this case. I continue to believe that *before the decision is made to terminate an employee's wages*, the employee is entitled to an opportunity to test the strength of the evidence "by confronting and cross-examining adverse witnesses and by presenting witnesses on [their] own behalf, whenever there are substantial disputes in testimonial evidence." Because the Court suggests that even in this situation due process requires no more than notice and an opportunity to be heard before wages are cut off, I am not able to join the Court's opinion in its entirety. . . .

JUSTICE BRENNAN, concurring in part and dissenting in part. . . . [Omitted.]

JUSTICE REHNQUIST, dissenting. . . .

We ought to recognize the totality of the State's definition of the property right in question, and not merely seize upon one of several paragraphs in a unitary statute to proclaim that in that paragraph the State has inexorably conferred upon a civil service employee something which it is powerless under the United States Constitution to qualify in the next paragraph of the statute. This practice ignores our duty under *Roth* to rely on state law as the source of property interests for purposes of applying the Due Process Clause of the Fourteenth Amendment. While it does not impose a federal definition of property, the Court departs from the full breadth of the holding in *Roth* by its selective choice from among the sentences the Ohio legislature chooses to use in establishing and qualifying a right.

Having concluded by this somewhat tortured reasoning that Ohio has created a property right in the respondents in this case, the Court naturally proceeds to inquire what process is "due" before the respondents may be divested of that right. This customary "balancing" inquiry conducted by the Court in this case reaches a result that is quite unobjectionable, but it seems to me that it is devoid of any principles which will either instruct or endure. The balance is simply an *ad hoc* weighing which depends to a great extent upon how the Court subjectively views the underlying interests at stake. The results in previous cases and in this case have been quite unpredictable. . . . The results from today's balance certainly do not jibe with the result in *Goldberg* or *Mathews v. Eldridge.*[7]

---

7. [Dissenting Court's Footnote 1] Today the balancing test requires a pretermination opportunity to respond. In *Goldberg* we required a full-fledged trial-type hearing, and in *Mathews* we

Notes and Questions

(1) Three theoretical approaches to procedural due process cases have emerged on the Supreme Court. The "unitary" theory assumes that *some* process is always "due" any time the government does anything that causes significant harm to a person. The unitary theory does not require an inquiry into whether "life, liberty, or property" is at stake, but rather assumes that the phrase "life, liberty, or property" is used in the Due Process Clause in a non-technical sense, as a phrase designed to capture the full range of interests of value to human beings. The theory is called "unitary" because it requires only one question to be answered in all due process cases: How much process is due? Is *Goldberg v. Kelly* an example of the unitary theory? At the time it was decided, it may have seemed so, but *Board of Regents v. Roth* clearly rejected the unitary approach, requiring first that a claimant demonstrate a concrete "life, liberty, or property" interest grounded in state or federal law. *See* Rodney A. Smolla, *The Reemergence of the Right-Privilege Distinction in Constitutional Law: The Price of Protesting Too Much*, 35 Stan. L. Rev. 69, 72 (1982); Mark Tushnet, *The Newer Property: Suggestions for the Revival of Substantive Due Process*, 1975 Sup. Ct. Rev. 261; William Van Alystne, *Cracks in "The New Property": Adjudicative Due Process in the Administrative State*, 62 Cornell L. Rev. 445 (1977).

(2) A second approach to procedural due process cases is the "positivist" theory. Under this theory, espoused by Chief Justice Rehnquist, in procedural due process cases involving governmentally created benefits, the entire problem is essentially a matter of contract between the government and the citizen. *See Arnett v. Kennedy*, 416 U.S. 134 (1974) (plurality opinion of Rehnquist, J.). The Rehnquist theory is thus a direct derivative of the "right-privilege" distinction of Justice Oliver Wendell Holmes. This is a "positivist" approach to due process, because the government, through positive law (such as statutes, regulations, or contracts entered into with recipients) decides both whether to bring an entitlement into existence in the first

---

declined to require any pretermination process other than those required by the statute. At times this balancing process may look as if it were undertaken with a thumb on the scale, depending upon the result the Court desired. For example, in *Mathews* we minimized the importance of the benefit to the recipient, stating that after termination he could always go on welfare to survive. Today, however, the Court exalts the recipient's interest in retaining employment; not a word is said about going on welfare. Conversely, in *Mathews* we stressed the interests of the State, while today, in a footnote, the Court goes so far as to denigrate the State's interest in firing a school security guard who had lied about a prior felony conviction.

Today the Court purports to describe the State's interest but does so in a way that is contrary to what the State has asserted in its briefs. The description of the State's interests looks more like a make-weight to support the Court's result. The decision of whom to train and employ is strictly a decision for the State. The Court attempts to ameliorate its ruling by stating that a State may always suspend an employee with pay, in lieu of predischarge hearing, if it determines that he poses a threat. This does less than justice to the State's interest in its financial integrity and its interest in promptly terminating an employee who has violated the conditions of his tenure, and ignores Ohio's current practice of paying back wages to wrongfully-discharged employees.

place, and how much procedural protection to include as part of the "package" that creates and defines the entitlement. Thus, for a public employee, the government decides how much job security the employee will receive in a particular governmental position, as well as how much procedural protection the employee is entitled to before he or she may be disciplined or terminated. The positivist theory essentially eliminates the Due Process Clause as a free-standing source of procedural protection. The only importance of the Due Process Clause under this approach is a command that the government abide by whatever procedural protections it has created. Chief Justice Rehnquist has never been able to attract a majority of the Court to this view, however, and it was explicitly rejected in *Loudermill*. For a critique of this approach, see Robert Rabin, *Job Security and Due Process: Monitoring Administrative Discretion Through a Reasons Requirement*, 44 U. CHI. L. REV. 60 (1976). For an interesting feminist approach to these issues, see Cynthia Farina, *Conceiving Due Process* 3 YALE J.L. & FEMINISM 189 (1991).

(3) The third approach to procedural due process is the "bifurcated theory," as exemplified by *Roth* and *Loudermill*. The theory is "bifurcated" because it creates a two-step analysis in procedural due process cases. The first question to be asked in all cases is whether the claimant has an "entitlement" to life, liberty, or property. The source of this entitlement is usually positive law — that is the holding of *Roth*. The bifurcated theory thus *starts out* resembling the "positivist" notions of Chief Justice Rehnquist. If no entitlement exists, the claimant is entitled to no due process at all, and the case is over. If an entitlement does exist, analysis proceeds to the second step: How much process is due? This is *not* a question answered by positive law, but is rather a "judicial" question to be answered by judges interpreting the requirements of the Due Process Clause itself. In determining "how much process is due," the Supreme Court has adopted, in *Mathews v. Eldridge*, 424 U.S. 319 (1976), a balancing test that requires courts to consider:

> First, the private interest that will be affected by the official action; second, the risk of an erroneous deprivation of such interest through the procedures used, and the probable value, if any, of additional or substitute procedural safeguards; and finally, the Government's interest, including the function involved and the fiscal and administrative burdens that the additional or substitute procedural requisites would entail.

Does this formula adequately capture the essence of procedural fairness? Or is its emphasis on accuracy and efficiency too cold, failing to take account of the interests in human dignity, participation, and catharsis that fair procedures also vindicate? *See* Jerry L. Mashaw, *The Supreme Court's Due Process Calculus for Administrative Adjudication in Mathews v. Eldridge: Three Factors in Search of a Theory of Value*, 44 U. CHI. L. REV. 28 (1976).

(4) Obviously, after *Roth*, a great deal hangs on whether the claimant is able to demonstrate that an "entitlement" exists. *Roth* is softened somewhat, however, by a companion case decided the same day, *Perry v. Sindermann*, 408 U.S. 593 (1972). Sindermann, like Roth, was a college teacher fired without a hearing. At Sindermann's

college, there *was* no formal tenure system. But Sindermann alleged that the college had a "de facto" tenure system, and that he had effectively acquired tenure through ten successive one-year contracts. The Supreme Court held that this stated a valid claim, and that Sindermann would be entitled to attempt to prove his de facto tenure theory at trial. Justice Stewart's opinion for the Court stated that:

> Property denotes a broad range of interests that is secured by "existing rules or understandings". . . . A person's interest in a benefit is a "property" interest for due process purposes if there are such rules or mutually explicit understandings that support his claim of entitlement to the benefit and that he may invoke at a hearing.

(5) In *Town of Castle Rock v. Gonzalez*, 545 U.S. 748 (2005), the Supreme Court held that the Due Process Clause was not violated when police officers, acting pursuant to official policy or custom, failed to respond to repeated reports over several hours that a woman's estranged husband had taken their three children in violation of her restraining order against the husband. Tragically, the husband murdered the children. The issue in the case was whether the plaintiff had a cognizable procedural due process claim because a Colorado statute established the state legislature's clear intent to require police to enforce retraining orders, thereby creating an "entitlement" to its enforcement. The Supreme Court held that no such entitlement existed. A benefit is not a protected entitlement, the Court reasoned, if officials have discretion to grant or deny it. Colorado law, the Court held, had not created a personal entitlement to enforcement of restraining orders. State law, the Court ruled, did not truly make such enforcement *mandatory*. To the contrary, a well established tradition of police discretion has long coexisted with apparently mandatory arrest statutes. Against the backdrop of that tradition, the Court held, a true mandate of police action would require some stronger indication than the Colorado statute's direction to "use every reasonable means to enforce a restraining order." Moreover, the purported property interest stemmed not from common law or from any contract, but merely from a state's statutory scheme. If the state had intended for this to rise to the level of an enforceable property interest, the Court reasoned, one would expect to see some indication of that in the statute itself. Finally, the Court held, even were the Court to think otherwise about Colorado's creation of an entitlement, it is not clear that an individual entitlement to enforcement of a restraining order could constitute a "property" interest for due process purposes. Such a right, the Court observed, would have no ascertainable monetary value and would arise incidentally, not out of some new species of government benefit or service, but out of a function that government actors have always performed — arresting people when they have probable cause.

Problem C

Alice Duncan is the Director of the Library at Freedonia State University Business School. She has been the Director for twenty years. Each year she is issued a one-year contract, which recites:

> The position of Director of the Library is a non-tenure position. It shall be renewed, in accordance with the procedures set forth in the By-Laws of the School of Business, except when termination is justified by good cause.

The By-Laws of the School of Business provide that, in the case of any non-tenured professional employee, including the Director of the Library: "Any decision to terminate shall be in the sole discretion of the Dean of the School of Business. In his or her discretion, the Dean may permit a hearing to determine if good cause for termination exists." The By-Laws in turn define "good cause" as "misfeasance or malfeasance in professional performance, as determined by the Dean."

Alice Duncan is terminated by the Dean following a budget dispute over budgetary allocations for the library. Without granting her a hearing, the Dean stated in a letter that her contract would not be renewed because, in his judgment, her insubordination in the budgetary process "was disruptive and not in the best interests of the School of Business." Duncan has an outstanding professional record as a librarian and is confident that several members of the faculty and outside experts would attest that she is among the best business school librarians in the nation. She is confident that, if she could just receive some kind of hearing, she would prevail. She comes to you for legal advice. How will you advise her? It is important to note that there is no contention that the Maryland regulation is infected with a racially discriminatory purpose or effect such as to make it inherently suspect.

§ 7.05 The Right to Bear Arms

District of Columbia v. Heller

United States Supreme Court
554 U.S. 570, 128 S. Ct. 2783; 171 L. Ed. 2d 637 (2008)

JUSTICE SCALIA delivered the opinion of the Court.

I

The District of Columbia generally prohibits the possession of handguns. It is a crime to carry an unregistered firearm, and the registration of handguns is prohibited. See D.C.Code §§ 7-2501.01(12), 7-2502.01(a), 7-2502.02(a)(4) (2001). Wholly apart from that prohibition, no person may carry a handgun without a license, but the chief of police may issue licenses for 1-year periods. See §§ 22-4504(a), 22-4506. District of Columbia law also requires residents to keep their lawfully owned firearms, such as registered long guns, "unloaded and dissembled or bound by a trigger lock or similar device" unless they are located in a place of business or are being used for lawful recreational activities. See § 7-2507.02.

Respondent Dick Heller is a D.C. special police officer authorized to carry a handgun while on duty at the Federal Judicial Center. He applied for a registration certificate for a handgun that he wished to keep at home, but the District refused. He thereafter filed a lawsuit in the Federal District Court for the District of Columbia seeking, on Second Amendment grounds, to enjoin the city from enforcing the bar on the registration of handguns, the licensing requirement insofar as it prohibits the carrying of a firearm in the home without a license, and the trigger-lock requirement insofar as it prohibits the use of "functional firearms within the home." . . .

II

We turn first to the meaning of the Second Amendment.

A

The Second Amendment provides: "A well regulated Militia, being necessary to the security of a free State, the right of the people to keep and bear Arms, shall not be infringed." In interpreting this text, we are guided by the principle that "[t]he Constitution was written to be understood by the voters; its words and phrases were used in their normal and ordinary as distinguished from technical meaning." *United States v. Sprague*, 282 U.S. 716, 731 (1931); see also *Gibbons v. Ogden*, 9 Wheat. 1, 188 (1824). Normal meaning may of course include an idiomatic meaning, but it excludes secret or technical meanings that would not have been known to ordinary citizens in the founding generation.

The two sides in this case have set out very different interpretations of the Amendment. Petitioners and today's dissenting Justices believe that it protects only the right to possess and carry a firearm in connection with militia service. Respondent argues that it protects an individual right to possess a firearm unconnected with service in a militia, and to use that arm for traditionally lawful purposes, such as self-defense within the home.

The Second Amendment is naturally divided into two parts: its prefatory clause and its operative clause. The former does not limit the latter grammatically, but rather announces a purpose. . . . Logic demands that there be a link between the stated purpose and the command. The Second Amendment would be nonsensical if it read, "A well regulated Militia, being necessary to the security of a free State, the right of the people to petition for redress of grievances shall not be infringed." That requirement of logical connection may cause a prefatory clause to resolve an ambiguity in the operative clause ("The separation of church and state being an important objective, the teachings of canons shall have no place in our jurisprudence." The preface makes clear that the operative clause refers not to canons of interpretation but to clergymen.) But apart from that clarifying function, a prefatory clause does not limit or expand the scope of the operative clause. . . .

1. Operative Clause.

a. "Right of the People."

The first salient feature of the operative clause is that it codifies a "right of the people." The unamended Constitution and the Bill of Rights use the phrase "right of the people" two other times, in the First Amendment's Assembly-and-Petition Clause and in the Fourth Amendment's Search-and-Seizure Clause. The Ninth Amendment uses very similar terminology ("The enumeration in the Constitution, of certain rights, shall not be construed to deny or disparage others retained by the people"). All three of these instances unambiguously refer to individual rights, not "collective" rights, or rights that may be exercised only through participation in some corporate body.

Three provisions of the Constitution refer to "the people" in a context other than "rights"—the famous preamble ("We the people"), §2 of Article I (providing that "the people" will choose members of the House), and the Tenth Amendment (providing that those powers not given the Federal Government remain with "the States" or "the people"). Those provisions arguably refer to "the people" acting collectively—but they deal with the exercise or reservation of powers, not rights. Nowhere else in the Constitution does a "right" attributed to "the people" refer to anything other than an individual right.

What is more, in all six other provisions of the Constitution that mention "the people," the term unambiguously refers to all members of the political community, not an unspecified subset. . . . We start therefore with a strong presumption that the Second Amendment right is exercised individually and belongs to all Americans.

b. "Keep and bear Arms."

Before addressing the verbs "keep" and "bear," we interpret their object: "Arms." The 18th-century meaning is no different from the meaning today. The 1773 edition of Samuel Johnson's dictionary defined "arms" as "weapons of offence, or armour of defence." 1 Dictionary of the English Language 107 (4th ed.) (hereinafter Johnson). Timothy Cunningham's important 1771 legal dictionary defined "arms" as "any thing that a man wears for his defence, or takes into his hands, or useth in wrath to cast at or strike another." 1 A New and Complete Law Dictionary (1771); see also N. Webster, American Dictionary of the English Language (1828) (reprinted 1989) (hereinafter Webster) (similar). The term was applied, then as now, to weapons that were not specifically designed for military use and were not employed in a military capacity. . . .

We turn to the phrases "keep arms" and "bear arms." Johnson defined "keep" as, most relevantly, "[t]o retain; not to lose," and "[t]o have in custody." Johnson 1095. Webster defined it as "[t]o hold; to retain in one's power or possession." No party has apprised us of an idiomatic meaning of "keep Arms." Thus, the most natural reading of "keep Arms" in the Second Amendment is to "have weapons."

The phrase "keep arms" was not prevalent in the written documents of the founding period that we have found, but there are a few examples, all of which favor viewing the right to "keep Arms" as an individual right unconnected with militia service. . . .

At the time of the founding, as now, to "bear" meant to "carry." See Johnson 161; Webster; T. Sheridan, A Complete Dictionary of the English Language (1796); 2 Oxford English Dictionary 20 (2d ed. 1989) (hereinafter Oxford). When used with "arms," however, the term has a meaning that refers to carrying for a particular purpose—confrontation. . . . Although the phrase implies that the carrying of the weapon is for the purpose of "offensive or defensive action," it in no way connotes participation in a structured military organization. From our review of founding-era sources, we conclude that this natural meaning was also the meaning that "bear arms" had in the 18th century. . . .

In any event, the meaning of "bear arms" that petitioners and Justice Stevens propose is not even the (sometimes) idiomatic meaning. Rather, they manufacture a hybrid definition, whereby "bear arms" connotes the actual carrying of arms (and therefore is not really an idiom) but only in the service of an organized militia. No dictionary has ever adopted that definition, and we have been apprised of no source that indicates that it carried that meaning at the time of the founding. But it is easy to see why petitioners and the dissent are driven to the hybrid definition. Giving "bear Arms" its idiomatic meaning would cause the protected right to consist of the right to be a soldier or to wage war — an absurdity that no commentator has ever endorsed. See L. Levy, Origins of the Bill of Rights 135 (1999). Worse still, the phrase "keep and bear Arms" would be incoherent. The word "Arms" would have two different meanings at once: "weapons" (as the object of "keep") and (as the object of "bear") one-half of an idiom. It would be rather like saying "He filled and kicked the bucket" to mean "He filled the bucket and died." Grotesque.

Petitioners justify their limitation of "bear arms" to the military context by pointing out the unremarkable fact that it was often used in that context — the same mistake they made with respect to "keep arms." It is especially unremarkable that the phrase was often used in a military context in the federal legal sources (such as records of congressional debate) that have been the focus of petitioners' inquiry. Those sources would have had little occasion to use it except in discussions about the standing army and the militia. And the phrases used primarily in those military discussions include not only "bear arms" but also "carry arms," "possess arms," and "have arms" — though no one thinks that those other phrases also had special military meanings. . . .

c. Meaning of the Operative Clause.

Putting all of these textual elements together, we find that they guarantee the individual right to possess and carry weapons in case of confrontation. This meaning is strongly confirmed by the historical background of the Second Amendment. We look to this because it has always been widely understood that the Second Amendment, like the First and Fourth Amendments, codified a pre-existing right. The very text of the Second Amendment implicitly recognizes the pre-existence of the right and declares only that it "shall not be infringed." . . .

There seems to us no doubt, on the basis of both text and history, that the Second Amendment conferred an individual right to keep and bear arms. Of course the right was not unlimited, just as the First Amendment's right of free speech was not. Thus, we do not read the Second Amendment to protect the right of citizens to carry arms for any sort of confrontation, just as we do not read the First Amendment to protect the right of citizens to speak for any purpose. Before turning to limitations upon the individual right, however, we must determine whether the prefatory clause of the Second Amendment comports with our interpretation of the operative clause.

2. Prefatory Clause.

The prefatory clause reads: "A well regulated Militia, being necessary to the security of a free State. . . ."

a. "Well-Regulated Militia."

In *United States v. Miller*, 307 U.S. 174, 179 (1939), we explained that "the Militia comprised all males physically capable of acting in concert for the common defense." That definition comports with founding-era sources. . . .

Petitioners take a seemingly narrower view of the militia, stating that "[m]ilitias are the state- and congressionally-regulated military forces described in the Militia Clauses (art. I, § 8, cls.15–16)." Although we agree with petitioners' interpretive assumption that "militia" means the same thing in Article I and the Second Amendment, we believe that petitioners identify the wrong thing, namely, the organized militia. Unlike armies and navies, which Congress is given the power to create ("to raise . . . Armies"; "to provide . . . a Navy," Art. I, § 8, cls. 12–13), the militia is assumed by Article I already to be in existence. Congress is given the power to "provide for calling forth the militia," § 8, cl. 15; and the power not to create, but to "organiz[e]" it — and not to organize "a" militia, which is what one would expect if the militia were to be a federal creation, but to organize "the" militia, connoting a body already in existence, ibid., cl. 16. . . .

b. "Security of a Free State."

The phrase "security of a free state" meant "security of a free polity," not security of each of the several States. . . .

3. Relationship between Prefatory Clause and Operative Clause

We reach the question, then: Does the preface fit with an operative clause that creates an individual right to keep and bear arms? It fits perfectly, once one knows the history that the founding generation knew and that we have described above. That history showed that the way tyrants had eliminated a militia consisting of all the able-bodied men was not by banning the militia but simply by taking away the people's arms, enabling a select militia or standing army to suppress political opponents. This is what had occurred in England that prompted codification of the right to have arms in the English Bill of Rights.

The debate with respect to the right to keep and bear arms, as with other guarantees in the Bill of Rights, was not over whether it was desirable (all agreed that it was) but over whether it needed to be codified in the Constitution. . . .

It is . . . entirely sensible that the Second Amendment's prefatory clause announces the purpose for which the right was codified: to prevent elimination of the militia. The prefatory clause does not suggest that preserving the militia was the only reason Americans valued the ancient right; most undoubtedly thought it even more important for self-defense and hunting. But the threat that the new Federal

Government would destroy the citizens' militia by taking away their arms was the reason that right — unlike some other English rights — was codified in a written Constitution. . . . Our interpretation is confirmed by analogous arms-bearing rights in state constitutions that preceded and immediately followed adoption of the Second Amendment. . . .

Justice Stevens relies on the drafting history of the Second Amendment — the various proposals in the state conventions and the debates in Congress. It is dubious to rely on such history to interpret a text that was widely understood to codify a pre-existing right, rather than to fashion a new one. But even assuming that this legislative history is relevant, JUSTICE STEVENS flatly misreads the historical record.

It is true, as JUSTICE STEVENS says, that there was concern that the Federal Government would abolish the institution of the state militia. That concern found expression, however, not in the various Second Amendment precursors proposed in the State conventions, but in separate structural provisions that would have given the States concurrent and seemingly non-pre-emptible authority to organize, discipline, and arm the militia when the Federal Government failed to do so. The Second Amendment precursors, by contrast, referred to the individual English right already codified in two (and probably four) State constitutions. The Federalist-dominated first Congress chose to reject virtually all major structural revisions favored by the Antifederalists, including the proposed militia amendments. Rather, it adopted primarily the popular and uncontroversial (though, in the Federalists' view, unnecessary) individual-rights amendments. The Second Amendment right, protecting only individuals' liberty to keep and carry arms, did nothing to assuage Antifederalists' concerns about federal control of the militia. . . .

[The majority next found that the interpretation of the Second Amendment by scholars, courts, and legislators, from immediately after its ratification through the late 19th century supports its interpretation of the Amendment.]

Justice Stevens places overwhelming reliance upon this Court's decision in *United States v. Miller*. . . . And what is, according to Justice Stevens, the holding of *Miller* that demands such obeisance? That the Second Amendment "protects the right to keep and bear arms for certain military purposes, but that it does not curtail the legislature's power to regulate the nonmilitary use and ownership of weapons."

Nothing so clearly demonstrates the weakness of JUSTICE STEVENS' case. *Miller* did not hold that and cannot possibly be read to have held that. The judgment in the case upheld against a Second Amendment challenge two men's federal convictions for transporting an unregistered short-barreled shotgun in interstate commerce, in violation of the National Firearms Act, 48 Stat. 1236. It is entirely clear that the Court's basis for saying that the Second Amendment did not apply was not that the defendants were "bear[ing] arms" not "for . . . military purposes" but for "nonmilitary use". Rather, it was that the type of weapon at issue was not eligible for Second Amendment protection: "In the absence of any evidence tending to show that the possession or use of a [short-barreled shotgun] at this time has some reasonable relationship to the preservation or efficiency of a well regulated militia, we cannot say that the Second Amendment guarantees the right to keep and bear such an instrument." 307 U.S., at 178. "Certainly," the Court continued, "it is not within judicial notice that this weapon is any part of the ordinary military equipment or that its use could contribute to the common defense." Ibid. Beyond that, the opinion provided no explanation of the content of the right.

This holding is not only consistent with, but positively suggests, that the Second Amendment confers an individual right to keep and bear arms (though only arms that "have some reasonable relationship to the preservation or efficiency of a well regulated militia"). Had the Court believed that the Second Amendment protects only those serving in the militia, it would have been odd to examine the character of the weapon rather than simply note that the two crooks were not militiamen. . . .

We may as well consider at this point (for we will have to consider eventually) what types of weapons *Miller* permits. Read in isolation, *Miller*'s phrase "part of ordinary military equipment" could mean that only those weapons useful in warfare are protected. That would be a startling reading of the opinion, since it would mean that the National Firearms Act's restrictions on machineguns (not challenged in *Miller*) might be unconstitutional, machineguns being useful in warfare in 1939. We think that *Miller*'s "ordinary military equipment" language must be read in tandem with what comes after: "[O]rdinarily when called for [militia] service [able-bodied] men were expected to appear bearing arms supplied by themselves and of the kind in common use at the time."307 U.S., at 179. The traditional militia was formed from a pool of men bringing arms "in common use at the time" for lawful purposes like self-defense. "In the colonial and revolutionary war era, [small-arms] weapons used by militiamen and weapons used in defense of person and home were one and the same." Indeed, that is precisely the way in which the Second Amendment's operative clause furthers the purpose announced in its preface. We therefore read *Miller* to say only that the Second Amendment does not protect those weapons not typically possessed by law-abiding citizens for lawful purposes, such as short-barreled shotguns. . . .

We conclude that nothing in our precedents forecloses our adoption of the original understanding of the Second Amendment. It should be unsurprising that such a significant matter has been for so long judicially unresolved. For most of our history, the Bill of Rights was not thought applicable to the States, and the Federal Government did not significantly regulate the possession of firearms by law-abiding citizens. Other provisions of the Bill of Rights have similarly remained unilluminated for lengthy periods. This Court first held a law to violate the First Amendment's guarantee of freedom of speech in 1931, almost 150 years after the Amendment was ratified, see *Near v. Minnesota ex rel. Olson*, 283 U.S. 697 (1931), and it was not until after World War II that we held a law invalid under the Establishment Clause, see *Illinois ex rel. McCollum v. Bd. of Educ. of School Dist. No. 71, Champaign Cty.*, 333 U.S. 203 (1948). . . .

III

Like most rights, the right secured by the Second Amendment is not unlimited. From Blackstone through the 19th-century cases, commentators and courts routinely explained that the right was not a right to keep and carry any weapon whatsoever in any manner whatsoever and for whatever purpose. . . . Although we do not undertake an exhaustive historical analysis today of the full scope of the Second Amendment, nothing in our opinion should be taken to cast doubt on longstanding prohibitions on the possession of firearms by felons and the mentally ill, or laws forbidding the carrying of firearms in sensitive places such as schools and government buildings, or laws imposing conditions and qualifications on the commercial sale of arms.

We also recognize another important limitation on the right to keep and carry arms. Miller said, as we have explained, that the sorts of weapons protected were those "in common use at the time." We think that limitation is fairly supported by the historical tradition of prohibiting the carrying of "dangerous and unusual weapons."

It may be objected that if weapons that are most useful in military service — M-16 rifles and the like — may be banned, then the Second Amendment right is completely detached from the prefatory clause. But as we have said, the conception of the militia at the time of the Second Amendment's ratification was the body of all citizens capable of military service, who would bring the sorts of lawful weapons that they possessed at home to militia duty. It may well be true today that a militia, to be as effective as militias in the 18th century, would require sophisticated arms that are highly unusual in society at large. Indeed, it may be true that no amount of small arms could be useful against modern-day bombers and tanks. But the fact that modern developments have limited the degree of fit between the prefatory clause and the protected right cannot change our interpretation of the right.

IV

We turn finally to the law at issue here. As we have said, the law totally bans handgun possession in the home. It also requires that any lawful firearm in the home be disassembled or bound by a trigger lock at all times, rendering it inoperable.

As the quotations earlier in this opinion demonstrate, the inherent right of self-defense has been central to the Second Amendment right. The handgun ban amounts to a prohibition of an entire class of "arms" that is overwhelmingly chosen by American society for that lawful purpose. The prohibition extends, moreover, to the home, where the need for defense of self, family, and property is most acute. Under any of the standards of scrutiny that we have applied to enumerated constitutional rights, banning from the home "the most preferred firearm in the nation to 'keep' and use for protection of one's home and family," would fail constitutional muster. . . .

In sum, we hold that the District's ban on handgun possession in the home violates the Second Amendment, as does its prohibition against rendering any lawful firearm in the home operable for the purpose of immediate self-defense. Assuming that Heller is not disqualified from the exercise of Second Amendment rights, the District must permit him to register his handgun and must issue him a license to carry it in the home.

We are aware of the problem of handgun violence in this country, and we take seriously the concerns raised by the many amici who believe that prohibition of handgun ownership is a solution. The Constitution leaves the District of Columbia a variety of tools for combating that problem, including some measures regulating handguns. But the enshrinement of constitutional rights necessarily takes certain policy choices off the table. These include the absolute prohibition of handguns held and used for self-defense in the home. Undoubtedly some think that the Second Amendment is outmoded in a society where our standing army is the pride of our Nation, where well-trained police forces provide personal security, and where gun violence is a serious problem. That is perhaps debatable, but what is not debatable is that it is not the role of this Court to pronounce the Second Amendment extinct. . . . *It is so ordered.*

JUSTICE STEVENS, with whom JUSTICE SOUTER, JUSTICE GINSBURG, and JUSTICE BREYER join, dissenting. . . .

The Second Amendment was adopted to protect the right of the people of each of the several States to maintain a well-regulated militia. It was a response to concerns raised during the ratification of the Constitution that the power of Congress to disarm the state militias and create a national standing army posed an intolerable threat to the sovereignty of the several States. Neither the text of the Amendment nor the arguments advanced by its proponents evidenced the slightest interest in limiting any legislature's authority to regulate private civilian uses of firearms. Specifically, there is no indication that the Framers of the Amendment intended to enshrine the common-law right of self-defense in the Constitution. . . .

The opinion the Court announces today fails to identify any new evidence supporting the view that the Amendment was intended to limit the power of Congress to regulate civilian uses of weapons. Unable to point to any such evidence, the Court stakes its holding on a strained and unpersuasive reading of the Amendment's text; significantly different provisions in the 1689 English Bill of Rights, and in various 19th-century State Constitutions; postenactment commentary that was available to the Court when it decided *Miller*; and, ultimately, a feeble attempt to distinguish *Miller* that places more emphasis on the Court's decisional process than on the reasoning in the opinion itself. . . .

The preamble to the Second Amendment makes three important points. It identifies the preservation of the militia as the Amendment's purpose; it explains that the militia is necessary to the security of a free State; and it recognizes that the militia must be "well regulated." In all three respects it is comparable to provisions in several State Declarations of Rights that were adopted roughly contemporaneously with the Declaration of Independence. Those state provisions highlight the importance members of the founding generation attached to the maintenance of state militias; they also underscore the profound fear shared by many in that era of the dangers posed by standing armies. . . .

The parallels between the Second Amendment and these state declarations, and the Second Amendment's omission of any statement of purpose related to the right to use firearms for hunting or personal self-defense, is especially striking in light of the fact that the Declarations of Rights of Pennsylvania and Vermont did expressly protect such civilian uses at the time. . . .

The centerpiece of the Court's textual argument is its insistence that the words "the people" as used in the Second Amendment must have the same meaning, and protect the same class of individuals, as when they are used in the First and Fourth Amendments. According to the Court, in all three provisions — as well as the Constitution's preamble, section 2 of Article I, and the Tenth Amendment — "the term unambiguously refers to all members of the political community, not an unspecified subset." But the Court itself reads the Second Amendment to protect a "subset" significantly narrower than the class of persons protected by the First and Fourth Amendments; when it finally drills down on the substantive meaning of the Second Amendment, the Court limits the protected class to "law-abiding, responsible citizens". But the class of persons protected by the First and Fourth Amendments is not so limited; for even felons (and presumably irresponsible citizens as well) may invoke the protections of those constitutional provisions. The Court offers no way to harmonize its conflicting pronouncements.

The Court also overlooks the significance of the way the Framers used the phrase "the people" in these constitutional provisions. In the First Amendment, no words define the class of individuals entitled to speak, to publish, or to worship; in that Amendment it is only the right peaceably to assemble, and to petition the Government for a redress of grievances, that is described as a right of "the people." These rights contemplate collective action. While the right peaceably to assemble protects the individual rights of those persons participating in the assembly, its concern is with action engaged in by members of a group, rather than any single individual. Likewise, although the act of petitioning the Government is a right that can be exercised by individuals, it is primarily collective in nature. For if they are to be effective, petitions must involve groups of individuals acting in concert.

Similarly, the words "the people" in the Second Amendment refer back to the object announced in the Amendment's preamble. They remind us that it is the collective action of individuals having a duty to serve in the militia that the text directly protects and, perhaps more importantly, that the ultimate purpose of the Amendment was to protect the States' share of the divided sovereignty created by the Constitution.

As used in the Fourth Amendment, "the people" describes the class of persons protected from unreasonable searches and seizures by Government officials. It is true that the Fourth Amendment describes a right that need not be exercised in any collective sense. But that observation does not settle the meaning of the phrase "the people" when used in the Second Amendment. For, as we have seen, the phrase means something quite different in the Petition and Assembly Clauses of the First Amendment. Although the abstract definition of the phrase "the people" could carry the same meaning in the Second Amendment as in the Fourth Amendment, the preamble of the Second Amendment suggests that the uses of the phrase in the First and Second Amendments are the same in referring to a collective activity. By way of contrast, the Fourth Amendment describes a right against governmental interference rather than an affirmative right to engage in protected conduct, and so refers to a right to protect a purely individual interest. As used in the Second Amendment, the words "the people" do not enlarge the right to keep and bear arms to encompass use or ownership of weapons outside the context of service in a well-regulated militia. . . .

Although the Court's discussion of these words treats them as two "phrases" — as if they read "to keep" and "to bear" — they describe a unitary right: to possess arms if needed for military purposes and to use them in conjunction with military activities. . . .

The term "bear arms" is a familiar idiom; when used unadorned by any additional words, its meaning is "to serve as a soldier, do military service, fight." 1 Oxford English Dictionary 634 (2d ed. 1989). . . . The Amendment's use of the term "keep" in no way contradicts the military meaning conveyed by the phrase "bear arms" and the Amendment's preamble. To the contrary, a number of state militia laws in effect at the time of the Second Amendment's drafting used the term "keep" to describe the requirement that militia members store their arms at their homes, ready to be used for service when necessary. The Virginia military law, for example, ordered that "every one of the said officers, non-commissioned officers, and privates, shall constantly keep the aforesaid arms, accoutrements, and ammunition, ready to be produced whenever called for by his commanding officer." Act for Regulating and Disciplining the Militia, 1785 Va. Acts ch. 1, §3, p. 2. "[K]eep and bear arms" thus perfectly describes the responsibilities of a framing-era militia member. . . .

When each word in the text is given full effect, the Amendment is most naturally read to secure to the people a right to use and possess arms in conjunction with service in a well-regulated militia. So far as appears, no more than that was contemplated by its drafters or is encompassed within its terms. Even if the meaning of the text were genuinely susceptible to more than one interpretation, the burden would remain on those advocating a departure from the purpose identified in the preamble and from settled law to come forward with persuasive new arguments or evidence. The textual analysis offered by respondent and embraced by the Court falls far short of sustaining that heavy burden. And the Court's emphatic reliance on the claim "that the Second Amendment . . . codified a pre-existing right," is of course beside the point because the right to keep and bear arms for service in a state militia was also a pre-existing right.

Indeed, not a word in the constitutional text even arguably supports the Court's overwrought and novel description of the Second Amendment as "elevat[ing] above all other interests" "the right of law-abiding, responsible citizens to use arms in defense of hearth and home."

The proper allocation of military power in the new Nation was an issue of central concern for the Framers. The compromises they ultimately reached, reflected in Article I's Militia Clauses and the Second Amendment, represent quintessential examples of the Framers' "splitting the atom of sovereignty."

Two themes relevant to our current interpretive task ran through the debates on the original Constitution. "On the one hand, there was a widespread fear that a national standing Army posed an intolerable threat to individual liberty and to the sovereignty of the separate States." *Perpich v. Department of Defense*, 496 U.S. 334, 340 (1990). . . . On the other hand, the Framers recognized the dangers inherent in relying on inadequately trained militia members "as the primary means of providing for the common defense," *Perpich*, 496 U.S., at 340; during the Revolutionary War, "[t]his force, though armed, was largely untrained, and its deficiencies were the subject of bitter complaint." Wiener, The Militia Clause of the Constitution, 54 Harv. L. Rev. 181, 182 (1940). In order to respond to those twin concerns, a compromise was reached: Congress would be authorized to raise and support a national Army and Navy, and also to organize, arm, discipline, and provide for the calling forth of "the Militia." U.S. Const., Art. I, §8, cls. 12–16. The President, at the same time, was empowered as the "Commander in Chief of the Army and Navy of the United States, and of the Militia of the several States, when called into the actual Service of the United States." Art. II, §2. But, with respect to the militia, a significant reservation was made to the States: Although Congress would have the power to call forth, organize, arm, and discipline the militia, as well as to govern "such Part of them as may be employed in the Service of the United States," the States respectively would retain the right to appoint the officers and to train the militia in accordance with the discipline prescribed by Congress. Art. I, §8, cl. 16.

But the original Constitution's retention of the militia and its creation of divided authority over that body did not prove sufficient to allay fears about the dangers posed by a standing army. For it was perceived by some that Article I contained a significant gap: While it empowered Congress to organize, arm, and discipline the militia, it did not prevent Congress from providing for the militia's *dis*armament. . . .

Madison, charged with the task of assembling the proposals for amendments sent by the ratifying States, was the principal draftsman of the Second Amendment. . . . [I]t is strikingly significant that Madison's first draft omitted any mention of non-military use or possession of weapons. Rather, his original draft repeated the essence of the two proposed amendments sent by Virginia, combining the substance of the two provisions succinctly into one, which read: "The right of the people to keep and bear arms shall not be infringed; a well armed, and well regulated militia being the best security of a free country; but no person religiously scrupulous of bearing arms, shall be compelled to render military service in person."

Madison's decision to model the Second Amendment on the distinctly military Virginia proposal is therefore revealing, since it is clear that he considered and rejected formulations that would have unambiguously protected civilian uses of firearms. When Madison prepared his first draft, and when that draft was debated and modified, it is reasonable to assume that all participants in the drafting process were fully aware of the other formulations that would have protected civilian use and possession of weapons and that their choice to craft the Amendment as they did represented a rejection of those alternative formulations.

Madison's initial inclusion of an exemption for conscientious objectors sheds reve-latory light on the purpose of the Amendment. It confirms an intent to describe a duty as well as a right, and it unequivocally identifies the military character of both. The objections voiced to the conscientious-objector clause only confirm the central meaning of the text. Although records of the debate in the Senate, which is where the conscientious-objector clause was removed, do not survive, the arguments raised in the House illuminate the perceived problems with the clause: Specifically, there was concern that Congress "can declare who are those religiously scrupulous, and prevent them from bearing arms." The ultimate removal of the clause, therefore, only serves to confirm the purpose of the Amendment — to protect against congressional disarmament, by whatever means, of the States' militias. . . .

The history of the adoption of the Amendment thus describes an overriding concern about the potential threat to state sovereignty that a federal standing army would pose, and a desire to protect the States' militias as the means by which to guard against that danger. But state militias could not effectively check the pros-pect of a federal standing army so long as Congress retained the power to disarm them, and so a guarantee against such disarmament was needed. As we explained in *Miller*: "With obvious purpose to assure the continuation and render possible the effectiveness of such forces the declaration and guarantee of the Second Amend-ment were made. It must be interpreted and applied with that end in view." 307 U.S., at 178. The evidence plainly refutes the claim that the Amendment was moti-vated by the Framers' fears that Congress might act to regulate any civilian uses of weapons. . . .

The brilliance of the debates that resulted in the Second Amendment faded into oblivion during the ensuing years, for the concerns about Article I's Militia Clauses that generated such pitched debate during the ratification process and led to the adoption of the Second Amendment were short lived.

In 1792, the year after the Amendment was ratified, Congress passed a statute that purported to establish "an Uniform Militia throughout the United States." 1 Stat. 271. The statute commanded every able-bodied white male citizen between the ages of 18 and 45 to be enrolled therein and to "provide himself with a good musket or firelock" and other specified weaponry. The statute is significant, for it confirmed the way those in the founding generation viewed firearm ownership: as a duty linked to military service. The statute they enacted, however, "was virtually ignored for more than a century," and was finally repealed in 1901.

The post-ratification history of the Second Amendment is strikingly similar. The Amendment played little role in any legislative debate about the civilian use of firearms for most of the 19th century, and it made few appearances in the decisions of this Court. . . .

In 1901 the President revitalized the militia by creating "'the National Guard of the several States,'" *Perpich*, 496 U.S., at 341, and nn. 9–10; meanwhile, the dominant understanding of the Second Amendment's inapplicability to private gun ownership continued well into the 20th century. . . . Thus, for most of our history, the invalidity of Second-Amendment-based objections to firearms regulations has been well settled and uncontroversial. Indeed, the Second Amendment was not even mentioned in either full House of Congress during the legislative proceedings that led to the passage of the 1934 Act. Yet enforcement of that law produced the judicial decision that confirmed the status of the Amendment as limited in reach to military usage. After reviewing many of the same sources that are discussed at greater length by the Court today, the *Miller* Court unanimously concluded that the Second Amendment did not apply to the possession of a firearm that did not have "some reasonable relationship to the preservation or efficiency of a well regulated militia." 307 U.S., at 178.

The key to that decision did not, as the Court belatedly suggests, turn on the difference between muskets and sawed-off shotguns; it turned, rather, on the basic difference between the military and nonmilitary use and possession of guns. Indeed, if the Second Amendment were not limited in its coverage to military uses of weapons, why should the Court in *Miller* have suggested that some weapons but not others were eligible for Second Amendment protection? If use for self-defense were the relevant standard, why did the Court not inquire into the suitability of a particular weapon for self-defense purposes? . . .

The Court concludes its opinion by declaring that it is not the proper role of this Court to change the meaning of rights "enshrine[d]" in the Constitution. But the right the Court announces was not "enshrined" in the Second Amendment by the Framers; it is the product of today's law-changing decision. The majority's exegesis has utterly failed to establish that as a matter of text or history, "the right of law-abiding, responsible citizens to use arms in defense of hearth and home" is "elevate[d] above all other interests" by the Second Amendment.

Until today, it has been understood that legislatures may regulate the civilian use and misuse of firearms so long as they do not interfere with the preservation of a well-regulated militia. The Court's announcement of a new constitutional right to own and use firearms for private purposes upsets that settled understanding, but leaves for future cases the formidable task of defining the scope of permissible regulations. Today judicial craftsmen have confidently asserted that a policy choice that denies a "law-abiding, responsible citize[n]" the right to keep and use weapons in the home for self-defense is "off the table." Given the presumption that most citizens are law abiding, and the reality that the need to defend oneself may suddenly arise in a host of locations outside the home, I fear that the District's policy choice may well be just the first of an unknown number of dominoes to be knocked off the table.

I do not know whether today's decision will increase the labor of federal judges to the "breaking point" envisioned by Justice Cardozo, but it will surely give rise to a far more active judicial role in making vitally important national policy decisions than was envisioned at any time in the 18th, 19th, or 20th centuries.

The Court properly disclaims any interest in evaluating the wisdom of the specific policy choice challenged in this case, but it fails to pay heed to a far more important policy choice — the choice made by the Framers themselves. The Court would have us believe that over 200 years ago, the Framers made a choice to limit the tools available to elected officials wishing to regulate civilian uses of weapons, and to authorize this Court to use the common-law process of case-by-case judicial lawmaking to define the contours of acceptable gun control policy. Absent compelling evidence that is nowhere to be found in the Court's opinion, I could not possibly conclude that the Framers made such a choice.

For these reasons, I respectfully dissent.

JUSTICE BREYER, with whom JUSTICE STEVENS, JUSTICE SOUTER, and JUSTICE GINSBURG join, dissenting. [Omitted]

Notes and Questions

(1) In an article analyzing the effect of *Heller*, Phillip Cook, Jens Ludwig, Adam Samaha, *Gun Control After Heller: Threats and Sideshows from a Social Welfare Perspective*, 56 U.C.L.A. L. REV. 1041 (2009), the authors provide a detailed portraiture of gun violence and gun ownership in America. They report that there are between 200–250 million firearms in private circulation in the United States, almost one for every adult, yet 75 percent of all American adults do not own a gun. Survey data they cite indicates that men own more guns than women, by a margin of 42% to 9%, with a total of 35% of all households having at least one gun. The prevalence of gun ownership varies significantly among different sectors of society. Only 13 percent of Massachusetts households have a gun, for example, compared to 60% in Mississippi. About 33% of privately held firearms are handguns. Using the year 2005 as their statistical sample for gun violence, the authors report that in 2005, a total of 30,694 people died in the United States as a result of gunfire, a figure that includes all homicides, suicides, and accidental shooting deaths.

(2) In *McDonald v. Chicago*, 561 U.S. 742 (2010), several suits were filed against Chicago and Oak Park in Illinois challenging their gun bans after the Supreme Court issued its opinion in *District of Columbia v. Heller*. The Supreme Court reversed the Seventh Circuit, holding that the Fourteenth Amendment makes the Second Amendment right to keep and bear arms for the purpose of self-defense applicable to the states. With Justice Samuel A. Alito writing for the majority, the Court reasoned that rights that are "fundamental to the Nation's scheme of ordered liberty" or that are "deeply rooted in this Nation's history and tradition" are appropriately applied to the states through the Fourteenth Amendment. The Court recognized in *Heller* that the right to self-defense was one such "fundamental" and

"deeply rooted" right. The Court reasoned that because of its holding in *Heller*, the Second Amendment applied to the states. Justice John Paul Stevens dissented. He disagreed that the Fourteenth Amendment incorporates the Second Amendment against the states. He argued that owning a personal firearm was not a "liberty" interest protected by the Due Process Clause. Justice Stephen G. Breyer, joined by Justices Ruth Bader Ginsburg and Sonia Sotomayor, also dissented. He argued that there is nothing in the Second Amendment's "text, history, or underlying rationale" that characterizes it as a "fundamental right" warranting incorporation through the Fourteenth Amendment.

(3) In *Caetano v. Massachusetts*, 136 S. Ct. 1027, 1027 (2016), Jamie Caetano was convicted of possession of a stun gun in Massachusetts state court. Caetano appealed and claimed her conviction violated her Second Amendment right to possess a stun gun in public for the purpose of self-defense, which was necessary to protect herself from her abusive ex-boyfriend. The Supreme Judicial Court of Massachusetts affirmed Caetano's conviction and held that a stun gun is not eligible for Second Amendment protection. In a per curiam opinion, the U.S. Supreme Court held that, although stun guns are unusual in nature and were not common during the enactment of the Second Amendment, they are included in the Second Amendment's protections. To hold otherwise, the Court reasoned, would be inconsistent with the Supreme Court's decision in *District of Columbia v. Heller*, which held that Second Amendment protections extend to arms that were not in existence at the time of the founding. Justice Samuel A. Alito, Jr. filed a concurring opinion in which he reiterated the importance of access to self-defense and the rights afforded by the Second Amendment. Justice Clarence Thomas joined in the concurring opinion.

(4) In *New York State Rifle & Pistol Association, Inc. v. Bruen*, 597 U.S. __, 142 S. Ct. 2111 (2022), the Court held that New York State's public carry law was unconstitutional. The statue provided that a license applicant who wants to carry a firearm outside his home or place of business must obtain an unrestricted license to have and carry a concealed pistol or revolver. To obtain that license, he must prove proper cause exists, which New York courts held requires that he can "demonstrate a special need for self-protection distinguishable from that of the general community." The Court relied heavily on its historical understanding of the Second Amendment and rejected the State's reliance on a governmental interest:

> In *Heller* and *McDonald*, we held that the Second and Fourteenth Amendments protect an individual right to keep and bear arms for self-defense. In doing so, we held unconstitutional two laws that prohibited the possession and use of handguns in the home. In the years since, the Courts of Appeals have coalesced around a "two-step" framework for analyzing Second Amendment challenges that combines history with means-end scrutiny. Today, we decline to adopt that two-part approach. In keeping with *Heller*, we hold that when the Second Amendment's plain text covers an individual's conduct, the Constitution presumptively protects that conduct. To justify its regulation, the government may not simply posit

that the regulation promotes an important interest. Rather, the government must demonstrate that the regulation is consistent with this Nation's historical tradition of firearm regulation. Only if a firearm regulation is consistent with this Nation's historical tradition may a court conclude that the individual's conduct falls outside the Second Amendment's "unqualified command."

To be sure, "[h]istorical analysis can be difficult; it sometimes requires resolving threshold questions, and making nuanced judgments about which evidence to consult and how to interpret it." *McDonald*, 561 U.S., at 803–804 (Scalia, J., concurring). But reliance on history to inform the meaning of constitutional text — especially text meant to codify a preexisting right — is, in our view, more legitimate, and more administrable, than asking judges to "make difficult empirical judgments" about "the costs and benefits of firearms restrictions," especially given their "lack [of] expertise" in the field.

The regulatory challenges posed by firearms today are not always the same as those that preoccupied the Founders in 1791 or the Reconstruction generation in 1868. Fortunately, the Founders created a Constitution — and a Second Amendment — "intended to endure for ages to come, and consequently, to be adapted to the various crises of human affairs." *McCulloch v. Maryland*, 4 Wheat. 316, 415 (1819). Although its meaning is fixed according to the understandings of those who ratified it, the Constitution can, and must, apply to circumstances beyond those the Founders specifically anticipated. When confronting such present-day firearm regulations, this historical inquiry that courts must conduct will often involve reasoning by analogy — a commonplace task for any lawyer or judge. Like all analogical reasoning, determining whether a historical regulation is a proper analogue for a distinctly modern firearm regulation requires a determination of whether the two regulations are "relevantly similar." C. Sunstein, *On Analogical Reasoning*, 106 Harv. L. Rev. 741, 773 (1993). And because "[e]verything is similar in infinite ways to everything else," one needs "some metric enabling the analogizer to assess which similarities are important and which are not," F. Schauer & B. Spellman, *Analogy, Expertise, and Experience*, 84 U. Chi. L. Rev. 249, 254 (2017). For instance, a green truck and a green hat are relevantly similar if one's metric is "things that are green." They are not relevantly similar if the applicable metric is "things you can wear." While we do not now provide an exhaustive survey of the features that render regulations relevantly similar under the Second Amendment, we do think that *Heller* and *McDonald* point toward at least two metrics: how and why the regulations burden a law-abiding citizen's right to armed self-defense. As we stated in *Heller* and repeated in *McDonald*, "individual self-defense is 'the central component' of the Second Amendment right." Therefore, whether modern and historical regulations impose a comparable burden on the right of armed self-defense and whether that burden is comparably justified are "central" considerations when engaging in an analogical inquiry. This does not mean that courts may engage in independent means.

To be clear, analogical reasoning under the Second Amendment is neither a regulatory straightjacket nor a regulatory blank check. On the one hand, courts should not "uphold every modern law that remotely resembles a historical analogue," because doing so "risk[s] endorsing outliers that our ancestors would never have accepted." On the other hand, analogical reasoning requires only that the government identify a well-established and representative historical analogue, not a historical twin. So even if a modern-day regulation is not a dead ringer for historical precursors, it still may be analogous enough to pass constitutional muster.

With these principles in mind, we turn to respondents' historical evidence. Throughout modern Anglo-American history, the right to keep and bear arms in public has traditionally been subject to well-defined restrictions governing the intent for which one could carry arms, the manner of carry, or the exceptional circumstances under which one could not carry arms. But apart from a handful of late 19th-century jurisdictions, the historical record compiled by respondents does not demonstrate a tradition of broadly prohibiting the public carry of commonly used firearms for self-defense. Nor is there any such historical tradition limiting public carry only to those law-abiding citizens who demonstrate a special need for self-defense. We conclude that respondents have failed to meet their burden to identify an American tradition justifying New York's proper cause requirement. Under *Heller*'s text-and-history standard, the proper-cause requirement is therefore unconstitutional.

Justice Barrett, concurring, added a possible refinement to the relevant historical evidence:

I join the Court's opinion in full. I write separately to highlight two methodological points that the Court does not resolve. First, the Court does not conclusively determine the manner and circumstances in which post-ratification practice may bear on the original meaning of the Constitution. Scholars have proposed competing and potentially conflicting frameworks for this analysis, including liquidation, tradition, and precedent. See, *e.g.*, Nelson, *Originalism and Interpretive Conventions*, 70 U. Chi. L. Rev. 519 (2003); McConnell, *Time, Institutions, and Interpretation*, 95 B.U. L. Rev. 1745 (2015). The limits on the permissible use of history may vary between these frameworks (and between different articulations of each one). To name just a few unsettled questions: How long after ratification may subsequent practice illuminate original public meaning? What form must practice take to carry weight in constitutional analysis? And may practice settle the meaning of individual rights as well as structural provisions? See Baude,

Constitutional Liquidation, 71 Stan. L. Rev. 1, 49–51 (2019) (canvassing arguments). The historical inquiry presented in this case does not require us to answer such questions, which might make a difference in another case.

Second and relatedly, the Court avoids another "ongoing scholarly debate on whether courts should primarily rely on the prevailing understanding of an individual right when the Fourteenth Amendment was ratified in 1868" or when the Bill of Rights was ratified in 1791. Here, the lack of support for New York's law in either period makes it unnecessary to choose between them. But if 1791 is the benchmark, then New York's appeals to Reconstruction-era history would fail for the independent reason that this evidence is simply too late (in addition to too little). So today's decision should not be understood to endorse freewheeling reliance on historical practice from the mid-to-late 19th century to establish the original meaning of the Bill of Rights. On the contrary, the Court is careful to caution "against giving post enactment history more weight than it can rightly bear."

Justice Breyer's dissenting opinion concluded:

We are bound by *Heller* insofar as *Heller* interpreted the Second Amendment to protect an individual right to possess a firearm for self-defense. But *Heller* recognized that that right was not without limits and could appropriately be subject to government regulation. 554 U.S., at 626–627. *Heller* therefore does not require holding that New York's law violates the Second Amendment. In so holding, the Court goes beyond *Heller*. It bases its decision to strike down New York's law almost exclusively on its application of what it calls historical "analogical reasoning." As I have admitted above, I am not a historian, and neither is the Court. But the history, as it appears to me, seems to establish a robust tradition of regulations restricting the public carriage of concealed firearms. To the extent that any uncertainty remains between the Court's view of the history and mine, that uncertainty counsels against relying on history alone. In my view, it is appropriate in such circumstances to look beyond the history and engage in what the Court calls means-end scrutiny. Courts must be permitted to consider the State's interest in preventing gun violence, the effectiveness of the contested law in achieving that interest, the degree to which the law burdens the Second Amendment right, and, if appropriate, any less restrictive alternatives.

Chapter 8

Religion

§ 8.01 What Does "Religion" Mean?

The Constitution uses the term "religion" or "religious" in several places. The First Amendment begins with the words: "Congress shall make no law respecting an establishment of religion, or prohibiting the free exercise thereof." Article VI, cl. 3 states: "The Senators and Representatives before mentioned, and the Members of the several State Legislatures, and all executive and judicial Officers, both of the United States and of the several States, shall be bound by Oath or Affirmation, to support this Constitution; but no religious Test shall ever be required as a Qualification to any Office or public Trust under the United States."

The United States Supreme Court has offered little guidance as to what "religion" means for constitutional purposes. In cases involving the Free Exercise Clause, the Court has made it clear that "religion" is not limited to formal religious sect, observing, "we reject the notion that to claim the protection of the Free Exercise Clause, one must be responding to the commands of a particular religious organization." *Frazee v. Illinois Dep't of Employment Sec.*, 489 U.S. 829, 834 (1989). Earlier cases seemed to emphasize traditional theistic religions centered on a belief in a Supreme Being. In 1890, the Court held that "[t]he term 'religion' has reference to one's views of his relations to his Creator, and to the obligations they impose of reverence for his being and character, and of obedience to his will." *Davis v. Beason*, 133 U.S. 333, 342 (1890). In the 1960s, however, the Court adopted a broader conception. In *Torcaso v. Watkins*, 367 U.S. 488, 495 n. 11 (1961), the Court held that First Amendment does not allow government to distinguish between religions that are centered on a belief in the existence of God and religions that do not. The Court noted, "Among religions in this country which do not teach what would generally be considered a belief in the existence of God are Buddhism, Taoism, Ethical Culture, Secular Humanism and others." In cases in which the Court was called on to interpret the "conscientious objector" exception to the military draft, the Court was increasingly expansive. *See United States v. Seeger*, 380 U.S. 163 (1965); *Welsh v. United States*, 398 U.S. 333 (1970). In focusing on the phrase "religious training and belief" as used to define the conscientious objector language in the military draft law, the Court adopted what came to be known as the "parallel belief" approach, which included "A sincere and meaningful belief which occupies in the life of its possessor a place parallel to that filled by the God of those admittedly qualifying for the exemption." *Seeger*, 380 U.S. at 176.

There is general agreement that the protection for "religion" in the Constitution means something *distinct*, however, from mere "philosophy" or "way of life." In *Wisconsin v. Yoder*, one of the most famous Free Exercise cases presented in this Chapter, the Supreme Court held that the practices of the Amish were "religious," contrasting the religion-based isolationist practices of the Amish with the philosophical views of Henry David Thoreau.

In the *Kennedy v. Bremerton School District* case, which is also presented in this Chapter, the Court opined on how the Establishment Clause, the Free Exercise Clause, and the Free Speech Clause of the First Amendment relate. Consider this key passage: "It is true that this Court and others often refer to the 'Establishment Clause,' the 'Free Exercise Clause,' and the 'Free Speech Clause' as separate units. But the three Clauses appear in the same sentence of the same Amendment: 'Congress shall make no law respecting an establishment of religion, or prohibiting the free exercise thereof; or abridging the freedom of speech.' A natural reading of that sentence would seem to suggest the Clauses have 'complementary' purposes, not warring ones where one Clause is always sure to prevail over the others." As you consider the focus of this Chapter, religion, and the focus of Chapter 9, speech, you may ask yourself whether you do or do not find this passage persuasive.

§ 8.02 Establishment of Religion

A. Rituals and Symbols in the Public Arena

Distinguishing the Public Arena from School Settings. The American constitutional debate over the "Establishment of Religion" has played out in two broad settings. There are first cases in the "public arena," by which is meant essentially every context *other than* education and schools. These cases involve challenges to government actions that allegedly "respect an establishment of religion." One branch of these public arena cases have largely involved litigation over religious rituals, such as prayers at the beginning of government activities such as meetings of town councils or legislatures. Another has involved the government use of symbols containing religious content, such as monuments or displays containing the Ten Commandments, or displays of creches (Nativity Scenes depicting the birth of Christ) or Menorahs during holiday seasons.

This Chapter examines the public arena cases separately from the education cases. As we will see, the Establishment Clause tends to be interpreted more strictly in the context of schools.

High, Low, and Medium Separationists. Supreme Court Justices, legal scholars, lawyers, and citizens have tended to fall into three camps.

"High Separationists" believe in fastidious separation of church and state, and would strike down virtually all references to religion or God in governmental rituals and symbols. President Teddy Roosevelt, for example, opposed the phrase "In

God We Trust" on currency. High Separations might object to the inclusion of the phrase "one nation, under God" in the Pledge of Allegiance, or the incantation "God Save the United States" at the commencement of a Supreme Court session. High separationists would certainly oppose the inclusion of a creche on government property during holiday season.

At the opposite end of the spectrum are "low separationists," who take a narrow view of the reach of the Establishment Clause. Low separationists tend to believe that the only core meaning of the Establishment Clause is the coercive taxation and support for one official "established" government religion. Justice Clarence Thomas, a strong low separationist, has opined that the Establishment Clause should be construed as only prohibiting the creation of a national federal religion, and that it ought not be understood as binding against the states at all.

For most of modern constitutional law history, however, neither "high separationists" nor "low separationists" have commanded a majority of the Supreme Court. Instead, decisions have been dominated by the views of "middle separationists," who are unwilling to strike down all rituals and symbols used by government that invoke religion, but will draw lines at some point when activities appear *too* religious.

The tests adopted by "middle separationists" are often less precise than those used by the Justices at the high or low extremes, leading to results that are often difficult to predict and reconcile. In two cases decided the same day, for example, the Supreme Court dealt with displays of the Ten Commandments, holding the display unconstitutional in one case, but constitutional in another.

In cases involving the display of creches, the Court has permitted displays that include other secular holiday symbols, such as reindeer, snowmen, or Santa Clause, but not those entirely religious. And as illustrated in the *Town of Greece* case, the Justices have been sharply divided over when prayers at legislative sessions or government meetings should or should not be permitted.

You will see that in more recent times, the center of gravity on the Court has shifted significantly. The Court has moved decidedly toward the "low separationist position," particularly in the general arena, outside of schools.

The Lemon Test. In 1971, the Supreme Court announced a three-part test for applying the Establishment Clause, in a case entitled *Lemon v. Kurtzman*, 403 U.S. 602 (1971): "First, the statute must have a secular legislative purpose; second, its principal or primary effect must be one that neither advances nor inhibits religion; finally, the statute must not foster an excessive government entanglement with religion." The *Lemon* test was "high separationist" test, and marked the apex of strict separation of church and state in American constitutional law. You will see that in two recent cases presented in this Chapter, *American Legion v. American Humanist Association*, and *Kennedy v. Bremerton School District*, the Court repudiated the *Lemon* test.

The Wall of Separation. Thomas Jefferson famously referred to a "wall of separation" between church and state. At least in the public arena, however, modern cases adopting the "middle separationist" approach are more a crooked and wavering line, with many seemingly inconsistent results. The cases involving the Ten Commandments and Creches are two exemplars of this seeming inconsistency.

The Ten Commandment Cases. In *Van Orden v. Perry*, 545 U.S. 677 (2005), and *McCreary County Kentucky v. American Civil Liberties Union of Kentucky*, 545 U.S. 844 (2005), decided the same day, the Court reached opposite conclusions with regard to displays of the Ten Commandments. Both decisions were decided by 5-4 votes. The difference was made by Justice Breyer, who voted against the Ten Commandments display in *McCreary*, but in favor of it in *Van Orden*.

In *McCreary*, the Court struck down the placing of displays of the Ten Commandments inside county courthouses. Assembled with the Commandments were framed copies of the Magna Carta, the Declaration of Independence, the Bill of Rights, the lyrics of the Star Spangled Banner, the Mayflower Compact, the National Motto, the Preamble to the Kentucky Constitution, and a picture of Lady Justice. The Court focused on the government's purpose, finding that it was religious, not secular.

In *Van Orden*, the Court held that the Establishment Clause was not violated by a display of the Ten Commandments in an outdoor area surrounding the Texas State Capitol in Austin. The Court observed:

> Whatever may be the fate of the *Lemon* test in the larger scheme of Establishment Clause jurisprudence, we think it not useful in dealing with the sort of passive monument that Texas has erected on its Capitol grounds. Instead, our analysis is driven both by the nature of the monument and by our Nation's history.

> In this case we are faced with a display of the Ten Commandments on government property outside the Texas State Capitol. Such acknowledgments of the role played by the Ten Commandments in our Nation's heritage are common throughout America. We need only look within our own Courtroom. Since 1935, Moses has stood, holding two tablets that reveal portions of the Ten Commandments written in Hebrew, among other lawgivers in the south frieze. Representations of the Ten Commandments adorn the metal gates lining the north and south sides of the Courtroom as well as the doors leading into the Courtroom. Moses also sits on the exterior east facade of the building holding the Ten Commandments tablets.

Justice Breyer, explaining his vote to uphold the Texas display, stated in a concurring opinion: "This display has stood apparently uncontested for nearly two generations. That experience helps us understand that as a practical matter of *degree* this display is unlikely to prove divisive. And this matter of degree is, I believe, critical in a borderline case such as this one."

The Creche Cases. In *Lynch v. Donnelly*, 465 U.S. 668 (1984), the Court held that a creche display did not violate the Establishment Clause. The Court described the setting:

Each year, in cooperation with the downtown retail merchants' association, the City of Pawtucket, Rhode Island, erects a Christmas display as part of its observance of the Christmas holiday season. The display is situated in a park owned by a nonprofit organization and located in the heart of the shopping district. The display is essentially like those to be found in hundreds of towns or cities across the Nation — often on public grounds — during the Christmas season. The Pawtucket display comprises many of the figures and decorations traditionally associated with Christmas, including, among other things, a Santa Claus house, reindeer pulling Santa's sleigh, candy-striped poles, a Christmas tree, carolers, cutout figures representing such characters as a clown, an elephant, and a teddy bear, hundreds of colored lights, a large banner that reads "SEASONS GREETINGS," and the crèche at issue here. All components of this display are owned by the City. The crèche, which has been included in the display for 40 or more years, consists of the traditional figures, including the Infant Jesus, Mary and Joseph, angels, shepherds, kings, and animals.

The majority opinion of the Court concluded: "To forbid the use of this one passive symbol — the crèche — at the very time people are taking note of the season with Christmas hymns and carols in public schools and other public places, and while the Congress and Legislatures open sessions with prayers by paid chaplains would be a stilted over-reaction contrary to our history and to our holdings. If the presence of the crèche in this display violates the Establishment Clause, a host of other forms of taking official note of Christmas, and of our religious heritage, are equally offensive to the Constitution."

In contrast, in *County of Allegheny v. American Civil Liberties Union Greater Pittsburgh Chapter*, 492 U.S. 573 (1989), the Court dealt with the constitutionality of two recurring holiday displays located on public property in downtown Pittsburgh. The first was a creche placed on the Grand Staircase of the Allegheny County Courthouse. The second was a Chanukah menorah placed just outside the City-County Building, next to a Christmas tree and a sign saluting liberty. A splintered Court held that the creche display was unconstitutional, reasoning that "unlike in *Lynch*, nothing in the context of the display detracts from the creche's religious message." However, the Court in *Allegheny* upheld the display of the Menorah. The Court reasoned that the Menorah had both a religious and secular message, and the *combined* display of a Menorah, made the overall display a secular, not religious message. Justice Blackmun's opinion for the Court contained these key passages:

> The display of the Chanukah menorah in front of the City-County Building may well present a closer constitutional question. The menorah, one must recognize, is a religious symbol: it serves to commemorate the miracle of the oil as described in the Talmud. But the menorah's message is not exclusively religious. The menorah is the primary visual symbol for a holiday that, like Christmas, has both religious and secular dimensions.

Moreover, the menorah here stands next to a Christmas tree and a sign saluting liberty. While no challenge has been made here to the display of the tree and the sign, their presence is obviously relevant in determining the effect of the menorah's display. The necessary result of placing a menorah next to a Christmas tree is to create an "overall holiday setting" that represents both Christmas and Chanukah — two holidays, not one.

The mere fact that Pittsburgh displays symbols of both Christmas and Chanukah does not end the constitutional inquiry. If the city celebrates both Christmas and Chanukah as religious holidays, then it violates the Establishment Clause. The simultaneous endorsement of Judaism and Christianity is no less constitutionally infirm than the endorsement of Christianity alone.

Conversely, if the city celebrates both Christmas and Chanukah as secular holidays, then its conduct is beyond the reach of the Establishment Clause. Because government may celebrate Christmas as a secular holiday, it follows that government may also acknowledge Chanukah as a secular holiday. Simply put, it would be a form of discrimination against Jews to allow Pittsburgh to celebrate Christmas as a cultural tradition while simultaneously disallowing the city's acknowledgment of Chanukah as a contemporaneous cultural tradition.

The Christmas tree, unlike the menorah, is not itself a religious symbol. The tree, moreover, is clearly the predominant element in the city's display.

In these circumstances, then, the combination of the tree and the menorah communicates, not a simultaneous endorsement of both Christian and Jewish faith, but instead, a secular celebration of Christmas coupled with an acknowledgment of Chanukah as a contemporaneous alternative tradition.

Town of Greece, New York v. Galloway

United States Supreme Court
572 U.S. 565, 134 S. Ct. 1811, 188 L. Ed. 2d 835 (2014)

JUSTICE KENNEDY delivered the opinion of the Court, except as to Part II-B.

The Court must decide whether the town of Greece, New York, imposes an impermissible establishment of religion by opening its monthly board meetings with a prayer. It must be concluded, consistent with the Court's opinion in *Marsh v. Chambers*, 463 U.S. 783 (1983), that no violation of the Constitution has been shown.

Greece, a town with a population of 94,000, is in upstate New York. For some years, it began its monthly town board meetings with a moment of silence. In 1999, the newly elected town supervisor, John Auberger, decided to replicate the prayer practice he had found meaningful while serving in the county legislature. Following the roll call and recitation of the Pledge of Allegiance, Auberger would invite a local clergyman to the front of the room to deliver an invocation. After the prayer,

Auberger would thank the minister for serving as the board's "chaplain for the month" and present him with a commemorative plaque. The prayer was intended to place town board members in a solemn and deliberative frame of mind, invoke divine guidance in town affairs, and follow a tradition practiced by Congress and dozens of state legislatures.

The town followed an informal method for selecting prayer givers, all of whom were unpaid volunteers. A town employee would call the congregations listed in a local directory until she found a minister available for that month's meeting. The town eventually compiled a list of willing "board chaplains" who had accepted invitations and agreed to return in the future. The town at no point excluded or denied an opportunity to a would-be prayer giver. Its leaders maintained that a minister or layperson of any persuasion, including an atheist, could give the invocation. But nearly all of the congregations in town were Christian; and from 1999 to 2007, all of the participating ministers were too.

Greece neither reviewed the prayers in advance of the meetings nor provided guidance as to their tone or content, in the belief that exercising any degree of control over the prayers would infringe both the free exercise and speech rights of the ministers. The town instead left the guest clergy free to compose their own devotions. The resulting prayers often sounded both civic and religious themes. Typical were invocations that asked the divinity to abide at the meeting and bestow blessings on the community:

> "Lord we ask you to send your spirit of servanthood upon all of us gathered here this evening to do your work for the benefit of all in our community. We ask you to bless our elected and appointed officials so they may deliberate with wisdom and act with courage. Bless the members of our community who come here to speak before the board so they may state their cause with honesty and humility. . . . Lord we ask you to bless us all, that everything we do here tonight will move you to welcome us one day into your kingdom as good and faithful servants. We ask this in the name of our brother Jesus. Amen."

Some of the ministers spoke in a distinctly Christian idiom; and a minority invoked religious holidays, scripture, or doctrine, as in the following prayer:

> "Lord, God of all creation, we give you thanks and praise for your presence and action in the world. We look with anticipation to the celebration of Holy Week and Easter. It is in the solemn events of next week that we find the very heart and center of our Christian faith. We acknowledge the saving sacrifice of Jesus Christ on the cross. We draw strength, vitality, and confidence from his resurrection at Easter. We pray for peace in the world, an end to terrorism, violence, conflict, and war. We pray for stability, democracy, and good government in those countries in which our armed forces are now serving, especially in Iraq and Afghanistan. Praise and glory be yours, O Lord, now and forever more. Amen."

Respondents Susan Galloway and Linda Stephens attended town board meetings to speak about issues of local concern, and they objected that the prayers violated their religious or philosophical views. At one meeting, Galloway admonished board members that she found the prayers "offensive," "intolerable," and an affront to a "diverse community." After respondents complained that Christian themes pervaded the prayers, to the exclusion of citizens who did not share those beliefs, the town invited a Jewish layman and the chairman of the local Baha'i temple to deliver prayers. A Wiccan priestess who had read press reports about the prayer controversy requested, and was granted, an opportunity to give the invocation.

Galloway and Stephens brought suit in the United States District Court for the Western District of New York. They alleged that the town violated the First Amendment's Establishment Clause by preferring Christians over other prayer givers and by sponsoring sectarian prayers, such as those given "in Jesus' name." They did not seek an end to the prayer practice, but rather requested an injunction that would limit the town to "inclusive and ecumenical" prayers that referred only to a "generic God" and would not associate the government with any one faith or belief.

II

In *Marsh v. Chambers,* the Court found no First Amendment violation in the Nebraska Legislature's practice of opening its sessions with a prayer delivered by a chaplain paid from state funds. The decision concluded that legislative prayer, while religious in nature, has long been understood as compatible with the Establishment Clause. As practiced by Congress since the framing of the Constitution, legislative prayer lends gravity to public business, reminds lawmakers to transcend petty differences in pursuit of a higher purpose, and expresses a common aspiration to a just and peaceful society. The Court has considered this symbolic expression to be a "tolerable acknowledgement of beliefs widely held," rather than a first, treacherous step towards establishment of a state church.

Marsh is sometimes described as "carving out an exception" to the Court's Establishment Clause jurisprudence, because it sustained legislative prayer without subjecting the practice to "any of the formal 'tests' that have traditionally structured" this inquiry. The Court in *Marsh* found those tests unnecessary because history supported the conclusion that legislative invocations are compatible with the Establishment Clause. The First Congress made it an early item of business to appoint and pay official chaplains, and both the House and Senate have maintained the office virtually uninterrupted since that time. When *Marsh* was decided, in 1983, legislative prayer had persisted in the Nebraska Legislature for more than a century, and the majority of the other States also had the same, consistent practice. Although no information has been cited by the parties to indicate how many local legislative bodies open their meetings with prayer, this practice too has historical precedent.

The Court's inquiry, then, must be to determine whether the prayer practice in the town of Greece fits within the tradition long followed in Congress and the state legislatures. Respondents assert that the town's prayer exercise falls outside that tradition and transgresses the Establishment Clause for two independent but mutually reinforcing reasons. First, they argue that *Marsh* did not approve prayers containing sectarian language or themes, such as the prayers offered in Greece that referred to the "death, resurrection, and ascension of the Savior Jesus Christ," and the "saving sacrifice of Jesus Christ on the cross." Second, they argue that the setting and conduct of the town board meetings create social pressures that force nonadherents to remain in the room or even feign participation in order to avoid offending the representatives who sponsor the prayer and will vote on matters citizens bring before the board. The sectarian content of the prayers compounds the subtle coercive pressures, they argue, because the nonbeliever who might tolerate ecumenical prayer is forced to do the same for prayer that might be inimical to his or her beliefs.

A

An insistence on nonsectarian or ecumenical prayer as a single, fixed standard is not consistent with the tradition of legislative prayer outlined in the Court's cases. The Court found the prayers in Marsh consistent with the First Amendment not because they espoused only a generic theism but because our history and tradition have shown that prayer in this limited context could "coexis[t] with the principles of disestablishment and religious freedom." The Congress that drafted the First Amendment would have been accustomed to invocations containing explicitly religious themes of the sort respondents find objectionable.

One of the Senate's first chaplains, the Rev. William White, gave prayers in a series that included the Lord's Prayer, the Collect for Ash Wednesday, prayers for peace and grace, a general thanksgiving, St. Chrysostom's Prayer, and a prayer seeking "the grace of our Lord Jesus Christ, &c." The decidedly Christian nature of these prayers must not be dismissed as the relic of a time when our Nation was less pluralistic than it is today. Congress continues to permit its appointed and visiting chaplains to express themselves in a religious idiom. It acknowledges our growing diversity not by proscribing sectarian content but by welcoming ministers of many creeds. See, e.g., 160 Cong. Rec. S1329 (Mar. 6, 2014) (Dalai Lama) ("I am a Buddhist monk — a simple Buddhist monk — so we pray to Buddha and all other Gods"); 159 Cong. Rec. H7006 (Nov. 13, 2013) (Rabbi Joshua Gruenberg) ("Our God and God of our ancestors, Everlasting Spirit of the Universe . . ."); 159 Cong. Rec. H3024 (June 4, 2013) (Satguru Bodhinatha Veylanswami) ("Hindu scripture declares, without equivocation, that the highest of high ideals is to never knowingly harm anyone"); 158 Cong. Rec. H5633 (Aug. 2, 2012) (Imam Nayyar Imam) ("The final prophet of God, Muhammad, peace be upon him, stated: 'The leaders of a people are a representation of their deeds'").

The contention that legislative prayer must be generic or nonsectarian derives from dictum in *County of Allegheny*, that was disputed when written and has been repudiated by later cases. There the Court held that a crèche placed on the steps of a county courthouse to celebrate the Christmas season violated the Establishment Clause because it had "the effect of endorsing a patently Christian message." Four dissenting Justices disputed that endorsement could be the proper test, as it likely would condemn a host of traditional practices that recognize the role religion plays in our society, among them legislative prayer and the "forthrightly religious" Thanksgiving proclamations issued by nearly every President since Washington. The Court sought to counter this criticism by recasting Marsh to permit only prayer that contained no overtly Christian references:

> "However history may affect the constitutionality of nonsectarian references to religion by the government, history cannot legitimate practices that demonstrate the government's allegiance to a particular sect or creed. . . . The legislative prayers involved in *Marsh* did not violate this principle because the particular chaplain had 'removed all references to Christ.'"

This proposition is irreconcilable with the facts of *Marsh* and with its holding and reasoning. *Marsh* nowhere suggested that the constitutionality of legislative prayer turns on the neutrality of its content.

To hold that invocations must be nonsectarian would force the legislatures that sponsor prayers and the courts that are asked to decide these cases to act as supervisors and censors of religious speech, a rule that would involve government in religious matters to a far greater degree than is the case under the town's current practice of neither editing or approving prayers in advance nor criticizing their content after the fact.

Our Government is prohibited from prescribing prayers to be recited in our public institutions in order to promote a preferred system of belief or code of moral behavior. *Engel v. Vitale,* 370 U.S. 421, 430 (1962). It would be but a few steps removed from that prohibition for legislatures to require chaplains to redact the religious content from their message in order to make it acceptable for the public sphere. Government may not mandate a civic religion that stifles any but the most generic reference to the sacred any more than it may prescribe a religious orthodoxy.

Respondents argue, in effect, that legislative prayer may be addressed only to a generic God. The law and the Court could not draw this line for each specific prayer or seek to require ministers to set aside their nuanced and deeply personal beliefs for vague and artificial ones. There is doubt, in any event, that consensus might be reached as to what qualifies as generic or nonsectarian. Honorifics like "Lord of Lords" or "King of Kings" might strike a Christian audience as ecumenical, yet these titles may have no place in the vocabulary of other faith traditions.

Because it is unlikely that prayer will be inclusive beyond dispute, it would be unwise to adopt what respondents think is the next-best option: permitting those religious words, and only those words, that are acceptable to the majority, even if they will exclude some. *Torcaso v. Watkins,* 367 U.S. 488, 495 (1961). The First Amendment is not a majority rule, and government may not seek to define permissible categories of religious speech. Once it invites prayer into the public sphere, government must permit a prayer giver to address his or her own God or gods as conscience dictates, unfettered by what an administrator or judge considers to be nonsectarian.

In rejecting the suggestion that legislative prayer must be nonsectarian, the Court does not imply that no constraints remain on its content. The relevant constraint derives from its place at the opening of legislative sessions, where it is meant to lend gravity to the occasion and reflect values long part of the Nation's heritage. Prayer that is solemn and respectful in tone, that invites lawmakers to reflect upon shared ideals and common ends before they embark on the fractious business of governing, serves that legitimate function. If the course and practice over time shows that the invocations denigrate nonbelievers or religious minorities, threaten damnation, or preach conversion, many present may consider the prayer to fall short of the desire to elevate the purpose of the occasion and to unite lawmakers in their common effort. That circumstance would present a different case than the one presently before the Court.

The tradition reflected in *Marsh* permits chaplains to ask their own God for blessings of peace, justice, and freedom that find appreciation among people of all faiths. That a prayer is given in the name of Jesus, Allah, or Jehovah, or that it makes passing reference to religious doctrines, does not remove it from that tradition. These religious themes provide particular means to universal ends. Prayer that reflects beliefs specific to only some creeds can still serve to solemnize the occasion, so long as the practice over time is not "exploited to proselytize or advance any one, or to disparage any other, faith or belief." *Marsh.*

The prayers delivered in the town of Greece do not fall outside the tradition this Court has recognized.

The prayer opportunity in this case must be evaluated against the backdrop of historical practice. As a practice that has long endured, legislative prayer has become part of our heritage and tradition, part of our expressive idiom, similar to the Pledge of Allegiance, inaugural prayer, or the recitation of "God save the United States and this honorable Court" at the opening of this Court's sessions. It is presumed that the reasonable observer is acquainted with this tradition and understands that its purposes are to lend gravity to public proceedings and to acknowledge the place religion holds in the lives of many private citizens, not to afford government an opportunity to proselytize or force truant constituents into the pews. That many appreciate these acknowledgments of the divine in our public institutions does not suggest that those who disagree are compelled to join the expression or approve its content. *West Virginia State Bd. of Ed. v. Barnette,* 319 U.S. 624, 642 (1943).

Ceremonial prayer is but a recognition that, since this Nation was founded and until the present day, many Americans deem that their own existence must be understood by precepts far beyond the authority of government to alter or define and that willing participation in civic affairs can be consistent with a brief acknowledgment of their belief in a higher power, always with due respect for those who adhere to other beliefs. The prayer in this case has a permissible ceremonial purpose. It is not an unconstitutional establishment of religion.

The town of Greece does not violate the First Amendment by opening its meetings with prayer that comports with our tradition and does not coerce participation by nonadherents.

JUSTICE ALITO, with whom JUSTICE SCALIA joins, concurring.

There can be little doubt that the decision in *Marsh* reflected the original understanding of the First Amendment. It is virtually inconceivable that the First Congress, having appointed chaplains whose responsibilities prominently included the delivery of prayers at the beginning of each daily session, thought that this practice was inconsistent with the Establishment Clause. And since this practice was well established and undoubtedly well known, it seems equally clear that the state legislatures that ratified the First Amendment had the same understanding. In the case before us, the Court of Appeals appeared to base its decision on one of the Establishment Clause "tests" set out in the opinions of this Court, but if there is any inconsistency between any of those tests and the historic practice of legislative prayer, the inconsistency calls into question the validity of the test, not the historic practice.

JUSTICE THOMAS, with whom JUSTICE SCALIA joins as to Part II, concurring in part and concurring in the judgment.

Except for Part II–B, I join the opinion of the Court, which faithfully applies *Marsh v. Chambers*. I write separately to reiterate my view that the Establishment Clause is "best understood as a federalism provision," *Elk Grove Unified School Dist. v. Newdow* (Thomas, J., concurring in judgment), and to state my understanding of the proper "coercion" analysis.

As an initial matter, the Clause probably prohibits Congress from establishing a national religion. Cf. D. Drakeman, Church, State, and Original Intent 260–262 (2010). The text of the Clause also suggests that Congress "could not interfere with state establishments, notwithstanding any argument that could be made based on Congress' power under the Necessary and Proper Clause." *Newdow* (opinion of Thomas, J.). The language of the First Amendment ("Congress shall make no law") "precisely tracked and inverted the exact wording" of the Necessary and Proper Clause ("Congress shall have power to make all laws which shall be necessary and proper"), which was the subject of fierce criticism by Anti–Federalists at the time of ratification.

Construing the Establishment Clause as a federalism provision accords with the variety of church-state arrangements that existed at the Founding. At least six States had established churches in 1789. Amar 32–33. New England States like Massachusetts, Connecticut, and New Hampshire maintained local-rule establishments whereby the majority in each town could select the minister and religious denomination (usually Congregationalism, or "Puritanism"). McConnell, *Establishment and Disestablishment at the Founding, Part I: Establishment of Religion*, 44 Wm. & Mary L. Rev. 2105, 2110 (2003); see also L. Levy, The Establishment Clause: Religion and the First Amendment 29–51 (1994) (hereinafter Levy). In the South, Maryland, South Carolina, and Georgia eliminated their exclusive Anglican establishments following the American Revolution and adopted general establishments, which permitted taxation in support of all Christian churches (or, as in South Carolina, all Protestant churches). See Levy 52–58; Amar 32–33. Virginia, by contrast, had recently abolished its official state establishment and ended direct government funding of clergy after a legislative battle led by James Madison. See T. Buckley, Church and State in Revolutionary Virginia, 1776–1787, pp. 155–164 (1977). Other States — principally Rhode Island, Pennsylvania, and Delaware, which were founded by religious dissenters — had no history of formal establishments at all, although they still maintained religious tests for office.

The Federalist logic of the original Establishment Clause poses a special barrier to its mechanical incorporation against the States through the Fourteenth Amendment. Unlike the Free Exercise Clause, which "plainly protects individuals against congressional interference with the right to exercise their religion," the Establishment Clause "does not purport to protect individual rights." *Newdow,* (opinion of Thomas, J.). Instead, the States are the particular beneficiaries of the Clause. Incorporation therefore gives rise to a paradoxical result: Applying the Clause against the States eliminates their right to establish a religion free from federal interference, thereby "prohibit[ing] exactly what the Establishment Clause protected."

Put differently, the structural reasons that counsel against incorporating the Tenth Amendment also apply to the Establishment Clause. To my knowledge, no court has ever suggested that the Tenth Amendment, which "reserve[s] to the States" powers not delegated to the Federal Government, could or should be applied against the States. To incorporate that limitation would be to divest the States of all powers not specifically delegated to them, thereby inverting the original import of the Amendment. Incorporating the Establishment Clause has precisely the same effect.

Even if the Establishment Clause were properly incorporated against the States, the municipal prayers at issue in this case bear no resemblance to the coercive state establishments that existed at the founding. "The coercion that was a hallmark of historical establishments of religion was coercion of religious orthodoxy and of financial support *by force of law and threat of penalty.*" *Lee v. Weisman,* 505 U.S. 577, 589 (1992) (Scalia, J., dissenting).

Thus, to the extent coercion is relevant to the Establishment Clause analysis, it is actual legal coercion that counts — not the "subtle coercive pressures" allegedly felt by respondents in this case.

JUSTICE BREYER, dissenting.

Having applied my legal judgment to the relevant facts, I conclude, like Justice KAGAN, that the town of Greece failed to make reasonable efforts to include prayer givers of minority faiths, with the result that, although it is a community of several faiths, its prayer givers were almost exclusively persons of a single faith. Under these circumstances, I would affirm the judgment of the Court of Appeals that Greece's prayer practice violated the Establishment Clause.

I dissent from the Court's decision to the contrary.

JUSTICE KAGAN, with whom JUSTICE GINSBURG, JUSTICE BREYER, and JUSTICE SOTOMAYOR join, dissenting.

For centuries now, people have come to this country from every corner of the world to share in the blessing of religious freedom. Our Constitution promises that they may worship in their own way, without fear of penalty or danger, and that in itself is a momentous offering. Yet our Constitution makes a commitment still more remarkable — that however those individuals worship, they will count as full and equal American citizens. A Christian, a Jew, a Muslim (and so forth) — each stands in the same relationship with her country, with her state and local communities, and with every level and body of government. So that when each person performs the duties or seeks the benefits of citizenship, she does so not as an adherent to one or another religion, but simply as an American.

I respectfully dissent from the Court's opinion because I think the Town of Greece's prayer practices violate that norm of religious equality — the breathtakingly generous constitutional idea that our public institutions belong no less to the Buddhist or Hindu than to the Methodist or Episcopalian. I do not contend that principle translates here into a bright separationist line. To the contrary, I agree with the Court's decision in *Marsh v. Chambers,* upholding the Nebraska Legislature's tradition of beginning each session with a chaplain's prayer. And I believe that pluralism and inclusion in a town hall can satisfy the constitutional requirement of neutrality; such a forum need not become a religion-free zone. But still, the Town of Greece should lose this case. The practice at issue here differs from the one sustained in *Marsh* because Greece's town meetings involve participation by ordinary citizens, and the invocations given — directly to those citizens — were predominantly sectarian in content. Still more, Greece's Board did nothing to recognize religious diversity: In arranging for clergy members to open each meeting, the Town never sought (except briefly when this suit was filed) to involve, accommodate, or in any way reach out to adherents of non-Christian religions. So month in and month out for over a decade, prayers steeped in only one faith, addressed toward members of the public, commenced meetings to discuss local affairs and distribute government benefits. In my view, that practice does not square with the First Amendment's promise that every citizen, irrespective of her religion, owns an equal share in her government.

I

To begin to see what has gone wrong in the Town of Greece, consider several hypothetical scenarios in which sectarian prayer — taken straight from this case's record — infuses governmental activities. None involves, as this case does, a proceeding that could be characterized as a legislative session, but they are useful to elaborate some general principles. In each instance, assume (as was true in Greece) that the invocation is given pursuant to government policy and is representative of the prayers generally offered in the designated setting:

- You are a party in a case going to trial; let's say you have filed suit against the government for violating one of your legal rights. The judge bangs his gavel to call the court to order, asks a minister to come to the front of the room, and instructs the 10 or so individuals present to rise for an opening prayer. The clergyman faces those in attendance and says: "Lord, God of all creation. We acknowledge the saving sacrifice of Jesus Christ on the cross. We draw strength from his resurrection at Easter. Jesus Christ, who took away the sins of the world, destroyed our death, through his dying and in his rising, he has restored our life. Blessed are you, who has raised up the Lord Jesus, you who will raise us, in our turn, and put us by His side. Amen." The judge then asks your lawyer to begin the trial.

- It's election day, and you head over to your local polling place to vote. As you and others wait to give your names and receive your ballots, an election official asks everyone there to join him in prayer. He says: "We pray this [day] for the guidance of the Holy Spirit as [we vote]. Let's just say the Our Father together. 'Our Father, who art in Heaven, hallowed be thy name; thy Kingdom come, thy will be done, on earth as it is in Heaven.'" And after he concludes, he makes the sign of the cross, and appears to wait expectantly for you and the other prospective voters to do so too.

- You are an immigrant attending a naturalization ceremony to finally become a citizen. The presiding official tells you and your fellow applicants that before administering the oath of allegiance, he would like a minister to pray for you and with you. The pastor steps to the front of the room, asks everyone to bow their heads, and recites: "[F]ather, son, and Holy Spirit — it is with a due sense of reverence and awe that we come before you [today] seeking your blessing. You are a wise God, oh Lord, as evidenced even in the plan of redemption that is fulfilled in Jesus Christ. We ask that you would give freely and abundantly wisdom to one and to all in the name of the Lord and Savior Jesus Christ, who lives with you and the Holy Spirit, one God for ever and ever. Amen."

I would hold that the government officials responsible for the above practices — that is, for prayer repeatedly invoking a single religion's beliefs in these settings — crossed a constitutional line. I have every confidence the Court would agree. And even Greece's attorney conceded that something like the first hypothetical (he was not asked about the others) would violate the First Amendment. Why?

The reason, of course, has nothing to do with Christianity as such. This opinion is full of Christian prayers, because those were the only invocations offered in the Town of Greece. But if my hypotheticals involved the prayer of some other religion, the outcome would be exactly the same. Suppose, for example, that government officials in a predominantly Jewish community asked a rabbi to begin all public functions with a chanting of the Sh'ma and V'ahavta. ("Hear O Israel! The Lord our God, the Lord is One. Bind [these words] as a sign upon your hand; let them be a symbol before your eyes; inscribe them on the doorposts of your house, and on your gates.") Or assume officials in a mostly Muslim town requested a muezzin to commence such functions, over and over again, with a recitation of the Adhan. ("God is greatest, God is greatest. I bear witness that there is no deity but God. I bear witness that

Muhammed is the Messenger of God.") In any instance, the question would be why such government-sponsored prayer of a single religion goes beyond the constitutional pale.

One glaring problem is that the government in all these hypotheticals has aligned itself with, and placed its imprimatur on, a particular religious creed. "The clearest command of the Establishment Clause," this Court has held, "is that one religious denomination cannot be officially preferred over another." *Larson v. Valente,* 456 U.S. 228, 244 (1982). Justices have often differed about a further issue: whether and how the Clause applies to governmental policies favoring religion (of all kinds) over non-religion . . . But no one has disagreed with this much:

> "[O]ur constitutional tradition, from the Declaration of Independence and the first inaugural address of Washington down to the present day, has ruled out of order government-sponsored endorsement of religion where the endorsement is sectarian, in the sense of specifying details upon which men and women who believe in a benevolent, omnipotent Creator and Ruler of the world are known to differ (for example, the divinity of Christ)."
> *Lee v. Weisman,* 505 U.S. 577, 641 (Scalia, J., dissenting).

See also *County of Allegheny v. American Civil Liberties Union, Greater Pittsburgh Chapter* [492 U.S. 573 (1989)] ("Whatever else the Establishment Clause may mean, [it] means at the very least that government may not demonstrate a preference for one particular sect or creed (including a preference for Christianity over other religions)"). By authorizing and overseeing prayers associated with a single religion — to the exclusion of all others — the government officials in my hypothetical cases (whether federal, state, or local does not matter) have violated that foundational principle. They have embarked on a course of religious favoritism anathema to the First Amendment.

And making matters still worse: They have done so in a place where individuals come to interact with, and participate in, the institutions and processes of their government. A person goes to court, to the polls, to a naturalization ceremony — and a government official or his hand-picked minister asks her, as the first order of official business, to stand and pray with others in a way conflicting with her own religious beliefs. Perhaps she feels sufficient pressure to go along — to rise, bow her head, and join in whatever others are saying: After all, she wants, very badly, what the judge or poll worker or immigration official has to offer. Or perhaps she is made of stronger mettle, and she opts not to participate in what she does not believe — indeed, what would, for her, be something like blasphemy. She then must make known her dissent from the common religious view, and place herself apart from other citizens, as well as from the officials responsible for the invocations. And so a civic function of some kind brings religious differences to the fore: That public proceeding becomes (whether intentionally or not) an instrument for dividing her from adherents to the community's majority religion, and for altering the very nature of her relationship with her government.

That is not the country we are, because that is not what our Constitution permits. Here, when a citizen stands before her government, whether to perform a service or request a benefit, her religious beliefs do not enter into the picture. Relying on that "unbroken" national tradition, *Marsh* upheld (I think correctly) the Nebraska Legislature's practice of opening each day with a chaplain's prayer as "a tolerable acknowledgment of beliefs widely held among the people of this country." And so I agree with the majority that the issue here is "whether the prayer practice in the Town of Greece fits within the tradition long followed in Congress and the state legislatures."

Where I depart from the majority is in my reply to that question. The town hall here is a kind of hybrid. Greece's Board indeed has legislative functions, as Congress and state assemblies do—and that means some opening prayers are allowed there. But much as in my hypotheticals, the Board's meetings are also occasions for ordinary citizens to engage with and petition their government, often on highly individualized matters. That feature calls for Board members to exercise special care to ensure that the prayers offered are inclusive—that they respect each and every member of the community as an equal citizen. But the Board, and the clergy members it selected, made no such effort. Instead, the prayers given in Greece, addressed directly to the Town's citizenry, were *more* sectarian, and *less* inclusive, than anything this Court sustained in *Marsh*. For those reasons, the prayer in Greece departs from the legislative tradition that the majority takes as its benchmark.

In 1790, George Washington traveled to Newport, Rhode Island, a longtime bastion of religious liberty and the home of the first community of American Jews. Among the citizens he met there was Moses Seixas, one of that congregation's lay officials. The ensuing exchange between the two conveys, as well as anything I know, the promise this country makes to members of every religion.

Seixas wrote first, welcoming Washington to Newport. He spoke of "a deep sense of gratitude" for the new American Government—"a Government, which to bigotry gives no sanction, to persecution no assistance—but generously affording to All liberty of conscience, and immunities of Citizenship: deeming every one, of whatever Nation, tongue, or language, equal parts of the great governmental Machine." Address from Newport Hebrew Congregation (Aug. 17, 1790), in 6 PGW 286, n. 1 (M. Mastromarino ed. 1996). The first phrase there is the more poetic: a government that to "bigotry gives no sanction, to persecution no assistance." But the second is actually the more startling and transformative: a government that, beyond not aiding persecution, grants "immunities of citizenship" to the Christian and the Jew alike, and makes them "equal parts" of the whole country.

Washington responded the very next day. Like any successful politician, he appreciated a great line when he saw one—and knew to borrow it too. And so he repeated, word for word, Seixas's phrase about neither sanctioning bigotry nor assisting persecution. But he no less embraced the point Seixas had made about equality of citizenship. "It is now no more," Washington said, "that toleration is spoken of, as if it was by the indulgence of one class of people" to another, lesser one. For "[a]ll possess alike immunities of citizenship." Letter to Newport Hebrew Congregation (Aug. 18, 1790), in 6 PGW 285. That is America's promise in the First Amendment: full and equal membership in the polity for members of every religious group, assuming only that they, like anyone "who live[s] under [the Government's] protection[,] should demean themselves as good citizens."

For me, that remarkable guarantee means at least this much: When the citizens of this country approach their government, they do so only as Americans, not as members of one faith or another. And that means that even in a partly legislative body, they should not confront government-sponsored worship that divides them along religious lines. I believe, for all the reasons I have given, that the Town of Greece betrayed that promise. I therefore respectfully dissent from the Court's decision.

American Legion v. American Humanist Association

United States Supreme Court
139 S. Ct. 2067 (2019)

JUSTICE ALITO announced the judgment of the Court and delivered the opinion of the Court with respect to Parts I, II-B, II-C, III, and IV, and an opinion with respect to Parts II-A and II-D, in which THE CHIEF JUSTICE, JUSTICE BREYER, and JUSTICE KAVANAUGH join.

Since 1925, the Bladensburg Peace Cross (Cross) has stood as a tribute to 49 area soldiers who gave their lives in the First World War. Eighty-nine years after the dedication of the Cross, respondents filed this lawsuit, claiming that they are offended by the sight of the memorial on public land and that its presence there and the expenditure of public funds to maintain it violate the Establishment Clause of the First Amendment.

Although the cross has long been a preeminent Christian symbol, its use in the Bladensburg memorial has a special significance. After the First World War, the picture of row after row of plain white crosses marking the overseas graves of soldiers who had lost their lives in that horrible conflict was emblazoned on the minds of Americans at home, and the adoption of the cross as the Bladensburg memorial must be viewed in that historical context. For nearly a century, the Bladensburg Cross has expressed the community's grief at the loss of the young men who perished, its thanks for their sacrifice, and its dedication to the ideals for which they fought. It has become a prominent community landmark, and its removal or radical alteration at this date would be seen by many not as a neutral act but as the manifestation of "a hostility toward religion that has no place in our Establishment Clause traditions." *Van Orden v. Perry* (Breyer, J., concurring in judgment). And contrary to respondents' intimations, there is no evidence of discriminatory intent in the selection of the design of the memorial or the decision of a Maryland commission to maintain it. The Religion Clauses of the Constitution aim to foster a society in which people of all beliefs can live together harmoniously, and the presence of the

Bladensburg Cross on the land where it has stood for so many years is fully consistent with that aim.

The cross came into widespread use as a symbol of Christianity by the fourth century, and it retains that meaning today. But there are many contexts in which the symbol has also taken on a secular meaning. Indeed, there are instances in which its message is now almost entirely secular.

A cross appears as part of many registered trademarks held by businesses and secular organizations, including Blue Cross Blue Shield, the Bayer Group, and some Johnson & Johnson products. Many of these marks relate to health care, and it is likely that the association of the cross with healing had a religious origin. But the current use of these marks is indisputably secular.

The image used in the Bladensburg memorial — a plain Latin cross — also took on new meaning after World War I. "During and immediately after the war, the army marked soldiers' graves with temporary wooden crosses or Stars of David" — a departure from the prior practice of marking graves in American military cemeteries with uniform rectangular slabs. G. Piehler, Remembering War the American Way 101 (1995). The vast majority of these grave markers consisted of crosses, and thus when Americans saw photographs of these cemeteries, what struck them were rows and rows of plain white crosses. As a result, the image of a simple white cross "developed into a 'central symbol'" of the conflict. Contemporary literature, poetry, and art reflected this powerful imagery.

After the 1918 armistice, the War Department announced plans to replace the wooden crosses and Stars of David with uniform marble slabs like those previously used in American military cemeteries. But the public outcry against that proposal was swift and fierce. Many organizations, including the American War Mothers, a nonsectarian group founded in 1917, urged the Department to retain the design of the temporary markers. When the American Battle Monuments Commission took over the project of designing the headstones, it responded to this public sentiment by opting to replace the wooden crosses and Stars of David with marble versions of those symbols. A Member of Congress likewise introduced a resolution noting that "these wooden symbols have, during and since the World War, been regarded as emblematic of the great sacrifices which that war entailed, have been so treated by poets and artists and have become peculiarly and inseparably associated in the thought of surviving relatives and comrades and of the Nation with these World War graves." This national debate and its outcome confirmed the cross's widespread resonance as a symbol of sacrifice in the war.

Recognition of the cross's symbolism extended to local communities across the country. In late 1918, residents of Prince George's County, Maryland, formed a committee for the purpose of erecting a memorial for the county's fallen soldiers. Among the committee's members were the mothers of 10 deceased soldiers. The committee decided that the memorial should be a cross and hired sculptor and architect John Joseph Earley to design it. Although we do not know precisely why the committee chose the cross, it is unsurprising that the committee — and many others commemorating World War I — adopted a symbol so widely associated with that wrenching event.

The completed monument is a 32-foot tall Latin cross that sits on a large pedestal. The American Legion's emblem is displayed at its center, and the words "Valor," "Endurance," "Courage," and "Devotion" are inscribed at its base, one on each of the four faces. The pedestal also features a 9 by 2.5-foot bronze plaque explaining that the monument is "Dedicated to the heroes of Prince George's County, Maryland who lost their lives in the Great War for the liberty of the world." The plaque lists the names of 49 local men, both Black and White, who died in the war. It identifies the dates of American involvement, and quotes President Woodrow Wilson's request for a declaration of war: "The right is more precious than peace. We shall fight for the things we have always carried nearest our hearts. To such a task we dedicate our lives."

In 2012, nearly 90 years after the Cross was dedicated and more than 50 years after the Commission acquired it, the American Humanist Association lodged a complaint with the Commission. The complaint alleged that the Cross's presence on public land and the Commission's maintenance of the memorial violate the Establishment Clause of the First Amendment.

If the *Lemon* Court thought that its test would provide a framework for all future Establishment Clause decisions, its expectation has not been met. In many cases, this Court has either expressly declined to apply the test or has simply ignored it.

This pattern is a testament to the *Lemon* test's shortcomings. As Establishment Clause cases involving a great array of laws and practices came to the Court, it became more and more apparent that the *Lemon* test could not resolve them.

For at least four reasons, the *Lemon* test presents particularly daunting problems in cases, including the one now before us, that involve the use, for ceremonial, celebratory, or commemorative purposes, of words or symbols with religious associations. Together, these considerations counsel against efforts to evaluate such cases under *Lemon* and toward application of a presumption of constitutionality for longstanding monuments, symbols, and practices.

First, these cases often concern monuments, symbols, or practices that were first established long ago, and in such cases, identifying their original purpose or purposes may be especially difficult.

The truth is that 70 years after the fact, there was no way to be certain about the motivations of the men who were responsible for the creation of the monument. And this is often the case with old monuments, symbols, and practices. Yet it would be inappropriate for courts to compel their removal or termination based on supposition.

Second, as time goes by, the purposes associated with an established monument, symbol, or practice often multiply. Take the example of Ten Commandments monuments, the subject we addressed in *Van Orden* and *McCreary*.

For believing Jews and Christians, the Ten Commandments are the word of God handed down to Moses on Mount Sinai, but the image of the Ten Commandments has also been used to convey other meanings. They have historical significance as one of the foundations of our legal system, and for largely that reason, they are depicted in the marble frieze in our courtroom and in other prominent public buildings in our Nation's capital.

The existence of multiple purposes is not exclusive to longstanding monuments, symbols, or practices, but this phenomenon is more likely to occur in such cases. Even if the original purpose of a monument was infused with religion, the passage of time may obscure that sentiment. As our society becomes more and more religiously diverse, a community may preserve such monuments, symbols, and practices for the sake of their historical significance or their place in a common cultural heritage.

Third, just as the purpose for maintaining a monument, symbol, or practice may evolve, "[t]he 'message' conveyed . . . may change over time." Consider, for example, the message of the Statue of Liberty, which began as a monument to the solidarity and friendship between France and the United States and only decades later came to be seen "as a beacon welcoming immigrants to a land of freedom."

With sufficient time, religiously expressive monuments, symbols, and practices can become embedded features of a community's landscape and identity. The community may come to value them without necessarily embracing their religious roots. The recent tragic fire at Notre Dame in Paris provides a striking example. Although the French Republic rigorously enforces a secular public square, the cathedral remains a symbol of national importance to the religious and nonreligious alike. Notre Dame is fundamentally a place of worship and retains great religious importance, but its meaning has broadened. For many, it is inextricably linked with the very idea of Paris and France. Speaking to the nation shortly after the fire, President Macron said that Notre Dame "is our history, our literature, our imagination. The place where we survived epidemics, wars, liberation. It has been the epicenter of our lives."

In the same way, consider the many cities and towns across the United States that bear religious names. Religion undoubtedly motivated those who named Bethlehem, Pennsylvania; Las Cruces, New Mexico; Providence, Rhode Island; Corpus Christi, Texas; Nephi, Utah, and the countless other places in our country with names that are rooted in religion. Yet few would argue that this history requires that these names be erased from the map. Or take a motto like Arizona's, "Ditat Deus" ("God enriches"), which was adopted in 1864, or a flag like Maryland's, which has included two crosses since 1904. Familiarity itself can become a reason for preservation.

Fourth, when time's passage imbues a religiously expressive monument, symbol, or practice with this kind of familiarity and historical significance, removing it may no longer appear neutral, especially to the local community for which it has taken on particular meaning. A government that roams the land, tearing down monuments with religious symbolism and scrubbing away any reference to the divine will strike many as aggressively hostile to religion. Militantly secular regimes have carried out such projects in the past, and for those with a knowledge of history, the image of monuments being taken down will be evocative, disturbing, and divisive.

These four considerations show that retaining established, religiously expressive monuments, symbols, and practices is quite different from erecting or adopting new ones. The passage of time gives rise to a strong presumption of constitutionality.

For example, few would say that the State of California is attempting to convey a religious message by retaining the names given to many of the State's cities by their original Spanish settlers—San Diego, Los Angeles, Santa Barbara, San Jose, San Francisco, etc. But it would be something else entirely if the State undertook to change all those names. Much the same is true about monuments to soldiers who sacrificed their lives for this country more than a century ago.

While the *Lemon* Court ambitiously attempted to find a grand unified theory of the Establishment Clause, in later cases, we have taken a more modest approach that focuses on the particular issue at hand and looks to history for guidance. Our cases involving prayer before a legislative session are an example.

Applying these principles, we conclude that the Bladensburg Cross does not violate the Establishment Clause.

As we have explained, the Bladensburg Cross carries special significance in commemorating World War I. Due in large part to the image of the simple wooden crosses that originally marked the graves of American soldiers killed in the war, the cross became a symbol of their sacrifice, and the design of the Bladensburg Cross must be understood in light of that background. That the cross originated as a Christian symbol and retains that meaning in many contexts does not change the fact that the symbol took on an added secular meaning when used in World War I memorials.

Not only did the Bladensburg Cross begin with this meaning, but with the passage of time, it has acquired historical importance. It reminds the people of Bladensburg and surrounding areas of the deeds of their predecessors and of the sacrifices they made in a war fought in the name of democracy. As long as it is retained in its original place and form, it speaks as well of the community that erected the monument nearly a century ago and has maintained it ever since. The memorial represents what the relatives, friends, and neighbors of the fallen soldiers felt at the time and how they chose to express their sentiments. And the monument has acquired additional layers of historical meaning in subsequent years. The Cross now stands among memorials to veterans of later wars. It has become part of the community.

The monument would not serve that role if its design had deliberately disrespected area soldiers who perished in World War I. More than 3,500 Jewish soldiers gave their lives for the United States in that conflict, and some have wondered whether the names of any Jewish soldiers from the area were deliberately left off the list on the memorial or whether the names of any Jewish soldiers were included on the Cross against the wishes of their families. There is no evidence that either thing was done, and we do know that one of the local American Legion leaders responsible for the Cross's construction was a Jewish veteran.

Notes and Questions

(1) In *McGowan v. Maryland*, 366 U.S. 420 (1961), the Court upheld Maryland's Sunday Blue Laws, which banned numerous labor, business, and commercial activities on Sunday. Despite the strongly religious origins of Sunday closing laws, the Court reasoned that, in modern times, such laws primarily served the secular purposes of setting aside a day for "rest, repose, recreation, and tranquility, a day which all members of the family and community have the opportunity to spend and enjoy together, a day on which there exists relative quiet and disassociation from the everyday intensity of commercial activities, a day on which people may visit friends and relatives who are not available during working days."

(2) In *Larkin v. Grendel's Den, Inc.*, 459 U.S. 116 (1982), the Court held that a Massachusetts law, which vested in churches and schools the power to veto applications for liquor licenses within a five-hundred-foot radius of the church or school, violated the Establishment Clause. The Court found that while the law had a valid secular purpose, it failed the "effect" and "entanglement" prongs of the *Lemon* test.

(3) In *Trump v. Hawaii*, 138 S. Ct. 2392 (2018), the Supreme Court upheld President Trump's controversial "travel ban," which critics characterized as an "anti-Muslim ban," restricting entry into the United States of persons from eight countries — Chad, Iran, Iraq, Libya, North Korea, Syria, Venezuela, and Yemen. In a 5-4 opinion written by Chief Justice Roberts, the Court rejected the assertion that the ban was an unconstitutional establishment of religion. The challengers to the ban relied heavily on various statements made by Mr. Trump while running for President, in which he spoke of banning Muslims, and various other statements made while President, that the challengers claimed tainted the President's actions. The majority rejected the claim. The Court's key passages reasoned:

> Plaintiffs argue that this President's words strike at fundamental standards of respect and tolerance, in violation of our constitutional tradition. But the issue before us is not whether to denounce the statements. It is instead the significance of those statements in reviewing a Presidential directive, neutral on its face, addressing a matter within the core of executive responsibility. In doing so, we must consider not only the statements of a particular President, but also the authority of the Presidency itself.

> The case before us differs in numerous respects from the conventional Establishment Clause claim. Unlike the typical suit involving religious displays or school prayer, plaintiffs seek to invalidate a national security directive regulating the entry of aliens abroad. Their claim accordingly raises a number of delicate issues regarding the scope of the constitutional right and the manner of proof. The Proclamation, moreover, is facially neutral

toward religion. Plaintiffs therefore ask the Court to probe the sincerity of the stated justifications for the policy by reference to extrinsic statements — many of which were made before the President took the oath of office. These various aspects of plaintiffs' challenge inform our standard of review.

The Proclamation is expressly premised on legitimate purposes: preventing entry of nationals who cannot be adequately vetted and inducing other nations to improve their practices. The text says nothing about religion. Plaintiffs and the dissent nonetheless emphasize that five of the seven nations currently included in the Proclamation have Muslim-majority populations. Yet that fact alone does not support an inference of religious hostility, given that the policy covers just 8% of the world's Muslim population and is limited to countries that were previously designated by Congress or prior administrations as posing national security risks.

B. Rituals and Symbols in School Settings

The school policy below was the policy at issue in *Santa Fe v. Doe*:

STUDENT ACTIVITIES:
PRE–GAME CEREMONIES AT FOOTBALL GAMES

The board has chosen to permit students to deliver a brief invocation and/ or message to be delivered during the pre-game ceremonies of home varsity football games to solemnize the event, to promote good sportsmanship and student safety, and to establish the appropriate environment for the competition.

Upon advice and direction of the high school principal, each spring, the high school student council shall conduct an election, by the high school student body, by secret ballot, to determine whether such a statement or invocation will be a part of the pre-game ceremonies and if so, shall elect a student, from a list of student volunteers, to deliver the statement or invocation. The student volunteer who is selected by his or her classmates may decide what message and/or invocation to deliver, consistent with the goals and purposes of this policy.

If the District is enjoined by a court order from the enforcement of this policy, then and only then will the following policy automatically become the applicable policy of the school district.

The board has chosen to permit students to deliver a brief invocation and/ or message to be delivered during the pre-game ceremonies of home varsity football games to solemnize the event, to promote good sportsmanship and student safety, and to establish the appropriate environment for the competition.

Upon advice and direction of the high school principal, each spring, the high school student council shall conduct an election, by the high school student body, by secret ballot, to determine whether such a message or invocation will be a part of the pre-game ceremonies and if so, shall elect a student, from a list of student volunteers, to deliver the statement or invocation. The student volunteer who is selected by his or her classmates may decide what statement or invocation to deliver, consistent with the goals and purposes of this policy. Any message and/or invocation delivered by a student must be nonsectarian and nonproselytizing.

Santa Fe Independent School District v. Doe

United States Supreme Court
530 U.S. 290, 120 S. Ct. 120, 2266, 147 L. Ed. 2d 295 (2000)

JUSTICE STEVENS delivered the opinion of the Court.

The first Clause in the First Amendment to the Federal Constitution provides that "Congress shall make no law respecting an establishment of religion, or prohibiting the free exercise thereof." In *Lee v. Weisman*, we held that a prayer delivered by a rabbi at a middle school graduation ceremony violated that Clause. Although this case involves student prayer at a different type of school function, our analysis is properly guided by the principles that we endorsed in *Lee*.

In this case the District first argues that this principle is inapplicable to its October policy because the messages are private student speech, not public speech. It reminds us that "there is a crucial difference between government speech endorsing religion, which the Establishment Clause forbids, and private speech endorsing religion, which the Free Speech and Free Exercise Clauses protect." We certainly agree with that distinction, but we are not persuaded that the pregame invocations should be regarded as "private speech."

These invocations are authorized by a government policy and take place on government property at government-sponsored school-related events. Of course, not every message delivered under such circumstances is the government's own. We have held, for example, that an individual's contribution to a government-created forum was not government speech. See *Rosenberger v. Rector and Visitors of Univ. of Va.*, 515 U.S. 819 (1995). Although the District relies heavily on *Rosenberger* and similar cases involving such forums, it is clear that the pregame ceremony is not the type of forum discussed in those cases. The Santa Fe school officials simply do not "evince either 'by policy or by practice,' any intent to open the [pregame ceremony] to 'indiscriminate use,' by the student body generally." *Hazelwood School Dist. v. Kuhlmeier*, 484 U.S. 260, 270 (1988). Rather, the school allows only one student, the same student for the entire season, to give the invocation. The statement or invocation, moreover, is subject to particular regulations that confine the content and topic of the student's message.

Granting only one student access to the stage at a time does not, of course, necessarily preclude a finding that a school has created a limited public forum. Here, however, Santa Fe's student election system ensures that only those messages deemed "appropriate" under the District's policy may be delivered. That is, the majoritarian process implemented by the District guarantees, by definition, that minority candidates will never prevail and that their views will be effectively silenced.

Recently, in *Board of Regents of Univ. of Wis. System v. Southworth*, 529 U.S. 217 (2000), we explained why student elections that determine, by majority vote, which expressive activities shall receive or not receive school benefits are constitutionally problematic:

> To the extent the referendum substitutes majority determinations for viewpoint neutrality it would undermine the constitutional protection the program requires. The whole theory of viewpoint neutrality is that minority views are treated with the same respect as are majority views. Access to a public forum, for instance, does not depend upon majoritarian consent. That principle is controlling here.

Like the student referendum for funding in *Board of Regents of Univ. of Wis. System v. Southworth*, 529 U.S. 217 (2000), this student election does nothing to protect minority views but rather places the students who hold such views at the mercy of the majority. Because "fundamental rights may not be submitted to vote; they depend on the outcome of no elections," *West Virginia Bd. of Ed. v. Barnette*, the District's elections are insufficient safeguards of diverse student speech.

In *Lee v. Weisman*, the school district made the related argument that its policy of endorsing only "civic or nonsectarian" prayer was acceptable because it minimized the intrusion on the audience as a whole. We rejected that claim by explaining that such a majoritarian policy "does not lessen the offense or isolation to the objectors. At best it narrows their number, at worst increases their sense of isolation and affront." Similarly, while Santa Fe's majoritarian election might ensure that most of the students are represented, it does nothing to protect the minority; indeed, it likely serves to intensify their offense.

Moreover, the District has failed to divorce itself from the religious content in the invocations. It has not succeeded in doing so, either by claiming that its policy is "'one of neutrality rather than endorsement'" or by characterizing the individual student as the "circuit-breaker" in the process. Contrary to the District's repeated assertions that it has adopted a "hands-off" approach to the pregame invocation, the realities of the situation plainly reveal that its policy involves both perceived and actual endorsement of religion.

In addition to involving the school in the selection of the speaker, the policy, by its terms, invites and encourages religious messages. The policy itself states that the purpose of the message is "to solemnize the event." A religious message is the most obvious method of solemnizing an event. Moreover, the requirements that the message "promote good citizenship" and "establish the appropriate environment for competition" further narrow the types of message deemed appropriate, suggesting that a solemn, yet nonreligious, message, such as commentary on United States foreign policy, would be prohibited. Indeed, the only type of message that is expressly endorsed in the text is an "invocation" — a term that primarily describes an appeal for divine assistance. In fact, as used in the past at Santa Fe High School, an "invocation" has always entailed a focused religious message. Thus, the expressed purposes of the policy encourage the selection of a religious message, and that is precisely how the students understand the policy. The results of the elections described in the parties' stipulation make it clear that the students understood that the central question before them was whether prayer should be a part of the pregame ceremony. We recognize the important role that public worship plays in many communities, as well as the sincere desire to include public prayer as a part of various occasions so as to mark those occasions' significance. But such religious activity in public schools, as elsewhere, must comport with the First Amendment.

The actual or perceived endorsement of the message, moreover, is established by factors beyond just the text of the policy. Once the student speaker is selected and the message composed, the invocation is then delivered to a large audience assembled as part of a regularly scheduled, school-sponsored function conducted on school property. The message is broadcast over the school's public address system, which remains subject to the control of school officials. It is fair to assume that the pregame ceremony is clothed in the traditional indicia of school sporting events, which generally include not just the team, but also cheerleaders and band members dressed in uniforms sporting the school name and mascot. The school's name is likely written in large print across the field and on banners and flags. The crowd will certainly include many who display the school colors and insignia on their school T-shirts, jackets, or hats and who may also be waving signs displaying the school name. It is in a setting such as this that "[t]he board has chosen to permit" the elected student to rise and give the "statement or invocation."

In this context the members of the listening audience must perceive the pregame message as a public expression of the views of the majority of the student body delivered with the approval of the school administration.

Furthermore, regardless of whether one considers a sporting event an appropriate occasion for solemnity, the use of an invocation to foster such solemnity is impermissible when, in actuality, it constitutes prayer sponsored by the school. And it is unclear what type of message would be both appropriately "solemnizing" under the District's policy and yet non-religious.

Most striking to us is the evolution of the current policy from the long-sanctioned office of "Student Chaplain" to the candidly titled "Prayer at Football Games" regulation. This history indicates that the District intended to preserve the practice of prayer before football games. The conclusion that the District viewed the October policy simply as a continuation of the previous policies is dramatically illustrated by the fact that the school did not conduct a new election, pursuant to the current policy, to replace the results of the previous election, which occurred under the former policy. Given these observations, and in light of the school's history of regular delivery of a student-led prayer at athletic events, it is reasonable to infer that the specific purpose of the policy was to preserve a popular "state-sponsored religious practice."

School sponsorship of a religious message is impermissible because it sends the ancillary message to members of the audience who are nonadherents "that they are outsiders, not full members of the political community, and an accompanying message to adherents that they are insiders, favored members of the political community." The delivery of such a message — over the school's public address system, by a speaker representing the student body, under the supervision of school faculty, and pursuant to a school policy that explicitly and implicitly encourages public prayer — is not properly characterized as "private" speech.

III

The District next argues that its football policy is distinguishable from the graduation prayer in *Lee* because it does not coerce students to participate in religious observances. Its argument has two parts: first, that there is no impermissible government coercion because the pregame messages are the product of student choices; and second, that there is really no coercion at all because attendance at an extracurricular event, unlike a graduation ceremony, is voluntary.

The reasons just discussed explaining why the alleged "circuit-breaker" mechanism of the dual elections and student speaker do not turn public speech into private speech also demonstrate why these mechanisms do not insulate the school from the coercive element of the final message. In fact, this aspect of the District's argument exposes anew the concerns that are created by the majoritarian election system. The parties' stipulation clearly states that the issue resolved in the first election was "whether a student would deliver prayer at varsity football games," and the controversy in this case demonstrates that the views of the students are not unanimous on that issue.

One of the purposes served by the Establishment Clause is to remove debate over this kind of issue from governmental supervision or control. We explained in *Lee* that the "preservation and transmission of religious beliefs and worship is a responsibility and a choice committed to the private sphere." The two student elections authorized by the policy, coupled with the debates that presumably must precede each, impermissibly invade that private sphere. The election mechanism, when considered in light of the history in which the policy in question evolved, reflects a device the District put in place that determines whether religious messages will be delivered at home football games. The mechanism encourages divisiveness along religious lines in a public school setting, a result at odds with the Establishment Clause.

The District further argues that attendance at the commencement ceremonies at issue in *Lee* "differs dramatically" from attendance at high school football games, which it contends "are of no more than passing interest to many students" and are "decidedly extracurricular," thus dissipating any coercion. Attendance at a high school football game, unlike showing up for class, is certainly not required in order to receive a diploma. Moreover, we may assume that the District is correct in arguing that the informal pressure to attend an athletic event is not as strong as a senior's desire to attend her own graduation ceremony.

There are some students, however, such as cheerleaders, members of the band, and, of course, the team members themselves, for whom seasonal commitments mandate their attendance, sometimes for class credit. The District also minimizes the importance to many students of attending and participating in extracurricular activities as part of a complete educational experience. To assert that high school students do not feel immense social pressure, or have a truly genuine desire, to be involved in the extracurricular event that is American high school football is "formalistic in the extreme." We stressed in *Lee* the obvious observation that "adolescents are often susceptible to pressure from their peers towards conformity, and that the influence is strongest in matters of social convention." High school home football games are traditional gatherings of a school community; they bring together students and faculty as well as friends and family from years present and past to root for a common cause. Undoubtedly, the games are not important to some students, and they voluntarily choose not to attend. For many others, however, the choice between whether to attend these games or to risk facing a personally offensive religious ritual is in no practical sense an easy one. The Constitution, moreover, demands that the school may not force this difficult choice upon these students for "[i]t is a tenet of the First Amendment that the State cannot require one of its citizens to forfeit his or her rights and benefits as the price of resisting conformance to state-sponsored religious practice."

Even if we regard every high school student's decision to attend a home football game as purely voluntary, we are nevertheless persuaded that the delivery of a pre-game prayer has the improper effect of coercing those present to participate in an act of religious worship.

The Religion Clauses of the First Amendment prevent the government from making any law respecting the establishment of religion or prohibiting the free exercise thereof. By no means do these commands impose a prohibition on all religious activity in our public schools. Thus, nothing in the Constitution as interpreted by this Court prohibits any public school student from voluntarily praying at any time before, during, or after the school day. But the religious liberty protected by the Constitution is abridged when the State affirmatively sponsors the particular religious practice of prayer.

We refuse to turn a blind eye to the context in which this policy arose, and that context quells any doubt that this policy was implemented with the purpose of endorsing school prayer.

The judgment of the Court of Appeals is, accordingly, affirmed.

CHIEF JUSTICE REHNQUIST with whom JUSTICE SCALIA and JUSTICE THOMAS join, dissenting.

The Court distorts existing precedent to conclude that the school district's student-message program is invalid on its face under the Establishment Clause. But even more disturbing than its holding is the tone of the Court's opinion; it bristles with hostility to all things religious in public life. Neither the holding nor the tone of the opinion is faithful to the meaning of the Establishment Clause, when it is recalled that George Washington himself, at the request of the very Congress which passed the Bill of Rights, proclaimed a day of "public thanksgiving and prayer, to be observed by acknowledging with grateful hearts the many and signal favors of Almighty God."

First, the Court misconstrues the nature of the "majoritarian election" permitted by the policy as being an election on "prayer" and "religion." To the contrary, the election permitted by the policy is a two-fold process whereby students vote first on whether to have a student speaker before football games at all, and second, if the students vote to have such a speaker, on who that speaker will be. It is conceivable that the election could become one in which student candidates campaign on platforms that focus on whether or not they will pray if elected. It is also conceivable that the election could lead to a Christian prayer before 90 percent of the football games. If, upon implementation, the policy operated in this fashion, we would have a record before us to review whether the policy, as applied, violated the Establishment Clause or unduly suppressed minority viewpoints. But it is possible that the students might vote not to have a pregame speaker, in which case there would be no threat of a constitutional violation. It is also possible that the election would not focus on prayer, but on public speaking ability or social popularity. And if student campaigning did begin to focus on prayer, the school might decide to implement reasonable campaign restrictions.

But the Court ignores these possibilities by holding that merely granting the student body the power to elect a speaker that may choose to pray, "regardless of the students' ultimate use of it, is not acceptable." The Court so holds despite that any speech that may occur as a result of the election process here would be private, not government, speech. The elected student, not the government, would choose what to say. Support for the Court's holding cannot be found in any of our cases. And it essentially invalidates all student elections. A newly elected student body president, or even a newly elected prom king or queen, could use opportunities for public speaking to say prayers. Under the Court's view, the mere grant of power to the students to vote for such offices, in light of the fear that those elected might publicly pray, violates the Establishment Clause.

Second, with respect to the policy's purpose, the Court holds that "the simple enactment of this policy, with the purpose and perception of school endorsement of student prayer, was a constitutional violation." But the policy itself has plausible secular purposes: "[T]o solemnize the event, to promote good sportsmanship and student safety, and to establish the appropriate environment for the competition."

The Court so concludes based on its rather strange view that a "religious message is the most obvious means of solemnizing an event." But it is easy to think of solemn messages that are not religious in nature, for example urging that a game be fought fairly. And sporting events often begin with a solemn rendition of our national anthem, with its concluding verse "And this be our motto: 'In God is our trust.'" Under the Court's logic, a public school that sponsors the singing of the national anthem before football games violates the Establishment Clause. Although the Court apparently believes that solemnizing football games is an illegitimate purpose, the voters in the school district seem to disagree. Nothing in the Establishment Clause prevents them from making this choice.

Finally, the Court seems to demand that a government policy be completely neutral as to content or be considered one that endorses religion. This is undoubtedly a new requirement, as our Establishment Clause jurisprudence simply does not mandate "content neutrality." That concept is found in our First Amendment speech cases and is used as a guide for determining when we apply strict scrutiny. For example, we look to "content neutrality" in reviewing loudness restrictions imposed on speech in public forums, and regulations against picketing. The Court seems to think that the fact that the policy is not content neutral somehow controls the Establishment Clause inquiry.

But even our speech jurisprudence would not require that all public school actions with respect to student speech be content neutral.

I would reverse the judgment of the Court of Appeals.

Kennedy v. Bremerton School District

United States Supreme Court
142 S. Ct. 2407 (2022)

JUSTICE GORSUCH delivered the opinion of the Court.

Joseph Kennedy lost his job as a high school football coach because he knelt at midfield after games to offer a quiet prayer of thanks. Mr. Kennedy prayed during a period when school employees were free to speak with a friend, call for a reservation at a restaurant, check email, or attend to other personal matters. He offered his prayers quietly while his students were otherwise occupied. Still, the Bremerton School District disciplined him anyway. It did so because it thought anything less could lead a reasonable observer to conclude (mistakenly) that it endorsed Mr. Kennedy's religious beliefs. That reasoning was misguided. Both the Free Exercise and Free Speech Clauses of the First Amendment protect expressions like Mr. Kennedy's. Nor does a proper understanding of the Amendment's Establishment Clause require the government to single out private religious speech for special disfavor. The Constitution and the best of our traditions counsel mutual respect and tolerance, not censorship and suppression, for religious and nonreligious views alike.

Joseph Kennedy began working as a football coach at Bremerton High School in 2008 after nearly two decades of service in the Marine Corps. Like many other football players and coaches across the country, Mr. Kennedy made it a practice to give "thanks through prayer on the playing field" at the conclusion of each game. In his prayers, Mr. Kennedy sought to express gratitude for "what the players had accomplished and for the opportunity to be part of their lives through the game of football." Mr. Kennedy offered his prayers after the players and coaches had shaken hands, by taking a knee at the 50-yard line and praying "quietly" for "approximately 30 seconds."

Initially, Mr. Kennedy prayed on his own. But over time, some players asked whether they could pray alongside him. Mr. Kennedy responded by saying, "This is a free country. You can do what you want." The number of players who joined Mr. Kennedy eventually grew to include most of the team, at least after some games. Sometimes team members invited opposing players to join. Other times Mr. Kennedy still prayed alone. Eventually, Mr. Kennedy began incorporating short motivational speeches with his prayer when others were present. Separately, the team at times engaged in pregame or postgame prayers in the locker room. It seems this practice was a "school tradition" that predated Mr. Kennedy's tenure. Mr. Kennedy explained that he "never told any student that it was important they participate in any religious activity." In particular, he "never pressured or encouraged any student to join" his postgame midfield prayers.

For over seven years, no one complained to the Bremerton School District about these practices.

The District placed Mr. Kennedy on paid administrative leave and prohibited him from participating, in any capacity, in football program activities. In a letter explaining the reasons for this disciplinary action, the superintendent criticized Mr. Kennedy for engaging in "public and demonstrative religious conduct while still on duty as an assistant coach" by offering a prayer following the games. The letter did not allege that Mr. Kennedy performed these prayers with students, and it acknowledged that his prayers took place while students were engaged in unrelated postgame activities. Additionally, the letter faulted Mr. Kennedy for not being willing to pray behind closed doors.

In a Q&A document provided to the public, the District admitted that it possessed no evidence that students have been directly coerced to pray with Kennedy. The Q&A also acknowledged that Mr. Kennedy had complied with the District's instruction to refrain from his "prior practices of leading players in a pre-game prayer in the locker room or leading players in a post-game prayer immediately following games." But the Q&A asserted that the District could not allow Mr. Kennedy to "engage in a public religious display." Otherwise, the District would "violate the Establishment Clause" because "reasonable students and attendees" might perceive the "district as endorsing religion."

While Mr. Kennedy received "uniformly positive evaluations" every other year of his coaching career, after the 2015 season ended in November, the District gave him a poor performance evaluation. The evaluation advised against rehiring Mr. Kennedy on the grounds that he failed to follow district policy regarding religious expression and failed to supervise student-athletes after games. Mr. Kennedy did not return for the next season.

Now before us, Mr. Kennedy renews his argument that the District's conduct violated both the Free Exercise and Free Speech Clauses of the First Amendment.

These Clauses work in tandem. Where the Free Exercise Clause protects religious exercises, whether communicative or not, the Free Speech Clause provides overlapping protection for expressive religious activities. That the First Amendment doubly protects religious speech is no accident. It is a natural outgrowth of the framers' distrust of government attempts to regulate religion and suppress dissent.

Under this Court's precedents, a plaintiff bears certain burdens to demonstrate an infringement of his rights under the Free Exercise and Free Speech Clauses. If the plaintiff carries these burdens, the focus then shifts to the defendant to show that its actions were nonetheless justified and tailored consistent with the demands of our case law.

That Mr. Kennedy has discharged his burdens is effectively undisputed. No one questions that he seeks to engage in a sincerely motivated religious exercise.

Nor does anyone question that, in forbidding Mr. Kennedy's brief prayer, the District failed to act pursuant to a neutral and generally applicable rule. A government policy will not qualify as neutral if it is "specifically directed at religious practice."

When it comes to Mr. Kennedy's free speech claim, our precedents remind us that the First Amendment's protections extend to "teachers and students," neither of whom "shed their constitutional rights to freedom of speech or expression at the schoolhouse gate." *Tinker* [*v. Des Moines Independent Community School Dist.*, 393 U.S. 503 (1969)].

To account for the complexity associated with the interplay between free speech rights and government employment, this Court's decisions in *Pickering* [*v. Board of Ed. of Township High School Dist. 205, Will Cty.*, 391 U.S. 563 (1968)], *Garcetti* [*v. Ceballos*, 547 U.S. 410 (2006)], and related cases suggest proceeding in two steps. The first step involves a threshold inquiry into the nature of the speech at issue. If a public employee speaks "pursuant to his or her official duties," this Court has said the Free Speech Clause generally will not shield the individual from an employer's control and discipline because that kind of speech is — for constitutional purposes at least — the government's own speech.

At the same time and at the other end of the spectrum, when an employee "speaks as a citizen addressing a matter of public concern," our cases indicate that the First Amendment may be implicated and courts should proceed to a second step. At this second step, our cases suggest that courts should attempt to engage in "a delicate balancing of the competing interests surrounding the speech and its consequences." Among other things, courts at this second step have sometimes considered whether an employee's speech interests are outweighed by "the interest of the State, as an employer, in promoting the efficiency of the public services it performs through its employees."

Applying these lessons here, it seems clear to us that Mr. Kennedy has demonstrated that his speech was private speech, not government speech. When Mr. Kennedy uttered the three prayers that resulted in his suspension, he was not engaged in speech "ordinarily within the scope" of his duties as a coach. He did not speak pursuant to government policy. He was not seeking to convey a government-created message. He was not instructing players, discussing strategy, encouraging better on-field performance, or engaged in any other speech the District paid him to produce as a coach.

Whether one views the case through the lens of the Free Exercise or Free Speech Clause, at this point the burden shifts to the District. Under the Free Exercise Clause, a government entity normally must satisfy at least "strict scrutiny," showing that its restrictions on the plaintiff's protected rights serve a compelling interest and are narrowly tailored to that end. See [*Church of the Lukumi Babalu Aye, Inc. v. City of Hialeah*, 508 U.S. 520 (1983)]. A similar standard generally obtains under the Free Speech Clause. See *Reed* [*v. Town of Gilbert*, 576 U.S. 155 (2015)]. The District, however, asks us to apply to Mr. Kennedy's claims the more lenient second-step *Pickering-Garcetti* test, or alternatively intermediate scrutiny. Ultimately, however, it does not matter which standard we apply. The District cannot sustain its burden under any of them.

As we have seen, the District argues that its suspension of Mr. Kennedy was essential to avoid a violation of the Establishment Clause. On its account, Mr. Kennedy's prayers might have been protected by the Free Exercise and Free Speech Clauses. But his rights were in "direct tension" with the competing demands of the Establishment Clause. To resolve that clash, the District reasoned, Mr. Kennedy's rights had to "yield."

But how could that be? It is true that this Court and others often refer to the "Establishment Clause," the "Free Exercise Clause," and the "Free Speech Clause" as separate units. But the three Clauses appear in the same sentence of the same Amendment: "Congress shall make no law respecting an establishment of religion, or prohibiting the free exercise thereof; or abridging the freedom of speech." A natural reading of that sentence would seem to suggest the Clauses have "complementary" purposes, not warring ones where one Clause is always sure to prevail over the others. See *Everson*.

To defend its approach, the District relied on *Lemon* and its progeny.

What the District and the Ninth Circuit overlooked, however, is that the "shortcomings" associated with this ambitious, abstract, and ahistorical approach to the Establishment Clause became so apparent that this Court long ago abandoned *Lemon* and its endorsement test offshoot.

In place of *Lemon* and the endorsement test, this Court has instructed that the Establishment Clause must be interpreted by "reference to historical practices and understandings." *Town of Greece*, 572; see also *American Legion*.

To be sure, this Court has long held that government may not, consistent with a historically sensitive understanding of the Establishment Clause, "make a religious observance compulsory." *Zorach v. Clauson*. [343 U.S. 306 (1952).] Government "may not coerce anyone to attend church," ibid., nor may it force citizens to engage in "a formal religious exercise," *Lee v. Weisman*. No doubt, too, coercion along these lines was among the foremost hallmarks of religious establishments the framers sought to prohibit when they adopted the First Amendment. Members of this Court have sometimes disagreed on what exactly qualifies as impermissible coercion in light of the original meaning of the Establishment Clause. But in this case Mr. Kennedy's private religious exercise did not come close to crossing any line one might imagine separating protected private expression from impermissible government coercion.

The absence of evidence of coercion in this record leaves the District to its final redoubt. Here, the District suggests that *any* visible religious conduct by a teacher or coach should be deemed—without more and as a matter of law—impermissibly coercive on students. In essence, the District asks us to adopt the view that the only acceptable government role models for students are those who eschew any visible religious expression.

Such a rule would be a sure sign that our Establishment Clause jurisprudence had gone off the rails. In the name of protecting religious liberty, the District would have us suppress it. Rather than respect the First Amendment's double protection for religious expression, it would have us preference secular activity. Not only could schools fire teachers for praying quietly over their lunch, for wearing a yarmulke to school, or for offering a midday prayer during a break before practice. Under the District's rule, a school would be required to do so. It is a rule that would defy this Court's traditional understanding that permitting private speech is not the same thing as coercing others to participate in it. See *Town of Greece*. It is a rule, too, that would undermine a long constitutional tradition under which learning how to tolerate diverse expressive activities has always been "part of learning how to live in a pluralistic society." We are aware of no historically sound understanding of the Establishment Clause that begins to make it necessary for government to be hostile to religion in this way. *Zorach v. Clauson*.

Meanwhile, this case looks very different from those in which this Court has found prayer involving public school students to be problematically coercive. In Lee, this Court held that school officials violated the Establishment Clause by including a clerical member who publicly recited prayers as part of an official school graduation ceremony because the school had in every practical sense compelled attendance and participation in a "religious exercise." In *Santa Fe Independent School Dist. v. Doe*, the Court held that a school district violated the Establishment Clause by broadcasting a prayer "over the public address system" before each football game. The Court observed that, while students generally were not required to attend games, attendance was required for "cheerleaders, members of the band, and, of course, the team members themselves." None of that is true here. The prayers for which Mr. Kennedy was disciplined were not publicly broadcast or recited to a captive audience. Students were not required or expected to participate. And, in fact, none of Mr. Kennedy's students did participate in any of the three October 2015 prayers that resulted in Mr. Kennedy's discipline.

Respect for religious expressions is indispensable to life in a free and diverse Republic—whether those expressions take place in a sanctuary or on a field, and whether they manifest through the spoken word or a bowed head. Here, a government entity sought to punish an individual for engaging in a brief, quiet, personal religious observance doubly protected by the Free Exercise and Free Speech Clauses of the First Amendment. And the only meaningful justification the government offered for its reprisal rested on a mistaken view that it had a duty to ferret out and suppress religious observances even as it allows comparable secular speech. The Constitution neither mandates nor tolerates that kind of discrimination. Mr. Kennedy is entitled to summary judgment on his First Amendment claims.

Justice Sotomayor, with whom Justice Breyer and Justice Kagan join, dissenting.

This case is about whether a public school must permit a school official to kneel, bow his head, and say a prayer at the center of a school event. The Constitution does not authorize, let alone require, public schools to embrace this conduct. Since *Engel v. Vitale*, 370 U.S. 421 (1962), this Court consistently has recognized that school officials leading prayer is constitutionally impermissible. Official-led prayer strikes at the core of our constitutional protections for the religious liberty of students and their parents, as embodied in both the Establishment Clause and the Free Exercise Clause of the First Amendment.

The Court now charts a different path, yet again paying almost exclusive attention to the Free Exercise Clause's protection for individual religious exercise while giving short shrift to the Establishment Clause's prohibition on state establishment of religion. To the degree the Court portrays petitioner Joseph Kennedy's prayers as private and quiet, it misconstrues the facts. The record reveals that Kennedy had a longstanding practice of conducting demonstrative prayers on the 50-yard line of the football field. Kennedy consistently invited others to join his prayers and for years led student athletes in prayer at the same time and location. The Court ignores this history. The Court also ignores the severe disruption to school events caused by Kennedy's conduct, viewing it as irrelevant because the Bremerton School District (District) stated that it was suspending Kennedy to avoid it being viewed as endorsing religion. Under the Court's analysis, presumably this would be a different case if the District had cited Kennedy's repeated disruptions of school programming and violations of school policy regarding public access to the field as grounds for suspending him. As the District did not articulate those grounds, the Court assesses only the District's Establishment Clause concerns. It errs by assessing them divorced from the context and history of Kennedy's prayer practice.

Today's decision goes beyond merely misreading the record. The Court overrules *Lemon v. Kurtzman*, and calls into question decades of subsequent precedents that it deems "offshoots" of that decision. In the process, the Court rejects longstanding concerns surrounding government endorsement of religion and replaces the standard for reviewing such questions with a new "history and tradition" test. In addition, while the Court reaffirms that the Establishment Clause prohibits the government from coercing participation in religious exercise, it applies a nearly toothless version of the coercion analysis, failing to acknowledge the unique pressures faced by students when participating in school-sponsored activities. This decision does a disservice to schools and the young citizens they serve, as well as to our Nation's longstanding commitment to the separation of church and state. I respectfully dissent.

Notes and Questions

(1) Note that the decision in *Kennedy v. Bremerton* traverses multiple areas of First Amendment law. We will examine the special rules governing the speech of government employees in Chapter 9. We will examine the conundrums presented by the Free Exercise Clause later in this chapter.

(2) In *McCollum v. Board of Education*, 333 U.S. 203 (1948), the Supreme Court held invalid as an establishment of religion an Illinois system under which school children, compelled by law to go to public schools, were freed from some hours of required school work on condition that they attend special religious classes held in the school buildings. Although the classes were taught by sectarian teachers neither employed nor paid by the state, the state did use its power to further the program by releasing some of the children from regular class work, insisting that those released attend the religious classes, and requiring that those who remained behind do some kind of academic work while the others received their religious training. The Court stated that: "Pupils compelled by law to go to school for secular education are released in part from their legal duty upon the condition that they attend the religious classes. This is beyond all question a utilization of the tax-established and tax-supported public school system to aid religious groups to spread their faiths. And it falls squarely under the ban of the First Amendment."

(3) In *Zorach v. Clauson*, 343 U.S. 306 (1952), the Supreme Court distinguished *McCollum* and upheld a New York City program that permitted its public schools to release students during the day so that they could leave public schools buildings and school grounds and go to religious centers for religious instruction or devotional exercises. Written requests for such "released time" were required from parents; churches made weekly reports to the schools with lists of students who were released but did not report for religious instruction. Justice Douglas wrote the opinion of the Court sustaining the released time program. In the course of his opinion, he made the following famous and provocative statement:

> We are a religious people whose institutions presuppose a Supreme Being. We guarantee the freedom to worship as one chooses. We make room for as wide a variety of beliefs and creeds as the spiritual needs of man deem necessary. We sponsor an attitude on the part of government that shows no partiality to any one group and that lets each flourish according to the zeal of its adherents and the appeal of its dogma. When the state encourages religious instruction or cooperates with religious authorities by adjusting the schedule of public events to sectarian needs, it follows the best of our traditions. For it then respects the religious nature of our people and accommodates the public service to their spiritual needs. To hold that it may not would be to

find in the Constitution a requirement that the government show a callous indifference to religious groups. That would be preferring those who believe in no religion over those who do believe. Government may not finance religious groups nor undertake religious instruction nor blend secular and sectarian education nor use secular institutions to force one or some religion on any person. But we find no constitutional requirement which makes it necessary for government to be hostile to religion and to throw its weight against efforts to widen the effective scope of religious influence. The government must be neutral when it comes to competition between sects. It may not thrust any sect on any person. It may not make a religious observance compulsory. It may not coerce anyone to attend church, to observe a religious holiday, or to take religious instruction. But it can close its doors or suspend its operations as to those who want to repair to their religious sanctuary for worship or instruction. No more than that is undertaken here.

In reply, Justice Black, dissenting, observed:

The Court's validation of the New York system rests in part on its statement that Americans are "a religious people whose institutions presuppose a Supreme Being." This was at least as true when the First Amendment was adopted; and it was just as true when eight Justices of this Court invalidated the released time system in *McCollum* on the premise that a state can no more "aid all religions" than it can aid one. It was precisely because Eighteenth Century Americans were a religious people divided into many fighting sects that we were given the constitutional mandate to keep Church and State completely separate. Colonial history had already shown that, here as elsewhere, zealous sectarians entrusted with governmental power to further their causes would sometimes torture, maim and kill those they branded "heretics," "atheists" or "agnostics." The First Amendment was therefore to insure that no one powerful sect or combination of sects could use political or governmental power to punish dissenters whom they could not convert to their faith.

Who has the better of the argument, Justice Douglas or Justice Black? Are we "a religious people whose institutions presuppose a Supreme Being"?

(4) In *Stone v. Graham*, 449 U.S. 39 (1980), the Court held that the display of a copy of the Ten Commandments on the walls of public classrooms violates the Establishment Clause.

(5) In earlier cases, the Court had "rejected unequivocally the contention that the Establishment Clause forbids only governmental preference of one religion over another." *School Dist. of Abington v. Schempp*, 374 U.S. 203, 216 (1963). In *Engel v. Vitale*, 370 U.S. 421, 436 (1962), one of the Court's early school prayer decisions, the Court struck down a New York law requiring reading of a "Regent's prayer" composed by New York officials to begin school days. While the prayer was generic and

non-denominational, the Court held the reading of an officially composed school prayer violated the Establishment Clause. The Court observed:

> It is true that New York's establishment of its Regents' prayer as an officially approved religious doctrine of that State does not amount to a total establishment of one particular religious sect to the exclusion of all others — that, indeed, the governmental endorsement of that prayer seems relatively insignificant when compared to the governmental encroachments upon religion which were commonplace 200 years ago. To those who may subscribe to the view that because the Regents' official prayer is so brief and general there can be no danger to religious freedom in its governmental establishment, however, it may be appropriate to say in the words of James Madison, the author of the First Amendment:

> [I]t is proper to take alarm at the first experiment on our liberties. Who does not see that the same authority which can establish Christianity, in exclusion of all other Religions, may establish with the same ease any particular sect of Christians, in exclusion of all other Sects? That the same authority which can force a citizen to contribute three pence only of his property for the support of any one establishment, may force him to conform to any other establishment in all cases whatsoever?

(6) In *Wallace v. Jaffree*, 472 U.S. 38 (1985), the Supreme Court held that an Alabama law that authorized a period of silence "for meditation or voluntary prayer" in public schools violated the Establishment Clause. The Court held that the intent behind the law was to "return prayer" to public schools, in violation of the Establishment Clause. The Court distinguished between a law that appeared to direct students to meditate or pray during an official moment of silence, and simply accommodating the rights of individual students to engage in their own voluntary prayer during random silent moments during the school day: "The legislative intent to return prayer to the public schools is, of course, quite different from merely protecting every student's right to engage in voluntary prayer during an appropriate moment of silence during the schoolday."

(7) In *Epperson v. Arkansas*, 393 U.S. 97 (1968), the Supreme Court reviewed an Arkansas statute that made it unlawful for an instructor to teach evolution or to use a textbook that referred to this scientific theory. Although the Arkansas anti-evolution law did not explicitly state its predominant religious purpose, the Court could found that, "[t]he statute was a product of the upsurge of 'fundamentalist' religious fervor" that had long viewed this particular scientific theory as contradicting the literal interpretation of the Bible. After reviewing the history of anti-evolution statutes, the Court determined that "there can be no doubt that the motivation for the [Arkansas] law was to suppress the teaching of a theory which, it was thought, 'denied' the divine creation of man." The Court found that there can be no legitimate state interest in protecting particular religions from scientific views "distasteful to them," and concluded "that the First Amendment does not permit the State to

require that teaching and learning must be tailored to the principles or prohibitions of any religious sect or dogma."

(8) In *Edwards v. Aguillard*, 482 U.S. 578 (1987), the Court extended *Epperson* to strike down a Louisiana law that mandated "balanced treatment" for "Creation Science" and "Evolution Science." In holding the law unconstitutional, The Court observed:

> The preeminent purpose of the Louisiana Legislature was clearly to advance the religious viewpoint that a supernatural being created human-kind. The term "creation science" was defined as embracing this particular religious doctrine by those responsible for the passage of the Creationism Act. Senator Keith's leading expert on creation science, Edward Boudreaux, testified at the legislative hearings that the theory of creation science included belief in the existence of a supernatural creator. The legislative history therefore reveals that the term "creation science," as contemplated by the legislature that adopted this Act, embodies the religious belief that a supernatural creator was responsible for the creation of humankind.

> Furthermore, it is not happenstance that the legislature required the teaching of a theory that coincided with this religious view. The legislative history documents that the Act's primary purpose was to change the science curriculum of public schools in order to provide persuasive advantage to a particular religious doctrine that rejects the factual basis of evolution in its entirety. The sponsor of the Creationism Act, Senator Keith, explained during the legislative hearings that his disdain for the theory of evolution resulted from the support that evolution supplied to views contrary to his own religious beliefs.

> Similarly, the Creationism Act is designed either to promote the theory of creation science which embodies a particular religious tenet by requiring that creation science be taught whenever evolution is taught or to prohibit the teaching of a scientific theory disfavored by certain religious sects by forbidding the teaching of evolution when creation science is not also taught. The Establishment Clause, however, "forbids alike the preference of a religious doctrine or the prohibition of theory which is deemed antagonistic to a particular dogma." Because the primary purpose of the Creationism Act is to advance a particular religious belief, the Act endorses religion in violation of the First Amendment.

In a caveat, however, the Court noted that "[w]e do not imply that a legislature could never require that scientific critiques of prevailing scientific theories be taught." That the First Amendment prohibits the posting of the Ten Commandments on a public school classroom wall, for example, does "not mean that no use could ever be made of the Ten Commandments, or that the Ten Commandments played an exclusively religious role in the history of Western Civilization." In a similar way, the Court argued, "teaching a variety of scientific theories about the origins of humankind to schoolchildren might be validly done with the clear secular intent of enhancing the effectiveness of science instruction. But because the primary purpose of the Creationism Act is to endorse a particular religious doctrine, the Act furthers religion in violation of the Establishment Clause."

C. Economic Aid to Religion

Everson v. Board of Education

United States Supreme Court
330 U.S. 1, 67 S. Ct. 504, 91 L. Ed. 711 (1947)

Mr. Justice Black delivered the opinion of the Court.

A New Jersey statute authorizes its local school districts to make rules and contracts for the transportation of children to and from schools. The appellee, a township board of education, acting pursuant to this statute authorized reimbursement to parents of money expended by them for the bus transportation of their children on regular buses operated by the public transportation system. Part of this money was for the payment of transportation of some children in the community to Catholic parochial schools. These church schools give their students, in addition to secular education, regular religious instruction conforming to the religious tenets and modes of worship of the Catholic faith. The superintendent of these schools is a Catholic priest.

The New Jersey statute is challenged as a "law respecting an establishment of religion." Whether this New Jersey law is one respecting the "establishment of religion" requires an understanding of the meaning of that language, particularly with respect to the imposition of taxes. Once again, therefore, it is not inappropriate briefly to review the background and environment of the period in which that constitutional language was fashioned and adopted.

A large proportion of the early settlers of this country came here from Europe to escape the bondage of laws which compelled them to support and attend government favored churches. The centuries immediately before and contemporaneous with the colonization of America had been filled with turmoil, civil strife, and persecutions, generated in large part by established sects determined to maintain their absolute political and religious supremacy.

The imposition of taxes to pay ministers' salaries and to build and maintain churches and church property aroused their indignation. It was these feelings which found expression in the First Amendment. No one locality and no one group throughout the Colonies can rightly be given entire credit for having aroused the sentiment that culminated in adoption of the Bill of Rights' provisions embracing religious liberty. But Virginia, where the established church had achieved a dominant influence in political affairs and where many excesses attracted wide public attention, provided a great stimulus and able leadership for the movement. The people there, as elsewhere, reached the conviction that individual religious liberty could be achieved best under a government which was stripped of all power to tax, to support, or otherwise to assist any or all religions, or to interfere with the beliefs of any religious individual or groups.

The movement toward this end reached its dramatic climax in Virginia in 1785–87 when the Virginia legislative body was about to renew Virginia's tax levy for the support of the established church. Thomas Jefferson and James Madison led the fight against this tax. Madison wrote his great *Memorial and Remonstrance* against the law. In it, he eloquently argued that a true religion did not need the support of law; that no person, either believer or non-believer, should be taxed to support a religious institution of any kind; that the best interest of a society required that the minds of men always be wholly free; and that cruel persecutions were the inevitable result of government-established religions. Madison's *Remonstrance* received strong support throughout Virginia, and the Assembly postponed consideration of the proposed tax measure until its next session. When the proposal came up for consideration at that session, it not only died in committee, but the Assembly enacted the famous "Virginia Bill for Religious Liberty" originally written by Thomas Jefferson.

This Court has previously recognized that the provisions of the First Amendment, in the drafting and adoption of which Madison and Jefferson played such leading roles, had the same objective and were intended to provide the same protection against governmental intrusion on religious liberty as the Virginia statute.

The "establishment of religion" clause of the First Amendment means at least this: Neither a state nor the Federal Government can set up a church. Neither can pass laws which aid one religion, aid all religions, or prefer one religion over another. Neither can force nor influence a person to go to or to remain away from church against his will or force him to profess a belief or disbelief in any religion. No person can be punished for entertaining or professing religious beliefs or disbeliefs, for church attendance or non-attendance. No tax in any amount, large or small, can be levied to support any religious activities or institutions, whatever they may be called, or whatever form they may adopt to teach or practice religion. Neither a state nor the Federal Government can, openly or secretly, participate in the affairs of any religious organizations or groups and vice versa. In the words of Jefferson, the clause against establishment of religion by law was intended to erect "a wall of separation between Church and State."

We must consider the New Jersey statute in accordance with the foregoing limitations imposed by the First Amendment. But we must not strike that state statute down if it is within the state's constitutional power even though it approaches the verge of that power. New Jersey cannot consistently with the "establishment of religion" clause of the First Amendment contribute tax-raised funds to the support of an institution which teaches the tenets and faith of any church. On the other hand, other language of the Amendment commands that New Jersey cannot hamper its citizens in the free exercise of their own religion.

Measured by these standards, we cannot say that the First Amendment prohibits New Jersey from spending tax-raised funds to pay the bus fares of parochial school pupils as a part of a general program under which it pays the fares of pupils attending public and other schools. It is undoubtedly true that children are helped to get to church schools. There is even a possibility that some of the children might not be sent to the church schools if the parents were compelled to pay their children's bus fares out of their own pockets when transportation to a public school would have been paid for by the State. The same possibility exists where the state requires a local transit company to provide reduced fares to school children including those attending parochial schools, or where a municipally owned transportation system undertakes to carry all school children free of charge. Moreover, state-paid policemen, detailed to protect children going to and from church schools from the very real hazards of traffic, would serve much the same purpose and accomplish much the same result as state provisions intended to guarantee free transportation of a kind which the state deems to be best for the school children's welfare. And parents might refuse to risk their children to the serious danger of traffic accidents going to and from parochial schools, the approaches to which were not protected by policemen. Similarly, parents might be reluctant to permit their children to attend schools which the state had cut off from such general government services as ordinary police and fire protection, connections for sewage disposal, public highways and sidewalks. Of course, cutting off church schools from these services, so separate and so indisputably marked off from the religious function, would make it far more difficult for the schools to operate. But such is obviously not the purpose of the First Amendment. That Amendment requires the state to be a neutral in its relations with groups of religious believers and non-believers; it does not require the state to be their adversary. State power is no more to be used so as to handicap religions, than it is to favor them.

This Court has said that parents may, in the discharge of their duty under state compulsory education laws, send their children to a religious rather than a public school if the school meets the secular educational requirements which the state has power to impose. It appears that these parochial schools meet New Jersey's requirements. The State contributes no money to the schools. It does not support them. Its legislation, as applied, does no more than provide a general program to help parents get their children, regardless of their religion, safely and expeditiously to and from accredited schools.

The First Amendment has erected a wall between church and state. That wall must be kept high and impregnable. We could not approve the slightest breach. New Jersey has not breached it here.

Affirmed.

Mr. Justice Rutledge, with whom Mr. Justice Frankfurter, Mr. Justice Jackson and Mr. Justice Burton agree, dissenting.

Not simply an established church, but any law respecting an establishment of religion is forbidden. The Amendment was broadly but not loosely phrased. It is the compact and exact summation of its author's views formed during his long struggle for religious freedom. In Madison's own words characterizing Jefferson's *Bill for Establishing Religious Freedom*, the guaranty he put in our national charter, like the bill he piloted through the Virginia Assembly, was "a Model of technical precision, and perspicuous brevity." Madison could not have confused "church" and "religion," or "an established church" and "an establishment of religion."

The Amendment's purpose was not to strike merely at the official establishment of a single sect, creed or religion, outlawing only a formal relation such as had prevailed in England and some of the colonies. Necessarily it was to uproot all such relationships. But the object was broader than separating church and state in this narrow sense. It was to create a complete and permanent separation of the spheres of religious activity and civil authority by comprehensively forbidding every form of public aid or support for religion. In proof the Amendment's wording and history unite with this Court's consistent utterances whenever attention has been fixed directly upon the question.

No provision of the Constitution is more closely tied to or given content by its generating history than the religious clause of the First Amendment. It is at once the refined product and the terse summation of that history. The history includes not only Madison's authorship and the proceedings before the First Congress, but also the long and intensive struggle for religious freedom in America, more especially in Virginia, of which the Amendment was the direct culmination. In the documents of the times, particularly of Madison, who was leader in the Virginia struggle before he became the Amendment's sponsor, but also in the writings of Jefferson and others and in the issues which engendered them is to be found irrefutable confirmation of the Amendment's sweeping content.

In view of this history no further proof is needed that the Amendment forbids any appropriation, large or small, from public funds to aid or support any and all religious exercises. But if more were called for, the debates in the First Congress and this Court's consistent expressions, whenever it has touched on the matter directly, supply it.

By contrast with the Virginia history, the congressional debates on consideration of the Amendment reveal only sparse discussion, reflecting the fact that the essential issues had been settled. Indeed the matter had become so well understood as to have been taken for granted in all but formal phrasing. Hence, the only enlightening reference shows concern, not to preserve any power to use public funds in aid of religion, but to prevent the Amendment from outlawing private gifts inadvertently by virtue of the breadth of its wording.

Does New Jersey's action furnish support for religion by use of the taxing power? Certainly it does, if the test remains undiluted as Jefferson and Madison made it, that money taken by taxation from one is not to be used or given to support another's religious training or belief, or indeed one's own. Today as then the furnishing of "contributions of money for the propagation of opinions which he disbelieves" is the forbidden exaction; and the prohibition is absolute for whatever measure brings that consequence and whatever amount may be sought or given to that end.

The funds used here were raised by taxation. The Court does not dispute nor could it that their use does in fact give aid and encouragement to religious instruction. It only concludes that this aid is not "support" in law. But Madison and Jefferson were concerned with aid and support in fact not as a legal conclusion "entangled in precedents." *Remonstrance*, Par. 3. Here parents pay money to send their children to parochial schools and funds raised by taxation are used to reimburse them. This not only helps the children to get to school and the parents to send them. It aids them in a substantial way to get the very thing which they are sent to the particular school to secure, namely, religious training and teaching.

Believers of all faiths, and others who do not express their feeling toward ultimate issues of existence in any creedal form, pay the New Jersey tax. When the money so raised is used to pay for transportation to religious schools, the Catholic taxpayer to the extent of his proportionate share pays for the transportation of Lutheran, Jewish and otherwise religiously affiliated children to receive their non-Catholic religious instruction. Their parents likewise pay proportionately for the transportation of Catholic children to receive Catholic instruction. Each thus contributes to "the propagation of opinions which he disbelieves" in so far as their religions differ, as to others who accept no creed without regard to those differences.

No one conscious of religious values can be unsympathetic toward the burden which our constitutional separation puts on parents who desire religious instruction mixed with secular for their children. They pay taxes for others' children's education, at the same time the added cost of instruction for their own. Nor can one happily see benefits denied to children which others receive, because in conscience they or their parents for them desire a different kind of training others do not demand.

But if those feelings should prevail, there would be an end to our historic constitutional policy and command. No more unjust or discriminatory in fact is it to deny attendants at religious schools the cost of their transportation than it is to deny them tuitions, sustenance for their teachers, or any other educational expense which others receive at public cost. Hardship in fact there is which none can blink. But, for assuring to those who undergo it the greater, the most comprehensive freedom, it is one written by design and firm intent into our basic law.

Two great drives are constantly in motion to abridge, in the name of education, the complete division of religion and civil authority which our forefathers made. One is to introduce religious education and observances into the public schools. The other, to obtain public funds for the aid and support of various private religious schools. In my opinion both avenues were closed by the Constitution. Neither should be opened by this Court. The matter is not one of quantity, to be measured by the amount of money expended. Now as in Madison's day it is one of principle, to keep separate the separate spheres as the First Amendment drew them; to prevent the first experiment upon our liberties; and to keep the question from becoming entangled in corrosive precedents. We should not be less strict to keep strong and untarnished the one side of the shield of religious freedom than we have been of the other.

Zelman v. Simmons-Harris

United States Supreme Court
536 U.S. 639, 122 S. Ct. 2460, 153 L. Ed. 2d 604 (2002)

CHIEF JUSTICE REHNQUIST delivered the opinion of the Court.

The State of Ohio has established a pilot program designed to provide educational choices to families with children who reside in the Cleveland City School District. The question presented is whether this program offends the Establishment Clause of the United States Constitution. We hold that it does not.

There are more than 75,000 children enrolled in the Cleveland City School District. The majority of these children are from low-income and minority families. Few of these families enjoy the means to send their children to any school other than an inner-city public school. For more than a generation, however, Cleveland's public schools have been among the worst performing public schools in the Nation.

It is against this backdrop that Ohio enacted, among other initiatives, its Pilot Project Scholarship Program.

The program provides two basic kinds of assistance to parents of children in a covered district. First, the program provides tuition aid for students in kindergarten through third grade, expanding each year through eighth grade, to attend a participating public or private school of their parent's choosing. §§ 3313.975(B) and (C) (1). Second, the program provides tutorial aid for students who choose to remain enrolled in public school. § 3313.975(A).

The tuition aid portion of the program is designed to provide educational choices to parents who reside in a covered district. Any private school, whether religious or nonreligious, may participate in the program and accept program students so long as the school is located within the boundaries of a covered district and meets statewide educational standards.

Tuition aid is distributed to parents according to financial need. Families with incomes below 200% of the poverty line are given priority and are eligible to receive 90% of private school tuition up to $2,250. For these lowest-income families, participating private schools may not charge a parental co-payment greater than $250. For all other families, the program pays 75% of tuition costs, up to $1,875, with no co-payment cap. These families receive tuition aid only if the number of available scholarships exceeds the number of low-income children who choose to participate. Where tuition aid is spent depends solely upon where parents who receive tuition aid choose to enroll their child. If parents choose a private school, checks are made payable to the parents who then endorse the checks over to the chosen school.

The tutorial aid portion of the program provides tutorial assistance through grants to any student in a covered district who chooses to remain in public school. Parents arrange for registered tutors to provide assistance to their children and then submit bills for those services to the State for payment. Students from low-income families receive 90% of the amount charged for such assistance up to $360. All other students receive 75% of that amount. The number of tutorial assistance grants offered to students in a covered district must equal the number of tuition aid scholarships provided to students enrolled at participating private or adjacent public schools.

The program has been in operation within the Cleveland City School District since the 1996–1997 school year. In the 1999–2000 school year, 56 private schools participated in the program, 46 (or 82%) of which had a religious affiliation. None of the public schools in districts adjacent to Cleveland have elected to participate. More than 3,700 students participated in the scholarship program, most of whom (96%) enrolled in religiously affiliated schools. Sixty percent of these students were from families at or below the poverty line. In the 1998–1999 school year, approximately 1,400 Cleveland public school students received tutorial aid. This number was expected to double during the 1999–2000 school year.

The program is part of a broader undertaking by the State to enhance the educational options of Cleveland's schoolchildren in response to the 1995 takeover. That undertaking includes programs governing community and magnet schools. Community schools are funded under state law but are run by their own school boards, not by local school districts. These schools enjoy academic independence to hire their own teachers and to determine their own curriculum. They can have no religious affiliation and are required to accept students by lottery. During the 1999–2000 school year, there were 10 start-up community schools in the Cleveland City School District with more than 1,900 students enrolled. For each child enrolled in a community school, the school receives state funding of $4,518, twice the funding a participating program school may receive.

Magnet schools are public schools operated by a local school board that emphasize a particular subject area, teaching method, or service to students. For each student enrolled in a magnet school, the school district receives $7,746, including state funding of $4,167, the same amount received per student enrolled at a traditional public school. As of 1999, parents in Cleveland were able to choose from among 23 magnet schools, which together enrolled more than 13,000 students in kindergarten through eighth grade. These schools provide specialized teaching methods, such as Montessori, or a particularized curriculum focus, such as foreign language, computers, or the arts.

There is no dispute that the program challenged here was enacted for the valid secular purpose of providing educational assistance to poor children in a demonstrably failing public school system. Thus, the question presented is whether the Ohio program nonetheless has the forbidden "effect" of advancing or inhibiting religion.

To answer that question, our decisions have drawn a consistent distinction between government programs that provide aid directly to religious schools, and programs of true private choice, in which government aid reaches religious schools only as a result of the genuine and independent choices of private individuals. While our jurisprudence with respect to the constitutionality of direct aid programs has "changed significantly" over the past two decades, our jurisprudence with respect to true private choice programs has remained consistent and unbroken. Three times we have confronted Establishment Clause challenges to neutral government programs that provide aid directly to a broad class of individuals, who, in turn, direct the aid to religious schools or institutions of their own choosing. Three times we have rejected such challenges.

Mueller v. Allen, 463 U.S. 388 (1983), *Witters v. Washington Dept. of Servs. for Blind*, 474 U.S. 481 (1986), and *Zobrest v. Catalina Foothills School Dist.*, 509 U.S. 1 (1993), thus make clear that where a government aid program is neutral with respect to religion, and provides assistance directly to a broad class of citizens who, in turn, direct government aid to religious schools wholly as a result of their own genuine and independent private choice, the program is not readily subject to challenge under the Establishment Clause. A program that shares these features permits government aid to reach religious institutions only by way of the deliberate choices of numerous individual recipients. The incidental advancement of a religious mission, or the perceived endorsement of a religious message, is reasonably attributable to the individual recipient, not to the government, whose role ends with the disbursement of benefits.

We believe that the program challenged here is a program of true private choice, consistent with *Mueller, Witters*, and *Zobrest*, and thus constitutional. As was true in those cases, the Ohio program is neutral in all respects toward religion. It is part of a general and multifaceted undertaking by the State of Ohio to provide educational opportunities to the children of a failed school district. It confers educational assistance directly to a broad class of individuals defined without reference to religion, *i.e.*, any parent of a school-age child who resides in the Cleveland City School District. The program permits the participation of *all* schools within the district, religious or nonreligious. Adjacent public schools also may participate and have a financial incentive to do so. Program benefits are available to participating families on neutral terms, with no reference to religion. The only preference stated anywhere in the program is a preference for low-income families, who receive greater assistance and are given priority for admission at participating schools.

Respondents suggest that even without a financial incentive for parents to choose a religious school, the program creates a "public perception that the State is endorsing religious practices and beliefs." But we have repeatedly recognized that no reasonable observer would think a neutral program of private choice, where state aid reaches religious schools solely as a result of the numerous independent decisions of private individuals, carries with it the *imprimatur* of government endorsement.

There also is no evidence that the program fails to provide genuine opportunities for Cleveland parents to select secular educational options for their school-age children. Cleveland schoolchildren enjoy a range of educational choices: They may remain in public school as before, remain in public school with publicly funded tutoring aid, obtain a scholarship and choose a religious school, obtain a scholarship and choose a nonreligious private school, enroll in a community school, or enroll in a magnet school. That 46 of the 56 private schools now participating in the program are religious schools does not condemn it as a violation of the Establishment Clause. The Establishment Clause question is whether Ohio is coercing parents into sending their children to religious schools, and that question must be answered by evaluating *all* options Ohio provides Cleveland schoolchildren, only one of which is to obtain a program scholarship and then choose a religious school.

Justice Souter speculates that because more private religious schools currently participate in the program, the program itself must somehow discourage the participation of private nonreligious schools. But Cleveland's preponderance of religiously affiliated private schools certainly did not arise as a result of the program; it is a phenomenon common to many American cities.

Respondents and Justice Souter claim that even if we do not focus on the number of participating schools that are religious schools, we should attach constitutional significance to the fact that 96% of scholarship recipients have enrolled in religious schools. They claim that this alone proves parents lack genuine choice, even if no parent has ever said so. We need not consider this argument in detail, since it was flatly rejected in *Mueller*, where we found it irrelevant that 96% of parents taking deductions for tuition expenses paid tuition at religious schools.

In sum, the Ohio program is entirely neutral with respect to religion. It provides benefits directly to a wide spectrum of individuals, defined only by financial need and residence in a particular school district. It permits such individuals to exercise genuine choice among options public and private, secular and religious. The program is therefore a program of true private choice. In keeping with an unbroken line of decisions rejecting challenges to similar programs, we hold that the program does not offend the Establishment Clause.

It is so ordered.

Justice O'Connor, concurring.

Justice Souter portrays this inquiry as a departure from *Everson*. A fair reading of the holding in that case suggests quite the opposite. Justice Black's opinion for the Court held that the "First Amendment requires the state to be a neutral in its relations with groups of religious believers and non-believers; it does not require the state to be their adversary." *Everson*. How else could the Court have upheld a state program to provide students transportation to public and religious schools alike? What the Court clarifies in these cases is that the Establishment Clause also requires that state aid flowing to religious organizations through the hands of beneficiaries must do so only at the direction of those beneficiaries. Such a refinement of the *Lemon* test surely does not betray *Everson*.

JUSTICE STEVENS, dissenting.

Is a law that authorizes the use of public funds to pay for the indoctrination of thousands of grammar school children in particular religious faiths a "law respecting an establishment of religion" within the meaning of the First Amendment? In answering that question, I think we should ignore three factual matters that are discussed at length by my colleagues.

First, the severe educational crisis that confronted the Cleveland City School District when Ohio enacted its voucher program is not a matter that should affect our appraisal of its constitutionality.

Second, the wide range of choices that have been made available to students *within the public school system* has no bearing on the question whether the State may pay the tuition for students who wish to reject public education entirely and attend private schools that will provide them with a sectarian education.

Third, the voluntary character of the private choice to prefer a parochial education over an education in the public school system seems to me quite irrelevant to the question whether the government's choice to pay for religious indoctrination is constitutionally permissible. Today, however, the Court seems to have decided that the mere fact that a family that cannot afford a private education wants its children educated in a parochial school is a sufficient justification for this use of public funds. . . .

JUSTICE SOUTER, with whom JUSTICE STEVENS, JUSTICE GINSBURG, and JUSTICE BREYER join, dissenting.

The applicability of the Establishment Clause to public funding of benefits to religious schools was settled in *Everson* which inaugurated the modern era of establishment doctrine. The Court stated the principle in words from which there was no dissent: "No tax in any amount, large or small, can be levied to support any religious activities or institutions, whatever they may be called, or whatever form they may adopt to teach or practice religion." The Court has never in so many words repudiated this statement, let alone, in so many words, overruled *Everson*.

How can a Court consistently leave *Everson* on the books and approve the Ohio vouchers? The answer is that it cannot. It is only by ignoring *Everson* that the majority can claim to rest on traditional law in its invocation of neutral aid provisions and private choice to sanction the Ohio law. It is, moreover, only by ignoring the meaning of neutrality and private choice themselves that the majority can even pretend to rest today's decision on those criteria.

Neutrality in this sense refers, of course, to evenhandedness in setting eligibility as between potential religious and secular recipients of public money. Thus, for example, the aid scheme in *Witters* provided an eligible recipient with a scholarship to be used at any institution within a practically unlimited universe of schools; it did not tend to provide more or less aid depending on which one the scholarship recipient chose, and there was no indication that the maximum scholarship amount would be insufficient at secular schools. Neither did any condition of Zobrest's interpreter's subsidy favor religious education.

In order to apply the neutrality test, then, it makes sense to focus on a category of aid that may be directed to religious as well as secular schools, and ask whether the scheme favors a religious direction. Here, one would ask whether the voucher provisions, allowing for as much as $2,250 toward private school tuition (or a grant to a public school in an adjacent district), were written in a way that skewed the scheme toward benefiting religious schools.

If the divisiveness permitted by today's majority is to be avoided in the short term, it will be avoided only by action of the political branches at the state and national levels. Legislatures not driven to desperation by the problems of public education may be able to see the threat in vouchers negotiable in sectarian schools. Perhaps even cities with problems like Cleveland's will perceive the danger, now that they know a federal court will not save them from it.

My own course as a judge on the Court cannot, however, simply be to hope that the political branches will save us from the consequences of the majority's decision. *Everson*'s statement is still the touchstone of sound law, even though the reality is that in the matter of educational aid the Establishment Clause has largely been read away. True, the majority has not approved vouchers for religious schools alone, or aid earmarked for religious instruction. But no scheme so clumsy will ever get before us, and in the cases that we may see, like these, the Establishment Clause is largely silenced. I do not have the option to leave it silent, and I hope that a future Court will reconsider today's dramatic departure from basic Establishment Clause principle.

JUSTICE BREYER, with whom JUSTICE STEVENS and JUSTICE SOUTER join, dissenting.

I write separately to emphasize the risk that publicly financed voucher programs pose in terms of religiously based social conflict. I do so because I believe that the Establishment Clause concern for protecting the Nation's social fabric from religious conflict poses an overriding obstacle to the implementation of this well-intentioned school voucher program.

With respect to government aid to private education, did not history show that efforts to obtain equivalent funding for the private education of children whose parents did not hold popular religious beliefs only exacerbated religious strife? The upshot is the development of constitutional doctrine that reads the Establishment Clause as avoiding religious strife, *not* by providing every religion with an *equal opportunity* (say, to secure state funding or to pray in the public schools), but by drawing fairly clear lines of *separation* between church and state — at least where the heartland of religious belief, such as primary religious education, is at issue.

Vouchers also differ in *degree*. The aid programs recently upheld by the Court involved limited amounts of aid to religion. But the majority's analysis here appears to permit a considerable shift of taxpayer dollars from public secular schools to private religious schools. That fact, combined with the use to which these dollars will be put, exacerbates the conflict problem. State aid that takes the form of peripheral secular items, with prohibitions against diversion of funds to religious teaching, holds significantly less potential for social division. In this respect as well, the secular aid upheld in *Mitchell* differs dramatically from the present case. Although it was conceivable that minor amounts of money could have, contrary to the statute, found their way to the religious activities of the recipients, that case is at worst the camel's nose, while the litigation before us is the camel itself.

Notes and Questions

The principles governing aid to religious schools are dramatically relaxed when the aid involves colleges and universities. At the college and university level, significant aid to religious universities is usually permitted unless the aid is to a university that is deemed "pervasively sectarian." The upshot of this principle was that a college or university that was religiously affiliated which was not so religious that religion pervasively infiltrated all of the school's activities could receive government grants generally available to higher education institutions, but a university in which religion pervaded all aspects of the university's culture would be disqualified. This principle tended to disqualify religious institutions that took religion very seriously, and arguably was itself a form of discrimination against the most devout. It is unclear whether the "pervasively sectarian" notion would be followed in the Supreme Court today. In *Mitchell v. Helms*, 530 U.S. 793 (2000), Justice Thomas, announcing the judgment of the Court in a plurality opinion joined by Chief Justice Rehnquist, Justice Scalia, and Justice Kennedy, argued that the religious nature of a recipient should not matter to the constitutional analysis, so long as the recipient adequately furthers the government's secular purpose:

> If a program offers permissible aid to the religious (including the pervasively sectarian), the areligious, and the irreligious, it is a mystery which view of religion the government has established, and thus a mystery what the constitutional violation would be. The pervasively sectarian recipient has not received any special favor, and it is most bizarre that the Court would, as the dissent seemingly does, reserve special hostility for those who take their religion seriously, who think that their religion should affect the whole of their lives, or who make the mistake of being effective in transmitting their views to children.

§ 8.03 Free Exercise of Religion

A. Discrimination or Hostility

Church of the Lukumi Babalu Aye, Inc. v. City of Hialeah. The Supreme Court has been adamant that the Free Exercise Clause is violated by laws that single out for especially disfavorable treatment a religious practice. Perhaps the most famous example is provided by *Church of the Lukumi Babalu Aye, Inc. v. City of Hialeah*, 508 U.S. 520 (1983). In *Lukumi*, the "animal sacrifice" case, the Supreme Court struck down an ordinance enacted by the city of Hialeah, Florida, prohibiting animal sacrifice. The Court found that the laws were enacted to target certain rituals of the Santeria religion. Many adherents of Santeria fled Cuba during the Castro regime and settled in Florida. In Santeria religious practice, animal sacrifices are performed at birth, marriage, and death rites, for the cure of the sick, for the initiation of new members and priests, and during an annual celebration. Animals sacrificed in Santeria rituals include chickens, pigeons, doves, ducks, guinea pigs, goats, sheep, and turtles. The animals are killed by the cutting of the carotid arteries in the neck. The sacrificed animal is cooked and eaten, except after healing and death rituals. In a sharp rebuke to Hialeah, the Court found that the ordinances had as their object the suppression of religion. The record, the Court held, demonstrated a pattern of animosity to Santeria adherents and their religious practices. The ordinances by their own terms targeted religious exercise, the Court noted, and the texts of the ordinances were gerrymandered with care to proscribe religious killings of animals but to exclude almost all secular killings (such as routine animal slaughter for food).

Masterpiece Cakeshop, Ltd. v. Colorado Civil Rights Commission. In *Masterpiece Cakeshop, Ltd. v. Colorado Civil Rights Commission*, 138 S. Ct. 1719 (2018), the Supreme Court invoked a finding of hostility toward religion to resolve a case posing a conflict between civil rights laws protecting persons from discrimination on the basis of sexual orientation and the asserted rights of a custom baker to refuse to make a custom wedding cake for a same-sex marriage. The case arose when Charlie Craig and David Mullins brought a claim under Colorado's public accommodations law when Jack Philipps, the owner of the Masterpiece Cakeshop, refused to make them a wedding cake for their same-sex wedding. Colorado's Civil Rights Commission held that Phillips' action was discrimination on the basis of sexual orientation, in violation of the Colorado Civil Rights law. It ruled that Phillips must stop refusing to make wedding cakes for same sex couples, and must instruct his employees (virtually all of whom were family members working in his small business) on why it was wrong to engage in such discrimination. Phillips argued that forcing him to bake the custom wedding cake was a form of "forced speech" violating his free speech rights, and also constituted a violation of his freedom of religion rights under the Free Exercise Clause. Phillips, an artist, considers his custom cakes to be a form of artistic expression honoring God, and sincerely believes that to engage in making a cake for a same-sex wedding would be contrary to God's will. Phillips explained to the couple that he would sell them any cake in his shop, but could not, consistent with his conscience, make them a wedding cake for a same-sex wedding, due to his religious scruples. In rejecting Phillips' free speech claim, the Colorado court concluded "that the act of designing and selling a wedding cake to all customers free of discrimination does not convey a celebratory message about same-sex weddings likely to be understood by those who view it." The court further concluded "that, to the extent that the public infers from a Masterpiece wedding cake a message celebrating same-sex marriage, that message is more likely to be attributed to the customer than to Masterpiece." Applying the Supreme Court's ruling in *Employment*

Division, Department of Human Resources v. Smith, the Colorado court also rejected Phillips' Free Exercise Claim, holding that the Colorado Civil Rights law was a neutral law of general applicability.

The Supreme Court of the United States accepted review. The Supreme Court avoided resolution of the principal conflict posed by the case, instead deciding the case in favor of Jack Phillips and the Masterpiece Cakeshop on the narrower ground that Colorado's decision against Phillips had been tainted by hostility toward religion. The 7-2 opinion, in which Justice Kennedy wrote for the Court, began by positing that in certain circumstances, such as in the case of religious clergy, it would be plain that First Amendment rights would prevail over conflicting civil rights laws. On the other hand, the Court observed, it was not clear that the same balance would be struck for the myriad other goods and services that might attend to the production of a wedding:

> When it comes to weddings, it can be assumed that a member of the clergy who objects to gay marriage on moral and religious grounds could not be compelled to perform the ceremony without denial of his or her right to the free exercise of religion. This refusal would be well understood in our constitutional order as an exercise of religion, an exercise that gay persons could recognize and accept without serious diminishment to their own dignity and worth. Yet if that exception were not confined, then a long list of persons who provide goods and services for marriages and weddings might refuse to do so for gay persons, thus resulting in a community-wide stigma inconsistent with the history and dynamics of civil rights laws that ensure equal access to goods, services, and public accommodations.

Moreover, the Court made it clear, it was plain "that Colorado law can protect gay persons, just as it can protect other classes of individuals, in acquiring whatever products and services they choose on the same terms and conditions as are offered to other members of the public." The Court also opined that "there are no doubt innumerable goods and services that no one could argue implicate the First Amendment."

But the claim by Phillips, the Court suggested, was not so easily dismissed. He had a sincere and deep religious aversion to engaging in what he believed was an endorsement of a wedding ceremony that was contrary to his religious beliefs. A decision in either direction had problems. To rule against Phillips appeared to burden sincerely held convictions, but a decision in his favor "would have to be sufficiently constrained, lest all purveyors of goods and services who object to gay marriages for moral and religious reasons in effect be allowed to put up signs saying 'no goods or services will be sold if they will be used for gay marriages,' something that would impose a serious stigma on gay persons."

Thus hinting that it was not at all clear how these issues ought to be resolved, the Court stated that "nonetheless, Phillips was entitled to the neutral and respectful consideration of his claims in all the circumstances of the case." The Court concluded that the neutral and respectful consideration to which Phillips was entitled was compromised. The Colorado "Civil Rights Commission's treatment of his case has some elements of a clear and impermissible hostility toward the sincere religious beliefs that motivated his objection." Grounding its finding of hostility toward religion in various comments made by officials in the course of adjudicating Phillips' claim, the Court ruled that Colorado's decision was tainted by animus toward religion that rendered it unconstitutional. As the Court explained:

> The Commission's hostility was inconsistent with the First Amendment's guarantee that our laws be applied in a manner that is neutral toward religion. Phillips was entitled to a neutral decisionmaker who would give full and fair consideration to his religious objection as he sought to assert it in all of the circumstances in which this case was presented, considered, and decided.

The Court warned, however, that its resolution of Phillips' case based on hostility toward religion did not dictate what the outcome would be in future cases that posed no such hostility. Resolution of those conflicts, the Court held, would await future litigation.

McDaniel v. Paty. In *McDaniel v. Paty*, 435 U.S. 618 (2018), the Court struck down a Tennessee statute disqualifying ministers from serving as delegates to the State's constitutional convention.

Trinity Lutheran Church of Columbia, Inc. v. Comer. In *Trinity Lutheran Church of Columbia, Inc. v. Comer*, 137 S. Ct. 2012 (2017), the Supreme Court held unconstitutional a Missouri policy that denied to the Trinity Lutheran Church a reimbursement grant available to nonprofit organizations that install playground surfaces made from recycled tires. The Court held that the denial violated the Free Exercise Clause of the First Amendment. The Court held that denying a generally available benefit solely on account of religious identity imposes a penalty on the free exercise of religion. As in *McDaniel*, the Court held, the Missouri policy expressly discriminated against otherwise eligible recipients by disqualifying them from a public benefit solely because of their religious character.

The Court rejected the claim that the Missouri law was justified under the principles established in *Locke v. Davey*, 540 U.S. 172 (2004). In *Locke*, the State of Washington created a scholarship program to assist high-achieving students with the costs of postsecondary education. Scholarship recipients were free to use state funds at accredited religious and nonreligious schools alike, but they could not use the funds to pursue a devotional theology degree. The Court distinguished *Locke* by reasoning that in *Locke*, Davey was not denied a scholarship because of who he was; he was denied a scholarship because of what he proposed to do.

In contrast, the Court held, "there is no question that Trinity Lutheran was denied a grant simply because of what it is — a church." Trinity Lutheran, the Court held, was put to the choice between being a church and receiving a government benefit, in violation of the Free Exercise Clause.

Espinoza v. Montana Department of Revenue. In *Espinoza v. Montana Department of Revenue*, 140 S. Ct. 2246 (2020), for example, the Court applied *Trinity Lutheran* to hold unconstitutional a decision of the Montana Supreme Court that applied the Montana Constitution in a manner that prevented the state's tuition assistance program from being applied to tuition at religious schools.

B. Neutral Laws That Burden Religion

Cases such as *Lukimi*, *Masterpiece Cakeshop*, *McDaniel*, and *Trinity Lutheran* demonstrate that the Supreme Court has adopted a virtual "zero tolerance" policy for laws that single out religions for disfavorable treatment. Efforts to directly regulate belief, or that discriminate against any particular sect or set of beliefs, or even against religion in general, will virtually always be struck down.

A far more vexing problem, however, is the question of what the proper constitutional doctrine should be in scrutinizing laws that are "neutral laws of general applicability" that nonetheless have the *effect* of substantially burdening the exercise of religion. Two lines of precedent have evolved. One approach is the tough-minded position that the Free Exercise Clause provides *zero* relief from generally applicable laws. Under this approach, most famously embraced in the *Reynolds* and *Employment Division* cases below, no viable claim for a violation of the Free Exercise Clause may be brought to challenge a general law that is neutral toward religion, but happens to substantially burden an adherent's free exercise of religion. In contrast, another line of cases, characterized most famously by cases such as *Sherbert* and *Yoder* below, subjects neutral laws of general applicability that substantially burden religion to the rigors of the "strict scrutiny" test, meaning that such laws may often be struck down.

Reynolds v. United States
United States Supreme Court
98 U.S. 145, 25 L. Ed. 244 (1878)

Mr. Chief Justice Waite delivered the opinion of the court.

On the trial, the plaintiff in error, the accused, proved that at the time of his alleged second marriage he was, and for many years before had been, a member of the Church of Jesus Christ of Latter-Day Saints, commonly called the Mormon Church, and a believer in its doctrines; that it was an accepted doctrine of that church "that it was the duty of male members of said church, circumstances permitting, to practise polygamy; . . . that this duty was enjoined by different books which the members of said church believed to be of divine origin, and among others the Holy Bible, and also that the members of the church believed that the practice of polygamy was directly enjoined upon the male members thereof by the Almighty God, in a revelation to Joseph Smith, the founder and prophet of said church; that the failing or refusing to practise polygamy by such male members of said church, when circumstances would admit, would be punished, and that the penalty for such failure and refusal would be damnation in the life to come."

Upon this proof he asked the court to instruct the jury that if they found from the evidence that he "was married as charged — if he was married — in pursuance of and in conformity with what he believed at the time to be a religious duty," that the verdict must be "not guilty." This request was refused, and the court did charge "that there must have been a criminal intent, but that if the defendant, under the influence of a religious belief that it was right, — under an inspiration, if you please, that it was right, — deliberately married a second time, having a first wife living, the want of consciousness of evil intent — the want of understanding on his part that he was committing a crime — did not excuse him; but the law inexorably in such case implies the criminal intent."

Congress cannot pass a law for the government of the Territories which shall prohibit the free exercise of religion. The first amendment to the Constitution expressly forbids such legislation. Religious freedom is guaranteed everywhere throughout the United States, so far as congressional interference is concerned. The question to be determined is, whether the law now under consideration comes within this prohibition.

The word "religion" is not defined in the Constitution. We must go elsewhere, therefore, to ascertain its meaning, and nowhere more appropriately, we think, than to the history of the times in the midst of which the provision was adopted. The precise point of the inquiry is, what is the religious freedom which has been guaranteed.

Amongst others, Mr. Madison prepared a "Memorial and Remonstrance," which was widely circulated and signed, and in which he demonstrated "that religion, or the duty we owe the Creator," was not within the cognizance of civil government. *Semple's Virginia Baptists, Appendix*. At the next session the proposed bill was not only defeated, but another, "for establishing religious freedom," drafted by Mr. Jefferson, was passed. In the preamble of this act religious freedom is defined; and after a recital "that to suffer the civil magistrate to intrude his powers into the field of opinion, and to restrain the profession or propagation of principles on supposition of their ill tendency, is a dangerous fallacy which at once destroys all religious liberty," it is declared "that it is time enough for the rightful purposes of civil government for its officers to interfere when principles break out into overt acts against peace and good order." In these two sentences is found the true distinction between what properly belongs to the church and what to the State.

Polygamy has always been odious among the northern and western nations of Europe, and, until the establishment of the Mormon Church, was almost exclusively a feature of the life of Asiatic and of African people. At common law, the second marriage was always void and from the earliest history of England polygamy has been treated as an offence against society. After the establishment of the ecclesiastical courts, and until the time of James I., it was punished through the instrumentality of those tribunals, not merely because ecclesiastical rights had been violated, but because upon the separation of the ecclesiastical courts from the civil the ecclesiastical were supposed to be the most appropriate for the trial of matrimonial causes and offences against the rights of marriage, just as they were for testamentary causes and the settlement of the estates of deceased persons.

In our opinion, the statute immediately under consideration is within the legislative power of Congress. It is constitutional and valid as prescribing a rule of action for all those residing in the Territories, and in places over which the United States have exclusive control. This being so, the only question which remains is, whether those who make polygamy a part of their religion are excepted from the operation of the statute. If they are, then those who do not make polygamy a part of their religious belief may be found guilty and punished, while those who do, must be acquitted and go free. This would be introducing a new element into criminal law. Laws are made for the government of actions, and while they cannot interfere with mere religious belief and opinions, they may with practices. Suppose one believed that human sacrifices were a necessary part of religious worship, would it be seriously contended that the civil government under which he lived could not interfere to prevent a sacrifice? Or if a wife religiously believed it was her duty to burn herself upon the funeral pile of her dead husband, would it be beyond the power of the civil government to prevent her carrying her belief into practice?

So here, as a law of the organization of society under the exclusive dominion of the United States, it is provided that plural marriages shall not be allowed. Can a man excuse his practices to the contrary because of his religious belief? To permit this would be to make the professed doctrines of religious belief superior to the law of the land, and in effect to permit every citizen to become a law unto himself. Government could exist only in name under such circumstances.

Judgment affirmed.

Sherbert v. Verner

United States Supreme Court
374 U.S. 398, 83 S. Ct. 1790, 10 L. Ed. 2d 965 (1963)

Mr. Justice Brennan delivered the opinion of the Court.

Appellant, a member of the Seventh-day Adventist Church was discharged by her South Carolina employer because she would not work on Saturday, the Sabbath Day of her faith. When she was unable to obtain other employment because from conscientious scruples she would not take Saturday work, she filed a claim for unemployment compensation benefits under the South Carolina Unemployment Compensation Act. The appellee Employment Security Commission, in administrative proceedings under the statute, found that appellant's restriction upon her availability for Saturday work brought her within the provision disqualifying for benefits insured workers who fail, without good cause, to accept "suitable work when offered by the employment office or the employer."

The door of the Free Exercise Clause stands tightly closed against any governmental regulation of religious *beliefs* as such, *Cantwell v. Connecticut*, 310 U.S. 296 (1940). Government may neither compel affirmation of a repugnant belief; nor penalize or discriminate against individuals or groups because they hold religious views abhorrent to the authorities; nor employ the taxing power to inhibit the dissemination of particular religious views. On the other hand, the Court has rejected challenges under the Free Exercise Clause to governmental regulation of certain overt acts prompted by religious beliefs or principles, for "even when the action is in accord with one's religious convictions, it is not totally free from legislative restrictions." *Braunfeld v. Brown*, 366 U.S. 599, 603 (1961). The conduct or actions so regulated have invariably posed some substantial threat to public safety, peace or order.

Plainly enough, appellant's conscientious objection to Saturday work constitutes no conduct prompted by religious principles of a kind within the reach of state legislation. If, therefore, the decision of the South Carolina Supreme Court is to withstand appellant's constitutional challenge, it must be either because her disqualification as a beneficiary represents no infringement by the State of her constitutional rights of free exercise, or because any incidental burden on the free exercise of appellant's religion may be justified by a "compelling state interest in the regulation of a subject within the State's constitutional power to regulate." *NAACP v. Button*, 371 U.S. 415, 438 (1963).

We turn first to the question whether the disqualification for benefits imposes any burden on the free exercise of appellant's religion. We think it is clear that it does. In a sense the consequences of such a disqualification to religious principles and practices may be only an indirect result of welfare legislation within the State's general competence to enact; it is true that no criminal sanctions directly compel appellant to work a six-day week. But this is only the beginning, not the end, of our inquiry. For "if the purpose or effect of a law is to impede the observance of one or all religions or is to discriminate invidiously between religions, that law is constitutionally invalid even though the burden may be characterized as being only indirect." *Braunfeld v. Brown*. Here not only is it apparent that appellant's declared ineligibility for benefits derives solely from the practice of her religion, but the pressure upon her to forego that practice is unmistakable. The ruling forces her to choose between following the precepts of her religion and forfeiting benefits, on the one hand, and abandoning one of the precepts of her religion in order to accept work, on the other hand. Governmental imposition of such a choice puts the same kind of burden upon the free exercise of religion as would a fine imposed against appellant for her Saturday worship.

Nor may the South Carolina court's construction of the statute be saved from constitutional infirmity on the ground that unemployment compensation benefits are not appellant's "right" but merely a "privilege." It is too late in the day to doubt that the liberties of religion and expression may be infringed by the denial of or placing of conditions upon a benefit or privilege.

Significantly South Carolina expressly saves the Sunday worshipper from having to make the kind of choice which we here hold infringes the Sabbatarian's religious liberty. When in times of "national emergency" the textile plants are authorized by the State Commissioner of Labor to operate on Sunday, "no employee shall be required to work on Sunday who is conscientiously opposed to Sunday work; and if any employee should refuse to work on Sunday on account of conscientious objections he or she shall not jeopardize his or her seniority by such refusal or be discriminated against in any other manner." S.C.Code, 64-4. No question of the disqualification of a Sunday worshipper for benefits is likely to arise, since we cannot suppose that an employer will discharge him in violation of this statute. The unconstitutionality of the disqualification of the Sabbatarian is thus compounded by the religious discrimination which South Carolina's general statutory scheme necessarily effects.

We must next consider whether some compelling state interest enforced in the eligibility provisions of the South Carolina statute justifies the substantial infringement of appellant's First Amendment right. The appellees suggest no more than a possibility that the filing of fraudulent claims by unscrupulous claimants feigning religious objections to Saturday work might not only dilute the unemployment compensation fund but also hinder the scheduling by employers of necessary Saturday work. But that possibility is not apposite here because no such objection appears to have been made before the South Carolina Supreme Court, and we are unwilling to assess the importance of an asserted state interest without the views of the state court. Nor, if the contention had been made below, would the record appear to sustain it; there is no proof whatever to warrant such fears of malingering or deceit as those which the respondents now advance. Even if consideration of such evidence is not foreclosed by the prohibition against judicial inquiry into the truth or falsity of religious beliefs — a question as to which we intimate no view since it is not before us — it is highly doubtful whether such evidence would be sufficient to warrant a substantial infringement of religious liberties. For even if the possibility of spurious claims did threaten to dilute the fund and disrupt the scheduling of work, it would plainly be incumbent upon the appellees to demonstrate that no alternative forms of regulation would combat such abuses without infringing First Amendment rights.

In holding as we do, plainly we are not fostering the "establishment" of the Seventh-day Adventist religion in South Carolina, for the extension of unemployment benefits to Sabbatarians in common with Sunday worshippers reflects nothing more than the governmental obligation of neutrality in the face of religious differences, and does not represent that involvement of religious with secular institutions which it is the object of the Establishment Clause to forestall. Nor does the recognition of the appellant's right to unemployment benefits under the state statute serve to abridge any other person's religious liberties. Nor do we, by our decision today, declare the existence of a constitutional right to unemployment benefits on the part of all persons whose religious convictions are the cause of their unemployment. This is not a case in which an employee's religious convictions serve to make him a nonproductive member of society. Finally, nothing we say today constrains the States to adopt any particular form or scheme of unemployment compensation. Our holding today is only that South Carolina may not constitutionally apply the eligibility provisions so as to constrain a worker to abandon his religious convictions respecting the day of rest. . . .

Mr. Justice Stewart, concurring in the result.

Although fully agreeing with the result which the Court reaches in this case, I cannot join the Court's opinion. This case presents a double-barreled dilemma, which in all candor I think the Court's opinion has not succeeded in papering over. The dilemma ought to be resolved.

I am convinced that no liberty is more essential to the continued vitality of the free society which our Constitution guarantees than is the religious liberty protected by the Free Exercise Clause explicit in the First Amendment and imbedded in the Fourteenth.

Yet what this Court has said about the Establishment Clause must inevitably lead to a diametrically opposite result. If the appellant's refusal to work on Saturdays were based on indolence, or on a compulsive desire to watch the Saturday television programs, no one would say that South Carolina could not hold that she was not "available for work" within the meaning of its statute. That being so, the Establishment Clause as construed by this Court not only *permits* but affirmatively *requires* South Carolina equally to deny the appellant's claim for unemployment compensation when her refusal to work on Saturdays is based upon her religious creed.

To require South Carolina to so administer its laws as to pay public money to the appellant under the circumstances of this case is thus clearly to require the State to violate the Establishment Clause as construed by this Court. This poses no problem for me, because I think the Court's mechanistic concept of the Establishment Clause is historically unsound and constitutionally wrong. And I think that the guarantee of religious liberty embodied in the Free Exercise Clause affirmatively requires government to create an atmosphere of hospitality and accommodation to individual belief or disbelief.

South Carolina would deny unemployment benefits to a mother unavailable for work on Saturdays because she was unable to get a babysitter. Thus, we do not have before us a situation where a State provides unemployment compensation generally, and singles out for disqualification only those persons who are unavailable for work on religious grounds. This is not, in short, a scheme which operates so as to discriminate against religion as such. But the Court nevertheless holds that the State must prefer a religious over a secular ground for being unavailable for work — that state financial support of the appellant's religion is constitutionally required to carry out "the governmental obligation of neutrality in the face of religious differences."

Yet in cases decided under the Establishment Clause the Court has decreed otherwise. It has decreed that government must blind itself to the differing religious beliefs and traditions of the people. With all respect, I think it is the Court's duty to face up to the dilemma posed by the conflict between the Free Exercise Clause of the Constitution and the Establishment Clause as interpreted by the Court.

My second difference with the Court's opinion is that I cannot agree that today's decision can stand consistently with *Braunfeld v. Brown*. The Court says that there was a "less direct burden upon religious practices" in that case than in this. With all respect, I think the Court is mistaken, simply as a matter of fact. The *Braunfeld* case involved a state *criminal* statute. The undisputed effect of that statute, as pointed out by Mr. Justice Brennan in his dissenting opinion in that case, was that "Plaintiff, Abraham Braunfeld, will be unable to continue in his business if he may not stay open on Sunday and he will thereby lose his capital investment." In other words, the issue in this case — and we do not understand either appellees or the Court to contend otherwise — is whether a State may put an individual to a choice between his business and his religion.

The impact upon the appellant's religious freedom in the present case is considerably less onerous. We deal here not with a criminal statute, but with the particularized administration of South Carolina's Unemployment Compensation Act. Even upon the unlikely assumption that the appellant could not find suitable non-Saturday employment, the appellant at the worst would be denied a maximum of 22 weeks of compensation payments. I agree with the Court that the possibility of that denial is enough to infringe upon the appellant's constitutional right to the free exercise of her religion. But it is clear to me that in order to reach this conclusion the court must explicitly reject the reasoning of *Braunfeld v. Brown*. I think the *Braunfeld* case was wrongly decided and should be overruled, and accordingly I concur in the result reached by the Court in the case before us.

Mr. Justice Harlan, whom Mr. Justice White joins, dissenting.

The South Carolina Supreme Court has . . . consistently held that one is not "available for work" if his unemployment has resulted not from the inability of industry to provide a job but rather from personal circumstances, no matter how compelling. . . . The fact that these personal considerations sprang from her religious convictions was wholly without relevance to the state court's application of the law. Thus in no proper sense can it be said that the State discriminated against the appellant on the basis of her religious beliefs or that she was denied benefits because she was a Seventh-day Adventist. She was denied benefits just as any other claimant would be denied benefits who was not "available for work" for personal reasons.

With this background, this Court's decision comes into clearer focus. What the Court is holding is that if the State chooses to condition unemployment compensation on the applicant's availability for work, it is constitutionally compelled to *carve out an exception* — and to provide benefits — for those whose unavailability is due to their religious convictions. Such a holding has particular significance in two respects.

First, despite the Court's protestations to the contrary, the decision necessarily overrules *Braunfeld v. Brown*. Clearly, any differences between this case and *Braunfeld* cut against the present appellant.

Second, the implications of the present decision are far more troublesome than its apparently narrow dimensions would indicate at first glance. The meaning of today's holding, as already noted, is that the State must furnish unemployment benefits to one who is unavailable for work if the unavailability stems from the exercise of religious convictions. The State, in other words, must *single out* for financial assistance those whose behavior is religiously motivated, even though it denies such assistance to others whose identical behavior (in this case, inability to work on Saturdays) is not religiously motivated.

It has been suggested that such singling out of religious conduct for special treatment may violate the constitutional limitations on state action. My own view, however, is that at least under the circumstances of this case it would be a permissible accommodation of religion for the State, if it *chose* to do so, to create an exception to its eligibility requirements for persons like the appellant. The constitutional obligation of "neutrality," is not so narrow a channel that the slightest deviation from an absolutely straight course leads to condemnation. There are too many instances in which no such course can be charted, too many areas in which the pervasive activities of the State justify some special provision for religion to prevent it from being submerged by an all-embracing secularism. . . .

I cannot subscribe to the conclusion that the State is constitutionally *compelled* to carve out an exception to its general rule of eligibility in the present case. Those situations in which the Constitution may require special treatment on account of religion are, in my view, few and far between, and this view is amply supported by the course of constitutional litigation in this area. Such compulsion in the present case is particularly inappropriate in light of the indirect, remote, and insubstantial effect of the decision below on the exercise of appellant's religion and in light of the direct financial assistance to religion that today's decision requires.

Wisconsin v. Yoder

United States Supreme Court
406 U.S. 205, 92 S. Ct. 1526, 32 L. Ed. 2d 15 (1972)

Mr. Chief Justice Burger delivered the opinion of the Court.

Respondents Jonas Yoder and Wallace Miller are members of the Old Order Amish religion, and respondent Adin Yutzy is a member of the Conservative Amish Mennonite Church. They and their families are residents of Green County, Wisconsin. Wisconsin's compulsory school-attendance law required them to cause their children to attend public or private school until reaching age 16 but the respondents declined to send their children, ages 14 and 15, to public school after they completed the eighth grade. The children were not enrolled in any private school, or within any recognized exception to the compulsory-attendance law, and they are conceded to be subject to the Wisconsin statute.

There is no doubt as to the power of a State, having a high responsibility for education of its citizens, to impose reasonable regulations for the control and duration of basic education. *See, e.g., Pierce v. Society of Sisters*, 268 U.S. 510, 534 (1925). Providing public schools ranks at the very apex of the function of a State. Yet even this paramount responsibility was, in *Pierce*, made to yield to the right of parents to provide an equivalent education in a privately operated system. There the Court held that Oregon's statute compelling attendance in a public school from age eight to age 16 unreasonably interfered with the interest of parents in directing the rearing of their offspring, including their education in church-operated schools. As that case suggests, the values of parental direction of the religious upbringing and education of their children in their early and formative years have a high place in our society. Thus, a State's interest in universal education, however highly we rank it, is not totally free from a balancing process when it impinges on fundamental rights and interests, such as those specifically protected by the Free Exercise Clause of the First Amendment, and the traditional interest of parents with respect to the religious upbringing of their children so long as they, in the words of *Pierce*, "prepare them for additional obligations."

In evaluating those claims we must be careful to determine whether the Amish religious faith and their mode of life are, as they claim, inseparable and interdependent. A way of life, however virtuous and admirable, may not be interposed as a barrier to reasonable state regulation of education if it is based on purely secular considerations; to have the protection of the Religion Clauses, the claims must be rooted in religious belief. Although a determination of what is a "religious" belief or practice entitled to constitutional protection may present a most delicate question, the very concept of ordered liberty precludes allowing every person to make his own standards on matters of conduct in which society as a whole has important interests. Thus, if the Amish asserted their claims because of their subjective evaluation and rejection of the contemporary secular values accepted by the majority, much as Thoreau rejected the social values of his time and isolated himself at Walden Pond, their claims would not rest on a religious basis. Thoreau's choice was philosophical and personal rather than religious, and such belief does not rise to the demands of the Religion Clauses.

Giving no weight to such secular considerations, however, we see that the record in this case abundantly supports the claim that the traditional way of life of the Amish is not merely a matter of personal preference, but one of deep religious conviction, shared by an organized group, and intimately related to daily living.

The impact of the compulsory-attendance law on respondents' practice of the Amish religion is not only severe, but inescapable, for the Wisconsin law affirmatively compels them, under threat of criminal sanction, to perform acts undeniably at odds with fundamental tenets of their religious beliefs. Nor is the impact of the compulsory-attendance law confined to grave interference with important Amish religious tenets from a subjective point of view. It carries with it precisely the kind of objective danger to the free exercise of religion that the First Amendment was designed to prevent. As the record shows, compulsory school attendance to age 16 for Amish children carries with it a very real threat of undermining the Amish community and religious practice as they exist today; they must either abandon belief and be assimilated into society at large, or be forced to migrate to some other and more tolerant region.

We turn, then, to the State's broader contention that its interest in its system of compulsory education is so compelling that even the established religious practices of the Amish must give way. Where fundamental claims of religious freedom are at stake, however, we cannot accept such a sweeping claim; despite its admitted validity in the generality of cases, we must searchingly examine the interests that the State seeks to promote by its requirement for compulsory education to age 16, and the impediment to those objectives that would flow from recognizing the claimed Amish exemption.

The State advances two primary arguments in support of its system of compulsory education. It notes, as Thomas Jefferson pointed out early in our history, that some degree of education is necessary to prepare citizens to participate effectively and intelligently in our open political system if we are to preserve freedom and independence. Further, education prepares individuals to be self-reliant and self-sufficient participants in society. We accept these propositions.

Whatever their idiosyncrasies as seen by the majority, this record strongly shows that the Amish community has been a highly successful social unit within our society, even if apart from the conventional "mainstream." Its members are productive and very law-abiding members of society; they reject public welfare in any of its usual modern forms. The Congress itself recognized their self-sufficiency by authorizing exemption of such groups as the Amish from the obligation to pay social security taxes.

The State, however, supports its interest in providing an additional one or two years of compulsory high school education to Amish children because of the possibility that some such children will choose to leave the Amish community, and that if this occurs they will be ill-equipped for life. The State argues that if Amish children leave their church they should not be in the position of making their way in the world without the education available in the one or two additional years the State requires. However, on this record, the argument is highly speculative. There is no specific evidence of the loss of Amish adherents by attrition, nor is there any showing that upon leaving the Amish community Amish children, with their practical agricultural training and habits of industry and self-reliance, would become burdens on society because of educational shortcomings.

The independence and successful social functioning of the Amish community for a period approaching almost three centuries and more than 200 years in this country are strong evidence that there is at best a speculative gain, in terms of meeting the duties of citizenship, from an additional one or two years of compulsory formal education.

The requirement of compulsory schooling to age 16 must therefore be viewed as aimed not merely at providing educational opportunities for children, but as an alternative to the equally undesirable consequence of unhealthful child labor displacing adult workers, or, on the other hand, forced idleness. The two kinds of statutes — compulsory school attendance and child labor laws — tend to keep children of certain ages off the labor market and in school; this regimen in turn provides opportunity to prepare for a livelihood of a higher order than that which children could pursue without education and protects their health in adolescence.

In these terms, Wisconsin's interest in compelling the school attendance of Amish children to age 16 emerges as somewhat less substantial than requiring such attendance for children generally. For, while agricultural employment is not totally outside the legitimate concerns of the child labor laws, employment of children under parental guidance and on the family farm from age 14 to age 16 is an ancient tradition that lies at the periphery of the objectives of such laws. There is no intimation that the Amish employment of their children on family farms is in any way deleterious to their health or that Amish parents exploit children at tender years. Any such inference would be contrary to the record before us. Moreover, employment of Amish children on the family farm does not present the undesirable economic aspects of eliminating jobs that might otherwise be held by adults.

Finally, the State argues that a decision exempting Amish children from the State's requirement fails to recognize the substantive right of the Amish child to a secondary education, and fails to give due regard to the power of the State as *parens patriae* to extend the benefit of secondary education to children regardless of the wishes of their parents.

Contrary to the suggestion of the dissenting opinion of Mr. Justice Douglas, our holding today in no degree depends on the assertion of the religious interest of the child as contrasted with that of the parents. It is the parents who are subject to prosecution here for failing to cause their children to attend school, and it is their right of free exercise, not that of their children, that must determine Wisconsin's power to impose criminal penalties on the parent. The dissent argues that a child who expresses a desire to attend public high school in conflict with the wishes of his parents should not *be* prevented from doing so. There is no reason for the Court to consider that point since it is not an issue in the case. The children are not parties to this litigation. The State has at no point tried this case on the theory that respondents were preventing their children from attending school against their expressed desires, and indeed the record is to the contrary.

Mr. Justice Powell and Mr. Justice Rehnquist took no part in the consideration or decision of this case.

Mr. Justice White, with whom Mr. Justice Brennan and Mr. Justice Stewart join, concurring.

I join the Court because the sincerity of the Amish religious policy here is uncontested, because the potentially adverse impact of the state requirement is great, and because the State's valid interest in education has already been largely satisfied by the eight years the children have already spent in school.

Mr. Justice Douglas, dissenting in part.

The Court's analysis assumes that the only interests at stake in the case are those of the Amish parents on the one hand, and those of the State on the other. The difficulty with this approach is that, despite the Court's claim, the parents are seeking to vindicate not only their own free exercise claims, but also those of their high-school-age children.

It is argued that the right of the Amish children to religious freedom is not presented by the facts of the case, as the issue before the Court involves only the Amish parents' religious freedom to defy a state criminal statute imposing upon them an affirmative duty to cause their children to attend high school.

First, respondents' motion to dismiss in the trial court expressly asserts, not only the religious liberty of the adults, but also that of the children, as a defense to the prosecutions. It is, of course, beyond question that the parents have standing as defendants in a criminal prosecution to assert the religious interests of their children as a defense. Although the lower courts and a majority of the Court assume an identity of interest between parent and child, it is clear that they have treated the religious interest of the child as a factor in the analysis.

Second, it is essential to reach the question to decide the case, not only because the question was squarely raised in the motion to dismiss, but also because no analysis of religious-liberty claims can take place in a vacuum. If the parents in this case are allowed a religious exemption, the inevitable effect is to impose the parents' notions of religious duty upon their children. Where the child is mature enough to express potentially conflicting desires, it would be an invasion of the child's rights to permit such an imposition without canvassing his views. As the child has no other effective forum, it is in this litigation that his rights should be considered. And, if an Amish child desires to attend high school, and is mature enough to have that desire respected, the State may well be able to override the parents' religiously motivated objections. . . .

Employment Division, Department of Human Resources v. Smith

United States Supreme Court
494 U.S. 872, 110 S. Ct. 1595, 108 L. Ed. 2d 876 (1990)

Justice Scalia delivered the opinion of the Court.

This case requires us to decide whether the Free Exercise Clause of the First Amendment permits the State of Oregon to include religiously inspired peyote use within the reach of its general criminal prohibition on use of that drug, and thus permits the State to deny unemployment benefits to persons dismissed from their jobs because of such religiously inspired use.

Oregon law prohibits the knowing or intention possession of a "controlled substance" unless the substance has been prescribed by a medical practitioner. Among the substances prohibited is the drug peyote.

Respondents Alfred Smith and Galen Black were fired from their jobs with a private drug rehabilitation organization because they ingested peyote for sacramental purposes at a ceremony of the Native American Church, of which both are members. When respondents applied to petitioner Employment Division for unemployment compensation, they were determined to be ineligible for benefits because they had been discharged for work-related "misconduct."

The free exercise of religion means, first and foremost, the right to believe and profess whatever religious doctrine one desires. Thus, the First Amendment obviously excludes all "governmental regulation of religious beliefs as such." *Sherbert v. Verner.* The government may not compel affirmation of religious belief, punish the expression of religious doctrines it believes to be false, impose special disabilities on the basis of religious views or religious status, or lend its power to one or the other side in controversies over religious authority or dogma.

But the "exercise of religion" often involves not only belief and profession but the performance of (or abstention from) physical acts: assembling with others for a worship service, participating in sacramental use of bread and wine, proselytizing, abstaining from certain foods or certain modes of transportation. It would be true, we think (though no case of ours has involved the point), that a state would be "prohibiting the free exercise [of religion]" if it sought to ban such acts or abstentions only when they are engaged in for religious reasons, or only because of the religious belief that they display.

Respondents in the present case, however, seek to carry the meaning of prohibiting the free exercise of religion one large step further. They contend that their religious motivation for using peyote places them beyond the reach of a criminal law that is not specifically directed at their religious practices, and that is concededly constitutional as applied to those who use the drug for other reasons

The only decisions in which we have held that the First Amendment bars application of a neutral, generally applicable law to religiously motivated action have involved not the Free Exercise Clause alone, but the Free Exercise Clause in conjunction with other constitutional protections, such as freedom of speech and of the press.

The present case does not present such a hybrid situation, but a free exercise claim unconnected with any communicative activity or parental right. Respondents urge us to hold, quite simply, that when otherwise prohibitable conduct is accompanied by religious convictions, not only the convictions but the conduct itself must be free from governmental regulation. We have never held that, and decline to do so now.

Respondents argue that even though exemption from generally applicable criminal laws need not automatically be extended to religiously motivated actors, at least the claim for a religious exemption must be evaluated under the balancing test set forth in *Sherbert v. Verner.* Under the *Sherbert* test, governmental actions that substantially burden a religious practice must be justified by compelling governmental interest. We have never invalidated any governmental action on the basis of the *Sherbert* test except the denial of unemployment compensation.

Even if we were inclined to breathe into *Sherbert* some life beyond the unemployment compensation field, we would not apply it to require exemptions from a generally applicable criminal law. The *Sherbert* test, it must be recalled, was developed in a context that lent itself to individualized governmental assessment of the reasons for the relevant conduct. A distinctive feature of unemployment compensation programs is that their eligibility criteria invite consideration of the particular circumstances behind an applicant's unemployment.

We conclude today that the sounder approach, and the approach in accord with the vast majority of our precedents, is to hold the test inapplicable to such challenges. The government's ability to enforce generally applicable prohibitions of socially harmful conduct, like its ability to carry out other aspects of public policy, "cannot depend on measuring the effects of governmental action on a religious objector's spiritual development."

The "compelling governmental interest" requirement seems benign, because it is familiar from other fields. But using it as the standard that must be met before the government may accord different treatment on the basis of race, is not remotely comparable to using it for the purpose asserted here. What it produces in those other fields — equality of treatment, and an unrestricted flow of contending speech — are constitutional norms; what it would produce here — a private right to ignore generally applicable laws — is a constitutional anomaly.

Nor is it possible to limit the impact of respondents' proposal by requiring a "compelling state interest" only when the conduct prohibited is "central" to the individual's religion. It is no more appropriate for judges to determine the "centrality" of religious beliefs before applying a "compelling interest" test in the free exercise field, than it would be for them to determine the "importance" of ideas before applying the "compelling interest" test in the free speech field.

If the "compelling interest" test is to be applied at all, then, it must be applied across the board, to all actions thought to be religiously commanded. Moreover, if "compelling interest" really means what it says (and watering it down here would subvert its rigor in the other fields where it is applied), many laws will not meet the test. Any society adopting such a system would be courting anarchy, but that danger increases in direct proportion to the society's diversity of religious beliefs, and its determination to coerce or suppress none of them. Precisely because "we are a cosmopolitan nation made up of people of almost every conceivable religious preference," and precisely because we value and protect that religious divergence, we cannot afford the luxury of deeming presumptively invalid, as applied to the religious objector, every regulation of conduct that does not protect an interest of the highest order. The rule respondents favor would open the prospect of constitutionally required religious exemptions from civic obligations of almost every conceivable kind.

Values that are protected against government interference through enshrinement in the Bill of Rights are not thereby banished from the political process. Just as a society that believes in the negative protection accorded to the press by the First Amendment is likely to enact laws that affirmatively foster the dissemination of the printed word, so also a society that believes in the negative protection accorded to religious belief can be expected to be solicitous of that value in its legislation as well. It is therefore not surprising that a number of States have made an exception to their drug laws for sacramental peyote use. But to say that a nondiscriminatory religious-practice exemption is permitted, or even that it is desirable, is not to say that it is constitutionally required, and that the appropriate occasions for its creation can be discerned by the courts. It may fairly be said that leaving accommodation to the political process will place at a relative disadvantage those religious practices that are not widely engaged in; but that unavoidable consequence of democratic government must be preferred to a system in which each conscience is a law unto itself or in which judges weigh the social importance of all laws against the centrality of all religious beliefs.

JUSTICE O'CONNOR, with whom JUSTICE BRENNAN, JUSTICE MARSHALL, and JUSTICE BLACKMUN join as to Parts I and II, concurring in the judgment.[1]

Although I agree with the result the Court reaches in this case, I cannot join its opinion. In my view, today's holding dramatically departs from well-settled First Amendment jurisprudence.

The Court today extracts from our long history of free exercise precedents the single categorical rule that "if prohibiting the exercise of religion is merely the incidental effect of a generally applicable and otherwise valid provision, the First Amendment has not been offended." Indeed, the Court holds that where the law is a generally applicable criminal prohibition, our usual free exercise jurisprudence does not even apply. To reach this sweeping result, however, the Court must not only give a strained reading of the First Amendment but must also disregard our consistent application of free exercise doctrine to cases involving generally applicable regulations that burden religious conduct.

The Court today interprets the Clause to permit the government to prohibit, without justification, conduct mandated by an individual's religious beliefs, so long as that prohibition is generally applicable. But a law that prohibits certain conduct — conduct that happens to be an act of worship for someone — manifestly does prohibit that person's free exercise of his religion. A person who is barred from engaging in religiously motivated conduct is barred from freely exercising his religion. Moreover, that person is barred from freely exercising his religion regardless of whether the law prohibits the conduct only when engaged in for religious reasons, only by members of that religion, or by all persons. It is difficult to deny that a law that prohibits religiously motivated conduct, even if the law is generally applicable, does not at least implicate First Amendment concerns.

---

1. [Court's footnote *] Although JUSTICE BRENNAN, JUSTICE MARSHALL, and JUSTICE BLACKMUN join Parts I and II of this opinion, they do not concur in the judgment.

The Court responds that generally applicable laws are "one large step" removed from laws aimed at specific religious practices. The First Amendment, however, does not distinguish between laws that are generally applicable and laws that target particular religious practices. Indeed, few States would be so naive as to enact a law directly prohibiting or burdening a religious practice as such. Our free exercise cases have all concerned generally applicable laws that had the effect of significantly burdening a religious practice. If the First Amendment is to have any vitality, it ought not be construed to cover only the extreme and hypothetical situation in which a State directly targets a religious practice. . . .

To say that a person's right to free exercise has been burdened, of course, does not mean that he has an absolute right to engage in the conduct. Under our established First Amendment jurisprudence, we have recognized that the freedom to act, unlike the freedom to believe, cannot be absolute. Instead, we have respected both the First Amendment's express textual mandate and the governmental interest in regulation of conduct by requiring the Government to justify any substantial burden on religiously motivated conduct by a compelling state interest and by means narrowly tailored to achieve that interest. The compelling interest test effectuates the First Amendment's command that religious liberty is an independent liberty, that it occupies a preferred position, and that the Court will not permit encroachments upon this liberty, whether direct or indirect, unless required by clear and compelling governmental interests "of the highest order."

To me, the sounder approach—the approach more consistent with our role as judges to decide each case on its individual merits—is to apply this test in each case to determine whether the burden on the specific plaintiffs before us is constitutionally significant and whether the particular criminal interest asserted by the State before us is compelling. Even if, as an empirical matter, a government's criminal laws might usually serve a compelling interest in health, safety, or public order, the First Amendment at least requires a case-by-case determination of the question, sensitive to the facts of each particular claim.

The Court today gives no convincing reason to depart from settled First Amendment jurisprudence. There is nothing talismanic about neutral laws of general applicability or general criminal prohibitions, for laws neutral toward religion can coerce a person to violate his religious conscience or intrude upon his religious duties just as effectively as laws aimed at religion. Although the Court suggests that the compelling interest test, as applied to generally applicable laws, would result in a "constitutional anomaly," the First Amendment unequivocally makes freedom of religion, like freedom from race discrimination and freedom of speech, a constitutional norm, not an anomaly.

Finally, the Court today suggests that the disfavoring of minority religions is an "unavoidable consequence" under our system of government and that accommodation of such religions must be left to the political process. In my view, however, the First Amendment was enacted precisely to protect the rights of those whose religious practices are not shared by the majority and may be viewed with hostility. The history of our free exercise doctrine amply demonstrates the harsh impact majoritarian rule has had on unpopular emerging religious groups such as Jehovah's Witnesses and the Amish.

I would therefore adhere to our established free exercise jurisprudence and hold that the State in this case has a compelling interest in regulating peyote use by its citizens and that accommodating respondents' religiously motivated conduct "will unduly interfere with fulfillment of the governmental interest." Accordingly, I concur in the judgment of the Court.

JUSTICE BLACKMUN, with whom JUSTICE BRENNAN and JUSTICE MARSHALL join, dissenting.

In weighing respondents' clear interest in the free exercise of their religion against Oregon's asserted interest in enforcing its drug laws, it is important to articulate in precise terms the state interest involved. It is not the State's broad interest in fighting the critical "war on drugs" that must be weighed against respondents' claim, but the State's narrow interest in refusing to make an exception for the religious, ceremonial use of peyote.

The State's interest in enforcing its prohibition, in order to be sufficiently compelling to outweigh a free exercise claim, cannot be merely abstract or symbolic. The State cannot plausibly assert that unbending application of a criminal prohibition is essential to fulfill any compelling interest, if it does not, in fact, attempt to enforce that prohibition. In this case, the State actually has not evinced any concrete interest in enforcing its drug laws against religious users of peyote. Oregon has never sought to prosecute respondents, and does not claim that it has made significant enforcement efforts against other religious users of peyote. The State's asserted interest thus amounts only to the symbolic preservation of an unenforced prohibition.

The fact that peyote is classified as a Schedule I controlled substance does not, by itself, show that any and all uses of peyote, in any circumstance, are inherently harmful and dangerous. The Federal Government, which created the classifications of unlawful drugs from which Oregon's drug laws are derived, apparently does not find peyote so dangerous as to preclude an exemption for religious use.

Notes and Questions

(1) In response to the Supreme Court's decision in *Smith*, Congress in 1993 passed the Religious Freedom Restoration Act of 1993. The law contained the bold declaration that:

> The purpose of the Religious Freedom Restoration Act of 1993 is: (1) to restore the compelling interest test as set forth in *Sherbert v. Verner*, 374 U.S. 398 (1963) and *Wisconsin v. Yoder*, 406 U.S. 205 (1972) and to guarantee its application in all cases where free exercise of religion is substantially burdened; and (2) to provide a claim or defense to persons whose religious exercise is substantially burdened by government.

The law contained a series of congressional findings that purport to pronounce the core values animating the Constitution's protection of freedom of religion. Congress found, the statute declared, that:

(1) the framers of the Constitution, recognizing free exercise of religion as an unalienable right, secured its protection in the First Amendment to the Constitution;

(2) laws "neutral" toward religion may burden religious exercise as surely as laws intended to interfere with religious exercise;

(3) governments should not substantially burden religious exercise without compelling justification;

(4) in *Employment Division v. Smith*, 494 U.S. 872 (1990) the Supreme Court virtually eliminated the requirement that the government justify burdens on religious exercise imposed by laws neutral toward religion; and

(5) the compelling interest test as set forth in prior federal court rulings is a workable test for striking sensible balances between religious liberty and competing prior governmental interests.

Section 3 of the Act provided that the "Government shall not substantially burden a person's exercise of religion even if the burden results from a rule of general applicability. . . ." The Act then contained a caveat, permitting the government to burden the free exercise of religion if it satisfies the classic "strict scrutiny test" familiar in constitutional adjudication:

Government may substantially burden a person's exercise of religion only if it demonstrates that application of the burden to the person —

(1) is in furtherance of a compelling governmental interest; and

(2) is the least restrictive means of furthering that compelling governmental interest.

(2) In *City of Boerne v. Flores*, 521 U.S. 507 (1997), the Supreme Court held that Congress lacked the power under §5 of the Fourteenth Amendment, to enact RFRA. The Court reasoned that because it had already held, in *Employment Division v. Smith*, that the strict scrutiny test did not apply to laws that substantially burden religion if they are neutral laws of general applicability, no federal constitutional right existed under the First Amendment in such cases. In turn, Congress lacked power to "enforce" the First Amendment, through the funnel of its power to "enforce" the Fourteenth Amendment, even though the First Amendment was "incorporated" against the states through the incorporation doctrine of the Fourteenth Amendment. In effect, the Court reasoned, it had already held that there were "zero" constitutional rights at issue, and Congress lacked enforcement power under the Fourteenth Amendment to enforce a "zero," or to attempt to create new constitutional rights that the Supreme Court had already rejected. The Court also held that RFRA was an attempt by Congress to simply overrule the Supreme Court's

interpretation of the First Amendment, and thus an afront to the Supreme Court's powers under *Marbury v. Madison.*

(3) While the decision in *Boerne v. Flores* struck down RFRA as applied to state and local governments, it did not strike down RFRA as applied to the *federal* government. Congress has the power to control the actions of federal agencies — which are creatures of Congress — and Congress may instruct federal agencies to not substantially burden religion unless the strict scrutiny test is satisfied. In *Gonzales v. O Centro Espirita Beneficente Uniao do Vegetal,* 546 U.S. 418 (2006), the Supreme Court held that the federal government violated the free exercise of religion rights guaranteed under RFRA. The case involved O Centro Espírita Beneficente Uniã do Vegetal (UDV), a Christian Spiritist sect based in Brazil, with an American branch of approximately 130 individuals. Central to the UDV's faith is receiving communion through *hoasca* (pronounced "wass-ca"), a sacramental tea made from two plants unique to the Amazon region. One of the plants, *psychotria viridis,* contains dimethyltryptamine (DMT), a hallucinogen whose effects are enhanced by alkaloids from the other plant, *banisteriopsis caapi.* Applying the strict scrutiny test imposed by RFRA, the Court held that the federal government's application of the federal drug laws to restrict access by the UDF to *hoasca* violated RFRA.

(4) Many states have enacted their own Religious Freedom Restoration Acts. Proposals for additional enactments of the so-called "mini-RFRAs" are pending in other states. The combination of the federal RFRA, which covers all federal government activity, and the fact that RFRA laws have been enacted in many states, means that in reality, the practical reach of the decision in *Employment Division v. Smith* has been significantly limited.

(5) If the decision in *Smith* was politically unpopular from the beginning, so too it has grown increasingly unpopular among Supreme Court Justices, leading to the distinct possibility that *Smith* will be overruled. Indeed, it may be not so much a question of whether *Smith* will be rejected but when. Not so clear, however, is what the Supreme Court would articulate as the governing doctrine *if* it rejects *Smith.* Consider, for example, the following observation from Justice Amy Coney Barrett:

> Petitioners, their amici, scholars, and Justices of this Court have made serious arguments that *Smith* ought to be overruled. While history looms large in this debate, I find the historical record more silent than supportive on the question whether the founding generation understood the First Amendment to require religious exemptions from generally applicable laws in at least some circumstances. In my view, the textual and structural arguments against *Smith* are more compelling. As a matter of text and structure, it is difficult to see why the Free Exercise Clause — lone among the First Amendment freedoms — offers nothing more than protection from discrimination. Yet what should replace *Smith*? The prevailing assumption seems to be that strict scrutiny would apply whenever a neutral and generally applicable law burdens religious exercise. But I am skeptical about

swapping *Smith*'s categorical antidiscrimination approach for an equally categorical strict scrutiny regime, particularly when this Court's resolution of conflicts between generally applicable laws and other First Amendment rights — like speech and assembly — has been much more nuanced.

Fulton v. City of Philadelphia, Pennsylvania, 141 S. Ct. 1868, 1882 (2021) (Barrett, J., concurring).

(6) Was the result in *Sherbert* consistent with the result in *Reynolds*? How, if at all, are the two cases different? Why was South Carolina required in *Sherbert* to demonstrate a "compelling state interest" to justify its regulation, rather than a "legitimate" or even "substantial" interest? What state interests would be considered "compelling" by the Court? Would proof of the "filing of fraudulent claims by unscrupulous claimants" satisfy the state's burden? Why not?

(7) Prior to the *Smith* decision, the Supreme Court had, in a series of cases, steadily expanded the principles of *Sherbert*. In *Thomas v. Review Bd., Ind. Empl. Sec. Div.*, 450 U.S. 707 (1981), the Court relied on *Sherbert* to reverse Indiana's refusal to pay unemployment benefits to a Jehovah's Witness who had quit his munitions factory job because of his religious objections to war. The state law denied benefits to "an individual who has voluntarily left his employment without good cause in connection with the work." In rejecting the Indiana court's characterization of Thomas as having made merely a "personal philosophical choice rather than a religious choice," the Chief Justice stated:

> Courts should not undertake to dissect religious beliefs because the believer admits that he is "struggling" with his position. . . . The narrow function of the reviewing court in this context is to determine whether there was an appropriate finding that petitioner terminated his work because of an honest conviction that such work was forbidden by his religion.

The Court found the "coercive impact" of the state scheme "indistinguishable from *Sherbert*." In *Hobbie v. Unemployment Appeals Commission of Florida*, 480 U.S. 136 (1987), the *employee* modified her religious beliefs after taking a job, converting to the Seventh-Day Adventist Church. The Court followed *Sherbert* and *Thomas* in overturning denial of employment benefits when she refused to work on her Sabbath. The majority found "no meaningful distinction among the situations of *Sherbert, Thomas*, and *Hobbie*." In each instance the employee was forced to choose between fidelity to religious belief and continued employment; the forfeiture of unemployment benefits for choosing the former over the latter brings unlawful coercion to bear on the employee's choice.

In *Frazee v. Illinois Dep't of Employment Security*, 489 U.S. 829 (1989), a unanimous Court reversed the state's determination that a free exercise exemption must be based on "a tenet or dogma of an established religious sect." Frazee was denied unemployment benefits because he declined Sunday work.

Although Frazee was not a member of a religious sect, he maintained that Sunday is the Lord's day for him because of his religious beliefs. Illinois attempted to

distinguish *Sherbet*, *Thomas*, and *Hobbie* on the fact that each of those claimants
was a member of a religious group. The Court was unimpressed:

> ... [N]one of those decisions turned on that consideration or on any
> tenet of the sect involved that forbade the work that the claimant refused
> to perform. Our judgments in those cases rested on the fact that each of the
> claimants had a sincere belief that religion required him or her to refrain
> from the work in question. Never did we suggest that unless a claimant
> belongs to a sect that forbids what his job requires, his belief, however sin-
> cere, must be deemed a purely personal preference rather than a religious
> belief. Indeed, [in] *Thomas*, there was disagreement among sect members
> as to whether their religion made it sinful to work in an armaments fac-
> tory; but we considered this to be an irrelevant issue and hence rejected the
> State's submission that unless the religion involved formally forbade work
> on armaments, Thomas' belief did not qualify as a religious belief. Because
> Thomas unquestionably had a sincere belief that his religion prevented him
> from doing such work, he was entitled to invoke the protection of the Free
> Exercise Clause.
>
> There is no doubt that "[o]nly beliefs rooted in religion are protected
> by the Free Exercise Clause," *United States v. Seeger*, 380 U.S. 163 (1965).
> Nor do we underestimate the difficulty of distinguishing between religious
> and secular convictions and in determining whether a professed belief is
> sincerely held. States are clearly entitled to assure themselves that there
> is an ample predicate for invoking the Free Exercise Clause. We do not face
> problems about sincerity or about the religious nature of Frazee's convic-
> tions, however. The courts below did not question his sincerity, and the
> State concedes it. Furthermore, the Board of Review characterized Frazee's
> views as "religious convictions," and the Illinois Appellate Court referred
> to his refusal to work on Sunday as based on a "personal professed reli-
> gious belief."

(8) According to the Court in *Sherbert*, South Carolina by statute may exempt the
Sunday worshipper from having to make the employment versus religious liberty
tradeoff. In *Braunfeld v. Brown*, 366 U.S. 599 (1961), the Court upheld a Sunday closing law because of the state interest in a uniform day of rest for all workers. Why
was the same rationale not adequate to support the state in *Sherbert*? In what respect
was the state's justification for its Sunday closing law greater than South Carolina's
reasons for its rule?

(9) Could the constitutional problems that gave rise to *Braunfeld* and *Sherbert* be
avoided by a state statute that provided: "No person who states that a particular day
of the week is observed as his Sabbath may be required by his employer to work on
such day. An employee's refusal to work his Sabbath shall not constitute grounds
for his dismissal"? Not according to the Court's 8-1 opinion in *Estate of Thornton v.
Caldor, Inc.*, 472 U.S. 703 (1985), where an identical Connecticut statute was struck
down as violative of the Establishment Clause. Because Connecticut dictated that

religious considerations "automatically control over all secular interests at the work-place" with no exception for especially burdened employers or employees who may be burdened by being required to work in place of Sabbath observers, its attempt to accommodate diverse Sabbath days ran afoul of the First Amendment principle that "no one [has] the right to insist that in pursuit of their own interests others must conform their conduct to his own religious necessities."

(10) In *Goldman v. Weinberger,* 475 U.S. 503 (1986), plaintiff, an Orthodox Jew who wore a yarmulke for religious reasons, challenged an Air Force regulation prohibiting the wearing of headgear. A closely divided Court held that the Free Exercise Clause did not prohibit application of the regulation notwithstanding its effect on plaintiff's religious beliefs. In so doing, the majority observed that its review of military regulations is "far more deferential than constitutional review of similar laws or regulations designed for civilian society."

(11) In *Smith,* the Court expresses an unwillingness to "breathe into *Sherbert* some life beyond the unemployment compensation field," and goes on to insist that not even *Sherbert* and its progeny require religious exemptions from "generally applicable law." Does *Smith* signal the impending doom of the *Sherbert* line of cases? How is *Church of the Lukumi Babalu Aye* different from *Smith*?

(12) The COVID pandemic led to government restrictions on the lives of virtually everyone in the United States. Some of those restrictions impacted religious worship, leading to challenges that reached the Supreme Court. The Court's first forays into the challenges upheld government restrictions. *See South Bay United Pentecostal Church v. Newsom,* 140 S. Ct. 1613 (2020); *Calvary Chapel Dayton Valley v. Sisolak*, 140 S. Ct. 2603 (2020). In *Roman Catholic Diocese of Brooklyn v. Cuomo*, 141 S. Ct. 63 (2020), however, the Court reversed course. The suit was brought by a Jewish Synagogue, Agudath Israel of America, and the Roman Catholic Diocese of Brooklyn, against New York Governor Andrew Cuomo, challenging Governor Cuomo's COVID-19 pandemic restrictions as applied to religious organizations. The applications for injunctive relief challenged an Executive Order issued by Governor Cuomo imposing severe restrictions on attendance at religious services in areas classified as "red" or "orange" zones. In red zones, no more than 10 persons could attend each religious service, and in orange zones, attendance was capped at 25. The Court held that the religious organizations made the required strong showing that the challenged restrictions violate "the minimum requirement of neutrality" to religion, reasoning that the New York regulations singled out religious organizations for more onerous treatment than other activities. The Court noted that in a red zone, while a synagogue or church may not admit more than 10 persons, businesses categorized as "essential" could admit as many people as they wished. Moreover, the list of "essential" businesses included things such as acupuncture facilities, camp grounds, garages, as well as many whose services are not limited to those that can be regarded as essential, such as all plants manufacturing chemicals and microelectronics and all transportation facilities. The disparate treatment, the Court observed, was even more striking in an orange zone. While attendance at houses of worship was limited

to 25 persons, the Court noted, even non-essential businesses in New York could decide for themselves how many persons to admit.

Problem A

You are a lawyer working as a policy analyst for the Governor of your State, which does not have a RFRA law. The Governor asks you for a cogent explanation of the pros and cons of RFRA laws, and your recommendation as to whether the Governor should or should not endorse passage of a RFRA law for your State.

§ 8.04 Religious Disputes in Secular Courts

The Ecclesiastical Abstention Doctrine. The First Amendment prohibits secular courts — state and federal courts — from resolving matters of religious theology or internal religious disputes. Religions often have their own tribunals and councils that resolve disputed issues of religious doctrine or disputes between members of the religious sect on matters relating to religious doctrine or conduct. Secular courts are barred by the First Amendment from reviewing or overturning such decisions. This First Amendment doctrine has roots in both the Establishment Clause and the Free Exercise Clause. It is sometimes called the "ecclesiastical abstention doctrine." This doctrine often involves property or contract disputes. Two rival factions within a church may each claim to own the church property, or each claim to be the proper leader of the church. The First Amendment does not bar *all* litigation in secular courts over church matters. If "neutral rules" of property law, or trust and estates law, or contract law, can be brought to bear to resolve a dispute, without any foray into theology or doctrine or internal religious principles, secular courts may adjudicate the dispute. In litigation over such matters, a threshold issue will often be whether the secular court may resolve the matter at all, or whether the dispute is too intertwined with theology or internal church matters for the court to adjudicate.

The Ministerial Exception. When religious entities are accused of violating civil rights laws, these First Amendment principles may also come into play. The Roman Catholic Church does not permit the ordination of women as priests. This appears on its face to be a straightforward violation of civil rights laws prohibiting gender discrimination. Yet it is clear that the civil rights laws governing gender discrimination will be overridden by the First Amendment. The Free Exercise Clause will plainly dictate that the criteria for ordaining a cleric must be left to the religious group itself, even if that criteria would normally be a violation of civil rights laws. This notion is often referred to as the "ministerial exception."

Hosanna-Tabor Evangelical Lutheran Church & School v. Equal Employment Opportunity Commission

United States Supreme Court
565 U.S. 171, 132 S. Ct. 694, 181 L. Ed. 2d 650 (2012)

CHIEF JUSTICE ROBERTS delivered the opinion of the Court.

Certain employment discrimination laws authorize employees who have been wrongfully terminated to sue their employers for reinstatement and damages. The question presented is whether the Establishment and Free Exercise Clauses of the First Amendment bar such an action when the employer is a religious group and the employee is one of the group's ministers.

Hosanna-Tabor Evangelical Lutheran Church and School is a member congregation of the Lutheran Church-Missouri Synod, the second largest Lutheran denomination in America. Hosanna-Tabor operated a small school in Redford, Michigan, offering a "Christ-centered education" to students in kindergarten through eighth grade.

The Synod classifies teachers into two categories: "called" and "lay." "Called" teachers are regarded as having been called to their vocation by God through a congregation. To be eligible to receive a call from a congregation, a teacher must satisfy certain academic requirements. One way of doing so is by completing a "colloquy" program at a Lutheran college or university. The program requires candidates to take eight courses of theological study, obtain the endorsement of their local Synod district, and pass an oral examination by a faculty committee. A teacher who meets these requirements may be called by a congregation. Once called, a teacher receives the formal title "Minister of Religion, Commissioned." A commissioned minister serves for an open-ended term; at Hosanna-Tabor, a call could be rescinded only for cause and by a supermajority vote of the congregation.

"Lay" or "contract" teachers, by contrast, are not required to be trained by the Synod or even to be Lutheran. At Hosanna-Tabor, they were appointed by the school board, without a vote of the congregation, to one-year renewable terms. Although teachers at the school generally performed the same duties regardless of whether they were lay or called, lay teachers were hired only when called teachers were unavailable.

Respondent Cheryl Perich was first employed by Hosanna-Tabor as a lay teacher in 1999. After Perich completed her colloquy later that school year, Hosanna-Tabor asked her to become a called teacher. Perich accepted the call and received a "diploma of vocation" designating her a commissioned minister.

Perich taught kindergarten during her first four years at Hosanna-Tabor and fourth grade during the 2003–2004 school year. She taught math, language arts, social studies, science, gym, art, and music. She also taught a religion class four days a week, led the students in prayer and devotional exercises each day, and attended a weekly school-wide chapel service. Perich led the chapel service herself about twice a year.

Perich became ill in June 2004 with what was eventually diagnosed as narcolepsy. Symptoms included sudden and deep sleeps from which she could not be roused. Because of her illness, Perich began the 2004–2005 school year on disability leave. On January 27, 2005, however, Perich notified the school principal, Stacey Hoeft, that she would be able to report to work the following month. Hoeft responded that the school had already contracted with a lay teacher to fill Perich's position for the remainder of the school year. Hoeft also expressed concern that Perich was not yet ready to return to the classroom.

On January 30, Hosanna-Tabor held a meeting of its congregation at which school administrators stated that Perich was unlikely to be physically capable of returning to work that school year or the next. The congregation voted to offer Perich a "peaceful release" from her call, whereby the congregation would pay a portion of her health insurance premiums in exchange for her resignation as a called teacher. Perich refused to resign and produced a note from her doctor stating that she would be able to return to work on February 22. The school board urged Perich to reconsider, informing her that the school no longer had a position for her, but Perich stood by her decision not to resign.

On the morning of February 22 — the first day she was medically cleared to return to work — Perich presented herself at the school. Hoeft asked her to leave but she would not do so until she obtained written documentation that she had reported to work. Later that afternoon, Hoeft called Perich at home and told her that she would likely be fired. Perich responded that she had spoken with an attorney and intended to assert her legal rights.

Following a school board meeting that evening, board chairman Scott Salo sent Perich a letter stating that Hosanna-Tabor was reviewing the process for rescinding her call in light of her "regrettable" actions. Salo subsequently followed up with a letter advising Perich that the congregation would consider whether to rescind her call at its next meeting. As grounds for termination, the letter cited Perich's "insubordination and disruptive behavior" on February 22, as well as the damage she had done to her "working relationship" with the school by "threatening to take legal action." The congregation voted to rescind Perich's call on April 10, and Hosanna-Tabor sent her a letter of termination the next day.

Perich filed a charge with the Equal Employment Opportunity Commission, alleging that her employment had been terminated in violation of the Americans with Disabilities Act. The ADA prohibits an employer from discriminating against a qualified individual on the basis of disability. It also prohibits an employer from retaliating "against any individual because such individual has opposed any act or practice made unlawful by the ADA or because such individual made a charge, testified, assisted, or participated in any manner in an investigation, proceeding, or hearing under the ADA."

The EEOC brought suit against Hosanna-Tabor, alleging that Perich had been fired in retaliation for threatening to file an ADA lawsuit.

The First Amendment provides, in part, that "Congress shall make no law respecting an establishment of religion, or prohibiting the free exercise thereof." We have said that these two Clauses "often exert conflicting pressures," *Cutter v. Wilkinson*, 544 U.S. 709 (2005), and that there can be "internal tension . . . between the Establishment Clause and the Free Exercise Clause," *Tilton v. Richardson*, 403 U.S. 672 (1971) (plurality opinion). Not so here. Both Religion Clauses bar the government from interfering with the decision of a religious group to fire one of its ministers.

Controversy between church and state over religious offices is hardly new. In 1215, the issue was addressed in the very first clause of Magna Carta. There, King John agreed that "the English church shall be free, and shall have its rights undiminished and its liberties unimpaired." The King in particular accepted the "freedom of elections," a right "thought to be of the greatest necessity and importance to the English church." J. Holt, Magna Carta App. IV, p. 317, cl. 1 (1965).

That freedom in many cases may have been more theoretical than real. See, e.g., W. Warren, Henry II 312 (1973) (recounting the writ sent by Henry II to the electors of a bishopric in Winchester, stating: "I order you to hold a free election, but forbid you to elect anyone but Richard my clerk"). In any event, it did not survive the reign of Henry VIII, even in theory. The Act of Supremacy of 1534, 26 Hen. 8, ch. 1, made the English monarch the supreme head of the Church, and the Act in Restraint of Annates, 25 Hen. 8, ch. 20, passed that same year, gave him the authority to appoint the Church's high officials. See G. Elton, The Tudor Constitution: Documents and Commentary 331–332 (1960). Various Acts of Uniformity, enacted subsequently, tightened further the government's grip on the exercise of religion. See, e.g., Act of Uniformity, 1559, 1 Eliz., ch. 2; Act of Uniformity, 1549, 2 & 3 Edw. 6, ch. 1. The Uniformity Act of 1662, for instance, limited service as a minister to those who formally assented to prescribed tenets and pledged to follow the mode of worship set forth in the Book of Common Prayer. Any minister who refused to make that pledge was "deprived of all his Spiritual Promotions." Act of Uniformity, 1662, 14 Car. 2, ch. 4.

Seeking to escape the control of the national church, the Puritans fled to New England, where they hoped to elect their own ministers and establish their own modes of worship. See T. Curry, The First Freedoms: Church and State in America to the Passage of the First Amendment 3 (1986); McConnell, *The Origins and Historical Understanding of Free Exercise of Religion*, 103 Harv. L. Rev. 1409, 1422 (1990). William Penn, the Quaker proprietor of what would eventually become Pennsylvania and Delaware, also sought independence from the Church of England. The charter creating the province of Pennsylvania contained no clause establishing a religion. See S. Cobb, The Rise of Religious Liberty in America 440–441 (1970).

Colonists in the South, in contrast, brought the Church of England with them. But even they sometimes chafed at the control exercised by the Crown and its representatives over religious offices. In Virginia, for example, the law vested the governor with the power to induct ministers presented to him by parish vestries, 2 Hening's Statutes at Large 46 (1642), but the vestries often refused to make such presentations and instead chose ministers on their own. See H. Eckenrode, Separation of Church and State in Virginia 13–19 (1910). Controversies over the selection of ministers also arose in other Colonies with Anglican establishments, including North Carolina. See C. Antieau, A. Downey, & E. Roberts, Freedom from Federal Establishment: Formation and Early History of the First Amendment Religion Clauses 10–11 (1964). There, the royal governor insisted that the right of presentation lay with the Bishop of London, but the colonial assembly enacted laws placing that right in the vestries. Authorities in England intervened, repealing those laws as inconsistent with the rights of the Crown. See *id.*, at 11; Weeks, Church and State in North Carolina, Johns Hopkins U. Studies in Hist. & Pol. Sci., 11th Ser., Nos. 5–6, pp. 29–36 (1893).

It was against this background that the First Amendment was adopted. Familiar with life under the established Church of England, the founding generation sought to foreclose the possibility of a national church. See 1 Annals of Cong. 730–731 (1789) (noting that the Establishment Clause addressed the fear that "one sect might obtain a pre-eminence, or two combine together, and establish a religion to which they would compel others to conform" (remarks of J. Madison)). By forbidding the "establishment of religion" and guaranteeing the "free exercise thereof," the Religion Clauses ensured that the new Federal Government — unlike the English Crown — would have no role in filling ecclesiastical offices. The Establishment Clause prevents the Government from appointing ministers, and the Free Exercise Clause prevents it from interfering with the freedom of religious groups to select their own.

Given this understanding of the Religion Clauses — and the absence of government employment regulation generally — it was some time before questions about government interference with a church's ability to select its own ministers came before the courts. This Court touched upon the issue indirectly, however, in the context of disputes over church property. Our decisions in that area confirm that it is impermissible for the government to contradict a church's determination of who can act as its ministers.

In *Watson v. Jones*, 13 Wall. 679, 20 L.Ed. 666 (1872), the Court considered a dispute between antislavery and proslavery factions over who controlled the property of the Walnut Street Presbyterian Church in Louisville, Kentucky. The General Assembly of the Presbyterian Church had recognized the antislavery faction, and this Court — applying not the Constitution but a "broad and sound view of the relations of church and state under our system of laws" — declined to question that determination. *Id.*, at 727. We explained that "whenever the questions of discipline, or of faith, or ecclesiastical rule, custom, or law have been decided by the highest of [the] church judicatories to which the matter has been carried, the legal tribunals must accept such decisions as final, and as binding on them." *Ibid.* As we would put it later, our opinion in Watson "radiates . . . a spirit of freedom for religious organizations, an independence from secular control or manipulation — in short, power to decide for themselves, free from state interference, matters of church government as well as those of faith and doctrine." *Kedroff v. Saint Nicholas Cathedral of Russian Orthodox Church in North America*, 344 U.S. 94 (1952).

Confronting the issue under the Constitution for the first time in *Kedroff*, the Court recognized that the "freedom to select the clergy, where no improper methods of choice are proven," is "part of the free exercise of religion" protected by the First Amendment against government interference. At issue in *Kedroff* was the right to use a Russian Orthodox cathedral in New York City. The Russian Orthodox churches in North America had split from the Supreme Church Authority in Moscow, out of concern that the Authority had become a tool of the Soviet Government. The North American churches claimed that the right to use the cathedral belonged to an archbishop elected by them; the Supreme Church Authority claimed that it belonged instead to an archbishop appointed by the patriarch in Moscow. New York's highest court ruled in favor of the North American churches, based on a state law requiring every Russian Orthodox church in New York to recognize the determination of the governing body of the North American churches as authoritative.

This Court reversed, concluding that the New York law violated the First Amendment. We explained that the controversy over the right to use the cathedral was "strictly a matter of ecclesiastical government, the power of the Supreme Church Authority of the Russian Orthodox Church to appoint the ruling hierarch of the archdiocese of North America." By "pass[ing] the control of matters strictly ecclesiastical from one church authority to another," the New York law intruded the "power of the state into the forbidden area of religious freedom contrary to the principles of the First Amendment."

Accordingly, we declared the law unconstitutional because it "directly prohibit[ed] the free exercise of an ecclesiastical right, the Church's choice of its hierarchy."

This Court reaffirmed these First Amendment principles in *Serbian Eastern Orthodox Diocese for United States and Canada v. Milivojevich*, 426 U.S. 696 (1976), a case involving a dispute over control of the American-Canadian Diocese of the Serbian Orthodox Church, including its property and assets. The Church had removed Dionisije Milivojevich as bishop of the American-Canadian Diocese because of his defiance of the church hierarchy. Following his removal, Dionisije brought a civil action in state court challenging the Church's decision, and the Illinois Supreme Court "purported in effect to reinstate Dionisije as Diocesan Bishop," on the ground that the proceedings resulting in his removal failed to comply with church laws and regulations.

Reversing that judgment, this Court explained that the First Amendment "permit[s] hierarchical religious organizations to establish their own rules and regulations for internal discipline and government, and to create tribunals for adjudicating disputes over these matters." When ecclesiastical tribunals decide such disputes, we further explained, "the Constitution requires that civil courts accept their decisions as binding upon them." We thus held that by inquiring into whether the Church had followed its own procedures, the State Supreme Court had "unconstitutionally undertaken the resolution of quintessentially religious controversies whose resolution the First Amendment commits exclusively to the highest ecclesiastical tribunals" of the Church.

Until today, we have not had occasion to consider whether this freedom of a religious organization to select its ministers is implicated by a suit alleging discrimination in employment. The Courts of Appeals, in contrast, have had extensive experience with this issue. Since the passage of Title VII of the Civil Rights Act of 1964, 42 U.S.C. §2000e et seq., and other employment discrimination laws, the Courts of Appeals have uniformly recognized the existence of a "ministerial exception," grounded in the First Amendment, that precludes application of such legislation to claims concerning the employment relationship between a religious institution and its ministers.

We agree that there is such a ministerial exception. The members of a religious group put their faith in the hands of their ministers. Requiring a church to accept or retain an unwanted minister, or punishing a church for failing to do so, intrudes upon more than a mere employment decision. Such action interferes with the internal governance of the church, depriving the church of control over the selection of those who will personify its beliefs. By imposing an unwanted minister, the state infringes the Free Exercise Clause, which protects a religious group's right to shape its own faith and mission through its appointments. According the state the power to determine which individuals will minister to the faithful also violates the Establishment Clause, which prohibits government involvement in such ecclesiastical decisions.

The EEOC and Perich acknowledge that employment discrimination laws would be unconstitutional as applied to religious groups in certain circumstances. They grant, for example, that it would violate the First Amendment for courts to apply such laws to compel the ordination of women by the Catholic Church or by an Orthodox Jewish seminary. According to the EEOC and Perich, religious organizations could successfully defend against employment discrimination claims in those circumstances by invoking the constitutional right to freedom of association — a right "implicit" in the First Amendment. *Roberts v. United States Jaycees*, 468 U.S. 609 (1984). The EEOC and Perich thus see no need — and no basis — for a special rule for ministers grounded in the Religion Clauses themselves.

We find this position untenable. The right to freedom of association is a right enjoyed by religious and secular groups alike. It follows under the EEOC's and Perich's view that the First Amendment analysis should be the same, whether the association in question is the Lutheran Church, a labor union, or a social club. That result is hard to square with the text of the First Amendment itself, which gives special solicitude to the rights of religious organizations. We cannot accept the remarkable view that the Religion Clauses have nothing to say about a religious organization's freedom to select its own ministers.

The EEOC and Perich also contend that our decision in *Employment Div., Dept. of Human Resources of Ore. v. Smith*, precludes recognition of a ministerial exception. In *Smith*, two members of the Native American Church were denied state unemployment benefits after it was determined that they had been fired from their jobs for ingesting peyote, a crime under Oregon law. We held that this did not violate the Free Exercise Clause, even though the peyote had been ingested for sacramental purposes, because the "right of free exercise does not relieve an individual of the obligation to comply with a valid and neutral law of general applicability on the ground that the law proscribes (or prescribes) conduct that his religion prescribes (or proscribes)."

It is true that the ADA's prohibition on retaliation, like Oregon's prohibition on peyote use, is a valid and neutral law of general applicability. But a church's selection of its ministers is unlike an individual's ingestion of peyote. *Smith* involved government regulation of only outward physical acts. The present case, in contrast, concerns government interference with an internal church decision that affects the faith and mission of the church itself. . . . The contention that *Smith* forecloses recognition of a ministerial exception rooted in the Religion Clauses has no merit.

Having concluded that there is a ministerial exception grounded in the Religion Clauses of the First Amendment, we consider whether the exception applies in this case. We hold that it does.

Every Court of Appeals to have considered the question has concluded that the ministerial exception is not limited to the head of a religious congregation, and we agree. We are reluctant, however, to adopt a rigid formula for deciding when an employee qualifies as a minister. It is enough for us to conclude, in this our first case involving the ministerial exception, that the exception covers Perich, given all the circumstances of her employment.

To begin with, Hosanna-Tabor held Perich out as a minister, with a role distinct from that of most of its members. When Hosanna-Tabor extended her a call, it issued her a "diploma of vocation" according her the title "Minister of Religion, Commissioned." She was tasked with performing that office "according to the Word of God and the confessional standards of the Evangelical Lutheran Church as drawn from the Sacred Scriptures." *Ibid.* The congregation prayed that God "bless [her] ministrations to the glory of His holy name, [and] the building of His church." In a supplement to the diploma, the congregation undertook to periodically review Perich's "skills of ministry" and "ministerial responsibilities," and to provide for her "continuing education as a professional person in the ministry of the Gospel."

Perich's title as a minister reflected a significant degree of religious training followed by a formal process of commissioning. To be eligible to become a commissioned minister, Perich had to complete eight college-level courses in subjects including biblical interpretation, church doctrine, and the ministry of the Lutheran teacher. She also had to obtain the endorsement of her local Synod district by submitting a petition that contained her academic transcripts, letters of recommendation, personal statement, and written answers to various ministry-related questions. Finally, she had to pass an oral examination by a faculty committee at a Lutheran college. It took Perich six years to fulfill these requirements. And when she eventually did, she was commissioned as a minister only upon election by the congregation, which recognized God's call to her to teach. At that point, her call could be rescinded only upon a supermajority vote of the congregation — a protection designed to allow her to "preach the Word of God boldly."

Perich held herself out as a minister of the Church by accepting the formal call to religious service, according to its terms. She did so in other ways as well. For example, she claimed a special housing allowance on her taxes that was available only to employees earning their compensation "'in the exercise of the ministry.'" App. 220 ("If you are not conducting activities 'in the exercise of the ministry,' you cannot take advantage of the parsonage or housing allowance exclusion" (quoting Lutheran Church-Missouri Synod Brochure on Whether the IRS Considers Employees as a Minister (2007)). In a form she submitted to the Synod following her termination, Perich again indicated that she regarded herself as a minister at Hosanna-Tabor, stating: "I feel that God is leading me to serve in the teaching ministry. . . . I am anxious to be in the teaching ministry again soon."

Perich's job duties reflected a role in conveying the Church's message and carrying out its mission. Hosanna-Tabor expressly charged her with "lead[ing] others toward Christian maturity" and "teach[ing] faithfully the Word of God, the Sacred Scriptures, in its truth and purity and as set forth in all the symbolical books of the Evangelical Lutheran Church." In fulfilling these responsibilities, Perich taught her students religion four days a week, and led them in prayer three times a day. Once a week, she took her students to a school-wide chapel service, and — about twice a year — she took her turn leading it, choosing the liturgy, selecting the hymns, and delivering a short message based on verses from the Bible. During her last year of teaching, Perich also led her fourth graders in a brief devotional exercise each morning. As a source of religious instruction, Perich performed an important role in transmitting the Lutheran faith to the next generation.

In light of these considerations — the formal title given Perich by the Church, the substance reflected in that title, her own use of that title, and the important religious functions she performed for the Church — we conclude that Perich was a minister covered by the ministerial exception. . . .

Justice Thomas, concurring.

I join the Court's opinion. I write separately to note that, in my view, the Religion Clauses require civil courts to apply the ministerial exception and to defer to a religious organization's good-faith understanding of who qualifies as its minister. . . . The question whether an employee is a minister is itself religious in nature, and the answer will vary widely. Judicial attempts to fashion a civil definition of "minister" through a bright-line test or multi-factor analysis risk disadvantaging those religious groups whose beliefs, practices, and membership are outside of the "mainstream" or unpalatable to some. Moreover, uncertainty about whether its ministerial designation will be rejected, and a corresponding fear of liability, may cause a religious group to conform its beliefs and practices regarding "ministers" to the prevailing secular understanding.

Notes and Questions

If it is plain that the ministerial exception would preclude a civil rights claim brought by a woman who claimed gender discrimination by a religious employer in a religion that refused to permit women clerics, and equally clear that a valid civil rights claim could be brought against the same organization for gender discrimination in the hiring of, say, a maintenance employee, where within the organization chart does the ministerial exception kick in? The Supreme Court in *Our Lady of Guadalupe School v. Morrissey-Berru*, 140 S. Ct. 2049 (2020), elaborated on the reach of the principle established in *Hosanna-Tabor*. *Our Lady of Guadalupe* involved two elementary school teachers at Roman Catholic schools who did not possess the title of "minister." The Court concluded, however, that title was not controlling for purposes of the ministerial exception. The Court explained that the "religious education and formation of students is the very reason for the existence of most private religious schools, and therefore the selection and supervision of the teachers upon whom the schools rely to do this work lie at the core of their mission." For courts to engage in judicial review of the way in which religious schools discharge those responsibilities, the Court concluded, "would undermine the independence of religious institutions in a way that the First Amendment does not tolerate." As the Court explained:

> When we apply this understanding of the Religion Clauses to the cases now before us, it is apparent that Morrissey-Berru and Biel qualify for the exemption we recognized in *Hosanna-Tabor*. There is abundant record evidence that they both performed vital religious duties. Educating and forming students in the Catholic faith lay at the core of the mission of the schools where they taught, and their employment agreements and faculty handbooks specified in no uncertain terms that they were expected to help the schools carry out this mission and that their work would be evaluated to ensure that they were fulfilling that responsibility. As elementary school teachers responsible for providing instruction in all subjects, including religion, they were the members of the school staff who were entrusted most directly with the responsibility of educating their students in the faith. And not only were they obligated to provide instruction about the Catholic faith, but they were also expected to guide their students, by word and deed, toward the goal of living their lives in accordance with the faith. They prayed with their students, attended Mass with the students, and prepared the children for their participation in other religious activities. Their positions did not have all the attributes of Perich's. Their titles did not include the term "minister," and they had less formal religious training, but their core responsibilities as teachers of religion were essentially the same. And both their schools expressly saw them as playing a vital part in carrying out the mission of the church, and the schools' definition and explanation of their roles is important. In a country with the religious diversity of the United States, judges cannot be expected to have a complete understanding

and appreciation of the role played by every person who performs a particular role in every religious tradition. A religious institution's explanation of the role of such employees in the life of the religion in question is important.

How far does this principle extend? Imagine, for example, a deeply religious sectarian university that treats virtually all aspects of its identity as infused with the university's spiritual mission. Would the ministerial exception extend to varsity athletic coaches? Counselors in the office of student affairs? Faculty?

Chapter 9

Freedom of Speech and Association

§ 9.01 Competing Conceptions of Freedom of Speech

A. Dueling Visions

As this Chapter bears witness, American free speech law is complex, a swirling miasma of specialized doctrines and multi-part tests. Cutting through all the dense doctrinal formulas, all of American free speech law can be distilled into a contest between two equally elegant and sublime visions of freedom of speech. In this Chapter, they are dubbed by the nicknames, the "Order and Morality Theory" and the "Marketplace Theory."

These two theories have competed for ascendancy in America, and world-wide. Although the American debate over the meaning of free speech began in earnest with the administration of President John Adams and the passage of the Alien and Sedition Acts (discussed in *New York Times Co. v. Sullivan*, later in this Chapter), the Supreme Court did not begin serious exploration of the meaning of freedom of speech until the World War I epoch. In the one hundred years since World War I, the Order and Morality Theory and Marketplace Theory have vied for control.

For roughly the first half of that hundred years, the Order and Morality Theory dominated. It is exemplified in the materials below by *Chaplinsky v. New Hampshire* (1942) and *Beauharnais v. Illinois* (1952). In *Chaplinsky*, Justice Frank Murphy captured, in just a few brilliant sentences, the soul of the Order and Morality Theory.

The Marketplace Theory in American law traces its pedigree to decisions of Justices Oliver Wendell Holmes and Louis Brandeis. In the case of Justice Holmes, the embrace of the Marketplace Theory was a work in progress. His early speech opinions were much more akin to the Order and Morality Theory, as evidenced by a series sending anti-war protestors to jail. Then everything changed with Holmes' extraordinary dissenting opinion in *Abrams v. United States* (1919). That opinion is a masterpiece, a work of literature. The Holmes' dissenting opinion in *Abrams* would be followed by the concurring opinion of Justice Brandeis in *Whitney v. California*, another judicial work of art.

In the 1960's, the Marketplace Theory began to turn the tail, and emerge as the dominant theory displacing the Order and Morality Theory. Yet it would be simplistic, and false, to claim that for roughly fifty years, the Order and Morality Theory controlled, and now the Marketplace Theory controls. A more accurate portraiture goes something like this: In the general open spaces in American society, the Marketplace Theory has now replaced the Order and Morality Theory. This is exemplified by many free speech doctrines that provide extraordinary protection for violent and graphically offensive speech. Yet there are many "special settings," which we might think of as "carve outs" from the general marketplace, in which the Order and Morality Theory still dominates. The principles governing speech in public schools, or the speech of government employees, are prime examples explored in this Chapter.

We begin the journey with an exploration of the two competing theories, through the vehicles of two cases on each side. The exemplars of the Order and Morality Theory are *Chaplinsky* and *Beauharnais*. The exemplars of the Marketplace Theory are the Holmes opinion in *Abrams* and the Brandeis opinion in *Whitney*.

B. The Order and Morality Theory

Chaplinsky v. New Hampshire

United States Supreme Court
315 U.S. 568, 62 S. Ct. 766, 86 L. Ed. 1031 (1942)

MR. JUSTICE MURPHY delivered the opinion of the Court.

Appellant, a member of the sect known as Jehovah's Witnesses, was convicted in the municipal court of Rochester, New Hampshire, for violation of Chapter 378, Section 2, of the Public Laws of New Hampshire:

> No person shall address any offensive, derisive or annoying word to any other person who is lawfully in any street or other public place, nor call him by any offensive or derisive name, nor make any noise or exclamation in his presence and hearing with intent to deride, offend or annoy him, or to prevent him from pursuing his lawful business or occupation.

The complaint charged that appellant "with force and arms, in a certain public place in said city of Rochester, to wit, on the public sidewalk on the easterly side of Wakefield Street, near unto the entrance of the City Hall, did unlawfully repeat, the words following, addressed to the complainant, that is to say, 'You are a God damned racketeer' and 'a damned Fascist and the whole government of Rochester are Fascists or agents of Fascists,' the same being offensive, derisive and annoying words and names."

[A]ppellant was found guilty and the judgment of conviction was affirmed by the Supreme Court of the State. . . .

There is no substantial dispute over the facts. Chaplinsky was distributing the literature of his sect on the streets of Rochester on a busy Saturday afternoon. Members of the local citizenry complained to the City Marshal, Bowering, that Chaplinsky was denouncing all religion as a "racket." Bowering told them that Chaplinsky was lawfully engaged, and then warned Chaplinsky that the crowd was getting restless. Some time later, a disturbance occurred and the traffic officer on duty at the busy intersection started with Chaplinsky for the police station, but did not inform him that he was under arrest or that he was going to be arrested. On the way, they encountered Marshal Bowering who had been advised that a riot was under way and was therefore hurrying to the scene. Bowering repeated his earlier warning to Chaplinsky who then addressed to Bowering the words set forth in the complaint.

Chaplinsky's version of the affair was slightly different. He testified that, when he met Bowering, he asked him to arrest the ones responsible for the disturbance. In reply, Bowering cursed him and told him to come along. Appellant admitted that he said the words charged in the complaint, with the exception of the name of the Deity. . . .

Appellant assails the statute as a violation of all three freedoms, speech, press and worship, but only an attack on the basis of free speech is warranted. The spoken, not the written, word is involved. And we cannot conceive that cursing a public officer is the exercise of religion in any sense of the term. But even if the activities of the appellant which preceded the incident could be viewed as religious in character, and therefore entitled to the protection of the Fourteenth Amendment, they would not cloak him with immunity from the legal consequences for concomitant acts committed in violation of a valid criminal statute. We turn, therefore, to an examination of the statute itself.

Allowing the broadest scope to the language and purpose of the Fourteenth Amendment, it is well understood that the right of free speech is not absolute at all times and under all circumstances. There are certain well-defined and narrowly limited classes of speech, the prevention and punishment of which have never been thought to raise any Constitutional problem. These include the lewd and obscene, the profane, the libelous, and the insulting or "fighting" words — those which by their very utterance inflict injury or tend to incite an immediate breach of the peace. It has been well observed that such utterances are no essential part of any exposition of ideas, and are of such slight social value as a step to truth that any benefit that may be derived from them is clearly outweighed by the social interest in order and morality. "Resort to epithets or personal abuse is not in any proper sense communication of information or opinion safeguarded by the Constitution, and its punishment as a criminal act would raise no question under that instrument." *Cantwell v. Connecticut*, 310 U.S. 296, 309 (1940). . . .

We are unable to say that the limited scope of the statute as thus construed contravenes the Constitutional right of free expression. It is a statute narrowly drawn and limited to define and punish specific conduct lying within the domain of state power, the use in a public place of words likely to cause a breach of the peace. . . . This conclusion necessarily disposes of appellant's contention that the statute is so vague and indefinite as to render a conviction thereunder a violation of due process. A statute punishing verbal acts, carefully drawn so as not unduly to impair liberty of expression, is not too vague for a criminal law. . . .

Nor can we say that the application of the statute to the facts disclosed by the record substantially or unreasonably impinges upon the privilege of free speech. Argument is unnecessary to demonstrate that the appellations "damn racketeer" and "damn Fascist" are epithets likely to provoke the average person to retaliation, and thereby cause a breach of the peace. . . .

Beauharnais v. Illinois

United States Supreme Court
343 U.S. 250, 72 S. Ct. 725, 96 L. Ed. 919 (1952)

MR. JUSTICE FRANKFURTER delivered the opinion of the Court.

The petitioner was convicted upon information in the Municipal Court of Chicago of violating s 224a of Division 1 of the Illinois Criminal Code, Ill.Rev.Stat.1949, c. 38, s 471. He was fined $200. The section provides:

> 'It shall be unlawful for any person, firm or corporation to manufacture, sell, or offer for sale, advertise or publish, present or exhibit in any public place in this state any lithograph, moving picture, play, drama or sketch, which publication or exhibition portrays depravity, criminality, unchastity, or lack of virtue of a class of citizens, of any race, color, creed or religion which said publication or exhibition exposes the citizens of any race, color, creed or religion to contempt, derision, or obloquy or which is productive of breach of the peace or riots.'

. . . We granted certiorari in view of the serious questions raised concerning the limitations imposed by the Fourteenth Amendment on the power of a State to punish utterances promoting friction among racial and religious groups.

The information, cast generally in the terms of the statute, charged that Beauharnais 'did unlawfully exhibit in public places lithographs, which publications portray depravity, criminality, unchastity or lack of virtue of citizens of Negro race and color and which exproses (sic) citizens of Illinois of the Negro race and color to contempt, derision, or obloquy.' The lithograph complained of was a leaflet setting forth a petition calling on the Mayor and City Council of Chicago 'to halt the further encroachment, harassment and invasion of white people, their property, neighborhoods and persons, by the Negro' Below was a call for 'One million self respecting white people in Chicago to unite' with the statement added that 'If persuasion and the need to prevent the white race from becoming mongrelized by the negro will not unite us, then the aggressions rapes, robberies, knives, guns and marijuana of the negro, surely will.' This, with more language, similar if not so violent, concluded with an attached application for membership in the White Circle League of America, Inc.

The testimony at the trial was substantially undisputed. From it the jury could find that Beauharnais was president of the White Circle League; that, at a meeting on January 6, 1950, he passed out bundles of the lithographs in question, together with other literature, to volunteers for distribution on downtown Chicago street corners the following day; that he carefully organized that distribution, giving detailed instructions for it; and that the leaflets were in fact distributed on January 7 in accordance with his plan and instructions. The court, together with other charges on burden of proof and the like, told the jury 'if you find that the defendant, Joseph Beauharnais, did manufacture, sell, or offer for sale, advertise or publish, present or exhibit in any public place the lithograph then you are to find the defendant guilty.' He refused to charge the jury, as requested by the defendant, that in order to convict they must find 'that the article complained of was likely to produce a clear and present danger of a serious substantive evil that rises for above public inconvenience, annoyance or unrest.' Upon this evidence and these instructions, the jury brought in the conviction here for review.

The statute before us is not a catchall enactment left at large by the State court which applied it. . . . It is a law specifically directed at a defined evil, its language drawing from history and practice in Illinois and in more than a score of other jurisdictions a meaning confirmed by the Supreme Court of that State in upholding this conviction. We do not, therefore, parse the statute as grammarians or treat it as an abstract exercise in lexicography. We read it in the animating context of well-defined usage, . . . and State court construction which determines its meaning for us. . . .

The Illinois Supreme Court tells us that § 224a 'is a form of criminal libel law.' . . . Moreover, the Supreme Court's characterization of the words prohibited by the statute as those 'liable to cause violence and disorder' paraphrases the traditional justification for punishing libels criminally, namely their 'tendency to cause breach of the peace.'

Libel of an individual was a common-law crime, and thus criminal in the colonies. Indeed, at common law, truth or good motives was no defense. In the first decades after the adoption of the Constitution, this was changed by judicial decision, statute or constitution in most States, but nowhere was there any suggestion that the crime of libel be abolished. Today, every American jurisdiction — the forty-eight States, the District of Columbia, Alaska, Hawaii and Puerto Rico — punish libels directed at individuals. 'There are certain well-defined and narrowly limited classes of speech, the prevention and punishment of which have never been thought to raise any Constitutional problem. These include the lewd and obscene, the profane, the libelous, and the insulting or 'fighting' words — those which by their very utterance inflict injury or tend to incite an immediate breach of the peace. It has been well observed that such utterances are no essential part of any exposition of ideas, and are of such slight social value as a step to truth that any benefit that may be derived from them is clearly outweighed by the social interest in order and morality. 'Resort to epithets or personal abuse is not in any proper sense communication of information or opinion safeguarded by the Constitution, and its punishment as a criminal act would raise no question under that instrument.' *Cantwell v. State of Connecticut*, 310 U.S. 296, 309 [1940].' Such were the views of a unanimous Court in *Chaplinsky v. State of New Hampshire*.

No one will gainsay that it is libelous falsely to charge another with being a rapist, robber, carrier of knives and guns, and user of marijuana. The precise question before us, then, is whether the protection of 'liberty' in the Due Process Clause of the Fourteenth Amendment prevents a State from punishing such libels—as criminal libel has been defined, limited and constitutionally recognized time out of mind—directed at designated collectivities and flagrantly disseminated.... But if an utterance directed at an individual may be the object of criminal sanctions, we cannot deny to a State power to punish the same utterance directed at a defined group, unless we can say that this a wilful and purposeless restriction unrelated to the peace and well-being of the State.

Illinois did not have to look beyond her own borders or await the tragic experience of the last three decades[1] to conclude that wilful purveyors of falsehood concerning racial and religious groups promote strife and tend powerfully to obstruct the manifold adjustments required for free, ordered life in a metropolitan, polyglot community. From the murder of the abolitionist Love-joy in 1837 to the Cicero riots of 1951, Illinois has been the scene of exacerbated tension between races, often flaring into violence and destruction. In many of these outbreaks, utterances of the character here in question, so the Illinois legislature could conclude, played a significant part. The law was passed on June 29, 1917, at a time when the State was struggling to assimilate vast numbers of new inhabitants, as yet concentrated in discrete racial or national or religious groups—foreign-born brought to it by the crest of the great wave of immigration, and Negroes attracted by jobs in war plants and the allurements of northern claims. Nine years earlier, in the very city where the legislature sat, what is said to be the first northern race riot had cost the lives of six people, left hundreds of Negroes homeless and shocked citizens into action far beyond the borders of the State. Less than a month before the bill was enacted, East St. Louis had seen a day's rioting, prelude to an out-break, only four days after the bill became law, so bloody that it led to Congressional investigation. A series of bombings had begun which was to culminate two years later in the awful race riot which held Chicago in its grip for seven days in the summer of 1919. Nor has tension and violence between the groups defined in the statute been limited in Illinois to clashes between whites and Negroes.

In the face of this history and its frequent obligato of extreme racial and religious propaganda, we would deny experience to say that the Illinois legislature was without reason in seeking ways to curb false or malicious defamation of racial and religious groups, made in public places and by means calculated to have a powerful emotional impact on those to whom it was presented. 'There are limits to the exercise of these liberties (of speech and of the press). The danger in these times from the coercive activities of those who in the delusion of racial or religious conceit

---

1. [Court's footnote 9] See, e.g., Loewenstein, *Legislative Control of Political Extremism in European Democracies*, 38 Col. L. Rev. 591 and 725; Riesman, *Democracy and Defamation*, 42 Col. L. Rev. 727 ...

would incite violence and breaches of the peace in order to deprive others of their equal right to the exercise of their liberties, is emphasized by events familiar to all. These and other transgressions of those limits the states appropriately may punish.' This was the conclusion, again of a unanimous Court, in 1940. *Cantwell v. State of Connecticut.*

It may be argued, and weightily, that this legislation will not help matters; that tension and on occasion violence between racial and religious groups must be traced to causes more deeply embedded in our society than the rantings of modern Know-Nothings. Only those lacking responsible humility will have a confident solution for problems as intractable as the frictions attributable to differences of race, color or religion. This being so, it would be out of bounds for the judiciary to deny the legislature a choice of policy, provided it is not unrelated to the problem and not forbidden by some explicit limitation on the State's power. That the legislative remedy might not in practice mitigate the evil, or might itself raise new problems, would only manifest once more the para-dox of reform. It is the price to be paid for the trial-and-error inherent in legislative efforts to deal with obstinate social issues. 'The science of government is the most abstruse of all sciences; if, indeed, that can be called a science which has but few fixed principles, and practically consists in little more than the exercise of a sound discretion, applied to the exigencies of the state as they arise. It is the science of experiment.' *Anderson v. Dunn*, 6 Wheat. 204, 226. Certainly the Due Process Clause does not require the legislature to be in the vanguard of science—especially sciences as young as human ecology and cultural anthropology. . . .

Long ago this Court recognized that the economic rights of an individual may depend for the effectiveness of their enforcement on rights in the group, even though not formally corporate, to which he belongs. . . . Such group-protection on behalf of the individual may, for all we know, be a need not confined to the part that a trade union plays in effectuating rights abstractly recognized as belonging to its members. It is not within our competence to confirm or deny claims of social scientists as to the dependence of the individual on the position of his racial or religious group in the community. It would, however, be arrant dogmatism, quite outside the scope of our authority in passing on the powers of a State, for us to deny that the Illinois Legislature may warrantably believe that a man's job and his educational opportunities and the dignity accorded him may depend as much on the reputation of the racial and religious group to which he willy-nilly belongs, as on his own merits. This being so, we are precluded from saying that speech concededly punishable when immediately directed at individuals cannot be outlawed if directed at groups with whose position and esteem in society the affiliated individual may be inextricably involved.

We are warned that the choice open to the Illinois legislature here may be abused, that the law may be discriminatorily enforced; prohibiting libel of a creed or of a racial group, we are told, is but a step from prohibiting libel of a political party.

Every power may be abused, but the possibility of abuse is a poor reason for denying Illinois the power to adopt measures against criminal libels sanctioned by centuries of Anglo-American law. 'While this Court sits' it retains and exercises authority to nullify action which encroaches on freedom of utterance under the guise of punishing libel. Of course discussion cannot be denied and the right, as well as the duty, of criticism must not be stifled.

The scope of the statute before us, as construed by the Illinois court, disposes of the contention that the conduct prohibited by the law is so ill-defined that judges and juries in applying the statute and men in acting cannot draw from it adequate standards to guide them.... Nor, thus construed and limited, is the act so broad that the general verdict of guilty on an indictment drawn in the statutory language might have been predicated on constitutionally protected conduct. On this score, the conviction here reviewed differs from those upset in *Stromberg v. People of State of California*, 283 U.S. 359 [1931]; *Thornhill v. State of Alabama*, 310 U.S. 88 [1940]; and *Terminiello v. City of Chicago*, 337 U.S. 1 [1949]. Even the latter case did not hold that the unconstitutionality of a statute is established because the speech prohibited by it raises a ruckus.

Libelous utterances not being within the area of constitutionally protected speech, it is unnecessary, either for us or for the State courts, to consider the issues behind the phrase 'clear and present danger.' Certainly no one would contend that obscene speech, for example, may be punished only upon a showing of such circumstances. Libel, as we have seen, is in the same class.

We find no warrant in the Constitution for denying to Illinois the power to pass the law here under attack. But it bears repeating — although it should not — that our finding that the law is not constitutionally objectionable carries no implication of approval of the wisdom of the legislation or of its efficacy. These questions may raise doubts in our minds as well as in others. It is not for us, however, to make the legislative judgment. We are not at liberty to erect those doubts into fundamental law.

Affirmed.

MR. JUSTICE BLACK, with whom MR. JUSTICE DOUGLAS concurs, dissenting.

... Today's case degrades First Amendment freedoms to the 'rational basis' level. It is now a certainty that the new 'due process' coverall offers far less protection to liberty than would adherence to our former cases compelling states to abide by the unequivocal First Amendment command that its defined freedoms shall not be abridged.

The Court's holding here and the constitutional doctrine behind it leave the rights of assembly, petition, speech and press almost completely at the mercy of state legislative, executive, and judicial agencies. ...

No rationalization on a purely legal level can conceal the fact that state laws like this one present a constant overhanging threat to freedom of speech, press and religion. Today Beauharnais is punished for publicly expressing strong views in favor of segregation. Ironically enough, Beauharnais, convicted of crime in Chicago, would probably be given a hero's reception in many other localities, if not in some parts of Chicago itself. Moreover, the same kind of state law that makes Beauharnais a criminal for advocating segregation in Illinois can be utilized to send people to jail in other states for advocating equality and nonsegregation. What Beauharnais said in his leaflet is mild compared with usual arguments on both sides of racial controversies.

We are told that freedom of petition and discussion are in no danger 'while this Court sits.' This case raises considerable doubt. Since those who peacefully petition for changes in the law are not to be protected 'while this Court sits,' who is? I do not agree that the Constitution leaves freedom of petition, assembly, speech, press or worship at the mercy of a case-by-case, day-by-day majority of this Court. I had supposed that our people could rely for their freedom on the Constitution's commands, rather than on the grace of this Court on an individual case basis. . . .

Mr. Justice Reed, with whom Mr. Justice Douglas joins, dissenting.

. . . These words — 'virtue,' 'derision,' and 'obloquy' — have neither general nor special meanings well enough known to apprise those within their reach as to limitations on speech. . . . Philosophers and poets, thinkers of high and low degree from every age and race have sought to expound the meaning of virtue, but each teaches his own conception of the moral excellence that satisfies standards of good conduct. Are the tests of the Puritan or the Cavalier to be applied, those of the city or the farm, the Christian or non-Christian, the old or the young? Does the Bill of Rights permit Illinois to forbid any reflection on the virtue of racial or religious classes which a jury or a judge may think exposes them to derision or obloquy, words themselves of quite uncertain meaning as used in the statute? I think not. A general and equal enforcement of this law would restrain the mildest expressions of opinion in all those areas where 'virtue' may be thought to have a role. Since this judgment may rest upon these vague and undefined words, which permit within their scope the punishment of incidents secured by the guarantee of free speech, the conviction should be reversed.

Mr. Justice Douglas, dissenting.

Hitler and his Nazis showed how evil a conspiracy could be which was aimed at destroying a race by exposing it to contempt, derision, and obloquy. I would be willing to concede that such conduct directed at a race or group in this country could be made an indictable offense. For such a project would be more than the exercise of free speech. Like picketing, it would be free speech plus.

I would also be willing to concede that even without the element of conspiracy there might be times and occasions when the legislative or executive branch might call a halt to inflammatory talk, such as the shouting of 'fire' in a school or a theatre.

My view is that if in any case other public interests are to override the plain command of the First Amendment, the peril of speech must be clear and present, leaving no room for argument, raising no doubts as to the necessity of curbing speech in order to prevent disaster.

The First Amendment is couched in absolute terms — freedom of speech shall not be abridged. Speech has therefore a preferred position 1 as contrasted to some other civil rights. For example, privacy, equally sacred to some, is protected by the Fourth Amendment only against unreasonable searches and seizures. There is room for regulation of the ways and means of invading privacy. No such leeway is granted the invasion of the right of free speech guaranteed by the First Amendment. Until recent years that had been the course and direction of constitutional law. Yet recently the Court in this and in other cases has engrafted the right of regulation onto the First Amendment by placing in the hands of the legislative branch the right to regulate 'within reasonable limits' the right of free speech. This to me is an ominous and alarming trend. The free trade in ideas which the Framers of the Constitution visualized disappears. In its place there is substituted a new orthodoxy — an orthodoxy that changes with the whims of the age or the day, an orthodoxy which the majority by solemn judgment proclaims to be essential to the safety, welfare, security, morality, or health of society. Free speech in the constitutional sense disappears. Limits are drawn — limits dictated by expediency, political opinion, prejudices or some other desideratum of legislative action. . . .

MR. JUSTICE JACKSON, dissenting.

. . . In this case, neither the court nor jury found or were required to find any injury to any person, or group, or to the public peace, nor to find any probability, let alone any clear and present danger, of injury to any of these. Even though no individuals were named or described as targets of this pamphlet, if it resulted in a riot or caused injury to any individual Negro, such as being refused living quarters in a particular section, house or apartment, or being refused employment, certainly there would be no constitutional obstacle to imposing civil or criminal liability for actual results. But in this case no actual violence and no specific injury was charged or proved.

The leaflet was simply held punishable as criminal libel per se irrespective of its actual or probable consequences. . . .

C. The Marketplace Theory

Abrams v. United States

United States Supreme Court
250 U.S. 616, 40 S. Ct. 17, 63 L. Ed. 1173 (1919)

MR. JUSTICE CLARKE delivered the opinion of the Court.

[T]he five plaintiffs in error, hereinafter designated the defendants, were convicted of conspiring to violate provisions of the Espionage Act . . . as amended May 16, 1918. . . .

Each of the first three counts charged the defendants with conspiring, when the United States was at war with the Imperial Government of Germany, to unlawfully utter, print, write and publish: In the first count, "disloyal, scurrilous and abusive language about the form of Government of the United States"; in the second count, language "intended to bring the form of Government of the United States into contempt, scorn, contumely, and disrepute"; and in the third count, language "intended to incite, provoke and encourage resistance to the United States in said war." The charge in the fourth count was that the defendants conspired "when the United States was at war with the Imperial German Government, . . . unlawfully and willfully, by utterance, writing, printing and publication, to urge, incite and advocate curtailment of production of things and products, to wit, ordnance and ammunition, necessary and essential to the prosecution of the war." The offenses were charged in the language of the act of Congress.

It was charged in each count of the indictment that it was a part of the conspiracy that the defendants would attempt to accomplish their unlawful purpose by printing, writing and distributing in the City of New York many copies of a leaflet or circular, printed in the English language, and of another printed in the Yiddish language, copies of which, properly identified, were attached to the indictment.

All of the five defendants were born in Russia. They were intelligent, had considerable schooling, and at the time they were arrested they had lived in the United States terms varying from five to ten years, but none of them had applied for naturalization. Four of them testified as witnesses in their own behalf, and of these, three frankly avowed that they were "rebels," "revolutionists," "anarchists," that they did not believe in government in any form, and they declared that they had no interest whatever in the government of the United States. The fourth defendant testified that he was a "socialist" and believed in "a proper kind of government, not capitalistic," but in his classification the Government of the United States was "capitalistic."

It was admitted on the trial that the defendants had united to print and distribute the described circulars and that five thousand of them had been printed and distributed about the 22d day of August, 1918. The group had a meeting place in New York City, in rooms rented by defendant Abrams, under an assumed name, and there the subject of printing the circulars was discussed about two weeks before the defendants were arrested. The defendant Abrams, although not a printer, on July 27, 1918, purchased the printing outfit with which the circulars were printed and installed it in a basement room where the work was done at night. The circulars were distributed, some by throwing them from a window of a building where one of the defendants was employed and others secretly, in New York City. . . .

On the record thus described it is argued, somewhat faintly, that the acts charged against the defendants were not unlawful because within the protection of that freedom of speech and of the press which is guaranteed by the First Amendment to the Constitution of the United States, and that the entire Espionage Act is unconstitutional because in conflict with that amendment.

This contention is sufficiently discussed and is definitely negatived in *Schenck v. United States*, 249 U.S. 47 (1919). . . .

The first of the two articles attached to the indictment is conspicuously headed, "The Hypocrisy of the United States and her Allies." After denouncing President

Wilson as a hypocrite and a coward because troops were sent into Russia, it proceeds to assail our government in general. . . .

Among the capitalistic nations Abrams testified the United States was included.

Growing more inflammatory as it proceeds, the circular culminates in:

The Russian Revolution cries: Workers of the World! Awake! Rise! Put down your enemy and mine!

Yes! Friends, there is only one enemy of the workers of the world and that is CAPITALISM.

This is clearly an appeal to the "workers" of this country to arise and put down by force the government of the United States which they characterize as their "hypocritical," "cowardly" and "capitalistic" enemy.

It concludes:

Awake! Awake, you Workers of the World!

REVOLUTIONISTS.

The second of the articles was printed in the Yiddish language and in the translation is headed, "Workers — Wake Up." After referring to "his Majesty, Mr. Wilson, and the rest of the gang; dogs of all colors!," it continues:

Workers, Russian emigrants, you who had the least belief in the honesty of *our* Government,

— which defendants admitted referred to the United States Government —

must now throw away all confidence, must spit in the face the false, hypocritic, military propaganda which has fooled you so relentlessly, calling forth your sympathy, your help, to the prosecution of the war.

The purpose of this obviously was to persuade the persons to whom it was addressed to turn a deaf ear to patriotic appeals in behalf of the government of the United States, and to cease to render it assistance in the prosecution of the war.

It goes on:

With the money which you have loaned, or are going to loan them, they will make bullets not only for the Germans, but also for the Workers Soviets of Russia. *Workers in the ammunition factories, you are producing bullets, bayonets, cannon, to murder not only the Germans, but also your dearest, best, who are in Russia and are fighting for freedom.*

It will not do to say, as is now argued, that the only intent of these defendants was to prevent injury to the Russian cause. Men must be held to have intended, and to be accountable for, the effects which their acts were likely to produce. Even if their primary purpose and intent was to aid the cause of the Russian Revolution, the plan of action which they adopted necessarily involved, before it could be realized, defeat of the war program of the United States, for the obvious effect of this appeal, if it should become effective, as they hoped it might, would be to persuade persons of character such as those whom they regarded themselves as addressing, not to aid government loans and not to work in ammunition factories, where their work would produce "bullets, bayonets, cannon" and other munitions of war, the use of which would cause the "murder" of Germans and Russians. . . .

This is not an attempt to bring about a change of administration by candid discussion, for no matter what may have incited the outbreak on the part of the defendant anarchists, the manifest purpose of such a publication was to create an attempt to defeat the war plans of the government of the United States, by bringing upon the country the paralysis of a general strike, thereby arresting the production of all munitions and other things essential to the conduct of the war. . . .

That the interpretation we have put upon these articles, circulated in the greatest port of our land, from which great numbers of soldiers were at the time taking ship daily, and in which great quantities of war supplies of every kind were at the time being manufactured for transportation overseas, is not only the fair interpretation of them, but that it is the meaning which their authors consciously intended should be conveyed by them to others is further shown by the additional writings found in the meeting place of the defendant group and on the person of one of them. One of these circulars is headed: "Revolutionists! Unite for Action!"

After denouncing the President as "Our Kaiser" and the hypocrisy of the United States and her Allies, this article concludes:

Socialists, Anarchists, Industrial Workers of the World, Socialists, Labor party men and other revolutionary organizations *Unite for Action* and let us save the Workers' Republic of Russia!

Know you lovers of freedom that in order to save the Russian revolution, we must keep the armies of the allied countries busy at home.

Thus was again avowed the purpose to throw the country into a state of revolution if possible and to thereby frustrate the military program of the government. . . .

The remaining article, after denouncing the President for what is characterized as hostility to the Russian revolution, continues:

We, the toilers of America, who believe in real liberty, shall *pledge ourselves*, in case the United States will participate in the bloody conspiracy against Russia, *to create so great a disturbance that the autocrats of America shall be compelled to keep their armies at home, and not be able to spare any for Russia.*

It concludes with this definite threat of armed rebellion:

If they will use arms against the Russian people to enforce their standard of order, *so will we use arms*, and they shall never see the ruin of the Russian Revolution.

These excerpts sufficiently show, that while the immediate occasion for this particular outbreak of lawlessness, on the part of the defendant alien anarchists, may have been resentment caused by our government sending troops into Russia as a strategic operation against the Germans on the eastern battle front, yet the plain purpose of their propaganda was to excite, at the supreme crisis of the war, disaffection, sedition, riots, and, as they hoped, revolution, in this country for the purpose of embarrassing and if possible defeating the military plans of the government in Europe. A technical distinction may perhaps be taken between disloyal and abusive language applied to the *form* of our government or language intended to bring the *form* of our government into contempt and disrepute, and language of like character and intended to produce like results directed against the President and Congress, the agencies through which that form of government must function in time of war. But it is not necessary to a decision of this case to consider whether such distinction is vital or merely formal, for the language of these circulars was obviously intended to provoke and to encourage resistance to the United States in the war, as the third count runs, and, the defendants, in terms, plainly urged and advocated a resort to a general strike of workers in ammunition factories for the purpose of curtailing the production of ordnance and munitions necessary and essential to the prosecution of the war as is charged in the fourth count. Thus it is clear not only that some evidence but that much persuasive evidence was before the jury tending to prove that the defendants were guilty as charged in both the third and fourth counts of the indictment and the judgment of the District Court must be

Affirmed.

MR. JUSTICE HOLMES, dissenting. . . .

I never have seen any reason to doubt that the questions of law that alone were before this Court in . . . *Schenck* were rightly decided. I do not doubt for a moment that by the same reasoning that would justify punishing persuasion to murder, the United States constitutionally may punish speech that produces or is intended to produce a clear and imminent danger that it will bring about forthwith certain substantive evils that the United States constitutionally may seek to prevent. The power undoubtedly is greater in time of war than in time of peace because war opens dangers that do not exist at other times.

But as against dangers peculiar to war, as against others, the principle of the right to free speech is always the same. It is only the present danger of immediate evil or an intent to bring it about that warrants Congress in setting a limit to the expression of opinion where private rights are not concerned. Congress certainly cannot forbid all effort to change the mind of the country. Now nobody can suppose that the surreptitious publishing of a silly leaflet by an unknown man, without more, would present any immediate danger that its opinions would hinder the success of the government aims or have any appreciable tendency to do so.

In this case sentences of twenty years imprisonment have been imposed for the publishing of two leaflets that I believe the defendants had as much right to publish as the Government has to publish the Constitution of the United States now vainly invoked by them. Even if I am technically wrong and enough can be squeezed from these poor and puny anonymities to turn the color of legal litmus paper; I will add, even if what I think the necessary intent were shown, the most nominal punishment seems to me all that possibly could be inflicted, unless the defendants are to be made to suffer not for what the indictment alleges but for the creed that they avow — a creed that I believe to be the creed of ignorance and immaturity when honestly held, as I see no reason to doubt that it was held here, but which, although made the subject of examination at the trial, no one has a right even to consider in dealing with the charges before the Court.

Persecution for the expression of opinions seems to me perfectly logical. If you have no doubt of your premises or your power and want a certain result with all your heart you naturally express your wishes in law and sweep away all opposition. To allow opposition by speech seems to indicate that you think the speech impotent, as when a man says that he has squared the circle, or that you do not care wholeheartedly for the result, or that you doubt either your power or your premises. But when men have realized that time has upset many fighting faiths, they may come to believe even more than they believe the very foundations of their own conduct that the ultimate good desired is better reached by free trade in ideas — that the best test of truth is the power of the thought to get itself accepted in the competition of the market, and that truth is the only ground upon which their wishes safely can be carried out. That at any rate is the theory of our Constitution. It is an experiment, as all life is an experiment. Every year if not every day we have to wager our salvation upon some prophecy based upon imperfect knowledge. While that experiment is part of our system I think that we should be eternally vigilant against attempts to check the expression of opinions that we loathe and believe to be fraught with death, unless they so imminently threaten immediate interference with the lawful and pressing purposes of the law that an immediate check is required to save the country. . . . Only the emergency that makes it immediately dangerous to leave the correction of evil counsels to time warrants making any exception to the sweeping command, "Congress shall make no law . . . abridging the freedom of speech." Of course I am speaking only of expressions of opinion and exhortations, which were all that were uttered here, but I regret that I cannot put into more impressive words my belief that in their conviction upon this indictment the defendants were deprived of their rights under the Constitution of the United States.

Mr. Justice Brandeis concurs with the foregoing opinion.

Whitney v. California

United States Supreme Court
274 U.S. 357, 47 S. Ct. 641, 71 L. Ed. 1095 (1927)

[Charlotte Anita Whitney was convicted of violating the California Criminal Syndicalism Act. The majority opinion of the Supreme Court affirmed her conviction, rejecting her constitutional defenses. Justice Brandeis concurred, largely because, as explained in the end of his opinion, Whitney had not properly raised her First Amendment defenses below. His opinion, while styled a concurrence, was in substance a dissent. It is one of the most famous opinions of Justice Brandeis' career, and a powerful argument for heightened protection for freedom of speech.]

Mr. Justice Brandeis, concurring.

Miss Whitney was convicted of the felony of assisting in organizing, in the year 1919, the Communist Labor Party of California, of being a member of it, and of assembling with it. These acts are held to constitute a crime, because the party was formed to teach criminal syndicalism. The statute which made these acts a crime restricted the right of free speech and of assembly theretofore existing. The claim is that the statute, as applied, denied to Miss Whitney the liberty guaranteed by the Fourteenth Amendment.

The felony which the statute created is a crime very unlike the old felony of conspiracy or the old misdemeanor of unlawful assembly. The mere act of assisting in forming a society for teaching syndicalism, of becoming a member of it, or assembling with others for that purpose is given the dynamic quality of crime. There is guilt although the society may not contemplate immediate promulgation of the doctrine. Thus the accused is to be punished, not for attempt, incitement or conspiracy, but for a step in preparation, which, if it threatens the public order at all, does so only remotely. The novelty in the prohibition introduced is that the statute aims, not at the practice of criminal syndicalism, nor even directly at the preaching of it, but at association with those who propose to preach it.

Despite arguments to the contrary which had seemed to me persuasive, it is settled that the due process clause of the Fourteenth Amendment applies to matters of substantive law as well as to matters of procedure. Thus all fundamental rights comprised within the term liberty are protected by the federal Constitution from invasion by the states. The right of free speech, the right to teach and the right of assembly are, of course, fundamental rights. These may not be denied or abridged. But, although the rights of free speech and assembly are fundamental, they are not in their nature absolute. Their exercise is subject to restriction, if the particular restriction proposed is required in order to protect the state from destruction or from serious injury, political, economic or moral. That the necessity which is essential to a valid restriction does not exist unless speech would produce, or is intended to produce, a clear and imminent danger of some substantive evil which the state constitutionally may seek to prevent has been settled.

It is said to be the function of the Legislature to determine whether at a particular time and under the particular circumstances the formation of, or assembly with, a society organized to advocate criminal syndicalism constitutes a clear and present danger of substantive evil; and that by enacting the law here in question the Legislature of California determined that question in the affirmative. The Legislature must obviously decide, in the first instance, whether a danger exists which calls for a particular protective measure. But where a statute is valid only in case certain conditions exist, the enactment of the statute cannot alone establish the facts which are essential to its validity. Prohibitory legislation has repeatedly been held invalid, because unnecessary, where the denial of liberty involved was that of engaging in a particular business. The powers of the courts to strike down an offending law are no less when the interests involved are not property rights, but the fundamental personal rights of free speech and assembly.

This court has not yet fixed the standard by which to determine when a danger shall be deemed clear; how remote the danger may be and yet be deemed present; and what degree of evil shall be deemed sufficiently substantial to justify resort to abridgment of free speech and assembly as the means of protection. To reach sound conclusions on these matters, we must bear in mind why a state is, ordinarily, denied the power to prohibit dissemination of social, economic and political doctrine which a vast majority of its citizens believes to be false and fraught with evil consequence.

Those who won our independence believed that the final end of the state was to make men free to develop their faculties, and that in its government the deliberative forces should prevail over the arbitrary. They valued liberty both as an end and as a means. They believed liberty to the secret of happiness and courage to be the secret of liberty. They believed that freedom to think as you will and to speak as you think are means indispensable to the discovery and spread of political truth; that without free speech and assembly discussion would be futile; that with them, discussion affords ordinarily adequate protection against the dissemination of noxious doctrine; that the greatest menace to freedom is an inert people; that public discussion is a political duty; and that this should be a fundamental principle of the American government.[2] They recognized the risks to which all human institutions are subject. But they knew that order cannot be secured merely through fear of punishment for its infraction; that it is hazardous to discourage thought, hope and imagination; that fear breeds repression; that repression breeds hate; that hate menaces stable

---

2. [Court's Footnote 3] *Compare* Thomas Jefferson: "We have nothing to fear from the demoralizing reasonings of some, if others are left free to demonstrate their errors and especially when the law stands ready to punish the first criminal act produced by the false reasonings; these are safer corrections than the conscience of the judge." Quoted by Charles A. Beard, *The Nation*, July 7, 1926, Vol. 123, p. 8. Also in first Inaugural Address: "If there be any among us who would wish to dissolve this union or change its republican form, let them stand undisturbed as monuments of the safety with which error of opinion may be tolerated where reason is left free to combat it."

government; that the path of safety lies in the opportunity to discuss freely supposed grievances and proposed remedies; and that the fitting remedy for evil counsels is good ones. Believing in the power of reason as applied through public discussion, they eschewed silence coerced by law — the argument of force in its worst form. Recognizing the occasional tyrannies of governing majorities, they amended the Constitution so that free speech and assembly should be guaranteed.

Fear of serious injury cannot alone justify suppression of free speech and assembly. Men feared witches and burnt women. It is the function of speech to free men from the bondage of irrational fears. To justify suppression of free speech there must be reasonable ground to fear that serious evil will result if free speech is practiced. There must be reasonable ground to believe that the danger apprehended is imminent. There must be reasonable ground to believe that the evil to be prevented is a serious one. Every denunciation of existing law tends in some measure to increase the probability that there will be violation of it. Condonation of a breach enhances the probability. Expressions of approval add to the probability. Propagation of the criminal state of mind by teaching syndicalism increases it. Advocacy of lawbreaking heightens it still further. But even advocacy of violation, however reprehensible morally, is not a justification for denying free speech where the advocacy falls short of incitement and there is nothing to indicate that the advocacy would be immediately acted on. The wide difference between advocacy and incitement, between preparation and attempt, between assembling and conspiracy, must be borne in mind. In order to support a finding of clear and present danger it must be shown either that immediate serious violence was to be expected or was advocated, or that the past conduct furnished reason to believe that such advocacy was then contemplated.

Those who won our independence by revolution were not cowards. They did not fear political change. They did not exalt order at the cost of liberty. To courageous, self-reliant men, with confidence in the power of free and fearless reasoning applied through the processes of popular government, no danger flowing from speech can be deemed clear and present, unless the incidence of the evil apprehended is so imminent that it may befall before there is opportunity for full discussion. If there be time to expose through discussion the falsehood and fallacies, to avert the evil by the processes of education, the remedy to be applied is more speech, not enforced silence. Only an emergency can justify repression. Such must be the rule if authority is to be reconciled with freedom. Such, in my opinion, is the command of the Constitution. It is therefore always open to Americans to challenge a law abridging free speech and assembly by showing that there was no emergency justifying it.

Moreover, even imminent danger cannot justify resort to prohibition of these functions essential to effective democracy, unless the evil apprehended is relatively serious. Prohibition of free speech and assembly is a measure so stringent that it would be inappropriate as the means for averting a relatively trivial harm to society. A police measure may be unconstitutional merely because the remedy, although effective as means of protection, is unduly harsh or oppressive. Thus, a state might, in the exercise of its police power, make any trespass upon the land of another a crime, regardless of the results or of the intent or purpose of the trespasser. It might, also, punish an attempt, a conspiracy, or an incitement to commit the trespass. But it is hardly conceivable that this court would hold constitutional a statute which punished as a felony the mere voluntary assembly with a society formed to teach that pedestrians had the moral right to cross uninclosed, unposted, waste lands and to advocate their doing so, even if there was imminent danger that advocacy would lead to a trespass. The fact that speech is likely to result in some violence or in destruction of property is not enough to justify its suppression. There must be the probability of serious injury to the State. Among free men, the deterrents ordinarily to be applied to prevent crime are education and punishment for violations of the law, not abridgment of the rights of free speech and assembly.

The California Syndicalism Act recites in section 4: "Inasmuch as this act concerns and is necessary to the immediate preservation of the public peace and safety, for the reason that at the present time large numbers of persons are going from place to place in this state advocating, teaching, and practicing criminal syndicalism, this act shall take effect upon approval by the Governor."

This legislative declaration satisfies the requirement of the Constitution of the state concerning emergency legislation. But it does not preclude inquiry into the question whether, at the time and under the circumstances, the conditions existed which are essential to validity under the federal Constitution. As a statute, even if not void on its face, may be challenged because invalid as applied the result of such an inquiry may depend upon the specific facts of the particular case. Whenever the fundamental rights of free speech and assembly are alleged to have been invaded, it must remain open to a defendant to present the issue whether there actually did exist at the time a clear danger, whether the danger, if any, was imminent, and whether the evil apprehended was one so substantial as to justify the stringent restriction interposed by the Legislature. The legislative declaration, like the fact that the statute was passed and was sustained by the highest court of the State, creates merely a rebuttable presumption that these conditions have been satisfied.

Whether in 1919, when Miss Whitney did the things complained of, there was in California such clear and present danger of serious evil, might have been made the important issue in the case. She might have required that the issue be determined either by the court or the jury. She claimed below that the statute as applied to her violated the federal Constitution; but she did not claim that it was void because there was no clear and present danger of serious evil, nor did she request that the existence of these conditions of a valid measure thus restricting the rights of free speech and assembly be passed upon by the court or a jury. On the other hand, there was evidence on which the court or jury might have found that such danger existed. I am unable to assent to the suggestion in the opinion of the court that assembling with a political party, formed to advocate the desirability of a proletarian revolution by mass action at some date necessarily far in the future, is not a right within the protection of the Fourteenth Amendment. In the present case, however, there was other testimony which tended to establish the existence of a conspiracy, on the part of members of the International Workers of the World, to commit present serious crimes, and likewise to show that such a conspiracy would be furthered by the activity of the society of which Miss Whitney was a member. Under these circumstances the judgment of the State court cannot be disturbed.

Our power of review in this case is limited not only to the question whether a right guaranteed by the federal Constitution was denied but to the particular claims duly made below, and denied. We lack here the power occasionally exercised on review of judgments of lower federal courts to correct in criminal cases vital errors, although the objection was not taken in the trial court. This is a writ of error to a state court. Because we may not inquire into the errors now alleged I concur in affirming the judgment of the state court.

Mr. Justice Holmes joins in this opinion.

Notes and Questions

(1) The dissenting opinion of Justice Holmes in *Abrams* was something of a turnabout for him. Justices Holmes had previously written three opinions from the same era affirming convictions of anti-war protestors, sending them to jail. The most famous of those opinions was *Schenck v. United States*, 249 U.S. 47 (1919), which was relied upon by the majority in *Abrams* in support of affirming Abrams' conviction. *Schenck* involved anti-war rhetoric and facts virtually identical to *Abrams*. Holmes wrote the opinion for the Court affirming Schenk's conviction. The Holmes opinion contained the following key passage:

> But it is said, suppose that that was the tendency of this circular, it is protected by the First Amendment to the Constitution. Two of the strongest expressions are said to be quoted respectively from well-known public men. It well may be that the prohibition of laws abridging the freedom of speech is not confined to previous restraints, although to prevent them may have been the main purpose. . . . We admit that in many places and in ordinary times the defendants in saying all that was said in the circular would have been within their constitutional rights. But the character of every act depends upon the circumstances in which it is done. . . . The most stringent protection of free speech would not protect a man in falsely shouting fire in a theatre and causing a panic. It does not even protect a man from an injunction against uttering words that may have all the effect of force. . . . The question in every case is whether the words used are used in such circumstances and are of such a nature as to create a clear and present danger that they will bring about the substantive evils that Congress has a right to prevent. It is a question of proximity and degree. When a nation is at war many things that might be said in time of peace are such a hindrance to its effort that their utterance will not be endured so long as men fight and that no Court could regard them as protected by any constitutional right. It seems to be admitted that if an actual obstruction of the recruiting service were proved, liability for words that produced that effect might be enforced.

The statute . . . punishes conspiracies to obstruct as well as actual obstruction. If the act, (speaking, or circulating a paper,) its tendency and the intent with which it is done are the same, we perceive no ground for saying that success alone warrants making the act a crime. . . .

While this passage did contain the "clear and present danger" test, a seemingly "pro-free speech" test, on closer reading, the Holmes opinion in *Schenck* was not very protective of free speech. His famous statement that the most stringent protection of free speech "would not protect a man in falsely shouting fire in a theatre and causing a panic" suggested that anti-war rhetoric uttered in time of war is equivalent to "falsely shouting fire." His opinion also suggested that Americans have diminished free speech protection during times of war, observing that when "a nation is at war many things that might be said in time of peace are such a hindrance to its effort that their utterance will not be endured so long as men fight." Finally, the *Shenck* opinion held that the mere *tendency* of speech to cause harm would be enough to cause it to forfeit constitutional protection. This mere "bad tendency" test seemed to undercut the "clear and present danger" language, and the "bad tendency" test was essentially identical to the "order and morality theory" later articulated in cases such as *Chaplinsky* and *Beauharnais*.

(2) In *Frohwerk v. United States*, 249 U.S. 204 (1919), Holmes wrote the opinion of the Supreme Court affirming the conviction of an obscure printer who circulated pro-German anti-war publications in Missouri. Holmes wrote that "on that record it is impossible to say that it might not have been found that the circulation of the paper was in quarters where a little breath would be enough to kindle a flame."

(3) In *Debs v. United States*, 249 U.S. 211 (1919), Holmes wrote for the Court in affirming the conviction of Eugene Debs, a prominent American labor leader, socialist, and political activist. Debs ran for President of the United States four times. He was famous for his oratory. While giving a speech in Canton, Ohio, Debs expressed sympathy for labor leaders who had been put in jail for opposing the military draft, praised the Russian Revolution, denounced a Supreme Court opinion striking down child labor laws, and asserted that socialism would triumph over capitalism. For his speech, he was arrested by federal authorities and charged with violation of the Espionage and Sedition Acts. Debs addressed the jury himself. "I have been accused of having obstructed the war," Debs told the jury. "I admit it. I abhor war. I would oppose the war if I stood alone." He was convicted and sentenced to ten years in a federal penitentiary. Justice Holmes' opinion for the Supreme Court, affirming Debs' conviction, relied on *Schenck*. It was enough, Holmes reasoned, "that if in that speech he used words tending to obstruct the recruiting service he meant that they should have that effect."

(4) While Holmes paid lip-service to *Schenk* in his *Abrams* dissent, lamely asserting that he had no reason to doubt *Schenck* "was rightly decided," there is no question that Holmes' dissent in *Abrams* represented a dramatic break with *Schenk*, *Frohwerk*, and *Debs*. What exactly caused this sudden conversion to the "marketplace theory" in so short a time remains a compelling legal mystery.

(5) Is speech advocating violent overthrow of the government inconsistent with notions about the process for arriving at truth and achieving change in our system? In a famous article, Judge Robert Bork argued that speech advocating the violent overthrow of government is essentially outside the social compact, making war on the Constitution itself, and undeserving of First Amendment protection. *See* Robert Bork, *Neutral Principles and Some First Amendment Problems*, 47 IND. L.J. 1 (1971). What about our own Declaration of Independence? Should such a document be protected "freedom of speech"?

(6) *Gitlow v. New York*, 268 U.S. 652 (1925), was an especially low point in free speech history. The case arose from the publication by Benjamin Gitlow, a member of the "Left Wing Section" of the Socialist Party in New York, of a document entitled "The Left Wing Manifesto," condemning "moderate socialism," and espousing "revolutionary socialism," "the class struggle," and "the power of the proletariat in action." In *Gitlow*, the Court worked a turn on the clear and present danger test by holding that a legislature could effectively "pre-certify" certain identified classes of speech as satisfying the requirement of proximity to a substantive issue the government has a right to prevent. The Court in *Gitlow* approved proscription of utterances which, "by their very nature, involve danger to the public peace and to the security of the State." If, as Bruce Springsteen says, "you can't start a fire without a spark," the Court in *Gitlow* was convinced that a "single revolutionary spark may kindle a fire that, smoldering for a time, may burst into a sweeping and destructive conflagration."

The Court in *Gitlow* did not require that foreseeable harm be demonstrated in each individual prosecution. Rather, the legislature could make a generic determination applicable to a broad class of speech, and thereby stop individuals from claiming that their particular speech posed no serious threats. Thus, the Court admonished, "when the legislative body has determined generally, in the constitutional exercise of its discretion, that utterances of a certain kind involve such danger of substantive evil that they may be punished, the question whether any specific utterance coming within the prohibited class is likely, in and of itself, to bring about the substantive evil, is not open to consideration."

Holmes and Brandeis dissented. It was impermissible, Holmes argued, to defer to legislative judgment on the question of whether a clear and present danger existed. He then took issue with the assertion that the Left Wing Manifesto for which Gitlow was convicted had gone beyond theory, to the level of "incitement." In a wonderfully compact and emphatic rejoinder, Holmes replied: "Every idea is an incitement." If all that is meant by "incitement" is that the speaker seeks to persuade, then the clear and present danger test is a meaningless sieve. Every idea, Holmes argued, "offers itself for belief, and if believed, it is acted on unless some other belief outweighs it, or some failure of energy stifles the movement at its birth." In a notable insight, Holmes explored the relation between expressions of opinion and incitement, and found that an incitement is often simply a narrower, more focused, more energetic and immediate form of opinion. "The only difference between the expression of an opinion and an incitement in the narrower sense is the speaker's enthusiasm for the result." But certainly, it is not permissible to censor opinion *merely* because it is passionate. "Eloquence may set fire to reason," Holmes admonished, and if in the long run, the views of radical socialists on the proper organization of the community are destined to become the dominant view, "they should be given their chance and have their way." In language reminiscent of his dissent in *Abrams*, Holmes dismissed the notion that Gitlow's manifesto created any imminent danger of violence as transparent and silly, writing that "whatever may be thought of the redundant discourse before us, it had no chance of starting a present conflagration."

(7) In the 1951 decision *Dennis v. United States*, 341 U.S. 494 (1951), the marketplace theory was still far from gaining acceptance. The case involved the convictions of eleven members of the American Communist Party for violating the Smith Act, a federal statute making it unlawful "to knowingly or willfully advocate, abet, advise, or teach the duty, necessity, desirability, or propriety of overthrowing or destroying any government in the United States by force or violence, or by assassination. . . ." The convictions were first appealed to the United States Court of Appeals for the Second Circuit in New York, and were affirmed by the Chief Judge of that court, Learned Hand. In his opinion affirming the convictions, Hand took the clear and present danger test, and purported to explain its meaning in new words. In each case, Hand maintained, courts must "ask whether the gravity of the 'evil,' discounted by its improbability, justifies such invasion of free speech as is necessary to avoid the danger." The Hand test sounded very convincing, but in several crucial respects, it was not the same as the prior Holmes-Brandeis versions of clear and present danger. What Hand had created was not a *proximity* test but a *probability* and *degree of risk* test, in which judges and juries are permitted to engage in a cost-benefit analysis in which the "gravity of the evil" and its "improbability" are assessed together, as interdependent factors, to produce a net risk factor that is then weighed against the incursion on free speech. This means that even speech with a relatively low probability of actually resulting in a danger may still be proscribed if the gravity of that danger is sufficiently high. Thus, whether the defendants in *Dennis* had any real prospect of overthrowing the government of the United States was not as important as the fact that the gravity of the potential harm for which they were convicted was catastrophic.

Indeed, Judge Hand's formula for assessing when it was permissible to impose liability for speech was no different than his formula for assessing when it was permissible to impose liability for all other forms of human activity. In a famous decision written during this same time period, *United States v. Carroll Towing Co.*, 159 F.2d 169 (2d Cir. 1947), for example, Hand was faced with the question of whether the owners of a ship were guilty of negligence. He expressed his analysis algebraically, stating that a party should be deemed negligent if the burden (B) of preventing the accident is less than the loss (L) multiplied by the probability (P) of its occurrence, or whether "B is less than PL."

In *Dennis*, Hand merely took his *Carroll Towing* formula and refitted it for the First Amendment. The invasion of free speech is the "burden" (B), and the key is whether it is less than the "gravity of the harm" (L) discounted by its improbability (P). Implicit in the Hand test in *Dennis*, therefore, was a postulate very unprotective of free speech: regulation of speech was not to be judged under any special methodology, but rather under the same standards applicable to any other form of conduct. Hand applied the same liability rules to speech as he applied to maintaining a tug boat.

Justice Vinson, writing the plurality opinion in *Dennis* for the Supreme Court, liked the Hand reformulation of clear and present danger, and adopted it as his own. With lavish praise, Vinson wrote that "as articulated by Chief Judge Hand, it is as succinct and inclusive as any other we might devise at this time. It takes into consideration those factors which we deem relevant, and relates their significance. More we cannot expect from words." Vinson then used the Hand test to affirm the convictions of the Communist leaders. The question of whether their speech posed any immediate danger to the country was finessed by instead emphasizing the gravity of the potential harm. The phrase "clear and present danger" he explained, "cannot mean that before the Government may act, it must wait until the putsch is about to be executed, the plans have been laid and the signal is awaited."

(8) As evidenced by *Beauharnais*, as late as 1952, the Order and Morality theory still appeared to reign, and the Marketplace Theory advanced by Holmes and Brandeis remained a minority view among Supreme Court Justices. There were some sporadic pre-1952 decisions that did appear to recognize growing protection for free speech. Two such cases were decided in 1937, *De Jonge v. Oregon*, 299 U.S. 353 (1937), and *Herndon v. Lowry*, 301 U.S. 242 (1937). In *De Jonge*, the defendant had been conducting a Communist Party meeting, open to the public, on workers' rights during a bitter maritime strike. No one at the meeting advocated any violence, but De Jonge was still convicted under Oregon's "Criminal Syndicalism" statute, which made his mere conducting of the meeting illegal. The Supreme Court overturned the conviction, and voided a law on the grounds that it violated the First Amendment. Nearly 150 years after the passage of the First Amendment, the Court finally held that a meaningful constitutional line existed separating peaceful from violent dissent.

The other key 1937 case vindicating freedom of speech was, quite fittingly, a case with powerful civil rights overtones, for in the coming decades, freedom of expression would be the strategic phalanx of the civil rights movement, changing America with appeals to conscience. In *Herndon*, the defendant Herndon was a black organizer for the Communist Party. Herndon traveled to Atlanta to recruit members to the Party, espousing a platform of equal rights for blacks, emergency relief for the poor, and unemployment insurance. A booklet Herndon carried advocated tactics of strikes, boycotts, and demonstrations. While Herndon did not cause any violence or advocate any violence, his themes were perceived as violent in Atlanta at the time, and he was convicted under *a slave insurrection* statute that forbade, "any attempt, by persuasion or otherwise, to induce others to join in any combined resistance to the lawful authority of the State." The causes of unemployment insurance, equal rights for blacks, and relief, at least if advanced through boycotts or demonstrations, were regarded as defiance of lawful authority. The Supreme Court overturned Herndon's conviction, holding that it violated the First Amendment.

(9) The Marketplace Theory did not begin its ascendancy until the 1960's, a decade in which a great deal changed in American culture and law. The Civil Rights Movement and the anti-Vietnam War protests fueled a free speech movement that also appeared to take hold in the jurisprudence of the Supreme Court of the United States. In many of the sections of this Chapter that follow, the dominance of the Marketplace Theory is evident. This includes the rules governing incitement, true threats, graphically vulgar or offensive speech, prior restraint doctrines, and the First Amendment principles that constrain tort liability for libel, invasion of privacy, and infliction of emotional distress, particularly in cases involving public officials and public figures.

(10) Yet it will also be seen that the Order and Morality theory is by no means entirely dead. The Order and Morality Theory still dominates in certain pockets of First Amendment law. The First Amendment principles governing obscenity are the most vivid example. The Order and Morality Theory also continues to dominate in certain sectors of society that are deemed outside the general marketplace. The *Chaplinsky* Order and Morality Theory still controls in special settings that constitute "carve outs" from the general marketplace, settings in which the wide-open freedom of the marketplace is displaced by an overriding interest in order or morality or both. The principles governing free speech in public schools, or free speech in the workplace, are prime examples. Citizens may be kicked out of schools or lose their jobs for speech that would be permitted in a public park, but not in a classroom or office.

§ 9.02 Speech and Lawless Activity

A. Incitement

Brandenburg v. Ohio

United States Supreme Court
395 U.S. 444, 89 S. Ct. 1827, 23 L. Ed. 2d 430 (1969)

PER CURIAM.

The appellant, a leader of a Ku Klux Klan group, was convicted under the Ohio Criminal Syndicalism statute for "advocat[ing] . . . the duty, necessity, or propriety of crime, sabotage, violence, or unlawful methods of terrorism as a means of accomplishing industrial or political reform" and for "voluntarily assembl[ing] with any society, group, or assemblage of persons formed to teach or advocate the doctrines of criminal syndicalism." . . . He was fined $1,000 and sentenced to one to 10 years imprisonment. The appellant challenged the constitutionality of the criminal syndicalism statute under the First and Fourteenth Amendments to the United States

Constitution, but the intermediate appellate court of Ohio affirmed his conviction without opinion. The Supreme Court of Ohio dismissed his appeal, *sua sponte*, "for the reason that no substantial constitutional question exists herein." It did not file an opinion or explain its conclusions. Appeal was taken to this Court, and we noted probable jurisdiction. . . . We reverse.

The record shows that a man, identified at trial as the appellant, telephoned an announcer-reporter on the staff of a Cincinnati television station and invited him to come to a Ku Klux Klan "rally" to be held at a farm in Hamilton County. With the cooperation of the organizers, the reporter and a cameraman attended the meeting and filmed the events. Portions of the films were later broadcast on the local station and on a national network.

The prosecution's case rested on the films and on testimony identifying the appellant as the person who communicated with the reporter and who spoke at the rally. The State also introduced into evidence several articles appearing in the film, including a pistol, a rifle, a shotgun, ammunition, a Bible, and a red hood worn by the speaker in the films.

One film showed 12 hooded figures, some of whom carried firearms. They were gathered around a large wooden cross, which they burned. No one was present other than the participants and the newsmen who made the film. Most of the words uttered during the scene were incomprehensible when the film was projected, but scattered phrases could be understood that were derogatory of Negroes and, in one instance, of Jews. Another scene on the same film showed the appellant, in Klan regalia, making a speech. The speech, in full, was as follows:

> This is an organizers' meeting. We have had quite a few members here today which are — we have hundreds, hundreds of members throughout the State of Ohio. I can quote from a newspaper clipping from the Columbus, Ohio *Dispatch*, five weeks ago Sunday morning. The Klan has more members in the State of Ohio than does any other organization. We're not a revengent [sic] organization, but if our President, our Congress, our Supreme Court, continues to suppress the white, Caucasian race, it's possible that there might have to be some revengeance [sic] taken.
>
> We are marching on Congress July the Fourth, four hundred thousand strong. From there we are dividing into two groups, one group to march on St. Augustine, Florida, the other group to march into Mississippi. Thank you.

The second film showed six hooded figures one of whom, later identified as the appellant, repeated a speech very similar to that recorded on the first film. The reference to the possibility of "revengeance" was omitted, and one sentence was added: "Personally, I believe the nigger should be returned to Africa, the Jew returned to Israel." Though some of the figures in the films carried weapons, the speaker did not.

 . . . [Our] decisions have fashioned the principle that the constitutional guarantees of free speech and free press do not permit a State to forbid or proscribe advocacy of the use of force or of law violation except where such advocacy is directed to inciting or producing imminent lawless action and is likely to incite or produce such action. . . .

Measured by this test, Ohio's Criminal Syndicalism Act cannot be sustained. The Act punishes persons who "advocate or teach the duty, necessity, or propriety" of violence "as a means of accomplishing industrial or political reform"; or who publish or circulate or display any book or paper containing such advocacy; or who "justify" the commission of violent acts "with intent to exemplify, spread or advocate the propriety of the doctrines of criminal syndicalism"; or who "voluntarily assemble" with a group formed "to teach or advocate the doctrines of criminal syndicalism." Neither the indictment nor the trial judge's instructions to the jury in any way refined the statute's bald definition of the crime in terms of mere advocacy not distinguished from incitement to imminent lawless action.

Accordingly, we are here confronted with a statute which, by its own words and as applied, purports to punish mere advocacy and to forbid, on pain of criminal punishment, assembly with others merely to advocate the described type of action. Such a statute falls within the condemnation of the First and Fourteenth Amendments. . . .

Reversed.

Mr. Justice Black, Concurring [Omitted].

Mr. Justice Douglas, concurring.

While I join the opinion of the Court, I desire to enter a *caveat*. . . .

. . . I see no place in the regime of the First Amendment for any "clear and present danger" test, whether strict and tight as some would make it, or free-wheeling as the Court in *Dennis* [*v. United States*, 183 F.2d 201 (2d Cir.) *aff'd*, 341 U.S. 494 (1951)] rephrased it.

When one reads the opinions closely and sees when and how the "clear and present danger" test has been applied, great misgivings are aroused. First, the threats were often loud but always puny and made serious only by judges so wedded to the *status quo* that critical analysis made them nervous. Second, the test was so twisted and perverted in *Dennis* as to make the trial of those teachers of Marxism an all-out political trial which was part and parcel of the cold war that has eroded substantial parts of the First Amendment. . . .

One's beliefs have long been thought to be sanctuaries which government could not invade. . . . I think that all matters of belief are beyond the reach of subpoenas or the probings of investigators. . . .

The line between what is permissible and not subject to control and what may be made impermissible and subject to regulation is the line between ideas and overt acts.

The example usually given by those who would punish speech is the case of one who falsely shouts fire in a crowded theatre.

This is, however, a classic case where speech is brigaded with action. . . . They are indeed inseparable and a prosecution can be launched for the overt acts actually caused. Apart from rare instances of that kind, speech is, I think, immune from prosecution. Certainly there is no constitutional line between advocacy of abstract ideas . . . and advocacy of political action. . . . The quality of advocacy turns on the depth of the conviction; and government has no power to invade that sanctuary of belief and conscience.

Notes and Questions

(1) In *Hess v. Indiana*, 414 U.S. 105 (1973) (*per curiam*), the Court set aside a conviction under Indiana's disorderly conduct statute. In so doing, the Court stated:

The events leading to Hess' conviction began with an antiwar demonstration on the campus of Indiana University. In the course of the demonstration, approximately 100 to 150 of the demonstrators moved onto a public street and blocked the passage of vehicles. When the demonstrators did not respond to verbal directions from the sheriff to clear the street, the sheriff and his deputies began walking up the street, and the demonstrators in their path moved to the curbs on either side, joining a large number of spectators who had gathered. Hess was standing off the street as the sheriff passed him. The sheriff heard Hess utter the word "fuck" in what he later described as a loud voice and immediately arrested him on the disorderly conduct charge. It was later stipulated that what appellant had said was "We'll take the fucking street later," or "We'll take the fucking street again." Two witnesses who were in the immediate vicinity testified, apparently without contradiction, that they heard Hess' words and witnessed his arrest. They indicated that Hess did not appear to be exhorting the crowd to go back into the street, that he was facing the crowd and not the street when he uttered the statement, that his statement did not appear to be addressed to any particular person or group, and that his tone, although loud, was no louder than that of the other people in the area.

. . . The Indiana Supreme Court placed primary reliance on the trial court's finding that Hess' statement "was intended to incite further lawless action on the part of the crowd in the vicinity of appellant and was likely to produce such action." . . . At best, however, the statement could be taken as counsel for present moderation; at worst, it amounted to nothing more than advocacy of illegal action at some indefinite future time. This is not sufficient to permit the State to punish Hess' speech. Under our decisions, "the constitutional guarantees of free speech and free press do not permit a State to forbid or proscribe advocacy of the use of force or of law violation except where such advocacy is directed to inciting or producing *imminent* lawless action and is likely to incite or produce such action." *Brandenburg v. Ohio*, 395 U.S. 444, 447 (1969). (Emphasis added.) . . . Since the uncontroverted evidence showed that Hess' statement was not directed to any person or group of persons, it cannot be said that he was advocating, in the normal sense, any action. And since there was no evidence, or rational inference from the import of the language, that his words were intended to produce, and likely to produce, disorder, those words could not be punished by the State on the ground that they had "a tendency to lead to violence."

(2) After *Brandenburg*, the Court repudiated the notion from *Gitlow* that deference was owed to legislative determinations that speech posed a clear and present danger. *See, e.g., Landmark Communications, Inc. v. Virginia*, 435 U.S. 829 (1978).

(3) Incitement cases often pose the conundrum of the "heckler's veto." When a speaker is acting lawfully, but is stirring up audience reaction against the speaker, what is the obligation of the police? May hecklers, by threatening to become violent, effectively silence the speaker, by forcing the police to arrest speaker? Or do the police have an obligation to protect the speaker and arrest the hecklers, even though that may require considerably more force, and possibly lead to uncontrolled violence?

The answer under the "Order and Morality" theory may allow the government to arrest the speaker. The Order and Morality theory, for example, would justify arresting or shutting down the racist and anti-Semitic white supremacists who descended on Charlottesville, Virginia in the summer of 2017, particularly at the infamous "Unite the Right Rally" that led to the tragic death of Heather Heyer.

The case of *Feiner v. New York*, 340 U.S. 315 (1951), for example, took place in 1951, still within the "Order and Morality" era. The case arose from an incident in which Irving Feiner was addressing an open-air meeting at the corner of South McBride and Harrison Streets in Syracuse, New York. Feiner was standing on a large wooden box on the sidewalk, addressing the crowd through a loudspeaker system attached to an automobile. The purpose of his speech was to urge people to attend a meeting to be held that evening at the Syracuse Hotel. During the course of his speech he made derogatory remarks about President Harry Truman, the American Legion, the Mayor of Syracuse, and other local political officials. Chief Justice Vinson, writing for the majority of the Supreme Court, described what happened next:

> The police officers made no effort to interfere with petitioner's speech, but were first concerned with the effect of the crowd on both pedestrian and vehicular traffic. They observed the situation from the opposite side of the street, noting that some pedestrians were forced to walk in the street to avoid the crowd. Since traffic was passing at the time, the officers attempted to get the people listening to petitioner back on the sidewalk. The crowd was restless and there was some pushing, shoving and milling around. One of the officers telephoned the police station from a nearby store, and then both policemen crossed the street and mingled with the crowd without any intention of arresting the speaker.
>
> At this time, petitioner was speaking in a "loud, high pitched voice." He gave the impression that he was endeavoring to arouse the Negro people

against the whites, urging that they rise up in arms and fight for equal rights. The statements before such a mixed audience "stirred up a little excitement." Some of the onlookers made remarks to the police about their inability to handle the crowd and at least one threatened violence if the police did not act. There were others who appeared to be favoring petitioner's arguments. Because of the feeling that existed in the crowd both for and against the speaker, the officers finally "stepped in to prevent it from resulting in a fight." One of the officers approached the petitioner, not for the purpose of arresting him, but to get him to break up the crowd. He asked petitioner to get down off the box, but the latter refused to accede to his request and continued talking. The officer waited for a minute and then demanded that he cease talking. Although the officer had thus twice requested petitioner to stop over the course of several minutes, petitioner not only ignored him but continued talking. During all this time, the crowd was pressing closer around petitioner and the officer. Finally, the officer told petitioner he was under arrest and ordered him to get down from the box, reaching up to grab him. Petitioner stepped down, announcing over the microphone that "the law has arrived, and I suppose they will take over now." In all, the officer had asked petitioner to get down off the box three times over a space of four or five minutes. Petitioner had been speaking for over a half hour.

On these facts, Feiner was convicted of breach of peace, and the Supreme Court sustained the conviction by a 6-3 vote. Chief Justice Vinson maintained that the "ordinary murmurings and objections of a hostile audience cannot be allowed to silence a speaker," and that "overzealous police officials" could not have "complete discretion to break up otherwise lawful public meetings," but insisted that "when as here the speaker passes the bounds of argument or persuasion and undertakes incitement to riot," the police may arrest the speaker to prevent a breach of peace.

In his dissent, Justice Black argued that Feiner had been "sentenced to the penitentiary for the unpopular views he expressed on matters of public interest while lawfully making a street-corner speech in Syracuse."

(4) As we will see, however, more modern cases reject the "heckler's veto" notion — in the sense that they side with the offensive or controversial speaker, and against the power of hecklers — even hecklers that may represent the views most decent people of good will believe in — to shut down the controversial speaker. The Supreme Court thus denounced the heckler's veto in *Reno v. American Civil Liberties Union*, 521 U.S. 844 (1997), dealing with offensive speech on the Internet.

(5) *Brandenburg* and its progeny often pose particularly difficult problems when efforts are made to impose civil liability on those who publish violent material that allegedly leads to violence or threats of violence. In the so-called "Hit Man case," *Rice v. Paladin Enterprises, Inc.*, 128 F.3d 233 (4th Cir. 1997), *cert. denied*, 573 U.S. 1074 (1998), the core of the plaintiffs' claim was that the publisher of the murder manual *Hit Man: A Technical Manual for Independent Contractors* had aided and

threatening the President. Again, however, threats against the President are not generally identified by reference to the content of any message that may accompany the threat, let alone any viewpoint, and there is no obvious correlation in fact between victim and message. Millions of statements are made about the President every day on every subject and from every standpoint; threats of violence are not an integral feature of any one subject or viewpoint as distinct from others. Differential treatment of threats against the President, then, selects nothing but special risks, not special messages. A content-based proscription of cross burning, on the other hand, may be a subtle effort to ban not only the intensity of the intimidation cross burning causes when done to threaten, but also the particular message of white supremacy that is broadcast even by nonthreatening cross burning.

I thus read *R.A.V.*'s examples of the particular virulence exception as covering prohibitions that are not clearly associated with a particular viewpoint, and that are consequently different from the Virginia statute. On that understanding of things, I necessarily read the majority opinion as treating *R.A.V.*'s virulence exception in a more flexible, pragmatic manner than the original illustrations would suggest. Actually, another way of looking at today's decision would see it as a slight modification of *R.A.V.*'s third exception, which allows content-based discrimination within a proscribable category when its "nature" is such "that there is no realistic possibility that official suppression of ideas is afoot." *R.A.V.* The majority's approach could be taken as recognizing an exception to *R.A.V.* when circumstances show that the statute's ostensibly valid reason for punishing particularly serious proscribable expression probably is not a ruse for message suppression, even though the statute may have a greater (but not exclusive) impact on adherents of one ideology than on others.

III

My concern here, in any event, is not with the merit of a pragmatic doctrinal move. For whether or not the Court should conceive of exceptions to *R.A.V.*'s general rule in a more practical way, no content-based statute should survive even under a pragmatic recasting of *R.A.V.* without a high probability that no "official suppression of ideas is afoot." I believe the prima facie evidence provision stands in the way of any finding of such a high probability here.

Virginia's statute provides that burning a cross on the property of another, a highway, or other public place is "prima facie evidence of an intent to intimidate a person or group of persons." Va.Code Ann. § 18.2-423 (1996). While that language was added by amendment to the earlier portion of the statute criminalizing cross burning with intent to intimidate, it was a part of the prohibitory statute at the time these respondents burned crosses, and the whole statute at the time of respondents' conduct is what counts for purposes of the First Amendment.

As I see the likely significance of the evidence provision, its primary effect is to skew jury deliberations toward conviction in cases where the evidence of intent to intimidate is relatively weak and arguably consistent with a solely ideological reason for burning. To understand how the provision may work, recall that the symbolic act of burning a cross, without more, is consistent with both intent to intimidate and intent to make an ideological statement free of any aim to threaten. One can tell the intimidating instance from the wholly ideological one only by reference to some further circumstance. In the real world, of course, and in real-world prosecutions, there will always be further circumstances, and the factfinder will always learn something more than the isolated fact of cross burning. Sometimes those circumstances will show an intent to intimidate, but sometimes they will be at least equivocal, as in cases where a white supremacist group burns a cross at an initiation ceremony or political rally visible to the public. In such a case, if the factfinder is aware of the prima facie evidence provision, as the jury was in respondent Black's case, the provision will have the practical effect of tilting the jury's thinking in favor of the prosecution. What is significant is not that the provision permits a factfinder's conclusion that the defendant acted with proscribable and punishable intent without any further indication, because some such indication will almost always be presented. What is significant is that the provision will encourage a factfinder to err on the side of a finding of intent to intimidate when the evidence of circumstances fails to point with any clarity either to the criminal intent or to the permissible one. The effect of such a distortion is difficult to remedy, since any guilty verdict will survive sufficiency review unless the defendant can show that, "viewing the evidence in the light most favorable to the prosecution, [no] rational trier of fact could have found the essential elements of the crime beyond a reasonable doubt." *Jackson v. Virginia*, 443 U.S. 307, 319 (1979). The provision will thus tend to draw nonthreatening ideological expression within the ambit of the prohibition of intimidating expression, as JUSTICE O'CONNOR notes.

To the extent the prima facie evidence provision skews prosecutions, then, it skews the statute toward suppressing ideas. Thus, the appropriate way to consider the statute's prima facie evidence term, in my view, is not as if it were an overbroad statutory definition amenable to severance or a narrowing construction. The question here is not the permissible scope of an arguably overbroad statute, but the claim of a clearly content-based statute to an exception from the general prohibition of content-based proscriptions, an exception that is not warranted if the statute's terms show that suppression of ideas may be afoot. Accordingly, the way to look at the prima facie evidence provision is to consider it for any indication of what is afoot. And if we look at the provision for this purpose, it has a very obvious significance as a mechanism for bringing within the statute's prohibition some expression that is doubtfully threatening though certainly distasteful.

It is difficult to conceive of an intimidation case that could be easier to prove than one with cross burning, assuming any circumstances suggesting intimidation are present. The provision, apparently so unnecessary to legitimate prosecution of intimidation, is therefore quite enough to raise the question whether Virginia's content-based statute seeks more than mere protection against a virulent form of intimidation. It consequently bars any conclusion that an exception to the general rule of *R.A.V.* is warranted on the ground "that there is no realistic [or little realistic] possibility that official suppression of ideas is afoot," Since no *R.A.V.* exception can save the statute as content based, it can only survive if narrowly tailored to serve a compelling state interest, a stringent test the statute cannot pass; a content-neutral statute banning intimidation would achieve the same object without singling out particular content.

IV

I conclude that the statute under which all three of the respondents were prosecuted violates the First Amendment, since the statute's content-based distinction was invalid at the time of the charged activities, regardless of whether the prima facie evidence provision was given any effect in any respondent's individual case. In my view, severance of the prima facie evidence provision now could not eliminate the unconstitutionality of the whole statute at the time of the respondents' conduct. I would therefore affirm the judgment of the Supreme Court of Virginia vacating the respondents' convictions and dismissing the indictments. Accordingly, I concur in the Court's judgment as to respondent Black and dissent as to respondents Elliott and O'Mara.

JUSTICE THOMAS, dissenting.

In every culture, certain things acquire meaning well beyond what outsiders can comprehend. That goes for both the sacred . . . and the profane. I believe that cross burning is the paradigmatic example of the latter.

I

Although I agree with the majority's conclusion that it is constitutionally permissible to "ban . . . cross burning carried out with intent to intimidate," I believe that the majority errs in imputing an expressive component to the activity in question. . . . In my view, whatever expressive value cross burning has, the legislature simply wrote it out by banning only intimidating conduct undertaken by a particular means. A conclusion that the statute prohibiting cross burning with intent to intimidate sweeps beyond a prohibition on certain conduct into the zone of expression overlooks not only the words of the statute but also reality.

A

"In holding [the ban on cross burning with intent to intimidate] unconstitutional, the Court ignores Justice Holmes' familiar aphorism that 'a page of history is worth a volume of logic.'" . . . "The world's oldest, most persistent terrorist organization is not European or even Middle Eastern in origin. Fifty years before the Irish Republican Army was organized, a century before Al Fatah declared its holy war on Israel, the Ku Klux Klan was actively harassing, torturing and murdering in the United States. Today . . . its members remain fanatically committed to a course of violent opposition to social progress and racial equality in the United States." M. Newton & J. Newton, *The Ku Klux Klan: An Encyclopedia*.

To me, the majority's brief history of the Ku Klux Klan only reinforces this common understanding of the Klan as a terrorist organization, which, in its endeavor to intimidate, or even eliminate those its dislikes, uses the most brutal of methods. Such methods typically include cross burning—"a tool for the intimidation and harassment of racial minorities, Catholics, Jews, Communists, and any other groups hated by the Klan." . . . For those not easily frightened, cross burning has been followed by more extreme measures, such as beatings and murder. J. Williams, *Eyes on the Prize: America's Civil Rights Years* 1954–1965, at 39 (1965). As the Government points out, the association between acts of intimidating cross burning and violence is well documented in recent American history. Indeed, the connection between cross burning and violence is well ingrained, and lower courts have so recognized. . . .

B

Virginia's experience has been no exception. In Virginia, though facing widespread opposition in 1920's, the KKK developed localized strength in the southeastern part of the Commonwealth where there were reports of scattered raids and floggings. . . .

. . . That in the early 1950's the people of Virginia viewed cross burning as creating an intolerable atmosphere of terror is not surprising: Although the cross took on some religious significance in the 1920's when the Klan became connected with certain southern white clergy, by the postwar period it had reverted to its original function "as an instrument of intimidation." W. Wade, *The Fiery Cross: The Ku Klux Klan in America* 185, 279 (1987). . . .

It strains credulity to suggest that a state legislature that adopted a litany of segregationist laws self-contradictorily intended to squelch the segregationist message. Even for segregationists, violent and terroristic conduct, the Siamese twin of cross burning, was intolerable. The ban on cross burning with intent to intimidate demonstrates that even segregationists understood the difference between intimidating and terroristic conduct and racist expression. It is simply beyond belief that, in passing the statute now under review, the Virginia legislature was concerned with anything but penalizing conduct it must have viewed as particularly vicious. Accordingly, this statute prohibits only conduct, not expression. And, just as one cannot burn down someone's house to make a political point and then seek refuge in the First Amendment, those who hate cannot terrorize and intimidate to make their point. In light of my conclusion that the statute here addresses only conduct, there is no need to analyze it under any of our First Amendment tests. . . .

Because I would uphold the validity of this statute, I respectfully dissent.

Notes and Questions

(1) One of the co-authors of the Casebook, Rodney Smolla, was the principal appellate lawyer in *Virginia v. Black*, and presented the oral argument before the United States Supreme Court on behalf of the cross-burners. On remand, the Supreme Court of Virginia affirmed the convictions of Elliott and O'Mara. *See Elliott v. Commonwealth*, 267 Va. 464 (2004).

(2) In *Counterman v. Colorado*, 143 S. Ct. 2106 (2023), the Supreme Court clarified the First Amendment standards defining the true threat doctrine. The case involved a defendant, the petitioner in the Supreme Court, named Billy Raymond Counterman. Counterman sent hundreds of Facebook messages to C.W., a Colorado singer-songwriter. C.W. maintained two Facebook profiles, one a public account for promoting her music and a second private account for personal use. The "relationship" between Counterman and C.W., was an entirely one-way. Counterman and C.W. had never actually met. C.W. wisely never once responded to Counterman. Instead, every time Counterman sent C.W. a message, she tried to block him. But the tactic failed. After each block, Counterman created a new Facebook page and messaged C.W. again. The messages ranged from weird and creepy to suggestive that Counterman was actively surveilling C.W. to more violent expressions of anger, including one message ending with the explicative "Die!" Counterman was convicted under a Colorado stalking statute, and sentenced to four and half years imprisonment. The Colorado courts, held that whether or not a statement constituted a true threat should be judged by an "objective" test, as measured by the ordinary reasonable person. Counterman appealed to the Supreme Court, claiming that his messages were protected by the First Amendment. The Court, in an opinion by Justice Kagan joined by Chief Justice Roberts and Justices Alito, Kavanaugh, and Jackson, vacated and remanded the conviction, holding that the objective standard applied by the Colorado courts did not provide sufficient protection for free speech. True threats of violence, the Court affirmed, "are outside the bounds of First Amendment protection and punishable as crimes." The Court held that the First Amendment still requires proof that the defendant had some subjective understanding of the threatening nature of his statements. The Court held that such a subjective understanding was required, but that a mental state of recklessness was sufficient. The Court held that the government must show that the defendant consciously disregarded a substantial risk that his communications would be viewed as threatening violence. Beyond that, however, the Court held, the government need not prove any more demanding form of subjective intent to threaten another. In a significant footnote, the Court addressed the difference between awareness of a communication's contents and awareness of its threatening nature. There was no question that the government must show awareness of the contents. The issue rather was whether what the rule should be when the defendant understands the content of the words but may not grasp that others would find them threatening.

(3) In *Planned Parenthood of the Columbia/Wilmette, Inc. v. American Coalition of Life Activists*, 290 F.3d 1058 (9th Cir. 2002) (en banc), the plaintiffs, who were principally providers of abortion services or entities providing counseling regarding abortion services, brought a suit for civil liability against anti-abortion activists who engaged in a range of virulent expression against abortion providers. In posters, pamphlets, and Internet postings, the activists accused abortion providers of "crimes against humanity," and offered money to persons who could provide information leading to the revocation of the abortion providers' medical licenses or to

anyone who could persuade them to cease performing abortions. The activists went beyond these forms of expression, however, making their attacks more personalized. In one poster, a specific abortion provider, Doctor Robert Christ, was featured by name, along with his photograph, and his work and home addresses. The activists began to assemble dossiers on various abortion providers, judges, and political leaders deemed supportive of abortion rights, which were dubbed the "Nuremberg Files." A web page included the names and addresses of doctors who performed abortions, and invited others to contribute additional names. The website marked the names of those already victimized by anti-abortion terrorists, striking through the names of those who had been murdered and graying out the names of the wounded. Neither the posters nor the website contained any explicit threats against the doctors. But the doctors knew that similar posters prepared by others had preceded clinic violence in the past. By publishing the names and addresses, the plaintiffs argued, the defendants had robbed the doctors of their anonymity and gave violent anti-abortion activists the information to find them. The doctors responded to this unwelcome attention by donning bulletproof vests, drawing the curtains on the windows of their homes and accepting the protection of United States Marshals. A group of doctors also sued the activists under a variety of state and federal laws. At the heart of all their causes of action, however, was the common supposition that the actions of the activists constituted threats against their lives. The Court of Appeals held, on these facts, that a jury could find that the actions of the defendants constituted a "true threat," and that a jury could award compensatory and punitive damages.

§ 9.03 Vulgar, Graphic, and Offensive Speech

A. Vulgarity

Cohen v. California

United States Supreme Court
403 U.S. 15, 91 S. Ct. 1780, 29 L. Ed. 2d 284 (1971)

MR. JUSTICE HARLAN delivered the opinion of the Court.

This case may seem at first blush too inconsequential to find its way into our books, but the issue it presents is of no small constitutional significance.

Appellant Paul Robert Cohen was convicted in the Los Angeles Municipal Court of violating that part of California Penal Code § 415 which prohibits "maliciously and willfully disturb[ing] the peace or quiet of any neighborhood or person . . . by . . . offensive conduct. . . ." He was given 30 days' imprisonment. The facts upon which his conviction rests are detailed in the opinion of the Court of Appeal of California, Second Appellate District, as follows:

> On April 26, 1968, the defendant was observed in the Los Angeles County Courthouse in the corridor outside of division 20 of the municipal court wearing a jacket bearing the words "Fuck the Draft" which were plainly

visible. There were women and children present in the corridor. The defendant was arrested. The defendant testified that he wore the jacket knowing that the words were on the jacket as a means of informing the public of the depth of his feelings against the Vietnam War and the draft.

The defendant did not engage in, nor threaten to engage in, nor did anyone as the result of his conduct in fact commit or threaten to commit any act of violence. The defendant did not make any loud or unusual noise, nor was there any evidence that he uttered any sound prior to his arrest. . . .

In affirming the conviction the Court of Appeal held that "offensive conduct" means "behavior which has a tendency to provoke *others* to acts of violence or to in turn disturb the peace," and that the State had proved this element because, on the facts of this case, "[i]t was certainly reasonably foreseeable that such conduct might cause others to rise up to commit a violent act against the person of the defendant or attempt to forcibly remove his jacket." . . . . The California Supreme Court declined review by a divided vote. We brought the case here . . . [and] now reverse. . . .

I

In order to lay hands on the precise issue which this case involves, it is useful first to canvass various matters which this record does *not* present.

The conviction quite clearly rests upon the asserted offensiveness of the *words* Cohen used to convey his message to the public. The only "conduct" which the State sought to punish is the fact of communication. Thus, we deal here with a conviction resting solely upon "speech." . . . Further, the State certainly lacks power to punish Cohen for the underlying content of the message the inscription conveyed. At least so long as there is no showing of an intent to incite disobedience to or disruption of the draft, Cohen could not, consistently with the First and Fourteenth Amendments, be punished for asserting the evident position on the inutility or immorality of the draft his jacket reflected. . . .

Appellant's conviction, then, rests squarely upon his exercise of the "freedom of speech" protected from arbitrary governmental interference by the Constitution and can be justified, if at all, only as a valid regulation of the manner in which he exercised that freedom, not as a permissible prohibition on the substantive message it conveys. This does not end the inquiry, of course, for the First and Fourteenth Amendments have never been thought to give absolute protection to every individual to speak whenever or wherever he pleases, or to use any form of address in any circumstances that he chooses. In this vein, too, however, we think it important to note that several issues typically associated with such problems are not presented here.

In the first place, Cohen was tried under a statute applicable throughout the entire State. Any attempt to support this conviction on the ground that the statute seeks to preserve an appropriately decorous atmosphere in the courthouse where Cohen was arrested must fail in the absence of any language in the statute that would have put appellant on notice that certain kinds of otherwise permissible speech or conduct would nevertheless, under California law, not be tolerated in certain places. . . . No fair reading of the phrase "offensive conduct" can be said sufficiently to inform the ordinary person that distinctions between certain locations are thereby created.

In the second place, as it comes to us, this case cannot be said to fall within those relatively few categories of instances where prior decisions have established the power of government to deal more comprehensively with certain forms of individual expression simply upon a showing that such a form was employed. This is not, for example, an obscenity case. Whatever else may be necessary to give rise to the States' broader power to prohibit obscene expression, such expression must be, in some significant way, erotic. . . . It cannot plausibly be maintained that this vulgar allusion to the Selective Service System would conjure up such psychic stimulation in anyone likely to be confronted with Cohen's crudely defaced jacket.

This Court has also held that the States are free to ban the simple use, without a demonstration of additional justifying circumstances, of so-called "fighting words," those personally abusive epithets which, when addressed to the ordinary citizen, are, as a matter of common knowledge, inherently likely to provoke violent reaction. *Chaplinsky v. New Hampshire*. . . . While the four-letter word displayed by Cohen in relation to the draft is not uncommonly employed in a personally provocative fashion, in this instance it was clearly not "directed to the person of the hearer.". . . . No individual actually or likely to be present could reasonably have regarded the words on appellant's jacket as a direct personal insult. Nor do we have here an instance of the exercise of the State's police power to prevent a speaker from intentionally provoking a given group to hostile reaction. Cf. *Feiner v. New York*, 340 U.S. 315 (1951). There is, as noted above, no showing that anyone who saw Cohen was in fact violently aroused or that appellant intended such a result.

Finally, in arguments before this Court much has been made of the claim that Cohen's distasteful mode of expression was thrust upon unwilling or unsuspecting viewers, and that the State might therefore legitimately act as it did in order to protect the sensitive from otherwise unavoidable exposure to appellant's crude form of protest. Of course, the mere presumed presence of unwitting listeners or viewers does not serve automatically to justify curtailing all speech capable of giving offense. . . . While this Court has recognized that government may properly act in many situations to prohibit intrusion into the privacy of the home of unwelcome views and ideas which cannot be totally banned from the public dialogue, . . . we have at the same time consistently stressed that "we are often 'captives' outside the sanctuary of the home and subject to objectionable speech.". . . . The ability of government, consonant with the Constitution, to shut off discourse solely to protect others from hearing it is, in other words, dependent upon a showing that substantial privacy interests are being invaded in an essentially intolerable manner. Any broader view of this authority would effectively empower a majority to silence dissidents simply as a matter of personal predilections.

In this regard, persons confronted with Cohen's jacket were in a quite different posture than, say, those subjected to the raucous emissions of sound trucks blaring outside their residences. Those in the Los Angeles courthouse could effectively avoid further bombardment of their sensibilities simply by averting their eyes. And, while it may be that one has a more substantial claim to a recognizable privacy interest when walking through a courthouse corridor than, for example, strolling through Central Park, surely it is nothing like the interest in being free from unwanted expression in the confines of one's own home. . . . Given the subtlety and complexity of the factors involved, if Cohen's "speech" was otherwise entitled to constitutional protection, we do not think the fact that some unwilling "listeners" in a public building may have been briefly exposed to it can serve to justify this breach of the peace conviction where, as here, there was no evidence that persons powerless to avoid appellant's conduct did in fact object to it, and where that portion of the statute upon which Cohen's conviction rests evinces no concern, either on its face or as construed by the California courts, with the special plight of the captive auditor, but, instead, indiscriminately sweeps within its prohibitions all "offensive conduct" that disturbs "any neighborhood or person. . . ."

II

Against this background, the issue flushed by this case stands out in bold relief. It is whether California can excise, as "offensive conduct," one particular scurrilous epithet from the public discourse, either upon the theory of the court below that its use is inherently likely to cause violent reaction or upon a more general assertion that the States, acting as guardians of public morality, may properly remove this offensive word from the public vocabulary.

The rationale of the California court is plainly untenable. . . . We have been shown no evidence that substantial numbers of citizens are standing ready to strike out physically at whoever may assault their sensibilities with execrations like that uttered by Cohen. There may be some persons about with such lawless violent proclivities, but that is an insufficient base upon which to erect, consistently with constitutional values, a governmental power to force persons who wish to ventilate their dissident views into avoiding particular forms of expression. The argument amounts to little more than the self-defeating proposition that to avoid physical censorship of one who has not sought to provoke such a response by a hypothetical coterie of the violent and lawless, the States may more appropriately effectuate that censorship themselves. . . .

The constitutional right of free expression is powerful medicine in a society as diverse and populous as ours. It is designed and intended to remove governmental restraints from the arena of public discussion, putting the decision as to what views shall be voiced largely into the hands of each of us, in the hope that use of such freedom will ultimately produce a more capable citizenry and more perfect polity and in the belief that no other approach would comport with the premise of individual dignity and choice upon which our political system rests. . . .

To many, the immediate consequence of this freedom may often appear to be only verbal tumult, discord, and even offensive utterance. These are, however, within established limits, in truth necessary side effects of the broader enduring values which the process of open debate permits us to achieve. That the air may at times seem filled with verbal cacophony is, in this sense not a sign of weakness but of strength. We cannot lose sight of the fact that in what otherwise might seem a trifling and annoying instance of individual distasteful abuse of a privilege, these fundamental societal values are truly implicated. . . .

Against this perception of the constitutional policies involved, we discern certain more particularized considerations that peculiarly call for reversal of this conviction. First, the principle contended for by the State seems inherently boundless. How is one to distinguish this from any other offensive word? Surely the State has no right to cleanse public debate to the point where it is grammatically palatable to the most squeamish among us. Yet no readily ascertainable general principle exists for stopping short of that result were we to affirm the judgment below. For, while the particular four-letter word being litigated here is perhaps more distasteful than most others of its genre, it is nevertheless often true that one man's vulgarity is another's lyric. Indeed, we think it is largely because governmental officials cannot make principled distinctions in this area that the Constitution leaves matters of taste and style so largely to the individual.

Additionally, we cannot overlook the fact, because it is well illustrated by the episode involved here, that much linguistic expression serves a dual communicative function: it conveys not only ideas capable of relatively precise, detached explication, but otherwise inexpressible emotions as well. In fact, words are often chosen as much for their emotive as their cognitive force. We cannot sanction the view that the Constitution, while solicitous of the cognitive content of individual speech, has little or no regard for that emotive function which, practically speaking, may often be the more important element of the overall message sought to be communicated. . . .

Finally, and in the same vein, we cannot indulge the facile assumption that one can forbid particular words without also running a substantial risk of suppressing ideas in the process. Indeed, governments might soon seize upon the censorship of particular words as a convenient guise for banning the expression of unpopular views. We have been able, as noted above, to discern little social benefit that might result from running the risk of opening the door to such grave results.

It is, in sum, our judgment that, absent a more particularized and compelling reason for its actions, the State may not, consistently with the First and Fourteenth Amendments, make the simple public display here involved of this single four-letter expletive a criminal offense. Because that is the only arguably sustainable rationale for the conviction here at issue, the judgment below must be

Reversed.

Mr. Justice Blackmun, with whom The Chief Justice and Mr. Justice Black join.

I dissent.

... Cohen's absurd and immature antic, in my view, was mainly conduct and little speech. ... Further, the case appears to me to be well within the sphere of *Chaplinsky v. New Hampshire* ... where Mr. Justice Murphy, a known champion of First Amendment freedoms, wrote for a unanimous bench. As a consequence, this Court's agonizing over First Amendment values seems misplaced and unnecessary. ...

Mr. Justice White concurs in [an omitted portion] of Mr. Justice Blackmun's dissenting opinion.

Federal Communications Commission v. Pacifica Foundation

United States Supreme Court
438 U.S. 726, 98 S. Ct. 3026, 57 L. Ed. 2d 1073 (1978)

Mr. Justice Stevens delivered the opinion of the Court (Parts I, II, III and IV-C) and an opinion in which The Chief Justice [Burger] and Mr. Justice Rehnquist joined (Parts IV-A and IV-B).

This case requires that we decide whether the Federal Communications Commission has any power to regulate a radio broadcast that is indecent but not obscene. A satiric humorist named George Carlin recorded a 12-minute monologue entitled "Filthy Words" before a live audience in a California theater. He began by referring to his thoughts about "the words you couldn't say on the public, ah, airwaves, um, the ones you definitely wouldn't say, ever." He proceeded to list those words [shit, piss, fuck, cunt, cocksucker, motherfucker, and tits] and repeat them over and over again in a variety of colloquialisms. The transcript of the recording [indicates] frequent laughter from the audience. ...

At about 2 o'clock in the afternoon on Tuesday, October 30, 1973, a New York radio station, owned by respondent Pacifica Foundation, broadcast the "Filthy Words" monologue. A few weeks later a man, who stated that he had heard the broadcast while driving with his young son, wrote a letter complaining to the Commission. ...

In its memorandum opinion the Commission stated that it intended to "clarify the standards which will be utilized in considering" the growing number of complaints about indecent speech on the airwaves. Advancing several reasons for treating broadcast speech differently from other forms of expression, the Commission found a power to regulate indecent broadcasting in two statutes: 18 U.S.C. §1464 (1976 ed.), which forbids the use of "any obscene, indecent, or profane language by means of radio communications," and 47 U.S.C. §303(g), which requires the Commission to "encourage the larger and more effective use of radio in the public interest. ..."

[T]he Commission concluded that certain words depicted sexual and excretory activities in a patently offensive manner, noted that they "were broadcast at a time when children were undoubtedly in the audience (i.e., in the early afternoon)," and that prerecorded language, with these offensive words "repeated over and over," was "deliberately broadcast." In summary, the Commission stated: "We therefore hold that the language as broadcast was indecent and prohibited by 18 U.S.C. [§] 1464. . . ."

IV

Pacifica makes two constitutional attacks on the Commission's order. First, it argues that the Commission's construction of the statutory language broadly encompasses so much constitutionally protected speech that reversal is required even if Pacifica's broadcast of the "Filthy Words" monologue is not itself protected by the First Amendment. Second, Pacifica argues that inasmuch as the recording is not obscene, the Constitution forbids any abridgment of the right to broadcast it on the radio.

A

The first argument fails because our review is limited to the question whether the Commission has the authority to proscribe this particular broadcast. As the Commission itself emphasized, its order was "issued in a specific factual context." That approach is appropriate for courts as well as the Commission when regulation of indecency is at stake, for indecency is largely a function of context — it cannot be adequately judged in the abstract. . . .

B

When the issue is narrowed to the facts of this case, the question is whether the First Amendment denies government any power to restrict the public broadcast of indecent language in any circumstances. For if the government has any such power, this was an appropriate occasion for its exercise.

The words of the Carlin monologue are unquestionably "speech" within the meaning of the First Amendment. It is equally clear that the Commission's objections to the broadcast were based in part on its content. The order must therefore fail if, as Pacifica argues, the First Amendment prohibits all governmental regulation that depends on the content of speech. Our past cases demonstrate, however, that no such absolute rule is mandated by the Constitution.

The classic exposition of the proposition that both the content and the context of speech are critical elements of First Amendment analysis is Mr. Justice Holmes' statement for the Court in *Schenck v. United States*:

> We admit that in many places and in ordinary times the defendants in saying all that was said in the circular would have been within their constitutional rights. But the character of every act depends upon the circumstances in which it is done. . . . The most stringent protection of free speech would not protect a man in falsely shouting fire in a theatre and causing a panic. It does not even protect a man from an injunction against uttering words that may have all the effect of force. . . . The question in every case is whether the words are used in such circumstances and are of such a nature as to create a clear and present danger that they will bring about the substantive evils that Congress has a right to prevent.

Other distinctions based on content have been approved in the years since Schenck. The government may forbid speech calculated to provoke a fight. See *Chaplinsky v. New Hampshire*. It may pay heed to the "'commonsense differences' between commercial speech and other varieties" *Bates v. State Bar of Arizona*, 433 U.S. 350, 381 (1977). It may treat libels against private citizens more severely than libels against public officials. See *Gertz v. Robert Welch, Inc.*, 418 U.S. 323 (1974). Obscenity may be wholly prohibited. *Miller v. California*. And only two Terms ago we refused to hold that a "statutory classification is unconstitutional because it is based on the content of communication protected by the First Amendment." *Young v. American Mini Theatres, Inc.*, 429 U.S. 873 (1976).

The question in this case is whether a broadcast of patently offensive words dealing with sex and excretion may be regulated because of its content. Obscene materials have been denied the protection of the First Amendment because their content is so offensive to contemporary moral standards. *Roth v. United States* [354 U.S. 476 (1957)]. But the fact that society may find speech offensive is not a sufficient reason for suppressing it. Indeed, if it is the speaker's opinion that gives offense, that consequence is a reason for according it constitutional protection. For it is a central tenet of the First Amendment that the government must remain neutral in the marketplace of ideas. If there were any reason to believe that the Commission's characterization of the Carlin monologue as offensive could be traced to its political content — or even to the fact that it satirized contemporary attitudes about four-letter words — First Amendment protection might be required. But that is simply not this case. These words offend for the same reasons that obscenity offends. Their place in the hierarchy of First Amendment values was aptly sketched by Mr. Justice Murphy when he said: "Such utterances are no essential part of any exposition of ideas, and are of such slight social value as a step to truth that any benefit that may be derived from them is clearly outweighed by the social interest in order and morality." *Chaplinsky v. New Hampshire*.

Although these words ordinarily lack literary, political, or scientific value, they are not entirely outside the protection of the First Amendment. Some uses of even the most offensive words are unquestionably protected. Indeed, we may assume, *arguendo*, that this monologue would be protected in other contexts. Nonetheless, the constitutional protection accorded to a communication containing such patently offensive sexual and excretory language need not be the same in every context. It is a characteristic of speech such as this that both its capacity to offend and its "social value," to use Mr. Justice Murphy's term, vary with the circumstances. Words that are commonplace in one setting are shocking in another. To paraphrase Mr. Justice Harlan, one occasion's lyric is another's vulgarity. Cf. *Cohen v. California*, 403 U.S. 15, 25.

In this case it is undisputed that the content of Pacifica's broadcast was "vulgar," "offensive," and "shocking." Because content of that character is not entitled to absolute constitutional protection under all circumstances, we must consider its context in order to determine whether the Commission's action was constitutionally permissible.

C

We have long recognized that each medium of expression presents special First Amendment problems. And of all forms of communication, it is broadcasting that has received the most limited First Amendment protection. Thus, although other speakers cannot be licensed except under laws that carefully define and narrow official discretion, a broadcaster may be deprived of his license and his forum if the Commission decides that such an action would serve "the public interest, convenience, and necessity." Similarly, although the First Amendment protects newspaper publishers from being required to print the replies of those whom they criticize, *Miami Herald Publishing Co. v. Tornillo*, 418 U.S. 241 (1974), it affords no such protection to broadcasters; on the contrary, they must give free time to the victims of their criticism. *Red Lion Broadcasting Co. v. FCC*, [395 U.S. 367 (1969)].

The reasons for these distinctions are complex, but two have relevance to the present case. First, the broadcast media have established a uniquely pervasive presence in the lives of all Americans. Patently offensive, indecent material presented over the airwaves confronts the citizen, not only in public, but also in the privacy of the home, where the individual's right to be left alone plainly outweighs the First Amendment rights of an intruder. Because the broadcast audience is constantly tuning in and out, prior warnings cannot completely protect the listener or viewer from unexpected program content. To say that one may avoid further offense by turning off the radio when he hears indecent language is like saying that the remedy for an assault is to run away after the first blow. One may hang up on an indecent phone call, but that option does not give the caller a constitutional immunity or avoid a harm that has already taken place.

Second, broadcasting is uniquely accessible to children, even those too young to read. Although Carlin's written message might have been incomprehensible to a first grader, Pacifica's broadcast could have enlarged a child's vocabulary in an instant. Other forms of offensive expression may be withheld from the young without restricting the expression at its source. Bookstores and motion picture theaters, for example, may be prohibited from making indecent material available to children. We held in *Ginsberg v. New York*, 404 U.S. 1027 (1972), that the government's interest in the "well-being of its youth" and in supporting "parents' claim to authority in their own household" justified the regulation of otherwise protected expression. The ease with which children may obtain access to broadcast material, coupled with the concerns recognized in *Ginsberg*, amply justify special treatment of indecent broadcasting.

It is appropriate, in conclusion, to emphasize the narrowness of our holding. This case does not involve a two-way radio conversation between a cab driver and a dispatcher, or a telecast of an Elizabethan comedy. We have not decided that an occasional expletive in either setting would justify any sanction or, indeed, that this broadcast would justify a criminal prosecution. The Commission's decision rested entirely on a nuisance rationale under which context is all-important. The concept requires consideration of a host of variables. The time of day was emphasized by the Commission. The content of the program in which the language is used will also affect the composition of the audience, and differences between radio, television, and perhaps closed-circuit transmissions, may also be relevant. As Mr. Justice Sutherland wrote, a "nuisance may be merely a right thing in the wrong place,—like a pig in the parlor instead of the barnyard." We simply hold that when the Commission finds that a pig has entered the parlor, the exercise of its regulatory power does not depend on proof that the pig is obscene.

The judgment of the Court of Appeals is reversed.

MR. JUSTICE POWELL, with whom MR. JUSTICE BLACKMUN joins, concurring in part and concurring in the judgment.

. . . In my view, the result in this case does not turn on whether Carlin's monologue, viewed as a whole, or the words that constitute it, have more or less "value" than a candidate's campaign speech. This is a judgment for each person to make, not one for the judges to impose upon him.

The result turns instead on the unique characteristics of the broadcast media, combined with society's right to protect its children from speech generally agreed to be inappropriate for their years, and with the interest of unwilling adults in not being assaulted by such offensive speech in their homes. Moreover, I doubt whether today's decision will prevent any adult who wishes to receive Carlin's message in Carlin's own words from doing so, and from making for himself a value judgment as to the merit of the message and words. . . .

MR. JUSTICE BRENNAN, with whom MR. JUSTICE MARSHALL joins, dissenting. . . .

For the second time in two years, see *Young v. American Mini Theatres, Inc.*, the Court refuses to embrace the notion, completely antithetical to basic First Amendment values, that the degree of protection the First Amendment affords protected speech varies with the social value ascribed to that speech by five Members of this Court. Moreover, as do all parties, all Members of the Court agree that the Carlin monologue aired by Station WBAI does not fall within one of the categories of speech, such as "fighting words," that is totally without First Amendment protection. This conclusion, of course, is compelled by our cases expressly holding that communications containing some of the words found condemnable here are fully protected by the First Amendment in other contexts. Yet despite the Court's refusal to create a sliding scale of First Amendment protection calibrated to this Court's perception of the worth of a communication's content, and despite our unanimous agreement that the Carlin monologue is protected speech, a majority of the Court nevertheless finds that, on the facts of this case, the FCC is not constitutionally barred from imposing sanctions on Pacifica for its airing of the Carlin monologue. This majority apparently believes that the FCC's disapproval of Pacifica's afternoon broadcast of Carlin's "Dirty Words" recording is a permissible time, place, and manner regulation. . . .

Whatever the minimal discomfort suffered by a listener who inadvertently tunes into a program he finds offensive during the brief interval before he can simply extend his arm and switch stations or flick the "off" button, it is surely worth the candle to preserve the broadcaster's right to send, and the right of those interested to receive, a message entitled to full First Amendment protection. . . .

The Court's balance, of necessity, fails to accord proper weight to the interests of listeners who wish to hear broadcasts the FCC deems offensive. It permits majoritarian tastes completely to preclude a protected message from entering the homes of a receptive, unoffended minority. No decision of this Court supports such a result. . . .

Because the Carlin monologue is obviously not an erotic appeal to the prurient interests of children, the Court, for the first time, allows the government to prevent minors from gaining access to materials that are not obscene, and are therefore protected, as to them. . . .

In concluding that the presence of children in the listening audience provides an adequate basis for the FCC to impose sanctions for Pacifica's broadcast of the Carlin monologue, the opinions of my Brother Powell, and my Brother Stevens, both stress the time-honored right of a parent to raise his child as he sees fit — a right this Court has consistently been vigilant to protect. Yet this principle supports a result directly contrary to that reached by the Court. [Our cases] hold that parents, *not* the government, have the right to make certain decisions regarding the upbringing of their children. As surprising as it may be to individual Members of this Court, some parents may actually find Mr. Carlin's unabashed attitude towards the seven "dirty words" healthy, and deem it desirable to expose their children to the manner in which Mr. Carlin defuses the taboo surrounding the words. Such parents may constitute a minority of the American public, but the absence of great numbers willing to exercise the right to raise their children in this fashion does not alter the right's nature or its existence. Only the Court's regrettable decision does that. . . .

As demonstrated above, neither of the factors relied on by both the opinion of my brother Powell and the opinion of my Brother Stevens — the intrusive nature of radio and the presence of children in the listening audience — can, when taken on its own terms, support the FCC's disapproval of the Carlin monologue. These two asserted justifications are further plagued by a common failing: the lack of principled limits on their use as a basis for FCC censorship. No such limits come readily to mind, and neither of the opinions constituting the Court serve to clarify the extent to which the FCC may assert the privacy and children-in-the-audience rationales as justification for expunging from the airways protected communications the Commission finds offensive. Taken to their logical extreme, these rationales would support the cleansing of public radio of any "four-letter words" whatsoever, regardless of their context. The rationales could justify the banning from radio of a myriad of literary works, novels, poems, and plays by the likes of Shakespeare, Joyce, Hemingway, Ben Jonson, Henry Fielding, Robert Burns, and Chaucer; they could support the suppression of a good deal of political speech, such as the Nixon tapes; and they could even provide the basis for imposing sanctions for the broadcast of certain portions of the Bible.

In order to dispel the specter of the possibility of so unpalatable a degree of censorship, and to defuse Pacifica's overbreadth challenge, the FCC insists that it desires only the authority to reprimand a broadcaster on facts analogous to those present in this case, which it describes as involving "broadcasting for nearly twelve minutes a record which repeated over and over words which depict sexual or excretory activities and organs in a manner patently offensive by its community's contemporary standards in the early afternoon when children were in the audience." The opinions of both my Brother Powell and my Brother Stevens take the FCC at its word, and consequently do no more than permit the Commission to censor the afternoon broadcast of the "sort of verbal shock treatment," involved here. To insure that the FCC's regulation of protected speech does not exceed these bounds, my Brother Powell is content to rely upon the judgment of the Commission while my Brother Stevens deems it prudent to rely on this Court's ability accurately to assess the worth of various kinds of speech. For my own part, even accepting that this case is limited to its facts, I would place the responsibility and the right to weed worthless and offensive communications from the public airways where it belongs and where, until today, it resided: in a public free to choose those communications worthy of its attention from a marketplace unsullied by the censor's hand. . . .

Mr. Justice Stewart, with whom Mr. Justice Brennan, Mr. Justice White, and Mr. Justice Marshall join, dissenting.

. . . I would hold [that] Congress intended, by using the word "indecent" in § 1464, to prohibit nothing more than obscene speech. Under that reading of the statute, the Commission's order in this case was not authorized, and on the basis I would affirm the judgment of the Court of Appeals.

Notes and Questions

Cohen is a prime example of the ascendency of the Marketplace Theory. *Pacifica*, in contrast, is an example of how the Order and Morality Theory retains dominance in certain "special settings." The specific special setting in *Pacifica* was broadcasting, such as radio and television, during hours in which children are likely to be watching or listening. We will see throughout this Chapter examples of what we might call the "Child's First Amendment." Free speech doctrines partaking of the Marketplace Theory applicable in the general marketplace in the "adult world" may at times be relaxed and supplanted by Order and Morality Theory principles when children are involved. The special rules governing speech in public schools provides another example. Typically, when speech is aimed at adults, the mere fact that children might be exposed to the speech is not enough to justify suppressing the speech. In *Cohen*, after all, children could see Cohen's jacket. Just as adults are told to look the other way when confronted with speech that offends them, parents may cover a child's ears, avert the child's gaze, or turn off the offending broadcast. Even so, *Pacifica* seemed to be grounded in the unique power that radio and television may have over children, speaking in terms of the pervasive influence of such media on children. Do you believe *Cohen* was rightly decided? *Pacifica*?

B. Graphically Offensive Speech

Texas v. Johnson

United States Supreme Court
491 U.S. 397, 109 S. Ct. 2533, 105 L. Ed. 2d 342 (1989)

JUSTICE BRENNAN delivered the opinion of the Court.

After publicly burning an American flag as a means of political protest, Gregory Lee Johnson was convicted of desecrating a flag in violation of Texas law. This case presents the question whether his conviction is consistent with the First Amendment. We hold that it is not.

I

While the Republican National Convention was taking place in Dallas in 1984, respondent Johnson participated in a political demonstration dubbed the "Republican War Chest Tour." As explained in literature distributed by the demonstrators and in speeches made by them, the purpose of this event was to protest the policies of the Reagan administration and of certain Dallas-based corporations. The demonstrators marched through the Dallas streets, chanting political slogans and stopping at several corporate locations to stage "die-ins" intended to dramatize the consequences of nuclear war. On several occasions they spray-painted the walls of buildings and overturned potted plants, but Johnson himself took no part in such activities. He did, however, accept an American flag handed to him by a fellow protestor who had taken it from a flag pole outside one of the targeted buildings.

The demonstration ended in front of Dallas City Hall, where Johnson unfurled the American flag, doused it with kerosene, and set it on fire. While the flag burned, the protestors chanted, "America, the red, white, and blue, we spit on you." After the demonstrators dispersed, a witness to the flag-burning collected the flag's remains and buried them in his backyard. No one was physically injured or threatened with injury, though several witnesses testified that they had been seriously offended by the flag-burning.

Of the approximately 100 demonstrators, Johnson alone was charged with a crime. The only criminal offense with which he was charged was the desecration of a venerated object in violation of Tex. Penal Code Ann. § 42.09(a)(3) (1989). After a trial, he was convicted, sentenced to one year in prison, and fined $2,000. The Court of Appeals for the Fifth District of Texas at Dallas affirmed Johnson's conviction, but the Texas Court of Criminal Appeals reversed, holding that the State could not, consistent with the First Amendment, punish Johnson for burning the flag in these circumstances. . . .

We granted *certiorari*, and now affirm.

II

Johnson was convicted of flag desecration for burning the flag rather than for uttering insulting words. This fact somewhat complicates our consideration of his conviction under the First Amendment. We must first determine whether Johnson's burning of the flag constituted expressive conduct, permitting him to invoke the First Amendment in challenging his conviction. *See, e.g., Spence v. Washington*, 418 U.S. 405 (1974). If his conduct was expressive, we next decide whether the State's regulation is related to the suppression of free expression. *See, e.g., United States v. O'Brien*, 391 U.S. 367 (1968). If the State's regulation is not related to expression, then the less stringent standard we announced in *United States v. O'Brien* for regulations of noncommunicative conduct controls. If it is, then we are outside of *O'Brien's* test, and we must ask whether this interest justifies Johnson's conviction under a more demanding standard. A third possibility is that the State's asserted interest is simply not implicated on these facts, and in that event the interest drops out of the picture.

The First Amendment literally forbids the abridgement only of "speech," but we have long recognized that its protection does not end at the spoken or written word. While we have rejected "the view that an apparently limitless variety of conduct can be labeled 'speech' whenever the person engaging in the conduct intends thereby to express an idea," we have acknowledged that conduct may be "sufficiently imbued with elements of communication to fall within the scope of the First and Fourteenth Amendments."

In deciding whether particular conduct possesses sufficient communicative elements to bring the First Amendment into play, we have asked whether [a]n intent to convey a particularized message was present, and [whether] the likelihood was great that the message would be understood by those who viewed it. . . .

Especially pertinent to this case are our decisions recognizing the communicative nature of conduct relating to flags. . . . That we have had little difficulty identifying an expressive element in conduct relating to flags should not be surprising. The very purpose of a national flag is to serve as a symbol of our country; it is, one might say, "the one visible manifestation of two hundred years of nationhood. . . ."

We have not automatically concluded, however, that any action taken with respect to our flag is expressive. Instead, in characterizing such action for First Amendment purposes, we have considered the context in which it occurred. In *Spence*, for example, we emphasized that Spence's taping of a peace sign to his flag was "roughly simultaneous with and concededly triggered by the Cambodian incursion and the Kent State tragedy." The State of Washington had conceded, in fact, that Spence's conduct was a form of communication, and we stated that "the State's concession is inevitable on this record."

The State of Texas conceded for purposes of its oral argument in this case that Johnson's conduct was expressive conduct, and this concession seems to us as prudent as was Washington's in *Spence*. Johnson burned an American flag as part — indeed, as the culmination — of a political demonstration that coincided with the convening of the Republican Party and its renomination of Ronald Reagan for President. The expressive, overtly political nature of this conduct was both intentional and overwhelmingly apparent. At his trial, Johnson explained his reasons for burning the flag as follows: "The American Flag was burned as Ronald Reagan was being renominated as President. And a more powerful statement of symbolic speech, whether you agree with it or not, couldn't have been made at that time. It's quite a just position [juxtaposition]. We had new patriotism and no patriotism." In these circumstances, Johnson's burning of the flag was conduct "sufficiently imbued with elements of communication," to implicate the First Amendment.

III

The government generally has a freer hand in restricting expressive conduct than it has in restricting the written or spoken word. It may not, however, proscribe particular conduct *because* it has expressive elements. "[W]hat might be termed the more generalized guarantee of freedom of expression makes the communicative nature of conduct an inadequate *basis* for singling out that conduct for proscription. A law *directed* at the communicative nature of conduct must, like a law directed at speech itself, be justified by the substantial showing of need that the First Amendment requires." It is, in short, not simply the verbal or nonverbal nature of the expression, but the governmental interest at stake, that helps to determine whether a restriction on that expression is valid.

Thus, although we have recognized that where "speech" and "nonspeech" elements are combined in the same course of conduct, a sufficiently important governmental interest in regulating the nonspeech element can justify incidental limitations on First Amendment freedoms, we have limited the applicability of *O'Brien*'s relatively lenient standard to those cases in which "the governmental interest is unrelated to the suppression of free expression." In stating, moreover, that *O'Brien*'s test "in the last analysis is little, if any, different from the standard applied to time, place, or manner restrictions," we have highlighted the requirement that the governmental interest in question be unconnected to expression in order to come under *O'Brien*'s less demanding rule.

In order to decide whether *O'Brien*'s test applies here, therefore, we must decide whether Texas has asserted an interest in support of Johnson's conviction that is unrelated to the suppression of expression. If we find that an interest asserted by the State is simply not implicated on the facts before us, we need not ask whether *O'Brien*'s test applies. The State offers two separate interests to justify this conviction: preventing breaches of the peace, and preserving the flag as a symbol of nationhood and national unity. We hold that the first interest is not implicated on this record and that the second is related to the suppression of expression.

A

Texas claims that its interest in preventing breaches of the peace justifies Johnson's conviction for flag desecration. However, no disturbance of the peace actually occurred or threatened to occur because of Johnson's burning of the flag.... The only evidence offered by the State at trial to show the reaction to Johnson's actions was the testimony of several persons who had been seriously offended by the flag-burning. The State's position, therefore, amounts to a claim that an audience that takes serious offense at particular expression is necessarily likely to disturb the peace and that the expression may be prohibited on this basis. Our precedents do not countenance such a presumption. On the contrary, they recognize that a principal "function of free speech under our system of government is to invite dispute. It may indeed best serve its high purpose when it induces a condition of unrest, creates dissatisfaction with conditions as they are, or even stirs people to anger." It would be odd indeed to conclude *both* that "if it is the speaker's opinion that gives offense, that consequence is a reason for according it constitutional protection," *and* that the government may ban the expression of certain disagreeable ideas on the unsupported presumption that their very disagreeableness will provoke violence.

Thus, we have not permitted the government to assume that every expression of a provocative idea will incite a riot, but have instead required careful consideration of the actual circumstances surrounding such expression, asking whether the expression "is directed to inciting or producing imminent lawless action and is likely to incite or produce such action." *Brandenburg v. Ohio*. To accept Texas' arguments that it need only demonstrate "the potential for a breach of the peace," and that every flag-burning necessarily possesses that potential, would be to eviscerate our holding in *Brandenburg*. This we decline to do. Nor does Johnson's expressive conduct fall within that small class of "fighting words" that are "likely to provoke the average person to retaliation, and thereby cause a breach of the peace." *Chaplinsky v. New Hampshire*. No reasonable onlooker would have regarded Johnson's generalized expression of dissatisfaction with the policies of the Federal Government as a direct personal insult or an invitation to exchange fisticuffs.

We thus conclude that the State's interest in maintaining order is not implicated on these facts. The State need not worry that our holding will disable it from preserving the peace. We do not suggest that the First Amendment forbids a State to prevent "imminent lawless action." And, in fact, Texas already has a statute specifically prohibiting breaches of the peace, which tends to confirm that Texas need not punish this flag desecration in order to keep the peace.

B

The State also asserts an interest in preserving the flag as a symbol of nationhood and national unity. In *Spence*, we acknowledged that the government's interest in preserving the flag's special symbolic value "is directly related to expression in the context of activity" such as affixing a peace symbol to a flag. We are equally persuaded that this interest is related to expression in the case of Johnson's burning of the flag. The State, apparently, is concerned that such conduct will lead people to believe either that the flag does not stand for nationhood and national unity, but instead reflects other, less positive concepts, or that the concepts reflected in the flag do not in fact exist, that is, we do not enjoy unity as a Nation. These concerns blossom only when a person's treatment of the flag communicates some message, and thus are related "to the suppression of free expression" within the meaning of *O'Brien*. We are thus outside of *O'Brien*'s test altogether.

IV

It remains to consider whether the State's interest in preserving the flag as a symbol of nationhood and national unity justifies Johnson's conviction.

As in *Spence*, "[w]e are confronted with a case of prosecution for the expression of an idea through activity," and "[a]ccordingly, we must examine with particular care the interests advanced by [petitioner] to support its prosecution." Johnson was not, we add, prosecuted for the expression of just any idea; he was prosecuted for his expression of dissatisfaction with the policies of this country, expression situated at the core of our First Amendment values.

Moreover, Johnson was prosecuted because he knew that his politically charged expression would cause "serious offense." If he had burned the flag as a means of disposing of it because it was dirty or torn, he would not have been convicted of flag desecration under this Texas law: federal law designates burning as the preferred means of disposing of a flag "when it is in such condition that it is no longer a fitting emblem for display," and Texas has no quarrel with this means of disposal. The Texas law is thus not aimed at protecting the physical integrity of the flag in all circumstances, but is designed instead to protect it only against impairments that would cause serious offense to others. Texas concedes as much. . . .

Whether Johnson's treatment of the flag violated Texas law thus depended on the likely communicative impact of his expressive conduct. Our decision in *Boos v. Barry* [485 U.S 312 (1988)], tells us that this restriction on Johnson's expression is content-based. In *Boos*, we considered the constitutionality of a law prohibiting "the display of any sign within 50 feet of a foreign embassy if that sign tends to bring that foreign government into 'public odium' or 'public disrepute.'" Rejecting the argument that the law was content-neutral because it was justified by "our international law obligation to shield diplomats from speech that offends their dignity," we held that "[t]he emotive impact of speech on its audience is not a 'secondary effect'" unrelated to the content of the expression itself.

According to the principles announced in *Boos*, Johnson's political expression was restricted because of the content of the message he conveyed. We must therefore subject the State's asserted interest in preserving the special symbolic character of the flag to "the most exacting scrutiny."

Texas argues that its interest in preserving the flag as a symbol of nationhood and national unity survives this close analysis. . . . The State's argument is not that it has an interest simply in maintaining the flag as a symbol of *something*, no matter what it symbolizes; indeed, if that were the State's position, it would be difficult to see how that interest is endangered by highly symbolic conduct such as Johnson's. Rather, the State's claim is that it has an interest in preserving the flag as a symbol of *nationhood* and *national unity*, a symbol with a determinate range of meanings. According to Texas, if one physically treats the flag in a way that would tend to cast doubt on either the idea that nationhood and national unity are the flag's referents or that national unity actually exists, the message conveyed thereby is a harmful one and therefore may be prohibited.

If there is a bedrock principle underlying the First Amendment, it is that the government may not prohibit the expression of an idea simply because society finds the idea itself offensive or disagreeable.

We have not recognized an exception to this principle even where our flag has been involved. . . .

In short, nothing in our precedents suggests that a State may foster its own view of the flag by prohibiting expressive conduct relating to it. To bring its argument outside our precedents, Texas attempts to convince us that even if its interest in preserving the flag's symbolic role does not allow it to prohibit words or some expressive conduct critical of the flag, it does permit it to forbid the outright destruction of the flag. The State's argument cannot depend here on the distinction between written or spoken words and nonverbal conduct. That distinction, we have shown, is of no moment where the nonverbal conduct is expressive, as it is here, and where the regulation of that conduct is related to expression, as it is here. . . .

Texas' focus on the precise nature of Johnson's expression, moreover, misses the point of our prior decisions: their enduring lesson, that the Government may not prohibit expression simply because it disagrees with its message, is not dependent on the particular mode in which one chooses to express an idea. If we were to hold that a State may forbid flag-burning wherever it is likely to endanger the flag's symbolic role, but allow it wherever burning a flag promotes that role — as where, for example, a person ceremoniously burns a dirty flag — we would be saying that when it comes to impairing the flag's physical integrity, the flag itself may be used as a symbol — as a substitute for the written or spoken word or a "short cut from mind to mind" — only in one direction. We would be permitting a State to "prescribe what shall be orthodox" by saying that one may burn the flag to convey one's attitude toward it and its referents only if one does not endanger the flag's representation of nationhood and national unity. . . . To conclude that the Government may permit designated symbols to be used to communicate only a limited set of messages would be to enter territory having no discernible or defensible boundaries. Could the Government, on this theory, prohibit the burning of state flags? Of copies of the Presidential seal? Of the Constitution? In evaluating these choices under the First Amendment, how would we decide which symbols were sufficiently special to warrant this unique status? To do so, we would be forced to consult our own political preferences, and impose them on the citizenry, in the very way that the First Amendment forbids us to do.

There is, moreover, no indication — either in the text of the Constitution or in our cases interpreting it — that a separate juridical category exists for the American flag alone. Indeed, we would not be surprised to learn that the persons who framed our

Constitution and wrote the Amendment that we now construe were not known for their reverence for the Union Jack. The First Amendment does not guarantee that other concepts virtually sacred to our Nation as a whole — such as the principle that discrimination on the basis of race is odious and destructive — will go unquestioned in the marketplace of ideas. We decline, therefore, to create for the flag an exception to the joust of principles protected by the First Amendment.

It is not the State's ends, but its means, to which we object. It cannot be gainsaid that there is a special place reserved for the flag in this Nation, and thus we do not doubt that the government has a legitimate interest in making efforts to "preserv[e] the national flag as an unalloyed symbol of our country." We reject the suggestion, urged at oral argument by counsel for Johnson, that the government lacks "any state interest whatsoever" in regulating the manner in which the flag may be displayed. Congress has, for example, enacted precatory regulations describing the proper treatment of the flag, and we cast no doubt on the legitimacy of its interest in making such recommendations. To say that the government has an interest in encouraging proper treatment of the flag, however, is not to say that it may criminally punish a person for burning a flag as a means of political protest. "National unity as an end which officials may foster by persuasion and example is not in question. The problem is whether under our Constitution compulsion as here employed is a permissible means for its achievement."

We are fortified in today's conclusion by our conviction that forbidding criminal punishment for conduct such as Johnson's will not endanger the special role played by our flag or the feelings it inspires. To paraphrase Justice Holmes, we submit that nobody can suppose that this one gesture of an unknown man will change our Nation's attitude towards its flag. . . .

We are tempted to say, in fact, that the flag's deservedly cherished place in our community will be strengthened, not weakened, by our holding today. Our decision is a reaffirmation of the principles of freedom and inclusiveness that the flag best reflects, and of the conviction that our toleration of criticism such as Johnson's is a sign and source of our strength. Indeed, one of the proudest images of our flag, the one immortalized in our own national anthem, is of the bombardment it survived at Fort McHenry. It is the Nation's resilience, not its rigidity, that Texas sees reflected in the flag — and it is that resilience that we reassert today.

The way to preserve the flag's special role is not to punish those who feel differently about these matters. It is to persuade them that they are wrong. . . . And, precisely because it is our flag that is involved, one's response to the flag-burner may exploit the uniquely persuasive power of the flag itself. We can imagine no more appropriate response to burning a flag than waving one's own, no better way to counter a flag-burner's message than by saluting the flag that burns, no surer means of preserving the dignity even of the flag that burned than by — as one witness here did — according its remains a respectful burial. We do not consecrate the flag by punishing its desecration, for in doing so we dilute the freedom that this cherished emblem represents.

V

Johnson was convicted for engaging in expressive conduct. The State's interest in preventing breaches of the peace does not support his conviction because Johnson's conduct did not threaten to disturb the peace. Nor does the State's interest in preserving the flag as a symbol of nationhood and national unity justify his criminal conviction for engaging in political expression. The judgment of the Texas Court of Criminal Appeals is therefore *affirmed*.

Justice Kennedy, concurring.

I write not to qualify the words Justice Brennan chooses so well, for he says with power all that is necessary to explain our ruling. I join his opinion without reservation, but with a keen sense that this case, like others before us from time to time, exacts its personal toll. This prompts me to add to our pages these few remarks. The case before us illustrates better than most that the judicial power is often difficult in its exercise. We cannot here ask another Branch to share responsibility, as when the argument is made that a statute is flawed or incomplete. For we are presented with a clear and simple statute to be judged against a pure command of the Constitution. The outcome can be laid at no door but ours.

The hard fact is that sometimes we must make decisions we do not like. We make them because they are right, right in the sense that the law and the Constitution, as we see them, compel the result. And so great is our commitment to the process that, except in the rare case, we do not pause to express distaste for the result, perhaps for fear of undermining a valued principle that dictates the decision. This is one of those rare cases. Our colleagues in dissent advance powerful arguments why respondent may be convicted for his expression, reminding us that among those who will be dismayed by our holding will be some who have had the singular honor of carrying the flag in battle. And I agree that the flag holds a lonely place of honor in an age when absolutes are distrusted and simple truths are burdened by unneeded apologetics.

With all respect to those views, I do not believe the Constitution gives us the right to rule as the dissenting Members of the Court urge, however painful this judgment is to announce. Though symbols often are what we ourselves make of them, the flag is constant in expressing beliefs Americans share, beliefs in law and peace and that freedom which sustains the human spirit. The case here today forces recognition of the costs to which those beliefs commit us. It is poignant but fundamental that the flag protects those who hold it in contempt.

For all the record shows, this respondent was not a philosopher and perhaps did not even possess the ability to comprehend how repellent his statements must be to the Republic itself. But whether or not he could appreciate the enormity of the offense he gave, the fact remains that his acts were speech, in both the technical and the fundamental meaning of the Constitution. So I agree with the Court that he must go free.

Chief Justice Rehnquist, with whom Justice White and Justice O'Connor join, dissenting....

The American flag . . . throughout more than 200 years of our history, has come to be the visible symbol embodying our Nation. It does not represent the views of any particular political party, and it does not represent any particular political philosophy. The flag is not simply another "idea" or "point of view" competing for recognition in the marketplace of ideas. . . . I cannot agree that the First Amendment invalidates the Act of Congress, and the laws of 48 of the 50 States, which make criminal the public burning of the flag. . . .

But the Court insists that the Texas statute prohibiting the public burning of the American flag infringes on respondent Johnson's freedom of expression. Such freedom, of course, is not absolute. . . .

Here it may equally well be said [as it was by a unanimous Court in *Chaplinsky*] that the public burning of the American flag by Johnson was no essential part of any exposition of ideas, and at the same time it had a tendency to incite a breach of the peace. Johnson was free to make any verbal denunciation of the flag that he wished; indeed, he was free to burn the flag in private. He could publicly burn other symbols of the Government or effigies of political leaders. He did lead a march through the streets of Dallas, and conducted a rally in front of the Dallas City Hall. He engaged in a "die-in" to protest nuclear weapons. He shouted out various slogans during the march, including: "Reagan, Mondale which will it be? Either one means World War III"; "Ronald Reagan, killer of the hour, Perfect example of U.S. power"; and "red, white and blue, we spit on you, you stand for plunder, you will go under." For none of these acts was he arrested or prosecuted; it was only when he proceeded to burn publicly an American flag stolen from its rightful owner that he violated the Texas statute.

The Court could not, and did not, say that Chaplinsky's utterances were not expressive phrases — they clearly and succinctly conveyed an extremely low opinion of the addressee. The same may be said of Johnson's public burning of the flag in this case; it obviously did convey Johnson's bitter dislike of his country. But his act, like Chaplinsky's provocative words, conveyed nothing that could not have been conveyed and was not conveyed just as forcefully in a dozen different ways. As with "fighting words," so with flag burning, for purposes of the First Amendment: It is "no essential part of any exposition of ideas, and [is] of such slight social value as a step to truth that any benefit that may be derived from [it] is clearly outweighed by the public interest in avoiding a probable breach of the peace." The highest courts of several States have upheld state statutes prohibiting the public burning of the flag on the grounds that it is so inherently inflammatory that it may cause a breach of public order.

The result of the Texas statute is obviously to deny one in Johnson's frame of mind one of many means of "symbolic speech." Far from being a case of "one picture being worth a thousand words," flag burning is the equivalent of an inarticulate grunt or roar that, it seems fair to say, is most likely to be indulged in not to express any particular idea, but to antagonize others. . . . The Texas statute deprived Johnson of only one rather inarticulate symbolic form of protest — a form of protest that was profoundly offensive to many — and left him with a full panoply of other symbols and every conceivable form of verbal expression to express his deep disapproval of national policy. Thus, in no way can it be said that Texas is punishing him because his hearers — or any other group of people — were profoundly opposed to the message that he sought to convey. Such opposition is no proper basis for restricting speech or expression under the First Amendment. It was Johnson's use of this particular symbol, and not the idea that he sought to convey by it or by his many other expressions, for which he was punished.

The Court concludes its opinion with a regrettably patronizing civics lecture, presumably addressed to the Members of both Houses of Congress, the members of the 48 state legislatures that enacted prohibitions against flag burning, and the troops fighting under that flag in Vietnam who objected to its being burned. . . . The Court's role as the final expositor of the Constitution is well established, but its role as a platonic guardian admonishing those responsible to public opinion as if they were truant school children has no similar place in our system of government. . . . Surely one of the high purposes of a democratic society is to legislate against conduct that is regarded as evil and profoundly offensive to the majority of people — whether it be murder, embezzlement, pollution, or flag burning.

Our Constitution wisely places limits on powers of legislative majorities to act, but the declaration of such limits by this Court "is, at all times, a question of much delicacy, which ought seldom, if ever, to be decided in the affirmative, in a doubtful case." Uncritical extension of constitutional protection to the burning of the flag risks the frustration of the very purpose for which organized governments are instituted. The Court decides that the American flag is just another symbol, about which not only must opinions pro and con be tolerated, but for which the most minimal public respect may not be enjoined. The government may conscript men into the Armed Forces where they must fight and perhaps die for the flag, but the government may not prohibit the public burning of the banner under which they fight. I would uphold the Texas statute as applied in this case.

JUSTICE STEVENS, dissenting.

As the Court analyzes this case, it presents the question whether the State of Texas, or indeed the Federal Government, has the power to prohibit the public desecration of the American flag. The question is unique. In my judgment rules that apply to a host of other symbols, such as state flags, armbands, or various privately promoted emblems of political or commercial identity, are not necessarily controlling. Even if flag burning could be considered just another species of symbolic speech under the logical application of the rules that the Court has developed in its interpretation of the First Amendment in other contexts, this case has an intangible dimension that makes those rules inapplicable.

A country's flag is a symbol of more than "nationhood and national unity." It also signifies the ideas that characterize the society that has chosen that emblem as well as the special history that has animated the growth and power of those ideas. The fleurs-de-lis and the tricolor both symbolized "nationhood and national unity," but they had vastly different meanings. The message conveyed by some flags — the swastika, for example — may survive long after it has outlived its usefulness as a symbol of regimented unity in a particular nation.

So it is with the American flag. It is more than a proud symbol of the courage, the determination, and the gifts of nature that transformed 13 fledgling Colonies into a world power. It is a symbol of freedom, of equal opportunity, of religious tolerance, and of goodwill for other peoples who share our aspirations. The symbol carries its message to dissidents both at home and abroad who may have no interest at all in our national unity or survival.

The value of the flag as a symbol cannot be measured. Even so, I have no doubt that the interest in preserving that value for the future is both significant and legitimate. Conceivably that value will be enhanced by the Court's conclusion that our national commitment to free expression is so strong that even the United States as ultimate guarantor of that freedom is without power to prohibit the desecration of its unique symbol. But I am unpersuaded. The creation of a federal right to post bulletin boards and graffiti on the Washington Monument might enlarge the market for free expression, but at a cost I would not pay. Similarly, in my considered judgment, sanctioning the public desecration of the flag will tarnish its value — both for those who cherish the ideas for which it waves and for those who desire to don the robes of martyrdom by burning it. That tarnish is not justified by the trivial burden on free expression occasioned by requiring that an available, alternative mode of expression — including uttering words critical of the flag — be employed.

It is appropriate to emphasize certain propositions that are not implicated by this case. The statutory prohibition of flag desecration does not . . . compel any conduct or any profession of respect for any idea or any symbol.

Nor does the statute violate "the government's paramount obligation of neutrality in its regulation of protected communication." The content of respondent's message has no relevance whatsoever to the case. The concept of "desecration" does not turn on the substance of the message the actor intends to convey, but rather on whether those who view the act will take serious offense. Accordingly, one intending to convey a message of respect for the flag by burning it in a public square might nonetheless be guilty of desecration if he knows that others — perhaps simply because they misperceive the intended message — will be seriously offended. Indeed, even if the actor knows that all possible witnesses will understand that he intends to send a message of respect, he might still be guilty of desecration if he also knows that this understanding does not lessen the offense taken by some of those witnesses. . . .

The case has nothing to do with "disagreeable ideas." It involves disagreeable conduct that, in my opinion, diminishes the value of an important national asset.

The Court is therefore quite wrong in blandly asserting that respondent "was prosecuted for his expression of dissatisfaction with the policies of this country, expression situated at the core of our First Amendment values." Respondent was prosecuted because of the method he chose to express his dissatisfaction with those policies. Had he chosen to spray paint — or perhaps convey with a motion picture projector — his message of dissatisfaction on the facade of the Lincoln Memorial, there would be no question about the power of the Government to prohibit his means of expression. The prohibition would be supported by the legitimate interest in preserving the quality of an important national asset. Though the asset at stake in this case is intangible, given its unique value, the same interest supports a prohibition on the desecration of the American flag.

The ideas of liberty and equality have been an irresistible force in motivating leaders like Patrick Henry, Susan B. Anthony, and Abraham Lincoln, schoolteachers like Nathan Hale and Booker T. Washington, the Philippine Scouts who fought at Bataan, and the soldiers who scaled the bluff at Omaha Beach. If those ideas are worth fighting for — and our history demonstrates that they are — it cannot be true that the flag that uniquely symbolizes their power is not itself worthy of protection from unnecessary desecration.

I respectfully dissent.

United States v. Stevens

United States Supreme Court
559 U.S. 460, 130 S. Ct. 1577, 176 L. Ed. 2d 435 (2010)

CHIEF JUSTICE ROBERTS delivered the opinion of the Court.

Congress enacted 18 U.S.C. §48 to criminalize the commercial creation, sale, or possession of certain depictions of animal cruelty. The statute does not address underlying acts harmful to animals, but only portrayals of such conduct. The question presented is whether the prohibition in the statute is consistent with the freedom of speech guaranteed by the First Amendment.

I

Section 48 establishes a criminal penalty of up to five years in prison for anyone who knowingly "creates, sells, or possesses a depiction of animal cruelty," if done "for commercial gain" in interstate or foreign commerce. §48(a). A depiction of "animal cruelty" is defined as one "in which a living animal is intentionally maimed, mutilated, tortured, wounded, or killed," if that conduct violates federal or state law where "the creation, sale, or possession takes place." §48(c)(1). In what is referred to as the "exceptions clause," the law exempts from prohibition any depiction "that has serious religious, political, scientific, educational, journalistic, historical, or artistic value." §48(b).

This case, however, involves an application of §48 to depictions of animal fighting. Dogfighting, for example, is unlawful in all 50 States and the District of Columbia, Respondent Robert J. Stevens ran a business, "Dogs of Velvet and Steel," and an associated Web site, through which he sold videos of pit bulls engaging in dogfights and attacking other animals. Among these videos were Japan Pit Fights and

Pick-A-Winna: A Pit Bull Documentary, which include contemporary footage of dogfights in Japan (where such conduct is allegedly legal) as well as footage of American dogfights from the 1960's and 1970's. A third video, Catch Dogs and Country Living, depicts the use of pit bulls to hunt wild boar, as well as a "gruesome" scene of a pit bull attacking a domestic farm pig. On the basis of these videos, Stevens was indicted on three counts of violating § 48.

. . . The jury convicted Stevens on all counts, and the District Court sentenced him to three concurrent sentences of 37 months' imprisonment, followed by three years of supervised release.

II

The Government's primary submission is that § 48 necessarily complies with the Constitution because the banned depictions of animal cruelty, as a class, are categorically unprotected by the First Amendment. We disagree.

The First Amendment provides that "Congress shall make no law . . . abridging the freedom of speech." "[A]s a general matter, the First Amendment means that government has no power to restrict expression because of its message, its ideas, its subject matter, or its content." *Ashcroft v. American Civil Liberties Union*, 535 U.S. 564, 573 (2002). Section 48 explicitly regulates expression based on content: The statute restricts "visual [and] auditory depiction[s]," such as photographs, videos, or sound recordings, depending on whether they depict conduct in which a living animal is intentionally harmed. As such, § 48 is "'presumptively invalid,' and the Government bears the burden to rebut that presumption." United States v. Playboy Entertainment Group, Inc., 529 U.S. 803, 817 (2000) (quoting *R.A.V. v. St. Paul*, 505 U.S. 377, 382 (1992)).

. . . The Government argues that "depictions of animal cruelty" should be added to the list. It contends that depictions of "illegal acts of animal cruelty" that are "made, sold, or possessed for commercial gain" necessarily "lack expressive value," and may accordingly "be regulated as *unprotected* speech." The claim is not just that Congress may regulate depictions of animal cruelty subject to the First Amendment, but that these depictions are outside the reach of that Amendment altogether — that they fall into a "'First Amendment Free Zone.'" *Board of Airport Comm'rs of Los Angeles v. Jews for Jesus, Inc.*, 482 U.S. 569, 574 (1987).

As the Government notes, the prohibition of animal cruelty itself has a long history in American law, starting with the early settlement of the Colonies. . . . But we are unaware of any similar tradition excluding *depictions* of animal cruelty from "the freedom of speech" codified in the First Amendment, and the Government points us to none.

The Government contends that "historical evidence" about the reach of the First Amendment is not "a necessary prerequisite for regulation today," and that categories of speech may be exempted from the First Amendment's protection without any long-settled tradition of subjecting that speech to regulation. Instead, the Government points to Congress's "'legislative judgment that . . . depictions of animals being intentionally tortured and killed [are] of such minimal redeeming value as to render [them] unworthy of First Amendment protection,'" and asks the Court to uphold the ban on the same basis. The Government thus proposes that a claim of categorical exclusion should be considered under a simple balancing test: "Whether a given category of speech enjoys First Amendment protection depends upon a categorical balancing of the value of the speech against its societal costs."

As a free-floating test for First Amendment coverage, that sentence is startling and dangerous. The First Amendment's guarantee of free speech does not extend only to categories of speech that survive an ad hoc balancing of relative social costs and benefits. The First Amendment itself reflects a judgment by the American people that the benefits of its restrictions on the Government outweigh the costs. Our Constitution forecloses any attempt to revise that judgment simply on the basis that some speech is not worth it. The Constitution is not a document "prescribing limits, and declaring that those limits may be passed at pleasure." *Marbury v. Madison,* 1 Cranch 137, 178, (1803).

. . . In *New York v. Ferber,* 458 U.S. 747 (1982), we noted that within these categories of unprotected speech, "the evil to be restricted so overwhelmingly outweighs the expressive interests, if any, at stake, that no process of case-by-case adjudication is required," because "the balance of competing interests is clearly struck." The Government derives its proposed test from these descriptions in our precedents.

But such descriptions are just that — descriptive. They do not set forth a test that may be applied as a general matter to permit the Government to imprison any speaker so long as his speech is deemed valueless or unnecessary, or so long as an ad hoc calculus of costs and benefits tilts in a statute's favor.

When we have identified categories of speech as fully outside the protection of the First Amendment, it has not been on the basis of a simple cost-benefit analysis. *In Ferber,* for example, we classified child pornography as such a category, 458 U.S., at 763. We noted that the State of New York had a compelling interest in protecting children from abuse . . . But our decision did not rest on this "balance of competing interests" alone. We made clear that *Ferber* presented a special case: The market for child pornography was "intrinsically related" to the underlying abuse, and was therefore "an integral part of the production of such materials, an activity illegal throughout the Nation." *Ferber* at 759, 761. . . .

Our decisions in *Ferber* and other cases cannot be taken as establishing a freewheeling authority to declare new categories of speech outside the scope of the First Amendment. Maybe there are some categories of speech that have been historically unprotected, but have not yet been specifically identified or discussed as such in our case law. But if so, there is no evidence that "depictions of animal cruelty" is among them. We need not foreclose the future recognition of such additional categories to reject the Government's highly manipulable balancing test as a means of identifying them.

III

Because we decline to carve out from the First Amendment any novel exception for § 48, we review Stevens's First Amendment challenge under our existing doctrine.

A

... [W]e granted the Solicitor General's petition for certiorari to determine whether 18 U.S.C. 48 is facially invalid under the Free Speech Clause of the First Amendment.

To succeed in a typical facial attack, Stevens would have to establish "that no set of circumstances exists under which [§ 48] would be valid," *United States v. Salerno*, 481 U.S. 739, 745 (1987), or that the statute lacks any "plainly legitimate sweep," *Washington v. Glucksberg*, 521 U.S. 702, 740, n. 7 (1997) (Stevens, J., concurring in judgments) ...

In the First Amendment context, however, this Court recognizes "a second type of facial challenge," whereby a law may be invalidated as overbroad if "a substantial number of its applications are unconstitutional, judged in relation to the statute's plainly legitimate sweep." *Washington State Grange v. Washington State Republican Party*, 552 U.S. 442, 449, n. 6 (2008). Stevens argues that § 48 applies to common depictions of ordinary and lawful activities, and that these depictions constitute the vast majority of materials subject to the statute. The Government makes no effort to defend such a broad ban as constitutional. Instead, the Government's entire defense of § 48 rests on interpreting the statute as narrowly limited to specific types of "extreme" material. As the parties have presented the issue, therefore, the constitutionality of § 48 hinges on how broadly it is construed. It is to that question that we now turn.

B

... We read § 48 to create a criminal prohibition of alarming breadth. To begin with, the text of the statute's ban on a "depiction of animal cruelty" nowhere requires that the depicted conduct be cruel. That text applies to "any ... depiction" in which "a living animal is intentionally maimed, mutilated, tortured, wounded, or killed." § 48(c)(1). "[M]aimed, mutilated, [and] tortured" convey cruelty, but "wounded" or "killed" do not suggest any such limitation.

... While not requiring cruelty, § 48 does require that the depicted conduct be "illegal." But this requirement does not limit § 48 along the lines the Government suggests. There are myriad federal and state laws concerning the proper treatment of animals, but many of them are not designed to guard against animal cruelty. Protections of endangered species, for example, restrict even the humane "wound[ing] or kill[ing]" of "living animal[s]." § 48(c)(1). Livestock regulations are often designed to protect the health of human beings, and hunting and fishing rules (seasons, licensure, bag limits, weight requirements) can be designed to raise revenue, preserve animal populations, or prevent accidents. The text of § 48(c) draws no distinction based on the reason the intentional killing of an animal is made illegal, and includes, for example, the humane slaughter of a stolen cow.

What is more, the application of § 48 to depictions of illegal conduct extends to conduct that is illegal in only a single jurisdiction. Under subsection (c)(1), the depicted conduct need only be illegal in "the State in which the creation, sale, or possession takes place, regardless of whether the . . . wounding . . . or killing took place in [that] State." A depiction of entirely lawful conduct runs afoul of the ban if that depiction later finds its way into another State where the same conduct is unlawful. This provision greatly expands the scope of § 48, because although there may be "a broad societal consensus" against cruelty to animals there is substantial disagreement on what types of conduct are properly regarded as cruel. Both views about cruelty to animals and regulations having no connection to cruelty vary widely from place to place.

In the District of Columbia, for example, all hunting is unlawful. . . . Other jurisdictions permit or encourage hunting, and there is an enormous national market for hunting-related depictions in which a living animal is intentionally killed. Hunting periodicals have circulations in the hundreds of thousands or millions . . . [but] because the statute allows each jurisdiction to export its laws to the rest of the country, § 48(a) extends to *any* magazine or video depicting lawful hunting, so long as that depiction is sold within the Nation's Capital.

C

The only thing standing between defendants who sell such depictions and five years in federal prison — other than the mercy of a prosecutor — is the statute's exceptions clause. Subsection (b) exempts from prohibition "any depiction that has serious religious, political, scientific, educational, journalistic, historical, or artistic value." The Government argues that this clause substantially narrows the statute's reach: News reports about animal cruelty have "journalistic" value; pictures of bullfights in Spain have "historical" value; and instructional hunting videos have "educational" value.

The Government's attempt to narrow the statutory ban, however, requires an unrealistically broad reading of the exceptions clause. As the Government reads the clause, any material with "redeeming societal value," [or] "at least some minimal value." But the text says "serious" value, and "serious" should be taken seriously. We decline the Government's invitation-advanced for the first time in this Court — to regard as "serious" anything that is not "scant."

Quite apart from the requirement of "serious" value in § 48(b), the excepted speech must also fall within one of the enumerated categories. Much speech does not. Most hunting videos, for example, are not obviously instructional in nature, except in the sense that all life is a lesson. According to Safari Club International and the Congressional Sportsmen's Foundation, many popular videos "have primarily entertainment value" and are designed to "entertai[n] the viewer, marke[t] hunting equipment, or increas[e] the hunting community."

In *Miller* we held that "serious" value shields depictions of sex from regulation as obscenity.... We did not, however, determine that serious value could be used as a general precondition to protecting *other* types of speech in the first place. *Most* of what we say to one another lacks "religious, political, scientific, educational, journalistic, historical, or artistic value" (let alone serious value), but it is still sheltered from government regulation.

Thus, the protection of the First Amendment presumptively extends to many forms of speech that do not qualify for the serious-value exception of §48(b), but nonetheless fall within the broad reach of §48(c).

D

Not to worry, the Government says [in its brief]: The Executive Branch construes §48 to reach only "extreme" cruelty and it "neither has brought nor will bring a prosecution for anything less." The Government hits this theme hard, invoking its prosecutorial discretion several times. But the First Amendment protects against the Government; it does not leave us at the mercy of *noblesse oblige*. We would not uphold an unconstitutional statute merely because the Government promised to use it responsibly.

This prosecution is itself evidence of the danger in putting faith in government representations of prosecutorial restraint. When this legislation was enacted, the Executive Branch announced that it would interpret §48 as covering only depictions "of wanton cruelty to animals designed to appeal to a prurient interest in sex." See Statement by President William J. Clinton upon Signing H.R. 1887, 34 Weekly Comp. Pres. Doc. 2557 (Dec. 9, 1999). No one suggests that the videos in this case fit that description. The Government's assurance that it will apply §48 far more restrictively than its language provides is pertinent only as an implicit acknowledgment of the potential constitutional problems with a more natural reading....

JUSTICE ALITO dissenting.

The Court strikes down in its entirety a valuable statute, 18 U.S.C. §48, that was enacted not to suppress speech, but to prevent horrific acts of animal cruelty — in particular, the creation and commercial exploitation of "crush videos," a form of depraved entertainment that has no social value. The Court's approach, which has the practical effect of legalizing the sale of such videos and is thus likely to spur a resumption of their production, is unwarranted....

As the Court of Appeals recognized, "the primary conduct that Congress sought to address through its passage [of §48] was the creation, sale, or possession of 'crush videos.'" A sample crush video, which has been lodged with the Clerk, records the following event:

> "[A] kitten, secured to the ground, watches and shrieks in pain as a woman thrusts her high-heeled shoe into its body, slams her heel into the kitten's eye socket and mouth loudly fracturing its skull, and stomps

repeatedly on the animal's head. The kitten hemorrhages blood, screams blindly in pain, and is ultimately left dead in a moist pile of blood-soaked hair and bone."

It is undisputed that the *conduct* depicted in crush videos may constitutionally be prohibited. All 50 States and the District of Columbia have enacted statutes prohibiting animal cruelty . . . These videos, which "often appeal to persons with a very specific sexual fetish," were made in secret, generally without a live audience, and "the faces of the women inflicting the torture in the material often were not shown, nor could the location of the place where the cruelty was being inflicted or the date of the activity be ascertained from the depiction." Thus, law enforcement authorities often were not able to identify the parties responsible for the torture.

. . . In light of the practical problems thwarting the prosecution of the creators of crush videos under state animal cruelty laws, Congress concluded that the only effective way of stopping the underlying criminal conduct was to prohibit the commercial exploitation of the videos of that conduct. And Congress' strategy appears to have been vindicated. We are told that "[b]y 2007, sponsors of § 48 declared the crush video industry dead. Even overseas Websites shut down in the wake of § 48."

The First Amendment protects freedom of speech, but it most certainly does not protect violent criminal conduct, even if engaged in for expressive purposes. Crush videos present a highly unusual free speech issue because they are so closely linked with violent criminal conduct. The videos record the commission of violent criminal acts, and it appears that these crimes are committed for the sole purpose of creating the videos. In addition, as noted above, Congress was presented with compelling evidence that the only way of preventing these crimes was to target the sale of the videos. Under these circumstances, I cannot believe that the First Amendment commands Congress to step aside and allow the underlying crimes to continue.

The most relevant of our prior decisions is *Ferber, 458 U.S. 747, which concerned child pornography. The Court there held that child pornography is not protected speech, and I believe that Ferber 's reasoning dictates a similar conclusion here. . . .*

It must be acknowledged that § 48 differs from a child pornography law in an important respect: preventing the abuse of children is certainly much more important than preventing the torture of the animals used in crush videos. . . . But while protecting children is unquestionably *more* important than protecting animals, the Government also has a compelling interest in preventing the torture depicted in crush videos.

The animals used in crush videos are living creatures that experience excruciating pain. Our society has long banned such cruelty, which is illegal throughout the country. . . .

For these reasons, I respectfully dissent.

Notes and Questions

(1) In United *States v. Alvarez*, 567 U.S. 709 (2012), the Supreme Court, in a plurality opinion written by Justice Kennedy and joined by Chief Justice Roberts, Justice Ginsburg, and Justice Sotomayor, struck down the Stolen Valor Act of 2005. *See* RODNEY SMOLLA, SMOLLA & NIMMER ON FREEDOM OF SPEECH § 3:7.50, *Attempting to criminalize mere "lies"— The Stolen Valor Act example* (2018 Edition).

As recounted by the Court: "In 2007, respondent attended his first public meeting as a board member of the Three Valley Water District Board. The board is a governmental entity with headquarters in Claremont, California. He introduced himself as follows: "I'm a retired marine of 25 years. I retired in the year 2001. Back in 1987, I was awarded the Congressional Medal of Honor. I got wounded many times by the same guy." All of this was false. As the plurality opinion of Justice Kennedy characterized it, the "statements were but a pathetic attempt to gain respect that eluded him." Alvarez was convicted of violating the Stolen Valor Act, which provided in pertinent part:

> (b) FALSE CLAIMS ABOUT RECEIPT OF MILITARY DECORATIONS OR MEDALS. — Whoever falsely represents himself or herself, verbally or in writing, to have been awarded any decoration or medal authorized by Congress for the Armed Forces of the United States . . . shall be fined under this title, imprisoned not more than six months, or both.

> (c) ENHANCED PENALTY FOR OFFENSES INVOLVING CONGRESSIONAL MEDAL OF HONOR. —

> (1) IN GENERAL. — If a decoration or medal involved in an offense under subsection (a) or (b) is a Congressional Medal of Honor, in lieu of the punishment provided in that subsection, the offender shall be fined under this title, imprisoned not more than 1 year, or both.

The plurality held that the list of categories of speech that may be regulated does not include any general exclusion of protection for false statements, a view compatible with the assumption that false statements are inevitable in a society committed to open discussion and debate. While there had been sound bites from many prior Supreme Court opinions seeming to indicate that false statements do not deserve constitutional protection, the plurality conceded, those quotations standing alone displace them from their proper context. The quotations, the plurality reasoned, all derived from cases discussing "defamation, fraud, or some other legally cognizable harm associated with a false statement, such as an invasion of privacy or the costs of vexatious litigation." While the element of falsity was relevant to the analysis of those cases, the plurality argued, it was not determinative. As the plurality saw it, the Court had never endorsed the categorical rule that false statements receive no First Amendment protection, and no prior decision had confronted a law that targeted "falsity and nothing more." The plurality rejected the attempt of the government to analogize the Stolen Valor Act to other laws in which restrictions on false speech are permissible, such as laws prohibiting lying to government officials, laws punishing perjury, or impersonating a government official. In each instance, the plurality maintained, societal interests going beyond the prevention of the falsehood itself were at stake. For example, perjured statements are not simply unprotected because they are false, but because they are "'at war with justice'" and may cause a court to render a "'judgment not resting on truth.'" Moreover, "[u]nlike speech in other contexts, testimony under oath has the formality and gravity necessary to remind the witness that his or her statements will be the basis for official governmental action, action that often affects the rights and liberties of others." Sworn testimony, the plurality reasoned, is thus distinct from the ordinary lie "simply intended to puff up oneself." Similarly, the plurality reasoned, laws prohibiting the impersonation of government officials serve to preserve the integrity of governmental processes. The plurality conceded, nonetheless, that First Amendment doctrine did not stand as an absolute bar to the identification of new categories of unprotected speech. Thus, "[a]lthough the First Amendment stands against any 'freewheeling authority to declare new categories of speech outside the scope of the First Amendment,' the Court has acknowledged that perhaps there exist 'some categories of speech that have been historically unprotected . . . but have not yet been specifically identified or discussed . . . in our case law.'" But prior to "exempting a category of speech from the normal prohibition on content-based restrictions," the plurality maintained, "the Court must be presented with 'persuasive evidence that a novel restriction on content is part of a long (if heretofore unrecognized) tradition of proscription.'"

The plurality in *Alvarez* found the broad sweep of the law to be one of its major infirmities. The law applied "to a false statement made at any time, in any place, to any person." If the government could label this speech a criminal offense, the plurality reasoned, such a holding "would endorse government authority to compile a list of subjects about which false statements are punishable." Invoking the imagery of George Orwell's classic novel Nineteen Eighty Four, the plurality declared that "[our] constitutional tradition stands against the idea that we need Oceania's Ministry of Truth. Invoking a kind of "falsity plus" test, the plurality emphasized the critical difference between penalizing falsehood merely because it is falsehood, and penalizing falsehood when it is uttered to obtain some material advantage.

In its analysis of the merits, the plurality recognized the significance of the government's proffered interest, agreeing that "[i]n periods of war and peace alike public recognition of valor and noble sacrifice by men and women in uniform reinforces the pride and national resolve that the military relies upon to fulfill its mission." The plurality found an insufficient link between the Government's interest in protecting the integrity of the military honors system and the Act's restriction on the false claims of liars. The government had produced no actual evidence that the public perception of military awards was diluted by false claims such as those made by Alvarez. In an important passage, the plurality also emphasized the importance of counterspeech in the balance, and the requirement that the government show that counterspeech will not work to vindicate its interests. Alvarez was ridiculed at the public meeting where he made the false claims, and later online. As the plurality proclaimed, the remedy for false speech is true speech: "The remedy for speech that is false is speech that is true. This is the ordinary course in a free society. The response to the unreasoned is the rational; to the uninformed, the enlightened; to the straight-out lie, the simple truth." Echoing Oliver Wendell Holmes, the plurality admonished that "[t]he theory of our Constitution is 'that the best test of truth is the power of the thought to get itself accepted in the competition of the market.'" In a classic restatement of First Amendment theory, the plurality observed:

> The First Amendment itself ensures the right to respond to speech we do not like, and for good reason. Freedom of speech and thought flows not from the beneficence of the state but from the inalienable rights of the person. And suppression of speech by the government can make exposure of falsity more difficult, not less so. Society has the right and civic duty to engage in open, dynamic, rational discourse. These ends are not well served when the government seeks to orchestrate public discussion through content-based mandates.

The plurality concluded that any true holders of the Medal who had heard of Alvarez's false claims "would have been fully vindicated by the community's expression of outrage, showing as it did the Nation's high regard for the Medal." The same, the plurality argued, could be said for the interest offered by the government; the American people do not need a criminal prosecution to express their esteem for their heroes. "Only a weak society needs government protection or intervention before it pursues its resolve to preserve the truth. Truth needs neither handcuffs nor a badge for its vindication."

The plurality also pointed to another simple expedient that would have largely vindicated the government's interest: a simple government-run database that listed all Congressional Medal of Honor winners. The plurality concluded by stating that the "Nation well knows that one of the costs of the First Amendment is that it protects the speech we detest as well as the speech we embrace." While most would find the speech of Alvarez contemptible, the plurality concluded, it was protected by the First Amendment.

Justice Breyer, joined by Justice Kagan, agreed with the judgment of the Court, concluding that the Stolen Valor Act violated the First Amendment, but rejected the plurality's analysis. Justice Breyer's opinion applied "intermediate scrutiny" review. Justice Breyer's opinion held up laws prohibiting trademark infringement as the closest analogy to the Stolen Valor Act. Just as trademark infringement may cause harm by inducing confusion among potential customers as to the source of goods, thereby "diluting the value of the mark to its owner, to consumers, and to the economy," he argued, "a false claim of possession of a medal or other honor creates confusion about who is entitled to wear it, thus diluting its value to those who have earned it, to their families, and to their country." Trademark laws, however, are focused on actual commercial harm. Much like the plurality, Justice Breyer ultimately settled on the principle that few, if any statutes simply prohibit the telling of a lie. And again, much like the plurality, Justice Breyer's opinion then went on to posit alternative avenues that would largely vindicate the government's proffered interests, concluding that "[t]he Government has provided no convincing explanation as to why a more finely tailored statute would not work."

Justice Alito, joined by Justices Scalia and Thomas, wrote a spirited dissent, holding out the valor of those who are awarded the Congressional Medal of Honor:

> Only the bravest of the brave are awarded the Congressional Medal of Honor, but the Court today holds that every American has a constitutional right to claim to have received this singular award. The Court strikes down the Stolen Valor Act of 2005, which was enacted to stem an epidemic of false claims about military decorations. These lies, Congress reasonably concluded, were undermining our country's system of military honors and inflicting real harm on actual medal recipients and their families.

Justice Alito argued that "the right to free speech does not protect false factual statements that inflict real harm and serve no legitimate interest." Applying that standard, he and his three dissenting colleagues would have upheld the law. His opinion included a number of constructions of the law that narrowed its reach. "First," he argued, "the Act applies to only a narrow category of false representations about objective facts that can almost always be proved or disproved with near certainty." Second, "the Act concerns facts that are squarely within the speaker's personal knowledge." Third, as he understood both the plurality and concurrence to concede, the law required proof beyond a reasonable doubt "that the speaker actually knew that the representation was false." Fourth, the law can be appropriately construed as applicable only to actual factual assertions, and not to expressions such as "dramatic performances, satire, parody, hyperbole, or the like." Finally, and perhaps most interestingly, Justice Alito argued that the law was "strictly viewpoint neutral." The law, he reasoned, applied to all false statements, without regard to any connection to a particular "political or ideological message."

(2) After the *Johnson* decision, Congress passed the Flag Protection Act of 1989, which provides in pertinent part:

> (a)(1) Whoever knowingly mutilates, defaces, physically defiles, burns, maintains on the floor or ground, or tramples upon any flag of the United States shall be fined under this title or imprisoned for not more than one year, or both.

> (2) This subsection does not prohibit any conduct consisting of the disposal of a flag when it has become worn or soiled.

> (b) As used in this section, the term "flag of the United States" means any flag of the United States, or any part thereof, made of any substance, of any size, in a form that is commonly displayed.

The constitutionality of that Act was challenged in *United States v. Eichman*, 496 U.S. 310 (1990). The Government contended that the Act is constitutional because, unlike the Texas statute addressed in *Johnson*, the federal law does not target expressive conduct on the basis of the content of the message. The Texas statute prohibited only those acts of flag desecration that offended onlookers. The federal law prohibited desecration without regard to the actor's motive or the likely effect on others. In *Eichman*, a majority of the Court rejected this distinction, holding the federal act unconstitutional. The Government's asserted interest is related to the suppression of free expression. The Act, therefore, suffers from the same fundamental flaw as the Texas statute: "it suppresses expression out of concern for its likely communicative impact."

§ 9.04 Content-Based, Viewpoint-Based, and Content-Neutral Regulation

A. Content and Viewpoint Discrimination

The Divide Between Content and Non-Content Regulation. With the ascendency of the Marketplace Theory, a key divide emerged. A central theme of modern First Amendment jurisprudence is the distinction between content-based speech regulation, and regulations that are content-neutral, impacting in some incidental way on speech, or regulating only the "modes" of communication, such as the time, the place, or the volume level of the expression.

Content Regulation. As a general matter, contemporary First Amendment doctrine treats content-based regulation of speech as presumptively invalid, and subject to the "strict scrutiny" test, placing high burdens on the government to justify its regulation. "Content-based laws — those that target speech based on its communicative content — are presumptively unconstitutional and may be justified only if the government proves that they are narrowly tailored to serve compelling state interests." *Reed v. Town of Gilbert*, Ariz., 135 S. Ct. 2218, 2226 (2015).

Viewpoint Regulation. Viewpoint regulation is a narrower concept than content regulation. When the government regulates on the basis of content, it often regulates in terms of broad subject matter categories. A law forbidding political speech within an airport, for example, would be content-based. Viewpoint regulation purports to ban or regulate a specific point-of-view *within* a content category, often "taking sides" in a debate. A law that made it legal to distribute Republican Party literature in airports, but not Democratic Party literature, would be viewpoint-based. Modern First Amendment doctrine is intensely antagonistic to view-point discrimination. The prohibition on such discrimination is virtually absolute. *See R.A.V. v. City of St. Paul*, 506 U.S. 377 (1992).

Heightened Scrutiny in the General Marketplace. One of the confusing aspects of modern First Amendment law is the place of tests such as "strict scrutiny," which apply to content-based regulation of speech, in relation to other tests that apply to specific doctrinal areas, such as "incitement" or "true threats." Modern First Amendment jurisprudence generally does not employ one omnibus doctrinal test for content-based and viewpoint-based regulation of speech in the general marketplace. Instead, discrete doctrinal tests and formulas have evolved to govern specific types of speech regulation. These various formulations, tailored to the particular contexts in which they arise, are all highly protective of speech, placing heavy burdens on the government before it may presume to abridge speech interests in the general marketplace. They include such doctrines as the "incitement" test protecting the advocacy of violence; the "actual malice" test protecting defendants in libel cases involving public officials and public figures; and the "heavy presumption" against prior restraints. One way to make sense of this complexity is to treat the strict scrutiny test as a sort of "default" standard that tends to be applied when no specialized standard is applicable. But when a specific test is applicable — for incitement or true threats or defamation, for example — then the specific test displaces the general strict scrutiny test.

Content-Neutral Regulation. Content-neutral regulations are generally reviewed by courts under less exacting standards. Content-neutral regulations arise in a number of contexts. One frequent context involves the "time, place, or manner" regulation of speech in public forums. These are rules that govern things such as when and where and how loud speech in a public forum, such a public park, may occur. These "time, place, or manner" regulations are not discussed in this section of this Chapter, but are deferred to the subsection dealing with public forum law. The two forms of content-neutral regulation discussed in this Chapter involve laws that are aimed at some regulatory purpose unrelated to the message of speech, but that incidentally burden speech — laws that are subjected to the *O'Brien* test, named after the case below, and situations in which speech is used to prove the element of a crime, or a penalty enhancement for a crime. As the *Wisconsin v. Mitchell* case below explains, the mere *evidentiary* use of speech to prove the element of some offense is not treated as a regulation of speech *at all*, and is entirely immune from First Amendment scrutiny.

B. Incidental Burdens on Speech and the *O'Brien* Principle

United States v. O'Brien

United States Supreme Court
391 U.S. 367, 88 S. Ct. 1673, 20 L. Ed. 2d 672 (1968)

Mr. Chief Justice Warren delivered the opinion of the Court.

On the morning of March 31, 1966, David Paul O'Brien and three companions burned their Selective Service registration certificates on the steps of the South Boston Courthouse. A sizable crowd, including several agents of the Federal Bureau of Investigation, witnessed the event. Immediately after the burning, members of the crowd began attacking O'Brien and his companions. An FBI agent ushered O'Brien to safety inside the courthouse. After he was advised of his right to counsel and to silence, O'Brien stated to FBI agents that he had burned his registration certificate because of his beliefs, knowing that he was violating federal law. He produced the charred remains of the certificate, which, with his consent, were photographed.

For this act, O'Brien was indicted, tried, convicted, and sentenced in the United States District Court for the District of Massachusetts. He did not contest the fact that he had burned the certificate. He stated in argument to the jury that he burned the certificate publicly to influence others to adopt his antiwar beliefs, as he put it, "so that other people would reevaluate their positions with Selective Service, with the armed forces, and reevaluate their place in the culture of today, to hopefully consider my position."

The indictment upon which he was tried charged that he "willfully and knowingly did mutilate, destroy, and change by burning . . . [his] Registration Certificate (Selective Service System Form No. 2). . . ."

I

When a male reaches the age of 18, he is required by the Universal Military Training and Service Act to register with a local draft board. He is assigned a Selective Service number, and within five days he is issued a registration certificate (SSS Form No. 2). Subsequently, and based on a questionnaire completed by the registrant, he is assigned a classification denoting his eligibility for induction, and "[a]s soon as practicable" thereafter he is issued a Notice of Classification (SSS Form No. 110). This initial classification is not necessarily permanent, and if in the interim before induction the registrant's status changes in some relevant way, he may be reclassified. After such a reclassification, the local board "as soon as practicable" issues to the registrant a new Notice of Classification.

Both the registration and classification certificates are small white cards, approximately 2 by 3 inches. The registration certificate specifies the name of the registrant, the date of registration, and the number and address of the local board with which he is registered. Also inscribed upon it are the date and place of the registrant's birth, his residence at registration, his physical description, his signature, and his Selective Service number. The Selective Service number itself indicates his State of registration, his local board, his year of birth, and his chronological position in the local board's classification record.

The classification certificate shows the registrant's name, Selective Service number, signature, and eligibility classification. It specifies whether he was so classified by his local board, an appeal board, or the President. It contains the address of his local board and the date the certificate was mailed. . . .

By the 1965 Amendment, Congress added to § 12(b)(3) of the 1948 Act the provision here at issue, subjecting to criminal liability not only one who "forges, alters, or in any manner changes" but also one who "knowingly destroys, [or] knowingly mutilates" a certificate. We note at the outset that the 1965 Amendment plainly does not abridge free speech on its face, and we do not understand O'Brien to argue otherwise. Amendment § 12(b)(3) on its face deals with conduct having no connection with speech. It prohibits the knowing destruction of certificates issued by the Selective Service System, and there is nothing necessarily expressive about such conduct. The Amendment does not distinguish between public and private destruction, and it does not punish only destruction engaged in for the purpose of expressing views.... A law prohibiting destruction of Selective Service certificates no more abridges free speech on its face than a motor vehicle law prohibiting the destruction of drivers' licenses, or a tax law prohibiting the destruction of books and records.

O'Brien nonetheless argues that the 1965 Amendment is unconstitutional in its application to him, and is unconstitutional as enacted because what he calls the "purpose" of Congress was "to suppress freedom of speech." We consider these arguments separately.

II

O'Brien first argues that the 1965 Amendment is unconstitutional as applied to him because his act of burning his registration certificate was protected "symbolic speech" within the First Amendment. His argument is that the freedom of expression which the First Amendment guarantees includes all modes of "communication of ideas by conduct," and that his conduct is within this definition because he did it in "demonstration against the war and against the draft."

We cannot accept the view that an apparently limitless variety of conduct can be labeled "speech" whenever the person engaging in the conduct intends thereby to express an idea. However, even on the assumption that the alleged communicative element in O'Brien's conduct is sufficient to bring into play the First Amendment, it does not necessarily follow that the destruction of a registration certificate is constitutionally protected activity. This Court has held that when "speech" and "nonspeech" elements are combined in the same course of conduct, a sufficiently important governmental interest in regulating the nonspeech element can justify incidental limitations on First Amendment freedoms. To characterize the quality of the governmental interest which must appear, the Court has employed a variety of descriptive terms: compelling; substantial; subordinating; paramount; cogent; strong. Whatever imprecision inheres in these terms, we think it clear that a government regulation is sufficiently justified if it is within the constitutional power of the Government; if it furthers an important or substantial governmental interest; if the governmental interest is unrelated to the suppression of free expression; and if the incidental restriction on alleged First Amendment freedoms is no greater than is essential to the furtherance of that interest. We find that the 1965 Amendment to §12(b)(3) of the Universal Military Training and Service Act meets all of these requirements, and consequently that O'Brien can be constitutionally convicted for violating it.

The constitutional power of Congress to raise and support armies and to make all laws necessary and proper to that end is broad and sweeping.... The power of Congress to classify and conscript manpower for military service is "beyond question."... Pursuant to this power, Congress may establish a system of registration for individuals liable for training and service, and may require such individuals within reason to cooperate in the registration system. The issuance of certificates indicating the registration and eligibility classification of individuals is a legitimate and substantial administrative aid in the functioning of this system. And legislation to insure the continuing availability of issued certificates serves a legitimate and substantial purpose in the system's administration.

O'Brien's argument to the contrary is necessarily premised upon his unrealistic characterization of Selective Service certificates. He essentially adopts the position that such certificates are so many pieces of paper designed to notify registrants of their registration or classification, to be retained or tossed in the wastebasket according to the convenience or taste of the registrant. Once the registrant has received notification, according to this view, there is no reason for him to retain the certificates. O'Brien notes that most of the information on a registration certificate serves no notification purpose at all; the registrant hardly needs to be told his address and physical characteristics. We agree that the registration certificate contains much information of which the registrant needs no notification. This circumstance, however, does not lead to the conclusion that the certificate serves no purpose, but that, like the classification certificate, it serves purposes in addition to initial notification. Many of these purposes would be defeated by the certificates' destruction or mutilation. Among these are:

1. The registration certificate serves as proof that the individual described thereon has registered for the draft. . . .

2. The information supplied on the certificates facilitates communication between registrants and local boards, simplifying the system and benefiting all concerned. . . .

3. Both certificates carry continual reminders that the registrant must notify his local board of any change of address, and other specified changes in his status. The smooth functioning of the system requires that local boards be continually aware of the status and whereabouts of registrants, and the destruction of certificates deprives the system of a potentially useful notice device.

4. The regulatory scheme involving Selective Service certificates includes clearly valid prohibitions against the alteration, forgery, or similar deceptive misuse of certificates. The destruction or mutilation of certificates obviously increases the difficulty of detecting and tracing abuses such as these. Further, a mutilated certificate might itself be used for deceptive purposes.

The many functions performed by Selective Service certificates establish beyond doubt that Congress has a legitimate and substantial interest in preventing their wanton and unrestrained destruction and assuring their continuing availability by punishing people who knowingly and wilfully destroy or mutilate them. . . .

We think it apparent that the continuing availability to each registrant of his Selective Service certificates substantially furthers the smooth and proper functioning of the system that Congress has established to raise armies. We think it also apparent that the Nation has a vital interest in having a system for raising armies that functions with maximum efficiency and is capable of easily and quickly responding to continually changing circumstances. For these reasons, the Government has a substantial interest in assuring the continuing availability of issued Selective Service certificates.

It is equally clear that the 1965 Amendment specifically protects this substantial governmental interest. We perceive no alternative means that would more precisely and narrowly assure the continuing availability of issued Selective Service certificates than a law which prohibits their wilful mutilation or destruction. . . . The 1965 Amendment prohibits such conduct and does nothing more. In other words, both the governmental interest and the operation of the 1965 Amendment are limited to the noncommunicative aspect of O'Brien's conduct. The governmental interest and the scope of the 1965 Amendment are limited to preventing harm to the smooth and efficient functioning of the Selective Service System. When O'Brien deliberately rendered unavailable his registration certificate, he wilfully frustrated this governmental interest. For this noncommunicative impact of his conduct, and for nothing else, he was convicted. . . .

III

O'Brien finally argues that the 1965 Amendment is unconstitutional as enacted because what he calls the "purpose" of Congress was "to suppress freedom of speech." We reject this argument because under settled principles the purpose of Congress, as O'Brien uses that term, is not a basis for declaring this legislation unconstitutional.

It is a familiar principle of constitutional law that this Court will not strike down an otherwise constitutional statute on the basis of an alleged illicit legislative motive. . . .

Inquiries into congressional motives or purposes are a hazardous matter. When the issue is simply the interpretation of legislation, the Court will look to statements by legislators for guidance as to the purpose of the legislature, because the benefit to sound decision-making in this circumstance is thought sufficient to risk the possibility of misreading Congress' purpose. It is entirely a different matter when we are asked to void a statute that is, under well-settled criteria, constitutional on its face, on the basis of what fewer than a handful of Congressmen said about it. What motivates one legislator to make a speech about a statute is not necessarily what motivates scores of others to enact it, and the stakes are sufficiently high for us to eschew guesswork. We decline to void essentially on the ground that it is unwise legislation which Congress had the undoubted power to enact and which could be reenacted in its exact form if the same or another legislator made a "wiser" speech about it. . . .

Accordingly, we vacate the judgment of the Court of Appeals, and reinstate the judgment and sentence of the District Court.

It is so ordered.

Mr. Justice Marshall took no part in the consideration or decision of these cases.

Mr. Justice Harlan, concurring.

. . . I wish to make explicit my understanding that . . . [the Court's holding] does not foreclose consideration of First Amendment claims in those rare instances when an "incidental" restriction upon expression, imposed by a regulation which furthers an "important or substantial" governmental interest and satisfies the Court's other criteria, in practice has the effect of entirely preventing a "speaker" from reaching a significant audience with whom he could not otherwise lawfully communicate. This is not such a case, since O'Brien manifestly could have conveyed his message in many ways other than by burning his draft card.

Mr. Justice Douglas, dissenting. [Omitted.]

C. Evidentiary Use of Speech to Prove the Elements of an Offense

Wisconsin v. Mitchell

United States Supreme Court
508 U.S. 476, 113 S. Ct. 2194, 124 L. Ed. 2d 436 (1993)

Chief Justice Rehnquist delivered the opinion of the Court.

Respondent Todd Mitchell's sentence for aggravated battery was enhanced because he intentionally selected his victim on account of the victim's race. The question presented in this case is whether this penalty enhancement is prohibited by the First and Fourteenth Amendments. We hold that it is not.

On the evening of October 7, 1989, a group of young black men and boys, including Mitchell, gathered at an apartment complex in Kenosha, Wisconsin. Several members of the group discussed a scene from the motion picture "Mississippi Burning," in which a white man beat a young black boy who was praying. The group moved outside and Mitchell asked them: "Do you all feel hyped up to move on some white people?" Shortly thereafter, a young white boy approached the group on the opposite side of the street where they were standing. As the boy walked by, Mitchell said: "You all want to fuck somebody up? There goes a white boy; go get him." Mitchell counted to three and pointed in the boy's direction. The group ran towards the boy, beat him severely, and stole his tennis shoes. The boy was rendered unconscious and remained in a coma for four days.

After a jury trial in the Circuit Court for Kenosha County, Mitchell was convicted of aggravated battery. That offense ordinarily carries a maximum sentence of two years' imprisonment. But because the jury found that Mitchell had intentionally selected his victim because of the boy's race, the maximum sentence for Mitchell's offense was increased to seven years under [a] provision [that] enhances the maximum penalty for an offense whenever the defendant "[i]ntentionally selects the person against whom the crime . . . is committed . . . because of the race, religion, color, disability, sexual orientation, national origin or ancestry of that person. . . ."

The Circuit Court sentenced Mitchell to four years' imprisonment for the aggravated battery.

Mitchell unsuccessfully sought postconviction relief in the Circuit Court. Then he appealed his conviction and sentence, challenging the constitutionality of Wisconsin's penalty-enhancement provision on First Amendment grounds. The Wisconsin Court of Appeals rejected Mitchell's challenge, but the Wisconsin Supreme Court reversed. The Supreme Court held that the statute "violates the First Amendment directly by punishing what the legislature has deemed to be offensive thought." It rejected the State's contention "that the statute punishes only the 'conduct' of intentional selection of a victim." According to the court, "[t]he statute punishes the 'because of' aspect of the defendant's selection, the reason the defendant selected the victim, the motive behind the selection." And under *R.A.V. v. St. Paul*, "the Wisconsin legislature cannot criminalize bigoted thought with which it disagrees."

The Supreme Court also held that the penalty-enhancement statute was unconstitutionally overbroad. It reasoned that, in order to prove that a defendant intentionally selected his victim because of the victim's protected status, the State would often have to introduce evidence of the defendant's prior speech, such as racial epithets he may have uttered before the commission of the offense. This evidentiary use of protected speech, the court thought, would have a "chilling effect" on those who feared the possibility of prosecution for offenses subject to penalty enhancement. Finally, the court distinguished antidiscrimination laws, which have long been held constitutional, on the ground that the Wisconsin statute punishes the "subjective mental process" of selecting a victim because of his protected status, whereas antidiscrimination laws prohibit "objective acts of discrimination." We granted certiorari because of the importance of the question presented and the existence of a conflict of authority among state high courts on the constitutionality of statutes similar to Wisconsin's penalty-enhancement provision.

We reverse.

Mitchell argues that we are bound by the Wisconsin Supreme Court's conclusion that the statute punishes bigoted thought and not conduct. There is no doubt that we are bound by a state court's construction of a state statute. *R.A.V.; New York v. Ferber*, 458 U.S. 747, 769, n. 24 (1982); *Terminiello v. Chicago*, 337 U.S. 1, 4 (1949). In *Terminiello*, for example, the Illinois courts had defined the term "breach of the peace," in a city ordinance prohibiting disorderly conduct, to include "stirs the public to anger . . . or creates a disturbance." We held this construction to be binding on us. But here the Wisconsin Supreme Court did not, strictly speaking, construe the Wisconsin statute in the sense of defining the meaning of a particular statutory word or phrase. Rather, it merely characterized the "practical effect" of the statute for First Amendment purposes. ("Merely because the statute refers in a literal sense to the intentional 'conduct' of selecting, does not mean the court must turn a blind eye to the intent and practical effect of the law — punishment of motive or thought.") This assessment does not bind us. Once any ambiguities as to the meaning of the statute are resolved, we may form our own judgment as to its operative effect.

The State argues that the statute does not punish bigoted thought, as the Supreme Court of Wisconsin said, but instead punishes only conduct. While this argument is literally correct, it does not dispose of Mitchell's First Amendment challenge. To be sure, our cases reject the "view that an apparently limitless variety of conduct can be labeled 'speech' whenever the person engaging in the conduct intends thereby to express an idea." *United States v. O'Brien*, 391 U.S. 367, 376 (1968); accord, *R.A.V.; Spence v. Washington*, 418 U.S. 405, 409 (1974) (per curiam); *Cox v. Louisiana*, 379 U.S. 536, 555 (1965). Thus, a physical assault is not by any stretch of the imagination expressive conduct protected by the First Amendment. *See Roberts v. United States Jaycees*, 468 U.S. 609, 628 (1984) ("[V]iolence or other types of potentially expressive activities that produce special harms distinct from their communicative impact ... are entitled to no constitutional protection"); *NAACP v. Claiborne Hardware Co.*, 458 U.S. 886, 916 (1982) ("The First Amendment does not protect violence").

But the fact remains that under the Wisconsin statute the same criminal conduct may be more heavily punished if the victim is selected because of his race or other protected status than if no such motive obtained. Thus, although the statute punishes criminal conduct, it enhances the maximum penalty for conduct motivated by a discriminatory point of view more severely than the same conduct engaged in for some other reason or for no reason at all. Because the only reason for the enhancement is the defendant's discriminatory motive for selecting his victim, Mitchell argues (and the Wisconsin Supreme Court held) that the statute violates the First Amendment by punishing offenders' bigoted beliefs.

Traditionally, sentencing judges have considered a wide variety of factors in addition to evidence bearing on guilt in determining what sentence to impose on a convicted defendant. The defendant's motive for committing the offense is one important factor. Thus, in many States the commission of a murder, or other capital offense, for pecuniary gain is a separate aggravating circumstance under the capital-sentencing statute.

But it is equally true that a defendant's abstract beliefs, however obnoxious to most people, may not be taken into consideration by a sentencing judge. *Dawson v. Delaware*, 503 U.S. 159 (1992). In *Dawson*, the State introduced evidence at a capital-sentencing hearing that the defendant was a member of a white supremacist prison gang. Because "the evidence proved nothing more than [the defendant's] abstract beliefs," we held that its admission violated the defendant's First Amendment rights. In so holding, however, we emphasized that "the Constitution does not erect a per se barrier to the admission of evidence concerning one's beliefs and associations at sentencing simply because those beliefs and associations are protected by the First Amendment." Thus, in *Barclay v. Florida*, 463 U.S. 939 (1983) (plurality opinion), we allowed the sentencing judge to take into account the defendant's racial animus towards his victim. The evidence in that case showed that the defendant's membership in the Black Liberation Army and desire to provoke a "race war" were related to the murder of a white man for which he was convicted. Because "the elements of racial hatred in [the] murder" were relevant to several aggravating factors, we held that the trial judge permissibly took this evidence into account in sentencing the defendant to death.

Mitchell suggests that *Dawson* and *Barclay* are inapposite because they did not involve application of a penalty-enhancement provision. But in *Barclay* we held that it was permissible for the sentencing court to consider the defendant's racial animus in determining whether he should be sentenced to death, surely the most severe "enhancement" of all. And the fact that the Wisconsin Legislature has decided, as a general matter, that bias-motivated offenses warrant greater maximum penalties across the board does not alter the result here. For the primary responsibility for fixing criminal penalties lies with the legislature.

Mitchell argues that the Wisconsin penalty-enhancement statute is invalid because it punishes the defendant's discriminatory motive, or reason, for acting. But motive plays the same role under the Wisconsin statute as it does under federal and state antidiscrimination laws, which we have previously upheld against constitutional challenge. *See Roberts v. Jaycees, Hishon v. King & Spalding*, 467 U.S. 69, 78 (1984); *Runyon v. McCrary*, 427 U.S. 160, 176 (1976). Title VII, for example, makes it unlawful for an employer to discriminate against an employee "because of such individual's race, color, religion, sex, or national origin." In *Hishon*, we rejected the argument that Title VII infringed employers' First Amendment rights. And more recently, in *R.A.V. v. St. Paul*, we cited Title VII (as well as 18 U.S. C. § 242 and 42 U.S. C. §§ 1981 and 1982) as an example of a permissible content-neutral regulation of conduct.

Nothing in our decision last Term in *R.A.V.* compels a different result here. That case involved a First Amendment challenge to a municipal ordinance prohibiting the use of "fighting words" that insult, or provoke violence, "on the basis of race, color, creed, religion or gender." Because the ordinance only proscribed a class of "fighting words" deemed particularly offensive by the city — *i.e.*, those "that contain . . . messages of 'bias-motivated' hatred," we held that it violated the rule against content-based discrimination. But whereas the ordinance struck down in *R.A.V.* was explicitly directed at expression (*i.e.*, "speech" or "messages," the statute in this case is aimed at conduct unprotected by the First Amendment.

Moreover, the Wisconsin statute singles out for enhancement bias-inspired conduct because this conduct is thought to inflict greater individual and societal harm. For example, according to the State and its amici, bias-motivated crimes are more likely to provoke retaliatory crimes, inflict distinct emotional harms on their victims, and incite community unrest. The State's desire to redress these perceived harms provides an adequate explanation for its penalty-enhancement provision over and above mere disagreement with offenders' beliefs or biases. As Blackstone said long ago, "it is but reasonable that among crimes of different natures those should be most severely punished, which are the most destructive of the public safety and happiness." 4 W. Blackstone, Commentaries 16.

Finally, there remains to be considered Mitchell's argument that the Wisconsin statute is unconstitutionally overbroad because of its "chilling effect" on free speech. Mitchell argues (and the Wisconsin Supreme Court agreed) that the statute is "overbroad" because evidence of the defendant's prior speech or associations may be used to prove that the defendant intentionally selected his victim on account of the victim's protected status. Consequently, the argument goes, the statute impermissibly chills free expression with respect to such matters by those concerned about the possibility of enhanced sentences if they should in the future commit a criminal offense covered by the statute. We find no merit in this contention.

The sort of chill envisioned here is far more attenuated and unlikely than that contemplated in traditional "overbreadth" cases. We must conjure up a vision of a Wisconsin citizen suppressing his unpopular bigoted opinions for fear that if he later commits an offense covered by the statute, these opinions will be offered at trial to establish that he selected his victim on account of the victim's protected status, thus qualifying him for penalty-enhancement. To stay within the realm of rationality, we must surely put to one side minor misdemeanor offenses covered by the statute, such as negligent operation of a motor vehicle; for it is difficult, if not impossible, to conceive of a situation where such offenses would be racially motivated. We are left, then, with the prospect of a citizen suppressing his bigoted beliefs for fear that evidence of such beliefs will be introduced against him at trial if he commits a more serious offense against person or property. This is simply too speculative a hypothesis to support Mitchell's overbreadth claim.

The First Amendment, moreover, does not prohibit the evidentiary use of speech to establish the elements of a crime or to prove motive or intent. Evidence of a defendant's previous declarations or statements is commonly admitted in criminal trials subject to evidentiary rules dealing with relevancy, reliability, and the like. Nearly half a century ago, in *Haupt v. United States*, 330 U.S. 631 (1947), we rejected a contention similar to that advanced by Mitchell here. Haupt was tried for the offense of treason, which, as defined by the Constitution (Art. III, § 3), may depend very much on proof of motive. To prove that the acts in question were committed out of "adherence to the enemy" rather than "parental solicitude," the Government introduced evidence of conversations that had taken place long prior to the indictment, some of which consisted of statements showing Haupt's sympathy with Germany and Hitler and hostility towards the United States. We rejected Haupt's argument that this evidence was improperly admitted. While "[s]uch testimony is to be scrutinized with care to be certain the statements are not expressions of mere lawful and permissible difference of opinion with our own government or quite proper appreciation of the land of birth," we held that "these statements . . . clearly were admissible on the question of intent and adherence to the enemy."

For the foregoing reasons, we hold that Mitchell's First Amendment rights were not violated by the application of the Wisconsin penalty-enhancement provision in sentencing him. The judgment of the Supreme Court of Wisconsin is therefore reversed, and the case is remanded for further proceedings not inconsistent with this opinion.

Notes and Questions

(1) A recurring problem in constitutional law is what to make of "neutral" laws that impact negatively on constitutional rights. In equal protection cases, rigorous "strict scrutiny" review is not triggered unless the classification at issue involves "purposeful" discrimination against a suspect class. When mere *de facto* discrimination occurs, the classification is analyzed under the highly deferential "rational basis" standard of review. Somewhat analogous problems exist in religion and speech cases. *Wisconsin v. Mitchell* and *United States v. O'Brien* represent two different approaches to this same sort of problem in the context of free speech jurisprudence. *O'Brien* is a "workhorse" case, cited hundreds of times each year by lower courts, and routinely used as the standard default test for most content-neutral regulation of speech. Under *O'Brien*, an "intermediate" standard of review is employed for laws that burden speech for reasons unrelated to the content of expression. Note that the *O'Brien* solution is a compromise different from the "all or nothing" debate between "strict scrutiny" and "rational basis" review that has characterized the Free Exercise Clause debate. One might ask why, for example, an *O'Brien*-style test has not evolved in religion cases.

(2) Why wasn't the *O'Brien* standard applied in *Mitchell*? The Court in *Mitchell* held that the mere "evidentiary" use of speech to prove a defendant's subjective state of mind does not penalize speech at all—or even implicate, in any meaningful sense, the First Amendment. Does *Mitchell* authorize the creation of "thought crimes"? Or is *Mitchell* a ruling that is virtually compelled under our constitutional system, because a contrary ruling in *Mitchell* would have made it impossible to sustain the constitutionality of civil rights laws? How does *Mitchell* square with *R.A.V. v. City of St. Paul*?

(3) The characterization of a law as content-neutral or content-based is enormously important, for it often effectively determines the outcome of First Amendment litigation. Content-based laws generally trigger heightened scrutiny in one of its manifestations, and when heightened scrutiny is applied, the odds are quite high that the law will be struck down. Content-neutral laws, on the other hand, qualify for significantly less rigorous levels of review, often resulting in judicial decisions upholding the regulations at issue. Content-neutral laws, however, by no means receive a "free pass" under the First Amendment. Indeed, as a logical matter, content-neutral regulation of speech is not invariably a "lesser offense" to free speech values. A sweeping content-neutral law, such as a complete ban on the posting of all signs or billboards anywhere within a city, for example, would actually stifle *more* expression than a content-based law that allowed some forms of expression but not others. For elaboration on the distinction between content-based and content-neutral laws, see generally Daniel Farber, *Content Regulation and the First*

Amendment: A Revisionist View, 68 GEO. L. REV. 727 (1980); Kenneth Karst, *Equality as a Central Principle in the First Amendment*, 43 CHI. L. REV. 20 (1975); Martin Redish, *The Content Distinction in First Amendment Analysis*, 34 STAN. L. REV. 113, 128 (1981); Paul B. Stephan, *The First Amendment and Content Discrimination*, 68 VA. L. REV. 203 (1982); Geoffrey Stone, *Content Regulation and the First Amendment*, 25 WM. & MARY L. REV. 189 (1983); RODNEY A. SMOLLA, FREE SPEECH IN AN OPEN SOCIETY, 43–69 (1992).

Problem B

Imagine that someone engages in a trespass and uses a can of spray paint to spray a swastika on the side of a synagogue. The perpetrator is prosecuted under a bias-crimes law similar to that in *Mitchell*. The *only* proof of his biased intent is the swastika on the synagogue wall. The defendant remains silent and does not testify. A jury, convinced that, because of the swastika, the defendant indeed committed the trespass with anti-Semitic intent, finds the defendant guilty of violating the bias crime law. On appeal, what result? Is the case controlled by *R.A.V., Black* or by *Mitchell*?

§ 9.05 Obscene and Pornographic Speech

A. Obscenity in the General Marketplace

Miller v. California

United States Supreme Court
413 U.S. 15, 93 S. Ct. 2607, 37 L. Ed. 2d 419 (1973)

MR. CHIEF JUSTICE BURGER delivered the opinion of the Court.

This is one of a group of "obscenity-pornography" cases being reviewed by the Court in a re-examination of standards enunciated in earlier cases involving what Mr. Justice Harlan called "the intractable obscenity problem." . . .

Appellant conducted a mass mailing campaign to advertise the sale of illustrated books, euphemistically called "adult" material. . . .

The brochures advertise four books entitled "Intercourse," "Man-Woman," "Sex Orgies Illustrated," and "An Illustrated History of Pornography," and a film entitled "Marital Intercourse." While the brochures contain some descriptive printed material, primarily they consist of pictures and drawings very explicitly depicting men and women in groups of two or more engaging in a variety of sexual activities, with genitals often prominently displayed.

I

This case involves the application of a State's criminal obscenity statute to a situation in which sexually explicit materials have been thrust by aggressive sales action upon unwilling recipients who had in no way indicated any desire to receive such materials. This Court has recognized that the States have a legitimate interest in prohibiting dissemination or exhibition of obscene material when the mode of dissemination carries with it a significant danger of offending the sensibilities of unwilling recipients or of exposure to juveniles....

II

This much has been categorically settled by the Court, that obscene material is unprotected by the First Amendment.... State statutes designed to regulate obscene materials [however] must be carefully limited.... As a result, we now confine the permissible scope of such regulation to works which depict or describe sexual conduct. That conduct must be specifically defined by the applicable state law, as written or authoritatively construed. A state offense must also be limited to works that, taken as a whole, appeal to the prurient interest in sex, which portray sexual conduct in a patently offensive way, and which, taken as a whole, do not have serious literary, artistic, political, or scientific value.

The basic guidelines for the trier of fact must be: (a) whether "the average person, applying contemporary community standards" would find that the work, taken as a whole, appeals to the prurient interest ... ; (b) whether the work depicts or describes, in a patently offensive way, sexual conduct specifically defined by the applicable state law; and (c) whether the work, taken as a whole, lacks serious literary, artistic, political, or scientific value.... If a state law that regulates obscene material is thus limited, as written or construed, the First Amendment values applicable to the States through the Fourteenth Amendment are adequately protected by the ultimate power of appellate courts to conduct an independent review of constitutional claims when necessary....

We emphasize that it is not our function to propose regulatory schemes for the States. That must await their concrete legislative efforts. It is possible, however, to give a few plain examples of what a state statute could define for regulation under part (b) of the standard announced in this opinion:

(a) Patently offensive representations or descriptions of ultimate sexual acts, normal or perverted, actual or simulated.

(b) Patently offensive representations or descriptions of masturbation, excretory functions, and lewd exhibition of the genitals.

Sex and nudity may not be exploited without limit by films or pictures exhibited or sold in places of public accommodation any more than live sex and nudity can be exhibited or sold without limit in such public places. At a minimum, prurient, patently offensive depiction or description of sexual conduct must have serious literary, artistic, political, or scientific value to merit First Amendment protection.... For example, medical books for the education of physicians and related personnel necessarily use graphic illustrations and descriptions of human anatomy. In resolving the inevitably sensitive questions of fact and law, we must continue to rely on the jury system, accompanied by the safeguards that judges, rules of evidence, presumption of innocence, and other protective features provide, as we do with rape, murder, and a host of other offenses against society and its individual members....

It is certainly true that the absence, since *Roth* [*v. United States*, 354 U.S. 476 (1957)], of a single majority view of this Court as to proper standards for testing obscenity has placed a strain on both state and federal courts. But today, for the first time since *Roth* was decided in 1957, a majority of this Court has agreed on concrete guidelines to isolate "hard core" pornography from expression protected by the First Amendment....

III

Under a National Constitution, fundamental First Amendment limitations on the powers of the States do not vary from community to community, but this does not mean that there are, or should or can be, fixed, uniform national standards of precisely what appeals to the "prurient interest" or is "patently offensive." These are essentially questions of fact, and our Nation is simply too big and too diverse for this Court to reasonably expect that such standards could be articulated for all 50 States in a single formulation, even assuming the prerequisite consensus exists. When triers of fact are asked to decide whether "the average person, applying contemporary community standards" would consider certain materials "prurient," it would be unrealistic to require that the answer be based on some abstract formulation. The adversary system, with lay jurors as the usual ultimate factfinders in criminal prosecutions, has historically permitted triers of fact to draw on the standards of their community, guided always by limiting instructions on the law. To require a State to structure obscenity proceedings around evidence of a *national* "community standard" would be an exercise in futility....

Nothing in the First Amendment requires that a jury must consider hypothetical and unascertainable "national standards" when attempting to determine whether certain materials are obscene as a matter of fact....

It is neither realistic nor constitutionally sound to read the First Amendment as requiring that the people of Maine or Mississippi accept public depiction of conduct found tolerable in Las Vegas, or New York City.... People in different States vary in their tastes and attitudes, and this diversity is not to be strangled by the absolutism of imposed uniformity. As the Court made clear ... the primary concern with requiring a jury to apply the standard of "the average person, applying contemporary community standards" is to be certain that, so far as material is not aimed at a deviant group, it will be judged by its impact on an average person, rather than a particularly susceptible or sensitive person — or indeed a totally insensitive one.... We hold that the requirement that the jury evaluate the materials with reference to "contemporary standards of the State of California" serves this protective purpose and is constitutionally adequate.

IV

The dissenting Justices sound the alarm of repression. But, in our view, to equate the free and robust exchange of ideas and political debate with commercial exploitation of obscene material demeans the grand conception of the First Amendment and its high purposes in the historic struggle for freedom.... The First Amendment protects works which, taken as a whole, have serious literary, artistic, political, or scientific value, regardless of whether the government or a majority of the people approve of the ideas these works represent. "The protection given speech and press was fashioned to assure unfettered interchange of *ideas* for the bringing about of political and social changes desired by the people," *Roth*. But the public portrayal of hard-core sexual conduct for its own sake, and for the ensuing commercial gain, is a different matter. . . .

Mr. Justice Douglas, dissenting.

. . . Today the Court retreats from the earlier formulations of the constitutional test and undertakes to make new definitions. This effort, like the earlier ones, is earnest and well intentioned. The difficulty is that we do not deal with constitutional terms, since "obscenity" is not mentioned in the Constitution or Bill of Rights. And the First Amendment makes no such exception from "the press" which it undertakes to protect nor, as I have said on other occasions, is an exception necessarily implied, for there was no recognized exception to the free press at the time the Bill of Rights was adopted which treated "obscene" publications differently from other types of papers, magazines, and books. So there are no constitutional guidelines for deciding what is and what is not "obscene." The Court is at large because we deal with tastes and standards of literature. What shocks me may be sustenance for my neighbor. What causes one person to boil up in rage over one pamphlet or movie may reflect only his neurosis, not shared by others. We deal here with a regime of censorship which, if adopted, should be done by constitutional amendment after full debate by the people. . . .

Obscenity — which even we cannot define with precision — is a hodge-podge. To send men to jail for violating standards they cannot understand, construe, and apply is a monstrous thing to do in a Nation dedicated to fair trials and due process.

III

While the right to know is the corollary of the right to speak or publish, no one can be forced by government to listen to disclosure that he finds offensive. . . . There is no "captive audience" problem in these obscenity cases. No one is being compelled to look or to listen. Those who enter newsstands or bookstalls may be offended by what they see. But they are not compelled by the State to frequent those places; and it is only state or governmental action against which the First Amendment, applicable to the States by virtue of the Fourteenth, raises a ban.

The idea that the First Amendment permits government to ban publications that are "offensive" to some people puts an ominous gloss on freedom of the press. That test would make it possible to ban any paper or any journal or magazine in some benighted place. The First Amendment was designed "to invite dispute," to induce "a condition of unrest," to "create dissatisfaction with conditions as they are," and even to stir "people to anger.". . . . The idea that the First Amendment permits punishment for ideas that are "offensive" to the particular judge or jury sitting in judgment is astounding. No greater leveler of speech or literature has ever been designed.

To give the power to the censor, as we do today, is to make a sharp and radical break with the traditions of a free society. The First Amendment was not fashioned as a vehicle for dispensing tranquilizers to the people. Its prime function was to keep debate open to "offensive" as well as to "staid" people. . . .

We deal with highly emotional, not rational, questions. To many the Song of Solomon is obscene. I do not think we, the judges, were ever given the constitutional power to make definitions of obscenity. If it is to be defined, let the people debate and decide by a constitutional amendment what they want to ban as obscene and what standards they want the legislatures and the courts to apply. Perhaps the people will decide that the path towards a mature, integrated society requires that all ideas competing for acceptance must have no censor. Perhaps they will decide otherwise. Whatever the choice, the courts will have some guidelines. Now we have none except our own predilections.

MR. JUSTICE BRENNAN with whom MR. JUSTICE STEWART and MR. JUSTICE MARSHALL join, dissenting. [Omitted.]

Paris Adult Theatre I v. Slaton

United States Supreme Court
413 U.S. 49, 93 S. Ct. 2628, 37 L. Ed. 2d 446 (1973)

MR. CHIEF JUSTICE BURGER delivered the opinion of the Court.

Petitioners are two Atlanta, Georgia, movie theaters and their owners and managers, operating in the style of "adult" theaters. On December 28, 1970, respondents, the local state district attorney and the solicitor for the local state trial court, filed civil complaints in that court alleging that petitioners were exhibiting to the public for paid admission two allegedly obscene films, contrary to Georgia Code Ann. § 26-2101. The two films in question, "Magic Mirror" and "It All Comes Out in the End," depict sexual conduct characterized by the Georgia Supreme Court as "hard core pornography" leaving "little to the imagination." . . .

We categorically disapprove the theory, apparently adopted by the trial judge, that obscene, pornographic films acquire constitutional immunity from state regulation simply because they are exhibited for consenting adults only. . . .

In particular, we hold that there are legitimate state interests at stake in stemming the tide of commercialized obscenity, even assuming it is feasible to enforce effective safeguards against exposure to juveniles and to passersby. Rights and interests "other than those of the advocates are involved." . . . These include the interest of the public in the quality of life and the total community environment, the tone of commerce in the great city centers, and, possibly, the public safety itself. The Hill-Link Minority Report of the Commission on Obscenity and Pornography indicates that there is at least an arguable correlation between obscene material and crime. Quite apart from sex crimes, however, there remains one problem of large proportions aptly described by Professor Bickel:

It concerns the tone of the society, the mode, or to use terms that have perhaps greater currency, the style and quality of life, now and in the future. A man may be entitled to read an obscene book in his room, or expose himself indecently there. . . . We should protect his privacy. But if he demands a right to obtain the books and pictures he wants in the market, and to foregather in public places—discreet, if you will, but accessible to all—with others who share his tastes, *then to grant him his right is to affect the world about the rest of us, and to impinge on other privacies.* Even supposing that each of us can, if he wishes, effectively avert the eye and stop the ear (which, in truth, we cannot), what is commonly read and seen and heard and done intrudes upon us all, want it or not.

But, it is argued, there are no scientific data which conclusively demonstrate that exposure to obscene material adversely affects men and women or their society. It is urged on behalf of the petitioners that, absent such a demonstration, any kind of state regulation is "impermissible." We reject this argument. It is not for us to resolve empirical uncertainties underlying state legislation, save in the exceptional case where that legislation plainly impinges upon rights protected by the Constitution itself. . . . Although there is no conclusive proof of a connection between antisocial behavior and obscene material, the legislature of Georgia could quite reasonably determine that such a connection does or might exist. In deciding *Roth*, this Court implicitly accepted that a legislature could legitimately act on such a conclusion to protect "*the social interest in order and morality.*"

. . . If we accept the unprovable assumption that a complete education requires the reading of certain books . . . and the well nigh universal belief that good books, plays, and art lift the spirit, improve the mind, enrich the human personality, and develop character, can we then say that a state legislature may not act on the corollary assumption that commerce in obscene books, or public exhibitions focused on obscene conduct, have a tendency to exert a corrupting and debasing impact leading to antisocial behavior? . . . The sum of experience, including that of the past two decades, affords an ample basis for legislatures to conclude that a sensitive, key relationship of human existence, central to family life, community welfare, and the development of human personality, can be debased and distorted by crass commercial exploitation of sex. Nothing in the Constitution prohibits a State from reaching such a conclusion and acting on it legislatively simply because there is no conclusive evidence or empirical data.

It is argued that individual "free will" must govern, even in activities beyond the protection of the First Amendment and other constitutional guarantees of privacy, and that government cannot legitimately impede an individual's desire to see or acquire obscene plays, movies, and books. We do indeed base our society on certain assumptions that people have the capacity for free choice. Most exercises of individual free choice—those in politics, religion, and expression of ideas—are explicitly protected by the Constitution. Totally unlimited play for free will, however, is not allowed in our or any other society. . . .

The States, of course, may follow such a "laissez-faire" policy and drop all controls on commercialized obscenity, if that is what they prefer, just as they can ignore consumer protection in the marketplace, but nothing in the Constitution *compels* the States to do so with regard to matters falling within state jurisdiction. . . .

It is asserted, however, that standards for evaluating state commercial regulations are inapposite in the present context, as state regulation of access by consenting adults to obscene material violates the constitutionally protected right to privacy enjoyed by petitioners' customers. Even assuming that petitioners have vicarious standing to assert potential customers' rights, it is unavailing to compare a theater open to the public for a fee, with the private home of *Stanley v. Georgia*, 394 U.S. 557 (1969) . . . and the marital bedroom of *Griswold v. Connecticut*.

Nothing . . . in this Court's decisions intimates that there is any "fundamental" privacy right "implicit in the concept of ordered liberty" to watch obscene movies in places of public accommodation.

If obscene material unprotected by the First Amendment in itself carried with it a "penumbra" of constitutionally protected privacy, this Court would not have found it necessary to decide *Stanley* on the narrow basis of the "privacy of the home," which was hardly more than a reaffirmation that "a man's home is his castle." . . .

It is also argued that the State has no legitimate interest in "control [of] the moral content of a person's thoughts," . . . . and we need not quarrel with this. But we reject the claim that the State of Georgia is here attempting to control the minds or thoughts of those who patronize theaters. Preventing unlimited display or distribution of obscene material, which by definition lacks any serious literary, artistic, political, or scientific value as communication, *Miller v. California* . . . is distinct from a control of reason and the intellect. . . . Where communication of ideas, protected by the First Amendment, is not involved, or the particular privacy of the home protected by *Stanley*, or any of the other "areas or zones" of constitutionally protected privacy, the mere fact that, as a consequence, some human "utterances" or "thoughts" may be incidentally affected does not bar the State from acting to protect legitimate state interests. . . . The fantasies of a drug addict are his own and beyond the reach of government, but government regulation of drug sales is not prohibited by the Constitution. . . .

Finally, petitioners argue that conduct which directly involves "consenting adults" only has, for that sole reason, a special claim to constitutional protection. Our Constitution establishes a broad range of conditions on the exercise of power by the States, but for us to say that our Constitution incorporates the proposition that conduct involving consenting adults only is always beyond state regulation, is a step we are unable to take. Commercial exploitation of depictions, descriptions, or exhibitions of obscene conduct on commercial premises open to the adult public falls within a State's broad power to regulate commerce and protect the public environment. The issue in this context goes beyond whether someone, or even the majority, considers the conduct depicted as "wrong" or "sinful." The States have the power to make a morally neutral judgment that public exhibition of obscene material, or commerce in such material, has a tendency to injure the community as a whole, to endanger the public safety, or to jeopardize, in Mr. Chief Justice Warren's words, the States' "right . . . to maintain a decent society." . . .

To summarize, we have today reaffirmed the basic holding of *Roth v. United States* . . . that obscene material has no protection under the First Amendment. . . . We have directed our holdings, not at thoughts or speech, but at depiction and description of specifically defined sexual conduct that States may regulate within limits designed to prevent infringement of First Amendment rights. We have also reaffirmed the holdings . . . that commerce in obscene material is unprotected by any constitutional doctrine of privacy. . . . In this case we hold that the States have a legitimate interest in regulating commerce in obscene material and in regulating exhibition of obscene material in places of public accommodation, including so-called "adult" theaters from which minors are excluded. In light of these holdings, nothing precludes the State of Georgia from the regulation of the allegedly obscene material exhibited in Paris Adult Theatre I or II, provided that the applicable Georgia law, as written or authoritatively interpreted by the Georgia courts, meets the First Amendment standards set forth in *Miller v. California*. . . . The judgment is vacated and the case remanded to the Georgia Supreme Court for further proceedings not inconsistent with this opinion and *Miller v. California*. . . .

Vacated and remanded.

MR. JUSTICE BRENNAN, with whom MR. JUSTICE STEWART and MR. JUSTICE MARSHALL join, dissenting. . . .

. . . [W]hile I cannot say that the interests of the State — apart from the question of juveniles and unconsenting adults — are trivial or nonexistent, I am compelled to conclude that these interests cannot justify the substantial damage to constitutional rights and to this Nation's judicial machinery that inevitably results from state efforts to bar the distribution even of unprotected material to consenting adults. . . . I would hold, therefore, that at least in the absence of distribution to juveniles or obtrusive exposure to unconsenting adults, the First and Fourteenth Amendments prohibit the State and Federal Governments from attempting wholly to suppress sexually oriented materials on the basis of their allegedly "obscene" contents. Nothing in this approach precludes those governments from taking action to serve what may be strong and legitimate interests through regulation of the manner of distribution of sexually oriented material. . . .

MR. JUSTICE DOUGLAS, dissenting. [Omitted.]

Notes and Questions

(1) The general principle that obscenity as defined in *Miller* and *Paris* receives no First Amendment protection is one of the most distinct vestiges of the Order and Morality Theory which remains alive and well in First Amendment doctrine. The doctrine that obscenity may be banned clearly derives from society's interest

in preserving "morality," and the prong of *Miller* that includes the absence of *serious* redeeming value strongly channels Justice Murphy's opinion in *Chaplinsky*, observing that certain categories of speech may claim no essential contribution to the exposition of ideas.

(2) Obscenity doctrine also runs contrary to the general Marketplace Theory dictum that persons confronted with offensive speech should simply avert their eyes and look the other way. Indeed, in *Paris*, only consenting adults who voluntarily entered the theatre as paying customers were exposed to the adult films—yet the Court found that the Theatre owners could still be prosecuted.

(3) The Supreme Court's modern treatment of obscene speech began with *Roth v. United States*, 354 U.S. 476 (1957). The Court, in an opinion by Justice Brennan, held that "obscenity is not within the area of constitutionally protected speech or press." *Roth* reduced First Amendment protection for obscenity to zero, but that did not end the issue, for the problem was then how to go about defining "obscene." Obscenity, the Court stated, did not include all sexual speech. Rather, obscenity "is material which deals with sex in a manner appealing to the prurient interest." By "prurient," the Court meant "material having a tendency to excite lustful thoughts." The Court elaborated on this by referring to the definition of "prurient" in *Webster's New International Dictionary* (Unabridged, 2d ed., 1949), which defined prurient, in pertinent part, as: "Itching; longing; uneasy with desire or longing; of persons, having itching, morbid, or lascivious longings; of desire, curiosity, or propensity, lewd. . . ."

(4) After *Roth*, the test for obscenity continued to evolve through *Miller* and *Paris Adult Theatre I*. In *Pope v. Illinois*, 481 U.S. 497 (1987), the Court clarified the *Miller* standard. Justice White, writing for the majority, stated that

> the first and second prongs of the *Miller* test—appeal to prurient interest and patent offensiveness—are issues of fact for the jury to determine applying contemporary community standards.

However, the third prong—whether the work, taken as a whole, lacks serious literary, artistic, or scientific value—is not determined by application of community standards:

> The proper inquiry is not whether an ordinary member of any given community would find serious literary, artistic, political or scientific value in allegedly obscene material, but whether a *reasonable person* would find such value in the material, taken as a whole. (Emphasis added.)

B. Obscenity in the Privacy of the Home

Stanley v. Georgia

United States Supreme Court

394 U.S. 557, 89 S. Ct. 1243, 22 L. Ed. 2d 542 (1969)

Mr. Justice Marshall delivered the opinion of the Court.

An investigation of appellant's alleged bookmaking activities led to the issuance of a search warrant for appellant's home. Under authority of this warrant, federal and state agents secured entrance. They found very little evidence of bookmaking activity, but while looking through a desk drawer in an upstairs bedroom, one of the federal agents, accompanied by a state officer, found three reels of eight-millimeter film. Using a projector and screen found in an upstairs living room, they viewed the films. The state officer concluded that they were obscene and seized them. Since a further examination of the bedroom indicated that appellant occupied it, he was charged with possession of obscene matter and placed under arrest. He was later indicted for "knowingly hav[ing] possession of . . . obscene matter" in violation of Georgia law. Appellant was tried before a jury and convicted. The Supreme Court of Georgia affirmed. . . .

Appellant raises several challenges to the validity of his conviction. We find it necessary to consider only one. Appellant argues here, and argued below, that the Georgia obscenity statute, insofar as it punishes mere private possession of obscene matter, violates the First Amendment, as made applicable to the States by the Fourteenth Amendment. For reasons set forth below, we agree that the mere private possession of obscene matter cannot constitutionally be made a crime. . . .

It is true that *Roth v. U.S.*, 354 U.S. 476 (1957), does declare, seemingly without qualification, that obscenity is not protected by the First Amendment. That statement has been repeated in various forms in subsequent cases. See, *e.g.*, *Smith v. California*, 361 U.S. 147, 152 (1959); *Jacobellis v. Ohio*, 378 U.S. 184, 186–187 (1964); *Ginsberg v. New York*, 390 U.S. 629, at 635 (1968). However, neither *Roth* nor any subsequent decision of this Court dealt with the precise problem involved in the present case. Roth was convicted of mailing obscene circulars and advertising, and an obscene book, in violation of a federal obscenity statute. The defendant in a companion case, *Alberts v. California*, 354 U.S. 476 (1957), was convicted of "lewdly keeping for sale obscene and indecent books, and [of] writing, composing and publishing an obscene advertisement of them. . . ." None of the statements cited by the Court in *Roth* for the proposition that "this Court has always assumed that obscenity is not protected by the freedoms of speech and press" were made in the context of a statute punishing mere private possession of obscene material; the cases cited deal for the most part with use of the mails to distribute objectionable material or with some form of public distribution or dissemination. Moreover, none of this Court's decisions subsequent to *Roth* involved prosecution for private possession of obscene materials. Those cases dealt with the power of the State and Federal Governments to prohibit or regulate certain public actions taken or intended to be taken with respect to obscene matter. . . .

In this context, we do not believe that this case can be decided simply by citing *Roth. Roth* and its progeny certainly do mean that the First and Fourteenth Amendments recognize a valid governmental interest in dealing with the problem of obscenity. But the assertion of that interest cannot, in every context, be insulated from all constitutional protections. Neither *Roth* nor any other decision of this Court reaches that far. As the Court said in *Roth* itself, "[c]easeless vigilance is the watchword to prevent . . . erosion [of First Amendment rights] by Congress or by the States. The door barring federal and state intrusion into this area cannot be left ajar; it must be kept tightly closed and opened only the slightest crack necessary to prevent encroachment upon more important interests." *Roth* and the cases following it discerned such an "important interest" in the regulation of commercial distribution of obscene material. That holding cannot foreclose an examination of the constitutional implications of a statute forbidding mere private possession of such material.

It is now well established that the Constitution protects the right to receive information and ideas. "This freedom [of speech and press] . . . necessarily protects the right to receive. . . ." This right to receive information and ideas, regardless of their social worth, is fundamental to our free society. Moreover, in the context of this case — a prosecution for mere possession of printed or filmed matter in the privacy of a person's own home — that right takes on an added dimension. For also fundamental is the right to be free, except in very limited circumstances, from unwanted governmental intrusions into one's privacy. . . .

These are the rights that appellant is asserting in the case before us. He is asserting the right to read or observe what he pleases — the right to satisfy his intellectual and emotional needs in the privacy of his own home. He is asserting the right to be free from state inquiry into the contents of his library. Georgia contends that appellant does not have these rights, that there are certain types of materials that the individual may not read or even possess. Georgia justifies this assertion by arguing that the films in the present case are obscene. But we think that mere categorization of these films as "obscene" is insufficient justification for such a drastic invasion of personal liberties guaranteed by the First and Fourteenth Amendments. Whatever may be the justifications for other statutes regulating obscenity, we do not think they reach into the privacy of one's own home. If the First Amendment means anything, it means that a State has no business telling a man, sitting alone in his own house, what books he may read or what films he may watch. Our whole constitutional heritage rebels at the thought of giving government the power to control men's minds.

And yet, in the face of these traditional notions of individual liberty, Georgia asserts the right to protect the individual's mind from the effects of obscenity. We are not certain that this argument amounts to anything more than the assertion that the State has the right to control the moral content of a person's thoughts. To some, this may be a noble purpose, but it is wholly inconsistent with the philosophy of the First Amendment. . . . Nor is it relevant that obscene materials in general, or the particular films before the Court, are arguably devoid of any ideological content. The line between the transmission of ideas and mere entertainment is much too elusive for this Court to draw, if indeed such a line can be drawn at all. Whatever the power of the state to control public dissemination of ideas inimical to the public morality, it cannot constitutionally premise legislation on the desirability of controlling a person's private thoughts.

Perhaps recognizing this, Georgia asserts that exposure to obscene materials may lead to deviant sexual behavior or crimes of sexual violence. There appears to be little empirical basis for that assertion. But more important, if the State is only concerned about printed or filmed materials inducing antisocial conduct, we believe that in the context of private consumption of ideas and information we should adhere to the view that "[a]mong free men, the deterrents ordinarily to be applied to prevent crime are education and punishment for violations of the law. . . ." Given the present state of knowledge, the State may no more prohibit mere possession of obscene matter on the ground that it may lead to antisocial conduct than it may prohibit possession of chemistry books on the ground that they may lead to the manufacture of homemade spirits.

It is true that in *Roth* this Court rejected the necessity of proving that exposure to obscene material would create a clear and present danger of antisocial conduct or would probably induce its recipients to such conduct. But that case dealt with public distribution of obscene materials and, as such, distribution is subject to different objections. For example, there is always the danger that obscene material might fall into the hands of children, see *Ginsberg v. New York*, or that it might intrude upon the sensibilities or privacy of the general public. No such dangers are present in this case.

Finally, we are faced with the argument that prohibition of possession of obscene materials is a necessary incident to statutory schemes prohibiting distribution. That argument is based on alleged difficulties of proving an intent to distribute or in producing evidence of actual distribution. We are not convinced that such difficulties exist, but even if they did we do not think that they would justify infringement of the individual's right to read or observe what he pleases. Because that right is so fundamental to our scheme of individual liberty, its restriction may not be justified by the need to ease the administration of otherwise valid criminal laws.

We hold that the First and Fourteenth Amendments prohibit making mere private possession of obscene material a crime. *Roth* and the cases following that decision are not impaired by today's holding. As we have said, the States retain broad power to regulate obscenity; that power simply does not extend to mere possession by the individual in the privacy of his home. Accordingly, the judgment of the court below is reversed and the case is remanded for proceedings not inconsistent with this opinion.

[The concurring opinions of Justices Black and Stewart are omitted.]

Notes and Questions

(1) What is the key to *Stanley*? Bear in mind that modern First Amendment doctrines declare that obscene speech receives *no* constitutional protection, because, as declared in *Roth v. United States*, it is "without redeeming social importance." If obscenity is not constitutionally protected speech, then how can the Constitution be understood to protect the right to its possession in the home? Is *Stanley* primarily a privacy case? If *Stanley* is essentially a privacy case, does its rationale require that other illegal activities also be protected inside the home, such as using illegal drugs?

(2) Consider the possibility that *Stanley* is a combination free speech/privacy case. "Speech crimes," such as the possession of obscene material, may be sufficiently different from other "victimless crimes," such as smoking marijuana or sodomy, to merit unique protection in the privacy of the home. *Stanley* may thus be a response to the intensified aura of "thought control" in prosecutions for mere possession of obscenity inside the home.

(3) Adult theatres have largely given way to the transmission of erotic material via satellite, cable television, and most prominently, the Internet. A person accessing hard-core obscenity that would be unprotected under *Miller v. California* from inside the home is protected under the doctrine of *Stanley v. Georgia*. Watching even hard-core *Miller* obscenity inside one's own dwelling cannot be made criminal, and it should not matter what the technical medium is (satellite, cable, or broadband) through which the material is accessed. In contrast, the *producers* of the material — a satellite or cable channel, or a Internet porn site, do not enjoy *Stanley* protection, and thus remain subject to prosecution under the principles of *Miller* and *Paris*. The fact that the Internet, particularly, is awash in pornographic sites does not mean such sites *could not* be prosecuted. Rather, it may simply reflect the judgment of most state and federal prosecutors that there are more important crimes to prosecute — much like simple possession of marijuana may not be prosecuted with vigor in modern times even though technically illegal in many jurisdictions, including under federal law. Prosecutors are *far* more likely, however, to seriously pursue both the purveyors and consumers of pornography portraying children and pornography pandering to children. The First Amendment principles governing pornography and the protection of children is explored in the following subsection of this Chapter.

C. Pornography and the Protection of Children

The Osborne v. Ohio Exception to Stanley v. Georgia. In *Osborne v. Ohio*, 495 U.S. 103 (1990), the Supreme Court held that the rule of *Stanley v. Georgia* protecting "home possession" of obscene material does *not* apply to possession of child pornography. *Osborne* involved an Ohio statute which, on its face, purported to prohibit the possession of "nude" photographs of minors. The Supreme Court recognized that depictions of nudity, without more, constitute protected expression. But as construed by the Ohio Supreme Court, the statute prohibited only "the possession or viewing of material or performance of a minor who is in a state of nudity, where such nudity constitutes a lewd exhibition or involves a graphic focus on the genitals, and where the person depicted is neither the child nor the ward of the person charged." By limiting the statute's operation in this manner, the Supreme Court held, "the Ohio Supreme Court avoided penalizing persons for viewing or possessing innocuous photographs of naked children." The Supreme Court also found it significant that the Ohio Supreme Court concluded that the state must establish scienter in order to prove a violation of the law. In distinguishing *Stanley*, the Court observed that in *Stanley*, Georgia primarily sought to proscribe the private possession of obscenity because it was concerned that obscenity would poison the minds of its viewers. The Court in *Stanley* responded by stating that "[w]hatever the power of the state to control public dissemination of ideas inimical to the public morality, it cannot constitutionally premise legislation on the desirability of controlling a person's private thoughts." The difference between possession of adult obscenity and the possession of child pornography, the *Osborne* Court asserted, was that in the case of regulation of possession of child pornography, the government need not rely solely on "a paternalistic interest in regulating [the defendant's] mind." Rather, observed the Court, the state enacted its law "in order to protect the victims of child pornography; it hopes to destroy a market for the exploitative use of children."

Ashcroft v. Free Speech Coalition

United States Supreme Court
535 U.S. 234, 122 S. Ct. 1389, 152 L. Ed. 2d 403 (2002)

Justice Kennedy delivered the opinion of the Court.

We consider in this case whether the Child Pornography Prevention Act of 1996 (CPPA), 18 U.S.C. § 2251 *et seq.*, abridges the freedom of speech. The CPPA extends the federal prohibition against child pornography to sexually explicit images that appear to depict minors but were produced without using any real children. The statute prohibits, in specific circumstances, possessing or distributing these images, which may be created by using adults who look like minors or by using computer imaging. The new technology, according to Congress, makes it possible to create realistic images of children who do not exist. See Congressional Findings, notes following 18 U.S.C. § 2251.

By prohibiting child pornography that does not depict an actual child, the statute goes beyond *New York v. Ferber*, which distinguished child pornography from other sexually explicit speech because of the State's interest in protecting the children exploited by the production process. See *id.*, at 758. As a general rule, pornography can be banned only if obscene, but under *Ferber*, pornography showing minors can be proscribed whether or not the images are obscene under the definition set forth in *Miller v. California. Ferber* recognized that "[t]he *Miller* standard, like all general definitions of what may be banned as obscene, does not reflect the State's particular and more compelling interest in prosecuting those who promote the sexual exploitation of children."

While we have not had occasion to consider the question, we may assume that the apparent age of persons engaged in sexual conduct is relevant to whether a depiction offends community standards. Pictures of young children engaged in certain acts might be obscene where similar depictions of adults, or perhaps even older adolescents, would not. The CPPA, however, is not directed at speech that is obscene; Congress has proscribed those materials through a separate statute. 18 U.S.C. §§ 1460–1466. Like the law in *Ferber*, the CPPA seeks to reach beyond obscenity, and it makes no attempt to conform to the *Miller* standard. For instance, the statute would reach visual depictions, such as movies, even if they have redeeming social value.

The principal question to be resolved, then, is whether the CPPA is constitutional where it proscribes a significant universe of speech that is neither obscene under *Miller* nor child pornography under *Ferber*.

I

. . . These images do not involve, let alone harm, any children in the production process; but Congress decided the materials threaten children in other, less direct, ways. Pedophiles might use the materials to encourage children to participate in sexual activity. "[A] child who is reluctant to engage in sexual activity with an adult, or to pose for sexually explicit photographs, can sometimes be convinced by viewing depictions of other children 'having fun' participating in such activity." Congressional Findings, note (3) following § 2251. Furthermore, pedophiles might "whet their own sexual appetites" with the pornographic images, "thereby increasing the creation and distribution of child pornography and the sexual abuse and exploitation of actual children." *Id.*, notes (4), (10)(B). Under these rationales, harm flows from the content of the images, not from the means of their production. In addition, Congress identified another problem created by computer-generated images: Their existence can make it harder to prosecute pornographers who do use real minors. See *id.*, note (6)(A). As imaging technology improves, Congress found, it becomes more difficult to prove that a particular picture was produced using actual children. To ensure that defendants possessing child pornography using real minors cannot evade prosecution, Congress extended the ban to virtual child pornography.

Section 2256(8)(C) prohibits a more common and lower tech means of creating virtual images, known as computer morphing. Rather than creating original images, pornographers can alter innocent pictures of real children so that the children appear to be engaged in sexual activity. Although morphed images may fall within the definition of virtual child pornography, they implicate the interests of real children and are in that sense closer to the images in *Ferber*. Respondents do not challenge this provision, and we do not consider it. . . .

The sexual abuse of a child is a most serious crime and an act repugnant to the moral instincts of a decent people. In its legislative findings, Congress recognized that there are subcultures of persons who harbor illicit desires for children and commit criminal acts to gratify the impulses . . .

As a general principle, the First Amendment bars the government from dictating what we see or read or speak or hear. The freedom of speech has its limits; it does not embrace certain categories of speech, including defamation, incitement, obscenity, and pornography produced with real children. While these categories may be prohibited without violating the First Amendment, none of them includes the speech prohibited by the CPPA. . . .

The CPPA prohibits speech despite its serious literary, artistic, political, or scientific value. The statute proscribes the visual depiction of an idea — that of teenagers engaging in sexual activity — that is a fact of modern society and has been a theme in art and literature throughout the ages. . . . It is, of course, undeniable that some youths engage in sexual activity before the legal age, either on their own inclination or because they are victims of sexual abuse.

Both themes — teenage sexual activity and the sexual abuse of children — have inspired countless literary works. William Shakespeare created the most famous pair of teenage lovers, one of whom is just 13 years of age. See Romeo and Juliet, act I, sc. 2, l. 9 ("She hath not seen the change of fourteen years"). In the drama, Shakespeare portrays the relationship as something splendid and innocent, but not juvenile. The work has inspired no less than 40 motion pictures, some of which suggest that the teenagers consummated their relationship. *E.g.*, Romeo and Juliet (B. Luhrmann director, 1996). Shakespeare may not have written sexually explicit scenes for the Elizabethan audience, but were modern directors to adopt a less conventional approach, that fact alone would not compel the conclusion that the work was obscene.

Contemporary movies pursue similar themes. Last year's Academy Awards featured the movie, Traffic, which was nominated for Best Picture. See *Predictable and Less So, the Academy Award Contenders*, N.Y. Times, Feb. 14, 2001, p. E11. The film portrays a teenager, identified as a 16-year-old, who becomes addicted to drugs. The viewer sees the degradation of her addiction, which in the end leads her to a filthy room to trade sex for drugs. The year before, American Beauty won the Academy Award for Best Picture. See *"American Beauty" Tops the Oscars*, N.Y. Times, Mar. 27, 2000, p. E1. In the course of the movie, a teenage girl engages in sexual relations with her teenage boyfriend, and another yields herself to the gratification of a middle-aged man. The film also contains a scene where, although the movie audience understands the act is not taking place, one character believes he is watching a teenage boy performing a sexual act on an older man.

Our society, like other cultures, has empathy and enduring fascination with the lives and destinies of the young. Art and literature express the vital interest we all have in the formative years we ourselves once knew, when wounds can be so grievous, disappointment so profound, and mistaken choices so tragic, but when moral acts and self-fulfillment are still in reach. Whether or not the films we mention violate the CPPA, they explore themes within the wide sweep of the statute's prohibitions. If these films, or hundreds of others of lesser note that explore those subjects, contain a single graphic depiction of sexual activity within the statutory definition, the possessor of the film would be subject to severe punishment without inquiry into the work's redeeming value. This is inconsistent with an essential First Amendment rule: The artistic merit of a work does not depend on the presence of a single explicit scene. See *Book Named "John Cleland's Memoirs of a Woman of Pleasure" v. Attorney General of Mass.*, 383 U.S. 413, 419 (1966) (plurality opinion) ("[T]he social value of the book can neither be weighed against nor canceled by its prurient appeal or patent offensiveness"). Under *Miller*, the First Amendment requires that redeeming value be judged by considering the work as a whole. Where the scene is part of the narrative, the work itself does not for this reason become obscene, even though the scene in isolation might be offensive. See *Kois v. Wisconsin*, 408 U.S. 229, 231 (1972) (*per curiam*). For this reason, and the others we have noted, the CPPA cannot be read to prohibit obscenity, because it lacks the required link between its prohibitions and the affront to community standards prohibited by the definition of obscenity.

The Government seeks to address this deficiency by arguing that speech prohibited by the CPPA is virtually indistinguishable from child pornography, which may be banned without regard to whether it depicts works of value. See *New York v. Ferber*, 458 U.S., at 761. Where the images are themselves the product of child sexual abuse, *Ferber* recognized that the State had an interest in stamping it out without regard to any judgment about its content . . . The production of the work, not its content, was the target of the statute. The fact that a work contained serious literary, artistic, or other value did not excuse the harm it caused to its child participants. It was simply "unrealistic to equate a community's toleration for sexually oriented materials with the permissible scope of legislation aimed at protecting children from sexual exploitation."

Ferber upheld a prohibition on the distribution and sale of child pornography, as well as its production, because these acts were "intrinsically related" to the sexual abuse of children in two ways. First, as a permanent record of a child's abuse, the continued circulation itself would harm the child who had participated. Like a defamatory statement, each new publication of the speech would cause new injury to the child's reputation and emotional well-being. Second, because the traffic in child pornography was an economic motive for its production, the State had an interest in closing the distribution network. "The most expeditious if not the only practical method of law enforcement may be to dry up the market for this material by imposing severe criminal penalties on persons selling, advertising, or otherwise promoting the product." Under either rationale, the speech had what the Court in effect held was a proximate link to the crime from which it came.

Later, in *Osborne v. Ohio*, 495 U.S. 103 (1990), the Court ruled that these same interests justified a ban on the possession of pornography produced by using children. "Given the importance of the State's interest in protecting the victims of child pornography," the State was justified in "attempting to stamp out this vice at all levels in the distribution chain." *Osborne* also noted the State's interest in preventing child pornography from being used as an aid in the solicitation of minors. The Court, however, anchored its holding in the concern for the participants, those whom it called the "victims of child pornography." It did not suggest that, absent this concern, other governmental interests would suffice.

In contrast to the speech in *Ferber*, speech that itself is the record of sexual abuse, the CPPA prohibits speech that records no crime and creates no victims by its production. Virtual child pornography is not "intrinsically related" to the sexual abuse of children, as were the materials in *Ferber*. While the Government asserts that the images can lead to actual instances of child abuse, the causal link is contingent and indirect. The harm does not necessarily follow from the speech, but depends upon some unquantified potential for subsequent criminal acts.

The Government says these indirect harms are sufficient because, as *Ferber* acknowledged, child pornography rarely can be valuable speech. ("The value of permitting live performances and photographic reproductions of children engaged in lewd sexual conduct is exceedingly modest, if not *de minimis*"). This argument, however, suffers from two flaws. First, *Ferber*'s judgment about child pornography was based upon how it was made, not on what it communicated. The case reaffirmed that where the speech is neither obscene nor the product of sexual abuse, it does not fall outside the protection of the First Amendment. ("[T]he distribution of descriptions or other depictions of sexual conduct, not otherwise obscene, which do not involve live performance or photographic or other visual reproduction of live performances, retains First Amendment protection").

The second flaw in the Government's position is that *Ferber* did not hold that child pornography is by definition without value. On the contrary, the Court recognized some works in this category might have significant value, but relied on virtual images — the very images prohibited by the CPPA — as an alternative and permissible means of expression: "[I]f it were necessary for literary or artistic value, a person over the statutory age who perhaps looked younger could be utilized. Simulation outside of the prohibition of the statute could provide another alternative." *Ferber*, then, not only referred to the distinction between actual and virtual child pornography, it relied on it as a reason supporting its holding. *Ferber* provides no support for a statute that eliminates the distinction and makes the alternative mode criminal as well. . . .

For the reasons we have set forth, the prohibitions of §§ 2256(8)(B) and 2256(8)(D) are overbroad and unconstitutional. Having reached this conclusion, we need not address respondents' further contention that the provisions are unconstitutional because of vague statutory language.

JUSTICE THOMAS, concurring in the judgment.

In my view, the Government's most persuasive asserted interest in support of the Child Pornography Prevention Act of 1996 (CPPA), 18 U.S.C. § 2251 *et seq.*, is the prosecution rationale — that persons who possess and disseminate pornographic images of real children may escape conviction by claiming that the images are computer-generated, thereby raising a reasonable doubt as to their guilt. At this time, however, the Government asserts only that defendants *raise* such defenses, not that they have done so successfully. In fact, the Government points to no case in which a defendant has been acquitted based on a "computer-generated images" defense. While this speculative interest cannot support the broad reach of the CPPA, technology may evolve to the point where it becomes impossible to enforce actual child pornography laws because the Government cannot prove that certain pornographic images are of real children. In the event this occurs, the Government should not be foreclosed from enacting a regulation of virtual child pornography that contains an appropriate affirmative defense or some other narrowly drawn restriction. . . .

JUSTICE O'CONNOR, with whom THE CHIEF JUSTICE and JUSTICE SCALIA join as to Part II, concurring in the judgment in part and dissenting in part.

The Court concludes, correctly, that the CPPA's ban on youthful-adult pornography is overbroad. In my view, however, respondents fail to present sufficient evidence to demonstrate that the ban on virtual-child pornography is overbroad. Because invalidation due to overbreadth is such "strong medicine," *Broadrick v. Oklahoma* [413 U.S. 601 (1973)], I would strike down the prohibition of pornography that "appears to be" of minors only insofar as it is applied to the class of youthful-adult pornography. . . .

I disagree with the Court, however, that the CPPA's prohibition of virtual-child pornography is overbroad. . . .

The Court concludes that the CPPA's ban on virtual-child pornography is overbroad. The basis for this holding is unclear. Although a content-based regulation may serve a compelling state interest, and be as narrowly tailored as possible while substantially serving that interest, the regulation may unintentionally ensnare speech that has serious literary, artistic, political, or scientific value or that does not threaten the harms sought to be combated by the Government. If so, litigants may challenge the regulation on its face as overbroad, but in doing so they bear the heavy burden of demonstrating that the regulation forbids a substantial amount of valuable or harmless speech. . . .

Although in my view the CPPA's ban on youthful-adult pornography appears to violate the First Amendment, the ban on virtual-child pornography does not. . . .

CHIEF JUSTICE REHNQUIST, with whom JUSTICE SCALIA joins in part, dissenting.

We normally do not strike down a statute on First Amendment grounds "when a limiting instruction has been or could be placed on the challenged statute." . . .

Other than computer generated images that are virtually indistinguishable from real children engaged in sexually explicitly conduct, the CPPA can be limited so as not to reach any material that was not already unprotected before the CPPA. . . .

This narrow reading of "sexually explicit conduct" not only accords with the text of the CPPA and the intentions of Congress; it is exactly how the phrase was understood prior to the broadening gloss the Court gives it today. Indeed, had "sexually explicit conduct" been thought to reach the sort of material the Court says it does, then films such as "Traffic" and "American Beauty" would not have been made the way they were.

Reno v. American Civil Liberties Union

United States Supreme Court
521 U.S. 844, 117 S. Ct. 2329, 138 L. Ed. 2d 874 (1997)

JUSTICE STEVENS delivered the opinion of the Court.

At issue is the constitutionality of two statutory provisions enacted to protect minors from "indecent" and "patently offensive" communications on the Internet. Notwithstanding the legitimacy and importance of the congressional goal of protecting children from harmful materials, we agree with the three-judge District Court that the statute abridges "the freedom of speech" protected by the First Amendment.

Sexually explicit material on the Internet includes text, pictures, and chat and "extends from the modestly titillating to the hardest-core."

II

The Telecommunications Act of 1996, Pub. L. 104-104, 110 Stat. 56, was an unusually important legislative enactment. . . . By contrast, Title V — known as the "Communications Decency Act of 1996 (CDA)" — contains provisions that were either added in executive committee after the hearings were concluded or as amendments offered during floor debate on the legislation. An amendment offered in the Senate was the source of the two statutory provisions challenged in this case . . .

The first, 47 U.S.C.A. § 223(a) (Supp. 1997), prohibits the knowing transmission of obscene or indecent messages to any recipient under 18 years of age. It provides in pertinent part:

"(a) Whoever —

(1) in interstate or foreign communications — . . .

(B) by means of a telecommunications device knowingly —

(i) makes, creates, or solicits, and

(ii) initiates the transmission of,

any comment, request, suggestion, proposal, image, or other communication which is obscene or indecent, knowing that the recipient of the communication is under 18 years of age, regardless of whether the maker of such communication placed the call or initiated the communication; . . .

(2) knowingly permits any telecommunications facility under his control to be used for any activity prohibited by paragraph (1) with the intent that it be used for such activity, shall be fined under Title 18, or imprisoned not more than two years, or both."

The second provision, § 223(d), prohibits the knowing sending or displaying of patently offensive messages in a manner that is available to a person under 18 years of age. It provides:

"(d) Whoever —

(1) in interstate or foreign communications knowingly —

(A) uses an interactive computer service to send to a specific person or persons under 18 years of age, or

(B) uses any interactive computer service to display in a manner available to a person under 18 years of age,

any comment, request, suggestion, proposal, image, or other communication that, in context, depicts or describes, in terms patently offensive as measured by contemporary community standards, sexual or excretory activities or organs, regardless of whether the user of such service placed the call or initiated the communication; or

(2) knowingly permits any telecommunications facility under such person's control to be used for an activity prohibited by paragraph (1) with the intent that it be used for such activity, shall be fined under Title 18, or imprisoned not more than two years, or both."

The breadth of these prohibitions is qualified by two affirmative defenses. One covers those who take "good faith, reasonable, effective, and appropriate actions" to restrict access by minors to the prohibited communications. §223(e)(5)(A). The other covers those who restrict access to covered material by requiring certain designated forms of age proof, such as a verified credit card or an adult identification number or code. §223(e)(5)(B) . . .

IV

In arguing for reversal, the Government contends that the CDA is plainly constitutional under three of our prior decisions: (1) *Ginsberg v. New York*, 390 U.S. 629 (1968); (2) *FCC v. Pacifica Foundation*, 438 U.S. 726 (1978); and (3) *Renton v. Playtime Theatres, Inc.*, 475 U.S. 41 (1986). A close look at these cases, however, raises, rather than relieves, doubts concerning the constitutionality of the CDA.

In *Ginsberg*, we upheld the constitutionality of a New York statute that prohibited selling to minors under 17 years of age material that was considered obscene as to them even if not obscene as to adults. We rejected the defendant's broad submission that "the scope of the constitutional freedom of expression secured to a citizen to read or see material concerned with sex cannot be made to depend on whether the citizen is an adult or a minor." In rejecting that contention, we relied not only on the State's independent interest in the well-being of its youth, but also on our consistent recognition of the principle that "the parents' claim to authority in their own household to direct the rearing of their children is basic in the structure of our society."

In four important respects, the statute upheld in *Ginsberg* was narrower than the CDA. First, we noted in *Ginsberg* that "the prohibition against sales to minors does not bar parents who so desire from purchasing the magazines for their children." Under the CDA, by contrast, neither the parents' consent-nor even their participation-in the communication would avoid the application of the statute. Second, the New York statute applied only to commercial transactions, whereas the CDA contains no such limitation. Third, the New York statute cabined its definition of material that is harmful to minors with the requirement that it be "utterly without redeeming social importance for minors." The CDA fails to provide us with any definition of the term "indecent" as used in § 223(a)(1) and, importantly, omits any requirement that the "patently offensive" material covered by § 223(d) lack serious literary, artistic, political, or scientific value. Fourth, the New York statute defined a minor as a person under the age of 17, whereas the CDA, in applying to all those under 18 years, includes an additional year of those nearest majority.

In *Pacifica*, we upheld a declaratory order of the Federal Communications Commission, holding that the broadcast of a recording of a 12-minute monologue entitled "Filthy Words" that had previously been delivered to a live audience "could have been the subject of administrative sanctions." The Commission had found that the repetitive use of certain words referring to excretory or sexual activities or organs "in an afternoon broadcast when children are in the audience was patently offensive" and concluded that the monologue was indecent "as broadcast." The respondent did not quarrel with the finding that the afternoon broadcast was patently offensive, but contended that it was not "indecent" within the meaning of the relevant statutes because it contained no prurient appeal. After rejecting respondent's statutory arguments, we confronted its two constitutional arguments: (1) that the Commission's construction of its authority to ban indecent speech was so broad that its order had to be set aside even if the broadcast at issue was unprotected; and (2) that since the recording was not obscene, the First Amendment forbade any abridgement of the right to broadcast it on the radio.

In the portion of the lead opinion not joined by Justices Powell and Blackmun, the plurality stated that the First Amendment does not prohibit all governmental regulation that depends on the content of speech. Accordingly, the availability of constitutional protection for a vulgar and offensive monologue that was not obscene depended on the context of the broadcast. Relying on the premise that "of all forms of communication" broadcasting had received the most limited First Amendment protection, the Court concluded that the ease with which children may obtain access to broadcasts, "coupled with the concerns recognized in *Ginsberg*," justified special treatment of indecent broadcasting.

As with the New York statute at issue in *Ginsberg*, there are significant differences between the order upheld in *Pacifica* and the CDA. First, the order in *Pacifica*, issued by an agency that had been regulating radio stations for decades, targeted a specific broadcast that represented a rather dramatic departure from traditional program content in order to designate when—rather than whether—it would be permissible to air such a program in that particular medium. The CDA's broad categorical prohibitions are not limited to particular times and are not dependent on any evaluation by an agency familiar with the unique characteristics of the Internet. Second, unlike the CDA, the Commission's declaratory order was not punitive; we expressly refused to decide whether the indecent broadcast "would justify a criminal prosecution." Finally, the Commission's order applied to a medium which as a matter of history had "received the most limited First Amendment protection," in large part because warnings could not adequately protect the listener from unexpected program content. The Internet, however, has no comparable history. Moreover, the District Court found that the risk of encountering indecent material by accident is remote because a series of affirmative steps is required to access specific material.

In *Renton*, we upheld a zoning ordinance that kept adult movie theatres out of residential neighborhoods. The ordinance was aimed, not at the content of the films shown in the theaters, but rather at the "secondary effects"—such as crime and deteriorating property values—that these theaters fostered. According to the Government, the CDA is constitutional because it constitutes a sort of "cyberzoning" on the Internet. But the CDA applies broadly to the entire universe of cyberspace. And the purpose of the CDA is to protect children from the primary effects of "indecent" and "patently offensive" speech, rather than any "secondary" effect of such speech. Thus, the CDA is a content-based blanket restriction on speech, and, as such, cannot be "properly analyzed as a form of time, place, and manner regulation."

These precedents, then, surely do not require us to uphold the CDA and are fully consistent with the application of the most stringent review of its provisions.

V

In *Southeastern Promotions, Ltd. v. Conrad*, 420 U.S. 546, 557 (1975), we observed that "[e]ach medium of expression . . . may present its own problems." Thus, some of our cases have recognized special justifications for regulation of the broadcast media that are not applicable to other speakers, see *Red Lion Broadcasting v. FCC*, 395 U.S. 367 (1969); *FCC v. Pacifica Foundation*, 438 U.S. 726 (1978). In these cases, the Court relied on the history of extensive government regulation of the broadcast medium, see, e.g., *Red Lion*, 395 U.S., at 399–400; the scarcity of available frequencies at its inception, see e.g., *Turner Broadcasting System, Inc. v. FCC*, 512 U.S. 622, 637–638 (1994); and its "invasive" nature, see *Sable Communications of Cal., Inc. v. FCC*, 492 U.S. 115, 128 (1989).

Those factors are not present in cyberspace. Neither before nor after the enactment of the CDA have the vast democratic fora of the Internet been subject to the type of government supervision and regulation that has attended the broadcast industry.[5] Moreover, the Internet is not as "invasive" as radio or television. The District Court specifically found that "[c]ommunications over the Internet do not 'invade' an individual's home or appear on one's computer screen unbidden. Users

---

5. [Court's Footnote 33] When *Pacifica* was decided, given that radio stations were allowed to operate only pursuant to federal license, and that Congress had enacted legislation prohibiting licensees from broadcasting indecent speech, there was a risk that members of the radio audience might infer some sort of official or societal approval of whatever was heard over the radio. No such risk attends messages received through the Internet, which is not supervised by any federal agency.

seldom encounter content 'by accident'." It also found that "[a]lmost all sexually explicit images are preceded by warnings as to the content," and cited testimony that "'odds are slim' that a user would come across a sexually explicit sight by accident."

We distinguished *Pacifica* in *Sable* on just this basis. In *Sable*, a company engaged in the business of offering sexually oriented prerecorded telephone messages (popularly known as "dial-a-porn") challenged the constitutionality of an amendment to the Communications Act that imposed a blanket prohibition on indecent as well as obscene interstate commercial telephone messages. We held that the statute was constitutional insofar as it applied to obscene messages but invalid as applied to indecent messages. In attempting to justify the complete ban and criminalization of indecent commercial telephone messages, the Government relied on *Pacifica*, arguing that the ban was necessary to prevent children from gaining access to such messages. We agreed that "there is a compelling interest in protecting the physical and psychological well-being of minors" which extended to shielding them from indecent messages that are not obscene by adult standards, but distinguished our "emphatically narrow holding" in *Pacifica* because it did not involve a complete ban and because it involved a different medium of communication. We explained that "the dial-it medium requires the listener to take affirmative steps to receive the communication. Placing a telephone call," we continued, "is not the same as turning on a radio and being taken by surprise by an indecent message."

Finally, unlike the conditions that prevailed when Congress first authorized regulation of the broadcast spectrum, the Internet can hardly be considered a "scarce" expressive commodity. It provides relatively unlimited, low-cost capacity for communication of all kinds. The Government estimates that "[a]s many as 40 million people use the Internet today, and that figure is expected to grow to 200 million by 1999." This dynamic, multifaceted category of communication includes not only traditional print and news services, but also audio, video, and still images, as well as interactive, real-time dialogue. Through the use of chat rooms, any person with a phone line can become a town crier with a voice that resonates farther than it could from any soapbox. Through the use of Web pages, mail exploders, and newsgroups, the same individual can become a pamphleteer. As the District Court found, "the content on the Internet is as diverse as human thought." We agree with its conclusion that our cases provide no basis for qualifying the level of First Amendment scrutiny that should be applied to this medium.

VI

. . . The vagueness of the CDA is a matter of special concern for two reasons. First, the CDA is a content-based regulation of speech. The vagueness of such a regulation raises special First Amendment concerns because of its obvious chilling effect on free speech. . . . . Second, the CDA is a criminal statute. . . .

The Government argues that the statute is no more vague than the obscenity standard this Court established in *Miller v. California*, 413 U.S. 15 (1973). But that is not so. In *Miller*, this Court reviewed a criminal conviction against a commercial vendor who mailed brochures containing pictures of sexually explicit activities to individuals who had not requested such materials. Having struggled for some time to establish a definition of obscenity, we set forth in *Miller* the test for obscenity that controls to this day . . .

Because the CDA's "patently offensive" standard (and, we assume *arguendo*, its synonymous "indecent" standard) is one part of the three-prong *Miller* test, the Government reasons, it cannot be unconstitutionally vague.

The Government's assertion is incorrect as a matter of fact. The second prong of the *Miller* test — the purportedly analogous standard — contains a critical requirement that is omitted from the CDA: that the proscribed material be "specifically defined by the applicable state law." This requirement reduces the vagueness inherent in the open-ended term "patently offensive" as used in the CDA. Moreover, the *Miller* definition is limited to "sexual conduct," whereas the CDA extends also to include (1) "excretory activities" as well as (2) "organs" of both a sexual and excretory nature.

VII

We are persuaded that the CDA lacks the precision that the First Amendment requires when a statute regulates the content of speech. In order to deny minors access to potentially harmful speech, the CDA effectively suppresses a large amount of speech that adults have a constitutional right to receive and to address to one another. That burden on adult speech is unacceptable if less restrictive alternatives would be at least as effective in achieving the legitimate purpose that the statute was enacted to serve.

In evaluating the free speech rights of adults, we have made it perfectly clear that "[s]exual expression which is indecent but not obscene is protected by the First Amendment." *Sable.* See also *Carey v. Population Services Int'l*, 431 U.S. 678, 701 (1977) ("[W]here obscenity is not involved, we have consistently held that the fact that protected speech may be offensive to some does not justify its suppression"). Indeed, *Pacifica* itself admonished that "the fact that society may find speech offensive is not a sufficient reason for suppressing it."

It is true that we have repeatedly recognized the governmental interest in protecting children from harmful materials. But that interest does not justify an unnecessarily broad suppression of speech addressed to adults. As we have explained, the Government may not "reduc[e] the adult population . . . to . . . only what is fit for children." *Denver* [*Area Educ. Telcoms. Consortium v. FCC*, 518 U.S. 727 (1996)] (quoting *Sable*). "[R]egardless of the strength of the government's interest" in protecting children, "[t]he level of discourse reaching a mailbox simply cannot be limited to that which would be suitable for a sandbox." *Bolger v. Youngs Drug Products Corp.*, 463 U.S. 60, 74–75 (1983). . . .

IX

. . . We agree with the District Court's conclusion that the CDA places an unacceptably heavy burden on protected speech, and that the defenses do not constitute the sort of "narrow tailoring" that will save an otherwise patently invalid unconstitutional provision. In *Sable*, we remarked that the speech restriction at issue there amounted to "'burn[ing] the house to roast the pig.'" The CDA, casting a far darker shadow over free speech, threatens to torch a large segment of the Internet community.

JUSTICE O'CONNOR, with whom THE CHIEF JUSTICE joins, concurring in the judgment in part and dissenting in part.

I write separately to explain why I view the Communications Decency Act of 1996 (CDA) as little more than an attempt by Congress to create "adult zones" on the Internet. Our precedent indicates that the creation of such zones can be constitutionally sound. Despite the soundness of its purpose, however, portions of the CDA are unconstitutional because they stray from the blueprint our prior cases have developed for constructing a "zoning law" that passes constitutional muster....

Notes and Questions

(1) In *United States v. Playboy Entertainment Group, Inc.*, 529 U.S. 803 (2000), the Supreme Court struck down § 505 of the Telecommunications Act of 1996, 47 U.S.C. § 561. Section 505 required cable television operators who provide channels "primarily dedicated to sexually-oriented programming" either to "fully scramble or otherwise fully block" those channels or to limit their transmission to hours when children are unlikely to be viewing, set by administrative regulation as the time between 10 p.m. and 6 a.m. The purpose of § 505 was to shield children from hearing or seeing images resulting from a phenomenon known as "signal bleed," in which some audio and visual portions of the scrambled programs are still discernable. Playboy, which operates several cable networks devoted to erotic programming, successfully challenged the statute, by demonstrating that alternative technologies, such as a regime in which viewers could order signal blocking on a household-by-household basis, presented an effective, less restrictive alternative to § 505.

Justice Scalia argued, in an interesting dissent, that in his view, the statute should have been upheld as a valid regulation of what he described as the "business of obscenity." As Justice Scalia put it:

> Playboy itself illustrates the type of business § 505 is designed to reach. Playboy provides, through its networks — Playboy Television, AdulTVision, Adam & Eve, and Spice — virtually 100% sexually explicit adult programming. For example, on its Spice network, Playboy describes its own programming as depicting such activities as "female masturbation/external," "girl/girl sex," and "oral sex/cunnilingus." As one would expect, given this content, Playboy advertises accordingly, with calls to "Enjoy the sexiest, hottest adult movies in the privacy of your own home." An example of the promotion for a particular movie is as follows: "Little miss country girls are aching for a quick roll in the hay! Watch southern hospitality pull out all the stops as these ravin' nymphos tear down the barn and light up the

big country sky." One may doubt whether — or marvel that — this sort of embarrassingly juvenile promotion really attracts what Playboy assures us is an "adult" audience. But it is certainly marketing sex. . . .

D. Erotic Dance Clubs, Public Nudity, and the Secondary Effects Doctrine

Erotic Dance Clubs. Erotic dance clubs that admit only adults are engaged in expressive activity protected under the First Amendment. Erotic dancing is not in itself hard-core obscenity meeting the test of *Miller v. California.*

Public Nudity. The orthodoxy is that there is no constitutional right to be nude in public. Sometimes courts explain this by stating that merely being in a state of nudity is not inherently "expressive" and therefore "speech" protected by the First Amendment. An alternative explanation is that government has a compelling governmental interest in societal norms regarding privacy, modesty, and dignity sufficient to require that people not appear stark naked in public. While there is widespread agreement that no constitutional right to be nude in public exists, there is less agreement over whether the Constitution allows government to define "nudity" differently for males and females. Modern laws governing nudity to not prohibit men from being topless, exposing their breasts. Most jurisdictions, however, treat a topless woman as engaging in prohibited public nudity. Challenges often involve beaches. Women plaintiffs have argued that if men are allowed be topless on a beach, women should be allowed to be topless on the beach as well. Lower courts have split over the resolution of these claims.

Nude Erotic Dancing. Some jurisdictions in the United States permit the dancers in erotic dance clubs to be entirely nude. Others prohibit dancers from exposing genitalia, but allow topless dancing. Still others prohibit all nude dancing, which typically require female dancers, for example, to wear tops or "pasties" partially covering their breasts. In *Barnes v. Glen Theatre, Inc.*, 501 U.S. 560 (1991), and *City of Erie v. Pap's A.M.*, 529 U.S. 277 (2000), the Supreme Court upheld limitations on nude erotic dancing. In neither case, however, was there a five-Justice majority opinion announcing a clear rationale. While nude dancing did involve expressive conduct, the plurality reasoned, it fell "only within the outer ambit of the First Amendment's protection." Even if Erie's public nudity ban had "some minimal effect on the erotic message by muting that portion of the expression that occurs when the last stitch is dropped, the dancers at Kandyland and other such establishments are free to perform wearing pasties and G-strings," the plurality observed, rendering any "incidental impact on the expressive element of nude dancing . . . *de minimus.*" The plurality also held that the city had an interest in preventing "harmful secondary effects" associated with nude dancing, such as the deterrence of crime and "the other deleterious effects caused by the presence of such an establishment in the neighborhood." Justice Stevens dissented, arguing that the ordinance was in fact content-based and aimed precisely at the erotic message conveyed by nude dancing.

Justice Souter wrote an opinion concurring in part and dissenting in part in which he argued that the City of Erie should have been forced to come forth with empirical evidence on the record actually establishing that such negative "secondary effects" were caused by clubs such as "Kandyland."

The Secondary Effects Doctrine. Municipalities often attempt to use zoning regulations to control sexually oriented expression, such as adult movie theatres, bookstores, or exotic dancing clubs, and these efforts have met with mixed results when challenged under the First Amendment. Because these efforts are often targeted toward only one type of expression—"adult entertainment" dealing with sex—they would appear to be content-based, triggering heightened scrutiny. In *City of Renton v. Playtime Theatres, Inc.*, 475 U.S. 41 (1986), the Supreme Court created what is known as the "secondary effects" doctrine, to justify application of the reduced scrutiny applied to content-neutral time, place, or manner regulations.

Renton involved an ordinance that prohibited the operation of adult movie theatres within 1,000 feet of residences, churches, parks, and schools. The effect was to exclude such theatres from approximately 94 percent of the land in the city. Of the remaining 520 acres, a substantial part was occupied by a sewage disposal and treatment plant, a horse racing track, a warehouse and manufacturing facilities, a Mobil Oil tank farm, and a fully developed shopping center. The city had thus, as a practical matter, largely zoned adult theatres out of existence. Since the ordinance applied to adult movie theatres only, it appeared on its face to be content-based, and to merit strict scrutiny review. The Court held: "At first glance, the Renton ordinance, like the ordinance in *Young*, does not appear to fit neatly into either the 'content-based' or the 'content-neutral' category. To be sure, the ordinance treats theatres that specialize in adult films differently from other kinds of theatres. Nevertheless, [the] City Council's 'predominate concerns' were with the secondary effects of adult theatres, and not with the content of adult films themselves."

These secondary effects were crime, injury to retail trade, depression of property values, and general deterioration in neighborhood quality, all of which were said to be caused by the existence of adult movie theatres. This analysis in turn made it possible for the Court to conclude that the ordinance satisfied the Court's definition of a content-neutral speech regulation, because the ordinance was "justified without reference to the content of the regulated speech." The analysis in *Renton* was a deviation from prior content-neutrality analysis. It was, of course, true that the city may have been primarily concerned with problems other than the "inherent" content of adult films, such as fears concerning prostitution or crime. In this sense the ordinance was much like most laws impacting on freedom of speech: The ultimate legislative goal was not censorship, but rather combating perceived social ills. Under the proper application of the *O'Brien* test, this ultimate goal should not have been what mattered—rather, the case should have turned on whether the regulation was geared to the communicative impact of the speech. In fairness to the Court, even on this "communicative impact" issue, the proper characterization was not free from doubt. Justice Rehnquist was correct in noting that the law did not fit easily within the traditional pigeonholes for content-neutral and content-based speech. For to the extent that the ordinance addressed the perceived correlation between adult theatres and problems such as prostitution or crime, the law was not based on "communicative impact" in the conventional sense. Nevertheless, the city had used content explicitly in drawing its ordinance — creating one zoning rule for theatres showing adult sex films and another zoning rule for all other theatres — and in that sense, there was simply no denying that the law was content-based. Never before the *Renton* case had the Court suggested that it would ever treat a law based explicitly on content as content-neutral merely because the justifications for the law did not relate to the suppression of speech. In that sense, *Renton* and its secondary effects test was a potentially portentous departure from existing First Amendment jurisprudence. *See* RODNEY SMOLLA, SMOLLA & NIMMER ON FREEDOM OF SPEECH § 9:19, *Content-neutrality and the peculiar case of the secondary effects doctrine — Genesis of the secondary effects doctrine: The Renton case* (2023 Edition).

§ 9.06 Free Speech and Tort Liability

A. Defamation

New York Times Company v. Sullivan

United States Supreme Court
376 U.S. 254, 84 S. Ct. 710, 11 L. Ed. 2d 686 (1964)

MR. JUSTICE BRENNAN delivered the opinion of the Court.

We are required in this case to determine for the first time the extent to which the constitutional protections for speech and press limit a State's power to award damages in a libel action brought by a public official against critics of his official conduct.

Respondent L. B. Sullivan is one of the three elected Commissioners of the City of Montgomery, Alabama. He testified that he was "Commissioner of Public Affairs and the duties are supervision of the Police Department, Fire Department, Department of Cemetery and Department of Scales." He brought this civil libel action against the four individual petitioners, who are Negroes and Alabama clergymen, and against petitioner the New York Times Company, a New York corporation which publishes the *New York Times*, a daily newspaper. A jury in the Circuit Court of Montgomery County awarded him damages of $500,000, the full amount claimed, against all the petitioners, and the Supreme Court of Alabama affirmed. . . .

Respondent's complaint alleged that he had been libeled by statements in a full-page advertisement that was carried in the *New York Times* on March 29, 1960. Entitled "Heed Their Rising Voices," the advertisement began by stating that "As the whole world knows by now, thousands of Southern Negro students are engaged in widespread non-violent demonstrations in positive affirmation of the right to live in human dignity as guaranteed by the U.S. Constitution and the Bill of Rights." It went on to charge that "in their efforts to uphold these guarantees, they are being met by an unprecedented wave of terror by those who would deny and negate that document that the whole world looks upon as setting the pattern for modern freedom. . . ." Succeeding paragraphs purported to illustrate the "wave of terror" by describing certain alleged events. The text concluded with an appeal for funds for three purposes: support of the student movement, "the struggle for the right-to-vote," and the legal defense of Dr. Martin Luther King, Jr., leader of the movement, against a perjury indictment then pending in Montgomery.

The text appeared over the names of 64 persons, many widely known for their activities in public affairs, religion, trade unions, and the performing arts. Below these names, and under a line reading "We in the South who are struggling daily for dignity and freedom warmly endorse this appeal," appeared the names of the four individual petitioners and of 16 other persons, all but two of whom were identified as clergymen in various Southern cities. The advertisement was signed at the bottom of the page by the "Committee to Defend Martin Luther King and the Struggle for Freedom in the South," and the officers of the Committee were listed.

Of the 10 paragraphs of text in the advertisement, the third and a portion of the sixth were the basis of respondent's claim of libel. They read as follows:

Third paragraph:

> In Montgomery, Alabama, after students sang "My Country, 'Tis of Thee" on the State Capitol steps, their leaders were expelled from school, and truckloads of police armed with shotguns and tear-gas ringed the Alabama State College Campus. When the entire student body protested to State authorities by refusing to re-register, their dining hall was padlocked in an attempt to starve them into submission.

Sixth paragraph:

> Again and again the Southern violators have answered Dr. King's peaceful protests with intimidation and violence. They have bombed his home almost killing his wife and child. They have assaulted his person. They have arrested him seven times — for "speeding," "loitering" and similar "offenses." And now they have charged him with "perjury" — a felony under which they could imprison him for ten years. . . .

Although neither of these statements mentions respondent by name, he contended that the word "police" in the third paragraph referred to him as the Montgomery Commissioner who supervised the Police Department, so that he was being accused of "ringing" the campus with police. He further claimed that the paragraph would be read as imputing to the police, and hence to him, the padlocking of the dining hall in order to starve the students into submission. As to the sixth paragraph, he contended that since arrests are ordinarily made by the police, the statement "They have arrested (Dr. King) seven times" would be read as referring to him; he further contended that the "They" who did the arresting would be equated with the "They" who committed the other described acts and with the "Southern violators." Thus, he argued, the paragraph would be read as accusing the Montgomery police, and hence him, of answering Dr. King's protests with "intimidation and violence," bombing his home, assaulting his person, and charging him with perjury. Respondent and six other Montgomery residents testified that they read some or all of the statements as referring to him in his capacity as Commissioner.

It is uncontroverted that some of the statements contained in the two paragraphs were not accurate descriptions of events which occurred in Montgomery. Although Negro students staged a demonstration on the State Capitol steps, they sang the National Anthem and not "My Country, 'Tis of Thee." Although nine students were expelled by the State Board of Education, this was not for leading the demonstration at the Capitol, but for demanding service at a lunch counter in the Montgomery County Courthouse on another day. Not the entire student body, but most of it, had protested the expulsion, not by refusing to register, but by boycotting classes on a single day; virtually all the students did register for the ensuing semester. The campus dining hall was not padlocked on any occasion, and the only students who may have been barred from eating there were the few who had neither signed a preregistration application nor requested temporary meal tickets. Although the police were deployed near the campus in large numbers on three occasions, they did not at any time "ring" the campus, and they were not called to the campus in connection with the demonstration on the State Capitol steps, as the third paragraph implied. Dr. King had not been arrested seven times, but only four; and although he claimed to have been assaulted some years earlier in connection with his arrest for loitering outside a courtroom, one of the officers who made the arrest denied that there was such an assault.

On the premise that the charges in the sixth paragraph could be read as referring to him, respondent was allowed to prove that he had not participated in the events described. . . .

Respondent made no effort to prove that he suffered actual pecuniary loss as a result of the alleged libel. . . .

The cost of the advertisement was approximately $4800, and it was published by the *Times* upon an order from a New York advertising agency acting for the signatory Committee. The agency submitted the advertisement with a letter from A. Philip Randolph, Chairman of the Committee, certifying that the persons whose names appeared on the advertisement had given their permission. Mr. Randolph was known to the *Times'* Advertising Acceptability Department as a responsible person, and in accepting the letter as sufficient proof of authorization it followed its established practice. . . . Each of the individual petitioners testified that he had not authorized the use of his name, and that he had been unaware of its use until receipt of respondent's demand for a retraction. The manager of the Advertising Acceptability Department testified that he had approved the advertisement for publication because he knew nothing to cause him to believe that anything in it was false, and because it bore the endorsement of "a number of people who are well known and whose reputation" he "had no reason to question." Neither he nor anyone else at the *Times* made an effort to confirm the accuracy of the advertisement, either by checking it against recent *Times* news stories relating to some of the described events or by any other means.

Alabama law denies a public officer recovery of punitive damages in a libel action brought on account of a publication concerning his official conduct unless he first makes a written demand for a public retraction and the defendant fails or refuses to comply. . . . Respondent served such a demand upon each of the petitioners. None of the individual petitioners responded to the demand, primarily because each took the position that he had not authorized the use of his name on the advertisement and therefore had not published the statements that respondent alleged had libeled him. The *Times* did not publish a retraction in response to the demand, but wrote respondent a letter stating, among other things, that "we . . . are somewhat puzzled as to how you think the statements in any way reflect on you," and "you might, if you desire, let us know in what respect you claim that the statements in the advertisement reflect on you." Respondent filed this suit a few days later without answering the letter. The *Times* did, however, subsequently publish a retraction of the advertisement upon the demand of Governor John Patterson of Alabama, who asserted that the publication charged him with "grave misconduct and . . . improper actions and omissions as Governor of Alabama and Ex-Officio Chairman of the State Board of Education of Alabama." When asked to explain why there had been a retraction for the Governor but not for respondent, the Secretary of the *Times* testified: "We did that because we didn't want anything that was published by the *Times* to be a reflection on the State of Alabama and the Governor was, as far as we could see, the embodiment of the State of Alabama and the proper representative of the State and, furthermore, we had by that time learned more of the actual facts which the ad purported to recite and, finally, the ad did refer to the action of the State authorities and the Board of Education presumably of which the Governor is the ex-officio chairman. . . ." On the other hand, he testified that he did not think that "any of the language in there referred to Mr. Sullivan. . . ."

Because of the importance of the constitutional issues involved, we granted the separate petitions for certiorari of the individual petitioners and of the *Times*. . . . We reverse the judgment. We hold that the rule of law applied by the Alabama courts is constitutionally deficient for failure to provide the safeguards for freedom of speech and of the press that are required by the First and Fourteenth Amendments in a libel action brought by a public official against critics of his official conduct. We further hold that under the proper safeguards the evidence presented in this case is constitutionally insufficient to support the judgment for respondent. . . .

[W]e consider this case against the background of a profound national commitment to the principle that debate on public issues should be uninhibited, robust, and wide-open, and that it may well include vehement, caustic, and sometimes unpleasantly sharp attacks on government and public officials. . . . The present advertisement, as an expression of grievance and protest on one of the major public issues of our time, would seem clearly to qualify for the constitutional protection. The question is whether it forfeits that protection by the falsity of some of its factual statements and by its alleged defamation of respondent. Authoritative interpretations of the First Amendment guarantees have consistently refused to recognize an exception for any test of truth — whether administered by judges, juries, or administrative officials — and especially one that puts the burden of proving truth on the speaker. . . .

[N]either factual error nor defamatory content suffices to remove the constitutional shield from criticism of official conduct, [and] the combination of the two elements is no less inadequate. This is the lesson to be drawn from the great controversy over the Sedition Act of 1798, 1 Stat. 596, which first crystallized a national awareness of the central meaning of the First Amendment. . . . That statute made it a crime, punishable by a $5,000 fine and five years in prison, "if any person shall write, print, utter or publish . . . any false, scandalous and malicious writing or writings against the government of the United States, or either house of the Congress . . . , or the President . . . , with intent to defame . . . or to bring them, or either of them, into contempt or disrepute; or to excite against them, or either or any of them, the hatred of the good people of the United States." The Act allowed the defendant the defense of truth, and provided that the jury were to be judges both of the law and the facts. Despite these qualifications, the Act was vigorously condemned as unconstitutional in an attack joined in by Jefferson and Madison. . . . Madison['s] . . . premise was that the Constitution created a form of government under which "The people, not the government, possess the absolute sovereignty." The structure of the government dispersed power in reflection of the people's distrust of concentrated power, and of power itself at all levels. This form of government was "altogether different" from the British form, under which the Crown was sovereign and the people were subjects. . . . The right of free public discussion of the stewardship of public officials was thus, in Madison's view, a fundamental principle of the American form of government.

Although the Sedition Act was never tested in this Court, the attack upon its validity has carried the day in the court of history. Fines levied in its prosecution were repaid by Act of Congress on the ground that it was unconstitutional. . . . Jefferson, as President, pardoned those who had been convicted and sentenced under the Act and remitted their fines. . . .

There is no force in respondent's argument that the constitutional limitations implicit in the history of the Sedition Act apply only to Congress and not to the States. It is true that the First Amendment was originally addressed only to action by the Federal Government, and that Jefferson, for one, while denying the power of Congress "to control the freedom of the press," recognized such a power in the States. . . . But this distinction was eliminated with the adoption of the Fourteenth Amendment and the application to the States of the First Amendment's restrictions. . . .

What a State may not constitutionally bring about by means of a criminal statute is likewise beyond the reach of its civil law of libel. The fear of damage awards under a rule such as that invoked by the Alabama courts here may be markedly more inhibiting than the fear of prosecution under a criminal statute. . . .

The state rule of law is not saved by its allowance of the defense of truth. . . . A rule compelling the critic of official conduct to guarantee the truth of all his factual assertions—and to do so on pain of libel judgments virtually unlimited in amount—leads to a comparable "self-censorship." Allowance of the defense of truth, with the burden of proving it on the defendant, does not mean that only false speech will be deterred. . . . Under such a rule, would-be critics of official conduct may be deterred from voicing their criticism, even though it is believed to be true and even though it is in fact true, because of doubt whether it can be proved in court or fear of the expense of having to do so. . . . The rule thus dampens the vigor and limits the variety of public debate. It is inconsistent with the First and Fourteenth Amendments.

The constitutional guarantees require, we think, a federal rule that prohibits a public official from recovering damages for a defamatory falsehood relating to his official conduct unless he proves that the statement was made with "actual malice"—that is, with knowledge that it was false or with reckless disregard of whether it was false or not. . . .

III

We hold today that the Constitution delimits a State's power to award damages for libel in actions brought by public officials against critics of their official conduct. Since this is such an action,[6] the rule requiring proof of actual malice is applicable. . . .

Since respondent may seek a new trial, we deem that considerations of effective judicial administration require us to review the evidence in the present record to determine whether it could constitutionally support a judgment for respondent. This Court's duty is not limited to the elaboration of constitutional principles; we must also in proper cases review the evidence to make certain that those principles have been constitutionally applied. . . .

Applying these standards, we consider that the proof presented to show actual malice lacks the convincing clarity which the constitutional standard demands, and hence that it would not constitutionally sustain the judgment for respondent under the proper rule of law. The case of the individual petitioners requires little discussion. Even assuming that they could constitutionally be found to have authorized the use of their names on the advertisement, there was no evidence whatever that they were aware of any erroneous statements or were in any way reckless in that regard. The judgment against them is thus without constitutional support.

---

6. [Court's Footnote 23] We have no occasion here to determine how far down into the lower ranks of government employees the "public official" designation would extend for purposes of this rule, or otherwise to specify categories of persons who would or would not be included. . . . Nor need we here determine the boundaries of the "official conduct" concept. It is enough for the present case that respondent's position as an elected city commissioner clearly made him a public official, and that the allegations in the advertisement concerned what was allegedly his official conduct as Commissioner in charge of the Police Department. . . .

As to the *Times*, we similarly conclude that the facts do not support a finding of actual malice. The statement by the *Times*' Secretary that, apart from the padlocking allegation, he thought the advertisement was "substantially correct," affords no constitutional warrant for the Alabama Supreme Court's conclusion that it was a "cavalier ignoring of the falsity of the advertisement, [from which] the jury could not have but been impressed with the bad faith of the *Times*, and its maliciousness inferable therefrom." The statement does not indicate malice at the time of the publication; even if the advertisement was not "substantially correct" — although respondent's own proofs tend to show that it was — that opinion was at least a reasonable one, and there was no evidence to impeach the witness's good faith in holding it. The *Times*' failure to retract upon respondent's demand, although it later retracted upon the demand of Governor Patterson, is likewise not adequate evidence of malice for constitutional purposes. Whether or not a failure to retract may ever constitute such evidence, there are two reasons why it does not here. First, the letter written by the *Times* reflected a reasonable doubt on its part as to whether the advertisement could reasonably be taken to refer to respondent at all. Second, it was not a final refusal, since it asked for an explanation on this point — a request that respondent chose to ignore. Nor does the retraction upon the demand of the Governor supply the necessary proof. It may be doubted that a failure to retract which is not itself evidence of malice can retroactively become such by virtue of a retraction subsequently made to another party. But in any event that did not happen here, since the explanation given by the *Times*' Secretary for the distinction drawn between respondent and the Governor was a reasonable one, the good faith of which was not impeached.

Finally, there is evidence that the *Times* published the advertisement without checking its accuracy against the news stories in the *Times*' own files. The mere presence of the stories in the files does not, of course, establish that the *Times* "knew" the advertisement was false, since the state of mind required for actual malice would have to be brought home to the persons in the *Times*' organization having responsibility for the publication of the advertisement. With respect to the failure of those persons to make the check, the record shows that they relied upon their knowledge of the good reputation of many of those whose names were listed as sponsors of the advertisement, and upon the letter from A. Philip Randolph, known to them as a responsible individual, certifying that the use of the names was authorized. There was testimony that the persons handling the advertisement saw nothing in it that would render it unacceptable under the *Times*' policy of rejecting advertisements containing "attacks of a personal character;" their failure to reject it on this ground was not unreasonable. We think the evidence against the *Times* supports at most a finding of negligence in failing to discover the misstatements, and is constitutionally insufficient to show the recklessness that is required for a finding of actual malice. . . .

We also think the evidence was constitutionally defective in another respect: it was incapable of supporting the jury's finding that the allegedly libelous statements were made "of and concerning" respondent. . . . There was no reference to respondent in the advertisement, either by name or official position. A number of the alleg-edly libelous statements — the charges that the dining hall was padlocked and that Dr. King's home was bombed, his person assaulted, and a perjury prosecution insti-tuted against him — did not even concern the police; despite the ingenuity of the arguments which would attach this significance to the word "They," it is plain that these statements could not reasonably be read as accusing respondent of personal involvement in the acts in question. The statements upon which respondent prin-cipally relies as referring to him are the two allegations that did concern the police or police functions: that "truckloads of police . . . ringed the Alabama State College Campus" after the demonstration on the State Capitol steps, and that Dr. King had been "arrested . . . seven times." These statements were false only in that the police had been "deployed near" the campus but had not actually "ringed" it and had not gone there in connection with the State Capitol demonstration, and in that Dr. King had been arrested only four times. The ruling that these discrepancies between what was true and what was asserted were sufficient to injure respondent's reputation may itself raise constitutional problems, but we need not consider them here. Although the statements may be taken as referring to the police, they did not on their face make even an oblique reference to respondent as an individual. . . . [T]o the extent that some of the witnesses thought respondent to have been charged with ordering or approving the conduct or otherwise being personally involved in it, they based this notion not on any statements in the advertisement, and not on any evidence that he had in fact been so involved, but solely on the unsupported assumption that, because of his official position, he must have been. . . . [T]he Supreme Court of Alabama . . . based its ruling on the proposition that:

> We think it common knowledge that the average person knows that munici-pal agents, such as police and firemen, and others, are under the control and direction of the city governing body, and more particularly under the direc-tion and control of a single commissioner. In measuring the performance or deficiencies of such groups, praise or criticism is usually attached to the official in complete control of the body. . . .

This proposition has disquieting implications for criticism of governmental conduct. . . . The present proposition would sidestep this obstacle by transmuting criticism of government, however impersonal it may seem on its face, into per-sonal criticism, and hence potential libel, of the officials of whom the government is composed. . . . Raising as it does the possibility that a good-faith critic of govern-ment will be penalized for his criticism, the proposition relied on by the Alabama courts strikes at the very center of the constitutionally protected area of free expres-sion. We hold that such a proposition may not constitutionally be utilized to estab-lish that an otherwise impersonal attack on governmental operations was a libel of an official responsible for those operations. Since it was relied on exclusively here, and there was no other evidence to connect the statements with respondent, the evidence was constitutionally insufficient to support a finding that the statements referred to respondent.

The judgment of the Supreme Court of Alabama is reversed and the case is remanded to that court for further proceedings not inconsistent with this opinion.

Reversed and remanded.

MR. JUSTICE BLACK, with whom MR. JUSTICE DOUGLAS joins (concurring).

. . . I base my vote to reverse on the belief that the First and Fourteenth Amendments not merely "delimit" a State's power to award damages to "public officials against critics of their official conduct" but completely prohibit a State from exercising such a power. The Court goes on to hold that a State can subject such critics to damages if "actual malice" can be proved against them. "Malice," even as defined by the Court, is an elusive, abstract concept, hard to prove and hard to disprove. The requirement that malice be proved provides at best an evanescent protection for the right critically to discuss public affairs and certainly does not measure up to the sturdy safeguard embodied in the First Amendment. Unlike the Court, therefore, I vote to reverse exclusively on the ground that the *Times* and the individual defendants had an absolute, unconditional constitutional right to publish in the *Times* advertisement their criticisms of the Montgomery agencies and officials. . . .

We would, I think, more faithfully interpret the First Amendment by holding that at the very least it leaves the people and the press free to criticize officials and discuss public affairs with impunity. . . . While our Court has held that some kinds of speech and writings, such as "obscenity," *Roth v. United States*, . . . and "fighting words," *Chaplinsky v. New Hampshire*, . . . are not expression within the protection of the First Amendment, freedom to discuss public affairs and public officials is unquestionably, as the Court today holds, the kind of speech the First Amendment was primarily designed to keep within the area of free discussion. To punish the exercise of this right to discuss public affairs or to penalize it through libel judgments is to abridge or shut off discussion of the very kind most needed. This Nation, I suspect, can live in peace without libel suits based on public discussions of public affairs and public officials. But I doubt that a country can live in freedom where its people can be made to suffer physically or financially for criticizing their government, its actions, or its officials. "For a representative democracy ceases to exist the moment that the public functionaries are by any means absolved from their responsibility to their constituents; and this happens whenever the constituent can be restrained in any manner from speaking, writing, or publishing his opinions upon any public measure, or upon the conduct of those who may advise or execute it." An unconditional right to say what one pleases about public affairs is what I consider to be the minimum guarantee of the First Amendment.

I regret that the Court has stopped short of this holding indispensable to preserve our free press from destruction.

MR. JUSTICE GOLDBERG, with whom MR. JUSTICE DOUGLAS joins (concurring in the result). . . .

In my view, the First and Fourteenth Amendments to the Constitution afford to the citizen and to the press an absolute, unconditional privilege to criticize official conduct despite the harm that may flow from excesses and abuses. The prized American right "to speak one's mind," . . . about public officials and affairs needs "breathing space to survive. . . ." The right should not depend upon a probing by the jury of the motivation of the citizen or press. The theory of our Constitution is that every citizen may speak his mind and every newspaper express its view on matters of public concern and may not be barred from speaking or publishing because those in control of government think that what is said or written is unwise, unfair, false, or malicious. In a democratic society, one who assumes to act for the citizens in an executive, legislative, or judicial capacity must expect that his official acts will be commented upon and criticized. Such criticism cannot, in my opinion, be muzzled or deterred by the courts at the instance of public officials under the label of libel. . . .

It may be urged that deliberately and maliciously false statements have no conceivable value as free speech. That argument, however, is not responsive to the real issue presented by this case, which is whether that freedom of speech which all agree is constitutionally protected can be effectively safeguarded by a rule allowing the imposition of liability upon a jury's evaluation of the speaker's state of mind. If individual citizens may be held liable in damages for strong words, which a jury finds false and maliciously motivated, there can be little doubt that public debate and advocacy will be constrained. And if newspapers, publishing advertisements dealing with public issues, thereby risk liability, there can also be little doubt that the ability of minority groups to secure publication of their views on public affairs and to seek support for their causes will be greatly diminished. . . .

This is not to say that the Constitution protects defamatory statements directed against the private conduct of a public official or private citizen. Freedom of press and of speech insures that government will respond to the will of the people and that changes may be obtained by peaceful means. Purely private defamation has little to do with the political ends of a self-governing society. The imposition of liability for private defamation does not abridge the freedom of public speech or any other freedom protected by the First Amendment. . . .

If liability can attach to political criticism because it damages the reputation of a public official as a public official, then no critical citizen can safely utter anything but faint praise about the government or its officials. The vigorous criticism by press and citizen of the conduct of the government of the day by the officials of the day will soon yield to silence if officials in control of government agencies, instead of answering criticisms, can resort to friendly juries to forestall criticism of their official conduct.

The conclusion that the Constitution affords the citizen and the press an absolute privilege for criticism of official conduct does not leave the public official without defenses against unsubstantiated opinions or deliberate misstatements. "Under our system of government, counterargument and education are the weapons available to expose these matters, not abridgment . . . of free speech. . . ." The public official certainly has equal if not greater access than most private citizens to media of communication. In any event, despite the possibility that some excesses and abuses may go unremedied, we must recognize that "the people of this nation have ordained in the light of history, that, in spite of the probability of excesses and abuses, [certain] liberties are, in the long view, essential to enlightened opinion and right conduct on the part of the citizens of a democracy. . . ." As Mr. Justice Brandeis correctly observed, "sunlight is the most powerful of all disinfectants."

For these reasons, I strongly believe that the Constitution accords citizens and press an unconditional freedom to criticize official conduct. It necessarily follows that in a case such as this, where all agree that the allegedly defamatory statements related to official conduct, the judgments for libel cannot constitutionally be sustained.

McKee v. Cosby

United States Supreme Court
139 S. Ct. 675 (2019)

JUSTICE THOMAS, concurring in the denial of certiorari.

In December 2014, petitioner Kathrine McKee publicly accused actor and comedian Bill Cosby of forcibly raping her some 40 years earlier. McKee contends that Cosby's attorney responded on his behalf by writing and leaking a defamatory letter. According to McKee, the letter deliberately distorts her personal background to "damage her reputation for truthfulness and honesty, and further to embarrass, harass, humiliate, intimidate, and shame" her. She alleges that excerpts of the letter were disseminated via the Internet and published by news outlets around the world.

McKee filed suit in federal court for defamation under state law, but her case was dismissed. Applying *New York Times Co. v. Sullivan*, and its progeny, the Court of Appeals concluded that, by disclosing her accusation to a reporter, McKee had "'thrust' herself to the 'forefront'" of the public controversy over "sexual assault allegations implicating Cosby" and was therefore a "limited-purpose public figure." Under this Court's First Amendment precedents, public figures are barred from recovering damages for defamation unless they can show that the statement at issue was made with "'actual malice' — that is, with knowledge that it was false or with reckless disregard of whether it was false or not." Like many plaintiffs subject to this "almost impossible" standard, McKee was unable to make that showing.

New York Times and the Court's decisions extending it were policy-driven decisions masquerading as constitutional law. Instead of simply applying the First Amendment as it was understood by the people who ratified it, the Court fashioned its own federal rules by balancing the "competing values at stake in defamation suits."

We should not continue to reflexively apply this policy-driven approach to the Constitution. Instead, we should carefully examine the original meaning of the First and Fourteenth Amendments. If the Constitution does not require public figures to satisfy an actual-malice standard in state-law defamation suits, then neither should we.

None of these decisions made a sustained effort to ground their holdings in the Constitution's original meaning. As the Court itself acknowledged, "the rule enunciated in the *New York Times* case" is "largely a judge-made rule of law," the "content" of which is "given meaning through the evolutionary process of common-law adjudication."

The constitutional libel rules adopted by this Court in New York Times and its progeny broke sharply from the common law of libel, and there are sound reasons to question whether the First and Fourteenth Amendments displaced this body of common law.

The common law of libel at the time the First and Fourteenth Amendments were ratified did not require public figures to satisfy any kind of heightened liability standard as a condition of recovering damages.

Far from increasing a public figure's burden in a defamation action, the common law deemed libels against public figures to be, if anything, more serious and injurious than ordinary libels.

These common-law protections for the "core private right" of a person's "uninterrupted enjoyment of his reputation" formed the backdrop against which the First and Fourteenth Amendments were ratified. Before our decision in *New York Times*, we consistently recognized that the First Amendment did not displace the common law of libel. As Justice Story explained,

> "The liberty of speech, or of the press, has nothing to do with this subject. They are not endangered by the punishment of libellous publications. The liberty of speech and the liberty of the press do not authorize malicious and injurious defamation."

There are sound reasons to question whether either the First or Fourteenth Amendment, as originally understood, encompasses an actual-malice standard for public figures or otherwise displaces vast swaths of state defamation law.

Historical practice further suggests that protections for free speech and a free press — whether embodied in state constitutions, the First Amendment, or the Fourteenth Amendment — did not abrogate the common law of libel.

As against this body of historical evidence, New York Times pointed only to opposition surrounding the Sedition Act of 1798. After discussing other opposition to the Act, the Court concluded that "the attack upon its validity has carried the day in the court of history."

The Court gleaned from this evidence a "broad consensus" that the First Amendment protects "criticism of government and public officials." And the Court further inferred that because the Act allowed truth to be offered as a defense and applied to defamatory statements, a libel law prohibiting only false defamation could still fail First Amendment scrutiny But constitutional opposition to the Sedition Act — a federal law directly criminalizing criticism of the Government — does not necessarily support a constitutional actual-malice rule in all civil libel actions brought by public figures. Madison did not contend that the Constitution abrogated the common law applicable to these private actions. Instead, he seemed to contemplate that "those who administer [the Federal Government]" retain "a remedy, for their injured reputations, under the same laws, and in the same tribunals, which protect their lives, their liberties, and their properties." Moreover, a central assumption of Madison's view was the historical absence of a national common law "pervading and operating through" each colony "as one society." Yet the Court elevated just such a rule to constitutional status in *New York Times.*

It is certainly true that defamation law did not remain static after the founding. For example, many States acted "by judicial decision, statute or constitution" during the early 19th century to allow truth or good motives to serve as a defense to a libel prosecution. But these changes appear to have reflected changing policy judgments, not a sense that existing law violated the original meaning of the First or Fourteenth Amendment.

In short, there appears to be little historical evidence suggesting that the *New York Times* actual-malice rule flows from the original understanding of the First or Fourteenth Amendment.

Like Justice White, I assume that *New York Times* and our other constitutional decisions displacing state defamation law have been popular in some circles, "but this is not the road to salvation for a court of law." We did not begin meddling in this area until 1964, nearly 175 years after the First Amendment was ratified. The States are perfectly capable of striking an acceptable balance between encouraging robust public discourse and providing a meaningful remedy for reputational harm. We should reconsider our jurisprudence in this area.

Notes and Questions

(1) Justice Neil Gorsuch joined forces with Justice Thomas in calling for reconsideration of *Sullivan* in *Berisha v. Lawson,* 141 S. Ct. 2424, 2425 (2021) (Gorsuch, J., dissenting from the denial of certiorari). Justice Gorsuch argued that the media landscape has changed dramatically since 1964. *Id., citing* David Logan, *Rescuing Our Democracy by Rethinking New York Times Co. v. Sullivan,* 81 Ohio St. L.J. 759, 794 (2020). Justice Gorsuch argued that that modern public discourse is battered by a perfect storm of technological and social changes, including the specter that given the dominance of social media, a person may become a public figure overnight.

(2) *New York Times Co. v. Sullivan* represents the intersection of many of the themes of modern constitutional law. *New York Times* is one of the great landmark cases in the history of freedom of speech, but it is also much more. It is, in many ways, a civil rights case, a case inextricably bound up in the struggle for racial justice led by heroic figures like Martin Luther King and Rosa Parks. For in the decade following *Brown v. Board of Education,* the South hung on stubbornly to its legacy of officially enforced racism. King, a student of the civil disobedience tactics of Thoreau and Gandhi, espoused a strategy of peaceful demonstrations and civil disobedience.

The American press was integral to that strategy. King wanted to hold the unjust laws of the South up to the larger American conscience. If the media could be punished with large libel verdicts for reporting on the civil rights movement, the effectiveness of the movement could be severely hampered. So too, if individuals and organizations around the nation who raised funds and generated support for the movement could be strapped with punishing verdicts for the statements made in fundraising or promotional materials, national support for the movement might be damaged. The trial in the *Times* case was heavily infected with racism. By the time the case reached the Supreme Court, a whole string of libel suits arising from the civil rights movement were popping up around Alabama, with the *Times*, CBS News, and individual reporters facing millions of dollars of libel verdicts. And so when seen from a civil rights perspective, the intervention of the Supreme Court seemed almost inevitable, for it could hardly allow state officials who were contumaciously undermining the principles of racial equality emanating from *Brown* to pervert the law of libel and use it as a vehicle for stifling dissent. In the last analysis, Justice Brennan's opinion in *New York Times Co. v. Sullivan* eloquently captures the essence of the American constitutional experience: that dynamic and vigorous debate, conducted generation through generation, over what it means to be American, to be committed to democracy, equality, tolerance, religious freedom, freedom of expression, and due process of law, to place our ultimate trust in "a profound national commitment to the principle that debate on public issues should be uninhibited, robust, and wide-open." For an historical overview of the *Times* case, and the many cases that it spawned, see Rodney A. Smolla, Suing the Press: Libel, the Media, and Power (1986). The definitive historical treatment of the case is Anthony Lewis, Make No Law: The Sullivan Case and the First Amendment (1991).

(3) The *Times* case also posed a subtle problem of state action. This was, ostensibly, a simple tort suit among private parties; this was not a governmental fine imposed on the paper for violating the criminal law. Yet the Court held the enforcement of the libel action through the state court system was sufficient to satisfy the state action requirement.

(4) The *Times* case also had powerful federalism overtones. The Alabama courts had done nothing more, remember, than enforce their state common law of libel. Tort rules had traditionally been purely the domain of state law. In order to vindicate the values of racial equality and freedom of speech threatened by the Alabama tort judgments, the Supreme Court had to "constitutionalize" one of the oldest and most venerable domains of state law, the common law of libel. *See generally* Harry Kalven, *The New York Times Case: A Note on the Central Meaning of the First Amendment*, 1964 Sup. Ct. Rev. 191; Anthony Lewis, *New York Times v. Sullivan Reconsidered: Time to Return to "The Central Meaning of the First Amendment,"* 83 Colum. L. Rev. 603 (1983); Rodney Smolla, *Let the Author Beware: The Rejuvenation of the American Law of Libel*, 132 U. Pa. L. Rev. 1 (1983).

(5) Following the decision in *New York Times v. Sullivan*, the Supreme Court embarked on a long series of First Amendment decisions further defining the

constitutional limitations on modern defamation law. *See generally* RODNEY SMOLLA, LAW OF DEFAMATION, ch. 1–3 (2018 ed.). The Supreme Court first expanded the coverage of the actual malice standard beyond suits brought by public officials, to include suits brought by "public figures." *Curtis Publishing Co. v. Butts*, 388 U.S. 130 (1967); *Associated Press v. Walker*, 389 U.S. 889 (1967). For a brief period, the Court flirted with going beyond *Butts* and *Walker*. In his opinion for a four-Justice plurality in *Rosenbloom v. Metromedia, Inc.*, 403 U.S. 29 (1971), Justice Brennan took the *New York Times* privilege one step further. He concluded that its protection should extend to defamatory falsehoods relating to private persons if the statements concerned matters of general or public interest. He abjured the suggested distinction between public officials and public figures on the one hand and private individuals on the other. He focused instead on society's interest in learning about certain issues: "If a matter is a subject of public or general interest, it cannot suddenly become less so merely because a private individual is involved, or because in some sense the individual did not 'voluntarily' choose to become involved."

(6) The plurality view in *Rosenbloom* was repudiated in 1974, however, in *Gertz v. Robert Welch, Inc.*, 418 U.S. 323 (1974). To this day, *Gertz* remains one of the canonical landmark decisions shaping American defamation law, establishing a critical First Amendment divide between public plaintiffs, including both public officials and public figures, on the one hand, and private figure plaintiffs on the other. The Court held that public official and public figure plaintiffs must establish actual malice to recover, but that states were free to allow private figure plaintiffs to recover as long as negligence was established. The Court held that "presumed damages" and "punitive damages" could not be recovered absent a showing of actual malice. This meant that in private figure cases in which there was no showing of actual malice, a plaintiff was required to prove "actual injury." This term, however, was broadly defined: "We need not define 'actual injury,' as trial courts have wide experience in framing appropriate jury instructions in tort actions. Suffice it to say that actual injury is not limited to out-of-pocket loss. Indeed, the more customary types of actual harm inflicted by defamatory falsehood include impairment of reputation and standing in the community, personal humiliation, and mental anguish and suffering. Of course, juries must be limited by appropriate instructions, and all awards must be supported by competent evidence concerning the injury, although there need be no evidence which assigns an actual dollar value to the injury."

(7) *Gertz* established two categories of public figures, the "all-purpose" or "general-purpose" public figures, by which the Court appeared to mean mega-celebrities, and the more common "limited-purpose" public figures. The key passage in *Gertz* stated: "That designation may rest on either of two alternative bases. In some instances an individual may achieve such pervasive fame or notoriety that he becomes a public figure for all purposes and in all contexts. More commonly, an individual voluntarily injects himself or is drawn into a particular public controversy and thereby becomes a public figure for a limited range of issues. In either case such persons assume special prominence in the resolution of public questions." The

Court went on to hold that Elmer Gertz, a well-known Chicago civil rights lawyer, was a *private figure* for purposes of defamation alleging that he was a communist or communist sympathizer.

(8) The Court in *Dun & Bradstreet, Inc. v. Greenmoss Builders, Inc.*, 472 U.S. 749 (1985), clarified that all of its First Amendment decisions altering common-law defamation doctrines were predicated on the supposition that the subject matter of the defamation involved issues of "public concern." The Court held that a routine defamation suit involving the credit-worthiness of a company was not a matter of public concern triggering First Amendment protection. In any defamation action, therefore, the First Amendment principles to be applied require a threshold two-step analysis. First, the *subject matter* of the defamation must be classified as a matter of public or private concern. If the subject matter is an issue of private concern, then no special First Amendment standards apply at all. If the subject matter is public concern, then the plaintiff must be classified as either private, requiring at least a showing of negligence, or public, requiring a showing of actual malice. Similarly, the rules requiring proof of "actual injury" unless the plaintiff proves actual malice only apply *if* the threshold gatekeeper requiring that the speech be on matters of public concern is first satisfied.

(9) When the speech involves matters of public concern, the plaintiff bears the burden of proving the statement was false, by a preponderance of the evidence. This is a reversal of the common-law rule, which placed the burden on the defendant to prove the truth of the statement. *Philadelphia Newspapers, Inc. v. Hepps*, 475 U.S. 767 (1986). The statement must be a factual statement about the defendant, and not mere name-calling, rhetorical hyperbole, or opinion. What matters is not whether the statement is *couched* in the verbiage of "opinion," but whether the statement implies facts that are objectively provable or disprovable as true or false. *Milkovich v. Lorain Journal Co.*, 497 U.S. 1 (1990).

B. False Light

The tort of false light invasion of privacy is defined in the Restatement Second of Torts as including these elements:

> One who gives publicity to a matter concerning another that places the other before the public in a false light is subject to liability to the other for invasion of his privacy, if
>
>> (a) the false light in which the other was placed would be highly offensive to a reasonable person, and
>
>> (b) the actor has knowledge of or acted in reckless disregard as to the falsity of the publicized matter and the false light in which the other would be placed.

The critical difference between defamation and false light is that defamation claims are predicated on *external* injury to reputation, though a plaintiff's *internal* anguish and distress are also recoverable as an element of damages, whereas false light claims focus entirely on a plaintiff's *internal* anguish and distress, as a result of suffering a falsehood that would be "highly offensive to a reasonable person." The Supreme Court has twice considered false light claims. In *Time, Inc. v. Hill*, 385 U.S. 374 (1967), the Supreme held that a false light claim involving "matters of public interest" was precluded "in the absence of proof that the material was published with knowledge of falsity or in reckless disregard of the truth." *Hill* was decided prior to *Gertz*, however, leaving unclear whether the dichotomy between public and private plaintiffs established in *Gertz* should also be applied to the false light tort. In *Cantrell v. Forest City Publishing Co.*, 419 U.S. 245 (1974), the Court found that on the facts of that case, actual malice had been established in any event, and stated that "[c]onsequently, this case presents no occasion to consider whether a State may constitutionally apply a more relaxed standard of liability for a publisher or broadcaster of false statements injurious to a private individual under a false-light theory of invasion of privacy, or whether the constitutional standard announced in *Time, Inc. v. Hill* applies to all false light cases."

C. Publication of Private Facts

The common law of torts recognizes a cause of action for the publication of private facts. In jurisdictions that recognize such a claim, the classic elements are the public disclosure of private facts, the disclosure of which would be highly offensive to a person of ordinary sensibilities. Both common-law doctrines and First Amendment principles, however, interpose a defense when the ostensibly private facts disclosed are "newsworthy." This tort is fundamentally different from defamation and false light, it should be emphasized, because the offending publication is by definition *true*, whereas for defamation and false light, the offending publication is *false*. This core invasion of privacy cause of action for disclosure of private facts rests on the supposition that there are certain *true* facts about a person's life that are nobody else's business, and the disclosure of those true facts may be tortious. Sometimes the common law tort principles applicable to this branch of invasion of privacy are augmented by statutory protections. There are laws, for example, that prohibit the publication of information about a victim of rape or sexual assault, without the victim's consent. There are also laws that prohibit trafficking in private information, such as laws prohibiting the publication of illegally intercepted telephone communications. These various common law and statutory forms of liability all exist in tension with the First Amendment. The materials below exhibit what is known and what is unknown regarding the First Amendment principles applicable to these issues.

Cox Broadcasting Corp. v. Cohn. In *Cox Broadcasting Corp. v. Cohn*, 420 U.S. 469 (1975), the father of a deceased rape victim sued under a private facts invasion of privacy theory for the publication of his daughter's name. Six youths were indicted for the murder and rape, and the crime and subsequent proceedings received substantial press coverage. The victim's name had not appeared in the press; a Georgia statute, in fact, made it a misdemeanor to publish or broadcast the name of a rape victim. A reporter learned of the victim's name by examining copies of the indictments, which were available for his inspection in the courtroom. The Georgia Supreme Court held that a common law cause of action for public disclosure of private facts had been stated. Even though it was the daughter's privacy that had been most directly invaded, the Georgia court held that the father had a valid claim in his own right because of the publication of his daughter's name. The U.S. Supreme Court reversed. Without reaching the question of whether the First Amendment always prohibits the imposition of liability for the publication of truthful facts, the Court held that the First Amendment at least prohibits the creation of tort liability for the publication of facts "obtained from public records — more specifically, from judicial records which are maintained in connection with a public prosecution which themselves are open to public inspection."

Florida Star v. B.J.F. The Supreme Court struck down a Florida statute in *Florida Star v. B.J.F.*, 491 U.S. 524 (1989), making it unlawful to print, publish, or broadcast in any instrument of mass communication the name, address, or other identifying fact of a victim of a sexual offense. After B.J.F. reported to the local sheriff that she was a victim of a robbery and rape, the police department prepared a report that identified her by her full name and then placed the report in its press room, where full access was available to the press. The newspaper *Florida Star* published this information verbatim, including the victim's full name. The rape victim sued, using a Florida law that protected the privacy of rape victims. The Supreme Court held that "if a newspaper lawfully obtains truthful information about a matter of public significance, then state officials may not constitutionally punish publication of the information, absent a need to further a state interest of the highest order." The Court concluded that although the state's interests in protecting the identity of rape victims was highly significant, they were not enough to limit the publishing of the information, because of the manner the newspaper obtained the information. It was the police department's fault that the information leaked, and the newspaper could not be punished for publishing true information of public concern that it obtained through no wrongdoing of its own.

Bartnicki v. Vopper. In *Bartnicki v. Vopper*, 532 U.S. 514 (2001), the Supreme Court held that federal and state statutes prohibiting the disclosure of information obtained through illegal interception of cellular phone messages was unconstitutional as applied to certain media and non-media defendants who received and disclosed to others tape recordings of the intercepted messages from anonymous sources. Congress enacted Title III of the Omnibus Crime Control and Safe Streets Act of 1968 to prohibit electronic eavesdropping. The law was amended in 1986 to include new technologies within its ambit, including cellular phones. The law prohibits not only the interception of electronic communications, but subsequent disclosure or use of the contents of the communication by any person knowing or having reason to know that the communication was obtained illegally.

Gloria Bartnicki was a principal labor negotiator for a teachers' union in Pennsylvania, the Pennsylvania State Education Association. Anthony Kane, a high school teacher at Wyoming Valley West High School, was president of the union. In May of 1993, Bartnicki and Kane had a telephone conversation concerning the ongoing labor negotiations with a local school board. Kane was speaking from a land phone at his house. Bartnicki was talking from her car, using her cellular phone. Strategies and tactics were discussed, including the possibility of a teacher strike. The talk was candid, and included some blunt down-and-dirty characterizations of their opponents in the labor controversy, at times getting personal. One of the school district's representatives was described as "too nice" another as a "nitwit" and still others as "rabble rousers." Among the opposition tactics that raised the ire of Bartnicki and Kane was the proclivity, in their view, of the school district to negotiate through the newspaper, attempting to pressure the teachers' union by leaks to the press. The papers had reported that the school district was not going to agree to anything more than a pay raise of three percent. As they discussed this position, Kane stated: "If they're not gonna move from three percent, we're gonna have to go to their, their homes . . . [t]o blow off their front porches, we'll have to do some work on some of those guys."

An unknown person intercepted the conversation, presumably using a scanner that picked up the cell phone transmissions, recording it on a cassette tape. An unknown person proceeded to place the tape in the mail box of the president of a local taxpayer's group that was opposed to the teachers' union and its bargaining positions, a man named Jack Yocum. Yocum listened to the tape, recognized the voices of Bartnicki and Kane, and took the tape to a local radio station talk show host, Frederick Vopper. Vopper received the tape in the spring of 1993, but waited until September 30 to broadcast it, which he did a number of times. At first, Vopper broadcast a part of the tape that revealed Bartnicki's phone numbers. She began to receive menacing calls, and was forced to change her numbers. The tape later was warped so that the numbers would be indistinguishable when it was played on the air. Yocum, who first received the tape, and Vopper, who played it on the radio, both realized that it had been intercepted from a cell phone, and that a scanner had probably been used to make the intercept. Other media outlets also received copies of the tape, including a newspaper in Wilkes-Barre, but no other broadcaster or publisher played the tape or disclosed its contents until the material on the tape was initially broadcast by Vopper. Once Vopper broke the story, however, secondary coverage of the events, including the contents of the tape, appeared in other media outlets. Invoking a federal statute and a very similar Pennsylvania law, Bartnicki and Kane sued Yocum, Vopper, and the radio stations that carried Vopper's show, for having used and disclosed the tape of their intercepted telephone conversation.

The Supreme Court, in an opinion written by Justice Stevens, held that the laws' prohibitions against intentional disclosure of illegally intercepted communication which the disclosing party knows or should know was illegally obtained were content-neutral laws of general applicability, and that application of those provisions against defendants violated their free speech rights, since the tape concerned a matter of public importance and defendants had played no part in the illegal interception. The purpose of the law, the Court explained, was to protect the privacy of wire, electronic, and oral communications, and it singled out such communications by virtue of the fact that they were illegally intercepted — by virtue of the source rather than the subject matter. On the other hand, the Court held, the prohibition against disclosures was still fairly characterized as a regulation of speech. The Court held that the first interest identified by the Government in support of the law — removing an incentive for parties to intercept private conversations — could not justify the statute. The normal method of deterring unlawful conduct, the Court argued, is to punish the person engaging in it, and it would be remarkable, the Court claimed, to hold that speech by a law-abiding possessor of information can be suppressed in order to deter conduct by a non-law-abiding third party. The Government's second interest — minimizing the harm to persons whose conversations have been illegally intercepted — was in the view of the Court considerably stronger. Privacy of communication, the Court accepted, is an important interest. Nevertheless, the Court reasoned, because the statements made by Bartnicki and Kane would have been matters of "public concern" had they been made in a public arena, they were also matters of concern when made in private conversation. Citing a long line of precedents granting the media a First Amendment right to print truthful information on matters of public concern that is "lawfully obtained," the Court held that the newsworthiness of the information revealed trumped the privacy rights of the parties to the conversation.

Significantly, Justice Breyer, in a concurring opinion joined by Justice O'Connor, took a much narrower view of matters, heavily emphasizing the fact that the conversation between Bartnicki and Kane appeared to contemplate violent and illegal action. In the views of those two concurring Justices, it was only this added element of illegality that provided the special circumstances that warranted application of a newsworthiness defense to the disclosure of the intercepted conversation.

Chief Justice Rehnquist, joined by Justices Scalia and Thomas dissented. The laws at issue, he argued, were content neutral, they sought to restrict only the disclosure of information that was illegally obtained in the first instance, they placed no restrictions on republication of material already in the public domain, they did not single out the media for especially disfavorable treatment, they utilized a scienter requirement to avoid being sprung to trap the unwary, and they promoted both the privacy interests and the free speech interests of those using devices such as cellular telephones.

D. Intrusion

The common-law tort of intrusion deals not with the subject matter of what is published by the defendant but with the method whereby the information is obtained. Intrusion is an extremely broad tort concept that is related to the action for trespass, but with the interests protected not limited to physical invasions. An intrusion consists of the intentional invasion of the solitude or seclusion of another in his or her private affairs or concerns, through either physical or nonphysical means. In the context of the media, intrusion is thus of concern as a news-gathering tort rather than a news dissemination tort. RODNEY SMOLLA, LAW OF DEFAMATION § 10:29. *Intrusion* (2nd ed. 2018).

Because intrusion does not turn on the publication of material, the First Amendment does not *directly* apply to the tort. First Amendment concerns tend to come into play when the media is found guilty of intrusion. A typical example would be a reporter engaging in undercover reporting, entering a business and surreptitiously recording what goes on inside. If the reporter or media outlet is sued, the defense will often be that the First Amendment should protect "newsgathering," and thus immunize the journalists from liability.

This defense typically fails, as courts apply the principle that the First Amendment does not immunize media outlets from generally applicable laws. In *Cohen v. Cowles Media Co.*, 501 U.S. 663 (1991), for example, the Supreme Court held that the press was not immunized from a breach of contract or promissory estoppel claim brought by a source against a media outlet for revealing the source's name, in violation of a promise to keep the identity of the source confidential. There is no First Amendment right to trespass on property, or to engage in intrusions. On the other hand, courts may choose to limit damages to the harm caused by the intrusion or trespass itself, as opposed to the harm flowing from the damage caused to the plaintiff from the publication of true facts uncovered from the surreptitious newsgathering. *Food Lion v. Capital Cities/ABC, Inc.*, 194 F.3d 505, 521 (4th Cir. 1999), for example, involved a suit brought by the North Carolina based grocery store chain to recover for injuries allegedly suffered due to ABC's undercover investigation of certain Food Lion operational practices and the subsequent broadcast of the story on "Prime Time Live," a popular weekly investigative news program. The court held that ABC had engaged in tortious activity, but that damages could not include the harm that flowed from the public's reaction to the broadcast, which revealed true video footage obtained from the undercover reporting. It is important to note, however, that if the footage shown had created a *false* impression — by selectively manipulating video footage to create a false impression — damages for defamation would have been permissible. Similarly, if the material broadcasted constituted a public revelation of private facts, liability for the damages caused by that branch of invasion of privacy would be permitted.

If reporters use deception to obtain footage of an accident victim inside a hospital room, for example, the journalists might be guilty of intrusion (the invasion of the patient's solitude inside the hospital room) and defamation (if a subsequent broadcast created a false defamatory impression — such as falsely creating the impression that the accident victim caused the accident) and publication of private facts (if the broadcast revealed some intimate private fact regarding the victim's medical history or health).

E. Appropriation and Right of Publicity

The Appropriation and Right of Publicity Torts. The prong of invasion of privacy, known as "the right of publicity," or "appropriation," lends common law or statutory protection to an individual's name or likeness. The Restatement (Second) of Torts states simply: "One who appropriates to his own use or benefit the name or likeness of another is subject to liability to another for invasion of privacy." Courts in the United States and England as far back as the 19th century held that it was tortious to use a person's photograph without his or her consent. The "right of publicity" or "appropriation" torts may be entirely common-law doctrines in some jurisdictions or may be replaced by statutes enacted to supplant the common-law action, or the common-law and statutory actions may co-exist side-by-side.

A great deal of First Amendment litigation arises from appropriation or right of publicity claims. The litigation typically involves a plaintiff whose name or likeness is used, without permission, in some form of expressive activity. If the use of the name or likeness is "newsworthy," the First Amendment will insulate the defendant from liability. In contrast, if the defendant has simply exploited the plaintiff's name or likeness for commercial purposes, no First Amendment defense will exist. To use a simple example, it would plainly be a violation of a famous athlete's right of publicity to use the athlete's picture to sell athletic wear. A photo of Lebron James cannot be used without his permission to sell basketball shoes. In contrast, the First Amendment protects a sports program on ESPN when it uses a photo of Lebron James without his permission in reporting a news story about Lebron James' performance in a basketball game. Many cases fall on the cusp of these issues, however, resulting in litigation posing close and difficult questions.

Zacchini v. Scripps-Howard Broadcasting Co. The United States Supreme Court decided a major right of publicity case in *Zacchini v. Scripps-Howard Broadcasting Co.*, 433 U.S. 562 (1977). *Zacchini*, playfully known to media lawyers as the "human cannonball case," involved the carnival act of the great Hugo Zacchini, whose human cannonball entertainment act consisted of being shot out of a cannon into a net, an act that took about 15 seconds from blast off to landing. A local television station covering the Ohio state fair recorded Zacchini's entire show and broadcast it on television, even though Zacchini specifically told the reporter not to record his act. Zacchini sued for violation of his common-law right of publicity, effectively asserting that he possessed an intellectual property right in his own show, and that it could not be broadcast in its entirety without his permission. The television station claimed a First Amendment right to broadcast the act, as a form of news coverage. The Supreme Court ruled against the station and in favor of Zacchini. The Court emphasized that the distinction between simply reporting on or describing the human cannonball act, which would have qualified as news coverage, and actually filming the entire routine and showing it to viewers. Somewhat akin to the fair use defense in copyright law, the Supreme Court thus drew a critical distinction between coverage or reporting on one hand, and broadcast of an "entire act" on the other. Also by analogy to copyright, the Supreme Court in *Zacchini* explained that the rejection of the First Amendment defense was consistent with the Constitution's overall scheme regarding the protection of intellectual property, and the theory that legal protection of intellectual property actually enhances the marketplace of ideas, by creating an economic incentive for creation and invention.

F. Infliction of Emotional Distress

Hustler Magazine v. Falwell

United States Supreme Court
485 U.S. 46, 108 S. Ct. 876, 99 L. Ed. 2d 41 (1988)

CHIEF JUSTICE REHNQUIST delivered the opinion of the Court.

Petitioner Hustler Magazine, Inc., is a magazine of nationwide circulation. Respondent Jerry Falwell, a nationally known minister who has been active as a commentator on politics and public affairs, sued petitioner and its publisher, petitioner Larry Flynt, to recover damages for invasion of privacy, libel, and intentional infliction of emotional distress. The District Court directed a verdict against respondent on the privacy claim, and submitted the other two claims to a jury. The jury found for petitioners on the defamation claim, but found for respondent on the claim for intentional infliction of emotional distress and awarded damages. We now consider whether this award is consistent with the First and Fourteenth Amendments of the United States Constitution.

The inside front cover of the November 1983 issue of Hustler Magazine featured a "parody" of an advertisement for Campari Liqueur that contained the name and picture of respondent and was entitled "Jerry Falwell talks about his first time." This parody was modeled after actual Campari ads that included interviews with various celebrities about their "first times." Although it was apparent by the end of each interview that this meant the first time they sampled Campari, the ads clearly played on the sexual double entendre of the general subject of "first times." Copying the form and layout of these Campari ads, Hustler's editors chose respondent as the featured celebrity and drafted an alleged "interview" with him in which he states that his "first time" was during a drunken incestuous rendezvous with his mother in an outhouse. The Hustler parody portrays respondent and his mother as drunk and immoral, and suggests that respondent is a hypocrite who preaches only when he is drunk. In small print at the bottom of the page, the ad contains the disclaimer, "ad parody—not to be taken seriously." The magazine's table of contents also lists the ad as "Fiction; Ad and Personality Parody."

Soon after the November issue of Hustler became available to the public, respondent brought this diversity action in the United States District Court for the Western District of Virginia against Hustler Magazine, Inc., Larry C. Flynt, and Flynt Distributing Co., Inc. Respondent stated in his complaint that publication of the ad parody in Hustler entitled him to recover damages for libel, invasion of privacy, and intentional infliction of emotional distress. The case proceeded to trial.[7] At the close of the evidence, the District Court granted a directed verdict for petitioners on the invasion of privacy claim. The jury then found against respondent on the libel claim, specifically finding that the ad parody could not "reasonably be understood as describing actual facts about [respondent] or actual events in which [he] participated." The jury ruled for respondent on the intentional infliction of emotional distress claim, however, and stated that he should be awarded $100,000 in compensatory damages, as well as $50,000 each in punitive damages from petitioners. Petitioners' motion for judgment notwithstanding the verdict was denied.

On appeal, the United States Court of Appeals for the Fourth Circuit affirmed the judgment against petitioners. The court rejected petitioners' argument that the "actual malice" standard of *New York Times Co. v. Sullivan* must be met before respondent can recover for emotional distress. The court agreed that because respondent is concededly a public figure, petitioners are "entitled to the same level of first amendment protection in the claim for intentional infliction of emotional distress that they received in [respondent's] claim for libel." But this does not mean that a literal application of the actual malice rule is appropriate in the context of an emotional distress claim. In the court's view, the *New York Times* decision emphasized the constitutional importance not of the falsity of the statement or the defendant's disregard for the truth, but of the heightened level of culpability embodied in the requirement of "knowing . . . or reckless" conduct. Here, the *New York Times* standard is satisfied by the state-law requirement, and the jury's finding, that the defendants have acted intentionally or recklessly.[8] The Court of Appeals then went on to reject the contention that because the jury found that the ad parody did not describe actual facts about respondent, the ad was an opinion that is protected by the First Amendment. As the court put it, this was "irrelevant," as the issue is "whether [the ad's] publication was sufficiently outrageous to constitute intentional infliction of emotional distress." Petitioners then filed a petition for rehearing en banc, but this was denied by a divided court. Given the importance of the constitutional issues involved, we granted certiorari.

This case presents us with a novel question involving First Amendment limitations upon a State's authority to protect its citizens from the intentional infliction of emotional distress. We must decide whether a public figure may recover damages for emotional harm caused by the publication of an ad parody offensive to him, and doubtless gross and repugnant in the eyes of most. Respondent would have us find that a State's interest in protecting public figures from emotional distress is

---

7. [Court's Footnote 1] While the case was pending, the ad parody was published in Hustler Magazine a second time.

8. [Court's Footnote 3] Under Virginia law, in an action for intentional infliction of emotional distress a plaintiff must show that the defendant's conduct (1) is intentional or reckless; (2) offends generally accepted standards of decency or morality; (3) is causally connected with the plaintiff's emotional distress; and (4) caused emotional distress that was severe.

sufficient to deny First Amendment protection to speech that is patently offensive and is intended to inflict emotional injury, even when that speech could not reasonably have been interpreted as stating actual facts about the public figure involved. This we decline to do.

At the heart of the First Amendment is the recognition of the fundamental importance of the free flow of ideas and opinions on matters of public interest and concern. "[T]he freedom to speak one's mind is not only an aspect of individual liberty—and thus a good unto itself—but also is essential to the common quest for truth and the vitality of society as a whole." *Bose Corp. v. Consumers Union of United States, Inc.*, 466 U.S. 485, 503–504 (1984). We have therefore been particularly vigilant to ensure that individual expressions of ideas remain free from governmentally imposed sanctions. The First Amendment recognizes no such thing as a "false" idea. *Gertz v. Robert Welch, Inc.*, 418 U.S. 323, 339 (1974). As Justice Holmes wrote, "when men have realized that time has upset many fighting faiths, they may come to believe even more than they believe the very foundations of their own conduct that the ultimate good desired is better reached by free trade in ideas — that the best test of truth is the power of the thought to get itself accepted in the competition of the market. . . ." *Abrams v. United States.*

The sort of robust political debate encouraged by the First Amendment is bound to produce speech that is critical of those who hold public office or those public figures who are "intimately involved in the resolution of important public questions or, by reason of their fame, shape events in areas of concern to society at large." Justice Frankfurter put it succinctly in *Baumgartner v. United States*, 322 U.S. 665 (1944), when he said that "[o]ne of the prerogatives of American citizenship is the right to criticize public men and measures." Such criticism, inevitably, will not always be reasoned or moderate; public figures as well as public officials will be subject to "vehement, caustic, and sometimes unpleasantly sharp attacks." "[T]he candidate who vaunts his spotless record and sterling integrity cannot convincingly cry 'Foul!' when an opponent or an industrious reporter attempts to demonstrate the contrary."

Of course, this does not mean that *any* speech about a public figure is immune from sanction in the form of damages. Since *New York Times Co. v. Sullivan* we have consistently ruled that a public figure may hold a speaker liable for the damage to reputation caused by publication of a defamatory falsehood, but only if the statement was made "with knowledge that it was false or with reckless disregard of whether it was false or not." False statements of fact are particularly valueless; they interfere with the truth-seeking function of the marketplace of ideas, and they cause damage to an individual's reputation that cannot easily be repaired by counterspeech, however persuasive or effective. But even though falsehoods have little value in and of themselves, they are "nevertheless inevitable in free debate," and a rule that would impose strict liability on a publisher for false factual assertions would have an undoubted "chilling" effect on speech relating to public figures that does have constitutional value. "Freedoms of expression require 'breathing space.'"

This breathing space is provided by a constitutional rule that allows public figures to recover for libel or defamation only when they can prove *both* that the statement was false and that the statement was made with the requisite level of culpability.

Respondent argues, however, that a different standard should apply in this case because here the State seeks to prevent not reputational damage, but the severe emotional distress suffered by the person who is the subject of an offensive publication. . . . In respondent's view, and in the view of the Court of Appeals, so long as the utterance was intended to inflict emotional distress, was outrageous, and did in fact inflict serious emotional distress, it is of no constitutional import whether the statement was a fact or an opinion, or whether it was true or false. It is the intent to cause injury that is the gravamen of the tort, and the State's interest in preventing emotional harm simply outweighs whatever interest a speaker may have in speech of this type.

Generally speaking the law does not regard the intent to inflict emotional distress as one which should receive much solicitude, and it is quite understandable that most if not all jurisdictions have chosen to make it civilly culpable where the conduct in question is sufficiently "outrageous." But in the world of debate about public affairs, many things done with motives that are less than admirable are protected by the First Amendment. In *Garrison v. Louisiana*, 379 U.S. 64 (1964), we held that even when a speaker or writer is motivated by hatred or ill will his expression was protected by the First Amendment:

> Debate on public issues will not be uninhibited if the speaker must run the risk that it will be proved in court that he spoke out of hatred; even if he did speak out of hatred, utterances honestly believed contribute to the free interchange of ideas and the ascertainment of truth.

Thus while such a bad motive may be deemed controlling for purposes of tort liability in other areas of the law, we think the First Amendment prohibits such a result in the area of public debate about public figures.

Were we to hold otherwise, there can be little doubt that political cartoonists and satirists would be subjected to damages awards without any showing that their work falsely defamed its subject. *Webster's* defines a caricature as "the deliberately distorted picturing or imitating of a person, literary style, etc. by exaggerating features or mannerisms for satirical effect." *Webster's New Unabridged Twentieth Century Dictionary of the English Language* 275 (2d ed. 1979). The appeal of the political cartoon or caricature is often based on exploitation of unfortunate physical traits or politically embarrassing events — an exploitation often calculated to injure the feelings of the subject of the portrayal. The art of the cartoonist is often not reasoned or evenhanded, but slashing and one-sided. One cartoonist expressed the nature of the art in these words:

> The political cartoon is a weapon of attack, of scorn and ridicule and satire; it is least effective when it tries to pat some politician on the back. It is usually as welcome as a bee sting and is always controversial in some quarters.

Long, *The Political Cartoon: Journalism's Strongest Weapon, The Quill* 56, 57 (Nov. 1962). Several famous examples of this type of intentionally injurious speech were drawn by Thomas Nast, probably the greatest American cartoonist to date, who was associated for many years during the post-Civil War era with Harper's Weekly. In the pages of that publication Nast conducted a graphic vendetta against William M. "Boss" Tweed and his corrupt associates in New York City's "Tweed Ring." It has been described by one historian of the subject as "a sustained attack which in its passion and effectiveness stands alone in the history of American graphic art." M. Keller, *The Art and Politics of Thomas Nast* 177 (1968). Another writer explains that the success of the Nast cartoon was achieved "because of the emotional impact of its presentation. It continuously goes beyond the bounds of good taste and conventional manners." C. Press, *The Political Cartoon* 251 (1981).

Despite their sometimes caustic nature, from the early cartoon portraying George Washington as an ass down to the present day, graphic depictions and satirical cartoons have played a prominent role in public and political debate. Nast's castigation of the Tweed Ring, Walt McDougall's characterization of Presidential candidate James G. Blaine's banquet with the millionaires at Delmonico's as "The Royal Feast of Belshazzar," and numerous other efforts have undoubtedly had an effect on the course and outcome of contemporaneous debate. Lincoln's tall, gangling posture, Teddy Roosevelt's glasses and teeth, and Franklin D. Roosevelt's jutting jaw and cigarette holder have been memorialized by political cartoons with an effect that could not have been obtained by the photographer or the portrait artist. From the viewpoint of history it is clear that our political discourse would have been considerably poorer without them.

Respondent contends, however, that the caricature in question here was so "outrageous" as to distinguish it from more traditional political cartoons. There is no doubt that the caricature of respondent and his mother published in Hustler is at best a distant cousin of the political cartoons described above, and a rather poor relation at that. If it were possible by laying down a principled standard to separate the one from the other, public discourse would probably suffer little or no harm. But we doubt that there is any such standard, and we are quite sure that the pejorative description "outrageous" does not supply one. "Outrageousness" in the area of political and social discourse has an inherent subjectiveness about it which would allow a jury to impose liability on the basis of the jurors' tastes or views, or perhaps on the basis of their dislike of a particular expression. An "outrageousness" standard thus runs afoul of our longstanding refusal to allow damages to be awarded because the speech in question may have an adverse emotional impact on the audience. And, as we stated in *FCC v. Pacifica Foundation*, 438 U.S. 726 (1978):

> [T]he fact that society may find speech offensive is not a sufficient reason for suppressing it. Indeed, if it is the speaker's opinion that gives offense, that consequence is a reason for according it constitutional protection. For it is a central tenet of the First Amendment that the government must remain neutral in the marketplace of ideas.

Admittedly, these oft-repeated First Amendment principles, like other principles, are subject to limitations. We recognized in *Pacifica Foundation*, that speech that is "'vulgar,' 'offensive,' and 'shocking'" is "not entitled to absolute constitutional protection under all circumstances." In *Chaplinsky v. New Hampshire*, we held that a State could lawfully punish an individual for the use of insulting "fighting" words — those which by their very utterance inflict injury or tend to incite an immediate breach of the peace." These limitations are but recognition of the observation in *Dun & Bradstreet, Inc. v. Greenmoss Builders, Inc.*, 472 U.S. 749, 758 (1985), that this Court has "long recognized that not all speech is of equal First Amendment importance." But the sort of expression involved in this case does not seem to us to be governed by any exception to the general First Amendment principles stated above.

We conclude that public figures and public officials may not recover for the tort of intentional infliction of emotional distress by reason of publications such as the one here at issue without showing in addition that the publication contains a false statement of fact which was made with "actual malice," i.e., with knowledge that the statement was false or with reckless disregard as to whether or not it was true. This is not merely a "blind application" of the *New York Times* standard, it reflects our considered judgment that such a standard is necessary to give adequate "breathing space" to the freedoms protected by the First Amendment.

Here it is clear that respondent Falwell is a "public figure" for purposes of First Amendment law.[9] The jury found against respondent on his libel claim when it decided that the Hustler ad parody could not "reasonably be understood as describing actual facts about [respondent] or actual events in which [he] participated." The Court of Appeals interpreted the jury's finding to be that the ad parody "was not reasonably believable," and in accordance with our custom we accept this finding. Respondent is thus relegated to his claim for damages awarded by the jury for the intentional infliction of emotional distress by "outrageous" conduct. But for reasons heretofore stated this claim cannot, consistently with the First Amendment, form a basis for the award of damages when the conduct in question is the publication of a caricature such as the ad parody involved here. The judgment of the Court of Appeals is accordingly

Reversed.

Justice Kennedy took no part in the consideration or decision of this case.

Justice White, concurring in the judgment.

As I see it, the decision in *New York Times Co. v. Sullivan* has little to do with this case, for here the jury found that the ad contained no assertion of fact. But I agree

---

9. [Court's Footnote 5] Neither party disputes this conclusion. Respondent is the host of a nationally syndicated television show and was the founder and president of a political organization formerly known as the Moral Majority. He is also the founder of Liberty University in Lynchburg, Virginia, and is the author of several books and publications. *Who's Who in America* 849 (44th ed. 1986–1987).

with the Court that the judgment below, which penalized the publication of the parody, cannot be squared with the First Amendment.

———————

Snyder v. Phelps. In *Snyder v. Phelps*, 562 U.S. 443 (2011), the Supreme Court dealt with the highly charged and notorious protests of the Westboro Baptist Church. The Westboro Church was founded by Fred Phelps in Topeka, Kansas, in 1955. The congregation believes that God hates and punishes the United States for its tolerance of homosexuality, particularly in America's military. For more than two decades, the Church has used, as a tactic for propagating its message, the picketing of military funerals. As the *Snyder* litigation reached the Supreme Court, the Church had picketed nearly 600 funerals. The Snyder case arose from a civil lawsuit brought by the family of Marine Lance Corporal Matthew Snyder, who was killed in Iraq in the line of duty. Phelps and the Westboro Church, following their standard tactics, set out to use Synder's funeral for one its protests. The funeral was set for a Catholic church in Westminster, Maryland, the Snyders' hometown. The time and location were printed in local newspapers. Phelps became aware of Matthew Snyder's funeral and decided to travel to Maryland with six other Westboro Baptist parishioners (two of his daughters and four of his grandchildren) to picket. On the day of the memorial service, Phelps and six of his fellow Church members picketed on public land adjacent to public streets near the Maryland State House, the United States Naval Academy, and Matthew Snyder's funeral. They carried signs with messages such as: "God Hates the USA/Thank God for 9/11," "America is Doomed," "Don't Pray for the USA," "Thank God for IEDs," "Thank God for Dead Soldiers," "Pope in Hell," "Priests Rape Boys," "God Hates Fags," "You're Going to Hell," and "God Hates You." The Westboro Church had, in advance, notified local law enforcement authorities of their protest plans. They complied with police instructions in staging their protests. The actual picketing took place within a 10-by-25-foot plot of public land adjacent to a public street, behind a temporary fence. This was a location approximately 1,000 feet from the church at which the funeral service was conducted. The protest lasted about 30 minutes. The funeral procession passed within 200 to 300 feet of the picket location. Albert Snyder, the father of Corporal Snyder, stated that he could see the tops of the picket signs, but not read their content. No protestors entered the church property or went to the cemetery. There was no use of profanity, and there was no violence associated with the event.

There was also an internet element to the case. Several weeks following the funeral, a member of the Westboro Church who had been one of the picketers at the Synder funeral posted on the Internet, on the Westboro web site, an attack on the Snyder family. The message was laced with religious denunciations of the Snyders, interspersed among lengthy Bible quotations. When Albert Snyder discovered the posting, which came to be known in the litigation by the nickname the "epic," his distress and sense of offense were understandably intensified. The epic played a role in the lower court litigation in the civil suit, but essentially dropped out of the case at the Supreme Court level. The Court marginalized the importance of the epic by relegating all mention of it to a footnote, stating that Snyder had not included any mention of the epic in his Petition for Certiorari, and had not devoted anything other than one paragraph of attention to it in his opening briefing before the Supreme Court. In a cryptic reference, the Court said simply that in light of these facts "and the fact that an Internet posting may raise distinct issues in this context, we decline to consider the epic in deciding this case."

Albert Synder brought a diversity suit in federal court based on Maryland state tort claims, including defamation, publicity given to private life, intentional infliction of emotional distress, intrusion upon seclusion, and civil conspiracy. The Westboro Church was granted summary judgment on the defamation and publicity given to private life claims, but the trial judge allowed the remaining three claims to proceed to a jury trial. At that trial Snyder described the intensity of his emotional injury, testifying that he was unable to separate the thought of his dead son from his thoughts of Westboro's picketing, and that he often becomes tearful, angry, and physically ill when he thinks about it. Snyder's personal testimony was in turn buttressed by expert witnesses, who explained that Snyder's emotional anguish had resulted in severe depression and had exacerbated Snyder's pre-existing health conditions. At the trial, the jury found for Snyder on his claims for intentional infliction of emotional distress, intrusion upon seclusion, and civil conspiracy claims. The jury awarded Snyder $2.9 million in compensatory damages and $8 million in punitive damages. The trial judge sustained the $2.9 million compensatory damages award, and but reduced the punitive damages award to $2.1 million. The United States Court of Appeals for the Fourth Circuit reversed, holding that the Church's expression was protected by the First Amendment.

The Supreme Court, in an opinion by Chief Justice Roberts, ruled 8-1 that the speech of the Westboro Church was insulated from liability by the First Amendment. Only Justice Alito dissented. The Court began its analysis by invoking the long line of Supreme Court cases holding that the First Amendment operates as a limiting force on state tort law claims involving freedom of expression, cases such as *Hustler Magazine, Inc. v. Falwell*. The key inquiry in this line of precedent, the Court held, was whether the speech falls within the class of expression deemed to be a matter of public concern. The public concern inquiry focuses on whether the expression may be fairly considered as relating to "any matter of political, social, or other concern to the community," or "is a subject of general interest and of value and concern to the public." Expression is not disqualified from being categorized as a matter of public concern merely because it is deemed inappropriate or controversial in character. To determine whether speech is of public or private concern, the Court explain, a court must independently examine the "content, form, and context," of the speech "as revealed by the whole record." The "content" of Westboro's signs, the Court held, plainly related to public, rather than private, matters. The placards highlighted issues of public import — the political and moral conduct of the United States and its citizens, the fate of the Nation, homosexuality in the military, and scandals involving the Catholic clergy. Westboro conveyed its views on those issues in a manner designed to reach as broad a public audience as possible. The Court held that even if a few of the signs were viewed as containing messages related to a particular individual, that would not alter the dominant theme of Westboro's public message. But what of the "context" of the speech, a military funeral? The Court was unwilling to hold that the mere fact that the Westboro Church chose to use Matthew Snyder's funeral as the launching pad for its expression did not transform the Church's speech from public to private. While it was true that the Church was in a sense exploiting the occasion of the funeral to heighten the attention paid to its message, and this may have been particularly hurtful to Snyder, this did not diminish the First Amendment protection that the Church's speech would otherwise enjoy. The Court conceded that the Church's speech could be subjected to reasonable time, place, or manner restrictions. It also noted that Maryland currently has a law restricting funeral picketing, but that law was not in effect at the time of the events. The Court said that in this posture, it would not opine on whether the restrictions in the Maryland law would be upheld as "reasonable time, place, or manner" regulations.

Against this backdrop, the Court reversed all the tort liability awards. The emotional distress claim, the Court held, could not stand, because the jury was permitted to award liability merely on the finding that the picketing was "outrageous." Following its prior decision in *Hustler*, the Court held that this was too subjective and unpredictable a standard to satisfy First Amendment principles. Such a standard posed too great a danger that the jury would punish Westboro for its views on matters of public concern. Nor, the Court held, could Snyder recover for the tort of intrusion upon seclusion. Snyder argued that he was a member of a captive audience at his son's funeral, and that the actions of the Church thus constituted an intrusion on his private space, because he could not leave his own son's funeral. The Court found this unpersuasive, noting that Westboro Church members stayed well away from the memorial service, that Snyder could see no more than the tops of the picketers' signs, and that there was no indication that the picketing interfered with the funeral service itself. Once the two substantive tort claims were deemed to be inconsistent with the First Amendment, it followed that the conspiracy claim based upon them would also fail.

The Court summarized its decision by noting that Westboro had been engaged in expressing its views on matters of public import on public property, in a peaceful manner, in full compliance with the guidance of local officials. The Church did not, in any literal sense, disrupt Mathew Snyder's funeral. The Church's strategic decision to picket Snyder's funeral did not alter the nature of its speech. Chief Justice Roberts' opinion concluded: "Speech is powerful. It can stir people to action, move them to tears of both joy and sorrow, and — as it did here — inflict great pain. On the facts before us, we cannot react to that pain by punishing the speaker. As a Nation we have chosen a different course — to protect even hurtful speech on public issues to ensure that we do not stifle public debate. That choice requires that we shield Westboro from tort liability for its picketing in this case."

Justice Alito wrote an impassioned dissent in *Snyder*. His opening statement framed his argument:

> Our profound national commitment to free and open debate is not a license for the vicious verbal assault that occurred in this case. Petitioner Albert Snyder is not a public figure. He is simply a parent whose son, Marine Lance Corporal Matthew Snyder, was killed in Iraq. Mr. Snyder wanted what is surely the right of any parent who experiences such an incalculable loss: to bury his son in peace. But respondents, members of the Westboro Baptist Church, deprived him of that elementary right. They first issued a press release and thus turned Matthew's funeral into a tumultuous media event. They then appeared at the church, approached as closely as they could without trespassing, and launched a malevolent verbal attack on Matthew and his family at a time of acute emotional vulnerability. As a result, Albert Snyder suffered severe and lasting emotional injury.

Notes and Questions

Since the *Times* case, the Court has decided several dozen cases involving libel, invasion of privacy, and infliction of emotional distress, applying First Amendment principles to these various torts. *Hustler Magazine v. Falwell* is among the most colorful in this line. The case is chronicled in Rodney A. Smolla, Jerry Falwell v. Larry Flynt: The First Amendment on Trial (1988). *See also* Paul LeBel, *Emotional Distress, the First Amendment, and "This Kind of Speech": A Heretical Perspective on Hustler Magazine v. Falwell*, 60 Colo. L. Rev. 315 (1989); Robert Post, *The Constitutional Concept of Public Discourse, Outrageous Opinion, Democratic Deliberation, and Hustler Magazine v. Falwell*, 103 Harv. L. Rev. 601 (1990); Rodney Smolla, *Emotional Distress and the First Amendment: An Analysis of Hustler v. Falwell*, 20 Ariz. L. Rev. 423 (1988).

§ 9.07 Prior Restraints

New York Times Company v. United States

United States Supreme Court
403 U.S. 713, 91 S. Ct. 2140, 29 L. Ed. 2d 822 (1971)

Per Curiam.

We granted certiorari . . . in these cases in which the United States seeks to enjoin the *New York Times* and the *Washington Post* from publishing the contents of a classified study entitled "History of U.S. Decision-Making Process on Viet Nam Policy."

"Any system of prior restraints of expression comes to this Court bearing a heavy presumption against its constitutional validity. . . ." The Government "thus carries a heavy burden of showing justification for the imposition of such a restraint. . . ." The District Court for the Southern District of New York in the *New York Times* case, . . .

and the District Court for the District of Columbia and the Court of Appeals for the District of Columbia Circuit, . . . in the *Washington Post* case held that the Government had not met that burden. We agree.

The judgment of the Court of Appeals for the District of Columbia Circuit is therefore affirmed. The order of the Court of Appeals for the Second Circuit is reversed, . . . and the case is remanded with directions to enter a judgment affirming the judgment of the District Court for the Southern District of New York. The stays entered June 25, 1971, by the Court are vacated. The judgments shall issue forthwith.

So ordered. . . .

Mr. Justice Black, with whom Mr. Justice Douglas joins, concurring.

I adhere to the view that the Government's case against the *Washington Post* should have been dismissed and that the injunction against the *New York Times* should have been vacated without oral argument when the cases were first presented to this Court. I believe that every moment's continuance of the injunctions against these newspapers amounts to a flagrant, indefensible, and continuing violation of the First Amendment. . . .

Our Government was launched in 1789 with the adoption of the Constitution. The Bill of Rights, including the First Amendment, followed in 1791. Now, for the first time in the 182 years since the founding of the Republic, the federal courts are asked to hold that the First Amendment does not mean what it says, but rather means that the Government can halt the publication of current news of vital importance to the people of this country.

In seeking injunctions against these newspapers and in its presentation to the Court, the Executive Branch seems to have forgotten the essential purpose and history of the First Amendment. When the Constitution was adopted, many people strongly opposed it because the document contained no Bill of Rights to safeguard certain basic freedoms. They especially feared that the new powers granted to a central government might be interpreted to permit the government to curtail freedom of religion, press, assembly, and speech. In response to an overwhelming public clamor, James Madison offered a series of amendments to satisfy citizens that these great liberties would remain safe and beyond the power of government to abridge. Madison proposed what later became the First Amendment in three parts, . . . one of which proclaimed: "The people shall not be deprived or abridged of their right to speak, to write, or to publish their sentiments; *and the freedom of the press, as one of the great bulwarks of liberty, shall be inviolable.*" The amendments were offered to *curtail* and *restrict* the general powers granted to the Executive, Legislative, and Judicial Branches two years before in the original Constitution. The Bill of Rights changed the original Constitution into a new charter under which no branch of government could abridge the people's freedoms of press, speech, religion, and assembly. Yet the Solicitor General argues and some members of the Court appear to agree that the general powers of the Government adopted in the original Constitution should be interpreted to limit and restrict the specific and emphatic guarantees of the Bill of Rights adopted later. I can imagine no greater perversion of history. Madison and the other Framers of the First Amendment, able men that they were, wrote in language they earnestly believed could never be misunderstood: "Congress shall make no law . . . abridging the freedom . . . of the press. . . ." Both the history and language of the First Amendment support the view that the press must be left free to publish news, whatever the source, without censorship, injunctions, or prior restraints.

In the First Amendment the Founding Fathers gave the free press the protection it must have to fulfill its essential role in our democracy. The press was to serve the governed, not the governors. The Government's power to censor the press was abolished so that the press would remain forever free to censure the Government. The press was protected so that it could bare the secrets of government and inform the people. Only a free and unrestrained press can effectively expose deception in government. And paramount among the responsibilities of a free press is the duty to prevent any part of the government from deceiving the people and sending them off to distant lands to die of foreign fevers and foreign shot and shell. In my view, far from deserving condemnation for their courageous reporting, the *New York Times*, the *Washington Post*, and other newspapers should be commended for serving the purpose that the Founding Fathers saw so clearly. In revealing the workings of government that led to the Vietnam War, the newspapers nobly did precisely that which the Founders hoped and trusted they would do. . . .

. . . [W]e are asked to hold that despite the First Amendment's emphatic command, the Executive Branch, the Congress, and the Judiciary can make laws enjoining publication of current news and abridging freedom of the press in the name of "national security." The Government does not even attempt to rely on any act of Congress. Instead it makes the bold and dangerously far-reaching contention that the courts should take it upon themselves to "make" a law abridging freedom of the press in the name of equity, presidential power and national security, even when the representatives of the people in Congress have adhered to the command of the First Amendment and refused to make such a law. . . . To find that the President has "inherent power" to halt the publication of news by resort to the courts would wipe out the First Amendment and destroy the fundamental liberty and security of the very people the Government hopes to make "secure." No one can read the history of the adoption of the First Amendment without being convinced beyond any doubt that it was injunctions like those sought here that Madison and his collaborators intended to outlaw in this Nation for all time.

The word "security" is a broad, vague generality whose contours should not be invoked to abrogate the fundamental law embodied in the First Amendment. The guarding of military and diplomatic secrets at the expense of informed representative government provides no real security for our Republic. The Framers of the First Amendment, fully aware of both the need to defend a new nation and the abuses of the English and Colonial Governments, sought to give this new society strength and security by providing that freedom of speech, press, religion, and assembly should not be abridged.

MR. JUSTICE DOUGLAS, with whom MR. JUSTICE BLACK joins, concurring. . . .

The Government says that it has inherent powers to go into court and obtain an injunction to protect the national interest, which in this case is alleged to be national security.

Near v. Minnesota ex rel. Olson, 283 U.S. 697 (1931), . . . repudiated that expansive doctrine in no uncertain terms.

The dominant purpose of the First Amendment was to prohibit the widespread practice of governmental suppression of embarrassing information. It is common knowledge that the First Amendment was adopted against the widespread use of the common law of seditious libel to punish the dissemination of material that is embarrassing to the powers-that-be. . . . The present cases will, I think, go down in history as the most dramatic illustration of that principle. A debate of large proportions goes on in the Nation over our posture in Vietnam. That debate antedated the disclosure of the contents of the present documents. The latter are highly relevant to the debate in progress.

Secrecy in government is fundamentally anti-democratic, perpetuating bureaucratic errors. Open debate and discussion of public issues are vital to our national health. On public questions there should be "uninhibited, robust, and wide-open" debate. *New York Times Co. v. Sullivan*. . . .

I would affirm the judgment of the Court of Appeals in the *Post* case, vacate the stay of the Court of Appeals in the *Times* case and direct that it affirm the District Court. . . .

MR. JUSTICE BRENNAN, concurring.

I

I write separately in these cases only to emphasize what should be apparent: that our judgments in the present cases may not be taken to indicate the propriety, in the future, of issuing temporary stays and restraining orders to block the publication of material sought to be suppressed by the Government. So far as I can determine, never before has the United States sought to enjoin a newspaper from publishing information in its possession. The relative novelty of the questions presented, the necessary haste with which decisions were reached, the magnitude of the interests asserted, and the fact that all the parties have concentrated their arguments upon the question whether permanent restraints were proper may have justified at least some of the restraints heretofore imposed in these cases. Certainly it is difficult to fault the several courts below for seeking to assure that the issues here involved were preserved for ultimate review by this Court. But even if it be assumed that some of the interim restraints were proper in the two cases before us, that assumption has no bearing upon the propriety of similar judicial action in the future. To begin with, there has now been ample time for reflection and judgment; whatever values there may be in the preservation of novel questions for appellate review may not support any restraints in the future. More important, the First Amendment stands as an absolute bar to the imposition of judicial restraints in circumstances of the kind presented by these cases.

II

The error that has pervaded these cases from the outset was the granting of any injunctive relief whatsoever, interim or otherwise. The entire thrust of the Government's claim throughout these cases has been that publication of the material sought to be enjoined "could," or "might," or "may" prejudice the national interest in various ways. But the First Amendment tolerates absolutely no prior judicial restraints of the press predicated upon surmise or conjecture that untoward consequences may result. Our cases, it is true, have indicated that there is a single, extremely narrow class of cases in which the First Amendment's ban on prior judicial restraint may be overridden. Our cases have thus far indicated that such cases may arise only when the Nation "is at war," . . . during which times "[n]o one would question but that a government might prevent actual obstruction to its recruiting service or the publication of the sailing dates of transports or the number and location of troops. . . ." Even if the present world situation were assumed to be tantamount to a time of war, or if the power of presently available armaments would justify even in peacetime the suppression of information that would set in motion a nuclear holocaust, in neither of these actions has the Government presented or even alleged that publication of items from or based upon the material at issue would cause the happening of an event of that nature. "[T]he chief purpose of [the First Amendment's] guaranty [is] to prevent previous restraints upon publication. . . ." Thus, only governmental allegation and proof that publication must inevitably, directly, and immediately cause the occurrence of an event kindred to imperiling the safety of a transport already at sea can support even the issuance of an interim restraining order. In no event may mere conclusions be sufficient: for if the Executive Branch seeks judicial aid in preventing publication, it must inevitably submit the basis upon which that aid is sought to scrutiny by the judiciary. And therefore, every restraint issued in this case, whatever its form, has violated the First Amendment — and not less so because that restraint was justified as necessary to afford the courts an opportunity to examine the claim more thoroughly. Unless and until the Government has clearly made out its case, the First Amendment commands that no injunction may issue.

Mr. Justice Stewart, with whom Mr. Justice White joins, concurring.

In the governmental structure created by our Constitution, the Executive is endowed with enormous power in the two related areas of national defense and international relations. This power, largely unchecked by the Legislative and Judicial branches, has been pressed to the very hilt since the advent of the nuclear missile age. For better or for worse, the simple fact is that a President of the United States possesses vastly greater constitutional independence in these two vital areas of power than does, say, a prime minister of a country with a parliamentary form of government.

In the absence of the governmental checks and balances present in other areas of our national life, the only effective restraint upon executive policy and power in the areas of national defense and international affairs may lie in an enlightened citizenry — in an informed and critical public opinion which alone can here protect the values of democratic government. For this reason, it is perhaps here that a press that is alert, aware, and free most vitally serves the basic purpose of the First Amendment. For without an informed and free press there cannot be an enlightened people.

Yet it is elementary that the successful conduct of international diplomacy and the maintenance of an effective national defense require both confidentiality and secrecy. Other nations can hardly deal with this Nation in an atmosphere of mutual trust unless they can be assured that their confidences will be kept. And within our own Executive departments, the development of considered and intelligent international policies would be impossible if those charged with their formulation could not communicate with each other freely, frankly, and in confidence. In the area of basic national defense the frequent need for absolute secrecy is, of course, self-evident.

I think there can be but one answer to this dilemma, if dilemma it be. The responsibility must be where the power is. If the Constitution gives the Executive a large degree of unshared power in the conduct of foreign affairs and the maintenance of our national defense, then under the Constitution the Executive must have the largely unshared duty to determine and preserve the degree of internal security necessary to exercise that power successfully. It is an awesome responsibility, requiring judgment and wisdom of a high order. I should suppose that moral, political, and practical considerations would dictate that a very first principle of that wisdom would be an insistence upon avoiding secrecy for its own sake. For when everything is classified, then nothing is classified, and the system becomes one to be disregarded by the cynical or the careless, and to be manipulated by those intent on self-protection or self-promotion. I should suppose, in short, that the hallmark of a truly effective internal security system would be the maximum possible disclosure, recognizing that secrecy can best be preserved only when credibility is truly maintained. But be that as it may, it is clear to me that it is the constitutional duty of the Executive — as a matter of sovereign prerogative and not as a matter of law as the courts know law — through the promulgation and enforcement of executive regulations, to protect the confidentiality necessary to carry out its responsibilities in the fields of international relations and national defense.

This is not to say that Congress and the courts have no role to play. Undoubtedly Congress has the power to enact specific and appropriate criminal laws to protect government property and preserve government secrets. Congress has passed such laws, and several of them are of very colorable relevance to the apparent circumstances of these cases. And if a criminal prosecution is instituted, it will be the responsibility of the courts to decide the applicability of the criminal law under which the charge is brought. Moreover, if Congress should pass a specific law authorizing civil proceedings in this field, the courts would likewise have the duty to decide constitutionality of such a law as well as its applicability to the facts proved.

But in the cases before us we are asked neither to construe specific regulations nor to apply specific laws. We are asked, instead, to perform a function that the Constitution gave to the Executive, not the Judiciary. We are asked, quite simply, to prevent the publication by two newspapers of material that the Executive Branch insists should not, in the national interest, be published. I am convinced that the Executive is correct with respect to some of the documents involved. But I cannot say that disclosure of any of them will surely result in direct, immediate, and irreparable damage to our Nation or its people. That being so, there can under the First Amendment be but one judicial resolution of the issues before us. I join the judgments of the Court.

Mr. Justice White, with whom Mr. Justice Stewart joins, concurring.

I concur in today's judgments, but only because of the concededly extraordinary protection against prior restraints enjoyed by the press under our constitutional system. I do not say that in no circumstances would the First Amendment permit an injunction against publishing information about government plans or operations. Nor, after examining the materials the Government characterizes as the most sensitive and destructive, can I deny that revelation of these documents will do substantial damage to public interests. Indeed, I am confident that their disclosure will have that result. But I nevertheless agree that the United States has not satisfied the very heavy burden that it must meet to warrant an injunction against publication in these cases, at least in the absence of express and appropriately limited congressional authorization for prior restraints in circumstances such as these.

. . . I am quite unable to agree that the inherent powers of the Executive and the courts reach so far as to authorize remedies having such sweeping potential for inhibiting publications by the press. Much of the difficulty inheres in the "grave and irreparable danger" standard suggested by the United States. If the United States were to have judgment under such a standard in these cases, our decision would be of little guidance to other courts in other cases, for the material at issue here would not be available from the Court's opinion or from public records, nor would it be published by the press. Indeed, even today where we hold that the United States has not met its burden, the material remains sealed in court records and it is properly not discussed in today's opinions. Moreover, because the material poses substantial dangers to national interests and because of the hazards of criminal sanctions, a responsible press may choose never to publish the more sensitive materials. To sustain the Government in these cases would start the courts down a long and hazardous road that I am not willing to travel, at least without congressional guidance and direction.

It is not easy to reject the proposition urged by the United States and to deny relief on its good-faith claims in these cases that publication will work serious damage to the country. But that discomfiture is considerably dispelled by the infrequency of prior-restraint cases. Normally, publication will occur and the damage be done before the Government has either opportunity or grounds for suppression. So here, publication has already begun and a substantial part of the threatened damage has already occurred. The fact of a massive breakdown in security is known, access to the documents by many unauthorized people is undeniable, and the efficacy of equitable relief against these or other newspapers to avert anticipated damage is doubtful at best. . . .

Congress has addressed itself to the problems of protecting the security of the country and the national defense from unauthorized disclosure of potentially damaging information. . . . It has not, however, authorized the injunctive remedy against threatened publication. It has apparently been satisfied to rely on criminal sanctions and their deterrent effect on the responsible as well as the irresponsible press. I am not, of course, saying that either of these newspapers has yet committed a crime or that either would commit a crime if it published all the material now in its possession. That matter must await resolution in the context of a criminal proceeding if one is instituted by the United States. In that event, the issue of guilt or innocence would be determined by procedures and standards quite different from those that have purported to govern these injunctive proceedings.

MR. JUSTICE MARSHALL, concurring.

It would . . . be utterly inconsistent with the concept of separation of powers for this Court to use its power of contempt to prevent behavior that Congress has specifically declined to prohibit. There would be a similar damage to the basic concept of these co-equal branches of Government if when the Executive Branch has adequate authority granted by Congress to protect "national security" it can choose instead to invoke the contempt power of a court to enjoin the threatened conduct. The Constitution provides that Congress shall make laws, the President execute laws, and courts interpret laws. *Youngstown Sheet & Tube Co. v. Sawyer*, 343 U.S. 579 (1952). It did not provide for government by injunction in which the courts and the Executive Branch can "make law" without regard to the action of Congress. It may be more convenient for the Executive Branch if it need only convince a judge to prohibit conduct rather than ask the Congress to pass a law, and it may be more convenient to enforce a contempt order than to seek a criminal conviction in a jury trial. Moreover, it may be considered politically wise to get a court to share the responsibility for arresting those who the Executive Branch has probable cause to believe are violating the law. But convenience and political considerations of the moment do not justify a basic departure from the principles of our system of government. . . .

MR. CHIEF JUSTICE BURGER, dissenting.

. . . In these cases, the imperative of a free and unfettered press comes into collision with another imperative, the effective functioning of a complex modern government and specifically the effective exercise of certain constitutional powers of the Executive. Only those who view the First Amendment as an absolute in all circumstances — a view I respect, but reject — can find such cases as these to be simple or easy. . . .

The newspapers make a derivative claim under the First Amendment; they denominate this right as the public "right to know"; by implication, the *Times* asserts a sole trusteeship of that right by virtue of its journalistic "scoop." The right is asserted as an absolute. Of course, the First Amendment right itself is not an absolute, as Justice Holmes so long ago pointed out in his aphorism concerning the right to shout "fire" in a crowded theater if there was no fire. . . . Conceivably such exceptions may be lurking in these cases and would have been flushed had they been properly considered in the trial courts, free from unwarranted deadlines and frenetic pressures. An issue of this importance should be tried and heard in a judicial atmosphere conducive to thoughtful, reflective deliberation, especially when haste, in terms of hours, is unwarranted in light of the long period the *Times*, by its own choice, deferred publication.

It is not disputed that the *Times* has had unauthorized possession of the documents for three to four months, during which it has had its expert analysts studying them, presumably digesting them and preparing the material for publication. During all of this time, the *Times*, presumably in its capacity as trustee of the public's "right to know," has held up publication for purposes it considered proper and thus public knowledge was delayed. No doubt this was for a good reason; the analysis of 7,000 pages of complex material drawn from a vastly greater volume of material would inevitably take time and the writing of good news stories takes time. But why should the United States Government, from whom this information was illegally acquired by someone, along with all the counsel, trial judges, and appellate judges be placed under needless pressure? After these months of deferral, the alleged "right to know" has somehow and suddenly become a right that must be vindicated instanter.

Would it have been unreasonable, since the newspaper could anticipate the Government's objections to release of secret material, to give the Government an opportunity to review the entire collection and determine whether agreement could be reached on publication? Stolen or not, if security was not in fact jeopardized, much of the material could no doubt have been declassified, since it spans a period ending in 1968. With such an approach — one that great newspapers have in the past practiced and stated editorially to be the duty of an honorable press — the newspapers and Government might well have narrowed the area of disagreement as to what was and was not publishable, leaving the remainder to be resolved in orderly litigation, if necessary. To me it is hardly believable that a newspaper long regarded as a great institution in American life would fail to perform one of the basic and simple duties of every citizen with respect to the discovery or possession of stolen property or secret government documents. That duty, I had thought — perhaps naively — was to report forthwith, to responsible public officers. This duty rests on taxi drivers, Justices, and the *New York Times*. The course followed by the *Times*, whether so calculated or not, removed any possibility of orderly litigation of the issues. If the action of the judges up to now has been correct, that result is sheer happenstance.

Our grant of the writ of certiorari before final judgment in the *Times* case aborted the trial in the District Court before it had made a complete record pursuant to the mandate of the Court of Appeals for the Second Circuit.

The consequence of all this melancholy series of events is that we literally do not know what we are acting on. . . .

MR. JUSTICE HARLAN, with whom THE CHIEF JUSTICE and MR. JUSTICE BLACKMUN join, dissenting. . . .

Both the Court of Appeals for the Second Circuit and the Court of Appeals for the District of Columbia Circuit rendered judgment on June 23. The *New York Times'* petition for certiorari, its motion for accelerated consideration thereof, and its application for interim relief were filed in this Court on June 24 at about 11 a.m. The application of the United States for interim relief in the *Post* case was also filed here on June 24 at about 7:15 p.m. This Court's order setting a hearing before us on June 26 at 11 a.m., a course which I joined only to avoid the possibility of even more peremptory action by the Court, was issued less than 24 hours before. The record in the *Post* case was filed with the Clerk shortly before 1 p.m. on June 25; the record in the *Times* case did not arrive until 7 or 8 o'clock that same night. The briefs of the parties were received less than two hours before argument on June 26.

This frenzied train of events took place in the name of the presumption against prior restraints created by the First Amendment. Due regard for the extraordinarily important and difficult questions involved in these litigations should have led the Court to shun such a precipitate timetable. In order to decide the merits of these cases properly, some or all of the following questions should have been faced:

> 1. Whether the Attorney General is authorized to bring these suits in the name of the United States. . . . This question involves as well the construction and validity of a singularly opaque statute — the Espionage Act, 18 U.S.C. § 793(e).

> 2. Whether the First Amendment permits the federal courts to enjoin publication of stories which would present a serious threat to national security. . . .

> 3. Whether the threat to publish highly secret documents is of itself a sufficient implication of national security to justify an injunction on the theory that regardless of the contents of the documents harm enough results simply from the demonstration of such a breach of secrecy.

> 4. Whether the unauthorized disclosure of any of these particular documents would seriously impair the national security.

> 5. What weight should be given to the opinion of high officers in the Executive Branch of the Government with respect to questions 3 and 4.

> 6. Whether the newspapers are entitled to retain and use the documents notwithstanding the seemingly uncontested facts that the documents, or the originals of which they are duplicates, were purloined from the

Government's possession and that the newspapers received them with knowledge that they had been feloniously acquired. . . .

7. Whether the threatened harm to the national security or the Government's possessory interest in the documents justifies the issuance of an injunction against publication in light of —

a. The strong First Amendment policy against prior restraints on publication;

b. The doctrine against enjoining conduct in violation of criminal statutes; and

c. The extent to which the materials at issue have apparently already been otherwise disseminated.

These are difficult questions of fact, of law, and of judgment; the potential consequences of erroneous decision are enormous. The time which has been available to us, to the lower courts, and to the parties has been wholly inadequate for giving these cases the kind of consideration they deserve. It is a reflection on the stability of the judicial process that these great issues — as important as any that have arisen during my time on the Court — should have been decided under the pressures engendered by the torrent of publicity that has attended these litigations from their inception.

Forced as I am to reach the merits of these cases, I dissent from the opinion and judgments of the Court. Within the severe limitations imposed by the time constraints under which I have been required to operate, I can only state my reasons in telescoped form, even though in different circumstances I would have felt constrained to deal with the cases in the fuller sweep indicated above. . . .

It is plain to me that the scope of the judicial function in passing upon the activities of the Executive Branch of the Government in the field of foreign affairs is very narrowly restricted. This view is, I think, dictated by the concept of separation of powers upon which our constitutional system rests. . . .

The power to evaluate the "pernicious influence" of premature disclosure is not, however, lodged in the Executive alone. I agree that, in performance of its duty to protect the values of the First Amendment against political pressures, the judiciary must review the initial Executive determination to the point of satisfying itself that the subject matter of the dispute does lie within the proper compass of the President's foreign relations power. . . . Moreover the judiciary may properly insist that the determination that disclosure of the subject matter would irreparably impair the national security be made by the head of the Executive Department concerned — here the Secretary of State or the Secretary of Defense — after actual personal consideration by that officer. . . .

But in my judgment the judiciary may not properly go beyond these two inquiries and redetermine for itself the probable impact of disclosure on the national security. . . .

Even if there is some room for the judiciary to override the Executive determination, it is plain that the scope of review must be exceedingly narrow. I can see no indication in the opinions of either the District Court or the Court of Appeals in the Post litigation that the conclusions of the Executive were given even the deference owing to an administrative agency, much less that owing to a co-equal branch of the Government operating within the field of its constitutional prerogative.

Accordingly, I would vacate the judgment of the Court of Appeals for the District of Columbia Circuit on this ground and remand the case for further proceedings in the District Court. Before the commencement of such further proceedings, due opportunity should be afforded the Government for procuring from the Secretary of State or the Secretary of Defense or both an expression of their views on the issue of national security. The ensuing review by the District Court should be in accordance with the views expressed in this opinion. And for the reasons stated above I would affirm the judgment of the Court of Appeals for the Second Circuit.

Pending further hearings in each case conducted under the appropriate ground rules, I would continue the restraints on publication. I cannot believe that the doctrine prohibiting prior restraints reaches to the point of preventing courts from maintaining the status quo long enough to act responsibly in matters of such national importance as those involved here.

Mr. Justice Blackmun, dissenting. . . .

The First Amendment, after all, is only one part of an entire Constitution. Article II of the great document vests in the Executive Branch primary power over the conduct of foreign affairs and places in that branch the responsibility for the Nation's safety. Each provision of the Constitution is important, and I cannot subscribe to a doctrine of unlimited absolutism for the First Amendment at the cost of downgrading other provisions. First Amendment absolutism has never commanded a majority of this Court. . . . What is needed here is a weighing, upon properly developed standards, of the broad right of the press to print and of the very narrow right of the Government to prevent. Such standards are not yet developed. The parties here are in disagreement as to what those standards should be. But even the newspapers concede that there are situations where restraint is in order and is constitutional. . . .

I therefore would remand these cases to be developed expeditiously, of course, but on a schedule permitting the orderly presentation of evidence from both sides, with the use of discovery, if necessary, as authorized by the rules, and with the preparation of briefs, oral argument, and court opinions of a quality better than has been seen to this point. . . .

I strongly urge, and sincerely hope, that these two newspapers will be fully aware of their ultimate responsibilities to the United States of America. . . . I hope that damage has not already been done. If, however, damage has been done, and if, with the Court's action today, these newspapers proceed to publish the critical documents and there results therefrom "the death of soldiers, the destruction of alliances, the greatly increased difficulty of negotiation with our enemies, the inability of our diplomats to negotiate," to which list I might add the factors of prolongation of the war and of further delay in the freeing of United States prisoners, then the Nation's people will know where the responsibility for these sad consequences rests.

Notes and Questions

(1) The Supreme Court's modern treatment of prior restraints began in *Near v. Minnesota*, 283 U.S. 697 (1931). The *Near* decision was a vigorous condemnation of prior restraints, but it did contain one sentence that arguably created a possible "national security exception" to the prohibition on prior restraints: "No one would question but that a government might prevent actual obstruction to its recruiting service or the publication of the sailing dates of transports or the number and location of troops." Did the Pentagon Papers case close this possible loophole? Or did the government in the case simply fail to prove that the secrets involved were genuine threats to national security?

(2) Prior restraints come in two classic forms. The first is an injunction issued by a court, the second is a licensure regime requiring advance approval by a government agency before material may be published. The Pentagon Papers case is an example of litigation involving an attempt to enjoin speech.

(3) *The Collateral Bar Rule*. When a defendant is prosecuted for disobeying a court order, the defendant is normally not permitted to challenge the legal merits of the court order. This is known as the "collateral bar" rule. The penalty for disobedience to a court order is a conviction for contempt of court. In the contempt trial, the only question is whether or not the defendant is guilty of contempt — whether or not he or she knowingly disobeyed the court order — and not whether the court order was legally valid or invalid. The legal validity of the court order is deemed to be "collateral" to the question of whether or not the defendant disobeyed the order, and the collateral bar rule prohibits litigating that question in the contempt proceeding. The collateral bar rule embodies a bedrock principle of American jurisprudence: court orders are sacrosanct; they are to be obeyed, right or wrong, until they are appealed and reversed by a higher court.

The point is vividly illustrated by *Shuttlesworth v. City of Birmingham*, 394 U.S. 147 (1969), and *Walker v. City of Birmingham*, 388 U.S. 307 (1967). In *Shuttlesworth*, the Supreme Court overturned the convictions of civil rights marchers who had marched through Birmingham in violation of an ordinance requiring a parade permit, on the grounds that the ordinance was unconstitutional in giving unbridled discretion to officials in determining who could or could not march. The Court stated that "a person faced with such an unconstitutional licensing law may ignore it and engage with impunity in the exercise of the right of free expression for which the law purports to require a license." In the *Walker* case, however, the Supreme Court upheld the convictions of Dr. Martin Luther King, Jr., and seven other black ministers for violating a court order from an Alabama court forbidding them from marching without first obtaining the parade permit required by the city ordinance. The Supreme Court refused to allow Dr. King and the other civil rights leaders to defend themselves in the contempt of court proceedings on the grounds that the court orders violated the First Amendment. The Court found it significant that Dr. King and the others had not sought to appeal the court order, but rather chose, literally, to take their assertion of its illegality to the streets. The marchers could not simply assume that the higher courts in Alabama would be prejudiced against them, or would fail to conscientiously apply the First Amendment. If they were rebuffed by the Alabama appellate courts, they could still appeal the court order to the U.S. Supreme Court. The marchers did not even try to use orderly judicial procedures. "This case would arise in quite a different constitutional posture if the petitioners, before disobeying the injunction, had challenged it in the Alabama courts, and had been met with delay or frustration of their constitutional claims." RODNEY SMOLLA, SMOLLA & NIMMER ON FREEDOM OF SPEECH, §15:73, *Procedural issues concerning prior restraints — Contempt of court and the collateral bar rule — Lessons of the Walker and Shuttlesworth decisions* (2023 ed.).

Problem C

You are legal counsel to a major news organization. A confidential source within the government is concerned that the President of the United States is about to approve the introduction of American troops to serve as trainers and advisers to assist in a war effort by the armed forces of a nation that is fighting against an invasion launched by Russia. The source is concerned that if the secret operation becomes known publicly, it could trigger World War III, by placing American forces in a directly adversarial conflict against Russian forces. The source believes that if the media organization reports that this plan is being considered, it would cause the plan to be scrapped, which the source believes is in the national interest. The source turns over to the news organization a memorandum to the President setting forth the proposed plan. The document is stamped as classified, and carries the very highest level of national security confidentiality. It is clear that in handing the document to the news organization, the source is violating federal national security laws.

The news organization would like legal and practical advice as to how it should proceed. At a meeting of the news organization's corporate board, chief editors, and most senior reporters, various options are being considered. A wide-ranging discussion ensues on the organization's moral and legal obligations. One editor suggests that the organization contact the government, tell the government it has the document in its possession, and listen to the government's reaction before deciding whether to broadcast or publish the story. At this point, people turn to you, the lawyer in the room, and ask, if the government finds out we have this information, what can it do to us? Could the government obtain a court order barring publication? Could we be thrown in jail if we publish it? What kind of advice will you give?

§ 9.08 Commercial Speech

44 Liquormart, Inc. v. Rhode Island

United States Supreme Court
517 U.S. 484, 116 S. Ct. 1495, 134 L. Ed. 2d 711 (1996)

Justice Stevens announced the judgment of the Court and delivered the opinion of the Court with respect to Parts I, II, VII, and VIII, an opinion with respect to Parts III and V, in which Justice Kennedy, Justice Souter, and Justice Ginsburg join, an opinion with respect to Part VI, in which Justice Kennedy, Justice Thomas, and Justice Ginsburg join, and an opinion with respect to Part IV, in which Justice Kennedy and Justice Ginsburg join.

Last Term we held that a federal law abridging a brewer's right to provide the public with accurate information about the alcoholic content of malt beverages is unconstitutional. *Rubin v. Coors Brewing Co.*, 115 S. Ct. 1585, 1593 (1995). We now hold that Rhode Island's statutory prohibition against advertisements that provide the public with accurate information about retail prices of alcoholic beverages is also invalid. Our holding rests on the conclusion that such an advertising ban is an abridgment of speech protected by the First Amendment and that it is not shielded from constitutional scrutiny by the Twenty-first Amendment.

I

In 1956, the Rhode Island Legislature enacted two separate prohibitions against advertising the retail price of alcoholic beverages. The first applies to vendors licensed in Rhode Island as well as to out-of-state manufacturers, wholesalers, and shippers. It prohibits them from "advertising in any manner whatsoever" the price of any alcoholic beverage offered for sale in the State; the only exception is for price tags or signs displayed with the merchandise within licensed premises and not visible from the street. The second statute applies to the Rhode Island news media. It contains a categorical prohibition against the publication or broadcast of any advertisements — even those referring to sales in other States — that "make reference to the price of any alcoholic beverages." . . .

II

Petitioners 44 Liquormart, Inc. (44 Liquormart), and Peoples Super Liquor Stores, Inc. (Peoples), are licensed retailers of alcoholic beverages. Petitioner 44 Liquormart operates a store in Rhode Island and petitioner Peoples operates several stores in Massachusetts that are patronized by Rhode Island residents. Peoples uses alcohol price advertising extensively in Massachusetts, where such advertising is permitted, but Rhode Island newspapers and other media outlets have refused to accept such ads. . . .

III

Advertising has been a part of our culture throughout our history. Even in colonial days, the public relied on "commercial speech" for vital information about the market. Early newspapers displayed advertisements for goods and services on their front pages, and town criers called out prices in public squares. See J. Wood, The Story of Advertising 21, 45–69, 85 (1958); J. Smith, Printers and Press Freedom 49 (1988). Indeed, commercial messages played such a central role in public life prior to the Founding that Benjamin Franklin authored his early defense of a free press in support of his decision to print, of all things, an advertisement for voyages to Barbados. Franklin, *An Apology for Printers*, June 10, 1731, reprinted in 2 *Writings of Benjamin Franklin* 172 (1907).

In accord with the role that commercial messages have long played, the law has developed to ensure that advertising provides consumers with accurate information about the availability of goods and services. In the early years, the common law, and later, statutes, served the consumers' interest in the receipt of accurate information in the commercial market by prohibiting fraudulent and misleading advertising. It was not until the 1970's, however, that this Court held that the First Amendment protected the dissemination of truthful and nonmisleading commercial messages about lawful products and services. *See generally* Kozinski & Banner, *The Anti-History and Pre-History of Commercial Speech*, 71 Texas L. Rev. 747 (1993).

In *Bigelow v. Virginia*, 421 U.S. 809 (1975), we held that it was error to assume that commercial speech was entitled to no First Amendment protection or that it was without value in the marketplace of ideas. The following Term in *Virginia Bd. of Pharmacy v. Virginia Citizens Consumer Council, Inc.*, 425 U.S. 748 (1976), we expanded on our holding in *Bigelow* and held that the State's blanket ban on advertising the price of prescription drugs violated the First Amendment.

Virginia Pharmacy Bd. reflected the conclusion that the same interest that supports regulation of potentially misleading advertising, namely the public's interest in receiving accurate commercial information, also supports an interpretation of the First Amendment that provides constitutional protection for the dissemination of accurate and nonmisleading commercial messages. We explained: "Advertising, however tasteless and excessive it sometimes may seem, is nonetheless dissemination of information as to who is producing and selling what product, for what reason, and at what price. So long as we preserve a predominantly free enterprise economy, the allocation of our resources in large measure will be made through numerous private economic decisions. It is a matter of public interest that those decisions, in the aggregate, be intelligent and well informed. To this end, the free flow of commercial information is indispensable."[10]

The opinion further explained that a State's paternalistic assumption that the public will use truthful, nonmisleading commercial information unwisely cannot justify a decision to suppress it:

---

10. [Court's Footnote 7] By contrast, the First Amendment does not protect commercial speech about unlawful activities. See *Pittsburgh Press Co. v. Pittsburgh Comm'n on Human Relations*, 413 U.S. 376 (1973).

"There is, of course, an alternative to this highly paternalistic approach. That alternative is to assume that this information is not in itself harmful, that people will perceive their own best interests if only they are well enough informed, and that the best means to that end is to open the channels of communication rather than to close them. If they are truly open, nothing prevents the 'professional' pharmacist from marketing his own assertedly superior product, and contrasting it with that of the low-cost, high-volume prescription drug retailer. But the choice among these alternative approaches is not ours to make or the Virginia General Assembly's. It is precisely this kind of choice, between the dangers of suppressing information, and the dangers of its misuse if it is freely available, that the First Amendment makes for us."

On the basis of these principles, our early cases uniformly struck down several broadly based bans on truthful, nonmisleading commercial speech, each of which served ends unrelated to consumer protection.[11] Indeed, one of those cases expressly likened the rationale that *Virginia Pharmacy Bd.* employed to the one that Justice Brandeis adopted in his concurrence in *Whitney v. California*, 274 U.S. 357 (1927). See *Linmark Associates, Inc. v. Willingboro*, 431 U.S. 85 (1977). There, Justice Brandeis wrote, in explaining his objection to a prohibition of political speech, that "the remedy to be applied is more speech, not enforced silence. Only an emergency can justify repression." *Whitney*, 274 U.S., at 377; see also *Carey v. Population Services Int'l*, 431 U.S. 678 (1977) (applying test for suppressing political speech set forth in *Brandenburg v. Ohio*, 395 U.S. 444 (1969)).

At the same time, our early cases recognized that the State may regulate some types of commercial advertising more freely than other forms of protected speech. Specifically, we explained that the State may require commercial messages to "appear in such a form, or include such additional information, warnings, and disclaimers, as are necessary to prevent its being deceptive," *Virginia Pharmacy Bd.*, and that it may restrict some forms of aggressive sales practices that have the potential to exert "undue influence" over consumers. See *Bates v. State Bar of Ariz.*, 433 U.S. 350 (1977).

Virginia Pharmacy Bd. attributed the State's authority to impose these regulations in part to certain "commonsense differences" that exist between commercial messages and other types of protected expression. Our opinion noted that the greater "objectivity" of commercial speech justifies affording the State more

---

11. [Court's Footnote 8] See *Bates v. State Bar of Ariz.*, 433 U.S. 350 (1977) (ban on lawyer advertising); *Carey v. Population Services Int'l*, 431 U.S. 678 (1977) (ban on contraceptive advertising); *Linmark Associates, Inc. v. Willingboro*, 431 U.S. 85 (1977) (ban on "For Sale" signs); *Virginia Bd. of Pharmacy v. Virginia Citizens Consumer Council, Inc.*, 425 U.S. 748 (1976) (ban on prescription drug prices); *Bigelow v. Virginia*, 421 U.S. 809 (1975) (ban on abortion advertising). Although *Linmark* involved a prohibition against a particular means of advertising the sale of one's home, we treated the restriction as if it were a complete ban because it did not leave open "satisfactory" alternative channels of communication.

freedom to distinguish false commercial advertisements from true ones, and that the greater "hardiness" of commercial speech, inspired as it is by the profit motive, likely diminishes the chilling effect that may attend its regulation.

Subsequent cases explained that the State's power to regulate commercial transactions justifies its concomitant power to regulate commercial speech that is "linked inextricably" to those transactions. *Friedman v. Rogers*, 440 U.S. 1 (1979); *Ohralik v. Ohio State Bar Ass'n*, 436 U.S. 447 (1978) (commercial speech "occurs in an area traditionally subject to government regulation . . ."). As one commentator has explained: "The entire commercial speech doctrine, after all, represents an accommodation between the right to speak and hear expression about goods and services and the right of government to regulate the sales of such goods and services." L. Tribe, *American Constitutional Law* § 12-15, p. 903 (2d ed. 1988). Nevertheless, as we explained in *Linmark*, the State retains less regulatory authority when its commercial speech restrictions strike at "the substance of the information communicated" rather than the "commercial aspect of [it] — with offerors communicating offers to offerees." See *Linmark*, 431 U.S., at 96; *Carey v. Population Services Int'l*, 431 U.S. 678, 701, n. 28 (1977).

In *Central Hudson Gas & Elec. Corp. v. Public Serv. Comm'n of N.Y.*, [447 U.S. 557 (1980),] we took stock of our developing commercial speech jurisprudence. In that case, we considered a regulation "completely" banning all promotional advertising by electric utilities. Our decision acknowledged the special features of commercial speech but identified the serious First Amendment concerns that attend blanket advertising prohibitions that do not protect consumers from commercial harms.

Five Members of the Court recognized that the state interest in the conservation of energy was substantial, and that there was "an immediate connection between advertising and demand for electricity." Nevertheless, they concluded that the regulation was invalid because the Commission had failed to make a showing that a more limited speech regulation would not have adequately served the State's interest.[12]

In reaching its conclusion, the majority explained that although the special nature of commercial speech may require less than strict review of its regulation, special concerns arise from "regulations that entirely suppress commercial speech in order to pursue a nonspeech-related policy." In those circumstances, "a ban on speech could screen from public view the underlying governmental policy." As a result, the Court concluded that "special care" should attend the review of such

---

12. [Court's Footnote 9] In other words, the regulation failed the fourth step in the four-part inquiry that the majority announced in its opinion. It wrote: "In commercial speech cases, then, a four-part analysis has developed. At the outset, we must determine whether the expression is protected by the First Amendment. For commercial speech to come within that provision, it at least must concern lawful activity and not be misleading. Next, we ask whether the asserted governmental interest is substantial. If both inquiries yield positive answers, we must determine whether the regulation directly advances the governmental interest asserted, and whether it is not more extensive than is necessary to serve that interest."

blanket bans, and it pointedly remarked that "in recent years this Court has not approved a blanket ban on commercial speech unless the speech itself was flawed in some way, either because it was deceptive or related to unlawful activity."[13]

IV

As our review of the case law reveals, Rhode Island errs in concluding that all commercial speech regulations are subject to a similar form of constitutional review simply because they target a similar category of expression. The mere fact that messages propose commercial transactions does not in and of itself dictate the constitutional analysis that should apply to decisions to suppress them. See *Rubin v. Coors Brewing Co.*, (Stevens, J., concurring in judgment).

When a State regulates commercial messages to protect consumers from misleading, deceptive, or aggressive sales practices, or requires the disclosure of beneficial consumer information, the purpose of its regulation is consistent with the reasons for according constitutional protection to commercial speech and therefore justifies less than strict review. However, when a State entirely prohibits the dissemination of truthful, nonmisleading commercial messages for reasons unrelated to the preservation of a fair bargaining process, there is far less reason to depart from the rigorous review that the First Amendment generally demands.

Sound reasons justify reviewing the latter type of commercial speech regulation more carefully. Most obviously, complete speech bans, unlike content-neutral restrictions on the time, place, or manner of expression, are particularly dangerous because they all but foreclose alternative means of disseminating certain information.

Our commercial speech cases have recognized the dangers that attend governmental attempts to single out certain messages for suppression. For example, in *Linmark*, we concluded that a ban on "For Sale" signs was "content based" and failed to leave open "satisfactory" alternative channels of communication. Moreover, last Term we upheld a 30-day prohibition against a certain form of legal solicitation largely because it left so many channels of communication open to Florida lawyers. *Florida Bar v. Went For It, Inc.*, 115 S. Ct. 2371 (1995). . . .

The special dangers that attend complete bans on truthful, nonmisleading commercial speech cannot be explained away by appeals to the "commonsense distinctions" that exist between commercial and noncommercial speech. Regulations that suppress the truth are no less troubling because they target objectively verifiable information, nor are they less effective because they aim at durable messages. As a result, neither the "greater objectivity" nor the "greater hardiness" of truthful,

---

13. [Court's Footnote 10] The Justices concurring in the judgment adopted a somewhat broader view. They expressed "doubt whether suppression of information concerning the availability and price of a legally offered product is ever a permissible way for the State to 'dampen' the demand for or use of the product." Indeed, Justice Blackmun believed that even "though 'commercial' speech is involved, such a regulation strikes at the heart of the First Amendment."

nonmisleading commercial speech justifies reviewing its complete suppression with added deference.

It is the State's interest in protecting consumers from "commercial harms" that provides "the typical reason why commercial speech can be subject to greater governmental regulation than noncommercial speech." *Cincinnati v. Discovery Network, Inc.*, 507 U.S. 410, 426 (1993). Yet bans that target truthful, nonmisleading commercial messages rarely protect consumers from such harms.[14] Instead, such bans often serve only to obscure an "underlying governmental policy" that could be implemented without regulating speech. In this way, these commercial speech bans not only hinder consumer choice, but also impede debate over central issues of public policy.[15]

Precisely because bans against truthful, nonmisleading commercial speech rarely seek to protect consumers from either deception or overreaching, they usually rest solely on the offensive assumption that the public will respond "irrationally" to the truth. The First Amendment directs us to be especially skeptical of regulations that seek to keep people in the dark for what the government perceives to be their own good. That teaching applies equally to state attempts to deprive consumers of accurate information about their chosen products:

> "The commercial market-place, like other spheres of our social and cultural life, provides a forum where ideas and information flourish. Some of the ideas and information are vital, some of slight worth. But the general rule is that the speaker and the audience, not the government, assess the value of the information presented. Thus, even a communication that does no more than propose a commercial transaction is entitled to the coverage of the First Amendment." See *Virginia State Bd. of Pharmacy* . . .

V

In this case, there is no question that Rhode Island's price advertising ban constitutes a blanket prohibition against truthful, nonmisleading speech about a lawful product. There is also no question that the ban serves an end unrelated to consumer protection. Accordingly, we must review the price advertising ban with "special care," *Central Hudson*, 447 U.S., at 566, n. 9, mindful that speech prohibitions of this type rarely survive constitutional review.

---

14. [Court's Footnote 11] In *Discovery Network*, we held that the city's categorical ban on commercial newsracks attached too much importance to the distinction between commercial and noncommercial speech. After concluding that the aesthetic and safety interests served by the newsrack ban bore no relationship whatsoever to the prevention of commercial harms, we rejected the State's attempt to justify its ban on the sole ground that it targeted commercial speech.

15. [Court's Footnote 12] This case bears out the point. Rhode Island seeks to reduce alcohol consumption by increasing alcohol price; yet its means of achieving that goal deprives the public of their chief source of information about the reigning price level of alcohol. As a result, the State's price advertising ban keeps the public ignorant of the key barometer of the ban's effectiveness: The alcohol beverages' prices.

The State argues that the price advertising prohibition should nevertheless be upheld because it directly advances the State's substantial interest in promoting temperance, and because it is no more extensive than necessary. Although there is some confusion as to what Rhode Island means by temperance, we assume that the State asserts an interest in reducing alcohol consumption.[16]

In evaluating the ban's effectiveness in advancing the State's interest, we note that a commercial speech regulation "may not be sustained if it provides only ineffective or remote support for the government's purpose." For that reason, the State bears the burden of showing not merely that its regulation will advance its interest, but also that it will do so "to a material degree." The need for the State to make such a showing is particularly great given the drastic nature of its chosen means — the wholesale suppression of truthful, nonmisleading information. Accordingly, we must determine whether the State has shown that the price advertising ban will significantly reduce alcohol consumption.

We can agree that common sense supports the conclusion that a prohibition against price advertising (footnote omitted), like a collusive agreement among competitors to refrain from such advertising, will tend to mitigate competition and maintain prices at a higher level than would prevail in a completely free market. Despite the absence of proof on the point, we can even agree with the State's contention that it is reasonable to assume that demand, and hence consumption throughout the market, is somewhat lower whenever a higher, noncompetitive price level prevails. However, without any findings of fact, or indeed any evidentiary support whatsoever, we cannot agree with the assertion that the price advertising ban will significantly advance the State's interest in promoting temperance.

Although the record suggests that the price advertising ban may have some impact on the purchasing patterns of temperate drinkers of modest means, 829 F. Supp., at 546, the State has presented no evidence to suggest that its speech prohibition will significantly reduce market-wide consumption.[17] Indeed, the District

16. [Court's Footnote 13] Before the District Court, the State argued that it sought to reduce consumption among irresponsible drinkers. In its brief to this Court, it equates its interest in promoting temperance with an interest in reducing alcohol consumption among all drinkers. The Rhode Island Supreme Court has characterized the State's interest in "promoting temperance" as both "the state's interest in reducing the consumption of liquor," and the State's interest in discouraging "excessive consumption of alcoholic beverages." A state statute declares the ban's purpose to be "the promotion of temperance and for the reasonable control of the traffic in alcoholic beverages."

17. [Court's Footnote 14] The appellants' stipulation that they each expect to realize a $100,000 benefit per year if the ban is lifted is not to the contrary. The stipulation shows only that the appellants believe they will be able to compete more effectively for existing alcohol consumers if there is no ban on price advertising. It does not show that they believe either the number of alcohol consumers, or the number of purchases by those consumers, will increase in the ban's absence. Indeed, the State's own expert conceded that "plaintiffs' expectation of realizing additional profits through price advertising has no necessary relationship to increased overall consumption." Moreover, we attach little significance to the fact that some studies suggest that people budget the amount of money that they will spend on alcohol. These studies show only that, in a competitive market,

Court's considered and uncontradicted finding on this point is directly to the contrary.[18] Moreover, the evidence suggests that the abusive drinker will probably not be deterred by a marginal price increase, and that the true alcoholic may simply reduce his purchases of other necessities.

In addition, as the District Court noted, the State has not identified what price level would lead to a significant reduction in alcohol consumption, nor has it identified the amount that it believes prices would decrease without the ban. Thus, the State's own showing reveals that any connection between the ban and a significant change in alcohol consumption would be purely fortuitous.

As is evident, any conclusion that elimination of the ban would significantly increase alcohol consumption would require us to engage in the sort of "speculation or conjecture" that is an unacceptable means of demonstrating that a restriction on commercial speech directly advances the State's asserted interest.[19] Such speculation certainly does not suffice when the State takes aim at accurate commercial information for paternalistic ends.

The State also cannot satisfy the requirement that its restriction on speech be no more extensive than necessary. It is perfectly obvious that alternative forms of regulation that would not involve any restriction on speech would be more likely to achieve the State's goal of promoting temperance. As the State's own expert conceded, higher prices can be maintained either by direct regulation or by increased taxation. Per capita purchases could be limited as is the case with prescription drugs. Even educational campaigns focused on the problems of excessive, or even moderate, drinking might prove to be more effective.

As a result, even under the less than strict standard that generally applies in commercial speech cases, the State has failed to establish a "reasonable fit" between its abridgment of speech and its temperance goal. *Board of Trustees, State Univ. of N.Y. v. Fox*, 492 U.S. 469, 480 (1989); see also *Rubin v. Coors Brewing Co.* (explaining that defects in a federal ban on alcohol advertising are "further highlighted by the availability of alternatives that would prove less intrusive to the First Amendment's protections for commercial speech"); *Linmark* (suggesting that the State use financial

---

people will tend to search for the cheapest product in order to meet their budgets. The studies do not suggest that the amount of money budgeted for alcohol consumption will remain fixed in the face of a market-wide price increase.

18. [Court's Footnote 15] Although the Court of Appeals concluded that the regulation directly advanced the State's interest, it did not dispute the District Court's conclusion that the evidence suggested that, at most, a price advertising ban would have a marginal impact on overall alcohol consumption.

19. [Court's Footnote 16] Outside the First Amendment context, we have refused to uphold alcohol advertising bans premised on similarly speculative assertions about their impact on consumption. *See Capital Cities Cable, Inc. v. Crisp*, 467 U.S. 691 (1984) (holding ban pre-empted by Federal Communications Commission regulations); *California Retail Liquor Dealers Ass'n v. Midcal Aluminum, Inc.*, 445 U.S. 97 (1980) (holding ban violated the Sherman Act). It would be anomalous if the First Amendment were more tolerant of speech bans than federal regulations and statutes.

incentives or counter-speech, rather than speech restrictions, to advance its interests). It necessarily follows that the price advertising ban cannot survive the more stringent constitutional review that *Central Hudson* itself concluded was appropriate for the complete suppression of truthful, nonmisleading commercial speech.

VI

The State responds by arguing that it merely exercised appropriate "legislative judgment" in determining that a price advertising ban would best promote temperance. Relying on the *Central Hudson* analysis set forth in *Posadas de Puerto Rico Associates v. Tourism Co. of P. R.*, 478 U.S. 328 (1986), and *United States v. Edge Broadcasting Co.*, 509 U.S. 418 (1993), Rhode Island first argues that, because expert opinions as to the effectiveness of the price advertising ban "go both ways," the Court of Appeals correctly concluded that the ban constituted a "reasonable choice" by the legislature. The State next contends that precedent requires us to give particular deference to that legislative choice because the State could, if it chose, ban the sale of alcoholic beverages outright. *See Posadas*, 478 U.S., at 345–346. Finally, the State argues that deference is appropriate because alcoholic beverages are so-called "vice" products. We consider each of these contentions in turn.

The State's first argument fails to justify the speech prohibition at issue. Our commercial speech cases recognize some room for the exercise of legislative judgment. See *Metromedia, Inc. v. San Diego*, 453 U.S. 490, 507–508 (1981). However, Rhode Island errs in concluding that *Edge* and *Posadas* establish the degree of deference that its decision to impose a price advertising ban warrants.

In *Edge*, we upheld a federal statute that permitted only those broadcasters located in States that had legalized lotteries to air lottery advertising. The statute was designed to regulate advertising about an activity that had been deemed illegal in the jurisdiction in which the broadcaster was located. Here, by contrast, the commercial speech ban targets information about entirely lawful behavior.

Posadas is more directly relevant. There, a five-Member majority held that, under the *Central Hudson* test, it was "up to the legislature" to choose to reduce gambling by suppressing in-state casino advertising rather than engaging in educational speech. Rhode Island argues that this logic demonstrates the constitutionality of its own decision to ban price advertising in lieu of raising taxes or employing some other less speech-restrictive means of promoting temperance.

The reasoning in *Posadas* does support the State's argument, but, on reflection, we are now persuaded that *Posadas* erroneously performed the First Amendment analysis. The casino advertising ban was designed to keep truthful, nonmisleading speech from members of the public for fear that they would be more likely to gamble if they received it. As a result, the advertising ban served to shield the State's anti-gambling policy from the public scrutiny that more direct, nonspeech regulation would draw. See *Posadas* (Brennan, J., dissenting).

Given our longstanding hostility to commercial speech regulation of this type, *Posadas* clearly erred in concluding that it was "up to the legislature" to choose suppression over a less speech-restrictive policy. The *Posadas* majority's conclusion on that point cannot be reconciled with the unbroken line of prior cases striking down similarly broad regulations on truthful, nonmisleading advertising when non-speech-related alternatives were available.

Because the 5-to-4 decision in *Posadas* marked such a sharp break from our prior precedent, and because it concerned a constitutional question about which this Court is the final arbiter, we decline to give force to its highly deferential approach.

Instead, in keeping with our prior holdings, we conclude that a state legislature does not have the broad discretion to suppress truthful, nonmisleading information for paternalistic purposes that the *Posadas* majority was willing to tolerate. As we explained in *Virginia Pharmacy Bd.*, "[i]t is precisely this kind of choice, between the dangers of suppressing information, and the dangers of its misuse if it is freely available, that the First Amendment makes for us."

We also cannot accept the State's second contention, which is premised entirely on the "greater-includes-the-lesser" reasoning endorsed toward the end of the majority's opinion in *Posadas*. There, the majority stated that "the greater power to completely ban casino gambling necessarily includes the lesser power to ban advertising of casino gambling." It went on to state that "*because* the government could have enacted a wholesale prohibition of [casino gambling] it is permissible for the government to take the less intrusive step of allowing the conduct, but reducing the demand through restrictions on advertising." The majority concluded that it would "surely be a strange constitutional doctrine which would concede to the legislature the authority to totally ban a product or activity, but deny to the legislature the authority to forbid the stimulation of demand for the product or activity through advertising on behalf of those who would profit from such increased demand." On the basis of these statements, the State reasons that its undisputed authority to ban alcoholic beverages must include the power to restrict advertisements offering them for sale.

In *Rubin v. Coors Brewing Co.* (1995), the United States advanced a similar argument as a basis for supporting a statutory prohibition against revealing the alcoholic content of malt beverages on product labels. We rejected the argument, noting that the statement in the *Posadas* opinion was made only after the majority had concluded that the Puerto Rican regulation "survived the *Central Hudson* test." Further consideration persuades us that the "greater-includes-the-lesser" argument should be rejected for the additional and more important reason that it is inconsistent with both logic and well-settled doctrine.

Although we do not dispute the proposition that greater powers include lesser ones, we fail to see how that syllogism requires the conclusion that the State's power to regulate commercial activity is "greater" than its power to ban truthful, nonmisleading commercial speech. Contrary to the assumption made in *Posadas*, we think it quite clear that banning speech may sometimes prove far more intrusive than banning conduct. As a venerable proverb teaches, it may prove more injurious to prevent people from teaching others how to fish than to prevent fish from being sold.[20] Similarly, a local ordinance banning bicycle lessons may curtail freedom far more than one that prohibits bicycle riding within city limits. In short, we reject the assumption that words are necessarily less vital to freedom than actions, or that logic somehow proves that the power to prohibit an activity is necessarily "greater" than the power to suppress speech about it.

As a matter of First Amendment doctrine, the *Posadas* syllogism is even less defensible. The text of the First Amendment makes clear that the Constitution presumes that attempts to regulate speech are more dangerous than attempts to regulate conduct. That presumption accords with the essential role that the free flow of information plays in a democratic society. As a result, the First Amendment directs that government may not suppress speech as easily as it may suppress conduct, and that speech restrictions cannot be treated as simply another means that the government may use to achieve its ends.

These basic First Amendment principles clearly apply to commercial speech; indeed, the *Posadas* majority impliedly conceded as much by applying the *Central Hudson* test. Thus, it is no answer that commercial speech concerns products and services that the government may freely regulate. Our decisions from *Virginia Pharmacy Bd.* on have made plain that a State's regulation of the sale of goods differs in kind from a State's regulation of accurate information about those goods. The distinction that our cases have consistently drawn between these two types of governmental action is fundamentally incompatible with the absolutist view that the State may ban commercial speech simply because it may constitutionally prohibit the underlying conduct.[21]

That the State has chosen to license its liquor retailers does not change the analysis. Even though government is under no obligation to provide a person, or the public, a particular benefit, it does not follow that conferral of the benefit may be conditioned on the surrender of a constitutional right. *See, e.g., Frost & Frost Trucking Co. v. Railroad Comm'n of Cal.*, 271 U.S. 583, 594 (1926). In *Perry v. Sindermann*, 408 U.S. 593 (1972), relying on a host of cases applying that principle during the preceding quarter-century, the Court explained that government "may not deny a benefit to a person on a basis that infringes his constitutionally protected interests — especially

---

20. [Court's Footnote 17] "Give a man a fish, and you feed him for a day. Teach a man to fish, and you feed him for a lifetime." The International Thesaurus of Quotations 646 (compiled by R. Tripp 1970).

21. [Court's Footnote 18] It is also no answer to say that it would be "strange" if the First Amendment tolerated a seemingly "greater" regulatory measure while forbidding a "lesser" one. We recently held that although the government had the power to proscribe an entire category of speech, such as obscenity or so-called fighting words, it could not limit the scope of its ban to obscene or fighting words that expressed a point of view with which the government disagrees. *R.A.V. v. St. Paul*, 505 U.S. 377 (1992). Similarly, in *Cincinnati v. Discovery Network, Inc.*, we assumed that States could prevent all newsracks from being placed on public sidewalks, but nevertheless concluded that they could not ban only those newsracks that contained certain commercial publications.

his interest in freedom of speech." That teaching clearly applies to state attempts to regulate commercial speech, as our cases striking down bans on truthful, nonmisleading speech by licensed professionals attest. *See, e.g., Bates v. State Bar of Ariz.; Virginia Bd. of Pharmacy v. Virginia Citizens Consumer Council, Inc.*, 425 U.S. 748 (1976).

Thus, just as it is perfectly clear that Rhode Island could not ban all obscene liquor ads except those that advocated temperance, we think it equally clear that its power to ban the sale of liquor entirely does not include a power to censor all advertisements that contain accurate and nonmisleading information about the price of the product. As the entire Court apparently now agrees, the statements in the *Posadas* opinion on which Rhode Island relies are no longer persuasive.

Finally, we find unpersuasive the State's contention that, under *Posadas* and *Edge*, the price advertising ban should be upheld because it targets commercial speech that pertains to a "vice" activity. The appellees premise their request for a so-called "vice" exception to our commercial speech doctrine on language in *Edge* which characterized gambling as a "vice." The respondents misread our precedent. Our decision last Term striking down an alcohol-related advertising restriction effectively rejected the very contention respondents now make.

Moreover, the scope of any "vice" exception to the protection afforded by the First Amendment would be difficult, if not impossible, to define. Almost any product that poses some threat to public health or public morals might reasonably be characterized by a state legislature as relating to "vice activity." Such characterization, however, is anomalous when applied to products such as alcoholic beverages, lottery tickets, or playing cards, that may be lawfully purchased on the open market. The recognition of such an exception would also have the unfortunate consequence of either allowing state legislatures to justify censorship by the simple expedient of placing the "vice" label on selected lawful activities, or requiring the federal courts to establish a federal common law of vice. For these reasons, a "vice" label that is unaccompanied by a corresponding prohibition against the commercial behavior at issue fails to provide a principled justification for the regulation of commercial speech about that activity. . . .

VIII

Because Rhode Island has failed to carry its heavy burden of justifying its complete ban on price advertising, we conclude that R.I. Gen. Laws §§ 3-8-7 and 3-8-8.1, as well as Regulation 32 of the Rhode Island Liquor Control Administration, abridge speech in violation of the First Amendment as made applicable to the States by the Due Process Clause of the Fourteenth Amendment. The judgment of the Court of Appeals is therefore reversed.

It is so ordered.

Justice Scalia, concurring in part and concurring in the judgment.

I share Justice Thomas's discomfort with the *Central Hudson* test, which seems to me to have nothing more than policy intuition to support it. I also share Justice

Stevens' aversion towards paternalistic governmental policies that prevent men and women from hearing facts that might not be good for them. On the other hand, it would also be paternalism for us to prevent the people of the States from enacting laws that we consider paternalistic, unless we have good reason to believe that the Constitution itself forbids them. I will take my guidance as to what the Constitution forbids, with regard to a text as indeterminate as the First Amendment's preservation of "the freedom of speech," and where the core offense of suppressing particular political ideas is not at issue, from the long accepted practices of the American people. *See McIntyre v. Ohio Elections Comm'n*, 115 S. Ct. 1511 (1995) (Scalia, J., dissenting). . . .

JUSTICE THOMAS, concurring in Parts I, II, VI, and VII, and concurring in the judgment.

In cases such as this, in which the government's asserted interest is to keep legal users of a product or service ignorant in order to manipulate their choices in the marketplace, the balancing test adopted in *Central Hudson Gas & Elec. Corp. v. Public Serv. Comm'n of N.Y.* should not be applied, in my view. Rather, such an "interest" is per se illegitimate and can no more justify regulation of "commercial" speech than it can justify regulation of "noncommercial" speech. . . .

I do not join the principal opinion's application of the *Central Hudson* balancing test because I do not believe that such a test should be applied to a restriction of "commercial" speech, at least when, as here, the asserted interest is one that is to be achieved through keeping would-be recipients of the speech in the dark.[22] Application of the advancement-of-state-interest prong of *Central Hudson* makes little sense to me in such circumstances. Faulting the State for failing to show that its price advertising ban decreases alcohol consumption "significantly," as Justice Stevens does, seems to imply that if the State had been more successful at keeping consumers ignorant and thereby decreasing their consumption, then the restriction might have been upheld. This contradicts *Virginia Pharmacy Bd.'s* rationale for protecting "commercial" speech in the first instance.

Both Justice Stevens and Justice O'Connor appear to adopt a stricter, more categorical interpretation of the fourth prong of *Central Hudson* than that suggested in some of our other opinions,[23] one that could, as a practical matter, go a long way toward the position I take. The State argues that keeping information about lower priced alcohol from consumers will tend to raise the total price of alcohol to consumers (defined as money price plus the costs of searching out lower priced alcohol), thus discouraging alcohol consumption. In their application of the fourth prong,

22. [Concurring Court's Footnote 2] In other words, I do not believe that a *Central Hudson*-type balancing test should apply when the asserted purpose is like the one put forth by the government in *Central Hudson* itself. Whether some type of balancing test is warranted when the asserted state interest is of a different kind is a question that I do not consider here.

23. [Concurring Court's Footnote 3] *E.g., Cincinnati v. Discovery Network* (commercial speech restrictions impermissible if alternatives are "numerous" and obvious).

both Justice Stevens and Justice O'Connor hold that because the State can ban the sale of lower priced alcohol altogether by instituting minimum prices or levying taxes, it cannot ban advertising regarding lower priced liquor. Although the tenor of Justice O'Connor's opinion (and, to a lesser extent, that of Justice Stevens's opinion) might suggest that this is just another routine case-by-case application of *Central Hudson*'s fourth prong, the Court's holding will in fact be quite sweeping if applied consistently in future cases. The opinions would appear to commit the courts to striking down restrictions on speech whenever a direct regulation (i.e., a regulation involving no restriction on speech regarding lawful activity at all) would be an equally effective method of dampening demand by legal users. But it would seem that directly banning a product (or rationing it, taxing it, controlling its price, or otherwise restricting its sale in specific ways) would virtually always be at least as effective in discouraging consumption as merely restricting advertising regarding the product would be, and thus virtually all restrictions with such a purpose would fail the fourth prong of the *Central Hudson* test. This would be so even if the direct regulation is, in one sense, more restrictive of conduct generally. In this case, for example, adoption of minimum prices or taxes will mean that those who, under the current legal system, would have happened across cheap liquor or would have sought it out, will be forced to pay more. Similarly, a State seeking to discourage liquor sales would have to ban sales by convenience stores rather than banning convenience store liquor advertising; it would have to ban liquor sales after midnight, rather than banning advertising by late-night liquor sellers; and so on.

The upshot of the application of the fourth prong in the opinions of Justice Stevens and of Justice O'Connor seems to be that the government may not, for the purpose of keeping would-be consumers ignorant and thus decreasing demand, restrict advertising regarding commercial transactions — or at least that it may not restrict advertising regarding commercial transactions except to the extent that it outlaws or otherwise directly restricts the same transactions within its own borders.[24] I welcome this outcome; but, rather than "applying" the fourth prong

---

24. [Concurring Court's Footnote 4] The two most obvious situations in which no equally effective direct regulation will be available for discouraging consumption (and thus, the two situations in which the Court and I might differ on the outcome) are: (1) When a law directly regulating conduct would violate the Constitution (e.g., because the item is constitutionally protected), or (2) when the sale is to occur outside the State's borders.

As to the first situation: Although the Court's application of the fourth prong today does not specifically foreclose regulations or bans of advertising regarding items that cannot constitutionally be banned, it would seem strange to hold that the government's power to interfere with transmission of information regarding these items, in order to dampen demand for them, is more extensive than its power to restrict, for the same purpose, advertising of items that are not constitutionally protected.

As to the second situation: When a State seeks to dampen consumption by its citizens of products or services outside its borders, it does not have the option of direct regulation. Here, respondent correctly points out that alternatives such as taxes will not be effective in discouraging sales to Rhode Island residents of lower priced alcohol outside the State, yet the Court strikes down the ban against price advertising even as applied to out-of-state liquor sellers such as petitioner Peoples

of *Central Hudson* to reach the inevitable result that all or most such advertising restrictions must be struck down, I would adhere to the doctrine adopted in *Virginia Pharmacy Bd.* and in Justice Blackmun's *Central Hudson* concurrence, that all attempts to dissuade legal choices by citizens by keeping them ignorant are impermissible. . . .

JUSTICE O'CONNOR, with whom THE CHIEF JUSTICE, JUSTICE SOUTER, and JUSTICE BREYER join, concurring in the judgment.

Rhode Island prohibits advertisement of the retail price of alcoholic beverages, except at the place of sale. The State's only asserted justification for this ban is that it promotes temperance by increasing the cost of alcoholic beverages. I agree with the Court that Rhode Island's price-advertising ban is invalid. I would resolve this case more narrowly, however, by applying our established *Central Hudson* test to determine whether this commercial-speech regulation survives First Amendment scrutiny. . . .

Given the means by which this regulation purportedly serves the State's interest, our conclusion is plain: Rhode Island's regulation fails First Amendment scrutiny. . . .

Notes and Questions

(1) Why is "commercial speech" deserving of any First Amendment protection at all? Many have argued that it should receive little or no protection under the Constitution, because advertising simply fails to vindicate any of the functions that are traditionally advanced to justify the special protection speech receives under the First Amendment. Thus, if one sees freedom of speech primarily as an aid to democratic self-governance, commercial speech may be perceived as not advancing the processes of democracy. *See* Thomas Jackson & John Jeffries, *Commercial Speech: Economic Due Process and the First Amendment*, 65 VA. L. REV. 1, 7–8 (1979) ("The first amendment guarantee of freedom of speech and press protects only certain identifiable values. Chief among them is effective self-government. Additionally, the first amendment may protect the opportunity for individual self-fulfillment through free expression. Neither value is implicated by governmental regulation of commercial speech."); Lillian BeVier, *The First Amendment and Political Speech: An Inquiry Into the Substance and Limits of Principle*, 30 STAN. L. REV. 299 (1978) (arguing against protection for

---

Super Liquor Stores. Perhaps Justice Stevens and Justice O'Connor would distinguish a situation in which a State had actually banned sales of lower priced alcohol within the State and had then, through a ban of advertising by out-of-state sellers, sought to keep residents ignorant of the fact that lower priced alcohol was legally available in other States.

The outcome in *Edge* may well be in conflict with the principles espoused in *Virginia Pharmacy Bd.* and ratified by me today. (In *Edge*, respondent did not put forth the broader principles adopted in *Virginia Pharmacy Bd.*, but rather argued that the advertising restriction did not have a sufficiently close fit under *Central Hudson*.) Because the issue of restrictions on advertising of products or services to be purchased legally outside a State that has itself banned or regulated the same purchases within the State is not squarely presented in this case, I will not address here whether the decision in *Edge* can be reconciled with the position I take today.

commercial speech, because it bears no relation to processes of politics and public decisionmaking). If one sees freedom of speech primarily as a vehicle for individual autonomy and self-fulfillment, commercial speech — at least when "spoken" through the artificial voices of inanimate corporations — does not seem to qualify as speech that lifts the human spirit of the speaker. *See* C. Edwin Baker, Human Liberty and Freedom of Speech 195–210 (1989); C. Edwin Baker, *Commercial Speech: A Problem in the Theory of Freedom*, 62 Iowa L. Rev. 1, 3 (1976) ("a complete denial of first amendment protection for commercial speech is not only consistent with, but required by, first amendment theory"). And if the oldest of free speech metaphors, "the marketplace of ideas," is one's primary justification for enhanced protection of speech, commercial speech again falls short, for its content seems largely devoid of anything that ought properly be called an "idea," or as some scholars maintain, much that can honestly be described as "information." Professors Ronald K.L. Collins and David M. Skover, for example, argue that the "logic of discourse" changes as modern advertising becomes less concerned with conveying information about products, and more concerned with conveying image and fantasy. Ronald K.L. Collins & David M. Skover, *Commerce and Communication*, 71 Tex. L. Rev. 697 (1992). Yet others have argued that commercial speech deserves high levels of protection. Justice Thomas in *44 Liquormart*, for example, appears to advance the idea that commercial speech should be protected under the same high standards that apply to political speech. *See also* Jeffrey Shaman, *Revitalizing the Clear-and-Present-Danger Test: Toward a Principled Interpretation of the First Amendment*, 22 Vill. L. Rev. 60 (1977) (arguing in favor of treating all speech as protected under rigorous heightened review standards, without regard to categories such as "commercial speech" or "libel"). Indeed, some have argued that commercial speech should presumptively enter the debate with full First Amendment protection. *See* Rodney A. Smolla, *Information, Imagery, and the First Amendment: A Case for Expansive Protection of Commercial Speech*, 71 Texas L. Rev. 777 (1993). *See also* Burt Neuborne, *A Rationale for Protecting and Regulating Commercial Speech*, 46 Brook. L. Rev. 437, 448–453 (1980) (arguing that commercial speech deserves greater protection than it currently receives to ensure that data necessary for economic and political decisionmaking is available); Martin H. Redish, *The First Amendment in the Marketplace: Commercial Speech and the Values of Free Expression*, 39 Geo. Wash. L. Rev. 429, 431 (1971) (arguing that certain commercial speech, such as informational and artistic advertising, should receive protection); Martin Redish, *What's Good for General Motors: Corporate Speech and the Theory of Free Expression*, 66 Geo. Wash. L. Rev. 235 (1998); Martin Redish, *First Amendment Theory and the Demise of the Commercial Speech Distinction: The Case of the Smoking Controversy*, 24 N. Ky. L. Rev. 553 (1997); Ronald D. Rotunda, *The Commercial Speech Doctrine in the Supreme Court*, 1976 U. Ill. L. Rev. 1080 (agreeing with the result of a recent Supreme Court case that seemed to reject a notion of affording a different protection for commercial speech and arguing that the distinction between commercial and noncommercial speech is untenable and unwise). For further reading, *see* Daniel Farber, *Commercial Speech and First Amendment Theory*, 74 Nw. U. L. Rev. 372 (1979); Alex Kozinski & Stuart Banner, *Who's Afraid of Commercial Speech?*,

76 Va. L. Rev. 627 (1990); Daniel H. Lowenstein, *"Too Much Puff": Persuasion, Paternalism and Commercial Speech*, 56 U. Cin. L. Rev. 1205 (1988); David F. McGowan, *A Critical Analysis of Commercial Speech*, 78 Cal. L. Rev. 359 (1990); Frederick Schauer, *Commercial Speech and the Architecture of the First Amendment*, 56 U. Cin. L. Rev. 1181 (1988); Steven Shiffrin, *The First Amendment and Economic Regulation: Away from a General Theory of the First Amendment*, 78 Nw. U. L. Rev. 1212 (1983).

(2) In commercial speech settings, the Supreme Court does not always apply the usually rigorous First Amendment norms that create a strong presumption against the constitutionality of forcing speakers to express views or associate with views against their will. Stated broadly, the First Amendment is normally understood to prevent the government from compelling individuals to express certain views. *See Wooley v. Maynard*, 430 U.S. 705, 714 (1977) (government may not force individual to display state motto, "Live Free or Die," on license plate); *West Virginia Board of Education v. Barnette*, 319 U.S. 624 (1943) (government may not force school children to salute flag). Similarly, the First Amendment often acts to prevent the government from compelling certain individuals to pay subsidies for speech to which they object. The Supreme Court in *Glickman v. Wileman Brothers & Elliott, Inc.*, 521 U.S. 457 (1997), however, rejected a First Amendment challenge to the constitutionality of a series of agricultural marketing orders that, as part of a larger regulatory marketing scheme, required producers of certain California tree fruit to pay assessments for generic product advertising. The Court in *Glickman* emphasized that the program imposed no restraint on the freedom of an objecting party to communicate its own message, did not compel an objecting party, a corporate entity, to itself to express views it disfavors, and did not compel the expression of political or ideological views, but merely participation in a financial program that generically promoted certain agricultural products. In contrast, in *United States v. United Foods, Inc.*, 533 U.S. 405 (2001), the Court reached a different result. In *United Foods*, a federal law, the Mushroom Promotion, Research, and Consumer Information Act, mandated that fresh mushroom handlers pay assessments used primarily to fund advertisements promoting mushroom sales. In *United Foods* the producer wanted to convey the message that its brand of mushrooms was superior to those grown by other producers. It objected to being charged for a contrary message, which appeared to be favored by a majority of producers, that tended to treat all mushrooms as similar. Unlike *Glickman*, in *United Foods*, the mandated assessments for generic advertising were not ancillary to a more comprehensive program restricting marketing autonomy in the agricultural products. Mushroom production is largely unregulated, and mushroom growers are not forced to associate as a group that makes cooperative decisions. In this context, the Court held, it violated the First Amendment to force the objecting mushroom producer to support speech by others to which the producer objected.

(3) In *Sorrell v. IMS Health Inc.*, 564 U.S. 552 (2011), the United States Supreme Court applied free speech doctrines to the practices of "data mining" and "detailing," processes through which pharmaceutical manufacturers promote their drugs.

Pharmacies receive what is called "prescriber-identifying information" when processing prescriptions. They in turn sell the information to "data miners." The data miners produce reports on prescriber behavior and lease their reports to pharmaceutical manufacturers. "Detailers" employed by pharmaceutical manufacturers then use the reports to refine their marketing tactics and increase sales to doctors. The state of Vermont sought to limit this practice, through passage of its Prescription Confidentiality Law, known as "Act 80." The Vermont statute provided that absent the prescriber's consent, prescriber-identifying information could not be sold by pharmacies and similar entities, disclosed by those entities for marketing purposes, or used for marketing by pharmaceutical manufacturers. There were certain limited exceptions. For example, the law allowed dissemination for "health care research." The Court, in an opinion written by Justice Kennedy, struck down the law, holding that it was a content-based and viewpoint based restriction on speech, thereby qualifying for heightened scrutiny. The principal line of battle in the Supreme Court was over the appropriate standard of review. Vermont argued that Act 80 was not a regulation of speech, but a commercial restriction on trafficking in a "commodity." The Court roundly rejected the state's argument. The Court held that the law, on its face, enacted a content-based and speaker-based restriction on speech. The law, the Court noted, prohibited the sale of information subject to exceptions that were based in large part on the content of a purchaser's speech. The law then prohibited the disclosure when pharmaceutical manufacturers used the information for marketing. The law thus targeted speech used for "marketing," with specific content, which was a content-based restriction. The Court emphasized that heightened scrutiny may be triggered by laws that burden speech based on its content, even though the law may not effect an outright ban on the speech. "Lawmakers may no more silence unwanted speech by burdening its utterance than by censoring its content." Vermont's law, the Court held, was animated by the state's policy disfavoring the use to which the information was being put. This made the law a regulation based on disagreement with the content of a message, thereby justifying heightened judicial scrutiny. "A government bent on frustrating an impending demonstration might pass a law demanding two years' notice before the issuance of parade permits. Even if the hypothetical measure on its face appeared neutral as to content and speaker, its purpose to suppress speech and its unjustified burdens on expression would render it unconstitutional." In an important elaboration on the connection between the broad antipathy toward content-based laws that is a central part of general First Amendment doctrine, and the specialized body of law governing commercial speech, the Court in *Sorrell* declared emphatically that "[c]ommercial speech is no exception." The Court, indeed, made a point of holding up commercial discourse as deserving of elevated constitutional protection, noting that, for many citizens, commercial information may be more important than political discussion. "A 'consumer's concern for the free flow of commercial speech often may be far keener than his concern for urgent political dialogue.'" This was particularly true when the information is related to medicine and health, the Court observed. The reality that consumers often care most about commercial information "has great relevance in the fields of medicine and public health, where information can save lives."

§ 9.09 Campaign Finance and the Political Process

Buckley v. Valeo. Modern First Amendment law dealing with the financing of political campaigns largely emanates from the Supreme Court's landmark decision in *Buckley v. Valeo*, 424 U.S. 1 (1976). The Court in *Buckley* drew a line between limits on contributions and limits on expenditures. Contributions are payments made to a political candidate or campaign fund or spent in coordination with the candidate's campaign organization. Expenditures, on the other hand, are sums spent directly by someone to foster a political cause. A candidate may, for example, spend his own money to advance his or her election. Similarly, an individual or corporation may independently advertise to promote or defeat a candidate, without the approval or cooperation of the candidate or his campaign. *Buckley* held that the First Amendment *barred* limits on *expenditures*. Citizens may spend as much as they want of their own money to elect themselves to office or to promote the election of someone else. In contrast, *Buckley* held that the First Amendment allows reasonable limitations on *contributions*. The core of *Buckley* was the supposition that expenditures implicate a core First Amendment right to engage in expressive activity. Contributions, however, pose a danger corruption and buying influence, and thus may be limited. In the aftermath of *Buckley*, the Supreme Court decided many cases fine-tuning the rules it established. The most controversial of those rulings was the decision in *Citizens United*.

Citizens United v. Federal Election Commission

United States Supreme Court
558 U.S. 310, 130 S. Ct. 876, 175 L. Ed. 2d 753 (2010)

Justice Kennedy delivered the opinion of the Court.

Federal law prohibits corporations and unions from using their general treasury funds to make independent expenditures for speech defined as an "electioneering communication" or for speech expressly advocating the election or defeat of a candidate. 2 U.S.C. § 441b. Limits on electioneering communications were upheld in *McConnell v. Federal Election Comm'n*, 540 U.S. 93 (2003). *The holding of McConnell* rested to a large extent on an earlier case, *Austin v. Michigan Chamber of Commerce*, 494 U.S. 652 (1990). *Austin* had held that political speech may be banned based on the speaker's corporate identity.

In this case we are asked to reconsider *Austin* and, in effect, *McConnell*. It has been noted that "*Austin* was a significant departure from ancient First Amendment principles," *Federal Election Comm'n v. Wisconsin Right to Life, Inc.*, 551 U.S. 449,

490 (2007). *(WRTL)* (Scalia, J., concurring in part and concurring in judgment). We agree with that conclusion and hold that *stare decisis* does not compel the continued acceptance of *Austin*. The Government may regulate corporate political speech through disclaimer and disclosure requirements, but it may not suppress that speech altogether. We turn to the case now before us.

I

A

Citizens United is a nonprofit corporation. It brought this action in the United States District Court for the District of Columbia. A three-judge court later convened to hear the cause. The resulting judgment gives rise to this appeal.

Citizens United has an annual budget of about $12 million. Most of its funds are from donations by individuals; but, in addition, it accepts a small portion of its funds from for-profit corporations.

In January 2008, Citizens United released a film entitled *Hillary: The Movie*. We refer to the film as *Hillary*. It is a 90-minute documentary about then-Senator Hillary Clinton, who was a candidate in the Democratic Party's 2008 Presidential primary elections. *Hillary* mentions Senator Clinton by name and depicts interviews with political commentators and other persons, most of them quite critical of Senator Clinton. *Hillary* was released in theaters and on DVD, but Citizens United wanted to increase distribution by making it available through video-on-demand.

B

Before the Bipartisan Campaign Reform Act of 2002 (BCRA), federal law prohibited-and still does prohibit-corporations and unions from using general treasury funds to make direct contributions to candidates or independent expenditures that expressly advocate the election or defeat of a candidate, through any form of media, in connection with certain qualified federal elections. . . .

II

Under this test, *Hillary* is equivalent to express advocacy. The movie, in essence, is a feature-length negative advertisement that urges viewers to vote against Senator Clinton for President. In light of historical footage, interviews with persons critical of her, and voiceover narration, the film would be understood by most viewers as an extended criticism of Senator Clinton's character and her fitness for the office of the Presidency. . . .

III

The First Amendment provides that "Congress shall make no law . . . abridging the freedom of speech." . . .

The law before us is an outright ban, backed by criminal sanctions. Section 441b makes it a felony for all corporations-including nonprofit advocacy corporations-either to expressly advocate the election or defeat of candidates or to broadcast electioneering communications within 30 days of a primary election and 60 days of a general election. Thus, the following acts would all be felonies under § 441b: The Sierra Club runs an ad, within the crucial phase of 60 days before the general election, that exhorts the public to disapprove of a Congressman who favors logging in national forests; the National Rifle Association publishes a book urging the public to vote for the challenger because the incumbent U.S. Senator supports a handgun ban; and the American Civil Liberties Union creates a Web site telling the public to vote for a Presidential candidate in light of that candidate's defense of free speech. These prohibitions are classic examples of censorship. . . .

Speech is an essential mechanism of democracy, for it is the means to hold officials accountable to the people. The right of citizens to inquire, to hear, to speak, and to use information to reach consensus is a precondition to enlightened self-government and a necessary means to protect it. The First Amendment "'has its fullest and most urgent application' to speech uttered during a campaign for political office." *Eu v. San Francisco County Democratic Central Comm.*, 489 U.S. 214, 223 (1989) (quoting *Monitor Patriot Co. v. Roy,* 401 U.S. 265 (1971)).

For these reasons, political speech must prevail against laws that would suppress it, whether by design or inadvertence. Laws that burden political speech are "subject to strict scrutiny," which requires the Government to prove that the restriction "furthers a compelling interest and is narrowly tailored to achieve that interest." . . . We shall employ it here.

Premised on mistrust of governmental power, the First Amendment stands against attempts to disfavor certain subjects or viewpoints. . . . As instruments to censor, these categories are interrelated: Speech restrictions based on the identity of the speaker are all too often simply a means to control content.

Quite apart from the purpose or effect of regulating content, moreover, the Government may commit a constitutional wrong when by law it identifies certain preferred speakers. By taking the right to speak from some and giving it to others, the Government deprives the disadvantaged person or class of the right to use speech to strive to establish worth, standing, and respect for the speaker's voice. The Government may not by these means deprive the public of the right and privilege to determine for itself what speech and speakers are worthy of consideration. The First Amendment protects speech and speaker, and the ideas that flow from each.

The Court has upheld a narrow class of speech restrictions that operate to the disadvantage of certain persons, but these rulings were based on an interest in allowing governmental entities to perform their functions. [Justice Kennedy points to exceptions in schools, prisons, and the military].

We find no basis for the proposition that, in the context of political speech, the Government may impose restrictions on certain disfavored speakers. Both history and logic lead us to this conclusion.

A

1

The Court has recognized that First Amendment protection extends to corporations. This protection has been extended by explicit holdings to the context of political speech. At least since the latter part of the 19th century, the laws of some States and of the United States imposed a ban on corporate direct contributions to candidates. Yet not until 1947 did Congress first prohibit independent expenditures by corporations and labor unions in § 304 of the Labor Management Relations Act 1947.

For almost three decades thereafter, the Court did not reach the question whether restrictions on corporate and union expenditures are constitutional. . . .

2

In *Buckley*, the Court addressed various challenges to the Federal Election Campaign Act of 1971 (FECA) as amended in 1974.

Before addressing the constitutionality of § 608(e)'s independent expenditure ban, *Buckley* first upheld § 608(b), FECA's limits on direct contributions to candidates. The *Buckley* Court recognized a "sufficiently important" governmental interest in "the prevention of corruption and the appearance of corruption."

The *Buckley* Court explained that the potential for *quid pro quo* corruption distinguished direct contributions to candidates from independent expenditures. The Court emphasized that "the independent expenditure ceiling . . . fails to serve any substantial governmental interest in stemming the reality or appearance of corruption in the electoral process. *Buckley* invalidated § 608(e)'s restrictions on independent expenditures, with only one Justice dissenting.

Less than two years after *Buckley,* [*First Nat. Bank of Boston v.*] *Bellotti*, [435 U.S. 765(1978),] reaffirmed the First Amendment principle that the Government cannot restrict political speech based on the speaker's corporate identity. *Bellotti* could not have been clearer when it struck down a state-law prohibition on corporate independent expenditures related to referenda issues:

"We thus find no support in the First . . . Amendment, or in the decisions of this Court, for the proposition that speech that otherwise would be within the protection of the First Amendment loses that protection simply because its source is a corporation that cannot prove, to the satisfaction of a court, a material effect on its business or property. . . . [That proposition] amounts to an impermissible legislative prohibition of speech based on the identity of the interests that spokesmen may represent in public debate over controversial issues and a requirement that the speaker have a sufficiently great interest in the subject to justify communication.

* * *

"In the realm of protected speech, the legislature is constitutionally disqualified from dictating the subjects about which persons may speak and the speakers who may address a public issue."

It is important to note that the reasoning and holding of *Bellotti* did not rest on the existence of a viewpoint-discriminatory statute. It rested on the principle that the Government lacks the power to ban corporations from speaking.

Bellotti did not address the constitutionality of the State's ban on corporate independent expenditures to support candidates. In our view, however, that restriction would have been unconstitutional under *Bellotti*'s *central principle: that the First Amendment does not allow political speech restrictions based on a speaker's corporate identity. See ibid.*

3

... *Austin* "uph[eld] a direct restriction on the independent expenditure of funds for political speech for the first time in [this Court's] history." There, the Michigan Chamber of Commerce sought to use general treasury funds to run a newspaper ad supporting a specific candidate. Michigan law, however, prohibited corporate independent expenditures that supported or opposed any candidate for state office. A violation of the law was punishable as a felony. The Court sustained the speech prohibition.

To bypass *Buckley* and *Bellotti,* the *Austin* Court identified a new governmental interest in limiting political speech: an antidistortion interest. *Austin* found a compelling governmental interest in preventing "the corrosive and distorting effects of immense aggregations of wealth that are accumulated with the help of the corporate form and that have little or no correlation to the public's support for the corporation's political ideas."

B

The Court is thus confronted with conflicting lines of precedent: a pre-*Austin* line that forbids restrictions on political speech based on the speaker's corporate identity and a post-*Austin* line that permits them. No case before *Austin* had held that Congress could prohibit independent expenditures for political speech based on the speaker's corporate identity.

1

As for *Austin*'s antidistortion rationale ... [it] cannot support § 441b.

If the First Amendment has any force, it prohibits Congress from fining or jailing citizens, or associations of citizens, for simply engaging in political speech. If the antidistortion rationale were to be accepted, however, it would permit Government to ban political speech simply because the speaker is an association that has taken on the corporate form. The Government contends that *Austin* permits it to ban corporate expenditures for almost all forms of communication stemming from a corporation If *Austin* were correct, the Government could prohibit a corporation from expressing political views in media beyond those presented here, such as by printing books. The Government responds "that the FEC has never applied this statute to a book," and if it did, "there would be quite [a] good as-applied challenge." This troubling assertion of brooding governmental power cannot be reconciled with the confidence and stability in civic discourse that the First Amendment must secure. . . .

Austin's antidistortion rationale would produce the dangerous, and unacceptable, consequence that Congress could ban political speech of media corporations. . . . Media corporations are now exempt from § 441b's ban on corporate expenditures. See 2 U.S.C. §§ 431(9)(B)(i), 434(f)(3)(B)(i). Yet media corporations accumulate wealth with the help of the corporate form, the largest media corporations have "immense aggregations of wealth," and the views expressed by media corporations often "have little or no correlation to the public's support" for those views. Thus, under the Government's reasoning, wealthy media corporations could have their voices diminished to put them on par with other media entities. There is no precedent for permitting this under the First Amendment.

The law's exception for media corporations is, on its own terms, all but an admission of the invalidity of the antidistortion rationale. And the exemption results in a further, separate reason for finding this law invalid: Again by its own terms, the law exempts some corporations but covers others, even though both have the need or the motive to communicate their views. The exemption applies to media corporations owned or controlled by corporations that have diverse and substantial investments and participate in endeavors other than news. So even assuming the most doubtful proposition that a news organization has a right to speak when others do not, the exemption would allow a conglomerate that owns both a media business and an unrelated business to influence or control the media in order to advance its overall business interest. At the same time, some other corporation, with an identical business interest but no media outlet in its ownership structure, would be forbidden to speak or inform the public about the same issue. This differential treatment cannot be squared with the First Amendment.

The censorship we now confront is vast in its reach. . . . By suppressing the speech of manifold corporations, both for-profit and nonprofit, the Government prevents their voices and viewpoints from reaching the public and advising voters on which persons or entities are hostile to their interests. Factions will necessarily form in our Republic, but the remedy of "destroying the liberty" of some factions is "worse than the disease." The Federalist No. 10. Factions should be checked by permitting them all to speak and by entrusting the people to judge what is true and what is false.

The nonprofit corporations, from presenting both facts and opinions to the public. This makes *Austin*'s antidistortion rationale all the more an aberration. . . .

When Government seeks to use its full power, including the criminal law, to command where a person may get his or her information or what distrusted source he or she may not hear, it uses censorship to control thought. This is unlawful. The First Amendment confirms the freedom to think for ourselves.

2

What we have said also shows the invalidity of other arguments made by the Government. For the most part relinquishing the antidistortion rationale, the Government falls back on the argument that corporate political speech can be banned in order to prevent corruption or its appearance. In *Buckley,* the Court found this interest "sufficiently important" to allow limits on contributions but did not extend that reasoning to expenditure limits.

. . . The *Buckley* Court, nevertheless, sustained limits on direct contributions in order to ensure against the reality or appearance of corruption. That case did not extend this rationale to independent expenditures, and the Court does not do so here.

. . . Limits on independent expenditures, such as § 441b, have a chilling effect extending well beyond the Government's interest in preventing *quid pro quo* corruption. The anticorruption interest is not sufficient to displace the speech here in question. Indeed, 26 States do not restrict independent expenditures by for-profit corporations. The Government does not claim that these expenditures have corrupted the political process in those States.

When *Buckley* identified a sufficiently important governmental interest in preventing corruption or the appearance of corruption, that interest was limited to *quid pro quo* corruption.

The appearance of influence or access, furthermore, will not cause the electorate to lose faith in our democracy. By definition, an independent expenditure is political speech presented to the electorate that is not coordinated with a candidate. The fact that a corporation, or any other speaker, is willing to spend money to try to persuade voters presupposes that the people have the ultimate influence over elected officials. . . .

. . . When Congress finds that a problem exists, we must give that finding due deference; but Congress may not choose an unconstitutional remedy. If elected officials succumb to improper influences from independent expenditures; if they surrender their best judgment; and if they put expediency before principle, then surely there is cause for concern. We must give weight to attempts by Congress to seek to dispel either the appearance or the reality of these influences. The remedies enacted by law, however, must comply with the First Amendment; and, it is our law and our tradition that more speech, not less, is the governing rule. An outright ban on corporate political speech during the critical preelection period is not a permissible remedy. Here Congress has created categorical bans on speech that are asymmetrical to preventing *quid pro quo* corruption.

3

The Government contends further that corporate independent expenditures can be limited because of its interest in protecting dissenting shareholders from being compelled to fund corporate political speech. This asserted interest, like *Austin's* antidistortion rationale, would allow the Government to ban the political speech even of media corporations. . . . Under the Government's view, that potential disagreement could give the Government the authority to restrict the media corporation's political speech. The First Amendment does not allow that power. There is, furthermore, little evidence of abuse that cannot be corrected by shareholders "through the procedures of corporate democracy."

Those reasons are sufficient to reject this shareholder-protection interest; and, moreover, the statute is both underinclusive and overinclusive. As to the first, if Congress had been seeking to protect dissenting shareholders, it would not have banned corporate speech in only certain media within 30 or 60 days before an election. A dissenting shareholder's interests would be implicated by speech in any media at any time. As to the second, the statute is overinclusive because it covers all corporations, including nonprofit corporations and for-profit corporations with only single shareholders. As to other corporations, the remedy is not to restrict speech but to consider and explore other regulatory mechanisms. The regulatory mechanism here, based on speech, contravenes the First Amendment.

4

We need not reach the question whether the Government has a compelling interest in preventing foreign individuals or associations from influencing our Nation's political process. . . .

C

Rapid changes in technology-and the creative dynamic inherent in the concept of free expression-counsel against upholding a law that restricts political speech in certain media or by certain speakers. . . .

Due consideration leads to this conclusion: *Austin,* 494 U.S. 652, should be and now is overruled. We return to the principle established in *Buckley* and *Bellotti* that the Government may not suppress political speech on the basis of the speaker's corporate identity. No sufficient governmental interest justifies limits on the political speech of nonprofit or for-profit corporations.

D

Austin is overruled, so it provides no basis for allowing the Government to limit corporate independent expenditures.

Given our conclusion we are further required to overrule the part of *McConnell* that upheld BCRA § 203's extension of § 441b's restrictions on corporate independent expenditures. The *McConnell* Court relied on the antidistortion interest recognized in *Austin* to uphold a greater restriction on speech than the restriction upheld in *Austin,* and we have found this interest unconvincing and insufficient. This part of *McConnell* is now overruled.

IV

A

Citizens United next challenges BCRA's disclaimer and disclosure provisions as applied to *Hillary* and the three advertisements for the movie.... Disclaimer and disclosure requirements may burden the ability to speak, but they "impose no ceiling on campaign-related activities," *Buckley* at 64, and "do not prevent anyone from speaking," *McConnell* at 201. The Court has subjected these requirements to "exacting scrutiny," which requires a "substantial relation" between the disclosure requirement and a "sufficiently important" governmental interest. *Buckley* at 64, 66; see *McConnell* at 231–232

In *Buckley,* the Court explained that disclosure could be justified based on a governmental interest in "provid[ing] the electorate with information" about the sources of election-related spending.

Although both provisions were facially upheld, the Court acknowledged that as-applied challenges would be available if a group could show a "'reasonable probability'" that disclosure of its contributors' names "'will subject them to threats, harassment, or reprisals from either Government officials or private parties.'"

For the reasons stated below, we find the statute valid as applied to the ads for the movie and to the movie itself.

B

Citizens United sought to broadcast one 30-second and two 10-second ads to promote *Hillary*. Under FEC regulations, a communication that "[p]roposes a commercial transaction" was not subject to 2 U.S.C. § 441b's restrictions on corporate or union funding of electioneering communications. 11 CFR § 114.15(b)(3)(ii). The regulations, however, do not exempt those communications from the disclaimer and disclosure requirements in BCRA §§ 201 and 311. See 72 Fed. Reg. 72901 (2007).

Citizens United argues that the disclaimer requirements in § 311 are unconstitutional as applied to its ads. It contends that the governmental interest in providing information to the electorate does not justify requiring disclaimers for any commercial advertisements, including the ones at issue here. We disagree.

... The Court has explained that disclosure is a less restrictive alternative to more comprehensive regulations of speech.

V

Modern day movies, television comedies, or skits on Youtube.com might portray public officials or public policies in unflattering ways.... Yet if a covered transmission during the blackout period creates the background for candidate ...

Some members of the public might consider *Hillary* to be insightful and instructive; some might find it to be neither high art nor a fair discussion on how to set the Nation's course; still others simply might suspend judgment on these points but decide to think more about issues and candidates. Those choices and assessments, however, are not for the Government to make. "The First Amendment underwrites the freedom to experiment and to create in the realm of thought and speech. Citizens must be free to use new forms, and new forums, for the expression of ideas. The civic discourse belongs to the people, and the Government may not prescribe the means used to conduct it." *McConnell* at 341. . . .

CHIEF JUSTICE ROBERTS, with whom JUSTICE ALITO joins, concurring.

The Court properly rejects that theory, and I join its opinion in full. The First Amendment protects more than just the individual on a soapbox and the lonely pamphleteer. I write separately to address the important principles of judicial restraint and *stare decisis* implicated in this case. . . .

JUSTICE SCALIA with whom Justice ALITO joins, and with whom JUSTICE THOMAS joins in part, concurring. [JUSTICE THOMAS does not join Part IV of the Court's opinion.]

I join the opinion of the Court.

I write separately to address Justice Steven's [opinion]. . . . This section of the dissent purports to show that today's decision is not supported by the original understanding of the First Amendment. The dissent attempts this demonstration, however, in splendid isolation from the text of the First Amendment. It never shows why "the freedom of speech" that was the right of Englishmen did not include the freedom to speak in association with other individuals, including association in the corporate form. . . .

JUSTICE STEVENS, with whom JUSTICE BREYER, and Justice SOTOMAYOR join, concurring in part and dissenting in part.

. . . The basic premise underlying the Court's ruling is its iteration, and constant reiteration, of the proposition that the First Amendment bars regulatory distinctions based on a speaker's identity, including its "identity" as a corporation. While that glittering generality has rhetorical appeal, it is not a correct statement of the law. Nor does it tell us when a corporation may engage in electioneering that some of its shareholders oppose. It does not even resolve the specific question whether Citizens United may be required to finance some of its messages with the money in its PAC. The conceit that corporations must be treated identically to natural persons in the political sphere is not only inaccurate but also inadequate to justify the Court's disposition of this case.

In the context of election to public office, the distinction between corporate and human speakers is significant. Although they make enormous contributions to our society, corporations are not actually members of it. They cannot vote or run for office. Because they may be managed and controlled by nonresidents, their interests may conflict in fundamental respects with the interests of eligible voters. The financial resources, legal structure, and instrumental orientation of corporations raise legitimate concerns about their role in the electoral process. Our lawmakers have a compelling constitutional basis, if not also a democratic duty, to take measures designed to guard against the potentially deleterious effects of corporate spending in local and national races. . . .

The majority's approach to corporate electioneering marks a dramatic break from our past.

Let us start from the beginning. The Court invokes "ancient First Amendment principles," and original understandings to defend today's ruling, yet it makes only a perfunctory attempt to ground its analysis in the principles or understandings of those who drafted and ratified the Amendment. Perhaps this is because there is not a scintilla of evidence to support the notion that anyone believed it would preclude regulatory distinctions based on the corporate form. To the extent that the Framers' views are discernible and relevant to the disposition of this case, they would appear to cut strongly against the majority's position. . . .

Today's decision is backwards in many senses. It elevates the majority's agenda over the litigants' submissions, facial attacks over as-applied claims, broad constitutional theories over narrow statutory grounds, individual dissenting opinions over precedential holdings, assertion over tradition, absolutism over empiricism, rhetoric over reality. Our colleagues have arrived at the conclusion that *Austin* must be overruled and that § 203 is facially unconstitutional only after mischaracterizing both the reach and rationale of those authorities, and after bypassing or ignoring rules of judicial restraint used to cabin the Court's lawmaking power. Their conclusion that the societal interest in avoiding corruption and the appearance of corruption does not provide an adequate justification for regulating corporate expenditures on candidate elections relies on an incorrect description of that interest, along with a failure to acknowledge the relevance of established facts and the considered judgments of state and federal legislatures over many decades.

Justice Thomas, concurring in part and dissenting in part.

I join all but Part IV of the Court's opinion.

Political speech is entitled to robust protection under the First Amendment. Section 203 of the Bipartisan Campaign Reform Act of 2002 (BCRA) has never been reconcilable with that protection. By striking down § 203, the Court takes an important first step toward restoring full constitutional protection to speech that is "indispensable to the effective and intelligent use of the processes of popular government." *McConnell v. Federal Election Comm'n,* 540 U.S. 93 (2003).

Congress may not abridge the "right to anonymous speech" based on the "'simple interest in providing voters with additional relevant information.'" In continuing to hold otherwise, the Court misapprehends the import of "recent events" that some *amici* describe "in which donors to certain causes were blacklisted, threatened, or otherwise targeted for retaliation." The Court properly recognizes these events as "cause for concern," *ibid.*, but fails to acknowledge their constitutional significance. In my view, *amici*'s submissions show why the Court's insistence on upholding

§§ 201 and 311 will ultimately prove as misguided (and ill fated) as was its prior approval of § 203. . . .

. . . I cannot endorse a view of the First Amendment that subjects citizens of this Nation to death threats, ruined careers, damaged or defaced property, or preemptive and threatening warning letters as the price for engaging in "core political speech, the 'primary object of First Amendment protection.'" *McConnell,* 540 U.S., at 264. Accordingly, I respectfully dissent from the Court's judgment upholding BCRA §§ 201 and 311.

§ 9.10 Public Forum Law

Widmar v. Vincent

United States Supreme Court
454 U.S. 263, 102 S. Ct. 269, 70 L. Ed. 2d 440 (1981)

JUSTICE POWELL delivered the opinion of the court.

This case presents the question whether a state university, which makes its facilities generally available for the activities of registered student groups, may close its facilities to a registered student group desiring to use the facilities for religious worship and religious discussion.

I

It is the stated policy of the University of Missouri at Kansas City to encourage the activities of student organizations. The University officially recognizes over 100 student groups. It routinely provides University facilities for the meetings of registered organizations. Students pay an activity fee of $41 per semester to help defray the costs to the University.

From 1973 until 1977 a registered religious group named Cornerstone regularly sought and received permission to conduct its meetings in University facilities. In 1977, however, the University informed the group that it could no longer meet in University buildings. The exclusion was based on a regulation, adopted by the Board of Curators in 1972, that prohibits the use of University buildings or grounds "for purposes of religious worship or religious teaching."

Eleven University students, all members of Cornerstone, brought suit to challenge the regulation. . . .

II

Through its policy of accommodating their meetings, the University has created a forum generally open for use by student groups. Having done so, the University has assumed an obligation to justify its discriminations and exclusions under applicable constitutional norms. The Constitution forbids a State to enforce certain exclusions from a forum generally open to the public, even if it was not required to create the forum in the first place. . . .

Here the UMKC has discriminated against student groups and speakers based on their desire to use a generally open forum to engage in religious worship and discussion. These are forms of speech and association protected by the First Amendment. In order to justify discriminatory exclusion from a public forum based on the religious content of a group's intended speech, the University must therefore satisfy the standard of review appropriate to content-based exclusions. It must show that its regulation is necessary to serve a compelling state interest and that it is narrowly drawn to achieve that end. . . .

III

The University [argues] that it cannot offer its facilities to religious groups and speakers on the terms available to other groups without violating the Establishment Clause of the Constitution of the United States. We agree that the interest of the University in complying with its constitutional obligations may be characterized as compelling. It does not follow, however, that an "equal access" policy would be incompatible with this Court's Establishment Clause cases. . . .

In this case two prongs of the [*Lemon v. Kurtzman*, 403 U.S. 602 (1971),] test are clearly met. Both the District Court and the Court of Appeals held that an open-forum policy, including nondiscrimination against religious speech, would have a secular purpose[25] and would avoid entanglement with religion. But the District Court concluded, and the University argues here, that allowing religious groups to share the limited public forum would have the "primary effect" of advancing religion.

The University's argument misconceives the nature of this case. The question is not whether the creation of a religious forum would violate the Establishment Clause. The University has opened its facilities for use by student groups, and the question is whether it can now exclude groups because of the content of their speech. In this context we are unpersuaded that the primary effect of the public forum, open to all forms of discourse, would be to advance religion.

We are not oblivious to the range of an open forum's likely effects. It is possible — perhaps even foreseeable — that religious groups will benefit from access to University facilities. But this Court has explained that a religious organization's enjoyment of merely "incidental" benefits does not violate the prohibition against the "primary advancement" of religion. *Committee for Public Education v. Nyquist*, 413 U.S. 756, 771 (1973). . . .

---

25. [Court's Footnote 10] It is the avowed purpose of UMKC to provide a forum in which students can exchange ideas. The University argues that use of the forum for religious speech would undermine this secular aim. But by creating a forum the University does not thereby endorse or promote any of the particular ideas aired there. Undoubtedly many views are advocated in the forum with which the University desires no association.

Because this case involves a forum already made generally available to student groups, it differs from those cases in which this Court has invalidated statutes permitting school facilities to be used for instruction by religious groups, but *not* by others. *See, e.g., McCollum v. Board of Education* [333 U.S. 203 (1948)]. In those cases the school may appear to sponsor the views of the speaker.

We are satisfied that any religious benefits of an open forum at UMKC would be "incidental" within the meaning of our cases. Two factors are especially relevant.

First, an open forum in a public university does not confer any imprimatur of state approval on religious sects or practices. As the Court of Appeals quite aptly stated, such a policy "would no more commit the University . . . to religious goals" than it is "now committed to the goals of the Students for a Democratic Society, the Young Socialist Alliance," or any other group eligible to use its facilities.

Second, the forum is available to a broad class of nonreligious as well as religious speakers; there are over 100 recognized student groups at UMKC. The provision of benefits to so broad a spectrum of groups is an important index of secular effect. If the Establishment Clause barred the extension of general benefits to religious groups, "a church could not be protected by the police and fire departments, or have its public sidewalk kept in repair." At least in the absence of empirical evidence that religious groups will dominate UMKC's open forum, we agree with the Court of Appeals that the advancement of religion would not be the forum's "primary effect." . . .

IV

Our holding in this case in no way undermines the capacity of the University to establish reasonable time, place, and manner regulations. Nor do we question the right of the University to make academic judgments as to how best to allocate scarce resources or "to determine for itself on academic grounds who may teach, what may be taught, how it shall be taught, and who may be admitted to study." Finally, we affirm the continuing validity of cases, that recognize a University's right to exclude even First Amendment activities that violate reasonable campus rules or substantially interfere with the opportunity of other students to obtain an education.

The basis for our decision is narrow. Having created a forum generally open to student groups, the University seeks to enforce a content-based exclusion of religious speech. Its exclusionary policy violates the fundamental principle that a state regulation of speech should be content-neutral, and the University is unable to justify this violation under applicable constitutional standards. . . .

JUSTICE STEVENS, concurring in the judgment.

As the Court recognizes, every university must "make academic judgments as to how best to allocate scarce resources." The Court appears to hold, however, that those judgments must "serve a compelling state interest" whenever they are based, even in part, on the content of speech. This conclusion apparently flows from the Court's suggestion that a student activities program — from which the public may be excluded — must be managed as though it were a "public forum." In my opinion, the use of the terms "compelling state interest" and "public forum" to analyze the question presented in this case may needlessly undermine the academic freedom of public universities.

Today most major colleges and universities are operated by public authority. Nevertheless, their facilities are not open to the public in the same way that streets and parks are. University facilities — private or public — are maintained primarily for the benefit of the student body and the faculty. In performing their learning and teaching missions, the managers of a university routinely make countless decisions based on the content of communicative materials. They select books for inclusion in the library, they hire professors on the basis of their academic philosophies, they select courses for inclusion in the curriculum, and they reward scholars for what they have written. In addition, in encouraging students to participate in extracurricular activities, they necessarily make decisions concerning the content of those activities.

Because every university's resources are limited, an educational institution must routinely make decisions concerning the use of the time and space that is available for extracurricular activities. In my judgment, it is both necessary and appropriate for those decisions to evaluate the content of a proposed student activity. I should think it obvious, for example, that if two groups of 25 students requested the use of a room at a particular time — one to view Mickey Mouse cartoons and the other to rehearse an amateur performance of Hamlet — the First Amendment would not require that the room be reserved for the group that submitted its application first. Nor do I see why a university should have to establish a "compelling state interest" to defend its decision to permit one group to use the facility and not the other. In my opinion, a university should be allowed to decide for itself whether a program that illuminates the genius of Walt Disney should be given precedence over one that may duplicate material adequately covered in the classroom. Judgments of this kind should be made by academicians, not by federal judges, and their standards for decision should not be encumbered with ambiguous phrases like "compelling state interest."

Thus, I do not subscribe to the view that a public university has no greater interest in the content of student activities than the police chief has in the content of a soapbox oration on Capitol Hill. A university legitimately may regard some subjects as more relevant to its educational mission than others. But the university, like the police officer, may not allow its agreement or disagreement with the viewpoint of a particular speaker to determine whether access to a forum will be granted. If a state university is to deny recognition to a student organization — or is to give it a lesser right to use school facilities than other student groups — it must have a valid reason for doing so.

In this case I agree with the Court that the University has not established a sufficient justification for its refusal to allow the Cornerstone group to engage in religious worship on the campus.

JUSTICE WHITE, dissenting [Omitted].

Frisby v. Schultz

United States Supreme Court
487 U.S. 474, 108 S. Ct. 2495, 101 L. Ed. 2d 420 (1988)

Justice O'Connor delivered the opinion of the Court.

Brookfield, Wisconsin, has adopted an ordinance that completely bans picketing "before or about" any residence. This case presents a facial First Amendment challenge to that ordinance.

I

Brookfield, Wisconsin, is a residential suburb of Milwaukee with a population of approximately 4,300. The appellees, Sandra C. Schultz and Robert C. Braun, are individuals strongly opposed to abortion and wish to express their views on the subject by picketing on a public street outside the Brookfield residence of a doctor who apparently performs abortions at two clinics in neighboring towns. Appellees and others engaged in precisely that activity, assembling outside the doctor's home on at least six occasions between April 20, 1985, and May 20, 1985, for periods ranging from one to one and a half hours. The size of the group varied from 11 to more than 40. The picketing was generally orderly and peaceful; the town never had occasion to invoke any of its various ordinances prohibiting obstruction of the streets, loud and unnecessary noises, or disorderly conduct. Nonetheless, the picketing generated substantial controversy and numerous complaints.

The Town Board therefore resolved to enact an ordinance to restrict the picketing. On May 7, 1985, the town passed an ordinance that prohibited all picketing in residential neighborhoods except for labor picketing. But after reviewing this Court's decision in *Carey v. Brown*, 447 U.S. 455 (1980), which invalidated a similar ordinance as a violation of the Equal Protection Clause, the town attorney instructed the police not to enforce the new ordinance and advised the Town Board that the ordinance's labor picketing exception likely rendered it unconstitutional. This ordinance was repealed on May 15, 1985, and replaced with the following flat ban on all residential picketing:

> It is unlawful for any person to engage in picketing before or about the residence or dwelling of any individual in the Town of Brookfield.

The ordinance itself recites the primary purpose of this ban: "the protection and preservation of the home" through assurance "that members of the community enjoy in their homes and dwellings a feeling of well-being, tranquility, and privacy." The Town Board believed that a ban was necessary because it determined that "the practice of picketing before or about residences and dwellings causes emotional disturbance and distress to the occupants . . . [and] has as its object the harassing of such occupants." The ordinance also evinces a concern for public safety, noting that picketing obstructs and interferes with "the free use of public sidewalks and public ways of travel." . . .

II

The antipicketing ordinance operates at the core of the First Amendment by prohibiting appellees from engaging in picketing on an issue of public concern. Because of the importance of "uninhibited, robust, and wide-open" debate on public issues, we have traditionally subjected restrictions on public issue picketing to careful scrutiny. Of course, "[e]ven protected speech is not equally permissible in all places and at all times."

To ascertain what limits, if any, may be placed on protected speech, we have often focused on the "place" of that speech, considering the nature of the forum the speaker seeks to employ. Our cases have recognized that the standards by which limitations on speech must be evaluated "differ depending on the character of the property at issue." Specifically, we have identified three types of fora: "the traditional public forum, the public forum created by government designation, and the nonpublic forum."

The relevant forum here may be easily identified: appellees wish to picket on the public streets of Brookfield. Ordinarily, a determination of the nature of the forum would follow automatically from this identification; we have repeatedly referred to public streets as the archetype of a traditional public forum. "[T]ime out of mind" public streets and sidewalks have been used for public assembly and debate, the hallmarks of a traditional public forum. Appellants, however, urge us to disregard these "cliches." They argue that the streets of Brookfield should be considered a nonpublic forum. Pointing to the physical narrowness of Brookfield's streets as well as to their residential character, appellants contend that such streets have not by tradition or designation been held open for public communication.

We reject this suggestion. Our prior holdings make clear that a public street does not lose its status as a traditional public forum simply because it runs through a residential neighborhood. . . .

In short, our decisions identifying public streets and sidewalks as traditional public fora are not accidental invocations of a "cliche," but recognition that "[w]herever the title of streets and parks may rest, they have immemorially been held in trust for the use of the public." No particularized inquiry into the precise nature of a specific street is necessary; all public streets are held in the public trust and are properly considered traditional public fora. Accordingly, the streets of Brookfield are traditional public fora. The residential character of those streets may well inform the application of the relevant test, but it does not lead to a different test; the antipicketing ordinance must be judged against the stringent standards we have established for restrictions on speech in traditional public fora:

> In these quintessential public for[a], the government may not prohibit all communicative activity. For the State to enforce a content-based exclusion it must show that its regulation is necessary to serve a compelling state interest and that it is narrowly drawn to achieve that end. . . . The State may

also enforce regulations of the time, place, and manner of expression which are content-neutral, are narrowly tailored to serve a significant government interest, and leave open ample alternative channels of communication.

. . . [T]he appropriate level of scrutiny is initially tied to whether the statute distinguishes between prohibited and permitted speech on the basis of content. . . . [W]e accept the lower courts' conclusion that the Brookfield ordinance is content-neutral. Accordingly, we turn to consider whether the ordinance is "narrowly tailored to serve a significant government interest" and whether it "leave[s] open ample alternative channels of communication."

Because the last question is so easily answered, we address it first. Of course, before we are able to assess the available alternatives, we must consider more carefully the reach of the ordinance. The precise scope of the ban is not further described within the text of the ordinance, but in our view the ordinance is readily subject to a narrowing construction that avoids constitutional difficulties. Specifically, the use of the singular form of the words "residence" and "dwelling" suggests that the ordinance is intended to prohibit only picketing focused on, and taking place in front of, a particular residence. As Justice White's concurring opinion recounts, the lower courts described the ordinance as banning "all picketing in residential areas." But these general descriptions do not address the exact scope of the ordinance and are in no way inconsistent with our reading of its text. "Picketing," after all, is defined as posting at a particular place, see *Webster's Third New International Dictionary* 1710 (1981), a characterization in line with viewing the ordinance as limited to activity focused on a single residence. Moreover, while we ordinarily defer to lower court constructions of state statutes, we do not invariably do so. We are particularly reluctant to defer when the lower courts have fallen into plain error, which is precisely the situation presented here. To the extent they endorsed a broad reading of the ordinance, the lower courts ran afoul of the well-established principle that statutes will be interpreted to avoid constitutional difficulties. . . . We instead construe the ordinance more narrowly. This narrow reading is supported by the representations of counsel for the town at oral argument, which indicate that the town takes, and will enforce, a limited view of the "picketing" proscribed by the ordinance. Thus, generally speaking, "picketing would be having the picket proceed on a definite course or route in front of a home." The picket need not be carrying a sign, but in order to fall within the scope of the ordinance the picketing must be directed at a single residence. Generally marching through residential neighborhoods, or even walking a route in front of an entire block of houses, is not prohibited by this ordinance. Accordingly, we construe the ban to be a limited one; only focused picketing taking place solely in front of a particular residence is prohibited.

So narrowed, the ordinance permits the more general dissemination of a message. As appellants explain, the limited nature of the prohibition makes it virtually self-evident that ample alternatives remain:

> Protestors have not been barred from the residential neighborhoods. They
> may enter such neighborhoods, alone or in groups, even marching. . . . They

may go door-to-door to proselytize their views. They may distribute literature in this manner . . . or through the mails. They may contact residents by
telephone, short of harassment.

We readily agree that the ordinance preserves ample alternative channels of communication and thus move on to inquire whether the ordinance serves a significant
government interest. We find that such an interest is identified within the text of the
ordinance itself: the protection of residential privacy.

"The State's interest in protecting the well-being, tranquility, and privacy of
the home is certainly of the highest order in a free and civilized society." *Carey v.
Brown.* Our prior decisions have often remarked on the unique nature of the home,
"the last citadel of the tired, the weary, and the sick," and have recognized that
"[p]eserving the sanctity of the home, the one retreat to which men and women
can repair to escape from the tribulations of their daily pursuits, is surely an
important value."

One important aspect of residential privacy is protection of the unwilling listener. Although in many locations, we expect individuals simply to avoid speech
they do not want to hear, the home is different. "That we are often 'captives' outside
the sanctuary of the home and subject to objectionable speech . . . does not mean we
must be captives everywhere." Instead, a special benefit of the privacy all citizens
enjoy within their own walls, which the State may legislate to protect, is an ability
to avoid intrusions. Thus, we have repeatedly held that individuals are not required
to welcome unwanted speech into their own homes and that the government may
protect this freedom.

It remains to be considered, however, whether the Brookfield ordinance is narrowly tailored to protect only unwilling recipients of the communications. A statute
is narrowly tailored if it targets and eliminates no more than the exact source of the
"evil" it seeks to remedy. A complete ban can be narrowly tailored, but only if each
activity within the proscription's scope is an appropriately targeted evil. For example, in [*Members of City Council v.*] *Taxpayers for Vincent*, 466 U.S. 789 (1984), we
upheld an ordinance that banned all signs on public property because the interest
supporting the regulation, an esthetic interest in avoiding visual clutter and blight,
rendered each sign an evil. Complete prohibition was necessary because "the substantive evil — visual blight — [was] not merely a possible by-product of the activity,
but [was] created by the medium of expression itself."

The same is true here. The type of focused picketing prohibited by the Brookfield
ordinance is fundamentally different from more generally directed means of communication that may not be completely banned in residential areas. In such cases
"the flow of information [is not] into . . . household[s], but to the public." Here, in
contrast, the picketing is narrowly directed at the household, not the public. The
type of picketers banned by the Brookfield ordinance generally do not seek to disseminate a message to the general public, but to intrude upon the targeted resident,
and to do so in an especially offensive way. Moreover, even if some such picketers

have a broader communicative purpose, their activity nonetheless inherently and offensively intrudes on residential privacy. . . .

In this case, for example, appellees subjected the doctor and his family to the presence of a relatively large group of protestors on their doorstep in an attempt to force the doctor to cease performing abortions. But the actual size of the group is irrelevant; even a solitary picket can invade residential privacy. . . .

The First Amendment permits the government to prohibit offensive speech as intrusive when the "captive" audience cannot avoid the objectionable speech. The target of the focused picketing banned by the Brookfield ordinance is just such a "captive." The resident is figuratively, and perhaps literally, trapped within the home, and because of the unique and subtle impact of such picketing is left with no ready means of avoiding the unwanted speech. . . . Accordingly, the Brookfield ordinance's complete ban of that particular medium of expression is narrowly tailored.

Of course, this case presents only a facial challenge to the ordinance. Particular hypothetical applications of the ordinance — to, for example, a particular resident's use of his or her home as place of business or public meeting, or to picketers present at a particular home by invitation of the resident — may present somewhat different questions. . . .

Because the picketing prohibited by the Brookfield ordinance is speech directed primarily at those who are presumptively unwilling to receive it, the State has a substantial and justifiable interest in banning it. The nature and scope of this interest make the ban narrowly tailored. The ordinance also leaves open ample alternative channels of communication and is content-neutral. Thus, largely because of its narrow scope, the facial challenge to the ordinance must fail. The contrary judgment of the Court of Appeals is

Reversed.

Justice White, concurring in the judgment. [Omitted].

Justice Brennan, with whom Justice Marshall joins, dissenting.

The Court today sets out the appropriate legal tests and standards governing the question presented, and proceeds to apply most of them correctly. Regrettably, though, the Court errs in the final step of its analysis, and approves an ordinance banning significantly more speech than is necessary to achieve the government's substantial and legitimate goal. Accordingly, I must dissent.

The ordinance before us absolutely prohibits picketing "before or about" any residence in the town of Brookfield, thereby restricting a manner of speech in a traditional public forum. Consequently, as the Court correctly states, the ordinance is subject to the well-settled time, place, and manner test: the restriction must be content and viewpoint neutral, leave open ample alternative channels of communication, and be narrowly tailored to further a substantial governmental interest.

Assuming one construes the ordinances as the Court does, I agree that the regulation reserves ample alternative channels of communication. I also agree with the

Court that the town has a substantial interest in protecting its residents' right to be left alone in their homes. It is, however, critical to specify the precise scope of this interest. The mere fact that speech takes place in a residential neighborhood does not automatically implicate a residential privacy interest. It is the intrusion of speech into the home or the unduly coercive nature of a particular manner of speech around the home that is subject to more exacting regulation. Thus, the intrusion into the home of an unwelcome solicitor or unwanted mail may be forbidden. Similarly, the government may forbid the intrusion of excessive noise into the home or, in appropriate circumstances, perhaps even radio waves. Similarly, the government may prohibit unduly coercive conduct around the home, even though it involves expressive elements. A crowd of protesters need not be permitted virtually to imprison a person in his or her own house merely because they shout slogans or carry signs. But so long as the speech remains outside the home and does not unduly coerce the occupant, the government's heightened interest in protecting residential privacy is not implicated.

The foregoing distinction is crucial here because it directly affects that last prong of the time, place, and manner text: whether the ordinance is narrowly tailored to achieve the governmental interest.... [T]he application of this test requires that the government demonstrate that the offending aspects of the prohibited manner of speech cannot be separately, and less intrusively, controlled. Thus here, if the intrusive and unduly coercive elements of residential picketing can be eliminated without simultaneously eliminating residential picketing completely, the Brookfield ordinance fails the Vincent test.

Without question there are many aspects of residential picketing that, if unregulated, might easily become intrusive or unduly coercive. Indeed, some of these aspects are illustrated by this very case. As the District Court found, before the ordinance took effect up to 40 sign-carrying, slogan-shouting protesters regularly converged on Dr. Victoria's home and, in addition to protesting, warned young children not to go near the house because Dr. Victoria was a "baby killer." Further, the throng repeatedly trespassed onto the Victorias' property and at least once blocked the exits to their home. Surely it is within the government's power to enact regulations as necessary to prevent such intrusive and coercive abuses. Thus, for example, the government could constitutionally regulate the number of residential picketers, the hours during which a residential picket may take place, or the noise level of such a picket. In short, substantial regulation is permitted to neutralize the intrusive or unduly coercive aspects of picketing around the home. But to say that picketing may be substantially regulated is not to say that it may be prohibited in its entirety. Once size, time, volume, and the like have been controlled to ensure that the picket is no longer intrusive or coercive, only the speech itself remains, conveyed perhaps by a lone, silent individual, walking back and forth with a sign. Such speech, which no longer implicates the heightened governmental interest in residential privacy, is nevertheless banned by the Brookfield law. Therefore, the ordinance is not narrowly tailored....

Justice Stevens, dissenting.

"GET WELL CHARLIE — OUR TEAM NEEDS YOU."

In Brookfield, Wisconsin, it is unlawful for a fifth grader to carry such a sign in front of a residence for the period of time necessary to convey its friendly message to its intended audience.

The Court's analysis of the question whether Brookfield's ban on picketing is constitutional begins with an acknowledgment that the ordinance "operates at the core of the First Amendment," and that the streets of Brookfield are a "traditional public forum." It concludes, however, that the total ban on residential picketing is "narrowly tailored" to protect "only unwilling recipients of the communications." The plain language of the ordinance, however, applies to communications to willing and indifferent recipients as well as to the unwilling. . . .

The picketing that gave rise to the ordinance enacted in this case was obviously intended to do more than convey a message of opposition to the character of the doctor's practice; it was intended to cause him and his family substantial psychological distress. As the record reveals, the picketers' message was repeatedly redelivered by a relatively large group — in essence, increasing the volume and intrusiveness of the same message with each repeated assertion. As is often the function of picketing, during the periods of protest the doctor's home was held under a virtual siege. I do not believe that picketing for the sole purpose of imposing psychological harm on a family in the shelter of their home is constitutionally protected. I do believe, however, that the picketers have a right to communicate their strong opposition to abortion to the doctor, but after they have had a fair opportunity to communicate that message, I see little justification for allowing them to remain in front of his home and repeat it over and over again simply to harm the doctor and his family. Thus, I agree that the ordinance may be constitutionally applied to the kind of picketing that gave rise to its enactment.

On the other hand, the ordinance is unquestionably "overbroad" in that it prohibits some communication that is protected by the First Amendment. The question, then, is whether to apply the overbreadth doctrine's "strong medicine," *see Broadrick v. Oklahoma*, 413 U.S. 601, 613 (1973), or to put that approach aside "and await further developments." In *Broadrick*, the Court framed the inquiry thusly:

> To put the matter another way, particularly where conduct and not merely speech is involved, we believe that the overbreadth of a statute must not only be real, but substantial as well, judged in relation to the statute's plainly legitimate sweep.

In this case the overbreadth is unquestionably "real." Whether or not it is "substantial" in relation to the "plainly legitimate sweep" of the ordinance is a more difficult question. My hunch is that the town will probably not enforce its ban against friendly, innocuous, or even brief unfriendly picketing, and that the Court may be right in concluding that its legitimate sweep makes its overbreadth insubstantial. But there are two countervailing considerations that are persuasive to me. The scope of the ordinance gives the town officials far too much discretion in making enforcement decisions; while we sit by and await further developments, potential picketers must act at their peril. Second, it is a simple matter for the town to amend its ordinance and to limit the ban to conduct that unreasonably interferes with the privacy of the home and does not serve a reasonable communicative purpose. Accordingly, I respectfully dissent.

Notes and Questions

(1) The Supreme Court has recognized distinct categories of public forums. There are "traditional" public forums, "designated" public forums, "limited" public forums, and "non-forums."

(2) The first, the "traditional" public forum, consists of places such as streets or parks which "have immemorially been held in trust for the use of the public and, time out of mind, have been used for purposes of assembly, communicating thoughts between citizens, and discussing public questions." *Perry Educational Ass'n v. Perry Local Educators' Ass'n*, 460 U.S. 37, 45 (1983), *quoting Hague v. CIO*, 307 U.S. 496, 515 (1939). Content-based regulation of speech in a traditional public forum is governed by principles of heightened scrutiny, such as the strict scrutiny test. Under these heightened scrutiny standards, attempts to regulate speech will usually be struck down. Content-neutral regulation of the time, place, and manner of speech in a traditional public forum is judged under a less rigorous interme-diate level test. Under this test "the government may impose reasonable restric-tions on the time, place, or manner of protected speech, provided the restrictions 'are justified without reference to the content of the regulated speech, that they are narrowly tailored to serve a significant governmental interest, and that they leave open ample alternative channels for communication of the information.'" *Ward v. Rock Against Racism*, 491 U.S. 781, 791 (1989). Time, place, or manner regula-tions deal with such characteristics as the location of the speech, the time of day the speech may take place, and the "manner," typically characteristics such as the loudness of the speech or the size of physical signs, unrelated to the content of the message.

(3) The second category of public forum is the "designated" public forum. This category consists of public property opened by the state for indiscriminate use as a place for expressive activity. If the government treats a piece of public property as if it were a traditional public forum, intentionally opening it up to the public at large for assembly and speech, then it will be bound by the same standards appli-cable to a traditional public forum. Content-based regulation of speech in a des-ignated public forum must thus satisfy the strict scrutiny test. As in the case of traditional public forums, content-neutral regulation of the time, place, or manner of speech in designated public forums is governed by the more relaxed time, place or manner test.

(4) The third category, the "limited" public forum, is sometimes treated as a third type of forum, and sometimes treated as a specialized version of the designated pub-lic forum. The limited forum is a forum reserved for certain topics, or certain users.

A state university law school, for example, might designate classroom spaces after class hours as available to members of the law school community who wish to meet on law-related topics.

(5) The fourth category is the "nonforum." Nonforums consist of publicly owned facilities that have been dedicated to use for either communicative or noncommunicative purposes, but that never have been designated for indiscriminate expressive activity by the general public. The "First Amendment does not guarantee access to property simply because it is owned or controlled by the government." *United States Postal Service v. Council of Greenburgh Civic Associations*, 453 U.S. 114, 129 (1981). The content-based regulation of speech in a nonforum is not governed by the strict scrutiny test, but by a "reasonableness" standard. The government "may reserve the forum for its intended purposes, *communicative or otherwise*, as long as the regulation of speech is reasonable and not an effort to suppress expression merely because public officials oppose the speaker's view." *Perry Education Ass'n v. Perry Local Educators' Ass'n*. Entire *classes* of speech thus may be excluded from a nonforum. Those classes may be identified by content, as long as the exclusion is reasonable in light of the purpose of the forum, and there is no discrimination among viewpoints *within* a class. "Control over access to a nonpublic forum can be based on *subject matter* and *speaker identity* so long as the distinctions drawn are reasonable in light of the purpose served by the forum and are viewpoint-neutral." *Cornelius v. NAACP Legal Defense and Educ. Fund*, 473 U.S. 788, 806 (1985). When such distinctions are made, the property is sometimes referred to as a "limited public forum," because access is limited to certain subjects or certain speakers. The critical inquiry in judging such selective access is whether the "differential access ... is reasonable because it is wholly consistent with the ... legitimate interest in preserving the property ... for the use to which it is 'lawfully dedicated.'" *Perry*.

§ 9.11 Government Speech

The Government Speech Doctrine. The government speech doctrine is a relatively new development in First Amendment law. The basic premise of the doctrine is that when the government is speaking in its own voice on issues, it is permitted to express particular viewpoints, and disparage other opposing viewpoints. The government's exercise of its own speech is immunized from First Amendment challenge in the courts. The government is entitled to condemn smoking, or condemn terrorism, for example, and is under no obligation to grant equal time to opposing viewpoints. It is now settled law that government speech is immune from First Amendment free speech scrutiny. The government speech doctrine does *not* immunize one particular species of government speech, however. Government speech that constitutes an establishment of religion (see Chapter 8) will violate the Establishment Clause. But insofar as routine Free Speech Clause challenges to government speech are concerned, the government is entitled to take positions of its own on issues, and cannot be challenged because the positions it takes constitute "viewpoint discrimination."

The government is entitled to its own viewpoints. If these basic principles are clear enough, however, their application in the real world is far less clear. The trick is to determine when expression should be deemed government speech, and when not. The cases below illustrate the efforts of the Court to divine the divide.

Shurtleff v. City of Boston

United States Supreme Court
142 S. Ct. 1583 (2022)

Justice Breyer delivered the opinion of the Court.

When the government encourages diverse expression — say, by creating a forum for debate — the First Amendment prevents it from discriminating against speakers based on their viewpoint. But when the government speaks for itself, the First Amendment does not demand airtime for all views. After all, the government must be able to "promote a program" or "espouse a policy" in order to function. The line between a forum for private expression and the government's own speech is important, but not always clear.

This case concerns a flagpole outside Boston City Hall. For years, Boston has allowed private groups to request use of the flagpole to raise flags of their choosing. As part of this program, Boston approved hundreds of requests to raise dozens of different flags. The city did not deny a single request to raise a flag until, in 2017, Harold Shurtleff, the director of a group called Camp Constitution, asked to fly a Christian flag. Boston refused. At that time, Boston admits, it had no written policy limiting use of the flagpole based on the content of a flag. The parties dispute whether, on these facts, Boston reserved the pole to fly flags that communicate governmental messages, or instead opened the flagpole for citizens to express their own views. If the former, Boston is free to choose the flags it flies without the constraints of the First Amendment's Free Speech Clause. If the latter, the Free Speech Clause prevents Boston from refusing a flag based on its viewpoint.

We conclude that, on balance, Boston did not make the raising and flying of private groups' flags a form of government speech. That means, in turn, that Boston's refusal to let Shurtleff and Camp Constitution raise their flag based on its religious viewpoint abridged their freedom of speech.

For years, since at least 2005, the city has allowed groups to hold flag-raising ceremonies on the plaza. Participants may hoist a flag of their choosing on the third flagpole (in place of the city's flag) and fly it for the duration of the event, typically a couple of hours.

In July 2017, Harold Shurtleff, the director of an organization called Camp Constitution, asked to hold a flagraising event that September on City Hall Plaza. The event would "commemorate the civic and social contributions of the Christian community" and feature remarks by local clergy. As part of the ceremony, the organization wished to raise what it described as the "Christian flag."

The first and basic question we must answer is whether Boston's flag-raising program constitutes government speech. If so, Boston may refuse flags based on viewpoint.

The First Amendment's Free Speech Clause does not prevent the government from declining to express a view. See *Pleasant Grove City v. Summum*, 555 U.S. 460 (2009). When the government wishes to state an opinion, to speak for the community, to formulate policies, or to implement programs, it naturally chooses what to say and what not to say. That must be true for government to work. Boston could not easily congratulate the Red Sox on a victory were the city powerless to decline to simultaneously transmit the views of disappointed Yankees fans. The Constitution therefore relies first and foremost on the ballot box, not on rules against viewpoint discrimination, to check the government when it speaks. The boundary between government speech and private expression can blur when, as here, a government invites the people to participate in a program. In those situations, when does government-public engagement transmit the government's own message? And when does it instead create a forum for the expression of private speakers' views?

In answering these questions, we conduct a holistic inquiry designed to determine whether the government intends to speak for itself or to regulate private expression. Our review is not mechanical; it is driven by a case's context rather than the rote application of rigid factors. Our past cases have looked to several types of evidence to guide the analysis, including: the history of the expression at issue; the public's likely perception as to who (the government or a private person) is speaking; and the extent to which the government has actively shaped or controlled the expression.

Considering these indicia in *Summum*, we held that the messages of permanent monuments in a public park constituted government speech, even when the monuments were privately funded and donated. In *Walker*, we explained that license plate designs proposed by private groups also amounted to government speech because, among other reasons, the State that issued the plates maintained direct control over the messages conveyed by "actively" reviewing designs and rejecting over a dozen proposals. [*Walker v. Texas Div., Sons of Confederate Veterans, Inc.*, 576 U.S. 200 (2015).]

Applying the government-speech analysis to this record, we find that some evidence favors Boston, and other evidence favors Shurtleff.

To begin, we look to the history of flag flying, particularly at the seat of government. Were we to consider only that general history, we would find that it supports Boston.

While this history favors Boston, it is only our starting point. The question remains whether, on the 20 or so times a year when Boston allowed private groups to raise their own flags, those flags, too, expressed the city's message. So we must examine the details of this flag-flying program.

As we have said, Boston allowed its flag to be lowered and other flags to be raised with some regularity. These other flags were raised in connection with ceremonies at the flagpoles' base and remained aloft during the events.

Compare the extent of Boston's control over flag raisings with the degree of government involvement in our most relevant precedents. In *Summum*, we emphasized that Pleasant Grove City always selected which monuments it would place in its park (whether or not the government funded those monuments), and it typically took ownership over them. In *Walker*, a state board maintained direct control over license plate designs by "actively" reviewing every proposal and rejecting at least a dozen.

The facts of this case are much closer to *Matal v. Tam*, 137 S. Ct. 1734 (2017). There, we held that trademarks were not government speech because the Patent and Trademark Office registered all manner of marks and normally did not consider their viewpoint, except occasionally to turn away marks it deemed "offensive." Boston's come-one-come-all attitude—except, that is, for Camp Constitution's religious flag—is similar.

Boston could easily have done more to make clear it wished to speak for itself by raising flags. Other cities' flag-flying policies support our conclusion. The City of San Jose, California, for example, provides in writing that its "flagpoles are not intended to serve as a forum for free expression by the public," and lists approved flags that may be flown "as an expression of the City's official sentiments."

All told, while the historical practice of flag flying at government buildings favors Boston, the city's lack of meaningful involvement in the selection of flags or the crafting of their messages leads us to classify the flag raisings as private, not government, speech—though nothing prevents Boston from changing its policies going forward.

Last, we consider whether Boston's refusal to allow Shurtleff and Camp Constitution to raise their flag amounted to impermissible viewpoint discrimination.

Boston acknowledges that it denied Shurtleff's request because it believed flying a religious flag at City Hall could violate the Establishment Clause.

Under our precedents, and in view of our government-speech holding here, that refusal discriminated based on religious viewpoint and violated the Free Speech Clause.

For the foregoing reasons, we conclude that Boston's flag-raising program does not express government speech. As a result, the city's refusal to let Shurtleff and Camp Constitution fly their flag based on its religious viewpoint violated the Free Speech Clause of the First Amendment.

It is so ordered.

Walker v. Texas Division, Sons of Confederate Veterans, Inc. In *Walker v. Texas Division, Sons of Confederate Veterans, Inc.*, 135 S. Ct. 752 (2015), the Supreme Court invoked the government speech doctrine to hold that the state of Texas could deny the request of the Sons of Confederate Veterans for a specialty license plate featuring the Confederate Flag. Poignantly and sadly, by an almost macabre coincidence, the opinion of the Court was issued on June 18, 2015, the very morning the nation awoke to the shocking news of the massacre of nine African Americans at the Emmanuel African Methodist Episcopal Church in Charleston, South Carolina, in which the perpetrator, Dylann Roof, brandished the Confederate Flag and symbols of apartheid from South Africa and Rhodesia in the course of his violent agenda of racism and hate. (The Charleston shootings led to a national outcry to take the Confederate Battle Flag down from the flagpole in front of the South Carolina Capitol, and weeks following the shooting, the flag was in fact removed.)

The opinion in *Walker* was written by Justice Breyer, and joined by Justices Thomas, Ginsburg, Kagan, and Sotomayer. One commentator noted that it was Justice Thomas, the Court's only African-American, who joined with the four liberal members of the Court to uphold Texas' policy. Justice Thomas defected from his more common allegiance to the more conservative members of the Court, perhaps because of his special personal experience with symbols of racism as an African-American child growing up in the South.[26]

---

26. *See* Garrett Epps, *Clarence Thomas Takes on a Symbol of White Supremacy*, THE ATLANTIC, June 18, 2015, at http://www.theatlantic.com/politics/archive/2015/06/clarence-thomas-confederate -flag/396281/:

> Why would Thomas cross over in the Sons of Confederate Veterans case? To state the obvious, Thomas is the Court's only African American. Much has been made of his rejection of contemporary civil-rights orthodoxy. But it is equally clear that Thomas retains vivid and bitter memories of his poverty-stricken childhood in the Jim Crow South — and that he retains a particular hatred for the symbols of Southern white supremacy.
>
> Thomas's most powerful moment on the bench occurred in a case concerning a similar symbol — the burning cross. The year was 2002; *Virginia v. Black* was a challenge to a Virginia criminal statute that forbade burning a cross with the intent to intimidate another person. . . .
>
> The state, and the federal government, were defending the cross ban as a regulation of "true threats," which the First Amendment does not protect. But Thomas interrupted this line of argument to ask, "[A]ren't you understating the — the effects of — of the burning cross? . . . [W]e had almost 100 years of lynching and activity in the South by the Knights of Camellia and — and the Ku Klux Klan, and this was a reign of terror and the cross was a symbol of that reign of terror. Was — isn't that significantly greater than intimidation or a threat?"
>
> Even on the audio, the impact of this comment is vivid. Rodney A. Smolla, who was representing the cross burners, remembered in a recent email: "I have never seen the atmosphere in a courtroom change so quickly. Justice Breyer, who sat next to Justice Thomas, put his arm on him, as if to say 'I feel your pain.' Justice Scalia was staring at Thomas with extraordinary intensity — the sense of empathy and support was virtually palpable. Justice Scalia's eyes left his friend Justice Thomas and he looked down and scowled at me, as I was only minutes from getting up to make my argument, and I immediately knew, from his look, that his views on the entire case had just pivoted, and that he

Texas, like many states, offers to automobile owners a choice between ordinary and specialty license plates. An individual or organization desiring a specialty plate may propose a plate design, typically including a slogan and some graphic image of symbol or logo. The Texas Department of Motor Vehicles Board must approve the design for it to become available to applicants willing to pay the additional fee for the plate. The Texas division of the Sons of Confederate Veterans proposed a specialty license plate design to the Texas DMV featuring a Confederate battle flag.

As the Court noted, there are three distinct ways a specialty plate may come into existence in Texas. The Texas state legislature may itself call for the development of a specialty license plate, as it did for plates expressing messages such as "Keep Texas Beautiful," "Mothers Against Drunk Driving," plates that honoring the Texas citrus industry, and plates that feature an image of the World Trade Center towers and the words "Fight Terrorism." A second avenue allows the Board of the DMV to approve a design proposal proposed by a state-designated private vendor. Examples include promoting the "Keller Indians" and plates with the slogan "Get it Sold with RE/MAX." Third, a nonprofit entity may propose a plate. Common examples include plates touting a university or its sports programs, or groups such as the Rotary. Texas law vests in the DMV Board the discretion, however, to reject a plate proposal, including rejection on the grounds that the plate "might be offensive to any member of the public."

The DMV Board denied the Confederate Veterans' application for a specialty plate featuring the Confederate Flag, reasoning that many persons were offended by the Confederate Flag, considering it a symbol of racism and hate.

The majority opinion written by Justice Breyer began with a proud pronouncement regarding the freedom the government enjoys to engage in content decisions when the government itself is speaking: "When government speaks, it is not barred by the Free Speech Clause from determining the content of what it says." Throughout its opinion, the Court in *Walker* relied heavily on its government speech decision in *Pleasant Grove City v. Summum*, 555 U.S. 460 (2009), in which the Court held that the government did not have to accept a privately donated religious monument on government property. The Court in *Walker* candidly admitted that, in its view, *Summun* created the appropriate frame for analysis. The government speech doctrine, the Court in *Walker* reasoned, "reflects the fact that it is the democratic electoral process that first and foremost provides a check on government speech." Thus, the Court observed that "government statements (and government actions and programs that take the form of speech) do not normally trigger the First Amendment rules designed to protect the marketplace of ideas." Drawing heavily on this notion of a political process check, the Court reasoned that the First Amendment protects the private rights of citizens to exercise free speech rights in order to influence

was about to come after me — which proved entirely prescient.") (quoting an email from Rodney Smolla).

government, which itself then may speak in a manner responsive to the mandate of the body politic.

As the Court saw it, this understanding of the First Amendment was essential to the very working of government, which otherwise would be paralyzed:

> Were the Free Speech Clause interpreted otherwise, government would not work. How could a city government create a successful recycling program if officials, when writing householders asking them to recycle cans and bottles, had to include in the letter a long plea from the local trash disposal enterprise demanding the contrary? How could a state government effectively develop programs designed to encourage and provide vaccinations, if officials also had to voice the perspective of those who oppose this type of immunization? "[I]t is not easy to imagine how government could function if it lacked th[e] freedom" to select the messages it wishes to convey.

The Court reasoned that any other rule would give citizens an untenably broad First Amendment veto over government policy. Even the rule against viewpoint discrimination is applied with a different lens when examining government speech, the Court in *Walker* observed, noting that the Court had "refused '[t]o hold that the Government unconstitutionally discriminates on the basis of viewpoint when it chooses to fund a program dedicated to advance certain permissible goals, because the program in advancing those goals necessarily discourages alternative goals.'"

The Court in *Walker* recognized only narrow possible exceptions to this principle. The Court noted that its rule was "not to say that a government's ability to express itself is without restriction," cautioning that "[c]onstitutional and statutory provisions outside of the Free Speech Clause may limit government speech." This phrasing was likely intended to acknowledge that constitutional provisions such as the Establishment Clause might limit government speech respecting an establishment of religion, or the Equal Protection Clause might limit speech discriminating against members of a particular racial group. So too, the Court in *Walker* acknowledged a potential carve-out from government speech principles when the government attempts to conscript private individuals to convey its message, noting that "the Free Speech Clause itself may constrain the government's speech if, for example, the government seeks to compel private persons to convey the government's speech." With these minor exceptions, however, "as a general matter, when the government speaks it is entitled to promote a program, to espouse a policy, or to take a position."

The Court held that the Texas specialty license plate program constituted government speech. "First, the history of license plates shows that, insofar as license plates have conveyed more than state names and vehicle identification numbers, they long have communicated messages from the States." States, the Court observed, "have used license plate slogans to urge action, to promote tourism, and to tout local industries." Texas had often engaged in such license plate messaging. Secondly, the Court reasoned, Texas license plate designs are often closely identified in the public mind with the State of Texas, including the facts that the state places the name "TEXAS" in large letters at the top of every plate, that requires Texas vehicle owners to display license plates, and all Texas license plate are issued by the state. Texas license plates, the Court reasoned, are "essentially, government IDs." Moreover, the private person or entity seeking a specialty plate, the Court reasoned, is likely to be intentionally playing on the suggestion that Texas has endorsed the message on the plate:

> Indeed, a person who displays a message on a Texas license plate likely intends to convey to the public that the State has endorsed that message. If not, the individual could simply display the message in question in larger letters on a bumper sticker right next to the plate. But the individual prefers a license plate design to the purely private speech expressed through bumper stickers. That may well be because Texas's license plate designs convey government agreement with the message displayed.

The Court in *Walker* also heavily emphasized the degree of direct control Texas maintained over the messages conveyed on its specialty plates, citing rules on design and the fact that the DMV "Board must approve every specialty plate design proposal before the design can appear on a Texas plate," an authority that had been actively exercised. The Court noted that Texas was free to take sides on the issues it chose to promote or not promote in exercising this approval:

> This final approval authority allows Texas to choose how to present itself and its constituency. Thus, Texas offers plates celebrating the many educational institutions attended by its citizens.... But it need not issue plates deriding schooling. Texas offers plates that pay tribute to the Texas citrus industry.... But it need not issue plates praising Florida's oranges as far better. And Texas offers plates that say "Fight Terrorism."... But it need not issue plates promoting al Qaeda.

The Court in *Walker* rejected the claim that the plates were private speech because the designs and slogans were proposed by private parties. The Court rejected the argument that the license plate regime constituted a public forum. Clearly the plates were not a traditional public forum, the Court reasoned, such as a street or a park. Nor did the plates program constitute a designated public forum, or a limited public forum, or even a nonforum. The program, rather, was not a forum of any sort at all, but the government engaged in its own speech:

> With respect to specialty license plate designs, Texas is not simply managing government property, but instead is engaging in expressive conduct. As we have described, we reach this conclusion based on the historical context, observers' reasonable interpretation of the messages conveyed by Texas specialty plates, and the effective control that the State exerts over the design selection process. Texas's specialty license plate designs "are meant to convey and have the effect of conveying a government message."... They "constitute government speech."

Having reached the conclusion that the Texas specialty plates constituted government speech, the Court rejected the Sons of Confederate Veterans' First Amendment challenge.

Justice Alito, joined by Chief Justice Roberts, and Justices Kennedy and Scalia, dissented. Justice Alito's dissent opened with the lament that "[t]he Court's decision passes off private speech as government speech and, in doing so, establishes a precedent that threatens private speech that government finds displeasing." Justice Alito argued that in First Amendment cases, "the distinction between government speech and private speech is critical." As Justice Alito saw it, the Court's holding that all the privately created messages on the many specialty plates issued by the State of Texas convey a government message could not possibly be correct. He offered this test:

> Here is a test. Suppose you sat by the side of a Texas highway and studied the license plates on the vehicles passing by. You would see, in addition to the standard Texas plates, an impressive array of specialty plates. (There are now more than 350 varieties.) You would likely observe plates that honor numerous colleges and universities. You might see plates bearing the name of a high school, a fraternity or sorority, the Masons, the Knights of Columbus, the Daughters of the American Revolution, a realty company, a favorite soft drink, a favorite burger restaurant, and a favorite NASCAR driver.
>
> As you sat there watching these plates speed by, would you really think that the sentiments reflected in these specialty plates are the views of the State of Texas and not those of the owners of the cars? If a car with a plate that says "Rather Be Golfing" passed by at 8:30 am on a Monday morning, would you think: "This is the official policy of the State—better to golf than to work"? If you did your viewing at the start of the college football season and you saw Texas plates with the names of the University of Texas's out-of-state competitors in upcoming games—Notre Dame, Oklahoma State, the University of Oklahoma, Kansas State, Iowa State—would you assume that the State of Texas was officially (and perhaps treasonously) rooting for the Longhorns' opponents? And when a car zipped by with a plate that reads "NASCAR—24 Jeff Gordon," would you think that Gordon (born in California, raised in Indiana, resides in North Carolina) is the official favorite of the State government?
>
> The Court says that all of these messages are government speech. It is essential that government be able to express its own viewpoint, the Court reminds us, because otherwise, how would it promote its programs, like recycling and vaccinations. So when Texas issues a "Rather Be Golfing" plate, but not a "Rather Be Playing Tennis" or "Rather Be Bowling" plate, it is furthering a state policy to promote golf but not tennis or bowling. And when Texas allows motorists to obtain a Notre Dame license plate but not a University of Southern California plate, it is taking sides in that long-time rivalry.

There is undeniable power to Justice Alito's dissent, and his assertion that the *Walker* Court's capacious interpretation of government speech threatens to take "a large and painful bite out of the First Amendment."

As powerful as Justice Alito's dissenting opinion was, there plainly are times in our constitutional law experience in which realism trumps idealism, and painful experience trumps painstaking application of doctrine. As the observations of Garrett Epps quoted above attest, as a lawyer, one of the co-authors of this Casebook, Rodney Smolla, personally witnessed this power of experience to bend logic and law in the cross-burning case in which he was lead counsel and oral advocate in the Supreme Court, *Virginia v. Black*. That case also involved a pernicious symbol of race hate, the burning cross, and that case also found Justice Thomas on the side of those who thought the state could treat such symbols as outside of normal First Amendment protection.

Matal v. Tam. In *Matal v. Tam*, 137 S. Ct. 1734 (2017), the Supreme Court held that the Patent and Trademark Office's denial of trademark registration to the rock group "The Slants" on the grounds that the term was disparaging to Asian-Americans was a violation of the First Amendment.[27] The Court's opinion, written by Justice Alito, explained that "slants" is a derogatory term for persons of Asian descent, and members of the band were Asian-Americans. "But the band members believe that by taking that slur as the name of their group, they will help to 'reclaim' the term and drain its denigrating force." The Patent and Trademark Office denied the application based on a provision of federal law prohibiting the registration of trademarks that may "disparage . . . or bring . . . into contemp[t] or disrepute" any "persons, living or dead." The government's action, the Court held, offended "a bedrock First Amendment principle: Speech may not be banned on the ground that it expresses ideas that offend."

The Court rejected the argument that trademark registration constitutes "government speech," which is exempt from First Amendment scrutiny. Government could not function if the First Amendment restricted government speech, the Court explained. To impose "a requirement of viewpoint-neutrality on government speech would be paralyzing." When a government entity embarks on a course of action, "it necessarily takes a particular viewpoint and rejects others." The First Amendment "does not require government to maintain viewpoint neutrality when its officers and employees speak about that venture."

Yet while the government speech doctrine is important — government could not function without it — the doctrine is also highly dangerous if misused. As the Court explained:

---

27. Disclosure: One of the co-authors of this Casebook, Rodney Smolla, was the principal drafter and co-lead counsel of an *amicus* brief in the Supreme Court, along with First Amendment attorney Floyd Abrams, arguing on behalf of the Slants and against the Patent and Trademark Office.

But while the government-speech doctrine is important — indeed, essential — it is a doctrine that is susceptible to dangerous misuse. If private speech could be passed off as government speech by simply affixing a government seal of approval, government could silence or muffle the expression of disfavored viewpoints. For this reason, we must exercise great caution before extending our government-speech precedents.

Observing the limited role of the Patent and Trademark Office in scrutinizing trademark applications, the Court determined that it was "far-fetched to suggest that the content of a registered mark is government speech." In the view of the Court, "[i]f the federal registration of a trademark makes the mark government speech, the Federal Government is babbling prodigiously and incoherently." Reviewing its prior government speech decisions, the Court concluded that "[t]rademarks are private, not government, speech."

§ 9.12 Government Funding

Rust v. Sullivan

United States Supreme Court
500 U.S. 173, 111 S. Ct. 1759, 114 L. Ed. 2d 233 (1991)

CHIEF JUSTICE REHNQUIST delivered the opinion of the Court.

These cases concern a facial challenge to Department of Health and Human Services (HHS) regulations which limit the ability of Title X fund recipients to engage in abortion-related activities. . . .

In 1970, Congress enacted Title X of the Public Health Service Act (Act) which provides federal funding for family-planning services. The Act authorizes the Secretary to "make grants to and enter into contracts with public or nonprofit private entities to assist in the establishment and operation of voluntary family planning projects which shall offer a broad range of acceptable and effective family planning methods and services." Grants and contracts under Title X must "be made in accordance with such regulations as the Secretary may promulgate." Section 1008 of the Act, however, provides that "[n]one of the funds appropriated under this subchapter shall be used in programs where abortion is a method of family planning." That restriction was intended to ensure that Title X funds would "be used only to support preventive family planning services, population research, infertility services, and other related medical, informational, and educational activities."

In 1988, the Secretary promulgated new regulations designed to provide "'clear and operational guidance' to grantees about how to preserve the distinction between Title X programs and abortion as a method of family planning." The regulations clarify, through the definition of the term "family planning," that Congress intended Title X funds "to be used only to support preventive family planning services." Accordingly, Title X services are limited to "preconceptional counseling, education, and general reproductive health care," and expressly exclude "pregnancy care (including obstetric or prenatal care)." The regulations "focus the emphasis of the Title X program on its traditional mission: The provision of preventive family planning services specifically designed to enable individuals to determine the number and spacing of their children, while clarifying that pregnant women must be referred to appropriate prenatal care services."

The regulations attach three principal conditions on the grant of federal funds for Title X projects. First, the regulations specify that a "Title X project may not provide counseling concerning the use of abortion as a method of family planning or provide referral for abortion as a method of family planning." Because Title X is limited to preconceptional services, the program does not furnish services related to childbirth. Only in the context of a referral out of the Title X program is a pregnant woman given transitional information. Title X projects must refer every pregnant client "for appropriate prenatal and/or social services by furnishing a list of available providers that promote the welfare of mother and unborn child." The list may not be used indirectly to encourage or promote abortion, "such as by weighing the list of referrals in favor of health care providers which perform abortions, by including on the list of referral providers health care providers whose principal business is the provision of abortions, by excluding available providers who do not provide abortions, or by 'steering' clients to providers who offer abortion as a method of family planning." The Title X project is expressly prohibited from referring a pregnant woman to an abortion provider, even upon specific request. One permissible response to such an inquiry is that "the project does not consider abortion an appropriate method of family planning and therefore does not counsel or refer for abortion."

Second, the regulations broadly prohibit a Title X project from engaging in activities that "encourage, promote or advocate abortion as a method of family planning." Forbidden activities include lobbying for legislation that would increase the availability of abortion as a method of family planning, developing or disseminating materials advocating abortion as a method of family planning, providing speakers to promote abortion as a method of family planning, using legal action to make abortion available in any way as a method of family planning, and paying dues to any group that advocates abortion as a method of family planning as a substantial part of its activities.

Third, the regulations require that Title X projects be organized so that they are "physically and financially separate" from prohibited abortion activities. To be deemed physically and financially separate, "a Title X project must have an objective integrity and independence from prohibited activities. Mere bookkeeping separation of Title X funds from other monies is not sufficient." The regulations provide a list of nonexclusive factors for the Secretary to consider in conducting a case-by-case determination of objective integrity and independence, such as the existence of separate accounting records and separate personnel, and the degree of physical separation of the project from facilities for prohibited activities.

Petitioners are Title X grantees and doctors who supervise Title X funds suing on behalf of themselves and their patients. Respondent is the Secretary of HHS. After the regulations had been promulgated, but before they had been applied, petitioners filed two separate actions, later consolidated, challenging the facial validity of the regulations and seeking declaratory and injunctive relief to prevent implementation of the regulations. Petitioners challenged the regulations on the grounds that they were not authorized by Title X and that they violate the First and Fifth Amendment rights of Title X clients and the First Amendment rights of Title X health providers....

Petitioners contend that the regulations violate the First Amendment by impermissibly discriminating based on viewpoint because they prohibit "all discussion about abortion as a lawful option—including counseling, referral, and the provision of neutral and accurate information about ending a pregnancy—while compelling the clinic or counselor to provide information that promotes continuing a pregnancy to term." They assert that the regulations violate the "free speech rights of private health care organizations that receive Title X funds, of their staff, and of their patients" by impermissibly imposing "viewpoint-discriminatory conditions on government subsidies" and thus "penaliz[e] speech funded with non-Title X monies." Because "Title X continues to fund speech ancillary to pregnancy testing in a manner that is not evenhanded with respect to views and information about abortion, it invidiously discriminates on the basis of viewpoint." Relying on *Regan v. Taxation with Representation of Wash.*, 461 U.S. 540 (1983), and *Arkansas Writers' Project, Inc. v. Ragland*, 481 U.S. 221, 234 (1987), petitioners also assert that while the Government may place certain conditions on the receipt of federal subsidies, it may not "discriminate invidiously in its subsidies in such a way as to 'ai[m] at the suppression of dangerous ideas.'"

There is no question but that the statutory prohibition contained in § 1008 is constitutional. In *Maher v. Roe*, 432 U.S. 464 (1977), we upheld a state welfare regulation under which Medicaid recipients received payments for services related to childbirth, but not for nontherapeutic abortions. The Court rejected the claim that this unequal subsidization worked a violation of the Constitution. We held that the government may "make a value judgment favoring childbirth over abortion, and ... implement that judgment by the allocation of public funds." Here the Government is exercising the authority it possesses under *Maher* and *Harris v. McRae*, 448 U.S. 917 (1980), to subsidize family planning services which will lead to conception and childbirth, and declining to "promote or encourage abortion." The Government can, without violating the Constitution, selectively fund a program to encourage certain activities it believes to be in the public interest, without at the same time funding an alternative program which seeks to deal with the problem in another way. In so doing, the Government has not discriminated on the basis of viewpoint; it has merely chosen to fund one activity to the exclusion of the other. "[A] legislature's decision not to subsidize the exercise of a fundamental right does not infringe the right." "A refusal to fund protected activity, without more, cannot be equated with the imposition of a 'penalty' on that activity." "There is a basic difference between direct state interference with a protected activity and state encouragement of an alternative activity consonant with legislative policy."

The challenged regulations implement the statutory prohibition by prohibiting counseling, referral, and the provision of information regarding abortion as a method of family planning. They are designed to ensure that the limits of the federal program are observed. The Title X program is designed not for prenatal care, but to encourage family planning. A doctor who wished to offer prenatal care to a project patient who became pregnant could properly be prohibited from doing so because such service is outside the scope of the federally funded program. The regulations prohibiting abortion counseling and referral are of the same ilk; "no funds appropriated for the project may be used in programs where abortion is a method of family planning," and a doctor employed by the project may be prohibited in the course of his project duties from counseling abortion or referring for abortion. This is not a case of the Government "suppressing a dangerous idea," but of a prohibition on a project grantee or its employees from engaging in activities outside of the project's scope.

To hold that the Government unconstitutionally discriminates on the basis of viewpoint when it chooses to fund a program dedicated to advance certain permissible goals, because the program in advancing those goals necessarily discourages alternative goals, would render numerous Government programs constitutionally suspect. When Congress established a National Endowment for Democracy to encourage other countries to adopt democratic principles, it was not constitutionally required to fund a program to encourage competing lines of political philosophy such as communism and fascism. Petitioners' assertions ultimately boil down to the position that if the government chooses to subsidize one protected right, it must subsidize analogous counterpart rights. But the Court has soundly rejected that proposition. Within far broader limits than petitioners are willing to concede, when the Government appropriates public funds to establish a program it is entitled to define the limits of that program.

Petitioners' reliance on these cases is unavailing, however, because here the Government is not denying a benefit to anyone, but is instead simply insisting that public funds be spent for the purposes for which they were authorized. The Secretary's regulations do not force the Title X grantee to give up abortion-related speech; they merely require that the grantee keep such activities separate and distinct from Title X activities. Title X expressly distinguishes between a Title X grantee and a Title X project. The grantee, which normally is a health-care organization, may receive funds from a variety of sources for a variety of purposes. The grantee receives Title X funds, however, for the specific and limited purpose of establishing and operating a Title X project. The regulations govern the scope of the Title X project's activities, and leave the grantee unfettered in its other activities. The Title X grantee can continue to perform abortions, provide abortion-related services, and engage in abortion advocacy; it simply is required to conduct those activities through programs that are separate and independent from the project that receives Title X funds.

In contrast, our "unconstitutional conditions" cases involve situations in which the Government has placed a condition on the recipient of the subsidy rather than on a particular program or service, thus effectively prohibiting the recipient from engaging in the protected conduct outside the scope of the federally funded program. In *FCC v. League of Women Voters of Cal.*, we invalidated a federal law providing that noncommercial television and radio stations that receive federal grants may not "engage in editorializing." Under that law, a recipient of federal funds was "barred absolutely from all editorializing" because it "is not able to segregate its activities according to the source of its funding" and thus "has no way of limiting the use of its federal funds to all noneditorializing activities." The effect of the law was that "a noncommercial educational station that receives only 1% of its overall income from [federal] grants is barred absolutely from all editorializing" and "barred from using even wholly private funds to finance its editorial activity." We expressly recognized, however, that were Congress to permit the recipient stations to "establish 'affiliate' organizations which could then use the station's facilities to editorialize with nonfederal funds, such a statutory mechanism would plainly be valid." Such a scheme would permit the station "to make known its views on matters of public importance through its nonfederally funded, editorializing affiliate without losing federal grants for its noneditorializing broadcast activities."

Similarly, in *Regan* we held that Congress could, in the exercise of its spending power, reasonably refuse to subsidize the lobbying activities of tax-exempt charitable organizations by prohibiting such organizations from using tax-deductible contributions to support their lobbying efforts. In so holding, we explained that such organizations remained free "to receive deductible contributions to support . . . nonlobbying activit[ies]." Thus, a charitable organization could create, under . . . the Internal Revenue Code of 1954 . . . an affiliate to conduct its nonlobbying activities using tax-deductible contributions, and at the same time establish . . . a separate affiliate to pursue its lobbying efforts without such contributions. Given that alternative, the Court concluded that "Congress has not infringed any First Amendment rights or regulated any First Amendment activity[; it] has simply chosen not to pay for [appellee's] lobbying." We also noted that appellee "would, of course, have to ensure that the § 501(c)(3) organization did not subsidize the § 501(c)(4) organization; otherwise, public funds might be spent on an activity Congress chose not to subsidize." The condition that federal funds will be used only to further the purposes of a grant does not violate constitutional rights. "Congress could, for example, grant funds to an organization dedicated to combating teenage drug abuse, but condition the grant by providing that none of the money received from Congress should be used to lobby state legislatures."

By requiring that the Title X grantee engage in abortion-related activity separately from activity receiving federal funding, Congress has, consistent with our teachings in *League of Women Voters* and *Regan*, not denied it the right to engage in abortion-related activities. Congress has merely refused to fund such activities out of the public fisc, and the Secretary has simply required a certain degree of separation from the Title X project in order to ensure the integrity of the federally funded program.

The same principles apply to petitioners' claim that the regulations abridge the free speech rights of the grantee's staff. Individuals who are voluntarily employed for a Title X project must perform their duties in accordance with the regulation's restrictions on abortion counseling and referral. The employees remain free, however, to pursue abortion-related activities when they are not acting under the auspices of the Title X project. The regulations, which govern solely the scope of the Title X project's activities, do not in any way restrict the activities of those persons acting as private individuals. The employees' freedom of expression is limited during the time that they actually work for the project; but this limitation is a consequence of their decision to accept employment in a project, the scope of which is permissibly restricted by the funding authority.

This is not to suggest that funding by the Government, even when coupled with the freedom of the fund recipients to speak outside the scope of the Government-funded project, is invariably sufficient to justify Government control over the content of expression. For example, this Court has recognized that the existence of a Government "subsidy," in the form of Government-owned property, does not justify the restriction of speech in areas that have "been traditionally open to the public for expressive activity," . . . Similarly, we have recognized that the university is a traditional sphere of free expression so fundamental to the functioning of our society that the Government's ability to control speech within that sphere by means of conditions attached to the expenditure of Government funds is restricted by the vagueness and overbreadth doctrines of the First Amendment. It could be argued by analogy that traditional relationships such as that between doctor and patient should enjoy protection under the First Amendment from Government regulation, even when subsidized by the Government. We need not resolve that question here, however, because the Title X program regulations do not significantly impinge upon the doctor-patient relationship. Nothing in them requires a doctor to represent as his own any opinion that he does not in fact hold. Nor is the doctor-patient relationship established by the Title X program sufficiently all encompassing so as to justify an expectation on the part of the patient of comprehensive medical advice. The program does not provide post conception medical care, and therefore a doctor's silence with regard to abortion cannot reasonably be thought to mislead a client into thinking that the doctor does not consider abortion an appropriate option for her. The doctor is always free to make clear that advice regarding abortion is simply beyond the scope of the program. In these circumstances, the general rule that the Government may choose not to subsidize speech applies with full force. . . .

Affirmed.

JUSTICE BLACKMUN, with whom JUSTICE MARSHALL joins, with whom JUSTICE STEVENS joins as to Parts II and III, and with whom JUSTICE O'CONNOR joins as to Part I, dissenting.

Until today, the Court never has upheld viewpoint-based suppression of speech simply because that suppression was a condition upon the acceptance of public funds. Whatever may be the Government's power to condition the receipt of its largess upon the relinquishment of constitutional rights, it surely does not extend to a condition that suppresses the recipient's cherished freedom of speech based solely upon the content or viewpoint of that speech. . . .

Nothing in the Court's opinion in *Regan v. Taxation with Representation of Washington* can be said to challenge this long-settled understanding. In *Regan*, the Court upheld a content-neutral provision of the Internal Revenue Code that disallowed a particular tax-exempt status to organizations that "attempt[ed] to influence legislation," while affording such status to veterans' organizations irrespective of their lobbying activities. Finding the case controlled by *Cammarano*, the Court explained: "The case would be different if Congress were to discriminate invidiously in its subsidies in such a way as to 'ai[m] at the suppression of dangerous ideas.' . . . We find no indication that the statute was intended to suppress any ideas or any demonstration that it has had that effect." . . .

It cannot seriously be disputed that the counseling and referral provisions at issue in the present cases constitute content-based regulation of speech. Title X grantees may provide counseling and referral regarding any of a wide range of family planning and other topics, save abortion.

The regulations are also clearly viewpoint based. While suppressing speech favorable to abortion with one hand, the Secretary compels antiabortion speech with the other. For example, the Department of Health and Human Services' own description of the regulations makes plain that "Title X projects are required to facilitate access to prenatal care and social services, including adoption services, that might be needed by the pregnant client to promote her well-being and that of her child, while making it abundantly clear that the project is not permitted to promote abortion by facilitating access to abortion through the referral process."

. . . .

In the cases at bar, the speaker's interest in the communication is both clear and vital. In addressing the family-planning needs of their clients, the physicians and counselors who staff Title X projects seek to provide them with the full range of information and options regarding their health and reproductive freedom. Indeed, the legitimate expectations of the patient and the ethical responsibilities of the medical profession demand no less. "The patient's right of self-decision can be effectively exercised only if the patient possesses enough information to enable an intelligent choice. . . . The physician has an ethical obligation to help the patient make choices from among the therapeutic alternatives consistent with good medical practice." . . .

Finally, it is of no small significance that the speech the Secretary would suppress is truthful information regarding constitutionally protected conduct of vital importance to the listener. One can imagine no legitimate governmental interest that might be served by suppressing such information. Concededly, the abortion debate is among the most divisive and contentious issues that our Nation has faced in recent years. "But freedom to differ is not limited to things that do not matter much. That would be a mere shadow of freedom. The test of its substance is the right to differ as to things that touch the heart of the existing order." . . .

Rosenberger v. Rector and Visitors of University of Virginia

United States Supreme Court
515 U.S. 819, 115 S. Ct. 2510, 132 L. Ed. 2d 700 (1995)

JUSTICE KENNEDY delivered the opinion of the Court.

The University of Virginia, an instrumentality of the Commonwealth for which it is named and thus bound by the First and Fourteenth Amendments, authorizes the payment of outside contractors for the printing costs of a variety of student publications. It withheld any authorization for payments on behalf of petitioners for the sole reason that their student paper "primarily promotes or manifests a particular belie[f] in or about a deity or an ultimate reality." That the paper did promote or manifest views within the defined exclusion seems plain enough. The challenge is to the University's regulation and its denial of authorization, the case raising issues under the Speech and Establishment Clauses of the First Amendment.

Petitioners' organization, Wide Awake Productions (WAP), qualified as a CIO. Formed by petitioner Ronald Rosenberger and other undergraduates in 1990, WAP was established "[t]o publish a magazine of philosophical and religious expression," "[t]o facilitate discussion which fosters an atmosphere of sensitivity to and tolerance of Christian viewpoints," and "[t]o provide a unifying focus for Christians of multicultural backgrounds." WAP publishes Wide Awake: A Christian Perspective at the University of Virginia.

A few months after being given CIO status, WAP requested the SAF to pay its printer $5,862 for the costs of printing its newspaper. The Appropriations Committee of the Student Council denied WAP's request on the ground that Wide Awake was a "religious activity" within the meaning of the Guidelines, i.e., that the newspaper promoted or manifested a particular belief in or about a deity or an ultimate reality

The necessities of confining a forum to the limited and legitimate purposes for which it was created may justify the State in reserving it for certain groups or for the discussion of certain topics. Once it has opened a limited forum, however, the State must respect the lawful boundaries it has itself set.

The SAF is a forum more in a metaphysical than in a spatial or geographic sense, but the same principles are applicable.

The University does acknowledge (as it must in light of our precedents) that "ideologically driven attempts to suppress a particular point of view are presumptively unconstitutional in funding, as in other contexts," but insists that this case does not present that issue because the Guidelines draw lines based on content, not viewpoint. As we have noted, discrimination against one set of views or ideas is but a subset or particular instance of the more general phenomenon of content discrimination. And, it must be acknowledged, the distinction is not a precise one. It is, in a sense, something of an understatement to speak of religious thought and discussion as just a viewpoint, as distinct from a comprehensive body of thought. The nature of our origins and destiny and their dependence upon the existence of a divine being have been subjects of philosophic inquiry throughout human history. We conclude, nonetheless, that here, as in *Lamb's Chapel*, viewpoint discrimination is the proper way to interpret the University's objections to Wide Awake. By the very terms of the SAF prohibition, the University does not exclude religion as a subject matter but selects for disfavored treatment those student journalistic efforts with religious editorial viewpoints. Religion may be a vast area of inquiry, but it also provides, as it did here, a specific premise, a perspective, a standpoint from which a variety of subjects may be discussed and considered. The prohibited perspective, not the general subject matter, resulted in the refusal to make third-party payments, for the subjects discussed were otherwise within the approved category of publications....

The University urges that, from a constitutional standpoint, funding of speech differs from provision of access to facilities because money is scarce and physical facilities are not. Beyond the fact that in any given case this proposition might not be true as an empirical matter, the underlying premise that the University could discriminate based on viewpoint if demand for space exceeded its availability is wrong as well. The government cannot justify viewpoint discrimination among private speakers on the economic fact of scarcity. Had the meeting rooms in *Lamb's Chapel* been scarce, had the demand been greater than the supply, our decision would have been no different. It would have been incumbent on the State, of course, to ration or allocate the scarce resources on some acceptable neutral principle; but nothing in our decision indicated that scarcity would give the State the right to exercise viewpoint discrimination that is otherwise impermissible.

Vital First Amendment speech principles are at stake here. The first danger to liberty lies in granting the State the power to examine publications to determine whether or not they are based on some ultimate idea and if so for the State to classify them. The second, and corollary, danger is to speech from the chilling of individual thought and expression. That danger is especially real in the University setting, where the State acts against a background and tradition of thought and experiment that is at the center of our intellectual and philosophic tradition. *See Healy v. James*, 408 U.S. 169, 180–181 (1972); *Keyishian v. Board of Regents, State Univ. of N.Y.*, 385 U.S. 589, 603 (1967); *Sweezy v. New Hampshire*, 354 U.S. 234, 250 (1957). In ancient Athens, and, as Europe entered into a new period of intellectual awakening, in places like Bologna, Oxford, and Paris, universities began as voluntary and spontaneous assemblages or concourses for students to speak and to write and to learn. *See generally* R. Palmer & J. Colton, *A History of the Modern World* 39 (7th ed. 1992). The quality and creative power of student intellectual life to this day remains a vital measure of a school's influence and attainment. For the University, by regulation, to cast disapproval on particular viewpoints of its students risks the suppression of free speech and creative inquiry in one of the vital centers for the nation's intellectual life, its college and university campuses. . . .

Before its brief on the merits in this Court, the University had argued at all stages of the litigation that inclusion of WAP's contractors in SAF funding authorization would violate the Establishment Clause. . . .

A central lesson of our decisions is that a significant factor in upholding governmental programs in the face of Establishment Clause attack is their neutrality towards religion.

The governmental program here is neutral toward religion. There is no suggestion that the University created it to advance religion or adopted some ingenious device with the purpose of aiding a religious cause. The object of the SAF is to open a forum for speech and to support various student enterprises, including the publication of newspapers, in recognition of the diversity and creativity of student life. The University's SAF Guidelines have a separate classification for, and do not make third-party payments on behalf of, "religious organizations," which are those "whose purpose is to practice a devotion to an acknowledged ultimate reality or deity." The category of support here is for "student news, information, opinion, entertainment, or academic communications media groups," of which Wide Awake was 1 of 15 in the 1990 school year. WAP did not seek a subsidy because of its Christian editorial viewpoint; it sought funding as a student journal, which it was.

The neutrality of the program distinguishes the student fees from a tax levied for the direct support of a church or group of churches. A tax of that sort, of course, would run contrary to Establishment Clause concerns dating from the earliest days of the Republic. The apprehensions of our predecessors involved the levying of taxes upon the public for the sole and exclusive purpose of establishing and supporting specific sects. The exaction here, by contrast, is a student activity fee designed to reflect the reality that student life in its many dimensions includes the necessity of wide-ranging speech and inquiry and that student expression is an integral part of the University's educational mission. This is a far cry from a general public assessment designed and effected to provide financial support for a church.

Government neutrality is apparent in the State's overall scheme in a further meaningful respect. The program respects the critical difference "between government speech endorsing religion, which the Establishment Clause forbids, and private speech endorsing religion, which the Free Speech and Free Exercise Clauses protect." In this case, "the government has not willfully fostered or encouraged" any mistaken impression that the student newspapers speak for the University. The University has taken pains to disassociate itself from the private speech involved in this case. The Court of Appeals' apparent concern that Wide Awake's religious orientation would be attributed to the University is not a plausible fear, and there is no real likelihood that the speech in question is being either endorsed or coerced by the State. . . .

To obey the Establishment Clause, it was not necessary for the University to deny eligibility to student publications because of their viewpoint. The neutrality commanded of the State by the separate Clauses of the First Amendment was compromised by the University's course of action. The viewpoint discrimination inherent in the University's regulation required public officials to scan and interpret student publications to discern their underlying philosophic assumptions respecting religious theory and belief. That course of action was a denial of the right of free speech and would risk fostering a pervasive bias or hostility to religion, which could undermine the very neutrality the Establishment Clause requires. There is no Establishment Clause violation in the University's honoring its duties under the Free Speech Clause.

The judgment of the Court of Appeals must be, and is, *reversed*.

JUSTICE SOUTER, with whom JUSTICE STEVENS, JUSTICE GINSBURG and JUSTICE BREYER join, dissenting.

The Court today, for the first time, approves direct funding of core religious activities by an arm of the State. It does so, however, only after erroneous treatment of some familiar principles of law implementing the First Amendment's Establishment and Speech Clauses, and by viewing the very funds in question as beyond the reach of the Establishment Clause's funding restrictions as such. Because there is no warrant for distinguishing among public funding sources for purposes of applying the First Amendment's prohibition of religious establishment, I would hold that the University's refusal to support petitioners' religious activities is compelled by the Establishment Clause. I would therefore affirm.

Legal Services Corporation v. Valezquez

United States Supreme Court
531 U.S. 533, 121 S. Ct. 1043, 149 L. Ed. 2d 63 (2001)

JUSTICE KENNEDY delivered the opinion of the Court.

In 1974, Congress enacted the Legal Services Corporation Act, 88 Stat. 378, 42 U.S.C. § 2996 et seq. The Act establishes the Legal Services Corporation (LSC) as a District of Columbia nonprofit corporation. LSC's mission is to distribute funds appropriated by Congress to eligible local grantee organizations "for the purpose of providing financial support for legal assistance in noncriminal proceedings or matters to persons financially unable to afford legal assistance."

LSC grantees consist of hundreds of local organizations governed, in the typical case, by local boards of directors. In many instances the grantees are funded by a combination of LSC funds and other public or private sources. The grantee organizations hire and supervise lawyers to provide free legal assistance to indigent clients. Each year LSC appropriates funds to grantees or recipients that hire and supervise lawyers for various professional activities, including representation of indigent clients seeking welfare benefits.

This suit requires us to decide whether one of the conditions imposed by Congress on the use of LSC funds violates the First Amendment rights of LSC grantees and their clients. For purposes of our decision, the restriction, to be quoted in further detail, prohibits legal representation funded by recipients of LSC moneys if the representation involves an effort to amend or otherwise challenge existing welfare law. As interpreted by the LSC and by the Government, the restriction prevents an attorney from arguing to a court that a state statute conflicts with a federal statute or that either a state or federal statute by its terms or in its application is violative of the United States Constitution.

Lawyers employed by New York City LSC grantees, together with private LSC contributors, LSC indigent clients, and various state and local public officials whose governments contribute to LSC grantees, brought suit in the United States District Court for the Southern District of New York to declare the restriction, among other provisions of the Act, invalid. . . . We agree that the restriction violates the First Amendment, and we affirm the judgment of the Court of Appeals.

I

From the inception of the LSC, Congress has placed restrictions on its use of funds. For instance, the LSC Act prohibits recipients from making available LSC funds, program personnel, or equipment to any political party, to any political campaign, or for use in "advocating or opposing any ballot measures." . . . The Act further proscribes use of funds in most criminal proceedings and in litigation involving nontherapeutic abortions, secondary school desegregation, military desertion, or violations of the Selective Service statute. Fund recipients are barred from bringing class-action suits unless express approval is obtained from LSC.

The restrictions at issue were part of a compromise set of restrictions enacted in the Omnibus Consolidated Rescissions and Appropriations Act of 1996, and continued in each subsequent annual appropriations Act. The relevant portion of § 504(a)(16) prohibits funding of any organization

> that initiates legal representation or participates in any other way, in litigation, lobbying, or rulemaking, involving an effort to reform a Federal or State welfare system, except that this paragraph shall not be construed to preclude a recipient from representing an individual eligible client who is seeking specific relief from a welfare agency if such relief does not involve an effort to amend or otherwise challenge existing law in effect on the date of the initiation of the representation.

The prohibitions apply to all of the activities of an LSC grantee, including those paid for by non-LSC funds. We are concerned with the statutory provision which excludes LSC representation in cases which "involve an effort to amend or otherwise challenge existing law in effect on the date of the initiation of the representation." . . .

II

The United States and LSC rely on *Rust v. Sullivan* as support for the LSC program restrictions. . . .

We upheld the law [in *Rust*] reasoning that Congress had not discriminated against viewpoints on abortion, but had "merely chosen to fund one activity to the exclusion of the other." . . . The Court in *Rust* did not place explicit reliance on the rationale that the counseling activities of the doctors under Title X amounted to governmental speech; when interpreting the holding in later cases, however, we have explained *Rust* on this understanding. We have said that viewpoint-based funding decisions can be sustained in instances in which the government is itself the speaker, see *Board of Regents of Univ. of Wis. System v. Southworth* [529 U.S. 217 (2000)] . . . or instances, like *Rust*, in which the government "used private speakers to transmit information pertaining to its own program." *Rosenberger v. Rector and Visitors of Univ. of Va.* [515 U.S. 819 (1995)]. . . .

Neither the latitude for government speech nor its rationale applies to subsidies for private speech in every instance, however. As we have pointed out, "[i]t does not follow . . . that viewpoint-based restrictions are proper when the [government] does not itself speak or subsidize transmittal of a message it favors but instead expends funds to encourage a diversity of views from private speakers."

Although the LSC program differs from the program at issue in *Rosenberger* in that its purpose is not to "encourage a diversity of views," the salient point is that, like the program in *Rosenberger*, the LSC program was designed to facilitate private speech, not to promote a governmental message. Congress funded LSC grantees to provide attorneys to represent the interests of indigent clients. In the specific context of § 504(a)(16) suits for benefits, an LSC funded attorney speaks on the behalf of the client in a claim against the government for welfare benefits. The lawyer is not the government's speaker. The attorney defending the decision to deny benefits will deliver the government's message in the litigation. The LSC lawyer, however, speaks on the behalf of his or her private, indigent client. . . .

The Government has designed this program to use the legal profession and the established Judiciary of the States and the Federal Government to accomplish its end of assisting welfare claimants in determination or receipt of their benefits. The advice from the attorney to the client and the advocacy by the attorney to the courts cannot be classified as governmental speech even under a generous understanding of the concept. In this vital respect this suit is distinguishable from *Rust*.

The private nature of the speech involved here, and the extent of LSC's regulation of private expression, are indicated further by the circumstance that the Government seeks to use an existing medium of expression and to control it, in a class of cases, in ways which distort its usual functioning. Where the government uses or attempts to regulate a particular medium, we have been informed by its accepted usage in determining whether a particular restriction on speech is necessary for the program's purposes and limitations. In *FCC v. League of Women Voters of Cal.*, the

Court was instructed by its understanding of the dynamics of the broadcast industry in holding that prohibitions against editorializing by public radio networks were an impermissible restriction, even though the Government enacted the restriction to control the use of public funds. The First Amendment forbade the Government from using the forum in an unconventional way to suppress speech inherent in the nature of the medium. In *Arkansas Ed. Television Comm'n v. Forbes*, [481 U.S. 221 (1987),] the dynamics of the broadcasting system gave station programmers the right to use editorial judgment to exclude certain speech so that the broadcast message could be more effective. And in *Rosenberger*, the fact that student newspapers expressed many different points of view was an important foundation for the Court's decision to invalidate viewpoint-based restrictions.

When the government creates a limited forum for speech, certain restrictions may be necessary to define the limits and purposes of the program. . . . The same is true when the government establishes a subsidy for specified ends. . . . As this suit involves a subsidy, limited forum cases such as *Perry*, *Lamb's Chapel* and *Rosenberger* may not be controlling in a strict sense, yet they do provide some instruction. Here the program presumes that private, nongovernmental speech is necessary, and a substantial restriction is placed upon that speech. At oral argument and in its briefs the LSC advised us that lawyers funded in the Government program may not undertake representation in suits for benefits if they must advise clients respecting the questionable validity of a statute which defines benefit eligibility and the payment structure. The limitation forecloses advice or legal assistance to question the validity of statutes under the Constitution of the United States. It extends further, it must be noted, so that state statutes inconsistent with federal law under the Supremacy Clause may be neither challenged nor questioned.

By providing subsidies to LSC, the Government seeks to facilitate suits for benefits by using the State and Federal courts and the independent bar on which those courts depend for the proper performance of their duties and responsibilities. Restricting LSC attorneys in advising their clients and in presenting arguments and analyses to the courts distorts the legal system by altering the traditional role of the attorneys in much the same way broadcast systems or student publication networks were changed in the limited forum cases we have cited. Just as government in those cases could not elect to use a broadcasting network or a college publication structure in a regime which prohibits speech necessary to the proper functioning of those systems, . . . it may not design a subsidy to effect this serious and fundamental restriction on advocacy of attorneys and the functioning of the judiciary.

LSC has advised us, furthermore, that upon determining a question of statutory validity is present in any anticipated or pending case or controversy, the LSC-funded attorney must cease the representation at once. This is true whether the validity issue becomes apparent during initial attorney-client consultations or in the midst of litigation proceedings. A disturbing example of the restriction was discussed during oral argument before the Court. It is well understood that when there are two reasonable constructions for a statute, yet one raises a constitutional question, the

Court should prefer the interpretation which avoids the constitutional issue. . . . Yet, as the LSC advised the Court, if, during litigation, a judge were to ask an LSC attorney whether there was a constitutional concern, the LSC attorney simply could not answer.

Interpretation of the law and the Constitution is the primary mission of the judiciary when it acts within the sphere of its authority to resolve a case or controversy. *Marbury v. Madison* ("It is emphatically the province and the duty of the judicial department to say what the law is"). An informed, independent judiciary presumes an informed, independent bar. Under § 504(a)(16), however, cases would be presented by LSC attorneys who could not advise the courts of serious questions of statutory validity. The disability is inconsistent with the proposition that attorneys should present all the reasonable and well-grounded arguments necessary for proper resolution of the case. By seeking to prohibit the analysis of certain legal issues and to truncate presentation to the courts, the enactment under review prohibits speech and expression upon which courts must depend for the proper exercise of the judicial power. Congress cannot wrest the law from the Constitution which is its source. "Those then who controvert the principle that the constitution is to be considered, in court, as a paramount law, are reduced to the necessity of maintaining that courts must close their eyes on the constitution, and see only the law."

The restriction imposed by the statute here threatens severe impairment of the judicial function. Section 504(a)(16) sifts out cases presenting constitutional challenges in order to insulate the Government's laws from judicial inquiry. If the restriction on speech and legal advice were to stand, the result would be two tiers of cases. In cases where LSC counsel were attorneys of record, there would be lingering doubt whether the truncated representation had resulted in complete analysis of the case, full advice to the client, and proper presentation to the court. The courts and the public would come to question the adequacy and fairness of professional representations when the attorney, either consciously to comply with this statute or unconsciously to continue the representation despite the statute, avoided all reference to questions of statutory validity and constitutional authority. A scheme so inconsistent with accepted separation-of-powers principles is an insufficient basis to sustain or uphold the restriction on speech.

It is no answer to say the restriction on speech is harmless because, under LSC's interpretation of the Act, its attorneys can withdraw. This misses the point. The statute is an attempt to draw lines around the LSC program to exclude from litigation those arguments and theories Congress finds unacceptable but which by their nature are within the province of the courts to consider.

The restriction on speech is even more problematic because in cases where the attorney withdraws from a representation, the client is unlikely to find other counsel. The explicit premise for providing LSC attorneys is the necessity to make available representation "to persons financially unable to afford legal assistance." There often will be no alternative source for the client to receive vital information respecting constitutional and statutory rights bearing upon claimed benefits. Thus, with respect to the litigation services Congress has funded, there is no alternative channel for expression of the advocacy Congress seeks to restrict. This is in stark contrast to *Rust*. There, a patient could receive the approved Title X family planning counseling funded by the Government and later could consult an affiliate or independent organization to receive abortion counseling. Unlike indigent clients who seek LSC representation, the patient in *Rust* was not required to forfeit the Government-funded advice when she also received abortion counseling through alternative channels. Because LSC attorneys must withdraw whenever a question of a welfare statute's validity arises, an individual could not obtain joint representation so that the constitutional challenge would be presented by a non-LSC attorney, and other, permitted, arguments advanced by LSC counsel.

Finally, LSC and the Government maintain that § 504(a)(16) is necessary to define the scope and contours of the federal program, a condition that ensures funds can be spent for those cases most immediate to congressional concern. In support of this contention, they suggest the challenged limitation takes into account the nature of the grantees' activities and provides limited congressional funds for the provision of simple suits for benefits. In petitioners' view, the restriction operates neither to maintain the current welfare system nor insulate it from attack; rather, it helps the current welfare system function in a more efficient and fair manner by removing from the program complex challenges to existing welfare laws.

The effect of the restriction, however, is to prohibit advice or argumentation that existing welfare laws are unconstitutional or unlawful. Congress cannot recast a condition on funding as a mere definition of its program in every case, lest the First Amendment be reduced to a simple semantic exercise. Here, notwithstanding Congress' purpose to confine and limit its program, the restriction operates to insulate current welfare laws from constitutional scrutiny and certain other legal challenges, a condition implicating central First Amendment concerns. In no lawsuit funded by the Government can the LSC attorney, speaking on behalf of a private client, challenge existing welfare laws. As a result, arguments by indigent clients that a welfare statute is unlawful or unconstitutional cannot be expressed in this Government-funded program for petitioning the courts, even though the program was created for litigation involving welfare benefits, and even though the ordinary course of litigation involves the expression of theories and postulates on both, or multiple, sides of an issue.

It is fundamental that the First Amendment "was fashioned to assure unfettered interchange of ideas for the bringing about of political and social changes desired by the people." *New York Times Co. v. Sullivan. . . .* There can be little doubt that the LSC Act funds constitutionally protected expression; and in the context of this statute there is no programmatic message of the kind recognized in *Rust* and which sufficed there to allow the Government to specify the advice deemed necessary for its legitimate objectives. This serves to distinguish § 504(a)(16) from any of the Title X program restrictions upheld in *Rust*, and to place it beyond any congressional funding condition approved in the past by this Court.

Congress was not required to fund an LSC attorney to represent indigent clients; and when it did so, it was not required to fund the whole range of legal representations or relationships. The LSC and the United States, however, in effect ask us to permit Congress to define the scope of the litigation it funds to exclude certain vital theories and ideas. The attempted restriction is designed to insulate the Government's interpretation of the Constitution from judicial challenge. The Constitution does not permit the Government to confine litigants and their attorneys in this manner.

We must be vigilant when Congress imposes rules and conditions which in effect insulate its own laws from legitimate judicial challenge. Where private speech is involved, even Congress' antecedent funding decision cannot be aimed at the suppression of ideas thought inimical to the Government's own interest.

For the reasons we have set forth, the funding condition is invalid. . . .

The judgment of the Court of Appeals is *Affirmed*.

JUSTICE SCALIA, with whom THE CHIEF JUSTICE, JUSTICE O'CONNOR, and JUSTICE THOMAS join, dissenting.

The LSC Act is a federal subsidy program, not a federal regulatory program, and "[t]here is a basic difference between [the two]." *Maher v. Roe*, 432 U.S. 464, 475 (1977). Regulations directly restrict speech; subsidies do not. Subsidies, it is true, may indirectly abridge speech, but only if the funding scheme is "'manipulated' to have a 'coercive effect'" on those who do not hold the subsidized position. . . . Proving unconstitutional coercion is difficult enough when the spending program has universal coverage and excludes only certain speech — such as a tax exemption scheme excluding lobbying expenses. The Court has found such programs unconstitutional only when the exclusion was "aimed at the suppression of dangerous ideas." . . . Proving the requisite coercion is harder still when a spending program is not universal but limited, providing benefits to a restricted number of recipients. . . . The Court has found such selective spending unconstitutionally coercive only once, when the government created a public forum with the spending program but then discriminated in distributing funding within the forum on the basis of viewpoint. . . . When the limited spending program does not create a public forum, proving coercion is virtually impossible, because simply denying a subsidy "does not 'coerce' belief," *Lyng v. Automobile Workers*, 485 U.S. 360, 369 (1988), and because the criterion of unconstitutionality is whether denial of the subsidy threatens "to drive certain ideas or viewpoints from the marketplace. . . . Absent such a threat, "the Government may allocate . . . funding according to criteria that would be impermissible were direct regulation of speech or a criminal penalty at stake." . . .

. . . The LSC Act, like the scheme in *Rust*, . . . does not create a public forum. Far from encouraging a diversity of views, it has always, as the Court accurately states, "placed restrictions on its use of funds". . . . Nor does §504(a)(16) discriminate on the basis of viewpoint, since it funds neither challenges to nor defenses of existing welfare law. The provision simply declines to subsidize a certain class of litigation . . . *Rust* thus controls these cases and compels the conclusion that § 504(a)(16) is constitutional.

The Court contends that *Rust* is different because the program at issue subsidized government speech, while the LSC funds private speech. . . . This is so unpersuasive it hardly needs response. If the private doctors' confidential advice to their patients at issue in *Rust* constituted "government speech," it is hard to imagine what subsidized speech would not be government speech. Moreover, the majority's contention that the subsidized speech in these cases is not government speech because the lawyers have a professional obligation to represent the interests of their clients founders on the reality that the doctors in *Rust* had a professional obligation to serve the interests of their patients. . . . Even respondents agree that "the true speaker in *Rust* was not the government, but a doctor."

The Court further asserts that these cases are different from *Rust* because the welfare funding restriction "seeks to use an existing medium of expression and to control it . . . in ways which distort its usual functioning." This is wrong on both the facts and the law. It is wrong on the law because there is utterly no precedent for the novel and facially implausible proposition that the First Amendment has anything to do with government funding that—though it does not actually abridge anyone's speech—"distorts an existing medium of expression." None of the three cases cited by the Court mentions such an odd principle. . . .

The only conceivable argument that can be made for distinguishing *Rust* is that there even patients who wished to receive abortion counseling could receive the nonabortion services that the Government-funded clinic offered, whereas here some potential LSC clients who wish to receive representation on a benefits claim that does not challenge the statutes will be unable to do so because their cases raise a reform claim that an LSC lawyer may not present. This difference, of course, is required by the same ethical canons that the Court elsewhere does not wish to distort. Rather than sponsor "truncated representation," Congress chose to subsidize only those cases in which the attorneys it subsidized could work freely. . . . And it is impossible to see how this difference from *Rust* has any bearing upon the First Amendment question, which, to repeat, is whether the funding scheme is "'manipulated' to have a 'coercive effect'" on those who do not hold the subsidized position. . . . It could be claimed to have such an effect if the client in a case ineligible for LSC representation could eliminate the ineligibility by waiving the claim that the statute is invalid; but he cannot. No conceivable coercive effect exists.

This has been a very long discussion to make a point that is embarrassingly simple: The LSC subsidy neither prevents anyone from speaking nor coerces anyone to change speech, and is indistinguishable in all relevant respects from the subsidy upheld in *Rust*. . . .

I respectfully dissent.

§ 9.13 Government Employees

A. Discipline Against Employees

Pickering v. Board of Education. In *Pickering v. Board of Education*, 391 U.S. (1968), the Court dealt with the question of whether a school board may constitutionally dismiss a high school teacher for openly criticizing the Board of Education on its allocation of funds between the school's athletic programs and its academic programs. Rather than treat the letter as an act of insubordination deserving a stiff disciplinary response, the Court held that this was a case of a teacher/citizen speaking out on issues of public concern upon which free and open debate is vital to informed decision making by the electorate, and that the Board's dismissal of the teacher thus violated the First Amendment.

Connick v. Myers. In *Connick v. Myers*, 461 U.S. 138 (1983), the Court dealt with the free speech of employees on matters that it deemed not relating to general discussion of issues of public interest or concern, but to "insubordination" within the hierarchy of the agency. The case involved Harry Connick, the District Attorney for Orleans Parish, Louisiana, and Sheila Myers, an Assistant District Attorney on Connick's staff. A dispute between Connick and Myers arose when Connick tried to transfer Myers to a different section of the criminal court. Myers prepared and distributed to the other assistants in the office a questionnaire concerning office transfer policy, office morale, the need for a grievance committee, their level of confidence in superiors, and whether they felt pressure from their superiors to work in political campaigns. Connick fired Myers, declaring the questionnaire an act of "insubordination." The Supreme Court upheld the termination. Justice White noted that "[f]or most of this century, the unchallenged dogma was that a public employee had no right to object to conditions placed upon the terms of employment — including those which restricted the exercise of constitutional rights." After acknowledging the Holmes position[28] and the persistence of the right/privilege distinction, however, Justice White explicitly rejected the distinction as a legitimate framework for analysis. Yet, Myers lost her case. The Court introduced a dichotomy between speech on matters of "public" concern and speech on matters of "private" concern. "When employee expression cannot be fairly considered as relating to any matter of political, social, or other concern to the community, government officials should enjoy wide latitude in managing their offices, without intrusive oversight by the judiciary in the name of the First Amendment."

Garcetti v. Ceballos. In *Garcetti v. Ceballos*, 547 U.S. 410 (2006), the Supreme Court, in a major elaboration on the First Amendment rules governing the speech of government employees, clarified and extended the principles emanating from its

---

28. Justice White quoted Holmes' opinion while on the Supreme Judicial Court of Massachusetts: "[A policeman] may have a constitutional right to talk politics, but he has no constitutional right to be a policeman." *McAuliffe v. Mayor of New Bedford*, 155 Mass. 216, 220, 29 N.E. 517, 517 (1892).

prior holdings in *Connick* and *Pickering*, holding that the First Amendment does not protect a government employee from discipline based on speech made pursuant to the employee's official duties. The case involved Richard Ceballos, who had been employed since 1989 as a deputy district attorney for the Los Angeles County District Attorney's Office. As recounted by the Court, Ceballos was a calendar deputy in the Pomona branch, and in this capacity he exercised certain supervisory responsibilities over other lawyers. In February 2000, a defense attorney contacted Ceballos about a pending criminal case. The defense attorney said there were inaccuracies in an affidavit used to obtain a critical search warrant. The attorney informed Ceballos that he had filed a motion to challenge the warrant, but he also wanted Ceballos to review the case. Ceballos did so, and determined the affidavit contained serious misrepresentations, and recommended dismissal of the case. The recommendation was reviewed in a meeting with Ceballos and various supervisors, and a decision was made to proceed with the case, despite the concerns expressed by Ceballos. The meeting allegedly became heated. Ceballos sued the office, claiming that in the aftermath of these events he was subjected to a series of retaliatory employment actions, such as reassignment from his calendar deputy position to a trial deputy position, transfer to another courthouse, and denial of a promotion. The Supreme Court, in an opinion by Justice Kennedy, began by acknowledging that the Supreme Court had long since jettisoned the unchallenged dogma that a public employee had no right to object to conditions placed upon the terms of employment — including those which restricted the exercise of constitutional rights. "The Court has made clear that public employees do not surrender all their First Amendment rights by reason of their employment," the Court noted. "Rather, the First Amendment protects a public employee's right, in certain circumstances, to speak as a citizen addressing matters of public concern." As summarized by *Pickering*, the problem in any case "is to arrive at a balance between the interests of the teacher, as a citizen, in commenting upon matters of public concern and the interest of the State, as an employer, in promoting the efficiency of the public services it performs through its employees."

The Court in *Garcetti* held that there are two inquiries to guide interpretation of the constitutional protections accorded to public employee speech. "The first requires determining whether the employee spoke as a citizen on a matter of public concern." If the answer to this analysis is negative, then the case is over — the employee has no First Amendment cause of action based on his or her employer's reaction to the speech. If, however, the answer is yes, then the possibility of a First Amendment claim arises, and the germane question becomes whether the relevant government entity had an adequate justification for treating the employee differently from any other member of the general public. As the Court elaborated: "This consideration reflects the importance of the relationship between the speaker's expressions and employment. A government entity has broader discretion to restrict speech when it acts in its role as employer, but the restrictions it imposes must be directed at speech that has some potential to affect the entity's operations." The driving rationale animating these principles is that when a citizen enters government service, the citizen by necessity must accept certain limitations on his or her freedom. At the same time, the Court in *Garcetti* explained, a citizen who works for the government is nonetheless a citizen. "The First Amendment limits the ability of a public employer to leverage the employment relationship to restrict, incidentally or intentionally, the liberties employees enjoy in their capacities as private citizens." So long as employees are speaking as citizens about matters of public concern, the Court cautioned, "they must face only those speech restrictions that are necessary for their employers to operate efficiently and effectively." The First Amendment interests at stake, the Court emphasized, "extend beyond the individual speaker." There is a public interest in "receiving the well-informed views of government employees engaging in civic discussion."

Applying these guiding principles, the Court turned to an analysis of Ceballos' First Amendment claim. It was not dispositive, the Court held, that Ceballos expressed his views inside his office, rather than publicly. "Employees in some cases may receive First Amendment protection for expressions made at work." Many citizens do much of their talking inside their respective workplaces, the Court observed, and it would not serve the goal of treating public employees like any member of the general public, to hold that all speech within the office is automatically exposed to restriction. The Court held that it wasn't automatically dispositive that Ceballos' speech concerned the subject matter of his employment, because the First Amendment protects some expressions related to the speaker's job. Rather, the Court held, the controlling factor in Ceballos' case was that his expressions were made pursuant to his duties as a calendar deputy. This "pursuant to duty" test was the Court's important elaboration on the *Connick/Pickering* line of decisions. In the words of the Court:

> That consideration — the fact that Ceballos spoke as a prosecutor fulfilling a responsibility to advise his supervisor about how best to proceed with a pending case — distinguishes Ceballos' case from those in which the First Amendment provides protection against discipline. We hold that when public employees make statements pursuant to their official duties, the employees are not speaking as citizens for First Amendment purposes, and the Constitution does not insulate their communications from employer discipline.

Ceballos wrote what he wrote, the Court elaborated, because that was what he was employed to do. "It is immaterial whether he experienced some personal gratification from writing the memo; his First Amendment rights do not depend on his job satisfaction. The significant point is that the memo was written pursuant to Ceballos' official duties."

As the Court in *Garcetti* saw it, restricting speech that owes its existence to a public employee's professional responsibilities does not infringe any liberties the employee might have enjoyed as a "private citizen." Rather, the restriction simply "reflects the exercise of employer control over what the employer itself has commissioned or created." Ceballos did not act as a citizen when he went about conducting his daily professional activities, such as supervising attorneys, investigating charges, and preparing filings, the Court reasoned. And in the same way, "he did not speak as a citizen by writing a memo that addressed the proper disposition of a pending criminal case. When he went to work and performed the tasks he was paid to perform, Ceballos acted as a government employee. The fact that his duties sometimes required him to speak or write did not mean his supervisors were prohibited from evaluating his performance." Employees "retain the prospect of constitutional protection for their contributions to the civic discourse," the Court held, but this "does not invest them with a right to perform their jobs however they see fit." Rather, the Court held, it was important to afford government employers sufficient discretion to manage their operations:

> Employers have heightened interests in controlling speech made by an employee in his or her professional capacity. Official communications have official consequences, creating a need for substantive consistency and clarity. Supervisors must ensure that their employees' official communications are accurate, demonstrate sound judgment, and promote the employer's mission. Ceballos' memo is illustrative. It demanded the attention of his supervisors and led to a heated meeting with employees from the sheriff's department. If Ceballos' superiors thought his memo was inflammatory or misguided, they had the authority to take proper corrective action.

The Court reasoned that any other rule would commit state and federal courts to a "new, permanent, and intrusive role, mandating judicial oversight of communications between and among government employees and their superiors in the course of official business." In explaining the theoretical underpinning for its ruling, the Court reasoned that employees who make public statements outside the course of performing their official duties "retain some possibility of First Amendment protection because that is the kind of activity engaged in by citizens who do not work for the government." In contrast, the Court explained, when a public employee speaks pursuant to employment responsibilities, "there is no relevant analogue to speech by citizens who are not government employees."

The Court concluded by responding to an argument made by Justice Souter, in dissent, that the rule announced by the Court would invite the squelching of the speech rights of public employees through the creation of excessively broad job descriptions. "Formal job descriptions often bear little resemblance to the duties an employee actually is expected to perform," the Court argued, "and the listing of a given task in an employee's written job description is neither necessary nor sufficient to demonstrate that conducting the task is within the scope of the employee's professional duties for First Amendment purposes." Secondly, the Court dealt with Justice Souter's argument that the decision could have important ramifications for academic freedom, at least as a constitutional value. "There is some argument that expression related to academic scholarship or classroom instruction implicates additional constitutional interests that are not fully accounted for by this Court's customary employee-speech jurisprudence," the Court conceded. The Court held, however, that it need not decide whether "the analysis we conduct today would apply in the same manner to a case involving speech related to scholarship or teaching."

Justice Stevens filed a dissenting opinion, as did Justice Souter, joined by Justices Stevens and Ginsburg. Justice Souter's opinion was particularly notable for its warning that the decision in *Garcetti* could have dire ramifications for academic freedom:

> This ostensible domain beyond the pale of the First Amendment is spacious enough to include even the teaching of a public university professor, and I have to hope that today's majority does not mean to imperil First Amendment protection of academic freedom in public colleges and universities, whose teachers necessarily speak and write "pursuant to official duties."

Justice Souter's point apparently hit home with the majority, which responded by especially noting that the holding in *Garcetti* could conceivably require modification in the context of speech related to scholarship or teaching.

Mt. Healthy City School District Board of Education v. Doyle. Once an employee demonstrates that he or she has been penalized for constitutionally protected expression, the state may still prevail if it is able to demonstrate that it would have taken the disciplinary action notwithstanding the protected expression. In *Mt. Healthy City School District Board of Education v. Doyle*, 429 U.S. 274 (1977), the Supreme Court established the matrix of shifting burdens. Once the employee speaker demonstrates that he or she engaged in constitutionally protected speech, and that such protected speech was a "substantial" or "motivating" factor in the disciplinary action taken, the burden shifts to the government to prove by a preponderance of the evidence that it would have taken the disciplinary action even in the absence of the protected expression.

Rankin v. McPherson. In *Rankin v. McPherson*, 438 U.S. 378 (1987), the Court held that the First Amendment was violated when a clerical employee in a county constable's office was discharged for remarking, after hearing of an attempt on the life of the President, "If they go for him again, I hope they get him." The Court held that McPherson's speech was expression on a matter of public concern. Then moving to the balancing test required under part two of the public employee speech doctrine, the Court found that the remark did not pose the sort of disruption that would justify dismissal. Would the same result obtain if the employee had been a law enforcement officer, not a clerical employee? Or what about a clerical employee within the Secret Service, which has as its mission the protection of the President?

B. Political Patronage

Branti v. Finkel

United States Supreme Court
445 U.S. 507, 100 S. Ct. 1287, 63 L. Ed. 2d 574 (1980)

Mr. Justice Stevens delivered the opinion of the Court.

The question presented is whether the First and Fourteenth Amendments to the Constitution protect an assistant public defender who is satisfactorily performing his job from discharge solely because of his political beliefs.

Respondents, Aaron Finkel and Alan Tabakman, commenced this action in the United States District Court for the Southern District of New York in order to preserve their positions as assistant public defenders in Rockland County, New York. Petitioner Branti's predecessor, a Republican, was appointed in 1972 by a Republican-dominated County Legislature. By 1977, control of the legislature had shifted to the Democrats and petitioner, also a Democrat, was appointed to replace the incumbent when his term expired. As soon as petitioner was formally appointed on January 3, 1978, he began executing termination notices for six of the nine assistants then in office. Respondents were among those who were to be terminated. With one possible exception, the nine who were to be appointed or retained were all Democrats and were all selected by Democratic legislators or Democratic town chairmen on a basis that had been determined by the Democratic caucus.

The District Court found that Finkel and Tabakman had been selected for termination solely because they were Republicans and thus did not have the necessary Democratic sponsors.

In *Elrod v. Burns*, 427 U.S. 347 (1976), the Court held that the newly elected Democratic Sheriff of Cook County, Ill., had violated the constitutional rights of certain non-civil-service employees by discharging them "because they did not support and were not members of the Democratic Party and had failed to obtain the sponsorship of one of its leaders."

Petitioner argues that *Elrod v. Burns* should be read to prohibit only dismissals resulting from an employee's failure to capitulate to political coercion. Thus, he argues that, so long as an employee is not asked to change his political affiliation or to contribute to or work for the party's candidates, he may be dismissed with impunity — even though he would not have been dismissed if he had had the proper political sponsorship and even though the sole reason for dismissing him was to replace him with a person who did have such sponsorship. Such an interpretation would surely emasculate the principles set forth in Elrod. While it would perhaps eliminate the more blatant forms of coercion described in Elrod, it would not eliminate the coercion of belief that necessarily flows from the knowledge that one must have a sponsor in the dominant party in order to retain one's job.

In sum, there is no requirement that dismissed employees prove that they, or other employees, have been coerced into changing, either actually or ostensibly, their political allegiance. To prevail in this type of an action, it was sufficient, as *Elrod* holds, for respondents to prove that they were discharged "solely for the reason that they were not affiliated with or sponsored by the Democratic Party."

Both opinions in *Elrod* recognize that party affiliation may be an acceptable requirement for some types of government employment. Thus, if an employee's private political beliefs would interfere with the discharge of his public duties, his First Amendment rights may be required to yield to the State's vital interest in maintaining governmental effectiveness and efficiency. In *Elrod*, it was clear that the duties of the employees — the chief deputy of the process division of the sheriff's office, a process server and another employee in that office, and a bailiff and security guard at the Juvenile Court of Cook County — were not of that character, for they were, as Mr. Justice Stewart stated, "nonpolicymaking, nonconfidential" employees.

As Mr. Justice Brennan noted in *Elrod*, it is not always easy to determine whether a position is one in which political affiliation is a legitimate factor to be considered. Under some circumstances, a position may be appropriately considered political even though it is neither confidential nor policymaking in character. As one obvious example, if a State's election laws require that precincts be supervised by two election judges of different parties, a Republican judge could be legitimately discharged solely for changing his party registration. That conclusion would not depend on any finding that the job involved participation in policy decisions or access to confidential information. Rather, it would simply rest on the fact that party membership was essential to the discharge of the employee's governmental responsibilities.

It is equally clear that party affiliation is not necessarily relevant to every policymaking or confidential position. The coach of a state university's football team formulates policy, but no one could seriously claim that Republicans make better coaches than Democrats, or vice versa, no matter which party is in control of the state government. On the other hand, it is equally clear that the Governor of a State may appropriately believe that the official duties of various assistants who help him write speeches, explain his views to the press, or communicate with the legislature cannot be performed effectively unless those persons share his political beliefs and party commitments. In sum, the ultimate inquiry is not whether the label "policymaker" or "confidential" fits a particular position; rather, the question is whether the hiring authority can demonstrate that party affiliation is an appropriate requirement for the effective performance of the public office involved.

Having thus framed the issue, it is manifest that the continued employment of an assistant public defender cannot properly be conditioned upon his allegiance to the political party in control of the county government. The primary, if not the only, responsibility of an assistant public defender is to represent individual citizens in controversy with the State.

Thus, whatever policymaking occurs in the public defender's office must relate to the needs of individual clients and not to any partisan political interests. Similarly, although an assistant is bound to obtain access to confidential information arising out of various attorney-client relationships, that information has no bearing whatsoever on partisan political concerns. Under these circumstances, it would undermine, rather than promote, the effective performance of an assistant public defender's office to make his tenure dependent on his allegiance to the dominant political party.

§ 9.14 Education

Morse v. Frederick

United States Supreme Court
551 U.S. 393, 127 S. Ct. 2618, 168 L. Ed. 2d 290 (2007)

CHIEF JUSTICE ROBERTS delivered the opinion of the Court.

At a school-sanctioned and school-supervised event, a high school principal saw some of her students unfurl a large banner conveying a message she reasonably regarded as promoting illegal drug use. Consistent with established school policy prohibiting such messages at school events, the principal directed the students to take down the banner. One student — among those who had brought the banner to the event — refused to do so. The principal confiscated the banner and later suspended the student. The Ninth Circuit held that the principal's actions violated the First Amendment, and that the student could sue the principal for damages.

Our cases make clear that students do not "shed their constitutional rights to freedom of speech or expression at the schoolhouse gate." *Tinker v. Des Moines Independent Community School Dist.* At the same time, we have held that "the constitutional rights of students in public school are not automatically coextensive with the rights of adults in other settings," *Bethel School Dist. No. 403 v. Fraser*, and that the rights of students "must be 'applied in light of the special characteristics of the school environment.'" *Hazelwood School Dist. v. Kuhlmeier.* Consistent with these principles, we hold that schools may take steps to safeguard those entrusted to their care from speech that can reasonably be regarded as encouraging illegal drug use. We conclude that the school officials in this case did not violate the First Amendment by confiscating the pro-drug banner and suspending the student responsible for it.

I.

On January 24, 2002, the Olympic Torch Relay passed through Juneau, Alaska, on its way to the winter games in Salt Lake City, Utah. The torchbearers were to proceed along a street in front of Juneau-Douglas High School (JDHS) while school was in session. Petitioner Deborah Morse, the school principal, decided to permit staff and students to participate in the Torch Relay as an approved social event or class trip. Students were allowed to leave class to observe the relay from either side of the street. Teachers and administrative officials monitored the students' actions.

Respondent Joseph Frederick, a JDHS senior, was late to school that day. When he arrived, he joined his friends (all but one of whom were JDHS students) across the street from the school to watch the event. Not all the students waited patiently. Some became rambunctious, throwing plastic cola bottles and snowballs and scuffling with their classmates. As the torchbearers and camera crews passed by, Frederick and his friends unfurled a 14-foot banner bearing the phrase: "BONG HiTS 4 JESUS." The large banner was easily readable by the students on the other side of the street.

Principal Morse immediately crossed the street and demanded that the banner be taken down. Everyone but Frederick complied. Morse confiscated the banner and told Frederick to report to her office, where she suspended him for 10 days. Morse later explained that she told Frederick to take the banner down because she thought it encouraged illegal drug use, in violation of established school policy. Juneau School Board Policy No. 5520 states: "The Board specifically prohibits any assembly or public expression that . . . advocates the use of substances that are illegal to minors. . . ." In addition, Juneau School Board Policy No. 5850 subjects "[p]upils who participate in approved social events and class trips" to the same student conduct rules that apply during the regular school program.

Frederick administratively appealed his suspension, but the Juneau School District Superintendent upheld it, limiting it to time served (8 days). In a memorandum setting forth his reasons, the superintendent determined that Frederick had displayed his banner "in the midst of his fellow students, during school hours, at a school-sanctioned activity." He further explained that Frederick "was not disciplined because the principal of the school 'disagreed' with his message, but because his speech appeared to advocate the use of illegal drugs."

The superintendent continued:

> The common-sense understanding of the phrase 'bong hits' is that it is a reference to a means of smoking marijuana. Given [Frederick's] inability or unwillingness to express any other credible meaning for the phrase, I can only agree with the principal and countless others who saw the banner as advocating the use of illegal drugs. [Frederick's] speech was not political. He was not advocating the legalization of marijuana or promoting a religious belief. He was displaying a fairly silly message promoting illegal drug usage in the midst of a school activity, for the benefit of television cameras covering the Torch Relay. [Frederick's] speech was potentially disruptive to the event and clearly disruptive of and inconsistent with the school's educational mission to educate students about the dangers of illegal drugs and to discourage their use.

Relying on our decision in *Fraser, supra*, the superintendent concluded that the principal's actions were permissible because Frederick's banner was "speech or action that intrudes upon the work of the schools." The Juneau School District Board of Education upheld the suspension. . . .

The District Court granted summary judgment for the school board and Morse, ruling that they were entitled to qualified immunity and that they had not infringed

Frederick's First Amendment rights. The court found that Morse reasonably interpreted the banner as promoting illegal drug use—a message that "directly contravened the Board's policies relating to drug abuse prevention." . . .

The Ninth Circuit reversed. Deciding that Frederick acted during a "school-authorized activit[y]," and "proceed[ing] on the basis that the banner expressed a positive sentiment about marijuana use," the court nonetheless found a violation of Frederick's First Amendment rights because the school punished Frederick without demonstrating that his speech gave rise to a "risk of substantial disruption." . . .

II.

At the outset, we reject Frederick's argument that this is not a school speech case—as has every other authority to address the question. . . . The event occurred during normal school hours. It was sanctioned by Principal Morse "as an approved social event or class trip," and the school district's rules expressly provide that pupils in "approved social events and class trips are subject to district rules for student conduct." Teachers and administrators were interspersed among the students and charged with supervising them. The high school band and cheerleaders performed. Frederick, standing among other JDHS students across the street from the school, directed his banner toward the school, making it plainly visible to most students. Under these circumstances, we agree with the superintendent that Frederick cannot "stand in the midst of his fellow students, during school hours, at a school-sanctioned activity and claim he is not at school." There is some uncertainty at the outer boundaries as to when courts should apply school-speech precedents, . . . but not on these facts.

III.

The message on Frederick's banner is cryptic. It is no doubt offensive to some, perhaps amusing to others. To still others, it probably means nothing at all. Frederick himself claimed "that the words were just nonsense meant to attract television cameras." But Principal Morse thought the banner would be interpreted by those viewing it as promoting illegal drug use, and that interpretation is plainly a reasonable one.

As Morse later explained in a declaration, when she saw the sign, she thought that "the reference to a 'bong hit' would be widely understood by high school students and others as referring to smoking marijuana." She further believed that "display of the banner would be construed by students, District personnel, parents and others witnessing the display of the banner, as advocating or promoting illegal drug use"— in violation of school policy. ("I told Frederick and the other members of his group to put the banner down because I felt that it violated the [school] policy against displaying . . . material that advertises or promotes use of illegal drugs.")

We agree with Morse. At least two interpretations of the words on the banner demonstrate that the sign advocated the use of illegal drugs. First, the phrase could be interpreted as an imperative: "[Take] bong hits . . ."—a message equivalent, as Morse explained in her declaration, to "smoke marijuana" or "use an illegal drug."

Alternatively, the phrase could be viewed as celebrating drug use — "bong hits [are a good thing]," or "[we take] bong hits" — and we discern no meaningful distinction between celebrating illegal drug use in the midst of fellow students and outright advocacy or promotion. . . .

The pro-drug interpretation of the banner gains further plausibility given the paucity of alternative meanings the banner might bear. The best Frederick can come up with is that the banner is "meaningless and funny." The dissent similarly refers to the sign's message as "curious," "ambiguous," "nonsense," "ridiculous," "obscure," "silly," "quixotic," and "stupid." Gibberish is surely a possible interpretation of the words on the banner, but it is not the only one, and dismissing the banner as meaningless ignores its undeniable reference to illegal drugs.

The dissent mentions Frederick's "credible and uncontradicted explanation for the message — he just wanted to get on television." But that is a description of Frederick's *motive* for displaying the banner; it is not an interpretation of what the banner says. The *way* Frederick was going to fulfill his ambition of appearing on television was by unfurling a pro-drug banner at a school event, in the presence of teachers and fellow students.

Elsewhere in its opinion, the dissent emphasizes the importance of political speech and the need to foster "national debate about a serious issue," as if to suggest that the banner is political speech. But not even Frederick argues that the banner conveys any sort of political or religious message. Contrary to the dissent's suggestion, this is plainly not a case about political debate over the criminalization of drug use or possession.

IV.

The question thus becomes whether a principal may, consistent with the First Amendment, restrict student speech at a school event, when that speech is reasonably viewed as promoting illegal drug use. We hold that she may.

In *Tinker*, this Court made clear that "First Amendment rights, applied in light of the special characteristics of the school environment, are available to teachers and students." *Tinker* involved a group of high school students who decided to wear black armbands to protest the Vietnam War. School officials learned of the plan and then adopted a policy prohibiting students from wearing armbands. When several students nonetheless wore armbands to school, they were suspended. The students sued, claiming that their First Amendment rights had been violated, and this Court agreed.

Tinker held that student expression may not be suppressed unless school officials reasonably conclude that it will "materially and substantially disrupt the work and discipline of the school." The essential facts of *Tinker* are quite stark, implicating concerns at the heart of the First Amendment. The students sought to engage in political speech, using the armbands to express their "disapproval of the Vietnam hostilities and their advocacy of a truce, to make their views known, and, by their example, to influence others to adopt them." Political speech, of course, is "at the core of what the First Amendment is designed to protect." *Virginia v. Black*, 538 U.S. 343 (2003). The only interest the Court discerned underlying the school's actions was the "mere desire to avoid the discomfort and unpleasantness that always accompany an unpopular viewpoint," or "an urgent wish to avoid the controversy which might result from the expression." *Tinker*. That interest was not enough to justify banning "a silent, passive expression of opinion, unaccompanied by any disorder or disturbance."

This Court's next student speech case concerned Matthew Fraser, who was suspended for delivering a speech before a high school assembly in which he employed what this Court called "an elaborate, graphic, and explicit sexual metaphor." . . .

The mode of analysis employed in *Fraser* is not entirely clear. The Court was plainly attuned to the content of Fraser's speech, citing the "marked distinction between the political 'message' of the armbands in *Tinker* and the sexual content of [Fraser's] speech." But the Court also reasoned that school boards have the authority to determine "what manner of speech in the classroom or in school assembly is inappropriate." (Brennan, J., concurring in judgment) ("In the present case, school officials sought only to ensure that a high school assembly proceed in an orderly manner. There is no suggestion that school officials attempted to regulate [Fraser's] speech because they disagreed with the views he sought to express").

We need not resolve this debate to decide this case. For present purposes, it is enough to distill from *Fraser* two basic principles. First, *Fraser's* holding demonstrates that "the constitutional rights of students in public school are not automatically coextensive with the rights of adults in other settings." Had Fraser delivered the same speech in a public forum outside the school context, it would have been protected. See *Cohen v. California*. In school, however, Fraser's First Amendment rights were circumscribed "in light of the special characteristics of the school environment." *Tinker*. Second, *Fraser* established that the mode of analysis set forth in *Tinker* is not absolute. Whatever approach *Fraser* employed, it certainly did not conduct the "substantial disruption" analysis prescribed by *Tinker*. See *Kuhlmeier*, 484 U.S., at 271, n.4 (disagreeing with the proposition that there is "no difference between the First Amendment analysis applied in *Tinker* and that applied in *Fraser*," and noting that the holding in *Fraser* was not based on any showing of substantial disruption).

Our most recent student speech case, *Kuhlmeier*, concerned "expressive activities that students, parents, and members of the public might reasonably perceive to bear the imprimatur of the school." Staff members of a high school newspaper sued their school when it chose not to publish two of their articles. The Court of Appeals analyzed the case under *Tinker*, ruling in favor of the students because it found no evidence of material disruption to classwork or school discipline. . . . This Court reversed, holding that "educators do not offend the First Amendment by exercising editorial control over the style and content of student speech in school-sponsored expressive activities so long as their actions are reasonably related to legitimate pedagogical concerns." *Kuhlmeier*.

Kuhlmeier does not control this case because no one would reasonably believe that Frederick's banner bore the school's imprimatur. The case is nevertheless instructive because it confirms both principles cited above. *Kuhlmeier* acknowledged that schools may regulate some speech "even though the government could not censor similar speech outside the school." And, like *Fraser*, it confirms that the rule of *Tinker* is not the only basis for restricting student speech....

Drawing on the principles applied in our student speech cases, we have held in the Fourth Amendment context that "while children assuredly do not 'shed their constitutional rights... at the schoolhouse gate,'... the nature of those rights is what is appropriate for children in school." *Vernonia School Dist. 47J v. Acton*, 515 U.S. 646 (1995). In particular, "the school setting requires some easing of the restrictions to which searches by public authorities are ordinarily subject."...

Even more to the point, these cases also recognize that deterring drug use by schoolchildren is an "important—indeed, perhaps compelling" interest. Drug abuse can cause severe and permanent damage to the health and well-being of young people:

> School years are the time when the physical, psychological, and addictive effects of drugs are most severe. Maturing nervous systems are more critically impaired by intoxicants than mature ones are; childhood losses in learning are lifelong and profound; children grow chemically dependent more quickly than adults, and their record of recovery is depressingly poor. And of course the effects of a drug-infested school are visited not just upon the users, but upon the entire student body and faculty, as the educational process is disrupted.

Just five years ago, we wrote: "The drug abuse problem among our Nation's youth has hardly abated since *Vernonia* was decided in 1995. In fact, evidence suggests that it has only grown worse." *Board of Education v. Earls*, 536 U.S. 822 (2002).

The problem remains serious today....

Congress has declared that part of a school's job is educating students about the dangers of illegal drug use. It has provided billions of dollars to support state and local drug-prevention programs....

Thousands of school boards throughout the country—including JDHS—have adopted policies aimed at effectuating this message. Those school boards know that peer pressure is perhaps "the single most important factor leading schoolchildren to take drugs," and that students are more likely to use drugs when the norms in school appear to tolerate such behavior. Student speech celebrating illegal drug use at a school event, in the presence of school administrators and teachers, thus poses a particular challenge for school officials working to protect those entrusted to their care from the dangers of drug abuse.

The "special characteristics of the school environment," and the governmental interest in stopping student drug abuse-reflected in the policies of Congress and myriad school boards, including JDHS—allow schools to restrict student expression that they reasonably regard as promoting illegal drug use. *Tinker* warned that schools may not prohibit student speech because of "undifferentiated fear or apprehension of disturbance" or "a mere desire to avoid the discomfort and unpleasantness that always accompany an unpopular viewpoint." The danger here is far more serious and palpable. The particular concern to prevent student drug abuse at issue here, embodied in established school policy, extends well beyond an abstract desire to avoid controversy.

Petitioners urge us to adopt the broader rule that Frederick's speech is proscribable because it is plainly "offensive" as that term is used in *Fraser*. We think this stretches *Fraser* too far; that case should not be read to encompass any speech that could fit under some definition of "offensive." After all, much political and religious speech might be perceived as offensive to some. The concern here is not that Frederick's speech was offensive, but that it was reasonably viewed as promoting illegal drug use.

Although accusing this decision of doing "serious violence to the First Amendment" by authorizing "viewpoint discrimination," the dissent concludes that "it might well be appropriate to tolerate some targeted viewpoint discrimination in this unique setting." Nor do we understand the dissent to take the position that schools are required to tolerate student advocacy of illegal drug use at school events, even if that advocacy falls short of inviting "imminent" lawless action. ("[I]t is possible that our rigid imminence requirement ought to be relaxed at schools"). And even the dissent recognizes that the issues here are close enough that the principal should not be held liable in damages, but should instead enjoy qualified immunity for her actions. Stripped of rhetorical flourishes, then, the debate between the dissent and this opinion is less about constitutional first principles than about whether Frederick's banner constitutes promotion of illegal drug use. We have explained our view that it does. The dissent's contrary view on that relatively narrow question hardly justifies sounding the First Amendment bugle.

School principals have a difficult job, and a vitally important one. When Frederick suddenly and unexpectedly unfurled his banner, Morse had to decide to act—or not act—on the spot. It was reasonable for her to conclude that the banner promoted illegal drug use—in violation of established school policy—and that failing to act would send a powerful message to the students in her charge, including Frederick, about how serious the school was about the dangers of illegal drug use. The First Amendment does not require schools to tolerate at school events student expression that contributes to those dangers.

The judgment of the United States Court of Appeals for the Ninth Circuit is reversed, and the case is remanded for further proceedings consistent with this opinion.

It is so ordered.

JUSTICE THOMAS, concurring.

The Court today decides that a public school may prohibit speech advocating illegal drug use. I agree and therefore join its opinion in full. I write separately to state my view that the standard set forth in *Tinker v. Des Moines Independent Community School Dist.*, is without basis in the Constitution. . . .

As this Court has previously observed, the First Amendment was not originally understood to permit all sorts of speech; instead, "[t]here are certain well-defined and narrowly limited classes of speech, the prevention and punishment of which have never been thought to raise any Constitutional problem." *Chaplinsky v. New Hampshire.* In my view, the history of public education suggests that the First Amendment, as originally understood, does not protect student speech in public schools. . . .

Because public schools were initially created as substitutes for private schools, when States developed public education systems in the early 1800's, no one doubted the government's ability to educate and discipline children as private schools did. Like their private counterparts, early public schools were not places for freewheeling debates or exploration of competing ideas. Rather, teachers instilled "a core of common values" in students and taught them self-control. . . .

Teachers instilled these values not only by presenting ideas but also through strict discipline. . . .

In short, in the earliest public schools, teachers taught, and students listened. Teachers commanded, and students obeyed. Teachers did not rely solely on the power of ideas to persuade; they relied on discipline to maintain order. . . .

As early as 1837, state courts applied the *in loco parentis* principle to public schools:

> "One of the most sacred duties of parents, is to train up and qualify their children, for becoming useful and virtuous members of society; this duty cannot be effectually performed without the ability to command obedience, to control stubbornness, to quicken diligence, and to reform bad habits. . . . The teacher is the substitute of the parent; . . . and in the exercise of these delegated duties, is invested with his power." *State v. Pendergrass*, 19 N.C. 365, 365–366, (1837).

Applying *in loco parentis*, the judiciary was reluctant to interfere in the routine business of school administration, allowing schools and teachers to set and enforce rules and to maintain order. . . .

Tinker effected a sea change in students' speech rights, extending them well beyond traditional bounds. . . .

Justice Black dissented, criticizing the Court for "subject[ing] all the public schools in the country to the whims and caprices of their loudest-mouthed, but maybe not their brightest, students." . . .

In light of the history of American public education, it cannot seriously be suggested that the First Amendment "freedom of speech" encompasses a student's right to speak in public schools. Early public schools gave total control to teachers, who expected obedience and respect from students. And courts routinely deferred to schools' authority to make rules and to discipline students for violating those rules. Several points are clear: (1) under *in loco parentis*, speech rules and other school rules were treated identically; (2) the *in loco parentis* doctrine imposed almost no limits on the types of rules that a school could set while students were in school; and (3) schools and teachers had tremendous discretion in imposing punishments for violations of those rules. . . .

I join the Court's opinion because it erodes *Tinker's* hold in the realm of student speech, even though it does so by adding to the patchwork of exceptions to the *Tinker* standard. I think the better approach is to dispense with *Tinker* altogether, and given the opportunity, I would do so.

JUSTICE ALITO, with whom JUSTICE KENNEDY joins, concurring.

I join the opinion of the Court on the understanding that (a) it goes no further than to hold that a public school may restrict speech that a reasonable observer would interpret as advocating illegal drug use and (b) it provides no support for any restriction of speech that can plausibly be interpreted as commenting on any political or social issue, including speech on issues such as "the wisdom of the war on drugs or of legalizing marijuana for medicinal use."

Speech advocating illegal drug use poses a threat to student safety that is just as serious, if not always as immediately obvious. As we have recognized in the past and as the opinion of the Court today details, illegal drug use presents a grave and in many ways unique threat to the physical safety of students. I therefore conclude that the public schools may ban speech advocating illegal drug use. But I regard such regulation as standing at the far reaches of what the First Amendment permits. I join the opinion of the Court with the understanding that the opinion does not endorse any further extension.

JUSTICE BREYER, concurring in the judgment in part and dissenting in part.

This Court need not and should not decide this difficult First Amendment issue on the merits. Rather, I believe that it should simply hold that qualified immunity bars the student's claim for monetary damages and say no more. . . .

JUSTICE STEVENS, with whom JUSTICE SOUTER and JUSTICE GINSBURG join, dissenting.

A significant fact barely mentioned by the Court sheds a revelatory light on the motives of both the students and the principal of Juneau-Douglas High School (JDHS). On January 24, 2002, the Olympic Torch Relay gave those Alaska residents a rare chance to appear on national television. As Joseph Frederick repeatedly explained, he did not address the curious message — "BONG HiTS 4 JESUS" — to his fellow students. He just wanted to get the camera crews' attention. Moreover, concern about a nationwide evaluation of the conduct of the JDHS student body would have justified the principal's decision to remove an attention-grabbing 14-foot banner, even if it had merely proclaimed "Glaciers Melt!" . . .

In my judgment, the First Amendment protects student speech if the message itself neither violates a permissible rule nor expressly advocates conduct that is illegal and harmful to students. This nonsense banner does neither, and the Court does serious violence to the First Amendment in upholding — indeed, lauding — a school's decision to punish Frederick for expressing a view with which it disagreed. . . .

Yet today the Court fashions a test that trivializes the two cardinal principles upon which *Tinker* rests. . . . The Court's test invites stark viewpoint discrimination. In this case, for example, the principal has unabashedly acknowledged that she disciplined Frederick because she disagreed with the pro-drug viewpoint she ascribed to the message on the banner, — a viewpoint, incidentally, that Frederick has disavowed. . . . "If there is a bedrock principle underlying the First Amendment, it is that the Government may not prohibit the expression of an idea simply because society finds the idea itself offensive or disagreeable." *Texas v. Johnson.*

It is also perfectly clear that "promoting illegal drug use," comes nowhere close to proscribable "incitement to imminent lawless action." *Brandenburg.* Encouraging drug use might well increase the likelihood that a listener will try an illegal drug, but that hardly justifies censorship:

"Every denunciation of existing law tends in some measure to increase the probability that there will be violation of it. Condonation of a breach enhances the probability. Expressions of approval add to the probability. . . . Advocacy of law-breaking heightens it still further. But even advocacy of violation, however reprehensible morally, is not a justification for denying free speech where the advocacy falls short of incitement and there is nothing to indicate that the advocacy would be immediately acted upon." *Whitney v. California*, (Brandeis, J., concurring).

No one seriously maintains that drug advocacy (much less Frederick's ridiculous sign) comes within the vanishingly small category of speech that can be prohibited because of its feared consequences. Such advocacy, to borrow from Justice Holmes, "ha[s] no chance of starting a present conflagration." *Gitlow v. New York.* . . .

The Court rejects outright these twin foundations of *Tinker* because, in its view, the unusual importance of protecting children from the scourge of drugs supports a ban on all speech in the school environment that promotes drug use. Whether or not such a rule is sensible as a matter of policy, carving out pro-drug speech for uniquely harsh treatment finds no support in our case law and is inimical to the values protected by the First Amendment. . . .

To the extent the Court independently finds that "BONG HiTS 4 JESUS" *objectively* amounts to the advocacy of illegal drug use — in other words, that it can *most* reasonably be interpreted as such — that conclusion practically refutes itself. This is a nonsense message, not advocacy. . . .

Among other things, the Court's ham-handed, categorical approach is deaf to the constitutional imperative to permit unfettered debate, even among high-school students, about the wisdom of the war on drugs or of legalizing marijuana for medicinal use. . . .

Although this case began with a silly, nonsensical banner, it ends with the Court inventing out of whole cloth a special First Amendment rule permitting the censorship of any student speech that mentions drugs, at least so long as someone could perceive that speech to contain a latent pro-drug message. Our First Amendment jurisprudence has identified some categories of expression that are less deserving of protection than others — fighting words, obscenity, and commercial speech, to name a few. Rather than reviewing our opinions discussing such categories, I mention two personal recollections that have no doubt influenced my conclusion that it would be profoundly unwise to create special rules for speech about drug and alcohol use.

The Vietnam War is remembered today as an unpopular war. During its early stages, however, "the dominant opinion" that Justice Harlan mentioned in his *Tinker* dissent regarded opposition to the war as unpatriotic, if not treason. . . . That dominant opinion strongly supported the prosecution of several of those who demonstrated in Grant Park during the 1968 Democratic Convention in Chicago, see *United States v. Dellinger*, 472 F.2d 340 (C.A.7 1972), and the vilification of vocal opponents of the war like Julian Bond, cf. *Bond v. Floyd*, 385 U.S. 116 (1966). In 1965, when the Des Moines students wore their armbands, the school district's fear that they might "start an argument or cause a disturbance" was well founded. *Tinker*. Given that context, there is special force to the Court's insistence that "our Constitution says we must take that risk; and our history says that it is this sort of hazardous freedom — this kind of openness — that is the basis of our national strength and of the independence and vigor of Americans who grow up and live in this relatively permissive, often disputatious, society." As we now know, the then-dominant opinion about the Vietnam War was not etched in stone.

Reaching back still further, the current dominant opinion supporting the war on drugs in general, and our antimarijuana laws in particular, is reminiscent of the opinion that supported the nationwide ban on alcohol consumption when I was a student. While alcoholic beverages are now regarded as ordinary articles of commerce, their use was then condemned with the same moral fervor that now supports the war on drugs. The ensuing change in public opinion occurred much more slowly than the relatively rapid shift in Americans' views on the Vietnam War, and progressed on a state-by-state basis over a period of many years. But just as prohibition in the 1920's and early 1930's was secretly questioned by thousands of otherwise law-abiding patrons of bootleggers and speakeasies, today the actions of literally millions of otherwise law-abiding users of marijuana, and of the majority of voters in each of the several States that tolerate medicinal uses of the product, lead me to wonder whether the fear of disapproval by those in the majority is silencing opponents of the war on drugs. Surely our national experience with alcohol should make us wary of dampening speech suggesting — however inarticulately — that it would be better to tax and regulate marijuana than to persevere in a futile effort to ban its use entirely.

Even in high school, a rule that permits only one point of view to be expressed is less likely to produce correct answers than the open discussion of countervailing views. *Whitney* (Brandeis, J., concurring); *Abrams* (Holmes, J., dissenting); *Tinker*.

In the national debate about a serious issue, it is the expression of the minority's viewpoint that most demands the protection of the First Amendment. Whatever the better policy may be, a full and frank discussion of the costs and benefits of the attempt to prohibit the use of marijuana is far wiser than suppression of speech because it is unpopular.

I respectfully dissent.

Notes and Questions

(1) It is arguable that poor Joseph Frederick blew his chances of winning the case when he responded, perhaps in typical teenager-caught-red-handed-and-confronted-by-an-authority-figure fashion, with what amounted to an "I didn't mean nothin'" defense. He called his message "meaningless and funny." This allowed Chief Justice Roberts an easy out of dismissing it as possible "gibberish," yet also as a serious call for the use of illegal drugs. Imagine how the case might have turned out if Frederick, when confronted, had been more fast on his feet, and said something like: "When I unfurled the banner BONG HiTS 4 JESUS, I was engaged in an existential religious and political commentary, suggesting, in a manner not unlike the manner in which in Christian traditions Jesus offered wine and invited his disciples to drink it in his memory, that marijuana — a substance essentially indistinguishable from wine for my generation — may also at times provide a channel to deeper spiritual awareness, an awareness that current political regimes and restrictive laws fail to properly respect, thus requiring their reformation." What if Frederick had said something like *that* to Principal Deborah Morse? Of course, the principal might have deemed him a smart-aleck, and not believed him. But what if he had back-up, such as social media posts or a journal essay expressing those views? Could that have changed the outcome of the case?

(2) The Supreme Court's journey from *Tinker* to *Frazer* to *Hazelwood* to *Morse* may seem confusing. The cases do, however, fall into a more or less coherent pattern. *Tinker* involved the passive wearing of an armband as a symbol of anti-war protest by a Middle School student, Mary Beth Tinker. The Court ruled that the actions of school officials disciplining her violated the First Amendment. The case took on legendary status in American culture. Many children read accounts of the case in their elementary or high school instruction. The Court in *Tinker* established a relatively demanding standard, requiring that to justify any discipline against a student in such circumstances, school officials demonstrate that the expression would cause substantial and material disruption to the operation of the school. *Tinker* is famous for its admonition that school children do not "shed their constitutional rights to freedom of speech or expression at the schoolhouse gate." In contrast, both *Frazer* and *Hazelwood* involved school-sponsored activities. The Court adopted a more lenient standard in those contexts, holding that greater deference was owed so school officials in such circumstances. *Hazelwood* thus explained: "Instead, we hold that educators do not offend the First Amendment by exercising editorial control over the style and content of student speech in school-sponsored expressive

activities so long as their actions are reasonably related to legitimate pedagogical concerns."

(3) The *Morse* case was a school-sponsored activity, but it was not particularly *pedagogical.* Perhaps that is why the majority opinion by Chief Justice Roberts did not adopt either the *Tinker* "substantial disruption" or the *Hazelwood* "pedagogical concerns" test. Instead, the opinion appeared to rest on the assumption that Joseph Frederick's speech could reasonably be interpreted as an exhortation to use illegal drugs. And in addition, a noted above, Frederick himself did not claim to have any other political or religious message in mind.

(4) Justice Alito, joined by Justice Kennedy, concurred in *Morse.* That concurrence is important, and arguably narrowed the reach of the majority opinion. Justice Alito stated that he (and Justice Kennedy) joined the majority only on the understanding that the decision "provides no support for any restriction of speech that can plausibly be interpreted as commenting on any political or social issue."

Problem D

Imagine that you are clerking for a newly appointed United States Supreme Court Justice. The Court has granted review in two cases in which students were suspended from school after they refused to obey the commands of school officials to cease engaging in expression and consolidated them for review and argument. In the first case, public high school officials refused to permit students to pass out buttons that said "I love boobies" at a display table at a student fair for student organizations, by a student group promoting public awareness regarding breast cancer. In the second case, school officials refused to permit a student to wear a t-shirt bearing the message "Drugs Suck" to school. When the students in each of the two cases refused to obey, they were suspended. The Justice for whom you are clerking asks you for a memorandum on the legal principles that should be applied to the two cases under existing precedent, as well as your recommendation as to how the cases should be decided, and why.

Mahanoy Area School District v. B.L. by & through Levy

Supreme Court of the United States
141 S. Ct. 2038 (2021)

JUSTICE BREYER delivered the opinion of the Court.

A public high school student used, and transmitted to her Snapchat friends, vulgar language and gestures criticizing both the school and the school's cheerleading team. The student's speech took place outside of school hours and away from the school's campus. In response, the school suspended the student for a year from the cheerleading team. We must decide whether the Court of Appeals for the Third Circuit correctly held that the school's decision violated the First Amendment. Although we do not agree with the reasoning of the Third Circuit panel's majority, we do agree with its conclusion that the school's disciplinary action violated the First Amendment.

B.L. (who, together with her parents, is a respondent in this case) was a student at Mahanoy Area High School, a public school in Mahanoy City, Pennsylvania. At the end of her freshman year, B.L. tried out for a position on the school's varsity cheerleading squad and for right fielder on a private softball team.

She did not make the varsity cheerleading team or get her preferred softball position, but she was offered a spot on the cheerleading squad's junior varsity team. B.L. did not accept the coach's decision with good grace, particularly because the squad coaches had placed an entering freshman on the varsity team.

That weekend, B.L. and a friend visited the Cocoa Hut, a local convenience store. There, B.L. used her smartphone to post two photos on Snapchat, a social media application that allows users to post photos and videos that disappear after a set period of time. B.L. posted the images to her Snapchat "story," a feature of the application that allows any person in the user's "friend" group (B.L. had about 250 "friends") to view the images for a 24 hour period.

The first image B.L. posted showed B.L. and a friend with middle fingers raised; it bore the caption: "Fuck school fuck softball fuck cheer fuck everything." The second image was blank but for a caption, which read: "Love how me and [another student] get told we need a year of jv before we make varsity but tha[t] doesn't matter to anyone else?" The caption also contained an upside-down smiley-face emoji.

B.L.'s Snapchat "friends" included other Mahanoy Area High School students, some of whom also belonged to the cheerleading squad. At least one of them, using a separate cellphone, took pictures of B.L.'s posts and shared them with other members of the cheerleading squad. One of the students who received these photos showed them to her mother (who was a cheerleading squad coach), and the images spread.

That week, several cheerleaders and other students approached the cheerleading coaches "visibly upset" about B.L.'s posts. Questions about the posts persisted during an Algebra class taught by one of the two coaches.

After discussing the matter with the school principal, the coaches decided that because the posts used profanity in connection with a school extracurricular activity, they violated team and school rules. As a result, the coaches suspended B.L. from the junior varsity cheerleading squad for the upcoming year. B.L.'s subsequent apologies did not move school officials. The school's athletic director, principal, superintendent, and school board, all affirmed B.L.'s suspension from the team. In response, B.L., together with her parents, filed this lawsuit in Federal District Court.

The District Court found in B.L.'s favor. It first granted a temporary restraining order and a preliminary injunction ordering the school to reinstate B.L. to the cheerleading team. In granting B.L.'s subsequent motion for summary judgment, the District Court found that B.L.'s Snapchats had not caused substantial disruption at the school. *Cf. Tinker v. Des Moines Independent Community School Dist.*, 393 U.S. 503 (1969).

We have made clear that students do not "shed their constitutional rights to freedom of speech or expression," even "at the school house gate." *Tinker.* But we have also made clear that courts must apply the First Amendment "in light of the special characteristics of the school environment." *Hazelwood School Dist. v. Kuhlmeier,* 484 U.S. 260 (1988). One such characteristic, which we have stressed, is the fact that schools at times stand *in loco parentis,* i.e., in the place of parents. See *Bethel School Dist. No. 403 v. Fraser,* 478 U.S. 675 (1986).

This Court has previously outlined three specific categories of student speech that schools may regulate in certain circumstances: (1) "indecent," "lewd," or "vulgar" speech uttered during a school assembly on school grounds; (2) speech, uttered during a class trip, that promotes "illegal drug use," *see Morse v. Frederick,* 551 U.S. 393 (2007); and (3) speech that others may reasonably perceive as "bear[ing] the imprimatur of the school," such as that appearing in a school-sponsored newspaper, see *Kuhlmeier.*

Finally, in *Tinker,* we said schools have a special interest in regulating speech that "materially disrupts classwork or involves substantial disorder or invasion of the rights of others." These special characteristics call for special leeway when schools regulate speech that occurs under its supervision.

Unlike the Third Circuit, we do not believe the special characteristics that give schools additional license to regulate student speech always disappear when a school regulates speech that takes place off campus. The school's regulatory interests remain significant in some off-campus circumstances. The parties' briefs, and those of amici, list several types of off-campus behavior that may call for school regulation. These include serious or severe bullying or harassment targeting particular individuals; threats aimed at teachers or other students; the failure to follow rules concerning lessons, the writing of papers, the use of computers, or participation in other online school activities; and breaches of school security devices, including material maintained within school computers.

Even B.L. herself and the amici supporting her would redefine the Third Circuit's off-campus/on-campus distinction, treating as on campus: all times when the school is responsible for the student; the school's immediate surroundings; travel en route to and from the school; all speech taking place over school laptops or on a school's website; speech taking place during remote learning; activities taken for school credit; and communications to school e-mail accounts or phones. And it may be that speech related to extracurricular activities, such as team sports, would also receive special treatment under B.L.'s proposed rule.

We are uncertain as to the length or content of any such list of appropriate exceptions or carveouts to the Third Circuit majority's rule. That rule, basically, if not entirely, would deny the off-campus applicability of Tinker's highly general statement about the nature of a school's special interests. Particularly given the advent of computer-based learning, we hesitate to determine precisely which of many school-related off-campus activities belong on such a list. Neither do we now know how such a list might vary, depending upon a student's age, the nature of the school's off-campus activity, or the impact upon the school itself. Thus, we do not now set forth a broad, highly general First Amendment rule stating just what counts as "off campus" speech and whether or how ordinary First Amendment standards must give way off campus to a school's special need to prevent, e.g., substantial disruption of learning-related activities or the protection of those who make up a school community.

We can, however, mention three features of off-campus speech that often, even if not always, distinguish schools' efforts to regulate that speech from their efforts to regulate on-campus speech. Those features diminish the strength of the unique educational characteristics that might call for special First Amendment leeway.

First, a school, in relation to off-campus speech, will rarely stand in loco parentis. The doctrine of in loco parentis treats school administrators as standing in the place of students' parents under circumstances where the children's actual parents cannot protect, guide, and discipline them. Geographically speaking, off-campus speech will normally fall within the zone of parental, rather than school-related, responsibility.

Second, from the student speaker's perspective, regulations of off-campus speech, when coupled with regulations of on-campus speech, include all the speech a student utters during the full 24-hour day. That means courts must be more skeptical of a school's efforts to regulate off-campus speech, for doing so may mean the student cannot engage in that kind of speech at all. When it comes to political or religious speech that occurs outside school or a school program or activity, the school will have a heavy burden to justify intervention.

Third, the school itself has an interest in protecting a student's unpopular expression, especially when the expression takes place off campus. America's public schools are the nurseries of democracy. Our representative democracy only works if we protect the "marketplace of ideas." This free exchange facilitates an informed public opinion, which, when transmitted to lawmakers, helps produce laws that reflect the People's will. That protection must include the protection of unpopular ideas, for popular ideas have less need for protection. Thus, schools have a strong interest in ensuring that future generations understand the workings in practice of the well-known aphorism, "I disapprove of what you say, but I will defend to the death your right to say it." (Although this quote is often attributed to Voltaire, it was likely coined by an English writer, Evelyn Beatrice Hall.)

Given the many different kinds of off-campus speech, the different potential school-related and circumstance-specific justifications, and the differing extent to which those justifications may call for First Amendment leeway, we can, as a general matter, say little more than this: Taken together, these three features of much off-campus speech mean that the leeway the First Amendment grants to schools in light of their special characteristics is diminished. We leave for future cases to decide where, when, and how these features mean the speaker's off-campus location will make the critical difference. This case can, however, provide one example.

Consider B.L.'s speech. Putting aside the vulgar language, the listener would hear criticism, of the team, the team's coaches, and the school — in a word or two, criticism of the rules of a community of which B.L. forms a part. This criticism did not involve features that would place it outside the First Amendment's ordinary protection. B.L.'s posts, while crude, did not amount to fighting words. And while B.L. used vulgarity, her speech was not obscene as this Court has understood that term. To the contrary, B.L. uttered the kind of pure speech to which, were she an adult, the First Amendment would provide strong protection.

Consider too when, where, and how B.L. spoke. Her posts appeared outside of school hours from a location outside the school. She did not identify the school in her posts or target any member of the school community with vulgar or abusive language. B.L. also transmitted her speech through a personal cellphone, to an audience consisting of her private circle of Snapchat friends. These features of her speech, while risking transmission to the school itself, nonetheless (for reasons we have just explained) diminish the school's interest in punishing B.L.'s utterance.

But what about the school's interest, here primarily an interest in prohibiting students from using vulgar language to criticize a school team or its coaches — at least when that criticism might well be transmitted to other students, team members, coaches, and faculty? We can break that general interest into three parts.

First, we consider the school's interest in teaching good manners and consequently in punishing the use of vulgar language aimed at part of the school community. The strength of this anti-vulgarity interest is weakened considerably by the fact that B.L. spoke outside the school on her own time.

B.L. spoke under circumstances where the school did not stand in loco parentis. And there is no reason to believe B.L.'s parents had delegated to school officials their own control of B.L.'s behavior at the Cocoa Hut. Moreover, the vulgarity in B.L.'s posts encompassed a message, an expression of B.L.'s irritation with, and criticism of, the school and cheerleading communities. Further, the school has presented no evidence of any general effort to prevent students from using vulgarity outside the classroom. Together, these facts convince us that the school's interest in teaching good manners is not sufficient, in this case, to overcome B.L.'s interest in free expression.

Second, the school argues that it was trying to prevent disruption, if not within the classroom, then within the bounds of a school-sponsored extracurricular activity. But we can find no evidence in the record of the sort of "substantial disruption" of a school activity or a threatened harm to the rights of others that might justify the school's action. Rather, the record shows that discussion of the matter took, at most, 5 to 10 minutes of an Algebra class "for just a couple of days" and that some members of the cheerleading team were "upset" about the content of B.L.'s Snapchats.

But when one of B.L.'s coaches was asked directly if she had "any reason to think that this particular incident would disrupt class or school activities other than the fact that kids kept asking . . . about it," she responded simply, "No." As we said in *Tinker*, "for the State in the person of school officials to justify prohibition of a particular expression of opinion, it must be able to show that its action was caused by something more than a mere desire to avoid the discomfort and unpleasantness that always accompany an unpopular viewpoint."

The alleged disturbance here does not meet *Tinker*'s demanding standard.

Third, the school presented some evidence that expresses (at least indirectly) a concern for team morale. One of the coaches testified that the school decided to suspend B.L., not because of any specific negative impact upon a particular member of the school community, but "based on the fact that there was negativity put out there that could impact students in the school." There is little else, however, that suggests any serious decline in team morale — to the point where it could create a substantial interference in, or disruption of, the school's efforts to maintain team cohesion. As we have previously said, simple "undifferentiated fear or apprehension . . . is not enough to overcome the right to freedom of expression." *Tinker*.

It might be tempting to dismiss B.L.'s words as unworthy of the robust First Amendment protections discussed herein. But sometimes it is necessary to protect the superfluous in order to preserve the necessary. *See Tyson & Brother v. Banton*, 273 U.S. 418, 447 (1927) (Holmes, J., dissenting). "We cannot lose sight of the fact that, in what otherwise might seem a trifling and annoying instance of individual distasteful abuse of a privilege, these fundamental societal values are truly implicated." *Cohen*.

Although we do not agree with the reasoning of the Third Circuit's panel majority, for the reasons expressed above, resembling those of the panel's concurring opinion, we nonetheless agree that the school violated B.L.'s First Amendment rights. The judgment of the Third Circuit is therefore affirmed.

It is so ordered.

Justice Alito, with whom Justice Gorsuch joins, concurring.

I start with this threshold question: Why does the First Amendment ever allow the free-speech rights of public school students to be restricted to a greater extent than the rights of other juveniles who do not attend a public school? As the Court recognized in *Tinker*, when a public school regulates student speech, it acts as an arm of the State in which it is located. Suppose that B.L. had been enrolled in a private school and did exactly what she did in this case — send out vulgar and derogatory messages that focused on her school's cheerleading squad. The Commonwealth of Pennsylvania would have had no legal basis to punish her and almost certainly would not have even tried. So why should her status as a public school student give the Commonwealth any greater authority to punish her speech?

Our cases involving the regulation of student speech have not directly addressed this question. All those cases involved either in-school speech or speech that was tantamount to in-school speech. And in those cases, the Court appeared to take it for granted that "the special characteristics of the school environment" justified special rules.

Why the Court took this for granted is not hard to imagine. As a practical matter, it is impossible to see how a school could function if administrators and teachers could not regulate on-premises student speech, including by imposing content-based restrictions in the classroom. In a math class, for example, the teacher can insist that students talk about math, not some other subject. In addition, when a teacher asks a question, the teacher must have the authority to insist that the student respond to that question and not some other question, and a teacher must also have the authority to speak without interruption and to demand that students refrain from interrupting one another. Practical necessity likewise dictates that teachers and school administrators have related authority with respect to other in-school activities like auditorium programs attended by a large audience.

Because no school could operate effectively if teachers and administrators lacked the authority to regulate in-school speech in these ways, the Court may have felt no need to specify the source of this authority or to explain how the special rules applicable to in-school student speech fit into our broader framework of free-speech case law. But when a public school regulates what students say or write when they are not on school grounds and are not participating in a school program, the school has the obligation to answer the question with which I began: Why should enrollment in a public school result in the diminution of a student's free-speech rights?

The only plausible answer that comes readily to mind is consent, either express or implied. The theory must be that by enrolling a child in a public school, parents consent on behalf of the child to the relinquishment of some of the child's free-speech rights.

This understanding is consistent with the conditions to which an adult would implicitly consent by enrolling in an adult education class run by a unit of state or local government. If an adult signs up for, say, a French class, the adult may be required to speak French, to answer the teacher's questions, and to comply with other rules that are imposed for the sake of orderly instruction.

When it comes to children, courts in this country have analyzed the issue of consent by adapting the common-law doctrine of *in loco* parentis. Under the common law, as Blackstone explained, "[a father could] delegate part of his parental authority . . . to the tutor or schoolmaster of his child; who is then in loco parentis, and has such a portion of the power of the parent committed to his charge, [namely,] that of restraint and correction, as may be necessary to answer the purposes for which he is employed." 1 W. Blackstone, Commentaries on the Laws of England 441 (1765).

Blackstone's explanation of the doctrine seems to treat it primarily as an implied term in a private employment agreement between a father and those with whom he contracted for the provision of educational services for his child, and therefore the scope of the delegation that could be inferred depended on "the purposes for which [the tutor or schoolmaster was] employed." *Ibid*. If a child was sent to a boarding school, the parents would not have been in a position to monitor or control the child's behavior or to attend to the child's welfare on a daily basis, and the schoolmaster would be regarded as having implicitly received the authority to perform those functions around the clock while the child was in residence. On the other hand, if parents hired a tutor to instruct a child in the home on certain subjects during certain hours, the scope of the delegation would be different. The tutor would be in charge during lessons, but the parents would retain most of their authority. In short, the scope of the delegation depended on the scope of the agreed-upon undertaking.

Today, of course, the educational picture is quite different. The education of children within a specified age range is compulsory, and States specify the minimum number of hours per day and the minimum number of days per year that a student must attend classes, as well as many aspects of the school curriculum. Parents are not required to enroll their children in a public school. They can select a private school if a suitable one is available and they can afford the tuition, and they may also be able to educate their children at home if they have the time and ability and can meet the standards that their State imposes. But by choice or necessity, nearly 90% of the students in this country attend public schools, and parents and public schools do not enter into a contractual relationship.

If *in loco parentis* is transplanted from Blackstone's England to the 21st century United States, what it amounts to is simply a doctrine of inferred parental consent to a public school's exercise of a degree of authority that is commensurate with the task that the parents ask the school to perform. Because public school students attend school for only part of the day and continue to live at home, the degree of authority conferred is obviously less than that delegated to the head of a late-18th century boarding school, but because public school students are taught outside the home, the authority conferred may be greater in at least some respects than that enjoyed by a tutor of Blackstone's time.

So how much authority to regulate speech do parents implicitly delegate when they enroll a child at a public school? The answer must be that parents are treated as having relinquished the measure of authority that the schools must be able to exercise in order to carry out their state-mandated educational mission, as well as the authority to perform any other functions to which parents expressly or implicitly agree — for example, by giving permission for a child to participate in an extracurricular activity or to go on a school trip.

The degree to which enrollment in a public school can be regarded as a delegation of authority over off-campus speech depends on the nature of the speech and the circumstances under which it occurs. I will not attempt to provide a complete taxonomy of off-premises speech, but relevant lower court cases tend to fall into a few basic groups. And with respect to speech in each of these groups, the question that courts must ask is whether parents who enroll their children in a public school can reasonably be understood to have delegated to the school the authority to regulate the speech in question.

One category of off-premises student speech falls easily within the scope of the authority that parents implicitly or explicitly provide. This category includes speech that takes place during or as part of what amounts to a temporal or spatial extension of the regular school program, e.g., online instruction at home, assigned essays or other homework, and transportation to and from school. Also included are statements made during other school activities in which students participate with their parents' consent, such as school trips, school sports and other extracurricular activities that may take place after regular school hours or off school premises, and after-school programs for students who would otherwise be without adult supervision during that time. Abusive speech that occurs while students are walking to and from school may also fall into this category on the theory that it is school attendance that puts students on that route and in the company of the fellow students who engage in the abuse. The imperatives that justify the regulation of student speech while in school — the need for orderly and effective instruction and student protection — apply more or less equally to these off-premises activities.

At the other end of the spectrum, there is a category of speech that is almost always beyond the regulatory authority of a public school. This is student speech that is not expressly and specifically directed at the school, school administrators, teachers, or fellow students and that addresses matters of public concern, including sensitive subjects like politics, religion, and social relations.

If a school tried to regulate such speech, the most that it could claim is that offensive off-premises speech on important matters may cause controversy and recriminations among students and may thus disrupt instruction and good order on school premises. But it is a "bedrock principle" that speech may not be suppressed simply because it expresses ideas that are "offensive or disagreeable." *Texas v. Johnson.*

This is true even if the student's off-premises speech on a matter of public concern is intemperate and crude. When a student engages in oral or written communication of this nature, the student is subject to whatever restraints the student's parents impose, but the student enjoys the same First Amendment protection against government regulation as all other members of the public.

Between these two extremes (i.e., off-premises speech that is tantamount to on-campus speech and general statements made off premises on matters of public concern) lie the categories of off-premises student speech that appear to have given rise to the most litigation. A survey of lower court cases reveals several prominent categories. I will mention some of those categories, but like the Court, I do not attempt to set out the test to be used in judging the constitutionality of a public school's efforts to regulate such speech.

One group of cases involves perceived threats to school administrators, teachers, other staff members, or students. Laws that apply to everyone prohibit defined categories of threats, but schools have claimed that their duties demand broader authority.

Another common category involves speech that criticizes or derides school administrators, teachers, or other staff members. Schools may assert that parents who send their children to a public school implicitly authorize the school to demand that the child exhibit the respect that is required for orderly and effective instruction, but parents surely do not relinquish their children's ability to complain in an appropriate manner about wrongdoing, dereliction, or even plain incompetence.

Perhaps the most difficult category involves criticism or hurtful remarks about other students. Bullying and severe harassment are serious (and age-old) problems, but these concepts are not easy to define with the precision required for a regulation of speech.

The present case does not fall into any of these categories. Instead, it simply involves criticism (albeit in a crude manner) of the school and an extracurricular activity. Unflattering speech about a school or one of its programs is different from speech that criticizes or derides particular individuals, and for the reasons detailed by the Court and by Judge Ambro in his separate opinion below, the school's justifications for punishing B.L.'s speech were weak.

There are more than 90,000 public school principals in this country and more than 13,000 separate school districts. The overwhelming majority of school administrators, teachers, and coaches are men and women who are deeply dedicated to the best interests of their students, but it is predictable that there will be occasions when some will get carried away, as did the school officials in the case at hand. If today's decision teaches any lesson, it must be that the regulation of many types of off-premises student speech raises serious First Amendment concerns, and school officials should proceed cautiously before venturing into this territory.

JUSTICE THOMAS dissenting.

While the majority entirely ignores the relevant history, I would begin the assessment of the scope of free-speech rights incorporated against the States by looking to "what 'ordinary citizens' at the time of [the Fourteenth Amendment's] ratification would have understood" the right to encompass. Cases and treatises from that era reveal that public schools retained substantial authority to discipline students. As I have previously explained, that authority was near plenary while students were at school.

Authority also extended to when students were traveling to or from school. See, *e.g., Lander v. Seaver*, 32 Vt. 114, 120 (1859). And, although schools had less authority after a student returned home, it was well settled that they still could discipline students for off-campus speech or conduct that had a proximate tendency to harm the school environment.

Perhaps the most familiar example applying this rule is a case where a student, after returning home from school, used "disrespectful language" against a teacher — he called the teacher "old" — "in presence of the [teacher] and of some of his fellow pupils." The Vermont Supreme Court held that the teacher could discipline a student for this speech because the speech had "a direct and immediate tendency to injure the school, to subvert the master's authority, and to beget disorder and insubordination."

The majority declines to consider any of this history, instead favoring a few pragmatic guideposts. This is not the first time the Court has chosen intuition over history when it comes to student speech. The larger problem facing us today is that our student-speech cases are untethered from any textual or historical foundation.

The Court's failure to explain itself in *Tinker* needlessly makes this case more difficult.

Perhaps there are good constitutional reasons to depart from the historical rule, and perhaps this Court and lower courts will identify and explain these reasons in the future. But because the Court does not do so today, and because it reaches the wrong result under the appropriate historical test, I respectfully dissent.

Notes and Questions

(1) Should schools play an "inculcation" function, transmitting civic values? Should schools, for example, attempt to mold students to be tolerant? Should schools teach students that it is wrong to be racist or sexist? If these are appropriate educational goals for a public school system in a pluralistic democracy, does it follow that schools may prohibit racist and sexist speech by students at school assemblies, and censor racist and sexist articles in a school newspaper? How can the teaching of such values — which necessarily involves the preference of one viewpoint (tolerance) over another viewpoint (intolerance) — be squared with the "neutrality principle" that generally prohibits the government from engaging in viewpoint-discrimination? Is there a special "child's First Amendment" more lax than the "adult First Amendment"?

(2) Concerns over racism or other forms of discrimination have led many school boards to enact measures against hate speech, including the wearing of certain symbols, such as the Confederate Flag, on school grounds. Similarly "hate speech" incidents on university campuses have led many universities, public and private, to adopt "hate speech codes" that are designed to ban various forms of hate speech in university settings. Generally, hate speech restrictions at the university level have met with hostility from courts. *See UWM Post v. Board of Regents of the University of Wisconsin*, 774 F. Supp. 1163 (E.D. Wis. 1991) (striking down hate speech code); *Doe v. University of Michigan*, 721 F. Supp. 852 (E.D. Mich. 1989) (same). *See also Iota XI Chapter of Sigma Chi Fraternity v. George Mason University*, 993 F.2d 386 (4th Cir. 1993) (holding that the First Amendment was violated by the imposition of disciplinary action against a college fraternity arising from allegedly offensive caricatures of a woman in blackface during a fraternity social event). At the high school and elementary school level, in contrast, the results have been more mixed, with courts showing a greater willingness to invoke the deference to school officials contemplated by Supreme Court decisions such as *Tinker, Hazelwood* and *Bethel* to allow restrictions, at least when school officials have been able to point to a record

of prior racial incidents and disturbances. *Scott v. School Board of Alachua County,* 324 F.3d 1246 (11th Cir. 2003) (sustaining ban on wearing of Confederate Flag where there was history of racial problems surrounding wearing of the Confederate Flag); *West v. Derby Unified School District No. 260,* 206 F.3d 1358 (10th Cir. 2000).

(3) Justice Breyer's opinion in *Mahanoy* was "vintage Justice Breyer," in that he eschewed adoption of any special test to guide schools in deciding when students could or could not be disciplined for speech off-campus on social media. Consider Justice Breyer's guidelines, as well as the other opinions in the case, in responding to Problem E below.

Problem E

You work for a law firm that represents a large public school district. The school district is one of the firm's most important clients. A senior partner at the firm assigns to you, a new associate, the following task: "Our client the school district has asked us to draft a policy for the school governing student conduct in the context of social media posts by students. I know the Supreme Court recently decided that f-bomb cheerleader case. I haven't read it myself—that's your job. Prepare a draft policy for the school, and then show me what you've drafted, and be ready to explain it to me, as well as to the school board."

§ 9.15 The Legal System

A. Reporting on Judicial Proceedings

Richmond Newspapers v. Virginia. In *Richmond Newspapers, Inc. v. Virginia,* 448 U.S. 555 (1980), the Supreme Court faced the question of whether the Constitution vested a right in the public and press to attend criminal trials. In an opinion by Chief Justice Burger, the Supreme Court ruled that absent an overriding interest articulated in findings, the trial of a criminal case must be open to the public. The Supreme Court examined the long tradition of granting public access to criminal trials in the United States, and determined that "from this unbroken, uncontradicted history, supported by reasons as valid today as in centuries past, we are bound to conclude that a presumption of openness inheres in the very nature of a criminal trial under our system of justice." Although noting that such a right of access was not specifically enumerated in the Constitution or Bill of Rights, the Court explained that:

> The Bill of Rights was enacted against the backdrop of the long history of trials being presumptively open.... In guaranteeing freedoms such as those of speech and press, the First Amendment can be read as protecting the right of everyone to attend trials so as to give meaning to those explicit guarantees.... Free speech carries with it some freedom to listen.... What this means in the context of trials is that the First Amendment guarantees of speech and press, standing alone, prohibit government from summarily closing courtroom doors.

B. Controlling the Speech of Lawyers

Gentile v. State Bar of Nevada. The Supreme Court in *Gentile v. State Bar of Nevada*, 501 U.S. 1030 (1991), considered a Nevada case in which an attorney was held to have violated a state supreme court rule ("Rule 177") prohibiting a lawyer from making extrajudicial statements to the press that he knows or reasonably should know will have a "substantial likelihood of materially prejudicing" an adjudicative proceeding. Dominic Gentile, the attorney, had held a press conference shortly after his client was indicted on criminal charges. Gentile read a prepared statement there and then responded to questions.

Gentile had contended that the First Amendment required a stricter standard be adhered to than the "substantial likelihood of material prejudice" standard used by the state of Nevada in determining whether an attorney may be disciplined for his speech. He claimed there should be a finding of "actual prejudice or a substantial and imminent threat to fair trial" before such steps were taken.

Chief Justice Rehnquist, writing for the Court on this issue, referred to the history of court regulation of admission to the practice of law and the exercise of court authority to discipline and to disbar lawyers whose conduct departed from prescribed standards. He then considered the dilemma presented by the need for impartial jurors who know as little as possible about the case and the need to inform people about proceedings in the criminal justice system. Chief Justice Rehnquist pointed out that First Amendment protections of speech and press have been held to require a showing of "clear and present danger" that a malfunction in the criminal justice system will occur before the government may prohibit media speech or publication about a particular trial. He then addressed the question of whether a lawyer representing a defendant in a criminal case is entitled to the same standard before being disciplined for speaking publicly about the case, or whether a state may punish that sort of speech under a less exacting standard. Rehnquist distinguished between parties to litigation and strangers to it, and held that lawyers are not protected by the First Amendment to the same extent as persons of other professions, deeming the "substantial likelihood of material prejudice" standard a constitutionally permissible balance between the First Amendment rights of attorneys in pending cases and the government interest in fair trials. Such a regulation is narrowly tailored, Rehnquist wrote, because it applies only to speech that is substantially likely to prejudice a trial; it is viewpoint-neutral; and it merely postpones an attorney's pronouncements until after the trial.

The Court also held, however, that the Nevada Supreme Court's interpretation of its Rule 177 was void for vagueness. Justice Kennedy wrote this part of the opinion for the Court, attacking the rule's safe harbor provision, rule 177(3). He explained that this section of the rule had misled Gentile into thinking that he could conduct the press conference without having to worry about violating the rule. The section provides that a lawyer "may state without elaboration ... the general nature of the ... defense." The Court held that this language was so vague it required lawyers attempting to abide by the rule to make their own interpretations of the rule. Kennedy pointed out that "general" and "elaboration" are both terms of degree with no settled usage in the interpretation of law, and that "[t]he lawyer has no principle for determining when his remarks pass from the safe harbor of the general to the forbidden sea of the elaborated."

The Court held that the words Gentile used during the press conference indicated that he was unable to determine which remarks were acceptable, but that he had made an effort to do so. On numerous occasions during the press conference, Gentile declined to answer reporters' questions seeking detailed comments, claiming that ethics prohibited him from elaborating. This demonstrated that Gentile had attempted to obey the rule and believed that his statements were protected by the safe harbor provision. The Court held that "[t]he fact Gentile was found in violation of the Rules after studying them and making a conscious effort at compliance demonstrates that Rule 177 creates a trap for the wary as well as the unwary," concluding that "the Rule is so imprecise that discriminatory enforcement is a real possibility."

§ 9.16 Anonymous Speech

Talley v. California. In *Talley v. California*, 362 U.S. 60 (1960), the Supreme Court observed that "[a]nonymous pamphlets, leaflets, brochures and even books have played an important role in the progress of mankind." The Court in *Talley* held that the First Amendment protected the distribution of unsigned handbills urging readers to boycott certain Los Angeles merchants who were allegedly engaging in discriminatory employment practices. Writing for the Court, Justice Black noted that "persecuted groups and sects from time to time throughout history have been able to criticize oppressive practices and laws either anonymously or not at all." Recalling England's abusive press licensing laws and seditious libel prosecutions, the Court in *Talley* admonished that even the arguments favoring the ratification of the Constitution advanced in the Federalist Papers were published under fictitious names.

McIntyre v. Ohio Elections Commission. In *McIntyre v. Ohio Elections Commission*, 514 U.S. 334 (1995), the Supreme Court examined an Ohio law prohibiting the distribution of anonymous campaign literature. The case arose from the actions of Margaret McIntyre, who distributed leaflets to persons attending a public meeting at the Blendon Middle School in Westerville, Ohio. At this meeting, the superintendent of schools planned to discuss an imminent referendum on a proposed school tax levy. The leaflets expressed Mrs. McIntyre's opposition to the levy. Nothing in the message was false, misleading, or libelous. McIntyre composed and printed the material on her home computer and paid a professional printer to make additional copies. Some of the handbills identified her as the author; others merely purported to express the views of "CONCERNED PARENTS AND TAX PAYERS." The Court, in an opinion by Justice Stevens, noted the long tradition of anonymous authorship, both in literature and politics.

Despite readers' curiosity and the public's interest in identifying the creator of a work of art, an author generally is free to decide whether or not to disclose her true identity. The decision in favor of anonymity may be motivated by fear of economic or official retaliation, by concern about social ostracism, or merely by a desire to preserve as much of one's privacy as possible. Whatever the motivation may be, at least in the field of literary endeavor, the interest in having anonymous works enter the marketplace of ideas unquestionably outweighs any public interest in requiring disclosure as a condition of entry. Accordingly, an author's decision to remain anonymous, like other decisions concerning omissions or additions to the content of a publication, is an aspect of the freedom of speech protected by the First Amendment.

To the extent that Ohio wished to guarantee truth in political discourse, the Court held, its regular election fraud and libel laws were sufficient to accomplish its objectives. While the Court was careful not to state that it necessarily approved the constitutionality of those election fraud provisions, they were evidence that Ohio has addressed directly the problem of election fraud, and thus had no need to encroach on the First Amendment freedom to publish with anonymity.

Unmasking Anonymous Internet Posts. Internet communication is often anonymous, conducted behind the facade of screen-names. Courts are sometimes asked to "unmask" the anonymous post, revealing the identity of the person or entity responsible. Defamation litigation poses a typical example. A would-be plaintiff defamed on the Internet will often not know the identity of the alleged defamer. One common tactic to deal with this problem is to file a suit against a "John Doe" defendant, and then serve a third-party subpoena against the Internet Service Provider from whose service the defamer appeared to have originated, seeking disclosure of the identity of the person behind the screen name. This process, often described as "unmasking," has generated a substantial body of law balancing the First Amendment right to engage in anonymous speech against the powerful social values favoring redress for defamation. Courts vary in the tests they apply in these unmasking cases. Four general approaches have emerged. They form a spectrum from standards that are very permissive in unmasking the anonymity of Internet users, to standards that require a high evidentiary showing before the unmasking is allowed. The approaches are typically described as (1) requiring only a minimal showing of a good faith basis that the plaintiff was the victim of actionable conduct, (2) requiring a party to show that its claim can survive a motion to dismiss, (3) requiring a prima facie showing that actionable conduct occurred, and (4) requiring a plaintiff to survive a hypothetical motion for summary judgment. RODNEY SMOLLA, LAW OF DEFAMATION, § 4:86.50, *Anonymity and the Internet* (2023 Edition).

§ 9.17   Forced Speech

303 Creative LLC v. Elenis

United States Supreme Court

143 S. Ct. 2298 (2023)

JUSTICE GORSUCH delivered the opinion of the Court.

Like many States, Colorado has a law forbidding businesses from engaging in discrimination when they sell goods and services to the public. Laws along these lines have done much to secure the civil rights of all Americans. But in this particular case Colorado does not just seek to ensure the sale of goods or services on equal terms. It seeks to use its law to compel an individual to create speech she does not believe. The question we face is whether that course violates the Free Speech Clause of the First Amendment.

Through her business, 303 Creative LLC, Lorie Smith offers website and graphic design, marketing advice, and social media management services. Recently, she decided to expand her offerings to include services for couples seeking websites for their weddings.

While Ms. Smith has laid the groundwork for her new venture, she has yet to carry out her plans. She worries that, if she does so, Colorado will force her to express views with which she disagrees. Ms. Smith provides her website and graphic services to customers regardless of their race, creed, sex, or sexual orientation. But she has never created expressions that contradict her own views for anyone — whether that means generating works that encourage violence, demean another person, or defy her religious beliefs by, say, promoting atheism. Ms. Smith does not wish to do otherwise now, but she worries Colorado has different plans. Specifically, she worries that, if she enters the wedding website business, the State will force her to convey messages inconsistent with her belief that marriage should be reserved to unions between one man and one woman. Ms. Smith acknowledges that her views about marriage may not be popular in all quarters. But, she asserts, the First Amendment's Free Speech Clause protects her from being compelled to speak what she does not believe. The Constitution, she insists, protects her right to differ.

The framers designed the Free Speech Clause of the First Amendment to protect the "freedom to think as you will and to speak as you think." *Boy Scouts of America v. Dale*, 530 U.S. 640, 660–661 (2000). By allowing all views to flourish, the framers understood, we may test and improve our own thinking both as individuals and as a Nation. For all these reasons, "[i]f there is any fixed star in our constitutional constellation," *West Virginia Bd. of Ed. v. Barnette*.

From time to time, governments in this country have sought to test these foundational principles. In *Barnette*, for example, the Court faced an effort by the State of West Virginia to force schoolchildren to salute the Nation's flag and recite the Pledge of Allegiance. If the students refused, the State threatened to expel them and fine or jail their parents. Some families objected on the ground that the State sought to compel their children to express views at odds with their faith as Jehovah's Witnesses. When the dispute arrived here, this Court offered a firm response. In seeking to compel students to salute the flag and recite a pledge, the Court held, state authorities had "transcend[ed] constitutional limitations on their powers."

A similar story unfolded in *Hurley v. Irish-American Gay, Lesbian and Bisexual Group of Boston*, Inc., 515 U.S. 557 (1995). There, veterans organizing a St. Patrick's Day parade in Boston refused to include a group of gay, lesbian, and bisexual individuals in their event. The group argued that Massachusetts's public accommodations statute entitled it to participate in the parade as a matter of law. Whatever state law may demand, this Court explained, the parade was constitutionally protected speech and requiring the veterans to include voices they wished to exclude would impermissibly require them to "alter the expressive content of their parade. The veterans' choice of what to say (and not say) might have been unpopular, but they had a First Amendment right to present their message undiluted by views they did not share.

Then there is *Boy Scouts of America v. Dale*. In that case, the Boy Scouts excluded James Dale, an assistant scoutmaster, from membership after learning he was gay. Mr. Dale argued that New Jersey's public accommodations law required the Scouts to reinstate him. The New Jersey Supreme Court sided with Mr. Dale, but again this Court reversed. The decision to exclude Mr. Dale may not have implicated pure speech, but this Court held that the Boy Scouts "is an expressive association" entitled to First Amendment protection. And, the Court found, forcing the Scouts to include Mr. Dale would "interfere with [its] choice not to propound a point of view contrary to its beliefs."

The Tenth Circuit held that the wedding websites Ms. Smith seeks to create qualify as "pure speech" under this Court's precedents. We agree. It is a conclusion that flows directly from the parties' stipulations. They have stipulated that Ms. Smith's websites promise to contain "images, words, symbols, and other modes of expression."

A hundred years ago, Ms. Smith might have furnished her services using pen and paper. Those services are no less protected speech today because they are conveyed with a "voice that resonates farther than it could from any soapbox." *Reno v. American Civil Liberties Union*. All manner of speech — from "pictures, films, paintings, drawings, and engravings," to "oral utterance and the printed word" — qualify for the First Amendment's protections; no less can hold true when it comes to speech like Ms. Smith's conveyed over the Internet.

We part ways with the Tenth Circuit only when it comes to the legal conclusions that follow. While that court thought Colorado could compel speech from Ms. Smith consistent with the Constitution, our First Amendment precedents laid out above teach otherwise. In *Hurley*, the Court found that Massachusetts impermissibly compelled speech in violation of the First Amendment. In *Dale*, the Court held that New Jersey intruded on the Boy Scouts' First Amendment rights when it tried to require the group to "propound a point of view contrary to its beliefs" by directing its membership choices. And in *Barnette*, this Court found impermissible coercion when West Virginia required schoolchildren to recite a pledge that contravened their convictions on threat of punishment or expulsion. Here, Colorado seeks to put Ms. Smith to a similar choice: If she wishes to speak, she must either speak as the State demands or face sanctions for expressing her own beliefs, sanctions that may include compulsory participation in "remedial training filing periodic compliance reports as officials deem necessary, and paying monetary fines. Under our precedents, that is enough, more than enough, to represent an impermissible abridgment of the First Amendment's right to speak freely.

Consider what a contrary approach would mean. Under Colorado's logic, the government may compel anyone who speaks for pay on a given topic to accept all commissions on that same topic — no matter the underlying message — if the topic somehow implicates a customer's statutorily protected trait. Seriously, that principle would allow the government to force all manner of artists, speechwriters, and others whose services involve speech to speak what they do not believe on pain of penalty. The government could require "an unwilling Muslim movie director to make a film with a Zionist message," or "an atheist muralist to accept a commission celebrating Evangelical zeal," so long as they would make films or murals for other members of the public with different messages. Equally, the government could force a male website designer married to another man to design websites for an organization that advocates against same-sex marriage. Countless other creative professionals, too, could be forced to choose between remaining silent, producing speech that violates their beliefs, or speaking their minds and incurring sanctions for doing so.

JUSTICE SOTOMAYOR, with whom JUSTICE KAGAN and JUSTICE JACKSON join, dissenting.

Five years ago, this Court recognized the "general rule" that religious and philosophical objections to gay marriage "do not allow business owners and other actors in the economy and in society to deny protected persons equal access to goods and services under a neutral and generally applicable public accommodations law." *Masterpiece Cakeshop, Ltd. v. Colorado Civil Rights Comm'n*, 584 U.S. __, __, 138 S. Ct. 1719, 201 L. Ed. 2d 35 (2018) (slip op., at 9). The Court also recognized the "serious stigma" that would result if "purveyors of goods and services who object to gay marriages for moral and religious reasons" were "allowed to put up signs saying 'no goods or services will be sold if they will be used for gay marriages.'"

Today, the Court, for the first time in its history, grants a business open to the public a constitutional right to refuse to serve members of a protected class. Specifically, the Court holds that the First Amendment exempts a website-design company from a state law that prohibits the company from denying wedding websites to same-sex couples if the company chooses to sell those websites to the public.

"What a difference five years makes." *Carson v. Makin*, 142 S. Ct. 1987, 2014 (2022) (SOTOMAYOR, J., dissenting). And not just at the Court. Around the country, there has been a backlash to the movement for liberty and equality for gender and sexual minorities. New forms of inclusion have been met with reactionary exclusion. This is heartbreaking. Sadly, it is also familiar. When the civil rights and women's rights movements sought equality in public life, some public establishments refused. Some even claimed, based on sincere religious beliefs, constitutional rights to discriminate. The brave Justices who once sat on this Court decisively rejected those claims.

Now the Court faces a similar test. A business open to the public seeks to deny gay and lesbian customers the full and equal enjoyment of its services based on the owner's religious belief that same-sex marriages are "false." The business argues, and a majority of the Court agrees, that because the business offers services that are customized and expressive, the Free Speech Clause of the First Amendment shields the business from a generally applicable law that prohibits discrimination in the sale of publicly available goods and services. That is wrong. Profoundly wrong. As I will explain, the law in question targets conduct, not speech, for regulation, and the act of discrimination has never constituted protected expression under the First Amendment. Our Constitution contains no right to refuse service to a disfavored group. I dissent.

Not only have public accommodations laws expanded to recognize more forms of unjust discrimination, such as discrimination based on race, sex, and disability, such laws have also expanded to include more goods and services as "public accommodations." What began with common inns, carriers, and smiths has grown to include restaurants, bars, movie theaters, sports arenas, retail stores, salons, gyms, hospitals, funeral homes, and transportation networks.

This broader scope, though more inclusive than earlier state public accommodations laws, is in keeping with the fundamental principle — rooted in the common law, but alive and blossoming in statutory law — that the duty to serve without unjust discrimination is owed to everyone, and it extends to any business that holds itself out as ready to serve the public. If you have ever taken advantage of a public business without being denied service because of who you are, then you have come to enjoy the dignity and freedom that this principle protects.

Lesbian, gay, bisexual, and transgender (LGBT) people, no less than anyone else, deserve that dignity and freedom. The movement for LGBT rights, and the resulting expansion of state and local laws to secure gender and sexual minorities' full and equal enjoyment of publicly available goods and services, is the latest chapter of this great American story.

LGBT people have existed for all of human history. And as sure as they have existed, others have sought to deny their existence, and to exclude them from public life. Those who would subordinate LGBT people have often done so with the backing of law. For most of American history, there were laws criminalizing same-sex intimacy. *Obergefell v. Hodges*, 576 U.S. 644, 660–661 (2015). "Gays and lesbians were [also] prohibited from most government employment, barred from military service, excluded under immigration laws, targeted by police, and burdened in their rights to associate." "These policies worked to create and reinforce the belief that gay men and lesbians" constituted "an inferior class."

Opponents of the Civil Rights Act of 1964 objected that the law would force business owners to defy their beliefs. They argued that the Act would deny them "any freedom to speak or to act on the basis of their religious convictions or their deep-rooted preferences for associating or not associating with certain classifications of people." Congress rejected those arguments.

Having failed to persuade Congress, opponents of Title II turned to the federal courts. In *Heart of Atlanta Motel* [*v. United States*, 379 U.S. 241 (1964)], one of several arguments made by the plaintiff motel owner was that Title II violated his Fifth Amendment due process rights by "tak[ing] away the personal liberty of an individual to run his business as he sees fit with respect to the selection and service of his customers." This Court disagreed, based on "a long line of cases" holding that "prohibition of racial discrimination in public accommodations" did not "interfere with personal liberty."

The unattractive lesson of the majority opinion is this: What's mine is mine, and what's yours is yours. The lesson of the history of public accommodations laws is altogether different. It is that in a free and democratic society, there can be no social castes. And for that to be true, it must be true in the public market. For the "promise of freedom" is an empty one if the Government is "powerless to assure that a dollar in the hands of [one person] will purchase the same thing as a dollar in the hands of a[nother]." *Jones v. Alfred H. Mayer Co.*, 392 U.S. 409, 443 (1968). Because the Court today retreats from that promise, I dissent.

Notes and Questions

(1) While the First Amendment is typically concerned with preventing government from restricting expression, it is also implicated when the government attempts to compel expression. The First Amendment generally prohibits government from forcing a speaker to profess statements or beliefs against the speaker's will. In addition to the cases cited in *303 Creative*, consider the following cases as well.

(2) In *Wooley v. Maynard*, 430 U.S. 705 (1977), the Supreme Court held that a Jehovah's Witness could not be compelled to display the motto "Live Free or Die" on his New Hampshire license plates. *Wooley v. Maynard*, like *Barnette*, is powerful authority for the proposition that the state cannot compel citizens to recite patriotic civic rituals or slogans. *Wooley* created a constitutional right for citizens to cover up the motto on their individual plates, and more broadly underscored the importance of the right not to speak under government compulsion.

(3) In *National Institute of Family & Life Advocates v. Becerra*, 138 S. Ct. 2361 (2018), the Supreme Court struck down provisions of the California Reproductive Freedom, Accountability, Comprehensive Care, and Transparency Act (FACT Act). The California law was enacted to regulate crisis pregnancy centers—pro-life centers that offer pregnancy-related services. The FACT Act required clinics that primarily serve

pregnant women to notify women that California provides free or low-cost services, including abortions, and give them a phone number to call. California claimed that its purpose was to make sure that state residents knew their rights and what health care services were available to them. In striking down the requirement that the clinics provide the required information, the Court, in an opinion written by Justice Thomas, observed that the "clinics must provide a government-drafted script about the availability of state-sponsored services, as well as contact information for how to obtain them. One of those services is abortion—the very practice that petitioners are devoted to opposing."

(4) In *Abood v. Detroit Board of Education*, 431 U.S. 209 (1977), the Supreme Court originally held that public employees could be forced to pay union dues even if they choose not to join the union and object to the positions the union takes in collective bargaining negotiations. *Abood* also held, however, that the Constitution requires that a union's expenditures for ideological causes not germane to its duties as a collective-bargaining representative be financed from charges, dues, or assessments paid by employees who do not object to advancing such causes and who are not coerced into doing so against their will by the threat of loss of governmental employment. An employee forced to pay union dues under *Abood* thus had the right to a rebate for the portion of the dues that subsidized ideological causes unrelated to the collective bargaining.

Abood's general rule allowing compulsory union dues was overruled in 2018 in *Janus v. American Federation of State, City & Municipal Employees, Council 31*, 138 S. Ct. 2448 (2018). In *Janus*, the Court partially overturned its prior decision in *Abood*. The Court in *Janus* held that the First Amendment is violated by laws that force public employees to subsidize a union, even if they choose not to join the union and strongly object to the positions the union takes in collective bargaining and related activities. The Court, in a five-four decision written by Justice Alito, held that *Abood* was poorly reasoned and has led to practical problems and abuse. The Court emphasized that it had "held time and again that freedom of speech 'includes both the right to speak freely and the right to refrain from speaking at all.'" Similar principles apply to the right not to associate. The Court held that "[c]ompelling individuals to mouth support for views they find objectionable violates that cardinal constitutional command, and in most contexts, any such effort would be universally condemned." The Court rejected the assertion that the pursuit of "labor peace," even if a compelling governmental interest, could justify the statute, in the absence of any showing that the law was necessary to ensure labor peace. The Court similarly rejected the assertion that "free rider" concerns could justify the law, noting that the "Petitioner strenuously objects to this free-rider label. He argues that he is not a free rider on a bus headed for a destination that he wishes to reach but is more like a person shanghaied for an unwanted voyage." The Court finally rejected the assertion that the line of precedent governing the speech of public employees emanating from *Pickering v. Board of Education* justified the rule, holding that the framework established by *Pickering* and its progeny was designed to deal with an entirely different

First Amendment problem—the balance of interests governing public employers and public employees implicated by the expressive activity of employees, and simply did not apply to the forced subsidy of speech problem posed by making public employees support a union they chose not to join or agree with.

(5) In *Board of Regents of the University of Wisconsin System v. Southworth*, 529 U.S. 217 (2000), the Supreme Court dealt with a First Amendment challenge to compelled student activity fees. The University of Wisconsin, like most colleges and universities, charged students a mandatory activity fee used to support campus services and extracurricular student activities. A group of students filed suit against the University, alleging that the fee violated their First Amendment rights by requiring them to fund activities that were offensive to their personal beliefs. The Supreme Court held that the First Amendment allowed the University to charge a mandatory student activity fee to fund extracurricular speech where the fund was administered in a viewpoint-neutral manner. At the outset, the Court drew a distinction between the university itself speaking, which would implicate principles governing speech by the government, and the student activity fee regime, which involved funding of speech engaged in by students. Finding that the University's purpose was to promote the free exchange of ideas and open discourse among students, the Court concluded that the viewpoint-neutrality standards developed in other areas of First Amendment law, particularly in public forum cases, should control analysis of the forced speech problems posed by the student activity fee. The Court distinguished the student activity fee from the *Abood* rebate rule. The notion of trying to determine what speech is or is not "germane" in the university setting made no sense, the Court reasoned, because in an academic setting, the state "undertakes to stimulate the whole universe of speech and ideas." Even asking what speech is germane would be antithetical to the very goal of a university, for "[i]t is not for the Court to say what is or is not germane to the ideas to be pursued in an institution of higher learning." The Court also rejected the idea of imposing a method of protecting objecting students, finding that any such method would be disruptive and expensive, rendering the program ineffective. Concluding that the First Amendment did not require the University to risk the program to protect objecting students, the Court held that the First Amendment's general prohibition on viewpoint discrimination was sufficient protection for the interests of objecting students.

§ 9.18 Freedom of Expressive Association

The Supreme Court has held that the First Amendment contains an implied right of "freedom of expressive association." The freedom of expressive association cases often overlap with the "forced speech" cases referenced in the last section. The right of expressive association has both an affirmative and negative dimension. The affirmative dimension grants individuals the right to form groups to collectively engage in expressive association. The negative dimension grants the members of those groups a correlate right to decide who may or may not be a member. The negative dimension might be called the right of "disassociation," the right of a private group to decide for itself what members it will include or exclude. The exercise of the right of disassociation may be in direct conflict with laws that forbid discrimination. If a group refuses to allow women, Jews, African-Americans, Roman Catholics, or gays and lesbians within its membership, for example, such exclusions may run afoul of anti-discrimination laws that prohibit discrimination on such grounds. One person's freedom of expressive association is another person's act of discrimination. When the claim of a right not to associate is grounded in religious beliefs, the claim takes on additional constitutional, statutory, and cultural intensity. In the aftermath of the Supreme Court's decision declaring bans on same-sex marriage unconstitutional, for example, a national debate ensued regarding the propriety of exempting those religiously opposed to same-sex marriage from anti-discrimination principles. Recall the Supreme Court's *Masterpiece Cakeshop* decision discussed in Chapter 8 (§ 8.03[A]) and the "ecclesiastical exemption" (§ 8.04). This tension has been the subject of numerous judicial decisions exploring the extent to which society's anti-discrimination policies, as manifest in civil rights laws or anti-discrimination policies enacted by government agencies, may trump the First Amendment right of disassociation, and vice-versa. The Supreme Court case law on the subject is split along several divides. In cases in which the private club or organization has a broad and diffuse membership, and the expressive content of the organization is relatively unfocused and amorphous, the Supreme Court has tended to subordinate the First Amendment disassociation right to the compelling governmental interest in the enforcement of civil rights laws.

The Rotary Club and Jaycees Cases. The decision in *Board of Directors of Rotary International v. Rotary Club of Duarte*, 481 U.S. 537 (1987), and *Roberts v. U.S. Jaycees*, 468 U.S. 609 (1984), involving Rotary Clubs and the Jaycees, are two early examples of civil rights norms trumping First Amendment free association values. In those cases, the Supreme Court held that state civil rights laws in Minnesota and California could force civic organizations such as the Rotary or Jaycees to accept women members. In *Roberts*, the Supreme Court articulated the following test, which appears to be a form of "strict scrutiny":

> The right to associate for expressive purposes is not, however, absolute. Infringements on that right may be justified by regulations adopted to serve compelling state interests, unrelated to the suppression of ideas, that cannot be achieved through means significantly less restrictive of associational freedoms.

In *Roberts*, the Court went on to hold that Minnesota had a compelling governmental interest in eliminating discrimination against women. In both the Rotary and Jaycees cases the Court did not regard the organizations as possessing very selective or strongly-held expressive agendas.

Hurley v. Irish-American Gay, Lesbian and Bisexual Group of Boston. In *Hurley v. Irish-American Gay, Lesbian and Bisexual Group of Boston*, 515 U.S. 557 (1995), the Supreme Court held that the First Amendment protected the right of a private group that managed and sponsored a St. Patrick's Day parade in South Boston to exclude gay and lesbian organizations from the march. The parade was conducted under the auspices of a private group, the Boston Allied War Veterans Council. The Council refused to permit a group of gay, lesbian, and bisexual descendants of Irish immigrants to participate in the parade. The gay, lesbian, and bisexual groups filed suit under the state public accommodations law, which prohibits "any distinction, discrimination or restriction on account of . . . sexual orientation . . . relative to the admission of any person to, or treatment in any place of public accommodation, resort or amusement." The Massachusetts Supreme Court affirmed the judgment of the trial court that the parade organizers were guilty of violating the state public accommodations law, rejecting the organizers' claim that application of the law to their actions in barring groups with messages they deemed incompatible with the theme of the parade would violate the First Amendment. The Supreme Court reversed, in a unanimous decision written by Justice Souter, holding that the First Amendment did indeed bar the application of the Massachusetts law to the parade organizers in these circumstances. The Massachusetts public accommodations law, the Court acknowledged served vital purposes and was, in most of its applications, fully consistent with the Constitution. The Court found, however, that the application of the law to control the content of a parade raised unique First Amendment concerns:

> In the case before us, however, the Massachusetts law has been applied in a peculiar way. Its enforcement does not address any dispute about the participation of openly gay, lesbian, or bisexual individuals in various units admitted to the parade. The petitioners disclaim any intent to exclude homosexuals as such, and no individual member of GLIB claims to have been excluded from parading as a member of any group that the Council has approved to march. Instead, the disagreement goes to the admission of GLIB as its own parade unit carrying its own banner. Since every participating unit affects the message conveyed by the private organizers, the state courts' application of the statute produced an order essentially requiring petitioners to alter the expressive content of their parade. Although the state courts spoke of the parade as a place of public accommodation, once the expressive character of both the parade and the marching GLIB contingent is understood, it becomes apparent that the state courts' application of the statute had the effect of declaring the sponsors' speech itself to be the public accommodation. Under this approach any contingent of protected individuals with a message would have the right to participate in petitioners' speech, so that the communication produced by the private organizers would be shaped by all those protected by the law who wished to join in with some expressive demonstration of their own. But this use of the State's power violates the fundamental rule of protection under the First Amendment, that a speaker has the autonomy to choose the content of his own message.

The Court clearly regarded the application of the state civil rights law to an expressive activity such as a parade as implicating First Amendment rights far more intense than the somewhat lame invocation of free association it had rejected in cases such as *Roberts* and *Rotary*.

Boy Scouts of America v. Dale. In *Boy Scouts of America v. Dale*, 530 U.S. 640 (2000), the Supreme Court held that New Jersey violated the First Amendment in applying a state civil rights law in a manner that forced the Boy Scouts to accept a gay Scoutmaster. Quoting from its prior decision in *Hurley*, the Court in *Dale* stated:

> We are not, as we must not be, guided by our views of whether the Boy Scouts' teachings with respect to homosexual conduct are right or wrong; public or judicial disapproval of a tenet of an organization's expression does not justify the State's effort to compel the organization to accept members where such acceptance would derogate from the organization's expressive message. "While the law is free to promote all sorts of conduct in place of harmful behavior, it is not free to interfere with speech for no better reason than promoting an approved message or discouraging a disfavored one, however enlightened either purpose may strike the government." *Hurley*, 515 U.S., at 579.

Christian Legal Society Chapter of the University of California, Hastings v. Martinez. In *Christian Legal Society Chapter of the University of California, Hastings v. Martinez*, 561 U.S. 661 (2010), the Supreme Court rejected a challenge by the Christian Legal Society to a policy of the Hastings Law School, a state university law school in San Francisco that is part of the University of California system. The policy, which the Supreme Court described as an "all-comers" policy, imposed an open membership rule on all officially recognized student groups, a rule that required the student group to accept all comers as voting members even if those individuals disagree with the mission of the group. The Hastings chapter of the Christian Legal Society, a national organization, required its members to sign a "Statement of Faith" and to live their lives according to certain tenets, including the principle that sexual activity should not occur outside of marriage between a man and a woman. Consistent with this belief, the Society would not accept gay and lesbian members, placing it in conflict with the nondiscrimination policy that Hastings mandated for all of its registered student organizations. The Christian Legal Society sought a waiver from Hastings, arguing that to force it to accept gay and lesbian members violated its First Amendment rights of freedom of speech and freedom of association, relying on decisions such as *Boy Scouts of America v. Dale*. The Supreme Court in *Christian Legal Society* acknowledged that the freedom of association recognized by prior decisions such as *Roberts* and *Boy Scouts* clearly presupposes a freedom not to associate.

By a 5-4 vote, in a decision written by Justice Ruth Bader Ginsburg, the Supreme Court rejected the Christian Legal Society's claim, holding that the Hastings Law School could require adherence to its all-comers nondiscrimination policy as a condition of official recognition as a registered student organization. Justice Ginsburg's opinion for the Court held that the First Amendment rights of the Christian Legal Society had to be measured in light of the special deference that courts pay to the pedagogical judgment of public universities in making judgments germane to the educational process, judgments that are not limited to the classroom, but that extend to extracurricular activities as well. Exclusion, Justice Ginsburg reasoned, has two sides. "Hastings, caught in the crossfire between a group's desire to exclude and students' demand for equal access, may reasonably draw a line in the sand permitting all organizations to express what they wish but no group to discriminate in membership."

The Court observed that just as Hastings would not allow its professors to teach only classes to those students who adhere to certain beliefs, it could reach the educational judgment that it should not grant official status to student groups who engage in similar discrimination. Moreover, the Court reasoned, it would be difficult for Hastings to police student groups to determine which forms of discrimination were truly belief-based, and which were mere cover for discrimination. The Court held that the Hastings Law School was entitled to reach the judgment that an all-comers policy would advance the valid educational goals of encouraging tolerance, conflict-resolutions skills, and a readiness to find common ground. Finally, the Court reasoned, the nondiscrimination policy followed by the Hastings Law School was consistent with the broader nondiscrimination policies of the State of California. Hastings, the Court reasoned, could make the judgment that it would not subsidize discrimination that ran contrary to the state's declared public policies.

The Court in *Christian Legal Society* made much of the fact that the Hastings policy did not force the Society to accept gay and lesbian members. It merely conditioned status as a registered student organization on such acceptance. The Christian Legal Society could still exist, and could even gain access to school facilities, and the use of chalkboards and bulletin boards to advertise Society events. All that the Hastings rule did was prevent the Society from receiving the other benefits that came with recognition as an official registered student organization, such as eligibility for funding assistance through the funds generated by required student fees, use of the Law School's name and logo, participation in a student organization fair, access to the Law School's official student services newsletter, and use of the Law School's e-mail service with an official Hastings organizational e-mail address. As the Court saw the matter, the Christian Legal Society could remain true to its principles if it chose, and reject these fringe benefits of official recognition, but still function within the Law School as an unofficial student organization or it could accept the benefits and agree to adhere to the Hastings policy.

Indeed, the Court appeared to concede that the First Amendment rights of the Christian Legal Society would have been violated if the government had forced the society to accept gay and lesbian members against its will, through an outright criminal prohibition. The Court noted, however, that "[i]n diverse contexts, our decisions have distinguished between policies that require action and those that withhold benefits." A less restrictive First Amendment standard applied, to the Hastings registered student organization program, the Court reasoned, because through it, Hastings was "dangling the carrot of subsidy, not wielding the stick of prohibition."

Justices Stevens and Kennedy both filed concurring opinions. Justice Kennedy's opinion ended with this statement:

> In addition to a circumstance, already noted, in which it could be demonstrated that a school has adopted or enforced its policy with the intent or purpose of discriminating or disadvantaging a group on account of its views, petitioner also would have a substantial case on the merits if it were shown that the all-comers policy was either designed or used to infiltrate the group or challenge its leadership in order to stifle its views. But that has not been shown to be so likely or self-evident as a matter of group dynamics in this setting that the Court can declare the school policy void without more facts; and if there were a showing that in a particular case the purpose or effect of the policy was to stifle speech or make it ineffective, that, too, would present a case different from the one before us.
>
> These observations are offered to support the analysis set forth in the opinion of the Court, which I join.

Justice Alito dissented, joined by Chief Justice Roberts and Justices Scalia and Thomas. Justice Alito wrote:

> The Court's treatment of this case is deeply disappointing. The Court does not address the constitutionality of the very different policy that Hastings invoked when it denied CLS's application for registration. Nor does the Court address the constitutionality of the policy that Hastings now purports to follow. And the Court ignores strong evidence that the accept-all-comers policy is not viewpoint neutral because it was announced as a pretext to justify viewpoint discrimination. Brushing aside inconvenient precedent, the Court arms public educational institutions with a handy weapon for suppressing the speech of unpopular groups — groups to which, as Hastings candidly puts it, these institutions "do not wish to . . . lend their name[s]."

§ 9.19 Journalism and the First Amendment

A. The Press Clause

The First Amendment contains a Press Clause. The text of the First Amendment thus reads: "Congress shall make no law . . . abridging the freedom of speech, or of the press. . . ." Does the Press Clause grant to the "press," the "media," special freedoms that are distinct from the freedom of speech guaranteed in the Speech Clause? Despite the fact that text of the First Amendment contains both Speech and Press Clauses, the Supreme Court has refused to grant any independent meaning to the Press Clause. The Court has effectively written the Press Clause out of the Constitution as a free standing guarantee, instead assuming that whatever rights members of the media enjoy, as individual journalists or as media entities, are simply identical — no greater and no less — than those enjoyed by all citizens and entities under the Speech Clause. This unwillingness to breathe independent life into the Press Clause has not been accepted by all Justices, lawyers, and scholars. The most famous proponent of treating the Press Clause as granting special protections to the institutional media was Justice Potter Stewart. His views are expressed below:

> It seems to me that the Court's approach to all these cases has uniformly reflected its understanding that the Free Press guarantee is, in essence, a structural provision of the Constitution. Most of the other provisions in the Bill of Rights protect specific liberties or specific rights of individuals: freedom of speech, freedom of worship, the right to counsel, the privilege against compulsory self-incrimination, to name a few. In contrast, the Free Press Clause extends protection to an institution. The publishing business is, in short, the only organized private business that is given explicit constitutional protection.
>
> This basic understanding is essential, I think to avoid an elementary error of constitutional law. It is tempting to suggest that freedom of the press means only that newspaper publishers are guaranteed freedom of expression. They *are* guaranteed that freedom, to be sure, but so are we all, because of the Free Speech Clause. If the Free Press guarantee meant no more than freedom of expression, it would be a constitutional redundancy. Between 1776 and the drafting of our Constitution, many of the state constitutions contained clauses protecting freedom of the press while at the same time recognizing no general freedom of speech. By including both guarantees in the First Amendment, the Founders quite clearly recognized the distinction between the two.
>
> It is also a mistake to suppose that the only purpose of the constitutional guarantee of a free press is to insure that a newspaper will serve as a neutral forum for debate, a "market place for ideas," a kind of Hyde Park corner for the community. A related theory sees the press as a neutral conduit of information between the people and their elected leaders. These theories, in my view, again give insufficient weight to the institutional autonomy of the press that it was the purpose of the Constitution to guarantee. . . .
>
> The primary purpose of the constitutional guarantee of a free press was a similar one: to create a fourth institution outside the Government as an additional check on the three official branches. . . .

Potter Stewart, *On the Press*, 26 HASTINGS L.J. 631, 633–634 (1975).[29]

---

29. Copyright © 1975 by Hastings Law Journal. Reprinted by permission.

Chief Justice Burger, on the other hand, wrote in *First National Bank of Boston v. Bellotti*, 435 U.S. 765 (1978) (concurring):

> The Court has not yet squarely resolved whether the Press Clause confers upon the "institutional press" any freedom from government restraint not enjoyed by all others.
>
> . . . [T]he history of the Clause does not suggest that the authors contemplated a "special" or "institutional" privilege. *See* David Lange, *The Speech and Press Clauses*, 23 UCLA L. Rev. 77, 88–99 (1975).
>
> Indeed most pre-First Amendment commentators "who employed the term 'freedom of speech' with great frequency, used it synonymously with freedom of the press. . . ."
>
> Those interpreting the Press Clause as extending protection only to, or creating a special role for, the "institutional press" must either (a) assert such an intention on the part of the framers for which no supporting evidence is available . . . ; (b) argue that events after 1791 somehow operated to "constitutionalize" this interpretation . . . ; or (c) candidly acknowledging the absence of historical support, suggest that the intent of the Framers is not important today. . . .
>
> To conclude that the Framers did not intend to limit the freedom of the press to one select group is not necessarily to suggest that the Press Clause is redundant. The Speech Clause standing alone may be viewed as a protection of the liberty to express ideas and beliefs, while the Press Clause focuses specifically on the liberty to disseminate expression broadly and "comprehends every sort of publication which affords a vehicle of information and opinion. . . ." Yet there is no fundamental distinction between expression and dissemination. The liberty encompassed by the Press Clause, although complementary to and a natural extension of Speech Clause liberty, merited special mention simply because it had been more often the object of official restraints. Soon after the invention of the printing press, English and continental monarchs, fearful of the power implicit in its use and the threat to Establishment thought and order—political and religious—devised restraints, such as licensing, censors, indices or prohibited books, and prosecutions for seditious libel, which generally were unknown in the pre-printing press era. Official restrictions were the official response to the new, disquieting idea that this invention would provide a means for mass communication.
>
> The second fundamental difficulty with interpreting the Press Clause as conferring special status on a limited group is one of definition. . . . The very task of including some entities within the "institutional press" while excluding others, whether undertaken by legislature, court, or administrative agency, is reminiscent of the abhorred licensing system of Tudor and Stuart England—a system the First Amendment was intended to ban

from this country. . . . Further, the officials undertaking that task would be required to distinguish the protected from the unprotected on the basis of such variables as content of expression, frequency or fervor of expression, or ownership of the technological means of dissemination. Yet nothing in this Court's opinions supports such a confining approach to the scope of Press Clause protection. . . .

Because the First Amendment was meant to guarantee freedom to express and communicate ideas, I can see no difference between the right of those who seek to disseminate ideas by way of a newspaper and those who give lectures or speeches and seek to enlarge the audience by publication and wide dissemination. "[T]he purpose of the Constitution was not to erect the press into a privileged institution but to protect all persons in their right to print what they will as well as to utter it. . . . [T]he liberty of the press is no greater and no less . . . than the liberty of every citizen of the Republic. . . ."

In short, the First Amendment does not "belong" to any definable category of persons or entities: It belongs to all who exercise its freedom.

The debate over whether to treat the Press Clause as containing special rights for the institutional press has taken on an even more difficult caste with the flourishing of the Internet. At one point in our culture, it might have been possible to determine who was or was not a member of the "media." With the Internet, however, there are millions of individuals and organizations who engage in reporting and the dissemination of information. Even if "the press" were granted special rights, it is difficult to discern a principled basis for determining who would or would not qualify as a member.

B. Access to Institutions and Events

While *Richmond Newspapers* recognized a general public right of access to criminal court proceedings, which incidentally benefited journalists, the Supreme Court has been generally unwilling to recognize any right of access to other institutions and events. The Court has refused to grant a right of access to prisons, for example. Nor has the Supreme Court ever recognized a right of access to military battlefields or the theatre of war. Quite often, administrative polices grant journalists such access. The American military, for example, is generally accommodating in providing the media with access to military campaigns. But these are accommodations voluntarily granted by government, not constitutionally guaranteed rights. In *Pell v. Procunier*, 417 U.S. 817 (1974), *Saxbe v. Washington Post Co.*, 417 U.S. 843 (1974), and *Houchins v. KQED, Inc.*, 438 U.S. 1 (1978), members of the press challenged prison regulations which forbade press and other media interviews with specific individual inmates. In none of the cases were the journalists successful.

C. Reporters' Privilege

Branzburg v. Hayes. In *Branzburg v. Hayes*, 408 U.S. 665 (1972), the Supreme Court
had before it four consolidated cases posing issues concerning assertions by journalists that they cannot be forced to testify or provide evidence in judicial proceedings obtained by them in the process of newsgathering. The justification for such an
assertion was the claim that the burden on newsgathering resulting from compelling reporters' disclosure outweighed any public interest in obtaining the information sought. The Court in *Branzburg* rejected, by a five-to-four vote, the claim of
reporters that they have a First Amendment right to refuse to testify or to refuse to
reveal the names of confidential sources in grand jury investigations. As narrowly
put by the Court, "The issue in these cases is whether requiring newsmen to appear
and testify before state or federal grand juries abridges the freedom of speech and
press guaranteed by the First Amendment. We hold that it does not." Sounding a
familiar theme, the Court in *Branzburg* declined to find in the First Amendment
for journalists a special "testimonial privilege that other citizens do not enjoy." The
Court was unmoved by the claim that recognition of such a privilege was essential
to safeguard the newsgathering function of the press:

> [W]e perceive no basis for holding that the public interest in law enforce-
> ment and in insuring effective grand jury proceedings is insufficient to
> override the consequential, but uncertain, burden on news gathering that
> is said to result from insisting that reporters, like other citizens, respond to
> relevant questions put to them in the course of a valid grand jury investiga-
> tion or criminal trial.

The majority stated that "the evidence fails to demonstrate that there would be a
significant constriction of the flow of news to the public if this Court reaffirms . . .
the testimonial obligations of newsmen."

Justice Lewis Powell joined the five-Justice majority in *Branzburg*. Justice Powell
also wrote a short concurring opinion, which stated:

> I add this brief statement to emphasize what seems to me to be the limited
> nature of the Court's holding. The Court does not hold that newsmen, sub-
> poenaed to testify before a grand jury, are without constitutional rights
> with respect to the gathering of news or in safeguarding their sources. Cer-
> tainly, we do not hold, as suggested in Mr. Justice Stewart's dissenting opin-
> ion, that state and federal authorities are free to "annex" the news media
> as "an investigative arm of government." The solicitude repeatedly shown
> by this Court for First Amendment freedoms should be sufficient assur-
> ance against any such effort, even if one seriously believed that the media —
> properly free and untrammeled in the fullest sense of these terms — were
> not able to protect themselves.

> As indicated in the concluding portion of the opinion, the Court states
> that no harassment of newsmen will be tolerated. If a newsman believes

that the grand jury investigation is not being conducted in good faith he is not without remedy. Indeed, if the newsman is called upon to give information bearing only a remote and tenuous relationship to the subject of the investigation, or if he has some other reason to believe that his testimony implicates confidential source relationship without a legitimate need of law enforcement, he will have access to the court on a motion to quash and an appropriate protective order may be entered. The asserted claim to privilege should be judged on its facts by the striking of a proper balance between freedom of the press and the obligation of all citizens to give relevant testimony with respect to criminal conduct. The balance of these vital constitutional and societal interests on a case-by-case basis accords with the tried and traditional way of adjudicating such questions.

In short, the courts will be available to newsmen under circumstances where legitimate First Amendment interests require protection.

Some lower courts interpreted Justice Powell's opinion as modifying the majority opinion, and drew on Justice Powell's opinion to establish a First Amendment balancing test creating a qualified privilege permitting journalists to refuse to reveal confidential sources obtained during news gathering. *See, e.g., United States v. Burke*, 700 F.2d 70 (2d Cir.), *cert. denied*, 464 U.S. 816 (1983) (reporter's qualified privilege in criminal, as well as civil cases, conditioned upon "clear and specific showing" that the information sought (1) is highly material and relevant, (2) is necessary or critical to the claim, and (3) is not obtainable from other available sources). More recently, however, the trend has been in the opposite direction, with lower courts refusing to treat Justice Powell's opinion as modifying the majority opinion in *Branzburg*. Those decisions have rejected the view that there is any First Amendment privilege immunizing a journalist from providing evidence or testimony that would be required of any other citizen. For example, the United States Court of Appeals for the District of Columbia Circuit in *In re Grand Jury Subpoena, Judith Miller*, 397 F.3d 964, 970 (D.C. Cir. 2005), rejected the First Amendment privilege in no uncertain terms:

> Unquestionably, the Supreme Court decided in *Branzburg* that there is no First Amendment privilege protecting journalists from appearing before a grand jury or from testifying before a grand jury or otherwise providing evidence to a grand jury regardless of any confidence promised by the reporter to any source. The Highest Court has spoken and never revisited the question. Without doubt, that is the end of the matter.

Shield Laws. Many states have passed statutes or created their own state-law based common-law or state constitutional law doctrines that provide some protection for the confidential sources or other materials produced in the process of newsgathering. These are often called "shield laws." The state provisions vary considerably in their scope and effect. There have been proposals to enact a federal shield law applicable in federal courts, but Congress has not passed such legislation.

Appendix

The Constitution of the United States of America

We the People of the United States, in Order to form a more perfect Union, establish Justice, insure domestic Tranquility, provide for the common defence, promote the general Welfare, and secure the Blessings of Liberty to ourselves and our Posterity, do ordain and establish this Constitution for the United States of America.

Article I.

SECTION 1. All legislative Powers herein granted shall be vested in a Congress of the United States, which shall consist of a Senate and House of Representatives.

SECTION 2. The House of Representatives shall be composed of Members chosen every second Year by the People of the several States, and the Electors in each State shall have the Qualifications requisite for Electors of the most numerous Branch of the State Legislature.

No Person shall be a Representative who shall not have attained to the Age of twenty five Years, and been seven Years a Citizen of the United States, and who shall not, when elected, be an Inhabitant of that State in which he shall be chosen.

Representatives and direct Taxes shall be apportioned among the several States which may be included within this Union, according to their respective Numbers, which shall be determined by adding to the whole Number of free Persons, including those bound to Service for a Term of Years, and excluding Indians not taxed, three fifths of all other Persons. The actual Enumeration shall be made within three Years after the first Meeting of the Congress of the United States, and within every subsequent Term of ten Years, in such Manner as they shall by Law direct. The Number of Representatives shall not exceed one for every thirty Thousand, but each State shall have at Least one Representative; and until such enumeration shall be made, the State of New Hampshire shall be entitled to chuse three, Massachusetts eight, Rhode Island and Providence Plantations one, Connecticut five, New York six, New Jersey four, Pennsylvania eight, Delaware one, Maryland six, Virginia ten, North Carolina five, South Carolina five, and Georgia three.

When vacancies happen in the Representation from any State, the Executive Authority thereof shall issue Writs of Election to fill such Vacancies.

The House of Representatives shall chuse their Speaker and other Officers; and shall have the sole Power of Impeachment.

SECTION 3. The Senate of the United States shall be composed of two Senators from each State, chosen by the Legislature thereof, for six Years; and each Senator shall have one Vote.

Immediately after they shall be assembled in Consequence of the first Election, they shall be divided as equally as may be into three Classes. The Seats of the Senators of the first Class shall be vacated at the Expiration of the second Year, of the second Class at the Expiration of the fourth Year, and of the third Class at the Expiration of the sixth Year, so that one third may be chosen every second Year; and if Vacancies happen by Resignation, or otherwise, during the Recess of the Legislature of any State, the Executive thereof may make temporary Appointments until the next Meeting of the Legislature, which shall then fill such Vacancies.

No Person shall be a Senator who shall not have attained to the Age of thirty Years, and been nine Years a Citizen of the United States, and who shall not, when elected, be an Inhabitant of the State for which he shall be chosen.

The Vice President of the United States shall be President of the Senate, but shall have no Vote, unless they be equally divided.

The Senate shall chuse their other Officers, and also a President pro tempore, in the Absence of the Vice President, or when he shall exercise the Office of President of the United States.

The Senate shall have the sole Power to try all Impeachments. When sitting for that Purpose, they shall be on Oath or Affirmation. When the President of the United States is tried the Chief Justice shall preside: And no Person shall be convicted without the Concurrence of two thirds of the Members present.

Judgment in Cases of Impeachment shall not extend further than to removal from Office, and disqualification to hold and enjoy any Office of honor, Trust or Profit under the United States: but the Party convicted shall nevertheless be liable and subject to Indictment, Trial, Judgment and Punishment, according to Law.

SECTION 4. The Times, Places and Manner of holding Elections for Senators and Representatives, shall be prescribed in each State by the Legislature thereof; but the Congress may at any time by Law make or alter such Regulations, except as to the Places of chusing Senators.

The Congress shall assemble at least once in every Year, and such Meeting shall be on the first Monday in December, unless they shall by Law appoint a different Day.

SECTION 5. Each House shall be the Judge of the Elections, Returns and qualifications of its own Members, and a Majority of each shall constitute a Quorum to do Business; but a smaller Number may adjourn from day to day, and may be authorized to compel the Attendance of absent Members, in such Manner, and under such Penalties as each House may provide.

Each House may determine the Rules of its Proceedings, punish its Members for disorderly Behaviour, and, with the Concurrence of two thirds, expel a Member.

Each House shall keep a Journal of its Proceedings, and from time to time publish the same, excepting such Parts as may in their Judgment require Secrecy; and the Yeas and Nays of the Members of either House on any question shall, at the Desire of one fifth of those Present, be entered on the Journal.

Neither House, during the Session of Congress, shall, without the Consent of the other, adjourn for more than three days, nor to any other Place than that in which the two Houses shall be sitting.

SECTION 6. The Senators and Representatives shall receive a Compensation for their Services, to be ascertained by Law, and paid out of the Treasury of the United States. They shall in all Cases, except Treason, Felony and Breach of the Peace, be privileged from Arrest during their Attendance at the Session of their respective Houses, and in going to and returning from the same; and for any Speech or Debate in either House, they shall not be questioned in any other Place.

No Senator or Representative shall, during the Time for which he was elected, be appointed to any civil Office under the Authority of the United States, which shall have been created, or the Emoluments whereof shall have been increased during such time; and no Person holding any Office under the United States, shall be a Member of either House during his Continuance in Office.

SECTION 7. All Bills for raising Revenue shall originate in the House of Representatives; but the Senate may propose or concur with amendments as on other Bills.

Every Bill which shall have passed the House of Representatives and the Senate, shall, before it become a Law, be presented to the President of the United States; If he approve he shall sign it, but if not he shall return it, with his Objections to that House in which it shall have originated, who shall enter the Objections at large on their Journal, and proceed to reconsider it. If after such Reconsideration two thirds of that House shall agree to pass the Bill, it shall be sent, together with the Objections, to the other House, by which it shall likewise be reconsidered, and if approved by two thirds of that House, it shall become a Law. But in all such Cases the Votes of both Houses shall be determined by Yeas and Nays, and the Names of the Persons voting for and against the Bill shall be entered on the Journal of each House respectively. If any Bill shall not be returned by the President within ten Days (Sunday excepted) after it shall have been presented to him, the Same shall be a Law, in like Manner as if he had signed it, unless the Congress by their Adjournment prevent its Return, in which Case it shall not be a Law.

Every Order, Resolution, or Vote to which the Concurrence of the Senate and House of Representatives may be necessary (except on a question of Adjournment) shall be presented to the President of the United States; and before the Same shall take Effect, shall be approved by him, or being disapproved by him, shall be repassed by two thirds of the Senate and House of Representatives, according to the Rules and Limitations prescribed in the Case of a Bill.

SECTION 8. The Congress shall have Power To lay and collect Taxes, Duties, Imposts and Excises, to pay the Debts and provide for the common Defence and general Welfare of the United States; but all Duties, Imposts and Excises shall be uniform throughout the United States;

To borrow Money on the credit of the United States;

To regulate Commerce with foreign Nations, and among the several States, and with the Indian Tribes;

To establish an uniform Rule of Naturalization, and uniform Laws on the subject of Bankruptcies throughout the United States;

To coin Money, regulate the Value thereof, and of foreign Coin, and fix the Standard of Weights and Measures;

To provide for the Punishment of counterfeiting the Securities and current Coin of the United States;

To establish Post Offices and post Roads;

To promote the Progress of Science and useful Arts, by securing for limited Times to Authors and Inventors the exclusive Rights to their respective Writings and Discoveries;

To constitute Tribunals inferior to the supreme Court;

To define and punish Piracies and Felonies committed on the high Seas, and Offenses against the Law of Nations;

To declare War, grant Letters of Marque and Reprisal, and make Rules concerning Captures on Land and Water;

To raise and support Armies, but no Appropriation of Money to that Use shall be for a longer Term than two Years;

To provide and maintain a Navy;

To make Rules for the Government and Regulation of the land and naval Forces;

To provide for calling forth the Militia to execute the Laws of the Union, suppress Insurrections and repel Invasions;

To provide for organizing, arming, and disciplining, the Militia, and for governing such Part of them as may be employed in the Service of the United States, reserving to the States respectively, the Appointment of the Officers, and the Authority of training the militia according to the discipline prescribed by Congress;

To exercise exclusive Legislation in all Cases whatsoever, over such District (not exceeding ten Miles square) as may, by Cession of particular States, and the Acceptance of Congress, become the Seat of the Government of the United States, and to exercise like Authority over all Places purchased by the Consent of the Legislature of the State in which the Same shall be, for the Erection of Forts, Magazines, Arsenals, dock-Yards, and other needful Buildings; — And

To make all Laws which shall be necessary and proper for carrying into Execution the foregoing Powers, and all other Powers vested by this Constitution in the Government of the United States, or in any Department or Officer thereof.

SECTION 9. The Migration or Importation of such Persons as any of the States now existing shall think proper to admit, shall not be prohibited by the Congress prior to the Year one thousand eight hundred and eight, but a Tax or duty may be imposed on such Importation, not exceeding ten dollars for each Person.

The Privilege of the Writ of Habeas Corpus shall not be suspended, unless when in Cases of Rebellion or Invasion the public Safety may require it.

No Bill of Attainder or ex post facto Law shall be passed.

No Capitation, or other direct Tax shall be laid, unless in Proportion to the Census of Enumeration herein before directed to be taken.

No Tax or Duty shall be laid on Articles exported from any State.

No Preference shall be given by any Regulation of Commerce or Revenue to the Ports of one State over those of another; nor shall Vessels bound to, or from, one State, be obliged to enter, clear or pay Duties in another.

No Money shall be drawn from the Treasury, but in Consequence of Appropriations made by Law; and a regular Statement and Account of the Receipts and Expenditures of all public Money shall be published from time to time.

No Title of Nobility shall be granted by the United States: And no Person holding any Office of Profit or Trust under them, shall, without the Consent of the Congress, accept of any present, Emolument, Office, or Title, of any kind whatever, from any King, Prince or foreign State.

SECTION 10. No State shall enter into any Treaty, Alliance, or Confederation; grant Letters of Marque and Reprisal; coin Money; emit Bills of Credit; make any Thing but gold and silver Coin a Tender in Payment of Debts; pass any Bill of Attainder, ex post facto Law, or Law impairing the Obligation of Contracts, or grant any Title of Nobility.

No State shall, without the Consent of the Congress, lay any Imposts or Duties on Imports or Exports, except what may be absolutely necessary for executing its inspection Laws: and the next Produce of all Duties and Imposts, laid by any State on Imports or Exports, shall be for the Use of the Treasure of the United States; and all such Laws shall be subject to the Revision and Controul of the Congress.

No State shall, without the Consent of Congress, lay any Duty of Tonnage, keep Troops, or Ships of War in time of Peace, enter into any Agreement or Compact with another State, or with a foreign Power, or engage in War, unless actually invaded, or in such imminent Danger as will not admit of delay.

Article II.

SECTION 1. The executive Power shall be vested in a President of the United States of America. He shall hold his Office during the Term of four Years, and, together with the Vice President, chosen for the same Term, be elected, as follows:

Each State shall appoint, in such Manner as the Legislature thereof may direct, a Number of Electors, equal to the whole Number of Senators and Representatives to which the State may be entitled in the Congress: but no Senator or Representative, or Person holding an Office of Trust or Profit under the United States, shall be appointed an Elector.

The Electors shall meet in their respective States, and vote by Ballot for two Persons, of whom one at least shall not be an Inhabitant of the same State with themselves. And they shall make a List of all the Persons voted for, and of the Number of Votes for each; which List they shall sign and certify, and transmit sealed to the Seat of the Government of the United States, directed to the President of the Senate. The President of the Senate shall, in the Presence of the Senate and House of Representatives, open all the Certificates, and the Votes shall then be counted. The Person having the greatest Number of Votes shall be the President, if such Number be a Majority of the whole Number of Electors appointed; and if there be more than one who have such Majority, and have an equal Number of Votes, then the House of Representatives shall immediately chuse by Ballot one of them for President; and if no Person have a Majority, then from the five highest on the List the said House shall in like Manner chuse the President. But in chusing the President, the Votes shall be taken by States, the Representation from each State having one Vote; a quorum for this Purpose shall consist of a Member or Members from two thirds of the States, and a Majority of all the States shall be necessary to a Choice. In every Case, after the Choice of the President, the Person having the greatest Number of Votes of the Electors shall be the Vice President. But if there should remain two or more who have equal Votes, the Senate shall chuse from them by Ballot the Vice President.

The Congress may determine the Time of chusing the Electors, and the Day on which they shall give their Votes; which Day shall be the same throughout the United States.

No Person except a natural born Citizen, or a Citizen of the United States, at the time of the Adoption of this Constitution, shall be eligible to the Office of President; neither shall any Person be eligible to that Office who shall not have attained to the Age of thirty five Years, and been fourteen Years a Resident within the United States.

In Case of the Removal of the President from Office, or of his Death, Resignation, or Inability to discharge the Powers and Duties of the said Office, the Same shall devolve on the Vice President, and the Congress may by Law provide for the Case of Removal, Death, Resignation or Inability, both of the President and Vice President, declaring what Officer shall then act as President, and such Officer shall act accordingly, until the Disability be removed, or a President shall be elected.

The President shall, at stated Times, receive for his Services, a Compensation, which shall neither be increased nor diminished during the Period for which he shall have been elected, and he shall not receive within that Period any other Emolument from the United States, or any of them.

Before he enter on the Execution of his Office, he shall take the following Oath or Affirmation: — "I do solemnly swear (or affirm) that I will faithfully execute the Office of President of the United States, and will to the best of my Ability, preserve, protect and defend the Constitution of the United States."

SECTION 2. The President shall be Commander in Chief of the Army and Navy of the United States, and of the Militia of the several States, when called into the actual Service of the United States; he may require the Opinion, in writing, of the principal Officer in each of the executive Departments, upon any Subject relating to the Duties of their respective Offices, and he shall have Power to grant Reprieves and Pardons for Offenses against the United States, except in Cases of Impeachment.

He shall have Power, by and with the Advice and Consent of the Senate, to make Treaties, provided two thirds of the Senators present concur; and he shall nominate, and by and with the Advice and Consent of the Senate, shall appoint Ambassadors, other public Ministers and Consuls, Judges of the supreme Court, and all other Officers of the United States, whose Appointments are not herein otherwise provided for, and which shall be established by Law: but the Congress may by Law vest the Appointment of such inferior Officers, as they think proper, in the President alone, in the Courts of Law, or in the Heads of Departments.

The President shall have Power to fill up all Vacancies that may happen during the recess of the Senate, by granting Commissions which shall expire at the End of their next Session.

SECTION 3. He shall from time to time give to the Congress Information of the State of the Union, and recommend to their Consideration such Measures as he shall judge necessary and expedient; he may, on extraordinary Occasions, convene both Houses, or either of them, and in Case of Disagreement between them, with Respect to the Time of Adjournment, he may adjourn them to such Time as he shall think proper; he shall receive Ambassadors and other public Ministers; he shall take Care that the Laws be faithfully executed, and shall Commission all the Officers of the United States.

SECTION 4. The President, Vice President and all Civil Officers of the United States, shall be removed from Office on Impeachment for, and Conviction of, Treason, Bribery, or other high Crimes and Misdemeanors.

Article III.

SECTION 1. The judicial Power of the United States, shall be vested in one supreme Court, and in such inferior Courts as the Congress may from time to time ordain and establish. The Judges, both of the supreme and inferior Courts, shall hold their Offices during good Behaviour, and shall, at stated Times, receive for their Services, a Compensation, which shall not be diminished during their Continuance in Office.

SECTION 2. The judicial Power shall extend to all Cases, in Law and Equity, arising under this Constitution, the Laws of the United States, and Treaties made, or which shall be made, under their Authority;—to all Cases affecting Ambassadors, other public Ministers and Consuls;—to all Cases of admiralty and maritime Jurisdiction;—to Controversies to which the United States shall be a Party;—to Controversies between two or more States;—between a State and Citizens of another State;—between Citizens of different States;—between Citizens of the same State claiming Lands under Grants of different States, and between a State, or the Citizens thereof, and foreign States, Citizens or Subjects.

In all Cases affecting Ambassadors, other public Ministers and Consuls, and those in which a State shall be Party, the Supreme Court shall have original Jurisdiction. In all the other Cases before mentioned, the supreme Court shall have appellate Jurisdiction, both as to Law and Fact, with such Exceptions, and under such Regulations as the Congress shall make.

The Trial of all Crimes, except in Cases of Impeachment, shall be by Jury; and such Trial shall be held in the State where the said Crimes shall have been committed; but when not committed within any State, the Trial shall be at such Place or Places as the Congress may by Law have directed.

SECTION 3. Treason against the United States, shall consist only in levying War against them, or in adhering to their Enemies, giving them Aid and Comfort. No Person shall be convicted of Treason unless on the Testimony of two Witnesses to the same overt Act, or on Confession in open Court.

The Congress shall have Power to declare the Punishment of Treason, but no Attainder of Treason shall work Corruption of Blood, or Forfeiture except during the Life of the Person attainted.

Article IV.

SECTION 1. Full Faith and Credit shall be given in each State to the public Acts, Records, and judicial Proceedings of every other State. And the Congress may by general Laws prescribe the Manner in which such Acts, Records and Proceedings shall be proved, and the Effect thereof.

SECTION 2. The Citizens of each State shall be entitled to all Privileges and Immunities of Citizens in the several States.

A Person charged in any State with Treason, Felony, or other Crime, who shall flee from Justice, and be found in another State, shall on Demand of the executive

Authority of the State from which he fled, be delivered up, to be removed to the State having Jurisdiction of the Crime.

No Person held to Service or Labour in one State, under the Laws thereof, escaping into another, shall, in Consequence of any Law or Regulation therein, be discharged from such Service or Labour, but shall be delivered up on Claim of the Party to whom such Service or Labour may be due.

SECTION 3. New States may be admitted by the Congress into this Union; but no new State shall be formed or erected within the Jurisdiction of any other State; nor any State be formed by the Junction of two or more States, or Parts of States, without the Consent of the Legislatures of the States concerned as well as of the Congress.

The Congress shall have Power to dispose of and make all needful Rules and Regulations respecting the Territory or other Property belonging to the United States; and nothing in this Constitution shall be so construed as to Prejudice any Claims of the United States, or of any particular State.

SECTION 4. The United States shall guarantee to every State in this Union a Republican Form of Government, and shall protect each of them against Invasion; and on Application of the Legislature, or of the Executive (when the Legislature cannot be convened) against domestic Violence.

Article V.

The Congress, whenever two thirds of both Houses shall deem it necessary, shall propose Amendments to this Constitution, or, on the Application of the Legislatures of two thirds of the several States, shall call a Convention for proposing Amendments, which, in either Case, shall be valid to all Intents and Purposes, as Part of this Constitution, when ratified by the Legislatures of three fourths of the several States, or by Conventions in three fourths thereof, as the one or the other Mode of Ratification may be proposed by the Congress; Provided that no Amendment which may be made prior to the Year One thousand eight hundred and eight shall in any Manner affect the first and fourth Clauses in the Ninth Section of the first Article; and that no State, without its Consent, shall be deprived of its equal Suffrage in the Senate.

Article VI.

All Debts contracted and Engagements entered into, before the Adoption of this Constitution, shall be as valid against the United States under this Constitution, as under the Confederation.

This Constitution, and the Laws of the United States which shall be made in Pursuance thereof; and all Treaties made, or which shall be made, under the Authority of the United States, shall be the supreme Law of the Land; and the Judges in every State shall be bound thereby, any Thing in the Constitution or Laws of any State to the Contrary notwithstanding.

The Senators and Representatives before mentioned, and the Members of the several State Legislatures, and all executive and judicial Officers, both of the United States and of the several States, shall be bound by Oath or Affirmation, to support this Constitution; but no religious Test shall ever be required as a Qualification to any Office or public Trust under the United States.

Article VII.

The Ratification of the Conventions of nine States, shall be sufficient for the Establishment of this Constitution between the States so ratifying the Same. . . .

ARTICLES IN ADDITION TO, AND AMENDMENT OF, THE CONSTITUTION OF THE UNITED STATES OF AMERICA, PROPOSED BY CONGRESS, AND RATIFIED BY THE SEVERAL STATES, PURSUANT TO THE FIFTH ARTICLE OF THE ORIGINAL CONSTITUTION.

Amendment I [1791].

Congress shall make no law respecting an establishment of religion, or prohibiting the free exercise thereof; or abridging the freedom of speech, or of the press; or the right of the people peaceably to assemble, and to petition the Government for a redress of grievances.

Amendment II [1791].

A well regulated Militia, being necessary to the security of a free State, the right of the people to keep and bear Arms, shall not be infringed.

Amendment III [1791].

No Soldier shall, in time of peace be quartered in any house, without the consent of the Owner, nor in time of war, but in a manner to be prescribed by law.

Amendment IV [1791].

The right of the people to be secure in their persons, houses, papers, and effects, against unreasonable searches and seizures, shall not be violated, and no

Warrants shall issue, but upon probable cause, supported by Oath or affirmation, and particularly describing the place to be searched, and the persons or things to be seized.

Amendment V [1791].

No person shall be held to answer for a capital, or otherwise infamous crime, unless on a presentment or indictment of a Grand Jury, except in cases arising in the land or naval forces, or in the Militia, when in actual service in time of War or public danger; nor shall any person be subject for the same offence to be twice put in jeopardy of life or limb; nor shall be compelled in any criminal case to be a witness against himself, nor be deprived of life, liberty, or property, without due process of law; nor shall private property be taken for public use, without just compensation.

Amendment VI [1791].

In all criminal prosecutions, the accused shall enjoy the right to a speedy and public trial, by an impartial jury of the State and district wherein the crime shall have been committed, which district shall have been previously ascertained by law, and to be informed of the nature and cause of the accusation; to be confronted with the witnesses against him; to have compulsory process for obtaining Witnesses in his favor, and to have the Assistance of Counsel for his defence.

Amendment VII [1791].

In Suits at common law, where the value in controversy shall exceed twenty dollars, the right of trial by jury shall be preserved, and no fact tried by a jury, shall be otherwise re-examined in any Court of the United States, than according to the rules of the common law.

Amendment VIII [1791].

Excessive bail shall not be required, nor excessive fines imposed, nor cruel and unusual punishments inflicted.

Amendment IX [1791].

The enumeration in the Constitution, of certain rights, shall not be construed to deny or disparage others retained by the people.

Amendment X [1791].

The powers not delegated to the United States by the Constitution, nor prohibited by it to the States, are reserved to the States respectively, or to the people.

Amendment XI [1798].

The Judicial power of the United States shall not be construed to extend to any suit in law or equity, commenced or prosecuted against one of the United States by Citizens of another State, or by Citizens or Subjects of any Foreign State.

Amendment XII [1804].

The Electors shall meet in their respective states and vote by ballot for President and Vice-President, one of whom, at least, shall not be an inhabitant of the same state with themselves; they shall name in their ballots the person voted for as President, and in distinct ballots the person voted for as Vice-President, and they shall make distinct lists of all persons voted for as President, and of all persons voted for as Vice-President, and of the number of votes for each, which lists they shall sign and certify, and transmit sealed to the seat of the government of the United States, directed to the President of the Senate; — The President of the Senate shall, in the presence of the Senate and House of Representatives, open all the certificates and the votes shall then be counted; — The person having the greatest number of votes for President, shall be the President, if such number be a majority of the whole number of Electors appointed; and if no person have such majority, then from the persons having the highest numbers not exceeding three on the list of those voted for as President, the House of Representatives shall choose immediately, by ballot, the President. But in choosing the President, the votes shall be taken by states, the representation from each state having one vote; a quorum for this purpose shall consist of a member or members from two-thirds of the states, and a majority of all the states shall be necessary to a choice. And if the House of Representatives shall not choose a President whenever the right of choice shall devolve upon them, before the fourth day of March next following, then the Vice-President shall act as President, as in the case of the death or other constitutional disability of the President — The person having the greatest number of votes as Vice-President, shall be the Vice-President, if such number be a majority of the whole number of Electors appointed, and if no person have a majority, then from the two highest numbers on the list, the Senate shall choose the Vice-President; a quorum for the purpose shall consist of two-thirds of the whole number of Senators, and a majority of the whole number shall be necessary to a choice. But no person constitutionally ineligible to the office of President shall be eligible to that of Vice-President of the United States.

Amendment XIII [1865].

SECTION 1. Neither slavery nor involuntary servitude, except as a punishment for crime whereof the party shall have been duly convicted, shall exist within the United States, or any place subject to their jurisdiction.

SECTION 2. Congress shall have power to enforce this article by appropriate legislation.

Amendment XIV [1868].

SECTION 1. All persons born or naturalized in the United States and subject to the jurisdiction thereof, are citizens of the United States and of the State wherein they reside. No State shall make or enforce any law which shall abridge the privileges or immunities of citizens of the United States; nor shall any State deprive any person of life, liberty, or property, without due process of law; nor deny to any person within its jurisdiction the equal protection of the laws.

SECTION 2. Representatives shall be apportioned among the several States according to their respective numbers, counting the whole number of persons in each State, excluding Indians not taxed. But when the right to vote at any election for the choice of electors for President and Vice President of the United States, Representatives in Congress, the Executive and Judicial officers of a State, or the members of the Legislature thereof, is denied to any of the male inhabitants of such State, being twenty-one years of age, and citizens of the United States, or in any way abridged, except for participation in rebellion, or other crime, the basis of representation therein shall be reduced in the proportion which the number of such male citizens shall bear to the whole number of male citizens twenty-one years of age in such State.

SECTION 3. No person shall be a Senator or Representative in Congress, or elector of President and Vice President, or hold any office, civil or military, under the United States, or under any State, who, having previously taken an oath, as a member of Congress, or as an officer of the United States, or as a member of any State legislature, or as an executive or judicial officer of any State, to support the Constitution of the United States, shall have engaged in insurrection or rebellion against the same, or given aid or comfort to the enemies thereof. But Congress may by a vote of two-thirds of each House, remove such disability.

SECTION 4. The validity of the public debt of the United States, authorized by law, including debts incurred for payment of pensions and bounties for services in suppressing insurrection or rebellion, shall not be questioned. But neither the United States nor any State shall assume or pay any debt or obligation incurred in aid of insurrection or rebellion against the United States, or any claim for the loss of emancipation of any slave; but all such debts, obligations and claims shall be held illegal and void.

SECTION 5. The Congress shall have power to enforce, by appropriate legislation, the provisions of this article.

Amendment XV [1870].

SECTION 1. The right of citizens of the United States to vote shall not be denied or abridged by the United States or by any State on account of race, color, or previous condition of servitude.

SECTION 2. The Congress shall have power to enforce this article by appropriate legislation.

Amendment XVI [1913].

The Congress shall have power to lay and collect taxes on incomes, from whatever source derived, without apportionment among the several States, and without regard to any census or enumeration.

Amendment XVII [1913].

The Senate of the United States shall be composed of two Senators from each State, elected by the people thereof, for six years; and each Senator shall have one vote. The electors in each State shall have the qualifications requisite for electors of the most numerous branch of the State legislatures.

When vacancies happen in the representation of any State in the Senate, the executive authority of such State shall issue writs of election to fill such vacancies: *Provided,* That the legislature of any State may empower the executive thereof to make temporary appointments until the people fill the vacancies by election as the legislature may direct.

This amendment shall not be so construed as to affect the election or term of any Senator chosen before it becomes valid as part of the Constitution.

Amendment XVIII [1919].

SECTION 1. After one year from the ratification of this article the manufacture, sale, or transportation of intoxicating liquors within, the importation thereof into, or the exportation thereof from the United States and all territory subject to the jurisdiction thereof for beverage purposes is hereby prohibited.

SECTION 2. The Congress and the several States shall have concurrent power to enforce this article by appropriate legislation.

SECTION 3. This article shall be inoperative unless it shall have been ratified as an amendment to the Constitution by the legislatures of the several States, as provided in the Constitution, within seven years from the date of the submission hereof to the States by the Congress.

Amendment XIX [1920].

The right of citizens of the United States to vote shall not be denied or abridged by the United States or by any State on account of sex.

Congress shall have power to enforce this article by appropriate legislation.

Amendment XX [1933].

SECTION 1. The terms of the President and Vice President shall end at noon on the 20th day of January, and the terms of Senators and Representatives at noon on the 3d day of January, of the years in which such terms would have ended if this article had not been ratified; and the terms of their successors shall then begin.

SECTION 2. The Congress shall assemble at least once in every year, and such meeting shall begin at noon on the 3d day of January, unless they shall by law appoint a different day.

SECTION 3. If, at the time fixed for the beginning of the term of the President, the President elect shall have died, the Vice President elect shall become President. If a President shall not have been chosen before the time fixed for the beginning of his term, or if the President elect shall have failed to qualify, then the Vice President elect shall act as President until a President shall have qualified; and the Congress may by law provide for the case wherein neither a President elect nor a Vice President elect shall have qualified, declaring who shall then act as President, or the manner in which one who is to act shall be selected, and such person shall act accordingly until a President or Vice President shall have qualified.

SECTION 4. The Congress may by law provide for the case of the death of any of the persons from whom the House of Representatives may choose a President whenever the right of choice shall have devolved upon them, and for the case of the death of any of the persons from whom the Senate may choose a Vice President whenever the right of choice shall have devolved upon them.

SECTION 5. Sections 1 and 2 shall take effect on the 15th day of October following the ratification of this article.

SECTION 6. This article shall be inoperative unless it shall have been ratified as an amendment to the Constitution by the legislatures of three-fourths of the several States within seven years from the date of its submission.

Amendment XXI [1933].

SECTION 1. The eighteenth article of amendment to the Constitution of the United States is hereby repealed.

SECTION 2. The transportation or importation into any State, Territory, or possession of the United States for delivery or use therein of intoxicating liquors, in violation of the laws thereof, is hereby prohibited.

SECTION 3. This article shall be inoperative unless it shall have been ratified as an amendment to the Constitution by conventions in the several States, as provided in the Constitution, within seven years from the date of the submission hereof to the States by the Congress.

Amendment XXII [1951].

SECTION 1. No person shall be elected to the office of the President more than twice, and no person who has held the office of President, or acted as President, for more than two years of a term to which some other person was elected President shall be elected to the office of the President more than once. But this Article shall not apply to any person holding the office of President when this Article was proposed by the Congress, and shall not prevent any person who may be holding the office of President, or acting as President, during the term within which this Article becomes operative from holding the office of President or acting as President during the remainder of such term.

SECTION 2. This article shall be inoperative unless it shall have been ratified as an amendment to the Constitution by the legislatures of three-fourths of the several States within seven years from the date of its submission to the States by the Congress.

Amendment XXIII [1961].

SECTION 1. The District constituting the seat of Government of the United States shall appoint in such manner as the Congress may direct:

A number of electors of President and Vice President equal to the whole number of Senators and Representatives in Congress to which the District would be entitled if it were a State, but in no event more than the least populous State; they shall be in addition to those appointed by the States, but they shall be considered, for the purposes of the election of President and Vice President, to be electors appointed by a State; and they shall meet in the District and perform such duties as provided by the twelfth article of amendment.

SECTION 2. The Congress shall have power to enforce this article by appropriate legislation.

Amendment XXIV [1964].

SECTION 1. The right of citizens of the United States to vote in any primary or other election for President or Vice President, for electors for President or Vice President, or for Senator or Representative in Congress, shall not be denied or abridged by the United States or any State by reason of failure to pay any poll tax or other tax.

SECTION 2. The Congress shall have power to enforce this article by appropriate legislation.

Amendment XXV [1967].

SECTION 1. In case of the removal of the President from office or of his death or resignation, the Vice President shall become President.

SECTION 2. Whenever there is a vacancy in the office of the Vice President, the President shall nominate a Vice President who shall take office upon confirmation by a majority vote of both Houses of Congress.

SECTION 3. Whenever the President transmits to the President pro tempore of the Senate and the Speaker of the House of Representatives his written declaration that he is unable to discharge the powers and duties of his office, and until he transmits to them a written declaration to the contrary, such powers and duties shall be discharged by the Vice President as Acting President.

SECTION 4. Whenever the Vice President and a majority of either the principal officers of the executive departments or of such other body as Congress may by law provide, transmit to the President pro tempore of the Senate and the Speaker of the House of Representatives their written declaration that the President is unable to discharge the powers and duties of his office, the Vice President shall immediately assume the powers and duties of the office as Acting President.

Thereafter, when the President transmits to the President pro tempore of the Senate and the Speaker of the House of Representatives his written declaration that no inability exists, he shall resume the powers and duties of his office unless the Vice President and a majority of either the principal officers of the executive departments or of such other body as Congress may by law provide, transmit within four days to the President pro tempore of the Senate and the Speaker of the House of Representatives their written declaration that the President is unable to discharge the powers and duties of his office. Thereupon Congress shall decide the issue, assembling within forty-eight hours for that purpose if not in session. If the Congress, within twenty-one days after receipt of the latter after Congress is required to assemble, determines by two-thirds vote of both Houses that the President is unable to discharge the powers and duties of his office, the Vice President shall continue to discharge the same as acting President; otherwise, the President shall resume the powers and duties of his office.

Amendment XXVI [1971].[1]

SECTION 1. The right of citizens of the United States, who are eighteen years of age or older, to vote shall not be denied or abridged by the United States or by any State on account of age.

SECTION 2. The Congress shall have power to enforce this article by appropriate legislation.

Amendment XXVII [1992].

No law, varying the compensation for the services of the Senators and Representatives, shall take effect, until an election of Representatives shall have intervened.

---

1. [The 26th Amendment was submitted to the States on March 23, 1971—three months after the Supreme Court decision holding unconstitutional the provisions of the Voting Rights Act Amendments of 1970 which had sought to authorize 18-year-olds to vote in state elections. See *Oregon v. Mitchell,* 400 U.S. 112 (1970). Three months later, on June 30, 1971, the ratification process was complete. — Ed.]

Index

A

Administrative Agencies
Delegation of powers to, 69–95
Due process in administrative review, 651

Administrative Review
Due process, 651

Articles of Confederation
Ratification of, 6

B

Bill of Rights
Precedent, as, 390
Privacy, right to, 580
Ratification of, 190, 381–89

Brown v. Board of Education
Equal Protection Clause, 479–84

C

Checks and Balances
(See Separation of Powers)

Civil Rights
Bill of Rights, 381–89
Equal protection (See Equal Protection)
Federal jurisdiction over civil rights
    actions, 304–320
State action doctrine, 408–39

Commerce Clause
Dormant commerce clause, 366–80
Dual sovereignty, 245
Historical background, 233

Intrastate regulation, 245–59
National Federation of Independent
    Business v. Sebelius, 351–65
New Deal legislation, 259–303

Congressional Powers
Commerce, regulation of (See Com-
    merce Clause)
Impeachment, 115–24
Necessary and Proper Clause, 350–65
Spending power, 350–65

D

Declaration of Independence
Ratification of, 6

Delegation of Powers
Executive branch, delegation of powers
    to
        Administrative agencies, 69–95
        Commander-in-chief, as, 55–69
        Emergency powers, 55–69
        Foreign relations, 125–40
        Legislative powers, 70–81
        War powers, 55–69, 140
Separation of powers and, 55
States, conferring powers to, 37–42

Due Process
Administrative review, 651
Fifth Amendment, 569
Fourteenth Amendment, 569
Privacy and right to be left alone,
    580

E

Elections

Campaign finance, 961–72

Political process, 961–72

Eleventh Amendment

Sovereign immunity, 198–231

Enemy Combatants

Detainment of, 143–58

Entitlements

Equal protection, 636

Equal Protection

Brown v. Board of Education, 479–84

Civil War Amendments

    Generally, 392

    Fourteenth Amendment, 381–89

    Thirteenth Amendment, 381–89

Entitlements and the negative constitu-

    tion, 636

Exclusion principle, 449

Fourteenth Amendment, 381–89

Gender classification

    Constitutional standard, 521–50

    Discriminatory intent or impact,

        650–56

Privacy, 580

Privileges and Immunities Clause,

    392–407

Racial classification

    Affirmative action, 496

    Constitutional standard, 465–87

    Definition of race, 465–87

    Discriminatory intent or impact,

        487–95

    Strict scrutiny test, 465–87

    Suspect standard for, 465–87

Slaughterhouse Cases, 392

Social and economic classification, 452

Thirteenth Amendment, 381–89

"We the People," 441

Executive Branch

Administrative agencies, 69–95

Appointment, 96–106

Clinton v. Jones, 121–23

Commander-in-chief, constitutional

    authority as, 55–69

Emergency powers, 55–69

Foreign relations, 125–40

Immunity, 115–24

Impeachment, 115–24

Judicial review, 23–36

Removal, 96–106

United States v. Nixon, 23–33

Veto

    Limitation on exercising, 81–95

    Line-item veto, 106–15

    Power to exercise, 81–95

War powers, 55–69, 140–59

F

Federalism

Generally, 183

Commerce, regulation of (See Com-

    merce Clause)

Effectiveness in government concept,

    183

Historical background

    Bill of Rights, 190, 381–92

    Constitution convention, 185

    Ratification, 188

    Tenth Amendment, 190, 195

Judiciary, 196

First Amendment

(See Freedom of Association; Freedom

    of Speech; Religion)

Fourteenth Amendment

Civil War Amendments, 392

Due process, 569–79

Equal protection, 441–568

Privacy, 580–635

Freedom of Association
(See also Freedom of Speech)
Generally, 1052

Freedom of Speech
(See also Freedom of Association)
Anonymous speech, 1044
Association, expressive, 1052
Campaign finance, 961–72
Commercial speech, 943–61
Competing conceptions of
    Dueling visions, 773
    Marketplace theory, 782–97
    Order and morality theory, 774–82
Content-based regulation
    Content discrimination, 858
    Element of offense, speech as,
        864–70
    Incidental burden on speech, 859–64
    O'Brien principle, 859–64
    Use of speech as element of offense,
        864–70
    Viewpoint discrimination, 858
Content-neutral regulation (See
    subhead: Content-based regulation)
Education, 1019–42
Expressive association, 1052
Forced speech, 1046
Government employees
    Discipline against employees,
        1012–16
    Political patronage, 1017–19
Government funding of speech,
    994–1011
Government speech, 984
Graphic speech (See subhead: Vulgar,
    graphic and offensive speech)
Journalism and the First Amendment
    Access to institutions and events,
        1060
    Press Clause, 1057
    Reporters' privilege, 1061

Lawless activity and speech
    Incitement, 797–803
    True threats, 804–24
Legal system and
    Lawyers, controlling speech of, 1043
    Reporting on judicial proceedings,
        1042
Obscenity
    Children, protection from pornogra-
        phy, 882–96
    Erotic dancing, 896–98
    General marketplace, in, 870–78
    Privacy of home, in, 879–82
    Public nudity, 896–98
    Secondary effects doctrine, 896–98
Offensive speech (See subhead: Vulgar,
    graphic and offensive speech)
Political process, 961–72
Pornography (see Subhead: Obscenity)
Prior restraint, 929–42
Public forum, 972–84
Tort liability
    Appropriation, 919
    Defamation, 898–913
    False light, 913
    Infliction of emotional distress,
        920–29
    Intrusion, 917
    Publication of private facts, 914
    Right of publicity, 919
Viewpoint discrimination (See sub-
    head: Content–based regulation)
Vulgar, graphic and offensive speech
    Graphically offensive speech, 836–58
    Obscenity (See subhead: Obscenity)
    Vulgarity, 824–35

G
Gun Control
(See Second Amendment)

H

History

Articles of Confederation, 6

Colonial period, 4

Common Sense, 5–6

Constitutional Convention of 1787, 6

Continental Congress, first, 5

Declaration of Independence, 6

Locke, John, philosophy of, 4, 48–49

Paine, Thomas, 5–6

Pre-Colonial constitutional theory, 4–6

Separation of powers, evolution of

American Revolution, 49

Constitutional Convention, 51

English heritage, 47

Social contract theory, 4

I

Independent Counsel

Oversight of, 96–100

J

Judiciary and Judicial Review

Case or controversy, 53, 159

Executive actions, review of, 23–36

Federalism, 196

Justiciability doctrine

Generally, 159

Political questions, 162–70

Ripeness, 176

Standing to sue, 170–72

Tyranny, 162

Marbury v. Madison, 13–22

State actions, 37–42

N

Necessary and Proper Clause

National Federation of Independent Business v. Sebelius, 351–65

Ninth Amendment

Right to privacy, 583–85

P

Privacy and Right to Be Left Alone

Due process, 580

Intrusion, 917

Publication of private facts, 914

R

Religion

Definition, 685–86

Disputes in secular courts, 762–72

Establishment of

Aid to, 725–36

Public arena

Religious symbols in, 686–708

Religious rituals in, 686–708

School settings

Religious symbols in, 708–25

Religious rituals in, 708–25

Free exercise

Discrimination against, 736–40

Hostility toward, 736–40

Neutral laws burdening, 740–62

Religious disputes in secular courts, 762–72

Right to Bear Arms

(See Second Amendment)

S

Second Amendment

Gun control, 8–12

Right to bear arms, 666–84

Separation of Powers

Appointment of officers, 96–106

Case or controversy dichotomy, 55

Current doctrine, 51

Delegation of powers to branches of government and, 53

Executive branch (See Executive Branch)

Executive privilege, 23–37

Foreign relations, 125–40

Historical background
    American Revolution, 49
    Constitutional Convention, 49
    English heritage, 47
Judicial review doctrine, 12–22
Removal of officers, 96–106
Sharing powers concept, 47, 52
Vesting of powers for branches of
    government, 47, 52
Veto power (See Veto Power)
War powers, 140–59

Sovereignty
Generally, 3
Brown v. Board of Education, 479–84
Immunity under Eleventh Amendment,
    198
Judicial review doctrine, 12–22

Spending Clause
*National Federation of Independent
    Business v. Sebelius*, 351–65

States
Commerce regulation
    Dormant commerce clause,
        366–80
    Dual sovereignty, 245–59
    Intrastate regulation, 245–59
Delegation of powers to states under
    Tenth Amendment, 195, 320–50
Judicial review of state actions,
    37–42
Sovereign immunity under Eleventh
    Amendment, 198

Supremacy Clause
Brown v. Board of Education, 479–84

T
Terrorism
Enemy combatants, detainment of,
    143–58
Presidential war powers, 55–69, 140

Thirteenth Amendment
Civil War Amendments, 392
Equal Protection, 381–90

U
United States v. Nixon
Executive privilege, in matter of, 23–37

V
Veto Power
Limitation on exercising, 70–95
Line-item veto, 106–15
Power to exercise, 81–95

W
War Powers
Separation of powers, 55–69, 140